MW01097708

THE EERDMANS CRITICAL COMMENTARY

†David Noel Freedman, *General Editor*

Astrid B. Beck, *Associate Editor*

THE EERDMANS CRITICAL COMMENTARY offers the best of contemporary Old and New Testament scholarship, seeking to give modern readers clear insight into the biblical text, including its background, its interpretation, and its application.

Contributors to the ECC series are among the foremost authorities in biblical scholarship worldwide. Representing a broad range of confessional backgrounds, authors are charged to remain sensitive to the original meaning of the text and to bring alive its relevance for today. Each volume includes the author's own translation, critical notes, and commentary on literary, historical, cultural, and theological aspects of the text.

Accessible to serious general readers and scholars alike, these commentaries reflect the contributions of recent textual, philological, literary, historical, and archaeological inquiry, benefiting as well from newer methodological approaches. ECC volumes are "critical" in terms of their detailed, systematic explanation of the biblical text. Although exposition is based on the original and cognate languages, English translations provide complete access to the discussion and interpretation of these primary sources.

COMMENTARY ON EXODUS

Thomas B. Dozeman

WILLIAM B. EERDMANS PUBLISHING COMPANY
GRAND RAPIDS, MICHIGAN / CAMBRIDGE, U.K.

Published 2009 by

Wm. B. Eerdmans Publishing Co.

2140 Oak Industrial Drive N.E., Grand Rapids, Michigan 49505 /

P.O. Box 163, Cambridge CB3 9PU U.K.

Printed in the United States of America

14 13 12 11 10 09   7 6 5 4 3 2 1

Library of Congress Cataloging-in-Publication Data

Dozeman, Thomas B.

Commentary on Exodus / Thomas B. Dozeman.

p.   cm. — (The Eerdmans critical commentary)

Includes bibliographical references (p.   ).

ISBN 978-0-8028-2617-6 (pbk.: alk. paper)

1. Bible. O.T. Exodus — Commentaries.   I. Title.

BS1245.53.D68   2009

222′.1207 — dc22

2009012685

www.eerdmans.com

To Mary

Contents

Contents

COMMENTARY

PART 1. THE POWER OF YAHWEH IN EGYPT (1:1–15:21)

Contents

Contents

PART 2. THE PRESENCE OF YAHWEH
IN THE WILDERNESS (15:22–40:38)

Contents

Contents

Preface

Many colleagues have contributed to the research and writing of this Commentary. I would like to thank my fellow researchers on the Pentateuch in the Society of Biblical Literature, who continually surprise me with new insights into old texts. The footnotes have been kept to a minimum. The bibliography is expanded beyond the footnotes, but also selected. The commentaries on Exodus by Brevard Childs, Cornelis Houtman, and William Propp were constant partners in my research and especially helpful resources in the history of interpretation, lexicography, and textual criticism. I regret that my manuscript was completed before the publication of William Propp's second volume, *Exodus 19-40* (The Anchor Yale Bible Commentary; Yale University Press, 2006), which I heartily recommend to readers.

I am especially grateful to my editor, David Noel Freedman. It was a pleasure to have such a seasoned scholar as an editor, who knew more about the book of Exodus than I. He graciously offered insights into the material, which I have often incorporated verbatim, while all the time encouraging my research even in those areas where he disagreed with me. What a gift!

I would like to thank Allen Myers for overseeing the Commentary from its early formation to its completion, and Linda Bieze for steering the volume through the editorial process.

I dedicate the Commentary to my wife, Mary R. Talen. Our ongoing conversations about biblical interpretation and her research in psychology always enrich my work.

THOMAS B. DOZEMAN

Abbreviations

AAR	American Academy of Religion
AB	Anchor Bible
ABD	*Anchor Bible Dictionary*
ABRL	Anchor Bible Reference Library
AcOr	*Acta Orientalia*
AJBA	*Australian Journal of Biblical Archaeology*
AJBI	*Annual of the Japanese Biblical Institute*
AJSL	*American Journal of Semitic Languages and Literature*
AnBib	Analecta Biblica
ANET	*Ancient Near Eastern Texts,* ed. J. B. Pritchard
AOAT	Alter Orient und Altes Testament
ASOR	American Schools of Oriental Research
ASORDS	American Schools of Oriental Research Dissertation Series
ASTI	*Annual of the Swedish Theological Institute*
ATANT	Abhandlungen zur Theologie des Alten und Neuen Testaments
ATD	Alte Testament Deutsch
BA	*Biblical Archaeologist*
BAR	*Biblical Archaeologist Reader*
BASOR	*Bulletin of the American Schools of Oriental Research*
BBB	Bonner biblische Beiträge
BDB	*Hebrew and English Lexicon of the Old Testament,* ed. F. Brown, S. R. Driver, and C. A. Briggs
BEATAJ	Beiträge zur Erforschung des Alten Testaments und des antiken Judentums
BETL	Bibliotheca Ephemeridum Theologicarum Lovaniensium
BevT	Beiträge zur evangelischen Theologie
BHS	Biblia Hebraica Stuttgartensia
Bib	*Biblica*
BibInt	*Biblical Interpretation*

BibOr	Biblica et Orientalia
BJS	Brown Judaic Studies
BKAT	Biblischer Kommentar: Altes Testament
BN	*Biblische Notizen*
BRev	*Biblical Review*
BWANT	Beiträge zur Wissenschaft vom Alten und Neuen Testament
BZ	*Biblische Zeitschrift*
BZAW	Beihefte zur Zeitschrift für die alttestamentliche Wissenschaft
CahRB	*Cahiers de la Revue Biblique*
CANE	*Civilizations of the Ancient Near East,* ed. J. M. Sasson
CAT	*Commentaire de l'Ancien Testament*
CBQ	*Catholic Biblical Quarterly*
CBQMS	Catholic Biblical Quarterly Monograph Series
ConBot	Coniectanea Biblica, Old Testament
CTA	*Corpus des tablettes en cunéiforms alphabétiques,* ed. A. Herdner
DtrH	Deuteronomistic History
EHS	Einleitung in die Heilige Schrift
ER	*Encyclopedia of Religion,* ed. M. Eliade
ETL	*Ephemerides Theologicae Lovanienses*
EvT	*Evangelische Theologie*
ExpTim	*Expository Times*
FAT	Forschungen zum Alten Testament
FB	Forschung zur Bibel
FCB	Feminist Companion to the Bible
FOTL	Forms of the Old Testament Literature
FRLANT	Forschungen zur Religion und Literatur des Alten und Neuen Testaments
GKC	*Gesenius' Hebrew Grammar,* ed. E. Kautzsch, trans. A. E. Cowley
HALOT	*The Hebrew and Aramaic Lexicon of the Old Testament,* ed. L. Koehler et al.
HAR	*Hebrews Annual Review*
HAT	Handbuch zum Alten Testament
HBT	Horizons in Biblical Theology
HKAT	Handkommentar zum Alten Testament
HS	*Historische Studien*
HSAT	Die Heilige Schrift des Alten Testaments
HSM	Harvard Semitic Monographs
HTR	*Harvard Theological Review*
HUCA	*Hebrew Union College Annual*
IB	*Interpreter's Bible*
IBC	Interpretation: A Bible Commentary for Teaching and Preaching
IBHS	International Bibliography of Historical Sciences
IBS	*Irish Biblical Studies*
ICC	International Critical Commentary

IDB	*Interpreter's Dictionary of the Bible*, ed. G. A. Buttrick
IDBSup	*Interpreter's Dictionary of the Bible*, Supplementary Volume
IEJ	*Israel Exploration Journal*
Int	*Interpretation*
JAAR	*Journal of the American Academy of Religion*
JANES	*Journal of the Ancient Near Eastern Society*
JANESCU	*Journal of the Ancient Near Eastern Society of Columbia University*
JAOS	*Journal of the American Oriental Society*
JBL	*Journal of Biblical Literature*
JCS	*Journal of Cuneiform Studies*
JEOL	*Jaarbericht. . . ex oriente lux*
JHNES	Johns Hopkins Near Eastern Studies
JJS	*Journal of Jewish Studies*
JNES	*Journal of Near Eastern Studies*
JPOS	*Journal of the Palestine Oriental Society*
JQR	*Jewish Quarterly Review*
JR	*Journal of Religion*
JSJSup	Journal for the Study of Judaism, Supplementary Series
JSNTSup	Journal for the Study of the New Testament, Supplementary Series
JSOT	*Journal for the Study of of the Old Testament*
JSOTSup	Journal for the Study of the Old Testament, Supplementary Series
JSS	*Journal of Semitic Studies*
JTS	*Journal of Theological Studies*
KEHAT	Kurzgefasstes exegetisches Handbuch zum Alten Testament
LSJ	*Greek-English Lexicon*, ed. H. G. Liddell, R. Scott, and H. S. Jones
LXX	Septuagint
MT	Masoretic Text
NCB	New Century Bible Commentary
NEB	New English Bible
NIV	New International Version
NJPS	Tanakh, New Jewish Publications Society translation
NRSV	New Revised Standard Version
OBO	Orbis Biblicus et Orientalis
OBS	Osterreichische Biblische Studien
OBT	Overtures to Biblical Theology
OLZ	*Orientalistische Literaturzeitung*
Or	*Orientalia*
OTL	Old Testament Library
OTS	*Old Testament Studies*
PJ	*Palästina-Jahrbuch*

PRU	*Le Palais Royal d'Ugarit*
PSB	*Princeton Seminary Bulletin*
QD	*Quaestiones Disputatae*
RB	*Revue Biblique*
ResQ	*Restoration Quarterly*
RevExp	*Review and Expositor*
Sam	Samaritan Pentateuch
SANT	Studien zum Alten und Neuen Testament
SBLASP	Society of Biblical Literature Abstracts and Seminar Papers
SBLDS	Society of Biblical Literature Dissertation Series
SBLMS	Society of Biblical Literature Monograph Series
SBLSCS	Society of Biblical Literature Septuagint and Cognate Studies
SBLSP	Society of Biblical Literature Seminar Papers
SBLSymS	Society of Biblical Literature Symposium Series
SBS	Stuttgarter Bibelstudien
SBT	Studies in Biblical Theology
ScEs	*Science et esprit*
ScrHier	*Scripta Hierosolymitana*
SEÅ	*Svensk Exegetisk Årsbok*
SJLA	Studies in Judaism in Late Antiquity
SJOT	*Scandinavian Journal of the Old Testament*
SJT	*Scottish Journal of Theology*
SOTSMS	Society for Old Testament Study Monograph Series
ST	*Studia Theologica*
StudBib	Studia Biblica
TB	Babylonian Talmud
TBL	*Theologische Blätter*
Tbü	Theologische Bücherei
TDNT	*Theological Dictionary of the New Testament,* ed. G. Friedrich and G. Kittel
TDOT	*Theological Dictionary of the Old Testament,* ed. G. J. Botterweck and H. Ringgren
TLZ	*Theologische Literaturzeitung*
TSK	*Theologische Studien und Kritiken*
TynBul	*Tyndale Bulletin*
TZ	*Theologische Zeitschrift*
UF	*Ugarit-Forschungen*
USFSHJ	University of South Florida Studies in the History of Judaism
VT	*Vetus Testamentum*
VTSup	Vestus Testamentum, Supplementary Series
VWGT	Veröffentlichungen der Wissenschaftlichen Gesellschaft für Theologie
WB	Die Welt der Bibel
WBC	Word Biblical Commentary

WMANT	Wissenschaftliche Monographien zum Alten und Neuen Testament
ZA	*Zeitschrift für Assyriologie und vorderasiatische Archäologie*
ZAW	*Zeitschrift für die alttestamentliche Wissenschaft*
ZBPV	*Zeitschrift des deutschen Palästina-Vereins*
ZKT	*Zeitschrift für Katholische Theologie*
ZTK	*Zeitschrift für Theologie und Kirche*

Introduction

TITLE

The book of Exodus is the second book in the Hebrew Bible. It is one of five books that make up the Torah or Pentateuch. The title "Exodus" derives from the title in Codex Alexandrinus of the Septuagint (LXX) version of the Hebrew Bible: "Exodus from Egypt" *(Exodos Aigyptou)*. In Jewish tradition the title consists of the opening words of the book: "And these are the names" *(wĕ'ēlleh šĕmôt)*. The title "Exodus" is the more common in Christian tradition. It emphasizes Israel's departure from Egypt and their salvation from slave labor, a central event in the first half of the book. The title does not adequately describe the content of the entire book, which includes stories of Israel's initial wilderness journey as well as the revelation of law and the tabernacle at Mount Sinai.

LITERATURE

The book of Exodus is an anthology of liturgy, law, and epic lore from many different periods of Israel's history. This insight has given rise to the study of genre in Exodus as interpreters seek to understand the diverse literary forms within the book as well as the method and purpose of their present composition.

The study of genre proceeds on two levels. At the smaller level, the focus is on individual stories and law codes. Many stories and laws in Exodus existed independently of their present context in the book. Interpreters seek to describe the literary character, the message, and the social function of the independent stories and laws to gain insight into their use within Exodus. At a larger level, the study of genre is applied to the entire book of Exodus and its relationship to the other books in the Pentateuch (Genesis, Leviticus, Numbers, and Deuteronomy) and in the Deuteronomistic History (DtrH: Joshua, Judges, Samuel, and Kings). The larger study of genre has demonstrated that several authors have contributed to the composition of Exodus, and that Exodus is part of a larger history, spanning at the very least the Pentateuch, and likely also the Deuteronomistic History. Interpreters seek to identify the anonymous authors, the time in which they lived, and the method and purpose of their writing.

INDIVIDUAL GENRES

Exodus contains a rich variety of literary forms, including poetry, law, cultic etiology, genealogy, and theophany. G. W. Coats has identified eighty-nine distinct genres of literature in Exodus, along with an additional twenty stereotyped formulas. The presence of so many fixed forms of literature indicates that Exodus is anything but a free composition. Yet the incorporation of established literary genres is undertaken in a creative manner in the composition of Exodus. Individual genres are employed by the authors of Exodus to address the central themes of divine identity, power, and presence (see below, "The Power and the Presence of Yahweh"), or to aid in defining the character of Moses (see below, "Leadership of Moses"). For example, the repeated use of the prophetic messenger speech when Moses addresses Pharaoh, "Thus said Yahweh," establishes his authority as Yahweh's representative and aids in defining his character.[1] The following four examples illustrate the range of literary genres in Exodus and how they are employed to develop the themes of divine power and presence in the book.

Hymns in Exodus 15

The power of Yahweh to save is explored in the two hymns in Exodus 15, the Song of the Sea (sometimes called the Song of Moses) in vv. 1-18 and the Song of Miriam in v. 21. Each celebrates the power of Yahweh as the Storm God, who uses nature to defeat enemies. There are many parallels between the image of Yahweh in the hymns and the Canaanite storm god Baal, who also wars against his enemies through the thunderstorm.[2] In *Studies in Ancient Yahwistic Poetry*, F. M. Cross and D. N. Freedman concluded that the two hymns are older than their surrounding narrative context and that they functioned independently in

1. G. W. Coats, *Exodus 1–18* (FOTL IIA; Grand Rapids: Eerdmans, 1999); eighty-nine is the number of entries in the glossary of genres, 155-74; the formulas are listed on 174-78.
2. For parallels and bibliography see T. B. Dozeman, "The Song of the Sea and Salvation History," in *On the Way to Nineveh: Studies in Honor of George M. Landes* (ed. S. L. Cook and S. C. Winter; ASOR 4; Atlanta: Scholars Press, 1999), 94-113.

the history of Israelite worship.[3] Of the two hymns, the Song of Miriam is often judged to be more ancient than the Song of the Sea. The Song of Miriam presents a celebration of divine power in a single poetic couplet:

> Sing to Yahweh, for he has triumphed gloriously;
> horse and rider he has thrown into the sea.

The victory war song states that God is powerful enough to destroy unnamed armies by drowning them in the chaotic sea. F. Crüsemann expresses the opinion of many scholars when he concludes that the Song of Miriam is an early example of the hymn form preserved in the Hebrew Bible. It praises Yahweh in the first line and gives the reason for praise in the second.[4] The poem represents reflection from ancient Israelite worship on the character and strength of divine power as overwhelming both unnamed political foes and the mythological sea.

The Song of the Sea in 15:1-18 is also judged to be an independent liturgy. Cross and Freedman, followed by D. A. Robertson, provide a catalogue of archaic forms of language, grammar, and orthography in the poem that separate the hymn from the surrounding narrative, suggesting that it too, like the Song of Miriam, represents an ancient liturgy.[5] Yet the Song of the Sea also contrasts to the Song of Miriam. It presents a more expanded interpretation of Yahweh's power as a song of victory. Pharaoh is identified as Yahweh's opponent (v. 4). The arrogance of Pharaoh is explored (v. 9). Yahweh's cosmic weapons of war are elaborated: they include his right hand (v. 6) and the breath of his nostrils (v. 8). And the chaotic sea is given location as the Red Sea in the first half of the poem (v. 4), before the poem turns its attention to Israel's future march through the desert and their eventual conquest of Canaan (vv. 13-18).

The hymns in Exodus 15 will require further interpretation in the commentary. Yet the present summary already indicates that Exodus includes independent poems on the theme of divine power. Moreover, comparison of the hymns suggests theological development. The Song of Miriam appears to be a core confession of divine power, expanded, refined, and historicized by the Song of the Sea. In the commentary I will demonstrate that the process of theological reflection and refinement continues in the composition of Exodus, from the poems to the narrative accounts of Yahweh's defeat of Pharaoh in Exodus 11–14.

---

3. F. M. Cross and D. N. Freedman, *Studies in Ancient Yahwistic Poetry* (SBLDS 21; Missoula, Mont.: Scholars Press, 1975), e.g., 5-6, 45-47.

4. F. Crüsemann, *Studien zur Formgeschichte von Hymnus und Danklied in Israel* (WMANT 32; Neukirchen-Vluyn: Neukirchener Verlag, 1969), 19-38.

5. Cross and Freedman, *Studies in Ancient Yahwistic Poetry*, 45-65; D. A. Robertson, *Linguistic Evidence in Dating Early Hebrew Poetry* (SBLDS 3; Missoula, Mont.: Scholars Press, 1972), esp. 28-31.

Theophany on the Mountain

The word "theophany" means "appearance of God." Biblical scholars use this term to identify a specific genre of literature, describing the appearance of God to Israel. J. Jeremias has identified the oldest form of theophany in ancient Israel as consisting of two parts: the approach of God is proclaimed at a time of crisis, and the reaction of nature is described through the imagery of a storm.[6] The Song of Deborah in Judg 5:4-5 provides illustration. In this poem Yahweh approaches from the desert region of Seir and Edom to aid Israel at a time of crisis, prompting the elements of nature to respond through storm imagery — the earth trembles, mountains quake, and the heavens pour out rain.

The theophany of Yahweh was also interpreted as an event that took place on a mountain. Storm imagery still accompanied the appearance of God, but in this account of theophany lightning and thunder were envisioned at the summit of a mountain. R. J. Clifford has clarified the prominent role of the storm imagery on the cosmic mountain in Canaanite mythology, where the appearance of Baal in his temple mountain also included the imagery of the thunderstorm.[7] The same imagery of theophany dominates in Exodus, with several accounts of God's appearance on the cosmic mountain in chaps. 19–24. Exodus 19:16-17 is one account of theophany on the mountain that may be older than its present narrative context. T. N. D. Mettinger notes that the verses assume God dwelling on the summit of the mountain, as compared to a more mobile presentation of the Deity descending and ascending from the mountain in the larger narrative context.[8] Yet the imagery in 19:16-17 has also changed from the oldest accounts of theophany as presented in Judg 5:4-5. The appearance of God to Israel is accompanied with the storm imagery of thunder and lightning, while the people tremble, rather than nature.

Exodus 24:10-11 may be another account of theophany that existed independently of its present narrative context. E. W. Nicholson notes the distinctive imagery, in which the leaders of Israel are envisioned as actually seeing the "God of Israel," while they eat and drink with the Deity at the summit of the di-

---

6. J. Jeremias, *Theophanie: Die Geschichte einer alttestamentlichen Gattung* (WMANT 10; Neukirchen-Vluyn: Neukirchener Verlag, 1965), 107-11; see also F. M. Cross, *Canaanite Myth and Hebrew Epic: Essays in the History of the Religion of Israel* (Cambridge: Harvard University Press, 1973), 164.

7. R. J. Clifford, *The Cosmic Mountain in Canaan and the Old Testament* (HSM 4; Cambridge: Harvard University Press, 1972).

8. T. N. D. Mettinger, *The Dethronement of Sabaoth: Studies in the Shem and Kabod Theologies* (ConBOT 18; Lund: Gleerup, 1982); see also T. B. Dozeman, *God on the Mountain: A Study of Redaction, Theology and Canon in Exodus 19–24* (SBLMS 37; Atlanta: Scholars Press, 1989).

vine mountain.[9] Feasting in the immediate presence of God is not a common motif in the Hebrew Bible. A notable exception is Isa 25:6, which describes a similar festival on the cosmic mountain before Yahweh. Feasting with God on the mountain is a motif from Canaanite religion. Baal also feasts in his temple on Mount Zaphon, suggesting that the writers of Exodus are incorporating mythological motifs from their broader cultural and religious environment.[10] The incorporation of ancient Near Eastern mythology continues in tradition. The Christian Eucharist conceived as a messianic banquet with God continues the same cultic mythology of feasting with the Deity in the cultic site.

The genre of divine theophany on the mountain plays a central role in developing the theme of divine presence in Exodus. Yahweh appears to Moses (Exod 3:1) and to Israel (24:13) on the unnamed "mountain of God." The mountain of theophany is also specifically named as Mount Sinai (e.g., 19:18) and as Mount Horeb (33:6) at different points in the book. Still other names for Yahweh's mountain of revelation outside Exodus include Mount Yahweh (Num 10:33) and Mount Zion (Ps 48:2). The variety of names for the mountain of theophany points to different interpretations of divine revelation in Israel's worship traditions. The distinct names for Yahweh's mountain of theophany in Exodus alert us to the fact that several interpretations of the nature of divine revelation and cultic presence have been incorporated into the story.

Sanctuary of God

In his study *God and Temple*, R. E. Clements argued that the center of ancient Israelite religion is Yahweh dwelling in a sacred cultic site.[11] The more recent research of J. Milgrom on the complex theologies of the sacred and the profane as well as the pure and the impure, which are associated with the temple in ancient Israel, reinforce the insight of Clements, alerting us to the important role of the sanctuary in Exodus.[12] There are indications that Exodus has incorporated several independent accounts of the sanctuary.

The tabernacle (Exodus 25–31, 35–40), the tent of meeting (33:7-11), and the Jerusalem temple are different forms of sacred dwellings. When Solomon

9. E. W. Nicholson, "The Interpretation of Exodus XXIV 9-11," *VT* 24 (1974): 77-97; idem, "The Antiquity of the Tradition in Exodus XXIV 9-11," *VT* 25 (1975): 69-79; idem, "The Origin of the Tradition in Exodus XXIV 9-11," *VT* 26 (1976): 148-60.

10. *CTA* 4.vi.1-64.

11. R. E. Clements, *God and Temple* (Philadelphia: Fortress, 1965).

12. J. Milgrom, *Leviticus 1–16* (AB 3; New York: Doubleday, 1991); idem, *Leviticus 17–22* (AB 3A; New York: Doubleday, 2000); and idem, *Leviticus 23–27* (AB 3B; New York: Doubleday, 2001).

completed the Jerusalem temple, he stated to Yahweh: "I have built you an exalted house, a place for you to dwell on earth" (1 Kgs 8:13). The same is true for the tabernacle. It is the place where Yahweh dwells on earth. Yahweh states to Moses: "Have [the Israelites] make me a sanctuary, so that I may dwell among them" (Exod 25:8). The architectural plans for the tabernacle are a pattern of God's heavenly home. Construction of the tabernacle will allow God to descend to the earth. Thus, as M. Eliade has demonstrated, the temple connects heaven and earth. It can even be conceived as the *axis mundi* — the central point of creation where heaven and earth link.[13] All communication with God is channeled through cultic rituals in the tabernacle.

Sacred dwellings are located on symbolic mountains, creating a close relationship between the themes "Theophany on the Mountain" and "Sanctuary of God." In Canaanite religion Baal's temple is on his sacred mountain, Zaphon, located in the north. Solomon's temple for Yahweh is on Mount Zion (Psalm 48). The tent of meeting in Exod 33:7-11 is associated with Mount Horeb, which is also the mountain of theophany in Deuteronomy 4–5 and in the story of Elijah (1 Kings 19). Jethro feasts with Moses on the "mountain of God" (Exodus 18). Numbers 10:33-34 identifies the desert mountain of God as Mount Yahweh, and the tabernacle is situated on Mount Sinai (Exod 24:15-18). Yahweh has many mountain homes.

The dominant role of the theophany of God on the mountain in the second half of Exodus becomes a magnet for biblical writers to incorporate independent genres describing the presence of God in the sanctuary. The reason, according to J. D. Levenson, is that the cosmic mountain discloses "the essential . . . relationship of YHWH to his people."[14] The account of the leaders "seeing the God of Israel" at the summit of the divine mountain in Exod 24:10-11 includes a description of a sanctuary. The vision of God by the elders gives way to temple imagery. The elders are located under blue sapphire stone, a common feature of temples in the ancient Near East. Baal's temple, for example, is also described with the terms "clarity of stone" *(ṭhr)*[15] and "pavement" *(lbnt)*.[16] After the leaders see God they perform the cultic rituals of eating and drinking with God. These details suggest that Exod 24:10-11 may be categorized as a description of a sanctuary in addition to its earlier classification as a theophany. The text illustrates the close relationship between the two genres of literature.

13. M. Eliade, *The Sacred and the Profane: The Nature of Religion* (trans. W. R. Trask; New York: Harcourt, Brace, 1959).

14. J. D. Levenson, *Sinai and Zion: An Entry into the Jewish Bible* (New York: Winston, 1985), 18.

15. *CTA* 4.v.81-82, 95-97.

16. *CTA* 4.v.73.

The identification of Yahweh's sanctuary as the tent of meeting in Exod 33:7-11 may also be an independent tradition, perhaps arising from a distinct Canaanite mythology of the sanctuary, as Clifford has argued.[17] It appears abruptly in its present narrative context, as a tent that Moses sets up outside the Israelite camp. This tent shrine contrasts to the Priestly tabernacle (chaps. 25–31, 35–40), which is constructed at the center of the Israelite camp. Moreover, the tent of meeting is associated with a distinct mountain of theophany — Mount Horeb (33:6) — as compared to the construction of the tabernacle at the base of Mount Sinai. The appearance of Yahweh in the tent of meeting is also unique. The act of revelation consists purely of divine speech to Moses, signaled by the descent of the pillar of cloud at the door of the tent of meeting.

The construction of Yahweh's sanctuary is central for developing the theme of divine presence in the second half of Exodus. The importance of the sanctuary is indicated by the detailed description of the Priestly tabernacle (chaps. 25–31, 35–40), which dominates the account of Yahweh's revelation at Mount Sinai (chaps. 19–24, 33–34). But, as we have seen, the dominant role of the tabernacle does not eclipse the other descriptions of Yahweh's sanctuary incorporated in Exodus.

Law Codes

Law played a central role throughout the history of the ancient Near East. Many law codes have been discovered. The most famous is the Code of Hammurabi, the Babylonian ruler.[18] Law codes like Hammurabi's are not intended to be complete. They provide the framework for legal decisions, but leave out many specific case laws. The administration of law in the ancient Near East resided ultimately with the king, but local officials and temple priests also acted as judges. Biblical law codes are similar to the ancient Near Eastern examples. They are not complete; many individual case laws are lacking.

Exodus contains law codes that explore the religious and ethical life of Israel. The laws do not mention the king as the leader who is ultimately responsible for the administration of law and justice. Rather, Moses is idealized as the lawgiver, while elders (chap. 18) aid in the administration of law. The authority of law rested ultimately with God. The Ten Commandments root the revelation of law in Yahweh (20:1-17). The theological role of covenant provides the link between religion and the administration of law. "Covenant" is a legal term in the ancient Near East, the Hebrew term *bĕrît* perhaps deriving from Akkadian

---

17. R. J. Clifford, "The Tent of El and the Israelite Tent of Meeting," *CBQ* 33 (1971): 221-27.
18. *ANET*, 163-80.

biritu, "fetter." The Israelites are envisioned as making a covenant with Yahweh at Mount Sinai (19:1-8; 24:3-8), which describes their relationship with God as a legal treaty.

The laws in Exodus are written in different styles. A. Alt distinguished two genres of law in the composition of the law codes.[19] *Casuistic* laws are written in the form of case law. Each law separates into two clauses. The first clause (the protasis) presents the situation or incident under examination. The second clause (the apodosis) states the consequences of the action. Exodus 22:1 provides an example: "*If* a man steals an ox . . . and sells it, *then* he must pay back five head of cattle." *Apodictic* law, by contrast, is categorical, not conditional. The command in 20:13, "You shall not kill," is apodictic.

The law codes in Exodus include the Decalogue (20:1-17), the Book of the Covenant (20:22–23:19), and the ritual law associated with the tabernacle (chaps. 25–31, 35–40). The law codes, or at least parts of them, were likely independent compositions. The Decalogue, for example, appears to have had a long literary development before reaching its present form in Exodus 20 (and in Deuteronomy 5), according to F.-L. Hossfeld.[20] Even without an interpretation of its earliest literary forms, a comparison between the two occurrences, Exodus 20 and Deuteronomy 5, indicates a history of commentary. Sabbath rest, for example, arises from the experience of the exodus in Deuteronomy 5, as compared to the act of creation in Exodus 20. The Book of the Covenant also contains several distinct compositions of law, including civil law in casuistic form (Exod 21:1–22:17) and religious, cultic, and moral instruction, some of which is written in apodictic form (22:18–23:19).

The law codes are woven into the account of divine revelation on Mount Sinai. The Decalogue is presented as a divine speech to the people of Israel. The Book of the Covenant and the cultic legislation of the tabernacle are revealed privately to Moses at the summit of the mountain. The careful distribution of the law codes indicates their important role for interpreting Exodus. The law codes provide a means for biblical authors to explore how humans live in the presence of God. Ritual law explores human conduct in the realm of the sacred, while ethical law outlines the social implications of living in the presence of God.

---

19. A. Alt, "The Origins of Israelite Law," in *Essays on Old Testament History and Religion* (trans. R. A. Wilson; Oxford: Basil Blackwell, 1966), 81-132.

20. F.-L. Hossfeld, *Der Dekalog: Seine späten Fassungen, die originale Komposition und seine Vorstufen* (OBO 45; Göttingen: Vandenhoeck & Ruprecht, 1982).

GENRE OF SALVATION HISTORY

The individual genres are woven into a larger story of salvation history, which is a difficult genre to evaluate. G. von Rad underscored the complex character of salvation history, noting the way in which it intertwines historical experience and cultic legend into a "canonical history" of election. He concluded that salvation history refers to a fixed pattern of God's saving actions that give identity to Israel as a nation. These include the promise of offspring and land to the ancestors, the exodus from Egypt, the wilderness wandering, the revelation at Mount Sinai, and the hope for a future life in the promised land of Canaan.[21]

T. L. Thompson rightly notes that salvation history must not be confused with the modern understanding of history. Modern history writing requires a critical evaluation of sources to represent past events. It does not allow for actions of the Deity to account for causes of events and their effects.[22] Salvation history, by contrast, is motivated by religious concerns. God remains the primary force behind the causes of events. Exodus touches on all of the themes of salvation history noted by von Rad, while focusing in particular on the exodus from Egypt and the revelation at Mount Sinai.

An investigation into three related topics will aid in defining the genre of salvation history. First, an interpretation of literary context will demonstrate that the genre of salvation history requires that Exodus be read with other books in the Torah and in the Former Prophets. The interpretation of literary context will also underscore the problems that arise from reading Exodus as an episode in a larger history. Second, a comparison of the genre of salvation history to ancient history writing will illustrate similarities between Greek and Hebrew history writing. The points of similarity will also clarify the different purposes of the biblical historians and the early Greek historians, which have raised the question of whether biblical literature conforms to the genre of ancient historiography. Third, an examination of the relationship of the story of the exodus to historical events will clarify the contrast between modern history writing and the book of Exodus.

---

21. For discussion of salvation history as a literary term for describing history writing see G. von Rad, *Old Testament Theology* (trans. D. M. G. Stalker; 2 vols.; New York: Harper & Row, 1962-1965), 1:126-29. For a broader discussion of salvation history as both a literary and theological construal see R. Gnuse, *"Heilsgeschichte" as a Model for Biblical Theology: The Debate Concerning the Uniqueness and Significance of Israel's Worldview* (College Theology Society Studies in Religion 4; Lanham, Md.: University Press of America, 1988).

22. T. L. Thompson, "Historiography (Israelite)," *ABD* 3:206-12.

Literary Context

Exodus is part of the five books of the Torah or Pentateuch, suggesting a close literary relationship between Genesis, Exodus, Leviticus, Numbers, and Deuteronomy. The antiquity of the literary formation of the Pentateuch (meaning a book in five parts) is not clear. Philo of Alexandria is aware of the Pentateuch in the first century c.e., as is Josephus.[23] J. Blenkinsopp suggests that the formation of the Pentateuch is evident already at Qumran in the second century b.c.e.[24] The plot of the Pentateuch recounts the origin of the Israelites within the framework of an extended migration initiated by God. The journey begins with Abraham, who leaves Ur of the Chaldeans upon receiving the divine promise that he would become a great nation and acquire a land of residency. The journey of Abraham develops into a national pilgrimage when his descendants escape from Egypt, traverse the desert, and reach the border of the promised land of Canaan. The story of Torah breaks off with the Israelite people not yet acquiring the land of divine promise.

The narrative sequence in Torah appears to flow seamlessly upon first reading. The account of creation and the ancestors (Genesis) brings the family of Jacob to Egypt, reuniting them with Joseph and setting the stage for the liberation of the Israelites from Egypt (Exodus). The exodus from Egypt launches the nation on a wilderness journey, where the people encounter God at the divine mountain, receive law, and construct the sanctuary (Exodus, Leviticus, Numbers). The story concludes with Moses recounting the events from Genesis through Numbers in Deuteronomy, before he dies at the end of Deuteronomy.

Yet a closer reading of the Torah raises questions about the literary context of Exodus. How closely is Exodus tied to the other books in the Torah, especially Deuteronomy, which repeats the entire story? Is Exodus related to the Former Prophets (Joshua, Judges, Samuel, and Kings), which recount the history of the Israelite people in the promised land as well as their loss of it in the exile? An overview of the textual traditions of the MT and LXX indicates that the questions of literary context were already occurring to the ancient writers. The chart in figure 1 on page 11 indicates which books in the MT and LXX begin with the conjunction "and," indicating a literary relationship to the preceding book, and which books lack the connection, suggesting at the very least a more distant literary relationship between the books.

The books lacking a conjunction in the MT are Genesis and Deuteronomy, resulting in a separation between Genesis–Numbers and Deuteronomy–2 Kings. The MT suggests a close literary relationship between the story of the

---

23. Philo, *Aet.* 19; Josephus, *C.Ap.* 1.37-41.

24. J. Blenkinsopp, *The Pentateuch: An Introduction to the First Five Books of the Bible* (ABRL; New York: Doubleday, 1992), 43-45.

Figure 1

Book	MT	LXX
Genesis	*bĕrē'šît,* "in the beginning"	*en archē,* "in the beginning"
Exodus	*we'ēlleh šĕmōt,* "**and** these are the names"	*tauta ta onomata,* "these are the names"
Leviticus	*wayyiqrā',* "**and** [Yahweh] called"	*kai anekalesen,* "**and** [the Lord] called"
Numbers	*waydabbēr,* "**and** [Yahweh] spoke"	*kai elalēsen,* "**and** [the Lord] spoke"
Deuteronomy	*'ēlleh haddĕbārîm,* "these are the words"	*houtoi hoi logoi,* "these are the words"
Joshua	*wayĕhî 'aḥărê môt mōšeh,* "**and** after the death of Moses"	*kai egeneto . . . ,* "**and** it happened . . ."
Judges	*wayyĕhî 'aḥărê môt yĕhôšuaʿ,* "**and** after the death of Joshua"	*kai egeneto . . . ,* "**and** it happened . . ."
Ruth		*kai egeneto . . . ,* "**and** it happened . . ."
MT: 1 Samuel LXX: 1 Kingdoms	*wayhî 'îš,* "**and** there was a man"	*anthrōpos ēn,* "there was a man"
MT: 2 Samuel LXX: 2 Kingdoms	*wayhî 'aḥărê môt šā'ûl,* "**and** it was after the death of Saul"	*kai egeneto . . . ,* "**and** it happened . . ."
MT: 1 Kings LXX: 3 Kingdoms	*wĕhammelek dāwid,* "**and** the king, David"	*kai ho basileus Dauid,* "**and** the king, David"
MT: 2 Kings LXX: 4 Kingdoms	*wayyipšaʿ mô'āb bĕyiśrā'ēl 'aḥărê môt 'aḥ'āb,* "**and** Moab rebelled after the death of Ahab"	*kai ēthetēsen Mōab . . . ,* "**and** Moab rebelled . . ."

ancestors in Genesis and the Israelite liberation from Egypt in Exodus. It also raises questions about the literary relationship between Exodus and Deuteronomy, with their distinct accounts of the liberation from Egypt and the revelation of law in the wilderness. Does Deuteronomy begin a version of salvation in the MT distinct from Exodus? Does the story line of Deuteronomy continue through the fall of the monarchy in Kings, as is indicated by the conjunction at the beginning of each book in the Former Prophets?

The books lacking a conjunction in the LXX are Genesis, Exodus, Deuteronomy, and 1 Samuel (= 1 Kingdoms in the LXX). The LXX suggests four broad divisions in the literature: (1) the ancestors (Genesis); (2) the exodus under the leadership of Moses; (3) the premonarchical period (Deuteronomy, Joshua, Judges, Ruth); and (4) the monarchical period (MT 1 Samuel–2 Kings = LXX 1-4 Kingdoms). The LXX supports the MT in underscoring a separation between Exodus and Deuteronomy. Thus it too raises the question of the literary relationship of the two books. But the LXX raises a further question about the relationship of Genesis and Exodus, since they also are not related with a conjunction. Is the history of the ancestors in Genesis distinct from the more nationally focused salvation of the Israelites under the leadership of Moses in Exodus–Numbers? And how do these two episodes relate to the Former Prophets, now also conceived as two distinct episodes?

The LXX and MT indicate three areas of research surrounding the literary context of Exodus: (1) the relationship of Exodus and Deuteronomy; (2) the broader literary relationship between Exodus and the Former Prophets; and (3) the connection between the story of the ancestors in Genesis and the account of Moses' liberation of the Israelite people in Exodus.

Exodus and Deuteronomy

The events of the exodus, the wilderness journey, and the revelation of the law codes at the mountain of God are presented twice, first in Exodus and a second time in Deuteronomy. The two accounts are written in different styles. Exodus is written in the third person narrative, while Deuteronomy is a first person speech by Moses, in which he recounts the past events of the exodus to the next generation of Israelites preparing to enter the promised land. The relationship between Exodus and Deuteronomy is one of the central literary problems of pentateuchal research in the modern period of biblical interpretation. The central role of this literary problem began with W. D. L. de Wette. E. Otto has recently reaffirmed its crucial role in understanding the composition of the Pentateuch and the Deuteronomistic History (Former Prophets).[25]

25. E. Otto, *Das Deuteronomium im Pentateuch und Hexateuch: Studien zur Literatur-*

De Wette established the paradigm for interpreting the literary relationship of Exodus and Deuteronomy. He concluded that the two accounts indicate different religious outlooks, written by different authors during distinct periods in the history of ancient Israel. This insight has provided a hallmark in the historical-critical study of Exodus, even though de Wette focused on the second body of law contained in Deuteronomy.[26]

De Wette noted that the story of Moses comes to an end at the close of Numbers. Moses' impending death is confirmed (Num 27:12-14), the land of Canaan is divided (26:52-56), and Joshua is appointed as successor (27:15-23). Then somewhat unexpectedly Deuteronomy begins the story anew, by repeating much of the material that occurs in Exodus, Leviticus, and Numbers. New law is given (Deuteronomy 4–5, 12–26), the story of the wilderness journey is retold (chaps. 1–3), the sin of the golden calf is described (chaps. 9–10), many specific laws repeat (Leviticus 26; Deuteronomy 28), Joshua is appointed a second time to succeed Moses (Deuteronomy 31), and God tells Moses again of his impending death (chaps. 31, 34). The repetitions suggest that the history of Moses is completed at the close of Numbers.

De Wette also pointed out that the style of the writing and the religious outlook in Deuteronomy were different from Exodus. He judged the language to be more reflective and theologically sophisticated than the literature in Genesis–Numbers. It contained distinctive phrases (i.e., "that you may live in the land that Yahweh our God gives you"). And the book presented a unique view of the cult, advocating worship at a single sanctuary (Deuteronomy 12). The demand for centralized worship meant that Passover became a national festival celebrated at the central temple (chap. 16). The command for centralized worship was at odds with the biblical portrait of Israel as having many sanctuaries throughout the Mosaic (i.e., Exod 20:24-26) and monarchical (i.e., Saul in 1 Samuel 13; David in 1 Samuel 21; and Solomon in 1 Kings 3) periods. As a consequence, de Wette argued that the books of Exodus and Deuteronomy were the product of separate authors, and that Deuteronomy was the later account.[27]

---

geschichte von Pentateuch und Hexateuch im Lichte des Deuteronomiumrahmens (FAT 30; Tübingen: Mohr Siebeck, 2000), 1-11.

26. W. M. L. de Wette, *Dissertatio critico-exegetica qua Deuteronomium a prioribus Pentateuchi Libris diversum, alius cuiusdam recentioris auctoris opus esse monstratur; quam ... auctoritate amplissimi philosophorum ordinis pro venia legendi AD XXVII* (Jena, 1805); idem, *Beiträge zur Einleitung in das Alte Testament* (Halle, 1806-7). For a detailed study of de Wette see John W. Rogerson, *W. M. L. de Wette, Founder of Modern Biblical Criticism: An Intellectual Biography* (JSOTSup 126; Sheffield: Sheffield Academic Press, 1992).

27. J. Wellhausen (*Prolegomena to the History of Ancient Israel* [trans. A. Menzies and J. Sutherland Black; 1883; repr. New York: Meridian, 1957], 4-5) describes de Wette as "the epoch-making pioneer of historical criticism." The reason, according to Wellhausen, is that de Wette

De Wette concluded that the earliest portions of Deuteronomy were written in the closing years of the monarchical period, during the Josianic reform (621 B.C.E.). The most important innovation of the Josianic reform was the centralization of worship (2 Kings 22–23) advocated in Deuteronomy. Thus this book with its command for one sanctuary and centralized worship must have been the "book of the law" (2 Kgs 22:8) that guided the reform of Josiah. Its original author, according to de Wette, wrote at the close of the monarchical period, with later writers adding even more literature in the exilic and postexilic periods.

De Wette's fixing of the date of Deuteronomy to the end of the monarchical period, and his assumption that Deuteronomy must be interpreted as a distinct version of the exodus, have influenced all subsequent interpretations of the book of Exodus. De Wette concluded that the Exodus was the older story and that Deuteronomy represents a later reinterpretation of Exodus. More recent interpreters have tended to reverse the literary relationship between Exodus and Deuteronomy, advocating that Deuteronomy is the older literary document, and that many portions of Exodus were composed by post-Deuteronomistic (so J. Van Seters) or post-Priestly (so Otto) authors.[28] Whether one follows the lead of de Wette or the more recent trend in interpretation in which the historical development of the literature is reversed, the relationship between the books of Exodus and Deuteronomy has become a central interpretive problem in modern commentaries on Exodus.

M. Noth is the most influential proponent of the hypothesis of de Wette.[29] He accentuated the difference between Exodus and Deuteronomy even more than de Wette, to the point where he introduced new terminology for interpreting the relationship of the two books. The literary context of Exodus must be restricted to the Tetrateuch, according to Noth, consisting of the first four books of the Hebrew Bible: Genesis, Exodus, Leviticus, and Numbers. Deuter-

---

perceived how "disconnected are the alleged starting-points of Israel's history and that history itself. The religious community set upon so broad a basis in the wilderness, with its sacred centre and uniform organization, disappears and leaves no trace as soon as Israel settles in a land of its own, and becomes, in any proper sense, a nation."

28. J. Van Seters (*The Life of Moses: The Yahwist as Historian in Exodus–Numbers* [Louisville: Westminster John Knox, 1994]) identifies the earliest author in Exodus as an exilic Yahwist, who is writing after the composition of Deuteronomy. Otto (*Deuteronomium im Pentateuch*) offers a different literary solution to the composition of Exodus, in which a series of redactors (the Hexateuch redactor and the Pentateuch redactor) are not only later than the composition of the entire book of Exodus, but also later than the P composition.

29. M. Noth, *A History of Pentateuchal Traditions* (trans. B. W. Anderson; Englewood Cliffs, N.J.: Prentice-Hall, 1972); idem, *Überlieferungsgeschichtliche Studien: Die sammelnden und bearbeitenden Geschichtswerke im Alten Testament* (2nd ed.; Tübingen: Max Niemeyer, 1957).

onomy introduced a separate corpus of literature, the Deuteronomistic History (DtrH), consisting of Joshua, Judges, Samuel, and Kings. Noth's description of a Tetrateuch and his argument that Deuteronomy must be combined with the Deuteronomistic History corresponds to the relationship of books in the MT. Central to Noth's hypothesis was the conclusion that there was no direct literary relationship between Exodus and Deuteronomy, at least one that could be attributed to the same author. For Noth this meant that there was no Deuteronomistic literature in the Tetrateuch. In reaching this conclusion Noth followed de Wette in accounting for the literary repetition in the Torah as a reinterpretation of the older account in Exodus in the later book of Deuteronomy.

Noth's hypothesis is very influential in the contemporary interpretation of Exodus, and I employ his terminology throughout the commentary, especially with regard to the term "Deuteronomistic History," to describe the literary composition that embraced Deuteronomy and the Former Prophets. But I do not follow Noth's strict literary separation between Exodus and Deuteronomy. In the commentary I explore a closer literary relationship between Exodus and Deuteronomy, indicating the presence of the same or at least closely related authors in the two books. In many cases I follow the lead of recent interpreters, who attribute the composition of Exodus to an author who is writing after the composition of Deuteronomy. In the commentary I explore Deuteronomistic themes throughout Exodus, including the call of Moses (Exodus 3), the festival of Passover or *Maṣṣôt* (chap. 13), the revelation of God on the mountain (chaps. 19–24), and the story of the golden calf (chap. 32).

The departure from Noth's hypothesis of restricting Deuteronomistic literature from the Tetrateuch follows the lead of recent interpretations. H. H. Schmid identified broad similarity in language, style, and literary forms between Exodus and Deuteronomy, concluding that each book reflected the influence of the prophetic tradition, especially evident in the use of Deuteronomistic language.[30] R. Rendtorff focused more narrowly on similar phrases that related Exodus and Deuteronomy, such as the divine promise of land.[31] E. Blum fashioned the new literary insights of Rendtorff into the hypothesis that Exodus must be more closely related in composition to Deuteronomy, identifying the books of Exodus and Deuteronomy as part of a broader *D Komposition (KD)*.[32]

30. H. H. Schmid, *Der sogenannte Jahwist: Beobachtungen und Fragen zur Pentateuchforschung* (Zurich: Theologischer Verlag, 1976).

31. R. Rendtorff, *The Problem of the Process of Transmission in the Pentateuch* (trans. J. J. Scullion; JSOTSup 89; Sheffield: Sheffield Academic Press, 1990); idem, "The 'Yahwist' as Theologian? The Dilemma of Pentateuchal Criticism," *JSOT* 3 (1977): 2-9.

32. E. Blum, *Die Komposition der Vätergeschichte* (WMANT 57; Neukirchen-Vluyn: Neukirchener Verlag, 1984); idem, *Studien zur Komposition des Pentateuch* (BZAW 189; Berlin: de Gruyter, 1990).

Blenkinsopp echoes many of the conclusions of Blum, employing instead the term "Deuteronomistic corpus."[33]

Yet Van Seters cautions that the similarity in language between Exodus and Deuteronomy should not overshadow clear literary differences. A central difference, according to him, is the identity of the ancestors. In Deuteronomy the ancestors are often the generation of the exodus, while in Exodus they are the patriarchs Abraham, Isaac, and Jacob. The differences between the books provide the basis for Van Seters to advocate a modified version of Noth's theory of the Tetrateuch, in which Genesis–Numbers is judged to be a later composition than Deuteronomy. Van Seters identifies the author as the exilic Yahwist historian, who reinterprets Deuteronomy in Genesis–Numbers, providing a new history of origins.[34] Otto represents a distinctive redaction-critical model of composition. He judges Van Seters's identification of a single post-Deuteronomistic historian to be too simple a hypothesis to account for the composition of Exodus or the Tetrateuch as a whole. He proposes, instead, multiple authors in the composition of Exodus, all of whom are post-Deuteronomistic and post-Priestly authors, whom he identifies as the hexateuchal and the pentateuchal redactors.[35] The theories of composition indicate the growing trend to date the composition of Exodus to the exilic and postexilic periods.

Exodus and the Former Prophets

Interpreters have suspected a literary relationship between Exodus and the Former Prophets from the outset of the modern historical-critical period of interpretation. Already in the *Theologico-Political Treatise*, B. de Spinoza concluded that the Pentateuch was part of a larger history, extending through Joshua, Judges, Samuel, and Kings.[36] The evidence for Spinoza was the connecting phrases between books: "as soon as he [the author] has related the life of Moses, the historian thus passes on to the story of Joshua: 'And it came to pass after Moses the servant of the Lord was dead, that God spoke to Joshua,' and so, in the same way, after the death of Joshua was concluded, he passes with identi-

---

33. Blenkinsopp, *Pentateuch*, e.g., 114.

34. J. Van Seters, *Prologue to History: The Yahwist as Historian in Genesis* (Louisville: Westminster John Knox, 1992); idem, *Life of Moses*, e.g., 47, 309, 457-68.

35. Otto, *Deuteronomium im Pentateuch*, 1-11.

36. Benedict de Spinoza, *A Theologico-Political Treatise Containing Certain Discussions Wherein Is Set Forth That Freedom of Thought and Speech Not Only May, Without Prejudice to Piety and the Public Peace, Be Granted; But Also May Not, Without Danger to Piety and the Public Peace, Be Withheld* (trans. R. H. M. Elwes; New York: Dover, 1951), 7. For discussion of Spinoza's use of Scripture see H.-J. Kraus, *Geschichte der historisch-kritischen Erforschung des Alten Testaments* (3rd ed.; Neukirchen-Vluyn: Neukirchener Verlag, 1982), 61-65.

cally the same transition and connection to the history of the Judges." Spinoza suspected Ezra (Ezra 7:10) to be the author of this history, which spans from Genesis through Kings. Contradiction between similar accounts in the histories of Chronicles and Genesis–Kings led Spinoza to conclude further that Ezra did not actually write the histories, but compiled them.[37]

The conclusions of Spinoza remain influential to subsequent interpreters, while also undergoing modification. Source critics like J. Wellhausen narrowed the focus from the entire corpus of the Former Prophets to the book of Joshua in tracing the literary connections to Exodus. Wellhausen came to the more restricted conclusion that Genesis–Joshua formed a literary corpus, which he described as a Hexateuch.[38] The Hexateuch narrated the history of the origin of Israel from the promise of land to the ancestors (Genesis) to its fulfillment in the conquest of the land (Joshua). The hypothesis of a Hexateuch remains influential for interpreting the relationship of Exodus to the Former Prophets.[39]

But as the work of Spinoza already indicated, the separation of Joshua from the remaining books of the Former Prophets poses a literary problem. The covenantal ceremonies at the close of Joshua (chaps. 23–24) indicate a significant transition in the history of Israel, but the story continues into Judges, creating literary relationships between Exodus and the larger corpus of the Former Prophets. A notable example is the notice of the death of a generation in Exodus (1:6) and in Judges (2:8-10). T. C. Vriezen first noted the strategic role of this repetition in the larger design of Genesis–2 Kings. His insight has been expanded by Van Seters, Blum, and K. Schmid.

D. N. Freedman introduced the literary category of a Primary History, an Enneateuch, consisting of the nine books from Genesis through Kings, to account for the literary relationships from the promise of land to the ancestors (Genesis) through the loss of the land in the exile (2 Kings). This literary evaluation echoes to some extent the insight of Spinoza.[40] Although interpreters debate the literary process by which the books of the Enneateuch were formed, there is a growing tendency to interpret Exodus within this large literary con-

---

37. *Treatise,* 133-39.

38. J. Wellhausen, *Die Composition des Hexateuch und der historischen Bücher des Alten Testaments* (3rd ed.; Berlin: Georg Reimer, 1899).

39. See, e.g., G. von Rad, "The Form-Critical Problem of the Hexateuch," in *The Problem of the Hexateuch and Other Essays* (trans. E. W. Trueman Dicken; New York: McGraw-Hill, 1966), 1-78; O. Eissfeldt, *The Old Testament: An Introduction* (trans. P. R. Ackroyd; New York: Harper & Row, 1965).

40. D. N. Freedman, "Pentateuch," *IDB* 3:711-27; idem, "Canon of the OT," *IDBSup,* 130-36; idem, *The Nine Commandments: Uncovering a Hidden Pattern of Crime and Punishment in the Hebrew Bible* (New York: Doubleday, 2000).

text. Blenkinsopp describes the literary boundaries of the Deuteronomistic corpus as extending from Genesis through 2 Kings.[41] Van Seters interprets an exilic Yahwist as combining the Tetrateuch with the Deuteronomistic History, which also requires Genesis–2 Kings to be read as a broad history by the time of the exilic period.[42] R. E. Friedman, too, relates the Enneateuch as a history, which for him takes shape already in the monarchical period.[43] E. Aurelius has examined the literary relationship between Exod 19:3b-8 and 2 Kgs 18:12, exploring the literary development of the material in the exilic period.[44] These few examples indicate that there is debate among current interpreters concerning the literary process that created an Enneateuch. At the very least the debate encourages an exploration of the literary relationship between Exodus and the Deuteronomistic History.

Exodus and Genesis

Modern interpreters of the Pentateuch have regularly raised questions about the relationship of Genesis and Exodus. Wellhausen noted the problems of narrative unity and style that arise from a comparison of Genesis and Exodus, not to mention the abrupt transition between the two books from family stories to a national epic.[45] But the tendency of modern interpreters has been to merge the story of the ancestors and the exodus into a single narrative by the same author(s). As a result the abrupt transition between the two books, as well as the changes in style, did not become the focus of interpretation. This judgment has continued even after the research of K. Galling identified the story of the ancestors and the exodus as separate traditions of election, which were combined later into their present literary form.[46] A. de Pury's subsequent study of the book of Hosea adds further support to the research of Galling. He concluded that the references to Jacob and to the exodus remain distinct in the formation of the book of Hosea, with the prophet using the exodus tradition to evaluate critically the Jacob tradition of origin.[47]

---

41. Blenkinsopp, *Pentateuch.*

42. Van Seters, *Prologue to History;* idem, *Life of Moses.*

43. R. E. Friedman, *The Hidden Book in the Bible* (San Francisco: HarperCollins, 1998).

44. E. Aurelius, *Zukunft jenseits des Gerichts: Eine redaktionsgeschichtliche Studie zum Enneateuch* (BZAW 319; Berlin: de Gruyter, 2003).

45. Wellhausen, *Composition,* 61 *et passim.*

46. K. Galling, *Die Erwählungstraditionen Israels* (BZAW 48; Giessen: de Gruyter, 1928).

47. A. de Pury, "Le cycle de Jacob comme légende autonome des origins d'Israël," in *Congress Volume: Leuven 1989* (ed. J. A. Emerton; VTSup 43; Leiden: Brill, 1991), 78-96; idem, "Osée et ses implications pour le débat actuel sur le Pentateuque," in *Le Pentateuque: Débats et recherches* (ed. P. Haudebert; LD 151; Paris: Cerf, 1992), 175-207.

The literary relationship between Genesis and Exodus has undergone further interpretation in recent studies on the Pentateuch. Following the lead of F. V. Winnett,[48] Van Seters accentuated the literary separation between Genesis and Exodus by examining the references to the ancestors in Deuteronomy, the Deuteronomistic History, Ezekiel, and Jeremiah.[49] He argued that the earliest references to the ancestors in Deuteronomy are to the exodus generation, not the patriarchal heroes Abraham, Isaac, and Jacob. He also noted that the earliest reference to the patriarch Abraham in the prophetic corpus is in the exilic writing of Ezekiel and Second Isaiah. He concluded that the merging of the generation of the exodus and the patriarchal ancestors in Genesis was a literary innovation in the exilic period by a Yahwist historian, indicating the late development of history writing in ancient Israel.

Rendtorff reinforced the conclusion of Van Seters, working in the opposite direction, from Genesis to Exodus. Rendtorff noted that the theme of promise of land to the ancestors was central to the formation of Genesis, but nearly absent from Exodus, where it is clustered at the outset, mainly in the commission of Moses: three times in the Priestly (P) History (Exod 2:24; 6:3, 8), four times in the Yahwistic (J) History (3:6, 15, 16; 4:5), with only two additional references later in the book (32:13; 33:1). He too concluded that the identification of the divine promise to the patriarchal ancestors, Abraham, Isaac, and Jacob, with the exodus generation was a late literary development. For Rendtorff the literary process was the work of a Deuteronomistic editor, who sought to relate the previously separate literary traditions ("complexes") of the patriarchs in Genesis with the story of the exodus.[50]

The insights of Van Seters and Rendtorff raise the question of whether the separation of the books of Genesis and Exodus in the LXX may reflect more than a minor textual difference and, instead, provide a window into a larger literary development in the formation of the Pentateuch. In this case the joining of Genesis and Exodus is at least as significant a literary problem in the formation of the Pentateuch as the relationship between Deuteronomy and Exodus–Numbers.

More recent interpreters have probed this question, arguing that the merging of Genesis and Exodus is the most significant literary development in the formation of the Pentateuch, overshadowing the problem of the relationship between Exodus and Deuteronomy that was so pivotal to Noth. T. Römer developed the thesis of Van Seters in a study of the theme of the ancestors in

---

48. F. V. Winnett, *The Mosaic Tradition* (Near and Middle East Series 1; Toronto: University of Toronto Press, 1949).

49. J. Van Seters, "Confessional Reformulation in the Exilic Period," *VT* 22 (1972): 448-59; more recently, idem, *Prologue to History,* 215-76.

50. Rendtorff, *Problem.*

Deuteronomy and related literature.[51] He extended the conclusion of Van Seters, arguing that the ancestor stories in Genesis were combined with the story of Moses only in the P History, not in the pre-P Yahwist, as Van Seters had concluded. K. Schmid has extended the argument, concluding that the ancestor stories in Genesis and the story of liberation by Moses must be interpreted as two distinct origin traditions of ancient Israel, both of which are centered on the promise of land.[52] Schmid follows Römer, placing the combination of the distinct accounts of origin in the postexilic period as the product of a post-P writer. The hypothesis has prompted Blum to restrict the literary boundaries of pre-P literature (designated KD) to Exodus–2 Kings, thus separating Genesis from Exodus until the P composition (designated KP).[53]

Origin traditions, writes F. V. Greifenhagen, recount the ethnogenesis of the Israelite people. Such traditions define the boundaries of group identity by employing selective perception and memory, fashioning aspects of historical experience into a founding mythology.[54] The ancestor stories in Genesis locate the origin of the Israelites in Babylon and present an indigenous account of land possession through peaceful negotiation. The story of Moses in Exodus, by contrast, locates the origin of the Israelites in Egypt. It emphasizes the formation of the people outside the land of promise, requiring holy war and conquest for the fulfillment of the promise of land possession. The combination of the two accounts results in a master narrative, in which the origin tradition of the ancestors in Babylon and the Moses tradition about Egyptian origins become episodes in the story of salvation history. This emerging line of research raises new questions about the relationship of Genesis and Exodus that I will explore in the commentary, especially whether the two traditions of origin are related before the P History (see below, "Authors").

51. T. Römer, *Israels Väter: Untersuchungen zur Väterthematik im Deuteronomium und in der deuteronomistischen Tradition* (OBO 99; Göttingen: Vandenhoeck & Ruprecht, 1990).

52. K. Schmid, *Erzväter und Exodus: Untersuchungen zur doppelten Begründung der Ursprünge Israels innerhalb der Geschichtsbücher des Alten Testaments* (WMANT 81; Neukirchen-Vluyn: Neukirchener Verlag, 1999). See also J. C. Gertz, *Tradition und Redaktion in der Exoduserzählung: Untersuchungen zur Endredaktion des Pentateuch* (Göttingen: Vandenhoeck & Ruprecht, 2000).

53. E. Blum, "Die literarische Verbindung von Erzvätern und Exodus: Ein Gespräch mit neueren Endredaktionshypothesen," in *Abschied vom Jahwisten: Die Komposition des Hexateuch in der jüngsten Diskussion* (ed. K. Schimd, J. C. Gertz, and M. Witte; BZAW 315; Berlin: de Gruyter, 2002), 119-56.

54. F. V. Greifenhagen, *Egypt on the Pentateuch's Ideological Map: Constructing Biblical Israel's Identity* (JSOTSup 361; Sheffield: Sheffield Academic Press, 2002), 256-60.

Ancient History Writing and Exodus

The overview of the literary context indicates that Exodus is part of a larger story, which begins broadly with the creation of the world before narrowing to the family stories of the ancestors in Genesis. The family stories in Genesis acquire a national perspective in the life of Moses in Exodus–Deuteronomy, which continues into the story of Israel's life in the land in the Deuteronomistic History. The interweaving of a divine creation, ancestral legends, epic accounts of salvation, and the chronicles of different kings results in a genre of literature that is difficult to describe. In the commentary I have characterized the book of Exodus as salvation history — a canonical story of Israel's divine election. But scholars have long since debated its proper description. Van Seters notes that it is not myth in the narrow understanding of the term, since the divine actions are confined for the most part to this world, rather than taking place in heaven.[55] But, as T. L. Thompson has indicated, salvation history does not conform well to the genre of history writing, at least in the modern sense of the term, where sources are critically evaluated by a strict rational standard in the recounting of past events.[56] Thus interpreters debate whether salvation history is an example of ancient history writing.

The Greek word *historia* means "inquiry" into the past as opposed to the mere retelling of accepted tales.[57] *Historia* has entered the modern study of history in several forms that must be distinguished in order to evaluate the genre of salvation history as ancient history writing. The word "historiography" describes a broad category of literature whose aim is to address current or past events or people. Van Seters notes that the term could potentially include many genres of literature, including tales, stories, prophetic oracles, and poems.[58] The result is that most books of the Hebrew Bible, including Exodus, fall under the umbrella of historiography. But such a broad definition is not sufficiently narrow to separate out "history as a form of the narration of past events."[59] It is the

55. See the discussion of J. Van Seters, "Myth and History: The Problem of Origins and Tradition and History: History as National Tradition," in *Histoire et conscience historique dans les civilisations du Proche-Orient Ancien* (ed. A. de Pury; Cahiers du Centre d'Études du Proche-Orient Ancien 5; Leuven: Peeters, 1989), 49-74; K. L. Sparks, "The Problem of Myth in Ancient Historiography," in *Rethinking the Foundations: Historiography in the Ancient World and in the Bible: Essays in Honour of John Van Seters* (ed. S. L. McKenzie and T. Römer; BZAW 294; Berlin: de Gruyter, 2000), 269-80.

56. Thompson, "Historiography (Israelite)," *ABD* 3:206.

57. M. I. Finley, "Introduction," *Thucydides: History of the Peloponnesian War* (Penguin Classics; London: Penguin, 1972), 14.

58. J. Van Seters, *In Search of History: Historiography in the Ancient World and the Origins of Biblical History* (New Haven: Yale University Press, 1983), 2.

59. Ibid., 1.

more narrow definition of ancient history writing that is our concern in the commentary, namely a genre of literature in which writers sought to explain the causes of their present circumstances by recounting the past. Van Seters encapsulates the more narrow concern of ancient history writing with the definition of J. Huizinga: "History is the intellectual form in which a civilization renders account to itself of its past."[60] Van Seters stresses that history writing is a distinct intellectual form of composition, aimed at explaining the causes of events, especially as they influence corporate or national identity.[61]

D. Edelman has sharpened the definition of ancient history writing in three ways. First, it is a narrative genre of current or past events and people, based on sources of information. Second, history writing creates meaning by attempting to answer the question, Why? How has the current situation of a people evolved? Third, history writing is concerned with the causes behind events. Thus there is a degree of critical evaluation in ancient history writing, both in the use of sources and in the quest to discover causation between events. The critical orientation separates the genre of history writing from mere antiquarian literature, in which authors simply collect and preserve past tradition. But, according to Edelman, ancient history writing must also be contrasted at least in degree to modern history writing.[62] The difference between ancient and modern history writing, she concludes, is the application or standard of critical evaluation. Unlike modern historians, ancient history writers allow for a wide range of sources to recount the past, including tales and oral reports. They also allow for both divine and human causation to account for events.[63] Salvation history incorporates many of the characteristics of ancient history writing.

The civilizations of the ancient Near East recounted their past in many

---

60. J. Huizinga, "A Definition of the Concept of History," in *Philosophy and History: Essays Presented to Ernst Cassirer* (ed. R. Klibansky and H. J. Paton; Oxford: Clarendon, 1936), 1-10. For critical evaluation of Huizinga see M. Brettler, *The Creation of History in Ancient Israel* (London: Routledge, 1995), 11; L. L. Grabbe, "Who Were the First Real Historians? On the Origins of Critical Historiography," in *Did Moses Speak Attic? Jewish Historiography and Scripture in the Hellenistic Period* (ed. L. L. Grabbe; JSOTSup 317; ESHM 3; Sheffield: Sheffield Academic Press, 2001), 156-81.

61. Van Seters, *In Search of History,* 2-5. B. Halpern (*The First Historians: The Hebrew Bible and History* [San Francisco: Harper & Row, 1988]) follows many aspects of Van Seters's definition. He accentuates the role of explanation, however, to include the author's intent in his definition of history writing (p. 8): "If the author . . . attempts knowingly to perpetrate on the readers a fraudulent reconstruction contradicted or unsupported by evidence, then the author is not engaged in writing history."

62. For critical discussion see Grabbe, "Who Were the First Real Historians?"

63. D. Edelman, "Clio's Dilemma: The Changing Face of History-Writing," in *Congress Volume: Oslo 1998* (ed. A. Lemaire and M. Sæbø; VTSup 80; Leiden: Brill, 2000), 247-55.

different ways. Van Seters notes a wide variety of forms, including royal inscriptions, king lists, omens, chronicles, historical epics celebrating victory in
war, annals, and dedication and commemorative inscriptions.[64] A. Kuhrt also
includes the additional genres of annals of military achievements and autobiog-
raphy as a means of social explanation, while also stressing the importance of
chronicles, especially the Babylonian Chronicles from the mid-eighth century
B.C.E. and later.[65] Many of these forms of literature appear in the Hebrew Bible,
but they do not provide an adequate model for the complex and extended narrative of salvation history, of which the book of Exodus is a part.

The Greeks provide a closer analogy to ancient Israelite history writing.
The earliest Greek writing is epic poetry from the ninth or eighth century B.C.E.
like Homer's *Iliad* and *Odyssey*. These epics are rooted in national pride, celebrating the honor and glory of national heroes. Greek prose writing emerged in
the sixth century B.C.E. with the Ionians. Anaximander of Miletus made a map
of the world in the mid-sixth century, accompanied with the relevant geographical information. Hecataeus of Miletus followed Anaximander, writing
first his *Genealogies*, an account of family histories, followed by *Periegesis*, a
travelogue of the lands of the world with ethnographic information.

The sixth-century prose tradition of geography and ethnography by the
early Greek logographers blossomed into the historiography of Herodotus a
century later.[66] M. Hadas notes the subjugation of the Ionians to the Persians as
an important cause for the transition from national epic to history writing:
"Epic, of which national pride is the lifeblood, could not survive in a subject
people." Instead: "The Ionians could only look to the remote past for their
heroes." As a result, Hadas concludes: "History . . . was looked to for the kind of
record of the past which epic had provided."[67]

Greek history writing included inherited traditions and legends, often organized and rationalized from a critical perspective. The ancient historians
sought to assess the causes of past actions and the responsibility for the present
state of affairs.[68] Herodotus sought to record the great deeds of the past and,
more particularly, to assess the causes of the wars between the Greeks and the
Persians.[69] His is a tragic history.[70] Whether tragedy or not, the content of an-

---

64. Van Seters, *In Search of History*, 55-208.

65. A. Kuhrt, "Israelite and Near Eastern Historiography," in *Congress Volume: Oslo 1998*,
ed. Lemaire and Sæbø, 257-79.

66. For discussion of the early Greek logographers see Van Seters, *In Search of History*, 9-18.

67. M. Hadas, *A History of Greek Literature* (New York: Columbia University Press, 1950),
65 *et passim*.

68. D. Lateiner, "Historiography (Greco-Roman)," *ABD* 3:212-19.

69. J. Romm, *Herodotus* (New Haven: Yale University Press, 1998).

70. Hadas, *History of Greek Literature*, 111-29.

cient history created images for transmission as tradition, forming a national or corporate identity. As E. Shils writes: "The promotion of a belief in continuity and identity with the national past, reverence for national heroes, the commemoration of founding events . . . were among the tasks laid on the teaching of national history."[71] Early Greek history writing reflects this aim. It sought to recount the causes of past events and institutions in order to provide identity by explaining present behavior, religious practice, and social circumstances.[72]

Salvation history, like early Greek history writing, is written in prose rather than poetry. It demonstrates an interest in antiquarian customs, but its organization, ethnographic interest, and development of themes go beyond the genre of antiquarian literature. The Pentateuch is especially concerned with the remote past, including the creation of the world (Genesis 1–11), the origin of the first ancestors from Babylon (Genesis 12–50), and the origin of the Israelite nation from Egypt (Exodus–Deuteronomy). The history of the kingdoms in the Former Prophets (Joshua–2 Kings) turns its attention to the more recent past. As is the case with early Greek history writing, the literature includes local records, epic lore, temple law, now organized around genealogy, chronology, and travelogue.

The exact relationship between ancient Israelite and Greek history writing is unclear because of debate surrounding the date of the earliest writing of history in ancient Israel. Biblical scholars have dated the pentateuchal narrative anywhere from the tenth to the second century B.C.E.[73] The earlier dates would place Israelite history writing significantly before the rise of Greek prose, while the later dates suggest a closer relationship with the development of Greek history writing. I assume a moderate date for the emergence of Israelite history writing, perhaps the late monarchical period at the earliest, but the most significant development occurs in the exilic and postexilic periods under Neo-Babylonian and especially Persian rule, not in the Hellenistic period, nor in the early monarchical period. The dating suggests a similar cultural environment for the emergence of Greek and Israelite history writing, as each group reacts to the new world order of Persian rule.[74] But a more specific literary influence is difficult to confirm.[75]

71. E. Shils, *Tradition* (Chicago: University of Chicago Press, 1981), 59. See also S. Grosby, *Biblical Ideas of Nationality Ancient and Modern* (Winona Lake, Ind.: Eisenbrauns, 2002).

72. Van Seters, *In Search of History*, 1-54; idem, "Myth and History."

73. Von Rad ("The Beginnings of Historical Writing in Ancient Israel," in *Problem of the Hexateuch*, 166-204, esp. 192-96) entertained a 10th-century date for the rise of history writing in ancient Israel, while L. P. Lemche ("The Old Testament — A Hellenistic Book?" in *Did Moses Speak Attic?* 287-318 = *SJOT* 7 [1993]: 163-93) advocates a 2nd-century date.

74. This is the view of A. Momigliano, "Persian Historiography, Greek Historiography, and Jewish Historiography," in *The Classical Foundations of Modern Historiography* (Sather Classical Lectures 54; Berkeley: University of California Press, 1990), 5-28.

75. For more detailed comparisons in literary images and language see J. P. Brown, *Israel and Hellas* (BZAW 231; Berlin: de Gruyter, 1995); in literary design and thematic development

A date for the rise of ancient Israelite history writing in the exilic and postexilic periods suggests that, like its Greek counterpart, Israelite history writing grew during a time of social subjugation under Neo-Babylonian and Persian rule. The story of salvation history in the Pentateuch does not celebrate national heroes or exhibit national pride. Rather, like early Greek histories, the Pentateuch looks to the past for heroes, while national pride is only a future hope when the Israelites enter the promised land of Canaan. Yet the similarities in outlook between Greek and Israelite history writing must not obscure important differences. A summary of their contrasts will provide focus for interpreting Exodus.

Greek history writing portrayed a critical spirit toward mythology and the epic legends of the gods. The role of gods in human affairs was not completely eliminated. Yet the critical spirit meant that the actions of the gods were not the central subject of history, because they did not provide reliable evidence for the causes of events. The concern with the reliability of evidence limited the focus of Greek historians. They did not trace history to the origin of the world, but examined instead the causes of more recent events.[76] Thus Herodotus avoids the story of the origin of the world, because it cannot be verified. He also states his intent to avoid investigating the business of the gods (*Hist.* 2.3.2; 2.65.2). The reason is that there is no way to distinguish true from false (2.23).[77] Thucydides is even more restrictive in probing the past.[78]

Ancient Israelite history writing shares the Greek critical spirit in evaluating past tradition. The actions of heroes like Moses are often mixed in motive. But the Israelite historians do not eliminate the action of God in human affairs as a reliable source of evidence. A. Momigliano concludes that history and religion become one for ancient Israelite historians. Their aim is to preserve a "truthful record of the events in which God showed his presence."[79] Thus, rather than a distinct enterprise from mythology, history becomes a religious duty for the biblical authors. As a consequence the writing of the past becomes a story of God's history of salvation toward the Israelites. The merging of history and reli-

see Van Seters, *In Search of History;* F. A. J. Nelson, *The Tragedy in History: Herodotus and the Deuteronomistic History* (JSOTSup 251; Sheffield: Sheffield Academic Press, 1997); Blenkinsopp, *Pentateuch;* R. N. Whybray, *The Making of the Pentateuch: A Methodological Study* (JSOTSup 53; Sheffield: Sheffield Academic Press, 1987), 221-42; and in editing see S. Mandell and D. N. Freedman, *The Relationship between Herodotus' History and Primary History* (USFSHJ 60; Atlanta: Scholars Press, 1993).

76. Momigliano, "Persian Historiography."

77. D. Lateiner, *The Historical Method of Herodotus* (Toronto: University of Toronto Press, 1989), 64-67.

78. A. Momigliano, "The Herodotean and the Thucydidean Tradition," in *Classical Foundations,* 29-53.

79. Momigliano, "Persian Historiography," 19-20.

gion into a salvation history separates ancient Israelite history writing from its Greek counterpart. The difference is crucial for interpreting Exodus.

Edelman states the difference between ancient and modern history writing as residing in the role of critical thinking.[80] Ancient history writers surpassed mere antiquarian interests, because they introduced a critical spirit in their use of sources and in the evaluation of causality. But, she adds, they differed from modern historians precisely in the same characteristic: in the application and standard of critical thinking with regard to sources and causation. The characterization of ancient Israelite history writing as salvation history underscores how far removed Exodus is from modern history writing, and even more importantly from ancient history writing. It shares aspects of the genre of ancient history writing, but as Momigliano concludes it also departs from the genre in its focus on divine causality. Herodotus wrote about the great and wonderful deeds of humans, including Greeks and barbarians (*Hist.* 1.1). The genre of salvation history alerts us to the insight that Yahweh is the central character throughout salvation history. Exodus is a story of Yahweh and his deeds of salvation, carried out by Moses, his servant. The personality of the most important hero in Exodus, Moses, is nearly absorbed into the Deity, when divine holiness radiates through his face after the revelation of law (Exod 34:29-35). The departure of salvation history from the more critical perspective of Greek historiography has prompted Römer to suggest the phrase "narrative history" to describe the story of salvation history. He describes narrative history as "the organization of material in a chronologically sequential order and the focusing of the content into a single coherent story, albeit with subplot."[81]

History and Exodus

A central question in the modern interpretation of Exodus concerns the historical background to the narrated events. Scholars have sought to determine whether there is a historical event of salvation from Egypt that has prompted the elaborate narrative of Exodus. The question concerning historical background has influenced the way in which Exodus has been interpreted, especially in the modern historical-critical period. A review of this important question will provide both methodological and theological focus for the commentary, illustrating

80. Edelman, "Clio's Dilemma," 253-55.
81. T. Römer, *The So-Called Deuteronomistic History: A Sociological, Historical and Literary Introduction* (London: T. & T. Clark, 2005), 37. The quotation of "narrative history" is from L. Stone, "The Revival of Narrative: Reflections on a New Old History," *Past and Present* 85 (1979): 3.

further that ancient history writing in general and salvation history in particular are not the same as modern history writing.

Evaluating the exodus from Egypt as history must begin with the witness of the biblical writers themselves. The biblical writers certainly wish to anchor the exodus from Egypt firmly in history. They date the event to the year 2666 (Exod 12:40-41) from the creation of the world, or year 1 (Gen 1:26-27). The construction of the tabernacle takes place in the year 2667 (Exod 40:1-2, 17). Biblical writers state further that the Israelite period of enslavement is 430 years (Exod 12:40-41), making their arrival in Egypt the year 2236 (Gen 47:9). Jacob and his family settle in a specific land within Egypt, Goshen (Gen 46:28; Exod 8:22; 9:26), also known as the "land of Rameses" (Gen 47:11). When the Israelites' guest status in Egypt turned into slavery, the biblical writers of the MT identify the cities of Pithom and Rameses (Exod 1:11; the LXX adds the city of On) as the product of their slave labor. During this period of time the Israelite population grows from the original family of Jacob to a nation of six hundred thousand men (Exod 12:37), making the total number of those leaving Egypt (including women and children) approximately two to three million persons, not counting the mixed multitude that accompanied the people upon their leaving Egypt (12:38).

The specific dates for the exodus, along with the careful numbering of the people, encourage a historical interpretation of the story. But the dates, the vague references to geography, and the unrealistic number of the group indicate that Exodus is not history. Goshen has not been clearly identified in the Delta region of Egypt.[82] Two to three million people in the Sinai desert would overwhelm the fragile environment. It is also impossible to interpret the biblical chronology as literal history or, for that matter, to translate the chronology of the biblical writers into the general Western system of dating (B.C.E. [Before the Common Era] and C.E. [the Common Era]. 1 Kings 6:1 provides some help. It states that the fourth year of King Solomon's reign was the 480th year after Israel left Egypt. The traditional Western dates for the reign of Solomon are approximately 960-922 B.C.E., making the fourth year of his reign 956 B.C.E. and the year of the exodus 1436 B.C.E. This chronology would place the Israelite exodus from Egypt under the 18th Dynasty of Egyptian rule, specifically during the reign of Thutmose III (1490-1436 B.C.E.). This date would associate the Israelite exodus with the Amorite migration into the ancient Near East described in Babylonian texts. But such an ethnic association conflicts with the biblical writ-

---

82. J. Van Seters, "The Geography of the Exodus," in *The Land That I Will Show You: Essays on the History and Archaeology of the Ancient Near East in Honour of J. Maxwell Miller* (ed. J. A. Dearman and M. P. Graham; JSOTSup 343; Sheffield: Sheffield Academic Press, 2001), 255-76; C. Meyers, *Exodus* (NCBC; Cambridge: Cambridge University Press, 2005), 5-7.

ers, who contrast themselves with Amorites (Gen 10:16; Numbers 21),[83] while the cities attributed to their construction are 19th Dynasty sites.

Other biblical chronologies yield different dates for the exodus, further complicating the quest for history. Genesis 15:13 states that Israel's time in Egypt was 400 years, not 430 years. Genesis 15:16 shortens their time in Egypt even further to three generations. The biblical system of dating may simply be formed for theological purposes. The 2,666 years from creation to the exodus is two-thirds of 4,000, which may be considered the period of time in a "world epoch." Blenkinsopp has argued that the fulfillment of this world epoch is the rededication of the temple under the Maccabees in 164 B.C.E.[84]

Exodus does not qualify as history. Yet the tradition that Yahweh saved Israel out of the land of Egypt has deep roots in the Hebrew Bible. Many scholars have argued that the two hymns in Exodus 15, the Song of the Sea in vv. 1-18 and the Song of Miriam in v. 21, are instances of ancient poetry. If this is so, then Exodus itself contains some of the oldest references to salvation as a defeat of the Egyptians. The prophet Hosea, whose career took place in the second half of the eighth century B.C.E., provides the earliest identification of Yahweh with Egypt outside the Pentateuch. F. I. Andersen and D. N. Freedman also see evidence of the exodus tradition in the book of Amos (Amos 3:1; 9:7), a contemporary of the prophet Hosea.[85] Hosea states that Egypt is the place of origin for Israel (Hos 2:15; 11:1), as well as the place of identity for Yahweh ("I am Yahweh your God from the land of Egypt"; Hos 12:9; 13:4). But the prophet is not familiar with the exodus as an event attached to the wilderness wandering tradition, in which Israel journeys for forty years through the desert as one stage in their history of salvation. In the six references to the wilderness in Hosea (Hos 2:3, 14-15; 9:10; 13:5, 15), the prophet uses the wilderness to signify Israel's loss of land. He does not refer to a past pilgrimage through the desert from Egypt to Canaan.[86]

Hosea prophesied to the northern kingdom of Israel, focusing specifically on the ritual practices of the Bethel cult (Hos 4:17; 12:2-6). The Bethel cult is also the setting for the oracles of the prophet Amos. This setting leads to the conclusion that the tradition of associating Yahweh with Egypt may have been centered in the worship practices of the northern kingdom of Israel, thus providing a contrast to worship practices in the southern temple of Jerusalem, where salvation was envisioned as Yahweh's enthronement on Mount Zion. A historical exodus

---

83. See J. Van Seters, "The Terms 'Amorite' and 'Hittite' in the Old Testament," *VT* 22 (1972): 64-81.

84. Blenkinsopp, *Pentateuch*, 47-50; see also Schmid, *Erzväter und Exodus*, 20-21.

85. F. I. Andersen and D. N. Freedman, *Amos* (AB 24A; New York: Doubleday, 1989), esp. the introduction, pp. 3-149.

86. T. B. Dozeman, "Hosea and the Wilderness Wandering Tradition," in *Rethinking the Foundations*, ed. McKenzie and Römer, 55-70.

from Egypt, however, cannot be determined from either the hymns in Exodus 15 or from the oracles of the prophet Hosea. The references to the exodus in Hosea suggest that the story of salvation history as recounted in Exodus had not yet been written, since it relates Israel's deliverance from Egypt with their subsequent journey through the wilderness, an event unknown to the prophet Hosea. The hymns in Exodus 15 and the book of Hosea do indicate that the tradition of salvation as a liberation from Egyptian rule is formative in the religious practice of Israel during the monarchical period.

Research on the history of an Israelite exodus from Egypt has branched out from the book of Exodus to include the broader study of archaeology and of ancient Near Eastern literature. There is no direct evidence that the Israelites dwelt in Egypt or that they escaped from slave labor. Scholars cite indirect evidence, however, that such an event might have been possible, although on a much smaller scale than the biblical story. The indirect evidence also lowers the dating by several centuries from the biblical chronology, since it points to the 19th rather than the 18th Dynasty of Egyptian rule. Reference to the city of Rameses (Exod 1:11) indicates the capital of Ramesses II (1290-1224 B.C.E.), the second pharaoh of Egypt during the 19th Dynasty. The Egyptian Papyrus Leiden 348 refers to the building of Piramesse and to the slave laborers, described as *'Apiru* — a term some scholars associate with the word "Hebrew."[87] The papyrus reads, "Distribute grain rations to the soldiers and to the *'Apiru* who transport stones to the great pylon of Rameses." Moreover, the Egyptian Papyri Anastasi provides insight into border crossings, migrations, and even runaway slaves during the thirteenth century B.C.E.[88]

The most interesting Egyptian evidence concerning the origin of Israel and their relationship to Egypt comes from the Merneptah Stele, composed during the fifth year of Merneptah's rule (ca. 1220 B.C.E.). Merneptah is the third pharaoh of the 19th Dynasty. He followed Ramesses II, ruling in 1224-1211 B.C.E. The Merneptah Stele has the oldest reference to Israel in the Egyptian records. In describing his military successes Merneptah writes: "Canaan has been plundered into every sort of woe; Ashkelon has been overcome; Gezer has been captured. Yano'am was made nonexistent; Israel is laid waste, his seed is not."[89] The

---

87. See N. P. Lemche, "Ḥabiru, Ḥapiru," *ABD* 3:6-10.

88. For discussion of the archaeological and literary evidence from Egypt for the exodus see E. S. Frerichs and L. H. Lesko, eds., *Exodus: The Egyptian Evidence* (Winona Lake, Ind.: Eisenbrauns, 1997); J. K. Hoffmeier, *Israel in Egypt: The Evidence for the Authenticity of the Exodus Tradition* (New York: Oxford University Press, 1997). For a review of the sociological evidence on the Shasu tent dwellers see Meyers, *Exodus*, 12–16. For a broad study of the influence of Egypt on Israel see D. B. Redford, *Egypt, Canaan, and Israel in Ancient Times* (Princeton: Princeton University Press, 1992).

89. *ANET*, 376-78.

Egyptian writing indicates that the middle three references (Ashkelon, Gezer, and Yano'am) are cities, and that the term "Israel" refers to a people, not a city or a particular place. The reference to Canaan is also not to a specific city, raising the question of the relationship between the terms "Canaan" and "Israel."[90] The Merneptah Stele indicates that an "Israelite" people could be identified in some way already in the thirteenth century B.C.E. But the evidence also tends to argue against the exodus from Egypt. Israel appears to be an indigenous group within Canaan who were the object of Egyptian conquest. As such they certainly would know firsthand Egyptian oppression. Not only Merneptah but also Ramesses II and Seti I (1305-1290 B.C.E.) made frequent military excursions into Palestine in order to tighten Egyptian control over the area during the 19th Dynasty.[91] But there is no indication that "Israelites" had recently fled Egypt, that a pharaoh died in the encounter, or that the people marched through the desert two to three million strong for an entire generation before their children conquered the land of Canaan.

The story of the defeat of Pharaoh and of his army in the Red Sea is a cultic legend, not history, perhaps associated with Bethel. It speaks to an ongoing political reality in the life of Israel. Egyptian rule loomed large in Israel's life from their earliest years, and it continued throughout their political history, giving the legend of the exodus from Egypt immediacy and continuing religious significance. Moreover, the ancient Israelite writers were also familiar with Egyptian customs and practices. Egyptian language influences the story of Exodus both in small details and in large events. The name "Moses" *(mōšeh),* for example, derives from the Egyptian word *msi,* a common theophoric element in proper names, meaning "son." The word appears on such names as Thut*mose,* "son of Thut," or Ptah*mose,* "son of Ptah." The "bulrush" *(gōme')* in which Moses is placed in Exod 2:3 may derive from the Egyptian word for "papyrus" *(g/kmy).* Even the plagues may be polemical actions against Egyptian gods, including Hapi, the god of the Nile; Osiris, the god of the dead; and Ra, the sun god. The influence of Egyptian culture on ancient Israelite writers may reach back to an experience of oppression in Egypt itself, but it need not.[92]

The reference to Pithom as one of the cities built by the Israelites may

90. So D. N. Freedman, private communication: "We must connect 'Canaan' with 'Israel,' because whatever their differences, to an outsider, a Canaanite and an Israelite would be indistinguishable: with the same physical characteristics and speaking the same language."

91. See the summary by I. Singer, "Egyptians, Canaanites, and Philistines in the Period of the Emergence of Israel," in *From Nomadism to Monarchy: Archaeological and Historical Aspects of Early Israel* (ed. I. Finkelstein and N. Na'aman; Jerusalem: Israel Exploration Society, 1994), 283-338.

92. See the discussion by B. Halpern, "The Exodus and the Israelite Historians," *Eretz Israel* 24 (Avraham Malamat volume; 1993): 89-95 (non-Hebrew section).

provide historical background for dating the composition of the story of the exodus. D. B. Redford noted that the name Pithom does not appear in hieroglyphic writing with the town determinative until after 600 B.C.E. This historical insight would place the author of the exodus in the late exilic period at the earliest.[93]

AUTHORS

The author of Exodus is not explicitly stated. Yet within the book both God and Moses are credited with writing. God writes laws (Exod 24:12), the architectural plans for the tabernacle (31:18), and the tablets containing the Ten Commandments (34:1). Moses writes instruction about holy war (17:14) and laws (24:4; 34:27-28). The song in 15:1-18 is also attributed to him. As a result, tradition has assigned the authorship of Exodus and the entire Pentateuch to Moses. The historical-critical study of the literature in the modern era has clarified that Exodus was not written by Moses or any other single author.

The identification of the anonymous authors, the time of their composition, and the method by which the literature was combined into a single history has dominated the interpretation of Exodus in the modern period. The central theory in the past century concerning the authorship of the Pentateuch, including Exodus, has been the Documentary Hypothesis. A description of the Documentary Hypothesis and its implications for interpreting the literature in Exodus will provide background for describing the method of interpretation in the commentary.

DOCUMENTARY HYPOTHESIS

The Documentary Hypothesis has provided biblical scholars with a model for identifying three anonymous authors in the composition of Exodus. The authors are entitled the Yahwist (J), the Elohist (E), and the Priestly writer (P). The work of each author is not confined to Exodus, but extends throughout the Tetrateuch (Genesis, Exodus, Leviticus, Numbers) and perhaps even to the book of Joshua. In addition the Documentary Hypothesis identifies the author of Deuteronomy as the Deuteronomist (D). Those who identify the anonymous

---

93. D. B. Redford, "Pithom," *Lexicon der Ägyptologie* (ed. W. Helck and W. Westendorf; Wiesbaden: Harrassowitz, 1982), 1054-58; idem, "Exodus I 11," *VT* 13 (1963): 401-18; idem, "An Egyptological Perspective on the Exodus Narrative," in *Egypt, Israel, Sinai: Archaeological and Historical Relationship in the Biblical Period* (ed. A. Rainey; Tel Aviv: Tel Aviv University Press, 1987), 137-61. See also Van Seters, "Geography."

pentateuchal authors as also responsible for the book of Joshua speak of a Hexateuch.

The three authors of Exodus (J, E, P) are evident where the same story (repetition) is told from different points of view (contradiction). Examples of stories containing both repetition and contradiction include the two names for the mountain of God (Sinai and Horeb), the two stories of the revelation of the divine name Yahweh (Exodus 3 and 6), several interpretations of the conflict at the Red Sea (chaps. 14–15), divergent law codes (chap. 20 and Deuteronomy 5), and different accounts of the appropriate sanctuary (i.e., the tent of meeting in Exodus 33, and the tabernacle in chaps. 25–31, 35–40). These and many other repetitions confirm the existence of several anonymous authors in the composition of Exodus with divergent views of God, community, and worship.

An important goal for interpreters employing the Documentary Hypothesis is to unravel the sources into their previously independent versions so that each can be interpreted separately from the others. In the process the narrated events of Exodus are not read for historical information about the Mosaic period, but to discern the social setting and religious outlook of the different authors writing centuries later. Careful interpretation of the individual sources, therefore, provides insight into the social, cultural, and religious circumstances of Israel's monarchical, exilic, and postexilic periods, the time when the sources were written. The authors are profiled in the following manner.

The titles J and E arise from the use of the divine names Yahweh (sometimes written "Jahweh" from the Latin, taken up also in English "Jehovah") and Elohim, especially in Genesis, but also in Exodus–Numbers. The advocates of the Documentary Hypothesis locate each source in the early monarchical period. The author of J was placed either in the time of the united monarchy of the tenth century or in the southern kingdom of Judah in the ninth to eighth century B.C.E. The J source begins with creation in Genesis 2, focusing on the garden of Eden. Its style is a terse but flowing narrative, free of formulaic phrases. Stories in the opening chapters of Genesis include Adam and Eve's expulsion from the garden of Eden, the murder of Abel by Cain, the flood, subsequent stories of Noah, and the tower of Babel. The ancestral literature is organized around the divine promise of land and descendants (Gen 12:1-3), a promise conceived as a covenant (Genesis 15). The J literature is also prominent in the story of Moses, including accounts of his birth and early years, the exodus, the revelation at Sinai, the wilderness wandering, and perhaps also stories of the conquest in Joshua.[94] As noted above, the J

---

94. See A. de Pury, "Yahwist ('J') Source," *ABD* 6:1012-20; H. W. Wolff, "The Kerygma of the Yahwist" (trans. W. A. Benware), *Int* 20 (1966): 129-58 (repr. in W. Brueggemann and H. W. Wolff, *The Vitality of Old Testament Traditions* [2nd ed.; Atlanta: John Knox, 1982], 41-66); R. B. Coote and D. R. Ord, *The Bible's First History* (Philadelphia: Fortress, 1989); Eissfeldt, *Introduction*, 199-204.

History was thought to reflect the renaissance under David and Solomon in the tenth century, or the religious outlook of the southern kingdom of Judah in the ninth to eighth centuries.

The author of E was thought to have written in the northern kingdom of Israel in the ninth to eighth centuries. The E source presents a prophetic interpretation of Israel's origins. Central examples include the second episode of Abraham falsely presenting Sarah as his sister to Abimelech of Gerar (Genesis 20), where Abraham is idealized as a prophet. The testing of Abraham in the divine command to sacrifice Isaac (Genesis 22) is considered an important story in the E source. Source critics also identify E in Exodus–Numbers. Examples include the use of the name Elohim in the call of Moses (Exodus 3) and in the theophany at Sinai (Exodus 19).[95] The prophetic perspective of E provides insight into the religious perspective of the northern kingdom of Israel.

The author of Deuteronomy is associated with the Josianic reform at the close of the monarchical period in the late seventh century. The D source is not a history but a law book.[96] It is confined to Deuteronomy, which divides between sermons and laws presented by Moses to Israel on the plains of Moab. The time span of the sermons is one day. Moses dies at the close of the day, giving Deuteronomy the character of a testimonial, as D. Olson has argued.[97] Central themes include covenant, the need for Israel to be distinct from surrounding nations, centralized worship, the importance of putting law above a king, and the danger of idolatry.[98] Deuteronomy is a polemical treatise that advocates the Israelites' exclusive loyalty to Yahweh over the other gods. The polemical rhetoric indicates the innovative nature of the message of monolatry, with the need for centralized worship (chap. 12).

The P writer is judged to be the latest to compose a history of Israel, sometime in the postexilic period. The P source is an independent account of Israelite origins, which uses the divine name Elohim in Genesis, hence its early designation as E^1. The P source is judged to be later than Deuteronomy, since it assumes the singular worship of Yahweh at a central cult. The absence of the polemical rhetoric that characterized Deuteronomy further reinforced the conclusion of the late composition of P.

The literary scope of the P source is debated. Some interpreters identify it

95. See A. W. Jenks, "Elohist," *ABD* 2:478-82; idem, *The Elohist and North Israelite Traditions* (SBLMS 22; Missoula, Mont.: Scholars Press, 1977).

96. The literature on Deuteronomy is vast. For an overview of the history of research see G. Braulik, *Das Deuteronomium* (2 vols.; NEB 15, 28; Würzburg: Echter Verlag, 1986-1992).

97. D. T. Olson, *Deuteronomy and the Death of Moses: A Theological Reading* (OBT; Minneapolis: Fortress, 1994).

98. M. Weinfeld, "Deuteronomy, Book of," *ABD* 2:168-83; idem, *Deuteronomy and the Deuteronomic School* (Oxford: Clarendon, 1972), passim; Eissfeldt, *Introduction*, 219-33.

as beginning with creation in Genesis 1 and continuing perhaps as far as the account of land distribution in Joshua 18–19. Wellhausen recognized the similarity in language and themes between portions of Joshua and the P source, yet he identified the literature in Joshua to be secondary to the P source.[99] T. Nöldeke extended the P source itself into Joshua.[100] Blenkinsopp represents a contemporary example of a similar interpretation.[101] Others limit the P source to the death of Moses announced in Num 27:12-23 and fulfilled in Deut 34:1-8. Noth advocated this position with his hypothesis of the Deuteronomistic History, a literary composition that included Deuteronomy + Joshua–2 Kings, that is distinct from the P Tetrateuch.[102] More recently interpreters have sought the ending of the P source in the revelation at Mount Sinai, either in the construction of the tabernacle[103] or in the ordination of the Aaronide priesthood in Leviticus 8–9.[104] The unifying thread throughout the different interpretations is that P literature is composed independently and only later combined with the other pentateuchal sources.

Interpreters also debate the literary character of the P source. Early critics separated law from narrative and identified only the narrative as the P source (Pg). P legal material was judged to be a supplement to the P source (designated Ps). Noth represents a later formulation of this position.[105] More recently interpreters have questioned the separation of law and narrative, arguing instead for a mixture of literary genres in the P source.[106] The style of the P History is formulaic.[107] Genealogies and dating organize the literature.[108] The central theme

---

99. Wellhausen, *Composition* (3rd ed. 1889), 118-36, esp. 130-31.

100. T. Nöldeke, *Untersuchungen zur Kritik des Alten Testaments* (Kiel, 1869), 1-144.

101. Blenkinsopp, *Pentateuch*, 237-39.

102. Noth, *History of Pentateuchal Traditions*, 8 *et passim*. See also K. Elliger, "Sinn und Ursprung der priesterlichen Geschichtserzählung," *ZTK* 49 (1952): 121-43; C. Frevel, *Mit Blick auf das Land die Schöpfung erinnern: Zum Ende der Priestergrundschrift* (Herders biblische Studien 23; Freiburg: Herder, 2000).

103. See, e.g., T. Pola, *Die ursprüngliche Priesterschrift: Beobachtungen zur Literarkritik und Traditionsgeschichte von Pg* (WMANT 70; Neukirchen-Vluyn: Neukirchener Verlag, 1995), who argues that the P source extended from creation (Gen 1:1–2:4a) to temple construction (Exod 25:1, 8a, 9; 29:45-46; 40:16, 17a, 33b).

104. E. Zenger, *Einleitung in das Alte Testament* (5th ed.; Studienbücher Theologie 1/1; Stuttgart: Kohlhammer, 2004), 169-71.

105. Noth, *History of Pentateuchal Traditions*, e.g., 8-11.

106. See Pola, *Ursprüngliche Priesterschrift*, 19-25 *et passim*; see also I. Knohl, *The Sanctuary of Silence: The Priestly Torah and the Holiness School* (Minneapolis: Fortress, 1995).

107. See the discussion of the important formulas in the P source in Pola, *Ursprüngliche Priesterschrift*, 116-46.

108. The P writer(s) organizes history around genealogy, as in the phrase, "These are the generations of the heavens and the earth" (Gen 2:4a). See the repetition of this phrase in Gen 5:1; 6:9; 10:1; 11:27, etc.

is the presence of God with Israel.[109] This theme is developed by relating world creation (Gen 1:1–2:4) and temple construction (Exodus 24, 25–31, 35–40).[110] Other important themes are the covenants with Noah (Genesis 9), Abraham (Genesis 17), and Israel (Exodus 2), which include the promise of land. The life of Moses in Exodus–Numbers is organized around the revelation (Exodus 25–31) and the construction of the tabernacle (Exodus 35–40), the creation of its sacrificial cultic system and priesthood (Leviticus), and the social organization of the wilderness camp (Numbers 1–10).[111] The P source reflects the social and religious changes of Israel during and after the exile, as a province under Persian rule, now organized as a theocracy.

The independent "sources" (J, E, P) were merged into their present form in the Pentateuch well into the postexilic period by editors (also called "redactors"). The editors who fashioned the Pentateuch were concerned to preserve and harmonize tradition. They were not formative or creative theologians in their own right. As a result advocates of the Documentary Hypothesis judged the present form of the Pentateuch, including Exodus, to lack a clear literary design. The goal of interpretation is to isolate the different sources. It is not to interpret the present form of the Pentateuch in general, or Exodus in particular. Propp's commentary on Exodus illustrates this view: according to him, the redactor is a scribe, but not an author. "His raw materials were already highly polished works of art, which he had but to transcribe."[112]

CURRENT STATE OF RESEARCH AND METHOD OF STUDY IN THE COMMENTARY

The research supporting the Documentary Hypothesis provides a starting point for my method of interpretation in this commentary. I interpret Exodus as the product of anonymous authors, not the work of Moses. Three lasting effects of the Documentary Hypothesis influence this commentary: (1) the identification of repetitions in the Pentateuch as a clue for profiling the anonymous authors, (2) the dating of Deuteronomy from the Josianic reform into the exilic period, and (3) the dating of the P literature later than Deuteronomy.

But I also depart from the Documentary Hypothesis. Three areas of re-

---

109. See, e.g., Blum, *Studien*, 287-332.

110. See esp. Pola, *Ursprüngliche Priesterschrift*.

111. See J. Milgrom, "Priestly ('P') Source," *ABD* 5:454-61; Eissfeldt, *Introduction*, 204-8; S. E. McEvenue, *The Narrative Style of the Priestly Writer* (AnBib 50; Rome: Pontifical Biblical Institute Press, 1971); R. B. Coote and D. R. Ord, *In the Beginning: Creation and the Priestly History* (Minneapolis: Fortress, 1991); J. Blenkinsopp, "The Structure of P," *CBQ* 38 (1976): 275-92.

112. W. H. C. Propp, *Exodus 1–18* (AB 2; New York: Doubleday, 1999), 52-53.

search have contributed to the breakdown of the Documentary Hypothesis: (1) the difficulty in identifying an E source, (2) the debate over the date of the J source and its relationship to Deuteronomy and the Deuteronomistic History, and (3) the literary character of the P material and its relationship to earlier tradition.

The Elusive Author of the Elohist Source

The identification of an anonymous author as the "Elohist" goes back nearly to the beginning of the historical-critical study of the Pentateuch. One of the earliest historical-critical interpreters of the Pentateuch, J. Astruc (1684-1766), identified two authors, A and B, based on the divine names Elohim and Yahweh. Astruc's "A" author could just as well have been called the "Elohist," since this author was identified by a preference for using the divine name Elohim. But the Elohist source of the Documentary Hypothesis came into focus only after the P source was identified and separated from the non-P uses of Elohim.

The Elohist source constitutes the non-P stories in which the name Elohim is used. Examples are sparse. As noted above they include Abraham's deception of Abimelech that Sarah was his sister and not his wife (Genesis 20), the sacrifice of Isaac (Genesis 22), the story of the midwives (Exod 1:15-21), and the meeting between Moses and Jethro (Exodus 18). This list of stories is not exhaustive, but it indicates a central problem confronting the Documentary Hypothesis: the scarcity of material in the Pentateuch that can be attributed to the Elohistic author.

Thus scholars debate whether there ever was an independent E source.[113] If such a document existed, most of the material is now lost, since so little of the literature attributed to it is evident. Those who favor the existence of an E source assume that most of the composition is absent from the Pentateuch.[114] Those who reject the hypothesis of an independent E source interpret the E stories as additions to the J History,[115] often designated as JE. The E source of the Documentary Hypothesis will play no role in this commentary. The stories traditionally attributed to it, such as the midwives in Exodus 1 or Moses' meeting with Jethro in Exodus 18, will be interpreted as distinct stories incorporated into a single history.

---

113. See the discussion by R. B. Coote, *In Defense of Revolution: The Elohist History* (Minneapolis: Fortress, 1991); R. K. Gnuse, "Redefining the Elohist," *JBL* 119 (2000): 201-20; A. Graupner, *Der Elohist: Gegenwart und Wirksamkeit des transzendenten Gottes in der Geschichte* (WMANT 97; Neukirchen-Vluyn: Neukirchener Verlag, 2002).

114. Jenks, "Elohist," *ABD* 2:478-82; idem, *Elohist.*

115. W. Rudolph, *Der "Elohist" von Exodus bis Josua* (BZAW 68; Berlin: Töpelmann, 1938).

The Exile and the Non-P History

The most recent debate among pentateuchal interpreters concerns the authorship and date of the Non-P History, which would be identified as J and E in the Documentary Hypothesis, especially its relationship to Deuteronomy (see above, "Literary Context"). Throughout the modern historical-critical period of interpretation there has been a strong consensus for dating the Non-P History to the early monarchical period. Thus it was viewed as preceding Deuteronomy in composition by several centuries. Wellhausen, a pioneer in the formation of the Documentary Hypothesis, placed the Non-P History (the J source) in the ninth-eighth century B.C.E. Later scholars like von Rad pushed its date to the tenth century B.C.E. In either case there was agreement that ancient Israel began to write historical narrative early in the monarchical period — if not during the renaissance of the united monarchy (10th century), then shortly thereafter (9th-8th century). Scholars debated questions of genre. Could such writing be called history, or were other categories such as epic, myth, legend, or folklore more appropriate?[116] (See above, "Ancient History Writing and Exodus.") Within this debate, however, there was general agreement that some form of history writing emerged during the early monarchical period, well before the composition of Deuteronomy.

The consensus influenced the interpretation of ancient Israelite religion in at least two ways. First, an early date for the Non-P History allowed interpreters to use it as an avenue for discerning the social and religious worldview of the united monarchy of David and Solomon.[117] Second, the presence of history writing during the early monarchical period also accentuated the uniqueness of Israel within its larger cultural setting, since no other contemporary culture had produced anything like the Non-P History.[118] The closest parallels to such history writing, as we have seen, appear much later in the ancient Near East. Early forms occur in the Babylonian Chronicles, dating from the mid-eighth century B.C.E. Closer parallels emerge with the early Greek historians like Herodotus, writing during the Persian period in the fifth century B.C.E. and later.[119]

Contemporary interpreters are increasingly arguing for a later date to the Non-P History. The central arguments surround its relationship to Deuteron-

---

116. For discussion of history writing see Thompson, "Historiography (Israelite)," *ABD* 3:206-12; Momigliano, *Classical Foundations of Modern Historiography.* For a summary of the myth-and-history debate see C. Kloos, *Yhwh's Combat with the Sea: A Canaanite Tradition in the Religion of Ancient Israel* (Leiden: Brill, 1986); J. W. Rogerson, *Myth in Old Testament Interpretation* (BZAW 134; Berlin: de Gruyter, 1974).

117. See, e.g., von Rad, *Problem of the Hexateuch,* 71-72.

118. For discussion see Gnuse, *Heilsgeschichte.*

119. For overview and comparison see Van Seters, *In Search of History.*

omy (D) and the Deuteronomistic History (DtrH: Joshua, Judges, Samuel, and Kings). Van Seters argued in 1983 that the Non-P History (identified by him as the Yahwist History) is later than Deuteronomy and the Deuteronomistic History.[120] He focused on the terminology and literary techniques in Genesis, Exodus, and Numbers, and the relationship of this literature to Deuteronomy and the Deuteronomistic History. In subsequent work he has included the comparative study of history writing to provide a broader basis for evaluating the development of literature in ancient Israel as it is reflected in the composition of the Pentateuch (see above, "Genre of Salvation History"). He concluded that comparison does not support the presence of the Non-P History in the early monarchical period of ancient Israel, since the genre of history writing in the complex form of the Pentateuch and the Deuteronomistic History emerges only late in the literary history of the ancient Near East.

In 1976 H. H. Schmid undertook a fresh literary study of J stories, terminology, and themes.[121] He discovered similarity between the Non-P literature in Genesis, Exodus, and Numbers and prophetic themes and genres in the Deuteronomistic History (e.g., the commissioning of Moses in Exodus 3–4 is a prophetic genre repeated in Judges and Samuel). He concluded that the "so-called" J literature was formed by Deuteronomic writers, accounting for the thematic emphasis on blessing, nationhood, and the promise of land (see above, "Literary Context"). He did not work out a clear framework for dating the literature.

Blum reached somewhat similar conclusions to Schmid, employing more tradition-historical methodology.[122] He too noted a literary relationship (a "profile") between the Non-P literature in Genesis–Numbers, Deuteronomy, and the Deuteronomistic History. He highlighted this network of linguistic and thematic connections by identifying the Non-P literature in Genesis–Numbers as the *D-Komposition (KD)*. The *KD* incorporates older traditions, but the author reflects the worldview of the Deuteronomistic tradition, presupposing Deuteronomy and the Deuteronomistic History. He concluded that the *KD* was likely written in the postexilic period as a supplement to Deuteronomy and the Deuteronomistic History, although he did not spell out the exact literary relationship between distinct blocks of literature. The *KD* provides a prelude to a larger history extending through the fall of the monarchy. It is intended to ground the faith of the Israelites in Abraham, while also providing a future orientation with the unfulfilled promise of land. Blum subsequently refined this conclusion, separating Genesis from the *KD* as a distinct story of origins, com-

---

120. Ibid.
121. Schmid, *Sogenannte Jahwist.*
122. Blum, *Studien.* See also Rendtorff, *Problem.*

bined with the story of Moses only in the P History.[123] (See above, "Literary Context.")

I will employ the term "Non-P" to describe the earliest history in the Pentateuch, which likely extends into the Deuteronomistic History. Debate over the best designation for the Non-P literature in the Pentateuch is far from settled. Van Seters continues to identify the exilic history as the Yahwist History. But it is important to realize that the Yahwist History of Van Seters has nothing to do with the Documentary Hypothesis. The anonymous author is not identified by the use of the divine name Yahweh. The history is not part of the social development of the monarchy under David and Solomon, but is actually critical of the monarchical period. And the history shares many of the perspectives of Deuteronomy and the Deuteronomistic History, providing a later reinterpretation of their central themes. Van Seters's use of the J History has been criticized as not reflecting clearly the breakdown of the Documentary Hypothesis. But as recent reviews of pentateuchal studies have illustrated, the term "J" has been used in a variety of ways throughout the history of the modern period of interpretation.[124] Thus C. Levin employs the term "the Yahwist" to identify a postexilic redaction of pentateuchal literature.[125] Others have preferred to restrict the term "J History" or "J Source" to the methodology of the Documentary Hypothesis, and therefore they have dropped the name altogether, as evidenced by Blum's designation *KD*, or Blenkinsopp's term "Deuteronomistic corpus."[126] These terms rightly emphasize the close literary relationship between the Non-P literature in Genesis–Numbers and Deuteronomy. But the literary designations "composition" by Blum or "corpus" by Blenkinsopp do not capture the genre of ancient history writing clarified by the comparative study of Van Seters.

The debate over the identification of the author indicates the dynamic character of pentateuchal studies at the present time. For this reason, I will employ the tentative title "Non-P" to identify the Non-P literature, following the lead of D. Carr.[127] The Non-P History shares many of the perspectives of Deuteronomy and the Deuteronomistic History, although each body of literature undergoes a distinct history of composition. In the commentary I will illustrate that the Non-P History in the Pentateuch includes diverse literature from many periods of Israel's history, organized by chronology, genealogy, and travelogue. A firm date for the Non-P History is not necessary for interpreting Exodus.

123. Blum, "Literarische Verbindung," 119-56.

124. J. L. Ska, "The Yahwist, a Hero with a Thousand Faces: A Chapter in the History of Modern Exegesis," in *Abschied vom Jahwisten*, ed. Gertz et al., 1-24.

125. C. Levin, *Der Jahwist* (FRLANT 157; Göttingen: Vandenhoeck & Ruprecht, 1993).

126. Blenkinsopp, *Pentateuch*, e.g., 114.

127. D. Carr, *Reading the Fractures of Genesis: Historical and Literary Approaches* (Louisville: Westminster John Knox, 1996), e.g., 143ff.

Deuteronomy is in formation as early as the late monarchical period. The Deuteronomistic History is likely written and revised in the exilic period. The exile may also be the date for the completion of the Non-P History, although the postexilic period is more likely, since in many places the Non-P History is clearly post-Deuteronomistic, for example, in the story of the golden calf, where Exodus 32 is later than Deuteronomy 9–10 and 1 Kings 12.[128]

The important point for interpreting the Non-P History is its close relationship to Deuteronomy and to the Deuteronomistic History. Although these bodies of literature do not represent a single, unified composition, they share a religious outlook in their late stages of composition, which makes it possible to read Genesis through Kings loosely as a broad history of salvation, which Freedman calls a Primary History.[129] Thus in the commentary I interpret the Non-P History as combining the promise to the ancestors in Genesis with the story of the exodus from Egypt in Exodus–Deuteronomy. The repetition of themes such as the death of a generation in Exod 1:6 and Judg 2:8-10, or the story of the golden calf in Exodus 32, Deuteronomy 9–10, and 1 Kings 12, also indicates that the author of the Non-P History relates pentateuchal literature to the Deuteronomistic History.

The central themes of the Non-P History can be summarized in the following manner. The Non-P History roots the promise of salvation in the ancestors, especially Abraham. The exodus is an event of liberation from Egyptian slavery, arising in part from the divine promise to Abraham. The exodus signifies the continuity of the divine promise to the patriarchs. The linking of the promise of land to the ancestors and the exodus also gives the Non-P History a future orientation, since the exodus requires the future conquest of the land of Canaan for completion. The crossings of the Red Sea and the Jordan River symbolize a two-part sequence in salvation history marked by the crossing of water, from Egypt into the wilderness, and from the wilderness into the land of promise. The repetition anchors the literary relationship between the Non-P History (Exodus 14) and the Deuteronomistic History (Joshua 3–5). Both bodies of literature provide tragic accounts of how the Israelite people failed to secure the promise of land. The Non-P History records the failure of the first generation of Israelites, those who undertook the journey through the wilderness, but lacked the faith to undertake holy war in a conquest of Canaan. The Deuteronomistic History records the failure of the Israelite monarchy; Israel loses the land because their kings abuse their power and reject the laws of Deuteronomy. Deuteronomy assumes a pivotal role between the Non-P History in the Pentateuch and the Deuteronomistic History. It represents the hope of a second generation

---

128. See Van Seters, *Life of Moses,* 290ff.
129. Freedman, "Pentateuch," *IDB* 3:711-27.

of Israelites in the wilderness. It contains the constitution for a nation-state in which monarchical power is restricted by law.

After the Exile and the P History

The Documentary Hypothesis advances two assumptions about the P History in Exodus. First, advocates of the Documentary Hypothesis argue that P originally existed as an independent source, even though it is presently interwoven with Non-P literature throughout the Pentateuch/Hexateuch (see the summary of the P source above, "Documentary Hypothesis"). The existence of a once independent P source is supported by the quantity of literary units in the Pentateuch/Hexateuch that share similar motifs and themes. The evidence far exceeds that of the E source. The P literature in Exodus includes the revelation of the divine name Yahweh (Exodus 6), a series of plagues (snakes, 7:6-13; gnats, 8:16-19; boils, 9:8-12), the Passover instruction (12:1-20), the story of manna (chap. 16), an account of the theophany on the mountain (24:15-18), and the revelation of the tabernacle (chaps. 25-31, 35–40).

Yet the once independent status of the P History is difficult to establish, because the reader encounters P literature as a supplement within the present structure of the Pentateuch/Hexateuch and not as an independent document. For this reason, in the commentary I will not reconstruct an independent P source as a starting point for interpretation. I will focus instead on the distinctive themes of the literature within the present narrative context. The methodology will allow for an interpretation of the particular view of the cult, society, and theology within the P History without advocating a firm position on its literary character prior to incorporation in the Pentateuch.

Second, the Documentary Hypothesis assumes that editors sought to preserve tradition by combining the P source with the other sources. Thus the editors were not creative theologians. This assumption raises a more pressing issue of methodology for the commentary. The implication is that the context of the P literature in Exodus lacks design. As a result, the literary context of the P stories has not been a central focus for interpretation by advocates of the Documentary Hypothesis.

I view the role of editors differently from the perspective of the Documentary Hypothesis. I assume intentional literary design in the distribution of P literature in shaping Exodus. The design may be the result of a P author, who is both using P tradition and composing literature, in which case the P History is a supplement of the Non-P History and a significant influence in creating the present structure of the Pentateuch. The implication of this hypothesis is that P literature in the Pentateuch/Hexateuch is not an independent source, but a supplement to a prior Non-P History, a position advocated by a number of recent interpreters.[130] The literary design, however, may be the product of a separate editor (a post-P redactor [Rp]), which would then require a separate designation for the once independent status of the P History (Pg).

In the commentary I will restrict the designation of P literature to the term "P History" in order to focus on the literary context of the P stories and law codes in Exodus. I assume that the author of the P History is aware of and dependent upon the Non-P History. Thus one aim of the commentary is to describe the literary relationship between the distinct bodies of literature, the Non-P and the P Histories. Careful attention to the literary context of the P literature will reveal a dynamic inner-biblical relationship with the Non-P History in Exodus, in which divergent interpretations of origin stories are related without being harmonized. The implication of the methodology is that Exodus contains a range of authoritative interpretations of salvation history, which force the reader to relate historically divergent traditions in the formation of the canon, as has been argued in slightly different ways by B. S. Childs and J. A. Sanders.[131]

The designation "P History" runs the risk of simplifying the P literature in Exodus. Past interpretations of the P literature have identified a history of composition in the literature, regardless of whether the reader works with the hypothesis of a P source. Interpreters have long argued for a history of composition in the P legislation,[132] some have even identified separate P documents,[133] while

---

130. See, e.g., Cross, *Canaanite Myth and Hebrew Epic*, 293-325; Rendtorff, *Problem*; J. Van Seters, "The Plagues of Egypt: Ancient Tradition or Literary Invention?" *ZAW* 98 (1986): 31-39; idem, "The Primeval Histories of Greece and Israel Compared," *ZAW* 100 (1988): 1-22; H. Utzschneider, *Das Heiligtum und das Gesetz: Studien zur Bedeutung der Sinaitischen Heiligtumstexts (Ex 25–40; Lev 8–9)* (OBO 77; Göttingen: Vandenhoeck & Ruprecht, 1988); Blum, *Studien*, 229-85; J. L. Ska, "La place d'Ex 6,2-8 dans la narration de l'exode," *ZAW* 94 (1982): 530-48; idem, "Quelques remarques sur Pg et la dernière rédaction du Pentateuque," in *Le pentateuque en question: Les origines et la composition des cinq premiers livres de la Bible à la lumière des recherches récentes* (ed. A. de Pury; MdB; Geneva: Labor et Fides, 1989), 95-125. For discussion see Pola, *Ursprüngliche Priesterschrift*, 29-31.

131. See B. S. Childs, *Introduction to the Old Testament as Scripture* (Philadelphia: Fortress, 1979), esp. 27-106; J. A. Sanders, *From Sacred Story to Sacred Texts* (Philadelphia: Fortress, 1987).

132. The identification of additions to the P source is evident already in the earliest source critics. Wellhausen, for example, identified the P portions of Joshua to be supplements to the P source (*Composition*, 130-32). Noth (*History of Pentateuchal Traditions*, e.g., 17-19) provides an extensive list of supplements (Ps) to the P source (Pg). Some scholars detect a more extensive history of interpretation within the P legislation (see, e.g., Knohl, *Sanctuary of Silence*).

133. Thus von Rad (*Die Priesterschrift im Hexateuch: Literarisch untersucht und theologisch gewertet* (BWANT 65; Stuttgart: Kohlhammer, 1934) identified two P sources. R. E. Friedman represents a contemporary version of the hypothesis of multiple P sources, advocating for a preexilic and a postexilic version of P. See his *The Exile and Biblical Narrative: The For-

more recently interpreters have described a series of post-P redactions.[134] The complex character of the P History is indicated in the variety of designations that emerge in modern literature, including Pg (Priestly source), Ps (Priestly supplements), and Rp (post-Priestly redactions, of which there can be several). In the commentary I highlight the more complex nature of the P History in the distinct exegetical sections, while maintaining a focus on the broad outline of a P corpus of literature.

The boundaries of the P History are debated (see above, "Documentary Hypothesis"). The literature is concentrated in the Tetrateuch, although there are signs of editing in Deuteronomy (e.g., the death of Moses in chap. 34) and in the Deuteronomistic History (e.g., the distribution of land in Joshua 18–19). The concentration of literature in Genesis through Numbers suggests that the P History is not tied as closely to the Deuteronomistic History as the Non-P History is, although it is equally critical of monarchical power. The P History envisions a sacerdotal society in the Mosaic age of the Pentateuch, not a monarchy. Salvation history is structured around the renewal of creation from Genesis 1, in contrast to the important role of conquest in the Non-P History. The P History envisions the history of Israel as a series of divine revelations, rather than as a sequence of acts of salvation (e.g., the progressive revelation of the divine name in Genesis 1, 17; Exodus 6; and the relationship of creation and temple construction in Genesis 1 and Exodus 25–31, 35–40). The exodus (Exodus 1–14) inaugurates the new creation, bringing back the lost structure of the Sabbath in the first wilderness story of manna (Exodus 16). The construction of the tabernacle (Exodus 25–31, 35–40), the formation of the sacrificial cult with its priestly personnel (Leviticus), and the establishment of a temple community (Numbers 1–10) offer an alternative vision of society to monarchical rule, providing a broad literary relationship between divine creation (Genesis 1) and the sacral community (Exodus 25–Numbers 10). The first generation of the Israelites dies in the wilderness, not because they fear the conquest of the promised land, but because they deny the goodness of the promised land (Numbers 13–15) and they resist the leadership of Moses and Aaron (Numbers 16–19). The P History progresses to the legislation regulating the land of Canaan (Numbers 26–36), before recounting the death of Moses and the close of the Mosaic age (Deuteronomy 34). The distribution of land (Joshua 18–19) also points the reader beyond the wilderness to the Israelites' future life in the land of Canaan.

---

mation of the Deuteronomistic and Priestly Works (HSM 22; Chico, Calif.: Scholars Press, 1981); idem, *Who Wrote the Bible?* (New York: Summit Books, 1987).

134. See, e.g., Römer, *Israel's Väter*; Schmid, *Erzväter und Exodus*; Gertz, *Tradition und Redaktion*; Otto, *Deuteronomium im Pentateuch*; R. Achenbach, *Die Vollendung der Tora: Studien zur Redaktionsgeschichte des Numeribuches im Kontext von Hexateuch und Pentateuch* (BZABR 3; Wiesbaden: Harrassowitz, 2002).

THE BOOK

Exodus is central to the Hebrew Bible. It probes the identity of Yahweh, the God of Israel, through two related themes: the character of divine power, and the nature of divine presence in this world. These two themes of Yahweh's power and presence go to the heart of ancient Israelite religion. It is not surprising, therefore, that Exodus contains many of the etiological stories for Israel's cultic practice, including circumcision, the death of the firstborn, the Passover, the Feast of Unleavened Bread, Firstfruits, Sabbath observance, as well as the building instructions for the sanctuary. As a story of Yahweh, Exodus is presented on a grand scale as a drama about kings, gods, and the forces of nature. Though written in prose, not poetry, the story is epic in content and scope.[135]

Exodus also contains the first part of the biography of Moses. Momigliano defines biography simply as "an account of the life of a man from birth to death."[136] The life of Moses provides a human story to parallel the grand drama of Yahweh's power over nations and descent into this world. The parallel stories of Yahweh and Moses intersect throughout Exodus. Each character is introduced lacking identity. Yahweh is absent at the outset of Exodus, requiring a series of self-introductions to Moses, to the Israelite people, and even to Pharaoh. Moses also lacks identity in the opening chapters of the book. He is born an Israelite, adopted into the Egyptian family of Pharaoh, and marries a Midianite, Zipporah. The formation of Israelite religion is tied closely to the clarification of Yahweh's identity and that of his servant Moses.

Thus Exodus is a story of the interdependence between divine identity and Mosaic authority. The absence of God in the life of the Israelite people and Moses' lack of identity create a problem of authority. The stories of Yahweh and Moses are interwoven, because the authority of Moses is dependent on the power of Yahweh to fulfill past promises of salvation to the ancestors.

THE POWER AND THE PRESENCE OF YAHWEH

Although intimately related throughout the entire book, the themes of divine power and presence take prominence at different stages in the story, allowing

135. "Epic" technically refers to a "long narrative poem in elevated style recounting the deeds of a legendary or historical hero." The primary examples are Homer's *Iliad* and *Odyssey*. Exodus is clearly a work of prose, not poetry, and therefore not an epic. My use of the term is limited to its legendary subject matter. For discussion of the definition of epic and its distinction from the biblical prose tradition see Van Seters, *In Search of History*, 18-31.

136. A. Momigliano, *The Development of Greek Biography* (Cambridge: Harvard University Press, 1993), 11.

for a loose division in the outline of Exodus. The first half of the book, Exod 1:1–15:21, explores the power of Yahweh to be faithful to past promises by saving Israel and leading them to the promised land. The biblical authors explore the power of Yahweh to save Israel, to influence other nations (the Egyptians), and to impact nature itself (the plagues, the control of light and darkness, and the splitting of the sea). The second half of the book, 15:22–40:38, describes the ways in which Yahweh is present with Israel in this world. Stories of travelogue through the wilderness, revelation of law from God's mountain home, eating and drinking with God on the divine mountain, and the construction of a sanctuary in the midst of the Israelite camp explore different channels by which Yahweh, the God of the ancestors, will now dwell with the Israelite nation. Geography reinforces the two-part division of Exodus. The theme of divine power is explored, for the most part, in the setting of the land of Egypt. The theme of divine presence is developed in the setting of the wilderness, as Israel journeys with God from Egypt to the promised land of Canaan. A brief summary of the events within the two parts of Exodus will provide further content to the themes of divine power and presence.

The Power of Yahweh: 1:1–15:21

The nature of divine power takes center stage in the first half of the book. Other themes and traditions are employed to probe the power of Yahweh to save Israel. The background to the events of Exodus is the divine promise to the ancestors from Genesis (e.g., Gen 12:1-9) that their offspring would become a great nation and one day also possess their own land. Events in Genesis do not allow for the fulfillment of this divine promise. Instead, Genesis ends with the family of Jacob migrating to Egypt because of famine in the land of Canaan. Exodus opens by recalling the divine promise to the ancestors when it states that the family of Jacob has grown into a great nation, fulfilling one aspect of the divine promise to the ancestors (Exod 1:7). But their vast population in the land of Egypt, not Canaan, threatens Pharaoh, prompting oppression and even genocide. The result is a paradoxical situation. The partial fulfillment of the divine promise creates suffering, not blessing, for Israel. Exodus 1 raises the central question for the first half of the book: Is Yahweh powerful enough to fulfill promises made to the Israelite ancestors in spite of the opposition of Pharaoh?

Exodus 1:1–15:21 narrates the conflict between Yahweh and Pharaoh over the fate of Israel. It is an epic battle between kings and gods. The weapons of war are the forces of nature. Yahweh summons reptiles, insects, and meteorological elements, including hail and darkness, in an initial assault on Pharaoh (chaps. 7–10). When these elements fail to persuade Pharaoh to release Israel from Egyptian slavery, the personification of death itself, described as "the destroyer," descends upon the land of Egypt in the pitch darkness of midnight, slaying all Egyptian firstborn children and animals (chaps. 11–12). Even the plague of death, however, does not dissuade Pharaoh from continuing the conflict. During the night he musters his army one last time and pursues the fleeing Israelites to the Red Sea (chap. 13), where Yahweh destroys him at dawn, this time using the sea itself as a weapon (chap. 14). The hymns in chap. 15 look back over the battlefield and answer the question raised in chap. 1: Yahweh is indeed a warrior God, possessing power over Pharaoh and over all the forces of nature.

The Presence of Yahweh: 15:22–40:38

The hymns in Exodus 15 also provide a change in focus from the exodus to the unfulfilled promise of land. Yahweh's power over Pharaoh leads to the confident conclusion that God will lead the Israelite people in a march through the wilderness, with images of conquest pointing to the fulfillment of the promise of land (15:13-18). The utopian vision of life in a land ruled by God introduces the theme of divine presence with Israel. Although never realized, the theme of divine presence in the promised land is central to the second half of Exodus. Instead of the promised land, the wilderness becomes the setting for exploring a variety of ways in which Yahweh dwells with Israel as they journey toward Canaan.

Exodus 15:22–40:38 describes Yahweh's leading of Israel into the desert after the defeat of Pharaoh in the Red Sea. The relationship of Yahweh and Israel is developed in two opening stories, the bitter water at Marah (15:22-27) and the absence of water at Rephidim (17:1-7). Both stories are initiated by crises over water in the wilderness. The crises allow for mutual testing between Yahweh and the Israelites. Yahweh tests Israel's faithfulness in the crisis of the contaminated water at Marah, promising the people healing from the polluted water in exchange for obedience. The absence of water at Rephidim, also identified as Massah/Meribah, provides the occasion for the Israelites to test Yahweh. They raise a question in this story that provides the central theme to the second part of Exodus: Is Yahweh in our midst or not? The miracle of water from the rock signifies God's initial positive answer to Israel's question.

The remainder of the wilderness stories in Exodus elaborate on the different ways that Yahweh will be present with Israel and what obligations Israel must assume in order to live in the presence of God. The miracle of manna (chap. 16) indicates one way in which God is present with Israel in this world. It also establishes the Israelites' obligation to observe Sabbath rest. The central event in the second half of Exodus is the revelation of Yahweh on Mount Sinai. Exodus 19–24 describes Yahweh's descent to the summit of Mount Sinai to reveal law and to make covenant with Israel. Exodus 25–40 focuses on Yahweh's sanctuary. The revelation of the tabernacle (chaps. 25–31) is halted when the Israelites worship the golden calf (chap. 32). God forgives Israel (34:1-10), issues new laws (34:11-29), and commissions the building of the tabernacle (chaps. 35–40). Exodus ends with Yahweh finally descending from Mount Sinai and entering the completed tabernacle on New Year's Day (40:1-2, 17), filling the sanctuary with fire and smoke (40:34-38).

The story of Yahweh's revelation to Israel in the wilderness is also told on an epic scale. The forces of nature change their role, however, from providing Yahweh with weapons of war to signaling the presence of God with Israel. Israel is repeatedly rescued from crises through miracles. Polluted water is purified, water is drawn from rock, and food falls from heaven. During the revelation of Yahweh at Mount Sinai natural forces like thunder, lightning, darkness, and fire also signal the nearness of God to Israel and its inherent danger to humans. Yet Exodus presents an incomplete story about the presence of Yahweh. The Israelites' initial question in the wilderness of whether Yahweh was with them (17:1-7) is not fully answered at the close of the book. God is present with Israel when the divine glory enters the tabernacle (40:34-38). But the promise of life with God in the land of Canaan remains a future hope.

LEADERSHIP OF MOSES

The epic drama of Yahweh's war with Pharaoh and the divine revelation to Israel on Mount Sinai also provide the background for the story of Moses, the central human character in the book. The life of Moses is a human drama paralleling the divine epic of war and revelation. Moses, like Yahweh, begins the story without clear identity. Moses is born during Pharaoh's initial genocide (Exodus 2). He miraculously survives this ordeal and even becomes adopted into the house of Pharaoh. Exodus traces his doubts, struggles, and successes in becoming Israel's leader. His story relates the two parts of the book, with their divergent themes of divine power and presence. The first part traces Moses' character development as the Israelites' savior in the liberation from Egypt, while the second half explores his role as mediator during the revelation of law at Mount Sinai.

Exodus 2–5 introduces the character of Moses, noting his mixed identity (he is both an Egyptian and an Israelite), his good intentions (he wishes to help his people Israel), and his violent nature (he kills impulsively). His early life experience with the Midianites in the wilderness foreshadows Israel's experience in the second half of Exodus. He is commissioned at the mountain of God (chaps. 3–4), he returns to Egypt to mediate for Yahweh in confronting Pharaoh (chap. 5), and he continues to represent Yahweh to Pharaoh during the sequence of the plagues (chaps. 7–10), including the plague of death (chaps. 11–12). In the process Moses emerges as the liberator of the Israelites. But he is also their mediator. He informs the people of their forgotten ancestral God, Yahweh (chap. 4). He instructs them in cultic practice (chap. 12). He leads them in their march from Egypt (chap. 13) and even through the Red Sea (chap. 14).

The character of Moses is further developed during Israel's wilderness march (chaps. 16–18), when complaints by Israel about their journey force him to intercede with Yahweh on their behalf. His mediatorial role is greatly expanded during the revelation of the law (chaps. 19–24) and in the construction of the tabernacle (chaps. 25–40). Through repeated trips to the summit of the mountain, Moses begins to model the offices of priest, prophetic teacher, and even scribe as he purifies Israel, teaches the people the covenant, and records divine law. Yet the portrayal of Moses in Exodus is incomplete. His character development progresses through the Pentateuch until his death at the conclusion of Deuteronomy, completing his biography from birth to death.

Non-P and P Histories

I will limit interpretation of Exodus for the most part to the identification of two bodies of literature, the Non-P History and the P History. Both histories were composed in the exile or later, although each contains literature from earlier periods in Israel's history. Both histories trace the origin of the Israelite people through the central events of salvation history (e.g., creation, ancestors, exodus, revelation at the mountain of God, and promise of land), linking the events through travelogue, chronology, and genealogy. Both histories are critical of the monarchical period. Finally, both histories present a new vision of the Israelite society through divinely revealed law codes.

Non-P History

The Non-P History begins with the Israelite slavery in Egypt (Exodus 1). Yahweh commissions Moses in the wilderness (chaps. 2–4), liberates the Israelites (chaps. 5–15), and leads them to the mountain of God (chaps. 16–18). Yahweh reveals law and establishes a covenant with the Israelites at the divine mountain (chaps. 19–24). The Israelites break the covenant by building the golden calf (chap. 32). Moses persuades Yahweh in the tent of meeting (chap. 33) to renew the covenant (chap. 34), concluding the literature of the Non-P History in Exodus. The following list provides a broad outline of the Non-P

History in Exodus. The introduction to each section of the commentary will include a more detailed identification of the literature.

1:6, 7*, 8-12	Pharaoh's Enforcement of Slave Labor
1:15-21	Pharaoh's Genocide and the Midwives
1:22–2:10	Birth of Moses
2:11-23a	Moses' Flight to Midian
3:1–4:18	Commission of Moses in the Wilderness
4:19–6:1	Failed Confrontation with Pharaoh
7:14–10:29*	Plagues
7:14-24*	Blood
7:25–8:15*	Frogs
8:20-32*	Flies
9:1-7	Death of Livestock
9:13-35*	Hail
10:1-20*	Locusts
10:21-29	Darkness
11:1–13:16*	Death of the Egyptian Firstborn and Passover
13:17–14:31*	Death of the Egyptian Army at the Red Sea
15:1-19	Song of the Sea
15:22-27	Bitter Water at Shur
16:1-36*	Manna
17:1-7	Water from the Rock
17:8-16	War against the Amalekites
18:1-27	Jethro and Moses
19:3-8a*	Proposal of Covenant
19:8b-19*	Revelation on the Mountain
20:1-20*	Revelation of the Decalogue
20:21–23:33	Revelation of the Book of the Covenant
24:3-8*	Covenant Ceremony
24:12-15a*; 31:18*	Tablets of Stone
32:1-35*	Golden Calf
33:1-11	Tent of Meeting
33:12-23	Mediation of Moses
34:1-35*	Renewal of Covenant

(* indicates that a section or verse contains both Non-P and P material)

The Non-P History in Exodus develops further the promise of the ancestors in Genesis. It progresses from the revelation of the tent of meeting (Exodus 33) and covenant renewal (chap. 34) to additional stories about Mosaic authority in the setting of the tent of meeting in Numbers 11–12, where the authority of

Moses is developed further in relationship to the elders and Aaron, themes first introduced in the commission of Moses (Exod 3:1–4:18).

P History

The P History opens with the theme of creation, emphasizing the fertility of the Israelite people (Exodus 1). Yahweh remembers the past covenant with the ancestors (chap. 2), commissions Moses (chaps. 6–7), and defeats Pharaoh, bringing the Egyptians to the knowledge of God (chaps. 8–15). Yahweh reveals the Sabbath to the Israelites in the wilderness (chap. 16), before the Glory of Yahweh appears on Mount Sinai (chaps. 19–24). The revelation of the tabernacle concludes the events at Mount Sinai in Exodus (chaps. 25–31, 35–40), linking world creation with temple construction. The following list provides a broad outline of P literature in Exodus. The introduction to each section of the commentary will include a more detailed identification of the P History.

1:1-5, 7*	Fertility of Israel
1:13-14	Violence of the Egyptian Oppression
2:23b-25	Divine Memory of Covenant
6:2–7:7	Commission of Moses in Egypt
7:8–10:29*	Plagues (Editing of the Plagues, Especially Blood and Frogs)
7:8-13	Snakes
8:16-19	Gnats
9:8-12	Boils
11:1–13:16*	Death of the Egyptian Firstborn and Passover (Editing to the Divine Announcement to Moses in 11:1-10*)
12:1-20	Passover and Feast of Unleavened Bread Legislation
12:40-51	Passover Legislation
13:17–14:31*	Death of the Egyptian Army at the Red Sea
15:20-21	Song of Miriam
16:1-36*; 17:1b	Manna
19:1-2*	Arrival at Mount Sinai
19:11b, 18, 20-25	Revelation on Mount Sinai
20:1-17*	Revelation of the Decalogue
24:15-18	Revelation of the Glory of Yahweh on Mount Sinai
25:1–31:17*	Revelation of the Tabernacle
31:18*	Tablets of Testimony
32:1-35*	Golden Calf
34:1-35*	Renewal of Covenant

35:1–40:38 Construction of the Tabernacle and Its Cult
(* indicates that a section or verse contains both Non-P and P material)

The P History in Exodus continues the themes of creation (Genesis 1) and covenant (Genesis 9, 17) from Genesis. The P History progresses from the revelation and construction of the tabernacle (Exodus 25–31, 35–40) to the ordination of the priesthood and formation of the tabernacle cult in Leviticus and the establishment of the wilderness camp in Numbers 1–10. Mount Sinai remains the setting for the revelation of the cult and community in Exodus 19–Numbers 10.

HISTORY OF INTERPRETATION

The events in Exodus have been the source for ongoing interpretation from the time of the ancient Israelites to the present. The process of interpretation begins already in the book itself. The study of genre indicated that the Song of Miriam (Exod 15:21) and the theophany of God on the mountain (19:16-17) were reinterpreted in the formation of the book. But reinterpretation is not confined to Exodus. The story of the exodus was also interpreted throughout the Hebrew Bible. The prophet Hosea, for example, interpreted the exodus from Egypt as the result of prophetic leadership (Hos 12:13). The exilic prophet Second Isaiah explored the mythical meaning of salvation from Egypt as a defeat of the sea monster (Isa 51:9-11), while the prophet Ezekiel viewed Israel's wilderness journey negatively, as a time of idolatry (Ezekiel 20). The events in Exodus thread their way throughout the entire Hebrew Bible.

Exodus was also influential in shaping the broader history of Judaism and Christianity. Early Jewish writers like Josephus and Philo of Alexandria reinterpreted the exodus and the life of Moses to a Hellenistic culture. In his *Life of Moses,* for example, Philo described the tutoring of Moses in arithmetic and geometry by the Greeks.[137] Hecataeus of Abdera interpreted the exodus as an expulsion of foreigners from Egypt to Greece, whose leader was Moses. The group founded colonies, one of which was Jerusalem.[138]

NT writers explored the meaning of Jesus' ministry and passion within the framework of the exodus. Jesus was called out of Egypt (Matt 2:15), underwent testing in the wilderness (Luke 4:1-12), and became the paschal lamb

137. *Moses* 1.21-23.

138. Diodorus Siculus 40.3.1-8. For discussion see M. Stern, ed., *Greek and Latin Authors on Jews and Judaism,* vol. 1: *From Herodotus to Plutarch* (2nd ed.; Jerusalem: Israel Academy of Sciences and Humanities, 1976); D. Mendels, "Hecataeus of Abdera and a Jewish *Patrios politeia* of the Persian Period (*Diodorus Siculus* 40.3)," in *Identity, Religion and Historiography: Studies in Hellenistic History* (JSPSup 24; Sheffield: Sheffield Academic Press, 1998), 334-51.

(John 19:36), while the early Christians were also identified with the wilderness generation of Israelites (1 Cor 10:1-13). The Passover Haggadah continues to propel the events of the exodus through time, interpreting the exodus to new generations of Jewish worshipers. In the commentary I explore selective passages in the history of Jewish and Christian interpretation that enrich the interpretation of Exodus.

OUTLINE AND FORMAT

The literary summary indicated a division in Exodus between the themes of divine power (1:1–15:21) and divine presence (15:22–40:38). The commentary follows this division. Each half of the book breaks down further into three episodes. The theme of divine power includes episodes on "Setting" (chaps. 1–2), "Characters" (3:1–7:7), and "Conflict" (7:8–15:21). The theme of divine presence includes episodes on "Journey" (15:22–18:27), "Revelation" (19:1–24:11), and "Sanctuary" (24:12–40:38).

Each of the six episodes separate between a general introduction and more detailed commentary. The introduction for each episode will outline the central themes, an overview of current research, the literature of the Non-P and P Histories, and a more canonical appraisal of the present literary structure. The use of an asterisk (*) next to a biblical text in the allocation of verses to authors indicates that a verse or a section of text includes literature from more than one author. The commentary will include a translation, notes, and a literary interpretation of the individual texts. The translation will indicate the P History with **boldface** print and the Non-P History with regular print. The notes will address syntactical problems and compare the Hebrew and Greek texts of Exodus, using the *Biblia Hebraica Stuttgartensia* based on the Leningrad Codex for the Masoretic Text (designated as MT; K. Elliger and W. Rudolph, *Biblia Hebraica Stuttgartensia.* Stuttgart: Deutsche Bibelgesellschaft, 1997), the Samaritan Pentateuch (designated as Sam; A. F. von Gall, *Der Hebraische Pentateuch der Sameritaner,* Giessen: Alfred Topelmann, 1918), and the A. Rahlfs edition of the Septuagint (designated as LXX; *Septuaginta. Id est Vetus Testamentum graece iuxta LXX interpretes.* Stuttgart: Württembergische Bibelanstalt, 1962). The literary interpretation will examine central motifs within distinct stories or laws, the literary structure of different scenes, and the relationship of the texts to the larger ancient Near Eastern literary tradition.

PART 1

The Power of Yahweh in Egypt
(1:1–15:21)

Setting (1:1–2:25)

INTRODUCTION

CENTRAL THEMES

Exodus 1–2 establishes the social and geographical setting for the salvation of the Israelites as one of oppression through slave labor and genocide in the land of Egypt. The oppression of the Israelites in the land of Egypt allows biblical authors to explore salvation as an experience of liberation from slavery. Indeed, the story of liberation has become the paradigm for a long history of political and social interpretations of salvation. G. V. Pixley provides a contemporary illustration, noting the privileged place of the exodus for oppressed urban and rural Christians in the Third World. The story of the exodus, writes Pixley, is the resource for oppressed people to discover that the "true God of their faith is the God who accompanies them in their struggle for liberation from modern tyrants who oppress and repress them as the Pharaoh did the Hebrews."[1]

The book of Exodus explores the themes of divine power and presence as a resource for liberation. But the themes are developed only indirectly in Exodus 1–2, since the story opens with the absence of God in the land of Egypt, and, hence, in the life of the Israelites. Years have transpired since Joseph ruled in the land of Egypt. Jacob and his sons have died. Yet the divine promise of fertility to Jacob (e.g., Gen 28:13-15) lingers, prompting a population explosion among the Israelites. The fertility of the Israelites underscores the power of divine promise, even when God is not an active character in the story.

The absence of God in Exodus 1–2 allows biblical writers to explore the

---

1. G. V. Pixley, *Exodus: A Liberation Perspective* (Maryknoll, N.Y.: Orbis, 1987); see also H. Bloom, ed., *Exodus: Modern Critical Interpretations* (New York: Chelsea House, 1987).

theme of power and oppression from a human perspective. The story moves quickly. Vignettes provide insight into a range of human responses to the effects of the divine promise on the Israelite population. As a result human power takes on many faces in chaps. 1–2, including Pharaoh, the taskmasters, the midwives, a Levite woman and her daughter, the daughter of Pharaoh, Moses, shepherds at the well in Midian, and Reuel and his daughters. Glimpses of the Deity emerge only indirectly through human actions of liberation.

The major opponent to the divine blessing is Pharaoh. He fears Israel's growth. His use of power is evil. He acts shrewdly in his interest to control the Israelite population through a series of oppressive actions, progressing from slave labor to genocide of male children. The oppression of Pharaoh is a catalyst in separating Israelites and Egyptians, and in the process the authors begin to define the identity of the Israelite nation.[2] Pharaoh's oppression becomes the object of satire.[3] The authors emphasize how easily Pharaoh can be subverted by actions of women functioning in the role of tricksters. The midwives fear God rather than Pharaoh, allowing the Israelite babies to be born. A Levite woman hides her son in a basket and sets him adrift in the Nile River. Even Pharaoh's daughter joins in the action by rescuing the child from the river and adopting him. The series of reversals carries a clear message. The power represented by Pharaoh is certainly dangerous to human well-being, but as an antidote to the power of divine promise it is futile. The fertility of the Israelites, so feared by Pharaoh, penetrates into his own family without his even knowing it.

Moses represents a far more ambiguous character than Pharaoh in his use of power. He is an Israelite, born a Levite, but adopted by Pharaoh's daughter. Biblical writers use the motif of adoption to explore how actions by Moses define his identity as an Egyptian and as an Israelite. The two stories immediately following the birth and rescue of Moses provide the core tension in the development of his character. The initial story recounts a failed attempt by Moses to save Israelites from oppression in killing an Egyptian. The next story tells of Moses' successful rescue of Reuel's daughters at the well in the land of Midian. Both stories underscore that Moses embodies the power to save. But this power is dangerous and leads to very different outcomes depending on Moses' different social context and geographical setting. In the land of Egypt Moses identifies with the Hebrews, but mirrors the brutality of Pharaoh. This story is about murder, prompting hostility from Israelites and Egyptians alike. But in the wilderness of Midian Moses emerges as a savior, even though he is identified as an Egyptian. This story is about deliverance, leading to hospitality and marriage. The biblical writers skill-

---

2. Greifenhagen, *Egypt*, 47-69.

3. For examples of irony see T. E. Fretheim, *Exodus* (IBC; Louisville: Westminster John Knox, 1991), 37; Meyers, *Exodus*, 42-43.

fully use the motif of adoption to underscore the close relationship between identity, action, and environment in the character development of Moses.

AUTHORS

Research

The identification of the authors in Exodus 1–2 has tended to focus on repetition, distinctive vocabulary, and gaps in the narrative logic of the literature. The most agreement among modern interpreters is in identifying the P author in 1:1-5, 7, 13-14; and 2:23b-25. The list of Jacob's sons in 1:1-5 is attributed to the P author because the phrase "and these are the names" is similar to the P writing style in Gen 46:8-27. The motifs "bearing fruit," "swarming," and "filling the land" repeat from the P creation story (Gen 1:28). The reference to hard service in Exod 1:13-14 anticipates legal language in Lev 25:43, 46, 53. And the motif of divine memory and covenant in Exod 2:23b-25 repeats earlier themes in the P History from the conclusion of the flood (Gen 9:8-17) and the covenant with Abraham (Genesis 17).[4]

The assessment of P literature has undergone revision in more recent evaluations of Exodus 1–2. F. V. Winnett questioned whether 1:7 was P literature, since the motifs of the Israelites "multiplying" and "becoming strong" are not characteristic of P literature, and they repeat frequently in the chapter (1:9, 12, 20) in the Non-P History. He concluded that the verse was a mixture of P and Non-P literature.[5] A number of recent interpreters have reinforced the literary insight of Winnett (e.g., Van Seters, Propp, P. Weimar, C. Levin), raising a question about the nature of P tradition.[6] Does P literature constitute a supplement to Non-P literature, thus accounting for the complex literary character of v. 7? Or must P literature be separated into two levels of tradition, a P source and a post-P redaction? Propp advocates the latter position, arguing that v. 7 and the list of Jacob's family in 1:1-5 constitute a post-P redaction, based on literary differences between Gen 46:26-27, a P text, and Exod 1:1-5, which he judges to be a post-P redaction. The result for Propp is the limitation of the P source in Exodus 1–2 to 1:13-14 and 2:23b-25, with a significant post-P redaction including 1:1-5 and 7.[7]

The interpretation of the Non-P literature in Exodus 1–2 has tended to fo-

---

4. See the summary in Childs, *Exodus*, 2-46.

5. Winnett, *Mosaic Tradition*, 16.

6. Van Seters, *Life of Moses*, 19-21; Propp, *Exodus 1–18*, 125-26; P. Weimar, *Untersuchungen zur priesterschriftlichen Exodusgeschichte:* (FB 9; Würzburg: Echter Verlag, 1973), 25-36; C. Levin, *Der Jahwist* (FRLANT 157; Göttingen: Vandenhoeck & Ruprecht, 1993), 313-16.

7. Propp, *Exodus 1–18*, 125-26.

cus on the separation of E and J literature. M. Noth singled out the story of the midwives (1:15-21) as E on the basis of the divine name Elohim and the phrase "king of Egypt" to describe the Pharaoh. He attributed the remainder of the narrative to J, including 1:8-12, 22; 2:1-23a, although he noted points of tension in the present form of the text, such as the role of Moses' sister (2:4, 7-10a*a*) in the story of his birth.[8]

The separation of the Non-P literature in Exodus 1–2 is debated, however, depending on the evaluation of the divine names Elohim and Yahweh, and more comprehensive literary theories about the composition of the Pentateuch. Propp continues to separate E (1:15-21) from J (1:22–2:23a) on the basis of divine names and the distinctive views of the population of the Israelite people. The unity of the J section (1:22–2:23a) is both thematic (the confusion surrounding Moses' ethnic identity) and literary (patterns of key motifs, such as the Hebrew root *yld*, distributed in groups of 7/8).[9] Other interpreters have moved away from the distinction of J and E. Winnett argued that the story of the midwives (1:15-21) requires the threat of the Israelite growth of population (1:8-12). He asks: "Are not these two stories interdependent parts of the same narrative?" The theme of hard labor (1:8-12) evolved into the theme of the genocide of male babies (1:15-21). The literary source for both episodes, according to Winnett, is the birth of Moses (2:1-10), with its theme of the hero who is cast away in infancy. The three stories cannot be separated into distinct literary sources. Such a hypothesis, of course, plays down the separation of the divine names as a marker of distinct sources.[10] Developing further Winnett's position, Van Seters reads the Non-P literature in Exodus 1–2 as the composition of a single Yahwist historian.[11]

The literary context of Exodus 1–2 has become an increasingly important factor in evaluating authorship. Van Seters points to numerous parallels between the Non-P literature in Exodus 1–2, Deuteronomy, and the Deuteronomistic History to identify an exilic Yahwist who is post-Deuteronomistic.[12] E. Blum has reinforced many of the same literary connections as Van Seters in describing *KD*, the Non-P body of literature that relates Exodus, Deuteronomy, and the Deuteronomistic History.[13] Examples of the literary parallels include the transition of generations (Gen 50:26; Exod 1:6-8; Judg 2:8-10), the increase of descendants (Gen 18:18; Exod 1:7, 9, 12, 20; Deut 7:1; 9:1; 11:23), the reference to storehouses (Exod 1:11; 1 Kgs 9:19), and the model of Moses as a political fugitive (Exod 2:11-23a; 1 Kgs 11:14-22).

8. M. Noth, *Exodus* (trans. J. S. Bowden; OTL; Philadelphia: Westminster, 1962), 20-28.
9. Propp, *Exodus 1–18*, 125-26.
10. Winnett, *Mosaic Tradition*, 16-29, quotation from 17.
11. Van Seters, *Life of Moses*, 15-34.
12. Ibid.
13. Blum, *Studien*.

Source critics have long recognized the loose connection between Exodus 1–2 and Genesis, although the relationship of the two books has not been a focus of interpretation. Noth wrote: "The introduction of the great theme 'The Exodus from Egypt' is connected briefly and loosely to the theme of the Patriarchs which has preceded it in the book of Genesis. We now have this connection only in the late formulation by P (vv. 1-7)."[14] Noth assumed that the original connection between Genesis and Exodus in the older sources was suppressed by the present position of the P literature, which allowed him to maintain the source-critical hypothesis, even though the older sources, according to Noth, presently lack a clear literary connection.

More recently interpreters have built on the insight of Noth. The loose relationship between Genesis and Exodus has taken on larger meaning, however, with the rejection of source criticism. The result is an emerging hypothesis concerning the formation of the Pentateuch in which the combination of the ancestral story of origin and the Mosaic account of salvation from Egypt become the central literary accomplishment in the formation of the Pentateuch. The problem of the relationship of Genesis and Exodus is evident in Propp's position; he attributes a significant role to the post-P redactor in the composition of 1:1-5, 7. Such a literary conclusion makes the most explicit connection between Genesis and Exodus the product of a very late author. The Documentary Hypothesis led Propp to conclude that the purpose of the post-P redaction was to provide an introduction to the book of Exodus.[15]

J. C. Gertz represents a literary analysis of the P and the post-P literature in Exodus 1–2 similar to that of Propp. He too limits the P literature to 1:7*, 13-14; 2:23a*b*-25, while expanding the role of a post-P final redactor of the Pentateuch to include 1:1-6, 8-10, 20b-21a.[16] But by not working within the framework of the Documentary Hypothesis, Gertz interprets the function of the P and the post-P literature as forging the literary relationship between the books of Genesis and Exodus, which represent independent origin traditions. Van Seters already suggested such a master narrative in the early 1970s, which he attributed to an exilic Yahwist. Blum's hypothesis of *KD* advanced in the mid- to late 1980s conforms to the argument of Van Seters, although he reaches his conclusion through more tradition-historical methodology. The interpretations by Gertz and Schmid in the late 1990s, however, advocate a later forging of the master narrative by the P author and by the post-P redactors.[17] This hypothesis has prompted Blum to qualify his literary de-

---

14. Noth, *Exodus,* 20.
15. Propp, *Exodus 1–18,* 125-26.
16. Gertz, *Tradition und Redaktion,* 349-87.
17. Schmid, *Erzväter und Exodus.*

scription of *KD,* the pre-P corpus of literature in Genesis–2 Kings, to exclude Genesis.[18]

The overview of the research on the authorship of Exodus 1–2 indicates the dynamic character of scholarship at the present time. Old hypotheses of authorship are being significantly revised or abandoned altogether. We have seen that the debate concerning the multiple authorship of Non-P literature (J and E) continues, and that there are new debates about P literature, especially its relationship to post-P authorship. We have also seen that the identification of authorship has branched out from a focus on internal problems in the style of the narrative, to the larger literary relationship of Exodus 1–2 to Genesis, on one hand, and to Deuteronomy and the Deuteronomistic History, on the other. The result is that the interpretation of Exodus 1–2 is related to broad questions about the literary formation of a Primary History, consisting of Genesis–2 Kings. My comments will address aspects of the ongoing debates about the multiple levels of authorship in the P and Non-P literature. The focus of interpretation, however, will remain at a more general level, seeking to distinguish the two histories, the Non-P History and the P History, both of which contain a history of composition.

Non-P and P Histories

The chart in figure 2 on page 61 identifies the literature of the Non-P and P Histories. The subsequent sections provide a summary of their distinct interpretations of the oppression of the Israelites in Egypt.

Non-P History

The Non-P author is most prominent in Exodus 1–2. The author begins the story by noting the death of Joseph and his entire generation (1:6), the continuing fertility of the Israelites, and more importantly the strength of the new generation of Israelites (1:7*). A new pharaoh, who is unfamiliar with Joseph, immediately takes center stage in three actions. He institutes slave labor to slow down the population growth and to weaken the Israelite people (1:8-12). He commands the midwives to kill all male Hebrew babies (1:15-21), and he makes a public proclamation that all male Hebrew babies should be thrown into the Nile, providing background for the birth story of Moses (1:22–2:10). The Non-P author is also responsible for the story of Moses' murder of the Egyptian (2:11-

18. E. Blum, "Die literarische Verbindung von Erzväter und Exodus: Ein Gespräch mit neueren Endredaktionshypothesen," in *Abschied vom Jahwisten,* ed. Gertz et al., 119-56.

Figure 2

Topic	Non-P History	P History
Israel in Egypt (1:1-7)		
1. Family of Jacob	—	1:1-5
2. Death of Joseph	1:6	—
3. Israelite Fertility	1:7*	1:7*
Pharaoh (1:8-21)		
1. Slave Labor	1:8-12	1:13-14
2. Genocide	1:15-21	—
Moses (1:22–2:22)		
1. Birth	1:22–2:10	—
2. Murder	2:11-15a	—
3. Flight to Midian	2:15b-22	—
Israel in Egypt (2:23-25)		
1. Death of Pharaoh	2:23a	—
2. Lament	—	2:23b-25

15a), his rescue of Reuel's daughters at the well, his marriage to Zipporah, the birth of a son, Gershom (2:15b-22), and most likely the death notice of the king of Egypt (2:23a). The literary structure of the Non-P History accentuates death as a sign of generational transition, and the increase of violence in history — a theme first introduced in the genealogy of Cain (Gen 4:17-26). The theme of death frames the episode. The death of Joseph and his generation opens the episode (Exod 1:6). The section concludes with the death of the oppressive pharaoh who did not know Joseph (2:23a).

P History

The P author adds a new opening (1:1-5, 7*) and closing (2:23b-25) to the Non-P History. Exodus 1:1-5, 7* relates the fertility of the Israelites to the creation of the world in Genesis 1. It also makes more explicit the divine promise of offspring to the ancestors as background to the story of the exodus. The closing episode stresses the theme of covenant from the P story of the flood (Gen 9:1-17) and from the divine promise to Abraham (Genesis 17). The P author concludes the episode with the notice that Yahweh remembered the covenant with the ancestors, thus firmly linking the story of the exodus with the promise to the patriarchs in Genesis. With the addition of Exod 1:13-14, the P author also underscores the violent and illegal nature of the Egyptian oppression.

LITERARY STRUCTURE

The Non-P History establishes the central themes in the opening episode, including the death of humans to signal generational transition and the absence of God from the life of the Israelites. Although not stated explicitly the divine promise of offspring to the ancestors lingers from Genesis through the fertility of the Israelites. But without the accompanying promise of land to provide a safe location for offspring, the fertility of the Israelites creates suffering and even death from the oppressive actions of Pharaoh, who fears their presence in his land.

The P History sharpens the themes from the Non-P History with a new introduction (1:1-5, 7*) and conclusion (2:23b-25) to the episode. Exodus 1:1-5 underscores the connection between the ancestral stories in Genesis and the national liberation of the Israelite nation in Exodus through genealogy (1:1-5). Exodus 1:7* expands the scope of the Israelite fertility with references to creation in Gen 1:28. Exodus 2:23b-25 gives voice to the suffering of the Israelite people with lament. The combination of the two histories yields the following four-part outline.

    I. Fertility of Israel (1:1-7)
   II. Fear of Pharaoh (1:8-21)
  III. Identity of Moses (1:22–2:22)
  IV. Human Lament (2:23-25)

COMMENTARY

FERTILITY OF ISRAEL (1:1-7)

¹:¹*And these are the names of the Israelites who came to Egypt. They came with Jacob, each with his household:* ²*Reuben, Simeon, Levi, and Judah,* ³*Issachar, Zebulun, and Benjamin,* ⁴*Dan and Naphtali, Gad and Asher.* ⁵*All the humans coming from Jacob's thigh were seventy humans. But Joseph was in Egypt.* ⁶*And Joseph died, and all of his brothers, and all that generation.* ⁷*Yet the Israelites* **bore fruit; they swarmed;** *they multiplied; and they became very, very strong,* **so that the land was filled with them.**

Notes

1:1 *And.* The MT begins with the conjunction *wě-*, while the LXX lacks a conjunction. The difference may provide insight into the relationship of Genesis and Exodus and the larger organization of the Pentateuch and the Deuteronomistic History in the distinct textual traditions. The lack of the conjunction in the LXX raises a question about the relationship between Genesis and Exodus. (See the overview of the MT and LXX in the introduction, "Literary Context").

Israelites. The Hebrew *běnê yiśrā'ēl* indicates both familial and national identity. Exodus 1:1 indicates a more familial context of descendants, prompting NRSV to translate "sons of Israel," as compared to 1:7, where NRSV translates the same phrase as "Israelites."

they came. The translation follows the MT, reading the phrase "with Jacob" in the second half of the verse in conjunction with the verb "they came." NRSV and NIV follow the LXX, placing "with Jacob" in the first half of the verse: "And these are the names of the sons of Israel who came to Egypt with Jacob."

1:2 *and Judah.* The translation follows the MT. The conjunction missing from the LXX suggests that Reuben, Simeon, Levi, Judah, Issachar, Zebulun, and Benjamin form one group, with Judah at the center, as compared to the two groups in the MT.

1:5 *humans.* The Hebrew *nepeš* repeats in the verse, indicating a human being or a living soul. The LXX is *psychai* ("lives, souls").

All the humans . . . But Joseph was in Egypt. The LXX reverses the order of v. 5, placing the reference to Joseph first in the verse ("But Joseph was in Egypt"), so that his name appears at the conclusion of the list of sons, followed by the number. 4QExod[b] lists Joseph with the sons of Jacob.[1] The textual traditions suggest confusion over the status of Joseph, perhaps also reflected in Gen 46:26-27, where the number of offspring changes depending on whether Joseph is included.

seventy humans. The LXX numbers the descendants at seventy-five, rather than seventy. 4QExod[b] and 4QGen-Exod[a] follow the LXX.

1:7 *multiplied.* The LXX has *chydaioi*, meaning "abundant," like Hebrew *rābbâ*, but the Greek word can also signify "common" or "vulgar," a meaning beyond the Hebrew.

Commentary

The fertility of the Israelite people is stated in v. 7. It establishes the central theme for the opening section of Exodus. The people of Israel have evolved into a great nation, fulfilling the divine prediction from Genesis even though God is absent.

1:1-5 The book of Exodus begins with a list of the sons of Jacob who migrated to Egypt. The P historian relates the books of Genesis and Exodus with this list. Three times in Genesis the sons of Jacob are specified: (1) the birth of the sons except Benjamin is given in Gen 29:31–30:22; (2) a full summary of Jacob's sons is provided after the birth of Benjamin in 35:23-26; and (3) a list of the sons who migrated to Egypt with Jacob along with their households occurs in 46:8-27. The sons are also enumerated in Jacob's blessing in Genesis 49. The lists are not the same. Only the first list (29:1–30:22) is organized by birth.

---

1. See F. M. Cross, *The Ancient Library of Qumran* (3rd ed.; Minneapolis: Fortress, 1995), 134-35.

Leah: Reuben, Simeon, Levi, and Judah
Bilhah, Rachel's servant: Dan and Naphtali
Zilpah, Leah's servant: Gad and Asher
Leah: Issachar, Zebulun, and a daughter Dinah
Rachel: Joseph

The other lists organize the sons by the arrangement of the mothers. For example, Leah's six sons are grouped together in all subsequent lists, and Rachel's sons precede those of Bilhah and Zilpah in Gen 35:23-26.

Repetition between Exod 1:1-5 and the preceding lists ties Genesis and Exodus together, while also advancing the plot of the story. The opening words of v. 1, "[And] these are the names of the sons of Israel" *(wĕʾēlleh šĕmôt bĕnê-yiśrāʾēl)*, repeats the similar phrase from Gen 46:8, the original list of Jacob's sons who migrate to Egypt (Gen 46:8-27). Both texts also place the number of Jacob's descendants at seventy persons. This number is repeated in Deut 10:22. Seventy persons may be a symbolic number for completeness in the MT tradition. Seventy sons are attributed to Gideon, the judge (Judg 8:30), and to King Ahab (2 Kgs 10:1). Moses also selects seventy elders to judge the people (Num 11:16). U. Cassuto notes the mythological background of the Canaanite goddess Atirat who also has seventy sons, perhaps implying perfection.[2] The LXX places the number of persons migrating to Egypt at seventy-five, the apparent source for the NT writers (see Acts 7:14).[3]

The order of the sons in Exod 1:2-4 does not follow Gen 46:8-27, but more closely resembles the list in Gen 35:23-26 (see fig. 3).

The differences have prompted interpreters to distinguish the author of Exod 1:1-5 from the P History, as a post-P redactor (Propp), or as an even later final redactor of the Pentateuch (J. C. Gertz).[4] I will interpret the literary unit within the larger context of the P History. In this setting the differences between the lists indicate that the P writer is adapting the literature to advance the plot of the story. First, the absence of Joseph in 1:1-5 is the result of his prior residency in Egypt, which is necessary for the context of the book of Exodus and stated explicitly in v. 5. Second, the change of reference to the family of Jacob is also noteworthy. Genesis 35:26 concludes the list of sons with the familial statement: "These are the sons of Jacob" *(ʾēlleh bĕnê-yaʿăqōb)*. This phrase fits the context of Gen 35:23-26, since the family of Jacob is complete with the birth of Benjamin in Gen 35:16-20. Exodus 1:1 provides a more national perspective to the same list with the

---

2. U. Cassuto, *Commentary on Exodus* (trans. I. Abrahams; Jerusalem: Magnes, 1967), 8.

3. Propp (*Exodus 1–18*, 121-22) expands the study of the number seventy in Canaanite literature, including the myth of Elkunirša.

4. Propp, *Exodus 1–18*, 125-26; Gertz, *Tradition und Redaktion*, 354-55.

Figure 3

	Gen 35:23-26	*Exod 1:2-4*
Leah:	Reuben	Reuben
	Simeon	Simeon
	Levi	Levi
	Judah	Judah
	Issachar	Issachar
	Zebulun	Zebulun
Rachel:	Joseph	—
	Benjamin	Benjamin
Bilhah:	Dan	Dan
	Naphtali	Naphtali
Zilpah:	Gad	Gad
	Asher	Asher

phrase "sons of Israel" *(běnê-yiśrā'ēl)*. The name "Israel" is given to Jacob in the Non-P History during his struggle with God at the Jabbok River (Gen 32:22-32) and again in the P History when Jacob returns to Bethel (35:9-15). The name Israel is used sparingly in the story of Jacob's migration to Egypt (42:5; 45:21; 46:5, 8; 50:25), including, as we have seen, in the list of his sons migrating to Egypt (46:8). The change in title between the original list of Jacob's sons in Gen 35:23-26 and in Exod 1:1 alerts the reader to a transition in subject matter from ancestral origins in Genesis to the beginning of the Israelite nation in Exodus.

1:6-7 Death and life are juxtaposed in these verses. Verse 6 recounts the death of Joseph, his brothers, and the entire generation. This verse is likely the Non-P historian's introduction to the exodus. Verse 7 notes the fertility of the Israelites with a variety of motifs, including "bearing fruit," "swarming," "multiplying," "becoming strong," and "filling the land." The density of motifs suggests the presence of both the Non-P and P historians (see the introduction to this section, "Authors: Research").

The references to Joseph's death and the passing of a generation in 1:6 do not reflect motifs from the P History. Thus v. 6 has traditionally been assigned to the Non-P source(s) of the Pentateuch. It is often designated as the beginning of Exodus in the J History. Verse 6 is noteworthy because it couples the death of Joseph with an entire generation *(dôr)*. T. C. Vriezen provided an important insight into the interpretation of v. 6 by noting a parallel to Judg 2:8-10, where the death of Joshua was also interwoven with the passing of a generation *(dôr)*.[5] The

---

5. T. C. Vriezen, "Exodusstudien: Exodus I," *VT* 17 (1967): 334-53, esp. 338.

repetition relates Exodus with the Deuteronomistic History, since each passage marks the death of a hero (Joseph, Joshua) and the death of an entire generation.

Judges 2:10 provides a parallel for interpreting Exod 1:6: "Moreover, that whole generation was gathered to their ancestors, and another generation grew up after them, who did not know Yahweh or the work that he had done for Israel." Judges 2:10 clarifies that the passing of a generation signifies the breakdown of tradition and memory. The generation after Joshua loses all knowledge of God. The same meaning is likely intended in Exod 1:6. The immediate context of 1:6, however, focuses more on the new pharaoh than on the people of Israel (1:8). He has forgotten Joseph. It is not until the call of Moses in Exodus 3 that the Israelites' loss of memory of God becomes a central topic that will require the self-introduction of Yahweh as the "God of the fathers."

The comparison of 1:6 and Judg 2:8-10 leads to an initial conclusion. The reference to the death of an entire generation *(dôr)* is more than a transition between Genesis and Exodus. It accentuates a break between the story of the ancestors and the deliverance from Egypt, at least as great as that between the books of Joshua and Judges. The generation after Joseph has lost knowledge of past tradition, which, in the present narrative context of Exodus, is the story of the ancestors in Genesis. Verse 6 may be a technique by which the Non-P author relates the ancestor stories in Genesis with the account of Moses in Egypt.[6] The motif of generational transition allows for the juxtaposition of the two accounts of origin, with only minimal repetition of motifs between the two bodies of literature.[7] The absence of God as an active character in Exodus 1–2 further underscores the separation from the stories of Genesis, where the Deity was imminent and active with the ancestors.

Van Seters noted a larger parallel between 1:6 and Josh 2:8-10 when the death notice of Joseph at the end of Genesis (Gen 50:26) and the rise of a new pharaoh in Egypt (Exod 1:8) are included.[8] The parallels are: (1) the death notice of the two heroes, Joseph and Joshua, both at the age of 110 years (Gen

---

6. See Schmid *(Erzväter und Exodus)* for discussion of the separate development of the ancestral stories in Genesis and the account of Moses' liberation of the Israelites in Exodus.

7. Rendtorff *(Problem)* has underscored the paucity of connecting motifs between the story of the ancestors and Moses.

8. Van Seters, *Life of Moses,* 17-18. Van Seters notes a further web of related motifs surrounding the bones of Joseph, which reappear at the close of Joshua (24:32). For Van Seters, the literary connections arise from a single author, an exilic Yahwist. But the authorship of Gen 50:22-26 and its relationship to Exod 1:6, 8-10 are debated. Blum *(Studien,* 363-64) identifies at least two authors in Gen 50:22-26. *KD* relates Gen 50:24 (the promise to the ancestors) to the death notice of Joseph (Exod 1:6); while a later editor (a "Joshua 24 editor") adds Gen 50:25-26a (the tradition of Joseph's bones), carrying the motif through to the end of the book of Joshua (24:29-32). Gertz *(Tradition und Redaktion,* 358-60) and Schmid *(Erzväter und Exodus,* 152-53) identify the author as a post-P redactor.

50:26a; Judg 2:8); (2) the burial notice for each hero: Joseph is embalmed (Gen 50:26b), and Joshua is buried in his tomb at Timnath-heres in Ephraim (Judg 2:9); (3) the death of a generation (Exod 1:6; Judg 2:10a); and (4) the break in continuity of tradition with the accompanying loss of memory: a new pharaoh does not know Joseph (Exod 1:8), and a new generation of Israelites do not know Yahweh (Judg 2:10b). When the context is expanded even further to include Exod 1:9-10 and Judg 2:11, a fifth parallel emerges concerning the actions of those who forget. Exodus 1:9-10 describes the oppressive actions of the new pharaoh, while Judg 2:11 laments the apostasy of the new generation of Israelites. The final parallel indicates the negative meaning in each story associated with the death of a generation. The passing of a generation signifies the loss of memory and the breakdown in the continuity of tradition. In Exodus it leads to violence by Pharaoh, and in Judges it results in evil acts of worship against Yahweh.

The parallels between Gen 50:26; Exod 1:6, 8-10; and Judg 2:6-11 indicate a literary relationship in the Non-P History between Genesis, Exodus, and the Deuteronomistic History. Childs concluded that the recurrence of the death notice from Gen 50:26 and Exod 1:6 has a dual function to point backward to the patriarchs and forward to the exodus.[9] The repetition of generational transition relates Exodus with the Deuteronomistic History. The interweaving of the ancestor stories in Genesis, the Egyptian oppression in Exodus, and the account of the Israelites' life in the land in the Deuteronomistic History creates a version of salvation history that includes two epochs. The first epoch of salvation history, according to J. C. Gertz, is the transition from the ancestors (Genesis) to Moses (Exodus); the second is the changeover from the generation of Joshua, who acquire the land through conquest (Joshua), to the rebellion of the Israelite people during the time of the judges (Judges).[10]

The literary design advocates a dark view of history. K. Schmid interprets the two-part structure as a tragic story of salvation history (Genesis–Joshua) and its downfall (Judges–2 Kings).[11] The repetition of generational change also suggests a parallel design to the two epochs: each period passes from an ideal time to a state of violence. In the first epoch the pacifism of the ancestors in Genesis, culminating in the peaceful life of Jacob's family in Egypt, gives way to slavery and oppression in the story of Moses in Exodus when the new pharaoh forgets Joseph. The successful liberation of the Israelite people from Egypt ushers in a new epoch of salvation history, which reaches an ideal when Joshua leads the Israelite people in the successful conquest of the land, culminating in

---

9. Childs, *Exodus*, 1-2.
10. Gertz, *Tradition und Redaktion*, 359.
11. Schmid, *Erzväter und Exodus*, 5-26 *et passim*.

a covenant between a unified Israelite people and Yahweh at the close of the book of Joshua (chap. 24). The book of Judges signals the downfall of the ideal portrayal of Israel in the second epoch, when a new generation forgets Yahweh, leading to their acts of apostasy, which are traced to the downfall of the kingdom in 2 Kings.

The reference to fertility in Exod 1:7 includes language from both the Non-P and P Histories. F. V. Winnett noted that the motifs "to multiply" (*rābbâ*) and "to become strong" (*'āṣam*) are not characteristic of the P author.[12] Furthermore, the motifs are presupposed in the following statement of Pharaoh, when he expresses his fear that the Israelites are multiplying and becoming strong (1:9). The word pair continues in the Non-P History in the summary of Pharaoh's slave labor (1:12) and again in the story of the midwives (1:20). The motifs of fertility and strength may be intended to recall the divine promise of offspring to the ancestors, which repeats in different forms to Abraham (Gen 12:1-4; 13:14-17; 15:5; 17:6-8; 22:17), Isaac (26:2-5), and Jacob (28:13-15; 35:11-13; 46:3-4). But the literary relationship is not explicit. Only once is the motif of strength noted in the sequence of promises to the ancestors, in the divine soliloquy in 18:18: "Shall I hide from Abraham what I am about to do [to Sodom and Gomorrah], seeing that Abraham shall become a great nation and powerful (*wĕ'āṣûm*)." The Hebrew verb *'āṣam* in Exod 1:7 may signify the continuing power of the divine promise, even though the new generation of Israelites (1:6) has forgotten it. What is emphasized in the Non-P History, however, is that the fertility of the Israelites accounts for the cruel treatment by the new pharaoh who has forgotten Joseph and now fears their strength.

The P historian emphasizes the fertility of the Israelites with language from the story of creation in Genesis 1. The P addition to Exod 1:7 recalls the divine blessing on the first humans in Gen 1:28, whom God commands to be fruitful (*pārâ*) and to fill (*mālē'*) the land (*'ereṣ*). The new generation of Israelites in Egypt fulfills all of these commands and more. They even swarm (*šāraṣ*) like the fish and birds in Gen 1:20. The language of fertility allows the P writer to create a repetition between the opening stories in Genesis and Exodus. The creation story recounts the beginning of all humanity. The fertility of Israel in Egypt signals the beginning of the Israelite nation, which has evolved from the genealogy of Jacob's family in Exod 1:1-5.

Finally, the juxtaposition of death and life in the present form of 1:6-7 is noteworthy. This combination is accentuated by the P writer's additions in v. 7. A similar juxtaposition occurs in Gen 35:16-26, a text that informs Exod 1:1-5. Genesis 35:16-26, like Exod 1:6-7, is a combination of literature from the Non-P and the

---

12. Winnett, *Mosaic Tradition*, 16. See also Van Seters, *Life of Moses*, 19; Propp, *Exodus 1–18*, 125-26. Cf. Gertz, *Tradition und Redaktion*, 352-54.

P Histories. The thematic focus of the Non-P author is the death of Rachel, as she gives birth to Benjamin, and the account of her burial (Gen 35:16-22). The P historian adds the list of Jacob's sons in Gen 35:23-26, moving the episode beyond the death of Rachel to the next generation. I have clarified that the P author repeats this list in Exod 1:1-5. But there is a progression in how the list is interpreted. The sons of Jacob represent the generation that dies, thus reinforcing the message of the Non-P author in 1:6. Yet the final word of the P author is not death (v. 6) but new life (v. 7), as it was in Gen 35:16-26. The Israelites are fertile and they give birth to a new generation. The explicit literary ties to the creation story accentuate the triumph of life over death in the P History, providing a countervoice to the Non-P History with its more tragic vision of salvation history, as a process whereby humans forget the past and act violently in the present.

FEAR OF PHARAOH (1:8-21)

¹ː⁸*Then a new king arose over Egypt, who did not know Joseph.* ⁹*And he said to his people, "Look, the Israelite people are more numerous and stronger than we.* ¹⁰*Come, let us deal shrewdly with him, lest he multiply, and in the event of war, even he be added to our enemies and fight against us, and go up from the land." ¹¹So they set over him taskmasters to oppress him with their forced labor. And he built the storage cities for Pharaoh: Pithom and Rameses. ¹²Yet as they oppressed him, he would multiply and he was breaking out. And the Egyptians dreaded the Israelites.* ¹³***And the Egyptians forced the Israelites to serve with violence.*** ¹⁴***And they made their lives bitter with hard service in mortar, in bricks, and in all kinds of fieldwork. All of their work they forced upon the Israelites with violence.***

¹⁵*And the king of Egypt said to the Hebrew midwives, one of whom was named Shiphrah and the second Puah,* ¹⁶*and he said, "When you aid the Hebrew women in birthing, and you see them on the birth stones, if he is a son, kill him, but if she is a daughter, she may live." ¹⁷But the midwives feared the God. And they did not do as the king of Egypt commanded them, and they let the boys live.*

¹⁸*Then the king of Egypt called to the midwives, and he said to them, "Why have you done this thing, and let the boys live?" ¹⁹And the midwives said to Pharaoh, "The Hebrew women are not like the Egyptian women. For they are teeming with life, and before the midwife comes to them, they give birth." ²⁰So God dealt well with the midwives, and the people multiplied and they became very strong. ²¹And because the midwives feared the God, he made houses for them.*

Notes

1:8 *a new king.* The LXX has *basileus heteros,* "another king."
1:9 *to his people . . . the Israelite people.* The MT repeats the word 'am in describing

both the Egyptians ("to his people") and the Israelites ("the Israelite people"). The LXX distinguishes the two groups by describing the Egyptians as *ethnos* (nation, people) and the Israelites as *genos* (possibly meaning "nation," but more likely "descendants, family").

1:10 *him.* The MT refers to the people in the collective singular. The LXX uses the plural pronoun, *autous.*

1:11 *Pithom and Rameses.* The LXX adds a third city, On, identified as Heliopolis.

1:12 *was breaking out.* The LXX underscores the threat of power that the fertility of the Israelites posed to the Egyptians, *ischyron sphodra sphodra,* "so they became very very strong."

1:15 *Hebrew midwives.* The MT reads "Hebrew" as an attributive adjective. In the LXX, by contrast, the word is a noun, *tais maiais tōn Hebraiōn.* The difference in syntax has contributed to debate over the ethnic identity of the midwives, whether they are Egyptians or Hebrews. See the commentary below.

1:16 *she may live.* For discussion of the form of the verb in the MT see GKC §67k. The LXX reads, *peripoieisthe auto,* "save her."

1:19 *teeming with life.* See Propp, who translates, "they are lively."[1]

1:21 *he made.* The MT lacks an explicit subject. The translation assumes God as subject from the preceding clause. The LXX reads, *epoiēsan heautais oikias,* "they [the midwives] made houses for themselves."

Commentary

The section describes the response of Pharaoh to the fertility of Israel. A new Pharaoh lacking knowledge of the past assumes the throne. He fears the fertility of the Israelites and seeks to stop it. Two stories probe the use of power for oppression. Exodus 1:8-14 is a story of slave labor aimed at limiting the birth rate of the Israelite people. Verses 15-21 intensify the abuse of power from slavery to genocide. The futility of such power is illustrated through a series of reversals.

1:8-14 Verse 8 sets the stage for the abuse of power by Pharaoh. It states that a new king arose in the land of Egypt, who did not know about Joseph. The "lack of knowledge" by the new pharaoh is crucial for the thematic development of the exodus. For the Non-P author, the motif of knowledge plays a restricted role in the opening chapters of Exodus. It develops from v. 6, where a transition in generation was already indicated. Verse 8 makes explicit that the transition of Egyptian rulers results in the loss of memory about Joseph and the Israelites. Genesis 41:37-40 provides insight into what the new pharaoh has forgotten. Past pharaohs knew that Joseph was "discerning" (*nābôn*), "wise" (*ḥākām*), and filled with "the spirit of God" (*rûaḥ 'ĕlōhîm*). This knowledge led to acts of hospitality toward Joseph and his entire family. For the Non-P author the new king's loss of memory sets the stage for the Israelite oppression. The P

1. Propp, *Exodus 1–18,* 136.

historian will expand the motif into a central theme for the exodus. The purpose of the exodus, according to the P writer, is to bring all of the Egyptians (e.g., Exod 7:5), including Pharaoh (e.g., 7:10), to the knowledge of God.

The speech of Pharaoh in 1:9-10 provides insight into his character. Without knowledge of the past, the wisdom that previous pharaohs saw in Joseph fades. In its place the new pharaoh sees the Israelites only as a military threat. In the process, "wise" actions *(ḥākām)* become perverted into "shrewd" ones *(nitḥakmâ).* Pharaoh states: "Come, we must deal shrewdly with them." The Hebrew *nitḥakmâ,* "deal shrewdly," is a Hithpael form of the verb *ḥakam,* "to be wise," but it carries negative connotations. The author of Ecclesiastes illustrates the negative meaning of the word, and, in the process, he also provides commentary on Pharaoh. He warns: "Neither be overwise [shrewd], why destroy yourself?" (Eccl 7:16).

The new pharaoh's decision to be shrewd is the first act in his self-destruction. He introduces a distinction between "his people" and the "people of Israel." He fears that the Israelites "are more numerous and stronger" than the Egyptians. Pharaoh fears not only the size *(rab)* of the Israelites, but also their strength *(ʿāṣûm).* The use of similar motifs in subsequent stories of the Non-P History indicates that the fear of Pharaoh concerns war. Similar language of fear is used to describe Israel's conquest of Canaan (Num 14:12; Deut 7:1; 9:1) and Balak's fear of the Israelites (Num 22:6).

Pharaoh makes the context of war explicit. He fears that Israel will war against the Egyptians by joining the side of their enemies. Such an action will result in Israel "going up from the land" *(wĕʿālâ min-hāʾāreṣ).* The fear that Israel might leave the country is somewhat odd, since the pharaoh fears their presence in the land. The Non-P author may be alluding to the exodus or more precisely to the Israelite possession of their own land. The possession of land as an outcome of the exodus is often described as an event in which "Yahweh brought Israel up from the land [of Egypt]" (see the commentary on 3:8, 17). The allusion may be the way by which the author points ahead to future events. The shrewdness of Pharaoh for the purpose of self-preservation sets in motion his own destruction and the eventual liberation of Israel, when they "go up from the land of Egypt."

The action of Pharaoh and its futility are outlined in vv. 11-12. Slave masters are appointed to oppress the Israelites with forced labor, supposedly to slow down their birth rate. The oppression of the Israelites as slaves fulfills the divine prediction to Abram in Gen 15:13. The thematic link to Genesis 15 also provides the outcome of Pharaoh's action. The point of the divine promise to Abram is not the slavery of his descendants, but their liberation and eventual return to Canaan.

Verses 11-12a state that the construction of Pithom and Rameses is accompanied by an increase in the birth rate of the Israelites. The Hebrew is more ominous than a simple reporting of their population growth. The Israelites not only multiply *(rābâ)*, they also break out *(pāraṣ)*. The Hebrew *pāraṣ* may signify population growth, prompting the translation "to spread out" (Gen 28:14). It can also have a more active meaning, in which the word describes a "breach in a wall" (2 Kgs 14:13) or the act of breaking through enemy lines during war (2 Sam 5:20). It is even used to signify the danger of the Divine during times of revelation (Exod 19:22, 24). The Israelites are not simply multiplying, they are "breaking out" in spite of the Egyptian oppression. The language of the Non-P author suggests two active forces pushing against each other: the Egyptian oppression and the Israelite fertility and strength.

For discussion of the cities Pithom and Rameses, see the introduction, "History and Exodus."

The Egyptian response in v. 12b is "dread" *(qûṣ)*, a form of fear that arises in the context of war. Ahaz, the king of Judah, dreads Rezin and Pekah when these kings lay siege to Jerusalem (Isa 7:16). Balak and the Moabites dread the Israelites as they marched toward Canaan (Num 22:2-3). Like the Egyptians, Balak and the Moabites fear the Israelites as opponents in war because of their fertility. Balak's solution to population control is not slave labor but divination. He hires the diviner Balaam to curse the Israelites, thus hoping to create an antidote to their fertility. Neither war nor divination is able to halt the Israelites' fertility, which, when interpreted in the context of Genesis, is the result of divine promise. It just keeps breaking through, creating dread in those who oppose it and exposing the paranoid character of those who act shrewdly to preserve their own power.

The P author adds vv. 13-14. These verses explore the legal background of the Egyptian oppression. Twice the P writer states that the Egyptian oppression was "violent" or "ruthless" *(pārek)*. Such treatment of slaves is a violation of the Jubilee law, outlined in detail by the P author in Leviticus 25 (vv. 43, 46, 53). Thus, according to the P writer, the forced labor is not only oppressive; it is illegal.

1:15-21 The story of the midwives represents an increased effort by Pharaoh to control the Israelite population. The progression is from slave labor to the killing of all male Hebrew babies. Verses 15-16 introduce the theme of the massacre of the male babies and the problem it poses for the midwives, the central characters in the episode. The text suggests that Pharaoh's instruction to kill the babies is secret. He addresses only the midwives for the Hebrew women, who are named Shiphrah ("Beauty") and Puah ("Splendor").

The story of the midwives is a tale of civil disobedience. The conflict is developed in 1:16-17 through a play on the words "to see" *(rā'â)* and "to fear" *(yārē')*, forms of which often sound similar in Hebrew. The Pharaoh instructs the midwives to kill every male Hebrew child, which they "see" born on the stones (v. 16). The "two stones" may indicate the place of birth (i.e., birthing stones) or the testicles of the male infants. The Non-P author establishes the conflict in the story by juxtaposing Pharaoh's instruction with the additional information that the midwives "fear the God." The reference to the Deity as "the God" is most likely a literary device. It is the more impersonal word for Deity in Hebrew, Elohim, as compared to the personal divine name, Yahweh, which has not yet been revealed to Moses (see Exodus 3). The use of the definite article in Hebrew, translated "the," makes the reference to the Deity even more remote.

The impersonal reference to the Deity fits the context of Exodus 1–2. The break between Genesis and Exodus, signifying the loss of memory, means that the midwives could not know the Deity as Yahweh at this point in the story, whether they are Egyptians or Israelites. The revelation of the more personal divine name Yahweh takes place in chap. 3. "The God" feared by the midwives is not revealed to them through worship. It is implanted in their conscience in the very act of being created as a human. Thus the story of the midwives has a background in the tradition of wisdom. It poses conscience against a tyrannical regime and raises the question: Will the midwives conform to the command of Pharaoh and act upon what they "see," namely the birth of Hebrew male babies condemned to death by the state? Or will they follow their conscience and act because they "feared the God"?

The midwives act on their fear of the God. Their actions provide guidelines for civil disobedience. The midwives disobey Pharaoh and allow the male babies to live (v. 17). They also lie to account for their actions (vv. 18-19). When Pharaoh inquires why his order is not being executed, the midwives play on his fear. They accentuate the difference between the Egyptians and the Israelites, first introduced by Pharaoh in 1:9. They state: "The Hebrew women are not like the Egyptian women." Then the midwives play upon the more primordial fear of Pharaoh, the explosive population growth of the Israelites: "[The Israelite women] are teeming with life, and before the midwife comes to them, they give birth." This is exactly what Pharaoh feared in the first place. The midwives are heroic characters in the opening episode. But not all commentators agree. John Calvin, for example, condemns their action as sin. The story illustrates, according to Calvin, that all human actions contain mixed motives, requiring divine grace for purification.[2]

Commentators have struggled to discern whether the midwives are Egyptian or Israelite.[3] Although their names are Semitic, the phrase "the He-

---

2. John Calvin, *The Four Last Books of Moses Arranged in the Form of a Harmony* (trans. C. W. Bingham; vol. 1; Grand Rapids: Eerdmans, 1950), 34-36.

3. The MT favors an interpretation of the midwives as Israelites and not Egyptians.

brew midwives" is ambiguous enough in the MT to allow for divergent interpretations. Are they "Hebrew midwives"? Or are they "midwives of the Hebrews"? The LXX reinforces the confusion by appearing to identify the midwives as Egyptians.

The Talmud favors the Hebrew identity of the midwives, going so far as to equate Shiphrah with Moses' mother, Jochebed, and Puah with Miriam (*b. Soṭah* 11b). Rashi also follows this line of interpretation. According to this reading, the midwives model Hebrew heroes who risked their lives to save the people of Israel. In Jewish legend Miriam even calls down God's wrath on Pharaoh for his evil plan.[4] God rewards the midwives with progeny, who belong to the house of Levi. The Hebrew identity of the midwives need not lead to their further identification with the mother of Moses and Miriam. Propp and C. Meyers support identifying the midwives as Hebrews. Propp writes of the midwives: "Their brave defiance of Pharaoh implies they are Hebrews themselves, not 'righteous gentiles.'"[5]

Josephus follows the LXX translation by identifying the midwives as Egyptians (*Ant.* 2.206). C. Houtman provides a contemporary illustration of the same interpretation, noting that the midwives are familiar with the birth process of Egyptian women (1:19), that Pharaoh at first gives the order only to a few Egyptians (1:22), and that the disobedience of two Egyptian women is more striking.[6] As Egyptians the midwives model the righteous gentile or perhaps the proselyte. N. Liebowitz summarizes this line of interpretation: "In the Bible the 'fear of God' is a demand made on every person created in His image. A gentile devoid of the fear of God is branded by the Bible as a traitor to his elementary obligations as a human being."[7]

The history of interpretation indicates the struggle by commentators to identify the ethnicity of the midwives. The emphasis on the identity of the midwives reflects the larger focus on ethnicity in the opening chapters of Exodus; out of fear Pharaoh introduces ethnicity negatively. The midwives blur

---

Rashbam, a twelfth-century c.e. Jewish commentator, represents the classical position of Jewish exegetes that the midwives are Israelites and not Egyptians. For discussion see the commentary by B. Jacob, *The Second Book of the Bible: Exodus* (trans. W. Jacob; Hoboken, N.J.: Ktav, 1992), 18. The LXX suggests that the midwives are Egyptians. Josephus (*Ant.* 2.206) represents an early example of this interpretation. For a summary of the grammatical issues involved in interpreting the syntax of the Hebrew see Schmidt, *Exodus*, 4-5.

4. L. Ginzberg, *The Legends of the Jews* (trans. H. Szold and P. Radin; 7 vols.; Philadelphia: Jewish Publication Society, 1909-1938), 2:251.

5. Propp, *Exodus 1–18*, 137; see also Meyers, *Exodus*, 36-37.

6. Houtman, *Exodus*, 1:251-52.

7. N. Liebowitz, *Studies in Shemot* (trans. A. Newman; 2 vols.; 1976; repr. Jerusalem: World Zionist Organization, Department for Torah Education and Culture in the Diaspora, 1981), 1:35.

the boundaries of separate ethnic identities. They could be either Hebrews or Egyptians without changing the underlying message of the story. When the midwives are identified as Egyptians they represent those who "fear God" (vv. 17, 21), thus providing a counterpoint to the fear of Pharaoh. But, since there is a break in tradition between Genesis and Exodus, along with the fact that God has been absent from the story until this point, the midwives' fear of God would be just as surprising from two Israelite women. The interpretation of the story does not depend on the ethnic identity of the midwives, but on the fact that they fear God more than Pharaoh. The Non-P author will continue to blur the line of ethnicity in those who possess an authentic fear of God/ Yahweh in the portrayal of Jethro and Zipporah at the mountain of God (Exodus 3–4, 18; Num 10:29-36), the positive portrayal of Balaam at the close of the wilderness journey (Numbers 22–24),[8] and even the Kenites in the promised land (Judges 1, 4).

Contemporary feminist interpreters shift the focus of identity from ethnicity to gender in evaluating the action of the midwives. As a result the midwives model the courage of women to oppose patriarchal oppression, represented by Pharaoh. The midwives, whether Hebrew or Egyptian, are tricksters who thwart the evil command of Pharaoh. Had Pharaoh known their cunning, writes P. Trible, he would have commanded all infant females to be killed.[9] "Their clever response to Pharaoh," writes R. Weems, "is not a lie, they simply do not tell the whole truth . . . a conventional weapon of the powerless, especially women in the Old Testament."[10] Not only are they cunning, the midwives also embody the theme of birth in Exodus, according to D. O'Donnel Setel: "They are the first to assist in the birth of the Israelite nation."[11] J. C. Exum sees the resistance of the midwives as a window into the heroic role of women throughout the opening chapters of Exodus. The book begins with a focus on women, including the mother and sister of Moses, and the daughter of Pharaoh. They defy oppression, give life, and model wisdom. And their actions determine the outcome of events.[12]

The word "Hebrew" (*'ibrît*) appears three times in the story of the midwives (Exod 1:15, 16, 19), providing commentary on the previous story of Pha-

---

8. For discussion of the positive portray of Balaam in the Non-P History see T. B. Dozeman, "Book of Numbers," *NIB* 2:169-202.

9. P. Trible, "Depatriarchalizing in Biblical Interpretation," *JAAR* 41 (1973): 34.

10. R. D. Weems, "The Hebrew Women Are Not like the Egyptian Women: The Ideology of Race, Gender and Sexual Reproduction in Exodus 1," *Semeia* 59 (1992): 29.

11. D. O'Donnel Setel, "Exodus," in *The Woman's Bible Commentary* (ed. C. A. Newsom and S. H. Ringe; Louisville: Westminster/John Knox, 1992), 30.

12. J. C. Exum, "'You shall let every daughter live'": A Study of Exodus 1:8–2:10," *Semeia* 28 (1983): 82.

raoh's oppression of the Israelites (1:8-14) in two ways. First, the word "Hebrew" separates the Israelites from the Egyptians as a distinct ethnic group. This distinction follows from Pharaoh's original separation of "his people" and the "people of Israel" (1:9).[13] The ethnic identification of the Israelites as "Hebrews" is not common in the Hebrew Bible. References to Abram (Gen 14:13) and Jonah (Jon 1:9) are two examples.

Second, the word "Hebrew" gives name to the experience of slavery imposed by Pharaoh. As slaves the Israelites are "Hebrews." The root meaning of the word is "to cross over." But this meaning raises more questions than answers. Is the "crossing over" the experience of salvation from Egypt? Scholars have sought to relate the word "Hebrew" to Akkadian *ḫa-pi-ru* (Sumerian SA.GAZ), a reference to fugitives and outlaws in the ancient Near East. But continued research has made a direct connection between the word "Hebrew" and "Hapiru" unlikely.[14]

The designation of some form of slavery or social alienation, however, is central to the word "Hebrew" in the Hebrew Bible. The Israelites are called Hebrews by other nations when they are in slavery to them, implying their lower social status or at least their status as the "other." There are also overtones of condescension when the word is placed in the mouth of non-Israelites. Potiphar's wife describes Joseph as a "Hebrew" when she accuses him of sexual assault (Gen 39:14, 17). The Philistines call the Israelites "Hebrews" when the Israelite people are under Philistine control (1 Sam 4:6, 9; 14:11, 21). Pharaoh's description of the Israelites as "Hebrews" indicates their low social status and objectifies their experience of slave labor. It may also imply his condescension.

The predominant use of the word "Hebrew" by non-Israelites prompted M. Sternberg to identify four patterns of meaning in the "Hebrewgram." When used in place of the word "Israelite" by a native speaker of a language other than Biblical Hebrew, the word "Hebrew" implies the superiority of the speaker and hostility toward the Israelites. Sternberg concludes that these dynamics continue even when Israelite characters use the term. Thus, if one Israelite addresses another and uses the term "Hebrew," the intent is to convey a foreign perspective on Israelites. The same is true when the narrator uses the term. The focus continues to be one of alienation between Israelites and another ethnic group.[15] The repeated use of "Hebrew" in the opening chapters of Exodus un-

13. See Greifenhagen, *Egypt*, 54-55.

14. For a summary of the research on this topic, along with the linguistic problems of relating the words "Hebrew" and "Hapiru," see N. P. Lemche, "Habiru, Hapiru," *ABD* 3:6-10; Meyers, *Exodus*, 12-16, 35-36.

15. M. Sternberg, *Hebrew between Cultures: Group Portraits and National Literature* (Indiana Studies in Biblical Literature; Bloomington: Indiana University Press, 1998), 1-89, esp. 85-87.

derscores the alienation and tension between Israelites and Egyptians, especially from the point of view of Egypt.

But the condescension of Pharaoh is not the last word on the identification of the Israelites as Hebrews. Once Yahweh takes an active role in the story, the word "Hebrew" defines the character of God. Yahweh is introduced both to the Israelites and to Pharaoh as "the God of the Hebrews" (Exod 3:18; 5:3; 7:16; 9:1, 13; 10:3). The Non-P historian is setting the stage for an interpretation of salvation as an experience of social reversal by the way in which the word "Hebrew" is woven into the story. G. V. Pixley captures this meaning when he interprets the exodus as a story of liberation.[16]

Exodus 1:20-21 provides the conclusion to the story of the midwives. The Deity Elohim enters the book of Exodus as an active character for the first time in v. 20. The civil disobedience of the midwives is rewarded: "So God dealt well with the midwives." As a consequence of the ethical action of the midwives, the Israelites continued to multiply *(rābâ)* and to increase in strength *('āṣam)*, fulfilling Pharaoh's original fear (1:9).

Verse 21 yields two interpretations, depending on the meaning of the second clause in the verse. All commentators agree that the opening clause translates: "And because the midwives feared the God." But the second clause is more ambiguous. The verb "to make" *('āśâ)* lacks a subject, and the word "houses" *(bāttîm)* is not altogether clear. The vast majority of interpreters read the closing verse as providing a positive ending to the risky action of the midwives. In this translation, "the God" is understood to be the subject of the verb "to make," and the word "houses" is interpreted metaphorically as a reference to families (see 1 Sam 25:28). Thus God rewards the midwives with families of their own. The NIV and NRSV represent this interpretation: "And because the midwives feared God, he [the God] gave them families of their own."

Rashbam takes the ending in a different direction as accentuating the dangers of civil disobedience. He interprets the subject of the verb "to make" as Pharaoh, and "the houses" as some form of house arrest, thus translating: "And because the midwives feared the God, he [Pharaoh] made houses for them." This interpretation would tie v. 21 more closely into the following verse, where Pharaoh is clearly identified as the subject of action, when he progresses from his secret instructions, directed only to the midwives, to a public announcement, aimed at all Egyptians, stating that the Hebrew male babies must be thrown into the Nile River.

16. Pixley, *On Exodus.*

IDENTITY OF MOSES (1:22–2:22)

^{1:22} *Then Pharaoh commanded all his people, saying, "You will throw every son that is born into the Nile, but you shall let every daughter live."*

^{2:1} *And a man from the house of Levi went and took a daughter of Levi.* ² *And the woman conceived and bore a son. And she saw him — that he was good — and she hid him for three months.* ³ *But she was not able to hide him any longer, and she took for him an ark of papyrus, she tarred it with tar and pitch, she set the boy in it, and she set it in the reeds on the edge of the Nile.* ⁴ *And his sister stationed herself at a distance to know what would happen to him.*

⁵ *Now the daughter of Pharaoh came down to bathe, and her attendants were walking on the bank of the Nile. She saw the ark in the midst of the reeds, and she sent her maid, and she took it.* ⁶ *She opened and saw him, the boy. Indeed, the child was crying, and she took pity on him. And she said, "This one is from the children of the Hebrews."*

⁷ *Then his sister said to the daughter of Pharaoh, "Shall I go and call for you a woman nursing from the Hebrews, and she can nurse the boy for you?"* ⁸ *And the daughter of Pharaoh said to her, "Go!" And the young girl went and called the mother of the boy.* ⁹ *The daughter of Pharaoh said to her, "Take this boy and nurse him for me. And I will give you your wage." And the woman took the boy, and she nursed him.* ¹⁰ *The boy grew, and she brought him to the daughter of Pharaoh, and he became a son to her. And she called his name "Moses," and she said, "for I drew him from the water."*

¹¹ *And it happened in those days Moses grew up. And he went out to his brothers, and he saw their forced labor. And he saw an Egyptian man striking a Hebrew man from among his brothers.* ¹² *And he turned thus and thus, and he saw that there was no one. And he struck the Egyptian, and he hid him in the sand.*

¹³ *And he went out on the second day and there were two Hebrew men fighting. And he said to the evil one, "Why did you strike your companion?"* ¹⁴ *And he said, "Who placed you as prince and judge over us? Do you intend to kill me, as you killed the Egyptian?" And Moses feared and he said, "Clearly the affair is known."*

¹⁵ *And Pharaoh heard of this affair, and he sought to kill Moses. And Moses fled from before Pharaoh, and he settled in the land of Midian, and he sat down by a well.* ¹⁶ *Now the priest of Midian had seven daughters. And they came and drew and filled the troughs to water their father's flock.* ¹⁷ *But shepherds came and drove them out. And Moses arose, and saved them, and watered their flock.* ¹⁸ *They went to Reuel, their father, and he said, "Why have you hastened to come today?"* ¹⁹ *And they said, "An Egyptian man rescued us from the hand of shepherds. He even drew water for us and watered the flock."* ²⁰ *And he said to his*

daughters, "Where is he? Why did you leave the man? Call him, so he may eat bread." ²¹And Moses agreed to settle with the man. And he gave his daughter, Zipporah, to Moses. ²²And she bore a son. And he called his name, Gershom, for he said, "I am an alien in a foreign land."

Notes

2:1 *went and took.* The MT does not explicitly state that the man married the woman (contra NRSV), but a marriage may be understood (see comment). The LXX adds the ambiguous phrase "and he had her" *(kai eschen autēn).*

2:6 *the child was crying.* The LXX adds "in the basket."

2:9 *take.* The Hebrew *hêlîkî* should read *hôlîkî.* GKC §69x suggests confusion with the following verb, *hēniqihû,* "nurse him."

2:11 *in those days.* The LXX underscores the passing of time with the phrase "many days" *(tais hēmerais tais pollais).*

a Hebrew from among his brothers. The LXX further identifies the "brothers of Moses" and the "Hebrews" as "Israelites."

2:12 *thus and thus.* The Hebrew phrase *kōh wākōh* could also be translated "this way and that way"; cf. LXX *hōde kai hōde.*

2:14 *prince and judge.* Propp translates the MT: "Who set you as a man *(lĕ'îš),* ruler *(śar)* and judge *(wĕšōpēṭ)* over us?"[1]

do you intend to kill me. The translation follows the LXX. The MT translates "to kill me are you saying?"

Commentary

The central event in Exodus 1–2 is the birth of Moses in 2:1-10. K. Schmid has argued that the story of the liberation of the Israelites from slavery originally began with the birth of Moses in Exodus 2.[2] Other interpreters suggest that the threatening birth story of Moses is the core tale that prompted ancient historians to add the additional stories of threat in chap. 1.[3] There is certainly a change in perspective between chaps. 1 and 2. The fertility of the Israelites has been a central but abstract theme in the opening stories of Exodus. The perspective has been panoramic, taking in the whole nation. The people are multiplying and even swarming like flies. The theme of fertility continues in this section, but the lens narrows to a single Israelite family, creating a more intimate story of birth, beginning with Moses (2:2) and ending with his son, Gershom (2:22).

The focus on a particular Levitical family allows for the character development of Moses. He is born during the third phase of Pharaoh's oppression of

---

1. Propp, *Exodus 1–18,* 161.

2. Schmid, *Erzväter und Exodus,* 152-59.

3. See, e.g., H. Gressmann, *Mose und seine Zeit: Ein Kommentar zu den Mose-Sagen* (FRLANT 1; Göttingen: Vandenhoeck & Ruprecht, 1912), 1-16; Winnett, *Mosaic Tradition,* 16-29; Coats, *Exodus,* 21-32.

the Israelites, in which all the Egyptians are called upon to kill the Israelite male babies (1:22–2:10). Thus his birth and rescue bridge the theme of Pharaoh's fear from the previous section. The ironic reversal of Moses' adoption into Pharaoh's family sets the stage for two stories that probe Moses' identity, the act of murder in Egypt (2:11-15a) and the rescue of Reuel's daughters in Midian (2:15b-22). These tales contrast death and life, recalling the same contrast from 1:6-7. The act of murder in the land of Egypt leads to hostility between Moses and his Israelite brothers and a death sentence from his adopted father, the pharaoh. The rescue of Reuel's daughters in the wilderness of Midian leads to hospitality, marriage, and new life through the birth of Moses' son.

1:22–2:10 The story of Moses' birth is told by the Non-P historian. The birth takes place under the shadow of Pharaoh's edict that all male children should be thrown into the Nile (1:22). In spite of the threatening situation, a Levite man takes a Levite woman and she bears a son. The syntax of 2:1-2 is ambiguous in a number of ways. First, the statement that "a man from the house of Levi went and took a daughter of Levi" suggests marriage. The NRSV even translates the Hebrew, which is literally "went and took," as "went and married." K. Schmid has argued that the phrase suggests Moses' illegitimate birth on analogy to the Legend of Sargon (see the commentary below).[4] But, as Blum has noted, the phrase is so general that it can also signify marriage.[5] Other ambiguities also arise. The notice suggests that the son is the first child born to the couple. Similar language is used to describe the birth of the first child born to Hosea and Gomer (Hos 1:3).[6] Later events in the story of Moses indicate otherwise, when an older sister enters the scene in v. 4. She takes an active role in vv. 7-10a, when the daughter of Pharaoh finds the baby boy. The sister may be a later embellishment to the story, accentuating the role of Miriam in the salvation of Moses.

The story of Moses' birth is rich in literary allusion. Once the son is born, the mother sees in v. 2 "that he is good" *(kî-ṭôb hû')*. For the Non-P author this expression most likely means that he is healthy. But when read in the larger context of the P History in the present context of the Hebrew Bible, links with Genesis 1 are forged. Seven times the goodness of creation is affirmed with the phrase, "God saw that it is good" *(kî-ṭôb)*. The context of the P History adds meaning to the birth story of Moses in the Non-P History, stressing that the Israelites as a whole and the Levite couple in particular were fruitful as God commanded in Genesis 1, and that Moses is "good" like the original

---

4. Schmid, *Erzvätern und Exodus*, 153.

5. Blum, "Literarische Verbindung," 146-47.

6. F. I. Andersen and D. N. Freedman, *Hosea* (AB 24; Garden City, N.Y.: Doubleday, 1980), 4, 197-98.

creation, further reinforcing the parallel between the beginning of Genesis and Exodus.

The mother hides the baby for three months in disobedience of Pharaoh's command. But eventually she floats him on the Nile in a basket *(tēbâ),* placing it in the reeds *(sûp)* at the edge of the river (Exod 2:3). References to other stories of chaotic water infuse the baby's river ordeal with overtones of judgment and salvation. The "basket" is an allusion to the flood in Genesis 6–9, where the same word is used to describe the vessel in which Noah escaped judgment. God states to Noah in Gen 6:14: "Make for yourself an ark *(tēbâ)."* The "reeds" of the Nile point in the other direction, to the future, not the past. They foreshadow Israel's impending salvation at the Red or Reed Sea *(yam-sûp).* Moses experiences many of the Israelites' key events of salvation in the opening chapters of Exodus. His river ordeal prefigures the Red Sea (Exodus 14). He encounters Yahweh on the mountain of God (chap. 3), where Israel will eventually meet God (chap. 19). And he experiences a divine attack (4:24-26) like God's attack on the Egyptians during the night of Passover (chap. 12).

Surprising events unfold in 2:4-10. The daughter of Pharaoh descends to the river for bathing with her retinue in vv. 5-6. They see the ark in the reeds, fetch it, open it, and recognize the crying baby as a Hebrew. Verse 6 plays on the Hebrew verb *ḥāmal,* which means to have compassion and to spare. The compassion of the daughter of Pharaoh is evident in her sparing the baby's life, an act of civil disobedience like that of the midwives. When the story is read without Moses' sister (vv. 4, 7-10a), the ending is immediate. It concludes in 2:10b with an etiological story about the name Moses.

Two etymologies are provided for the name Moses *(mōšeh).* The first underscores the adoption of Moses by Pharaoh's daughter through the wordplay between "son" in Hebrew *(ben)* and in Egyptian *(mose).* The name Moses is Egyptian. The Egyptian verb *msy* means "to be born," and the noun *ms* means "a son." The word is used in the names of the pharaohs, such as Thut*mose.* Thut or Thoth is the name of the Egyptian moon god, represented as an ibis or baboon, and associated with wisdom, writing, and wise government. The name Thutmose means "son of Thut." The wordplay between Egyptian *ms* and the name "Moses" is likely intended to function in a similar manner as in the name Thutmose: in the story of Moses *mōšeh* now conveys adoption. Exodus 2:10b could be paraphrased: "He became her son *(ben).* And she named him 'Son' *(mōšeh)."* But when the name Moses is compared to the name Thutmose, it becomes clear that the divine component is missing in the former, as D. N. Freedman notes: "In the case of Moses, his name is typically hypocoristic, meaning that the divine component has been left out, but it is understood. The same is true of many biblical names, including the patriarchs, Isaac, Jacob, and the latter's son, Joseph. Only the verbal component of the name is given, but the divine name — usually El in these early times — is understood, and occasionally (in other names) given. In the case of Moses, we may speculate that his full name included the name of one of the Egyptian gods."[7]

A second interpretation emphasizes Moses' salvation from the river. The daughter of Pharaoh states: "I drew him *(māšâ)* out of the water." This etymology frees the name Moses of its Egyptian origin, locating it instead in the Hebrew verb "to draw out." According to this interpretation "Moses" means "drawer from water." A passive form of the verb would better conform to the details of Moses' birth (i.e., "one drawn from the water"), but the active meaning may be pointing ahead to Moses' role at the well in Midian or to his leading Israel through the water. Most scholars agree that Moses' name is Egyptian, and that the Hebrew etymology and derivation represent a later, popular interpretation. The two etymologies for the name Moses may be the result of different writers, but that possibility is difficult to confirm.[8]

The sister of Moses takes an active role in 2:4, 7-10a. She is unnamed in the story, as are Moses' mother and father. She is described as both "sister" to Moses (vv. 4, 7) and as a "young woman" (v. 8). Thus she too is a Levite. The sister adds an interesting turn of events to the adoption of Moses. She does not save Moses from the water, but she is present at his rescue and influences the outcome of the story. She negotiates with the daughter of Pharaoh so that Moses' mother raises him and even nurses him, thus pulling Moses into the orbit of his Hebrew parents.[9] Only after Moses is grown does his Hebrew mother turn him over to the daughter of Pharaoh for adoption. The complex relationship of Hebrew and Egyptian women in raising Moses adds intrigue to the story, while also laying the foundation for the theme of Moses' identity as both Egyptian and Hebrew, which becomes central in his character development (see 2:11-22).

The offer of wages to Moses' mother by Pharaoh's daughter may be no more than an ironic twist to the plot of the tale. The mother now gets paid for taking care of her son, who should have been killed. But it may also be a criticism of the slavery imposed by Pharaoh. Women have played a subversive and a critical role over against Pharaoh throughout the opening stories of Exodus.

---

7. Private communication.

8. B. O. Long (*The Problem of Etiological Narrative in the Old Testament* [BZAW 108; Berlin: Töpelmann, 1968], 5-10) identifies two forms of etymological etiologies. The present form of Exod 2:10b conforms to Form I in that (a) the act of naming is narrated in the historical tense ("She called his name Moses") and (b) it is followed by an explanation ("for she said, 'I drew him from the water'"). The wordplay in the opening phrase of v. 10b conforms loosely to Form II. This form is (a) "always introduced by the Hebrew phrase עַל־כֵּן ['therefore']" (absent from Exod 2:10b), and (b) "the act of naming is not narrated. Rather, the formula expresses a logical inference" to the story through wordplay ("He became her son. And she named him Moses").

9. For discussion of wet nurses see Meyers, *Exodus*, 40-42.

The exchange of service for wages may be another instance of civil disobedience, where women provide a countermodel to Pharaoh.

The P historian names the Levite couple and the sister of Moses in Num 26:59. Moses' father is Amram, his mother Jochebed, and his sister Miriam (see the commentary on 6:14-27). The P author's identification of Miriam as Moses' sister provides a new dimension to the story of Moses' birth and rescue from the Nile. Naming the sister links the birth story of Moses to the Song of Miriam in Exod 15:20-21. This does not mean that the P historian is the author of the individual stories of Miriam or of Moses' unnamed sister. These stories may have been unrelated before the P historian's identification. Miriam is not identified as Moses' sister in 15:20-21, and the sister of Moses in 2:1-10 is not identified as Miriam. But the P historian forges these links by identifying Miriam as Moses' sister through a genealogy. Once they are made, they cannot be ignored in interpreting the present form of the story. The result is that Miriam, the sister of Moses, frames the story of salvation in chaps. 1–15, witnessing two events of rescue from water: Moses from the Nile River and Israel from the Red Sea. Miriam's power in both stories resides in her speech. She is idealized as a prophetess. At the Nile River she persuades the daughter of Pharaoh to hire Moses' mother as a wet nurse. At the Red Sea Miriam interprets the salvation of Israel through song. Miriam's prophetic ability later comes into conflict with the prophetic role of Moses in Numbers 12.[10]

The birth and rescue of Moses also conforms to a common legend in the ancient Near East in which a hero is abandoned, set adrift in water, and eventually adopted. The most striking parallel to the story of Moses is the Legend of Sargon.[11] Sargon is the child of a priestess prohibited from conceiving a child. She disobeys, conceives Sargon in secret, and floats the baby on the river in a vessel of reeds. Sargon is rescued from the river and adopted by Akki, the water drawer, who raises him as a gardener; eventually Sargon becomes king of Akkad. The secret birth of Sargon and his adoption may cover over a family genealogy that is less than royal. H. Gressmann long ago noted problems of legitimacy with the absence of the father's name.[12] B. Lewis concurs, noting that the motifs of abandonment and adoption emphasize the mysterious origin of Sargon and his humble beginnings, not royal genealogy.[13] Lewis is also likely correct that the story of Sargon is intended to represent the prototype of the

10. See C. V. Camp, *Wise, Strange and Holy: The Strange Woman and the Making of the Bible* (JSOTSup 320; Sheffield: Sheffield Academic Press, 2000), 227-78.

11. *ANET,* 119. See the more detailed study by B. Lewis, *The Sargon Legend* (ASORDS 4; Cambridge: ASOR, 1980). Lewis identifies no fewer than sixty-four versions of the story of the abandoned hero.

12. Gressmann, *Mose und seine Zeit,* 8-10.

13. Lewis, *Sargon Legend,* 249 *et passim.*

ideal king in Mesopotamian tradition by idealizing the deeds of Sargon. It is the heroic actions of Sargon, not his genealogy, that account for his rise to power. The tale is, to use a phrase from B. S. Childs, a "rags-to-riches" story.[14] The continued prominence of the tale from its likely eighth-century B.C.E. composition is evident in its central role in Herodotus's account of the birth and rescue of Cyrus, the Persian king.[15]

The parallels between the Legend of Sargon and Moses' birth story include anonymous parents from the priestly class, an illegal if not illegitimate birth, a river ordeal, rescue, adoption, the protection of women, and as we will see an emphasis on the heroic deeds of Moses. The similarities suggest that the Non-P historian also wishes to explore the identity of Moses. Indeed, the theme of identity is woven throughout the early stories of Moses. The naming of Moses by the daughter of Pharaoh suggests an adoption, compounded by the subterfuge of how he was nursed, while the actions of Moses in the opening two stories of his life, the murder of the Egyptian (2:11-15a) and his life in Midian (2:15b-22), will probe the relationship between his deeds and his identity.

The departure from the heroic pattern in the birth story of Moses provides the point of view of the Non-P historian for interpreting the theme of Moses' identity. The first departure is in the reshaping of the birth story to maintain the clear ethnic identity of Moses. The expected pattern of the birth legend is the early anonymity of the infant, who remains incognito until becoming an adult and assuming a role of leadership. But in the case of Moses his identity is never lost. Pharaoh's daughter recognizes him as a Hebrew immediately in the river before adopting him, exclaiming: "This one is from the children of the Hebrews" (2:6). Moses even remains in the care of his Hebrew mother, solidifying his genealogical origin even further (2:9). Ethnic separation between Egyptians and Hebrews is clearly maintained in the opening chapters of Exodus, and this is also true of Moses. Thus Coats is certainly correct when he concludes that the birth story of Moses is not intended to make Moses an Egyptian, but to place him in an Egyptian culture.[16]

The second departure from the heroic legend has more to do with the literary context of the Non-P History than the reshaping of the birth story itself. As noted above, the expected pattern of the heroic legend is a rags-to-riches story, in which the hero rises from the threat of death and anonymity to public leadership. The structure of Moses' birth story is inverted. Moses is, indeed, exalted into the family of Pharaoh, but only momentarily before he returns to the

---

14. Childs, *Exodus*, 10.

15. *Hist.* 1.107ff. See H. Zlotnick-Sivan, "Moses the Persian? Exodus 2, the 'Other' and Biblical 'Mnemohistory,'" *ZAW* 116 (2004): 189-205.

16. Coats, *Exodus*, 44.

status of a hunted slave, when Pharaoh seeks his life (2:15). Many interpret the inverted structure against the backdrop of the Israelite slavery and the need for Moses to become a savior of slaves; for example, Propp writes: "Whereas the typical hero eventually leaves his lowly environment to assume his rightful glory, Moses flees the Pharaonic court to discover his path first among the desert nomads and later among slaves."[17] The social focus of slavery is certainly an important theme in Moses' preparation for leadership. The inversion of hierarchy in his idealization fits the larger thematic development of the exodus, in which salvation is the destruction of royalty and liberation of slaves. The identity of Moses will be explored further through his actions in the next two stories, 2:11-15a and 15b-22.

The heroic birth of Moses has played a central role in the history of interpretation. It is expanded in early Jewish interpretation.[18] The threat of Pharaoh against the male Israelite babies is intensified through dreams and foretelling. Pharaoh dreams that Egypt is outweighed on a balance by a goat, indicating that an Israelite child would destroy the country.[19] Josephus states that scribes warn Pharaoh of the birth of this child,[20] while another rabbinic tradition attributes the forewarning to astrologers.[21] The intensification of the threat to Pharaoh is accompanied by a more miraculous birth of Moses. His birth is accompanied by light.[22] The mother of Moses, Jochebed, is over one hundred years old at the time of birth, yet her beauty and fertility are restored in giving birth to Moses.[23] Her delivery of Moses is painless.[24] And she gives birth in the seventh month of pregnancy.[25] "A seventh months delivery in pagan or Jewish or Christian sources," according to D. Allison, "betokens a divine origin or a conception supernaturally assisted."[26]

The author of the Gospel of Matthew builds on the legend of Moses to describe the birth of Jesus.[27] The Gospel account is strongly influenced by early

---

17. Propp, *Exodus 1–18*, 158.

18. See R. E. Brown, *The Birth of the Messiah: A Commentary on the Infancy Narratives in the Gospels of Matthew and Luke* (ABRL; New York: Doubleday, 1993), 110-19 *et passim*; A. Kensky, "Moses and Jesus: The Birth of the Savior," *Judaism* 165 (1993): 43-49; Ginzberg, *Legends*, 2:262-65.

19. *Tg. Yer. I* on Exod 1:15.

20. *Ant.* 2.205.

21. *b. Sanh.* 101a.

22. *b. Soṭah* 12a.

23. *b. B. Bat.* 120a.

24. *b. Soṭah* 12a.

25. *Tg. Yer.* on Exod 2:2. See Ginzberg, *Legends*, 5:397 n. 44, for further references.

26. D. Allison, *The New Moses: A Matthean Typology* (Minneapolis: Fortress, 1993), 150.

27. See ibid., 140-65; Brown, *Birth of the Messiah*, 110-19 *et passim*; U. Luz, *Matthew 1–7: A Commentary* (trans. W. C. Linss; Minneapolis: Augsburg, 1989), 127-55.

Jewish interpretation, as is evident in the central role of astrology and the magi to predict a supernatural birth. Yet the account of Moses' birth in Exodus also retains an influential role in the Gospel of Matthew, especially in exploring the destructive power of evil, often accompanying an act of divine salvation. Each story includes a series of similar motifs, the slaughter of babies, the flight of the hero, and the return of the hero only after the death of the evil tyrant.[28]

Both the birth of Moses and the birth of Jesus probe conflict over power. Even though each story centers on an unexpected rescue of the hero, the abuse of power by the ruler unleashes unimaginable evil. Both stories use the fanatical fear of a powerful ruler to explore how acts of salvation can be accompanied by senseless suffering. I have highlighted the dread of Pharaoh at the growth of the Israelites, leading to his desperate act of genocide. Herod, the king, replaces Pharaoh in Matthew's birth story of Jesus. He too enacts an infanticide on the male babies of Bethlehem. Like Pharaoh, his action is rooted in a paranoid quest for power, cloaked in shrewd acts of deception. Herod works in secret with the magi as Pharaoh sought to do with the midwives. Both kill ruthlessly to maintain power.

The result in both stories is the paradox that salvation and slaughter often accompany each other. The slaughter is, moreover, anything but heroic. Childs writes: "The grim reality is that even when redemption finally comes, it is accompanied, not by the heroic martyrdom of the brave partisan, but by the senseless murder of children."[29] The Christian liturgical calendar has memorialized this paradox: the birth of Jesus (Christmas, December 25) is followed immediately by the Feast of the Holy Innocents (December 28). This is the feast memorializing the slaughter of the babies in Bethlehem. The interweaving of salvation and senseless suffering in the birth stories of Moses and Jesus becomes the paradigm of the martyr in Christian tradition. Yet the unresolved paradox is a reminder that religious experience raises as many questions about the world and divine providence as it provides answers.

2:11-15a The first story of Moses as an adult is a tale of failed leadership. The Non-P author sketches Moses' initial inclination toward violence, how such action influences his identity and undermines his authority. The message is that violence begets violence. The Non-P historian states the same message at the outset of the history in the story of Cain's murder of Abel, and in the genealogy of Cain, which culminates in the boast of Lamech over killing a boy (Genesis 4). In approximately seventy words in Exod 2:11-15a, the Non-P writer re-

---

28. The parallels include the genocide (Exod 1:15-16; Matt 2:16-18), the flight of the hero (Exod 2:15; Matt 2:13-15), and the eventual return after the death of the ruler (Exod 4:19-20; Matt 2:19-20).

29. Childs, *Exodus*, 25.

counts no fewer than three murders (an Egyptian kills a Hebrew, Moses kills the Egyptian, and a Hebrew kills another Hebrew), before concluding the episode with Moses fleeing for his life under a death sentence by Pharaoh. The story is structured into three scenes: Moses murders an Egyptian (vv. 11-12), Moses fails to mediate a conflict between two Hebrews (vv. 13-14a), and Moses fears for his life, fleeing from Egypt to escape a death sentence by Pharaoh (vv. 14b-15a).

Verses 11-12 narrate the murder of an Egyptian by Moses. The scene is told from Moses' point of view. He identifies himself as an Israelite. Twice in the two verses Hebrews are described as his "brothers." When venturing out one day Moses sees the "hard labor" of the Israelites (1:11; 2:11), recalling the initial act of slave labor by Pharaoh. But the slavery is now intensified. Moses sees an Egyptian striking a Hebrew man. The Hebrew word "to strike" *(nākâ)* is violent, often indicating a blow that results in death. After ensuring secrecy, Moses responds in kind, striking *(nākâ)* the Egyptian. The opening scene ends with Moses burying the corpse in the sand to conceal the murder. The Hebrew word "to bury" *(ṭāman)* means both "to bury" and "to hide." Although Moses seeks to liberate Hebrews, his first act as an adult is a violent murder performed in secret, recalling the private instructions of Pharaoh toward the midwives.

Verses 13-14a tell of Moses' initial encounter with Israelites. It is told from the point of view of the Hebrews. The scene begins as a repetition of the first. Moses goes out *(yāṣā', vv. 11, 13)* the next day. This time he sees two Hebrews struggling *(nāṣâ)*. The Hebrew verb *nāṣâ* does not necessarily indicate a fight to the death. But three features of Moses' response suggest that the conflict results in murder. First, Moses addresses the Hebrew man as "the one in the wrong." Childs concludes that the Hebrew is technical legal language indicating guilt.[30] Second, the question of Moses, "Why are you hitting your fellow Hebrew?" employs the same Hebrew verb *(nākâ)* used to describe the Egyptian's assault on the Hebrew slave (v. 11) and Moses' attack on the Egyptian (v. 12). All of these actions likely describe deadly blows. The alternative is that the same verb has different meaning in three consecutive verses. Third, the combination of the verbs "to struggle" *(nāṣâ)* and "to strike" *(nākâ)* indicates murder in the tale of the wise woman of Tekoa, who recounts to King David the struggle *(nāṣâ)* of her two sons when one is struck *(nākâ)* by the other in the field, an act of murder (2 Sam 14:6).

The point of emphasis in the second scene is the response by the Hebrew man to Moses in Exod 2:14a. He questions the authority of Moses: "Who placed you as prince and judge over us?" And he indicates his knowledge that Moses is a murderer: "Do you intend to kill me, as you killed the Egyptian?" Scholars de-

---

30. Ibid., 30.

bate whether the Hebrew views Moses as an Egyptian or as a fellow Israelite. The reference to Moses as a "ruler" *(śar)* is the same word used to describe the Egyptian taskmasters (1:11), suggesting that perhaps the Hebrew views Moses as an Egyptian. Some scholars argue the reverse on the basis of verisimilitude. The Hebrew views Moses as a fellow Israelite, because a Hebrew slave would not address an Egyptian with such disrespect. One wonders, however, whether this tale was intended to conform to a strict social verisimilitude. The ambiguity of the story concerning the identity of Moses is perhaps the most telling point of all. Whether Moses is viewed as an Israelite or an Egyptian, his actions define him as a murderer, placing him squarely in the world of Pharaoh. The Hebrew slave, a fellow murderer, knows this fact about Moses, and he rejects Moses' attempt to be a leader who mediates conflict. There is no authority in murder.

Verses 14b-15a conclude the tale. Murder has already located Moses in the world of Pharaoh. His actions at the close of the episode confirm his lack of moral authority. Moses' initial statement to the Hebrew slave was an attempt to provide moral leadership for others through asking why one friend would strike another (v. 13). Whatever moral authority Moses had hoped to convey through this question disappears when the murderer reveals that Moses is himself a murderer. The realization that his secret act of murder was now public information changes Moses' behavior. He ceases to be a moral mediator for others and begins to fear for his own preservation. Such fear was first introduced by Pharaoh, starting the cycle of violence in the opening chapters of Exodus. It is not surprising, therefore, that the story concludes where it originally began, with Pharaoh. He hears the news that Moses has committed murder and he seeks to kill him.

Moses' killing of the Egyptian has prompted interpreters to discern his motive. The phrase "he turned thus and thus" holds the key to motive. I have stressed the secret nature of the murder, but such a reading does not reflect the range of interpretation. The *Mekilta* states that the phrase indicates Moses' complete devotion to the Israelites. According to the *Mekilta,* "He turned thus and thus" interprets the previous verse, where it states that Moses looked out upon the burden of the Israelites. "Thus because he devoted himself with his whole soul to Israel they were called his." The interpretation of the *Mekilta* does not address the killing of the Egyptian.[31] Other midrashic interpretations do address the circumstances and the act of killing in detail. One reading suggests that "he turned thus and thus" indicates Moses' quest for justice.[32] When none was forthcoming he decided to act himself, but not before consulting the an-

---

31. *Mekilta Shirata* 1.35-64.

32. For a modern example of this interpretation see Jacob, *Exodus,* 37-38, who notes Isa 59:15-16 as a parallel. See also Cassuto, *Exodus,* 22.

gels. Only then did Moses kill the Egyptian by pronouncing the divine name.[33] For Calvin the act of "turning thus and thus" indicated hesitation on the part of Moses to risk his security in an act of divinely appointed deliverance. Such hesitation was a sign of weak faith, requiring divine mercy.[34]

Philo stresses Moses' control of his emotions, his tight rein on his passions, and the power of reason guiding his actions. There is no mention of Moses "turning thus and thus" in Philo's interpretation. The killing of the Egyptian was a deliberate and just action by Moses. It was a "righteous deed," according to Philo, because "one who lived to destroy men should himself be destroyed."[35] This line of interpretation is also followed in Stephen's speech in Acts 7:23-29. The interpretation in Heb 11:23-28 omits the killing altogether, focusing instead on Moses' choice to give up wealth and status in order to take on the suffering of the Israelites. But N. Leibowitz also provides a more critical interpretation of Moses' actions from the *Midrash of the Passing of Moses,* where Moses' request not to die is denied him because of his slaying of the Egyptian.[36]

2:15b-22   The transition to the story of Moses in Midian is immediate, indicating the close tie between the first two stories of Moses' early adulthood. Verse 15b states in rapid succession that Moses fled from Pharaoh, arrived in the land of Midian, and sat by a well. Midian represents both a geographical location and a people in biblical tradition. According to Gen 25:1-6 the Midianite people are descendants of Abraham through his wife Keturah. Midianites reappear as traders in the Joseph story (Gen 37:25-36) traveling from Gilead to Egypt. The land of Midian is difficult to locate. The Midianites are associated loosely with the Moabites (Gen 36:35; Num 22:4, 7; 31:8), suggesting a territory in southern Transjordan. G. Mendenhall concludes from archaeological evidence that the land of Midian was located in the region east of the Gulf of Aqaba.[37] E. Axel Knauf is less sure about the historical location of the Midianites.[38] What is clear is that biblical writers locate the land of Midian in the wilderness outside the land of Egypt.

The two stories of Moses' early adult life highlight different aspects of his innate ability to be a deliverer. In the previous story Moses saw oppression and initiated liberation by killing an Egyptian. Although intended as justice, the act was overly violent. The words used to describe Moses' action revolve around death. Moses "strikes" *(nākâ)* the Egyptian and "buries" *(ṭāman)* the corpse.

---

33. Ginzberg, *Legends,* 2:277-82.
34. Calvin, *Harmony,* 1:46-50.
35. *Mos.* 1.40-44.
36. Leibowitz, *Studies in Shemot,* 1:44-46.
37. G. Mendenhall, "Midian," *ABD* 4:815-18; see also Meyers, *Exodus,* 12-16.
38. E. A. Knauf, *Midian: Untersuchungen zur Geschichte Palästinas und Nordarabiens am Ende des 2 Jahrtausens v. Chr.* (Wiesbaden: Harrassowitz, 1988).

The Hebrew man describes this act as "killing" *(hārag).* At the well in Midian Moses sees another act of oppression. This time shepherds drive away *(gāraš)* the daughters of Reuel from the well, preventing them from watering their animals. The words describing Moses' action in Midian emphasize life, not death. He "saves" *(yāšaʿ)* the women (Exod 2:17). In contrast to the Hebrew man who called Moses a "killer," the daughters describe his action on their behalf as a "rescue" *(nāṣal),* even though they identify him as an Egyptian, not a Hebrew (v. 19). Salvation as a rescue is not free of violence. It signifies deliverance from a threatening situation. Yahweh promises such liberation for Israel in 3:8 and 6:6. It takes place on the night of Passover.

The episode of Moses at the well in Midian is filled with literary allusion. Moses' act of drawing water recalls the etymology of his name, "water drawer." Drawing water for the daughters of Reuel repeats the previous actions by women who drew Moses from the river. Propp suggests that Moses may be "returning the protection he received from women in 1:22–2:10."[39] The verbs "to save" and "to rescue" will play a central role in Exodus. Moses' act of salvation *(yāšaʿ)* at the well prefigures Yahweh's salvation of Israel at the Red Sea (14:13, 30; 15:2). The verb "to rescue" *(nāṣal,* in the Hiphil) occurs nine times in Exodus (2:19; 3:8; 5:23; 6:6; 12:27; 18:4, 8, 9, 10). The distribution indicates that the motif is closely associated with Moses and his Midianite father-in-law. It is introduced by the daughters of Reuel to describe the action of Moses at the well in the land of Midian (2:19). The motif returns when Moses is reunited with his Midianite father-in-law in the wilderness, where both characters describe Yahweh's deliverance of Israel as a rescue from the Egyptians (18:4, 8, 9, 10).

The change in geographical setting from Egypt to the wilderness of Midian marks the shift in topic from murder and death to life and marriage. The introduction of the well prepares for the change in theme. Coats identified the setting of the well as a typical feature for stories of marriage.[40] Abraham's servant finds Rebekah, Isaac's wife, at a well (Genesis 24). Jacob meets Rachel at a well (Genesis 29). Now Moses meets the seven daughters of Reuel at the well in Midian, suggesting an imminent marriage. Moses rescues the women from the shepherds. And Reuel shows hospitality that does, indeed, lead to Moses' marriage with Zipporah, one of Reuel's seven daughters, and the birth of a son, Gershom (Exod 2:21-22).

The narrative of Moses' marriage and the birth of his son is sparse, only two verses. An additional tradition of Moses' marriage to a Cushite woman appears in Num 12:1. A second son, Eliezer, is mentioned in passing in Exod 18:4. Biblical writers do not emphasize the descendants of Moses, as they do with the ancestors

39. Propp, *Exodus 1–18,* 175.
40. Coats, *Exodus,* 31-32.

Abraham (Gen 25:1-18) and Jacob (Gen 29:1–30:24), or with the priestly line (Exod 6:14-25). The most likely reason is Moses' unique role in the Pentateuch as the mediator of Torah (for discussion on the genealogy of Moses see 6:14-27).[41] It is not an office that repeats in Scripture, requiring offspring for its continuation. The divine speech in Numbers 12 underscores the point, emphasizing Moses' special status as compared to other prophets or even to Aaron and Miriam.

The reticence of biblical writers to explore the descendants of Moses is evident in the etiologies provided at the birth of Gershom. There are two in v. 22. Both provide commentary on Moses, not Gershom. The first etiology derives from the name Gershom. The etymology is uncertain. It may combine the word "resident alien" *(gēr)* with the word "there" *(šām),* although the spelling in Hebrew is not exact. A more likely explanation is that Gershom includes the consonants of the verb "to drive out" *(gāraš),* the action of the shepherds against the daughters of Reuel, prompting the rescue of Moses. In this case the name Gershom recalls the first instance in which Moses saves. A second etiology defines the status of Moses as a resident alien in Midian. "I have become an alien *(gēr)* in a foreign land."

HUMAN LAMENT (2:23-25)

²:²³ *And it happened in those many days the king of Egypt died. And the Israelites moaned from their servitude.* **And they cried out. And their cry for help went up to God from their servitude.** ²⁴ *And God heard their groan.* **And God remembered his covenant with Abraham, with Isaac, and with Jacob.** ²⁵ *And God saw the Israelites.* **And God knew.**

Notes

2:23 *And it happened in those many days.* The phrase also occurred in 2:11a, where the MT and the LXX diverged. But in 2:23 the MT conforms to the LXX, which underscores the passing of "many days" in each of the temporal clauses.

they cried out. There is no object to the cry of the Israelites. Instead, their groan finds its own way to God. The LXX follows the MT reading *(aneboēsan,* "they cried out").

2:25 *and God knew.* The MT has no object for the divine knowledge, creating a parallel with the Israelite cry in v. 23. The LXX departs from the MT, interpreting the verb "to know" in the passive ("he made himself known," *egnōsthē)* and adding "to them" *(autois),* meaning the Israelites. The result is a different reading, in which the Israelite people become the object of the divine revelation.

41. F. Crüsemann, *The Torah: Theology and Social History of Old Testament Law* (trans. A. W. Mahnke; Minneapolis: Fortress, 1996), 60-61.

Commentary

The P historian is responsible for the introduction (1:1-5, 7*) and the conclusion (2:23b-25) to chaps. 1–2. The introduction underscored the partial fulfillment of the divine promise to the ancestors. The fertility of Israel in Egypt, not Canaan, sets the stage for suffering, not blessing. The conclusion underscores the suffering of Israel through the language of human lament.

2:23a   The Non-P historian may be the author of the opening clause in v. 23a, "during that long period, the king of Egypt died." In the MT the phrase is tied to 4:19: "Go and return to Egypt, for all the men seeking your life have died." The LXX creates a verbatim repetition: "After those many days the king of Egypt died." The result of the repetition is that the call of Moses (3:1–4:18) is framed by a resumptive repetition, a type of repetition that often frames an insertion. The repetition between 2:23a and 4:19 may indicate that the call of Moses in 3:1–4:18 is an embellishment to the plot of the Non-P History. The Non-P historian uses the passage of time and the death of the original tyrant in v. 23a to advance the story of Moses. The death of the king of Egypt who sought Moses' life provides transition to the call of Moses in 3:1–4:18, setting the stage for the hero's return to Egypt. In the Non-P History the oppression of the Israelite nation recedes in order to tell the story of Moses.

2:23b-25   The P historian uses the passage of time to focus anew on the people of Israel and their ongoing suffering. The message of the P author is that individual tyrants may die, but oppression continues. The language and the syntax of the Israelites' situation in v. 23 are important for interpretation. Twice the P author refers to the fact of the slavery of the Israelite people. But the focus is more on Israel's psychological and social condition in slavery. The people groan (Niphal of 'ānaḥ) under their slavery. Animals groan when they have no pasture or grain (Joel 1:18). Humans groan when the wicked rule (Prov 29:2). Even the roads leading to Jerusalem groan at the absence of God and the inability of the Israelites to perform religious festivals (Lam 1:4, 8, 11). All of these images — the lack of basic sustenance, political oppression, and the absence of religion — inform the groaning of Israel.

The condition of oppression prompts a cry for help by the Israelites, but their cry lacks an object. The Hebrew verb "to cry out" *(zā'aq)* without an object is unusual, signifying desperation. It introduces David's wail: "O my son Absalom! My son, my son Absalom! If only I had died instead of you — O Absalom, my son, my son!" (2 Sam 19:4). The verb without object occurs again in Tamar's anguish after being raped by Amnon: "She put her hand on her head and went away, weeping aloud as she went" (2 Sam 13:19). More often the verb "to cry out" is used in human lament specifically addressed to Yahweh in a situation of distress. Israel cries out to Yahweh for salvation from the king of Aram

(Judg 3:9), the king of Moab (Judg 3:15), and the Midianites (Judg 6:6). The psalmist states that the ancestors cried out to Yahweh and were saved (Ps 22:5).

The absence of an object to Israel's cry underscores the anguish of their situation and most likely their lack of knowledge of God. They are unable to employ the language of lament properly, because like Pharaoh they too have lost all knowledge of their past life with God (Exod 1:6). They simply "cry out." But "their cry for help" takes on a life of its own and works its way to God.

The P historian changes the mood of the opening chapters with 2:24-25. God has not been an active character in the story up to this point. But the "groan" of the Israelite people awakens the Deity to a flurry of activity. God becomes the subject of four verbs. God "hears" the groan. God "remembers" the past covenant with the ancestors (in the P History God makes covenant with Abraham in Genesis 17). Divine memory is first introduced in the P History during the flood when God remembers Noah (Gen 8:1). God "looked" on the Israelites. And God "comes to knowledge." The NIV translates the closing phrase, "and [God] was concerned with them," while NRSV reads, "God took notice of them." The Hebrew is significantly different from these translations. It simply states: "And God knew." There is no object qualifying what God knows. It is the LXX version that adds the object, "them." In the MT version the P author leaves the reader with a question at the close of the introduction to Exodus: What is it that God knows? The reader must continue into the commission of Moses in 3:1–7:7 for an answer to the question.

Characters (3:1–7:7)

INTRODUCTION

CENTRAL THEMES

The most significant development in this section is the entry of Yahweh into the story as an active character. The absence of Yahweh from Exodus 1–2 allowed biblical authors to explore the themes of power and identity from a human perspective, thus setting the stage for the story of the exodus. Pharaoh and the women provided insight into a range of human responses to the divinely induced fertility of the Israelites. Moses emerged as the central character in this section. The biblical authors explored in particular the ambiguity of human power through the character of Moses. His lack of identity and changing family situations, from Hebrew, to Egyptian, and finally to Midianite, provided the diverse settings for biblical authors to examine the close tie between action and identity in the hero.

The introduction of Yahweh dominates 3:1–7:7, shifting the focus from the social, political, and geographical setting in chaps. 1–2 to an examination of characters. Yahweh is introduced without a clear identity, creating a parallel to the opening stories of Moses, where the hero also lacked identity. When Yahweh enters the scene in 3:1–7:7 the biblical authors explore two related themes with regard to the divine character. The first is to identify Yahweh. Who is this God? What is the past history of this God? How powerful is this God in relationship to Israel, other nations, and nature? And how will this God act in the future? The two commissions of Moses (3:1–4:18; 6:2–7:7) provide answers to these questions. The God appearing to Moses is the same God who made promises to Abraham, Isaac, and Jacob and led them in their migrations in the promised land. Yahweh's awareness of the Israelite suffering and concern for their liberation are spelled out in detail (3:5-10; 6:2-8). The character of God is also developed with the revelation of the divine name, Yahweh (3:13-15; 6:2-8). Once Yahweh enters the story, the Deity orchestrates all action, commissioning Moses to rescue the Israelites (3:10), providing Moses with signs of power and persuasion (4:1-17), introducing Aaron (4:14-17, 27-31), predicting the outcome of events (4:21-23; 7:1-7), and even attacking Moses in the wilderness (4:24-26).

The second goal in the section is to define all other characters in relationship to Yahweh. The relationships separate into three groups: the people of God (the ancestors, Moses, the Israelites, the elders, and Aaron), the opponents of God (Pharaoh and the Egyptians), and the allies of God (Jethro and the Midianites). The special status of Moses and the close ties between his story and the story of Yahweh suggest that he should be separated out from the category "people of God" as a unique hero.

The relationship of Yahweh and Moses dominates in 3:1–7:7. The central event in the section is the encounter between Moses and God at the mountain of the God. Moses emerges as the leader of the Israelite people. The ambiguity surrounding Moses' identity, so prominent in the opening scene, is refashioned around the theme of authority when Moses encounters Yahweh on the mountain of God. Twice he is commissioned to rescue the Israelites (3:9-12; 6:2-8). All revelation of Yahweh is channeled through Moses, and as a consequence the theme of Mosaic authority runs throughout the section. Moses doubts his own authority (4:10-13; 6:28-30). The "belief" (*'āman*) of the Israelites in Moses is a repeated motif (4:1-17), as is the need for recognition of his authority by the Egyptians (7:5).

The divine commission of Moses relates the character of God and Moses to such a degree that the self-revelation of Yahweh and Mosaic authority become inseparable in Exodus. The book will trace the parallel development of Yahweh and Moses until the two are nearly merged into one character, when the glory of Yahweh radiates through the face of Moses after the revelation of law at the divine mountain (34:29-35). Exodus 3:1–7:7 is the first step in that process. The lack of a clear identity for both Yahweh and Moses in Exodus sets the stage for something new in history that will disrupt the established social and political order represented by Egypt and more particularly by Pharaoh. J. Assmann argues that the sense of newness, accompanied by social disruption, is the essence of the myth of the exodus. He concludes further that the characters of Yahweh and Moses represent a revolution, not an evolution, in world history and religion.[1]

The Israelites are also defined more clearly with the appearance of

---

1. J. Assmann, *Moses the Egyptian: The Memory of Egypt in Western Monotheism* (Cambridge: Harvard University Press, 1997), 1-8.

Yahweh. Yahweh is the God of Moses' father (3:6), the God of the Israelite ancestors in Egypt (3:15), and the God of the patriarchs Abraham, Isaac, and Jacob (3:6, 16; 4:5), having made covenant with them and promising them the land of Canaan (6:4). Yahweh identifies the Israelites as "the people of God" (3:7, 10; 6:7) and as the firstborn offspring of God (4:22). The elders are important representatives of the Israelites. Yahweh singles them out to Moses (3:16). If the "officials" who oversee the slave labor in the opening confrontation with Pharaoh are also the elders (5:1–6:1), then they model the conflict of faith in weighing allegiance between the competing power of Pharaoh and Yahweh.

Pharaoh emerges as the opponent of Yahweh. Pharaoh and Egypt represent the old world order of kings, polytheism, and social oppression.[2] The commission of Moses places Yahweh in conflict with Pharaoh as the God of the Hebrews, implying both a social class and an ethnic group. Moses as Yahweh's representative is to bring out the Israelites from the oppression of Pharaoh (3:10). Yahweh predicts that Pharaoh will resist (4:21; 7:3-4). The opposition between Yahweh and Pharaoh is stated most clearly in their initial meeting (5:1–6:1). The scene revolves around conflicting prophetic messenger formulas: "Thus said Yahweh/Pharaoh" *(kōh-'āmar yhwh/par'ōh).* The episode begins when Moses and Aaron deliver a message to Pharaoh: "Thus said Yahweh, 'Let my people go, so that they may hold a festival to me in the wilderness'" (5:1). The response of Pharaoh is first condescension: "Who is Yahweh?" (5:2). Then the messengers of Pharaoh counter the demand of Yahweh with increased oppression: "Thus said Pharaoh, I will not give you any more straw." The standoff sets the stage for the conflict between Pharaoh and Yahweh in the following episode (7:8–15:21).

The Midianites are allies of Yahweh in the rescue of the Israelites. They play a minimal yet important role in the story. In the previous scene the Midianites offered hospitality to Moses that led to his marriage with Zipporah (2:15-22). In this scene Moses receives his commission from Yahweh in the land of Midian (3:1). When Moses is instructed by Yahweh to return to Egypt, Jethro, the father-in-law of Moses, sends him away in peace (4:18). Then on the journey to Egypt Zipporah rescues Moses from a divine attack by circumcising her son as a means of warding off God and thus saving Moses' life (4:24-26). The Midianites are neither the people of God nor the opponents of God. They are allies of God. In contrast to Pharaoh, they are able to discern divine revelation. They even know rituals that influence divine action.

2. Ibid.

Authors

Research

Interpreters employ a range of methodologies to identify the anonymous authors in 3:1–7:7. The language, the changes in literary style, and the repetitions have received the most attention in the modern period of interpretation. The divine names Yahweh and Elohim have played a crucial role in identifying authors. But interpreters have also branched out to study the genres of theophany and prophetic commissioning throughout the Hebrew Bible as a resource for comparison. They have examined themes in the Hebrew Bible to profile the authors, such as the divine promise to the ancestors and the identification of Yahweh with the God of the fathers.

The most prominent repetition in 3:1–7:7 is the commission of Moses. Twice he is commanded to rescue the Israelite people from Egypt: first in the wilderness (3:1–4:18), and a second time in the land of Egypt (6:2–7:7). This repetition is the starting point for the identification of multiple, anonymous authors in the composition of 3:1–7:7. Interpreters are nearly unanimous in attributing the second commission, 6:2–7:7, to the P author. The first commission of Moses (3:1–4:18), the story of his return to Egypt (4:19-31), and the initial confrontation with Pharaoh (5:1–6:1) are identified with Non-P author(s). The review of research will follow this division, summarizing first the research identifying the Non-P authorship, and second the problems surrounding P authorship. The focus of debate concerning Non-P authorship in 3:1–6:1 is whether the story separates into two sources, J and E, or is the product of a single author. Interpreters also detect a history of composition in the P account of the commission of Moses in Egypt, 6:2–7:7, and in portions of 3:1–6:1.

Non-P Authorship of 3:1–6:1

S. McEvenue provides a starting point for evaluating the composition of 3:1–6:1.[3] He has listed a number of possible breaks in narrative continuity that may suggest multiple authors, including: (1) the change of divine names, Yahweh and Elohim; (2) the repetition of God's acknowledgment of the Israelite slavery in 3:7 and 9; (3) the break in narrative flow in the revelation of the divine name, Yahweh, between 3:13 and 15 created by 3:14; (4) the abrupt introduction of the

---

3. S. McEvenue, *Interpreting the Pentateuch* (Old Testament Series 4; Collegeville, Minn.: Liturgical Press, 1990), 3-13; idem, "The Speaker(s) in Ex 1–15," in *Biblische Theologie und gesellschaftlicher Wandel: Für Norbert Lohfink, SJ* (ed. G. Braulik et al.; Freiburg: Herder, 1993), 220-36.

elders in 3:16-20 after the revelation of the divine name introducing new vocabulary; (5) the elaboration of the motif of faith in 4:5 and 8-9; (6) the reference to Moses' staff in 4:17; and (7) the repetition of Moses' departure from Midian in 4:18-20. To this list we might add: (8) the identification of the God of Moses' father with the God of the Israelite ancestors, Abraham, Isaac, and Jacob (3:6, 15, 16; 4:5);[4] (9) the appearance of Aaron at the conclusion of the commission of Moses (4:13-16, 27-31), including his presence with Moses in the confrontation with Pharaoh (5:1–6:1);[5] and (10) the cluster of stories recounting Moses' return to Egypt, especially the divine prediction of the events of the exodus in 4:21-23 and the divine attack in 4:24-26.

Interpreters debate the number of authors in 3:1–6:1 based in part on the evaluation of literary unity or coherence. Is it possible to read 3:1–6:1 as the product of a single author? Or do the tensions require the identification of several authors to account for the changing literary style and range of motifs in the story? If more than one author is identified, how do the distinct compositions relate in the present form of the text? Are there two accounts of the same story now interwoven as in source criticism with the identification of the J and E authors? Or are individual literary units added to the work of a primary author as in supplementary criticism? An examination of the past research on the divine names and the literary character of the commission of Moses (3:1–4:18) will illustrate the contrasting methods of interpretation and their implications for identifying the Non-P author(s). The complexity and age of the literature make all literary judgments tentative and open to revision.

The diverse references to the Deity (e.g., the Messenger of Yahweh, God, the God, Yahweh) prior to the revelation of the name Yahweh in 3:13-15 have received the most attention in the modern period of interpretation as a sign of multiple authorship. The divine name Elohim (translated "God") occurs in 3:1, 4, 6, 11, 12, 13, 14, 15; while the name Yahweh is used in 3:2 (Messenger of Yahweh), 4, 7, 15. The different divine names are especially important for interpreters working within the framework of the Documentary Hypothesis, who seek to identify J and E sources (see, among the many examples, Noth, W. H. Schmidt, Childs, McEvenue, Propp).[6] The occurrence of both names in v. 4 requires that it be separated between J (v. 4a) and E (v. 4b), while the similar mixing of names in v. 15 can be attributed to E, since it represents the revelation of the name Yahweh. The result is two versions of Moses' encounter with the Deity: the J author (3:2-4a, 5, 7-8) and the E author (3:1, 4b, 6, 9-15).

---

4. Blenkinsopp, *Pentateuch*, 117.

5. Noth, *Exodus*, 46, 51.

6. Ibid., 30-35; Schmidt, *Exodus*, 106-11 *et passim*; Childs, *Exodus*, 52-53; McEvenue, *Interpreting the Pentateuch*, 3-13; Propp, *Exodus 1–18*, 190-94.

The J author recounts the appearance of the Messenger of Yahweh in the burning bush (v. 2), the declaration of holy ground (vv. 3-4a, 5), and Yahweh's announcement to deliver the Israelites from Egypt to a land flowing with milk and honey (vv. 7-8). The J version would also include the divine commission that Moses seek out the elders of Israel (3:16-22) and the series of objections by Moses, ending with the inclusion of Aaron in his mission (4:1-16). The E author describes Moses on the mountain of God (v. 1), the address of Elohim to Moses (v. 4b), the identification of the Deity as the God of the ancestors (v. 6), along with the commission of Moses, his objection, and the revelation of the divine name Yahweh (vv. 9-15). Most source critics identify the J source as the base text with supplements from E. Noth attributes 3:1ab*a*, 2-4a, 5, 7-8, 16-23; 4:1-27* to the J source, with the role of Aaron representing a secondary addition to the narrative, and he assigned 3:1b*b*, 4b, 6, 9-15; 4:17, 18, 20b to the E source.[7] Propp has recently departed from this judgment, reading the P source as the primary document, requiring a less significant role for the divine names (J: 3:2-4a, 5, 8, 9, 21-22; 4:19-20a, 24-26; and E: 3:1, 4b, 6, 7, 10-15, 16-20; 4:1-17, 18, 20b, 21-23, 27-31).[8]

Literary problems linger from the identification of J and E sources based on the distribution of the divine names in Exodus 3. Blum argues that the story is too compressed to preserve sources, as is perhaps most evident in the separation of 3:4.[9] A variety of solutions have been offered to account for the present distribution of the divine names with varying degrees of success. K. Berge sees tensions in the text suggesting multiple authors, but he also concludes that the problem of the divine names cannot be resolved by source criticism. He offers the tentative conclusion that the Messenger of Yahweh in v. 2 is likely a later insertion to the story.[10] K. Schmid notes that the name Yahweh is associated with the verb "to see/to appear" ($r\bar{a}$'$\hat{a}$; 3:2, 4, 7, 16; 4:1, 5), reinforcing the themes of perception, revelation, and authority in the commission of Moses and providing a contrast to the name Elohim.[11] Cassuto built on the theme of perception in the commission of Moses to argue that the divine names reflect points of view in the narrative. The omniscient narrator employs the name Yahweh, while Moses' perception of the Deity is indicated through the name Elohim,

---

7. Noth, *Exodus*, 33-34, 38-47. In *A History of Pentateuchal Traditions*, 30, 36, Noth attributes Exod 4:1-4(5), 6, 7 (8, 9), 10-12 (13-16), 19, 20a (21-23), 24-26 (27, 28), 29 (30-31) to J; and Exod 4:17, 18, 20b to E.

8. Propp, *Exodus 1–18*, 190-94.

9. Blum, *Studien*, 24.

10. K. Berge, *Reading Sources in a Text: Coherence and Literary Criticism in the Call of Moses: Models, Methods, Micro-Analysis* (Arbeiten zu Text und Sprache in Alten Testament 54; St. Ottilien: EOS Verlag, 1997), 61-70.

11. Schmid, *Erzväter und Exodus*, 191; see already Cassuto, *Exodus*, 32; now also Gertz, *Tradition und Redaktion*, 266-69.

emphasizing the breakdown of tradition and memory from 1:6.[12] The absence of Yahweh from chaps. 1–2 adds strength to the literary argument, although aspects of this reading are forced, as in the abrupt shift from Yahweh to Elohim in 3:4. Blum detects literary design in the distribution of the divine names in 3:2-4, culminating in the identification of Yahweh as "the God" *(hā'ĕlōhîm)*. Schmid broadens the literary argument, suggesting a focus on Elohim prior to the revelation in 3:15 (3:4, 6, 11, 12, 13, 14) as compared to its use in apposition to Yahweh afterward (3:15, 16, 18; 4:5).[13]

F. Kohata questioned why the use of Elohim continues after Exodus 3, if the narrative strategy of the E source culminates in the revelation of the divine name Yahweh in 3:13-15.[14] The interplay between Yahweh and Elohim appears throughout the Non-P narrative of Exodus (e.g., chaps. 18, 19, 24). The continuing use of both names is all the more striking when compared to the P History, where the name El Shaddai gives way to Yahweh in 6:2-8, without reappearing again. Kohata attributes the literary problem of the continued use of Elohim in the Non-P history to a later editor of the E source. F. V. Winnett saw the same problem but moved in a different direction to conclude that the use of the divine name Elohim is not part of an E source in Exodus. Instead he notes that Elohim is clustered in literature associated with the mountain of God/Elohim (see chaps. 3, 4, 18, 19, 24), thus accounting for many of its occurrences beyond chap. 3.[15] The literary solution of Winnett implies a single author who has incorporated distinct literary traditions into one narrative, rather than the two continuous narratives of the J and E authors. A number of recent interpreters have also followed the literary solution of Winnett, although they diverge in their evaluation of the process of composition and in the degree of unity attributed to the present narrative. The interpreters include Blum (the *D-Komposition*), C. Levin (the Yahwist redactor), Blenkinsopp (the Deuteronomistic corpus), and Van Seters (the Yahwist historian).[16]

The debate over the authorship of 3:1–6:1 is not limited to the distribution of the divine names Yahweh and Elohim, and their role in the process of composition. An additional literary problem emerges at the conclusion of Moses' commission, where his departure from Midian is stated twice in 4:18-20. First, Moses decides to return to Egypt and tells his father-in-law Jethro, who blesses him in 4:18. Then in 4:19 Yahweh commands Moses to return to Egypt, inform-

---

12. Cassuto, *Exodus*, 30-40; see also Jacob, *Exodus*, 51-53.

13. Schmid, *Erzväter und Exodus*, 191-92.

14. F. Kohata, *Jahwist und Priesterschrift in Exodus 3–14* (BZAW 166; Berlin: de Gruyter, 1986), 29; see also Van Seters, *Life of Moses*, 36, 46-47.

15. Winnett, *Mosaic Tradition*, 20-29.

16. Blum, *Studien*; idem, *Vätergeschichte*; Levin, *Jahwist*; Blenkinsopp, *Pentateuch*; Van Seters, *Life of Moses*.

ing him that the persons seeking his life in Egypt have now died. It is this repetition, not the divine names, that is the starting point for Noth's identification of the J and E sources. The J author recounts the return of Moses to Egypt at the command of Yahweh (4:19) with his wife and family (4:20a), while the E author describes Moses deciding on his own to depart from Midian (4:18), which he does alone taking the "staff of God" (4:20b).

The source-critical solution to the twice-told departure of Moses is complicated by an additional repetition between 2:15, 23a, and 4:19. The divine statement in 4:19: "all the persons seeking your life are dead" *(mētû kol-hā'ănāšîm haměbaqšîm 'et-napšekā)* recalls the conclusion to the story of Moses' murder of the Egyptian in 2:15, when Pharaoh was described as seeking Moses' life *(wayěbaqqēš lahărōg 'et-mōšeh),* which prompted his flight to Midian. The death of the king of Egypt is noted in 2:23a, "and it happened in those many days the king of Egypt died." The material in 2:15 and 2:23a is repeated in 4:19. The repetition is not exact, since the king of Egypt is not explicitly mentioned in 4:19. Yet the similarities led Noth to write: "The narrative of Moses' encounter with God (Ex. *3:1ff.) . . . seems to have been inserted." The reason, according to Noth, is that "Yahweh's command to return in Ex. 4:19 strikingly contains no reference to a commission given to Moses."[17] Instead 4:19 simply notes the passing of time and the death of Moses' enemies.

The literary connections between 2:15, 23a, and 4:19 led Noth to conclude that there was an earlier version of the story of Moses that lacked his divine commission at the mountain of God and led instead directly into his encounter with Pharaoh in 5:1–6:1. The evidence for an insertion is stronger in the LXX, since it frames 3:1–4:18 with a resumptive repetition, adding the death notice of the king of Egypt from 2:23a to 4:19: "after those many days the king of Egypt died" *(meta de tas hēmeras tas pollas ekeinas eteleutēsen ho basileus Aigyptou).* Resumptive repetitions, according to C. Kuhl, bracket insertions.[18] Yet, even on the basis of the more general repetition in the MT, Noth concluded that the commission of Moses was a late addition into the J source. His early dating of the sources allowed Noth to maintain both the hypothesis of a literary insertion and a source-critical solution for identifying authorship.

But with the abandonment of the source-critical hypothesis and the later dating of the narrative literature, the identity of the author of the commission of Moses in 3:1–4:18 has undergone reevaluation, with many interpreters advocating a single author rather than two parallel sources. The isolation of the commission of Moses, 3:1–4:18, in content and in syntax has reinforced this conclusion. The commission of Moses introduces new content to the opening

---

17. Noth, *History of Pentateuchal Traditions,* 203 n. 549.
18. C. Kuhl, "Die 'Wiederaufname' — ein literarkritisches Prinzip?" *ZAW* 64 (1952): 1-11.

chapters of Exodus. W. H. Schmidt underscores the complexity of the episode, noting five important themes: (1) the theophany of God on the cosmic mountain; (2) the instruction or commission of Moses; (3) the promise of rescue from Egypt; (4) the revelation of the divine name Yahweh; and (5) the identification of Yahweh with the God of the ancestors.[19] K. Schmid would expand the list to include (1) the motif of faith and (2) the idealization of Moses as a prophet.[20] And, as Blenkinsopp has underscored, the most central theme of all is the promise of land.[21] The combination of themes indicates the pivotal role of the commission of Moses in the composition of the Pentateuch and also its literary relationship with the Deuteronomistic History. Its themes stretch back into the story of the ancestors in Genesis, while also anticipating the conquest of land in the book of Joshua.

H. H. Schmid argued that the language of the commission and its form reflect the prophetic influence of the Deuteronomistic History. He noted, for example, that the commission of Moses is similar to that of Gideon in Judges 6 and to that of the prophet Jeremiah (chap. 1), while the divine proclamation of seeing the misery of the people (Exod 3:7) repeats in Deuteronomy (26:7) and in the Deuteronomistic History (2 Kgs 14:26). The imagery of the promised land as "broad and wide" and as "flowing with milk and honey" also reflects the language of Deuteronomy, as does the list of the indigenous population of the land.[22]

Blum extended the work of Schmid, arguing that the commission of Moses is a free composition within the *D-Komposition (KD)*, serving a broad literary purpose.[23] This exilic or postexilic author reinterprets prophetic accounts of revelation from the book of Hosea (e.g., Hos 1:9 and 12:10) and Ezekiel 20, accounting for the complexity of themes in Exod 3:1–4:18. The result is a pivotal role to the commission of Moses relating broadly with ancestral literature in Genesis (Gen 12:10-12; 15:1-21; 50:22-24), the larger story of the exodus (Exod 11:1-3; 12:21-27; 13:3-16; 14:1-31), while also anticipating themes in the Deuteronomistic History, although Blum is not clear about the ending of this literary corpus.[24]

Van Seters, building on the work of M. Rose, identifies the author of 3:1–4:18 as an exilic Yahwist historian, who reinterprets the commissioning of leaders in the Deuteronomistic History (e.g., Judges 6 and 1 Samuel 9–10), by em-

---

19. Schmidt, *Exodus*, 106-7.

20. Schmid, *Erzväter und Exodus*, 195-97.

21. Blenkinsopp, *Pentateuch*, 109-11.

22. Schmid, *Sogenannte Jahwist*, 19-29.

23. Blum, *Studien*, 40.

24. Ibid., 22-28. See the modifications of this hypothesis in idem, "Literarische Verbindung," 119-56.

ploying the self-introduction of the Deity in the commission of Moses. The aim of the Yahwist historian, according to Van Seters, is to relate the story of the exodus with the patriarchal stories in Genesis.[25]

K. Schmid reaches a similar position concerning the purpose of the commission of Moses, as an episode aimed at relating the ancestral literature in Genesis with the story of the exodus. But he identifies the author as a post-P editor, dependent on the P version of the commission of Moses in 6:2–7:7. He underscores in particular the close relationship between Genesis 15; Exod 3:1–4:18; and Joshua 24. All three texts interpret salvation from a prophetic perspective, emphasizing themes of faith, God as savior from death, and the promise of the land as oath.[26]

P Authorship of 3:1–7:7

The P authorship of 6:2–7:7 is identified from the language and from the literary style. The name of God as El Shaddai recalls the P account of the covenant with Abraham in Genesis 17. The emphasis on Aaron and the genealogy of Levi reflect concerns of the P author. But interpreters debate the history of composition. The genealogy in Exod 6:14-27 is likely an insertion into the commission of Moses. Propp notes that the opening phrase in v. 14, "these are the heads of their fathers' house," may have once headed an independent document.[27] Moreover, the genealogy is framed with a resumptive repetition in 6:10-12 and 28-30, further indicating its addition to the narrative.[28] Childs concludes that the genealogy now serves to introduce Aaron into the commission of Moses.[29]

There is some debate over the unity of 6:1-12; for example, Kohata concludes that v. 8 is a Deuteronomistic addition: "I will bring you to the land, to which I raised my arm to give to Abraham, to Isaac, and to Jacob. And I will give it to you as an inheritance, I am Yahweh." She argued that the phrase "to which I raised my arm" reflects the tradition of the promise of land as oath in Deuteronomistic literature.[30] But T. Römer and J. Lust have demonstrated that the language of "lifting up the hand/arm" reflects a Priestly point of view already evident in Ezekiel.[31] Thus interpreters in general read the second com-

---

25. Van Seters, *Life of Moses,* 39. See M. Rose, *Deuteronomist und Jahwist: Untersuchungen zu den Beruhrungspunkten beider Literaturwerke* (ATANT 67; Zurich: Theologischer Verlag, 1981), 9-11, 89, *et passim.*

26. Schmid, *Erzväter und Exodus,* 209-12 et passim.

27. Propp, *Exodus 1–18,* 275.

28. See Noth, *Exodus,* 58-59; Schmidt, *Exodus,* 296; Blum, *Studien,* 231.

29. See Childs, *Exodus,* 111-12.

30. Kohata, *Jahwist,* 28-41.

31. Römer, *Israels Väter,* 504-6; J. Lust, "Exodus 6,2-8 and Ezekiel," in *Studies in the Book*

mission of Moses as reflecting the concerns of the P author. I. Knohl is a departure from this consensus, arguing that the entire section belongs to the Holiness Code, a post-P author, while Gertz identifies three authors: the original P narrative (6:2-5, 6*, 7-12; 7:1-2, 4-7), an addition to P (6:13-30), and the post-P redactor of the Pentateuch (6:6bb; 7:3).[32]

The presence of P literature in the first commission of Moses, 3:1–6:1, has long been a topic of research. Interpreters question whether the signs given to Moses (4:1-9) and the presence of Aaron (4:13-16, 27-31; 5:1–6:1) indicate P or post-P authorship because of similarities to the P account of the plagues.

In 4:1-9 Yahweh presents Moses with three signs *('ōtôt)* to confirm his authority: transforming his staff into a snake (4:2-5), changing his healthy hand into a leprous one (4:6-7), and instructions for turning the water of the Nile into blood (4:9). Verses 5 and 8-9 indicate that the signs are meant to instill faith (Hiphil of *'āman)* in the Israelite people in the authority of Moses. The debate over authorship centers on the direction of dependence between the signs in 4:1-9 and the P plagues.

Some detect the influence of P literature in the signs, suggesting post-P authorship (e.g., K. Schmid, Blum, Gertz, Otto). The reasons are varied. The order of the signs given to Moses follows the order of the plagues in the present form of the text, suggesting the dependence of 4:1-9 on the P History. The motif of faith is a late addition to the Pentateuch, relating prophetic presentations of Abraham (Genesis 15), Moses (Exod 3:1–4:17), and Joshua (Joshua 24). The repetition of specific motifs suggests further that Exod 4:1-9 is reinterpreting the P plagues: the underworld snake, *tannîn* (7:8-13), is reinterpreted as a local creature, *nāḥāš* (4:2-4); the turning of water into blood fits the setting of Egypt (7:14-24), but is out of place in the wilderness (4:9); and the motif of dry ground *(yabbāšâ)* is a late addition to the story of the exodus.[33]

Others argue that the P author has reinterpreted 4:1-9, emphasizing the role of Aaron in the plagues (e.g., Noth, Propp, W. H. Schmidt, Van Seters). They note differences between the P account of the plagues and the signs to Moses. Verses 1-9 focus on the authority of Moses and the faith of the elders, as compared to the focus on Aaron and Pharaoh in the P History. Moses' staff becomes a snake *(nāḥāš)*, not a water serpent *(tannîn)*, as is the case in 7:8-13. The

---

of Exodus: Redaction — Reception — Interpretation (ed. Marc Vervenne; BETL 126; Leuven: Leuven University Press, 1996), 209-24.

32. I. Knohl, *The Sanctuary of Silence: The Priestly Torah and the Holiness School* (Minneapolis: Fortress, 1995); Gertz, *Tradition und Redaktion*, 237-54.

33. For more detailed interpretations see Schmid, *Erzväter und Exodus*, 203-5; Gertz, *Tradition und Redaktion*, 313-15; Blum, "Literarische Verbindung," 134; and esp. E. Otto, "Die nachpriesterschriftliche Pentateuchredaktion im Buch Exodus," in *Studies in the Book of Exodus,* ed. Vervenne, 103-6.

leprosy of Moses' hand does not repeat in the plague cycle. And the acts of power are called signs *('ōtôt)* in 4:1-9 as compared to wonders *(môpĕtîm)* in the P version of the plagues.[34]

The comparison of motifs is important for identifying the literary dependence. But it is less helpful in determining the direction of the inner-biblical interpretation. The different form of the signs and their sequence do, however, provide additional clues for identifying the author. The first two signs are in a different form from the third one. The first two signs are acted out: the staff of Moses is changed into a snake and reversed (4:2-5), and his healthy hand becomes leprous and is cured (4:6-8). The third sign, changing the water of the Nile into blood (4:9), is not acted out. It remains a divine prediction of a future event.

The difference in form is carried over into the meaning of the signs. The first two signs convey a message distinct from the third. The snake/staff of the first sign (4:2-5) likely indicates healing, a symbolic meaning of the snake in the ancient Near East.[35] The source of healing, however, is not in the snake. Moses is presented as fleeing from its danger. The power to heal is rather in Moses' ability to reverse the sign and change the snake back into his staff. The second sign (4:6-8) conveys the same message. Mosaic authority resides in the reversal of the leprosy, underscoring once again the power of Moses to heal. The emphasis on a reversal in the signs idealizes Moses as a healer, not as a wonder-worker. The third sign (4:9) departs from the previous two. The power of Moses is not in a reversal signifying healing, but in the destructive action itself, when Moses will pollute the Nile River into blood. In this sign Moses is a wonder-worker who transforms nature.[36]

There are three problems with interpreting the signs to Moses as dependent on the P plagues. The first is the absence of the motif of leprosy in the P plague cycle. Why would a post-P author include the sign of leprosy if the intention is to reinterpret the P plagues in 4:1-9? The second problem is that the changing of the Nile River into blood is not restricted to the P version of the plague. It is also the first plague in the Non-P History (see the commentary on 7:14-25). The third problem is that Aaron is a wonder-worker in the P plagues and not a healer as is the case in the first two signs given to Moses. The three problems are an obstacle

34. See Noth, *Exodus,* 45-46; Schmidt, *Exodus,* 195-96; Van Seters, *Life of Moses,* 55-58.

35. See, e.g., J. F. Borghouts, "Witchcraft, Magic, and Divination in Ancient Egypt," *CANE* 3:1775-85; for more specific evaluation of the Israelite cult see Lohfink, "'I am Yahweh, your Physician' (Exodus 15:26): God, Society and Human Health in a Postexilic Revision of the Pentateuch (Exod. 15:25b, 26)," in *Theology of the Pentateuch: Themes of the Priestly Narrative and Deuteronomy* (trans. L. M. Maloney; Minneapolis: Fortress, 1994), 35-95, esp. 63-71.

36. See Van Seters, *Life of Moses,* 57 n. 68, who describes such action as "metamorphoses," referring to Ovid, *Metamorphoses.*

for interpreting the P account of the plagues as the literary source for the signs to Moses in 4:1-9. It is possible, however, to account for the form, the number, and the sequence of the signs to Moses in the Non-P History.

The three signs given to Moses in 4:1-9 are acted out in reverse order in the Non-P account of the exodus and the wilderness journey, developing in the process the character of Mosaic authority that was first introduced in the wilderness commission (3:1–4:18). The third sign, the changing of the Nile River into blood in 4:9, is the first of the signs to be fulfilled in the Non-P History. It is fulfilled in the first plague in the Non-P History (7:14-24*), which begins a sequence of action that will culminate in the destruction of Pharaoh and the Egyptian army at the Red Sea (Exodus 14*). The third sign contains no reversal, unlike the first two signs, because it indicates the power to save through the destruction of the enemy, not through the healing of the Israelite people. The third sign illustrates the destructive power of Moses' commission against Pharaoh and the Egyptians. Yet even the destruction of the Egyptians develops the theme of Moses' wilderness commission, since it will culminate in the Israelite people "believing" in Moses and in Yahweh at the Red Sea (14:31).

The first and second signs are characterized by an act of reversal in order to explore the healing power of Moses in the wilderness journey of the Israelite people. The theme of healing is introduced in the opening story of the wilderness journey, when the Israelites are promised health at Marah with the divine self-revelation: "I am Yahweh, your healer" (15:22-26). Divine healing in this story is a reward for obedience to the law (15:25b-26) revealed in Exodus 19–34. Exodus 15:22-26 indicates that healing is a central theme throughout the wilderness journey. The healing power of Moses is demonstrated in the second half of the wilderness journey (Numbers 11–21) after the revelation of the law (Exodus 19–34), when Moses acts out the signs of healing from his commission. Moses performs the second sign, leprosy (4:6-8), when he cures the leprosy of Miriam (Numbers 12).[37] He demonstrates the first sign, the snake, when he re-

---

37. The mixture of themes (Moses' marriage to the Cushite woman and the unique role of Mosaic authority) and characters (Miriam and Aaron) indicates a history of composition in Numbers 12. M. Noth (*Numbers: A Commentary* [trans. J. D. Martin; OTL; Philadelphia: Westminster, 1968], 92-93) concluded that a literary division was not possible, but that the correspondence between Numbers 12 and the insertions of prophetic authority in Numbers 11 (vv. 14-17, 24b-30) suggested a later insertion into J. For arguments in favor of pre-P dating see Levin (*Jahwist*, 375), JE; Van Seters (*Life of Moses*, 234-39), the exilic Yahwist history (J); Blum (*Studien*, 76-85), KD. For arguments in favor of a post-P date see T. Römer, "Das Buch Numeri und das Ende des Jahwisten: Anfragen zur 'Quellenscheidung' im vierten Buch des Pentateuch," in *Abschied vom Jahwisten*, ed. Gertz, 215-27, esp. 225-27; idem, "Nombres 11–12 et la question d'une redaction deutéronomique dans le Pentateuque," in *Deuteronomy and Deuteronomic Literature: Festschrift C. H. W. Brekelmans* (ed. M. Vervenne and J. Lust; BETL 133; Leuven: Leuven University Press, 1997), 481-98.

verses the deadly bite of the seraphim with the construction of Nehoshet, the copper snake, at the conclusion of the wilderness journey (Num 21:4-9). The healing power of Moses takes place in both stories through intercessory prayer, which Aurelius has argued is crucial in the characterization of Moses as a healer in the Deuteronomistic tradition, not in the P History.[38]

The signs in Exod 4:1-9 are not dependent on the P History. Instead they outline the essential structure of the exodus and the wilderness journey in the Non-P History. The prediction (4:9) of the first plague (7:14-24) leads to the "faith" of the people in Moses and in Yahweh (14:31) at the conclusion of the exodus. The idealization of Moses as a healer (4:2-8) is demonstrated at strategic locations, which frame the second half of the wilderness journey (Numbers 12 and 21:4-9) in the Non-P History. It is the P author who partially reinterprets the signs of Moses to accentuate the role of Aaron in the plagues. The P reinterpretation is similar in both cases. Aaron performs the sign before Pharaoh, not the Israelite people, while the meaning of the sign is no longer a unique act of healing but a demonstration of power, conforming to the central theme of the P commission of Moses to bring Pharaoh and the Egyptians to the knowledge of Yahweh (7:5). Moreover, the demonstrations of power by Aaron are not unique, but are repeated by the Egyptian magicians.

The debate over P authorship is even more acute in 4:10-17, because of the sudden appearance of Aaron in the wilderness (4:13-16, 27-31) and in the initial confrontation with Pharaoh (5:1–6:1). The P author fashions the commission of Moses to accentuate the importance of Aaron (6:2–7:7), while also including him in the plague cycle (see the commentary). Indeed, most references to Aaron in the Pentateuch occur in the P History, where his portrayal as high priest is developed in detail. Thus the question arises whether the sudden appearance of Aaron in the wilderness is not evidence of P or post-P authorship to expand the role of Aaron from priest to prophetic teacher and to include him in the initial confrontation with Pharaoh (e.g., H. Valentin, Blum, K. Schmid, Otto, Gertz).

The problem with attributing 4:10-17 to a P or post-P author is that Aaron appears in texts that have no relationship to P literature. The clearest example is the war against the Amalekites in 17:8-16, where Aaron and Hur assist Moses. Aaron and Hur are also assigned a leadership role over the people in 24:14, although only Aaron plays a role in the construction of the golden calf (Exodus 32; Deut 9:20).[39] Aaron is not a priest in these stories. Nor is Aaron a priest in

38. Aurelius, *Fürbitter Israels*, 153-56, 173-74, *et passim*.

39. See Valentin, *Aaron*, 365-406, for a more extensive list of texts in which Aaron occurs in a less defined role than as high priest, including his presence with Moses before Pharaoh (Exod 5:1, 4, 20; 12:31), his relation to Miriam as brother (15:20), and his feasting with Jethro and the elders (18:12). Aaron is also summoned by Yahweh during theophany (19:24), and he feasts

Exod 4:13-16. He is identified as a Levite and as the brother of Moses, but he functions as a prophet, not a priest. A. Cody concluded that Aaron is polyvalent in these stories, taking on different characteristics in the distinct stories, prior to his reinterpretation in the P History.[40] Noth agreed: "new and different things continued to be related" to Aaron, until his early presentations were superseded by the P author.[41] Thus both Cody and Noth assign the portrayal of Aaron in 4:10-17 to a pre-P author (see also Childs, Propp, Van Seters, W. H. Schmid). I will also interpret 4:10-17 as an episode within the Non-P History.

The research on 3:1–7:7 indicates its important role in the composition of the Pentateuch. The twice-told commission of Moses is a pivotal text, relating themes throughout the Primary History of Genesis–2 Kings. The selective overview of scholarship confirms the multiple authorship of 3:1–7:7. But it also underscores the ambiguity of the more precise identification of the authors, or the exact history of composition of the literature. The distribution of the divine names in 3:1–6:1 resists a satisfactory solution, leaving open the character of the earliest stories of Moses and the exodus. A similar ambiguity emerges in the latest literary contributions, raising questions about the authorship of the signs of Moses and the presence of Aaron in 4:1-18. I will return to aspects of the debate over authorship in 3:1–7:7, although the focus of interpretation will remain on the Non-P and P Histories.

Non-P and P Histories

The review of research has clarified that Moses is commissioned twice to rescue the Israelites (3:1–4:18; 6:2–7:7). The commissions differ in language, literary style, and point of view. Their most prominent difference, however, is in setting. Moses is first commissioned in the wilderness in the Non-P History (3:1–4:18) and a second time in the land of Egypt in the P History (6:2–7:7). Thus geography emerges as an important feature for interpreting the two commissions of Moses. The Non-P History presents a two-part story of Moses' commission at the divine mountain in the wilderness (3:1–4:18) and his failed confrontation with Pharaoh (4:19–6:1). The P History supplies a second commission of Moses in the land of Egypt (6:2–7:7). The Non-P and P versions result in two commissions with similar motifs, including the revelation of the divine name Yahweh (3:13-15; 6:2-8), objections by Moses because of his inability to speak (4:10-12;

---

before Yahweh on the divine mountain with Nadab, Abihu, and the seventy elders (24:1, 9), both portraits of Aaron that correspond more closely to the P History.

40. A. Cody, *A History of Old Testament Priesthood* (AnBib 35; Rome: Pontifical Biblical Institute, 1969), 150.

41. Noth, *History of Pentateuchal Traditions*, 181.

6:12, 30), and the inclusion of Aaron in the commission of Moses (4:10-16; 7:1-2). The stories are presently separated by Moses' failure to liberate the Israelites in his initial encounter with Pharaoh (4:19–6:1).

Non-P History

The wilderness commission of Moses in the Non-P History (3:1–4:18) is aimed at the Israelites, especially the elders. Yahweh commands Moses to address the Israelites (3:15) and to seek out the elders (3:16). Exodus 1:6 provides the background for the commission. The death of Joseph's generation indicated a loss of memory about God and past tradition, requiring that Moses inform the Israelite people about Yahweh. Thus Yahweh, like Moses, enters the story of the exodus lacking identity. The commission of Moses is intended to clarify the identity of Yahweh to the Israelite people in three ways: (1) to reestablish the name Yahweh to Moses and to the Israelite people after the break in tradition (3:13-15); (2) to identify Yahweh as the God of their ancestors, Abraham, Isaac, and Jacob (3:6, 15); and (3) to assure Moses and the Israelite people that Yahweh is present with them (3:12, 14). But when Yahweh commissions Moses, he objects, noting first his lack of identity (3:11) and second God's lack of identity (3:13), before confessing his inability to speak (4:10). Moses doubts his skill to persuade the elders of the divine promise of rescue or of his authority. The central problem in the Non-P account of Moses' commission is the "belief" of the elders (4:1, 5, 8 [twice], 9). The Israelites and their leaders have no basis to believe in the authority of Moses or his divine commission.

The revelation of the divine name Yahweh is a first step in laying a foundation for the Israelites to believe in Moses and in Yahweh (3:13-15). The emphasis in the Non-P History is less on the revelation of a new name than on the equation of Yahweh, the God of Moses' father, with the God of Abraham, Isaac, and Jacob. In this way the Non-P History merges the story of salvation in Exodus with the ancestors in Genesis. When Moses continues to resist the divine commission, the miraculous signs are further demonstrations of his authority intended to create belief among the Israelites (4:1-9). The signs initially achieve their intended effect with the Israelite people believing in Moses and the power of his signs (4:31). But the failed confrontation with Pharaoh (5:1–6:1) indicates how fleeting the faith of the Israelites is as long as they dwell under the oppression of Pharaoh in the land of Egypt.

The faith of the Israelite people in the Non-P History will require the same setting of the wilderness as the commission of Moses. Thus when Pharaoh rejects the message of Moses, "Yahweh requires a festival in the wilderness" (5:1), the "officials," who are likely Israelites, identify themselves as "servants of Pharaoh" (5:15-16) in seeking relief from the increased oppression. The point of emphasis in the Non-P History is that the Israelites, like Moses, require the wilderness setting to achieve a firm faith in Yahweh and in the authority of Moses. The confrontation at the Red Sea, a wilderness location in the Non-P History (14:31), and the revelation at the mountain of God (19:9) provide the proper environment for nurturing faith in the wilderness.

Repetitions within the narrative indicate a history of composition within the Non-P History. The review of research has indicated the literary tensions within the narrative. The divine concern over the Israelite oppression occurs twice in 3:7-8 and 9-10. In vv. 7-8 Yahweh states: "I have indeed seen the misery of my people in Egypt. I have heard them crying out." Then the Deity repeats the message in v. 9: "And now the cry of the Israelites has reached me, and I have seen the way the Egyptians are oppressing them." The commission of Moses and the identity of God as the Deity of the ancestors are also stated twice in 3:10-15 and 16-22. These repetitions and perhaps even the different uses of the names of God, Yahweh and Elohim, may indicate diverse stories now incorporated in the Non-P History. Thus it is important to recognize that the Non-P History is a compilation of stories, providing distinct points of view on the narrated events. Whatever may have been the precise history of composition, the different stories share an emphasis on the wilderness setting as the important location for the commission of Moses, along with a focus on the Israelites, not the Egyptians.

The Non-P History also narrates the wilderness journey of Moses from Midian to the land of Egypt (4:18-31). The narrative is uneven from the outset. The departure of Moses is stated twice (4:18-20). Yahweh predicts the outcome of events to Moses (4:21-23) before attacking him (4:24-26). Moses is saved from the divine attack when Zipporah, his Midianite wife, wards off the Deity with a bloody foreskin (4:24-26). Moses then meets Aaron in the wilderness before proclaiming Yahweh's impending rescue to the Israelites (4:27-31). The initial confrontation with Pharaoh in the Non-P History is a failure. Pharaoh's rejection of the claims of Yahweh upon the Israelites (5:1-14) results in two complaint stories: the first by the Israelite officials (5:15-21), and the second by Moses (5:22–6:1).

P History

The P historian adds a second commission of Moses (6:2–7:7) after his initial failure in the land of Egypt (5:1–6:1). The commission includes many of the themes from the wilderness commission of Moses in the Non-P History. There is a revelation of the divine name Yahweh (6:2; cf. 3:13-15), along with the announcement of rescue (6:2-8; cf. 3:8; 5:3) from hard labor (6:5, 6, 9; cf. 5:9, 11, 15, 16, 18, 21) and forced labor (cf. 2:11; 5:4, 5). But the circumstances of the revelation are changed. The God of the ancestors is not forgotten as in the previous commission. Instead there is an evolution in the name of God from El Shaddai to Yahweh. The commission in the land of Egypt also repeats the promise of salvation (6:3-8), adding new motifs about covenant and divine memory first introduced in 2:23b-25. But the motif of the "belief" of the Israelites is absent. In its place the P author underscores the need for the Egyptians "to acknowledge" Yahweh, building on a theme that is also central to the prophet Ezekiel, who also called both Israel (e.g., Ezek 6:6-7, 14; 7:4) and the nations (Ezek 25:7, 11, 17) to acknowledge Yahweh. The central theme of the P version of Moses' commission is stated at the conclusion by Yahweh: "The Egyptians will know that I am Yahweh when I stretch out my hand against Egypt and bring the Israelites out of it" (Exod 7:5).

The change in focus from the Israelites to the Egyptians is introduced in the objection of Moses (6:12). His inability to speak is no longer an obstacle to instilling belief in the Israelites. It is the rejection by Pharaoh that Moses fears. Exodus 6:28–7:7 focuses exclusively on this problem. The revelation of the divine name Yahweh reappears aimed at Pharaoh (6:29). Moses is to address the king of Egypt, but objects because of a speech defect (6:30). Yahweh's concluding speech to Moses (7:1-5) counters the objection, providing an outline of what the effects of the exodus will be on the land of Egypt, on Pharaoh, and on the Egyptian people, not the Israelites, nor their wilderness experience of Yahweh. Moses will appear as a god to Pharaoh, and Aaron as a prophet (7:1). Pharaoh will resist, allowing Yahweh to increase signs in the land of Egypt (7:3). The Israelites' leaving Egypt will be an act of judgment on the land of Egypt. God concludes: "The Egyptians will know that I am Yahweh" (7:5).

The P author constructs a polemical interpretation of the exodus aimed at bringing the Egyptians to the knowledge of Yahweh. The land of Egypt is the important setting for the story, not the wilderness. The Egyptians must know that Yahweh is the God who rules even their land. The Israelites must also come to the knowledge of Yahweh. But for the P author the Israelites' recognition of Yahweh does not arise from the exodus, nor does it take place in the land of Egypt. It occurs in the wilderness with the construction of the tabernacle and the formation of the priesthood at Mount Sinai (Exodus 29). The polemical perspective of the P History infuses the story of the exodus with a more universal dimension concerning the scope and power of Yahweh not simply as the God of the Israelites but as the Deity who also rules the land of Egypt. The universal perspective of the P History is reminiscent of the exilic prophet Second Isaiah (see Isaiah 40–55), who also probes the power of Yahweh in world history.

LITERARY STRUCTURE

The relationship of the Non-P and P Histories in Exod 3:1–7:7 follows the strategy of chaps. 1–2, where blocks of material are inserted promoting a new or extended interpretation of events.[42] The P author framed chaps. 1–2 with a new introduction (1:1–7*) and conclusion (2:23b-25). Exodus 2:23b-25 serves a dual purpose, also functioning as the introduction to the following section (3:1–7:7). As a result, the P History (2:23b-25 and 6:2–7:7) now frames the commission of Moses in the Non-P History (3:1–6:1).

The repetition of the motifs of covenant and divine memory in the P History (2:24-25; 6:4-5) underscores the literary relationship between 2:23b-25 and 6:2–7:7. The repetition has led many interpreters to conclude that the P History was once an independent source or history. But, as Cross noted, such a hypothesis means that Moses appears in Exodus without introduction, requiring, at the very least, the assumption that a large section of the P History is now missing.[43] The need for such gaps in the P History and the close ties to the present narrative context have prompted J. L. Ska to conclude that the P account of Moses' commission is an insertion into the Non-P History. He notes links in language between 6:2–7:7 and 3:1–6:1, such as hard labor (5:9, 11, 15, 18, 21; 6:5, 6, 9), slave labor (2:11; 5:4, 5; 6:6-7), and salvation as rescue (3:8; 5:3; 6:6). He further concludes that the divine speech to Moses in 6:2-8 is an oracle of response, presupposing the events of the failed mission of Moses in 5:1–6:1.[44]

The literary position of 6:2–7:7 creates two revelations of the divine name Yahweh, 3:13-15 and 6:2-8. Recent studies have explored, in particular, how Yahweh undergoes development when the Non-P and P versions are read sequentially from the initial revelation of the name in 3:13-15 to the second in 6:2-8. T. L. Thompson suggests that the sequence is intended to advance a new form of "inclusive Yahwism."[45] The present sequence of the stories certainly accentuates a development in the identity of Yahweh. The first revelation of the name, 3:13-15, focuses more on the identification of Yahweh, the God of the exodus, with the God of the ancestors. The revelation progresses from a general

---

42. See also Blum, *Studien*, 235.

43. Cross, *Canaanite Myth and Hebrew Epic*, 301. See also Blum, *Studien*, 229-31.

44. J. L. Ska, "La place d'Ex 6,2-8 dans la narration de l'exode," *ZAW* 94 (1982): 530-48; see also idem, "Quelques remarques sur Pg et la dernière rédaction du Pentateuque," in *Le Pentateuque en question* (ed. A. de Pury; MdB; Geneva: Labor et Fides, 1989), 95-125.

45. See, e.g., T. L. Thompson, "How Yahweh Became God: Exodus 3 and 6 and the Heart of the Pentateuch," *JSOT* 68 (1995): 57-74; C. Seitz, "The Call of Moses and the 'Revelation' of the Divine Name: Source-Critical Logic and Its Legacy," in *Theological Exegesis: Essays in Honor of Brevard S. Childs* (ed. C. Seitz and K. Green-McCreight; Grand Rapids: Eerdmans, 1999), 145-67.

identification of Yahweh with the ancestors, stated as a question by Moses (v. 13), to the more explicit listing of Abraham, Isaac, and Jacob in the divine response (v. 15). The relationship of Yahweh to the ancestors is present from the outset in 6:2-8. The focus of this revelation shifts more explicitly to the divine names of God, El Shaddai and Yahweh, exploring in a more pointed manner the character and evolution of the Deity in the change of names. When the two commissions are read in sequence, there is a development in theme. Exodus 3:13-15 clarifies the relationship between God and the Israelites. Yahweh, the God of the exodus, is also the God of the ancestors, Abraham, Isaac, and Jacob. Exodus 6:2-8 sharpens the attributes of Yahweh, clarifying that El Shaddai is also Yahweh. Finally, the two texts explore the full range of Yahweh's power over evil. Yahweh is able to rescue the Israelites from Egypt (3:1–7:7) and bring the Egyptians to the knowledge of his power (6:2–7:7).

The geographical setting of the two commissions is also important for interpreting the literary structure of the canonical text. The separate settings of the wilderness and the land of Egypt are crucial for interpretation, providing the springboard for divergent interpretations of Moses' commission. The setting of the wilderness in the Non-P history identifies the divine name Yahweh in relationship to the Israelites and their salvation. The setting of Egypt in the P History explores the power of God in the broader relationship of the Egyptians and Pharaoh, the opponents of Yahweh. The juxtaposition of the Non-P (3:1–4:18) and P (6:2–7:7) versions of the commission, as events framing the failure of Moses' initial confrontation with Pharaoh (4:19–6:1), allows for two points of view on the power of Yahweh and the significance of the exodus without requiring the reader to harmonize them. The exodus will force the Egyptians to acknowledge the power of Yahweh in the land of Egypt (the P History) and it will bring the Israelites into the wilderness, where they will acquire faith in Yahweh and in Moses (the Non-P History).

The distinct settings of the commissions of Moses, with their separate themes, provide the initial clue that geography plays an active role in the thematic development of both the Non-P and P Histories. The chart in figure 4 on page 114 illustrates how the distinct settings for the commissions of Moses are carried through to the confrontation at the Red Sea.

The account of the confrontation at the Red Sea in the Non-P History is preceded by the notice that the Israelites encamp at Etham (13:20), a location at the "edge of the wilderness," making the defeat of Pharaoh at the Red Sea a wilderness event.[46] Thus in the Non-P History the confrontation at the Red

---

46. See G. W. Coats, "The Traditio-Historical Character of the Reed Sea Motif," *VT* 17 (1967): 253-65; idem, "The Wilderness Itinerary," *CBQ* 34 (1972): 135-52; idem, "An Exposition for the Wilderness Traditions," *VT* 22 (1972): 288-95; Dozeman, *God at War*, 42-54.

Figure 4

Non-P History	*P History*
COMMISSION OF MOSES (3:1–4:18)	**COMMISSION OF MOSES** (6:2–7:7)
SETTING: WILDERNESS	SETTING: LAND OF EGYPT
THEME: FAITH OF ISRAEL (4:1-9)	THEME: EGYPTIAN ACKNOWLEDGMENT OF YAHWEH (7:5)
RED SEA CONFRONTATION (14:1-31)	**RED SEA CONFRONTATION** (14:1-31)
SETTING: WILDERNESS	SETTING: LAND OF EGYPT
Etham (13:20)	**Pi-hariroth** (14:1-2)
Edge of the wilderness	Turn back, between Migdol and sea, before Baal-zephon
THEME: FAITH OF ISRAEL (14:31)	THEME: EGYPTIAN ACKNOWLEDGMENT OF YAHWEH (14:18)

Sea is the first experience of the Israelite people in the wilderness. Indeed, the story is focused on them. The destruction of Pharaoh reveals the power of Yahweh to the Israelites, recalling Moses' initial confrontation with God in the same setting (3:1–4:18). Moreover, the result of the destruction of Pharaoh is that the Israelites begin to acquire faith in Moses and in Yahweh (14:31), developing the theme that was first introduced in Moses' wilderness commission (4:1-9). The P History changes the setting of the Red Sea, adding the new location of Pi-hariroth (14:1-2).[47] The P author states that the Israelites arrived at Pi-hariroth by "turning back." The reversing of direction after the wilderness setting of Etham suggests that they reenter the land of Egypt and leave the wilderness. As a result, the Red Sea is a location in the land of Egypt in the P History, corresponding to the setting of Moses' commission in 6:2–7:7. The shift in geographical setting is accompanied by a change in theme from the faith of the Israelite people (14:31) to the Egyptian acknowledgment of Yahweh's power (14:18).

The role of geography in 3:1–7:7 yields a three-part structure to the scene: the commission of Moses in the wilderness, the failed confrontation with Pharaoh, and the commission of Moses in Egypt. The commissions of Moses mirror each other, separating into the same two-part structure: the identity of Yahweh, and the authority of Moses. The result is the following outline for the commentary.

---

47. See Childs, *Exodus,* 220.

I. Commission of Moses in the Wilderness (3:1–4:18)
   A. Identity of Yahweh (3:1-15)
   B. Authority of Moses (3:16–4:18)
II. Failed Confrontation with Pharaoh (4:19–6:1)
   A. Wilderness Journey (4:19-31)
   B. Failure to Rescue (5:1–6:1)
III. Commission of Moses in Egypt (6:2–7:7)
   A. Identity of Yahweh (6:2-9)
   B. Authority of Moses (6:10–7:7)

COMMENTARY

Commission of Moses in the Wilderness (3:1–4:18)

3:1 *And Moses was herding the flock of Jethro, his father-in-law, the priest of Midian. And he drove the flock into the far side of the wilderness, and he came to the mountain of God, toward Horeb.* 2 *And the Messenger of Yahweh appeared to him in a flame of fire from the midst of the bush. And he saw. Indeed, the bush is burning with fire, but the bush is not consumed.*

3 *And Moses said, "I must turn aside to see this great vision. Why is the bush not burned up?"*

4 *And Yahweh saw that he turned aside to see. And God called to him from the midst of the bush. And he said, "Moses, Moses."*

And he said, "Here I am."

5 *And he said, "Do not approach here! Remove your sandals from your feet, because the place on which you are standing, it is holy ground."* 6 *And he said, "I am the God of your father, God of Abraham, God of Isaac, and God of Jacob." And Moses hid his face, because he was afraid to gaze at the God.*

7 *And Yahweh said, "I have observed the torment of my people in Egypt. And their cry I have heard from his taskmasters, because I know his pain.* 8 *And I have descended to rescue him from the hand of Egypt and to bring him up from that land to a good and broad land, to a land flowing with milk and honey, to the place of the Canaanite, the Hittite, the Amorite, the Perizzite, the Hivite, and the Jebusite.* 9 *And now, indeed, the cry of the Israelites has come to me, and I have also seen the suffering with which the Egyptians make them suffer.* 10 *And now, go, and I will send you to Pharaoh. Bring out my people, the Israelites, from Egypt!"*

11 *And Moses said to the God, "Who am I that I should go to Pharaoh, and that I will lead the Israelites from Egypt?"*

12 *And he said, "For I will be with you. And this is for you a sign that I sent*

you. When you bring out the people, the Israelites, from Egypt, you will serve the God on this mountain."

¹³ And Moses said to the God, "Indeed, I come to the Israelites and I say to them, 'The God of your fathers sent me to you.' And they say to me, 'What is his name?' What will I say to them?"

¹⁴ And God said to Moses, "I will be who I will be." And he said, "Thus you will say to the Israelites, 'I will be' sent me to you."

¹⁵ And God said further to Moses, "Thus you will say to the Israelites, 'Yahweh, the God of your fathers, the God of Abraham, the God of Isaac, and the God of Jacob sent me to you. This is my name forever. This is my memorial for all generations.'

¹⁶ Go and gather the elders, and you will say to them, 'Yahweh the God of your fathers appeared to me, God of Abraham, Isaac, and Jacob,' saying, 'I am very aware of you and what has been done to you in Egypt.' ¹⁷ I say, 'I will bring you up from the torment of Egypt to the land of the Canaanite, and the Hittite, and the Amorite, and the Perizzite, and the Hivite, and the Jebusite, to a land flowing with milk and honey.'

¹⁸ And they will listen to your voice. And you, and the elders of Israel, will come to the king of Egypt. And you will say to him, 'Yahweh, the God of the Hebrews, has met with us. And now let us go a journey of three days into the wilderness, so that we can sacrifice to Yahweh, our God.' ¹⁹ But I know that the king of Egypt will not let you go, except by a strong hand. ²⁰ And I will send out my hand and I will strike Egypt with all my wonders, which I will do in his midst. And after that he will send you out. ²¹ And I will give this people favor in the eyes of Egypt. And it will happen that you will go out and you will not go out empty. ²² Each woman will request from her neighbor and from the resident alien in her house vessels of silver and vessels of gold, and clothing. And you will place them on your sons and on your daughters. And you will plunder Egypt."

⁴:¹ And Moses answered and he said, "And suppose they do not believe me. And they do not listen to my voice, but they say, 'Yahweh did not appear to you.'"

² And Yahweh said to him, "What is this in your hand?"

And he said, "A staff."

³ And he said, "Throw it on the ground." And he threw it on the ground, and it became a snake. And Moses fled from it.

⁴ And Yahweh said to Moses, "Send out your hand and seize its tail." And he sent out his hand and he grasped it. And it became a staff in his palm. ⁵ "So that they may believe that Yahweh, the God of their fathers, God of Abraham, God of Isaac, and God of Jacob, appeared to you."

⁶ And Yahweh said further to him, "Bring your hand in your breast." And he brought his hand in his breast. And he took it out, and indeed, his hand was leprous, like snow. ⁷ And he said, "Return your hand to your breast." And he returned

his hand to his breast. And he took it out, and indeed, it returned like his flesh.
8 *"And it will be that if they do not believe you and will not listen to the voice of the
first sign, they will believe the voice of the second sign.* 9 *And it will be, if they will
not believe even these two signs, and they will not listen to your voice, then you
will take from the water of the Nile and pour [it] on dry ground. And the water
that you will take from the Nile will become blood on the dry ground."*

10 *And Moses said to Yahweh, "O, my Lord, I am not a speaker, neither yesterday, nor the day before, nor since your speaking to your servant. But I am heavy
of mouth and heavy of tongue."*

11 *And Yahweh said to him, "Who makes a mouth for humans? Or who
makes dumb or deaf, clear-sighted or blind? Is it not I, Yahweh?* 12 *Now, go, and I
will be with your mouth and teach you what you will speak."*

13 *And he said, "O, my Lord, send, please, by the hand you send."*

14 *And Yahweh became angry with Moses, and he said, "Is there not Aaron
your brother, the Levite? I know that he can speak. Even now he is approaching to
meet you, and he will see you and rejoice in his heart.* 15 *And you will speak to
him, and you will place the words in his mouth. But I will be with your mouth and
with his mouth. And I will teach you both what you will do.* 16 *He will speak for
you to the people. And it will be that he will become as a mouth for you, but you
will become as God for him.* 17 *But this staff you will take in your hand, with which
you will do the signs."*

4:18 *And Moses went and he returned to Jethro, his father-in-law, and he said
to him, "I must go and return to my brothers, who are in Egypt, and I must see if
they still live." And Jethro said to Moses, "Go in peace."*

Notes

3:1 *the far side of the wilderness.* The Hebrew preposition *'aḥar* ("beyond") is unusual.
  The MT is followed by Sam. The LXX employs *hypo* with the accusative to express
  motion toward an object. Wevers concludes that if one's orientation is to the east,
  the phrase indicates the western part of the desert: "What Exod [i.e., LXX] is saying is that Moses brought the sheep way down below, i.e. into the far reaches of, the
  desert where Horeb lay."[1] The awkward syntax in both the MT and LXX is likely
  intended to indicate fantastic geography, meaning locations of mystery at the
  edges of everyday human experience, where unexpected events occur.[2]
toward Horeb. The phrase continues the emphasis on fantastic geography at the edge
  of human experience (see above). Horeb, *ḥōrēb*, is both a wilderness region and a
  divine mountain in the Non-P History, Deuteronomy, and the Deuteronomistic

---

1. J. W. Wevers, *Notes on the Greek Text of Exodus* (SBLSCS 30; Atlanta: Scholars Press,
1990), 25.

2. For discussion of the genre of the fantastic see T. Todorov, *The Fantastic: A Structural
Approach to the Literary Genre* (trans. R. Howard; Ithaca: Cornell University Press, 1975).

History (see the commentary).[3] The translation "toward Horeb" results from the directional *he* on Horeb, *ḥōrēbâ,* which, when separated from the mountain of God, emphasizes more the general locale for the divine residence than the specific residence itself. Thus the MT and Sam create a literary relationship between the mountain of God and its location at (or in) the region of Horeb, without fully merging the two descriptions. The result is the continuation of geographical imagery, in which Moses moves from the wilderness to the more remote desert region (Horeb) at the edge of human experience, where God resides. The Hebrew could be translated: "And he drove the flock beyond the wilderness, and he came to the mountain of God, toward the desert." The LXX removes the literary allusion, eliminating the reference to the mountain of God, and instead identifying the divine residence as Mount Horeb *(eis to oros chōrēb).*

3:2 *Messenger of Yahweh.* The LXX reads, *angelos kyriou,* "angel of the Lord."

3:3 *burned up.* The MT employs the verb *bāʿar,* "to burn," with *lōʾ,* normally translated "not," hence the translation, "Why is the bush not burned up?" The sentence, however, contradicts the statement in v. 2, "The bush is burning *(bāʿar)* with fire." The LXX resolves the contradiction with different verbs, *kaietai* (burning) and *katekaieto* (burned up). D. N. Freedman resolves the problem of the MT by reading Hebrew *lōʾ* as an asseverative rather than a negative, translating, "why the bush was burning brightly."[4]

3:4 *Yahweh saw that he turned aside to see. And God called to him.* The Sam departs from the MT by employing *ʾĕlōhîm,* "God," in both references to the Deity. The LXX unifies the references in the other direction, employing *kyrios,* "Lord," suggesting Hebrew *yhwh.* Blum suggests that the juxtaposition of the names Yahweh and Elohim may be the result of dittography.[5]

3:7 *his taskmasters . . . his pain.* The LXX employs the plural, *autōn,* "their taskmasters . . . their pain."

3:8 *I have descended.* The MT is past tense, *wāʾērēd,* as compared to the future in Sam, *wʾrdh,* "I will descend."

Canaanite . . . Jebusite. The LXX and Sam add "the Girgashite," bringing the six-member list of indigenous nations to seven. The MT employs the seven-member list in Deut 7:1 in a different order.

3:9 *indeed.* The MT *hinnēh* could also be translated "see" in this verse and in v. 13.[6]

3:10 *Pharaoh.* The LXX adds "the king of Egypt."

3:11 *to Pharaoh . . . from Egypt.* The LXX reads, "Pharaoh, the king of Egypt . . . from the land of Egypt."

3:12 *and he said.* The LXX reads, "and God said."

3:13 *indeed.* This is the third occurrence of Hebrew *hinnēh* in the MT marking transitions in the story: 3:2 (when Moses sees the burning bush), 3:9 (when God com-

---

3. L. Perlitt, "Sinai und Horeb," in *Beiträge zur Alttestamentlichen Theologie: Festschrift für Walther Zimmerli* (ed. H. Donner et al.; Göttingen: Vandenhoeck & Ruprecht, 1977), 302-22.

4. Private communication.

5. Blum, *Studien,* 25.

6. Schmidt, *Exodus,* 104-5.

missions Moses), 3:13 (the inquiry of Moses into the divine name). The LXX differs from the MT, translating in 3:2 with *kai*, lit. "and," and in 3:9, 13 with *idou*, "behold."

3:14 *I will be who I will be.* The LXX reads, *egō eimi ho ōn*, "I am the one who is." According to Wevers the participle is simply an attempt to render the Hebrew into acceptable Greek and "not a philosophic statement."[7]

3:17 *Canaanite . . . Jebusite.* The LXX and Sam add "the Girgashite." See the translation note on 3:8.

3:18 *king of Egypt.* The LXX has "Pharaoh, king of Egypt."
Yahweh, the God of the Hebrews. The LXX omits "Yahweh."

3:19 *king of Egypt.* The LXX reads, "Pharaoh, king of Egypt."

4:1 *Yahweh.* The LXX reads, *ho theos*, "the God."

4:5 *so that.* The syntax is difficult, since the verse is a purpose clause without a clear antecedent.

4:9 The repetition of *wĕhāyâ* ("and it will happen/be") in the MT to describe the water from the Nile River changing to blood is eliminated in the LXX.

4:10 *speaker.* The MT *'îš dĕbārîm* could also be translated "a man of words." For discussion of the syntax see GKC §128t. The LXX departs from the MT: *ouch hikanos eimi*, "I am incapable."

4:13 *send, by the hand you send.* The LXX reads, *procheirisai dynamenon allon, hon aposteleis*, "appoint another who is able," perhaps carrying through the earlier reading from 4:10, in which Moses states that he is "incapable."

4:17 *but.* The MT *wĕ'et-hammaṭṭeh* is disjunctive, "but the staff," thus separating Moses' staff from the role of Aaron as speaker. Cf. the LXX *kai*, lit. "and," also "but."

4:18 *Jethro.* The MT reads, *yeter* (Jether), as compared to *ytrw* (Jethro) in Sam.

Commentary

The episode separates into two parts, 3:1-15 and 3:16–4:18. Each section is organized around the motif of divine commission. The Deity commands Moses in 3:10: "And now, go, and I will send you to Pharaoh. Bring out my people, the Israelites, from Egypt." There are two additional commissions in the second section. The first in 3:16 marks the transition between the two scenes: "Go and gather the elders, and you will say to them." An additional commission occurs in 4:12: "Now go, and I will be with you as you speak and will instruct you what to say." The two sections are interwoven by the repeated resistance of Moses to the divine commission (3:11; 4:1, 10, 13), indicating that 3:1–4:18 is a literary unit in the Non-P History. Both sections explore the related themes of divine identity and Mosaic authority, with 3:1-15 focusing more on the former and 3:16–4:18 on the latter theme. Exodus 3:1-15 addresses the problem of the divine identity after the break in tradition from the time of the ancestors (1:6). The section also explores the ability of God to be present with the Israelite people during their diaspora in Egypt. Exodus 3:16–4:18 raises the related problem of the authority

7. Wevers, *Notes*, 34.

of Moses in proclaiming Yahweh's imminent salvation, when the experience of the Israelites is of slavery suggesting divine abandonment, not salvation.

Identity of Yahweh (3:1-15)

Many interpreters have recognized a commissioning form in this section. W. H. Schmidt locates the central features of the form in 3:10-12, including: the commission (v. 10), the objection (v. 11), the reassurance (v. 12a), and the sign (v. 12b).[8] This form repeats in a wide variety of literature recounting the commission of charismatic and prophetic heroes like Gideon (Judg 6:14-17), Saul (1 Samuel 9–10), and Jeremiah (Jer 1:4-10). N. Habel expanded the literary pattern of the commission to include Exod 3:1-12.[9] He argued that the commission of Moses begins with a divine confrontation with the person (3:1-4a). An introductory word (3:4b-9) sets the stage for a specific commission or task (3:10). The hero objects to the commission (3:11), allowing for a divine reassurance (3:12a) and finally a sign (3:12b). The repetition of motifs between the divine reassurance of presence in v. 12a, "I will be with you" *(kî-'ehyeh 'immāk),* and the play on the divine name in v. 14, "I will be who I will be" *('ehyeh 'ăšer 'ehyeh),* indicates that the section must be extended beyond v. 12 through the revelation of the name Yahweh in 3:15.

The genre of the commission is important for interpretation. N. Habel described the form as a call narrative. But others have rightly qualified the genre as a commission rather than a call, since the hero does not assume an office but is given a specific task to perform. Childs pointed out that the genre indicates an identification of Moses with the prophetic office.[10] He noted further that the ancient writers are self-conscious of this form, since narrative tensions indicating possible literary expansions remain within the genre of the commission narrative, such as the repetition of Yahweh acknowledging the Israelites' oppression (3:7-8 and 9).[11] The commission of Moses in the wilderness accentuates his role as a prophetic and charismatic leader, not as a priest. This imagery will be carried through in the presentation of Aaron (4:13-16), who also functions in a prophetic role.

The genre of commission, however, does not adequately describe the opening encounter between God and Moses. The commission, already identified as 3:10-12, could be expanded to include v. 9, since this verse provides the circumstances giving rise to Moses' task. But 3:9-12 is framed by accounts of di-

---

8. Schmidt, *Exodus,* 123-30.
9. N. Habel, "The Form and Significance of the Call Narratives," *ZAW* 77 (1965): 297-323.
10. Childs, *Exodus,* 55.
11. Ibid., 53.

vine self-revelation in 3:1-8 and 13-15. Verse 6 includes a divine self-identification to Moses: "I am the God of your father." Verses 13-15 extend the genre through the introduction of the divine name Yahweh. The mixing of genres in 3:1-15 provides a point of departure for interpretation. The commission of Moses (3:9-12) is at the heart of the episode, but the point of focus is the identity of Yahweh (3:1-8 and 13-15).

3:1-8   The opening scene of Moses' wilderness commission has been categorized as a theophany and as a cultic etiology. Gertz has noted that the initial exchange between God and Moses repeats language from Jacob's theophany at Beer-sheba in Gen 46:1-5.[12] The similarities include: (1) the address of the Deity to the human protagonist with a repetition of the name, "Jacob, Jacob" and "Moses, Moses"; (2) prompting the response, "Here I am" (Gen 46:2; Exod 3:4). Both encounters (3) progress to a divine self-revelation, in which the Deity is revealed as the God of the father (Gen 46:3; Exod 3:6). And (4) each text moves to a proclamation, which indicates that God is able to be present in Egypt, using language of migration and return (Gen 46:3-4; Exod 3:7-8). God promises Jacob: "I myself will go down (*yārad*) with you to Egypt, and I will also bring you up again (Hiphil of *ʿālâ*)." The promise to Jacob provides the background for God's opening address to Moses: "And I have come down (*yārad*) to rescue him from the hand of Egypt and to bring him up (Hiphil of *ʿālâ*) from that land" (3:8).

H. Gressmann argued long ago that Moses' encounter with God also contains features of a cultic etiology.[13] The motifs include the identification of holy ground (3:5), requiring Moses to remove his sandals, and the imagery of fire associated with the burning bush (3:2). The association of the bush with an eternal flame signifies holiness, as with, for example, the holy fire on the altar (Lev 10:1-2) or the fire from heaven that Elijah calls down on the altar on Mount Carmel (1 Kgs 18:38). The focus on a holy place ties the experience of Moses to Joshua (Josh 5:13-15). M. Rose has concluded that the account of Joshua is similar to vision reports in the ancient Near East, which predict success in war, rather than the genre of a cultic etiology.[14] There may be aspects of the same function in Exod 3:1-8. Images of war linger in the background when the encounter is read in conjunction with the commission of Moses to rescue the Israelite people in 3:9-10 and with the prediction of success in 3:21-22. Both passages contain images of war. But Moses' encounter also reflects aspects of a cultic etiology in the Non-P History, emphasizing the sacred character of the

12. Gertz, *Tradition und Redaktion*, 237-54. For Gertz the repetitions are confined to Exod 3:4b, 6a, which he attributed to the post-P final redactor, who is forging the links to the story of the ancestors in Genesis.

13. Gressmann, *Mose und seine Zeit*, 21-56, esp. 23-38; see also Levin, *Jahwist*, 326-33.

14. Rose, *Deuteronomist und Jahwist*, 57-64, 83-88.

divine mountain. The cultic imagery associated with the mountain points ahead to the revelation of law and the establishment of the tent of meeting on the same site in Exodus 32–34.[15]

The emphasis in v. 1 is the setting. The scene opens with a portrait of Moses, tending the sheep of his father-in-law, Jethro, the priest of Midian (see the commentary on 4:18-26 for discussion of Jethro and the Midianites as allies of God in the salvation of the Israelites). The point of departure for the divine encounter is Moses' arrival at "the mountain of God" *(har hā'ĕlōhîm)*, located in the "far side of the wilderness" *('aḥar hammidbār)*. The setting is both geographical and symbolic. In ancient Near Eastern religion, the gods live on mountains. The mountain home of a god is cosmic in scale, reaching to heaven and providing a way for the deity to be present on earth. Temples are built on the site of a cosmic mountain to provide sanctuary for the god on earth. A. R. George provides illustration of the relationship between mountain imagery and sanctuaries from the Akkadian lexicon for temples, including *é.ḫur.saĝ.galam.(ma)*, "House, Skillfully-Built Mountain," a description of a temple to Enlil at Nippur; *e.kur*, "House, Mountain," another temple of Enlil at Nippur; and *é.kur.igi.ĝál*, "House, Mountain Endowed with Sight," a shrine dedicated to Enlil and Ninlil at Nippur.[16] The following song, containing a dialogue between Nanna and Ningal, provides further illustration of the close relationship between temples and mountains:

In your *house on high*, in your beloved *house*,
I will come to live,
O Nanna, up above in your cedar perfumed *mountain*.

The writers of the Hebrew Bible are firmly anchored in the mythological tradition of associating temples with mountains. The prophet Micah illustrates the close relationship between cosmic mountains and temples when he envisions "the mountain of the temple of Yahweh" (Mic 4:1; see also 2 Chr 33:15). Once Yahweh dwells in "the mountain of the temple," it becomes a holy site. In another passage Yahweh refers to the temple as "the mountain of my holiness" (Isa 65:11).

The Non-P author mixes geography and religious symbolism in the wilderness commission of Moses. Moses is located in the wilderness, associated with the land of Midian. Yet he is also situated on the "mountain of God," which

15. See Otto ("Nachpriesterschriftliche Pentateuchredaktion," 61-111) for the important role of law as background for reading the commission of Moses. Otto, however, attributes the authorship to a post-P redactor.
16. A. R. George, *The Temples of Ancient Mesopotamia* (Mesopotamian Civilizations; Winona Lake, Ind.: Eisenbrauns, 1993), 100 no. 480, 116 no. 677, 117 no. 683.

locates him in a sacred place (see notes on 3:1). The blending of geography and religious symbolism has prompted interpreters to identify the genre as a cultic legend and the setting as representing a cosmic mountain, which connects heaven and earth. The "mountain of God" is also the location where Aaron meets Moses (4:27), where Jethro sacrifices with Moses and the leaders of Israel (18:5), and where the leaders of Israel feast with Yahweh (24:13). The "mountain of God" is not a common designation for Yahweh's mountain home in the history of Israelite religion. More frequent is Mount Zion, the hill upon which the Jerusalem temple is built (Psalm 48). It is "chief among the mountains" (Mic 4:1) and "beautiful in elevation" (Ps 48:2), providing power and authority to the Israelite kings (Psalm 2).

There may be an early tradition of locating Yahweh's mountain home in the desert, which is characterized in modern biblical scholarship as the "March in the South" tradition of theophany. W. F. Albright noted that in the blessing of Moses (Deuteronomy 33), one of the older poems in the Hebrew Bible, Yahweh dwells on Mount Paran, a location in the southern desert associated with Seir and Teman (Deut 33:2; see also Hab 3:3). He concluded that the desert homes of Yahweh preserve an early tradition of theophany and divine rescue, in which Yahweh would appear from this southern wilderness region to save Israel at the time of crisis.[17] The tradition is preserved and even accentuated by both the Non-P and P Histories. Both accounts organize the wilderness journey of the Israelites around the desert mountains of Horeb and Sinai and not Mount Zion, the location for the Jerusalem temple during the monarchical period. The desert location for God's dwelling in both the Non-P and P Histories indicates a rejection of the monarchical emphasis of Mount Zion (see the commentary on Exod 24:12–40:38 on the topic of the tent of meeting and the tabernacle).

The more general reference, "mountain of God," may represent an independent tradition of Yahweh's dwelling place on earth, taken over by the Non-P historian. Winnett reached this conclusion, noting that a separate tradition of theophany accounts for the distribution of the divine name Elohim in Exodus

---

17. The early traditions of Yahweh's mountain home include Judg 5:5; Ps 68:9, 18; Deut 33:2; and Hab 3:3. For discussion see W. F. Albright, "The Earliest Form of Hebrew Verse," *JPOS* 2 (1922): 69-86; idem, "The Song of Deborah in Light of Archaeology," *BASOR* 66 (1936): 30; idem, "A Catalogue of Early Hebrew Lyric Poems," *HUCA* 23 (1950-1951): 14-24; idem, "The Psalm of Habakkuk," in *Studies in Old Testament Prophecy: Presented to Theodore H. Robinson* (ed. H. H. Rowley; Edinburgh: T. & T. Clark, 1950), 1-18; idem, *Yahweh and the Gods of Canaan: A Historical Analysis of Two Contrasting Faiths* (1968; repr. Garden City, N.Y.: Doubleday, 1969). In addition to Albright, see Cross and Freedman, *Studies in Ancient Yahwistic Poetry*, 13-21, 97-122; Cross, *Canaanite Myth and Hebrew Epic*, 99-105; Clifford, *Cosmic Mountain*, 100-110; A. L. Eric, *The Lord Rose Up from Seir: Studies in the History and Traditions of the Negev and Southern Judah* (ConBOT 25; Lund: Almqvist & Wiksell, 1987).

(e.g., chaps. 3, 4, 18, 24).[18] Noth also identified an independent mountain of God tradition associated with the Midianites.[19] This research underscores the compositional character of the Non-P History as including diverse literary traditions. But the mountain of God also acquires a distinctive function in the Non-P History. It becomes the setting for theophany and cultic rituals, which take place without a sanctuary. In the literary design of the Non-P History, the sanctuary is not present until Exodus 33 with the appearance of the tent of meeting, after which the designation "mountain of God" ceases in the story of Moses. Thus all ritual and cultic meals on the mountain of God function as a prologue to the establishment of the tent of meeting. The designation "mountain of God" returns one time in the larger context of the Primary History (Genesis–2 Kings) to describe Elijah's wilderness encounter with God in 1 Kgs 19:8. Elijah's theophany also lacks a clear cultic setting, while making literary allusions to "Horeb" as a desert region in much the same way as the account of Moses in Exod 3:1-4 (see below).

Moses' initial encounter with God is filled with literary allusions to the more prominent desert mountains of Yahweh, Horeb and Sinai. The reference to Horeb in 3:1 may be explicit, although it need not be. The NIV and NRSV translations of v. 1 illustrate a direct identification of the mountain of God and Mount Horeb: "He [Moses] led the flock to the far side of the desert and came to Horeb, the mountain of God." The Hebrew word *ḥōrēb* means "desolate and dry." The form of the word in this verse, with a locative ending *(ḥōrēbâ)* indicating direction, may signify a more general translation, in which the "mountain of God" is located in the desolate desert. Mount Horeb becomes the home of Yahweh in Deuteronomy (Deut 1:2, 6, 19). It is the site for the revelation of the Decalogue (Deut 4:10, 15; 5:2), the sin of the golden calf (Deut 9:8), and the making of covenant (Deut 29:1). Mount Horeb also plays a role in the Non-P History as the location of the tent of meeting (Exod 33:6).

The bush in Exod 3:2 provides an allusion to the sacred site of Sinai. The Hebrew word for "bush" *(sĕneh)* employs the same consonants, *s* and *n*, as the word "Sinai" *(sînay),* suggesting at the very least a wordplay. The allusion to Sinai may be to a general region, as is the case with the phrase "toward Horeb." Sinai is already a sacred location in the "March in the South" theophany tradition, where, as noted above, it is a region associated with Seir, Teman, and Paran (Judg 5:5; Deut 33:2). The "wilderness of Sinai" also functions as the general region for the revelation of God in the Non-P History (Exod 19:2), continuing the same imagery as the older "March in the South" theophany tradition.

It is the P History, however, that emphasizes Sinai as the divine mountain

---

18. Winnett, *Mosaic Tradition,* 16-29.
19. Noth, *History of Pentateuchal Traditions,* 136-41.

of revelation and the setting for the tabernacle cult. The P History contains twenty-nine of the thirty-six references to Sinai in the Pentateuch. The P writer describes Sinai as a region fourteen times: (1) the wilderness of Sinai is referred to twice in the itinerary list of Numbers 33, a text with possible P editing (33:15, 16);[20] four times in texts referring to the itinerary (Exod 16:1; 19:1, 2; Num 10:12); eight times as the place where cultic worship must be observed (the first public worship [Lev 7:38], Passover [Num 9:1, 5], the place of census [Num 1:1, 19; 3:4, 14; 26:64]). The P writer designates the divine home as Mount Sinai at a number of important junctures: the mountain of theophany (Exod 19:11, 18, 20, 23), the location of the Glory of Yahweh (24:16; 31:18), the mountain of covenant renewal (34:2, 4, 29, 32), and the location for cultic instructions (Lev 7:38; 25:1; 26:46; Num 28:6) (see the commentary on Exodus 19–24).

God appears to Moses in the form of the "Messenger of Yahweh." The NIV, NRSV, and NJPS translate "the angel of the LORD," following the LXX. The MT is more ambiguous, indicating simply the "Messenger of Yahweh" (*mal'āk yhwh*). The divine messenger is often indistinguishable from God. Verse 2 employs the phrase "Messenger of Yahweh" (see also Gen 16:7, 9; 22:11, 15). Other titles include "the Messenger of God" (*mal'āk hā'ĕlōhîm*, Gen 21:17; 31:11), and simply "a messenger" (*māl'āk*, Exod 23:20). All the titles occur in Exodus. The "Messenger of Yahweh" appears to Moses (3:2). The "Messenger of God" leads Israel at the Red Sea (14:19). And God promises Moses "a messenger" to lead the Israelites (23:20; 33:2; cf. "my messenger," 23:23).

The divine messenger functions in one of two ways, depending on the geographical setting.[21] In the land of Canaan the messenger usually wages holy war for the Israelites (e.g., 1 Sam 29:9; 2 Kgs 19:35), but at times against them (e.g., Judg 2:1-7). The holy war function of the messenger is promised to Moses in Exod 23:20, 23; and 33:2. In the wilderness setting the messenger rescues and leads people. The appearance of the Messenger of Yahweh to Moses is for the purpose of rescuing the Israelites. His divine confrontation with the Messenger of Yahweh creates literary relationships between Exodus, Genesis, and the Deuteronomistic History. The wilderness setting of Moses recalls the experience of Hagar, the first person rescued by the messenger in the wilderness (Gen 16:7-14). The scene also anticipates the story of Gideon, where the Messenger of Yahweh appears to commission the judge to rescue the Israelites from the Midianite oppression (Judg 6:11-17).

The response of Moses to the divine confrontation provides insight into

---

20. Dozeman, "Numbers," in *NIB* 2:250-54.

21. T. W. Mann, *Divine Presence and Guidance in Israelite Traditions: The Typology of Exaltation* (Johns Hopkins Near Eastern Studies; Baltimore: Johns Hopkins University Press, 1977).

his character. He acknowledges the event: "Indeed, the bush is burning with fire, but the bush is not consumed." The setting of the divine mountain with an eternal flame in a bush is the most explicit sign of the Deity possible in the Hebrew Bible. Yet Moses does not recognize the significance. His response is simply curiosity over the unusual phenomenon: "I must turn aside to see this great vision. Why is the bush not burned up?" Moses, like the entire generation of the Israelites, has lost all knowledge of God (see Exod 1:6). The proper response to such an explicit appearance of the Deity is to fear God and to turn away from the sight. Moses performs these acts of reverence (3:6), but only after God rescues him from the potential danger of trespassing on holy ground. The Messenger of Yahweh warns: "The place *(māqôm)* where you are standing, it is holy ground *('admat-qōdeš hû')*" (3:5). The designation "holy ground" is unusual in the Hebrew Bible, occurring only one other time: in Zech 2:12 it refers to the land of Israel. The word "place" *(māqôm)* often implies a sanctuary. "The place of the name" in Deuteronomy, for example, indicates the sanctuary (Deut 12:14). The use of the word "place" in the P literature may even refer to a special section of the sanctuary (Exod 29:31). The combination of the word "place" with "holy ground" suggests that the Non-P author is fashioning an etiology for a sanctuary to be fulfilled when the Israelite people encounter God at the same mountain (chaps. 19–34).

The aim of the opening encounter between the Messenger of Yahweh and Moses is to identify God. Exodus 3:6-8 provides the initial information. Many interpreters limit the divine self-identification to v. 6: "I am the God of your father, the God of Abraham, the God of Isaac, and the God of Jacob." But the parallel to the story of Jacob in Gen 46:1-5 (see above) indicates that it includes vv. 6-8. The parallels underscore that the Deity appearing before Moses is not only the God of the father (Gen 46:3 and Exod 3:6), but also a God who promised to be present with Jacob in Egypt, employing the imagery of migration down to Egypt and a return (Gen 46:4 and Exod 3:7-8). Exodus 3:7-8 completes the parallel to Jacob's encounter with God at Beer-sheba. The statement of divine perception in v. 7 indicates God's presence with the Israelite people in Egypt: "I have observed *(rā'ōh rā'îtî)* the torment of my people in Egypt. And their cry from his taskmasters I have heard, because I know his pain." The unusual use of the singular "his" ("his taskmasters" and "his pain") may refer to Jacob in Gen 46:1-5, linking the nation with the ancestor. The initial identification of God also repeats the imagery of migration, now refashioned as the language of salvation: "I have come down to rescue him from the hand of Egypt and to bring him up from that land to a good and broad land" (Exod 3:8; see Gen 46:4). The parallels indicate that the divine identification to Moses includes all of Exod 3:6-8.

The initial identification of God is with Moses' ancestors in 3:6. But the identification is perplexing because it moves from a more personal reference, "the God of your father," to a national focus, "the God of Abraham, the God of Isaac, and the God of Jacob." The personal identification is not altogether clear. The "God of a father" usually refers to the Deity of a clan. When God appears to Isaac he states: "I am the God of Abraham your father" (Gen 26:24; see also Gen 31:5). The initial identification of God may also be limited in scope to Moses' father. A similar identification repeats in the Song of the Sea. If the hymn is interpreted in the context of the Non-P History, making the voice of the psalmist Moses, then the praise of Yahweh as "the God of my father" (*ʾĕlōhê ʾābî;* Exod 15:2) would yield the same meaning. The father of Moses is the Levite from his birth story (2:1), who remains unnamed in the Non-P History, but is later identified as Amram in the P genealogy (6:20).

The identification of God with Moses' father and with the patriarchal ancestors Abraham, Isaac, and Jacob fits only loosely together. Van Seters concluded that the merging of the God of Moses' father with the patriarchs Abraham, Isaac, and Jacob is an innovation by the author of 3:1–4:18, whom he identified as the exilic Yahwist historian. The aim of this historian, according to Van Seters, is to bridge the story of Moses and the exodus with the story of the ancestors in Genesis.[22] In his study of the promise of land to the ancestors in Genesis, R. Rendtorff reached the same interpretation, concluding that the theme of the "God of the fathers" in Exodus 3, identified as the patriarchs Abraham, Isaac, and Jacob, was a late development in the formation of the literature. He noted that the reference to Abraham, Isaac, and Jacob is infrequent in the story of Moses and is clustered at the outset of Exodus, three times in the P History (2:24; 6:3, 8) and four times in the Non-P literature (3:6, 15, 16; 4:5). The three patriarchs are mentioned only two other times in Exodus (32:13; 33:1). Rendtorff concluded that the insertion of the promise to the ancestors in the story of Moses introduced a new interpretation. The point of focus is no longer the reception of the promise by the ancestors, as was the case in Genesis, but the continuity of divine revelation from the time of the patriarchs to the exodus generation of Israelites.[23]

Van Seters reached his conclusion working in the opposite direction from Rendtorff. He recognized that the ancestors in Ezekiel (20:5-6) and Jeremiah (2:4-5) are the generation of the exodus, not the patriarchs from Genesis. Coupled with this he noted that the earliest reference to Abraham in the prophetic corpus was in the exilic book of Ezekiel (33:24), where the context is the future possession of the land: "Abraham was only one man, yet he got possession of the land; but we are many; the land is surely given to us." Abraham also be-

---

22. J. Van Seters, "Confessional Reformulation in the Exilic Period," *VT* 22 (1972): 448-59.
23. Rendtorff, *Problem.*

comes more central in the literature of Second Isaiah, where imagery similar to Ezekiel appears: "Look to Abraham your father and to Sarah who bore you; for he was but one when I called him, but I blessed him and made him many" (Isa 51:2). Van Seters concluded that the promise of land to the ancestors in the earliest tradition of Deuteronomy and throughout the Deuteronomic tradition focused on the generation of the exodus. The merging of the ancestors of the exodus with the patriarchal ancestors Abraham, Isaac, and Jacob was the work of the exilic Yahwist historian. Van Seters writes: "In the period of the exile, there was a conscious confessional shift from Yahweh as the God of the exodus to Yahweh as the God of the patriarchs and to base God's covenantal promises on identity with them."[24] Exodus 3:1–4:18 thematizes this confessional reformulation, according to Van Seters, as a new myth of origin.

The research on the God of the fathers in Exodus indicates that the divine promise to the patriarchs focuses on the land. The land becomes the point of focus in the self-identification of God to Moses in 3:6-8. The initial revelation of the Deity in v. 6, as the God of Abraham, Isaac, and Jacob, is followed in vv. 7-8 by the promise of land. Verses 7-8 are a brief summary of salvation history. God will rescue the Israelites (v. 7) in order to give them a land of their own (v. 8). The rescue of God in v. 7 (*nāṣal* in the Hiphil) is the same word that characterized Moses' deliverance of Jethro's daughters at the well (2:19), indicating a reversal from a situation of oppression. The emphasis in 3:7-8, however, is on the promise of the land of Canaan as the goal of the divine rescue. The expression in v. 8, "to bring [the Israelites] up (Hiphil of *ʿālâ*) from that land," is about acquiring the land of Canaan, not leaving Egypt.[25] The "going up" or "aliyah" of the Israelites indicates immigration or land possession, as it continues to do in contemporary Israeli society. When the departure or the exodus from Egypt is the point of emphasis, biblical writers use the expression, "to go out (*yāṣāʾ*) of the land" (see the commentary on chap. 13). The exodus will become the point of focus in the commission of Moses (3:9-12). But in God's self-introduction to Moses the promise of land takes center stage. The prediction of the Israelites "going up from the land" is followed by a detailed description of the land of promise.

God reveals to Moses the utopian character of the promised land. It is a good and broad land. Its abundant fertility is expressed with the image "flowing with milk and honey," a common description in Deuteronomy (Deut 6:3; 11:9; 26:9, 15; 27:3; 31:20). Milk most likely refers to goats' milk. Honey is probably

---

24. Van Seters, "Confessional Reformulation," 456; see also idem, *Prologue to History*, 227-45; idem, *Life of Moses*, 35-50.

25. See the study by J. Wijngaards, "הוציא and העלה: A Twofold Approach to the Exodus," *VT* 15 (1965): 91-102.

produced from dates or grapes, not bees. In his study of eschatological imagery, Gressmann underscored the utopian character of the expression, noting that milk and honey are the food of the gods in Greek tradition.[26] The Israelite prophets use similar imagery to describe the messianic age (Amos 9:13; Joel 3:18). In Exodus the phrase does not appear to be messianic, but it does suggest utopian images of paradise, requiring divine revelation to Moses. Yahweh must tell Moses about the land of Canaan (3:8, 17) before he is able to convey the information to the Israelites as cultic instruction (13:5).

Paradise is not unpopulated. Yahweh lists six nations as the indigenous inhabitants of the land, the Canaanites, Hittites, Amorites, Perizzites, Hivites, and Jebusites. Variations of the list occur twenty-seven times in the Hebrew Bible.[27] The number of nations ranges from two (Gen 13:7) to twelve (Gen 15:19-21), creating conflicting borders to the promised land. The twelve-nation list envisions the promised land as encompassing much of the ancient Near East, from Egypt to the Euphrates River. The six-nation list in Exod 3:8 is the most common, appearing eleven times.[28] It divides between three nations whose history is recoverable (the Canaanites, Amorites, and Hittites) and three obscure groups (the Perizzites, Hivites, and Jebusites). The six-nation list envisions the promised land as a smaller territory confined to Syria-Palestine. The story of the spies provides a partial geographical distribution (Num 13:29). The Canaanites live by the sea and along the Jordan River, while the Hittites, Amorites, and Jebusites dwell in the hill country. Yet it is doubtful whether any of the nations reflect the historical circumstances of the Non-P writer.[29] They appear to be stereotyped, used to represent foreign gods and nations who pose a threat to the worship of Yahweh. The Non-P historian underscores the need for the Israelites to remain separate from the indigenous nations, conquering them upon entry into the promised land in order to remain faithful to Yahweh (see the commentary on 23:20-33).

3:9-12 God's awareness of the Israelite oppression in Egypt is stated twice in 3:7-9. God first reveals to Moses in v. 7: "I have observed the torment of my people in Egypt. And their cry I have heard from his taskmasters, because I know his pain." Then in v. 9 the Deity repeats the message: "And now, indeed, the cry of the Israelites has come to me, and I have also seen the suffering with which the Egyptians make them suffer." S. McEvenue writes of the repetition:

---

26. H. Gressmann, *Der Ursprung der israelitisch-jüdischen Eschatologie* (Göttingen: Vandenhoeck & Ruprecht, 1905), 205.

27. For the complete list of the indigenous nations see T. Ishida, "The Structure and Historical Implications of the Lists of Pre-Israelite Nations," *Bib* 60 (1979): 461-62.

28. Exod 3:8, 17; 23:23; 33:2; 34:11; Deut 20:17; Josh 9:1; 11:3; 12:8; Judg 3:5; Neh 9:8.

29. J. Van Seters, "The Terms 'Amorite' and 'Hittite' in the Old Testament," *VT* 22 (1972): 67-72; cf. Ishida, "Structure and Historical Implications," 461-90.

Figure 5

Text	Exod	Josh	2 Sam
Revelation	3:6-8	14:6-9	7:27
Ground for Action; *wĕʿattâ,* "and now"	3:9	14:10-11	7:28
Action; *wĕʿattâ,* "and now"	3:10-12	14:12	7:29

"Verse 9 after v. 8 sits there either portraying God as senile, or showing a break in the text."[30] For McEvenue and all source critics the repetition indicates originally distinct versions of the story.

M. Greenberg, followed by Blum, provides the starting point for an interpretation that addresses the literary function of the repetition.[31] The interpretation requires comparison between the divine commission of Moses (3:7-10), the prayer of David (2 Sam 7:27-29), and the message of Caleb to Joshua (Josh 14:6-12). See figure 5 above.

The three stories share a similar structure in which an instance of revelation progresses to a specific action. The middle section of the form provides transition stating the reason or ground for the action. Both the reason for the action and the action itself are introduced with the phrase "and now" *(wĕʿattâ).* The form can be illustrated in the prayer of David. 2 Samuel 7:27-29 begins with David recounting the revelation of his election as king: "For you, O Yahweh of hosts, have made this revelation to your servant" (v. 27). The revelation moves to a concrete request in v. 29 requiring a specific divine act: "And now *(wĕʿattâ)* may it please you to bless the house of your servant." Verse 28 provides the transition from the election of David to the request for the divine act of blessing: "And now *(wĕʿattâ),* O Yahweh God, you are God and your words are true, and you have promised." The message of Caleb adapts the form from a prayer to a claim on land. Caleb recounts a past revelation to Joshua in Josh 14:6-9: "You know what Yahweh said to Moses." This revelation is the background for action in Josh 14:12: "And now *(wĕʿattâ)* give me this hill country." Verse 10 provides transition from the revelation to the specific action: "And now *(wĕʿattâ),* as you see Yahweh has kept me alive." The significant point of transition in both of these texts is the shift from revelation to the ground for action marked by the phrase "and now."

The same structure is at work in Exod 3:6-12, although it is now adapted to a

30. McEvenue, "Speaker(s) in Ex 1–15," 226-27.
31. M. Greenberg, *Understanding Exodus* (Melton Research Center Series 2; New York: Behrman House, 1969), 99; Blum, *Studien,* 11. Both writers also argued for a chiastic pattern to the repetition between Exod 3:7 and 9.

story of divine commission rather than a prayer (2 Sam 7:27-29) or a legal claim on land (Josh 14:6-12). Exodus 3:6-12 divides between the self-introduction of God (3:6-8) and the commission of Moses (3:9-12). God's statement to Moses in v. 7, "I have observed the torment of my people," is part of the divine self-revelation to Moses in 3:6-8. It provides insight into the character of God. But the repetition of this motif in v. 9 is no longer the self-revelation of God. It is rather the beginning of Moses' commission (3:9-12). Verse 9 provides the grounds or rationale for action, signaled by the emphatic "and now": "And now *(wĕʿattâ)* the cry of the Israelites has come to me." The rationale for action requires a specific act, the commission of Moses in v. 10: "And now *(wĕʿattâ)* go!" The repetition between 3:7 and 9 may reflect distinct accounts of the commission, but in the present structure of the story they mark the transition from divine self-revelation (3:6-8) to the commission of Moses (3:9-12). The present form of 3:6-12, with the three-part structure of revelation (vv. 6-8), ground for action (v. 9), and action (vv. 10-12), suggests moreover that the Non-P historian is fashioning the story into a pattern that repeats in the Deuteronomistic History.[32]

I have already clarified that the self-revelation of God in 3:6-8 focuses on the promise of land. The commission for Moses in 3:9-12 is not about the promise of land. It focuses rather on the exodus from Egypt. Three times the exodus formula is used: "to bring out (Hiphil of *yāṣāʾ*) the Israelites from Egypt" (3:10, 11, 12; see the commentary on Exodus 13 for a more detailed interpretation of the exodus formula). The exodus formula occurs first in the divine commission itself. God states to Moses: "I am sending you to Pharaoh to bring out *(yāṣāʾ)* my people the Israelites from Egypt" (3:10). Moses' objection arises from his ambiguous identity. He states: "Who am I?" But he also repeats the exodus formula: "that I should . . . bring the Israelites out of Egypt" (3:11).

The divine reassurance in v. 12a is a promise of presence: "I will be with you" *(ʾehyeh ʿimmāk)*, implying if not success then at least the ability of God to be present with Moses in Egypt. Finally, God provides a sign to Moses in v. 12b, repeating the exodus formula a third time: "When you have brought the people out of Egypt, you will worship God on this mountain." The commission of Moses in 3:9-12 is about the exodus. It is not about the entrance into the promised land. The Non-P History separates these themes between Moses and Joshua.

The sign to Moses in v. 12a presents a problem. Signs are a means for humans to test the reliability of a divine commission. They are an extension of the objection to a call. Gideon, for example, asks for a sign in his commission (Judg 6:11-17). God does not offer him one. Gideon states to God: "If now I have found favor in your eyes, give me a sign that it is really you talking to me" (Judg

---

32. Examples of the general pattern include 1 Sam 24:20-22; 25:26-27; 26:19-20; 2 Sam 2:6-7; 19:10-11; 1 Kgs 8:25-26.

6:17). The sign to Moses is not a sign at all. It is a divine prediction about the future. The need for God to initiate a sign to Moses underscores yet again his lack of knowledge of tradition. Moses does not know enough about the process of divine commissioning to finish his own call narrative by testing through a sign. God must do it for him. The remainder of Moses' wilderness commission is a sequence of signs, meant to answer his objection and to confirm his authority as Yahweh's commissioned messenger to the Israelites (Exod 4:1-17).

3:13-15   The wilderness commission of Moses returns to the theme of divine identity in 3:13-15. The objections of Moses provide the transition in theme. The first objection of Moses underscored his lack of identity: "Who am I that I should go to Pharaoh?" (v. 11a). It brings forth the divine reassurance that God would be present in Egypt with Moses: "I will be with you" (v. 12a). The promise of divine presence in Egypt sets the stage for the change in focus from the commission of Moses (3:9-12) back to the identity of God (3:13-15). The second objection of Moses focuses directly on God's identity. Moses poses the objection by creating a hypothetical situation: "Indeed, I come to the Israelites and I say to them, 'The God of your fathers sent me to you.' And they say to me, 'What is his name?' What will I say to them?" (v. 13). The question repeats the personal revelation to Moses from 3:6, in which God was identified as "the God of his father." The hypothetical character of Moses' objection introduces a national perspective for exploring the identity of God. The question places the problem of God's identity outside Moses' personal experience and into the context of the nation. Who are you in relation to the nation of Israel? The repetition indicates that the divine response in 3:14-15 to Moses' question about the nation is an extension of the private self-revelation of God to Moses in 3:6-8. The separation between private revelation to Moses and public revelation to the nation will continue throughout the revelation of law in the Non-P History (19-34) and in Deuteronomy. It provides the basis for the exploration of Mosaic authority in the Non-P History.

The divine response to Moses in 3:14-15 is one of the most extensively interpreted texts in the Hebrew Bible. The verses include three statements by God:

(v. 14a) And God said to Moses, "I will be who I will be" (*'ehyeh 'ăšer 'ehyeh*)

(v. 14b) And he said, "Thus you will say to the Israelites, 'I will be' (*'ehyeh*) sent me to you."

(v. 15) And God said further to Moses, "Thus you will say to the Israelites, 'Yahweh (*yhwh*), the God of your fathers, the God of Abraham, the God of Isaac, and the God of Jacob, sent me to you.' This is my name forever. This is my memorial for all generations."

When 3:6-8 and 3:13-15 are read together there is a progression in the Deity's self-introduction from Moses to the nation. God is first identified in a personal revelation to Moses as the God of his father and the God of the patriarchs Abraham, Isaac, and Jacob (3:6). Moses places this new information in the larger context of the entire Israelite nation with the question: "Indeed, I come to the Israelites and I say to them, 'The God of your fathers sent me to you.' And they say to me, 'What is his name?' What will I say to them?" (3:13). Verse 15 contains the divine response to Moses' question. In providing the name Yahweh, God is identifying with the entire Israelite nation. The national scope of the name Yahweh is indicated by the repetition of the theme, "God of the father," now in the plural form rather than the singular form, to Moses. Moses is to identify Yahweh to the Israelites as "the God of your fathers and the God of Abraham, the God of Isaac, and the God of Jacob."

Van Seters concluded that the identification of Yahweh with the God of the ancestors in Genesis and the God of the fathers of the exodus generation is the point of the wilderness commission of Moses, since it merges the story of the ancestors in Genesis with the story of Moses. The name Yahweh is not a new name in this interpretation, since it has been used from the outset of the Non-P History (see already Genesis 4). It is, rather, the reintroduction of the divine name Yahweh to the exodus generation of the Israelites, which is necessary because of the break in tradition that was noted in Exod 1:6: "And Joseph died, and all of his brothers, and all that generation." The rupture in tradition provides a clear break between Genesis and Exodus, which underscores that the promise of land to the ancestors is unfulfilled to the exodus generation of Israelites. Van Seters characterizes this merging of traditions as a confessional reformulation of tradition in the exilic period, which focuses on the unfulfilled promise of the land. The unfulfilled promise of land gives the story of salvation history a future orientation in the Non-P History. The result is that God is now obligated to act in the ongoing salvation of the Israelite people, because of the oath to the ancestors in Genesis.

Verse 14 shifts in focus from the God of the fathers to a more direct reflection on the name Yahweh through wordplay on the Hebrew verb "to be" *(hāyâ).* Interpreters judge v. 14 to be a later addition, perhaps as an attempt to introduce more speculative reflection on the meaning of the Deity.[33] The reason for judging the verse a later addition is that v. 14 does not address directly the question of Moses in v. 13. Propp comments on this ambiguity, questioning whether the verse is revelation or obfuscation, yet in the end he attributes its composition to the author of the E source, thus assuming the unity of 3:13-15.[34]

---

33. See the review of scholarship in Childs, *Exodus,* 60-70; Schmidt, *Exodus,* 169-77.
34. Propp, *Exodus 1–18,* 224-26.

Whether an addition or the literary creation of the Non-P author, the combination of vv. 14 and 15 relates the themes of divine presence and the God of the father(s). The two themes were introduced together in the private revelation to Moses in 3:6-8. The theme of the God of the father(s) begins the self-revelation (v. 6). And the theme of divine presence in Egypt concludes the section when God states to Moses: "I have come down to rescue them [the Israelites] from the hand of Egypt" (v. 8). The theme of divine presence is further developed in God's reassurance to Moses: "I will be with you" (3:12). The divine reassurance is stated using the first person form of the verb, "I will be" *('ehyeh)*. The book of Hosea provides comparison. When God threatens to withdraw from the Israelite people in Hos 1:9 the Deity states: "For you are not my people, and I will not be *('ehyeh)* to you." F. I. Andersen and D. N. Freedman translate the phrase in Hosea as the name of God: "For you are not my people, and I am not *Ehyeh* for you."[35]

The threefold repetition of the verb "I will be" in Exod 3:14 suggests a further extension of the theme of divine presence and its association with the divine name. The expression "I will be" occurs twice in the *Idem per Idem* of v. 14a: "I will be what I will be" *('ehyeh 'ăšer 'ehyeh)*. The repetition of the verb in the *Idem per Idem* construction is for emphasis.[36] It is followed by yet a third occurrence in v. 14b, when the Deity repeats, "I will be *('ehyeh)* sent me to you," recalling the language of Hos 1:9.

The aim of Exod 3:14, to advance the theme of divine presence through reflection on the meaning of the divine name, continues in the history of translation, especially in v. 14a. The LXX provides an ancient example, when it eliminates the *Idem per Idem* construction to translate: "I am the one who is" *(egō eimi ho ōn)*. The reflection on the meaning of the divine name Yahweh continues into the present. Two prominent modern translations are the declarative, "I am who I am," and the causative, "I cause to be what I cause to be."[37] The difference between the two translations is the emphasis on God as creator in the causative translation, a theme that comes to center stage in the divine response to Moses in 4:11: "Who makes a mouth for humans? Or who makes dumb or deaf, clear-sighted or blind? Is it not I, Yahweh?"

35. Andersen and Freedman, *Hosea*, 4. See other instances of the phrase "I will be" in Jer 11:4 and Ezek 11:20.

36. See T. C. Vriezen, "'*Ehje 'ser 'ehje*,'" in *Festschrift Alfred Bertholet* (ed. W. Baumgartner et al.; Tübingen: Mohr, 1950), 498-512; J. R. Lundbom, "God's Use of the *Idem per Idem* to Terminate Debate," *HTR* 71 (1978): 193-201.

37. For the declarative see, e.g., NRSV, NIV. The causative translation was first proposed by P. Haupt, "Der Name Jahwe," *OLZ* 12 (1909): 211-14; and followed by W. F. Albright, "The Name of Yahweh," *JBL* 43 (1924): 370-78; and G. R. Driver, "The Original Form of the Name 'Yahweh,'" *ZAW* 46 (1928): 7-25.

The divine name Yahweh is revealed to Moses in 3:15. W. H. Schmidt notes that the verse rests somewhat uneasily in its present narrative context with the additional introduction: "And God said further *(ʿôd)* to Moses."[38] The history of interpretation has emphasized the verbal character of the play on the divine name Yahweh. The name may be an early form of the Hebrew verb "to be" *(hwh)* and not a noun, as one would expect.[39] W. F. Albright, supported by Freedman, interpreted the name *yhwh* as a hypocoristic form of an original theophoric sentence, Yahweh-El, with a causative meaning, "Let El create."[40]

The revelation of the divine name to Moses evolves through two stages in the story, playing with its verbal character. God responds initially to Moses in v. 14 by stating the verb "to be" in the first person with the phrase: "I will be who I will be" *(ʾehyeh ʾăšer ʾehyeh)*. When read from this point of view the focus in 3:15 is not the theme of the God of the fathers, but the verbal character of the divine name Yahweh, in which the Hebrew consonants *yhwh* are read as the third person masculine singular form of the verb "to be," translated "he is." The verbal character of the name Yahweh places the focus of God's name on actions for the Israelites and not on God's independent being or essence. The verbal focus emphasizes the theme of divine presence in the divine reassurance to Moses: "I will be with you." The LXX may have moved the focus of the name back to God's being with the translation: "I am the one who is." But in the MT the verbal background to the divine name Yahweh suggests that God cannot be discerned through contemplation of the name itself. The same point is made in Jacob's struggle with the nocturnal being, when he is denied the name of his opponent (Gen 32:22-32), also a story in the Non-P History.

The name Yahweh in Exod 3:15 actually creates an incomplete sentence that poses a question: "'He is' . . . what?" The answer requires further reading in Exodus and indeed in the entire Primary History, which records the future actions of Yahweh for Israel. The content of the divine verbal name is contained in the actions of God for Israel. By reading on in the Non-P History the question posed by the name receives an answer: "'He is' savior, healer, revealer, covenant maker, and so on." But, as the interpretation of Van Seters underscores, the first insight into the divine name concerns the past, not the future. Yahweh, the God appearing to Moses and the Israelites in Egypt, is also the God of the ancestors Abraham, Isaac, and Jacob (3:15). Yahweh is rooted in the past. Moreover, God reveals to Moses that the name Yahweh is eternal. Yahweh may be rooted in the past as the God of the father(s), but the everlasting qual-

---

38. Schmidt, *Exodus,* 132-33.

39. Albright, "Name of Yahweh," 370-78.

40. D. N. Freedman, "The Name of the God of Moses," *JBL* 79 (1960): 151-56. For bibliography see Childs, *Exodus,* 60-71; Schmidt, *Exodus,* 169-80.

ity of the name also signifies the faithfulness of God's actions toward Israel into the future.

The divine name Yahweh is known in tradition as the Tetragrammaton, referring to the four consonants, *Y-H-W-H*. In Jewish tradition, before the Common Era (the era of Judaism and Christianity), uttering the divine name became a religious taboo. This religious development has influenced the writing of the Hebrew Bible. The four consonants of the divine name, *yhwh*, lack their original vowels. Scholars are left to reconstruct an original pronunciation of the name based on a study of comparative Semitic languages. A common vocalization of the name is "Yahweh," with the vowels *a* and *e*, the form I use throughout this commentary. To ensure that the Tetragrammaton would not be pronounced the Masoretes inserted the vowels from the word *'ădōnāy*, "my Lord," into the consonants *yhwh*. Their intention was that whenever the reader saw the Tetragrammaton, he or she would say *'ădōnāy*. The insertion of the vowels from the word *'ădōnāy* yields the name *YeHoWaH* for the Tetragrammaton (the first "a" becomes an "e" in Hebrew because of rules of phonology). This vocalization appears as "Jehovah" in the KJV (through Latin the Hebrew *y* is transliterated as *j*, and *w* as *v*). The NIV, NRSV, NJPS, and most other English versions translate the name Yahweh as "Lord." The English "God" translates Hebrew *'ĕlōhîm* (Elohim) or variations of this word (e.g., *'ēl*, El).

The name Yahweh also appears twice in Exodus in a shortened form, "Yah." The first is at the outset of the Song of the Sea, "my strength and my power is Yah" (15:2), and the second is in the closing line of the war against the Amalekites, "the test of Yah" (17:16). The shortened form also occurs in names, such as Elijah, "My El is Yah," and in the cultic formula *Hallelujah*, "praise Yah."

Authority of Moses (3:16–4:18)

The wilderness commission of Moses (3:1–4:18) changes in emphasis from the identity of God (3:1-15) to the authority of Moses (3:16–4:18). Mosaic authority is prophetic in character and aimed at the Israelites. The story introduces the theme of Mosaic authority in two scenes with different characters: 3:16–4:9 explores Mosaic authority in relation to the elders; while 4:10-17 changes the focus to Aaron in a prophetic role. The first scene (3:16–4:9) confirms the absence of Mosaic authority and the need to equip Moses with signs aimed especially at the elders. Exodus 4:1 states the central theme as "belief" (*'āman*) in Moses, which means listening (*šāmaʿ*) to his voice (*qôl*). The phrase "listening to the voice" is a reference to the law in Deuteronomy (e.g., 5:22; 15:5; 26:17; 28:1, 45, 62; 30:20), and the same meaning is present in the Non-P History. The motif will reappear at the outset of the wilderness journey in Exod 15:26 signifying God's voice as law. But it will become increasingly intermingled with

Moses' voice in the experience of theophany when the people appoint him to mediate law for them (19:9, 19; 20:18-20).[41] The second scene with Aaron (4:10-17) continues the emphasis on prophetic authority and clarifies the unique role of Moses as a god-like figure and the subordinate role of Aaron as a prophetic teacher.

The theme of Mosaic authority, conceived as charisma, returns in the Non-P History, after the revelation of law (Exodus 19–34) when the people resume their wilderness journey in Numbers 11–12. The motif of leprosy relates the stories. The second sign of Mosaic authority in Exod 4:6-7 is his ability to heal leprosy, which Moses performs on Miriam in Num 12:10-15. The relationship goes beyond theme to structure, with both stories dividing between the elders (Exod 3:16–4:9; Numbers 11) and Aaron in a prophetic role (Exod 4:10-17; Numbers 12). The parallel structure reveals development in the theme of Mosaic authority in the Non-P History. The absence of Mosaic authority among the elders in 3:16–4:9 is fulfilled in Numbers 11, when seventy elders receive a portion of Moses' spirit. The unique character of Moses' authority, as a god to Aaron's prophet, first established in 4:10-17, is confirmed in a divine oracle to Aaron and Miriam in Num 12:6-8 within the tent of meeting, the designation for the sanctuary in the Non-P History. Aaron and Miriam may be prophets, but only Moses speaks directly with God — in that role he is unique. The emphasis on Moses' special relationship with God as one who speaks directly with the Deity relates the Non-P History and Deuteronomy.

3:16–4:9 The topic of Mosaic authority in relationship to the elders of Israel *(ziqnê-yiśrā'ēl)* begins in 3:16-22 with the divine command that Moses gather them together (v. 16) and announce their impending deliverance (v. 17), which is followed by a divine prediction of the events (vv. 18-22). The scene concludes in 4:1-9 when God equips Moses with signs signifying his authority. The absence of a specific reference to the elders in 4:1-9 may indicate a later expansion of the story.

The command in v. 16 repeats the name Yahweh, the identification of God with the "God of the fathers," and the further identification with the patriarchs Abraham, Isaac, and Jacob. The emphasis in the command, however, is on the experience of Moses, not on the identity of God. The verb "to see" is stated in the passive, placing the focus on Moses and the authority of his experience, not on the identity of God. He is to inform the elders: "Yahweh, the God of your fathers, *appeared to me (nir'â 'ēlay)*." The literary style indicates the change in theme from the identity of God to the authority of Moses, which will continue in the objection of Moses. It is the need to persuade the elders of the authenticity of his experience that will prompt Moses' objection in 4:1: "They will say,

---

41. See Otto, "Nachpriesterschriftliche Pentateuchredaktion," 61-100.

'Yahweh did not appear to you'" *(lō'-nir'â 'ēleykā),* which calls forth the divine response in 4:5, "They will believe that Yahweh appeared to you" *(nir'â 'ēleykā).*

The theme of Mosaic authority is explored specifically in relationship to the elders of Israel in the Non-P History. They will reappear at important junctures in the history: as the "officials" during the first confrontation with Pharaoh (5:1–6:1), to receive Passover instructions (12:21-27), at the mountain of God with Jethro (Exodus 18), in making covenant (19:7), on the mountain of God for the cultic meal (24:9-11), and as recipients of Moses' spirit in the wilderness journey when they assume a charismatic office of leadership as judges and inspired interpreters of tradition (Numbers 11). The close relationship between the Non-P History and Deuteronomy is evident in the role of the elders throughout the latter book (e.g., Deut 19:12; 21:2, 3; 22:15; 31:9).

The introduction of the elders separates into two sections, Exod 3:16-17 and 18-22. First, Yahweh commands Moses to address the elders to inform them of the content of his commission (3:16-17). Many themes repeat in this section, from Moses' initial encounter with God, including the identity of Yahweh as the God of the fathers (see 3:6, 13-15), the divine concern over the Israelite oppression (see 3:7, 9), and the promise of land with the same utopian vision of fertility and the list of the indigenous nations (see 3:8). The repetitions underscore the close literary relationship between chaps. 3 and 4 as constituting a single account of the commission of Moses in the wilderness.

Second, Yahweh instructs Moses to take the elders with him to Pharaoh to request the release of the Israelites for worship in the wilderness (3:18-22). New themes appear in this section. Worship of Yahweh requires a three-day journey into the wilderness. A journey of three days marks significant events in the wilderness travel of the Israelites. After the defeat of Pharaoh at the Red Sea, Israel's arrival at the wilderness of Shur is a three-day journey (15:22). The Israelites' departure from Mount Yahweh (yet another name for the mountain of God) after the revelation of the law is also a three-day journey (Num 10:33).

Three additional motifs are introduced in Exod 3:18-22, all reflecting a background in war and anticipating the ensuing conflict between Yahweh and Pharaoh. First, Yahweh informs Moses that Pharaoh will resist, requiring Yahweh to act "with a mighty hand" *(běyād ḥăzāqâ).* The "hand of God" underscores the theme of divine power and the conflict between God and Pharaoh that is central to the exodus. The motif occurs frequently in Deuteronomy in reference to the exodus from Egypt (e.g., Deut 5:15; 6:21; 7:8, 19). The root of the word "mighty" *(ḥzq)* takes on a variety of meanings in the story of the exodus. When used as an adjective to describe the hand of Yahweh it is a term of salvation. But as a verb it is often used to describe the heart of Pharaoh, translated "to harden," as in the conclusion to the first plague: "Yet Pharaoh's heart became hard" *(ḥāzaq,* Exod 7:13). Often, as in this example, Pharaoh hardens his own heart (see also the conclusion to the plagues of blood [7:22] and gnats [8:19]). But eventually Yahweh takes over and hardens Pharaoh's heart (e.g., boils [9:12], hail and fire [9:35], locusts [10:20], darkness [10:27], culminating in the death of the Egyptian firstborn [11:10]). Yahweh's overpowering of Pharaoh in the act of hardening his heart is one sign of Yahweh's "mighty hand."

Second, Yahweh also predicts "wonders" *(niplāʾôt)* performed among the Egyptians causing them to send out the Israelites from their land. The "wonders" of God are frequently mentioned in the Psalms as the basis for praise by the worshiper (e.g., Pss 72:18; 98:1). Thus Yahweh's wonders are normally signs of salvation recognized by the people of Yahweh, not by the opponents of God (see also Exod 34:10; Josh 3:5). But in this passage the wonders of God are the plagues aimed at the Egyptians, not the Israelites. They are weapons of war by which Yahweh will strike the Egyptians, forcing them to send out the Israelites from their land.

Third, the war background is further underscored when God foretells that the Israelites will plunder the Egyptians of their jewelry, gold, and clothing (Exod 3:21-22). The word "to plunder" *(nāṣal* in the Piel) connotes images of booty taken in battle. The command to plunder or to despoil the Egyptians is repeated in 11:2-3 and executed in 12:35-36, indicating Yahweh's victory over Pharaoh and the Egyptian people. The theme returns one other time in Exodus, when the Israelites plunder themselves of silver and gold in the construction of the golden calf (32:1-6). The act of building the golden calf is described as self-plundering because after this event the people no longer wear jewelry. The absence of jewelry indicates an aniconic view of worship, perhaps symbolizing a rejection of the icon of the golden calf. Worship without symbols is associated with Mount Horeb (33:6), the mountain of revelation in Deuteronomy (e.g., Deuteronomy 4–5).

4:1-9 Moses objects to the divine commission in 4:1 even after he is equipped with the name Yahweh. He fears that the elders will not believe that God appeared to him. With this objection the theme of the "belief" *(ʾāman)* of the elders in Moses takes center stage. The verb *ʾāman* occurs three times (4:1, 8, 9). His objection also introduces the inseparable relationship between Mosaic authority and the revelation of Yahweh conceived as law. The NIV and NRSV translate Moses' objection: "What if they do not believe me or listen to me?" The Hebrew can be rendered in English more literally: "What if they do not believe (Hiphil of *ʾāman*) in me and they do not listen *(šāmaʿ)* to my voice *(qôl)*." The phrase "listening to the voice of Moses" becomes interchangeable with the act of "listening to the voice of Yahweh" in the Non-P History. The purpose of theophany in the Non-P History is for the people to hear the voice of God as revealed law, which is possible only through the speech of Moses (15:26; 19:9, 19; 20:18-20). Deuteronomy continues the same emphasis on theophany as an experience of sound, not sight (see Deut 4:12, 33; 5:4, 22), which is then channeled as law through the voice of Moses.

The objection of Moses prompts God to equip him with three magical powers in Exod 4:2-9 identified as signs (*'ōtôt*, v. 9) that confirm his authority. First, God infuses the staff of Moses with supernatural power, so that it can be transformed into a snake (*nāḥāš*) and back into a staff. God's power over the staff/snake may symbolize royal power, since the staff indicates royalty and the snake is a protector of Pharaoh. More likely the snake indicates Yahweh's power to heal, another symbolic meaning of the snake in the ancient Near East. The emphasis on healing is not in the snake, however. Moses is presented as fleeing from its danger. Rather, the power to heal is in Moses' ability to reverse the sign and change the snake back into his staff. This power, moreover, is unique to Moses. He acts out this sign in the concluding story of the wilderness journey (Num 21:4-9), when he reverses the deadly bite of the seraphim snakes by constructing Nehoshet, the copper snake, which is able to heal the Israelite people from the poisonous venom (Num 21:4-9). Aurelius has emphasized that the power of Moses to heal resides in his ability to intercede through prayer.[42] The people plead with Moses: "Pray to Yahweh to take away the serpents from us" (Num 21:7). The healing of the Israelite people fulfills one of the initial self-revelations of God to the Israelites in the wilderness at Shur: "I am Yahweh, your healer" (Exod 15:26).

The magical staff may be a transformation of Moses' shepherd staff, or it may be Yahweh's staff. It is called the "staff of God" when Moses sets out on his journey back to Egypt (4:20). Many gods possess a staff in the ancient Near East. The Canaanite god Baal, for example, has two magical clubs used in battle (*CTA* 1.2.IV.11-25). The motif of a wizard's staff will return in the first plague of the P History, when Aaron and the Egyptian magicians transform their staffs into a sea monster, known as *tannîn* (7:8-13). The conflict between Aaron and the Egyptian magicians is limited to changing their staffs into a snake. They do not reverse the process as in the sign to Moses.

The second sign provided to Moses is the transformation of his hand from healthy flesh to leprous and its cure (4:6-7), perhaps indicating Yahweh's power over death. The Hebrew word usually translated "leprosy" signifies a wide range of skin diseases requiring seclusion (see Leviticus 13–14). It is not Hansen's disease, the modern form of leprosy. The point of this sign, like the previous one, is the reversal, underscoring the power to heal that is unique to Moses. Moses illustrates the power to heal when he cures Miriam from "leprosy" (Numbers 12) through intercessory prayer: "And Moses cried out to Yahweh, 'O God, please heal her!'" (Num 12:13). Thus both of the signs given to

---

42. Aurelius, *Fürbitter Israels*, 127-60.

Moses are acted out subsequently in the wilderness journey, and they are exercised through intercessory prayer. J. Assmann has noted that the motif of leprosy repeats in many of the later Hellenistic accounts of Moses and the exodus, suggesting a strong relationship between this motif and the retelling of the story of Moses in the Hellenistic period.[43]

Third, Moses is given the power to turn the water of the Nile to blood (Exod 4:9), a direct link to the impending plagues (7:14-24). In contrast to what God did with the preceding two signs, God only predicts the power of this sign as a later act in the land of Egypt. The setting of the wilderness precludes the acting out of the sign by Moses. There is an additional contrast. The emphasis of the sign is not on the reversal but on the action itself. Thus the third sign points ahead in the story, beyond the initial meeting of Moses with the Israelite people to the first plague in the Non-P History, when Moses changes the water of the Nile into blood (7:14-24). It presupposes the confrontation with Pharaoh (5:1–6:1), when his refusal to send out the people leads the officers of the Israelites to doubt the authority of Moses (5:15-21) after their initial belief in him (4:31).

The third sign also indicates that the plagues in the Non-P History remain focused on the Israelites and therefore lack the polemical character of the P History, in which they are intended to bring the Egyptians to the knowledge of God (7:5). The Non-P author confirms a different focus for the plague cycle in 10:1-2a in stating that they are intended to bring the Israelite people to knowledge of God, the opposite conclusion of the P historian. The third sign to Moses becomes the second plague in the P History, where the first plague is the changing of Aaron's staff into the sea monster. Moreover, the editorial changes in the P History make Aaron the protagonist in the second plague of changing water into blood, rather than Moses (the P additions to the plague of turning water into blood include 7:16b, 17ab, 19-20a*a*, 21b, 22a, b*b*; see the commentary on 7:14-24).

4:10-18 The commission of Moses in the wilderness is extended through one additional scene by two further objections, both of which focus on Moses' inability to speak. Verses 10-12 introduce the theme of eloquence, and vv. 13-17 extend the topic of prophetic authority. The result of Moses' final two objections is that Aaron is introduced into the Non-P History as a prophet. The commission of Moses in the wilderness concludes with the notice of his departure from Midian in 4:18.

Moses presents five objections to Yahweh in 3:1–4:18. The first focused on himself, especially his lack of identity: "Who am I, that I should go to Pharaoh and bring the Israelites out of Egypt?" (3:11). The second addressed the identity

---

43. Assmann, *Moses the Egyptian*, 23-54.

of Yahweh as the God of the ancestors: "If the Israelites ask your name, what do I tell them?" (3:13). The third raised the problem of the elders' belief: "They will not believe me and they will not listen to my voice" (4:1). Now Moses' fourth (4:10) and fifth (4:13) objections come full circle and focus once again on himself, this time his inability to speak adequately.

Moses states his fourth objection in 4:10: "O, my Lord, I am not a speaker, neither yesterday, nor the day before, nor since your speaking to your servant. But I am heavy of mouth and heavy of tongue." Commentators speculate on what is meant by "heavy of mouth and heavy of tongue." Is it a speech defect? The text is unclear. The point of emphasis is the divine response in 4:11-12. The parallel between Moses' wilderness commission in 3:9-12 and the prophetic call form has already indicated the idealization of Moses as a prophet in the Non-P History. The call narrative is used to authenticate prophets (e.g., Jeremiah) and charismatic leaders (e.g., Gideon). Such leadership is based on personal charisma, often requiring persuasive speech. Moses is the most persuasive speaker in all of Scripture, since he is the transmitter of Torah. Yet his final objection reveals that he is not by nature eloquent. Moses' objection, that he lacks rhetorical skills, sets the stage for the divine reply that charisma, the power of personal leadership and persuasive speech, comes from God; it does not reside innately in humans.

The Non-P historian explores the nature of charismatic power in a divine speech of disputation in 4:11-12. Yahweh responds to the objection of Moses by underscoring the creative power of God: "Who makes mouth for humans? Or who makes dumb or deaf, clear-sighted or blind? Is it not I, Yahweh?" W. H. Schmidt notes that the disputation speech begins with a rhetorical question, introduced by such words as "who" *(mî)* or "where" *('êpōh)*.[44] The content of the disputation often focuses on the power of God as creator. The appearance of God to Job provides comparison, "Where *('êpōh)* were you when I laid the foundation of the earth? Tell me, if you have understanding. . . . Who *(mî)* determined its measurements?" (Job 38:4-5). The questions are intended to accentuate the creative power of God. The same is true in God's response to Moses. The parallels to Job underscore the background of this language in the wisdom tradition.[45] The disputation speech also places the Non-P History in the larger context of exilic prophetic literature. Second Isaiah employs the disputation speech to underscore the creative power of Yahweh even during the Israelites' experience of the exile. The prophet despairs, concluding that humans are no more than grass (Isa 40:6). God disputes such despair through the imagery of creation: "Who has measured the waters?" (40:12). "Who has directed the spirit

---

44. Schmidt, *Exodus,* 201-2.
45. Childs (*Exodus,* 78) notes the close parallel to Ps 94:9.

of Yahweh?" (40:13). "Who taught him knowledge?" (40:14). Despair based on human experience does not adequately probe the power of God, who is able to create new things, even out of the situation of the exile.

The imagery of creation in the divine disputation to Moses is focused more narrowly on persuasive speech. God claims the power to create and to destroy speech in commissioning Moses: "Now, go, and I will be with your mouth and teach you what you will speak" (Exod 4:12). The assertion that God creates prophetic speech also appears in the exilic literature of Second Isaiah, where the prophet is called from the womb (Isa 49:1-5). The commission of the prophet Jeremiah provides an even closer parallel to the commission of Moses. Jeremiah is also commissioned in the womb: "Before I formed you in the womb I knew you" (Jer 1:5). But his commission, like the story of Moses, moves to an objection in which he notes his inability to speak: "O, my Lord, Yahweh, I do not know how to speak" (Jer 1:6). The objection leads to the declaration that Yahweh is the creator of speech. God touches the mouth of the prophet, stating: "Now I have put my words in your mouth" (Jer 1:9).[46]

Finally, in his fifth objection, Moses just pleads his case: "O, my Lord, send, by the hand you send" (Exod 4:13). The syntax of this final statement is awkward in Hebrew: Is Moses acquiescing to the commission or unwilling to go? Whatever the exact meaning, Yahweh becomes angry and states: "Is there not *(hălō')* Aaron, your brother, the Levite?" (4:14). The phrase "is there not" *(hălō')* repeats God's self-identification at the close of the disputation speech: "Is it not *(hălō')* I, Yahweh?" (4:11). The parallel suggests that both questions function rhetorically.

The identification of Aaron is noteworthy. The syntax is unexpected, according to H. Valentin. The order of the identification of Aaron, from "brother" *('āḥ)* to "the Levite" *(hallēwî)*, raises questions about his relationship to Moses and his religious function in the Non-P History. The ambiguity begins with the interpretation of the word "brother." The problem is that the P History has fashioned the word to mean the nuclear family of Amram, whose children include Moses, Aaron, and Miriam (6:20; 7:1-2). Thus the word "brother" as a description of Aaron in the P History would mean "sibling." This designation continues in the later description of the priesthood (28:1, 4, 41). Some interpreters judge the description of Aaron as "brother" in 4:14 to indicate a post-P author, who is building on the familial relationship of Aaron and Moses from the P History. This is the position of Valentin, who states that the aim of the author is to accentuate the teaching office of the Aaronide priesthood in the postexilic period (see Lev 10:11).

46. See Van Seters, *Life of Moses*, 61; Gertz, *Tradition und Redaktion*, 31-39; Schmidt, *Exodus*, 201-2; Childs, *Exodus*, 78-79.

But the term "brother" also plays a role in the Non-P History, where it has a more general meaning, signifying the entire Israelite nation as opposed to Egyptians. Thus Moses identifies with the Israelite people in 2:11 as his "brothers." Exodus 1:6 may provide transition and background for the broader meaning of the term in the Non-P History: "Joseph died, and all his brothers, and the whole generation." The verse provides transition in the meaning of "brother" from the nuclear family of Joseph ("all his brothers") to the nation ("the whole generation"). The more general meaning of "brother" is also intended in 32:27 when Moses commands the Levites to slaughter their "brothers" in the camp after the incident of the golden calf. The narrator concludes that they killed three thousand of the people (*'am*), a collective term for the Israelites. The Non-P author most likely intends the same broad meaning of "brother" in the description of Aaron (4:14) corresponding to its meaning in the earlier description of Moses (2:11) and in the later actions of the Levites (32:27). It is also the intended meaning four verses later in 4:18 when Moses announces to Jethro: "I must go and return to my brothers (*'aḥay*), who are in Egypt."

The point of emphasis of the divine reply to Moses is not that Aaron is a "brother," but that he is "the Levite." The title conflicts with the view of Aaron in the P History, where Levites are separated from the Aaronide priests as subordinate assistants in the cult (Numbers 3–4, 8). In the Non-P History the title "the Levite" designates an office of teaching. Aaron speaks the words that Yahweh teaches (*yārâ*) Moses (4:15). W. H. Schmidt points to parallels in Deuteronomy (33:10), in Chronicles (2 Chr 17:8ff.), and in Nehemiah (8:7ff.).[47] Deuteronomy provides more detail on the teaching function of Levitical priests (Deut 24:8-9), their care of Torah (31:9-13, 25), and their ability to convey covenant curses (27:1-26).

The Levites are separated from the elders in Moses' wilderness commission. The two groups are introduced in the second half of the commission, which develops the theme of Mosaic authority (Exod 3:16–4:9). The elders are introduced in 3:16–4:9 to develop the theme of the belief in the authority of Moses. The introduction of Aaron, the Levite, is contained in 4:10-17, where the theme is no longer the "belief" in Mosaic authority. Rather it is the need to convey Mosaic authority to the people through teaching.

The distinction between the elders and Aaron is further developed when the theme of Mosaic authority returns in Numbers 11–12. The texts are once again clearly separated, with the elders functioning in Numbers 11 and Aaron in Numbers 12. In Numbers 11 the elders acquire an office of leadership when they

---

47. Schmidt, *Exodus*, 204. See also Valentin, *Aaron*, 128-29; Van Seters, *Life of Moses*, 62. See Propp, *Exodus 1–18*, 214, for an early dating to this section; and Gertz, *Tradition und Redaktion*, 321-28, for arguments supporting the post-P authorship.

receive Mosaic authority directly from God and even acquire momentarily the charismatic power of Moses to become prophets (Num 11:25). Numbers 12, by contrast, separates Aaron (and Miriam) from Moses, underscoring the latter's unique status before God as the only person to speak directly to the Deity. The clairvoyance of Aaron and Miriam is indirect at best, arising from visions and dreams (Num 12:6-8).[48] The introduction of Aaron in Exod 4:13-16 reinforces the same point. He and the Levites do not directly possess Mosaic authority themselves, even though they teach it. The Deity makes this clear in appointing Aaron to assist Moses in 4:14-16. He is singled out for his eloquence in speaking. But he functions in a subordinate role to Moses. Yahweh speaks only through Moses in the Non-P History. Moses will function as a god to Aaron. Aaron, in turn, will be Moses' spokesperson to the Israelites conveying the divine instruction (*yārâ* in the Hiphil, v. 15), a reference to law or Torah in the Non-P History (see 15:25; 24:12). Deuteronomy 17:10-11 outlines the role of the priests to instruct the people.

The wilderness commission of Moses concludes in Exod 4:17-18. God commands Moses to take his staff with him and to perform the signs from 4:1-9. Exodus 4:18 records the departure of Moses from Midian. Moses informs his father-in-law, Jethro, of his intention to return to Egypt to inquire about the Israelite people. Yet the departure of Moses is recorded twice in 4:18 and 19 (see "Authors: Research"). In the commentary I have separated the repetition to designate the literary boundaries of the wilderness commission of Moses. Both notices provide transition from Moses' encounter with God at the divine mountain to his wilderness journey to Egypt. The first notice, 4:18, emphasizes Moses' Midianite family. The second notice, 4:19, shifts the focus to Moses' Israelite family ("his brothers"), while also making reference indirectly to his Egyptian family ("those seeking his life have died").

FAILED CONFRONTATION WITH PHARAOH (4:19–6:1)

[4:19] *And Yahweh said to Moses in Midian, "Go and return to Egypt, for all the men seeking your life have died."* [20] *And Moses took his wife and his sons and he mounted them on the donkey, and he returned to the land of Egypt. And Moses took the staff of the God in his hand.*
[21] *And Yahweh said to Moses, "As you go to return to Egypt, see all the wonders that I placed in your hand, and do them before Pharaoh. But I will harden his*

---

48. Miriam may represent other competing prophetic groups in the postexilic period. See U. Rapp, *Mirjam: Eine feministisch-rhetorische Lektüre der Mirjamtexte in der hebräischen Bibel* (BZAW 317; Berlin: de Gruyter, 2002).

heart, and he will not send out the people. ²²*And you will say to Pharaoh, 'Thus said Yahweh: My son, my firstborn, is Israel.* ²³*And I say to you, Send out my son, so that he can serve me. And if you refuse to send him out, indeed, I will kill your son, your firstborn.'"*

²⁴*And it happened on the way at the place where they spent the night, Yahweh met him and sought to kill him.* ²⁵*And Zipporah took a flint. And she cut the foreskin of her son. And she touched his feet, and she said, "For a bridegroom of blood are you to me."* ²⁶*And he let them alone. Then she said, "Bridegroom of blood for circumcision."*

²⁷*And Yahweh said to Aaron, "Go and meet Moses in the wilderness." And he went and he encountered him at the mountain of God. And he kissed him.* ²⁸*And Moses told Aaron all the words of Yahweh, which he sent him, and all the signs, which he commanded him.*

²⁹*And Moses and Aaron went and they gathered together all the elders of the Israelites.* ³⁰*And Aaron spoke all the words that Yahweh had spoken to Moses. And he did the signs in the eyes of the people.* ³¹*And the people believed. And they heard that Yahweh was aware of the Israelites, and that he saw their torment. And they bowed and they worshiped.*

^{5:1}*Afterward Moses and Aaron entered and said to Pharaoh, "Thus said Yahweh, God of Israel, 'Send out my people so they can keep a festival to me in the wilderness.'"*

²*And Pharaoh said, "Who is Yahweh, that I should listen to his voice to send out the Israelites? I do not know Yahweh. And, moreover, the Israelites I will not send out."*

³*And they said, "The God of the Hebrews encountered us. Let us go a journey of three days into the wilderness, so that we may sacrifice to Yahweh our God, lest he strike us with plague or with sword."*

⁴*And the king of Egypt said to them, "Why, Moses and Aaron, do you slacken the people from their work? Go to your forced labor!"* ⁵*And Pharaoh said, "Indeed, many now are the people of the land. Return them to their forced labor!"*

⁶*And on that day Pharaoh commanded the taskmasters and his officers, saying,* ⁷*"You will no longer give the people straw for bricks as yesterday and the day before. They will go and collect straw for themselves.* ⁸*But the number of bricks that they made yesterday and the day before, place on them. Do not deduct from them, because they are slack. Therefore they cry out, saying, 'Let us go and sacrifice to our God.' Make the work heavy on the men. Let them do it and not look to words of deceit."*

¹⁰*And the taskmasters of the people and his officers went out and they said to the people, saying, "Thus said Pharaoh, 'I will not give you straw.* ¹¹*You go and take for yourselves straw from wherever you find, for your work will not be lessened at all.'"*

¹²*And the people scattered throughout the land of Egypt to collect stubble for brick.* ¹³*But the taskmasters harangued, saying, "Complete your work, a day's work in its day, as when there was the straw."* ¹⁴*And the officers of the Israelites, whom the taskmasters of Pharaoh placed over them, were beaten, saying, "Why have you not completed either yesterday or today your prescribed amount of bricks as yesterday and the day before?"*

¹⁵*And the officers of the Israelites went and they cried to Pharaoh, saying, "Why do you do this to your servants?* ¹⁶*No straw has been given to your servants. Yet they are saying to us, 'Make bricks!' Indeed, your servants are being beaten and you have sinned against your people."*

¹⁷*And he said, "Slackers, you are slack! Therefore, you are saying, 'Let us go and worship Yahweh.'* ¹⁸*And now go and work. Straw will not be given to you, yet the full measure of bricks you will give."*

¹⁹*The officers of the Israelite saw themselves in trouble in the saying, "Do not deduct from your bricks, a day's work in its day."* ²⁰*And they encountered Moses and Aaron stationed to meet them when they went out from Pharaoh.* ²¹*And they said to them, "May Yahweh look on you and judge, since you have made our scent stink in the eyes of Pharaoh and in the eyes of his servants to place a sword in their hand to kill us."*

²²*And Moses returned to Yahweh and he said, "My Lord, why did you bring this evil on this people? Was it for this that you sent me?* ²³*Ever since I came to Pharaoh to speak in your name, he has treated this people badly. And you have certainly not rescued your people."*

⁶:¹*And Yahweh said to Moses, "Now you will see what I will do to Pharaoh. For by a strong hand he will send them out, and by a strong hand he will drive them out from his land."*

Notes

4:19 *and Yahweh said to Moses in Midian.* The LXX adds, "after those many days the king of Egypt died" (*meta de tas hēmeras tas pollas ekeinas eteleutēsen ho basileus Aigyptou*), creating a repetition with 2:23a.

4:23 *to send him out.* The LXX reads, "to send them (*autous*) out."

4:24 *Yahweh.* The LXX reads, *angelos kyriou,* "the angel of the Lord." Wevers speculates that the LXX has sought to "mitigate the harshness of the account."[1]

4:25 *she touched his feet.* The antecedent to "his" is unclear in the MT, whether Moses, his son, or Yahweh. The LXX replaces "she touched" with "she fell down at" (*prosepesen*) and eliminates "his" in reference to feet. The result is: "She fell down at the feet." But Wevers rightly concludes: "One still does not know whether it refers to Moses or the angel or to her son."[2]

---

1. Wevers, *Notes*, 55.
2. Ibid.

for a bridegroom of blood are you to me. The LXX departs significantly from the MT: *Estē to haima tēs peritomēs tou paidiou mou,* "The blood of the circumcision of my son stands."

4:26 *bridegroom of blood for circumcision.* The LXX departs from the MT. See previous note.

4:30 *that Yahweh had spoken to Moses.* The LXX reads, "which the God *(ho theos)* had spoken to Moses."

4:31 *and they heard.* The LXX reads, *echarē,* "they rejoiced."

Yahweh. The LXX reads, *ho theos,* "the God."

5:1 *keep a festival.* The MT *ḥāgag* implies a religious pilgrimage with a festival celebration.

5:2 *Who is Yahweh.* The LXX reads, *Tis estin,* "Who is he?"

5:3 *to Yahweh our God.* The LXX reads, *tō theō,* "to God."

with plague or with sword. The LXX reads, *thanatos,* "death," for MT "plague."

5:4 *many now are the people of the land.* The syntax of the MT suggests that the "people of the land" are the Israelites. The Sam turns the sentence into a comparison, making the "people of the land" Egyptians: "And Pharaoh said, 'Indeed, they are greater now than the people of the land *(rbym 'th m'm h'rṣ).'*"

5:6 *officers.* The MT *šōṭĕrāyw* means "officers" or "scribes." The LXX reads, *grammateusin,* "scribes." The range of meaning, from officers to scribes, influences the identity of the "officers," whether they are Egyptian or Israelite. See the commentary.

5:7 *you will no longer.* The MT *tō'sipûn* is written with an aleph, suggesting the root *'sp* ("gather, collect"), although the translation assumes the root *ysp* ("add to, increase"), as in Sam. The LXX follows the Sam reading: "Do not continue to give" *(prostethēsesthe didonai).*

5:9 *let them do it.* The LXX reads, *merimnatōsan tauta,* "they will look at it," repeating the same verb in the following sentence, *mē merimnatōsan en logois kenois,* "and they will not look at false/empty words."

5:14 *and the officers of the Israelites.* The LXX describes officers as *grammateis,* "scribes," and identifies their ethnicity as Israelites, adding *tou genous* ("and the scribes of the race of the Israelites"). See also 5:6.

either yesterday or today . . . as yesterday and the day before. The MT does not separate the two phrases, but reads: "Why have you not completed your prescribed amount of bricks either yesterday or today as yesterday and the day before?"

5:16 *you have sinned against your people.* The MT, *wĕḥāṭā't 'ammekā,* lacks the preposition, *lĕ,* "against." The Hebrew, *ḥāṭā't,* rendered in the second person rather than the third, implies a moral offense, hence the translation, "sin," as in the statement of Pharaoh in Exod 9:27, "I sinned this time." The LXX translates, *adikēseis oun ton laon sou,* "So you will treat your people unjustly." The LXX is reflected in the NRSV, "You are unjust to your own people."

5:19 *saw themselves in trouble.* The Hebrew is awkward, translating lit. "saw themselves in evil."

in the saying. The MT reads "saying" *(lē'mōr)* as does the LXX *(legontes).* The translation indicates a reference to past speech, not direct discourse.

5:21 *Yahweh.* The LXX reads *ho theos,* "the God."

since. Hebrew *'ăšer* is translated as an independent relative, serving in the larger verbal clause as an object, thus indicating the content of what Yahweh is to judge (see *IBHS* §19.3.c).

5:22 *was it for this.* The MT *lāmmâ zeh* could be translated "Why this?" The LXX reads, *hina ti apestalkas me.*

Commentary

The twice-told departure of Moses in 4:18-19 prepares for the confrontation with Pharaoh (4:19–6:1), which separates into two parts: 4:19-31 is an account of Moses' wilderness journey to Egypt and his report to the Israelite people of Yahweh's imminent salvation; 5:1–6:1 narrates Moses' initial failed confrontation with Pharaoh, which provides a prelude to the story of the plagues.

Wilderness Journey (4:19-31)

The central theme in the wilderness journey of Moses is kinship, explored through the family relationships of the hero, Moses. Moses has three different family relationships in Exodus. He is born to an Israelite family (2:1); he is adopted into the Egyptian family of Pharaoh (2:10); and he marries into the Midianite family of Jethro (2:21). The twice-told account of Moses' departure (4:18-19) refers to all three relationships. Motifs of kinship play a role in the individual stories of Moses' journey. The geography of his journey from Midian to Egypt provides the setting for the theme of kinship in the individual stories. The theme of family relationships begins with the description of Moses leaving Midian accompanied by his wife Zipporah and his sons (4:19-20). It continues in the divine speech declaring the Israelite people to be God's firstborn (4:21-23). The divine attack on Moses further advances the theme of family (4:24-26) before Aaron enters the story in 4:27-31.

The portrayal of Moses' family in 4:19-31 conflicts with other accounts of his nuclear family. For example, the reference to the "sons" of Moses in 4:20 is plural, yet the reader learns about the two sons of Moses, Gershom and Eliezer, only in 18:4. Exodus 18 also assumes that Moses traveled alone to Egypt and only later was united with his Midianite family (18:1-4). The contradictions between these stories indicate that the Non-P History is a conflation of several traditions surrounding the Midianite background of Moses. It also reinforces the importance of family relations as a theme in 4:19-31. The theme is important enough for the Non-P historian to tolerate the conflict in narrative logic in the larger story of Moses. The overall aim of the author in fashioning the multiple images of family in 4:19-31 is to reestablish Moses' Israelite identity. The goal is achieved through the motif of a journey conceived as a rite of passage from Moses' Midianite family to his Israelite family. The central event in the rite of passage is the attack by Yahweh (4:24-26), in which paradoxically it is Moses' Midianite wife Zipporah who provides the ritual protection, creating a close bond between Midianites and Israelites in the Non-P History.

4:19-20 Moses' return to Egypt begins with the Midianites. The wilderness commission of Moses concludes with a portrait of Jethro in 4:18. Moses approaches his father-in-law stating his need to return and to inquire of his "brothers," a reference to the Hebrews. This statement begins the process of separating Moses from the Midianites in the Non-P History. The sparse information provided by Moses to Jethro hardly appears to be an act of deception, as suggested by Propp.[3] The blessing of Jethro reinforces a positive interpretation of Moses' transition from Midian to Egypt. The divine command for Moses to return in 4:19 appears out of place, but it provides continuity with 2:23a, where the death of the king of Egypt was noted (see "Authors: Research"). The indirect reference to the king of Egypt also calls the reader's attention to the third family of Moses, his previous adoption into the house of Pharaoh. Moses departs with his Midianite family, including Zipporah and, most likely, two sons (see 18:1-4). In addition to his family Moses also leaves Midian with two possessions, one from Jethro, a donkey, and another from Yahweh, "the staff of God." Both indicate his improved status from his initial arrival in the land of Midian when he fled the death threat of Pharaoh, his adopted Egyptian father.

The Midianites play a special role in Exodus as allies of Yahweh. They are closely associated with the two wilderness revelations of Yahweh at the mountain of God, initially to Moses (3:1–4:17) and then to the Israelites (Exodus 19–Numbers 10). The diagram in figure 6 on page 151 illustrates the distribution of the Midianite stories in the Non-P History and shows that stories about the Midianites frame Moses' wilderness commission (Exod 3:1–4:17). The revelation of Yahweh to Moses is introduced with a positive story about the Midianites in 2:15-22. The land of Midian provides a safe haven for Moses in fleeing from Pharaoh. The Midianite family of Jethro offers Moses hospitality, which leads to his marriage with Zipporah. The land of Midian is also the setting for the appearance of Yahweh on the mountain of God (3:1). The wilderness commission of Moses (3:1–4:17) is followed by two additional stories about the Midianites in 4:18-26. Upon hearing of his commission, Jethro blesses Moses (4:18-20). Then, when Moses begins his journey, Zipporah, his Midianite wife, rescues him from a divine attack in the wilderness (4:24-26).

The wilderness revelation of Yahweh to the Israelites on the mountain of God (Exodus 19–Numbers 10) is also framed by stories about the Midianites in the Non-P History. The story of Jethro on the mountain of God in Exodus 18

3. Propp, *Exodus 1–18*, 215.

Figure 6

Wilderness Revelation to Moses on the Mountain of God

2:15-22	3:1–4:17	4:18-26
MIDIAN	REVELATION	MIDIAN
Moses' flight to Midian and marriage into the family of Reuel	to Moses on the mountain of God	Moses' departure from Jethro, with blessing
		Moses is rescued from the divine attack by Zipporah

Wilderness Revelation to the Israelites on the Mountain of God

18:1-27	19-34	Num 10:29-32
MIDIAN	REVELATION	MIDIAN
Sacrifice with Jethro on the mountain of God	to Israel on the mountain of God	Israelite departure from Hobab ben-Reuel
Moses receives legal advice from his father-in-law		

provides an introduction to the revelation of Yahweh in chaps. 19–34. Jethro interprets the Israelite flight from Egypt as the salvation of Yahweh (18:10-11), while offering sacrifices to God (18:12). The revelation of Yahweh to the Israelite people follows chap. 18. It includes the theophany of God (chap. 19), which establishes the covenant (chap. 24) and forms the Israelite cult (chaps. 32–34). The revelation of Yahweh to the Israelites is followed in the Non-P History by further stories about the Midianites (Num 10:29-32). This time Moses requests his father-in-law, here named Hobab ben-Reuel, to lead them in their wilderness journey to the promised land of Canaan. When he declines, Yahweh assumes the leadership of the Israelites (Num 10:33-36).

Thus the stories about the Midianites frame the two accounts of divine revelation at the mountain of God. In the process the Midianites emerge as a people with close ties to Yahweh and who possess special knowledge of religious rituals. The mountain of God is either in or at least near their land (Exod 3:1). Moses' father-in-law, Jethro, is a priest, who shows hospitality to Moses (2:15-22). He possesses the power to bless Moses upon hearing of his divine commission (4:18). Moses' wife, Zipporah, is skilled in rituals that save him from a divine attack (4:24-26). Jethro is also clairvoyant, recognizing the power of Yahweh in the rescue of the Israelites from Egypt, which leads to his interpretation of the event for the elders of Israel (18:10-11). In addition, Jethro is skilled in cultic rituals and in sacrifice (18:12). He advises Moses on judicial matters (18:13-27). Finally, Moses requests that his father-in-law serve as the guide in their wilderness march and offers him a share in the future salvation of Yahweh (Num 10:29-32).

The literary role of the Midianites in Exodus has raised questions about the history of Israelite religion. Biblical scholars have speculated that the worship of Yahweh may have originated in Midianite culture and only later was it adopted by the Israelites in the land of Canaan.[4] The evidence arises in part from archaic poetry, which preserves glimpses of tradition that do not correspond with the story line of the Pentateuch. Early traditions identify the home of Yahweh as the southern Transjordanian desert (see the commentary on 3:1). Yahweh is the "one of Sinai," who journeys from Seir and marches from the land of Edom during times of crisis to rescue the Israelites in the land of Canaan (Judg 5:4-5; Deut 33:2).[5] The location of the land of Midian is unclear from the biblical stories, but it too may be associated with the same desert region as the early poems about Yahweh's residence.

A further complication in unraveling the history of Israelite religion is the equation of the Midianites with the Kenites outside Exodus. Twice in Judges the Kenites are identified as the in-laws of Moses (Judg 1:16; 4:11), not the Midianites. The father-in-law of Moses is named Hobab, not Jethro (Judg 4:11). Yet the names, the ethnic groups, and their regional homes are intermixed. Both groups dwell in the southern desert, the Midianites in southern Transjordan and the Kenites at Arad (Judg 1:16). Jethro and Hobab share the name Reuel (Num 10:29). And Hobab is identified as both a Midianite (Num 10:29) and a Kenite (Judg 4:11).[6] The biblical accounts of Moses' Midianite father-in-law include a range of distinct folk literature. Albright sought to harmonize the divergent traditions into a single account by arguing that the distinct names for Moses' Midianite father-in-law actually represent two generations. Thus the reference to Hobab in Num 10:29 is to the son of Reuel.[7]

The Kenites are descendants of Cain (Gen 4:17-24). They represent cultural heroes and itinerant smiths (the name Cain is related to the verb "to forge"). The image of the Kenites as metallurgists may reflect historical circumstances surrounding their occupation, or it may carry a symbolic message about cultural assimilation. P. McNutt has demonstrated that metallurgy can

---

4. See B. Halpern, "Kenites," *ABD* 4:17-22.

5. See F. M. Cross and D. N. Freedman, *Studies in Ancient Yahwistic Poetry* (SBLDS 21; Missoula, Mont.: Scholars Press, 1975), 13-27, 97-122.

6. H. Seebass, *Numeri* (BKAT IV/2; Neukirchen-Vluyn: Neukirchener Verlag, 2003), 21-23.

7. W. F. Albright, "Jethro, Hobab and Reuel in Early Hebrew Tradition," *CBQ* 25 (1963): 1-11.

represent cultural intermixing in ancient literature, the forging of two different elements into new objects.[8] The Kenite/Midianites fill this role in the area of religion in Exodus. They are allies of God, forging a new form of Yahwistic worship by aiding Moses and the Israelites in the wilderness.

The questions surrounding the history of Israelite religion are intriguing, but in the end probably irresolvable. What emerges is a complex web of folk traditions about the desert and the non-Israelite origin of Yahwistic worship, known in biblical scholarship as the Kenite Hypothesis.[9] More certain is an interpretation of the Midianites as a literary theme in Exodus. The Midianites complicate the character of Yahweh. They are a wilderness people, distinct from the indigenous nations of the land of Canaan (see the list in Exod 3:8), who must be destroyed by conquest. The Midianites, by contrast, appear to have knowledge of Yahweh that is independent of Moses and the Israelites. They are not the founders of Yahwistic religion in the Non-P History. Yahweh is clearly the God of the Israelite ancestors, calling Abram from Ur (Gen 12:1-4). Yet the religious insight of the Midianites (offspring of Abraham and Keturah, Gen 25:1-6) prevents Yahweh from being exclusively a national God, limited to the Israelites.

The heroic role of the midwives, who feared God more than Pharaoh, already suggested the theme of Yahweh's relationship to the nations. But the Midianites advance the theme beyond the midwives' general fear of God. The Midianites possess a special understanding of God as the Deity Yahweh. And they transmit their religious knowledge to Moses, once he encounters Yahweh on the mountain of God. Jethro returns to lead the Israelites in worship at the mountain of God (Exodus 18). Balaam, the seer, reinforces the same theme at the close of the Israelite wilderness journey, when he too demonstrates an intimate knowledge of Yahweh independent of the Israelite cult or history of salvation (Numbers 22–24).[10] The uneasiness of exploring divine relationships outside the boundaries of the Israelites is evident in the P History, where both the Midianites and Balaam are killed in an act of war sanctioned by Yahweh (Numbers 31).

4:21-23 Yahweh advances the theme of kinship in this section beyond distinct human groups to include the divine family by proclaiming the Israelite people his firstborn. The speech includes an interpretation of the exodus. God refers to the previous "signs" given to Moses (4:1-9), now described as "wonders" to be performed before Pharaoh, not before the people of Israel. The meaning of the divine instruction to Moses is not immediately clear. The word

---

8. P. McNutt, *The Forging of Israel: Iron Technology, Symbolism, and Tradition in Ancient Society* (Social World of Biblical Antiquity Series 8; Sheffield: Almond Press, 1990).

9. See Childs, *Exodus*, 221-26.

10. See Dozeman, "Numbers," 170-95.

"wonders" *(mōpĕtîm)* is used by the P author to frame the plague cycle, describing the initial episode where Aaron and the Egyptian magicians turn their staffs into snakes (7:3, 9) and the death of the Egyptian firstborn (11:9, 10). The repetition in the P History suggests upon first reading that the P author composed this speech. The phrase "in signs and in wonders" *(bĕ'ōtōt ûbĕmōpĕtîm)* is a common expression in Deuteronomy (e.g., Deut 4:34; 6:22; 13:2, 3; 26:8; 28:46) in reference to the salvation from Egypt. The compound phrase, however, is absent from 4:21-23. The story of the man of God in 1 Kings 13, who proclaims an oracle against the altar at Bethel, employs the motif of a "wonder" to develop the theme of true and false prophecy (1 Kgs 13:3, 5). The wonder in this story is the destruction of the altar confirming the truth of the oracle of the man of God. This parallel provides a closer analogy to Exod 4:21-23. It suggests that the wonders confirm the truth of Moses' message and his authority as God's representative to Pharaoh. Thus the divine speech to Moses is not about the faith of the Israelites. It is about God's power over Pharaoh.

Yahweh predicts the failure of the wonders and states that he would harden Pharaoh's heart. The hardening of Pharaoh's heart (see the commentary on 3:19-20) signifies resistance to God. Pharaoh will not listen to the request of God or Moses to release the Israelites (e.g., 7:13). The divine claim to be the agent of the hardening is less deterministic than it appears upon first reading (see the commentary on 3:19). The hardening evolves in the course of the conflict between Yahweh and Pharaoh. Initially Pharaoh hardens his own heart in resisting God's claim on Israel (snakes, 7:13; blood, 7:22; gnats, 8:19). Eventually, however, God overpowers Pharaoh, conceding his stance of resistance and in the process becoming the agent of the hardening (boils, 9:12; hail and fire, 9:35; locusts, 10:20; darkness, 10:27; culminating in the death of the Egyptian firstborn, 11:10). The evolution of the motif underscores the interactive process involved in the hardening of Pharaoh's heart.

The divine prediction to harden the heart of Pharaoh probably refers to the death of the Egyptian firstborn, since it is followed by the divine claim that Israel is Yahweh's firstborn *(bĕkōr)*. The firstborn status of Israel is a new motif to the story, expanding the theme of family relations in this section. The firstborn status of the Israelites signifies kinship between Yahweh and the Israelites. It provides background for the subsequent death of the Egyptian firstborn (see the commentary on chap. 12) and the divine claim on all the Israelite firstborn (see the commentary on 13:1-2).

4:24-26 The newly proclaimed kinship tie between Yahweh and Moses' family is acted out in this section. Zipporah plays the central role in the story, rescuing the person under attack from God. The exact details of the episode, however, are impossible to determine because of the lack of proper names to identify the role of each participant. The ambiguity begins in 4:24. During the night Yahweh seeks to kill one of the male family members — it is unclear whether it is the son or Moses. The attack may represent Yahweh's claim on the firstborn, or it may result from the absence of circumcision of either Moses or his son.

Zipporah stops the attack in 4:25 by circumcising her son, presumably Gershom, and warding off the Deity with the bloody foreskin. The word for "knife" *(ṣōr)* indicates a flint knife, common for circumcision in the ancient Near East. The act of cutting the son's foreskin is described with the Hebrew verb *kārat* (lit. "to cut"), a word used to indicate covenant relationships (e.g., Gen 15:18), rather than the expected term *mûl,* "to circumcise." Zipporah takes the foreskin and "touches his feet." The word "feet" is most likely a euphemism for genitals. The action of Zipporah as a rescuer suggests that Moses is the object of the divine attack, since his salvation by women is a central theme in the opening chapters of Exodus (see also the midwives, his mother and sister, and the daughter of Pharaoh). The NIV and NRSV translations also indicate that Moses is the object of her action: "And Zipporah . . . touched Moses' feet with it [the foreskin]." The NJPS is more ambiguous: "and [she] touched his legs with it." The Hebrew is unclear whose genitals she touches, Moses' or perhaps she refers symbolically to God. Zipporah's statement: "For a bridegroom of blood are you to me," eliminates Gershom as the object of her action.

The phrase "bridegroom of blood" probably indicates marriage. The Hebrew word *ḥātān* means "a male relative by marriage," usually indicating a son-in-law. The Arabic *ḥtn* means "to circumcise" and "to protect." Perhaps all of these meanings are playing a role in the story. Zipporah's act of circumcision protects by warding off the Deity and, as noted, it may create or confirm a familial relationship with the Deity. The identification of Yahweh as the "God of the fathers" has been a central theme throughout the opening chapters of Exodus. If Yahweh is the object of her action, the story underscores the familial bond between Yahweh and the family of Moses, hence the allusion to covenant. Yahweh has also just proclaimed a familial relationship with Israel in the previous speech (4:21-23). If Moses is the object of Zipporah's action, the story may represent the protection of Moses through the circumcision of his son. But it may also reflect an ancient understanding of circumcision as a rescue of the firstborn from the divine claim upon his life.

What is clear in the story is that Zipporah, the Midianite, performs the proper ritual to appease the Deity and to protect her family. In the process she passes on the ritual knowledge to Moses and hence to the Israelites. The closing verse (4:26) indicates that the story functioned at one time as an etiology for infant circumcision. As a cultic legend the story tells of a transfer of circumcision from the religious practice of the Midianites to the Israelites through Zipporah, the Midianite wife of Moses.

The story also plays an important role in the present context of Exodus. Twice in Exodus Yahweh is presented as a destroyer. God seeks to kill Moses or Gershom in 4:24-26, and "the destroyer" kills the Egyptian firstborn in chap. 12. The two stories are related. Both explore Yahweh's claim on firstborn, introduced in 4:22. The historical and religious background of the divine claim on firstborn is not clear from the biblical text, especially whether the claim required the sacrifice of the firstborn. The prophet Ezekiel acknowledges the ritual practice, but separates it from the Deity as a law that was "not good" (Ezek 20:25-26). Genesis 22 is a polemical story against the practice in the Non-P History. Exodus 13:1-2 states that Yahweh claims all firstborn animals and humans, suggesting a possible tradition of child sacrifice. Rescue from the divine attack in both stories requires special cultic rituals associated with blood. The blood of the Passover lamb protects the Israelite firstborn from death in Exodus 12. The blood from the circumcision of Gershom protects Moses or Gershom from the attack by Yahweh.

The exact meaning of Zipporah's ritual action is no longer clear. What stands out is that it is Zipporah, not Moses, who knows the special rituals of protection and that in performing them she rescues Moses from the attack of Yahweh. In this act she is the final female rescuer of Moses. Her rescue is not an escape from the social tyranny of Pharaoh. Instead, her knowledge of religious ritual about Yahweh, associated with Jethro the Midianite (Exodus 18), allows Moses to live safely in the wilderness with God, his divine father (see 15:2).

4:27-31 This section shifts the focus from Moses' Midianite family to his Israelite family by referring to Aaron. Aaron was introduced as the brother of Moses at the close of Moses' wilderness commission (4:14-17). Aaron returns in 4:27-31, providing a transition to Moses' role as the representative of Yahweh in claiming the Israelite people (5:1–6:1). Aaron is instructed to meet Moses in the wilderness (4:27; cf. 4:14). Moses informs Aaron of his encounter with God (4:28; cf. 4:15). Aaron speaks for Moses to the Israelites (4:29-30; cf. 4:16). Aaron performs the signs given to Moses (4:30), which creates a literary tension with 4:17, where Moses is instructed to perform the signs. Finally, the people believe in Moses (4:31; cf. 4:1, 8, 9). The Israelite belief in Moses in the land of Egypt is fleeting, however. It will disappear at the first resistance of Pharaoh. The motif will return when the Israelites first enter the wilderness at the Red Sea (14:31) and later encounter Yahweh at the divine mountain (19:9).

Failure to Rescue (5:1–6:1)

The initial confrontation with Pharaoh separates into three scenes. The story opens with Pharaoh's rejection of Yahweh's claim upon the Israelites (5:1-14). The failure of Moses to rescue the Israelite people leads to complaints, first by the Israelite officers (5:15-21) and second by Moses (5:22–6:1).

5:1-14   The initial confrontation pits Pharaoh against Yahweh, with the Israelite elders in the middle of the conflict. Moses and Aaron are presented as messengers of Yahweh to Pharaoh in 5:1. The clause "Thus said Yahweh" is prophetic speech, indicating that the prophet is a spokesperson for God who brings an announcement to a king or to the people of Israel (e.g., Amos 5:3, 4). The idealization of Moses as a prophetic messenger is rooted in his commission in the wilderness (Exod 3:1–4:17) and it continues throughout the events of the exodus (e.g., 7:17; 8:1; 9:4).

Pharaoh's response, "I do not know Yahweh" (5:2), fits the larger context in which Yahweh must be revealed anew to the Israelites. Pharaoh could not possibly know the identity of Yahweh. His speech is also contemptuous, however, implying his superiority to Yahweh: "Who is Yahweh? . . . I will not send out the Israelites." Moses and Aaron answer Pharaoh by identifying Yahweh with the Israelite slaves as "the God of the Hebrews" (5:3; see the commentary on 1:15-16 for the meaning of "Hebrew" as "slave"). They add that Yahweh requires a three-day journey into the wilderness for worship (see 3:18). They conclude by stating that the failure of the Israelites to respond to the divine demand for worship carries the threat of punishment in the form of plagues or a sword, recalling the divine attack of Moses (4:24-26).

Pharaoh's response continues in 5:4-9. The section begins as an address to Moses and Aaron, but shifts to a more private speech addressed to the "taskmasters" *(nōgĕśîm)* and the "officers" *(šōṭĕrîm)*. The "taskmasters" are most likely Egyptians, while the "officers" appear to be Israelites. Deuteronomy 1:15 describes Israelite officers as leaders of the people, and 16:18 identifies such persons as judges. The same Hebrew word, *šōṭēr,* also means "scribe," deriving from Akkadian *šaṭāru,* "to write." The Non-P historian identifies the officers as the elders in Num 11:16 in the divine command to Moses: "Gather for me seventy of the elders of Israel, whom you know to be the elders of the people and *officers* over them."

The identification of the elders as the officers is important for interpreting the confrontation with Pharaoh. They emerge as the central characters in the initial confrontation between Yahweh and Pharaoh, thus developing the theme of faith in Moses that was introduced in Exod 3:16–4:9. Yahweh designated the elders as the object of Moses' commission (3:16, 18). Their belief in Moses is central in establishing his authority (4:1, 5, 8, 9). The closing portrait of the Israelite people upon hearing of the revelation of Yahweh was their belief in Moses and the act of worship (4:31). It is unclear whether the elders are included in the scene. The reference to all the Israelites may include the elders, but they are not specifically mentioned. Exodus 5:1-14 indicates that the elders have a special role with Pharaoh. They are part of his private group in planning a response to Yahweh. Pharaoh shares his fear with the elders that the growth of the Israelites poses a threat to Egypt. The Israelites are many. They may even have come to outnumber the "people of the land," a technical term for land-owners, in this case the Egyptians.

Pharaoh commands the taskmasters and the Israelite elders (the "offi-cers") to intensify the Israelite oppression by making the people gather their own straw for construction without decreasing their work quota. Pharaoh states that the increased labor is intended to demonstrate that the message of Moses and Aaron was a lie. The Hebrew word for "lie" *(šeqer)* indicates false prophecy in Jeremiah (e.g., Jer 5:31; 14:14; 20:6), recalling the prophetic role of Moses and Aaron as messengers of Yahweh. The dual role of the elders, as lead-ers of the Israelite people who must believe in the imminent salvation of Yahweh and the authority of Moses, and as part of Pharaoh's planning group, raises the question of their loyalty, thus advancing the motif of "faith" in the Non-P History.

The question of loyalty is further complicated with the public proclama-tion in Exod 5:10-14. The elders, along with the Egyptian taskmasters, are pre-sented as delivering the message of Pharaoh in the form of a prophetic messen-ger announcement, "Thus said Pharaoh." Pharaoh requires an equal amount of building without providing straw, setting the stage for a conflict between Yahweh and Pharaoh. The use of the prophetic messenger speech by represen-tatives of Yahweh and Pharaoh frames the confrontation initially as one of equals. The elders are caught in the middle of the conflict. The scene ends with their being beaten by the Egyptian taskmasters for failing to meet their building quota (5:14).

5:15-21 The elders complain that their situation has worsened. Their ac-tions and their speech raise questions of loyalty. They "cry out," employing the language of lament used in addressing Yahweh. But their lament is directed to Pharaoh, not Yahweh. Three times they identify themselves as "servants" of Pharaoh (5:15-16) and once as Pharaoh's "own people" (5:16). If they were in-cluded in the initial belief in Moses and in the worship of Yahweh in 4:31, their statement is now an abrupt reversal. Yet the scene closes with the elders calling on Yahweh to judge the action of Moses and Aaron, whom they accuse of hav-ing put them in peril of death. They now "stink," meaning most likely that the Egyptians hold the Israelites in contempt (see the reversal of the motif in the plagues of blood [7:18, 21] and frogs [8:6, 14]). They are vulnerable to the point of death because of their present circumstance. The complaint of the elders will intensify in the wilderness journey with the development of the murmuring motif (see the commentary on the journey, 15:22–18:27).

5:22-6:1 Moses turns to Yahweh to register his own complaint, ques-tioning again his authority. The complaint of Moses in 5:22-23 relates the ac-tions of Yahweh and Pharaoh through repetition of the word "mistreat" *(rāʿaʿ,*

"to do badly"). Yahweh mistreated the people by sending Moses, prompting Pharaoh to mistreat the people through increased slave labor. Moses' conclusion is that Yahweh has not rescued his people, a denial of the divine promise (cf. 3:8). Moses will repeat this complaint in Num 11:10-15, accusing Yahweh of not fulfilling the divine promise of presence (cf. Exod 3:12).

Yahweh addresses the complaint of Moses in 6:1. The divine response also links the actions of Yahweh and Pharaoh, this time through repetition of the phrase "a mighty hand" (*yād ḥăzāqâ;* see also 3:19). Yahweh's mighty hand on Pharaoh will force him to "drive out" Israel from his land with his own "mighty hand." Salvation, as an act of "driving out" (*gāraš*) by either Pharaoh or the Egyptians, is repeated by Yahweh in 11:1 and fulfilled in 12:39. The word also recalls the name Gershom (2:22) and the action of the shepherds prompting Moses to rescue the women at the well in Midian (2:17). Salvation in this instance is not Yahweh's direct liberation of the Israelites as either a defeat of the Egyptians or an escape from Egypt. It is, rather, Yahweh's ability to overwhelm the will of Pharaoh, so that he himself expels the Israelite people from the land of Egypt by "driving them out." The exodus as an expulsion of the Israelite people by the Egyptians is at the core of the tradition. It is noteworthy that it repeats in the Hellenistic histories, where the cause of the expulsion is the contamination of Egypt from the leprosy of the Israelites.[11]

COMMISSION OF MOSES IN EGYPT (6:2–7:7)

6:2 And God spoke to Moses, and said to him, "I am Yahweh. 3 And I appeared to Abraham, to Isaac, and to Jacob as El Shaddai. But my name Yahweh I did not make known to them. 4 And I also established my covenant with them to give to them the land of Canaan, the land of their sojourning in which they resided as aliens. 5 And I also heard the groan of the Israelites from the Egyptians forcing them to work. And I remembered my covenant. 6 Therefore, say to the Israelites, 'I am Yahweh, and I will bring you out from under the forced labor of Egypt. And I will rescue you from their work service. And I will redeem you with an outstretched arm and with great judgments. 7 And I will take you to myself as a people. And I will be to you as God. And you will know that I am Yahweh your God, who brought you from under the forced labor of Egypt. 8 I will bring you to the land, to which I raised my arm to give to Abraham, to Isaac, and to Jacob. And I will give it to you as an inheritance. I am Yahweh.'" 9 And Moses spoke thus to the Israelites. But they did not listen to Moses, because of a depressed spirit and hard work.

---

11. For a summary of the Hellenistic histories see Assmann, *Moses the Egyptian*, 23-54.

¹⁰*And Yahweh spoke to Moses, saying,* ¹¹*"Go and speak to Pharaoh, king of Egypt, so that he sends out the Israelites from his land."*

¹²*And Moses spoke before Yahweh, saying, "If the Israelites did not listen to me, how would Pharaoh listen to me, since I am uncircumcised of lips?"*

¹³*And Yahweh spoke to Moses and to Aaron. And he commanded them concerning the Israelites and Pharaoh, king of Egypt, to bring out the Israelites from the land of Egypt.*

¹⁴*These are the heads of their fathers' house: the sons of Reuben, the firstborn of Israel: Hanoch, Pallu, Hezron, and Carmi. These are the families of Reuben.* ¹⁵*And the sons of Simeon: Jemuel, Jamin, Ohad, Jachin, Zohar, and Shaul, the son of a Canaanite. These are the families of Simeon.* ¹⁶*And these are the names of the sons of Levi, by their genealogies: Gershon, Kohath, and Merari. And the years of life of Levi were 137 years.* ¹⁷*The sons of Gershon: Libni and Shimei, by their families.* ¹⁸*And the sons of Kohath: Amram, Izhar, Hebron, and Uzziel. And the years of life of Kohath were 133 years.* ¹⁹*And the sons of Merari: Mahli and Mushi. These are the families of the Levites by their genealogies.* ²⁰*And Amram took Jochebed, his aunt, to be his wife. And she bore for him Aaron and Moses. And the years of life of Amram were 137 years.* ²¹*And the sons of Izhar: Korah, Nepheg, and Zichri.* ²²*And the sons of Uzziel: Mishael, Elzaphan, and Sithri.* ²³*And Aaron took Elisheba, the daughter of Amminadab and the sister of Nahshon, to be his wife. And she bore for him Nadab and Abihu, Eleazar and Ithamar.* ²⁴*And the sons of Korah: Assir, Elkanah, and Abiasaph. These are the families of the Korahites.* ²⁵*And Eleazar, the son of Aaron, took for himself one of the daughters of Putiel to be his wife. And she bore for him Phinehas. These are the heads of the fathers of the Levites according to their families.*

²⁶*That is the very Aaron and Moses, to whom Yahweh said, "Bring out the Israelites from the land of Egypt by their regiments."* ²⁷*They are the ones who spoke to Pharaoh king of Egypt to bring out the Israelites from Egypt. That is the very Moses and Aaron.*

²⁸*And it happened on the day that Yahweh spoke to Moses in the land of Egypt,* ²⁹*Yahweh spoke to Moses, saying, "I am Yahweh. Speak to Pharaoh, king of Egypt, all that I speak to you."*

³⁰*And Moses said before Yahweh, "If I have uncircumcised lips, how will Pharaoh listen to me?"*

⁷:¹*And Yahweh said to Moses, "See, I made you a god to Pharaoh, and Aaron, your brother, will be your prophet.* ²*You will speak all that I will command you. And Aaron, your brother, will speak to Pharaoh, and he will send out the Israelites from his land.* ³*But I will harden the heart of Pharaoh, and I will multiply my signs and my wonders in the land of Egypt.* ⁴*But Pharaoh will not listen to you, and I will lay my hand on Egypt and I will bring out my*

regiment, my people, the Israelites, from the land of Egypt with great judg-
ments. ⁵*And the Egyptians will know that I am Yahweh when I stretch out my*
hand on Egypt. And I will bring out the Israelites from their midst."

⁶*And Moses and Aaron did as Yahweh commanded them. Thus they did.*
⁷*And Moses was a son of 80 years and Aaron was a son of 83 years when they*
spoke to Pharaoh.

Notes

6:3 *El Shaddai.* The LXX *theos ōn autōn,* "God, being of them," departs significantly
from the MT and Sam, thus eliminating the name El Shaddai. Wevers translates
the LXX: "I appeared to Abram and Isaac and Jacob (as) being their God."[1]

6:12 *how would Pharaoh listen.* The Hebrew particle *'êk* may signify a real question or
an exclamation (see *IBHS* §18.4d). When the particle is used with the imperfect it
indicates a reproach or even mocking (GKC §148). The syntax of *hēn . . . 'êk* also
occurs in 6:30.

6:12 *since I am uncircumcised of lips.* The LXX provides a more general description of
Moses' ability to communicate as lacking *logos* (*egō de alogos eimi;* "I am lacking in
eloquence").

6:26 *Yahweh.* The LXX reads, *ho theos,* "the God."

by their regiments. The LXX reads, *syn dynamei autōn,* "with their force/army," underscoring further the military imagery of the exodus from Egypt.

Commentary

The P account of the commission of Moses in Egypt (6:2–7:7) follows the structure of the wilderness account (3:1–4:17). It too separates between sections focused on the identity of God (6:2-9; cf. 3:1-15) and the authority of Moses (6:10–
7:7; cf. 3:16–4:17). The P account also identifies the Deity by mixing the genres
of divine self-revelation (6:2-5; cf. 3:1-8, 13-15) with the divine commission that
Moses rescue the Israelite people (6:6-8; cf. 3:9-12). The loss of the divine name
Yahweh through the breakdown of tradition in the Non-P History is reinterpreted in the P History as an evolution in the divine name from El Shaddai to
Yahweh. The mixing of the genres of divine self-revelation and the commission
of Moses allows for an identification of the God of the exodus with the patriarchal ancestors, as was also the case in the wilderness account.

The P account of Moses' commission also changes in emphasis from the
identity of God (6:2-9) to the authority of Moses (6:10–7:7). The transition is
signaled by Moses' statement that he is not a persuasive speaker. His objection
is stated twice (6:10-13 and 28-30) with the result that the authority of Moses is
developed in two stages following the pattern of his wilderness commission,
where his authority was developed first in relation to the elders (3:16–4:9) and

---

1. Wevers, *Notes,* 73.

Figure 7

Commission of Moses in the Wilderness: *Commission of Moses in Egypt:*
3:1–4:17   *6:2–7:7*

IDENTITY OF YAHWEH

Self-Revelation:	3:1-8	Self-Revelation:	6:2-5
Commission:	3:9-10	Commission:	6:6-8
Objection:	3:11		
Reassurance:	3:12		
Self-Revelation:	3:13-15		

AUTHORITY OF MOSES

Moses and the Elders:	3:16–4:9	Moses and Phinehas:	6:10-27
Moses and Aaron:	4:10-17	Moses and Aaron:	6:28–7:7

second in relationship to Aaron, considered a prophet (4:10-17). The first objection of Moses, "I am uncircumcised of lips" (6:12), is followed by a divine speech directed to Moses and Aaron, which, in turn, introduces the genealogy of Phinehas (6:14-27). The parallel structure between the two commissions of Moses suggests that Phinehas replaces the elders (3:16–4:9) as the representative of Mosaic authority in the P commission. The second objection of Moses, "If I have uncircumcised lips, how will Pharaoh listen to me?" (6:30), allows for the repetition of Aaron as the prophet of Moses (4:10-17), while changing the context of prophetic speech from the belief of the Israelite people in God and in Moses to the Egyptians' acknowledgment of Yahweh.

The diagram in figure 7 above illustrates the similar structure of the two commissions of Moses. The parallel structure of the two commissions of Moses suggests that the P account is dependent on the Non-P wilderness version. The genre of the commission is rooted in the prophetic office. It explores the authority of charismatic leadership, not the authority of the priest. The genre requires the audience to encounter directly the hero's power. They must be persuaded through experience. The interplay of objection and divine reassurance is equally crucial to the genre, since it clarifies that the charismatic power of the hero originates with God and not with the personal strength of the hero. Exodus 3:1–4:17 fulfills these expectations. The motif of faith requires the Israelites to experience firsthand Moses' signs of authority (4:1-9), while the objections of Moses underscore that his charismatic power derives from God, not from his personal strength.

The P account of Moses' commission follows the form of the genre while lacking the essential characteristics. The authority of Moses is not rooted in the prophetic office, it is not affirmed experientially through signs, and it does not require the faith of the Israelite people. Mosaic authority is noncharismatic in the P account of his commission. It is established objectively through the P genealogy. Phinehas represents the continuation of Mosaic authority in the P account of Moses' commission as a right of birth, not as an act of faith. The objective, noncharismatic character of Moses' commission is further evident in his objections. They fulfill the form of the genre of a commission, but again they lack function. The first objection of Moses has nothing to do with charismatic authority, or with the hero's fear in fulfilling a mission. It is a statement focused as much on past actions as on the fear of future inadequacies: "The Israelites would not listen to me; how then should Pharaoh heed me?" (6:12). The objection does not even warrant a direct divine response. There is no reassurance of divine presence linked to the objection of Moses. The second objection (6:30) allows for a redefinition of Aaron's prophetic function from the people of Israel (4:10-17) to the Egyptian nations (7:1-5). The comparisons suggest that the P author is following the prophetic genre of 3:1–4:17 to designate the Aaronide priesthood, not the elders, as the representatives of Mosaic authority, while defining prophetic authority in the larger setting of the nations.

Identity of Yahweh (6:2-9)

The name Yahweh is revealed to Moses a second time in this section, indicating a different author from the revelation in 3:1-6, 13-22. Exodus 6:2-9 is written by the P historian, who places the event in the land of Egypt, as compared to the Non-P historian's account of a wilderness confrontation between Moses and Yahweh. The section is unified by the repeated self-introduction of Yahweh (6:2, 6, 8), while also splitting its focus between the self-revelation of Yahweh (vv. 2-5) and the commission of Moses (vv. 6-8). The section concludes with the fulfillment of the commission by Moses (v. 9). The command (vv. 6-8) and fulfillment (v. 9) pattern is common in the P History (see its repeated use in Numbers 1–10).

The motifs in Exod 6:2-9 provide literary links to the larger P History, to the account of Moses' commission in the Non-P History, and to Ezekiel. The self-revelation of Yahweh (6:2), the theme of covenant (6:4), the divine memory (6:5), and the reference to the land of sojourning (6:4) recall the revelation to Abraham in Genesis 17 and the notice of divine awareness of the Israelites in Exod 2:23b-25. J. L. Ska has argued that the motifs of hard labor (6:5, 9) and slave labor (6:6, 7) relate the commission of Moses with the Non-P History (see 5:4, 5, 9, 11, 15). Ska also interprets the genre of 6:2-8 as a divine disputation, presupposing the initial failure of Moses in 5:1–6:1.[2]

---

2. Ska, "Place d'Ex 6,2-8"; idem, "Quelques remarques sur Pg," 97-107.

P. Weimar and J. Lust note a series of literary parallels to Ezekiel. Weimar notes that the passive construction of the verb "to be known" in 6:3, "I did not make myself known to them," is a common expression in Ezekiel (see especially Ezek 20:5).[3] Lust notes an increase in parallels to Ezekiel in the commission of Moses (Exod 6:6-8), beginning with the phrase "therefore say" *(lākēn 'ĕmōr)*, which often introduces a public oracle in Ezekiel (e.g., Ezek 11:16, 17; 12:23, 28; 20:30; 36:22). Other parallels include salvation as an act of redemption *(gā'al,* Exod 6:6; Ezek 11:15), the phrase "lifting the hand" (Exod 6:8; Ezek 20:28, 42; 47:13ff.), and reference to the land as a heritage *(môrāšâ;* Exod 6:8; Ezek 11:15; 25:4, 10; 33:24; 36:2, 3, 5).[4]

6:2-5 The self-revelation of Yahweh to Moses opens with the proclamation: "I am Yahweh" *('ănî yhwh)*. The phrase is a central motif in the P History and occurs three times in this section alone (6:2, 6, 8). The phrase has been researched broadly. M. Greenberg demonstrated that it may function as an oath and that similar expressions are attributed to deities throughout the ancient Near East. The Egyptian god Khnum is introduced with the phrase: "I am Khnum, your creator." The Assyrian goddess Ishtar states: "I am Ishtar, of Arbela, O Esarhaddon."[5] W. Zimmerli concluded that the phrase is a cultic formula in ancient Israel indicating the self-introduction of God as creator and savior.[6] The literature of the exilic prophet Second Isaiah indicates that the phrase is a reply to Israel's doubts about the divine ability to save (Isa 41:4; 44:6) and a response to the cry for help (Isa 42:8). In addition to its use in Second Isaiah, the self-introduction of Yahweh is also used frequently in Ezekiel, where it occurs 82 times (e.g., Ezek 5:13, 15, 17). The phrase is limited to one occurrence in the Non-P History (Exod 15:26).

The P historian employs the self-introduction of Yahweh in a variety of contexts. It recalls the self-revelation to Abraham, "I am El Shaddai" (Gen 17:1), indicating a progression in revelation. The self-introduction of Yahweh is sometimes accompanied with a further qualification, "your God" or "their God." The self-introduction of Yahweh occurs during the plagues (e.g., Exod 7:17; 8:22; 10:2), the instruction for Passover (12:12), the confrontation at the Red Sea (14:4, 18), on the wilderness journey, during the revelation of Sabbath (16:12), and frequently during the revelation of the tabernacle cult at Mount Sinai (e.g., 29:46; 31:13; Lev 11:44-45; 18:2, 4, 5, 6, 21, 30). On the basis of the wide range of occurrences K. Elliger concluded that the self-introduction of Yahweh confirms the power of God in deeds of salvation for the Israelites and in actions

---

3. Weimar, *Untersuchungen,* 102-3.
4. Lust, "Exodus 6,2-8," 214-22; Römer, *Israels Väter,* 504-6.
5. Greenberg, *Understanding Exodus,* 130-33.
6. W. Zimmerli, "I Am Yahweh," in *I Am Yahweh* (trans. D. W. Stott; ed. W. Brueggemann; Atlanta: John Knox, 1982), 1-28.

against their enemies.[7] This is certainly the case in the present passage, where Yahweh affirms his intention to save the Israelites (Exod 6:2-8) and, in the process, to overpower Pharaoh (6:11-13, 29; 7:5). Finally, Sarna has rightly noted that the self-introduction of Yahweh does not indicate a new revelation of the name Yahweh.[8] Its use in ancient Near Eastern religions confirms that the self-introduction of a deity assumes a prior knowledge of the god on the part of the recipient. This is also true in the P History. Many of the occurrences of the formula imply that either Pharaoh (e.g., 8:22) or the Israelites (e.g., 10:2) know the name Yahweh.

Yet in 6:2-5 the P author does intend for the self-introduction of Yahweh to function as a new revelation of the divine name. God states that the ancestors did not know the name Yahweh but were limited in their knowledge of God to the divine name El Shaddai, translated in NIV and NRSV as "God Almighty," and in NJPS as "El Shaddai." The meaning of the divine name El Shaddai has long puzzled scholars. The treatment of the name in the LXX, *theos ōn autōn,* "God, being of them," indicates that the name presented a problem already to the ancient writers and translators. El means "God," and may indicate the high god in the Canaanite pantheon. "Shaddai" may indicate a connection with mountains,[9] suggesting the translation "God of the mountain," although its more primary meaning is "breast." Cross has traced connections to an Amorite storm god, Ilu Amurru, and to the Canaanite god El.[10] The name refers to a group of gods *(šdyn)* in the Balaam text from Deir ʿAlla, where they appear to influence the weather. Yet neither etymology nor comparative religion provides a clear avenue for interpretation. The larger context of the P History provides better clues.

In the P History El Shaddai is a distinct manifestation of God to the patriarchs Abram and Jacob. The creator God, Elohim (Genesis 1), appeared to the ancestors as El Shaddai when they were resident aliens, making covenant and promising them a land of their own. The result of God's appearance to Abram and Jacob is the transformation of the human participants, which is signaled by their change of names: Abram becomes Abraham and Jacob becomes Israel. The first appearance of God as El Shaddai is to Abram in Gen 17:1. The story begins with the formula of the divine self-introduction: "I am El Shaddai." The manifestation of God as El Shaddai to Abram is associated with covenant: "I will confirm my covenant between me and you." El Shaddai promises Abram both progeny and the land of Canaan, which results in his change of name to

---

7. K. Elliger, "Ich bin der Herr — euer Gott," in *Kleine Schriften zum Alten Testament* (TBü 32; Munich: Chr. Kaiser, 1966), 213-16.

8. Sarna, *Exodus,* 31.

9. See Houtman, *Exodus,* 1:100-101.

10. Cross, *Canaanite Myth and Hebrew Epic,* 52-60.

Abraham, meaning he would be a father of many nations. El Shaddai does not appear to Isaac. Instead Isaac repeats the covenant promise of El Shaddai to Jacob (28:3), who later receives a similar revelation as Abraham, only this time at Bethel (35:9-11).[11] The revelation of El Shaddai to Jacob begins with the same formula of the divine self-introduction: "I am El Shaddai." The promises of progeny and land are repeated to Jacob, who then also undergoes a name change from Jacob to Israel.

The revelation of El Shaddai to the patriarchs provides the background for interpreting the revelation of the name Yahweh to Moses in the P account of his commission. There are a number of similarities between the appearance of El Shaddai to the ancestors and that of Yahweh to Moses. The appearance of Yahweh to Moses is in the form of the divine self-introduction, "I am Yahweh," recalling the earlier appearances of El Shaddai to the patriarchs Abram and Jacob. The appearance of Yahweh is also associated with covenant and the promise of land, providing a parallel in content to the theophany of El Shaddai to the ancestors. The revelation of the name Yahweh to Moses is based explicitly on the prior covenant with the ancestors. The Deity states to Moses that it is the divine memory of covenant (Exod 6:5) that has prompted the appearance of Yahweh to Moses. The Deity also tells Moses that the content of the covenant is the promise of land (6:4). Thus there is continuity in form (the divine self-introduction) and in theme (the promise of land, covenant) between the appearance of El Shaddai to the ancestors and Yahweh to Moses.

But there is also an important difference. The Deity undergoes a change of name in the commission of Moses, from El Shaddai to Yahweh, rather than the human heroes in the stories of the ancestors. Moses does not undergo a change of name like Abram (Abraham) or Jacob (Israel), when El Shaddai made covenant with them and promised them land. Rather, in remembering the covenant with the ancestors, the Deity, El Shaddai, now becomes Yahweh: "I am Yahweh. I appeared to Abraham, to Isaac, and to Jacob as El Shaddai. But my name Yahweh I did not make known to them." What accounts for this reversal in the story of the divine self-introduction to Moses? Why must the Deity undergo a change of name rather that the human hero? The clearest reason for the reversal is the Israelite oppression in Egypt. The slave status of the Israelites is a new social condition, which draws out a new dimension of the Deity in the P History. El Shaddai must become Yahweh in order to fulfill the covenant promises to the ancestors, which now required the leading of the Israelite people out of Egyptian slavery. Yahweh is not a distinct God from El Shaddai according to

11. Jacob repeats the name El Shaddai as a blessing (Gen 43:14) and he refers to the revelation of Gen 35:11 (Gen 48:3). El Shaddai also occurs in the poem entitled "The Blessing of Jacob," specifically in the blessing of Joseph (Gen 49:22-26, esp. v. 25).

the P author any more than El Shaddai was distinct from the creator, Elohim, or Abraham was a different character from Abram. Rather the groaning of the Israelites under slave labor (2:23b-25; 6:5) has called forth a new aspect of the creator God, Elohim, and the covenantal God, El Shaddai, now signified by the name Yahweh, whose characteristics are described in vv. 6-9.[12] The common theme in the names Elohim, El Shaddai, and Yahweh is the promise of land.

6:6-9 Yahweh's commission to Moses in 6:6-8 is framed with the self-introduction, "I am Yahweh" (6:6, 8). The content of the commission is a series of seven predictions by Yahweh that define the character of the new name, Yahweh. Each announcement is a divine action to save the Israelites. The number seven is significant in the P history often symbolizing completeness. God creates in seven days (Genesis 1), Moses ascends the mountain to receive the plans for the tabernacle on the seventh day (Exod 24:15-18), God delivers seven speeches to Moses to describe the plans for the tabernacle (Exodus 25–31), and the central month for worship in the P liturgical calendar is the seventh (Leviticus 23; Numbers 28–29). The seven acts of salvation in Exod 6:6-8 are stated in the first person, "I am," or "I will," recalling the self-introduction of Yahweh and providing definition for the new name. When read together they outline the salvation of the Israelites from slave laborers to residents in their own land.

1. I will bring you out from under the yoke of the Egyptians.
2. I will rescue you from slavery.
3. I will redeem you with an outstretched arm and with mighty acts of judgment.
4. I will take you as my own people.
5. I will be your God.
6. I will bring you to the land I swore with uplifted hand to give to Abraham, to Isaac, and to Jacob.
7. I will give it to you as a possession.

The first three statements provide insight into the character of Yahweh as savior. The P author employs words and phrases that are closely associated with the Israelites' exodus from Egypt. Some themes repeat from the wilderness commission of Moses. The declaration of Yahweh "to bring out" the Israelites from Egypt, employing Hebrew *yaṣa'* (in the Hiphil), is a standard reference to the Israelite liberation from Egyptian slavery and a central theme of the wilder-

---

12. See the discussion on El Shaddai by A. de Pury, "Abraham: The Priestly Writer's 'Ecumenical' Ancestor," in *Rethinking the Foundations: Historiography in the Ancient World and in the Bible: Essays in Honour of John Van Seters* (ed. S. L. McKenzie and T. Römer; BZAW 294; Berlin: de Gruyter, 2000), 163-82.

ness commission of Moses (see 3:10-12; see the commentary on chap. 13). Salvation from Egyptian oppression as a divine "rescue" (*nāṣōṣ* in the Hiphil) also occurs in 3:8. Salvation as "redemption" (*gāʾōṣā* by God is a new theme, indicating a restoration of lost property (see the one other occurrence in 15:13). The term may reflect the context of covenant stressed in the P History. The fourth and fifth statements anticipate the revelation of God at Mount Sinai in the wilderness, since it is the location where the Israelites become the people of God and where they finally achieve knowledge of God (29:44-46). The final two statements provide continuity with the past covenant to the ancestors, recalling El Shaddai's promise of land, while also pointing the reader ahead to the conclusion of the P History.

Moses fulfills the commission immediately in v. 9. But the Israelites reject the message based on their present experience (6:9) as compared to 4:31, where they believe in Moses and worship Yahweh. Their rejection sets the stage for a change in theme from the identity of God to the authority of Moses.

Authority of Moses (6:10–7:7)

The focus on the authority of Moses in the P version of his commission arises from his objection to the commission, which parallels the wilderness version in the Non-P History. The point of focus changes, however, from the faith of the elders to the obedience of Pharaoh. The section separates into three parts: the commission and Moses' objection (6:10-13), the genealogy of Phinehas (6:14-27), and a repetition of the commission and Moses' objection (6:28–7:7).

6:10-13 Moses receives a second commission in the P History. His first commission was directed to the Israelites: "Therefore, say to the Israelites" (6:6-8). The second commission is now aimed at Pharaoh: "Go and speak to Pharaoh" (6:10-11). The double commission follows the pattern of the Non-P History, in which a first commission of Moses (3:9-12) was followed by a second focused on the elders (3:16-22). The P History follows the two-part structure of the commission of Moses in the Non-P History, but changes the focus in the second commission from the elders to Pharaoh.

The role of Aaron represents a further change between the Non-P and P Histories. Whereas Aaron was included at the end of Moses' commission in the Non-P History in the role of prophet, in the P History Aaron is embedded in the commission from the outset, replacing the leadership role of the elders in Non-P History. The change in leadership is signaled in the objection of Moses in v. 12, when he claims his inability to speak persuasively, which in the P History is directed not to the elders but to Pharaoh: "If the Israelites did not listen to me, how would Pharaoh listen to me, since I am uncircumcised of lips?" The objection creates a repetition with the commission in the Non-P History (4:10).

A closer reading suggests that the P History is dependent on the structure of the Non-P History, since the objection has no function or force in 6:12. Indeed, the Deity does not even respond to it. Instead, the following verse simply assumes the presence of Aaron in the commission of Moses: "And Yahweh spoke to Moses and Aaron" (v. 13). The result is that the commission of Moses in the P History is also the commission of Aaron. The two characters are interwoven into a single office by genealogy.

6:14-27   The prominent role of the genealogy in the commission of Moses provides a clue into the nature of Mosaic authority in the P History. The authority of Moses is not developed through charismatic signs of power experienced directly by the Israelites. Mosaic authority in the P History is rather the objective genealogy of Moses, where the focus is on Aaron and more particularly his grandson Phinehas. The genealogy may consist of portions from several distinct texts, all of which have been woven into the present narrative context. The call of Moses and Aaron (6:13, 28-29) and the objection of Moses (6:12, 30) frame the genealogy (6:14-27), providing narrative context. The bracketing emphasizes Aaron, not Moses, suggesting that the purpose of the genealogy is to legitimate his descendants as the official priesthood of the Yahweh cult, and thus as the tradition bearers of Mosaic authority.

There is also a tension in the genealogy between vv. 14-15 and vv. 16-25. The former section provides the genealogy of Jacob's first two sons, while the latter portion develops the genealogy of Levi through Phinehas. The different points of view may indicate that previously independent genealogies are combined in the P History. The second genealogy, vv. 16-25, represents the traditional division of the Levitical clans into the three houses of Gershon, Kohath, and Merari. This structure is the most prominent tradition of the Levites in the Hebrew Bible. It is first stated in the family genealogy of Gen 46:11. It reappears in the census of the Levites in Numbers 3 and again in 1 Chr 5:27–6:34. The standard three-part division of the house of Levi originates in the exilic period. The Hebrew Bible has preserved a glimpse into an older structure of the Levitical priesthood in Num 26:58a, where the house of Levi is separated into five clans, rather than three: Libnites, Hebronites, Mahlites, Mushites, and Korahites. The divergent genealogies have given rise to research on the historical development of the Israelite priesthood in the preexilic period and the identification of the priestly clans represented by the distinct descendants. The Mushite clan in particular has attracted special interest as possibly representing the priestly line of Moses. Wellhausen, followed by K. Mühlenbrink, speculated that Moses and the Mushite priesthood were associated with the Shiloh cult.[13]

---

13. Wellhausen, *Prolegomena*, 151-61; K. Mühlenbrink, "Die levitischen Überlieferung des Alten Testaments," *ZAW* 12 (1934): 184-231.

Cross extended this line of research, identifying preexilic conflicts between Aaronide and Mushite priests that are preserved in the stories of the wilderness (Numbers 12, 16–17; Lev 10:1-7).[14]

Genealogies play a prominent role in ancient historiography. Ancient king lists evolved into more complex genealogies in order to indicate the origin of a people and the evolution of their city, tribe, or nation.[15] Genealogy in ancient history writing is unlike contemporary genealogy, which seeks historical accuracy. Ancient genealogies are socially constructed fictions intended to explain relationships or to legitimate the status of an individual hero or a particular group. For this reason two genealogies of the same person may vary greatly depending on the aim of the author.

For example, the Non-P (Gen 4:17-24) and the P (5:1-32) authors provide different genealogies of Cain to conform to their distinct views of history. The Non-P author provides a dark view of history as increasing in violence. The evolution of violence is evident in the genealogy of Cain. Although his descendants produce all aspects of higher culture including the construction of cities (Cain, Enoch), the musical arts (Jubal), and metallurgy (Tubal-cain), the Non-P author concludes that the accomplishments of civilization rest in the end on violence, symbolized by Lamech, who boasts of killing a boy: "I have killed a man for wounding me, a young man for striking me" (4:23). The P author sees more hope in history and reaffirms the image of God in humans through the same genealogy. He begins the genealogy: "When God created humans he made them in the likeness of God" (5:1). The lingering image of God in humanity results in a different portrait of Cain's ancestor Lamech. In the P genealogy he does not boast about killing a boy, instead he looks for the relief from suffering through his son Noah: "Out of the ground that Yahweh curses this one shall bring us relief from our work and from the toil of our hand" (5:29). The Gospels of Matthew (Matt 1:1-17) and Luke (Luke 3:23-38) also provide conflicting genealogies of Jesus. The author of Matthew relates Jesus to Abraham, thereby emphasizing his Jewish identity, while the author of Luke takes his genealogy back to Adam to underscore the universal significance of Jesus. The genealogies not only focus on different origins in tracing the identity of Jesus, they also run in opposite directions with differences in ancestry after the generation of David.

Ancient genealogies are constructed to serve a larger literary and sociological purpose for their authors. The social background of the genealogies in the P History suggests that the loss of land in the exile is important and that the emergence of the Aaronide priesthood into a leadership role is most central of

14. Cross, *Canaanite Myth and Hebrew Epic*, 195-215.
15. See the study by R. R. Wilson, *Genealogy and History in the Biblical World* (Yale Near Eastern Researches 7; New Haven: Yale University Press, 1977).

all. The genre of the genealogy assumes a prominent role in the P History. The P History is organized by a genealogy, described as *tôlĕdôt*, meaning "the begettings," deriving from the Hebrew verb *yālad*, "to beget." The history begins with the genealogy of heaven and earth (Gen 2:4) and of the first human, Adam (5:1), before narrowing in scope through Noah (6:9), Shem (10:1), Terah, the father of Abraham (11:27), Isaac (25:19), Jacob (37:2), and finally ending with Aaron and Moses (Num 3:1). The use of genealogy to provide such an overarching structure indicates its important role in the composition of the P History.[16] The interpretation of Exod 6:14-27 must also be placed within the larger structure of the P History. The specific individuals mentioned in a genealogy, their relationships, and any additional commentary provided by the author aid in the interpretation.

A genealogy is best interpreted backward. Genealogies are written from the perspective of the final character, usually to legitimate that person or the group represented by the person. The genealogy structuring the P History ends with Aaron and Moses (Num 3:1). Although Aaron precedes Moses, he is the central person, indicating that the P History is written with an eye on the Israelite priesthood. The genealogy beginning with the heavens and the earth (Gen 2:4) and the first human, Adam (Gen 5:1), is actually the family tree of the Aaronide priests, legitimating their role as leaders in the Israelite cult.

The genealogy in Exod 6:14-27 also appears to be focused on Moses and Aaron. Verse 13 states that Moses and Aaron received a commission from Yahweh, while v. 26 mentions both characters at the close of the genealogy, but in reverse order, emphasizing Aaron over Moses. Most commentators have noted the emphasis on Aaron, concluding that the aim of the P author is to legitimate Aaron as a hero of the exodus along with Moses. This certainly appears to be the case. But the last person named in the genealogy is Phinehas, the grandson of Aaron.

Commentators suggest that Phinehas is included to introduce all the high priests that are mentioned in the Pentateuch. Phinehas follows Aaron and Eleazar in the office of the high priest in the Pentateuch, assuming leadership at the close of the wilderness journey, when he wages a holy war against the Midianites (Numbers 31). His inclusion in the genealogy may carry an additional message about the Midianites. The indigenous nations of Canaan represent a religious threat to the Israelites according to the Non-P author (see Exod 3:8). They must be destroyed. But the wilderness nation of the Midianites assumes a very different position. The Midianites played a central religious role in the Non-P historian's account of Moses' wilderness commission (2:15-22; 3:1–4:26). By extending the genealogy of Aaron to Phinehas, the P author intro-

---

16. See Blenkinsopp, *Pentateuch*, 58-60, 99-109.

Figure 8

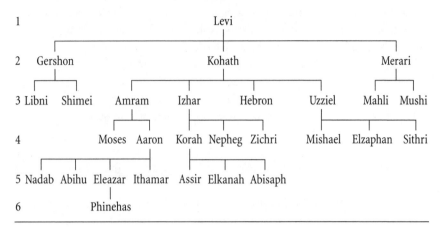

duces the character who will destroy the Midianites for polluting the cult of Yahweh. The genealogy of Phinehas may contain the P author's commentary on the Non-P version of Moses' commission, especially the role of the Midianites as allies of Yahweh.

The structure of the genealogy and the additional commentary included by the P author affirm the central focus on the Aaronide priesthood. The basic form of a genealogy consists of names and the intergenerational relationship between them. For example, the P author introduces the ancestor Levi as having three sons, Gershon, Kohath, and Merari (6:16), and Gershon as having two sons, Libni and Shimei (6:17). When the genealogy of Levi is read from this limited perspective, six generations emerge (see fig. 8 above).

The structure indicates the important position of Phinehas. He is the only character mentioned in the sixth generation of descendants from Levi. Additional information provided by the P author further accentuates his position. The P author provides the age of three characters, Levi (137 years), Kohath (133 years), and Amram (137 years), emphasizing the ancestry of Aaron. Then, beginning with the father of Aaron, Amram, the P author also includes the name of the wife: Amram married Jochebed, his father's sister; Aaron married Elisheba, the daughter of Amminadab and the sister of Nahshon; and Eleazar married one of the daughters of Putiel. The recording of the mothers further accentuates the status of Phinehas.

When read against the background of the exile, Phinehas, the sixth generation, represents the postexilic community, since the fourth and fifth generations are those who undertake the wilderness journey, which signifies the experience of the exile. Aaron represents the generation of the exodus itself, those who begin the wilderness journey but fail to enter the promised land. Eleazar is the high priest for the second generation who journey in the wilderness and enter the promised land. Phinehas is the high priest for the third generation of Israelites who must create a new life in the promised land. This is the audience of the P author.

Scholars have raised two further questions about the selectivity of characters in the genealogy of 6:14-25. The first is the insertion of information in the fifth generation of descendants about the Korahite clans, Assir, Elkanah, and Abiasaph (6:24). The fifth generation represents the second generation of Israelites who journey in the wilderness. Moses, Aaron, and Korah are part of the fourth generation, representing those who experienced the exodus from Egypt but lost the gift of the promised land. Korah is important in the P History because he represented the most significant challenge to the Aaronide priests from within the clan of Levi. During the wilderness journey, the Korahites claim equal status with Aaron (Numbers 16), requiring the intercession of Yahweh to authenticate the role of Aaron as high priest (Numbers 17). Their inclusion in the genealogy may be related to the conflict in Numbers 16. The inclusion of Phinehas, as the only representative of the sixth generation, reinforces the conclusion of the narrative in Numbers 16–17, that the Aaronide line of priests are specially chosen by Yahweh as the representatives of Mosaic authority.

The second puzzle concerning the characters in the genealogy is the inclusion of Reuben (Exod 6:14) and Simeon (6:15). The P writer listed all the tribes at the outset of the book of Exodus (1:1-5), raising the question of why only the two tribes of Reuben and Simeon are now incorporated in 6:14-27. The selection may be the result of the birth order of the sons: Levi is the third son, after Reuben and Simeon. Another possible reason may be the role of the Reubenites in the subsequent wilderness journey, where the exclusive role of Aaron as priest is challenged. The Reubenites Dathan and Abiram are included in the Korahite challenge to the leadership of Aaron (Numbers 16). Perhaps their inclusion in the genealogy is intended to point to the same story, in which case the inclusion of Reubenites is a polemic by the P author. But this leaves the tribe of Simeon as a problem, since no persons from this tribe are mentioned in Numbers 16.

A sociological reason for the inclusion of Reuben and Simeon may be indicated in the comment by the P author that their descendants are the "heads of their fathers' house" *(roʾšê bêt-ʾăbōtām)*. The Hebrew phrase *bêt ʾābōt* translates literally as "house of fathers," not "families" as in NIV. The NRSV translates, "ancestral houses"; NJPS, "respective clans." The word "family" is also used in the genealogy, "These are the families of Reuben" (6:14), and "These are the families of the Levites, according to their genealogies" (6:19). The confusion in translation arises from the fluidity of the words to describe overlapping social groups. Both the words *mišpāḥâ* (usually translated "family") and *bayit* (lit.

"house") can describe small social or kinship units. The key for interpreting the *bêt 'ābōt*, however, is not translation, but the social group represented by the phrase, especially in the postexilic period, the time of the P History.

J. Weinberg concluded that in the Second Temple, or postexilic, period the term *bêt 'ābōt* designated lay groups organized around temples for economic purposes. He concluded that the *bêt 'ābōt* signified an agnate group, meaning members related by male descent. But such kinship relationships could be either real or fictional. Thus genealogies tracing the "descendants" in a *bêt 'ābōt* may indicate a social coalition of unrelated individuals, rather than a family tree. The tendency, writes Freedman, is for such groups to blend into kinship groups over time.[17] Membership in a *bêt 'ābōt*, according to Weinberg, was essential for economic prosperity and for successful leadership. The books of Ezra and Nehemiah indicate that such temple communities or *bêt 'ābōt* assumed a prominent role in Judah at the time of the P author.[18] The research suggests that the P writer may be addressing such a temple community, indicating a relationship between the Aaronide priests and the lay leadership of the *bêt 'ābōt*, composed of clans identified with Reuben and Simeon. This interpretation moves in the opposite direction of the previous solution to the selective listing of the two tribes in the genealogy. The nonpriestly members are not the object of a polemic, but members of a coalition with the Aaronide priests.

6:28–7:7 The final section of the P account of Moses' commission begins with a series of repetitions between 6:10-13 and 6:28–7:2. The repetitions include the divine command that Moses go to Pharaoh (6:10 and 29) and Moses' objection that he is unable to speak (6:12 and 30). The divine response to the first objection simply includes Aaron in the commission, "Yahweh spoke to Moses and Aaron" (6:13). Thus when God outlines the role of Aaron as prophet after the second objection of Moses (7:1-2), it appears out of place. The genealogy has already underscored the important role of Aaron, even reversing the order of their names in 6:26: "It is this same Aaron and Moses to whom Yahweh said." The role of Aaron as prophet in 7:1-2 suggests that the P historian is reinterpreting the Non-P History. The demonstration of Mosaic authority in Aaron is no longer the ability to teach the law to the Israelites (so 4:13-16). It is rather Aaron's ability to mediate the message of liberation to Pharaoh (7:2). In the P History this mediation is in the form of magical actions set over against the Egyptian magicians.

The commission of Moses in the P History concludes with the divine prediction of the outcomes of events (7:3-5), creating a counterpart to the similar

---

17. Private communication.

18. J. Weinberg, *The Citizen-Temple Community* (trans. Daniel L. Smith-Christopher; JSOTSup 151; Sheffield: Sheffield Academic Press, 1992).

speech to Moses in the wilderness (4:21-23). The prediction includes Pharaoh's resistance to the commission as a hard heart, causing signs and wonders, judgment upon the Egyptians, the exodus of the Israelite people, and the Egyptians' acknowledgment of Yahweh.

The P author's account of the hardening of Pharaoh's heart introduces two new interpretations of the exodus. First, the exodus will occur with acts of judgment, mighty deeds that prove the power of Yahweh. Similar motifs occur in Ezekiel (Ezek 14:21). The "judgment" of Yahweh is most likely a reference to the death of the Egyptian firstborn, since the P author repeats the motif in describing this event (see Exod 12:12). Second, the exodus will bring the Egyptians to the knowledge of God. Yahweh's demand for recognition is stated with the formula consisting of the verb "to know" (*yāda'*) used in conjunction with the causal particle "that" *(kî)*, resulting in the phrase: "So that you/they may know that." Zimmerli concluded that recognition of Yahweh is always preceded by concrete divine actions that are public and momentary. These actions provided the basis for recognition.[19] In the P History the public actions are the plagues aimed at the Egyptians. The theme of knowledge is carried through the confrontation between Yahweh and Pharaoh. One aim of the plagues and the exodus in the P History is to bring Pharaoh and the Egyptians to the knowledge of Yahweh (see 7:5, 17; 8:10, 22; 9:14; 10:2; 11:7), which is fulfilled with Yahweh's victory at the Red Sea (14:8, 18).

Exodus 7:6-7 states that Moses and Aaron execute the divine command at the ages of eighty and eighty-three, respectively. The P author often provides the age of heroes at important junctures in their lives. Noah is five hundred years old when he has children before the flood (Gen 5:32) and six hundred years old at the end of the flood (8:13). Abram is ninety-nine years old when God appears to him as El Shaddai (17:1), one hundred at the birth of Isaac (21:5), and one hundred and seventy-five when he dies (25:7). Jacob dies at age one hundred and forty-seven (47:28) and Joseph at one hundred and ten (50:22). Cassuto notes that the age of Moses in the P History creates tension with his portrayal in Exodus 2, which suggests a younger person.

---

19. W. Zimmerli, "Knowledge of God According to the Book of Ezekiel," in *I Am Yahweh*, 71-87.

Conflict (7:8–15:21)

INTRODUCTION

CENTRAL THEMES

Exodus 7:8–15:21 returns to the theme of power first introduced in chaps. 1–2. In the opening chapters of Exodus the power of God was evident only indirectly through the fertility of the Israelites, a lingering effect of the divine promise to the ancestors. The population explosion of the Israelites allowed the biblical authors to explore a range of human responses to the power of God without introducing Yahweh into the story as an active character. Pharaoh emerged as a sharply defined character in chaps. 1–2 opposed to the power of God. He perceived himself to be shrewd, he feared the growth of the Israelites, and he instituted acts of oppression to combat the power of the divine promise at work in the growth of the Israelite population.

The opposition between Yahweh and Pharaoh intensifies in Exodus from an indirect to a direct confrontation. In chaps. 1–2 the tension between the two characters was only indirect. The women, including the midwives, Moses' mother and sister, and even Pharaoh's daughter, represent the power of the divine promise over against Pharaoh, and their actions as agents of God are often performed unwittingly, since only the midwives are explicitly described as fearing God. The women resist Pharaoh by playing subversive roles in undermining his power. Their actions created an ironic and satirical story demonstrating the ease by which Pharaoh's plans could be subverted.

Exodus 7:8–15:21 narrates the direct conflict between Yahweh and Pharaoh over the fate of the Israelites as a war between kings. The participation of Yahweh in war suggests that the story of the exodus is in the tradition of holy war. F. Schwally stated that Israelite warfare was holy because the people saw

176

themselves as a federation constituted around the Warrior God Yahweh. Thus Israel was Yahweh's military host. The act of warfare was sacramental, while war itself was closely linked to cultic practices.[1] The closing hymns in Exodus 15 certainly celebrate the power of Yahweh through the imagery of war. Yahweh destroys "the horse and its rider," hurling them "into the sea" (15:21). Yahweh is even proclaimed to be a "warrior" (15:3). Also the actions of Yahweh become closely linked with worship practices, including the Passover and the Feast of Unleavened Bread (chap. 12). The Israelite act of "despoiling" the Egyptians also involves the people in war as Yahweh's military host taking booty after a victory (12:35-36). The Israelites are even described as a military host, "armed for battle," as they march out of Egypt (14:8). These motifs reinforce an interpretation of the exodus as a story of holy war.

Yet the conflict between Yahweh and Pharaoh also departs from the tradition of holy war in a significant way. Holy war focuses on the people of Israel. The act of war probes their courage and faith to participate in a life-and-death situation trusting that Yahweh fights along with them. The book of Joshua provides an example of holy war. Joshua is called to be courageous and not to fear as the leader of the Israelites (Josh 1:6). Throughout the stories of war in Joshua the focus is on the Israelite nation and their faithfulness in following Yahweh against more powerful nations.

The story of the exodus focuses on Yahweh, not the Israelites. Once Moses employs a war oracle, encouraging the Israelites not to fear the approaching Egyptian army (Exod 14:13). But for the most part the story of the exodus is not about the faithfulness and courage of the Israelites. Exodus 3:1–4:17 indicates that the "faith" of the Israelites, and along with it holy war, are themes reserved for the wilderness setting and eventually the land of Canaan. The land of Egypt is the setting for Yahweh's deliverance. Salvation from Egypt is certainly a story of war, but the conflict is between Yahweh and Pharaoh, not between the Israelites and the Egyptians. The focus on Yahweh does not conform to other stories of holy war, where the Israelites assume center stage (e.g., Numbers 31; Deuteronomy 20; Joshua 6–9).

The war between Yahweh and Pharaoh takes on epic proportions. The plagues are both weapons of war and signs of Yahweh's power over nature aimed at defeating Pharaoh. The plagues progress through the elements of nature, from water (the snake or sea monster) to land (gnats from the earth), and finally to air (boils from ashes thrown into the air) as Yahweh assaults Pharaoh. Yahweh emerges in the sequence of the plagues as the Storm God hurling hail-

---

1. F. Schwally, *Der heilige Krieg im alten Israel* (Semitische Kriegsaltertümer 1; Leipzig: Dieterich, 1901). For further discussion on the topic of holy war see G. von Rad, *Holy War in Ancient Israel* (trans. M. J. Dawn; Grand Rapids: Eerdmans, 1991), 39-134.

stones on the land of Egypt. When the weapons of nature fail to persuade Pharaoh to release the Israelites, Yahweh narrows and intensifies the attack, first by killing the Egyptian firstborn and then by destroying the Egyptian army in the Red Sea. The Song of the Sea interprets the theme of power, declaring that Yahweh is a warrior, worthy of praise, because of his victory over Pharaoh.

The focus on Yahweh allows the biblical authors to explore how God exercises power in the world. The introduction of characters in Exod 3:1–7:7 provides the framework for the biblical authors to explore the nature of Yahweh's power through the divine interaction with the secondary characters. Two perspectives on power loom in the background.[2] The first is that Yahweh exerts power unilaterally in the world. From this perspective Yahweh is the only active agent in the story, forcing his will on all persons in order to achieve his goals. The will of God is not influenced by other characters. Yahweh simply forges ahead in the story, independently, to defeat Pharaoh and to achieve the liberation of the Israelites. The secondary characters are incapable of influencing God or the outcome of events. The exercise of unilateral power is like fate, since the outcome of events is predetermined by Yahweh. As a result Yahweh does not undergo change in the events of the story.

The second perspective on power is that Yahweh exerts his will only in relationship with other characters. From this perspective Yahweh is both an active force in the world and influenced by other characters and events. The response of Pharaoh, the intercession of Moses, and the role of the Israelites are capable of changing the outcome of the story, because Yahweh exerts power in relationship to other characters. When power is exerted through relationships the will of God undergoes change, depending on the events in the unfolding story.[3]

The two perspectives on power raise a series of interpretive questions that I will deal with in the commentary. Does Yahweh exert force independently of humans in the story of the exodus, making the outcome of events predetermined? Is the exodus a story about fate with the ending firmly fixed at the outset? Or do other characters interact with God in the story of the exodus and in the process influence the outcome of events? Are Moses, Pharaoh, the Israelites, and the Egyptians able to shape the outcome of the story by how they respond

---

2. For discussion of the two forms of power, unilateral and relational, see B. Loomer, "Two Kinds of Power," *Criterion* 15 (1976): 12-29. For more broadly based discussion of power in the Hebrew Bible see N. Lohfink, "Literaturverzeichnis," in *Gewalt und Gewaltlosigkeit im Alten Testament* (ed. N. Lohfink; QD 96; Freiburg: Herder, 1983), 15-50; J. P. M. Walsh, *The Mighty from Their Thrones: Power in the Biblical Tradition* (OBT 21; Philadelphia: Fortress, 1987). For a more detailed study of power in the story of the exodus see T. B. Dozeman, *God at War: Power in the Exodus Tradition* (New York: Oxford University Press, 1996).

3. See Loomer, "Two Kinds of Power."

to God, making Yahweh open to change through time? These questions probe the nature of Yahweh's power in the world, the central theme of the following commentary on 7:8–15:21.

AUTHORS

Travel Notices

The two commissions of Moses in 3:1–7:7 provide the starting point for identifying the Non-P and the P Histories in 7:8–15:21. Geography emerged as an important difference in the two commissions. The Non-P History locates the commission of Moses in the wilderness (3:1–4:18), the P account in the land of Egypt (6:2–7:7). The literary design of the commissions indicates the active role of setting in the distinct interpretations of Moses' commission, the reason for his objection, and the goal of the exodus. The diagram in figure 9 on page 180 summarizes the different interpretations of the commission of Moses in the Non-P and P Histories.

In the Non-P History Moses is alone in the wilderness to receive his commission. The content of his commission is aimed at the Israelites, especially the elders (3:16). Moses' objection centers on their lack of belief in his authority (4:1, 5, 8, 9). Yahweh predicts that the exodus will bring the Israelites into the wilderness, where they will acquire faith in Moses.

In the P History the commission of Moses occurs in the land of Egypt. Moses remains the recipient of the commission, but Aaron is also closely associated with the call. The genealogy at the center of the commission is of Phinehas, the grandson of Aaron, not Moses (6:14-25). The objection of Moses is not about the lack of belief by the Israelites or the elders, but the resistance of Pharaoh to the demand that he release the people (6:30). The goal of the exodus remains the liberation of the Israelites from the land of Egypt. But the P author introduces a new and more polemical motif aimed at Pharaoh and the Egyptians: they must recognize that Yahweh is the God ruling over the land of Egypt (7:5).

The setting continues to influence the presentation of the exodus and the wilderness journey in the Non-P and P Histories. Both histories track the departure of the Israelite people from Egypt into the wilderness with travel notices described by Coats and later by G. I. Davies as "itineraries."[4] The organiza-

---

4. See G. W. Coats, "The Wilderness Itinerary," *CBQ* 34 (1972): 135-52; G. I. Davies, *The Way of the Wilderness: A Geographical Study of the Wilderness Itineraries in the Old Testament* (SOTSMS 5; Cambridge: Cambridge University Press, 1979); M. D. Oblath, *The Exodus Itinerary Sites: Their Locations from the Perspective of the Biblical Sources* (Studies in Biblical Literature 55; New York: Peter Lang, 2004), 77-169.

Figure 9

Commission of Moses	Non-P History (3:1–4:17)	P History (6:2–7:7)
Setting	Wilderness	Land of Egypt
Commission	To lead Israel out of Egypt into the wilderness	To demand that Pharaoh let the Israelites leave Egypt
Objection of Moses	Disbelief of the elders	Resistance of Pharaoh
Outcome of the exodus	Belief of the Israelites	Egyptians' recognition of Yahweh's power

tion of ancient histories with travelogues is not unusual. Davies has noted that the expedition of ancient armies is recorded with itinerary notices. The Assyrian Annals, for example, contain itineraries of military campaigns with lengthy descriptions of topography and foreign customs, which relate the Assyrians to their neighboring cultures (e.g., the Sargon Geography).[5] The inclusion of the itineraries in the Non-P and P Histories may also be for the purpose of infusing the literature with the imagery of a military march.[6] Itineraries are also important devices in the writing of ancient history. Geography plays a prominent role in the development of Greek historiography. Van Seters notes that the forerunners of Herodotus were geographers (e.g., Anaximander and Hecataeus).[7]

Coats has argued further that the itinerary notices provide an important structural framework for interpreting both the exodus and the wilderness wandering.[8] They organize the Pentateuch. The first travel notice occurs in 12:37: "And the Israelites journeyed from Rameses to Succoth." Once they are introduced, the itineraries continue to organize the remainder of the story of the exodus, the wilderness journey, and even the entry into Canaan.

The exodus story includes the following locations in the journey out of

5. The Sargon Geography traces the conquest of Sargon of Akkad to describe the boundaries of his empire, which include the entire expanse of the earth's surface. The document is based on legendary materials organized as lists of place-names mixed with legendary information about the reign of Sargon of Akkad. For interpretation and a translation of the documents see W. Horowitz, *Cosmic Geography* (Mesopotamian Civilizations 8; Winona Lake: Eisenbrauns, 1998), 67-95.

6. G. I. Davies, "The Wilderness Itineraries: A Comparative Study," *TynBul* 25 (1974): 46-81.

7. See, e.g., the study of J. S. Romm, *The Edges of the Earth in Ancient Thought: Geography, Exploration, and Fiction* (Princeton: Princeton University Press, 1992).

8. Coats, "Wilderness Itinerary," 147-48; G. I. Davies, "The Wilderness Itineraries and the Composition of the Pentateuch," *VT* 33 (1983): 1-13.

Egypt: Rameses, Succoth (12:37), Etham (13:20), Pi-hahiroth (14:1-2). The wilderness journey includes the follow locations: Shur (15:22), Elim (15:27), Sin (16:1), Rephidim (17:1), Sinai (19:1-2), Sinai (Num 10:12), Mount Yahweh (Num 10:33), Taberah (11:1-3), Kibroth-hattaavah (11:35), Hazeroth (11:35; 12:16), Paran (12:16; 13:3, 26), Kadesh/Zin (13:26; 20:1), Mount Hor (20:22), Edom (21:10-20), the land of the Amorites (21:25, 31), the plains of Moab (22:1; 26:3; 31:12; 35:1), Shittim (25:1). The entry of the Israelites into the promised land includes Gilgal (Josh 4:19).

The abrupt change in location, the disruption in the sequence of travel, and the confusion in the setting indicate the presence of more than one author in the arrangement of the itinerary notices. The exodus from Egypt includes the divine command that the Israelites "turn around" and encamp at Pi-hahiroth (Exod 14:1-2), indicating an abrupt change in location. With regard to the sequence of travel the wilderness journey presents a number of problems in narrative logic. The isolation of the oasis at Elim (15:27) suggests its possible subordination to the setting of Sin (16:1) for the story of manna. The two locations for the Israelite departure after the revelation of law from Sinai (Num 10:12) and from Mount Yahweh (Num 10:33) indicate a contradiction in setting, as does the confusion over the setting of the spy story, which takes place at Kadesh/Zin (Num 13:26) and at Paran (Num 13:3, 26). The problem surrounding the setting of the spy story is compounded by a separate account of the arrival of the Israelites at Kadesh/Zin toward the end of the wilderness journey (Num 20:1). The problems in the sequence of the itinerary notices increase with a comparison to Numbers 33, which contains a separate version of the travel sequence of the exodus and the wilderness journey.[9] The evidence of multiple au-

---

9. Davies ("Wilderness Itineraries and Composition," 6) notes that the parallels between Numbers 33 and the itinerary notices throughout Exodus and Numbers are so close that some form of literary relationship must be presupposed. Scholars differ at this point, however. M. Noth ("Der Wallfahrtsweg zum Sinai," *PJ* 36 [1940]: 5-28) argued that Numbers 33 is a late compilation of isolated itineraries from Exodus and Numbers. Cross (*Canaanite Myth and Hebrew Epic,* 308-9) argues for just the reverse relationship, that Numbers 33 is the base document for the construction of the itineraries in Exodus and Numbers. He is followed by Davies, "Wilderness Itineraries: Comparative Study," 50-51, 60-70; idem, "Wilderness Itineraries and Composition," 6-7; idem, "The Wilderness Itineraries and Recent Archaeological Research," in *Studies in the Pentateuch* (ed. J. A. Emerton; VTSup 41; Leiden: Brill, 1990), 171-74. The difference between Cross and Davies is that for Cross Numbers 33 is the basis for Priestly tradition in Exodus and Numbers, while for Davies Numbers 33 is the basis for a pre-Priestly (i.e., Deuteronomistic) version of the itineraries in Exodus and Numbers, with the Priestly influence in Numbers 33 the result of a later redaction. Both Noth and Cross agree that the most likely origin of Numbers 33 concerns a list of pilgrimage stations, while Davies looks instead to royal military records from ancient Near Eastern Assyrian archives. For a literary comparison of the itineraries in Exodus and Numbers and in Numbers 33 see Dozeman, "Numbers," *NIB* 2:244-53.

thors is clear from the many points of tension in the sequence of travel. Yet the identification of the authors has continued to pose a problem for modern interpreters because the travel notices do not fit a single literary form.[10]

The itinerary notices present a range of historical and literary problems that exceed the scope of this commentary. My aim here is to identify places where the P author has influenced the travel sequence of the Israelites in order to provide a distinct interpretation of events from the Non-P History. For this limited goal there is evidence that the P author has changed the travel sequence of the Non-P History in three places: (1) the confrontation at the Red Sea (Exodus 12–14); (2) the sequence of travel from Elim (15:27) to Sinai (19:1-2); (3) the location of the spy story (Numbers 13–15).

The three settings are associated with the central themes of the exodus, the revelation of law, and the loss of the land by the first generation of Israelites to leave Egypt. Below I will summarize the itinerary structure of the exodus (Exodus 12–14) and the spy story (Numbers 13–15) to provide an overview of the distinct itinerary structures of the Non-P and P Histories. The travel sequence from Elim to Sinai will be described in the commentary on the journey, 15:22–18:27.

Exodus

The distinct settings for the commission of Moses continue to influence the account of the confrontation at the Red Sea in the Non-P and P Histories. The

---

10. Modern interpreters have offered a variety of solutions to account for the history of composition of the itineraries. M. Haran ("Exodus, The" *IDBSup,* 304-10, esp. 309-10) offers a source-critical interpretation of the itineraries. Other solutions include Noth (*History of Pentateuchal Traditions,* 220-27, esp. 224-26), who questions whether the itineraries might not be independent, but in the end interprets them within the framework of J and P; as does Cross (*Canaanite Myth and Hebrew Epic,* 307-21), who also attributes many texts to P (Exod 12:37a; 13:20; 14:1; 15:22a; 16:1; 17:1a; 19:2; Num 10:12; 20:1a, 22; 21:10; 22:1), with the remainder of the references belonging to either E or J. Coats ("Wilderness Itinerary," 135-52) and J. T. Walsh ("From Egypt to Moab: A Source Critical Analysis of the Wilderness Itinerary," *CBQ* 39 [1977]: 20-33) argue for a more independent development to the growth of the itineraries over against narrative sources. They differ, however, in that Coats sees more unity to the itineraries in their present form as compared to Walsh, who identifies three distinct itinerary chains. Davies ("Wilderness Itineraries and Composition") also interprets the development of the itinerary notices more independently with only a few locations attributed to P (Exod 14:2? 19:1; Num 10:12; 20:1aα; 22:1). For analysis of the itineraries from a geographical perspective see Davies, *Way of the Wilderness,* 62-93; H. Cazelles, "Les localisations de l'Exode et la critique littéraire," in *Autour de l'Exode* (Sources bibliques; Paris: Gabalda, 1987), 189-231. For review of the itinerary notices in relation to recent archaeology see Davies, "Wilderness Itineraries and Recent Archaeological Research," in *Studies in the Pentateuch,* ed. Emerton, 161-75, who concludes that recent archaeological research does little to support a historical and geographical reconstruction of Israel's wilderness travels.

confrontation at the Red Sea takes place in the wilderness in the Non-P History corresponding to the wilderness commission of Moses in 3:1–4:17. The event is located in the land of Egypt in the P History, as was the commission of Moses in 6:2–7:7. The different settings for the defeat of Pharaoh emerge from an interpretation of the itinerary notices in the Non-P and P Histories, which trace the journey of the Israelites out of Egypt (chaps. 12–14).

There are two itinerary notices in the Non-P History. They share a similar form and are related in content. Third person narration describes the Israelite pilgrimage from one location to another, with the references overlapping to form a chain: the Israelites journeyed from Rameses to Succoth (12:37); after leaving Succoth they camped at Etham (13:20).

The Israelite journey in the Non-P History from Rameses through Succoth (12:37) to Etham (13:20) brings the people to the "edge of the wilderness" (13:20). The reference suggests that the location for the conflict at the Red Sea is the wilderness, not the land of Egypt. This was the conclusion of Coats, who also concluded that the defeat of Pharaoh at the Red Sea takes place in the wilderness in the Non-P History.[11] Other evidence for the wilderness setting is the additional reference to the wilderness road of the exodus as the way by which the Israelites reach Etham: "the wilderness road of the Red Sea" (13:18). The murmuring of the Israelite people at the approach of the Egyptian army is an action that is also associated exclusively with the wilderness. The people complain to Moses in 14:11: "Is it because there are no graves in Egypt that you took us to die in the wilderness?" Coats has clarified that the murmuring motif is part of the wilderness wandering stories and not a feature of the exodus.[12] The murmuring of the Israelites describes their resistance to the leadership of Moses in the wilderness journey. The act of murmuring idealizes slavery in the land of Egypt over the risk of following Moses in the wilderness.

The murmuring of the Israelites at the Red Sea (14:10ff.), the travel on the "wilderness road of the Red Sea" (13:18), and the setting of Etham "at the edge of the wilderness" (13:20) indicate that the confrontation at the Red Sea is the first event in the wilderness wandering for the Non-P historian. The wilderness setting is important to the author. It frames the story of the exodus as the location for

---

11. G. W. Coats, "The Traditio-Historical Character of the Reed Sea Motif," *VT* 17 (1967): 253-65; idem, "Wilderness Itinerary," 135-52; idem, "An Exposition for the Wilderness Traditions," *VT* 22 (1972): 288-95. Lohfink (*Theology of the Pentateuch*, 37 n. 5) disagrees with the interpretation of Coats: "The stratum that most strongly shapes the definitive image, the priestly historical narrative, made the miracle at the sea the climax of the exodus event." This statement does not disconfirm the insight of Coats. It simply illustrates the strategy of the Priestly author to place both the commission of Moses and the confrontation at the Red Sea in Egypt.

12. G. W. Coats, *Rebellion in the Wilderness: The Murmuring Motif in the Wilderness Traditions of the Old Testament* (Nashville: Abingdon: 1968).

the commission of Moses (3:1–4:17) and the defeat of Pharaoh (13:17–14:31). The wilderness commission of Moses introduced the motif of the "faith" of the Israelites in Moses, and the defeat of Pharaoh at the Red Sea concludes with the motif. Thus the wilderness is the setting where the Israelites acquire faith in Moses (14:31) as Yahweh predicted in the wilderness commission of Moses (4:1, 5, 8, 9).

The confrontation at the Red Sea takes place in the land of Egypt in the P History. The P author achieves the change in setting by adding an itinerary stop of Pi-hahiroth in 14:1-2. The form of this travel notice indicates its separate authorship from the Non-P History. It is a divine speech to Moses, not information provided by the narrator as in the Non-P History. The instruction is disconnected from any of the encampments in the Non-P History. Thus the P author disrupts the chain of stopping points in the Non-P History with a new divine command to Moses in order to change the location of the Red Sea from the wilderness to the land of Egypt: "Then Yahweh said to Moses, 'Tell the Israelites to turn back and encamp near Pi-hahiroth'" (14:1-2).[13] As a result, the destruction of the Egyptian army is the last event in the land of Egypt in the P History and not the first event in the wilderness journey of the Israelites as in the Non-P History. Childs also notes the change of focus in the P History. He too concludes: "P views the event at the sea in connection with the exodus from Egypt." He adds: "The wilderness wanderings do not begin until after the sea."[14] The setting of the land of Egypt for the confrontation at the sea corresponds to the divine prediction in the P version of Moses' commission that the Egyptians would come to knowledge of Yahweh from the events of the exodus (7:5; 14:18).

The distinct travel sequence in the Non-P and P Histories and their relation to the separate accounts of the commission of Moses can be illustrated as in figure 10 on page 185 (see also the commentary on 3:1–7:7).

Loss of the Land

The loss of the promised land by the first generation of Israelites to leave Egypt is central to both the Non-P and P Histories. The account is contained in the story of the spies in Numbers 13–15. The two histories diverge on the cause for the loss of the promised land. The distinctive interpretations are embedded in divergent travel routes through the wilderness.[15] The two travel routes can be illustrated as in figure 11 on page 186.

The sequence of travel in the Non-P History begins with the Israelite departure from Mount Yahweh on a three-day journey (Num 10:33) through

13. Cf. Davies, "Wilderness Itineraries and Composition."
14. Childs, *Exodus*, 222-23.
15. See also Davies, "Wilderness Itineraries and Composition"; B. A. Levine, *Numbers 1–20* (AB 4B; New York: Doubleday, 1993), 48-72.

Figure 10

Non-P History	P History
COMMISSION OF MOSES (3:1–4:17)	**COMMISSION OF MOSES** (6:2–7:7)
SETTING: WILDERNESS	SETTING: LAND OF EGYPT
THEME: FAITH OF ISRAEL (4:1-9)	THEME: EGYPTIAN ACKNOWLEDGMENT OF YAHWEH (7:5)
RED SEA CONFRONTATION (14:1-31)	**RED SEA CONFRONTATION** (14:1-31)
SETTING: WILDERNESS	SETTING: LAND OF EGYPT
Etham (13:20)	**Pi-hahiroth** (14:2)
"Edge of the wilderness"	"Turn back, between Migdol and Sea, before Baal-zephon"
THEME: FAITH OF ISRAEL (14:31)	THEME: EGYPTIAN ACKNOWLEDGMENT OF YAHWEH (14:18)

Taberah (11:1-3) to Kibroth-hattaavah, the location for the complaint about meat, before the people travel to Hazeroth (11:35). Kadesh/Zin is an important setting in the Non-P History, even though it lacks a clear itinerary notice in the present form of the text. The Israelites arrive at Kadesh in the second year of the exodus. It is the setting for the story of the spies, when the generation of the exodus loses the land (13:21, 26), because they fear to undertake holy war (13:22-24, 26-30; 14:2-4). Kadesh/Zin remains the setting for the challenge to Moses' leadership by Dathan and Abiram (chap. 16) and an unsuccessful negotiation with the king of Edom to cross his land (20:14-21). The Israelites leave Kadesh/Zin in the Non-P History at the close of their wilderness journey (20:22).[16]

The P author changes the sequence of travel after the revelation of law, creating a series of contradictions about the location of the Israelite people. In the P History the Israelites depart from Sinai (Num 10:12), rather than Mount Yahweh. Their next significant stopping point is Paran. This is stated at the outset of their journey from Sinai in 10:12: "Then the Israelites set out by stages from the wilderness of Sinai, and the cloud settled down in the wilderness of Paran." It repeats immediately preceding the spy story in 12:16: "After that the people set out from Hazeroth, and camped in the wilderness of Paran." The repetition indicates that Paran is firmly established as the location for the spy story in the P History, creating confusion in the present form of the story. The new location is accompanied by a distinctive interpretation for the loss of the land. It is no longer the fear of holy war as it is in the Non-P History, but the failure of

---

16. See Dozeman, "Numbers."

Figure 11

Non-P History:	*P History:*
Kadesh Sequence of Travel	*Paran Sequence of Travel*

REVELATION OF LAW (Exod 19–34)	REVELATION OF LAW (Exod 19–Num 9)
	Departure: Sinai to Paran (Num 10:12)
Departure: from Mount Yahweh (Num 10:33) (three days' journey)	
Taberah (Num 11:1-3)	
Kibroth-hattaavah to Hazeroth (Num 11:35)	
	Hazeroth to Paran (Num 12:16)
KADESH/ZIN (Num 13:21, 26)	**PARAN** (Num 13:3, 26)
— Spy Story (Num 13–15)	— Spy Story (Num 13–15)
— Dathan and Abiram Rebellion (Num 16)	— Korah Rebellion (Num 16–19)
— Negotiation with Edom (Num 20:14-21)	
	To Kadesh/Zin (Num 20:1)

the people to judge the land "good" (13:31-33). The insertion of Paran by the P author results in the Israelites arriving at Kadesh only at the end of their wilderness journey (20:1), creating still further confusion with the sequence of travel in the Non-P History.

The summary of the travel sequence surrounding the exodus and the loss of the land illustrates the important role of geographical setting in developing the central themes of the Non-P and P Histories. The exodus (Exodus 12–14) and the loss of land (Numbers 13–15) take place at different locations in the two histories. In each case the geographical setting is the springboard for divergent interpretations of the events. The summary also indicates that the P History is dependent on the Non-P History. The insertion of Pi-hahiroth, as the setting for the confrontation at the Red Sea, requires the travel sequence of the Non-P History. The same is true for the setting of the spy story. The P author has inserted the location of Paran into the more complete travel sequence in the Non-P History. The same literary relationship is also evident in the travel sequence from Elim to Sinai in Exod 15:27–19:1 (see the commentary on the journey, 15:22–18:27). The diagram in figure 12 on pages 187-88 provides an overview of the travel notices in the Non-P and P Histories and a listing of the stories that are associated with each location.

Figure 12	
Non-P History: **Travel Itinerary**	**P History:** **Additions and Changes in Locations**
Rameses (12:37)	
Succoth (12:37)	
Etham (13:20) Edge of wilderness RED SEA CONFRONTATION IN WILDERNESS (chap. 14)	**#1 Pi-hahiroth** (14:1-2) Turn back, between Migdol and sea, before Baal-zephon RED SEA CONFRONTATION IN EGYPT (chap. 14)
Shur (15:22) Three-day journey into wilderness DISEASED WATER (15:23-26)	
Elim (15:27) Twelve Springs/Seventy Palm Trees MANNA IN WILDERNESS	**#2 Wilderness of Sin** (arrival — 16:1) Between Elim and Sinai MANNA IN WILDERNESS **Wilderness of Sin** (departure — 17:1a)
Rephidim (17:1b) No water WATER FROM THE ROCK AT HOREB (17:2-7) WAR AGAINST AMALEK (17:8-16) JETHRO, MOUNTAIN OF GOD, WORSHIP, JUDGES (chap. 18)	
Wilderness of Sinai (19:2) REVELATION ON MOUNTAIN OF GOD (Exod 19–34)	REVELATION ON MOUNTAIN OF GOD (Exod 19–Num 10)
From Mount Yahweh (Num 10:33) Three-day journey COMPLAINT AT TABERAH (Num 11:1-3)	**From wilderness of Sinai** (Num 10:12) (to Paran)
Kibroth-hattaavah (Num 11:35) COMPLAINT OVER FOOD/SEVENTY ELDERS (Num 11:4-34)	

Hazeroth (Num 11:35) CONFLICT OVER MOSES' PROPHETIC LEADERSHIP (Num 12)	**Hazeroth** (Num 12:16)
Kadesh/Zin (Num 13:26) SPY STORY (Num 13–14) DATHAN AND ABIRAM'S REBELLION (Num 16) MESSAGE TO EDOM AND EDOMITE REJECTION (Num 20:14-21)	**#3 Paran** (Num 12:16; 13:3, 26) SPY STORY (Num 13–15) KORAH'S REBELLION (Num 16–19) **Kadesh/Zin** (Num 20:1) SIN OF MOSES (Num 20:2-13)
Mount Hor (Num 20:22) WAR WITH KING OF ARAD AT HORMAH (Num 21:1-3)	DEATH OF AARON (Num 20:22-29)

Journey around Edom
 	
  1. Red Sea road (Num 21:4)
  2. Oboth (Num 21:10-20)
  3. Iye-abarim (wilderness bordering Moab)
  4. Wadi Zered
  5. Other side of Arnon (wilderness bordering Amorites and Moabites)
  6. Beer (well, wilderness)
  7. Mattanah
  8. Nahaliel
  9. Bamoth
10. Pisgah in fields of Moab	

Land of Amorites (Num 21:25, 31) DEFEAT OF SIHON AND OG (Num 21:21-35) BALAK AND BALAAM (Num 22–24)	**#4 Plains of Moab** (Num 22:1)
Shittim (Num 25:1) INTERMARRIAGE WITH MOABITES (Num 25:1-5) SPYING JERICHO (Josh 2:1) CROSSING JORDAN RIVER (Josh 3:1)	INTERMARRIAGE WITH MIDIANITES (Num 25:6-18) **Plains of Moab** (Num 26:3; 31:12; 35:1) SECOND CENSUS (Num 26) INHERITANCE LAW AND CULTIC CALENDAR (Num 27–30, 36) WAR AGAINST MIDIAN (Num 31) BOUNDARIES OF LAND OF CANAAN (Num 34) LEVITICAL CITIES (Num 35) DEATH OF MOSES (Deut 34:1-8)
Gilgal (Josh 4:19)	

Non-P and P Histories

The account of the conflict between Yahweh and Pharaoh in 7:8–15:21 contains material from several different authors. The hymns attributed to Moses (15:1-18) and to Miriam (15:21) are likely independent liturgies by separate authors (see the introduction, "Individual Genres: Hymns in Exodus 15"). The cultic instructions concerning the Passover, the Feast of Unleavened Bread, and the divine claim on the firstborn (chaps. 12–13) represent central rituals in the history of Israelite worship. My comments will highlight a range of interpretations regarding the authorship of the festivals. Yet the focus of interpretation will remain on identifying the Non-P and P Histories in 7:8–15:21. Figure 13 on page 190 identifies the literature of the Non-P and P Histories. The narrative of the exodus is aimed at the Israelites in the Non-P History. The story explores the power of Yahweh as the Israelites' savior through a two-stage conflict, which is intended to bring the Israelites into the wilderness (Exod 5:1, 3; 7:16; 8:27). The initial conflict is the plagues, 7:14–10:20. The second is the defeat of Pharaoh, 10:21–14:31. The second conflict progresses from Egypt to the wilderness, where the Israelites see the dead Egyptians on the shore of the Red Sea and acquire faith in Yahweh and in Moses (14:31). The following summary provides an overview of the Non-P History.

Non-P History

Initial Confrontation in the Non-P History

The elimination of the P literature (see "P History" below) allows for the identification of the plagues in the Non-P History. The six plagues are organized in pairs emphasizing different elements of nature.

First Pair: Water

A. Turning the Nile into blood (7:14-16a, 17a*a*, b, 18, 20a*b*-21, 22b*a*, 23-24, excluding references to Aaron)

B. Frogs that emerge from the Nile (7:25–8:4; 8:8-10a*b*, 11-15a*a*; excluding references to Aaron)

Second Pair: Land

A. Flies infest the ground of Egypt (8:20-22a, 23-32; excluding references to Aaron)

B. Death of cattle in the fields of Egypt (9:1-7)

Third Pair: Air

A. Hail falls from the sky (9:13-14a, 15-28, 29a, b*a*, 30-35a; excluding references to Aaron)

B. Locusts are blown in on the east wind (10:1-2a, 3-20; excluding references to Aaron)

Figure 13

Topic	Non-P History	P History
Initial Confrontation (7:8–10:20)		
1. Sea dragon	———	7:8-13
2. Water to blood	7:14-16a, 17a*a*, b, 18, 20a*b*-21a, 22b*a*, 23-24	7:16b, 17a*b*, 19-20a*a*, 21b, 22a, b*b*
3. Frogs	7:25; 8:1-4, 8-10a*b*, 11-15a*a*	8:5-7, 8a*a* (Aaron), 10b*b*, 12a*a* (Aaron), 15a*b*, b
4. Gnats	———	8:16-19
5. Flies	8:20-22a, 23-32	8:22b, 25a*b* (Aaron)
6. Death of cattle	9:1-7	———
7. Boils	———	9:8-12
8. Hailstorm	9:13-14a, 15-28, 29a, b*a*, 30-35a	9:14b, 27a*a* (Aaron), 29b*b*, 35b
9. Locusts	10:1-2a, 3-20	10:2b, 3a*a* (Aaron), 8a*a* (Aaron), 16a*a* (Aaron)
Defeat of Pharaoh (10:21–14:31)		
1. Darkness	10:21-29	———
2. Death of the Egyptian firstborn	11:1-7a, 8; 12:21-27, 29-39; 13:3-16	11:7b, 9-10; 12:1-20, 28, 40-51; 13:1-2
3. Destruction of the Egyptian army at the Red Sea	13:17-18a, 19, 20; 14:5-7, 8a, 9a, 10-16a*a*, b, 19a, 20a*a*, 21a, 22a, 23-24a*a*, 24b-29a, 30-31	13:18b, 21-22; 14:1-4, 8b, 9b, 16a*b*, 17-18, 19b, 20a*b*, b, 21b, 22b, 24a*b*, 29b
Celebration of Victory (15:1-21)		
1. Song of Moses	15:1-18	
2. Song of Miriam		15:19-21

In the commentary I will highlight points of tension in the plagues, which suggest that the Non-P History contains literature from more than one author. L. Schmidt, for example, builds on the tensions to identify two authors in the literature, the author of a J History (J) and a subsequent author, identified as the Jehovist (JE). Schmidt concluded that the J History consists of four plagues (blood, frogs, flies, and locust). The Jehovist (JE), according to Schmidt, created the cycle of six plagues by adding cattle and hail.[17] The detailed reconstruction of the history of composition sought by Schmidt goes beyond the aims of this commentary, which limits the focus to the Non-P and P Histories.[18]

The structure of the plagues in the Non-P History can be illustrated with the diagram in figure 14 on page 192. The diagram allows for several conclusions concerning the plagues in the Non-P History. First, the plagues tend to follow an eight-part pattern including (1) the introduction, in which Yahweh commands Moses to meet Pharaoh; (2) the address by Moses to Pharaoh, always in the form of a prophetic messenger speech, "Thus said Yahweh"; (3) the conditions are presented to Pharaoh for avoiding the plague; (4) the plague; (5) the concessions by Pharaoh; (6) the intercession by Moses; (7) the reversal of the plague in response to the intercession by Moses; and (8) the conclusion noting Pharaoh's resistance.

Second, the announcements by Moses advance themes from his wilderness commission (3:1–4:17), especially the divine command that the Israelites worship Yahweh. In each plague Moses states Yahweh's demand that Pharaoh "send out" the Israelites for the purpose of worship. Three times the wilderness is specifically mentioned as the location for worship (5:1-3; 7:16; 8:27). Pharaoh resists the demands of Moses by hardening his heart. Pharaoh's resistance is described with the word "to harden" *(ḥāzaq)* in the initial plague of blood and final plague of locust; while the word "to be heavy" *(kābēd)* is employed in the middle four plagues of frogs, flies, cattle, and hail. Pharaoh's hardening of his heart results in his refusing "to send out" the Israelites.

Third, the introductions reinforce the earlier conclusion that the plagues are grouped in pairs in the Non-P History, and that each pair of actions begins at dawn. The first plague in each pair (blood, flies, hail) begins with the divine command to Moses that he "stand" or "station himself" *(nāṣab/yāṣab)* before Pharaoh in the "morning" *(bōqer)*. The second plague in each pair (frogs, cattle, locust) begins with the more abrupt command that Moses "go/approach" *(bô')* Pharaoh.

---

17. L. Schmidt, *Beobachtungen zu der Plagenerzählung in Exodus VII 14-XI 10* (StudBib 4; Leiden: Brill, 1990), 58-77.

18. For more detailed evaluation see Dozeman, *God at War.*

Figure 14

(X marks the presence of a motif; – marks the absence of a motif)

	First Pair		Second Pair		Third Pair	
	Blood 7:14-24	Frogs 7:25–8:15	Flies 8:20-32	Cattle 9:1-7	Hail 9:13-35	Locusts 10:1-20
Intro	Stand *(nāṣab)* in the morning *(bōqer)*	Go *(bô')*	Stand *(nāṣab)* in the morning *(bōqer)*	Go *(bô')*	Stand *(nāṣab)* in the morning *(bōqer)*	Go *(bô')*
Messenger Formula	X	X	X	X	X	X
Condition	X	X	X	X	X	X
Plague	X	X	X	X	X	X
Concession by Pharaoh	–	X	X	–	X	X
Intercession by Moses	–	X	X	–	X	X
Reversal of Plague	–	X	X	–	X	X
Resistance of Pharaoh	X	X	X	X	X	X

DEFEAT OF PHARAOH IN THE NON-P HISTORY

The Non-P History includes the following three events. The first scene is the imposition of darkness over the land of Egypt (10:21-29). Darkness provides the setting for the subsequent events. The second scene is the death of the Egyptian firstborn (11:1-7a, 8; 12:21-27, 29-39; 13:3-16). The story is carefully orchestrated by time and by geography. It begins in the city of Rameses with the divine announcement to Moses (11:1-7a, 8). Moses instructs the elders of the Israelites on the rite of Passover as a means for protecting their firstborn from death (12:21-27). The death of the Egyptian firstborn follows precisely at midnight prompting the Israelites to depart from Egypt (12:29-39). The Israelites journey from the city of Rameses to Succoth, where Moses provides further instruction on the Feast of Unleavened Bread (13:3-10) and on the divine claim upon the first-born males (13:11-16). The third scene is the destruction of the Egyptian army in the Red Sea (13:17-18a, 19, 20; 14:5-7, 8a, 9a, 10-16aa, b, 19a, 20aa, 21a, 22a, 23-24aa, 24b-29a, 30-31). This story is also organized by time and by geography. The events progress through the night until the Egyptian army is destroyed at the break of dawn after a journey from Succoth to Etham, a location on the edge of the wilderness, making the conflict at the Red Sea the first event in the Israelites' wilderness journey, as Coats has argued.[19]

The defeat of Pharaoh in the Non-P History stands apart from the cycle of the plagues. As a result, the death of the Egyptian firstborn and the destruction of the Egyptian army in the Red Sea represent intensification in the conflict between Yahweh and Pharaoh from the cycle of the plagues. The first indication of this development is that the intercessory role of Moses recedes from its prominent place in the sequence of the plagues. Moses no longer presents Pharaoh with conditions for avoiding the death of the Egyptian firstborn or the destruction of his army at the Red Sea. Instead, Yahweh announces inevitable actions against Pharaoh and the Egyptian nation.

The second sign of intensification is signaled by a reversal of the temporal sequence of events between the cycle of the plagues and the defeat of Pharaoh. The instructions to Moses in the plague cycle include two forms. Moses is commanded to stand *(nāṣab/yāṣab)* before Pharaoh in the morning *(bōqer)* and to approach *(bô')* Pharaoh. Repetition indicates that the plagues are grouped in pairs and that divine actions against Pharaoh begin at dawn in each cycle of the plague. The destruction of Pharaoh, 10:21–14:31, reverses the pattern of the plague cycle. It begins in darkness, not light (10:21-29). And it concludes at dawn (14:27), with the destruction of the Egyptian army (14:28), the last event in the series, not the first, as was the case in the plague cycle.

The third indication of intensification is the journey of the Israelites from Egypt to the wilderness. The people were stationary in the cycle of the plagues. But during the defeat of Pharaoh they journey from the city of Rameses, the location for the midnight death of the Egyptian firstborn, to Etham, "at the edge of the wilderness," where they enter the Red Sea at dawn. Although the encampment of the Israelites at several locations creates tension with the temporal chronology of a single night of activity, the two structures merge at the Red Sea. The defeat of Pharaoh and the Israelite crossing of the sea come together at dawn. The merging of the two structures fulfills the divine prediction to Moses in his wilderness commission that the Israelites would acquire faith in him through the events of the exodus (3:18; 14:31).

19. See n. 11 above.

CELEBRATION OF VICTORY IN THE NON-P HISTORY

The Song of the Sea (15:1-18) likely provided transition in the Non-P History. It looks backward to celebrate the defeat of Pharaoh (15:1-12). And it also points the reader ahead to provide an overview of the wilderness journey and the future conquest of the land of Canaan (15:13-17).

P History

The P historian presents a polemical version of the exodus, aimed at the Egyptians. It explores the power of Yahweh as creator and the influence of God over the nations. Thus in the P History, the exodus is reinterpreted as a divine judgment against Pharaoh (7:4). The Israelite nation is not excluded as a focus in the P History. They too will know Yahweh from the event (6:7; 10:2b). But the emphasis falls on Pharaoh and the Egyptian nation. Yahweh states to Moses: "The Egyptians will know that I am Yahweh, when I stretch out my hand on Egypt. And I will bring out the Israelites from their midst" (7:5). The plague cycle, 7:7–10:28, represents the initial effort to bring about the knowledge of Yahweh in the land of Egypt. The plagues represent signs and wonders to the Egyptians (7:3). The defeat of Pharaoh in the Red Sea, 10:21–14:31, achieves the goal of knowledge. Yahweh states to Moses: "And the Egyptians will know that I am Yahweh when I gain glory over Pharaoh, his chariots, and his horsemen" (14:18).

INITIAL CONFRONTATION IN THE P HISTORY

The commission of Moses in the P History, 6:2–7:7, provides a point of departure for identifying the P version of the plagues. Central motifs in the commission of Moses include the divine recollection of covenant (6:4-5); the divine self-disclosure, "I am Yahweh" (6:6, 7, 8, 29; 7:5), resulting in the recognition of divine power, "so that you may know that I am Yahweh" (6:7; 7:5); Pharaoh's resistance to Yahweh indicated by the motif of "not listening" (*šāmaʿ*, 6:9, 12, 30; 7:4); and the prominent role of Aaron (6:23, 25, 26, 27; 7:1, 2). The repetition of these motifs in the plague cycle aids in identifying the P History.

The P historian adds three plagues to the cycle: the sea dragon (7:8-13), the gnats (8:16-19), and the boils (9:8-12). The plagues repeat motifs from the P version of Moses' commission. Aaron emerges as a central character in all three plagues. The resistance of Pharaoh is noted in each case as not "listening" (*šāmaʿ*). Moreover, each plague is structured as a divine command and fulfillment, a common pattern in the P History. The most distinctive characteristic of the plagues in the P History is that they are presented as a competition between

Figure 15			
	Snakes (7:8-13)	**Gnats (8:16-19)**	**Boils (9:8-12)**
Divine command	To Aaron Content: staff into sea dragon (vv. 8-9)	To Aaron Content: gnats from the earth (v. 16)	To Moses Content: boils from soot in air (vv. 8-9)
Protagonist of the event	Aaron (v. 10)	Aaron (v. 17)	Moses (v. 10)
Response of magicians	1. Present 2. Repeat the event 3. No interpretation (vv. 11-12)	1. Present 2. Unable to repeat 3. Interpretation: "Finger of God" (vv. 18-19a)	1. Not present 2. No attempt 3. No interpretation (v. 11)
Resistance of Pharaoh and fulfillment of divine prediction	1. Pharaoh hardens his heart 2. Pharaoh did not listen 3. "As Yahweh said" (v. 13b)	1. Pharaoh hardens his heart 2. Pharaoh did not listen 3. "As Yahweh said" (v. 19b)	1. Yahweh hardens Pharaoh's heart 2. Pharaoh did not listen 3. "As Yahweh said" (v. 12)

Aaron and Moses and the Egyptian magicians. The diagram in figure 15 above highlights their similar four-part structure.

The three plagues are stereotyped. (1) Yahweh addresses Moses and Aaron and commands one or the other to perform a miraculous sign with his staff, (2) which they do. (3) The action by Aaron and Moses prompts (initially) a similar action by the Egyptian magicians. (4) Each plague ends with a summary of how Pharaoh would not listen to the sign, thus fulfilling a divine prediction. It is also noteworthy that there are no conditions presented to Pharaoh in any of these plagues. Instead they focus more on magical powers produced by Aaron or Moses and at least initially by the Egyptian magicians.

Comparison also brings to light thematic development (see "Central Themes"). There is progression from Aaron (the sea dragon and gnats) to Moses (boils) as the person executing the sign. The role of the magicians also changes. They initially transform their staffs into sea dragons, as Aaron does, but when their power fails to produce gnats they recognize the power of God at work. By the third plague, boils, the magicians are unable even to be in the presence of Moses. Pharaoh's resistance also undergoes transformation. In the first two plagues he hardens his own heart. But by the third plague Yahweh becomes the agent of the hardening.

The distribution of the three P plagues within the Non-P History is im-

portant for interpretation. The cycle of the plagues in the Non-P History separates into three pairs, (1) blood (7:14-24) and frogs (7:25–8:15); (2) flies (8:20-32)
and cattle (9:1-7); and (3) hail (9:13-35) and locusts (10:1-20). The P historian has
distributed the plagues of the sea dragon, gnats, and boils as introductions to
the paired plagues in the Non-P History, thus creating the present form of the
plague cycle (see below, "Literary Structure: Initial Confrontation"). As introductions, the plagues of the sea dragon, gnats, and boils provide the
hermeneutical lens by which the P author supplements and edits the Non-P cycle of the plagues.

The P interpretation of the plagues, as signs and as a contest of magical
power between Aaron and the magicians, is carried over into the cycle of
plagues in the Non-P History. The P author thoroughly reworks the first pair of
plagues in the Non-P History, blood and frogs. The P author adds the following
motifs to the plague of blood (7:14-24): the statement that Pharaoh has not listened (7:16b), the recognition motif aimed at Pharaoh (7:17ab), the magical
competition between Aaron and the magicians (7:19-20aa), and a conclusion
that the magicians could perform the same wonder (7:22a) and that Pharaoh
would not listen, fulfilling a divine prediction (7:22bb). The P author adds the
following motifs to the plague of frogs (7:25–8:15): the competition between
Aaron and the magicians (8:5-7), the addition of Aaron (8:8aa; 12aa), the recognition motif aimed at Pharaoh (8:10bb), and the conclusion that Pharaoh would
not listen (8:15aa) and how this fulfilled a divine prediction (8:15b).

The P author adds far fewer motifs to the second (flies and cattle) and
third (hail and locust) pair of plagues in the Non-P History. The plague of flies
(8:20-32) receives the recognition motif aimed at Pharaoh (8:22b) and a reference to Aaron (8:25ab). There are no additions to the death of the Egyptians'
cattle (9:1-7). The third pair of plagues includes the following additions by the P
author. To the plague of hail (9:13-35) the P author adds the recognition motif
aimed at Pharaoh (9:14b), a reference to Aaron (9:27aa), a second recognition
motif aimed at Pharaoh (9:29b), and a concluding notice indicating Pharaoh's
refusal to listen as a fulfillment of a divine prediction (9:35bb). To the plague of
locusts (10:1-20) the P author adds only the recognition motif aimed at the Israelites (10:2b) and references to Aaron (10:3aa, 8aa, 16aa).

The summary of the P additions to the Non-P History indicates how unevenly the motifs have been inserted. Both the plagues of blood (7:14-24) and of
frogs (7:25–8:15) have been extensively expanded by the P author to include a
confrontation between Aaron and the Egyptian magicians, a refusal of Pharaoh
"to listen" to the sign, and a notice of how Pharaoh's obstinacy fulfilled divine
predictions. The result is that the plagues of blood and frogs conform to the introductory plague of snakes, where both Aaron and the magicians perform the
same events. The three plagues represent the first cycle of action in the P His-

tory where the focus is on water. The competition between Aaron and the magicians ceases when the latter group is unable to produce gnats from the ground. It is at this juncture in the story that the P additions to the plagues in the Non-P History decrease. The result of the P editing is an intensification of the plague cycle. The action progresses from a near equal competition between Aaron and the magicians in cycle one (the sea dragon, blood, frogs) where the focus is on water, to the clear superiority of Aaron over the magicians in cycle two (gnats, flies, death of livestock) where the competition switches to the land. The competition with the Egyptian magicians is absent when Moses replaces Aaron in the third cycle (boils, hail, locust), drawing upon the power of Yahweh from the air.

The P author also inserts the recognition motif ("so that you may know that . . .") into the plague cycle and into the larger story of the exodus. The motif occurs twice in the P version of the commission to Moses (6:2–7:7), once with the Israelites as the object (6:7) and once with the Egyptians (7:5). The P author repeats the motif in the account of the destruction of the Egyptian army at the Red Sea, where it is directed both times toward the Egyptians (14:4, 18). Zimmerli has demonstrated that the recognition motif has a polemical intent, especially when it is combined with the self-introduction of God: "I am Yahweh." Public, concrete actions by God actively challenge humans to acknowledge Yahweh.[20] The framing of the exodus with the recognition motif in the commission to Moses and in the defeat of the Egyptians at the Red Sea indicates the central role of this motif in the P History. The significance has been explored by many scholars, including Z. Zevit, M. Greenberg, and J. Krašovec.[21] All agree that the motif is intended to be polemical and that it includes both a didactic role of teaching and a revelatory function of confronting a person or a group with the presence and power of God.

The recognition motif also occurs throughout the plague cycle. The motif is repeated six times in the plagues (7:17a*b*; 8:10b*b*; 22b; 9:14b; 29b*b*; 10:2b) and once in the announcement of the death of the Egyptian firstborn (11:7b). The diagram in figure 16 on page 198 lists the occurrences of the recognition motif and (in italics) to whom the call for recognition is directed: Pharaoh, Egypt, or Israel.

20. W. Zimmerli, "Knowledge of God According to the Book of Ezekiel," in *I Am Yahweh* (trans. D. W. Stott; ed. W. Brueggemann; Atlanta: John Knox, 1982), 83-87; idem, "The Word of Divine Self-Manifestation (Proof-Saying): A Prophetic Genre," in *I Am Yahweh*, 99-110.

21. Z. Zevit, "The Priestly Redaction and Interpretation of the Plague Narrative in Exodus," *JQR* 66 (1975): 193-211; Greenberg, *Understanding Exodus*, 169-73; J. Krašovec, "Unifying Themes in Ex 7, 8-11, 10," in *Pentateuchal and Deuteronomistic Studies: Papers Read at the XIIIth IOSOT Congress, Leuven 1989* (ed. Chr. Brekelmans and J. Lust; BETL 94; Leuven: Leuven University Press, 1990), 47-66.

Figure 16				
Introduction (6:2–7:7)	Cycle 1 (7:8–8:15)	Cycle 2 (8:16–9:7)	Cycle 3 (9:8–10:20)	Cycle 4 (10:21–14:31)
Israel (6:7) *Egypt* (7:5)	Introduction: sea dragon	Introduction: gnats	Introduction: boils	Introduction: darkness
	Blood *Pharaoh* (7:17ab)	Flies *Pharaoh* (8:22b)	Hail *Pharaoh* (9:14b) *Pharaoh* (9:29bb)	Firstborn *Pharaoh/Egypt* (11:7b)
	Frogs *Pharaoh* (8:10bb)	Cattle	Locusts *Israel* (10:2b)	Red Sea *Egypt* (14:4) *Egypt* (14:18)

Many scholars assign the recognition motif in the cycle of the plagues to the Non-P History, designated as either the J historian (Childs, Hyatt, Coats) or even an E author (Propp).[22] There are strong literary reasons for this conclusion. First, the recognition motif is aimed at Pharaoh throughout the plague cycle, not the Egyptians, as is the case in the P version of the commission to Moses and the account of the defeat of Pharaoh in the Red Sea. Second, the recognition motif in the plague cycle can be interpreted as providing a response to Pharaoh's opening statement to Moses in 5:2: "Who is Yahweh, that I should obey him and let Israel go? *I do not know Yahweh and I will not let Israel go.*" The response of Pharaoh is part of the Non-P History.

But there are also strong reasons for attributing all of the occurrences of the recognition motif to the P author. First, the P author uses the motif in the commission of Moses. It is absent from the Non-P version of Moses' commission.[23] Even the response of Pharaoh in 5:2 is not an instance of the recognition

22. Childs, *Exodus*, 131; J. P. Hyatt, *Exodus* (NCB; 1971; repr. Grand Rapids: Eerdmans, 1983), 48-49; Coats, *Exodus*, 71; Propp, *Exodus 1–18*, 287-354.

23. The syntax of the formula does not provide criteria for identifying two authors. There is a wide variation in how the formula is introduced (*lĕma'an* in Exod 8:10, 22 [MT 6, 18]; 9:29; 11:7; *bĕzō't* in 7:17; *ba'ăbûr* in 9:14). There is also variation in the person and number of the verbs (second person plural suffix forms occur in 6:7; 10:2; a second person plural prefix form is used in 11:7; second person singular prefix forms occur in 7:17; 8:10, 22 [MT 6, 18]; 9:14, 29; finally, third person plural suffix forms occur in 7:5; 14:4, 18). The variations, however, yield no distinctive patterns that would signal different authors. This conclusion also includes the instances where the recognition motif ("so that you may know that") functions independently of the motif of self-introduction ("I am Yahweh"), since these occurrences (frogs, 8:10b; hail, 9:14b, 29b; and death to firstborn, 11:7b) tend to enhance the interpretation of the exodus in relation to creation, and thus fit best within the P History.

motif. Second, the content of the recognition motif throughout the plague cycle tends to underscore Yahweh's power as creator, a central concern of the P author. Pharaoh must learn that Yahweh is God (blood, 7:17a*b*), that there is no god like Yahweh (frogs, 8:10b*b*), that Yahweh dwells in the land of Egypt (flies, 8:22b), that there is no god like Yahweh in all the earth (hail, 9:14b), and that the earth belongs to Yahweh (9:29b*b*). Third, the recognition motif continues to play a central role in the P History beyond the events of the exodus, where the focus shifts from the Egyptians to the Israelites. The recognition of Yahweh is aimed primarily at the Egyptians during the events of the exodus (with the exception of 10:2b). But it is aimed at the Israelites once the people leave Egypt and journey with Yahweh in the wilderness. The need for the Israelites to recognize Yahweh is tied closely to cultic events, including manna (16:6, 12), the revelatory function of the tabernacle cult (29:46), Sabbath (31:13), and the Feast of Booths (Lev 23:42-43), all stories in the P History. The motif is absent from the Non-P History.

Defeat of Pharaoh in the P History

The P History presents a distinctive version of the defeat of Pharaoh, Exod 10:21–14:31. The defeat of Pharaoh in the P History follows the three-part structure of Non-P History. But the P History relates the defeat of Pharaoh more closely with the cycle of plagues, in contrast to the Non-P History, which tended to separate the two sections. The result, as D. McCarthy and J.-L. Ska have demonstrated, is that the defeat of Pharaoh becomes a fourth cycle of the plagues.[24]

The P History includes the following literature in 10:21–14:31:

The first scene, the imposition of darkness (10:21-29), undergoes no changes or additions by the P author.

The second scene, the death of the Egyptian firstborn (11:1–13:16), receives two additions from the P historian. First, the announcement of the death of the Egyptian firstborn is brought into conformity with the central motifs from the P version of the plagues (11:7b, 9-10). The recognition motif aimed at Pharaoh (v. 7b) is inserted. The character of Aaron is added to the episode. And the resistance of Pharaoh is described as "not listening" (vv. 9-10). Second, the P author adds an extended interpretation of the Passover and the Feast of Unleavened Bread (12:1-20, 28, 40-51).

The third scene, the destruction of the Egyptian army in the Red Sea (13:17–14:31), undergoes extensive revision by the P author. Five motifs provide contrast to the Non-P History allowing for the identification of the P literature. The first and most significant is the change in geography noted earlier. The P

---

24. D. J. McCarthy, "Plagues and the Sea of Reeds: Exodus 5–14," *CBQ* 27 (1965): 336-47; J.-L. Ska, "Les plaies d'Égypte dans le récit sacerdotal (P^g)," *Bib* 60 (1979): 23-35.

author relocates the confrontation at the Red Sea from Etham in the Non-P History (13:20) to Pi-hahiroth (14:1-4, 8b). As a result, the death of the Egyptian army is the last event in the land of Egypt, not the first event in the wilderness. Second, the change in geography signals a new interpretation of the event. The destruction of the Egyptian army acquires the polemical perspective from the plague cycle in the P History. The Egyptians will recognize the power of Yahweh from the confrontation at the Red Sea (14:17-18). Third, the divine leading of the Israelites is also distinctive in the P History. The people are guided out of Egypt by the pillar of cloud (13:21-22; 14:19b, 20ab, b, 24ab), not directly by God (13:17-18a) or by the Messenger of the God (14:19a), as is the case in the Non-P History. Fourth, the description of the Israelites leaving Egypt is also transformed. The people marched out boldly in the P History, armed for battle (13:18b; 14:8b). The Non-P historian states the opposite, that the Israelites were not yet ready for war (13:17-18a). Fifth, Yahweh's power over the sea is also described in a unique way by the P author, with distinct mythological overtones. Yahweh splits the sea, creating walls of water (14:21b, 22b, 29b), as compared to the Non-P account, where the water is dried up by an east wind (14:21a).

CELEBRATION OF VICTORY IN THE P HISTORY

The Song of Miriam, 15:20-21, is an independent poem. But in its present narrative context it provides commentary on the P interpretation of the exodus.

LITERARY STRUCTURE

The interweaving of the Non-P and P Histories has created ambiguity in the canonical form of the story, giving rise to extensive debate over the literary design of Yahweh's conflict with Pharaoh in 7:8–15:21. In a summary I will highlight points of debate. I will underscore the ways in which the divergent interpretations of the Non-P and P Histories have been preserved in the canonical text. I will also illustrate the influential role of the P author in creating the present literary structure. The summary will follow the three-part sequence identified in the previous section on "Authors": the initial confrontation (7:8–10:20), the defeat of Pharaoh (10:21–14:31), and the celebration of the victory (15:1-21).

Initial Confrontation (7:8–10:20)

The number of the plagues and the scope of the present form of the text are debated among scholars. The plague of the sea dragon (7:8-13) is interpreted by

Figure 17

Cycle 1	Cycle 2	Cycle 3	*Prelude to* *Each Plague in Cycle*
1. Blood	4. Flies	7. Hail	Warning: "in the morning"
2. Frogs	5. Livestock	8. Locusts	Warning: "in approaching"
3. Gnats	6. Boils	9. Darkness	Warning: none

some as an introduction to the plague cycle, not as a plague itself.[25] Others debate the character of darkness (10:21-29), whether it is a plague or an introduction to the report of the death of the Egyptian firstborn.[26] The most notable solution is the long tradition of structuring the plague cycle in groups of three, beginning with the plague of blood, not the sea dragon, and culminating with the death of the Egyptian firstborn as the climax.[27] The structure results in nine plagues, yielding the pattern 3 + 3 + 3 + 1, when the death of the Egyptian firstborn is added. I have slightly adapted Cassuto's structure of the nine plagues in figure 17 above.[28]

The problem with this structure is that it does not include the initial action of Aaron turning his staff into a sea dragon (7:8-13) within the plague cycle, even though this action clearly includes many of the motifs from both the plagues of gnats (8:16-19) and boils (9:8-12). A further argument for the inclusion of the story of the sea dragon in the plague cycle is that all three plagues (the sea dragon, gnats, and boils) present a contest between Aaron and the Egyptian magicians, with Pharaoh's resistance indicated as his "not listening." Thus the exclusion of the first confrontation between Aaron and the magicians from the plague cycle is a weakness in this literary solution for interpreting the canonical form of the plague cycle.

Ska has provided another solution to the present form of the text. He suggested that a division within 7:1-5 provides the clue to a two-part structure of

---

25. See, e.g., Childs, *Exodus*, 151-53.

26. See W. Rudolph, *Der "Elohist" von Exodus bis Josua* (BZAW 68; Berlin: Töpelmann, 1938), 21.

27. See, e.g., Cassuto, *Exodus*, 92-93; Greenberg, *Understanding Exodus*, 171-72; S. E. Loewenstamm, *The Tradition of the Exodus in Its Development* (trans. B. J. Schwartz; Perry Foundation for Biblical Research in the Hebrew University; Jerusalem: Magnes, 1992), 35; Zevit, "Priestly Redaction," 193; J. Kegler, "Zu Komposition und Theologie der Plagenerzählungen," in *Die Hebräische Bibel und ihre zweifache Nachgeschichte* (ed. E. Blum et al.; Neukirchen-Vluyn: Neukirchener Verlag, 1990), 61. See Blum, *Studien*, 242-56, for the most recent discussion of this structure.

28. Cassuto, *Exodus*, 93.

Figure 18

Cycle 1 (7:8–8:15)	Cycle 2 (8:16–9:7)	Cycle 3 (9:8–10:20)
Nature: Water	*Nature: Land*	*Nature: Air*
Introduction: Aaron; sea dragon (7:8-13)	Introduction: Aaron; gnats (8:16-19)	Introduction: Moses; boils (9:8-12)
blood (7:14-24)	flies (8:20-32)	hail (9:13-35)
frogs (7:25–8:15)	cattle (9:1-7)	locust (10:1-20)

the plague cycle and the exodus. Exodus 7:1-5 contains Yahweh's announcement of the exodus in the P commission to Moses. The subject matter of 7:1-4a*a* is Yahweh's prediction of multiplying miraculous signs. It anticipates the plagues in 7:7–11:10. Exodus 7:4a*b*-5 is Yahweh's prediction of mighty acts. It shifts the focus to judgment, executed in 12:1–14:31.[29] Ska recognizes that the plague of the sea dragon must be included in the plague cycle, but this division does not recognize the introductory role of the sea dragon, gnats, and boils in the cycle of the plagues.

The plague of the sea dragon will be interpreted as the first plague in the cycle. Darkness may qualify as a plague, but it will be interpreted under the heading "The Defeat of Pharaoh," because it introduces the setting of darkness for the death of the Egyptian firstborn at midnight. Thus the initial conflict between Yahweh and Pharaoh consists of nine plagues, including the sea dragon (7:8-13), blood (7:14-24), frogs (7:25–8:15 [MT 7:25–8:11]), gnats (8:16-19 [MT 12-15]), flies (8:20-32 [MT 16-28]), death of livestock (9:1-7), boils (9:8-12), hail (9:13-35), and locusts (10:1-20). The plagues represent the initial confrontation between Yahweh and Pharaoh. They explore the power of Yahweh over nature in the land of Egypt and how Yahweh employs this power against Pharaoh. T. E. Fretheim has captured the role of the plagues in Exodus by describing them as ecological signs of historical disaster.[30]

I organize the initial confrontation between Yahweh and Pharaoh into three cycles of three plagues each, following the structure imposed by the P History. I read the plagues of sea dragon, the gnats, and the boils as introductions to three cycles, each consisting of three plagues. The introduction to each cycle reinforces an element of nature in the progression of the plagues: the sea dragon underscores the element of *water*; gnats are associated with the *land,* and boils with the *air*. The outline of the plague cycle emerges as in figure 18 above.

29. Ska, "Plaies d'Égypte."

30. Fretheim, *Exodus,* 108; idem, "The Plagues as Ecological Signs of Historical Disaster," *JBL* 110 (1991): 385-96.

The outline indicates that the plagues of the sea dragon (7:8-13), the gnats (8:16-19), and the boils (9:8-12) provide an introduction to each section, which includes an additional pair of plagues. The introductory plagues increase in intensity in two ways. First, they progress through the elements of nature from water (the sea dragon) to land (gnats from the earth) and finally to air (boils from ashes thrown into the air). Second, there is a development in the central characters. Aaron is the protagonist in the introductory plagues of the first two cycles. Aaron turns his staff into a sea dragon (7:8-13) and he brings forth gnats from the earth (8:16-19). The Egyptian magicians play an active role over against Aaron. In the first plague they too change their staffs into sea dragons. But in the plague of gnats the Egyptian magicians are unable to perform the same wonder. Their inability to produce the plague opens their eyes to the power of God in the action of Aaron. They state to Pharaoh concerning the gnats: "This is the finger of God" (8:19). Moses replaces Aaron in the introductory plague of the third cycle by creating boils from the soot in the air (9:8-12). The Egyptian magicians fade from the story at this point. They are unable even to stand before Moses at the outset of the third cycle of plagues, because they too now suffer from boils.

Defeat of Pharaoh (10:21–14:31)

Exodus 10:21–14:31 separates into three scenes, following the pattern of the cycle of plagues. The plague of darkness (10:21-29) introduces two subsequent actions by Yahweh, the death of the Egyptian firstborn (11:1–13:16) and the defeat of the Egyptian army at the Red Sea (13:17–14:31). The defeat of Pharaoh yields two structures only loosely related in the present form of the story: one structure emerges from the time frame of the story, and the other arises from the geography of the Israelite journey. The sequence of time focuses on Yahweh's power over nature as the Deity defeats Pharaoh in one night of action by controlling light, darkness, and the sea. The geography of the story traces the Israelites through a series of encampments over a more extended period of time emphasizing Yahweh's power over history.[31]

Night of Death and Yahweh's Power over Nature

Yahweh's defeat of Pharaoh includes three actions in one night, progressing from midnight to dawn. The plague of darkness (10:21-29) sets the stage for the death of the Egyptian firstborn at midnight (*baḥăṣî hallaylâ*, 12:29-36). The

---

31. For more detailed study of the two structures see Dozeman, *God at War*.

conflict continues through the night when Pharaoh pursues the Israelites to the Red Sea (14:1-18). The destruction of the Egyptian army is carefully choreographed into three stages. During the night (*kol-hallāyĕlâ*, 14:20) the Messenger of the God and the pillar of cloud separate the Egyptian army and the Israelites, while Yahweh dries up the Red Sea (14:19-23). At the final watch of the night (*bĕ'ašmōret habbōqer,* 14:24) Yahweh attacks the Egyptian army as they pursue the Israelites into the Red Sea (14:24-25). At dawn (*lipnôt bōqer,* 14:27) Yahweh destroys the Egyptian army (14:26-31). Many psalms reflect a similar liturgical background, in which a night vigil (Psalms 17; 27; 63) culminates in an experience of salvation at dawn (Psalm 46).[32] The same pattern informs the Christian liturgy of Easter, which also progresses through a night vigil leading to the celebration of salvation at dawn.

The single night of action emphasizes Yahweh's power over nature as a weapon to defeat Pharaoh. Yahweh controls the primordial forces of light and darkness. The thematic focus on nature ties the defeat of Pharaoh into the cycle of the plagues. The relationship to the plague cycle goes beyond theme to include form: the defeat of Pharaoh with its three-part structure extends the pattern of the plagues from three to four cycles (see fig. 19). As figure 19 illustrates, the defeat of Pharaoh, like the previous three cycles of the plagues, consists of an introductory plague followed by two additional actions. The plague of darkness continues the progression in intensity established in the plague cycle. Moses, not Aaron, communicates the plague. The Egyptian magicians are now absent altogether. Yahweh's power over nature is extended to include the primordial forces of light and darkness and even the sea itself. Such power is used to bring death to the Egyptian firstborn and to the Egyptian army. As a result the fourth cycle is intended to bring the conflict between Yahweh and Pharaoh to conclusion.

Pilgrimage from Egypt and Yahweh's Power over History

Yahweh's defeat of Pharaoh is also organized by geography. A series of encampments trace the escape of the Israelites from the land of Egypt into the wilderness. Coats describes the sequence of encampments as itinerary notices (see above, "Authors: Travel Notices").[33] M. S. Smith has clarified that the motif of travel is liturgical. It structures the exodus as a pilgrimage.[34] On the basis of the

---

32. J. W. McKay, "Psalms of Vigil," *ZAW* 91 (1979): 229-47; J. Ziegler, "Die Hilfe Gottes 'am Morgen,'" in *Alttestamentliche Studien: Friedrich Nötscher zum 60. Geburtstag* (ed. H. Junker and J. Botterweck; BBB 1; Bonn: Peter Hanstein, 1950), 281-88.

33. Coats, "Wilderness Itinerary," 129-42.

34. M. S. Smith, *The Pilgrimage Pattern in Exodus* (JSOTSup 239; Sheffield: Sheffield Academic Press, 1997).

Figure 19

Cycle 1 (7:8–8:15) Nature: water	*Cycle 2* (8:16–9:7) Nature: land	*Cycle 3* (9:8–10:20) Nature: air	*Cycle 4* (10:21–14:31) Nature: light/dark
Introduction: Aaron; sea dragon	Introduction: Aaron; gnats	Introduction: Moses; boils	Introduction: Moses; darkness
blood	flies	hail	Death of firstborn; time: midnight
frogs	cattle	locusts	Defeat of army; time: dawn

work of V. Turner, S. Ackerman compares the sequence of travel to a rite of passage.[35] The motif of pilgrimage creates tension with the chronology, since it suggests a story of many days, rather than a single night.

The sequence of itinerary stops includes Rameses, Succoth, Etham, and Pi-hahiroth, before the Israelites cross the Red Sea. The plague of darkness, the death of the Egyptian firstborn, and the Israelite observance of Passover/Feast of Unleavened Bread occur at Rameses, in the land of Egypt (12:37). The Israelites then journey to Succoth (12:37) during the same night, where they encamp and receive further instruction on the meaning of the Passover, the Feast of Unleavened Bread, and even new law concerning Yahweh's claim on firstborn (12:43-51; 13:1-16). The encampment at Succoth does not conform to the temporal organization of the episode, in which the events progressed rapidly from midnight to dawn. But, as the list indicates, Succoth is only the first of two additional encampments, Etham (13:20) and Pi-hahiroth (14:1-2), before the destruction of the Egyptian army in the Red Sea at dawn. The sequence of events suggests that the journey out of Egypt takes many days, not simply a few hours.

The sequence of the itinerary notices serves a theological purpose in Exodus.[36] M. S. Smith has recently explored the important role of pilgrimage in worship and liturgy and its influence in the formation of the book of Exodus.[37] The very first itinerary stop, Succoth, illustrates the creative mix of history, leg-

---

35. S. Ackerman, "Why Is Miriam also Among the Prophets? (And Zipporah among the Priests?)," *JBL* 121 (2002): 47-80; V. Turner, *The Ritual Process: Structure and Anti-Structure* (Ithaca: Cornell University Press, 1969).

36. For discussion of the problem of historical reconstruction associated with the itinerary notices see Davies, "Wilderness Itineraries and Recent Archaeological Research"; Oblath, *Exodus Itinerary Sites*.

37. Smith, *Pilgrimage Pattern*.

end, and liturgy suggested by the encampments. Succoth may refer to a city in Egypt *(ṭkw).* But it also signifies a religious festival, the Feast of Tabernacles or Booths (Lev 23:33-43), a yearly celebration of the Israelite's wilderness trek. The journey of the Israelites represents their pilgrimage of faith in following Yahweh through the desert to the promised land of Canaan. The central role of pilgrimage creates the paradigm of salvation history.[38] It symbolizes Yahweh's power over history. Worship, within the paradigm of the pilgrimage from Egypt to the promised land, becomes an act of memory in which one generation passes along the story of salvation history to the next generation (Exod 12:21-27; 13:1-16).[39]

Celebration of Victory (15:1-21)

Exodus 15:1-21 contains the celebration of Yahweh's victory over Pharaoh. Moses and the Israelites sing a hymn in vv. 1-18. The first two strophes celebrate Yahweh's power over nature in defeating Pharaoh at the Red Sea (15:1-6, 7-12). The hymn changes focus in the third episode (15:13-16) to accentuate the Israelite pilgrimage in the wilderness and Yahweh's power in history. The hymn concludes with a vision of Yahweh ruling over the Israelite nation (15:17-18). Miriam and the women of Israel provide their own hymn in 15:21. They turn the reader's attention away from the pilgrimage into the wilderness and back to Egypt. Miriam's song is limited to Yahweh's power over nature in defeating the Egyptian army. The Song of Miriam provides a conclusion to the story of the exodus in Exodus 1–15.

The conflict between Yahweh and Pharaoh in 7:8–15:21 separates into the following three episodes:

I. 7:8-10:20 Initial Confrontation
II. 10:21–14:31 Defeat of Pharaoh
III. 15:1-21 Celebration of Victory

---

38. See Dozeman, *God at War,* 44-46.

39. J. Blenkinsopp, "Memory, Tradition, and the Construction of the Past in Ancient Israel," in *Treasures Old and New: Essays in the Theology of the Pentateuch* (Grand Rapids: Eerdmans, 2004), 1-17; M. S. Smith, *The Memoirs of God: History, Memory, and the Experience of the Divine in Ancient Israel* (Minneapolis: Fortress, 2004), 140-51.

COMMENTARY

INITIAL CONFRONTATION (7:8–10:20)

The description "plagues" for the divine actions in 7:8–10:20 does not capture the full range of meaning in the events. Hebrew *deber,* "plague," describes the death of cattle (9:3) and lightning (9:24). It is reinforced in 9:14, when all of the actions of Yahweh are described as "blows" *(maggēpōt),* and when the death of the Egyptian firstborn is announced in 11:1 as one final "strike" *(negaʿ).* A range of Hebrew verbs reinforces the imagery of conflict associated with plagues. Yahweh "strikes" *(nāgap)* the Egyptians with frogs (7:27) and by killing their firstborn (12:23, 27). And God "smites" *(nākâ)* the Egyptians by turning the Nile into blood (7:17), and by sending frogs (7:25), gnats (8:13), and hail (9:15). But these actions are also instances of revelation. Thus the plagues are "wonders" *(môpĕtîm,* 7:3, 9, 11:9, 10) and "signs" *('ōtōt,* 7:3; 8:23; 10:1, 2), revealing the power and character of Yahweh to Pharaoh and the Egyptians (7:3; 8:23; 11:9-10) and to the Israelites (10:1-2).

The cycle of the plagues follows loosely from the commissioning of Moses in 3:1–7:7. Yahweh predicts the plagues in 4:21-23, stating to Moses: "As you go to return to Egypt, see all the wonders that I placed in your hand, and do them before Pharaoh." The prediction provides a clear introduction to the plague cycle, but it also raises a problem of interpretation. It implies that Moses is equipped to perform the plagues, when he is not. Yahweh does provide Moses with three signs in 4:1-9, turning his staff into a snake, transforming water into blood, and inflicting leprosy on his hand. Two of the events also occur in the plague cycle (the sea dragon and blood). But the signs given to Moses are meant for the Israelites, not Pharaoh. Moses and Aaron may perform them before the elders of Israel in 4:29-31, while Moses also demonstrates the signs at later points in the wilderness journey (Numbers 12; 21:4-9).

The cycle of plagues evolves from the initial confrontation between Yahweh and Pharaoh in Exod 5:1–6:1, where the demand by Yahweh for the release of the Israelites and the refusal by Pharaoh set the stage for a conflict between the two characters. The plagues build on this initial confrontation elaborating the nature and scope of the conflict between Yahweh and Pharaoh. The three cycles of the plagues explore the power of Yahweh over the elements of nature, including water (episode one, 7:8–8:15), land (episode two, 8:16–9:7), and air (episode three, 9:8–10:20) (see above, "Literary Structure"). Fretheim concluded that the cycle of the plagues, with its emphasis on nature, advances a theology of creation.[1] Central to this theology is the ancient Near Eastern belief

---

1. Fretheim, *Exodus,* 105-12.

that the morality of the king influences the well-being of creation and the fertility of the land.[2] As a result a king who oppresses his subjects risks the ecological ruin of his country.

The intertwining of human morality and the well-being of the land is a hallmark of the Israelite prophets.[3] Hosea states: "The land mourns" and "the beasts of the field, the birds of the air, and fish of the sea are dying," because humans are acting immorally (Hos 4:1-3). Amos also describes drought and even "pestilence after the manner of Egypt" (Amos 4:9) sent by Yahweh as a result of immoral action. Joel too equates an invasion of locusts with the divine judgment (Joel 1–2), a motif that will also appear in the plague cycle. The oracles of Hosea, Amos, and Joel indicate that human oppression has ecological consequences. It can undo creation.

The plagues on the land of Egypt are the result of the breakdown in the moral order because of the actions of Pharaoh. Fretheim writes: "Pharaoh's oppressive, anti-life measures against Israel are anticreational, striking at the point where God was beginning to fulfill the creational promise of fruitfulness in Israel."[4] He notes that the motifs of blessing and fertility in Genesis 1 repeat in the opening verses of Exodus (see Gen 1:28 and Exod 1:7). The plagues signify the undoing of creation for the Egyptians as a result of Pharaoh's actions. The breakdown of creation progresses through "every tree," "all the fruit," and "the whole land," until darkness engulfs the land of Egypt.

Propp cautions that the theme of anticreation is not as explicit as Jer 4:23-26, where the land regressed to darkness and "waste and void" recalling Gen 1:1-2. He adds that certain plagues (blood, frogs, biting insects, and boils) lack the scope of a cosmological event. The plagues may not envision the return to chaos as explicitly as Jeremiah, but creation is certainly a central theme, especially its relationship with the moral character of the king. The resistance of Pharaoh to the demand of Yahweh that he release the Israelites results in ecological disaster to his kingdom. The officials of Pharaoh finally state to him during the plague of locusts: "Do you not yet know that Egypt is perished?" (Exod 10:7). Z. Zevit rightly concludes that at the end of the plague cycle Egypt is pictured as a "land in which creation is undone."[5]

The plague cycle receives surprisingly little interpretation in biblical tradition. It is the subject of two psalms. Psalm 78 reflects the perspective of the Non-P History recounting the plagues as actions directed toward the Israelites with the aim of instilling faith in them. Psalm 105 is more reminiscent of the P

2. See H. Frankfort, *Kingship and the Gods* (Chicago: University of Chicago Press, 1978), 310-12.

3. See K. Koch, *The Prophets* (trans. M. Kohl; 2 vols.; Philadelphia: Fortress, 1982-1984).

4. Fretheim, *Exodus*, 106.

5. Zevit, "Priestly Redaction," 220.

History recounting the plagues as public displays of power aimed at the Egyptians. Neither psalm follows the form or sequence of the pentateuchal histories, suggesting fluidity in the tradition of the plagues.

Psalm 78 recounts the history of the Israelite people as a series of rebellions. The psalm is intended as intergenerational teaching about the past, hidden deeds of Yahweh (Ps 78:2-4). The theme of intergenerational teaching again recalls the perspective of the Non-P History (12:24-27; 13:1-16). The plagues may be mentioned in v. 12 before they are enumerated in vv. 40-55. The poetic structure makes the exact number of the plagues unclear. S. Loewenstamm counts seven: blood, flies and frogs, locusts, hail, cattle pestilence, pestilence on humans, death of the firstborn.[6] The message of Psalm 78 is that the Israelites rebelled in the wilderness forgetting the miracles of Yahweh on their behalf.

Psalm 105 is a hymn celebrating the past, public actions of Yahweh. It recounts tradition as a source of praise, not as a warning against rebellion. The plagues are one source for praise. They are not "hidden things from old" (Ps 78:2). They are judgments performed publicly in "all the earth" (Ps 105:5-7), sharing the point of view of the P historian. The recounting of the plagues includes yet another sequence. Scholars debate the exact number.[7] Loewenstamm concludes the following: darkness, blood, frogs, swarms and lice, hail, locusts, slaying firstborn.[8] The recounting of the plagues is aimed at the Egyptians: "[Moses and Aaron] performed his miraculous signs among them [the Egyptians], his wonders in the land of Ham" (Ps 105:27). The focus on the Israelite rebellion in Psalm 78 is absent. In its place are public demonstrations of Yahweh's power "in all the earth."

The plagues are also mentioned in a number of sermons and prayers. Moses refers to the signs performed by Yahweh (Deut 11:3; 13:2) as do Joshua (Josh 24:5) and Ezra (Neh 9:10). Josephus (*Vita* 2.293) and Philo (*Mos.* 1.146) interpret the plagues as occasions for instruction of the Israelite people. In Jewish legend the plagues parallel the cruel treatment of the Israelites.[9] In the NT the sermon of Stephen continues the tradition of Moses, Joshua, and Ezra, referring to the plagues as "wonders" and "miraculous signs" (Acts 7:36). The apostle Paul provides a unique midrash on Exod 9:16 in Rom 9:17, transforming the motif of Pharaoh's hardened heart to account for the rejection of the Jews to the mission of Jesus. This interpretation recalls Psalm 78. Revelation 16 is more in the tradition of Psalm 105, where the plagues are public, cosmological events, performed before the nations, signaling the end of time.

---

6. S. E. Loewenstamm, *The Evolution of the Exodus Tradition* (trans. B. J. Schwartz; Jerusalem: Magnes, 1992), 88.

7. B. Margulis, "The Plague Tradition in Ps 105," *Bib* 50 (1969): 491-96.

8. Loewenstamm, *Evolution of Exodus Tradition*, 184-88.

9. Ginzberg, *Legends*, 2:345-47.

Episode One: Water (7:8–8:15)

The first cycle of plagues focuses on water. Aaron changes his staff into a snake or, better, the sea dragon (*tannîn*, 7:8-13). Next he and Moses transform the water of the Nile into blood (7:14-24). The third plague is an invasion of frogs, which progresses from the water to the land (7:25–8:15).

Sea Dragon (7:8-13)

⁷:⁸*And Yahweh said to Moses and to Aaron, saying,* ⁹*"When Pharaoh speaks to you, saying, 'Give your wonder,' you will say to Aaron, 'Take your staff and throw it before Pharaoh.' It will become a sea dragon."* ¹⁰*And Moses and Aaron came to Pharaoh and they did so, as Yahweh commanded. And Aaron threw his staff before Pharaoh and before his servants. And it became a sea dragon.*

¹¹*Pharaoh also called to the wise men and to the sorcerers. And they also, the magical priests of Egypt, did so with their secret enchantments.* ¹²*And each threw his staff and they became sea dragons. And the staff of Aaron swallowed their staffs.* ¹³*The heart of Pharaoh hardened. And he would not listen to them as Yahweh had spoken.*

Notes

7:9 *wonder*. The Sam (*'wt 'w mwpt*) and the LXX (*sēmeion ē teras*) read "sign or wonder."

Aaron. The LXX includes "your brother."

sea dragon. The MT and Sam use the word *tannîn*, the sea monster (Gen 1:20-21) or the sea dragon (Isa 27:1) in the Hebrew Bible. The LXX conveys the same meaning with the word *drakōn*, "water snake" or "dragon." Compare the more ambiguous translation in NRSV, "snake."

It will become. The MT *yĕhî* can also be translated "let it be," making the final clause a continuation of the words of Moses, rather than a divine prediction of the event. The translation follows the repetition of the phrase in 7:10.

7:10 *servants*. The LXX reads *therapontōn*, which also means "servants," but can signify medical caretakers, as in Eng. "therapist."

7:11 *sorcerers*. The LXX employs Greek *pharmakous* for Hebrew *mĕkaššĕpîm*, continuing the medical emphasis from the previous verse. A *pharmakeus* is one who uses drugs for spells, witchcraft, or healing (note Eng. "pharmacist").

the magical priests. Hebrew *ḥarṭummîm* is of Egyptian origin.[10] The LXX reads *hoi epaoidoi*, from *epaeidō*, suggesting incantation through song, most likely for the purpose of healing.

---

10. Jean-Michel de Tarragon, "Witchcraft, Magic, and Divination in Canaan and Ancient Israel," *CANE* 3:2076.

secret enchantments. The LXX continues the medicinal imagery by repeating the reference to pharmacy, *pharmakeiais.*

7:13 *hardened.* Here the LXX translates Hebrew *ḥāzaq* as *katischysen*, "overpowered" "prevailed." Wevers notes that it is the only occurrence of this Greek word for Hebrew *ḥāzaq* in the LXX. All other instances of *ḥāzaq* are translated *sklērynō*, "to harden."[11]

Commentary

The P author has composed the plagues of the sea dragon (7:8-13), the gnats (8:16-19), and the boils (9:8-12). Some scholars conclude that the account of Aaron turning his staff into the sea dragon is not a plague, because there is no request for Pharaoh to release the Israelites. Childs, for example, suggests that the event lies outside the plague cycle, providing an introduction to the events. He concludes that the central theme of this episode is to establish the authority of Moses.[12] But there is a problem with this reading. Moses is not prominent in this story. Furthermore the absence of a demand for Pharaoh to release the Israelites does not indicate that the story stands outside the plague cycle, since none of the P plagues contain such a demand.

The plague of the sea dragon is the first act in the plague cycle. Its central theme is the transformation of Aaron's staff into the *tannîn*, "sea monster." The motif of the sea provides the introduction to two subsequent plagues also associated with water, turning the Nile into blood and the infiltration of frogs from the water onto the land. Like the P plagues of gnats (8:16-19) and boils (9:8-12), the plague of the sea dragon follows a four-part structure, including divine commission (vv. 8-9), the event (v. 10), an action by the magicians (vv. 11-12), and resistance by Pharaoh fulfilling a divine prediction (v. 13).

7:8-9   Yahweh predicts to Moses and Aaron that Pharaoh will request a "wonder" *(môpēt)* from them. With this motif the P writer provides a connection to the prediction of the death of the firstborn in the Non-P History (4:21-23), where future plagues were also described as wonders. The wonder in the P story of 7:8-13 is that when Aaron throws down his staff it will become the sea dragon, *tannîn.*

The P author identifies the *tannîn* in the creation mythology of Genesis 1, when, on the fifth day, God commands the waters to bring forth creatures (Gen 1:20). On this day God also creates the "great sea monsters" (*hattannînim haggĕdōlîm*, Gen 1:21). The NIV translation, "So God created the great creatures of the sea," does not capture the meaning of the Hebrew. A better translation is NRSV, "So God created the great sea monsters." Hebrew *tannîn* is described

---

11. Wevers, *Notes*, 98.

12. Childs, *Exodus*, 151-53. See also W. Janzen, *Exodus* (Believers Church Bible Commentary; Waterloo, Ont.: Herald, 2000), 115-17.

more precisely as the dragon in the Hebrew Bible (Isa 27:1; 51:9; Job 7:12), accounting for the translation "sea dragon." The sea dragon often represents cosmological forces of chaos in the ancient Near East. In Canaanite religion the sea god, Yamm, is the personified opponent of the god of life, Baal. Also in Babylonian religion the chaotic water goddess, Tiamat, opposes the creator god, Marduk. Isaiah 27:1 associates the *tannîn* with Leviathan, the sea dragon, who will one day be destroyed by Yahweh. Ezekiel, by contrast, mythologizes Pharaoh as the "sea monster" (Ezek 29:3-7).

The staff of Aaron is introduced in this story. It must be distinguished from Moses' staff, introduced in Exod 4:2, 4, 17, and also identified as the "staff of God" (4:20; 17:9). Both staffs have magical power. Each turns into a snake, although of different types. Moses' staff turns into a land snake, *nāḥāš* (4:3), while, as we have seen, Aaron's staff turns into the sea dragon. Both Aaron and Moses employ their staffs during the plague cycle. Moses commands Aaron to strike the Nile (7:19) and to bring forth frogs from the water (8:5). Aaron also uses his staff to bring gnats from the earth (8:16 17). Moses uses his staff to change the water of the Nile into blood (7:17), to bring a hailstorm (9:23) and locusts (10:13) on the Egyptians, and to part the Red Sea (14:16). The magical staff of Moses also brings victory in war during the wilderness journey (17:8-16), while Aaron's staff grows buds in the tabernacle, confirming his authority as high priest (Numbers 17).

7:10-13 The action of Aaron prompts Pharaoh to call three groups: wise men or sages *(ḥăkāmîm)*, sorcerers *(mĕkaššĕpîm)*, and magicians *(ḥarṭummê miṣrayim)*. The category of sage is common in both Egypt and Israel. Sages assume a leadership role in Deut 1:13. The Egyptian sages are called to interpret Pharaoh's dream in the story of Joseph (Gen 41:8). The designation of sorcerers is not common in the Hebrew Bible. They are mentioned in Dan 2:2 as dream interpreters, and they are condemned in Deut 18:10. Both the sages and the sorcerers play no role in the story. Rather, it is the third category, the magicians, who take on a central role in the P interpretation of the plagues. They reappear in the plagues of blood (Exod 7:22), frogs (8:7), gnats (8:18-19), and boils (9:11). Their power is described as "secret arts" *(lahăṭîm)* — the lore and enchantments that sustain Egyptian religion and culture.

The Hebrew term for the magicians, *ḥarṭummîm,* is an Egyptian title for the "chief ritualist" *(hrj-tp)* of magic and divination. Magic is central to Egyptian religion and culture. Its purpose, according to J. F. Borghouts, is to avert danger and to protect. The power of magic is rooted in its antiquity. Heka, the personification of magic, states: "I am he whom the Sole Lord made before two things came into being on earth. . . . I am charged with the protection of what the Sole Lord has ordained." Magic sustained the order of creation by warding off elements of chaos. And, writes Borghouts: "Because magic was regarded as a defensive weapon, its use was tantamount to an act of war. . . . A magician would be called a 'warrior.'" There were levels of magicians and degrees of magical power in Egypt. Local magicians could devise simple spells. But the "chief ritualists," the magicians confronting Aaron, were the "true professional theologians."[13] They were connected with the "House of Life," the repository of all sacred and secret traditions that sustained Egyptian society.[14]

The opening confrontation between Aaron and the Egyptian magicians is not a "cheap, juggler's trick."[15] The power of the Egyptian magicians is not for the purpose of producing supernatural wonders. Their power is a weapon of protection. The ability of the Egyptian magicians to conjure up the sea dragon with their magical staffs signifies a primordial confrontation about the control of chaos in the land of Egypt. That the Egyptian magicians have access to the same cosmic power as Aaron indicates the intensity of the conflict that is to follow. Yet the P author also provides a glimpse of the end with the comment that Aaron's staff/snake swallowed *(bālaʿ)* the others, perhaps an image of their undoing. The same imagery of being swallowed up by the *tannîn* is used to describe the Israelite exile in Jer 51:34, which might also provide commentary on the effect of the plagues on the Egyptians:

"Nebuchadrezzar king of Babylon has devoured us,
he has thrown us into confusion,
he has made us an empty jar.
Like a sea dragon he has swallowed us.

7:13   Pharaoh concludes the opening confrontation with acts of resistance. His heart is hard (see the commentary on 3:19-20; 4:21-23). And he refuses to listen, thus fulfilling the divine prediction.

Turning the Water into Blood (7:14-24)

7:14 *And Yahweh said to Moses, "The heart of Pharaoh is heavy, he refuses to send out the people.* 15 *Go to Pharaoh in the morning, as he is going out to the water. And you will station yourself to meet him on the edge of the Nile. And the staff, which was changed into a snake, you will take in your hand.* 16 *And you will say to him, 'Yahweh the God of the Hebrews sent me to you, saying, "Send out my people, so that they can serve me in the wilderness."* **But you have not listened until**

13. J. F. Borghouts, "Witchcraft, Magic, and Divination in Ancient Egypt," *CANE* 3:1775-85. Quotations from 1776, 1777, 1784.

14. See also H. te Velde, "Theology, Priests, and Worship in Ancient Egypt," *CANE* 3:1731-49.

15. Childs, *Exodus*, 152.

now. ¹⁷ **Thus said Yahweh, "By this you will know that I am Yahweh."** *See, with the staff that is in my hand, I am striking the water, which is in the Nile. And it will turn to blood.* ¹⁸*And the fish that are in the Nile will die, and the Nile will stink. And the Egyptians will not be able to drink water from the Nile.'"*

¹⁹**And Yahweh said to Moses, "Say to Aaron, 'Take your staff, and stretch your hand on the water of Egypt, on its rivers, its canals, and on its ponds, and on all the reservoirs of its waters, so that they become blood. And there will be blood in the entire land of Egypt, and in the wood and in the stones.'"**

²⁰**And Moses and Aaron did so, as Yahweh commanded.** *And he raised the staff, and he struck the water, which was in the Nile before Pharaoh and before his servants. And all the water that was in the Nile turned to blood.* ²¹*And the fish that were in the Nile died, and the Nile stunk, and the Egyptians were not able to drink water from the Nile.* **And the blood was in the entire land of Egypt.**

²²**But the magical priests also did so with their secret enchantments.** *And the heart of Pharaoh was hardened,* **and he did not listen to them, as Yahweh had spoken.** ²³*And Pharaoh turned and he entered his house. And he did not set his heart even to this.* ²⁴*And all the Egyptians dug for water to drink around the Nile, because they were not able to drink from the water of the Nile.*

Notes

7:14 *is heavy.* Hebrew *kābēd* occurs in the LXX as *bebarētai*, "is weighed down, depressed."

7:15 *to the water.* The Sam *hmym*, "water," lacks the accusative ending signifying direction in the MT *hammaymāh*.

into a snake. Hebrew *nāḥāš* repeats the sign from 4:2-4 and contrasts to the sea dragon in 7:8-13. The LXX uses *ophis*, "serpent," as compared to *drakōn* in 7:8-13.

7:19 *Aaron.* The LXX adds "your brother" after "Aaron."

ponds. Hebrew *'ăgam* means a swamp or pool of reeds. The LXX *ta helē* means "marshland."

reservoirs. Hebrew *miqweh*, "ditch" or "reservoir," is rendered *synestēkos* in the LXX, the perfect participle of *synistēmi*, likely referring to cisterns made by humans. The *miqweh* in Gen 1:10 suggests a more primordial meaning, the "sea."

in the wood and in the stones. The image may be primordial, in which case the polluted water progresses from the Nile, to the ponds, to the primordial sea *(miqweh)*, and finally making its way into wood and stone. Many translations add "vessels," although it is absent from both the MT and the LXX. In this case the progression of the pollution is from nature to human receptacles. The pollution of blood moves from the Nile, to its tributaries (ponds), to the human-made canals (reservoirs), and finally to human vessels of wood and stone containing water.

7:23 *and he did not set his heart even to this.* Hebrew *šît lēb*, "to set the heart," is not common in the Hebrew Bible. In Prov 24:32 and 1 Sam 4:20 it means "to consider."

The LXX underscores this meaning by translating Hebrew *lēb* with *nous,* "mind," rendering the MT: *kai ouk epestēsen ton noun autou oude epi toutō,* "he paid no attention even to this." The MT relates the action of Pharaoh and its consequence for the Egyptians through the repetition of sounds. The description of Pharaoh, "he did not set *(wĕlō'-šat)* his heart," leads to the Egyptians' inability "to drink" *(lištôt).*

Commentary

The transformation of water into blood separates into three parts: a divine command (vv. 14-19), the execution of the event (vv. 20-22a), and the response of Pharaoh (vv. 22b-24). Both the Non-P and the P authors follow the three-part structure of the story. But each presents a distinct interpretation of the plague. The Non-P History includes 7:14-16a, 17a*a*, b, 18, 20a*b*-21a, 22b*a*, 23-24; and the P History consists of 7:16b, 17a*b*, 19-20a*a*, 21b, 22a, b*b* (see above, "Authors").

The turning of water into blood is the first plague in the Non-P History. It immediately follows the exchange between Yahweh and Moses in 5:22–6:1, where Moses accused Yahweh of not saving the Israelites, prompting Yahweh to predict the plagues. The plague is also connected to the third sign given to Moses in 4:1-9. The account of the plague includes the command of Yahweh that Moses strike the Nile with his staff turning it into blood (7:14-16a, 17b-18), the execution of the command by Moses (7:20a*b*-21a), and Pharaoh's resistance (7:23-24). The Non-P History focuses exclusively on Moses and the power of his staff. Aaron is absent. The content and scope of the plague is that the Nile River is turned into blood, killing the fish and becoming undrinkable for humans. The central theme is that Pharaoh release the Israelites from their slave labor for worship in the wilderness.

The turning of water into blood is the second plague in the P History. It follows the confrontation between Aaron and the magicians concerning the sea dragon (7:8-13). The P literature includes the command (7:16b, 17a*b*, 19), the execution of the event (7:20a*a*, 21b, 22b*a*), and Pharaoh's resistance (7:22b*b*). The distribution indicates that the P History is intended to reinterpret the Non-P History. The additions expand the theme and bring the structure of the story into conformity with the initial confrontation between Aaron and the Egyptian magicians. The P author also adds an additional purpose for the plague. The demand for Pharaoh to release the Israelites from slave labor will bring Pharaoh to the knowledge of Yahweh (7:16b, 17a*b*). In addition the P author includes a second divine command shifting the focus from Moses to Aaron, and expanding the scope of the plague to include all water in the land of Egypt (7:19). Thus in the P interpretation Aaron, not Moses, executes the plague with his staff (7:20a*a*, 21b) and the Egyptian magicians respond with a similar action (7:22a). Finally the resistance of Pharaoh is indicated by his not "listening," a term favored by the P author (7:22b*b*; see 7:13).

7:14-19 The Non-P account of the plague of blood makes frequent reference to earlier literature. Yahweh's statement in v. 14 about Pharaoh's refusal to send out the Israelites follows from the initial confrontation in 5:1–6:1. Pharaoh's resistance is now characterized as a "heavy heart," a motif that will repeat in the plagues of frogs (8:15), flies (8:32), cattle (9:12), and hail (9:34). The divine demand in 7:16 that the Israelites be allowed to worship in the desert is a repetition from 5:1. And the magical staff of Moses mentioned in 7:15 and 17 is the same one used to produce the land snake, *nāḥāš,* in 4:3-5. Only now it becomes a weapon against the Egyptians and not a sign to instill faith in the Israelites (see 4:5).

Moses is instructed to transform the Nile River into blood. Scholars have sought to interpret this action as a seasonal reddening of the water in the Nile River. But the details of the story argue against such a naturalistic reading. The water is undrinkable and the fish even die. The story takes on significance in the broader context of Egyptian religion. The Nile River is divine, personified as the god Hapi. Its yearly flooding is a source of life in Egypt, associated with the god Osiris, the divine father of the pharaoh. The transformation of the Nile River into blood is an attack against the Egyptian gods. It also renders the land of Egypt ritually impure. The Egyptians themselves use such imagery to signify catastrophe: "The River is blood. . . . The people thirst for water."[16]

The time of the confrontation is important. Yahweh commands Moses in v. 15 to meet Pharaoh at dawn *(bōqer).* Similar confrontations at dawn occur in the plagues of flies (8:20) and hail (9:13). The final confrontation at dawn is the destruction of the Egyptian army in the Red Sea (14:27). (See above, "Literary Structure.") The emphasis on dawn may signify a nocturnal revelation to Moses. Yahweh appears to Samuel at night (1 Samuel 3). It also suggests a liturgical background to the plague cycle and the defeat of Pharaoh at the Red Sea, in which events of salvation take place at break of day. Psalms 17, 27, and 63 describe night vigils. And Ps 46:5 celebrates the salvation of Yahweh "at break of day."

The P author changes the focus of the plague from Moses to Aaron and expands the scope of the plague in v. 19. Thus Aaron, not Moses, turns water into blood with his staff. The action of Aaron results in a more cosmological event. Not only the Nile River but all the rivers, canals, and ponds in Egypt turn to blood. Indeed, "all their gathered water" *(kol-miqwēh mêmêhem)* turned to blood, according to the P author. The translation "reservoirs" does not capture the scope of the plague. The same phrase in Gen 1:10 suggests a more primordial meaning. In the creation story the P author identifies the "gathered water" as "sea" in distinction from dry land. The same expansion in scope is evident in the P writer's version of the flood story (Genesis 6–9). What is a regional inundation

16. *ANET,* 441.

of rain in the Non-P History (Gen 7:17, 22-23) becomes a cosmological flood in the P History (Gen 7:18-21, 24). In the P interpretation of the plagues Aaron first conjures up the sea dragon with his staff (Exod 7:8-13) and then he transforms the sea itself into blood. The pollution of water by blood even extends to all containers. As a result blood replaced water "in the entire land of Egypt."

The P author also adds a polemical purpose to the event in v. 17a*b*. For the P author it is not enough that the Israelites escape from Egypt and worship Yahweh in the desert. Pharaoh must also recognize the power of Yahweh. Moses states to Pharaoh: "By this you will know that I am Yahweh" (7:17a*b*). The need for Pharaoh and the Egyptians to acknowledge Yahweh was introduced by the P author in 7:5, and the motif continues throughout the plague cycle (frogs, 8:10b*b*; flies, 8:22b; hail, 9:14b; locusts, 10:2b).

7:20-22a Moses and Aaron execute the divine command. Yet the action in vv. 20-21a is described in the singular. One person, most likely Moses, raises his staff and strikes the water, since the result corresponds to the Non-P account of the plague. Only the Nile River turns to blood. The fish die and the river itself "stinks" *(bā'aš)*. The defilement of the Nile River recalls the Israelites' condition before Pharaoh (5:21). The plague is bringing about a reversal, which will continue into the plague of frogs (8:10, 14), when not only the Nile River but also the land of Egypt will stink.

The P author adds two motifs to the event in 7:21b-22a. Blood was not limited to the Nile River, but "was everywhere in Egypt," a repetition of v. 19. And the Egyptian magicians counter by performing the similar action through their own secret arts. The transformation of water into blood, according to the P author, is a standoff between Aaron and the Egyptian magicians. Both sides have control over the sea dragon and the sea.

7:22b-24 Pharaoh assumes center stage in the final scene. The power of Yahweh looms in the background with the notice that divine prediction has been fulfilled. Yet Pharaoh remains in control of his destiny. He is the subject of the verbs: he refuses to listen, he hardens his heart, he turns away from Moses and goes to his palace. The closing scene is one of catastrophe, separating the retreating Pharaoh from his subjects. The Egyptians are described as digging wells in search of water, recalling the Egyptian text noted earlier: "The River is blood. . . . The people thirst for water."[17]

Frogs (7:25–8:15 [MT/LXX 7:25–8:11])

7:25 Seven days were filled after Yahweh struck the Nile. 8:1 (7:26) And Yahweh said to Moses, "Approach Pharaoh and say to him, 'Thus said Yahweh: "Send out my peo-

---

17. Ibid.

ple, so that they may serve me. 8:2 (7:27)*If you refuse to send out, indeed, I am plaguing all your boundary with frogs.* 8:3 (7:28)*And the Nile will breed frogs, and they will come up and they will enter into your house, and into your bedroom, and into your bed, and into the house of your servants, and on your people, and into your ovens, and into your kneading bowls.* 8:4 (7:29)*On you, on your people, and on all your servants the frogs will come up."''*

8:5 (8:1)**And Yahweh said to Moses, "Say to Aaron, 'Stretch out your hand with our staff on the rivers, on the canals, and on the ponds. And bring up frogs on the land of Egypt.'"** 6 (2)**And Aaron stretched out his hand over the water of Egypt. And the frogs came up and covered the land of Egypt.** 7 (3)**And the magical priests did so with their secret enchantments. And they brought up frogs on the land of Egypt.**

8 (4)*And Pharaoh called to Moses* **and to Aaron**. *And he said, "Pray to Yahweh, that he turn away the frogs from me and from my people. Then I will send out the people, so they can sacrifice to Yahweh."*

9 (5)*And Moses said to Pharaoh, "You may prevail over me. When should I pray for you, and for your servants, and for your people to cut off the frogs from you and from your houses? They will be left only in the Nile."*

10 (6)*And he said, "Tomorrow."*

And he said, "As you say, **so that you may know that there is no one like Yahweh our God.** 11 (7)*The frogs will turn away from you, and from your houses, and from your servants, and from your people. They will remain only in the Nile."*

12 (8)*Moses* **and Aaron** *went out from Pharaoh. And Moses cried out to Yahweh concerning the frogs, which he had placed on Pharaoh.* 13 (9)*And Yahweh did according to the word of Moses. And the frogs died from the houses, from the yard, and from the fields.* 14 (10)*And they heaped them up in heaps. And the land stank.* 15 (11)*And when Pharaoh saw that there was relief, he made his heart heavy,* **and he would not listen to them as Yahweh had spoken**.

Notes

8:2 (7:27) *I am plaguing.* The MT participle *nōgēp* is rendered in the LXX with the finite verb *typtō*, "to strike," rather than the more common *patassō*. For distribution of the Greek words see Wevers.[18]

all of your boundary. The LXX also renders Hebrew *gĕbûl* as "boundary," but in the plural, *ta horia.* Cf. NRSV "your whole country."

8:5 (1) *Aaron.* The LXX adds "your brother" after "Aaron."

on the canals. See 7:19.

8:7 (3) *magical priests.* The LXX adds, "of Egypt."

8:8 (4) *pray to Yahweh.* The LXX has "pray for me *(peri emou)* to the Lord."

8:9 (5) *You may prevail over me.* The MT *hitpā'ēr 'ālay* is difficult. The Hithpael of

---

18. Wevers, *Notes,* 106.

pā'ar with *'al* means "to show one's glory before." Is the phrase confrontational or polite? NRSV represents the latter meaning, "kindly tell me." The LXX is certainly less polite, but hardly confrontational, *taxai pros me,* "arrange for me when."

8:14 (10) *in heaps.* The MT *ḥomārim ḥomārim* derives from the measurement *ḥōmer,* "homer." The phrase in this form occurs only in this verse. A somewhat similar phrase appears in a saying of Samson, "with the jawbone of a donkey, heaps upon heaps *(ḥǎmôr ḥāmōrātāyim)*" (Judg 15:16). The LXX renders the phrase here in Exodus *thēmōnias, thēmōnisa,* "heaps, heaps."

Commentary

The plague of frogs completes the first cycle of plagues focused on water. The plague of frogs separates into three parts. Yahweh provides instruction for the plague (7:25–8:5). The action is performed (8:6-7). And there is an extended section exploring the response of Pharaoh (8:8-15). But unlike the previous plague of turning the water into blood, the Non-P and the P Histories diverge in their structure. The Non-P History includes 7:25; 8:1-4, 8-10b*a*, 11-15a*b*; and the P History consists of 8:5-7, 8a*a*, 10b*b*, 12a*a*, 15a*b*, b (see above, "Authors").

The Non-P History divides between the divine command to Moses (7:25–8:4) and the response of Pharaoh (8:8-15). The central theme is that Pharaoh release the Israelites for worship. The story does not narrate the actual plague. Instead the effects of the plague are recounted in the divine statement to Moses, when he is informed that there would be a breakdown of boundary between the water and the land with the swarming of frogs from the Nile River to the land of Egypt. The focus of the plague is on Pharaoh, especially his deceitful response to Moses. Unlike the plague of blood, the frogs penetrate Pharaoh's palace, his bedroom, and even his bed. He seeks relief from Moses through deceit, promising to release the Israelites. The motif of deceit underscores Pharaoh's control of his fate in the plague of frogs.

The P History brings the account of the plague of frogs into conformity with the story of the sea dragon (7:8-13) and the plague of blood (7:14-24), adding Aaron and the magicians to the confrontation. In addition to transferring the execution of the plague from Moses to Aaron, the P author also expands the scope of the event from the Nile River to all rivers and canals in the land of Egypt (8:5) in a similar manner as the plague of blood. The P author departs from the structure of the Non-P story by including Aaron's execution of the plague and the counterresponse by the magicians (8:6-7), completing the confrontation between Aaron and the magicians in the first cycle of plagues. Finally the P author also adds stock motifs to the response of Pharaoh. The theme is again expanded beyond the release of the Israelites for worship, so that the purpose of the plague is to bring Pharaoh to knowledge of Yahweh (8:10b). The resistance of Pharaoh is the result of his "not listening," thus fulfilling divine prediction (8:15a*b*, b).

7:25–8:5 A seven-day period transpires between the plagues of blood and frogs. The period of time may indicate defilement of the Nile River. Seven days is often the required time for purification from defilement (e.g., Num 19:10b-13). Yahweh commands Moses "to approach" *(bô')* Pharaoh with a message. Yahweh employs similar language in the plagues of cattle (9:1) and locusts (10:1). The command to approach provides contrast to the three plagues in which Moses is instructed to station himself before Pharaoh at dawn (blood, 7:15; flies, 8:20; and hail, 9:13).

The message of Moses to Pharaoh is fashioned in the form of a prophetic speech: "Thus said Yahweh." The content is a repetition from the plague of blood. Moses commands Pharaoh to release the Israelites for worship. Refusal will result in an attack by Yahweh. Yahweh states: "I am plaguing all your boundary *(gĕbûl)*." Two interpretations of this phrase are possible. Both emphasize the scope of the plague. The first interpretation designates the entire domain of the land of Egypt, as is reflected in NIV: "all of your country" (see also Josh 13:23, 27; Judg 19:29; 2 Sam 21:5). Thus all of Egypt will be plagued by frogs. A second interpretation places the scope of the plague in a cosmological context. Hebrew *gĕbûl*, "boundary," is also used to describe divine creation. Psalm 104 provides an example. The psalm is strongly influenced by Egyptian religion and may even be an Egyptian hymn in origin, the Hymn of Amenhotep IV.[19] Psalm 104 celebrates the creative power of Yahweh through architectural imagery. Yahweh stretches out the heavens like a tent, lays beams to hold water, and sets the mountains on their foundations. The result of the divine creation is the establishment of boundary *(gĕbûl)* between water and land, which cannot be crossed (Ps 104:9). The invasion of frogs from the Nile River into the land of Egypt may indicate the breakdown of the creation order as it is envisioned in Psalm 104, since the frogs cross the boundary between water and land. The same language returns in the plague of locusts where the border between air and land is crossed (Exod 10:4, 14, 19).

But why frogs? They are mentioned in the Hebrew Bible only in this story and in the two psalms that refer to the plagues (Pss 78:45; 105:30). No single answer emerges. The frogs may simply fit the literary needs of the Non-P author. They are associated with the water, yet they are also mobile allowing for an invasion of water creatures on to the land of Egypt. The frogs are also unclean for consumption according to Israelite food laws (Leviticus 11), thus introducing the theme of defilement into the story. The invasion of frogs into ovens and on cooking utensils reinforces the theme of defilement, as does the conclusion in 8:8-11 that the land of Egypt "stunk" from the frogs.

---

19. *ANET*, 370-71. For parallels between Psalm 104 and the Egyptian hymn see L. Allen, *Psalms 101–150* (WBC 21; Waco: Word, 1983), 28-31.

Other interpretations of the frogs have also been offered. There may have been a yearly inundation of frogs from the Nile River, suggesting the theme to the Non-P author. Or the frogs may represent a religious polemic. The Egyptian goddess Heket was portrayed with a frog's head. She was associated with life, particularly in assisting the god Khnum in the birth of humans.[20] The invasion of the frogs into Pharaoh's palace, his bedroom, and even onto his bed as a plague, rather than the blessing of life, may be a statement against the Egyptian goddess. The invasion of frogs into the bed of Pharaoh is equally a polemic against the god Bes. He is the god of the bedroom, associated with fertility and the protection of the family — especially at night and during the birth of children.[21] Or it may be a polemical statement against Pharaoh. Does the Non-P author wish to allude to the death of the Egyptian firstborn? Is the invasion of frogs into Pharaoh's bed a harbinger of the death of the Egyptian firstborn? Perhaps. The P author certainly strengthens a polemical reading, introducing the Egyptian gods through the warning: Pharaoh must know "that there is no [god] like Yahweh, our God" (8:10b*b*; see 7:17 for the comment on the recognition formula).

The P author adds Aaron to the plague in 8:5. As was the case in the plague of blood, a divine command to Moses is transferred to Aaron, who is instructed to perform the plague with his magical staff. The scope of the plague is also expanded from the Nile River (8:3) to include all the rivers, canals, and ponds in Egypt, a repetition of 7:19.

8:6-7   Only the P author narrates the actual event. The narration allows for the continuation of the confrontation between Aaron and the Egyptian magicians. Aaron performs the plague by stretching his staff over the waters of Egypt, not just the Nile River. Once again the magicians perform the same act by means of their secret lore. They too bring up frogs from the water onto the land of Egypt.

The confrontation between Aaron and the Egyptian magicians over the power to control water through the first cycle of plagues is more or less a standoff. Each has access to the sea dragon. Each has the ability to transform water into blood. And now each is able to bring frogs from the water onto the land. The only difference between the power of Aaron and the magicians in the entire first cycle of plagues occurred in the first plague when Aaron's sea dragon swallowed the sea monsters of the Egyptian magicians.

8:8-15   Pharaoh takes center stage in the plague of frogs. The previous plague of blood did not penetrate into the house of Pharaoh. And, as a consequence, it ended abruptly with Pharaoh retreating to his house. The plague of frogs is a development in the intensity of the divine attack on Pharaoh. Frogs

20. Cassuto, *Exodus*, 101.
21. Te Velde, *CANE* 3:1736-40.

fill Pharaoh's house, his bedroom, and even his bed. He is no longer able to retreat from the plague, and this gives rise to an extended exchange between Pharaoh and Moses.

The exchange between Pharaoh and Moses underscores the freedom of Pharaoh to determine the nature and extent of the conflict with Yahweh. Pharaoh begins the interaction by requesting that Moses "pray" (Hiphil of '*ātar*) to Yahweh, an initial acknowledgment of the power of Yahweh (compare 5:2). The request also allows for the development of Moses as an intercessor. He will intercede through prayer two more times to halt a plague (flies, 8:29-30; and locusts 10:17-18). But Pharaoh is deceitful, a character trait established in the opening chapters of Exodus. He promises to release the Israelites for worship, specifically sacrifice, if Moses would pray for him.

The response of Moses in v. 9 appears odd upon first reading: "You may prevail over me. When should I pray for you?" (see NIV: "I leave to you the honor of setting the time for me to pray for you." And NRSV: "Kindly tell me when I am to pray for you"). The Hebrew verb *pā'ar* means "to show one's glory." Propp interprets the statement as "mock humility" by Moses.[22] Childs suggests that Moses is giving Pharaoh an advantage by letting him determine the exact time in which the plague of frogs would be removed.[23] Cassuto asserts that the response underscores Moses' complete trust in Yahweh.[24] But the focus of the exchange is as much on Pharaoh as it is on Moses. The impact of Moses' statement is that Pharaoh is given complete control of the situation. He is allowed to determine the outcome of the plague. The plague of frogs is not a predetermined event in the Non-P History. Pharaoh is an active participant in determining his own fate.

Pharaoh chooses the following day for the reversal of the plague of frogs. Moses intercedes by crying out to Yahweh, the only instance of this action in the plague cycle. Moses will cry to Yahweh for the Israelites in the wilderness (15:25; 17:4). As a result of Moses' intercession, the frogs are restricted once again to their habitat in the Nile River. Those on land die, creating a "stink" or pollution. The plagues of blood and frogs result in the pollution of both the Nile River and the land of Egypt (see the pollution of the Nile River in the previous plague, 7:21). The closing scene underscores the deceit of Pharaoh. When Pharaoh saw relief, he (not Yahweh) "hardened" (Hiphil of *kābēd*) his heart (8:15).

The P author adds several motifs to the exchange between Pharaoh and Moses. Aaron is woven into the event in 8:8. The intercession of Moses is intended to teach Pharaoh that there is no god like Yahweh (8:10b; see the discus-

22. Propp, *Exodus 1–18*, 326.
23. Childs, *Exodus*, 156.
24. Cassuto, *Exodus*, 103.

sion of this motif in the introduction to 7:8–15:21, "Authors: The P History"). And Pharaoh's resistance is indicated as his "not listening" *(šāma')*, which fulfills a divine prediction (8:15b).

Episode Two: Land (8:16–9:7)

The second cycle focuses directly on the land and its inhabitants. First, Aaron brings forth gnats from the "dust of the earth" *('ăpar hā'āreṣ)* (8:16-19). Second, the biting insects or flies infest the "ground" *(hā'ădāmâ)* of the Egyptians, but not the "land of Goshen" *('ereṣ gōšen)* where the Israelites live (8:20-32). Third, all the Egyptian livestock of the field *(běmiqněkā 'ăšer baśśādeh)* are killed (9:1-7).

Gnats (8:16-19 [MT/LXX 12-15])

8:16 (12)*And Yahweh said to Moses, "Say to Aaron, 'Stretch out your staff and strike the dust of the earth, so that it may become gnats in all the land of Egypt.'"*

17 (13)*And they did so. And Aaron stretched his hand with his staff. And he struck the dust of the earth. And there were gnats on humans and on animals. All the dust of the earth was gnats in all the land of Egypt.*

18 (14)*And the magical priests did so with their secret enchantments to bring forth gnats. But they were not able. And the gnats were on humans and on animals.* 19 (15)*And the magical priests said to Pharaoh, "It is the finger of God." But the heart of Pharaoh was hardened and he did not listen to them, as Yahweh spoke.*

Notes

8:16 (12) *your staff.* The LXX includes a reference to the staff and Aaron's hand, "stretch out your staff with your hand."

gnats. The MT *kinnām*, "gnat, lice," is rendered in the LXX *skniphes*, "an insect found under the bark of trees, eaten by the woodpecker," or "an insect that attacks vines." Note the phrase *ho sknips en chōra*, "a flea at home!" (LSJ 1613).

8:17 (13) *All the dust of the earth was gnats in all the land of Egypt.* The LXX qualifies, *kai en panti chōmati tēs gēs egenonto hoi skniphes en pasē gē Aigyptou*, "and in all the dust of the ground, there were gnats in all the land of Egypt."

Commentary

The P author writes about the plague of gnats to begin the second cycle of plagues as the sea dragon began the first cycle (7:8-13). The two plagues share a similar four-part structure: the divine instruction (8:16), the event (8:17), the response by the magicians (8:18), and the resistance by Pharaoh fulfilling divine prediction (8:19).

8:16-17   The divine instruction to Moses centers on Aaron and his staff. Aaron is commanded to strike the "dust of the earth" (*'ăpar hā'āreṣ*). The phrase occurs three times in these two verses. The motif indicates a change of focus in the elements of nature from water to land. The result of Aaron's action is that gnats emerge from the dust of the earth and spread out over all of the land of Egypt. Hebrew *kinnām*, translated "gnats," is unclear. It may signify lice, sand fleas, or mosquitoes. What is clear is that they originate from dust, not water. They represent a plague from dry land. Dry ground or dust is the substance from which humans are created (Gen 2:7). But in this plague dust brings biting creatures that torment animals and humans. There may be a religious polemic in the story. Dry ground is significant in Egyptian religion, represented by the god Geb, who, with his consort Nut (the sky), give life to Osiris. "Barley is grown 'on the ribs of Geb,' and the harvest is 'what the Nile causes to grow on the back of Geb,'"[25] not gnats. Whether the P author has the Egyptian deity in mind is difficult to determine. The P instructions for Passover (12:12) state that the judgment is against the Egyptian gods.

8:18-19   The Egyptian magicians attempt to counteract the plague as in the previous plagues. But there is progression in the role of the magicians within the plague cycle. They were equal to Aaron during the plagues associated with water in cycle one. But when the focus shifts to land they are unable to produce the same magic.

Verse 18 suggests initially that the Egyptian magicians will counteract the plague of Aaron. The language is stereotyped from the previous plagues: "And the Egyptians did the same with their secret arts" (7:11, 22; 8:7). Then the text takes a turn, underscoring the magicians' inability to perform the same action. They are not able to protect through their magic (see the commentary on 7:8-13). As a result, gnats infest animals and humans, signifying a progression in the intensity of the plagues.

The inability of the Egyptian magicians to counteract Aaron prompts speech. They advise or perhaps warn Pharaoh that the action of Aaron "is the finger of God." The finger of God may be associated with the arm or hand of God, perhaps symbolized in the staff of Aaron. It may also indicate that the magical power is beyond the written lore of the Egyptian magicians. The finger of God is associated with divine writing and secret instruction to Moses in 31:18 concerning the tabernacle. The statement indicates an acknowledgment of the power of God by the magicians. They will not return in the two remaining plagues of cycle two, where the focus is directed to the land.

---

25. Frankfort, *Kingship and the Gods*, 181-90.

Pharaoh lacks the insight of the magicians. He rejects their advice. He hardens his heart, and refuses to listen *(šāmaʿ)*, fulfilling a divine prediction to Moses.

Flies (8:20-32 [MT/LXX 16-28])

8:20 (16) *And Yahweh said to Moses, "Rise early in the morning and station yourself before Pharaoh, as he is going toward the water. And you will say to him, 'Thus said Yahweh, Send out my people, so that they may worship me.* 21 (17) *For if you do not send out my people, indeed, I am sending on you, on your servants, on your people, and on your houses, flies. And the houses of Egypt and even the ground, upon which they are, will be filled with the flies.* 22 (18) *But I will separate on that day the land of Goshen, upon which my people stand,* **so that you may know that I am Yahweh in the midst of the land.** 23 (19) *I will place a separation between my people and between your people. This sign will be tomorrow.'"*

24 (20) *And Yahweh did so. And heavy swarms of flies came into the house of Pharaoh, and the houses of his servants. And in all the land of Egypt the land was corrupted because of the flies.*

25 (21) *And Pharaoh called to Moses* **and to Aaron.** *And he said, "Go, sacrifice to your God in the land."*

26 (22) *And Moses said, "It is not right to do so, because an abomination of Egypt we will sacrifice to Yahweh our God. Thus we will sacrifice an abomination of Egypt before their eyes. Will they not stone us?* 27 (23) *A journey of three days we will go into the wilderness, and we will sacrifice to Yahweh our God as he may say to us."*

28 (24) *And Pharaoh said, "I will send you and you will sacrifice to Yahweh your God in the wilderness. Only do not go far! Pray for me!"*

29 (25) *And Moses said, "Indeed, when I go out from you, I will pray to Yahweh. And he will turn away the flies from Pharaoh, from his servants, from his people tomorrow. Only, let not Pharaoh continue to deceive, not sending the people out to sacrifice to Yahweh."*

30 (26) *And Moses went out from Pharaoh, and he prayed to Yahweh.* 31 (27) *And Yahweh did according to the word of Moses. And the flies turned away from Pharaoh, from his servants, and from his people. Not one remained.* 32 (28) *But Pharaoh made his heart heavy even this time, and he did not send out the people.*

Notes

8:21 (17) *flies.* Hebrew *ʿārōb* is unclear as to the type of insect. The LXX *kynomuian* is more precise, indicating "dog *(kyno)* fleas *(muian)*."

8:22 (18) *that I am Yahweh in the midst of the land.* The LXX expands the statement, *hoti egō eimi kyrios ho kyrios pasēs tēs gēs,* "that I am Lord, the Lord of all the land."

8:23 (19) *separation.* The meaning of Hebrew *pĕdut* is uncertain. It may mean redemption (Pss 111:9; 130:7; Isa 50:2). The LXX has *diastolēn*, "distinctness, discrimination."

this sign will be tomorrow. The LXX adds *epi tēs gēs*, "on the earth."

8:24 (20) *was corrupted.* Hebrew *tiššāḥēt*, a Niphal, indicates both destruction and defilement (Gen 6:11). The LXX *exōlothreuthē* emphasizes only total destruction.

8:27 (23) *he may say.* The modal sense of Hebrew *yō'mar* is rendered as a past tense in the LXX, *eipen*, "he said."

8:28 (24) *pray for me.* The LXX adds "to the Lord."

8:29 (25) *to deceive.* Hebrew *hātal* also conveys the sense of mocking. The LXX *exapatēsai* focuses more narrowly on deceit.

Commentary

The plague of flies separates into three sections: the divine instruction to Moses (8:20-23), the event (8:24), and the response of Pharaoh (8:25-32). The story is from the Non-P author. The central theme is that Pharaoh release the Israelites for worship in the wilderness, a repetition from the plagues of blood and frogs. Resistance to Yahweh's demand carries the threat that flies will ruin the land of Egypt. The threat indicates a shift in the elements of nature in the Non-P History from water in the previous plagues of blood and frogs to the land. The flies are not associated with the Nile River. They infest the ground (*'ădāmâ*, 8:21). The story focuses on Pharaoh's response to the plague, especially his deceitful character.

The P author adds little to the account. The insertion of the plague of gnats (8:16-19) as the introduction to the second cycle of plagues reinforces the transition from water to land in the Non-P History. But the standard motifs of the plagues from the P History are absent. Aaron does not perform the plague. The magicians do not enter the stage. And Pharaoh's resistance to the divine demand is not indicated with the motif of his refusing "to listen." Aaron is mentioned in passing (8:25ab), a possible addition by the P author. The description of the land of Egypt as being "ruined" may also be an addition by the P author. The polemical motif that Pharaoh must come to knowledge of Yahweh from the event (8:22b) is the clearest indication of an addition by the P author (see above, "P History").

8:20-23 Yahweh commands Moses to meet Pharaoh at dawn *(bōqer).* The emphasis on dawn repeats in the plagues of blood (7:14-24) and hail (9:13-35). The speech of Moses is cast in the form of a prophetic messenger speech: "Thus said Yahweh" (see also the plagues of blood, frogs, cattle, hail, and locusts). The divine demand is for Pharaoh to release the Israelites for worship (see also blood, 7:16; and frogs, 8:1). Refusal by Pharaoh carries the threat of flies. Hebrew *'ārōb* has a root meaning of "mixture." It is limited to this story and the two references to the plague in the Psalms (Pss 78:45; 105:31). The translation "flies" is provisional. Some form of biting insect is intended. They originate from the ground *('ădāmâ),* indicating that the breakdown of the cosmological order in Egypt is progressing from water to land. The flies will infest Pharaoh, his officers, and his people by infiltrating their houses.

The shift in focus from water to land is accompanied by a new motif in 8:22-23, a distinction between the land of Goshen where the Israelites live and the remainder of the land of Egypt. The land of Goshen, perhaps an area in the eastern half of the Delta (Gen 46:28-29, 33-34; 47:1-6, 11), will not be infested with the flies. The distinction that is introduced by Yahweh in Exod 8:23, "I will place a separation between my people and between your people," carries the meaning of redemption in Hebrew *(pĕdūt).* Yahweh will redeem the Israelites from the plague of flies. The redemption of the Israelites, not the plague of flies, is a "sign" *('ōt).* Previous "signs" in Exodus have been directed to Moses (3:12) and to the Israelite elders (4:8, 9, 17, 28, 30). It is not clear whether the Non-P author intends for the redemption of the Israelites to be a sign aimed at Pharaoh or the Israelites. The P author removes any ambiguity by placing the focus squarely on Pharaoh with the addition of the divine recognition formula in v. 22b: Pharaoh, not the Israelites, must know that "I am Yahweh in the midst of the land."

8:24 There is intensification in the execution of the plague. Moses changed the water of the Nile River into blood with his staff (7:20-21). The next plague, the plague of frogs, did not narrate the actual plague, moving instead from divine announcement (8:1-4) to Pharaoh's response (8:8-15). Now, in the plague of flies, it is Yahweh who performs the action. The flies infest the Egyptian houses. But worse, the land of Egypt is ruined.

The Hebrew root *šht,* describing the ruin of the land of Egypt, is common in the Hebrew Bible. It signifies destruction, corruption, spoil, and decay of people (Hos 11:9), plants (Nah 2:3), buildings (Jer 48:18), and land (Josh 22:33). Thus for something or someone "to be ruined" may indicate brokenness (destruction) or defilement (spoil).

The particular form of Hebrew *šāhat,* "to ruin," a Niphal, in 8:24 has a passive meaning that occurs only five times in the Hebrew Bible. The clearest parallel to the plague of flies is the P writer's introduction to the flood story (Gen 6:9-21), where the land is also described as "ruined," prompting Yahweh to destroy it with the flood (Gen 6:11). The reason for the ruin of the land in the flood story is the violent action of humans. Other uses of the word "to ruin" emphasize defilement and pollution. Jeremiah 13:7 describes a soiled linen garment as "ruined," while in Jer 18:4 a damaged pot on the potter's wheel is equally "corrupted." Ezekiel 20:44 explicitly associates defilement *(ṭāmē')* with "ruin." The parallels provide a framework for interpretation. The ruin of the land of Egypt is a result of Pharaoh's violent actions against the Israelites. Such action by the king has ecological effects on his land, defiling it in this case through the infestation of the flies.

8:25-32 The response of Pharaoh to the different plagues builds in complexity. Pharaoh's initial reaction to the plague of blood was to retreat into his house (7:23). His reaction to the plague of frogs was more extensive (8:8-15). Pharaoh tricked Moses to intercede through prayer to halt the plague of frogs with the promise of releasing the Israelites. The trickery of Pharaoh continues in the plague of flies. It is expanded into two cycles of action, an initial exchange between Moses and Pharaoh (8:25-27) and a repetition of Pharaoh's request for intercessory prayer (8:28-32).

The initial exchange between Pharaoh and Moses (8:25-27) begins with a summons from Pharaoh. He commands Moses (and Aaron) to sacrifice in the land (8:25). The response of Moses in vv. 26-27 is ironic, given that the land of Egypt is defiled. He states that the Israelite sacrifices will be "detestable" to the Egyptians, requiring that the Israelites journey into the wilderness to worship. Herodotus repeatedly underscores the strict purity laws of the Egyptians, providing some context for the concern of Moses that the Israelites would be offensive in their sacrifice, resulting in further persecution.[26]

Hebrew *tôʿēbâ*, translated "detestable" or "abomination," has a cultic meaning. It occurs frequently in Deuteronomy to emphasize the exclusive claims of Yahweh upon the Israelites and their need to keep separate from other nations and other gods. Wearing silver and gold like the other nations (Deut 7:25-26), inquiring of other gods (12:31), and imitating any of the practices of foreigners (18:12) are "detestable" actions. The use of this phrase in the response of Moses may underscore the separation of Israelites and Egyptians. In the wisdom tradition, an "abomination" is any act that is hypocritical. Weinfeld writes: "It is this two-facedness or false pretension assumed when dealing with one's fellow man or in the execution of one's sacrificial dues that is an abomination to God."[27] The meaning of the term in the wisdom tradition also suggests an ironic interpretation, as commentary on Pharaoh whose actions throughout the book of Exodus are two-faced. The exchange between Moses and Pharaoh concludes with Pharaoh allowing the Israelites to worship in the desert, with the paradoxical provision that they not journey too far.

The second exchange between Moses and Pharaoh (Exod 8:28-32) returns to the topic of intercession, introduced in the plague of frogs. Pharaoh requests that Moses intercede through prayer. Moses agrees, but cautions Pharaoh not to

26. *Hist.* 2.18, 38-41.

27. M. Weinfeld, *Deuteronomy and the Deuteronomic School* (Oxford: Clarendon, 1972), 268-69.

mock him or Yahweh by continuing to deceive though broken promises. Hebrew *hātal*, "to mock through deception," is also used to describe the trickery of Laban against Jacob (Gen 31:7). But Pharaoh does trick Moses yet again. Once Yahweh removes the flies at the request of Moses Pharaoh hardens his heart and does not send out the Israelites.

Death of Animals (9:1-7)

⁹:¹*And Yahweh said to Moses, "Approach Pharaoh and speak to him, 'Thus said Yahweh the God of the Hebrews, Send out my people, so that they may worship me. ²For if you refuse to send out, and yet you hold them, ³indeed, the hand of Yahweh is on your cattle in the field, on the horses, on the donkeys, on the camels, on the herds, and on the flock — a very heavy plague. ⁴And Yahweh will separate between the cattle of the Israelites and between the cattle of the Egyptians. And from all that belongs to the Israelites nothing will die.'" ⁵Yahweh set an appointed time, saying, "Tomorrow, Yahweh will do this thing in the land." ⁶And Yahweh did this thing on the morrow. And all the cattle of the Egyptians died. But from the cattle of the Israelites not one died. ⁷And Pharaoh sent out, and, indeed, from the cattle of the Israelites not one died. Yet the heart of Pharaoh was heavy and he did not send out the people.*

Notes

9:3 *a very heavy plague.* Hebrew *deber* means "plague." The LXX has "death" *(thanatos)* in place of "plague." The MT plays with the root *dbr* throughout the story. Yahweh commands Moses in v. 1 to speak *(wĕdibbartā)*. The message in v. 3 is about the plague *(deber)*. Moses warns Pharaoh in v. 4 that not one "thing" *(dābār)* of the Israelites will die. And vv. 5-6 state twice that Yahweh performs the event *(dābār)*.

9:5 *Yahweh set an appointed time.* The LXX departs from the MT *yhwh*, employing *ho theos*, "the God," rather than the expected *kyrios*. The LXX renders Hebrew *mô'ēd*, "appointed time," as *horon*, "boundary, landmark, limit."

Commentary

The episode is short, separating into three parts: the divine announcement of the plague to Moses (9:1-5), the event (9:6), and the response of Pharaoh (9:7). The death of animals, like the plagues of gnats and flies, is directed to the land. The plague is targeted against the beasts of the field. The plague is part of the Non-P History. There are no additions to the story by the P author.

9:1-5 Most of the plague consists of Yahweh's instruction to Moses. The language of the divine instruction differs from previous speeches in the plague cycle in that the Deity is referred to for the most part in the third person, not in the first person. The form of the announcement, however, includes many of the features that appear in the other plagues within the Non-P History. Moses is commanded "to approach" *(bô')* Pharaoh (v. 1). The instructions to Moses are presented in the form of a prophetic messenger speech: "Thus said Yahweh." The central theme is that Pharaoh release the Israelites for worship (v. 1). And refusal carries the threat of the plague (vv. 2-3).

The content of the plague is outlined in vv. 4-5. The action of Yahweh is called a "plague" *(deber)* for the first time, suggesting perhaps intensification. The death of animals in the field is the second action of Yahweh aimed at the land. The species to be killed are horses, donkeys, camels, cattle, sheep, and goats. Naturalistic interpretations of the plague have been suggested. Sarna argues that the death of animals is the result of anthrax stemming from the death of frogs.[28] But the plague is certainly meant to function in the broader cosmological context of religion. The deification of cattle, cattle worship, and the Egyptian belief in the sacred bulls may lie behind the plague.[29] The death of the animals will result from a direct action by the "hand of Yahweh," as was the case in the plague of flies (8:24). There is no mediation through Moses.

Yahweh spells out two additional features of the plague. First, the distinction between Goshen, the land of the Israelites, and the remainder of Egypt is maintained in the death of animals. No Israelite livestock will die. Second, the time of the plague is emphasized. Yahweh states specifically that the plague will occur "tomorrow." The designation for the time of the plague by Yahweh is a reversal from the plague of frogs, when Pharaoh determined the time sequence of events (see 7:25–8:15, esp. 8:9-10).

9:6 Yahweh executes the plague, killing "all the livestock" of the Egyptians. The emphasis is on the magnitude of the action and the contrast to the Israelites, where not a single animal dies. The desire to provide an absolute contrast creates an internal literary problem when Egyptian livestock return in the plague of hail (9:19).

9:7 The response of Pharaoh takes a new turn in this story. He sends officials to examine the Israelite livestock. They report that none of the Israelite animals have died as compared to the wholesale slaughter of the Egyptian livestock. But not even this evidence persuades Pharaoh to release the Israelites for worship. He refuses the demand of Yahweh by hardening his heart.

---

28. Sarna, *Exodus*, 44-45.
29. Frankfort, *Kingship and the Gods*, 162-80.

Episode Three: Air (9:8–10:20)

The third cycle focuses on air. The plague of boils originates from soot thrown into the air (9:8-12). The heavens rain down hailstones (9:13-35). And the locusts invade on the east wind (10:1-20).

Boils (9:8-12)

⁹:⁸*And Yahweh said to Moses and to Aaron, "Take for yourselves soot of the kiln to fill the hollow of both hands, and Moses will dust it toward heaven before Pharaoh.* ⁹*And it will become powder on all the land of Egypt. And it will become on humans and on animals boils, inflamed blisters on all the land of Egypt."* ¹⁰*And they took the soot of the kiln and they stood before Pharaoh. And Moses dusted it toward heaven. And there were boils, inflamed blisters on humans and on animals.* ¹¹*But the magical priests were not able to stand before Moses on account of the boils. For the boils were on the magical priests and on all the Egyptians.* ¹²*Yahweh hardened the heart of Pharaoh. And he would not listen to them, as Yahweh had spoken to Moses.*

Notes

9:9 *inflamed blisters.* The MT *pōrēaḥ ʾăbaʿbuʿōt* translates more lit. "blisters sprouting." The verb *pāraḥ* conveys botanical imagery of a tree budding or flowering. The LXX employs *anazeousai,* "to bubble, break out, and boil over."

Commentary

The P author writes the story of the plague of boils. The account follows the stereotyped pattern of the plagues of the sea dragon (7:8-13) and the gnats (8:16-19) separating into four parts: the divine commission (vv. 8-9), the event (v. 10), the action of the magicians (v. 11), and the resistance by Pharaoh fulfilling the divine command (v. 12). The specific motifs indicate intensification in the plague cycle from land to air. Other signs of intensification include: Moses replaces Aaron in performing the action; the magicians are afflicted with the plague, and thus unable even to stand before Moses; and for the first time Yahweh hardens Pharaoh's heart.

   9:8-9 The divine instructions to Moses are precise. Many of the words are limited to this story or confined to the P purity legislation. Moses is to fill the palm of his hands *(hōpen)* with soot *(pîaḥ)* from a kiln and throw it toward heaven *(haššāmaymâ).* The command suggests liturgical and cultic action. The imagery of filling the palms occurs in Ezekiel when coals from beneath the cherubim signal the departure of Yahweh from the Jerusalem temple (Ezek 10:2). Aaron also fills his palms with incense from the altar when he presents a sin offering for himself on the Day of Atonement (Lev 16:12). The reference to soot is limited to this text. The effects of the action will be the breaking out *(pārah)* of boils *(šĕḥîn)*. The plague must be interpreted in the larger context of P purity law in Lev 13:18-23, where the same language occurs. Open, festering boils render a person unclean. Thus according to the P writer the plague of boils will advance contamination of the water and the land of Egypt to humans and animals. The transmission of pollution takes place through the air.

9:10 There is progression in the P writer's organization of the plague cycle. Aaron is the protagonist in the first two cycles. He turns his staff into the sea dragon and he strikes the ground with his staff, bringing forth the gnats. But Moses is the protagonist when the focus shifts to the air. Moses throws the soot toward heaven in the presence of Pharaoh, resulting in boils on animals and humans. The P author is explicit in stating that the boils render the Egyptians unclean. They are open wounds that bubble or blister *('ăba'bu'ōt)*.

9:11 The shift from Aaron to Moses is accompanied by a progression in the role of the magicians. Their magical power is defensive. It is meant to protect Pharaoh and the land of Egypt (see the commentary on 7:10-13). The magicians were able to counter the power of Aaron during the plagues in cycle one, where the focus was on water. They were unable to protect Egypt when the focus shifted to land (8:16-19), although they themselves were not affected by the plague. Now the magicians are unable to protect even themselves from the action of Moses. They do not appear before Moses because they are covered with running boils. The P writer is most likely making a polemical statement about the power of the professional Egyptian magicians to heal. The history of medical knowledge and medical training for healers and magicians was most likely located in the House of Life. The affliction of boils on the magicians suggests that the plague has penetrated to the heart of the Egyptian magic.[30] The magicians do not appear again in Exodus.

9:12 Yahweh not only penetrates into the very core of the Egyptian world of magic, he also invades the will of Pharaoh. In this plague Yahweh hardens Pharaoh's heart, giving him over to his resistance. This is the first time that Yahweh is the subject of the hardening. In all previous cases Pharaoh controlled his own destiny. With the breakdown of all Egyptian magic Pharaoh loses the ability to stand over against Yahweh. The scene closes with the stereotyped phrase that Pharaoh would not listen, thus fulfilling the divine prediction.

---

30. K. R. Weeks, "Medicine, Surgery, and Public Health in Ancient Egypt," *CANE* 3:1789.

Hail (9:13-35)

⁹:¹³ *And Yahweh said to Moses, "Rise early in the morning and station yourself before Pharaoh. And you will say to him, 'Thus said Yahweh, the God of the Hebrews: "Send out my people so they may worship me.* ¹⁴*For this time I am sending all of my blows against your heart, and against your servants, and against your people* **so that you will know that there is no one like me in all the land**. ¹⁵*For now I could have sent my hand, and struck you, and your people with the plague. And you would be effaced from the land.* ¹⁶*But for this I have let you stand, so that I could show you my power, in order to declare my name in all the land.* ¹⁷*Yet you continue to be haughty against my people without sending them out.* ¹⁸*Indeed, at this time tomorrow, I am going to rain down very heavy hail, the like of which has not been in Egypt from the day of its having been founded until now.* ¹⁹*Now send out and protect your cattle, and everything of yours in the field. All humans and animals found in the field, and not gathered into the house, will have the hail fall on them, and they will die."'"*

²⁰*And each one from the servants of Pharaoh who feared the word of the Yahweh rushed his servants and his cattle into the houses.* ²¹*And each one who did not set his heart to the word of Yahweh left his servants and his cattle in the field.*

²²*And Yahweh said to Moses, "Stretch your hand toward heaven, so that there is hail in all the land of Egypt, on humans, and on animals, and on all plants of the field in the land of Egypt."* ²³*And Moses stretched his staff toward heaven. And Yahweh gave thunder and hail. And fire came toward earth. And Yahweh rained down hail on the land of Egypt.* ²⁴*And there was hail, and fire flaring in the midst of the hail, very heavy, the like of which has not occurred in all of the land of Egypt from when it became a nation.* ²⁵*And the hail struck in all the land of Egypt and everything that was in the field, from humans to animals. The hail struck all the plants of the field, and all the trees of the field shattered.* ²⁶*Only in the land of Goshen, where the Israelites were, there was no hail.*

²⁷*And Pharaoh sent out and he called to Moses* **and to Aaron**, *and he said to them, "I sinned this time. Yahweh is the just one, and I and my people are the wicked ones.* ²⁸*Pray to Yahweh, enough of the thunder of God and hail! Let me send you out, so that you need not continue to stand."*

²⁹*And Moses said to him, "When I go out of the city, I will spread my hands to Yahweh, and the thunder will cease and the hail will be no longer,* **so that you may know that the land belongs to Yahweh**. ³⁰*You and your servants, I know that you do not yet fear before Yahweh God."*

(³¹*Now the flax and the barley were struck down, for the barley was ripe and the flax was in bud.* ³²*But the wheat and the spelt were not struck down, because they were late.)*

[33] *And Moses went out of the city from with Pharaoh. And he stretched his hands to Yahweh. And the thunder and the hail ceased. And rain no longer fell to the earth.* [34] *And when Pharaoh saw that the rain, and the hail, and the thunder ceased, he continued to sin. And he made his heart heavy, he and his servants.* [35] *And the heart of Pharaoh was hardened, and he did not send out the Israelites, as Yahweh had spoken by the hand of Moses.*

Notes

9:14 *my blows.* Hebrew *maggēpōtay* is rendered in the LXX *synantēmata mou*, "my occurrence."

9:16 *so that I could show you my power.* The LXX reads, "so that I might show my power in you." In the MT Pharaoh is the object of Yahweh's display of power, while in the LXX Pharaoh becomes the means by which Yahweh displays power.

9:18 *until now.* The LXX has *heōs tēs hēmeras tautēs*, "until this day."

9:19 *now send out and protect.* The MT *wĕʿattâ šĕlaḥ hāʿēz* is written in the LXX, *nyn oun kataspeuson synagagein*, "now therefore, hasten to gather."

9:21 *who did not set his heart.* The LXX reads, *hos de mē proseschen tē dianoia*, "who did not set the mind." Cf. 7:23, where the LXX translates the same Hebrew phrase as *ouk epestēsen ton noun autou*, to describe Pharaoh.

9:27 *this time.* The LXX reads, *to nyn*, "now."

9:28 *pray to Yahweh.* The LXX adds *peri emou*, "for me."

enough of the thunder of God and hail. The LXX changes the statement of exclamation in the MT so that Pharaoh states the content of the prayer, *kai pausasthō tou genēthēnai phōnas theou kai chalazan kai pyr*, "and may the thunder of God and the hail and fire cease to be."

9:29 *and the hail will be no longer.* The LXX adds *ho hyetos*, "the rain."

9:31 *bud.* Hebrew *gibʿōl* is rendered in the LXX *spermatizon*, "sown."

Commentary

The plague of hail divides into three parts: the divine announcement of the plague (vv. 13-21), the event (vv. 22-26), and the response of Pharaoh (vv. 27-35). The plague includes many of the motifs from previous plagues in the Non-P History (blood, frogs, flies, and cattle). Yahweh addresses Moses, not Aaron (v. 13). Moses is commissioned to speak as Yahweh's prophetic messenger: "Thus said Yahweh" (v. 13). The central theme is that Pharaoh must release the Israelites for worship (v. 13). Refusal by Pharaoh is accompanied by the threat of a plague, this time hail from heaven (v. 18). Moses initiates the plague with an action of his staff (v. 23). The Israelites are separated from the Egyptians (v. 26), thus avoiding the destructive power of the storm. Pharaoh requests an intercessory prayer from Moses (v. 28). And, upon the cessation of the plague, Pharaoh hardens his heart (v. 35).

But the plague of hail also includes many new motifs suggesting intensification. The most significant development is that Yahweh is presented as the Storm God. The imagery of the storm god is more common in ancient Mesopotamia and in Syria-Palestine than in Egypt.[31] One reason is that the thunderstorm is central to the agricultural cycle in Syria-Palestine. The flooding of the Nile River controls the agricultural cycle in Egypt.[32] The flooding of the Nile River influences religious rituals associated with the worship of Hapi, the god of the river, and Osiris, who also dwells in the river. But neither of these deities is a storm god.

The Canaanite god Baal is the god of the thunderstorm. His representation includes images of fertility and war. Baal wages war with his lightning bolts against the forces of death (the god Mot) and chaos (the god Yamm). And he brings forth life through the storm rains. His enthronement is proclaimed in the land through the claps of thunder in the storm.[33] In the mythology of the storm god Baal, the thunderstorm is an event of revelation, a celebration of life, and a proclamation of political victory and power. Baal is revealed in the seasonal storm, and his enthronement indicates political rule over his kingdom (see further comment on 15:1-17).

Ancient Israelites also worshiped Yahweh as the God of the thunderstorm.[34] Psalm 29 celebrates the revelation of Yahweh in the storm.[35] The voice of Yahweh is the thunder (v. 3). Bolts of lightning flash out from Yahweh as weapons striking the earth (v. 7). And Yahweh, like Baal, is the "rider of the clouds," meaning the God of the thunderstorm who sustains life in his kingdom (see also v. 8).[36] The imagery of the storm god suggests an invasion of Yahweh into the land of Egypt through the plague of hailstorm. The point of emphasis in the plague is on war. The frozen hailstones are not the life-giving power of the rain. Yahweh describes them as weapons of war in Job 38. The hailstorm destroys all humans, animals, and agriculture in its path. Yahweh states that the storm will result in the power of Yahweh becoming evident to Pharaoh and the name of Yahweh will be proclaimed in the land (v. 16). The divine prediction emphasizes both the revelation of Yahweh to Pharaoh and the political conquest of Pharaoh by Yahweh.

The P author adds little to the story of the hailstorm. The central motifs of

31. See M. S. Smith, "Myth and Mythmaking in Canaan and Ancient Israel," *CANE* 3:2031-41.

32. Frankfort, *Kingship and the Gods,* 85-86, 181-95; C. J. Eyre, "The Agricultural Cycle, Farming, and Water Management in the Ancient Near East," *CANE* 1:175-89.

33. *ANET,* 129-42.

34. J. Day, *God's Conflict with the Dragon and the Sea: Echoes of a Canaanite Myth in the Old Testament* (University of Cambridge Oriental Studies 35; Cambridge: Cambridge University Press, 1990); idem, "Baal," *ABD* 1:545-49; Cross, *Canaanite Myth and Hebrew Epic.*

35. See P. C. Craigie, *Psalms 1–50* (WBC 19; Waco: Word, 1983), 241-49; H.-J. Kraus, *Psalms 1–59: A Commentary* (trans. H. C. Oswald; Continental Commentary; Minneapolis: Augsburg, 1988), 344-51.

36. Yahweh is described in Ps. 68:4 as the "rider on the clouds," as is Baal in *CTA* 2.iv.8.

the P author, including the active role of Aaron and the response of the magicians, are absent. Aaron is included once in the story when Pharaoh summons both him and Moses (v. 27). More significantly the P author emphasizes both the revelation of Yahweh and the divine conquest of Egypt by inserting the recognition formula twice — the divine demand that Pharaoh come to knowledge of God from the event. This motif is a constant element in the P author's interpretation of the exodus (6:7; 7:5, 17a*b*; 8:10b*b*, 22b; 9:14b, 29b*b*; 10:2b; 11:7b; 14:4, 18). The first instance underscores the revelatory power of the event: Pharaoh must learn that there is no god like Yahweh in all the land (9:14b). The second occurrence stresses the motif of conquest: Pharaoh must learn that the land itself belongs to Yahweh (v. 29b).

9:13-21   The opening instructions of Yahweh to Moses are more extensive than in any previous plague. Many of the motifs from the previous plagues appear. The plague of hail begins with the divine command that Moses meet Pharaoh at dawn (see also the plagues of blood and flies). He must present Pharaoh with Yahweh's demand that the Israelites be allowed to leave Egypt in order to worship. But there are also new motifs. The intensification of the plague is indicated in v. 14, when Yahweh states: "For this time I am sending all of my blows against your heart." The P writer extends the divine speech in order to detail the effects of the plague on Pharaoh: he will know "that there is no one like me in all the land." The incomparability of Yahweh was also proclaimed to Pharaoh in the plague of frogs (8:10).

Further commentary on the power of Yahweh follows in vv. 15-16. The Egyptians could have been destroyed by now, states Yahweh. The purpose for prolonging the conflict has been to demonstrate divine power, and thus proclaim the name *(šēm)* of Yahweh in the land of Egypt. The power of Yahweh is associated with holy war in Exodus. Moses recalled Yahweh's victory over Pharaoh and deliverance of Israel as an event of great power executed through Yahweh's mighty hand (32:11). The victory hymn in Exodus 15 uses the same language (v. 6). Psalm 29:4 also extols the voice of Yahweh in the thunderstorm as strong.

The victory of Yahweh in the land of Egypt will establish the divine name in the land first revealed to Moses during his commission (3:15). The events of the exodus can be interpreted as an unfolding revelation of the divine name. And once revealed the name must be feared (20:7). The Psalms and Deuteronomy establish a theology of the name Yahweh. The name is great and terrible (Ps 99:3), and a source of blessing for the Israelites (Deut 28:8-11). The name resides in the cult (Deuteronomy 12), providing access to God and a source of praise (Ps 22:22-23).[37]

---

37. See T. N. D. Mettinger, *The Dethronement of Sabaoth: Studies in the Shem and Kabod Theologies* (trans. F. H. Cryer; ConBOT 18; Lund: Gleerup, 1992).

The terrible plague is hail *(bārād)*. Most of the references to hail in the Hebrew Bible occur in this plague (17 times) or in texts that refer to this event (Exod 10:5, 12, 15; Pss 78:48; 105:32). The references to the hailstorm outside the plague story provide important background for interpretation. The hailstorm is associated with Yahweh as the Storm God. Yahweh informs Job that hail and snow are stored by the Deity for battle (Job 38:22). Psalm 18:13-14 describes such an event. Yahweh thunders from heaven, shoots his arrows against the enemy, and scatters them with hailstones and bolts of lightening. The result is that the very foundations of the earth are laid bare (v. 15). The same imagery is applied to Egypt. The hailstorm is an invasion of Yahweh into the land of Egypt. The hailstorm also penetrates to the very foundation of the kingdom of Egypt. Nothing like it every happened before in the history of the kingdom of Egypt.

The intensity of the hailstorm prompts two new motifs in vv. 19-21. First, Yahweh warns Pharaoh to bring in all livestock from the fields to spare them from death, creating tension with the previous plague, since the animals are already dead. The divine concern for animals also concludes the book of Jonah, in which God states that the many cattle in Nineveh provide one reason for sparing the city from destruction. Second, a separation is introduced among the Egyptians between those who brought in their livestock and those who did not.

9:22-26 Moses executes the plague with his magical staff. He stretches his staff toward heaven to commence the attack of the Storm God. The attack includes thunder, hail, and lightning similar to the description of Ps 18:13-14 (see also Isa 28:2, 17). For the first time humans are killed along with all animals in the open fields. Crops and trees are destroyed. But Goshen, the residence of the Israelites, is spared the attack.

9:27-35 The response of Pharaoh repeats many of the motifs from the previous plagues. He requests intercessory prayer from Moses to halt the plague (see the plagues of frogs and flies). Moses performs the request, stating that the halting of the plague will teach Pharaoh that the land of Egypt belongs to Yahweh (v. 29). Moses also states that he knows Pharaoh does not fear Yahweh. Indeed, when the plague ceases Pharaoh resists Yahweh's demand that he release the Israelites. He hardens his heart. Pharaoh's confession of sin *(ḥāṭā'ti)* is a new motif. The word means "missing the mark." The extended speech of Pharaoh provides additional commentary. He states that Yahweh is just, while he is evil.

The time of the plague is clarified in vv. 31-32 perhaps because the agricultural cycle of the Egyptians is different from the Israelites in Syria-Palestine. The seasons in Egypt are determined by the flooding of the Nile River, not by the rain or the thunderstorm. There are three seasons in Egypt, each lasting approximately four months. The first season is Akhet, the Season of Inundation, when the Nile River overflows. Akhet begins in June/July. The second season is Peroyet, the Season of Coming-Forth, referring either to the fields emerging from flood or perhaps the sprouting of plants. Peroyet begins in October/November. The third season is Shomu, the Season of Deficiency, referring to the lack of water and the time of harvest. Shomu begins in Feb/March. The insertion of the time in vv. 31-32 locates the plague of hail during the season of Shomu preparing the reader for the spring festival of Passover.[38]

Pharaoh resists the demands of Yahweh in vv. 34-35. He hardens his heart yet again, only this time it is described as "sin." Thus the initial attack of Yahweh as the Storm God does not persuade Pharaoh to release the Israelites. The motif of Yahweh as the warring Storm God will continue through the defeat of Pharaoh at the Red Sea, which will conclude with the hymn of victory in 15:1-18, which praises Yahweh as the Warrior God.

Locusts (10:1-20)

10:1 *And Yahweh said to Moses, "Approach Pharaoh, for I have made his heart heavy, and the heart of his servants, so that I may place these my signs in his midst* ²*and that you may declare in the ears of your children and your children's children how I dealt ruthlessly with Egypt and my signs I placed among them.* **Then you will know that I am Yahweh."**

³*And Moses* **and Aaron** *approached Pharaoh, and* **they** *said to him, "Thus said Yahweh, the God of the Hebrews, 'How long will you refuse to humble yourself before me?* ⁴*For, if you refuse to send out my people, indeed, I am bringing tomorrow locusts in your borders.* ⁵*And it will cover the face of the earth. And no one will be able to see the earth. And it will eat the last of the remnant remaining to you from the hail. And it will eat all your sprouting trees from the field.* ⁶*They will fill your house and the houses of all your servants, and the houses of all Egyptians, which your fathers and your fathers' fathers did not see, from the day of their being on the ground until this day.'" And he turned and he went out from with Pharaoh.*

⁷*And the servants of Pharaoh said to him, "How long will this be a snare to us. Send out the men, so they may worship Yahweh their God. Do you not yet know that Egypt is perished?"*

⁸*Moses* **and Aaron** *were brought back to Pharaoh. And he said to them, "Go and worship Yahweh, your God. Who and who are going?"*

⁹*And Moses said, "With our young and with our old we will go. With our flocks and with our herds we will go, for it is a festival of Yahweh for us."*

¹⁰*And he said* **to them,** *"Yahweh would certainly be with you, if I sent out*

---

38. Frankfort, *Kingship and the Gods*, 367 n. 3.

you and your youth, for evil is before your face. ¹¹*Not so! The men shall go and serve Yahweh, for that is what you are seeking." And* **they** *were driven from the face of Pharaoh.*

¹²*And Yahweh said to Moses, "Stretch out your hand on the land of Egypt with locusts, so that it ascends on the land of Egypt and eats all the plants of the land, everything which the hail left." ¹³And Moses stretched his staff over the land of Egypt, and Yahweh drove an east wind on the land all that day and the night, and when it was morning, the east wind carried the locusts. ¹⁴And the locusts as-cended on all the land of Egypt, and they rested on the entire border of Egypt, very heavy. Before it there was never such locusts like it, and after it there will never be so again. ¹⁵It covered the face of all the land, so that the land became dark. And it ate all the plants of the land, and all the fruit of the trees, which the hail left. No green was left on the tree, on the plant of the field, and on all the land of Egypt.*

¹⁶*And Pharaoh rushed to call Moses* **and Aaron**. *And he said, "I sinned against Yahweh, your God, and against you. ¹⁷Now, raise up my sin only this time, and pray to Yahweh, your God, that he turn away from me only this death." ¹⁸And he went out from with Pharaoh, and he prayed to Yahweh. ¹⁹And Yahweh re-versed a very strong west wind. And it raised up the locusts, and drove them to-ward the Red Sea. Not one of the locusts remained in all the boundary of Egypt. ²⁰And Yahweh hardened the heart of Pharaoh. And he would not send out the Is-raelites.*

Notes

10:1 *And Yahweh said to Moses.* The LXX adds *legōn*, "saying."

so that I may place these my signs in his midst. The LXX removes the Deity as the sub-ject of the clause: *hina hexēs epelthē ta sēmeia tauta ep' autous*, "so that these signs might fall in succession on them."

10:2 *how I dealt ruthlessly.* The LXX reads, *hosa empepaicha*, "how I mocked."

10:7 *so they may worship Yahweh their God.* The LXX omits "Yahweh."

do you not yet know that Egypt is perished. Hebrew *hăṭerem tēdaʿ* is rendered in the LXX *eidenai boulei*, "do you wish to experience." Wevers interprets the phrase ironically in the LXX: "The servants themselves understand that Egypt is already destroyed, ἀπόλωλεν; only Pharaoh seems not to realize that Egypt is finished. The locust plague was the final coup de grace."[39]

10:9 *for it is a festival of Yahweh for us.* The LXX adds *tou theou hēmōn*, "our God."

10:10 *Yahweh would certainly be with you, if I sent out you and your youth.* The LXX reads, *Estō houtōs, kyrios meth' hymōn; kathoti apostellō hymas, mē kai tēn aposkeuēn hymōn?* "May the Lord be with you; in what manner should I send you, with your household possessions?"

10:12 *with locusts.* The MT places the reference to the locusts in the sentence describ-

---

39. Wevers, *Notes*, 148.

ing the action of Moses. The LXX places the locusts in the following sentence as the subject, "And let the locusts ascend. . . ."

10:13 *an east wind.* The LXX reads, *ho anemos ho notos,* "the south wind." Wevers writes, "To an Alexandrian an east wind producing locusts would not make much sense."[40]

10:15 *became dark.* The more mythological meaning of the MT *ḥāšak* is rendered in the LXX *ephtharē,* "was destroyed." The darkness of the locusts in the MT prefigures the coming darkness, *ḥōšek,* in 10:21, where the LXX also translates *skotos.*

10:17 *only this time.* Hebrew *'ak happa'am* is conveyed in the LXX *eti nyn.*

only. Hebrew *raq* is absent from the LXX.

10:18 *to Yahweh.* The LXX reads, *pros ton theon,* "to God."

10:19 *west wind.* The LXX reads, *apo thalassēs,* "from the sea." Wevers writes, "This makes sense to an Alexandrian; a wind from the sea is either north or west; such a wind toward the ἐρυθρὰν θάλασσαν ('Red Sea') would have to be from the west and slightly north."[41]

in all the boundary of Egypt. The LXX reads, *en pasē gē Aigyptou,* "in all the land of Egypt."

Commentary

The plague of locusts divides into three general sections: the announcement of the plague (vv. 1-12), the event (vv. 13-15), and the response of Pharaoh (vv. 16-20). The three-part structure is similar to other plagues in the Non-P history, but the details within each section are different, especially in the opening announcement of the plague. The divine speech to Moses is shortened (vv. 1-2) and in its place Moses presents an extended speech to Pharaoh (vv. 3-6), which is followed by yet another speech to Pharaoh from his own people (v. 7). The central theme of the plague remains the divine demand that Pharaoh release the Israelites for worship (v. 3). But the point of emphasis shifts to the question of "how long" Pharaoh will continue to resist. Moses confronts Pharaoh with this question (v. 3), as do his own people (v. 7). The P author includes Aaron in the events (vv. 3a*a*, 8a*a*, 16a*a*) and also adds the recognition motif, this time aimed at the Israelites, not Pharaoh (v. 2b). The plague of locusts departs from the pattern of the previous plagues by referring explicitly to the preceding plague of hail. The locusts "devoured everything that was left after the hail" (10:5, 15).

The inner-biblical reference between the plagues of hail and locusts suggests that the pair of plagues should be interpreted as a single action of Yahweh in two stages. Thus the locusts continue the attack of Yahweh, the Storm God, which began with the assault of hailstones, lightning, and thunder. The broader

40. Ibid., 152.
41. Ibid., 154.

use of locusts in the Hebrew Bible reinforces this interpretation. Locusts represent divine judgment on the land. They are one of the curses of covenant disobedience (Deut 28:38). Solomon prays that Yahweh will forgive the Israelites of their sin when the locusts invade the land (1 Kgs 8:37 = 2 Chr 6:28). Even the invasion of other nations is likened to a plague of locusts (Judg 6:5; 7:12), suggesting divine judgment.

The locusts take on cosmological significance in the book of Joel, which is most likely their meaning in the plague cycle. The invasion of locusts is a sign of the terrible Day of Yahweh to the prophet Joel. He writes in 1:4: "What the locust swarm has left, the great locusts have eaten. What the great locusts have left, the young locusts have eaten. What the young locusts have left, other locusts have eaten." The locusts are not simply a natural disaster; they are also a sign of cosmological judgment. The prophet calls the Israelites to "wake up" (v. 5). The people must see the portent. "For the Day of Yahweh is near; it will come like destruction from the Almighty" (v. 15). As judgment, the Day of Yahweh is envisioned as darkness. The prophet Amos proclaims: "Woe to you who long for the Day of Yahweh. Why do you long for the Day of Yahweh? That day will be darkness, not light" (Amos 5:18). Darkness also follows the plague of locusts in the story of the exodus.

The plague of locusts is a cosmological judgment. Locusts continue the attack of Yahweh, the Storm God, against Pharaoh and the land of Egypt. They invade from the air, just as the hailstones fell from heaven. And, as is the case in Joel, the locusts are a portent of coming events that represent the terrible Day of Yahweh for the Egyptians. They turn the ground "black" (Exod 10:15). The locusts are the final portent for the Egyptians. The subsequent events represent the Day of Yahweh itself. The locusts will be followed by cosmological darkness (10:21-29). Darkness will intensify until the Egyptian firstborn are killed at midnight (Exodus 12). And the Day of Yahweh concludes with the destruction of the Egyptian army in the Red Sea at dawn (Exodus 14).

10:1-12 The introductory section of the plague of locusts consists of four speeches or dialogues. First, there is a divine speech to Moses (vv. 1-2). Yahweh has now hardened the heart of Pharaoh and his officials. The purpose is to instruct the Israelites through the signs/wonders. The emphasis is on intergenerational instruction. Children and grandchildren must be told of Yahweh's acts of salvation. The Non-P author will continue the emphasis on intergenerational teaching in the context of the Passover (12:26; 13:14-15) and the Festival of Unleavened Bread (13:8). The emphasis continues into Deuteronomy and the Deuteronomistic History to underscore the importance of law (Deut 6:4-25) and the crossing of the Jordan River (Joshua 4). The P author adds the Recognition Formula to the divine speech (v. 2b). Yahweh concludes the speech to Moses by stating that the Israelites "must know that I am Yahweh."

Such knowledge will require the revelation of the tabernacle cult for the P writer (see the commentary on Exodus 29).

Second, Moses addresses Pharaoh with the demands of Yahweh (vv. 3-6). This is a departure from previous plagues, where Yahweh would outline demands to Moses, leaving the reader to assume the transmission of the message to Pharaoh. Moses (and Aaron) "approach" *(bô')* Pharaoh (see also the plagues of frogs and livestock). Moses addresses Pharaoh as Yahweh's prophetic messenger: "Thus said Yahweh." He demands the release of the Israelites for worship. The emphasis of his address is on the continued resistance of Pharaoh. "How long" will Pharaoh continue to resist Yahweh, the God of the Hebrews? Refusal to send out the Israelites will prompt the worst attack of locusts in the history of the Egyptian nation.

Third, the separation of the Egyptians from Pharaoh initiated in the plague of hail (9:20) continues. The Egyptian officials repeat the question of Moses (v. 7). "How long" will Pharaoh continue to resist? Egypt is destroyed. They plead with Pharaoh to let the Israelites serve Yahweh.

Fourth, there is an exchange between Pharaoh and Moses (vv. 8-12). This is a new element in the plague cycle. Dialogue between Moses and Pharaoh has tended to take place after a plague, not before. Pharaoh allows Moses to worship Yahweh, but he questions who must go (v. 8). Moses states that all must go because their worship is a *hag* to Yahweh, meaning "a pilgrimage festival" (v. 9). Pharaoh refuses to send out the women and the children. The scene ends when he drives out *(gāraš)* Moses from his presence. The motif of "driving out" Moses foreshadows the exodus event when the Egyptian people will "drive out" the Israelites from their midst (12:39). Yahweh predicts the expulsion twice (6:1; 11:1).

10:13-15 Moses initiates the plague by striking his staff on the ground. But Yahweh actually brings in the plague of locusts by driving *(nihag)* an east wind *(rûaḥ haqqādîm)*. The east wind blows from the desert (Hos 13:15) all night and day bringing locusts on the land of Egypt. The result is the devastation of all green plants in the land of Egypt. The same east wind returns at the Red Sea to dry up the water (14:21).

10:16-20 The response of Pharaoh follows the pattern of previous plagues in the Non-P history. Pharaoh requests an intercessory prayer to halt the plague (vv. 16-17). He also confesses his sin (see the plague of hail). Moses intercedes, halting the plague (vv. 18-19). The literary connection to the final confrontation at the Red Sea is continued in this section. Yahweh changes the direction of the wind from the east to the west blowing the locusts into the Red Sea. But Pharaoh's heart is hardened (v. 20), this time by Yahweh. The active role of Yahweh in hardening the heart of Pharaoh indicates progression and intensification in the plague cycle.

DEFEAT OF PHARAOH (10:21–14:31)

Exodus 10:21–14:31 separates into three episodes. The plague of darkness (10:21-29) provides the introduction to two subsequent actions by Yahweh, the death of the Egyptian firstborn (11:1–13:16) and the destruction of the Egyptian army in the Red Sea (13:17–14:31). The three-part structure extends the cycles of plagues from three to four suggesting continuity with the preceding section, 7:8–10:20 (see above, "Literary Structure"). The two sections are also related through similar themes. The power of Yahweh remains at center stage. The demand of Yahweh that Pharaoh release the Israelites for worship retains a prominent role. And the plagues continue. The traditional interpretation of darkness and the death of the Egyptian firstborn as plagues in the Passover Haggadah, for example, reinforces a reading that emphasizes continuity between the initial plagues and the defeat of Pharaoh.

A number of literary developments indicate intensification from the initial plagues to the defeat of Pharaoh. First, the display of Yahweh's power is elevated. Yahweh acts more directly against Pharaoh and the Egyptians, and, as a result, the intercessory role of Moses recedes somewhat, especially in the death of the Egyptian firstborn. Also, Yahweh's power over nature increases. The initial confrontation between Yahweh and Pharaoh explored the power of God over water, land, and air. The defeat of Pharaoh will demonstrate Yahweh's control over the more primordial powers of light and darkness, human life and death, and the sea.

Second, there is a reversal of time in the sequence of action. The defeat of Pharaoh progresses from darkness to dawn. The plague of darkness sets the stage for the death of the Egyptian firstborn at midnight before the episode ends with the destruction of Pharaoh and his army at dawn (see above, "Non-P History"). The previous three cycles of plagues progressed in the opposite direction, always beginning with dawn.

Third, the Israelites become active participants in the story as compared to their passive role in the previous cycle of plagues. They now participate in their redemption. They begin their pilgrimage with God, journeying from Rameses to Succoth, Etham, Pi-hahiroth, and through the Red Sea. The Israelites also participate through cultic rituals that protect them from Yahweh's assault on the Egyptians. The observance of the Passover, the Feast of Unleavened Bread, and the divine claim on firstborn signal intensification and thus a distinction between the defeat of Pharaoh and the previous cycle of plagues. The rituals also provide a means for the Israelites to recall and to reenact the defeat of Pharaoh. The central question of the Passover Haggadah — "Why is this night different from all other nights?" — reinforces the interpretation of Pharaoh's defeat as a development beyond the previous plague cycle.

Darkness (10:21-29)

¹⁰:²¹*And Yahweh said to Moses, "Stretch out your hand toward heaven, so that there is darkness on the land — a darkness that is felt." ²²And Moses stretched his hand toward heaven, and there was total darkness in all the land of Egypt, three days. ²³Each person could not see his brother, and no one could rise from his place, for three days. But, for all the Israelites, there was light where they lived.*

²⁴*And Pharaoh called to Moses and he said, "Go, serve Yahweh! Only your flocks and your herds shall be detained. Even your children may go with you."*

²⁵*And Moses said, "Also you must give into our hand sacrifices and burnt offerings, so that we can make to Yahweh, our God. ²⁶And also our cattle must go with us. And not a hoof must remain, for from them we will take to worship Yahweh our God. But we do not know how we should worship Yahweh until our arrival there."*

²⁷*And Yahweh hardened the heart of Pharaoh. And he refused to send them out. ²⁸And Pharaoh said to him, "Away from me! Guard yourself, that you do not again see my face. For on the day you see my face, you will die."*

²⁹*And Moses said, "You said so. I will never again see your face."*

Notes

10:21 *darkness.* Hebrew ḥōšek, "darkness," is rendered in the LXX *skotos*, often indicating the darkness of death and of the netherworld.

a darkness that is felt. The phrase is difficult. Hebrew *māšaš* means "to feel through, grope," with darkness as the subject. The LXX indicates the same meaning, *psēlapheton skotos*. Propp suggests a possible original phrase, *ûmiṣrayim yĕmaš(ĕ)šû (ba)ḥōšek*, "and Egypt will grope in the dark."[1]

10:22 *total darkness.* Hebrew *'ăpēlâ* is rendered in the LXX *gnophos thyella*, a much more meteorological image of a "dark cloud" and a "hurricane."

10:23 *from his place.* The somewhat ambiguous Hebrew *mittaḥtāyw*, "from underneath him," is clarified in the LXX as *koitēs autou*, "his bed."

10:24 *serve Yahweh.* The LXX adds "your God."

10:28 *that you do not again see my face.* The MT has the preposition *'el*, "to," but with some textual support (see *BHS*) I revocalize as *'al*, "not."

Commentary

The plague of darkness separates into three parts. The story begins with a divine command to Moses that he stretch his hand to heaven and conjure up darkness over the land of Egypt. The execution of the command commences immediately without announcement (vv. 21-23). An exchange between Pharaoh and Moses about the conditions for the Israelite departure from Egypt follows

1. Propp, *Exodus 1–18*, 306.

(vv. 24-26). The story closes with the notice that Yahweh hardened Pharaoh's heart, this time prompting a threat against Moses (vv. 27-29).

There are a number of unique developments in the story that have puzzled interpreters, creating difficulty in identifying the author. Some motifs repeat from the previous plagues in the Non-P History. The central role of Moses, not Aaron, an act of stretching out his hand to bring a plague, the exchange between Moses and Pharaoh about the conditions for the Israelite departure, and the hardening motif all fit the Non-P History. But other motifs raise questions. The plague of darkness lacks an introduction that Moses "stand" before Pharaoh in the "morning," or for that matter the more abrupt command that he simply "go" to Pharaoh. In addition there is no message from Moses to Pharaoh demanding the release of the Israelites for worship, nor are there any conditions by which Pharaoh could avoid the plague of darkness. Also the story does not end with the notice that Pharaoh's heart was hardened. Instead it includes an additional speech by Pharaoh, a threat to Moses, which foreshadows the forthcoming events.

The absence of any conditions to Pharaoh has prompted some interpreters to assign the plague of darkness to the P author.[2] But the problem with such an interpretation is that the plague of darkness lacks the identifying motifs of the P author: Aaron, his staff, the Egyptian magicians, and the concluding formula describing Pharaoh's resistance as "not listening." The plague of darkness is a story in the Non-P History, but tension between vv. 24-26, 28-29 and vv. 21-23, 27 suggests the addition of motifs over time. Childs concludes that the plague of darkness (vv. 21-23) and the motif of hardening (v. 27) are a continuation of the plague of locusts and distinct from 10:24-26, 28-29, which include the exchange between Pharaoh and Moses and the death threat of Pharaoh.[3]

The motifs of continuity and the points of departure with the previous plagues provide the clue for interpreting the plague of darkness in its present narrative context. The plague of darkness is not simply one more plague in the assault on Pharaoh. It is, rather, a transition to the death of the Egyptian firstborn. Darkness sets the stage for the midnight act of death, thus providing an introduction to the defeat of Pharaoh.

10:21-23 Rudolph suggested that darkness is not really a plague. It is more like a "wonder," he concluded.[4] Cassuto advanced a naturalistic interpretation, suggesting a sandstorm that shut out the sun and thus darkened the land of Egypt.[5] But the language used to describe the darkness, the role of the

---

2. See Noth, *Exodus,* 83; Van Seters, *Life of Moses,* 107-8. Both assign portions of the plague of darkness to the P author (vv. 21-23, 27).

3. Childs, *Exodus,* 131.

4. Rudolph, *Elohist,* 21.

5. Cassuto, *Exodus,* 129-30.

Storm God in creating darkness, and the central place of the sun in Egyptian religion indicate that darkness is neither a wonder nor a natural catastrophe. It is a supernatural and primordial event, signaling the advent of the Day of Yahweh and thus the beginning of the end to the conflict between Yahweh and Pharaoh.

First, the Hebrew word for "darkness" *(ḥōšek)* requires interpretation to determine the nature of the plague. The Hebrew words for "darkness" and "night" *(laylâ)* are used infrequently with each other in the Hebrew Bible. Psalm 104:20 states that God brings darkness and it becomes night. Psalm 139:11-12 uses "darkness" and "night" interchangeably. Perhaps most significantly the creation story in Genesis 1 names darkness as night (Gen 1:5). But it would be a mistake to interpret the plague of darkness as a reference to the night. "Darkness" has a more primordial meaning than night in most of its occurrences in the Hebrew Bible. The opposite of darkness is not day; it is light itself. Light and darkness are primordial qualities of creation in opposition. The creation of these opposites penetrates to the very core of the creator's power. Yahweh proclaims: "I am Yahweh, and there is no other. I form the light and create darkness" (Isa 45:6-7). Compare Genesis 1, where darkness exists prior to an act of creation by Yahweh (Gen 1:2). The naming of darkness as night in Genesis 1 may reflect the P author's attempt to contain the primordial power of darkness within the structure of creation.

The study of Hebrew *ḥōšek* makes it difficult to imagine just what the Non-P author is describing. The plague of darkness is not the night. It is the absence of all light. Genesis 1:2 provides a partial window into the nature of the darkness when it pictures uncreated chaos as "dark" *(ḥōšek),* "wet" *(tĕhôm),* and "formless" *(tōhû wābōhû).* The image suggests an oil slick or something comparable. But the darkness in Exod 10:21-29 lacks water. It is associated with the air. Moses is instructed to raise his hand toward heaven in order to conjure up the darkness. All light is eliminated. The Egyptians are unable even to make artificial light in their homes through fire. They are reduced to "groping" in this darkness. The imagery suggests something like a black hole where light is not simply absent but consumed. The plague of darkness is even more difficult to imagine because within this "black hole" the individual houses of the Israelites are lit up. They shine like stars in a black hole. However we might imagine the scene, the picture is not of an extended evening, but of the undoing of creation itself.[6] Light, a primordial element of creation, is consumed by darkness. The scene is filled with foreboding.

Second, the description of darkness also incorporates imagery of the Storm God. The plagues of hail and locusts have already developed the imagery

---

6. Fretheim, *Exodus,* 129-30.

of Yahweh as the Storm God attacking the Egyptians. Hail is the weapon of the Storm God, and locusts signify an impending divine judgment on the Day of Yahweh. The additional description of darkness in v. 22 as "total darkness" (*ḥōšek-'ăpēlâ*) relates the plague with prophetic descriptions of the Day of Yahweh as an occasion of judgment by Yahweh, the Storm God. The Day of Yahweh in Joel is a day of darkness (*ḥōšek*) and gloom (*'ăpēlâ*). Similar imagery occurs in Amos (5:20), Zephaniah (1:15), and Isaiah (8:22; 58:10; 59:9). The prophetic parallels indicate that darkness is the beginning of the Day of Yahweh. The plague of darkness advances the assault of Yahweh, the Storm God, on Egypt, which began with the plagues of hail and locusts. It signals a transition from a sign of impending doom to the Day of Yahweh itself. The Day of Yahweh will progress through the death of the Egyptian firstborn and the destruction of the Egyptian army in the Red Sea.

Third, the plague of darkness is an attack on the very core of Egyptian religion. According to S. Quirke, "The sun embodies for the Egyptians more than power in heaven or power over earth; the daily guarantee of sunrise after the sunset of yesterday offered a bright and tangible promise of resurrection, and for this reason the sun-god was considered the central and original power of creation."[7] The name of the sun god is Ra in Egyptian religion, and it is often combined with Horus, the god embodying power over the earth. The combined name Ra-Horakhty, "the sun god, the Horus of the horizon," celebrated the primordial power of the sun in the rising and the setting. A common Coffin Text illustrates the power of the sun-god,

> Incantation for coming forth by day in the necropolis:
> the word took form, all was mine, when I existed alone;
> I am Ra in his first appearances, when he shines forth from the horizon;
> I am the great god who took form of himself, who created his names,
> lord of Enneads, who has no opponent among the gods; yesterday is
> mine, and I know tomorrow.[8]

The plague of darkness is a direct assault upon Ra-Horakhty. The three-day length of the plague (v. 22) underscores the power of Yahweh to eliminate sunrise and sunset, to remove yesterday and tomorrow. There is no resurrection, no happy ending to the plague of darkness for the Egyptian people. The assault on Ra-Horakhty is equally the undoing of Pharaoh, for as king of Egypt he is the sun priest. A temple text of Luxor praises Pharaoh as the one who knows the manifestations of Ra and who even lives in heaven like Ra-Horakhty,

---

7. S. Quirke, *Ancient Egyptian Religion* (London: British Museum Press, 1992), 22-23.
8. Coffin Text 335.

knowing the secret portal through which the great god brings forth the dawn on the horizon.[9]

10:24-26 The exchange between Pharaoh and Moses repeats themes from the previous plagues. Pharaoh initially allows the Israelites to leave Egypt in order to worship, but he places restrictions upon them. This time all humans may leave, but not the livestock. The restriction by Pharaoh is unacceptable to Moses. He states that the Israelites must take livestock in order to sacrifice to Yahweh. This is the second time that sacrifice to Yahweh is a motif in the plague cycle. The first was during the plague of flies (8:24-28), where the concern was that the Israelites not offend the Egyptians with their sacrifice. The focus shifts in the plague of darkness from the Egyptians to the demands of Yahweh. All livestock must accompany the Israelites because they do not yet know how to worship Yahweh.

10:27-29 Pharaoh does not reply to the argument of Moses. Instead Yahweh hardens Pharaoh's heart, building on the intensification of Yahweh's control over Pharaoh first introduced in the plague of locusts. The final exchange between Pharaoh and Moses indicates that the plague of darkness is an introduction to the subsequent events. The exchange is filled with irony and foreboding. Pharaoh threatens Moses with death the next time they see each other. The threat plays off the setting of darkness and blindness that permeates the story and that will intensify with the death of the Egyptian firstborn. Light will not return in the story until the sun rises at the Red Sea. But it will bring the death of Pharaoh, not Moses.

Death of the Egyptian Firstborn (11:1–13:16)

The central event in this section is the death of the Egyptian firstborn at midnight. It is announced in 11:1-10 and fulfilled in 12:29-36, resulting in the Israelite departure from Egypt in 12:37-42. The parallel structure of the announcement (11:1-10) and the fulfillment (12:29-36) can be illustrated as in the diagram in figure 20 on page 249. The diagram also illustrates that the death of the Egyptian firstborn is a compact story. Every item predicted by Yahweh is fulfilled in a few verses. But the story is a core event in the history of Israelite worship attracting extensive commentary. As a result the death of the Egyptian firstborn now provides the etiology for three distinct rituals, the divine claim on the firstborn (13:1-2, 11-16), the Passover (12:1-13, 21-28, 40-51), and the Feast of Unleavened Bread (12:14-20; 13:3-10). The merging of the three rituals around the death of the Egyptian firstborn is crucial to the formation of the narrative.

9. R. B. Parkinson, *Voices from Ancient Egypt: An Anthology of Middle Kingdom Writings* (Oklahoma Series in Classical Culture; Norman: University of Oklahoma Press, 1991), 38-39.

Figure 20

Announcement (11:1-10)	*Shared Motifs*	*Fulfillment* (12:29-36)
(A) Midnight	Time	(A') Midnight
(B) Every firstborn in the land of Egypt will die	Content	(B') Yahweh struck down all the firstborn in Egypt
(C) From Pharaoh to the female slaves and livestock	Scope	(C') From Pharaoh to the prisoner and livestock
(D) Great cry	Outcome	(D') Great cry
(E) Officials will plead for the Israelites to leave		(E') Departure from Egypt

The divine claim on the Israelite firstborn is tied closely to the plot of the exodus. The theme of the firstborn status of the Israelites frames the death of the Egyptian firstborn. Yahweh claimed the Israelites as firstborn in 4:21-23 predicting the death of the Egyptian firstborn. The theme reappears after the death of the Egyptian firstborn in the instruction of Moses at Succoth, 13:1-2, 11-16. The slaughter of the Egyptian firstborn provides the occasion for a divine demand that the Israelites consecrate their firstborn male livestock and children to Yahweh.

The Feast of Unleavened Bread also evolves from the events of the exodus. Yahweh predicts that the Egyptians would plead for the Israelites to leave their land after the death of the Egyptian firstborn (11:8), resulting in the Israelites actually being driven out of Egypt in great haste (11:1). The divine prediction is fulfilled in 12:29-36. Death permeates the land of Egypt after the divine attack, and the Egyptians beg the Israelites to leave. They drive out the Israelites so fast that the people are forced to take bread dough without yeast. The description of the Israelites evacuating Egypt during the night with kneading bowls slung over their shoulders accentuates the power of Yahweh over the Egyptians. The action gives rise to the legislation of the Feast of Unleavened Bread in 12:14-20 and 13:3-10 as a ritual commemoration of the Israelite departure from Egypt.

The Passover emerges as the central ritual associated with the death of the Egyptian firstborn. The Passover instruction dominates the story. The blood of the paschal lamb protects the Israelites from the midnight plague of death, and its ritual requirements are carefully outlined. Yahweh provides Moses with in-

structions about the Passover (12:1-20). Moses instructs the elders of the Israelites about the Passover (12:21-28). Then Yahweh returns to the topic with further instructions to Moses, outlining who might participate in the Passover
(12:40-51).

The divine claim on the firstborn, the Feast of Unleavened Bread, and the
Passover all play a role in the Non-P and P Histories. But they are related in different ways reflecting divergent cultic calendars and interpretations of the exodus.

Non-P History

The Non-P History consists of 11:1-7a, 8, 12:21-27, 29-39; 13:3-16. There are no divine instructions to Moses in the Non-P History to inform him of the rituals of
Passover, the Feast of Unleavened Bread, or the divine claim on the firstborn.
Instead, all of the cultic instructions are speeches by Moses to the Israelites. He
conveys directly the instruction without receiving divine teaching. This contrasts to the role of Moses in the plague cycle, where he would regularly receive
divine instruction.[10] The Non-P History divides into two sections separated by
distinct locations.

The first section focuses on the death of the Egyptian firstborn and the
Passover at Rameses in Egypt. It begins with the divine announcement of the
impending plague (11:1-7a, 8). Moses prepares the elders of Israel for the
plague by introducing the rite of Passover as a form of protection (12:21-27).
The first section closes with the narration of the death of the Egyptian firstborn (12:29-36). The second section begins with the travel notice that the Israelites journeyed from Rameses to Succoth (12:37-39), where Moses instructs
the Israelites in the Feast of Unleavened Bread and Yahweh's claim on the firstborn (13:3-16).

Geography is important to the structure of the Non-P History. The observance of the Passover and the Feast of Unleavened Bread are separated by the
itinerary notice in 12:37, which indicates that the Israelites journeyed from
Rameses to Succoth. Thus the instructions for Passover and its observance take
place in Rameses prior to the death of the Egyptian firstborn, as compared to
the instructions for the Feast of Unleavened Bread and the divine claim on the
firstborn, which take place at Succoth after the event. The change in geography
indicates that the Passover and the Feast of Unleavened Bread are brought together in the Non-P History, but they are not merged into one festival. The set-

---

10. Gertz (*Tradition und Redaktion*, 259-60) argues that the portrayal of Moses teaching
without prior divine instruction in Exod 12:21-27 and 13:3-16 indicates that the texts are post-
Priestly compositions dependent on the divine instruction to Moses in 12:1-20 and 13:1-2.

ting also signifies that the Feast of Unleavened Bread is tied more closely to the divine claim on the Israelite firstborn, since these two actions take place at the same location.

The sequencing of the festivals in the Non-P History at different locations accentuates salvation history. The Passover sacrifice at Rameses commemorates the night in which the Israelites were spared from death (12:21-27). The Feast of Unleavened Bread (13:3-10) at Succoth memorializes the exodus from Egypt. The divine claim on the firstborn points to the completion of the exodus pilgrimage, when the Israelites enter the promised land of Canaan (13:11-16). The commemoration of all three festivals is in the form of a catechism, in which an elder teaches a youth by answering questions (see the commentary on 12:21-27).[11] The reappearance of similar catechisms during the revelation of the law on the plains of Moab (Deut 6:4-25, esp. vv. 7 and 20-25) and at the crossing of the Jordan River at Gilgal (Joshua 4, esp. vv. 6b-7 and 21-24) reinforces the conclusion that the catechisms are intended to create a salvation-historical perspective for the cultic traditions of the Israelites. The distribution of the catechisms also suggests a literary relationship between the Non-P History, Deuteronomy, and the Deuteronomistic History.[12]

P History

The P History consists of 11:7b, 9-10; 12:1-20, 28, 40-51; 13:1-2. The P History follows the structure of the Non-P History (see above, "Authors"). But it provides a distinct interpretation of the death of the Egyptian firstborn by inserting a series of divine instructions to Moses and Aaron. The most significant literary change is that all cultic instruction becomes divine speech to Moses and Aaron, as compared to the absence of divine instruction in the Non-P History, where Moses, not Yahweh, taught the Israelites. The specific additions of the P author include the following:

First, the divine announcement of the plague is brought into conformity with the P interpretation of the plague cycle. The demand for the recognition of Yahweh (11:7b), the indication of Pharaoh's resistance as "not listening" (v. 9), and the presence of Aaron (v. 10) are central motifs in the P History.

Second, the teaching of the Passover by Moses to the elders (12:21-27) is prefaced with divine instruction to Moses and Aaron (12:1-20) and followed by the notice that the instructions were fulfilled (12:28), a common practice in the P History. The content of the divine instruction presents a distinct interpreta-

---

11. See J. A. Soggin, "Kultätiologische Sagen und Katechese im Hexateuch," *VT* 10 (1960): 341-47; Long, *Problem of Etiological Narrative*, 65-69, 81-83.
12. Dozeman, *God at War*, 54-60.

tion of the festivals from the Non-P History merging the Passover and the Feast of Unleavened Bread into a single celebration at Rameses (12:1-20, 28).

Third, the distinction between the Passover and the Feast of Unleavened Bread is blurred even further when Yahweh presents additional instruction on the Passover to Moses and Aaron at Succoth (12:40-51).

Fourth, the divine claim on the firstborn in 13:1-2 provides an introduction to the instruction of Moses on the Feast of Unleavened Bread (13:3-10) and the divine claim on the Israelite firstborn (13:11-16).

The observance of the religious festivals takes effect immediately in the P History and is not restricted to the Israelites' future life in the land of Canaan, as is the case in the Non-P History. The wilderness generation of the Israelites will observe the Passover and the Feast of Unleavened Bread immediately after the revelation of the law at Mount Sinai (Num 9:1-14). The divine claim on the firstborn will affect the organization of the wilderness tabernacle and camp through the formation of a separate class of sacred personnel, the Levites (Numbers 3, 8).

The death of the Egyptian firstborn (Exod 11:1–13:16) is structured in the following manner:

I. Events at Rameses (11:1–12:36)
   A. Announcement of the Death of the Egyptian Firstborn (11:1-10)
   B. Divine Instruction about Passover and Feast of Unleavened Bread (12:1-20)
   C. Mosaic Instruction about Passover (12:21-28)
   D. Death of the Egyptian Firstborn (12:29-36)
II. Events at Succoth (12:37–13:16)
   A. Journey from Rameses to Succoth (12:37-42)
   B. Divine Instruction about Passover (12:43-51)
   C. Divine Instruction about the Israelite Firstborn (13:1-2)
   D. Mosaic Instruction about Feast of Unleavened Bread and the Firstborn (13:3-16)

Events at Rameses (11:1–12:36)

Exodus 12:37-42 is a travel notice stating that the Israelites journeyed from Rameses to Succoth. Although the Israelites are associated with the land of Goshen in the plague cycle (8:22; 9:26), they actually leave Rameses during the night of the death of the Egyptian firstborn. The central ritual event at Rameses is the institution of the Passover. My comments will illustrate that the Non-P and the P Histories provide separate interpretations of the Passover, even though they are loosely combined into a sequence. The episode is structured around the divine announcement of the death of the Egyptian firstborn (11:1-10) and its fulfillment (12:29-36). The plot frames two teachings on the Passover: a divine speech to Moses and Aaron (the P History, 12:1-20), and the instruction of Moses to the elders of the Israelites (the Non-P History, 12:21-27).

Announcement of the Death of the Egyptian Firstborn (11:1-10)

11:1 *And Yahweh said to Moses, "Yet one blow I will bring against Pharaoh and against the Egyptians. After this he will send you out from here. And when he sends out completely, he will expel you from here. ²Speak now in the ears of the people that each man request from his neighbor and each woman from her neighbor vessels of silver and vessels of gold."*

³And Yahweh gave the people favor in the eyes of the Egyptians. Indeed, the man Moses was very great in the land of Egypt, in the eyes of the servants of Pharaoh and in the eyes of the people. ⁴And Moses said, "Thus said Yahweh, 'At midnight I am going out in the midst of Egypt. ⁵And all the firstborn of the Egyptians will die, from the firstborn of Pharaoh, who sits on his throne, to the firstborn of the female slave, who is behind the hand-mill, and all the firstborn of animals. ⁶And there will be a great cry in all the land of Egypt, the like of which has not been and will not be again. ⁷But to all the Israelites a dog will not growl with his tongue from human to animal, **so that you may know that Yahweh separates between Israelites and Egyptians.'** *⁸And all these your servants will come down to me and bow to me, saying, 'Go out, you and all the people who are at your feet.' And afterward, I will go out." And he went out from with Pharaoh in hot anger.*

⁹And Yahweh said to Moses, **"Pharaoh will not listen to you, so that my wonders may be multiplied in the land of Egypt." ¹⁰And Moses and Aaron did all these wonders before Pharaoh. And Yahweh hardened the heart of Pharaoh, and he did not send out the Israelites from his land.**

Notes

11:1 *and when he sends out completely.* Hebrew *kālâ* is difficult. The LXX translates, *syn panti,* "with everything," from Hebrew *kol.* The LXX also interprets the phrase with the following clause, *syn panti ekbalei hymas,* "he will drive you out with everything." Wevers notes that the meaning of the LXX is that Pharaoh will send out everything of the Israelites, as compared to past attempts to retain cattle, or children, or women.[13]

11:4 *at midnight.* Hebrew *kaḥăṣōt hallaylâ* is lit. "the divide of the night."

11:7 *a dog will not growl.* The idiomatic Hebrew, *lō' yeḥĕraṣ-keleb lĕšōnô,* "a dog will not

---

13. Wevers, *Notes,* 162.

sharpen his tongue," is rendered in the LXX, *ou gryxei kyōn tē glōssē autou*, "a dog will not mutter his tongue."

11:8 *bow to me.* Hebrew *wěhištaḥăwwû* normally means "to worship." The LXX renders the word *proskyneō*, also suggesting worship. The translation "to bow" suggests obeisance to Moses, the assumed reference for "to me," who then leaves in anger (v. 8b). According to this reading the divine speech to Pharaoh would end in v. 7. But note the absence of any change in subject from the divine speech in 11:4-7, which raises the question of whether Yahweh is still conveying a message to Pharaoh in v. 8. In this case the servants of Pharaoh go out and worship Yahweh, while also requesting the Deity to leave the land of Egypt. The LXX reinforces this reading by adding "Moses" as the subject of the final clause and including the particle *de* to indicate a change in subject, *exēlthen de Mōysēs apo pharaō meta thymou*, "Then Moses left Pharaoh with anger."

11:9 *my wonders.* The LXX expands the Hebrew to *ta sēmeia kai ta terata*, "signs and wonders."

Commentary

The proclamation of the death of the Egyptian firstborn is in three sections. Yahweh announces the plague to Moses providing instructions for the Israelites to acquire goods from the Egyptians (vv. 1-3). Moses tells Pharaoh what will happen employing the prophetic messenger formula: "Thus said Yahweh" (vv. 4-8). The conclusion is a divine prediction of Pharaoh's resistance and a summary statement, indicating that Moses and Aaron performed all the wonders of Yahweh before Pharaoh (vv. 9-10).

There is a history of composition in 11:1-10, exceeding the Non-P (vv. 1-7a, 8) and P (vv. 7b, 9-10) Histories. Past interpreters have struggled with two related literary problems in the Non-P History. The first is the structure of 11:2-8. To whom is Moses speaking? He is instructed to address the Israelites in vv. 2-3, but when he conveys the divine message in vv. 4-8 Pharaoh is the addressee of the speech. Interpreters debate which of the speeches is a latter addition, the instructions for the Israelites (vv. 2-3) or the divine messenger speech to Pharaoh (vv. 4-8). The second problem is the relationship between the plague of darkness (10:21-29) and the announcement of the death of the Egyptian firstborn. How could Moses be speaking to Pharaoh when he was just threatened with death if he ever appeared again before the king? Scholars offer a wide range of solutions to answer these questions.

Wellhausen represents the classic source-critical solution. The different audiences represent different literary sources. The instruction for the Israelites in 11:1-3 is the E version of the story and the announcement to Pharaoh in 11:4-8 is the J account of events, with vv. 9-10 being P. Noth offered a different literary solution. He attributed all of vv. 1-8 to J, but concluded that vv. 7b-8, the verses addressing Pharaoh explicitly, are a later addition. Thus according to Noth the divine announcement concerning the plague of death was originally addressed to the Israelites, not Pharaoh, to prepare them for the Passover. Noth's interpretation resolved the problem of Moses reappearing before Pharaoh after the plague of darkness, but his solution is unlikely. All previous occasions in which Moses employs the divine messenger speech, "Thus said Yahweh," are addressed to Pharaoh, not the Israelites, suggesting that Pharaoh is also the intended object of the speech in 11:4-8.

The Non-P author's account of the announcement of the death of the Egyptian firstborn includes motifs that cannot be harmonized. Although I am including both the instruction for the Israelites (vv. 2-3) and the announcement to Pharaoh (vv. 4-7a, 8) within the Non-P History, the two motifs indicate a history of composition. The instruction for the Israelites to acquire possessions from the Egyptian people disrupts to some degree the announcement to Pharaoh. And the conclusion of Moses' announcement to Pharaoh in v. 8 also creates confusion. It is unclear whether Moses is predicting that Pharaoh's servants will worship him, or whether Yahweh is now the speaker. These tensions are difficult to resolve, especially the address to the Israelites in vv. 2-3. Yet this speech in particular is important in the Non-P History. The despoiling of the Egyptians of their possessions represents booty in war, signifying the defeat of the Egyptians. This motif is woven throughout the Non-P History. It is first introduced in the commission of Moses (3:21-22) and it is fulfilled when the Israelites leave Egypt (12:35-36). It returns one final time when the Israelites despoil themselves of their possessions by worshiping the golden calf (32:1-6).

The relationship of the plague of darkness to the announcement of the death of the Egyptian firstborn is not as problematic as past scholars suggest, once the criterion of verisimilitude is relinquished. The story is not history. The plague cycle and the defeat of Pharaoh are cultic legends progressing from a nocturnal setting for the death of the Egyptian firstborn to the death of the Egyptian army at dawn. The plague of darkness establishes the setting for the announcement of the death of the Egyptian firstborn. The announcement is part of an epiphany of darkness that will culminate at midnight (12:29-36). Pharaoh does not see the face of Moses in the announcement of the death of the Egyptian firstborn (11:4-7a, 8), creating irony in the story. Pharaoh is only able to see the face of Moses when it is dawn at the Red Sea (14:27), where he, not Moses, is destroyed. The irony is that Pharaoh's death threat to Moses seals his own death at the Red Sea.

11:1-3 Yahweh states that there will be one last plague. It will force Pharaoh to "drive out" *(gāraš)* the Israelites from the land of Egypt. Hebrew *gāraš*, "to drive out," occurs eleven times in Exodus in three different contexts. The first is in the orbit of the exodus (6:1; 10:11; 11:1; 12:39), where the term must be interpreted in relationship to the divine command that Pharaoh "send out" the

Israelites for worship. The point of emphasis in this usage is that the power of Yahweh overwhelms even the will of Pharaoh. As a result the exodus becomes an act of Pharaoh, not Yahweh. Pharaoh and the Egyptians drive out the Israelites. A second use of the term is in conquest stories, where Yahweh or his Messenger is described as "driving out" the inhabitants of the land (23:28, 29, 30, 31; 33:2; 34:11). Here the power of Yahweh does not overwhelm the will of opponents. Rather Yahweh overpowers through conflict. Victory in the conquest stories is an act of Yahweh. The third context is the idealization of Moses in the opening chapters of Exodus (2:17), where he overpowers opponents.

Exodus 11:2-3 is divine instruction for the Israelites. They must "request" *(šā'al)* vessels of silver and vessels of gold from the Egyptians. Their success is assured because Yahweh "will give the people favor in the eyes of the Egyptians." The announcement is fulfilled in 12:35-36 when the Israelites request vessels of silver, vessels of gold, and clothing after the death of the Egyptian firstborn, which they are given because of their favored status. This process is described as the "despoiling" *(waynaṣṣĕlû)* of the Egyptians in 12:36.

Scholars debate the meaning of the divine instruction to the Israelites. Th. C. Vriezen concluded that the motif signifies the positive relationship that existed between the Egyptians and the Israelites.[14] Others add that Hebrew *šā'al,* "to request," in this context indicates a desire on the part of the Israelites to borrow the valuables from the Egyptians.[15] Interpreters differ on whether the Egyptians (1) were tricked by the Israelites,[16] (2) had high regard for the Israelites,[17] or (3) gave their possessions because it was a legal requirement that released slaves not leave empty-handed.[18]

But there are strong reasons for reading the divine instruction to the Israelites as an act of war. Yahweh predicted the military defeat of the Egyptians in introducing the motif of Egyptian favor toward the Israelites in 3:21-22: "I will strike the Egyptians," states Yahweh, "And I will make the Egyptians favorably disposed toward this people, so that when you leave you will not go empty-handed." Similar imagery of conflict is also suggested in 11:2-3 by the peculiar form of the motif of Israel's favored status with the Egyptians. It does not occur

14. Th. C. Vriezen, "A Reinterpretation of Exodus 3:21-22 and Related Texts, Exod 11:2f., 12:35f., and Ps 105:37f. (Gen 15:4b)," *JEOL* 23 (1973-1974): 393 n. 5.

15. See Noth, *Exodus,* 93; G. W. Coats, "Despoiling the Egyptians," *VT* 18 (1968): 453; D. Daube, *The Exodus Pattern in the Bible* (All Souls Studies 2; London: Faber & Faber, 1963), 57; J. Morgenstern, "The Despoiling of the Egyptians," *JBL* 68 (1949): 4.

16. Coats, "Despoiling the Egyptians," 453.

17. Noth, *Exodus,* 94; D. J. McCarthy, "Plagues and Sea of Reeds: Exodus 5–14," *JBL* 85 (1966): 147.

18. Daube, *Exodus Pattern,* 55-58; Greenberg, *Understanding Exodus,* 86-87, 168; Cassuto, *Exodus,* 44.

in the expected form: "Israel found *(māṣā')* favor in the eyes of the Egyptians." Instead, it states: "Yahweh gave *(nātan)* the Israelites favor in the eyes of the Egyptians" (see also 3:21). The traditional form implies that the favored status of a person arises from his or her character. Noah (Gen 6:8) and Moses (Exod 33:12) find favor in the eyes of Yahweh because of their character. But in 11:2-3 Yahweh, not the Israelites, influences the perspective of the Egyptians. Coats writes: "The formula . . . shows that the basis for the Israelites' favor in the eyes of the Egyptians does not lie in the object . . . (i.e., the people), but in the initiation of the subject (i.e., God)."[19] The emphasis is not on the relationship between the Israelites and the Egyptians, but on the power of God to bring about reversal in the event of liberation.[20] The request for possessions from the Egyptians is an act of plunder, signifying military defeat. As a result, 12:36 describes the Egyptian people as "despoiled." The use of the word in 2 Chr 20:25 provides a parallel, where the taking of booty from a defeated enemy is also described as despoiling. "The point of the tradition," writes Childs, "focuses on God's plan for the Israelites to leave Egypt as victors from a battle."[21]

11:4-8 The prophetic messenger speech of Moses is addressed to Pharaoh. It is an announcement of impending death. All the firstborn male children and cattle of the Egyptians will be killed. The time of the plague is stated precisely. It will occur at midnight. The Hebrew translates literally as "the divide of the night" *(kaḥăṣōt hallaylâ)*. In his study of fairy-tale motifs in the Hebrew Bible, H. Gunkel noted that the night is the time of demons, when evil power rules.[22] The night is the time of terror (Ps 91:5) and weeping (Ps 30:5). Pestilence stalks in the night (Ps 91:6). The ancestor Jacob is attacked in the night (Gen 32:22-32). J. Ziegler notes that divine rescue from these situations takes place at dawn.[23] God helps when the morning dawns (Ps 46:5). It is the time of divine grace (Ps 90:14). A prophetic liturgy in Isaiah 33 foretells the demise of the destroyer, when Yahweh's arm of salvation appears in the morning light (Isa 33:1-2). The contrasts between night and day, terror and rescue, and destruction and salvation raise the question of how to interpret the plague of death at midnight: "the divide of the night." Does it represent a descent into the

---

19. Coats, "Despoiling the Egyptians," 453-54.

20. See the discussion by D. N. Freedman and J. R. Lundbom, *"nātan," TDOT* 6:22-36, esp. 23, who also note how the causative construction of the formula concerning favor is restricted in its application to Yahweh.

21. Childs, *Exodus,* 177.

22. H. Gunkel, *The Folktale in the Old Testament* (trans. M. D. Rutter; Sheffield: Almond, 1987), 86.

23. J. Ziegler, "Die Hilfe Gottes 'am Morgen,'" in *Alttestamentliche Studien: Friedrich Nötscher zum 60. Geburtstag Gewidmet* (ed. H. Junker and G. Botterweck; BBB 1; Bonn: Peter Hanstein, 1950), 281-88.

darkest terror of the night, "the witching hour," or is it the moment of turning, the halfway point when night begins its ascent to dawn?

The structure of Pharaoh's defeat in Exod 10:21–14:31 has been carefully constructed around the contrast between light and dark and night and day. The ambiguity of midnight is important to the story. It is a moment between the times, representing both the terror of darkness and the turning point of the night. For Pharaoh and the Egyptians midnight inaugurates a sequence of death that will conclude at dawn in the Red Sea. Sunrise brings the final epiphany of death for the Egyptians when they will recognize Yahweh in the rising sun. There is most certainly a polemic against the Egyptian sun god, Ra, in the story. For the Israelites midnight is the turning point toward dawn, the first event in their rescue, which will culminate in salvation at sunrise. Other instances of "midnight" emphasize this latter meaning, though risk is involved. Samson undertakes a surprise escape at midnight to save his life (Judg 16:3), while Ruth's salvation through Boaz begins with her midnight tryst. The NT continues the motif with the parable of the delayed bridegroom, who finally arrives at midnight (Matt 25:6).

The two perspectives on midnight are developed through a series of contrasts and reversals. Moses predicts a great cry by the Egyptians (Exod 11:6) as compared to the previous cry of the Israelites at the outset of the story (3:7, 9). The cry will exceed any previous agony in the land of Egypt, thus concluding a sequence of unique and incomparable catastrophes that included the hailstorm (9:18, 24) and the plague of locusts (10:6, 14). The land of Goshen, by contrast, will remain so calm that not even the lowly dogs will bark. The reversals are completed when divine speech intrudes into the message of Moses in 11:8, perhaps displacing Moses as mediator. If Yahweh emerges as the speaker, v. 8 becomes a divine prediction that the Egyptians will "bow down," an act of worship begging the Deity to leave the land of Egypt along with the Israelites. A reference to the anger of Moses completes the speech.

11:9-10 The P author adds a conclusion to the announcement repeating motifs from the plague cycle. Yahweh predicts Pharaoh's resistance as "not listening." The reason for the resistance was to multiply wonders in the land of Egypt, a repetition from 7:3. Verse 10 indicates the fulfillment of the mission of Moses and Aaron and the continued resistance of Pharaoh.

Divine Instruction about Passover and the Feast of Unleavened Bread (12:1-20)

¹²:¹*And Yahweh said to Moses and to Aaron in the land of Egypt, saying,* ²*"This month is for you the beginning of months. It will be the first month of the year.* ³*Speak to the entire congregation of Israel, saying, 'On the tenth of*

this month, they must take for themselves each a kid for the house of the father, a kid for the house. ⁴*If the house is too small for a kid, then it and the nearest neighbor to the house will take according to the number of persons. You will divide the kid according to the number of persons eating it.* ⁵*The kid will be for you a perfect male, one year old. You may take it from the sheep or from the goats.* ⁶*And it will be for you an observance until the fourteenth day of this month. All the assembly of the congregation of Israel will slaughter it at twilight.* ⁷*And they will take from the blood and place on the two doorposts and on the lintel on the house in which they will eat it.* ⁸*And they will eat the meat in this night, roasted over fire, and they will eat it with unleavened bread and bitter herbs.* ⁹*Do not eat from it raw or boiled in water, but roasted over fire, its head with its legs and its inner organs.* ¹⁰*And leave none of it until morning. Whatever remains from it until morning, you will burn in fire.* ¹¹*And thus you will eat it, your hips bound, your sandals on your feet, and your staff in your hand. And you will eat it in haste. It is the Passover for Yahweh.*

¹²*"And I will cross over the land of Egypt on this night. And I will strike all of the firstborn in the land of Egypt, from humans to animals. And on all the gods of Egypt, I will make a judgment; I am Yahweh.* ¹³*And the blood will be for you a sign on the houses in which you are. And I will see the blood and I will pass over you. And the attack of destruction will not be against you, when I strike the land of Egypt.*

¹⁴*"And this night will be for you a memorial, and you will celebrate it as a festival to Yahweh throughout your generations, an eternal statute you will celebrate it.* ¹⁵*Seven days you will eat unleavened bread. Indeed, on the first day you will remove leaven from your houses, for anyone eating leaven, that person's life will be cut off from the Israelites from the first day until the seventh day.* ¹⁶*On the first day a holy assembly and on the seventh day a holy assembly will be for you. No work will be done in them, except what is eaten for that person's life, only that will be done for you.* ¹⁷*You will observe the Unleavened Bread, for on this very day, I brought your host out from the land of Egypt. And you will observe this day throughout your generations, an eternal statute.* ¹⁸*On the first month, on the fourteenth day of the month at evening you will eat unleavened bread, until the twenty-first day of the month at evening.* ¹⁹*Seven days leaven will not be found in your houses, for anyone eating leaven, that person's life will be cut off from the congregation of the Israelites, from the resident alien and the native of the land.* ²⁰*You will eat no leaven. In all of your dwellings you will eat unleavened bread."*

Notes

12:2 *beginning of months.* Hebrew *rō'š ḥodāšîm* is lit. "head of the months"; cf. LXX *archē mēnōn*, "beginning of months."

12:3 *a kid.* The LXX renders Hebrew *śeh* as *probaton*, also indicating a variety of four-legged animals, including cattle, although the reference to sheep dominates.

12:6 *an observance.* Hebrew *mišmeret* could also be translated "obligation." The LXX employs the participle of *diatēreō*, "to watch closely, observe."

all the assembly of the congregation of Israel. The Hebrew includes the terms *qāhāl*, "assembly," and *'ēdâ*, "congregation." The terms usually occur alone in separate contexts. The LXX often translates "assembly" as *ekklēsia* (see Deut 31:3) and "congregation" as *synagōgē*. But in this case "assembly" is rendered *plēthos*, "great number, multitude."

12:8 *and they will eat it with unleavened bread and bitter herbs.* Hebrew *ûmaṣṣôt 'al-mĕrōrîm yō'kĕluhû* translates, "and unleavened bread with bitter herbs they will eat it," as does the LXX, *kai azyma epi pikridōn edontai.* The translation follows Num 9:11, where the instruction repeats, placing the preposition *'al* with "unleavened bread," *'al-maṣṣôt ûmĕrōrîm yō'kĕluhû.*

12:9 *inner organs.* The LXX has *endosthiois* (= *entosthious*), "intestines, entrails."

12:10 *leave none of it until morning.* The LXX adds *kai ostoun ou syntripsete ap' autou,* "and a bone you shall not break from it," perhaps reflecting the additional instruction in 12:46.

12:11 *your hips bound.* The image is likely of clothing bound for travel. Cf. LXX *hai osphyes hymōn periezōsmenai,* "the lower part of your back embraced/surrounded."

12:13 *the attack of destruction.* The LXX renders Hebrew *negep lĕmašḥît* as *plēgē tou ektribēnai,* "the plague of destruction."

12:14 *and you will celebrate it as a festival to Yahweh.* The Eng. "celebrate" and "festival" derive from the same word in Hebrew, *ḥāgag,* indicating a religious celebration with pilgrimage. The Hebrew translates more lit. as "you will make a pilgrimage, it is a pilgrimage festival to Yahweh." The LXX *heortazō,* "to celebrate," does not indicate a pilgrimage; rather, *kai heortasete autēn heortēn kyriō* means: "and you will celebrate it, as a festival to the Lord."

12:15 *you will remove leaven from your houses, for anyone eating leaven.* The Hebrew uses two different words to refer to leaven, *śĕ'ōr* and *ḥāmēṣ.* The LXX renders both terms *zymēn.*

12:18 *at evening . . . at evening.* The LXX reads, *aph' hesperas . . . heōs hesperas,* "from evening . . . until evening."

Commentary

The interpretation of the Passover and the Feast of Unleavened Bread in the P History separates into three parts: vv. 1-2 provide instruction for a new cultic calendar; vv. 3-13 outline the ritual of the Passover; and vv. 14-20 describe the Feast of Unleavened Bread (also known as *Maṣṣôt*).

The Passover was not originally associated with the exodus. Wellhausen placed the ritual in the context of the divine demand for a sacrifice of first-born.[24] L. Rost speculated that the original setting of Passover was in semi-nomadic culture and that the blood of the lamb functioned to protect against the dangers of migration.[25] J. B. Segal sought a setting within a New Year Festival.[26] J. Pedersen concluded that the association between Passover and the exodus was early in the cultic history of the Israelites, while others see the historical interpretation of the festival as late in the monarchical period.[27]

The references to the Passover in the Hebrew Bible provide little insight into its practice before it was historicized in the story of the exodus.[28] Many of the references occur in late cultic calendars (Deuteronomy 16; Leviticus 23; Numbers 28; and Ezek 45:18-25) and in histories from the late monarchical and

---

24. Wellhausen, *Prolegomena*, 83-120.

25. L. Rost, "Weidewechsel und altisraelitischer Festkalender," *ZDPV* 66 (1943): 205-15.

26. J. B. Segal, *The Hebrew Passover from the Earliest Times to A.D. 70* (London Oriental Series 12; London: Oxford University Press, 1963).

27. J. Pedersen, "Passahfest und Passahlegende," *ZAW* 52 (1934): 161-75; cf. E. Kutsch, "Erwägungen zur Geschichte der Passafeier und des Massotfestes," *ZTK* 55 (1958): 1-35.

28. The debate over the relationship of the Passover and the exodus is extensive in contemporary scholarship. Noth (*Exodus*, 87) favored an early relationship between the Passover and the exodus tradition. He was influenced in part by Pedersen, "Passahfest und Passahlegende"; idem, "The Crossing of the Reed Sea and the Paschal Legend," in *Israel: Its Life and Culture* (trans. A. I. Fausbøll; 4 vols. in 2; London: Oxford University Press, 1926-1940), 3/4:728-37. Noth (*Exodus*, 93) concluded that the merging of the Passover and firstborn was well established already by the formation of a preexilic Yahwistic History. Cf. Wellhausen, *Prolegomena*, 83-92, who argued that the Passover was a late addition to the exodus traditions. In *Composition*, 75, Wellhausen argued that Exod 12:21-27 was a late addition to JE.

The secondary literature on the topic is vast and wide-ranging. See Kutsch, "Erwägungen zur Geschichte"; G. Fohrer, *Überlieferung und Geschichte des Exodus: Eine analyse von Ex 1–15* (BZAW 91; Berlin: Töpelmann, 1964), 82-83, 91-97; H. Schmid, *Mose: Überlieferung und Geschichte* (BZAW 110; Berlin: Töpelmann, 1968), 44-45; Childs, *Exodus*, 184, 191-92; Otto, "Plagenzyklus," 13-27; J. Van Seters, "The Place of the Yahwist in the History of Passover and Massot," *ZAW* 95 (1983): 167-83, esp. 167-75; idem, *Life of Moses*, 113-27; J. C. Rylaarsdam, "The Book of Exodus," *IB* 1:923; M. Haran, "The Passover Sacrifice," in *Studies in the Religion of Ancient Israel* (VTSup 23; Leiden: Brill, 1972), 89, 93-95; Hyatt, *Exodus*, 136-37; Kohata, *Jahwist und Priesterschrift*, 267; Norin, *Er spaltete das Meer*, 176; B. N. Wambacq, "Les origines de la Pasah israélite," *Bib* 57 (1976): 206-24; S. Boorer, *The Promise of the Land as Oath: A Key to the Formation of the Pentateuch* (BZAW 205; Berlin: de Gruyter, 1992), 153-57 *et passim*; J. Schreiner, "Exodus 12,21-23 und das israelitische Pascha," in *Studien zum Pentateuch: Festschrift für W. Kornfeld* (ed. G. Braulik; Vienna: Herder, 1977), 79; Gertz, *Tradition und Redaktion*, 29-73. For an overview of the research see P. Laaf, *Die Pascha-Feier Israels: Eine literarkritische und überlieferungsgeschichtliche Studie* (BBB 36; Bonn: Peter Hanstein, 1970); R. Schmitt, *Exodus und Passa; Ihr Zusammenhang im Alten Testament* (2nd ed.; OBO 7; Göttingen: Vandenhoeck & Ruprecht, 1982); J. B. Segal, *The Hebrew Passover from the Earliest Times to A.D. 70* (London Oriental Series 12; London: Oxford University Press, 1963).

exilic periods. Josiah is credited with instituting Passover as a national festival in the Deuteronomistic History (2 Kgs 23:21-23). No mention is made of the exodus or the Feast of Unleavened Bread in the story of Josiah. In the Chronicler's History, by contrast, Hezekiah (2 Chronicles 30) and Josiah (2 Chronicles 35) celebrate both the Passover and the Feast of Unleavened Bread. Scholars have sought clues to possible earlier celebrations of Passover in Exod 12:21-23 and in Josh 5:10-12. The description of Israelite families in Exod 12:21-23 remaining in their houses until morning does not fit the narrative context, suggesting that it may represent an independent tradition incorporated into the Non-P History. Some scholars judge the association of the Passover with firstfruits in Josh 5:10-12 to be a clue to its early setting and practice.[29]

The Passover is clearly historicized into the exodus in the P History, where it is merged with the Feast of Unleavened Bread. Thus the change in topic from the Passover to the Feast of Unleavened Bread does not indicate two separate festivals in the P History. They represent one festival of seven days' duration celebrated at Rameses. Several features of the instruction indicate their unity. The literary structure of Exod 12:1-20 presents the seamless observance of one feast, not two. The command in 12:14, "This is a day you are to commemorate," is unclear. It may refer to the preceding instruction about the Passover or to the following description of the Feast of Unleavened Bread. Childs writes of the ambiguity: "The passage views passover and *maṣṣôt* as part of the one redemptive event."[30] Exodus 12:8 confirms this conclusion. The Passover sacrifice and the unleavened bread are eaten together. The dates further cement the merging of the two festivals. The Passover takes place in month 1, day 14 at twilight (12:6), while the Feast of Unleavened Bread lasts seven days from month 1, day 14 through day 21 (12:18). In the P History the Passover/Feast of Unleavened Bread is a single, seven-day feast. It is a yearly ritual by which the Israelites protect themselves from death.

12:1-2 The P interpretation of the Passover is presented as a divine speech to Moses and Aaron. Yahweh states that the death of the Egyptian firstborn and the Israelite exodus from Egypt will change time for the Israelites, requiring a new calendar. The exodus will signal the first month of the year for the Israelites. Repetition of the words "month" and "first" stress that the divine decree is an innovation, a change in how the Israelites reckon time. The NRSV translation of v. 2 conveys the repetition: "This month will mark for you the beginning of months; it shall be the first month of the year for you." The legislation for the Passover is specifically located "in the land of Egypt," the location of

---

29. H.-J. Kraus, *Worship in Israel: A Cultic History of the Old Testament* (trans. G. Buswell; Richmond: John Knox, 1966).

30. Childs, *Exodus*, 197.

Yahweh's assault on the Egyptians. The Passover protects the Israelites from death in Egypt.

Scholars are unsure what the reference to month 1 means for the P author, since the New Year (Rosh Hashanah) is identified as month 7, day 1 in the P liturgical calendars of Leviticus 23 and Numbers 28-29. Propp speculates that there may have been two New Years in the P calendar, one in the fall (month 7 [September-October]) focusing on agriculture, and another in the spring (month 1 [March-April]) focusing on the exodus.[31] B. Jacob suggests that the reference to month 1 in Exod 12:1-2 is not a New Year at all, but is only intended to signal "the counting of months."[32] The lunar focus may be intended to emphasize the power of God in history as compared to a solar calendar based on the equinox. The solar calendar would highlight the power of God in creation marking the cycles of agriculture. Jacob writes concerning the reference to month 1 in 12:2: "Beginning with this month, Israel shall count all others in sequence, so that it may remain as a memorial of the great miracle, in this way whenever any month was mentioned, the miracle of . . . redemption will always be remembered through association."

The language associated with the calendar in 12:1-2 suggests change, raising a question about the relationship of the P system of dating to earlier calendars, such as 23:14-17 or Deuteronomy 16. The word "month" (*ḥōdeš*) employed by the P writer means "new moon." It replaces an older word for "month" (*yeraḥ*) and "moon" (*yārēaḥ*). Also the numbering of months, such as "the first," contrasts to older texts in which the months are named Abib, Bul, Ziv, and Ethanim. The dating of Solomon's temple in the Deuteronomistic History reflects the older calendar, where the months are named. The author states in 1 Kgs 6:37-38 that the foundation of the temple is laid "in the month of Ziv," and that the temple was completed "in the month of Bul." The designation "month 1" in 12:1-2 replaces the earlier names for the months. But even this form of naming the months undergoes change within the P tradition under the influence of the Babylonian calendar. For example, month 1 is named Nisan (Neh 2:1), probably meaning "firstfruits."

The use of "month 1" to date an event intertwines the divine instruction for the Passover with other significant events in the P History. Three references to month 1 provide insight into the theological perspective of the P author: (1) the conclusion of the flood (Gen 8:13), month 1, day 1 (New Year's Day); (2) the exodus from Egypt (12:1-2), month 1; (3) the construction of the tabernacle (40:2, 17), month 1, day 1 (New Year's Day). These events begin new eras in the P History. The system of dating by the P author is not historical in the mod-

---

31. Propp, *Exodus 1–18*, 386-87.
32. Jacob, *Exodus*, 292-93.

ern sense of the term. Rather, dating and chronology provide insight into the P theology. The exodus is a watershed event in the P History. It ushers in a new age of salvation, signified as month 1, and it also influences the counting of years (i.e., the construction of the tabernacle is year 2 after the exodus). This is similar to the later distinction between B.C. and A.D. in classical Christian chronology, where the birth of Jesus organizes time for the followers of Christ.

Two differences among the three stories also indicate progression in the P History. First, the manner in which the dates are established indicates a progression in revelation and cultic history. The end of the flood in Gen 8:13 is dated impersonally by the narrator. There is no divine decree to Noah underscoring the significance of the end of the flood and anchoring the date into a liturgical calendar. Indeed, there is no cult for Noah. In contrast to the flood, Yahweh decrees the dates of the exodus and the completion of the tabernacle. The divine decrees are revelation to Moses that shape time and inform the rhythm of Israelite worship. The progression from impersonal dating to divine decree indicates a development in revelation and cultic history from the time of Noah to the age of Moses.

The second difference is New Year's Day. The end of the flood and the building of the tabernacle are specifically dated to New Year's Day, month 1, day 1. Genesis 8:13 states that the flood ended "by the first day of the first month." And Yahweh commands Moses in Exod 40:2 to set up the tabernacle "on the first day of the first month." The repetition indicates progress in the P History from the precultic age of Noah to the cultic community of the Israelites encamped at Mount Sinai. The reference to month 1 in 12:1-2 without reference to day 1 indicates that the exodus provides the transition from the age of Noah to the age of the tabernacle cult, but it is not itself a New Year's Day.

12:3-5 The section describes the selection of the Passover animal. The instruction for the Passover is addressed to the "congregation of Israel" *('ădat yiśrā'ēl)*. Hebrew *'ēdâ* indicates the religious character of the group rather than family ties. The Hebrew noun *'ēdâ* derives from the verb *yā'ad*, meaning "to appoint," "to meet," or "to gather by appointment" for worship. "Appointed days" are religious festivals (Gen 1:14). The tent of meeting, *'ōhel mō'ēd*, also described as the "tabernacle" *(miškān)* by the P author, derives from the same verb. Thus the "congregation" is the group of people gathered round the tent of meeting. It is the act of gathering that defines the group. By using this term in Exod 12:3 the P writer anticipates the wilderness cult of the tabernacle.

The Passover sacrifice is a "kid" *(śeh),* either a lamb or a goat (see v. 5). The "kid" is used in a range of sacrifices including the burnt offering (Gen 22:7), the sin offering (Lev 12:8), and the guilt offering (Lev 5:7). It also had value in the act of redemption (Exod 13:13). The animal is to be selected on the tenth day of the month. The specific reference to the tenth day may provide a balance to Yom Kippur, the Day of Atonement, the tenth day of the seventh month in the P calendar.

The Passover sacrifice is celebrated in the home according to the P author. Exodus 12:3 states that each "father's house" is to take a "kid." The phrase "house of the father" first appeared in the P genealogy of Phinehas (6:14-27) indicating a broad social unit. The specific reference to "households" in 12:3 suggests a more narrow meaning, most likely a single "family." Verse 4 specifies a provision in case a family is too small to consume an entire "kid." One family may join another and celebrate Passover together. The instruction has prompted two interpretations: households are combined by proximity (the LXX reading) or by size, meaning the combination of households is determined by an equal number of persons in each (the most likely MT reading). In either case the emphasis is that there must be enough people to consume the Passover sacrifice in one night. Any portion remaining must be destroyed before morning.

The location of the Passover in the home is significant for two reasons. First, the Passover is a family feast for the P author, not a national festival. The Passover does not require a pilgrimage to the central sanctuary of the kingdom. The family orientation of the Passover contrasts to Deuteronomy (Deut 16:2), the Deuteronomistic History (with its account of the Josianic reform in 2 Kings 23), and most likely the Non-P History (when it is read in conjunction with the Deuteronomistic History), where the Passover becomes a national feast, celebrated at the central temple under Josiah. Second, as a family ritual the Passover is one of only two sacrifices in the P History that are separated from the altar of the sanctuary. The other sacrifice is the slaughter of the red heifer outside the wilderness camp and thus also separated from the tabernacle (Numbers 19). Both rituals protect the Israelites from death. The Passover protects from the midnight slaughter of the firstborn. It is regularized in the calendar and associated with the exodus from Egypt. The ashes of the red heifer protect from the more random experience of individual death resulting in corpse contamination. The two rituals allow the Israelites and their firstborn to remain in the community of God.

12:5-10 The ritual, slaughter, and consumption of the Passover sacrifice is described in this section. Verse 5 states that the "kid" must be a one-year-old male, without blemish, selected on the tenth day of the month. The care of the "kid" from the tenth to the fourteenth day is described as an "obligation" (*mišmeret*) for the Israelites. The word may mean nothing more than "guarding" the animal for the designated period of time. But it may also indicate ritual duties. Other uses of this term in the P History suggest some form of ritual action or duty.

The P writer frequently uses the term "obligation" to describe the cultic duties of the Levites (Num 3:7, 8, 32, 36, 38; 4:31, 32; 18:3, 4) and the Aaronide priests (18:5, 8). The staff of Aaron, which buds in the sanctuary to confirm his appointment as priest, is an "obligation" to the rebellious Levites who challenged his authority (17:25). The cultic associations of the term "obligation" are also evident when it is used to describe the Israelites. The gathering of manna for Sabbath (Exod 16:23), the omer of manna collected by Aaron and placed "before Yahweh" (16:32-34), and the requirement that the Israelites observe the movement of the cloud over the tabernacle in their wilderness journey (Num 9:19, 23) are all "obligations" for the Israelites. Finally the ashes of the red heifer are an "obligation" for the water of cleansing (Num 19:9).

The references suggest that the "obligation" of the Israelites concerning the Passover "kid" from days 10-14 has cultic meaning, but a more specific interpretation is not possible. No further information is provided. The P calendars in Leviticus 23 and Numbers 28–29 make no mention of any ritual process surrounding the Passover sacrifice on the tenth day of the month. The rabbis puzzled over the unique reference to day 10 in Exod 12:3, prompting a distinction between the *Pesaḥ Miẓrayim* (the Passover in Egypt) and the *Pesaḥ Dorot* (the Passover of Ages). They surmised that the obligation from days 10-14 in the Passover in Egypt was circumcision.[33]

Verses 6-7 provide instruction for the slaughter of the Passover victim and for the placing of the blood around the doorway of each Israelite house. The slaughter is not a sacrifice *(zebah)* for the P author, though it is for the Non-P historian (12:27) and for the author of Deuteronomy (Deut 16:2). The law of blood in Leviticus 17 states that sacrifice can take place only at the altar before the priest and that the blood of sacrifices must be sprinkled on the altar. The reason for the strict regulation is that "the life of a creature is in the blood" (Lev 17:14). The shedding of blood is a pollutant that defiles creation, as Cain's murder of Abel illustrates: Abel's blood cries out from the ground (Gen 4:10). The sacrificial cult is an antidote to the pollution of blood, just as a vaccine often contains the virus it is designed to destroy. Sprinkling blood on the altar during sacrifice is an antitoxin to the violence of shedding blood (Leviticus 4, 5, 7). It is a way of giving the life back to God. Anyone violating this law is guilty of bloodshed, carrying the penalty of excommunication or death (Lev 17:14).

The law of blood indicates how uneasily the ritual of the Passover fits within the larger teaching on sacrifice in the P History. The slaughter of the Passover victim certainly mimics a sacrifice in action, if not in name, and blood is placed on the doorway of a house as it is on the altar. The setting of the story, as an event in Egypt prior to the formation of the tabernacle cult, does not provide a satisfactory explanation for the tension, since the ritual of the Passover is an "eternal statute" to be observed throughout history according to the P author.

---

33. Leibowitz, *Studies in Shemot*, 1:193-202.

The tension between the ritual of Passover and sacrifice aids its interpretation within the P History. The instruction that the slaughter of the Passover victim occurs "between the two evenings" (*bên hāʿarbāyim*, v. 6) may mean twilight, the time between sunset and darkness, thus providing the paradigm for all future observances. Yet, in the present context of the exodus story, it is already dark. All light, including fire, has been eliminated in the plague of darkness (10:21-29). The absence of light indicates a cosmological battle. Yahweh, the Storm God, is attacking the land of Egypt. Death is on the horizon. It has enveloped the land. The only oases from the consuming darkness are the individual Israelite houses. Each is lit up in the sea of darkness (10:23). They now become the setting for the drama of the Passover.

The point of emphasis in the slaughter of the Passover victim is on the houses, not on the individual Israelites. Recall the warning of God to Cain: sin crouches at the doorway. It desires to enter (Gen 4:7). The doorway is the point of vulnerability, the threshold into a home. Each Israelite house must be protected from the ensuing plague of death by placing the blood of the Passover victim on its frame, including the doorposts and the lintel. The blood on the doorpost invites comparison to the tabernacle altar, even through the Passover is not a sacrifice. It cannot atone like a sacrifice at the altar of the tabernacle, nor is it even aimed at individual Israelites, as a sacrifice would be. Instead, the blood of the Passover victim protects each Israelite house. The blood on the doorpost is apotropaic, a Greek word meaning "to turn away." The Passover wards off death, it guards the inner space of each house, and it allows the Israelite firstborn to survive the night (see Exod 12:13). But the blood of the Passover victim is not redemptive. It does not atone for humans.

Exodus 12:8-10 describes the slaughter of the Passover victim and its manner of consumption. The text is constructed in a chiasm progressing from night to morning.

> A   Time — night (time of consumption)
>> B   Instruction — roasted with unleavened bread and bitter herbs
>>> C   Prohibitions — not raw, not boiled
>> B′ Instruction — roasted with head, shank, and inner organs
> A′ Time — morning (elimination of the victim)

The prohibitions against eating the Passover victim "raw" or "boiled" (C) are at the center of the instruction. The injunction to roast the meat (B, B′) frames the prohibitions. And the time frame of the ritual is strictly limited to one night. The meal cannot progress into the next day (A, A′).

The prohibitions at the center are difficult to interpret. The consumption of raw meat is not a topic in the Hebrew Bible. Hebrew *nāʾ*, "raw," occurs only in this text. The boiling of meat, by contrast, is described in a number of texts. In fact, in Deut 16:7 the instructions are to boil the Passover victim, not roast it. The instruction for the Passover in 2 Chr 35:13 conflates the P instruction and Deut 16:7 by describing the preparation of the animal as both boiled and roasted.

In the P legislation the boiling and consumption of meat in sacrifice is infrequent. Most meat is placed directly on the altar's fire and turned into smoke for Yahweh. It is not consumed by humans, but becomes a pleasing aroma for God. Yet in three instances Yahweh commands that meat be boiled and consumed by priests: during the ordination of priests (29:31; Lev 8:31), in the sin offering (Lev 6:28), and to release a nazirite from the vow (Num 6:19). In each instance the consumption of boiled meat indicates a transformation in the participants. The priests pass from the profane world to the sacred world to assume their office. The Israelites are purged from sin through offering. And the nazirite also passes from the sacred to the profane world.

The texts within the P History that describe the consumption of boiled meat by priests suggest two reasons for the prohibition against boiling the Passover victim in 12:9. First, in the P History the Passover is celebrated in homes, apart from the sanctuary without a priest. Meat is boiled only at the sanctuary. Second, there is no transformation of the human participants in the Passover rite. The Passover is an apotropaic ritual. The ritual averts evil, thus protecting homes from the invasion of death by turning it away. The Passover does not redeem or transform the participants.

C. Lévi-Strauss has demonstrated that cooking carries symbolic meaning.[34] The categories of "raw" versus "cooked" meat represent a fundamental contrast in human experience between nature and society, between the wild and the domestic, and even between death and life. He concluded that cooking is a form of mediation between these poles. One reason for the formative role of cooking is that it represents control over fire. The act of cooking marks the transition from wild nature, where meat is consumed raw, to the domesticated life in society, where meat is cooked. The insight of Lévi-Strauss provides another perspective for interpreting the Passover in the P History.

The dual prohibition against raw and boiled meat in 12:9 provides commentary on the literary setting of the story. The prohibition is a rejection of both nature and culture. The Passover victim is not to be eaten raw, nor is it to be butchered and boiled, requiring the separation of its organs with proper utensils and cultic rituals. Instead it is to be roasted directly over the fire with the un-

---

34. C. Lévi-Strauss, *The Raw and the Cooked: Introduction to a Science of Mythology* (trans. J. and D. Weightman; New York: Harper & Row, 1969), 64-65, 164, *et passim*. See also G. S. Kirk, *Myth: Its Meaning and Functions in Ancient and Other Cultures* (Cambridge: Cambridge University Press, 1970).

usual requirement that the head, shank, and intestines be included. Reference to "roasted" meat is used only one other time in the Hebrew Bible, in a satire against idols (Isa 44:16). Thus the act of cooking as roasting is unique, even more so in that the entire victim, head and intestines, is placed directly over the fire. Roasting suggests a liminal state between the raw and the boiled, mirroring the present circumstances of the story where both nature and civilization are undone by darkness. Death rules during the night of Passover; neither nature nor society can withstand its assault. Roasting the Passover victim is an act of mediation, providing a means of transition through the night of death. The Passover victim cannot be taken into the next day, while any remaining meat must be destroyed. Even time changes for those who survive the night of death. Survival through the nightmare marks month 1, a new beginning.

The accompanying food (Exod 12:8) and the manner in which the Israelites are to eat the Passover victim (12:11) reinforce the transitional function of the Passover meal. "Bitter herbs" *(mĕrōrîm)* are a plant, most likely a variety of lettuce. The noun can also indicate the quality of "bitterness," pain, and humiliation (see Lam 3:15; Job 13:26), recalling the Israelite oppression in Egypt (Exod 1:14). Propp suggests a possible apotropaic function as well.[35] Also, for the P author, unleavened bread symbolizes the Israelites' departure from the bitterness of Egypt (12:17). The meal is to be eaten in anticipation of a hasty exit with cloak tucked into the belt, sandals on the feet, and the walking staff in hand.

12:11-13   The verses contain the P interpretation of the Passover meal. The meal is named "the Passover to Yahweh." The Hebrew verb *pāsaḥ* means "to limp," "to pass over," or perhaps, "to protect" (see Isa 31:5). The word acquires significance from the setting. The state of darkness is important for interpretation; it indicates that the ritual of Passover addresses destruction and death and the role of Yahweh in relationship to these forces. The night of death includes three actions by Yahweh signifying warfare. The P author states that Yahweh will "pass through" *('ābar)* the land of Egypt, "strike down" *(nākâ)* every firstborn male human and animal, and "judge" *(šāpaṭ)* the Egyptian gods. "Passing through," or better "crossing over," a country often signals conquest. The refrain in Exod 15:16 celebrates the conquest of the four nations, Philistia, Edom, Moab, and the inhabitants of Canaan. The verb "to strike down" describes the annihilation of an enemy in battle (see 17:6). And the shift from humans to gods as the object of judgment indicates that the warfare in Egypt is cosmological in scope.

Yahweh's assault on the land of Egypt, its people, and its gods is presented as an epiphany of darkness, punctuated with the revelation of the divine name, "I am Yahweh" (see the commentary on 6:2-18). Yahweh is engaged in a cosmo-

---

35. Propp, *Exodus 1–18,* 394.

logical battle against darkness, social evil, and other gods. In this battle the P author states twice that Yahweh strikes down the Egyptians. The death of the Egyptian firstborn results from a "plague" that enters the Egyptian homes "to destroy" the firstborn. The Non-P author is more ambiguous on this point, attributing a more independent power to a personified "destroyer" (12:23) who slaughters the firstborn, rather than directly attributing this act to Yahweh. The blood of the Passover victim on the door of a house, according to the P author, will protect its occupants from the slaughter because Yahweh will "pass over" *(pāsaḥ)* each house (v. 13). As a result the plague accompanying Yahweh's assault will not enter blood-marked houses to destroy the firstborn within them. The blood of the Passover victim becomes a perennial "sign" for the Israelites, like the rainbow (Gen 9:12), circumcision (Gen 17:11), and Sabbath (Exod 31:13).

12:14-20 The Passover and the Feast of Unleavened Bread are merged into one feast in the P History celebrated at Rameses. The reference to "this day" in v. 14 is the one festival of Passover/Unleavened Bread, most likely the first day of the feast, day 14. The day is a "memorial" *(zikkārôn)*. The only other day memorialized in the P History is month 7, day 1, New Year's Day (Lev 23:24). Other memorials in the P History include the stones in the ephod of the high priest (Exod 28:12, 29; 39:7), the bronze censers of rebellious priests nailed to the door of the tabernacle (Num 16:39-40), and the gold given to the cult (Num 31:54). There is one memorial sacrifice, when the jealousy of a husband is recounted (Num 5:15, 18). The Feast of Unleavened Bread memorializes the Israelite exodus from Egypt (Exod 12:14, 17) when Yahweh brought out the people in their military divisions (see 13:18). The Feast of Unleavened Bread begins with the Passover meal on month 1, day 14 at evening and continues for seven days through day 21 (12:18). It requires "sacred assemblies" on the first and seventh days with no work (12:16).

The unification of the Passover/Feast of Unleavened Bread creates ambiguity at a number of points in the story, indicating that the desire to establish the etiological setting of the festival takes precedence over the narrative logic of the story.

First, there is tension in the overall plot of the narrative. The death of the Egyptian firstborn occurs in one night resulting in the Israelites' leaving Egypt. The Passover meal conforms to the plot, but not the combination of the Passover/Feast of Unleavened Bread. The one feast takes seven days, yet Pharaoh and the Egyptian army must be destroyed at dawn.

Second, it is not altogether clear how the two feasts connect in practice. Passover is celebrated in houses within the setting of the family. Yet the Feast of Unleavened Bread is a pilgrimage *(ḥag)* festival, requiring larger "sacred assemblies" on the first and seventh days. This tension has prompted some interpreters to identify a history of composition between the legislation for Passover (12:1-13) and Feast of Unleavened Bread (12:14-20).

Third, the instructions for the Feast of Unleavened Bread actually presuppose the Israelite possession of the land of Canaan. Both the alien and the native-born Israelite are required to observe the Feast of Unleavened Bread (12:19) upon penalty of being "cut off" from the congregation of the Israelites. These social categories presuppose the Israelites' residency in Canaan. Exodus 12:1-13 does not state who is able to participate in the Passover, but vv. 43-51 clarify that an alien must be circumcised to participate in the meal, making participation voluntary. The laws of Passover/Feast of Unleavened Bread are permanently binding (12:14).

Mosaic Instruction about Passover (12:21-28)

^{12:21}*And Moses called to the elders of the Israelites, and he said to them, "Draw out and take for yourselves from the small herd for your families, and slaughter the Passover.* ²²*And you will take a bundle of hyssop and dip in the blood that is in the bowl. And you will touch the lintel and the two doorposts from the blood in the bowl. And you will not go out, each from the door of his house, until morning.* ²³*And Yahweh will cross over to strike the Egyptians, and he will see the blood on the lintel and on the two doorposts. And Yahweh will pass over the door, and he will not allow the destroyer to enter into your house to strike.* ²⁴*You will observe this word as a statute for you and for your children forever.* ²⁵*And when you enter the land in which Yahweh will give you as he spoke, you will observe this service.* ²⁶*And when your children will say to you, 'What is this service for you?'* ²⁷*And you will say, 'It is the sacrifice of Passover for Yahweh, when he passed over the houses of the Israelites in Egypt in his striking the Egyptians, but our houses he rescued.'" And the people bowed down and worshiped.* ²⁸***And the Israelites went and did as Yahweh commanded Moses and Aaron. They did so.***

Notes

12:21 *And Moses called to the elders of the Israelites.* The LXX reads, *pasan gerousian huiōn Israel,* "to all the elders of the sons of Israel."

from the small herd. The LXX renders Hebrew *ṣōʾn* as *probaton,* "a sheep."

12:22 *the blood that is in the bowl . . . from the blood in the bowl.* Hebrew *bassāp,* translated "in the bowl," is rendered in the LXX *para tēn thyran,* "on the threshold," suggesting, perhaps, that the container of blood is placed in the doorway.

12:23 *And Yahweh will cross over to strike the Egyptians . . . And Yahweh will pass over the door.* The Hebrew employs distinct verbs, *ʿābar,* "to cross over," and *pāsaḥ,* "to pass over." The LXX repeats the same verb, *parerchomai,* "to pass by."

12:25 *this service.* Hebrew *hāʿăbōdâ* is somewhat unusual. The LXX translates, *latreia,* "the service of a hired slave," which can also have religious meaning, "to serve the gods with prayers and sacrifices."

Commentary

The Non-P interpretation of the Passover is presented as a teaching by Moses in 12:21-27. Moses describes the rite of the Passover in vv. 21-23. He adds additional teaching on the Passover in vv. 24-27a in the form of a catechism with questions and answers. The instruction concludes with worship in v. 27b, a repetition from 4:31. Verse 28 indicates that the Israelites fulfilled the divine commands concerning Passover, pointing back to Yahweh's previous instruction to Moses in 12:1-20.

12:21-23 The Passover instruction in vv. 21-23 may be an ancient rite incorporated into the Non-P History. Scholars suspect the antiquity of vv. 21-23 because of the obscurity of the word *pesaḥ,* "passover,"[36] the role of the demonic destroyer,[37] the night setting,[38] the apotropaic blood rite,[39] the absence of a particular cultic location, [40] and the use of hyssop.[41] Yet debate has also continued concerning the antiquity of the rite, its original setting, and the relationship between Passover and the exodus (see the commentary on 12:1-20). Not all agree on the antiquity of the unit. Van Seters, for example, interprets the sacrificial language in vv. 21-22 ("slaughter," "hyssop," "dipping," and "basin") as indicating that 12:21-27 is part of the P History, in which case 12:1-28 would be a single literary unit.[42] Gertz argues, instead, that 12:21-27 has incorporated cultic language from Deuteronomy and the P History, indicating that the composition of the passage is post-P.[43]

The independent character of the cultic instruction in 12:21-23 is reinforced by tensions in its present narrative context and by comparison to the teaching on the Passover in Deuteronomy. The focus on the family does not correspond to Deuteronomy 16, where the Passover is interpreted as a national festival to be observed at a central sanctuary. And the instruction for the Israelites to remain in their houses until morning in 12:22 conflicts with the chronology of the Non-P History, where the journey out of Egypt commences during

---

36. G. Gerleman ("Was heisst פֶּסַח?" *ZAW* 88 [1976]: 409-13) argues that the primary meaning is "to strike against violently, rebound." O. Keel ("Erwägungen zum Sitz im Leben des vormosaischen Pascha und zur Etymologie von פֶּסַח," *ZAW* 84 [1972]: 414-34) argues instead that it means "to walk with a limp." For an overview of the problems see Kraus, *Worship in Israel,* 45-47.

37. Noth, *Exodus,* 91-92.

38. Haran, "Passover Sacrifice," 89.

39. Kraus, *Worship in Israel,* 46.

40. E. Otto and T. Schramm, *Festival and Joy* (trans. J. L. Blevins; Biblical Encounters Series; Nashville: Abingdon, 1980), 13.

41. Ibid.

42. Van Seters, *Life of Moses,* 114-19. Van Seters also identifies the phrase "ordinance for you and your offspring forever" in v. 24 as a further indication of Priestly authorship.

43. Gertz, *Tradition und Redaktion,* 38-56.

the night in the wake of the final midnight plague of death. If the Passover ritual was originally independent, it was probably limited to vv. 21-22. Reference to Yahweh passing over to strike the Egyptians in v. 23 would be an addition to accommodate the ritual to the narrative context of the exodus.

Moses addresses the "elders of Israel" with the Passover instruction in v. 21. The book of Deuteronomy and the Deuteronomistic History provide background on the role of elders. The elders receive the law from Moses (Deut 31:9) and they judge the people in Deuteronomy (Deut 19:12; 21:2, 3, 4; 22:15; 25:7). Elders assume a variety of leadership roles in the Deuteronomistic History, including the choosing of a king (1 Sam 8:4). Elders also assume a leadership role in the Non-P History. Moses is commissioned to address the elders at the outset of Exodus (Exod 3:16, 18), which he does upon reaching Egypt (4:29). The elders are singled out to receive legal instruction concerning the Passover as in Deuteronomy. And elders continue in a leadership role throughout the Non-P History to judge the people and to receive law. They witness the miracle of water at Massah (17:5-6), they are commissioned as judges (18:12), they accompany Moses on the mountain of God (24:1, 9, 14), and eventually seventy of the elders even receive a portion of Moses' spirit (Num 11:25).

The Passover victim must be taken from the small herd (*ṣō'n*, v. 21), sheep or goats, thus overlapping in meaning with the P description of a "kid" (12:3). Also, like the P instruction, the setting for Passover is the family. The family setting raises a question about the relationship of 12:21-23 to Deuteronomy (Deut 16:2) and to the Deuteronomistic History (2 Kings 23), in which the Passover is a national pilgrimage festival celebrated at a central shrine. The Non-P History may simply provide a distinct interpretation from Deuteronomy and the Deuteronomistic History, closer to that of the P History (see Leviticus 23; Numbers 28–29). The reason for the divergent interpretation, as noted above, may be that vv. 21-23 represent an ancient rite taken over by the Non-P author. But the description of Passover can also be read in conjunction with Deuteronomy and the Deuteronomistic History, in which case there is an evolution in the celebration of the Passover. The family setting anchors the ritual in the exodus. But the aim of the history is the national observance under Josiah. The corporate character of the Passover as a festival outside the family orbit is underscored in the first observance in the promised land (Josh 5:10-12). It is prescribed as a national festival in Deuteronomy 16 to be celebrated at the central sanctuary. And it is finally enacted under Josiah at the close of the Deuteronomistic History as a national festival at Jerusalem (2 Kings 23).

The point of emphasis for the slaughter in the ritual of the Passover is the power of the blood in v. 22. It is placed in a bowl and applied to the doorframe with hyssop. The reference to hyssop is a distinct element from the P interpretation. It likely refers to marjoram *(Orgianum Maru)*. Hyssop is instrumental in cleansing or absolving humans from skin disease (Lev 14:4) and from corpse contamination (Num 19:18). H.-J. Kraus notes the cleansing power attributed to the shrub. He cites a Babylonian prayer to Marduk and Ps 51:7. The former reads: "May the tamarisks cleanse me, the . . . -growth release me, the palm pulp blot out my sins; may the basin of holy water of Ea and Asariluchi bring me good luck!" The latter states: "Cleanse me with hyssop, and I will be clean; wash me and I will be whiter than snow."[44] It is unclear whether the reference to hyssop means that the Non-P author intends the blood of the Passover victim to cleanse the participants. The description of the Passover as a sacrifice in Exod 12:27 may indicate a cleansing function. Yet the focus remains on the house, not the participants. No one is allowed to venture outside the house. The blood will protect those inside from death.

The destruction of the Egyptians is stated in both the Non-P (12:23) and P (12:13) Histories. But the syntax of each verse suggests different interpretations. In the P History Yahweh is the source of destruction: "And I will see the blood and I will pass over you. And the attack of destruction will not be against you, when I strike the land of Egypt." But in the Non-P History the word "destroy" is stated with a definite article *(hammašḥît),* translated "the destroyer," indicating a separate power: "He [Yahweh] will not permit *the destroyer* to enter your houses." In the Non-P History the destroyer, not Yahweh, is warded off by the blood of the Passover victim. The personification of the destroyer relates the Non-P History to the Deuteronomistic History and to exilic prophetic literature. The Deuteronomistic History shows transition in the use of the term. The destroyer refers to humans (1 Sam 13:17 and 14:15). But the destroyer is also personified in 2 Sam 24:10-17, where it is merged with the Messenger of Yahweh *(hammal'āk)* as a source of punishment and death, resulting from David's census. The "Hill of Destruction" *(lĕhar-hammašḥît)* is the location for child sacrifice (2 Kgs 23:13), recalling the same theme in the Passover. See the similar interchange between human and divine power in reference to the destroyer in exilic prophetic literature (Jer 4:7; 5:26; 51:1, 25; Ezek 5:16; 9:1-11; 25:15; Isa 54:16). The blood of the Passover victim wards off an independent destroyer, not Yahweh, in the Non-P History.

12:24-27   The cultic instruction in vv. 24-27 employs distinctive language from vv. 21-23, which is similar in style to Deuteronomy and portions of the Deuteronomistic History.[45] The command to observe a law or ritual as a statute forever (v. 24; Deut 12:28; Josh 4:7) and the description of the land as a future gift (v. 25; Deut 6:4-25) prompted Wellhausen to identify the author as the Deuteronomist, rather than the Yahwist or the Elohist of classical source

---

44. Kraus, *Psalms 1–59*, 504-5.
45. See already Wellhausen, *Composition*, 74-76.

criticism. The literary judgment of Wellhausen has influenced subsequent interpreters. Noth, for example, also attributes the composition of vv. 24-27 to the author of the Deuteronomistic History.[46] But not all agree. Lohfink noted that vv. 24-27a lack the lengthy style of fully developed Deuteronomistic rhetoric with its tendency for repetition and elaborate syntax. He concluded that vv. 24-27a was an early independent speech (proto-Deuteronomic), whose similarity to later Deuteronomistic tradition arises from its use in a similar cultic sphere.[47] S. Boorer evaluated the partial similarity between vv. 24-27a and the P instruction of Passover to argue that 12:21-27 is an addition occurring sometime after Deuteronomy and before the P History.[48] Van Seters, on the other hand, attributes the unit to the P author,[49] while Gertz identifies a combination of motifs from Deuteronomy and the P History, suggesting a post-P author for 12:21-27.[50]

The emphasis on Moses as a teacher and orator conforms to the development of his character in the Non-P History. The presentation also corresponds to the role of heroes in Deuteronomy and the Deuteronomistic History who make speeches at transitional points in the story. The device is important to the structure of Deuteronomy, which is presently fashioned as sermons by Moses, and it continues into the Deuteronomistic History as, for example, in the speech of Joshua at the crossing of the Jordan River and at the close of book of Joshua. Moses is distinct from subsequent heroes, however, in that the

---

46. Noth, *Exodus*, 97-98. Noth designated vv. 24-27a as a Deuteronomistic supplement, to which v. 24b was a later addition.

47. N. Lohfink, *Das Hauptgebot: Eine Untersuchung literarischer Einleitungsfragen zu Dtn 5-11* (AnBib 20; Rome: Pontifical Biblical Institute, 1962), 122. Lohfink identified a series of stylistic differences between Exod 12:24-27 and Deuteronomistic rhetoric: "to observe" in v. 24; the singular use of "statute" in v. 24; the use of Israel as the subject in the reference to the future possession of the land in v. 25; the combination of "to observe" with "service" in v. 25; the cultic use of "service" in v. 25; and the use of "to say" rather than "to request" in introducing the child's question concerning the meaning of Passover. For interpretations supporting the conclusion of Lohfink see J. Loza, "Les catéchèses étiologiques dans l'Ancien Testament," *RB* 78 (1971): 481-500 esp. 484-87; M. Caloz, "Exode, XIII, 3-16 et son rapport au Deutéronome," *RB* 75 (1968): 5-62; A. Reichert, "Israel, The Firstborn of God: A Topic of Early Deuteronomic Theology," in *Proceedings of the Sixth World Congress of Jewish Studies* (3 vols.; ed. A. Shinan; Jerusalem: World Union of Jewish Studies, 1977), 1:341-49, esp. 345; M. Weinfeld, *Deuteronomy 1–11* (AB 5; New York: Doubleday, 1991), 328-29. See Chr. Brekelmans, "Die sogenannten deuteronomischen Elemente in Gen.-Num: Ein Beitrag zur Vorgeschichte des Deuteronomiums," in *Volume du Congrès: Genève 1965* (VTSup 15; Leiden: Brill, 1966), 89-96, who outlines three criteria for identifying proto-Deuteronomic material in the Tetrateuch. For a response to the methodology see Dozeman, *God at War*, 48-51.

48. Boorer, *Promise of Land*, 161-65.

49. Van Seters, *Life of Moses*, 114-19.

50. Gertz, *Tradition und Redaktion*.

Figure 21

Text:	Exod 12:21-27	Exod 13:1-16	Deut 6:4-25	Joshua 4
Event:	Death of Egyptian firstborn	Exodus from Egypt	Promulgation of law	Entrance into the land
Speaker:	Moses	Moses	Moses	Joshua
Catechetical instruction				
Question:	Passover	*Maṣṣôt*/Firstlings	Deuteronomic Law	Twelve Stones
Answer:	Israel spared plague of death	Israel led from Egypt/Egyptian firstborn killed	Promise of land to the ancestors	Triumph of Yahweh over Sea/River

subject matter of his speech contains the instruction for the central festival of Passover.[51]

The most distinct literary feature of 12:24-27 is the intergenerational instruction in the form of a catechism. The genre appears for the first time in the institution of the Passover at Rameses (12:24-27), but it repeats immediately in the presentation of the Feast of Unleavened Bread and the divine claim on the firstborn at Succoth (13:8, 14-15). The repetition of this form indicates the relationship between 12:21-27 and 13:3-16. J. A. Soggin has clarified the cultic setting of the form, while also noting its further repetition in the giving of law in Deuteronomy (Deut 6:20-25) and during the crossing of the Jordan River (Josh 4:6b-7a, 21-24).[52] The repetition reinforces the conclusion of Wellhausen that the instruction of the Passover in Exod 12:21-27 has close literary ties with Deuteronomy and the Deuteronomistic History. The diagram in figure 21 illustrates the distribution of the catechisms, their setting, the speaker, and the content of the instruction in the Non-P History, Deuteronomy, and the Deuteronomistic History.

Verse 24 indicates that the instruction of the Passover is a permanent statute, thus changing the perspective from the present to the future, from the night

51. See Weinfeld, *Deuteronomy and the Deuteronomic School*, 10-58, esp. 32-45, who discusses the role of oration in the Deuteronomistic tradition. He describes Exod 12:21-27 as liturgical oration. For additional commentary on the use of oration to create point of view in Deuteronomy and in the Deuteronomistic History see R. Polzin, *Moses and the Deuteronomist: A Literary Study of the Deuteronomic History* (part one; New York: Seabury, 1980).

52. Soggin, "Kultätiologische Sagen," 341-47. For further discussion of the form of catechetical instruction see J. Loza, "Les catéchèses étiologiques dans l'Ancien Testament," *RB* 78 (1971): 481-500; Long, *Problem of Etiological Narrative*, 78-79; Dozeman, *God at War*, 54-60 (with additional bibliography).

of death in Egypt to the subsequent observance of the Passover in the promised land. Verse 25 develops explicitly the change in focus by stating that the ritual of Passover is intended for the Israelites' future life in the land: "When you enter the land that Yahweh will give you as he spoke, you will observe this service." When the Non-P History is read in conjunction with Deuteronomy and the Deuteronomistic History the next observance of the Passover is, indeed, at Gilgal, after the Israelites cross the Jordan River to enter the land of Canaan (Josh 5:10-12). In the P History, by contrast, the Passover is observed immediately in the wilderness (Numbers 9), at the close of the revelation of law at Mount Sinai.

The restriction for the celebration of Passover in the Non-P History to the Israelites' future life in the promised land means that the observance of the Passover becomes disconnected from its originating experience in Egypt, the inevitable problem of historicizing cultic ritual. To overcome the problem of time, participation in the Passover includes intergenerational education and memory through the ritual of the questions and the answers, which comprise the celebration of the feast. Exodus 12:26-27 provides the paradigm. A child in the Passover ritual is instructed to ask: "What does this ceremony mean to you?" The question is not simply curiosity. It is certainly pedagogy, as Sarna notes.[53] And, as Soggin clarified, it is also a ritual.[54] The question requires a response, thus interpreting the ritual. B. O. Long has underscored further the etiological function of the text, thus relating the participants in the ritual with the originating event.[55]

All the aspects of the catechism, pedagogy, ritual, and etiology continue in the Jewish service of the Passover Haggadah, which is also structured in the format of intergenerational teaching through questions and answers. The Passover Seder progresses through a series of questions and answers. There are four questions during the second cup of the Seder meal: "Why is this night different from all other nights?" The paschal lamb, the unleavened bread, and the bitter herbs *(mārōr)* are all introduced with questions: What is the meaning? What is the origin? And what does it teach us? The questions require a response from the participants, activating memory, which recalls and actively shapes the original event of salvation. The Christian Eucharist follows many of the same liturgical principles. It too is an *anamnesis,* an activation of memory to participate in a past event of salvation. With such a view of memory, tradition itself is released from the constraints of the past, becoming, as I. Stavinsky defined it: "A living force that animates and informs the present."[56]

---

53. Sarna, *Exodus,* 60.
54. Soggin, "Kultätiologische Sagen."
55. Long, *Problem of Etiological Narrative,* 82-83.
56. The definition of tradition comes from I. Stravinsky's 1939-1940 Harvard Lectures. See R. Taruskin, *Stravinsky and the Russian Traditions: A Biography of the Works Through*

The response in v. 27 includes two interpretations of the Passover both of which are distinct from the teaching on the Passover in the P History. First, the Passover is a sacrifice to Yahweh, implying that it is burned at an altar.[57] This interpretation corresponds to Deuteronomy (Deut 16:2), where the Passover is a national festival to be observed at a central shrine and thus burned on the altar. Second, the Passover ritual "delivers" each house marked by blood. Hebrew *nāṣal* is used to describe the divine rescue of the Israelite people in the commission of Moses (3:8). For the P author, the Passover is not a sacrifice and it does not rescue. It only protects the participants from death. The Non-P historian and Deuteronomy interpret the ritual differently. The Passover is a sacrifice to Yahweh and it has the power to rescue. The instructions end with the Israelites worshiping (v. 27a), a repetition of their response to Moses upon his initial return from the wilderness (4:31).

Finally, the language in vv. 24-27 ties into larger themes in the story of the exodus. Hebrew *ʿăbōdâ*, meaning "work," "service" (including slavery), and "worship," is an unusual designation for a festival, yet it fits the larger context of the exodus. The Israelites served Pharaoh in slave labor (1:14), while liberation for the Israelites was the divine demand that Pharaoh release the people from slavery for worship or service to Yahweh (7:16; 8:1; 9:1, 13; 10:3). The observance of Passover as a "work" (*ʿăbōdâ*) is part of the larger thematic developed of the Hebrew term in the Non-P History.[58]

12:28 The P author provides a conclusion to the instruction of the Passover and the Feast of Unleavened Bread by noting that the Israelites performed all the commandments. The verse also results in a literary structure organized around divine command and fulfillment, a typical feature of the P History. The divine commands to Moses and Aaron in 12:1-20 are fulfilled in 12:28. The book of Numbers provides further examples of the same structure. Sections are organized with a stereotypical introduction, "Yahweh spoke to Moses . . ." (Num 2:1; 3:5, 14, 40, 44; 4:1, 17, 21), and conclude with a notice of fulfillment, "as Yahweh had commanded Moses" (2:34; 3:51; 4:37, 41, 45, 49; 5:4; 8:4, 22; 9:20-23).

The structure of divine command and fulfillment allows the P author to frame, incorporate, and subordinate the Non-P account of the Passover to the P interpretation, without harmonizing the two versions. The instruction for the Passover is the divine speech to Moses and Aaron (Exod 12:1-20). Once the P version is in place, the Non-P account in 12:21-27 must be interpreted as an

"*Mavra*" (Berkeley: University of California Press, 1996). See also Blenkinsopp, "Memory, Tradition," 1-17; Mark S. Smith, *Memoirs of God* (Minneapolis: Fortress, 2004).

57. G. Anderson, "Sacrifice and Sacrificial Offerings (OT)," *ABD* 5:872-73.

58. For arguments favoring the proto-Deuteronomic character of the literary unit see Lohfink, *Hauptgebot*, 121-22; Boorer, *Promise of Land*, 154-55. For a summary with further bibliography see Dozeman, *God at War*, 48-51.

abridgement of the preceding material. When the P author concludes the section in v. 28, indicating the fulfillment of the divine command, the reader assumes that the Israelites observed the Feast of Unleavened Bread with the Passover at Rameses, because of the divine instruction in 12:1-20. Yet in the Non-P History the Feast of Unleavened Bread is not mentioned in 12:21-27. Instead, it is celebrated separately at Succoth (13:3-10).

The success of the P author in subordinating the Non-P interpretation is evident in the commentary of Rambam, who concluded that Moses' instruction in 12:21-27 was meant to be a briefer treatment of the main points in Yahweh's speech in 12:1-20.[59] The rabbinic interpretation illustrates how the divine instruction of the P interpretation of the Passover takes precedence in the present form of the text. It provides the full description of the Passover. The Non-P interpretation is read as an abbreviated summary of Yahweh's instruction to Moses.

Death of the Egyptian Firstborn (12:29-36)

12:29 *And at midnight Yahweh struck all the firstborn in the land of Egypt, from the firstborn of Pharaoh, who dwelt on his throne, to the firstborn of the prisoner who was in the house of the pit, and every firstborn animal.* 30 *And Pharaoh arose that night, and all his servants, and all the Egyptians. And there was a great cry in Egypt, because there was not a house in which there was not death.* 31 *And he called to Moses and to Aaron at night, and he said, "Arise, go out from the midst of my people, both you and the Israelites. Go, serve Yahweh, as you spoke!* 32 *Both your flocks and your herds take, as you spoke! Go and bless me also!"* 33 *The Egyptians pressed upon the people to hasten in sending them out from the land, because they said, "We are all dead!"*

34 *And the people picked up their dough before its leavening, their dough pans wrapped in their clothes on their shoulder.* 35 *But the Israelites did as Moses spoke, and they requested from the Egyptians vessels of silver and vessels of gold, and clothes.* 36 *Now Yahweh gave the people favor in the eyes of the Egyptians and they lent to them. And they despoiled the Egyptians.*

Notes

12:29 *at midnight.* Hebrew *baḥăṣî hallaylâ* translates more lit., "at the middle of the night." See also LXX *mesousēs tēs nyktos.*

in the house of the pit. The insertion of "house" in the MT is unclear. Perhaps it is intended to relate to v. 30, "because there was *not a house* in which there was not death." The reference to a house is absent from v. 29 in the LXX, which has only *en*

59. See Leibowitz, *Studies in Shemot,* 1:193-202.

tō lakkō, "in the cistern," but present in v. 30, *ou gar ēn oikia*, "for there was not a house."

12:31 *serve Yahweh.* The LXX adds *tō theō hymōn*, "your God."

12:33 *in sending them out.* Hebrew *lĕšallĕḥām* is intensified in the LXX, *ekballein autous*, "to drive them out," which is closer to Hebrew *gāraš* (cf. 11:1).

12:36 *and they lent to them.* Hebrew *wayyaš'ilûm* is the Hiphil of *šā'al*, "to ask." The LXX translates, *kai echrēsan autois*, "and they furnished them."

and they despoiled the Egyptians. Hebrew *waynaṣṣĕlû* is the Piel of *nāṣal*, which basically means "to rescue" (i.e., 3:8).

Commentary

The Egyptian firstborn are killed in this section. The action fulfills the divine announcement from 11:4-8 repeating many of the same motifs (see fig. 20 at the outset of the commentary on 11:1–13:16). Verse 29 attributes the attack directly to Yahweh. Death invades every Egyptian home at midnight creating a loud cry, a reversal of the Israelite cry under slavery (2:23; 3:7, 9; 5:8, 15). The invasion of death into the Egyptian homes is universal, from Pharaoh's palace to the prison house.

The penetration of a plague into Pharaoh's house recalls the opening plagues of blood and frogs. Pharaoh was able to retreat into his home initially during the plague of blood (7:23), but frogs invaded his bedroom in the next plague (8:3). Now death invades his home. Jeremiah warns the Israelites of the invasion of death into the house through the window, "cutting off children from the streets" (Jer 9:21). The invasion of frogs into the palace prompted Pharaoh's initial response to Moses (Exod 8:8-15), a request for intercessory prayer in exchange for the release of the Israelites. Once the plague was halted, however, Pharaoh reversed his decision. The same deception continues through the plagues of flies (8:28-32), hail (9:27-35), and locusts (10:16-20). But now after the death to the Egyptian firstborn Pharaoh capitulates to Moses. No intercessory prayer is requested, nor is there deception. Instead he requests a blessing (12:32). Blessing and health are closely associated in the Hebrew Bible. Perhaps Pharaoh is requesting a reversal of the plague's curse. D. Daube provides another interpretation associating the blessing with the release of slaves as stated in Deut 15:18: "Do not consider it a hardship to set your servant free, because his service to you these six years has been worth twice as much as that of a hired hand. And Yahweh your God will bless you in everything you do."[60]

Pharaoh's deception throughout the plague cycle was indicated at the conclusion of each plague. The most common description of his resistance to the demands of Yahweh and Moses was that his heart was hard *(ḥāzaq)* and, consequently, he would not send out *(šālaḥ)* the Israelites from Egypt. Pha-

---

60. Daube, *Exodus Pattern*, 52-53.

raoh's capitulation to Moses in vv. 31-32 avoids this language. But the description of the Egyptians in v. 33 includes the language indicating a reversal. The motif of hardening is now used to describe their urgent pleading of the Israelite to leave quickly: "The Egyptians pressed upon the people *(hāzaq)* to hasten in sending them out *(šalah)* from the land."

Exodus 12:34 describes the haste of the Israelite departure. It is not originally a reference to the Festival of Unleavened Bread requiring the seven-day observance. The bread dough, *bāṣēq,* does not indicate the absence of leaven, but dough from flour in which the leavening process has not yet occurred (2 Sam 13:8; Jer 7:18; Hos 7:4). The dough is taken so fast that it is not able to leaven. The image of haste is reinforced by the manner in which utensils are gathered. The kneading trough is wrapped in a sleeping mantle and thrown over the shoulder. The focus on clothing may serve a ritual function, perhaps symbolizing the transitional nature of the festival. The imagery of the hasty departure fulfills the divine prediction to Moses in Exod 11:1, and the Israelites are driven out of Egypt. Exodus 12:35-36 returns to the motif of the despoiling of the Egyptians. Yahweh predicted twice to Moses (see the commentary on 3:21-22; 11:2-3) that the Israelites would not leave Egypt empty-handed, but with spoils of war.

Events at Succoth (12:37–13:16)

The first encampment of the Israelites is at Succoth. Exodus 12:37-42 provides a transition to the new location. Two sections follow. Exodus 12:43-51 outlines who may participate in the Passover. Exodus 13:1-16 shifts in subject matter from the Passover to the divine claim on the firstborn and the instruction for the Feast of Unleavened Bread.

Journey from Rameses to Succoth (12:37-42)

[12:37] *And the Israelites journeyed from Rameses to Succoth, about six hundred thousand foot soldiers, besides children.* [38] *And also a mixed group went up with them, flocks and herds, very many cattle.* [39] *And they baked the dough, which they brought out from Egypt, circular cakes of unleavened bread; it was not leavened, because they were driven out by the Egyptians, and they were not able to linger, and they could not even make for themselves provisions.*

[40] **And the residence of the Israelites, in which they dwelt in Egypt, was four hundred and thirty years.** [41] **And at the end of the four hundred and thirty years, on this very day, all the hosts of Yahweh went out from the land of Egypt.** [42] **It is a night of observance for Yahweh to bring them out from the land**

*of Egypt. This night is to Yahweh an observance for all the Israelites through-
out their generations.*

Notes

12:38 *foreigners went up with them.* Hebrew *ʿēreb* indicates "mixed company," as does
LXX *epimiktos.* The imagery may be of an army on the move.[61]

very many cattle. Hebrew *miqneh kābēd mĕʾōd,* "very heavy cattle," most likely indicates their great number, not their size.

12:40 *And the residence of the Israelites, in which they dwelt in Egypt, was four hundred
and thirty years.* The LXX adds *en gē Aigyptō kai en gē Chanaan,* "in the land of
Egypt and in the land of Canaan," thus changing the time of 430 years for the Isra-
elite sojourn in Egypt to include the entire patriarchal age. The Sam reflects the
LXX, reversing the order, *yšbw bʾrṣ knʿn wbʾrṣ mṣrym:* "they dwelt in the land of
Canaan and in the land of Egypt."

12:42 *observance.* Hebrew *šimmurîm* is well translated in the LXX *prophylakē,* "a guard
in front," related to Eng. "prophylactic," "tending to prevent or ward off," thus underscoring the apotropaic character of the rite.

Commentary

The section intertwines both Non-P and P literature. The Non-P History describes the departure from Egypt and its participants (vv. 37-39). The P History
dates the time in which the Israelites dwelt in Egypt while adding further commentary on the character of the departure and the mood of the night (vv. 40-
42).

12:37-39 Exodus 12:37 is the first itinerary notice. It anchors the point of
departure of the Israelite exodus at Rameses (see above, "Authors"). The departure from Rameses is described with the verb "to journey . . . from" *(nāsaʿ mē-),*
a standard feature of the itinerary notices (e.g., 12:37; 13:20; 15:22).[62] A firm location of Rameses is debated. Many archaeologists identify the city with
Piramesse, a location in the northeastern Delta at Katana-Qantir. Piramesse
was the residency of the pharaohs in the 19th and 20th Dynasties. The city was
plundered by the pharaohs of the 21st and 22nd Dynasties.[63] The biblical authors associate the Israelite slave labor with this city (1:11), and as a result it becomes the point of origin for the pilgrimage from Egypt, even though the Israelites are also associated with Goshen in the plague cycle.

The Israelites journey to Succoth. No verb is used to indicate their arrival
at Succoth. This is unusual in the itinerary notices. Although a verbal sentence
is expected, the particular description of how the Israelites reach their destina-

---

61. Wevers, *Notes,* 188.
62. See Coats, "Wilderness Itinerary," 135-52.
63. E. F. Wente, "Rameses," *ABD* 5:617-18.

tion varies widely in the itinerary notices. A range of verbs and prepositions are employed, including "to camp at," "to go out to," and "to enter in." The encampment at Succoth presents even more problems for historical geography than Rameses. The Hebrew word may refer to an Egyptian city, Tjeku *(ṯkw),* identified as the modern Tell el-Maskhuta. This location would place Succoth approximately a one-day journey from Rameses.[64]

The identity of Succoth is complicated by the use of this name in the Hebrew Bible. Two distinct geographical locations are presented in the biblical texts. The exodus from Egypt locates Succoth in Egypt (12:37; Num 33:5-6). Yet the story of Jacob (Gen 33:17) and stories about the judges place Succoth on the east side of the Jordan (Josh 13:27; Judg 8:5-17). M. D. Oblath writes of Succoth: "It is consistently placed somewhere within the Jordan River Valley, possibly between Shechem and the Jabbok River."[65] To complicate matters further, Succoth may also be a reference to the Festival of Booths (= Hebrew *sukkôt,* Lev 23:33-43), making the first encampment a metaphorical reference to worship in the wilderness. The Feast of Booths memorializes the exodus from Egypt. M. Harris writes of the Festival of Booths or Tabernacles: "Jews are to dwell in succot so that they 'may know' that God 'made the children of Israel to dwell in booths when I brought them out of the land of Egypt'(Lev 23:43)."[66]

Exodus 12:37-38 provides information on the number and character of the people leaving Egypt. The number of Israelites leaving Egypt is huge: six hundred thousand males, plus women and children, making the total over two million. A literal reading is impossible. A theological or metaphorical meaning to the number six hundred thousand is possible but difficult to decipher. Numbers certainly carry significance in the Hebrew Bible. The P writer employs similarly large numbers in Numbers 1, where the Israelite males total 603,551. Scholars have explored astronomy,[67] gematria (a process of valuation in which letters from the alphabet have a certain numerical worth),[68] the measurements of the temple,[69] and the possible misunderstanding of the numerical value of Hebrew *'elep,* "thousand," to interpret the precise number of Israelite males leaving Egypt.[70] All are possible, none is sure. The last solution, the misunder-

---

64. J. A. H. Seely, "Succoth," *ABD* 6:217-18. See the reference in *ANET,* 259.

65. Oblath, *Exodus Itinerary Sites,* 98.

66. M. Harris, *Exodus and Exile: The Structure of the Jewish Holidays* (Minneapolis: Fortress, 1992), 65.

67. M. Barnouin, "Les recensements du livre des Nombres et l'astronomie babylonienne," *VT* 27 (1977): 280-303.

68. G. Fohrer, *Introduction to the Old Testament* (trans. D. E. Green; Nashville: Abingdon, 1968), 184.

69. P. J. Budd, *Numbers* (WBC 5; Waco: Word, 1984), 8-9.

70. G. Mendenhall, "The Census Lists of Numbers 1 and 26," *JBL* 77 (1958): 52-66.

standing of the numerical value of Hebrew *'elep*, first advanced by G. Mendenhall, moves in the opposite direction of the more theological or symbolically oriented solutions. The large number certainly indicates at the very least that the divine promise of fertility, so important at the outset of the story (Exodus 1–2), is now fulfilled in spite of the oppression instituted by Pharaoh.

12:40-42 A "mixed group" also joins the journey. Hebrew *'ēreb*, "mixed group," is used to describe weaving (Lev 13:53). It indicates a broader group leaving Egypt than the Israelite nation. Verse 39 reinforces the hasty departure of the group by reference to cakes not yet leavened.

The P History dates the length of the Israelite stay in Egypt to 430 years in 12:40-42. Other dates for the period of Egyptian sojourn include four generations (Gen 15:16) and 400 years (Gen 15:13). The LXX describes the entire period of the ancestors and the Israelite oppression in Egypt as 430 years, as does the Sam. The period of 430 years likely carries meaning for the P author. But, like so many other numbers, interpretation is difficult. The period of the sojourn in Egypt is calculated one other time. 1 Kings 6:1 states that Solomon built the temple 480 years after the Israelite exodus from Egypt. The temple of Solomon stands for about 400 years before it is destroyed, based on the accumulated dates of the Israelite monarchs (which are somewhat less than 400 years). The roughly similar period of time suggests some form of inner-biblical interpretation between the time of the Egyptian sojourn and the monarchical period.[71] The parallel may carry a critique of the monarchical period: both life in Egypt and life under the monarchs constitute oppression. The P History advocates a ruling priesthood rather than a king. But such an interpretation is conjecture at best.

The P writer adds two further descriptions of the night of Passover. The first is that the Israelites march out as a military host. The second is that the night of the Passover is characterized by vigilance. Yahweh kept vigil over the Israelites, and the Israelites are now required to keep vigil by observing the Passover throughout their generations. The instruction to observe the Passover is not restricted to the land of Canaan, as in the Non-P History. The wilderness generation observes the Passover already in Numbers 9 at the conclusion to the revelation of the law at Mount Sinai.

Divine Instruction about Passover (12:43-51)

¹²:⁴³ *And Yahweh said to Moses and to Aaron, "This is the statute of Passover: No foreigner may eat it.* ⁴⁴*And, concerning every slave purchased with silver, if you circumcise him, then he may eat it.* ⁴⁵*The temporary resident or a hired worker may not eat it.* ⁴⁶*In one house it will be eaten. You will not bring out-*

---

71. Blenkinsopp, *Pentateuch*, 47-50.

side from the house any of the flesh. You will not break any of its bones. [47] *The entire congregation of the Israelites must do it.* [48] *And if a resident alien so-journs with you, and he wishes to do Passover to Yahweh, every male must be circumcised, and then he may draw near to do it. He will be as a native resi-dent of the land. But no one uncircumcised may eat it.* [49] *There will be one law to the native resident and to the resident alien, who sojourns in your midst."* [50] *And all the Israelites did as Yahweh commanded Moses and Aaron. They did so.* [51] *And on this very day Yahweh brought out the Israelites from the land of Egypt according to their hosts.*

Notes

12:43 *foreigner.* Hebrew *ben-nēkār* is lit. "son of a stranger"; LXX has *allogenēs,* "a per-son of another race."

12:44 *slave.* For Hebrew *ʿebed,* "servant, slave," the LXX has *oiketēn,* "household slave."

12:45 *temporary resident.* For Hebrew *tôšāb* the LXX has *paroikos,* "neighbor."

hired worker. The LXX renders Hebrew *śākîr* as *misthōtos,* "one hired for fixed wages."

12:48 *resident alien.* Hebrew *gēr* indicates a specific social group. The LXX *prosēlytos* likely suggests a similar social situation, even though the term later indicates a proselyte. For discussion see Wevers.[72]

native resident of the land. The LXX renders Hebrew *ʿezraḥ hāʾāreṣ* as *ho autochthōn tēs gēs,* "one sprung from the land itself, indigenous."

12:49 *native resident.* Hebrew *ʿezraḥ* repeats v. 48; the LXX introduces a new term, *enchōriō,* "a trueborn, someone of the country."

Commentary

The P History returns to the topic of the Passover and the exodus. Verses 43-49 outline the persons who would be acceptable participants in the Passover ritual, and vv. 50-51 describe the departure of the Israelite people from Egypt.

12:43-49 The section separates into three parts. Verses 43-45 and 47-49 describe who is able to participate in the Passover. The center, v. 46, provides further information on the Passover victim. Verse 46 states that no bones may be broken and the meat may not be taken outside the house. The taboo against broken bones is not immediately apparent. It is applied to Jesus, the paschal lamb, in John 19:36. The prohibition against leaving the house repeats earlier in-struction from the Non-P History (12:22), but absent from the previous P litera-ture (12:1-13).

The majority of 12:43-49 provides commentary on the notice in the Non-P History that the departure out of Egypt included both Israelites and a "mixed group" (12:38). The clarification concerning participants is offered as a divine speech to Moses and Aaron, a common literary feature in the P History. The

---

72. Wevers, *Notes,* 193.

perspective of the divine speech is from the Israelites' life in the promised land, not their present state as homeless pilgrims. The P writer delineates the nature of the mixed group, sorting out those who may participate in the Passover. The Passover is a family ritual in the P History. Thus by clarifying who is allowed to participate in the ritual of Passover, the section also states who might be included in the family or "congregation." The communal nature of the festival is underscored in v. 47 with the command that "the whole congregation of the Israelites" must celebrate the Passover. Circumcision is key to participation in the Passover and to entry into the congregation.

Five groups are distinguished from native Israelites. Verses 43-45 address the status of the foreigner *(nokrî)*, the temporary resident or client *(tôšāb)*, the purchased slave *('ebed)*, the hired worker *(śākîr)*; vv. 47-49 focus exclusively on the resident alien *(gēr)*. The groups share two common characteristics: they lack the inalienable right to own land and they are separated from the Israelite family structure. The differences among the groups are not clear. The purchased slave can be separated most easily from among the other groups because of his slave status. Such a person can be incorporated into the ritual of the Passover on condition of circumcision. The other groups probably overlap. All designate non-Israelites who reside for different reasons among the Israelite people in the land of Israel. Thus the instruction anticipates the Israelites' future life in the land. The resident alien may simply be a person from one of the other categories who resides for a more extended time among Israelites. This person is singled out as able to participate in the Passover upon condition of circumcision. Such a person has equal protection under the law (v. 49).[73] The alien assumes a special position in the Hebrew Bible. Moses identifies himself as a resident alien (2:22). And the Israelites are also characterized as sojourners or resident aliens in Yahweh's land (Lev 25:23).

12:50-51 Verse 50 provides a conclusion, noting the fulfillment of the divine command. Verse 51 marks the time of the exodus from Egypt with the phrase "on this very day," a common phrase in the P History (see Gen 17:23 and Exod 12:17), which is used to note significant events. The nature of the departure suggests a military march, with the people marching in military formation as a host.

Divine Instruction about the Firstborn (13:1-2)

13:1 *And Yahweh spoke to Moses, saying,* [2] *"Sanctify to me every firstborn, opening every womb among the Israelites, in humans and in animals. It is mine."*

---

73. See C. J. H. Wright, *God's People in God's Land: Family, Land, and Property in the Old Testament* (Grand Rapids: Eerdmans, 1990), 99-103.

Notes

13:2 *every firstborn, opening every womb.* Hebrew *kol-bĕkôr,* "every firstborn," followed
by *peṭer kol-reḥem,* "opening every womb," indicates a women's firstborn son. The
verb *pāṭar* means "to escape, set free" (see *CTA* 16.vi.8). Propp writes: "*Peṭer* may
mean '(the act of) loosening,' and then, by extension, 'that which loosens.'"[74] The
LXX renders *bĕkôr* and *peṭer* as two nouns in apposition, *prōtotokon prōtogenes,*
both indicating firstborn.

Commentary

Exodus 13:1-2 is the first statement of the divine claim on the Israelite firstborn.
I have assigned the instruction to the P History, but there is debate over the literary context of the verses. B. S. Childs concluded that 13:1-2 functions as a superscription for the subsequent teaching by Moses in 13:3-16.[75] Those who disagree with Childs note that the P superscription contains no teaching on the
Feast of Unleavened Bread, which is the central theme in 13:3-10, and therefore
cannot be an introduction to the following law.[76] The emphasis on the firstborn
in 13:1-2, rather than the Feast of Unleavened Bread, is likely intentional by the
P author, since the P teaching on the Feast of Unleavened Bread is already completed in 12:1-20, where the two festivals, Passover and Unleavened Bread, are
merged into one feast. The exclusive focus on the firstborn in 13:1-2 subordi-
nates the additional instruction on the Feast of Unleavened Bread in 13:3-10 by
pointing ahead to the subsequent teaching about the firstborn in 13:11-16.

The technique by which the P author inserts 13:1-2 as a new introduction
to 13:3-16 follows the pattern of the P additions to the plague cycle and to the
teaching on Passover. The three plagues in the P History, the sea dragon, the
gnats, and the boils, were inserted as introductions to the separate cycles of the
plagues. The divine instruction about the Passover and the Feast of Unleavened
Bread in 12:1-20 was also inserted as an introduction to the additional instruction on Passover in 12:21-27. In both instances the P material influences the interpretation of the following literature. The divine claim on the firstborn in
13:1-2 repeats the same technique. It too provides the point of focus for reading
13:3-16. In all of these instances, the new introduction of the P author becomes

74. Propp, *Exodus 1–18,* 421.

75. Childs, *Exodus,* 202-4. In assigning Exod 13:1-2 to the P History, scholars note the
change in number from the singular (13:1-2) to the plural (13:3-16), the form of the introduction
in v. 1 compared to other introductions in the P History (14:1; 25:1; 30:11; etc.), and the repetition
of the language of sanctification (the Hiphil of *qādaš*) in the P History (Num 3:13; 8:17). But
Kohata (*Jahwist und Priesterschrift,* 274) has noted that the Hiphil of *qādaš* is also used in Deut
15:19, while Noth (*Exodus,* 101) is less sure of separating vv. 1-2 from vv. 3-16 in spite of changes
with regard to singular and plural.

76. Durham, *Exodus,* 177.

the hermeneutical lens for the interpretation. The literary technique indicates that the P History takes prominence in the canonical text, even though it is dependent on the Non-P History. The P historian's interpretation of the Passover and the Feast of Unleavened Bread, as a single festival, overrides the interpretation in the Non-P History where the two festivals are separated, with the Passover observed at Rameses, apart from the observance of the Feast of Unleavened Bread at Succoth.

The divine claim on the firstborn is central to the P History (see the commentary on 13:11-16). The reference to the firstborn in 13:1-2 is in relationship to mothers, not fathers. It is the firstborn "to open the womb." The restriction is even narrower, since it is limited to firstborn males. The claim is historicized in the P History. It arises as a result of the survival of the Israelite firstborn during the death of the Egyptian firstborn. The divine claim applies to both humans and animals. It is in effect immediately in the P History, thus applying to the Israelites in the wilderness. It is not postponed until the Israelites enter the promised land, as in the Non-P History. As a result, the divine claim on the firstborn is crucial to the organization of the wilderness camp of the Israelites (Numbers 1–8). The application of the law outside the land of Canaan may be aimed at Jews of the Diaspora in the exilic and postexilic periods.

The central command of Yahweh to Moses in 13:1-2 is that the firstborn must be consecrated. The act of consecration (*qādaš*) indicates a transfer from the profane to the sacred sphere. Such a transfer is necessary for serving Yahweh. God is holy and humans are profane. The root meaning of the verb "to consecrate" is to set apart and thus to make holy. The ordination of the priesthood in Exodus 29 illustrates the complexity required to consecrate a human for divine service. The process requires rites of purification and atonement through sacrifice, as well as proper vestments, resulting in a restriction of action. No such rituals are outlined in 13:1-2 even though the claim is in effect immediately. The reason is that the divine claim on the firstborn will be transferred to the Levites in the P History creating a separate class in Israelite society between the priesthood and the laity. Numbers 3:11-13 describes the role of the Levites as substitutes for the Israelite firstborn, while Num 8:5-26 outlines the complex procedures required for their transfer from the profane to the sacred sphere. As a result, the Israelite firstborn are redeemed from their obligation to Yahweh. The obligation of lay Israelites in exchange for their firstborn is a temple tax. The Levites provide service to Yahweh and to the Aaronide priesthood in place of the firstborn.[77]

---

77. See Dozeman, "Numbers," *NIB* 2:50-51, 80-82.

Mosaic Instruction on the Feast of Unleavened Bread and the Firstborn (13:3-16)

¹³:³ *And Moses said to the people, "Remember this day, on which you came out from Egypt, from the house of slavery, for with a strong hand Yahweh brought you out from this. Therefore leaven will not be eaten.* ⁴ *Today you are going out, in the month of Abib.* ⁵ *And when Yahweh brings you into the land of the Canaanite, the Hittite, the Amorite, the Hivite, and the Jebusite, which he promised to your fathers to give to you, a land flowing with milk and honey, you must perform this service in this month.* ⁶ *Seven days you will eat unleavened bread, and on the seventh [there shall be] a festival to Yahweh.* ⁷ *Unleavened bread will be eaten seven days. Leaven will not be seen among you, and leaven will not be seen in your borders.* ⁸ *And you will tell your children on that day, saying, 'This is because of what Yahweh did for me in my going out of Egypt.'* ⁹ *And it will be for you as a sign on your hand, and a memorial between your eyes, so that the law of Yahweh will be in your mouth, because with a strong hand Yahweh brought you out from Egypt.* ¹⁰ *And you will observe this statue at its appointed time from days to days.*

¹¹ *"And when Yahweh brings you to the land of the Canaanite, as he promised to you and to your fathers, and he gives it to you,* ¹² *every first opening of the womb will belong to Yahweh. Every first opening of an animal, which is male, belongs to Yahweh.* ¹³ *Every first opening of a donkey you will redeem with a kid. But if you do not redeem it, then you will break its neck.* ¹⁴ *And when your son asks you tomorrow, saying, 'What is this?' You will say to him, 'With a strong hand Yahweh brought me out from Egypt, from the house of slavery.* ¹⁵ *And when Pharaoh hardened to send us out, Yahweh killed all the firstborn in the land of Egypt, from the firstborn of humans to the firstborn of animals. Therefore I sacrifice to Yahweh every first male opening the womb. But every firstborn of my sons I redeem.'* ¹⁶ *And this will be a sign on our hand, and a mark between your eyes, because with a strong hand Yahweh brought you out of Egypt."*

Notes

13:4 *today*. Hebrew *hayyôm* is rendered in the LXX *en gar tē sēmeron*, "for in this day." Wevers notes the unusual construction, limited in the Pentateuch to Deut 4:4.[78]

13:8 *This is because of what Yahweh did for me in my going out of Egypt*. The LXX adds *kyrios ho theos*, "the Lord God." See also vv. 9, 11.

13:10 *at its appointed time*. Hebrew *lĕmô'ădāh* designates festivals (see Gen 1:14); see LXX *kata kairous hōrōn*, "according to the times of the seasons."

from days to days. Hebrew *mîyāmîm yāmîmâ* may indicate "year" rather than "day" (see Judg 11:40).

13:12 *every first opening of an animal*. The Hebrew includes reference to a litter, *wĕkol-*

---

78. Wevers, *Notes*, 196.

peṭer šeger bĕhēmâ, "every first opening of the litter of cattle." The LXX translates, *ek tōn boukoliōn ē en tois ktēnesin sou,* "from the cattle or in your herd."

13:16 *a mark between your eyes.* Hebrew *ṭôṭāpōt* may indicate something concrete, such as a headdress, or phylacteries, meaning small square leather boxes containing slips inscribed with scriptural passages and worn on the left arm and forehead during prayer. The LXX translates, *asaleuton,* "immovable," suggesting a more metaphorical meaning.

Commentary

Moses provides cultic instruction at Succoth on two topics: 13:3-10 is instruction about the Feast of Unleavened Bread, and 13:11-16 outlines the divine requirement concerning firstborn. The language of the instruction repeats many themes from the Non-P History and Deuteronomy, including the list of the indigenous nations of Canaan (13:5; see 3:8, 17; Deut 1:7; 7:1; 20:17; Josh 3:10; 5:1; 9:1; 11:1-3, etc.), the description of Egypt as the "house of slavery" (Exod 13:3, 14; see Deut 5:6; 6:12; 8:14; 13:10), the call for Israel "to remember" (Exod 13:3; see Deut 7:18; 24:9; 25:17, etc.), the description of the land as "flowing with milk and honey" (Exod 13:5; see Deut 6:3; 11:9; 26:9, 15, etc.), the "strong arm" of God (Exod 13:9; see Deut 3:24; 4:34; 5:15; 6:21; 7:8, 19; 9:26; 11:2; 26:8, etc.), the older Canaanite calendrical reckoning with the month of Abib (Exod 13:4; see Deut 16:1), and specific references to phylacteries (Exod 13:9, 16; Deut 6:8-9; 11:18-20).[79]

The themes are organized around the catechism, requiring intergenerational teaching, which first appeared in Moses' instruction about the Passover in 12:21-27. Exodus 13:8 is a shortened form of the catechism stating simply that the Feast of Unleavened Bread must be taught to children; while 13:14-16 includes the complete form as in 12:26-27 with both the question from the child and the answer from the adult. B. O. Long has demonstrated that the two sec-

---

79. The Deuteronomistic character of Exod 13:3-16 has long since been recognized. Yet debate has continued concerning its literary unity and its relationship to Deuteronomy. Wellhausen (*Composition,* 73) assigned vv. 1-2 to P and vv. 3-16 to Deuteronomistic tradition. For a similar analysis see Hyatt, *Exodus,* 141-42; Childs, *Exodus,* 184, 202-4; or with slight variation Fohrer, *Überlieferung und Geschichte,* 86-89, who assigns vv. 3-16 to D and designates vv. 1-2 as a later redactional addition in the traditions of either D and P. Moving in a somewhat different direction, Noth (*Exodus,* 101-2) argued that the Deuteronomistic character of 13:3-16 was the result of a redaction of earlier distinct traditions. Beer (*Exodus,* 60) takes the analysis of Noth one step further, dividing the unit into Priestly (vv. 11-16) and Deuteronomistic (vv. 3-10) literature. F. Michaeli (*Le livre de l'Exode* [CAT 2; Paris: Delachaux et Niestlé, 1974], 111) describes the unit as ancient tradition in the spirit of J with Deuteronomistic additions. Cf. Van Seters ("Place of the Yahwist," 175-76), who argues that the unit is unified and the product of a late (exilic) Yahwist; while Gertz (*Tradition und Redaktion,* 57-72) attributes the entire text to a post-Priestly redactor. See also W. Fuss, *Die deuteronomistische Pentateuchredaktion in Exodus 3–17* (BZAW 126; Berlin: de Gruyter, 1972), 289-90; Blum, *Studien,* 35-36, 167-68.

tions, 13:3-10 and 11-16, share similar motifs, including the promise of land (vv. 5, 11), the catechism (vv. 8, 14-15), a sign (vv. 9, 14), and the reference to the exodus (vv. 9, 16).[80]

13:3-10   The Feast of Unleavened Bread. This section is a speech by Moses to the Israelite people, containing the interpretation of the Feast of Unleavened Bread in the Non-P History. The instruction relates the Feast of Unleavened Bread to the exodus (vv. 3-4, 8-9). The general instruction on the Feast of Unleavened Bread frames the teaching in vv. 3 and 10. The observance of the Feast of Unleavened Bread is an act of "memory" (*zākar,* v. 3), which requires "observance" (*šāmar*) of a statute (*ḥuqqâ*) through time (v. 10). The teaching of Moses in vv. 4-9 provides the details of the ritual. The time of the festival is the month of Abib (v. 4; see the commentary on 12:1-2). The duration of the festival is seven days (vv. 6-7). The ritual of intergenerational teaching is an important feature of the liturgy (v. 8). The continuing significance of the liturgy is indicated by its description as a sign (v. 9) of the exodus, which will function when the people acquire the promised land (v. 5).

The Feast of Unleavened Bread is firmly anchored in the exodus in both the Non-P and P Histories. But the historicizing of the ritual into the exodus is likely a late development in the history of Israelite worship. Wellhausen established the framework for the modern study of the Feast of Unleavened Bread. He speculated that the observance of unleavened bread was ancient, most likely pre-Israelite. And he judged the cultic calendar in 23:14-17 to be the earliest reference to the Feast of Unleavened Bread, where it is one of three pilgrimage feasts described in Hebrew as a *ḥag.*[81] The Feast of Unleavened Bread (*ḥag hammaṣṣôt*) occurred in the spring, during the month of Abib. It was a seven-day feast, followed by the Feast of Harvest (*ḥag haqqāṣîr*) associated with the firstfruits of planting, a one-day feast approximately fifty days after the Feast of Unleavened Bread. The third pilgrimage was the Feast of Ingathering (*ḥag hā'āsip*), a seven-day harvest festival in the fall of the year. The three feasts are tied to the agricultural cycle. The calendar indicates that the Feast of Unleavened Bread was originally a spring festival of planting, not associated with Passover. Noth suggested that the absence of leaven was rooted in the requirement that the first bread of the New Year be eaten in its natural state, that is, unleavened.[82]

J. Halbe questioned the agricultural setting of the Feast of Unleavened Bread. He noted that the date, Abib, is not really the appropriate time for a harvest festival and that a pilgrimage resulting in a seven-day ritual would be un-

80. Long, *Problem of Etiological Narrative,* 69-83.
81. Wellhausen, *Prolegomena,* 83-120.
82. Noth, *Exodus,* 97.

likely for such a celebration.[83] B. N. Wambacq provided further support for the conclusion of Halbe, noting that the fixed date for the Feast of Unleavened Bread conflicts with an agricultural feast, which would vary in time depending on the harvest.[84] And Propp raised further questions about the grain used for the festival. New grain, he notes, cannot be ground but would instead be roasted. The grinding of grain suggests the use of the old crop, which would further detach the festival from the agricultural cycle. For Propp the unleavened bread is a ritual of riddance aimed at purging impure leaven from bread in the spring of the year.[85] The research indicates that the identification of the origin of the ritual of Unleavened Bread remains obscure.

Wellhausen also influenced the interpretation of the Feast of Unleavened Bread in the story of the exodus. He argued that the Passover and the Feast of Unleavened Bread were originally separate rituals not associated with the exodus. The historicizing of the Passover and the Feast of Unleavened Bread, as an event growing out of the Israelites' salvation from Egypt, was a development in the late monarchical period, first evident in Deuteronomy. He judged the Non-P accounts of the Passover (12:21-27) and the Feast of Unleavened Bread and the sacrifice of the firstborn (13:3-16) to be late additions to the narrative of the exodus, likely by a Deuteronomistic author.[86]

The combination of the Feast of Unleavened Bread with the Passover and their further association with the exodus continue to be debated, influencing the identification of the author of 12:21-27 and 13:3-16. H.-J. Kraus represents the trend to identify an earlier date for the merging of Passover and the Feast of Unleavened Bread, which he locates in the liturgical practice at Gilgal, preserved in Josh 5:10-12.[87] The earlier dating for the combination of the two festivals and their association with the exodus has prompted more complex proposals for the composition of 13:3-16. Noth agreed with Wellhausen about the Deuteronomistic character of 13:3-16, but he added that it was the result of a redaction of earlier distinct traditions.[88] F. Michaeli agreed, describing the unit as ancient tradition in the spirit of J with Deuteronomistic additions.[89] Childs also identifies the author of 13:3-16 as "the Deuteronomist," but he too indicates that the author is passing on tradition. The trend in interpretation among these

---

83. J. Halbe, "Erwägungen zu Ursprung und Wesen des Massotfestes," *ZAW* 87 (1975): 324-46.

84. B. N. Wambacq, "Les Massot," *Bib* 61 (1980): 31-53.

85. Propp, *Exodus 1–18*, 429-34.

86. Wellhausen, *Composition*, 74-76; idem, *Prolegomena*, 83-120.

87. H.-J. Kraus, "Zur Geschichte des Passah-Massot-Festes im Alten Testament," *EvT* 18 (1958): 47-58; idem, "Gilgal: Ein Beitrag zur Kultusgeschichte Israels," *VT* 1 (1951): 181-99.

88. Noth, *Exodus*, 101-2.

89. Michaeli, *Exode*, 111.

scholars is to allow for a more complex formation of 13:3-16, while avoiding a detailed description of the process of composition.

Lohfink sought to describe the process of composition more clearly by locating the "Deuteronomistic style" of 13:3-16 within the broader development of the tradition that is reflected in Deuteronomy. He noted a number of peculiarities in style between 13:3-16 and the rhetoric of Deuteronomy to argue for the early composition of 13:3-16, which he described as proto-Deuteronomic. The unique literary features include the phrase "out of Egypt" as opposed to the phrase "out of the land of Egypt"; the predominance of the syntactical form *běḥōzeq yād*, "with a strong arm," in 13:3, 14, 16 as opposed to the more common phrase in Deuteronomy, *běyād ḥăzāqâ*, "with a strong arm," which occurs only in Exod 13:9; the use of "Yahweh" rather than "Yahweh, your God"; the particular form of the table of nations with only five members rather than seven as in Deut 7:1; and the form of the reference to the fathers in 13:5, 11.[90]

The approach of Lohfink to the composition of 13:3-16 has prompted new theories of the formation of the Passover and the Feast of Unleavened Bread. Boorer, for example, has argued on the basis of a comparison between 13:3-16 and 34:18-20 that the instructions concerning the Feast of Unleavened Bread in 13:4, 6a and the firstborn in 13:12, 13, 15b are older traditions that have been reframed by later writers (13:3, 5, 6b-9, 11, 14, 16). This framing is pre-Deuteronomistic, and it occurs independently of the Passover legislation in 12:21-27. The result is a three-part reconstruction of the cultic history of the exodus from (1) Unleavened Bread/firstborn to (2) the Passover and the Feast of Unleavened Bread loosely connected with firstborn becoming isolated and finally (3) the Passover and the Feast of Unleavened Bread as one unified festival with firstborn removed.[91]

The tradition-historical recovery of the early formation of the Passover and the Feast of Unleavened Bread has undergone revision. E. Kutsch represents a return to the view of Wellhausen, calling into question the ability of interpreters to recover an extended tradition-historical development of the festivals as advocated by Kraus.[92] Literary critics have also questioned whether the rhetorical style of the instruction in 13:3-16 allows for the complex literary history described by Lohfink and others. Blum has returned to the more general literary judgment of Wellhausen, identifying 13:3-16 as an episode within the *D-Komposition (KD)*.[93] Van Seters includes the entire account within the exilic

90. Lohfink, *Hauptgebot*, 122-23. For an expansion of the arguments of Lohfink see Caloz, "Exode, XIII, 3-16 et son rapport au Deutéronome," 5-62. Cf. Fuss, *Deuteronomistische Pentateuchredaktion*, 289-90; Blum, *Studien*, 35-36, 167-68.

91. Boorer, *Promise of Land*, 129-43, 188-202.

92. Kutsch, "Erwägungen zur Geschichte," 1-35.

93. Blum, *Studien*, 35-36.

Yahwist History without identifying a more complex history of composition.[94] Gertz follows the same trend of simplifying the history of the composition of 13:3-16 by identifying the author as a post-P final redactor of the Pentateuch.[95]

The origin and circumstances for the combination of the Passover and the Feast of Unleavened Bread remain unresolved. But it is clear that the Feast of Unleavened Bread is combined with the Passover and historicized with the exodus by the time of the exile. Cultic reform under Josiah (2 Kgs 23:21-23) includes the celebration of the Passover, but not the Feast of Unleavened Bread. The Feast of Unleavened Bread is combined with the Passover and firmly historicized with the exodus in the cultic calendar in Deuteronomy 16 (see also Josh 5:10-12). The exact process of cultic transformation remains unclear because of difficulty in dating the present form of the calendar in Deuteronomy 16. But the literary parallels noted above provide the basis for incorporating the Feast of Unleavened Bread in Exod 13:3-10 within the Non-P History.

In the Non-P History, the Passover and the Feast of Unleavened Bread celebrate distinct aspects of the salvation of the Israelite people from Egypt. The Feast of Unleavened Bread commemorates the act of leaving the land of Egypt, as compared to the Passover, which is tied more closely to the death of the Egyptian firstborn (12:21-27). The act of leaving Egypt is foremost in the instruction. It frames the teaching in vv. 3 and 9, while also repeating in vv. 4 and 8. Moses begins the instruction by commanding the people "to remember" (*zākar*) the day on which "Yahweh brought you out" (*yāṣā'* in the Hiphil). The same teaching returns at the conclusion of the instruction in v. 9: the Israelites are to celebrate the Feast of Unleavened Bread, "because with a strong hand Yahweh brought you out from Egypt." Blum notes that the teaching on the Feast of Unleavened Bread is intended to provide a cultic etiology for the narrative account of the Israelite expulsion from Egypt in 12:33 and 39.[96]

The central word to describe the exodus from Egypt is the verb "to go out" (*yāṣā'*). It occurs not less than five times in 13:3-10. Moses states to the people that on this very day the people "came out of Egypt" (v. 3; see also vv. 4, 8) because Yahweh "brought them out" (v. 3; see also v. 9). J. Wijngaards has identified the statement of divine leading from Egypt as a standard confessional formula, which he describes as the "exodus motif." It consists of the phrase: "Yahweh brought us out of Egypt." This confession uses stereotyped language, including the causative (Hiphil) form of the verb *yāṣā'*, "to go out," with Yahweh

---

94. Van Seters, *Life of Moses*, 119-22.

95. Gertz, *Tradition und Redaktion*, 58-67.

96. Blum, *Studien*, 37. Cf. Gertz, *Tradition und Redaktion*, 59, who relates the designation "this day" to Exod 12:40-42 in the P History, which becomes one factor in identifying the author of 13:3-16 as post-Priestly.

as the subject and Israel as the object.[97] The noncausative (Qal) form of the verb "to go out" can be a technical term for the going out of a slave, while the causative form of the verb can express release from prison. Thus the "exodus motif" has overtones of social oppression and probably "expresses a strict liberation from slavery."[98] The motif is so important in the faith of ancient Israel that it becomes one of the defining characteristics of Yahweh. The Decalogue begins: "I am Yahweh your God, who brought you out of Egypt, out of the house of slavery" (20:2).

Salvation as divine liberation may have deep roots in Israel's cultic practice. Emerging forms of the motif occur in older poetry. Psalm 68:7 and 2 Sam 22:49 use the expression to signify how God brought about a reversal (usually in the context of war), which is celebrated as a liberating act of salvation. Psalm 68:7 describes God as "going out" in the imagery of a military march to save the Israelites: "O God, when you went out before your people." 2 Samuel 22:49 describes the defeat of an enemy as a divine liberation: "God . . . brought me out from my enemies."

The emphasis on liberation associated with the exodus motif is also central to Deuteronomy. Yahweh is described as "having brought out" Israel with a strong hand (Deut 6:21; 7:8; 9:26), with a strong hand and an outstretched arm (5:15; 7:19), and with his presence and great power (4:37). Other uses of the motif describe the place or situation from which Israel was rescued: Israel was "brought out" from the iron furnace (4:20), from slavery (5:6; 6:12; 8:14; 13:5), from the hand of Pharaoh (7:8), from the Egyptians (4:20, 37; 6:21; 9:26; 23:4; 26:8), and from the land of Egypt (5:6; 6:12; 8:14; 13:5, 10; 20:1).

The Non-P History shares the perspective of Deuteronomy. The Feast of Unleavened Bread commemorates liberation through the imagery of leaving Egypt. The liberation is a release from slavery brought about by Yahweh's mighty hand (Exod 13:3). The festival is to be commemorated in the month of Abib (v. 4; see Deut 16:1) through intergenerational teaching (Exod 13:8; see the catechisms in 12:26-27; 13:14-15; Deut 6:4-25; and Josh 4:6-7, 20-24). And it is a pilgrimage feast lasting seven days.

The instruction on the Feast of Unleavened Bread also indicates that its observance will take effect when the Israelites enter the promised land of Ca-

---

97. W. J. Wijngaards, "הוציא and העלה: A Twofold Approach to the Exodus," *VT* 15 (1965): 92; idem, *The Formulas of the Deuteronomic Creed (Dt. 6/20-23; 26/5-9)* (Pontificia Univeristas Gregoriana; Tilburg: A. Reijnen, 1963); idem, *The Dramatization of Salvific History in the Deuteronomic Schools* (OTS 16; Leiden: Brill, 1969). See also B. S. Childs, "Deuteronomic Formulae of the Exodus Tradition," in *Hebräische Wortforschung: Festschrift zum 80. Geburtstag von Walter Baumgartner* (ed. B. Hartmann et al.; VTSup 16; Leiden: Brill, 1967), 30-39; H. D. Preuss, "*yāṣā*," *TDOT* 6:20-49.

98. H. D. Preuss, "*bôʾ*," *TDOT* 2:233.

naan. Exodus 13:5 establishes the future setting for the observance of the Feast of Unleavened Bread, stating that it is to be observed "when Yahweh brings you into the land." Thus unlike Passover at Rameses, the Feast of Unleavened Bread is not celebrated at Succoth, only its instructions are given at this location. The acquiring of land, which provides the basis for the festival, is guaranteed by a divine promise: "Which he [Yahweh] promised to your fathers to give you."

Boorer has demonstrated that the promise of land is also a confessional formula, which repeats throughout the Non-P History, Deuteronomy, and the Deuteronomistic History. The phrase is composed of the causative form of the verb "to enter" *(bôʾ)* to indicate the divine leading into the land, the verb "to give" *(nātan)* to signify the divine gift of the land, and the verb "to promise" or "to swear" (Niphal of *šbʿ*) to underscore that the land is the fulfillment of a divine promise to the ancestors.[99] The confession can be translated in the following manner: "When Yahweh brings you into the land . . . which he swore to [you and] your ancestors to give you." The promise of land is accompanied in v. 5 with a list of the indigenous nations that the Israelites will defeat (see the commentary on 3:6-7; and 23:20-33).

The promise of the land as oath is an important motif in the Non-P History (e.g., 13:5, 11; 32:13; 33:1; Num 11:12; 14:23; 32:11) and in the subsequent literature of Deuteronomy (Deut 1:8, 35; 6:10, 18, 23; 7:13; 8:1; 10:11, etc.) and the Deuteronomistic History (Josh 1:6; 5:6; 21:43). The promise of land with oath also relates the account of the exodus in the Non-P History with the story of the ancestors in Genesis. The promise of land first appears to Abram without the divine oath (Gen 12:7). The promise of land with the divine guarantee through an oath appears for the first time to Isaac in Gen 26:2-4. This promise also introduces the intergenerational character of the divine promise of land, which is central to the teaching of Moses in Exod 13:3-10. The book of Genesis closes with Joseph repeating the same promise to his brothers (Gen 50:24), again emphasizing the intergenerational character of the divine promise of land.

13:11-16 Divine Claim of the Firstborn. The teaching of the law of the firstborn shifts in emphasis from the exodus to the fulfillment of the promise of land. The promise of land repeats in vv. 11 and 14. The repetition of the promise of land provides the structure for the overall teaching. The first section, vv. 11-13, states the law of the firstborn. Verse 11 provides the future setting of the law in the promised land. Verse 12 states the general law that Yahweh claims the firstborn. And v. 13 provides qualifications for fulfilling the law through substitution and redemption. The second section, vv. 14-16, introduces the ritual commemorating the divine claim on the firstborn as a catechism. Verse 14a

---

99. See Boorer, *Promise of Land*; Wijngaards, "הוציא and העלה," 92. For further discussion and more complete bibliography see Dozeman, *God at War*, 81 n. 80.

again emphasizes the future setting of the ritual in the promised land. Verses 14b-15 outline the ritual with the intergenerational teaching in the form of questions and answers. Verse 16 provides a conclusion by historicizing the divine claim on the firstborn in the event of the exodus.

The interpretation of the divine claim on the Israelite firstborn is difficult for two reasons. The theme of the firstborn is subordinated to the Passover and the Feast of Unleavened Bread in the present form of the text. And the teaching concerning the firstborn throughout the Hebrew Bible is not clear. The language in 13:1-2 suggests child sacrifice, but it is not stated explicitly. Exodus 22:29-30 confirms the sacred status of the firstborn, again suggesting child sacrifice. Yahweh states: "You must give me the firstborn of your sons." The divine attack against Moses or Gershom in 4:24-25 may also represent a divine claim on the firstborn.

The sacrifice of the firstborn was likely practiced by the Israelites.[100] The Deuteronomistic History contains stories of child sacrifice by Israelite judges (Jephthah, Judg 11:34-40), neighboring kings (the king of Moab, 2 Kgs 3:27), and Israelite kings (Ahaz, 2 Kgs 16:3; Manasseh, 2 Kgs 21:6). The ritual is localized in the Valley of Hinnom on the outskirts of Jerusalem (2 Kgs 23:10). Child sacrifice is condemned in late prophetic literature suggesting its role in the Israelite cult. The exilic prophet Ezekiel writes: "You took your sons and your daughters, whom you had borne to me and sacrificed them as food to the idols" (Ezek 16:20-21; see also Jer 7:31; 19:5; 32:35). The story of Abraham's binding of Isaac, known in tradition as the *Akedah,* may also be a polemic against child sacrifice, advocating the substitution of a ram for the child (Genesis 22).

The Non-P and P Histories also advocate different forms of substitution to redeem firstborn humans. The P History presents the divine claim on the firstborn in Exod 13:1-2. As noted above, the substitution for the divine claim on the firstborn in the P History gives rise to the class of the Levites described in Numbers 3 and 8. The substitution of the firstborn in the Non-P History is described in Exod 13:11-16. Moses states the law of the firstborn in vv. 11-13. It begins with the promise of land as oath indicating the restriction of the law to the Israelites' future life in the land (v. 11). The restriction of the law to the land of Canaan suggests an association with the Festival of Firstfruits, also known as Weeks (see Deut 26:1-15). The central content of the law is the divine claim on the firstborn and the need for the Israelites to substitute for firstborn human males. The Non-P historian introduces the motif of substitution for firstborn males in the *Akedah.*

100. See J. D. Levenson, *The Death and Resurrection of the Beloved Son: The Transformation of Child Sacrifice in Judaism and Christianity* (New Haven: Yale University Press, 1993), 3-52 *et passim;* A. Green, *The Role of Human Sacrifice in the Ancient Near East* (ASORDS 1; Missoula, Mont.: Scholars Press, 1977), 156-87.

The Non-P historian includes additional legal guidelines for the substitution of firstborn males in Exod 13:11-16. Verse 12 states the general requirement: all male firstborn must "be passed over" to Yahweh. The law is similar to the P History in 13:1-2. Firstborn status is defined in relation to the mother. The Hebrew verb ʿābar, "to pass over," indicates transfer of ownership from the profane to the sacred in this context. The firstborn males are a divine possession. Whether divine ownership implies their sacrifice is unclear, but it is implied by the exceptions to the law in v. 13. Donkeys and humans can be "redeemed" *(pādâ)*. The Hebrew term is an economic one, meaning bought out of slavery. Indentured Israelites can be redeemed (21:8). A firstborn male donkey must be killed by breaking its neck, if it is not redeemed. All firstborn male humans must be redeemed. The price of redemption is not stated in the Non-P History. The P History provides precise economic guidelines: human redemption costs five shekels (Num 3:46-48). The law of the firstborn is memorialized through intergenerational teaching like the Passover and the Feast of Unleavened Bread (see the commentary on 12:21-27).

Destruction of the Egyptian Army in the Red Sea (13:17–14:31)

The conflict between Yahweh and Pharaoh over the fate of the Israelites climaxes in this section. The magnitude of the conflict is underscored by the role of nature. Nature already played an important role in the plague cycle where Yahweh demonstrated control over water, land, and air. The final confrontation explores Yahweh's power over the chaotic sea itself to destroy Pharaoh and his army. Yahweh controls the sea with his breath. He splits the sea in two. He is even able to dry up the sea, allowing the Israelites to pass through safely. At the same time, Yahweh has the power to reverse the process in order to destroy the Egyptian army.

The story of Yahweh's control over the sea is influenced by liturgical motifs from ancient Near Eastern religion where the sea represents the forces of nature at war with the god of creation. The Canaanite god of fertility, Baal, wars against the chaotic forces of sea and river, the god Yamm-Nahar (Yamm = "sea" and Nahar = "river").[101] The defeat of the god Yamm-Nahar signals the victory of order, creation, and fertility in Canaanite religion. The Babylonian god Marduk splits the sea monster, Tiamat, as the initial act of creation in the myth *Enuma Elish.*[102] The representation of the sea, as the absence of order, continues in a less mythological form in ancient Near Eastern and in Greek literature

---

101. *CTA* 2 is the story of Baal's conflict with Yamm-Nahar.
102. See *ANET,* 60-72.

through the use of "Ocean." "Ocean" does not signify a god. Rather it represents the boundary of structured civilization and the limit of human experience.[103] The tradition of the sea in the story of the exodus suggests more the tradition of "Ocean" than the presentation of a deity over against Yahweh.

The ancient Israelite writers know the tradition of the chaotic sea outside the story of the exodus. The sea is often an opponent to God representing chaotic forces that seek to undo creation. Isaiah 27:1 associates the sea *(yām)* with the sea dragon *(tannîn)*, the serpent *(nāḥāš)*, and Leviathan *(liwyātān)*. The passage celebrates Yahweh's punishment of the sea monster. Job too identifies the sea *(yām)* with the sea dragon (Job 7:12) and with Rahab *(rāhāb)*, "the Boisterous One," who functions much like Leviathan (Job 9:13).[104] The primeval waters are also described as the deep *(tĕhôm;* Ps 33:6-7; Prov 8:27-29) and the "many waters" *(mayim rabbîm;* Hab 3:8-15), which Yahweh controls at the time of creation.[105] Psalm 74:12-14 weaves together many of the mythological motifs of the sea in celebrating the creative power of Yahweh to break Sea (Yamm, the sea god), to shatter the head of the sea dragons, and to crush the heads of Leviathan. The temple of Solomon also symbolizes God's control of the sea with the huge bronze bowl, known as the molten sea (1 Kgs 7:23-26). Psalm 89:9-10 provides commentary: Yahweh rules the raging sea. When its waves rise, Yahweh crushes them like Rahab. Yahweh scatters the enemy with his mighty arm. Such a display of strength reveals the power of God as the creator (89:11) and the faithfulness of God as savior (89:8).

The mythology of the sea is also historicized by biblical writers. The book of Isaiah describes the army of the enemy as "the roaring of the sea" (Isa 5:30) and the "roaring of the many waters" (17:13). The prophets Jeremiah and Ezekiel also historicize the mythology of the chaotic sea. Jeremiah 51:34 describes the Babylonian king Nebuchadrezzar as the sea monster because of the destruction of Judah and the exile of the Israelite people. Ezekiel 32:1-16 equates the defeat of Pharaoh to the destruction of the great sea monster.

The most prominent use of the mythology of the sea, however, is to describe the exodus.[106] Isaiah 51:9-11 refers to the exodus from Egypt as the time

---

103. For illustrations from Greek writing see Romm, *Edges of the Earth;* and for ancient Near Eastern examples see W. Horowitz, *Mesopotamian Cosmic Geography* (Mesopotamian Civilizations; Winona Lake, Ind.: Eisenbrauns, 1998).

104. Day, *God's Conflict;* idem, "Rahab," *ABD* 5:610-11. Other references to Rahab include Psalms 87; 89; Isa 30:7; 51:9.

105. Day, *God's Conflict;* C. L. Seow, "The Deep," *ABD* 2:125-26. See the work of H. Gunkel, *Creation and Chaos in the Primeval Era and the Eschaton* (trans. K. W. Whitney Jr.; Grand Rapids: Eerdmans, 2006).

106. See Day, *God's Conflict.*

when Yahweh defeated the sea monster, Rahab, by drying up the sea. Isaiah 43:16 celebrates the power of God as savior and creator by describing Yahweh as the one "who makes a way in the sea, a path in the mighty waters," suggesting the imagery of the exodus. Isaiah 11:15-16 echoes the same theme, only the sea in this text is described as River *(nāhār),* recalling the close association of Sea-River (Yamm-Nahar) in Canaanite mythology. In Isaiah 11 the splitting of the river results in seven channels of water (echoing the seven heads of Leviathan), rather than the two walls of water in Exodus 14. Psalm 114 also memorializes God's power over sea and river. The sea flees before the presence of God and the Jordan River turns back.

The Non-P and the P Histories also employ the mythology of the chaotic sea to describe the final conflict between Yahweh and Pharaoh. Like the exilic prophets Second Isaiah, Jeremiah, and Ezekiel, the Non-P and P authors historicize the mythology of the sea. Pharaoh, not the sea, is the opponent of Yahweh. The sea is a weapon used to destroy Pharaoh. The Non-P and P Histories employ different traditions of the chaotic sea to describe the destruction of Pharaoh. The Non-P History reflects the Canaanite myth of Baal and Yamm-Nahar, while the P History is influenced more by the Babylonian myth of Marduk, who splits Tiamat. The combination of the two interpretations creates repetition in the present form of Exod 13:17–14:31. The sea is both dried up by an east wind and split in two. Despite their different interpretations the Non-P and P Histories follow a similar three-part structure:

   I. The Israelite Journey to the Sea (13:17–14:4)
  II. The Pursuit by Pharaoh (14:5-14)
 III. The Destruction of Pharaoh and the Egyptian Army in the Red Sea (14:15-31)

Non-P History

The Non-P History consists of 13:17-18a, 19-20; 14:5-7, 8a, 9a, 10-16a*a*, b, 19a, 20a*a*, 21a, 22a, 23-24a*a*, 24b-29a, 30-31. Geography continues to play an important role in the story. The episode begins with an account of the Israelite journey to the sea. The trek from Succoth is indirect, avoiding the land of the Philistines, because the Israelites are not yet ready for war (13:17-18a). The people finally encamp at Etham, a location on the edge of the wilderness (13:20). The result of the location of Etham is that the conflict at the Red Sea takes place in the wilderness in the Non-P History, not in the land of Egypt.

The pursuit by Pharaoh shifts between the point of view of the Egyptians and the Israelites. Pharaoh changes his mind and gathers his army in pursuit (14:5-7, 8a, 9a). The Israelites fear the approach of Pharaoh and complain to

Moses about their present condition (14:10-14). They state their preference for slavery in Egypt to the risk of freedom in the wilderness. Their complaint is known as the wilderness murmuring tradition (see the introduction to 15:22–18:27). It repeats throughout the Non-P History. The murmuring motif is a rejection both of Yahweh's salvation and of Moses' authority, the very thing that Moses feared in the Non-P version of his commission (3:1–4:18).

The destruction of Pharaoh at the Red Sea includes two cycles of action that progress through the night (see above, "Authors"). Each cycle begins with a divine command to Moses to influence the flow of water in the Red Sea.

Cycle one: Yahweh dries up the sea with an east wind during the night (14:15-16a, 21a). The Messenger of Yahweh leads the Israelites (14:19a, 20a). The Israelites cross the Red Sea on dry ground, with the Egyptians pursuing them (14:22a, 23). The cycle concludes with Yahweh beginning to attack the Egyptian army at the morning watch (14:24a, b, 25).

Cycle two: Yahweh returns the water to its natural flow, destroying the Egyptian army in the sea at daybreak (14:26-29a). The episode concludes with the Israelites seeing the dead soldiers, fearing Yahweh, and believing in Moses (14:30-31), fulfilling the divine promise to Moses in his commission.

The central motif of the Non-P History is the drying up of the Red Sea and the entrance into it of the Israelite people on dry ground. The entrance into the Red Sea is a rite of passage, which further launches the Israelite people on their wilderness pilgrimage. The same actions occur at the end of the Israelite journey when Yahweh dries up the Jordan River allowing the people to cross into the promised land of Canaan on dry ground (Joshua 3–4). A. Lauha noted that the Red Sea and the Jordan River are related events framing the wilderness journey.[107]

Coats has built on the work of Lauha.[108] He noted that the drying up of the Red Sea functions as a doorway for the Israelites to march into the wilderness. Coats agreed with Lauha that the event is interwoven with the book of Joshua, where the crossing of the Red Sea is first recounted in the spy story (Joshua 2) and again in the catechism of Josh 4:21-24, where the relationship between the two bodies of water is made explicit: "Yahweh your God dried up the waters of the Jordan for you until you crossed over, as Yahweh your God did to

---

107. A. Lauha, "Das Schilfsmeermotiv im Alten Testament," in *Congress Volume: Bonn 1962* (VTSup 9; Leiden: Brill, 1963), 32-46.

108. G. W. Coats, "The Traditio-Historical Character of the Reed Sea Motif," *VT* 17 (1967): 253-65; idem, "The Song of the Sea," *CBQ* 31 (1969): 1-17; idem, "An Exposition for the Wilderness Tradition," *VT* 22 (1972): 289-95; idem, "A Structural Transition in Exodus," *VT* 22 (1972): 129-42; idem, "The Sea Tradition in the Wilderness Theme: A Review," *JSOT* 12 (1979): 2-8. See also B. S. Childs, "A Traditio-Historical Study of the Reed Sea Tradition," *VT* 20 (1970): 406-18.

Figure 22

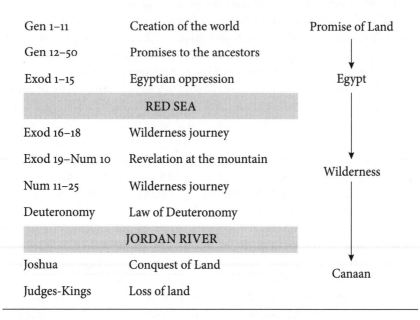

Gen 1–11	Creation of the world	Promise of Land
Gen 12–50	Promises to the ancestors	
Exod 1–15	Egyptian oppression	Egypt
RED SEA		
Exod 16–18	Wilderness journey	
Exod 19–Num 10	Revelation at the mountain	Wilderness
Num 11–25	Wilderness journey	
Deuteronomy	Law of Deuteronomy	
JORDAN RIVER		
Joshua	Conquest of Land	Canaan
Judges–Kings	Loss of land	

the Red Sea, which he dried up for us until we crossed over." The dual event is meant to demonstrate the strength of Yahweh.[109]

Cross has shown that the merging of the Red Sea and the Jordan River motifs incorporates the mythological influence of Baal's conflict with the Sea (Yamm) and the River (Nahar).[110] In the Non-P History, the Canaanite myth provides a framework for interpreting salvation as the wilderness pilgrimage from the exodus out of Egypt (Red Sea) to the conquest of the promised land (Jordan River). The structure can be illustrated with the diagram in figure 22 above.

This diagram provides the background for a comparison of the Red Sea and the Jordan River in the Non-P History. Each describes the Israelite people passing through a body of water on dry ground *(yabbāšâ)*. Yet the two events are not the same. Most notable is the different description of the people's movement through the water. The Israelites "enter" *(bôʾ;* 14:16, 22, 29; 15:19) the Red Sea; while they "cross" *(ʿābar)* the Jordan River. The motif of crossing the Jordan River occurs not fewer than twenty-two times. The ark of Yahweh (Josh

109. See T. B. Dozeman, "The *yam-sûp* in the Exodus Tradition and in the Crossing of the Jordan River," *CBQ* 58 (1996): 407-16.

110. Cross, *Canaanite Myth and Hebrew Epic,* e.g., 121ff.

Figure 23

	Red Sea	**Jordan River**
Setting	Exodus from Egypt	Conquest of the land
Focus of the story	Faith of Israel	Nations and holy war
Rite of passage	"to enter" *(bô')* the sea on dry ground	"to cross" *('ābar)* the Jordan on dry ground

3:11; 4:11), the people (1:11; 3:1, 4, 14, 16, 17 [twice]; 4:1, 7, 10, 11, 13, 22, 23 [twice]), the leaders of the tribes (4:5), the tribes east of the Jordan (1:14; 4:12), and even the cultic stones (4:3, 8) are described as crossing the Jordan River.[111] A. R. Hulst states that the verb "to cross over" has theological meaning in Deuteronomy. It signifies actions that must take place, if the Israelites are to achieve the divine promise of the land at the end of their wilderness march.[112] The frequent repetition of this word in the story of the crossing of the Jordan River reinforces the same meaning.

The use of separate motifs to describe the Israelite people passing through the Red Sea and the Jordan River indicates that the two events form a single rite of passage in the Non-P History framing the wilderness journey as noted above by Lauha, Coats, and Cross. The "entrance" into the Red Sea signals the moment when the people of Israel acquire faith in Moses and in Yahweh, fulfilling the divine prediction in the commission of Moses (Exod 3:1–4:18). The faith of the Israelite people at the Red Sea marks the beginning of their pilgrimage launching them on the wilderness journey. It is for this reason that the confrontation at the Red Sea is located in the wilderness in the Non-P History. The crossing of the Jordan River marks the end of the wilderness journey, when the Israelite people enter the promised land of Canaan prepared to undertake holy war against the indigenous nations. The separate themes of the two stories are illustrated in the diagram in figure 23.

P History

The P History includes 13:18b, 21-22; 14:1-4, 8b, 9b, 16ab, 17-18, 19b, 20ab, b, 21b, 22b, 24ab, 29b. The P History presents a distinct interpretation of the confrontation at the Red Sea. The changes begin with the Israelite journey to the Red Sea. Unlike the Non-P History, where the Israelites were not ready for war, the

---

111. See Dozeman, *God at War*, 64-65.

112. A. R. Hulst, "Der Jordan in den alttestamentlichen Überlieferungen," *OTS* 14 (1965): 162-88.

P History states that the people were prepared for battle (13:18b). Another contrast is that the people are led by the pillar of cloud, rather than by the Messenger of Yahweh (13:21-22). The changes continue in the P History, when the people encamp at Pi-hahiroth (14:1-4), having turned back at Etham. Thus the setting for the confrontation at the Red Sea is shifted from the wilderness, associated with Etham, to the land of Egypt in the P History, signified by the reversal of direction required to reach Pi-hahiroth. The confrontation at the Red Sea in the P History is the final and decisive conflict between Yahweh and Pharaoh in the land of Egypt, not the first event in the Israelites' wilderness pilgrimage as in the Non-P History.

The description of Pharaoh's pursuit of the Israelites reinforces changes from the previous section in the P History. The P author states that the Israelites are not timid but march out boldly (14:8b), reinforcing once again that the confrontation between the two forces takes place at Pi-hahiroth (14:9b), not Etham.

The destruction of Pharaoh in the sea also undergoes reinterpretation in the P History. Most notably the sea is split in the P History (14:16ab, 21b), resulting in two walls of water (14:22b, 29b). The imagery incorporates the Babylonian myth of creation noted above, *Enuma Elish,* where the splitting of chaotic sea is the decisive victory of Marduk over Tiamat, inaugurating creation. Yahweh's splitting of the Red Sea suggests that the exodus is also an act of creation in the P History. The pillar of cloud and fire continues to lead the Israelites (14:19b, 20ab, b, 24ab). The P History also adds a new interpretation to the event in 14:17-18, fulfilling the divine prediction to Moses from his commission in 7:1-5 that the destruction of Pharaoh would bring the Egyptians to the knowledge of Yahweh.

The change in the setting for the confrontation at the Red Sea and the introduction of the motifs of creation by conflict from *Enuma Elish* sever the close relationship between the exodus and the conquest in the Non-P History. When the Israelite people turn around at Etham to reach Pi-hahiroth, the confrontation at the Red Sea becomes the final event of salvation in the land of Egypt. Thus in the P History, the confrontation at the Red Sea does not require the crossing of the Jordan River for completion. It is, rather, a climactic event signaling a new era in world history. The motif of the splitting of the sea further reinforces the separation between the exodus and the conquest by encouraging a comparison to the original creation in Genesis 1, which also emphasized the process of separation and splitting. Thus in the P History the defeat of Pharaoh at the Red Sea is an act of creation for the Israelite people. And, like the original creation of the world in Genesis 1, the splitting of the Red Sea has universal significance. The universal focus of the P History is evident in the change of theme from the Non-P History. The central theme of the

P History is not the faith of the Israelite people, but the acknowledgment of Yahweh's power by the Egyptians.[113]

Israelite Journey to the Sea (13:17–14:4)

[13:17] *And when Pharaoh sent out the people, God did not lead them [by] the way of the land of the Philistines, even though it was near, because God said, "Lest the people repent in their seeing war, and they return to Egypt."* [18] *God turned the people aside on the way of the wilderness of the Red Sea.* **As an army in five parts, the Israelites went up from the land of Egypt.** [19] *And Moses took the bones of Joseph with him, for he had made the Israelites swear, saying, "God will become very aware of you, and you must take up my bones from here with you."*

[20] *And they journeyed from Succoth, and they encamped at Etham, on the edge of the wilderness.* [21] **And Yahweh was going before them by day in the pillar of cloud to lead them in the way, and by night in a pillar of fire to give them light, to go day and night.** [22] **The pillar of cloud would not depart by day and the pillar of fire by night before the people.**

[14:1] **And Yahweh spoke to Moses, saying,** [2] **"Speak to the Israelites, that they turn back and they camp before Pi-hahiroth, between Migdol and the sea, before Baal-zephon, opposite it, you will camp by the sea.** [3] **And Pharaoh will say of the Israelites, 'They are wandering in confusion in the land, the wilderness has closed them in.'** [4] **And I will harden the heart of Pharaoh, and he will pursue after them. And I will gain glory over Pharaoh and over all his army. And the Egyptians will know that I am Yahweh." And they did so.**

Notes

13:17 *way.* Hebrew *derek* could be translated more precisely in this context as "road," as in the LXX, *hodon.*

13:18 *the Red Sea.* The translation follows the LXX, *tēn erythran thalassan.* Hebrew *yam-sûp* may also indicate the Red Sea. The word *sûp,* however, designates "reeds" or "rushes," perhaps from Egyptian *twf(y),* meaning "reed" or "papyrus."[114] For further interpretation of Hebrew *yam-sûp,* see the commentary on 13:17-20.

as an army in five parts. Hebrew *waḥămušîm* is a military term, designating an army in five parts: vanguard, lead, body, and two wings. See also Josh 1:14; 4:12; Judg 7:11; and Num 32:17. The LXX departs significantly from the Hebrew, designating the group of Israelites leaving Egypt as the fifth generation, *pemptē de genea.*

13:21 *And Yahweh.* The LXX has *ho de theos,* "and the God."

---

113. For more detailed discussion of the literary design of the P History with bibliography see Dozeman, *God at War,* 104-10, 175-77.

114. See W. A. Ward, "The Semitic Biconsonantal Root *SP* and the Common Origin of Egyptian *ČWF* and Hebrew *SûP:* "Marsh(-Plant)," *VT* 24 (1965): 395-98.

pillar of fire to give them light. The LXX lacks "to give them light."

13:22 *before the people.* The LXX adds *pantos tou laou,* "all the people."

14:2 *before Pi-hahiroth.* Hebrew *pî haḥîrōt,* "mouth of *ḥyrt,*" a place name, is rendered in the LXX, *apenanti tēs epauleōs,* "before the farm/homestead." Wevers states that the phrase describes an unwalled settlement, while Propp translates, "before the sheepfold."[115] Both the MT and the LXX agree that the Israelites turn back from Etham, at the edge of the wilderness. The location returns in the itinerary list of Num 33:7-8, where the MT and the LXX are in closer agreement in designating the name of the location: LXX, *epi stoma Eiroth* (v. 7) and *Eiroth* (v. 8); MT, *pî haḥîrōt* (v. 7), and *haḥîrōt* (v. 8). In Numbers 33, however, the location precedes the Red Sea by several itinerary stops, since the Red Sea appears between Elim and the wilderness of Sin (Num 33:10-11; cf. Exod 16:1-2).

14:4 *the Egyptians will know.* The LXX adds *pantes,* thus "all the Egyptians will know."

Commentary

The journey of the Israelite people to the Red Sea is complex in structure. The episode separates into two parts: 13:17-20 and 13:21–14:4. The two sections represent in general the Non-P History (13:17-20) and the P History (13:21–14:4). Each section includes a description of the divine leading of the Israelite people. God leads in the Non-P History (13:17-18). The pillar of cloud leads in the P History (13:21-22). Each section also includes the location of the confrontation at the Red Sea. The event takes place at Etham in the Non-P History (13:20) and at Pi-hahiroth in the P History (14:1-4). But the separation of the authors on the basis of two distinct sections breaks down when the P author includes the statement in 13:18b that the Israelite people left Egypt prepared for war, which conflicts with the Non-P author, who states the opposite in 13:17-18a. The people were not ready for war. My comments will follow the two sections, 13:17-20 and 13:21–14:4.

13:17-20 The exodus takes place under the direct leadership of God in 13:17-20. Three times the leadership of God is stated: "God did not lead them on the way of the land of the Philistines" (v. 17a); "God said" (v. 17b); and "God turned the people aside" (v. 18).

Exodus 13:17-18a, 20 introduces a series of roads and place names to describe the leadership of God. The Israelites travel from Succoth to Etham. Alternative travel routes are juxtaposed, the "way of the land of the Philistines" and "the way of the wilderness of the Red Sea." Neither route is clear. M. D. Oblath concludes: "With no firm indication as to the author's fixed perspective, we cannot state the starting point of the journey with any certainty."[116] The "way of the land of the Philistines" is likely a reference to the trading route

---

115. Wevers, *Notes,* 208; Propp, *Exodus 1-18,* 465.
116. Oblath, *Exodus Itinerary Sites,* 100.

along the Mediterranean Sea from the Nile Delta to Megiddo extending on into Asia Minor and Mesopotamia. It is a direct route into Canaan, yet it is avoided because of the threat of war. The Israelites are not yet ready for battle in the Non-P History. In view of this God directs the Israelites on the second route, "the way of the wilderness of the Red Sea." If the location determines the direction in phrases, then the Israelites journey toward the Red Sea.

The locations of the journey out of Egypt in the Non-P History include Succoth, Etham, and the Red Sea (13:18, 20). Succoth is clearly associated with Egypt in 13:20 and in the itinerary list of Num 33:6. In other biblical texts Succoth is associated more closely with the Jordan River. It is part of the territory of Gad (Josh 13:27), and it is also associated with Penuel in the story of Gideon (Judg 8:4-9). As noted in the introduction it also carries religious significance as the name of the festival, *Sukkot,* Feast of Booths, which commemorates the wilderness journey of the Israelite people. Etham only occurs in the context of the exodus, once in 13:20 and twice in Num 33:6-7. In both instances, Etham is associated with the wilderness. Exodus 13:20 states: "They [the Israelites] set out from Succoth, and camped at Etham, on the edge of the wilderness." Numbers 33:6 repeats the same information identifying Etham as situated "on the edge of the wilderness." This information is crucial to the Non-P History. It places the confrontation at the Red Sea in the wilderness.

The Red Sea is perhaps the most debated geographical location in the story of the exodus. The term "Red Sea" translates Hebrew *yam-sûp.* The translation is debated. The Hebrew term is used three times in the story of the exodus, twice in the Non-P History (13:18; 15:22) and once in the Song of the Sea (15:4; see also 10:19). Scholars debate the meaning of the phrase. There may be a mythological background to the term. N. Snaith noted that the context of the hymn in 15:4-5 is less focused on geography than on creation mythology conceived as a fight against the chaotic sea monster. The hymn in 15:5 refers to "the deeps" and "depths," which is the name for the primeval waters (see Gen 1:2), not a specific road or body of water. The result is a progression in the poetic lines of Exod 15:4-5 from "the sea" to the *yam-sûp* to the great primeval Sea, which has been "God's enemy since before the foundation of the world."[117] The mythological context of the Song of the Sea prompted Snaith to interpret Hebrew *bĕyam-sûp* as "that distant scarcely known sea away to the south, of which no man knew the boundary. It was the sea at the end of the land."[118] B. Batto reinforced this interpretation noting a similar use of *bĕyam-sûp* in the Song of Jonah (Jonah 2:6). Batto translates Hebrew *yam-sûp* as "Sea of Extinction."[119]

117. N. H. Snaith, "ים‑סוֹף: The Sea of Reeds: The Red Sea," *VT* 15 (1965): 395-98.
118. Ibid., 397.
119. B. Batto, "The Reed Sea: *Requiescat in Pace*," *JBL* 102 (1983): 27-35.

Such a translation places the *yam-sûp* in the context of "Ocean" in ancient Near Eastern and Greek literature, which also signifies the most extreme boundary of civilization or the edge of the world.

The Non-P History encourages a geographical interpretation designating the *yam-sûp* as a road (Exod 13:18; see also Num 14:25; 21:4; Deut 1:40; 2:1), although the identification of the road is unknown. The *yam-sûp* is also a body of water with a specific location (Exod 15:22; see also Num 33:10-11; Judg 11:16). The trend toward more realistic geography in the Non-P History intertwines the mythical imagery of creation and combat in Exod 15:4 with a salvation-historical perspective. The geographical emphasis in the Non-P History has given rise to further debate over the intended body of water, with modern interpreters arguing for the Gulf of Elath, the Gulf of Suez, or perhaps both.[120]

The process of historicizing Hebrew *yam-sûp* further complicated its meaning, which is reflected in the history of translation. The translation "Red Sea" is based on the LXX *erythra thalassa,* "Red Sea." A competing translation, "Reed Sea," is also common going back to early commentators like Jerome and Rashi. They reasoned that when Hebrew *sûp* is used alone it designates "reeds" or "rushes," as is evident in the story of Moses' rescue from the Nile River. His mother placed him in the "reeds" *(sûp).* The translation "Reed Sea" received support in more recent scholarship when Hebrew *sûp* was considered a loan-word from Egyptian *twf(y),* meaning "reed" or "papyrus." The debates result in a variety of translations for *yam-sûp,* including "Sea of Extinction," "Reed Sea," and "Red Sea."

The debate over translation has focused on historical geography to determine the route of Israel's exodus in the Non-P History. Scholars argue that the Reed Sea designates a different body of water further north than the Red Sea (i.e., the Gulf of Suez); or, as noted above, some even advocate that the Red Sea refers to two bodies of water (the Gulf of Elath and the Gulf of Suez). But this line of interpretation, with its focus on historical geography, does not capture the central message of the Non-P History with regard to the confrontation at the Red Sea. The Non-P History certainly intends to historicize the tradition of the sea. But the intention of the author is to maintain the mythological background of *yam-sûp* already evident in the Song of the Sea. The larger structure of the Non-P History, with its organization around the Red Sea and the Jordan River, supports a reading that is not limited to historical geography, since the word pair recalls the mythical combat between the gods Baal and Yamm-Nahar. The historicizing of the Red Sea in the Non-P History indicates a rite of passage

120. See J. Simons, *The Geographical and Topographical Texts of the Old Testament: A Concise Commentary in XXXII Chapters* (Leiden: Brill, 1959), §§423-27b; Davies, *Way of the Wilderness,* 70-74; Oblath, *Exodus Itinerary Sites,* 98-106.

for the Israelite pilgrimage into the wilderness. The event takes place at Etham, the first location in the wilderness. The next location after the Israelites enter the Red Sea is the wilderness of Shur, a journey of three days into the wilderness (15:22-26). The Red Sea is balanced in the Non-P History by a similar rite of passage, when the Israelites cross the Jordan River to enter the land of Canaan (see Josh 4:20-24). The association of Succoth with both the Red Sea and the Jordan River further reinforces the perspective of religious geography.[121]

The Israelites journey out of Egypt with the bones of Joseph (Exod 13:19), fulfilling his dying wish to be buried in Canaan. The motif of Joseph's bones provides an overarching literary design in the Non-P History, linking Genesis, the story of Moses and the exodus (Exodus–Deuteronomy), and the conquest of the land under Joshua (Joshua). Joseph requests that his bones be removed at the conclusion of Genesis, predicting on his deathbed God's further rescue of the Israelite people (Gen 50:24-25). The notice in Exod 13:19 that Joseph's bones were taken from Egypt during the exodus provides transition to the story of covenant renewal at Shechem during the end of Joshua's career (Josh 24:32). Joseph is buried at Shechem in the land that Jacob purchased from the descendants of Hamor. J. Gertz argues that the motif of Joseph's bones is a late addition to the literature by a post-P redactor, which is reflecting the burial practices of the Diaspora Jews.[122]

The P History provides a different portrait of the Israelite departure from Egypt in Exod 13:18b. In the Non-P History the Israelites will acquire faith in Moses only at the Red Sea. They lack faith as they leave Egypt, requiring God to protect them from war in their journey from Succoth to Etham. Even at the Red Sea the Israelites will not acquire the kind of faith necessary to undertake holy war. In the Non-P History the first generation of Israelites to leave Egypt never acquire this faith (Numbers 13–14). It is reserved for the second generation who will cross the Jordan River with Joshua to conquer the land (Joshua 3–5). The P History presents the opposite view of the exodus. The people leave Egypt as a military garrison, prepared for battle. Hebrew *ḥămušîm,* "an army in five parts," describes their organization with a military term (see translation note on 13:18).

13:21–14:4 The P author makes two additional changes to the account of the Israelite journey to the Red Sea. Exodus 13:20-21 describes the divine leading of the people more indirectly as the pillar of cloud, rather than the direct leading of God (13:17-18). The P author also shifts the confrontation at the Red Sea back into Egypt in 14:1-4.

Exodus 13:21-22 introduces the divine leading of the Israelites in the wil-

121. For discussion of religious geography as compared to historical geography see C. C. Park, *Sacred Worlds: An Introduction to Geography and Religion* (London: Routledge, 1994).
122. See Gertz, *Tradition und Redaktion,* 358-70.

derness as a pillar of cloud by day and a pillar of fire by night. The imagery of fire likely symbolizes the divine presence in the cloud, a common metaphor for divinity in the ancient Near East. The pillar of cloud is associated with the tent of meeting in the Hebrew Bible (33:7-11), a sanctuary where God would descend in a cloud or a pillar of cloud to deliver oracles. The tent of meeting may be an ancient form of revelation, perhaps with roots in Canaanite religion (see the commentary on 33:7-11). The high god of the Canaanite pantheon, El, is described as dwelling in a tent where he receives the divine assembly.[123]

The tent of meeting is important in both the Non-P and P Histories. Moses receives oracles in the tent of meeting in the Non-P History. This tent is located outside the Israelite camp (33:7-11; see also Num 11:14-17, 24-30; 12; and Deut 31:14-15). The revelation in the tent of meeting is accompanied by a divine descent in a cloud or a pillar of cloud. Moses would receive oral revelation from God at the door of the tent, while Joshua is described as dwelling in the shrine. The tent of meeting is also identified with the tabernacle in the P History (e.g., Exodus 25–30). The tabernacle and the tent of meeting are combined nearly one hundred times in the P History to describe the sanctuary located at the center of the Israelite camp, not outside the camp as in the Non-P History. Thus the pillar of cloud leading the Israelites in 13:21-22 could be associated with either the Non-P or P Histories.

Yet it is the P History that develops the role of the cloud as the wilderness guide of the Israelites, not the Non-P History where God either leads directly (13:17-18a) through the Messenger of the God (14:19a) or by means of the ark (Num 10:33-35). T. W. Mann clarifies the additional function of the pillar of cloud as a divine guide in holy war. He notes the close relationship between the cloud (*'rpt*) and messengers (*ǵlmm*) in the courtly retinue of Baal (*CTA* 5.v.6-11). He concludes that the pillar of cloud in the story of the exodus carries holy war imagery that is similar to the function of the Messenger of Yahweh. Both indicate divine military escorts.[124] The role of the fiery cloud to lead the Israelites in their wilderness march is repeated at crucial junctures in the P History at the completion of the tabernacle/tent of meeting (see the commentary on 40:36-38) and when the Israelite camp is established (Num 9:15-23).

Exodus 14:1-4 shifts the setting for the confrontation at the Red Sea. Yahweh commands Moses to reverse the direction of the Israelite march and encamp at Pi-hahiroth, apparently a location within the territory of Egypt. A more detailed setting is added: Pi-hahiroth lies between Migdol, a Hebrew word mean-

---

123. R. J. Clifford, "The Tent of El and the Israelite Tent of Meeting," *CBQ* 33 (1971): 221-27; T. W. Mann, "The Pillar of Cloud in the Reed Sea Narrative," *JBL* 90 (1971): 19-24.

124. Mann, "Pillar of Cloud." See also P. D. Miller Jr., "Fire in the Mythology of Canaan and Israel," *CBQ* 27 (1965): 257.

ing "tower," and the sea opposite Baal-zephon, the name of the Canaanite deity. The locations of Pi-hahiroth and Baal-zephon are limited to the story of the exodus (14:2, 9) and the itinerary list in Num 33:7. Migdol also occurs in Exod 14:2 and Num 33:7 and in the books of Jeremiah (46:14) and Ezekiel (29:10; 30:6), where the location is associated with the land of Egypt. The change of direction locates the Israelite people in the territory of Egypt, not in the wilderness.

The change of location is accompanied by a shift in focus from the escape of the Israelites in the Non-P History to the confrontation between Yahweh and Pharaoh in the P History. The purpose for the change of direction is to draw Pharaoh into one final confrontation. Yahweh will harden Pharaoh's heart to pursue the Israelites one last time, leading to his destruction. As a result God will gain glory over Pharaoh, while the Egyptians will come to the knowledge of Yahweh, fulfilling the divine prediction to Moses in his commission in the P History (7:5).

Pursuit by Pharaoh (14:5-14)

14:5 *And it was reported to the king of Egypt that the people fled. And the heart of Pharaoh and his servants was changed toward the people, and they said, "What is this we did, that we sent out the Israelites from our service?"* 6 *And he gathered his chariots, and his people he took with him.* 7 *And he took six hundred chosen chariots, and all the chariots of Egypt, and the third officer over all of it.* 8 *And Yahweh hardened the heart of Pharaoh, king of Egypt. And he pursued after the Israelites.* **But the Israelites went out with raised arm.** 9 *And the Egyptians pursued them, and overtook them encamped by the sea, all the horse chariotry of Pharaoh, his horsemen, and his army,* **at Pi-hahiroth, before Baal-zephon.**

10 *But as Pharaoh drew near, the Israelites lifted up their eyes, and there were the Egyptians journeying after them. And they feared greatly. The Israelites cried out to Yahweh,* 11 *and they said to Moses, "Is it because there are no graves in Egypt that you took us to die in the wilderness? What is this you did to us to bring us out of Egypt?* 12 *Is this not the word that we spoke to you in Egypt, saying, 'Let us alone, that we may serve the Egyptians, for it is better for us to serve the Egyptians than our dying in the wilderness'?"*

13 *And Moses said to the people, "Do not fear! Stand firm, and see the salvation of Yahweh, which he will do for you today. For, as you saw the Egyptians today, you will never again see them, ever.* 14 *Yahweh will fight for you, but you will keep still."*

Notes

14:7 *and the third officer.* Hebrew *šālišim* is translated in the LXX *tristatas*, "one who stands next to the king and queen; vizier." The context suggests a third man on the chariot (so BDB 1026), but extensive research has questioned this conclusion.[125] Ezekiel 23:15 and 23 identify the term with a heroic warrior. See the commentary.

over all of it. Hebrew *'al-kullô* is translated in the LXX, *epi pantōn,* meaning perhaps that the third officers commanded the entire army.

14:9 *all the horse chariotry of Pharaoh.* Hebrew *kol-sûs rekeb par'ōh* is separated into two categories in the LXX, *kai pasa hē hippos kai ta harmata Pharaō,* "all the cavalry and the chariots of Pharaoh."

14:11 *in Egypt.* The LXX adds *gē,* "land of," before "Egypt."

14:13 *the salvation of Yahweh.* The LXX has *tēn sōtērian tēn para tou theou,* "the salvation of God."

Commentary

The exodus from Egypt is told from contrasting points of view in this section. Verses 5-9 explore the exodus from the perspective of Pharaoh and his officials. Verses 10-14 describe the same event from the point of view of the Israelite people. The episode is part of the Non-P History in which the Israelite people leave Egypt lacking faith and unprepared for war. The P History includes only two motifs: the description of the Israelite people leaving Egypt "with raised arm" (v. 8b) and the location of the conflict at Pi-hahiroth (v. 9b).

14:5-9   Verses 5-6 provide insight into Pharaoh, here described as the king of Egypt, and his officials. Verse 5a provides transition from the death of the Egyptian firstborn, noting the change of heart in Pharaoh and his officials regarding the sending out of the Israelite people. The change of mind of Pharaoh and of his officials refers to the expulsion of the Israelites (12:30-32). But the description of a change in attitude about the sending out of the Israelites from Egypt also ties the confrontation at the Red Sea into the plague cycle. The statement that Yahweh also hardened the heart of Pharaoh in v. 8 further reinforces the literary relationship to the plagues.

The initial speech of Pharaoh to his people at the outset of Exodus in 1:8-10 also provides a strong literary parallel to 14:5-6. The speech of Pharaoh in 1:8-10 launches the events of the exodus. It provided the point of view of Pharaoh and his people with regard to the Israelites. In fact, it is the only other text in the book of Exodus that explores point of view in this way. In 1:8-10 the king of Egypt is introduced as the Pharaoh who has forgotten Joseph and now seeks to act shrewdly against the Israelite population. He advises his people to control the Israelite population, to keep them from warring against the Egyptians, and to stop them from leaving the land of Egypt. The speech in 1:8-10 accentuates the threat of the Israelite population giving rise to the stories of genocide. Exodus 14:5-6 advances the theme of war and the exodus from 1:8-10. The quo-

---

125. B. A. Mastin, "Was the *šālîš* the Third Man in the Chariot?" in *Studies in the Historical Books of the Old Testament* (ed. J. A. Emerton; VTSup 30; Leiden: Brill, 1979), 125-54.

tation in 14:5 provides the point of view: "What is this we did, that we sent out the Israelites from our service?" The concern of Pharaoh and his officials is the loss of service resulting from the exodus, not the fear of war as stated in 1:8-10. The P History provides a different point of view in 14:3 in a divine speech. In this case Pharaoh misinterprets the exodus as a confused wandering, thinking that the Israelite people have become entrapped in the land of Egypt by the wilderness.

Pharaoh views the exodus as a "flight" *(bārah),* which requires a military solution. That v. 7 introduces the Egyptian military for the first time in the book of Exodus indicates intensification. Moreover, the focus is on the chariots. Repetition underscores the strength of the force: "six hundred chosen chariots, all the chariots of Egypt." The final line of v. 7 suggests that each chariot has three officers *(wĕšālišim).* M. A. Littauer and J. H. Crouwel note that Egyptian chariots tended to have two riders, not three, as was the case with the Hittites. Three-person chariots appear in Assyrian reliefs of the ninth and eighth centuries B.C.E.[126] Cross and Freedman translate the same word in 15:4 as "troops."[127]

The P author characterizes the Israelites' departure from Egypt in 14:8b as an event that they undertake "with raised arm." The phrase repeats in Num 33:3 to describe the exodus. The phrase indicates that the exodus in the P History is an act of intention that is undertaken with power. The phrase is used in the P legislation in Num 15:30 to indicate an intentional action of a person, as compared to the unintentional breaking of a law. The P History also repeats the setting of Pi-hahiroth in Exod 14:9b.

14:10-14   The point of view concerning the exodus changes from Pharaoh to the Israelites who watch the approach of the Egyptian army. The section includes a complex interaction between the Israelites, Yahweh, and Moses, which extends through v. 15, even though v. 15 also introduces the confrontation at the sea.

A   The cry of the Israelites to Yahweh (v. 10)
   B   The complaint of the Israelites to Moses (vv. 11-12)
   B′   The response of Moses to the complaint (vv. 13-14)
A′   The response of Yahweh to the cry of Moses (v. 15)

The center of the literary unit is the exchange between the Israelites (B) and Moses (B′). The Israelites fear the approach of Pharaoh and they complain to Moses, preferring slavery in Egypt to the risk of freedom in the wilderness.

---

126. M. A. Littauer and J. H. Crouwel, "Chariots," *ABD* 1:888-92. See also the translation note on v. 7 above.

127. Cross and Freedman, *Studies in Ancient Yahwistic Poetry,* 58.

Their complaint is characterized as the murmuring motif.[128] It is repeated throughout the wilderness journey (see the commentary on 15:22–18:27). The content of their complaint reinforces the setting of the wilderness as the location for the confrontation at the Red Sea: "Is it because there are no graves in Egypt that you took us to die *in the wilderness?*" The people have left the land of Egypt and they await the arrival of the Egyptian army in the wilderness. Moses responds with a word of assurance in the form of a war oracle. E. W. Conrad separates the war oracle into the following parts: a word of assurance, "Do not be afraid!"; a directive that the people "Stand firm!"; a prediction that they will see the salvation of Yahweh; and the clarification that Yahweh will fight for the people requiring that they "Keep still!" The war oracle indicates both victory over an enemy (2 Chr 20:17-20) and the revelation of God in the event (1 Sam 12:16-18).[129]

The outer ring of the structure, the cry of the Israelites in Exod 14:10 (A) and the divine response to the cry in 14:15 (A′), has puzzled interpreters. The problem is that the response of Yahweh is directed to Moses, not the Israelites: "Why are you [Moses] crying to me?" Moses does not cry to Yahweh in this scene. It is as though Yahweh has forgotten the setting and the circumstances of the story. And, to make matters worse, the divine response is a complaint against Moses, at the very moment when he is the ideal of faithfulness. Moses has just countered the Israelite complaint with the war oracle, assuring the people of Yahweh's power and faithfulness.

The structure of the section suggests that the divine speech in v. 15 is directed at the Israelites, not Moses. It is a response to their complaint about the risks of the wilderness. The channeling of the divine complaint through Moses accentuates his role as mediator between God and the people in the wilderness journey. Yahweh speaks directly to the Israelites only once in the wilderness to deliver the Ten Commandments on Mount Sinai. It so terrifies the Israelites that they choose Moses to mediate for them permanently (20:18-20). (See the commentary on 15:22–18:27 for the interpretation of Moses as mediator in the wilderness.)

Destruction of Pharaoh and the Egyptian Army in the Red Sea (14:15-31)

14:15 *And Yahweh said to Moses, "Why do you cry to me? Speak to the Israelites that they journey out.* 16 *But you raise your staff, and stretch out your arm over the*

---

128. Coats, *Rebellion in the Wilderness.*
129. E. W. Conrad, *Fear Not Warrior: A Study of 'al tîrā' Pericopes in the Hebrew Scriptures* (BJS 75; Chico, Calif.: Scholars Press, 1985), 143-45.

sea, **and split it**. And the Israelites will enter into the midst of the sea on dry ground. [17]But I will harden the heart of the Egyptians, and they will enter after them. **And I will gain glory over Pharaoh, over all his army, over his chariots, and over his horsemen.** [18]**And the Egyptians will know that I am Yahweh, when I gain glory over Pharaoh, over his chariots, and over his horsemen.**"

[19]And the Messenger of the God journeyed, going before the camp of the Israelites. And he went behind them. **And the pillar of cloud journeyed ahead of them, and stood behind them.** [20]And it came between the camp of the Egyptians and the camp of the Israelites. **And there was the cloud and the darkness. And it lit up the night.** And this one did not draw near to this one all the night.

[21]And Moses stretched his arm on the sea. And Yahweh pushed the sea with a strong east wind all night. And he turned the sea into dry ground, **and the water was split.** [22]And the Israelites entered into the midst of the sea on dry ground. **But the water was for them a wall on their right and on their left.** [23]And the Egyptians pursued and entered after them, all the horses of Pharaoh, his chariots, and his horsemen, into the midst of the sea.

[24]And at the morning watch Yahweh looked down toward the camp of the Egyptians **in the pillar of fire and cloud,** and he confused the camp of the Egyptians. [25]And he turned aside the wheel of his chariots and he caused it to drive with difficulty. And the Egyptian said, "I must flee from before the Israelites, for Yahweh is the fighter for them against Egypt."

[26]And Yahweh said to Moses, "Stretch out your arm on the sea, so that the water returns on the Egyptians, on his chariots, and on his horsemen."

[27]And Moses stretched out his arm on the sea, and the sea returned to its original course at break of day. But the Egyptians were fleeing to meet it. And Yahweh shook off the Egyptians in the midst of the sea. [28]And the water returned and covered the chariot, the horsemen, and all the army of Pharaoh, who entered after them into the sea. Not one of them remained. [29]But the Israelites went on dry ground in the midst of the sea, **and the water was for them a wall on their right and on their left.**

[30]And Yahweh saved on that day the Israelites from the arm of the Egyptians. [31]And the Israelites saw the great arm, which Yahweh did in Egypt. And the people feared Yahweh. And they believed in Yahweh and in Moses, his servant.

Notes

14:17 *but I will harden*. The Hebrew syntax conveys an immediacy and an intensity, *wa'ănî hinnî měḥazēq*, "and I, behold me hardening."

the heart of the Egyptians. The LXX has *tēn kardian Pharaō kai tōn Aigyptiōn pantōn*, "the heart of Pharaoh and all the Egyptians."

14:18 *the Egyptians*. The LXX has *pantes hoi Aigyptioi*, "all the Egyptians."

14:20 *And there was the cloud and the darkness. And it lit up the night.* The imagery of the MT is of the cloud (*'ānān*) creating light (*wayyā'er*) in the midst of the darkness (*ḥōšek*) and the night (*hallaylâ*). The reference to "darkness" in Hebrew *wayhî he'ānān wĕhaḥōšek* recalls the darkness (*ḥōšek*) from 10:21-29, the story that introduces the section 10:21–14:31. The LXX presents the opposite image, of complete darkness with no light, *kai egeneto skotos kai gnophos, kai diēlthen hē nyx,* "And there was darkness and gloom, and the night came through." For discussion of the distinct imagery see Gressmann.[130] The conflicting images may be the result of the history of composition. The Non-P History envisions total darkness, limiting the divine leading to the Messenger of the God. The P History introduces the imagery of the cloud, which contains fire during the night, perhaps leading the Israelites.

14:24 *and he confused the camp of the Egyptians.* Hebrew *wayyāhām* also indicates fear or panic. See NRSV: "and threw the Egyptian army into panic."

14:25 *and he turned aside the wheel.* The translation assumes Yahweh as the subject of the action. The action of Yahweh on the wheels of chariots is unclear. The translation "turned aside" assumes Hebrew *sûr.* The Sam writes *wy'sr,* "to bind," suggesting that the wheels were clogged or locked. The LXX *synedēsen,* "tied together," is similar to the Sam. For discussion see Propp.[131]

14:27 *at break of day.* Hebrew *lipnôt bōqer* is lit. "turning of morning."

and Yahweh shook off the Egyptians in the midst of the sea. The LXX translates Hebrew *wayna'ēr,* "he shook off," as *exetinaxen,* which indicates shaking off dust from clothing. The LXX creates a wordplay between Moses stretching out his arm over the sea, *exeteinen de Mōysēs tēn cheira epi tēn thalassan,* and Yahweh shaking off the Egyptians into the sea, *kai exetinaxen kyrios tous Aigyptious meson tēs thalassēs.*

14:31 *they believed in Yahweh.* The LXX has *tō theō,* "the God," rather than *kyrios,* "Lord."

Commentary

The final confrontation at the Red Sea occurs in two stages, each initiated by divine command. First, Yahweh commands Moses to control the Red Sea, allowing for the escape of the Israelites, while also setting the stage for the initial attack against the Egyptian army (14:15-25). Second, Yahweh instructs Moses to release the control of the sea, returning it to its natural flow and destroying the Egypt army (14:26-29). The two cycles are carefully orchestrated by time. The first cycle takes place during the night (v. 21, *kol-hallaylâ*) and it continues until the first watch of the night (v. 24, *wayhî bĕ'ašmōret habbōqer*). The second cycle occurs at daybreak (v. 27, *lipnôt bōqer*). The second section concludes with an interpretation of the destruction of the Egyptian army in the Red Sea (14:30-31).

14:15-25 The first cycle of action is the most extensive. The Non-P His-

---

130. Gressmann, *Mose und seine Zeit,* 109 n. 1.
131. Propp, *Exodus 1–18,* 500.

tory focuses especially on the entrance of the Israelites into the Red Sea on dry ground. The divine complaint against Moses (v. 15) provides a transition to the command that the Israelites journey toward the sea. The magical staff of Moses assumes a prominent role in the confrontation at the sea (see chap. 4). Moses is commanded to dry up the sea, allowing the Israelites to march into it (14:16). The P writer adds that the sea was split in two by Moses (v. 16a). The P author also adds an extended speech by Yahweh to Moses in vv. 17b-18, which predicts the outcome of the event on Pharaoh and the Egyptian army. The prediction repeats motifs from the commission of Moses in the P History (7:1-5). Yahweh will gain glory over Pharaoh, and the Egyptians will come to the knowledge of Yahweh from the event.

Exodus 14:19-20 is an interlude in the first cycle, describing the leading of God at the Red Sea. The Non-P History identifies the divine presence as the Messenger of the God *(mal'ak hā'ĕlōhîm)*. The Messenger first appeared to Moses during his wilderness commission at the mountain of God, where it was described as the Messenger of Yahweh (3:2). The Messenger now returns. The primary function of the Messenger is to lead Israel in their wilderness journey. But during the confrontation at the Red Sea the Messenger moves behind the Israelites (v. 19), separating the camp of the Egyptians from the camp of the Israelites (v. 20a). The Messenger of the God reappears as the wilderness guide of the Israelites during the revelation of law at the mountain of God (32:34; 33:2). God also promises that the Messenger will wage holy war for the Israelites in their future conquest of the promised land (23:20).

The P History states that the presence of God is the pillar of cloud (*'ammûd he'ānān*, 14:19b, 20b), first introduced in 13:21-22. Like the Messenger of the God, the main function of the pillar of cloud is to lead the people in their wilderness journey (13:21-22). But at the Red Sea it too is stationed behind the people (v. 19b). The P author further describes the role of the cloud during the confrontation at the Red Sea in v. 20b: "And there was the cloud and the darkness. And it lit up the night. And this one did not draw near to this one all the night." But what exactly is the cloud doing? The confusing description of the event has prompted extensive commentary by past interpreters. In classical Jewish interpretation, the side of the cloud facing the Egyptians is dark, while the side facing the Israelites is light. However the P writer intends to picture the cloud, the result is that Yahweh separates the Israelites and the Egyptians during the night. Thus the P History agrees with the Non-P History that there is no battle between the Israelites and the Egyptians. Rather the confrontation at the sea is between Yahweh and Pharaoh, as Moses stated in the war oracle of 14:13-14.

Moses fulfills the divine command in 14:21-25. He raises his staff, prompting Yahweh to send an east wind on the sea all night. The sea is both split in two and dried up. The Israelites enter the sea on dry ground with walls of water on each side. Verses 24-25 describe the initial attack of Yahweh on the Egyptian army during the time of the first morning watch. The text is not altogether clear. The MT indicates that Yahweh "turned aside" *(sûr)* the wheels of the Egyptian chariots. The LXX employs a different verb, "to bind," suggesting that the chariot wheels were clogged. The motif of turning aside fits the larger context of the exodus. Three times Pharaoh had requested of Moses that he pray to Yahweh to "turn aside" a plague (frogs, 8:8; flies, 8:31; and locusts, 10:17). The turning aside of the Egyptian chariots is a reversal from the previous uses, bringing destruction, not relief, upon the Egyptians. The Egyptians recognize the power of Yahweh in the event and they attempt to flee.

14:26-29 The second cycle of action moves quickly to a conclusion. The action takes place at daybreak. Yahweh commands Moses to reverse the flow of the sea (14:26). Moses fulfills the command (14:27-29), resulting in the destruction of the entire army. The verses contrast the experience of the Egyptian army and the Israelites. The army of the Egyptians now consists of chariots and horsemen. They are pictured as running head-on into the returning sea. The Israelites, by contrast, walked *(hālak)* on dry ground in the midst of the sea.

14:30-31 The closing verses provide an interpretation of the event. The destruction of the Egyptian army is not simply another plague. It is an event of salvation, as Moses predicted in the war oracle: "You will see the salvation of Yahweh" (14:13). The episode concludes with a play on the similar sounding words in Hebrew "to see" *(rā'â)* and "to fear" *(yārē')*. The Israelites "see" the dead bodies on the shore, prompting their "fear" of Yahweh. The people also believe *('āman)* in Yahweh and in Moses, fulfilling the commission of Moses in the Non-P History (see 4:1, 5, 8-9, 31).

CELEBRATION OF VICTORY (15:1-21)

15:1 *Then Moses and the Israelites sang this song to Yahweh, and they said, saying:*

"I will sing to Yahweh, for he acted supremely;
horse and his rider he hurled into the sea.

2 My strength and my power is Yah;
and he has become for me salvation.

This is my God, and I will praise him;
the God of my father, and I will exalt him.

3 Yahweh is a man of war;
Yahweh is his name.

⁴*The chariots of Pharaoh and his army he threw into the sea;*
and the chosen of his third officers were sunk in the Red Sea.

⁵*The depths covered them;*
they descended into the depths like a stone.

⁶*Your right hand, Yahweh, strong in might;*
your right hand, Yahweh, shatters the enemy.

⁷*And in the greatness of your majesty you threw down your adversary;*
you sent out your wrath, it consumed them like straw.

⁸*And with the wind of your nostrils water piled up;*
floods stood up like a heap;
the depths curdled to the heart of the sea.

⁹*The enemy said,*
'I will pursue, I will overtake,
I will divide spoil.
My life will be full of them,
I will draw my sword,
my arm will dispossess them.'

¹⁰*You blew with your wind, Sea covered them;*
they sank like lead in the mighty waters.

¹¹*Who is like you among the gods, Yahweh?*
Who is like you, majestic in holiness,
awesome of praise, worker of wonder?

¹²*You stretched out your right hand;*
Earth swallowed them.

¹³*You led in your steadfast love the people whom you redeemed;*
you guided in your strength to your holy abode.

¹⁴*Peoples heard, they trembled.*
Pangs seized the inhabitants of Philistia.

¹⁵*Then the chiefs of Edom were terrified.*
The leaders of Moab, trembling seized them.
All the inhabitants of Canaan melted.

¹⁶*Terror and dread fell upon them;*
at your great arm they became silent like a stone.

Until your people cross over, Yahweh,
until the people, whom you conceived, cross over.

¹⁷ *You will bring them in and plant them on the mountain of your inheritance,*
the place for your dwelling that you made, Yahweh,
the sanctuary, my Lord, that your arm established.

¹⁸ *Yahweh will reign forever and ever."*

¹⁹ *When the horse of Pharaoh, with his chariots and his horsemen entered into the sea, Yahweh returned on them the water of the sea. But the Israelites walked on dry ground in the midst of the sea.* ²⁰ ***And Miriam, the prophetess, the sister of Aaron, took the drum in her hand. And all the women went out after her with drums and with dances.*** ²¹ ***And Miriam answered them,***

"Sing to Yahweh, for he acted supremely;
horse and his rider he hurled into the sea."

Notes

15:1 *Then Moses and the Israelites sang*. The sentence is intended to provide a narrative context for the song in 15:1b-18. The prefixed form of the verb, *yāšîr*, normally translated "will sing," is rendered in the past. Waltke and O'Connor write: "The prefix conjugation is used to represent a real situation which arises as a consequence of some other situation" (*IBHS* §31.6.3). In this case the song is a response to the narrated events in Exodus 14. I. Rabinowitz concludes that the syntax, *'āz*, "then," with the prefixed form of the verb *šîr*, is intended to relate more closely the narrated events and the song.[1] The literary effect is that the song is sung while the Israelites see the dead Egyptians on the shore of the sea.

I will sing. Hebrew *'āšîrâ* is cohortative and could also be translated "Let me sing" or "I would sing." The LXX has the plural, *aisōmen*, "we will sing"; while the Sam *'šrw* may translate, "make sing!" Cross and Freedman suggest a conflation in the Sam of *'āšîrâ* and *šîrû*.

for he acted supremely. The Hebrew infinitive absolute with finite verb, *gā'ōh gā'â*, is rendered in the LXX with a finite verb and adverb, *endoxōs gar dedoxastai*, "for he glorified gloriously." In both instances Yahweh/the Lord is the subject. The Sam departs significantly from the MT in making the "gentile" the subject, *ky gwy g'h*, "for a gentile was arrogant/exalted," perhaps referring to Pharaoh/Egypt.

horse and his rider. For the Hebrew participle *rōkĕbô*, "his rider," the LXX has *anabatēn*, "chariot," suggesting Hebrew *rekeb*, prompting the translation "horse and chariotry."[2] See also the study by S. Mowinckel, who notes historical problems surrounding the reference to cavalry, thus also preferring the translation "chariotry."[3]

1. I. Rabinowitz, "'āz Followed by Imperfect Verb-Form in Preterite Contexts: A Redactional Device in Biblical Hebrew," *VT* 34 (1984): 53-62.

2. P. Haupt, "Moses' Song of Triumph," *AJSL* 20 (1904): 149-72; Cross and Freedman, *Studies in Ancient Yahwistic Poetry*, 54.

3. S. Mowinckel, "Drive and/or Ride in O.T.," *VT* 12 (1962): 278-99, esp. 278, 284-85.

15:2 *my strength and my power is Yah; and he has become for me salvation.* The MT *ʿozzî wĕzimrāt yāh wayhî-lî lîšûʿâ* is lit. "my strength and the power of Yah, he has become for me salvation." The Sam *ʿzy wzmrty wyhy ly lyšwʿh* omits the MT reference to "Yah," a shortened form for "Yahweh," while adding the first person suffix to *wzmrty,* "my power," resulting in the translation, "my strength and my power; and he has become for me salvation." My translation retains the reference to "Yah" in the MT, while also including the first person suffix on *wzmrty.* Freedman concludes that the absence of the suffix in the MT may be an instance of the suffix on *ʿzy* serving double duty, or the *yod* at the beginning of "Yah" may represent the suffix on *zimrāt.*[4] The LXX renders the two lines as one, following more closely the Sam by omitting the reference to "Yah," yet it also lacks the first person suffixes, *boēthos kai skepastēs egeneto moi eis sōtērian,* "a help and a protector he became for me salvation." The poetic lines also appear in Isa 12:2b and Ps 118:14.

power. Hebrew *zimrāt* is problematic. It may mean "glory" or "music," "protection," or the designation of Yahweh as a protective Deity.[5] The word pair *ʿāz* and *zimrâ* also occurs in the Ugaritic literature, *ʿz* and *dmr* (= *zmr*), leading S. I. L. Norin to favor the meaning "defense" rather than "praise."[6]

This is my God, and I will praise him. Hebrew *zeh ʾēlî wĕʾanwēhû* is rendered in the LXX as *houtos mou theos, kai doxasō auton,* "this is my God, and I will glorify him." The meaning of Hebrew *wĕʾanwēhû* is debated. Cross and Freedman relate it to Arabic *nwy,* "to look or gaze ardently at." The Hiphil form in Hebrew would then translate as "I will admire."[7] M. Dahood favors "to adorn," from Ugaritic *šnwy.*[8] Propp suggests the root *nwh,* "high, eminence."[9]

the God of my father. P. D. Miller interprets the phrase as a reference to the ancestral tribal or clan deity, adding that it may be the oldest attestation of the identification of Yahweh and the God of the fathers.[10] H. Spieckermann identifies the line as an apostrophic reference to God.[11]

The problem of language in v. 2 affects larger questions of genre. H. Schmidt ar-

---

4. D. N. Freedman, "Strophe and Meter in Exodus 15," in *Pottery, Poetry, and Prophecy: Studies in Early Hebrew Poetry* (Winona Lake, Ind.: Eisenbrauns, 1980), 200.

5. See, respectively, E. Loewenstamm, "The Lord Is My Strength and My Glory," *VT* 19 (1969): 464-70; S. B. Parker, "Exodus XV 2 Again," *VT* 21 (1971): 373-79; M. L. Barré, "My Strength and My Song in Exod 15:2," *CBQ* 54 (1992): 623-37.

6. See *Ugaritica* V:553; Norin, *Er spaltete das Meer*; Cross and Freedman, *Studies in Ancient Yahwistic Poetry,* 55, who also favor the meaning "protection, defense."

7. Cross and Freedman, *Studies in Ancient Yahwistic Poetry,* 56; Cross, *Canaanite Myth and Hebrew Epic,* 127 n. 52.

8. M. Dahood, "Exodus 15,2 *ʾanwēhû* and Ugaritic *šnwt,*" *Bib* 59 (1978): 260-61.

9. Propp, *Exodus 1–18,* 514.

10. P. D. Miller Jr., *The Divine Warrior in Early Israel* (HSM 5; Cambridge: Harvard University Press, 1973), 114.

11. H. Spieckermann, *Heilsgegenwart: Eine Theologie der Psalmen* (FRLANT 148; Göttingen: Vandenhoeck & Ruprecht, 1989), 96 n. 2.

gued that v. 2 is the key for interpreting the hymn as a liturgy of the individual.[12] Cross and Freedman note problems with the context and poetic meter to eliminate the verse from an original form of the hymn.[13] J. D. W. Watts agrees, adding that the confession of personal faith is out of place in the larger context of vv. 1b and 3b-5 with the description of Yahweh's victory over Pharaoh's forces.[14] But J. Muilenburg argued that v. 2 fits its present context because of the first person praise in vv. 1b and 2 and the focus on the divine name in vv. 2-3.[15] J. Jeremias speculates whether the thanksgiving of the individual in v. 2 may have entered into the Song of the Sea in much the same way as creation mythologies were used in the more intimate context of birthing.[16]

15:3 *Yahweh is a man of war.* The MT *'îš milḥāmâ,* "man of war," appears in the Sam as *gbwr bmlḥmh,* "a hero in war." The LXX goes in yet a different direction, *kyrios syntribōn polemous,* "the Lord shatters wars," which reverses the imagery from the action of war to its end.

Yahweh is his name. The LXX *kyrios onoma autō* could be translated "the Lord is the name to him."

15:4 *And the chosen of his third officers were sunk.* The passive form of Hebrew *ṭubbĕ'û* is rendered in the LXX as the active *katepontisen,* "he sank," making God the subject as in the previous line.

in the Red Sea. Hebrew *yam-sûp* could be translated "Sea of Reeds" or even "Sea at the End." The latter translation arises from the mythological context of the poem. N. H. Snaith noted that the context of 15:4-5 is not about geography but creation mythology, especially creation conceived as a fight against the monster of chaos. Snaith noted that the words "the deeps" *(tĕhōmōt)* and "depths" *(mĕṣōlōt)* in 15:5, in conjunction with "sea" and "the Red Sea" in 15:4, result in a progression from "the sea" *(yām)* to the *yam-sûp,* and, finally, to the great primeval sea *(tĕhôm),* which has been "God's enemy since before the foundation of the world." The mythological context led Snaith to conclude that Hebrew *yam-sûp* means "that distant scarcely known sea away to the south, of which no man knew the boundary. It was the sea at the end of the land." The meaning "sea at the end of the land" prompted Snaith to revocalize *sûp* to *sôp* (which in Hebrew means "end").[17] B. Batto extended the work of Snaith, arguing that Hebrew *sûp* could mean "end" or "extinc-

12. H. Schmidt, "Das Meerlied: Ex 15 2-19," *ZAW* 49 (1931): 63-64.

13. Cross and Freedman, *Studies in Ancient Yahwistic Poetry,* 54-55.

14. J. D. W. Watts, "The Song of the Sea — Ex XV," *VT* 7 (1957): 374.

15. J. Muilenburg, "A Liturgy on the Triumphs of Yahweh," in *Hearing and Speaking the Word: Selections from the Works of James Muilenburg* (ed. T. F. Best; Scholars Press Homage Series; Chico, Calif.: Scholars Press, 1984), 157. For similar arguments see A. J. Hauser, "Two Songs of Victory: A Comparison of Exodus 15 and Judges 5," in *Directions in Biblical Hebrew Poetry* (ed. E. R. Follis; JSOTSup 40; Sheffield: Sheffield Academic Press, 1987), 282 n. 5.

16. J. Jeremias, *Das Königtum Gottes in den Psalmen: Israels Begegnung mit dem kanaanäischen Mythos in den Jahwe-König-Psalmen* (FRLANT 141; Göttingen: Vandenhoeck & Ruprecht, 1987), 98.

17. Snaith, "Sea of Reeds."

tion," without revocalization, based on the word pair *yām* and *yam-sûp* in the Song of Jonah (Jon 2:4, 6), where a geographical interpretation of *yam-sûp* is unlikely.[18]

15:5 *the depths covered them*. Hebrew *těhōmōt* could also be translated "abyss, flood," designating the mythological waters. Snaith writes: "The word *tehôm* does not refer to the depths of any natural sea. This is the depths of the primeval ocean, of Tiamat the great sea monster."[19] The LXX reads, *pontō ekalypsen autous*, "with the sea he [God] covered them," continuing the emphasis on the Deity as the subject of the verbs (see v. 4).

covered them. Hebrew *yěkasyumû*, "[the depths] covered them," represents an archaic form, preserving the final *yod* of the root and the suffix *-mû*.[20] The prefixed form is likely a *yaqtul* preterite, conveying past meaning in conformity with the predominance of past tense verbs in the larger literary context.

15:6 *Your right hand, Yahweh, strong in might*. The final *yod* in Hebrew *ne'dārî* presents a problem. The form is a Niphal masculine participle, likely referring to the feminine *yāmîn*, "right hand," but possibly to "Yahweh."[21] The word is rendered in the LXX by the passive *dedoxastai*, "has been magnified." W. L. Moran would revocalize the word as an infinitive absolute to account for the *yod*,[22] while Cross and Freedman identify it as an old genitive case ending translating, "the One-to-be-feared," and noting Ugaritic *adr*, "vast, noble" (see, e.g., *CTA* 16.i.8).[23]

Your right hand, Yahweh, shatters the enemy. Hebrew *tir'aṣ* could refer to "right hand" as a third feminine singular form, or to "Yahweh" as a second masculine singular form resulting in the translation, "your right hand, Yahweh, you shatter the enemy." The tense of *tir'aṣ* could be present/future or a *yaqtul* preterite as in NRSV, "your right hand, O Lord, shattered the enemy." The LXX also translates the line in the past tense, *hē dexia sou cheir, kyrie, ethrausen echthrous*, "your right hand, Lord, shattered the enemy." My translation has tentatively retained the present tense to reflect the character of v. 6 as a refrain.

15:7 *And in the greatness of your majesty you threw down your adversary*. C. Cohen separates vv. 7a and b, arguing that v. 7a is part of a three-line staircase parallelism beginning in v. 6.[24]

15:8 *And with the wind of your nostrils water piled up*. Hebrew *ne'ermû* could derive from a root meaning "to heap up" or "to be shrewd or crafty." J. Goldin notes several early translations that favor the latter meaning by describing the waters as be-

---

18. Batto, "Reed Sea"; idem, *Slaying the Dragon: Mythmaking in the Biblical Tradition* (Louisville: Westminster/John Knox, 1992).

19. Snaith, "Sea of Reeds," 397.

20. Cross and Freedman, *Studies in Ancient Yahwistic Poetry*, 58.

21. Ibid., 59.

22. W. L. Moran, "The Hebrew Language in Its Northwest Semitic Background," in *The Bible and the Ancient Near East: Essays in Honor of William Foxwell Albright* (ed. G. E. Wright; Garden City, N.Y.: Doubleday, 1967), 67.

23. Cross and Freedman, *Studies in Ancient Yahwistic Poetry*, 59.

24. C. Cohen, "Studies in Early Israelite Poetry I: An Unrecognized Case of Three-Line Staircase Parallelism in the Song of the Sea," *JANES* 7 (1975): 13-17.

coming wise.[25] Indeed, there is a degree of personification of the water in the larger context of the hymn. But the emphasis on the divine wind suggests the former meaning, in which the action of the waters is a result of God's blowing upon it. The LXX *diestē* provides a distinct interpretation of the waters separating, perhaps in conformity with the P account of the splitting of the sea (14:22b).

floods stood up. Hebrew *nōzĕlîm,* "floods," could also be translated "streams," as in Isa 44:3, *kî 'eṣṣāq-mayim 'al-ṣāmē' wĕnōzĕlîm 'al-yabbāšâ,* "for I will pour water on the thirsty ground, and streams on the dry ground." The LXX translates, *hydata,* "water."

like a heap. Hebrew *nēd* is uncommon, appearing here, in Josh 3:13, 16; and Ps 78:13. It may be related to Arabic *nadd,* "hill." A more concrete translation of the Hebrew would be "like a dam." The LXX translates, *teichos,* "wall," suggesting again the imagery from the P narrative account (Exod 14:21-22).

the depths curdled to the heart of the sea. The meaning of Hebrew *qāpĕ'û,* "thicken, condense, curdle," is debated. The word occurs elsewhere only in Zech 14:6; Zeph 1:12 (dregs of wine); and Job 10:10 (curdling of cheese). Is the imagery one of solidification recounting the P account of the confrontation at the sea (so Childs),[26] or of a raging sea (so Cross, who translates, "the deeps foamed in the heart of the sea").[27] The LXX suggests the former by repeating the verb *epage,* "to become still, congealed" from the previous line, where the word translated Hebrew *niṣṣĕbû,* "stood up." But the LXX has tended to reflect the P account of the confrontation at the sea through v. 8 over against the MT. The poetry resists a clear resolution.

15:9 *will dispossess them.* The LXX renders Hebrew *tôrîšēmô* as *kyrieusei,* "will rule/dominate," without suffix. Cross and Freedman read the form as an enclitic *mem* rather than the pronominal suffix "them."[28] When retained, "them" signifies the adversary.

15:10 *they sank.* Hebrew *ṣālălû* is a hapax legomenon likely meaning "they sank."[29] The LXX translates, *edysan,* "they went down."

in the mighty waters. H. G. Mays notes that there is likely cosmological imagery in the phrase.[30]

15:11 *majestic in holiness.* Hebrew *ne'dār baqqōdeš* is plural in the LXX, *dedoxasmenos en hagiois,* "glorified among the holy ones." See Cross and Freedman for a similar translation of the Hebrew.[31] Miller notes that the same translation, "holy ones," is also possible if *baqqōdeš* is read as a collective.[32]

25. J. Goldin, *The Song at the Sea* (New Haven: Yale University Press, 1971), 165.

26. Childs, *Exodus,* 243.

27. Cross, *Canaanite Myth and Hebrew Epic,* 128 n. 59.

28. Cross and Freedman, *Studies in Ancient Yahwistic Poetry,* 61.

29. Ibid.

30. H. G. Mays, "Some Cosmic Connotations of *Mayim Rabbîm,* 'Many Waters,'" *JBL* 74 (1955): 17.

31. Cross and Freedman, *Studies in Ancient Yahwistic Poetry,* 61.

32. See, e.g., P. D. Miller Jr., "Two Critical Notes on Psalm 68 and Deuteronomy 33," *HTR* 57 (1964): 241.

awesome of praise. Cross and Freedman translate *těhillōt* "praiseworthy acts."³³ The LXX has *thaumastos en doxais*, "wonderful in glory [or glorious deeds]."

15:12 *You stretched out your right hand, Earth swallowed them.* Hebrew *'eres*, "earth," most likely signifies the underworld.³⁴ Verse 12 is transitional in the poem. The content remains on the destruction of the Egyptians, placing the verse in the larger context of 15:1-11 as a concluding summary of the destruction. In this setting note the repetition of Yahweh's right hand from the refrain in v. 6. Verse 12 also anticipates the final strophe. The shift from the sea to the earth in the second line not only underscores the death of the Egyptians but also prepares for imagery of divine leading. For more detailed discussion of the transitional character of v. 12 see Freedman or Propp.³⁵

15:13 *to your holy abode.* Hebrew *něwēh*, which I translated "abode," has a broader meaning, including "pasture" and "tent." The LXX translates, *eis katalyma hagion sou*, "to your holy inn/lodge," removing the pastoral imagery of the Hebrew.

15:14 *The peoples heard, they trembled.* Hebrew *'ammîm* is translated in the LXX by *ethnē*, "nations." Their reaction in the LXX, moreover, is one of anger, *ōrgisthēsan*, "they became angry," as opposed to the image of fear in the MT. The change in perspective to describe the reaction of the peoples in vv. 14-16 parallels the words of the enemy in v. 9. The result is that both the confrontation at the sea (vv. 1-12) and the journey to the land (vv. 13-17) shift to the point of view of the "other" to accentuate the power of Yahweh.

15:15 *chiefs of Edom were terrified.* The image of terror in Hebrew *nibhălû*, "to be disturbed, terrified," is rendered in the LXX by *espeusan*, "they hurried," perhaps suggesting their flight from the Israelite people.

leaders of Moab. Hebrew *'êlê mô'āb*, "rams of Moab," becomes "rulers" in the LXX, *archontes*.

15:16 *fell.* The MT *tippōl* could also be read *tappîl*, "you cast down."³⁶ The LXX *epipesoi* is an imprecation, "cast down."

cross over. Hebrew *'ābar*, "to cross over," is associated not with the narrative of the Red Sea (Exodus 14), but with that of the Jordan River (Joshua 3–5; see the commentary). The meaning of the term in the poem, however, cannot be restricted to the narrative accounts, since much of the language of the poem is distinct from the surrounding narrative. Various scholars discuss the motif of crossing and the relationship that is created between the Red Sea and the Jordan River.³⁷

you conceived. Hebrew *qānîtā*, "you conceived/created," suggests imagery of procreation (see Ugaritic *qny*, and the divine identification in Gen 14:19, 22). Cf. NRSV "whom you acquired," which is also a possible meaning of the verb. The LXX translates, *ektēsō*, "created." See especially the parallel in Deut 32:6.

---

33. Cross and Freedman, *Studies in Ancient Yahwistic Poetry*, 61.

34. See Cross, *Canaanite Myth and Hebrew Epic*, 129 n. 62; Smith, *Pilgrimage Pattern*, 210.

35. Freedman, *Pottery*, 209-11; Propp, *Exodus 1–18*, 528-31.

36. Cross and Freedman, *Studies in Ancient Yahwistic Poetry*, 63.

37. Cross, *Canaanite Myth and Hebrew Epic*, 141; Batto, *Slaying the Dragon*, 136-44; Dozeman, "*Yam-sûp*"; Propp, *Exodus 1–18*, 537-39.

15:17 *You will bring them in and plant them.* Hebrew *tĕbi'ēmô wĕtiṭṭā'ēmô* could also be translated "may you bring them in and plant them." Cross translates in the past tense positing a cultic setting in which the acquisition of land is celebrated.[38]

on the mountain of your inheritance. Hebrew *bĕhar nahălātĕkā* has a parallel in Ugaritic literature, *ǧr nhlt, CTA* 3.C.27; 3.D.64) as a description of Baal's temple. Cf. NRSV: "on the mountain of your own possession." There is debate whether the reference is to the temple, the land, or both.[39]

the place for your dwelling. The imagery of the Hebrew most likely concerns the throne of God. For a parallel to Hebrew *mākôn lĕšibtĕkā* see Ugaritic *ksu ṯbth*, "seat of the throne," *CTA* 1.iii.1; 3.f12-13. See the discussion by Propp.[40]

the sanctuary, my Lord, that your arm established. Hebrew *miqdāš* designates any sanctuary. The geographical imagery of v. 17 has given rise to debate over the location of the sanctuary. Is the pastoral imagery the most prominent feature, suggesting the desert sanctuary at Sinai, or does the language point to Zion or to Gilgal?[41]

15:19 *when.* Hebrew *kî*, translated "when," indicates a temporal clause. Waltke and O'Connor (*IBHS* §38.7a) note that the *kî* is used in temporal clauses to indicate situations that are contemporary, hence the Song of the Sea (15:1b-18) and the Song of Miriam (15:21) may have been sung concurrently. Hebrew *kî* could also be translated causally, "for," in which case v. 19 would provide the ending to the preceding Song of the Sea.

15:20 *drum.* Hebrew *tōp* can also be translated "tambourine." The LXX *tympanōn* means "kettledrum."

dances. Hebrew *mĕḥōlōt* likely derives from *ḥwl*, "to whirl, writhe."[42] The LXX translates, *chorōn*, "dance," as a public religious gesture.

Commentary

There are two songs in 15:1-21, the Song of the Sea (15:1b-18) and the Song of Miriam (15:21b). Both songs celebrate the deliverance of the Israelites at the sea. There is no indication that the songs were associated with Moses or Miriam in their original composition. Yet both are now thoroughly embedded in the larger narrative context. Each song has an introduction naming the singers as Moses and Miriam. The introductions function much like psalm titles, in which songs become associated with events in the life of a hero.[43] The two

---

38. Cross, *Canaanite Myth and Hebrew Epic*, 125.

39. See Wijngaards, *Dramatization*, 82-84.

40. Propp, *Exodus 1–18*, 542-43.

41. For Sinai see D. N. Freedman, "Early Israelite History in the Light of Early Israelite Poetry," in *Pottery, Poetry, and Prophecy*, 136-38. For Zion see Blenkinsopp, *Introduction to the Pentateuch*, 159-60; Mettinger, *Dethronement of Sabaoth*, 26-28. For Gilgal see Cross, *Canaanite Myth and Hebrew Epic*, 123 n. 37.

42. E. Poethig, "The Victory Song Tradition of the Women of Israel" (Ph.D. diss.; Union Theological Seminary, New York, 1985), 50-66.

43. B. S. Childs, "Psalm Titles and Midrashic Exegesis," *JSS* 16 (1971): 137-50; idem, "Mid-

songs conclude the story of the conflict between Pharaoh and Yahweh (7:8–15:21) in their present narrative setting. First, Moses and the Israelites sing a song to Yahweh in 15:1-18, the Song of the Sea; and then Miriam and the women sing a song in 15:19-21, the Song of Miriam.

Exodus 15:1a indicates that the Song of the Sea is the immediate response by Moses and the Israelites to the death of the Egyptian army. I. Rabinowitz has underscored the close relationship between the song and the narrated events in Exodus 14 that results from the introduction in 15:1a: "Then (*'āz*) Moses and the Israelites sang." The word *'āz* is a poetic device creating immediacy between the Song of the Sea and the narrated events (see the note on 15:1 above).[44] The literary effect is that the song is sung while Moses and the Israelites see the dead Egyptians on the shore of the sea. The narrative clarifies that this is the moment when the Israelite people acquire faith in Moses and in Yahweh (14:31). Thus the Song of the Sea may be read as giving voice to the newly acquired faith of the Israelites, providing a conclusion to the account of Yahweh's defeat of Pharaoh, while also advancing the theme of faith first introduced in the wilderness commission of Moses (3:1–4:18).

Exodus 15:19-21a is narrative, which separates the Song of the Sea (15:1b-18) and the Song of Miriam (15:21b). Verse 19 can be read as a temporal clause indicating that the two songs occur at the same time (see the note above on v. 19). The content in v. 19 also anchors the Song of Miriam in the narrated events of Exodus 14. The verse repeats the description of the Egyptian army as including horse (14:9, 23), chariots (14:6, 7, 17, 23, 26, 28) and horsemen (14:9, 17), and it recounts the imagery of the Egyptians entering the sea, which leads to their death as opposed to the Israelites, who walked in the midst of the sea on dry ground (14:16b, 22a, 29a). The repetition of the motif allows for the introduction of Miriam, who sings her song as a response (15:21b).

The identification of the genre of the two songs has influenced interpretations of the function of the poems in the present narrative context. Interpreters debate whether the poems are hymns of thanksgiving or victory songs. F. Crüsemann argued that the Song of Miriam is an ancient form of the hymn, while the Song of the Sea is mixed in form reflecting for the most part the hymn of the individual.[45] Noth also described the Song of Miriam as a hymn and the Song of the Sea as a hymn with elements of the thanskgiving form.[46] Childs provides no evaluation of the genre of the Song of Miriam, but he also characterizes

---

rash and the Old Testament," in *Understanding the Sacred Text: Essays in Honor of Morton S. Enslin* (ed. J. Reumann; Valley Forge, Pa.: Judson Press, 1972), 47-59.

44. Rabinowitz, "'*āz* Followed by Imperfect."

45. F. Crüsemann, *Studien zur Formgeschichte von Hymnus und Danklied in Israel* (WMANT 32; Neukirchen-Vluyn: Neukirchener Verlag, 1969), 19-38.

46. Noth, *Exodus*, 123.

the Song of the Sea as a hymn, noting that it is directed solely to the praise of God and that it implies a cultic setting.[47] The cultic setting of the hymn suggested by Childs follows earlier interpreters, such as P. Haupt or S. Mowinckel, who identified the Song of the Sea as an enthronement hymn.[48] J. D. W. Watts continued the interpretation of Mowinckel, noting the strong parallels between the Song of the Sea and the "Yahweh is King" psalms (Psalms 93–99).[49]

The mixing of hymnic elements in the Song of the Sea noted by Crüsemann and Noth is developed by a number of interpreters. H. Schmidt described the Song of the Sea as including both hymnic (vv. 6, 7, 11) and ballad (vv. 3-5, 8-10, 12-13, 14-17) styles.[50] G. Beer also distinguished between the hymn (vv. 2, 3, 6, 7, 11, 12) and the ballad (vv. 4, 5, 8-10, 13-17).[51] J. Muilenburg added the further distinction between hymnic refrains (vv. 6, 11, 16cd), hymnic confessional speech (vv. 2-3, 7-8, 12-13), and epic narrative (vv. 4-5, 9-10, 14-16).[52] Coats does not identify a unified genre in the Song of the Sea, yet he describes it in broad terms as a hymn of praise.[53] M. Howell adds to the discussion of genre by employing the terminology of C. Westermann, distinguishing between declarative (vv. 6 7, 11) and descriptive (vv. 4-5, 8-10, 12) praise in the first part of the Song of the Sea.[54]

The Song of the Sea and the Song of Miriam are also identified as victory songs. Muilenburg gives voice to this line of interpretation: "The Song [of the Sea] contains another primary motif [apart from the genre of the hymn]. It is the celebration of Yahweh's victory and belongs to the substantial literature gathered about the wars of Yahweh."[55] The Song of Miriam is characterized even more strongly as a victory song. Mowinckel argued that the short couplet provides the paradigm for the victory song.[56] Cross and Freedman describe both the Song of Miriam and the Song of the Sea as victory songs.[57] M. Brenner extends the form-critical research on the victory song, noting that the phrase in 15:2, "and he has become for me salvation," is a statement of help by an ally in

---

47. Childs, *Exodus,* 250.

48. P. Haupt, "Moses' Song of Triumph," *AJSL* 20 (1904): 149-72; S. Mowinckel, *The Psalms in Israel's Worship* (trans. D. R. Ap-Thomas; 2 vols.; Nashville: Abingdon, 1962), 1:126.

49. Watts, "Song of the Sea," 378.

50. Schmidt, "Meerlied," 61.

51. Beer, *Exodus,* 80.

52. Muilenburg, *Hearing,* 155. See also Freedman, *Pottery,* 188 *et passim,* who follows Muilenburg especially with regard to the refrains.

53. Coats, "Song of the Sea," 7-8.

54. M. Howell, "Exodus 15,1b-18," *ETL* 65 (1989): 1-34, esp. 32-33. See also C. Westermann, *Praise and Lament in the Psalms* (trans. K. R. Crim and R. N. Soulen; Atlanta: John Knox Press, 1981), 31 *et passim.*

55. Muilenburg, *Hearing,* 153.

56. Mowinckel, *Psalms,* 2:26-27.

57. Cross and Freedman, *Studies in Ancient Yahwistic Poetry,* 45.

war (2 Sam 10:11). The imagery of Yahweh in the two poems reinforces further the genre of the victory song: Yahweh is a warrior (v. 3a); he hurls the chariots into the sea (vv. 4a and 21b), destroys the enemy (vv. 6b, 12), and expresses fierce anger (vv. 7, 8a).[58]

E. Poethig has presented the most detailed identification of the tradition of the victory song, focusing in particular on the role of women, which is central in the Song of Miriam. She notes parallels between the Song of Miriam (15:20-21), the account of the women who meet Saul and David returning from battle (1 Sam 18:6), and the role of the daughter of Jephthah (Judg 11:34). In each case women "go out" *(yāṣā')* to meet the victorious army singing with drum *(tôp)* and chorus *(mĕḥōlōt).* The song of victory is included in 1 Sam 18:6 as a short couplet providing a further point of comparison with the Song of Miriam.[59] The Song of Deborah in Judges 5 is also cited as a parallel to the victory songs in 15:1-21, providing comparison to the longer Song of the Sea associated with Moses in the present form of the text. According to M. L. Brenner, the shared motifs of women celebrating victory in war indicate that the parallels extend beyond the songs to their present narrative context. In view of this he concluded that the composer of the present narrative context of 15:1-21 also intended the two poems be read as victory songs.[60]

The identification of the Song of Moses and the Song of Miriam as victory songs raises a series of questions about their function in Exodus 15:1-21. First, the victory song celebrates a heroic warrior. The women in 1 Sam 18:6, for example, celebrate the exploits of Saul and especially David. But the Song of Moses and the Song of Miriam focus exclusively on the Deity. J. W. Watts concluded that the victory songs in 15:1-21 are modified with elements of the hymn form.[61] The mixed form of the poems accounts for the debate over genre. A second problem is that the Song of the Sea is attributed to Moses and the Israelites, not Miriam and the women, thus departing from the tradition of the women singing the victory song. P. Trible questions whether Moses may not have displaced Miriam as the singer of the Song of the Sea.[62] Third, the relationship between the two victory songs is further complicated by the near repe-

---

58. M. L. Brenner, *The Song of the Sea: Ex 15:1-21* (BZAW 195; Berlin: de Gruyter, 1991), 36-38.

59. Poethig, "Victory Song Tradition," 31-68, 85-90, *et passim.*

60. Brenner, *Song of the Sea,* 36-39.

61. J. W. Watts, *Psalm and Story: Inset Hymns in Hebrew Narrative* (JSOTSup 139; Sheffield: Sheffield Academic Press, 1992), 54.

62. P. Trible, "Subversive Justice: Tracing the Miriamic Traditions," in *Justice and the Holy: Essays in Honor of Walter Harrelson* (ed. D. A. Knight et al.; Atlanta: Scholars Press, 1989), 99-109; idem, "Bringing Miriam out of the Shadows," in *A Feminist Companion to Exodus to Deuteronomy* (ed. A. Brenner; FCB 1/6; Sheffield: Sheffield Academic Press, 1994), 166-86, esp. 169-73.

tition between 15:1b and 21b. The Song of the Sea begins as a statement of praise in the first person: "I will sing to Yahweh for he acted supremely. The horse and its rider he has hurled into the sea" (15:1b). The Song of Miriam repeats the opening verse of the Song of the Sea as a call to praise in the second person: "Sing to Yahweh for he acted supremely. The horse and its rider he has hurled into the sea" (15:21). J. G. Janzen raises the question that has puzzled many interpreters: How does the second person call to praise in 15:21b relate to the first person praise of Yahweh in 15:1b?[63]

Interpreters offer a variety of solutions to account for the narrative context of the songs in 15:1-21. Many interpretations in the modern period arise from the history of composition. H. Schmidt interpreted the repetition of 15:1b and 21b as a double tradition of the victory song, which he separated between the E (15:1, 19) and J (15:21) sources. He judged 15:2-18 to be a liturgy, which was added later to the narrative context.[64] Few have followed the lead of Schmidt, but many others seek a resolution to the repetition of 15:1b and 21b in the history of composition. Crüsemann has argued that the Song of Miriam is an ancient form of the hymn and that it is older than the Song of the Sea.[65] Noth also evaluated the Song of Miriam as the older song and the Song of the Sea as a later addition to the text.[66]

Noth's interpretation of the history of composition was placed in the broader context of the history of religion by feminist interpreters, who trace the development of patriarchal religion in the formation of 15:1-21. R. Burns explored the role of women in Israel's early cultic tradition based on the antiquity of the Song of Miriam.[67] Trible also advocated the antiquity of the Song of Miriam as a window for exploring the role of women in early Israelite tradition. The dominance of Moses and the Song of the Sea in the present form of the text indicates a more patriarchal form of Yahwism, according to Trible, accounting for the suppression of the Song of Miriam as an anticlimax.[68] Cross and Freedman move in a different direction also based on the history of composition. They argue that both the Song of Miriam and the Song of the Sea are ancient hymns and that the Song of Miriam (15:21b) is the title, the incipit, for the more extended Song of the Sea.[69] In view of this liter-

---

63. J. G. Janzen, "Song of Moses, Song of Miriam: Who Is Seconding Whom?" in *Feminist Companion to Exodus to Deuteronomy*, ed. Brenner, 187-99 (repr. from *CBQ* 54 [1992]: 211-20).

64. Schmidt, "Meerlied," 59-66.

65. Crüsemann, *Studien zur Formgeschichte*, 19-38.

66. Noth, *Exodus*, 121-26.

67. R. Burns, *Has the Lord Indeed Spoken Only through Moses? A Study of the Biblical Portrait of Miriam* (SBLDS 84; Atlanta: Scholars Press, 1987).

68. Trible, "Subversive Justice," 99-109.

69. Cross, *Canaanite Myth and Hebrew Epic*, 123-24.

ary development, they describe 15:1-18 as the Song of Miriam rather than the Song of the Sea.[70]

Interpreters are increasingly turning to the present literary design of 15:1-21 to explain the relationship of the Song of the Sea and the Song of Miriam.[71] The most prominent interpretation is that the two poems are related as song and antiphonal response.[72] Propp has underscored that short songs in the second person, like the Song of Miriam, may have functioned as refrains in antiphonal singing (see also Num 21:7). Thus he concludes that the Song of Miriam may be an antiphon to the Song of the Sea in the cultic practice of ancient Israel, accounting for the presence of the two hymns in Exod 15:1-21. This is also the conclusion of Fretheim, who writes that the repetition created by the Song of Miriam serves "to reinforce the thanksgiving voiced by the people as a whole" in the Song of the Sea.[73] Brenner presents the same interpretation attributing the authorship of both the Song of the Sea and the Song of Miriam to postexilic Levitical priests.[74] Janzen reverses the function of the two songs, arguing that the Song of Moses (15:1-18), with its praise of Yahweh in the first person, is the response to the Song of Miriam, in which the Israelites are called upon to praise Yahweh.[75]

The interpretation of the Song of Miriam (15:21b) as an antiphonal response to the Song of the Sea (15:1b-18) provides insight into the present structure of the two victory songs at the conclusion of the account of Yahweh's conflict with Pharaoh (7:8–15:21). They punctuate the drama that developed throughout the sequence of the plagues. But the function of the repetition goes beyond form to include the content of the victory songs. The two victory songs represent distinct interpretations of the exodus. The Song of the Sea interprets salvation as an exodus and a conquest. The structure of the song moves from the present destruction of the enemy (15:1-12) to God's leading of the Israelites through nations, which results in their arriving eventually at the divine abode (15:13-18). The Song of Miriam anticipates neither the wilderness journey nor the conquest of the land of Canaan. Her celebration of salvation is limited to Egypt and the destruction of the army in the sea.

Interpreters agree that it is not possible to identify the composition of the victory songs with the Non-P and P authors. Yet the content of the two hymns

70. Cross and Freedman, *Studies in Ancient Yahwistic Poetry,* 45-65.

71. See Watts, *Psalm and Story,* 41-62; Janzen, "Song of Moses."

72. B. W. Anderson, "The Song of Miriam Poetically and Theologically Considered," in *Directions in Biblical Hebrew Poetry,* ed. Follis, 285-96; Brenner, *Song of the Sea,* 40; F. van Dijk-Hemmes, "Some Recent Views on the Presentation of the Song of Miriam," in *Feminist Companion to Exodus to Deuteronomy,* ed. Brenner, 200-206.

73. Fretheim, *Exodus,* 161.

74. Brenner, *Song of the Sea,* 40.

75. Janzen, "Song of Moses," 187-99.

corresponds to the interpretation of the exodus in the Non-P and P Histories. The Non-P History, like the Song of the Sea, interprets salvation as an exodus and a conquest, marked by the crossing of the Red Sea and the Jordan River. The Song of the Sea reinforces the interpretation of the Non-P History.[76] Moses celebrates the past event of the exodus (15:1-12), but he also looks ahead to the divine leading of the Israelite people and to the conquest of the land of Canaan (15:13-18), relating the books of Exodus and Joshua. The Song of Miriam corresponds to the interpretation of the exodus in the P History, where the defeat of Pharaoh was the final conflict in Egypt, unrelated to a future conquest of the land. The P History advanced this interpretation by changing the location of the confrontation at the sea from Etham, at the edge of the wilderness, to Pi-hahiroth (14:1-4), which required that the people turn around and thus reenter Egypt. The change in setting plays down the relationship between the exodus and the conquest in the Non-P History.

The Song of Miriam may be an antiphon to the Song of the Sea in the Israelite cult. But in its present narrative context it also reinforces the interpretation of the exodus in the P History, in which the defeat of Pharaoh is the final and decisive event in the land of Egypt. It is noteworthy that the placement of the Song of Miriam, after the Song of the Sea, disrupts the progression from the exodus to the conquest in the Song of the Sea, in the same way that the narrative insertion of Pi-hahiroth in the P History (14:1-4) changed the location for the conflict at the sea in the Non-P History. In both instances the effect is to turn the reader's attention away from the future conquest and back to Egypt, as the location for the decisive act of salvation by Yahweh. The Song of Miriam, like the P History, views the conflict at the sea as the decisive victory of Yahweh unrelated to a subsequent conquest of the promised land.

The two victory hymns are also pivotal to the structure of Exodus, connecting the two themes of divine power and presence. Exodus 1:1–15:21 explores the power of Yahweh to save the Israelites from Egyptian slavery. The plot is centered on the conflict between Yahweh and Pharaoh and the setting is the land of Egypt. Exodus 15:22–40:38 shifts the theme to the presence of Yahweh with the Israelite people. The plot progresses from the conflict between Yahweh and Pharaoh to the pilgrimage of the Israelite people, and the setting changes from the land of Egypt to the wilderness and the mountain of God. The Song of the Sea and the Song of Miriam are a response of faith by the people at the point of transition in the book.[77] S. Ackerman describes this point of transition as a liminal moment in the narrative.[78] Both hymns celebrate the display of divine

---

76. Childs, *Exodus,* 249.
77. Ibid., 248-49.
78. Ackerman, "Why Is Miriam Also Among the Prophets?" 71.

power, when Yahweh hurled the horse and its rider into the sea, providing commentary on the exodus. The Song of the Sea, in particular, provides a transition to the theme of divine presence in the second half of Exodus. The final strophe of the hymn, 15:13-18, includes a confession about Yahweh's leading of the Israelites and planting them in the place of divine rule. M. S. Smith reinforces the transitional role of the Song of the Sea, writing that 15:1-12 is attached to the triumph of Yahweh in the first half of Exodus, while 15:13-18 anticipates "the period of the journey following the victory at the Sea."[79]

Song of the Sea (15:1-18)

Yahweh's victory over Pharaoh at the sea is celebrated as an event of holy war. Miller writes: "Yahweh the warrior, 'terrible in glorious deeds,' is nowhere more vividly described than here in the Song of the Sea."[80] M. C. Lind adds: "There is no question but that the exercise of military power is the theme of this poem." The theme is stated in the description of Yahweh as a warrior (v. 3). Lind notes that the act of war is stated succinctly in vv. 4 and 7: Yahweh casts Pharaoh's army in the sea by means of his messengers, "his majesty" and "his fury." The victory is total. But there is also the unique feature of the theme of holy war that has been evident throughout the narrative account of the exodus. The Israelites are not involved in the conflict, and, thus, it is not a battle in the conventional sense.[81] As Cross has demonstrated, the imagery of the Song of the Sea also departs from the narrative accounts of the Non-P and P Histories. There is no crossing of the sea on dry ground in the Song of the Sea. Instead, Yahweh destroys the enemy in the sea, sending them to the underworld.[82]

The literary style of the Song of the Sea varies widely. God is referred to both in the third (vv. 1-5, 18) and in the second (vv. 6-17) person. The poetry is mixed in style, including hymn (vv. 2, 3, 6, 7, 11), ballad (vv. 4-5, 8-10, 13-17), and refrains (vv. 6, 11, 16b).[83] The personal proclamation of praise in vv. 2-3 is not clearly integrated into the poem, which has prompted Cross and Freedman to argue that v. 2 is not part of the original poem. Muilenburg, on the other hand, argued that v. 2 fits its present context, because of the first person praise in vv.

79. Smith, *Pilgrimage Pattern*, 190-91, 205-18.

80. Miller, *Divine Warrior*, 113.

81. M. C. Lind, *Yahweh Is a Warrior: The Theology of Warfare in Ancient Israel* (Scottdale, Pa.: Herald, 1980), 49; see also S.-M. Kang, *Divine War in the Old Testament and in the Ancient Near East* (BZAW 177; Berlin: de Gruyter, 1989), 114-25.

82. Cross, *Canaanite Myth and Hebrew Epic*, 131-37.

83. For an overview of scholarship see T. B. Dozeman, "The Song of the Sea and Salvation History," in *On the Way to Nineveh: Studies in Honor of George M. Landes* (ed. S. L. Cook and S. C. Winter; ASOR 4; Atlanta: Scholars Press, 1999), 94-113.

1b and 2 and the focus on the divine name in vv. 2-3 (see the Notes).[84] The song also shifts in perspective and in tone. What begins as a hymn of the individual, celebrating Yahweh's past victory at the sea (vv. 1-12), changes in time and in topic to describe the Israelites' wilderness journey and eventual arrival at Yahweh's cult (vv. 13-18).

J. Jeremias summarized the following contrasts in theme and in topic between the two halves of the Song of the Sea: the first half of the poem focuses on (1) Yahweh alone, (2) in a battle event, (3) where the enemy is destroyed in the sea, (4) culminating in divine victory and kingship, while the focus in vv. 13-17 is on (1) Israel, (2) being led on a journey by Yahweh, (3) through nations that are specifically named, (4) culminating in their arrival at the cult.[85] The change in voice, style, and temporal perspective prompted Muilenburg to designate the genre of the poem simply as a liturgy.[86] Others have sought to account for the changes in style through a history of composition especially with regard to the final strophe, vv. 13-18.[87]

The variations in the literary style of the Song of Sea have given rise to different evaluations of the structure of the poem. Many interpreters focus on the themes of the poem, noting the contrast between the defeat of the enemy in the sea at the outset and the divine leading of the Israelite people at the conclusion. The focus of debate from this perspective is to determine the point of transition between the two themes, especially with regard to v. 12: "You stretched out your right hand; Earth swallowed them." Cross represents many interpreters in evaluating v. 12 as a concluding coda, thus separating the song between vv. 1-12, the confrontation at the sea, and vv. 13-18, the divine leading of the Israelite people through the desert and to the land.[88] M. S. Smith agrees, noting a parallelism between vv. 12 and 18, with each short verse closing sections of the poem.[89] Beer argued, however, that the poem divides between vv. 1-

---

84. Muilenburg, *Hearing,* 157. For similar arguments see Hauser, "Two Songs of Victory," 282 n. 5.

85. Jeremias, *Königtum Gottes,* 99.

86. Muilenburg, *Hearing,* 151-69.

87. For a variety of solutions regarding the history of composition of the Song of the Sea, especially with regard to the final strophe, vv. 13-18, see Watts, "Song of the Sea," 371-80; Coats, "Song of the Sea," 1-17; E. Zenger, "Tradition und Interpretation in Exodus XV 1-21," in *Congress Volume: Vienna 1980* (ed. J. A. Emerton; VTSup 32; Leiden: Brill, 1981), 452-83; T. C. Butler, "'Song of the Sea': Exodus 15:1-18: A Study in the Exegesis of Hebrew Poetry" (Ph.D. diss., Vanderbilt, 1971), 102-99; Norin, *Er spaltete das Meer,* 77-107; H. Spieckermann, *Heilsgegenwart: Eine Theologie der Psalmen* (FRLANT 148; Göttingen: Vandenhoeck & Ruprecht, 1989), 96-115; Dozeman, "Song of the Sea," 94-113.

88. Cross, *Canaanite Myth and Hebrew Epic,* 125-26. See also Childs, *Exodus,* 250-51; Brenner, *Song of the Sea.*

89. Smith, *Pilgrimage Pattern,* 211.

10 and 11-18. Verses 11-12 begin the second part of the hymn, according to Beer, with v. 12 referring to the story of Korah who is swallowed by the "earth" (Num 16:30-31) rather than the destruction of the Egyptian army in the sea.[90] R. Alter also makes the transition from the confrontation at the sea to the wilderness leading at v. 12, while noting that the verse functions in a transitional way.[91]

The evaluation of the poetic design of the Song of the Sea is also influenced by the refrains in vv. 6, 11, 16b, which, as indicators of structure, yield an organization of three or more strophes. Muilenburg identified three strophes, each ending with a refrain: vv. 2-6, 7-11, 12-16. The strophes share a similar progression in language, consisting of confession (vv. 2-3, 7-8, 12-14), epic narrative (vv. 4-5, 9-10, 15-16a), and the hymnic refrain (vv. 6, 11, 16b).[92] Freedman refined the poetic analysis of Muilenburg to include the exodium in vv. 1-2, providing an introduction to the song; the opening in vv. 3-5 with the refrain (v. 6); the first strophe in vv. 7-10 with refrain (v. 11); the second strophe in vv. 12-16a with refrain (v. 16b); and the ending in vv. 17-18 (with v. 21b). Freedman also refined the poetic structure of the Song of the Sea through the study of its metrical patterns, using the common poetic technique of syllable counting to evaluate the length of the lines and their balance throughout the poem.[93]

The Song of the Sea is rich in literary allusion to the Canaanite mythology of the storm god Baal. The battle between Baal and Yamm-Nahar, the brother of Baal and the sea god, is central to the mythology. In the Canaanite mythology Baal's victory over the chaotic sea god Yamm-Nahar (*CTA* 2) leads to the construction of a temple, the conquest of cities to create an empire, and finally to Baal's enthronement in his sanctuary on Mount Zaphon (*CTA* 3–4). The Song of the Sea follows the pattern of Baal's conflict with Yamm-Nahar. It too progresses from conflict to enthronement on a divine mountain, and it includes an account of conquest to create an empire. Yahweh's victory over Pharaoh in the sea (15:1-12) leads to the conquest of people (15:13-16) and the enthronement of God on the "mountain of inheritance," a cosmological image for the sanctuary (15:17-18). The Song of the Sea even includes phrases from the mythology of Baal. Yahweh's victory over the enemy leads to the proclamation of an eternal kingship, "Yahweh will reign forever and ever!" (15:18), as it does for Baal (*CTA* 2.iv.10, 32).[94] The designation of Yahweh's sanctuary as "the mountain of inheri-

---

90. Beer, *Exodus*, 82.

91. R. Alter, *The Art of Biblical Poetry* (New York: Basic Books, 1985), 54-55.

92. Muilenburg, *Hearing*, 155-63.

93. Freedman, "Strophe and Meter in Exodus 15," 187-227. See Butler, "Song of the Sea," 51-52, for an overview of the variety of interpretations with regard to metrical patterns.

94. The research comparing the Song of the Sea and Canaanite mythology is rich. For more detailed comparison see Cross, *Canaanite Myth and Hebrew Epic*, 112-44; C. Kloos, *Yhwh's Combat with the Sea: A Canaanite Tradition in the Religion of Ancient Israel* (Leiden: Brill, 1986);

tance" and "the place of dwelling" (Exod 15:17) is also applied to the temples of Canaanite gods (*CTA* 1.iii.1; 3.F.16; 4.viii.12-13). These phrases indicate that the focus of the hymn is on Yahweh's sanctuary. Propp rightly concludes that the Song of the Sea could be called the "Song of the Mountain," since the divine enthronement in the sanctuary on the holy mountain is the climax of the liturgy.[95]

Finally the language of the Song of the Sea is noteworthy because of its concentration of ancient linguistic forms. The poem employs an archaic use of the prefixed *(yaqtul)* form of the verb with past meaning that is present in Ugaritic literature but uncommon in Classical Hebrew. Examples of the *yaqtul* form of the verb with past meaning include the description of waters in v. 5, "the depths covered *(yĕkasyumû)* them"; and of the earth in v. 12, "Earth swallowed *(tiblā'ēmô)* them." The verbs used to characterize the nations in vv. 14-15 and to celebrate the Israelite march in the refrain of v. 16b have also been identified as further instances of the *yaqtul* form, although the meaning is less clear in these instances from the context. The older form of the third person plural pronominal suffix, *-mw*, is used throughout the poem on verbs (vv. 5, 7, 9, 10, 12, 15, 17). The archaic form of the relative pronoun *zû* appears in vv. 13 and 16. Still other examples of archaic style include the preservation of a final *yod* in an open syllable in v. 6 *(ne'dārî)* and the use of the enclitic *mem* on the preposition *kĕ* in vv. 5 and 8.

Cross and Freedman, followed by D. A. Robertson, date the Song of the Sea to the premonarchical period of Israel in part on the basis of the archaic style. They identify the Song of the Sea with a larger corpus of ancient poetry, including Judges 5, Deuteronomy 33, 2 Samuel 22 (= Psalm 18), and Habakkuk 3.[96] J. Day questions whether linguistic forms and comparison to Ugaritic literature provide a sound basis for dating.[97] Brenner notes that many archaic forms, such as the pronominal suffix *-mw* or the relative pronoun *zû*, occur in later literature extending into the postexilic period, and may therefore reflect literary style rather than dating.[98] The debate introduces the problem of distinguishing between genuinely archaic literature and the archaizing style of later writers. The important debate surrounding this topic should not obscure the striking concentration of archaic linguistic forms in the Song of the Sea, which sepa-

---

Day, *God's Conflict*; M. S. Smith, *The Early History of God: Yahweh and the Other Deities in Ancient Israel* (San Francisco: Harper & Row, 1990), 41-79.

95. Propp, *Exodus 1–18*, 562.

96. Cross and Freedman, *Studies in Ancient Yahwistic Poetry*, esp. 45-65; D. A. Robertson, *Linguistic Evidence in Dating Early Hebrew Poetry* (SBLDS 3; Missoula, Mont.: Scholars Press, 1972).

97. Day, *God's Conflict*, 100 *et passim*; see also Butler, "Song of the Sea," 217-20.

98. Brenner, *Song of the Sea*, 34-36.

rates the poem from the narrative and calls attention to the pivotal role of the victory song in the literary structure of Exodus.

15:1-3 The opening verse states the theme of the first half of the song, vv. 1-12, which is the defeat of the army in the sea.[99] The song opens in the first person: "I will sing." Similar motifs repeat in v. 2, "I will praise," and "I will exalt." The literary context identifies the singer with Moses regardless of the use of the song in other cultic settings. Four times in v. 2 the first person suffix "my" is used to modify Yahweh, here spelled in a shortened form, "Yah." Four confessions about the character of Yahweh and the relationship of God to the singer result: (1) Yahweh is "my strength and song." The translation "song" for Hebrew *zimrāt* is possible, meaning that Yahweh is praiseworthy. But many interpreters prefer the translation "strength" or "protection," from Ugaritic *dmr*, "to be strong."[100] (2) Yahweh "has become my salvation." The motif relates the hymn with the close of the narrative (14:30). (3) Yahweh is "my God." And (4) Yahweh is "my father's God." The motif of Yahweh as the ancestral Deity first occurred in the commission of Moses (2:24; 3:6, 15, 16; 6:3). The predications add to the identity of Yahweh, which was first revealed to Moses in his wilderness commission (3:1–4:18).

There is progression in the four predications about Yahweh. The display of divine strength in victory over the enemy leads to the insight that the victory is salvation (see the similar statements in Isa 12:2 and Ps 118:14). The insight prompts a confession that Yahweh is the God of the psalmist in the present moment and the ancestral God from the past. The four predications in v. 2 lead to the conclusion in v. 3 that Yahweh is a "man of war" (see also Isa 42:13). The relationship between the phrase "man of war" and "the name" of God in v. 3 suggests that the quality of "warrior" is embedded into the name Yahweh. The cycle of the plagues and the emphasis on Yahweh as the Storm God in the events of the exodus certainly reinforce such an interpretation. The title "Yahweh Sabaoth" ("Yahweh of hosts") also suggests military imagery (see Isa 48:2).

15:4-12 The identification of Yahweh in vv. 1-3 leads to the description of the enemy's defeat at the sea. The two refrains, vv. 6 and 11, indicate that Yahweh is victorious over earthly (v. 6) and cosmic (v. 11) forces. Verses 4-5, 7, and 9 describe the arrogance of the enemy and his defeat. The arrogance of the enemy is emphasized through boasting in the first person: "I will pursue, I will overtake, I will divide spoil. My life will be full of them, I will draw my sword, my arm will dispossess them" (v. 9). The victory of Yahweh over the army is accentuated by the first refrain: "Your right hand, Yahweh, strong in might; your right hand, Yahweh, shatters the enemy."

---

99. Zenger, "Tradition und Interpretation," 452-83, esp. 468-69.
100. Barré, "My Strength."

Verses 8 and 10 indicate Yahweh's power over the sea. The sea is described in v. 10 as "mighty," *mayim 'addîrîm*. It even becomes the subject of verbs, suggesting that the sea is personified to some degree: "waters *(mayim)* pile up," "the deep waters *(tĕhōmōt)* congealed," and "sea *(yām)* covered them." But the emphasis is certainly on Yahweh's power over the sea, since the imagery stresses control over water. The "piling up" (Niphal of *'āram*) of the sea influences its flow, perhaps through damming. The "congealing" *(qāpā')* of the sea may be some form of curdling (see Zeph 1:12; Job 10:10) or even solidification (like the walls of water in the P History).[101] Whatever the intended image the enemy sinks like lead when the breath of Yahweh blows on the sea, prompting the second refrain: "Who among the gods is like you, O Yahweh?" The question is rhetorical, since no god is like Yahweh, majestic in holiness (or perhaps "mighty among the holy ones," meaning other gods), awesome in glory, and a wonder worker (see the prediction of "wonders" in 3:20).

The victory of Yahweh at the sea ends in v. 12 with a change in imagery from the sea to the earth. The earth swallows the enemy when Yahweh extends his right hand, a repeat of the metaphor from the refrain in v. 6. The reference to the earth, rather than the sea, may provide a transition to the second half of the song, where the imagery changes from the setting of the sea to the divine leading through the land.[102] But the earth may also indicate the underworld, accentuating the earlier proclamation that the enemy sank like lead to the bottom of the sea.[103] The earth also swallows Korah, Dathan, and Abiram as punishment for rebelling against Moses (Num 16:30-34).[104] Citing *Memar Marqah* 2:8, Propp notes that all the elements of nature participate in the destruction of the enemy: fire from the nose of God, wind from the breath of God, the sea covers the enemy, and finally even the earth swallows them — a fitting conclusion to the central role of nature throughout the cycle of the plagues and the defeat of Pharaoh.[105]

15:13-18 The imagery changes from conflict at the sea to the divine leading of the Israelite people. The motifs of guidance and temple construction (vv. 13, 17) frame the account of a future conquest (vv. 14-16a), culminating with the refrain: "until your people pass by, O Yahweh, until the people you bought pass by" (v. 16b). The poem concludes with a proclamation of Yahweh's eternal kingship (v. 18).

Verses 13 and 17 establish the central theme of the section, which is

---

101. For curdling see Cross, *Canaanite Myth and Hebrew Epic,* 128-29. For solidifying see Childs, *Exodus,* 243.

102. Muilenburg, *Hearing,* 164.

103. Cross, *Canaanite Myth and Hebrew Epic,* 129.

104. Dozeman, "Numbers," 138-39.

105. Propp, *Exodus 1–18,* 529.

Yahweh's leading of the Israelites to the divine sanctuary as an act of election. The election of the Israelite people is signaled by the words "redeem," "steadfast love," and "inheritance." Both verses divide between motifs of divine leading and the sanctuary.

Verse 13 describes Yahweh as leading *(nāḥâ)* and guiding *(nāhal)*. The Israelites are characterized as a redeemed people (see the P version of the commission to Moses, 6:6-8). The verbs of leading convey pastoral images of herding. The shepherding of God is associated with fidelity, *ḥesed*, translated in NRSV as "steadfast love," and in NIV as "unfailing love." The word may indicate covenantal obligation. The goal of the journey is the divine sanctuary, the "holy abode." Hebrew *něwēh*, translated "abode," continues the pastoral imagery, suggesting a shepherd's abode or even a pasture land of rest.

Verse 17 develops images of divine leading from v. 13, changing the perspective of time from the past to the future. The shepherding of Yahweh will terminate when Yahweh brings the Israelites into the domain of the divine rule and plants them there. This event has not yet happened in the hymn. It is a confession about the future. Yahweh's domain is the divine temple described as the "mountain of inheritance," the "place of dwelling," and the "sanctuary" established by God's own hands. Scholars have sought to identify Yahweh's temple with a more specific location, ranging from Sinai/Horeb, Kadesh, Gilgal, and Jerusalem. The imagery of the sanctuary incorporates the mythology of the divine mountain. Baal's temple is also located on the "mountain of inheritance." It is also the "place of his dwelling," implying the enthronement of God. But, unlike the mythology of Baal, the enthronement of Yahweh in the temple and the residency of the Israelites in the domain of Yahweh's rule remain a future hope, not a present reality. Verse 18 reinforces the future orientation of the liturgy by proclaiming the coming reign of Yahweh, not his present rule.

Verses 14-16 provide the perspective of the nations in Syria-Palestine to the victory of Yahweh at the sea. The nations include Philistia, Edom, Moab, and the rulers of Canaan. Their reaction provides the counterpart to the enemy in v. 9. The response of the nations in vv. 14-16 is strikingly different than the enemy in v. 9. The enemy at the sea was arrogant envisioning an easy victory over the Israelite. The arrogance leads to his ruin, since in the end he sinks like a stone in the sea (v. 5). The reaction of the nations to the divine leading of the Israelites after the exodus is the opposite of the enemy's arrogance at the sea. The nations are disturbed (Niphal of *bāhal*, v. 15) by the message of the exodus. They tremble *(rā'ad*, v. 15) and quake *(rāgaz*, v. 14). They experience anguish like birth pangs *(ḥîl*, v. 14), along with terror *('êmâ*, v. 16) and dread *(paḥad*, v. 16). They even melt away *(môg*, v. 15). As a result, they stand "still as a stone" as the Israelite people pass by (v. 16b). The reaction of the nations contains common motifs from the tradition of holy war. Joshua 2:9 and 24 also describe the fear of the nations at the approach of the Israelites as terror *('êmâ)*. They too melt away *(môg)*. Deuteronomy 2:25 also characterizes the fear of the nations during the Israelite conquest as trembling *(rā'ad)*, as experiencing anguish like birth pangs *(ḥîl)*, and as being in dread *(paḥad)*.

The refrain in v. 16b, "until your people pass by, O Yahweh," continues the imagery of conquest. "Pass by" renders the Hebrew verb *'ābar*, "to cross over." The tense of the verb is debated. Cross translates in the past, identifying the verb as an example of the archaic *yaqtul* form. He rightly notes that Josh 10:13 provides a parallel, where the preposition *'ad*, "until," is also combined with the prefixed form of the Hebrew verb to indicate past time.[106] But the use of the imperfect with *'ad* more frequently indicates future meaning (Isa 22:14; Hos 10:12).[107] A. R. Hulst concluded that the verb takes on theological meaning in Deuteronomy to signify action that must take place if the Israelites are to achieve the divine promise of the land at the end of their wilderness journey (e.g., Deut 4:26; 9:1). The motif of crossing over is central to the story of the Jordan River, which begins the conquest of the promised land (Joshua 1–5).[108] The verb occurs twenty-two times in the story of the Jordan River crossing. The ark of the covenant (Josh 3:11; 4:11), the people (1:11; 3:1, 4, 14, 16, 17 [twice]; 4:1, 7, 10, 11, 13, 22, 23 [twice]), the leaders of the tribes (4:5), the tribes east of the Jordan (1:14; 4:12), and even the cultic stones (4:3, 8) are described as crossing the Jordan River for conquest. This term is avoided in the story of the confrontation at the Red Sea, where the Israelites are described instead as "entering" *(bô',* Exod 14:16, 22) the sea, not crossing it. Only once is the verb "to cross over" associated with the Red Sea, in the speech of Joshua during the crossing of the Jordan River, where the emphasis is on the conquest of the land (Josh 4:22-23).

The Song of the Sea reflects the perspective of salvation history. It has

---

106. Cross, *Canaanite Myth and Hebrew Epic*, 130 n. 67. See also Smith, *Pilgrimage Pattern*, 220-21.

107. The use of the imperfect with *'ad* occurs three times in the Pentateuch: two times in poetry (Num 23:24; Exod 15:16), and once in narrative (Gen 38:11). Genesis 38:11 is a reference to the future (Tamar is encouraged by Judah to remain a widow until Shelah grows up). And the Balaam oracle uses the construction to make a general characterization of Israel (Israel is likened both to a lioness and a lion, who does not lie down until it devours its prey). There are two occurrences in the Deuteronomistic History: Josh 10:13, where the meaning is past, and 2 Sam 10:5, where the meaning is future (David commands the men with half-shaven beards to remain at Jericho until their beards grow back). The construction occurs six times in the poetry of Isaiah (22:14; 26:20; 32:15; 42:4; 62:1, 7), where it always has future meaning. Still other occurrences throughout the Hebrew Bible reinforce the future meaning of this construction (Hos 10:12; Pss 57:1; 94:13; 110:1; 132:5; 141:10). Only in Ps 73:17 could past meaning possibly be attributed to the construction, but even here a frequentative meaning is probably more appropriate (the psalmist understands the way of the wicked every time he enters the sanctuary).

108. Hulst, "Jordan."

historicized the mythology of Baal's conflict with the sea god Yamm into a story of the Israelite exodus and conquest, reinforcing the interpretation of the exodus in the Non-P History. The exodus is the defeat of the enemy in the sea. It is a past event, celebrated in the first part of the Song of the Sea. The conquest of the nations in Syria-Palestine and the enthronement of Yahweh in his temple on his holy mountain remain a future hope. The wilderness journey of the Israelite people also relates the exodus and the conquest in the Non-P History. The Song of the Sea provides a snapshot of the story of salvation history in the Non-P History, during the liminal moment of transition at the Red Sea.

Song of Miriam (15:19-21)

The Song of Miriam reinforces the theme of holy war. It repeats the account of the destruction of the Egyptian army from the first half of the Song of the Sea (vv. 1-12), not the leading of the Israelite people to the divine abode in the second half of the poem (vv. 13-18). The Song of Miriam is a response to the Song of the Sea. It is a call to praise in the second person (15:21b), which repeats the first person praise of 15:1b. In the present context, the first person praise in 15:1b is most clearly the voice of Moses, even though the introduction (15:1a) also includes the Israelites. When the call to praise by Miriam is read as a response to the praise of Moses, it is her song that calls forth the language of faith from the people of Israel. They are to respond to the voice of Moses, with a similar confession of Yahweh's power to save.

The placement of the Song of Miriam goes beyond its function as an antiphonal response to the Song of Moses. It also provides the final commentary on the story of the exodus. Women have functioned in the role of saviors throughout the opening stories of Moses. The midwives rescue Moses from Pharaoh's death threat at the moment of his birth, his mother hides him in the ark on the river, and the daughter of Pharaoh adopts him. Zipporah also rescues Moses from the death threat of Yahweh in the wilderness. Miriam expands the role of women as saviors at the conclusion of the exodus. She assumes a prophetic role by leading the entire nation of Israel in the language of faith. As P. Trible has noted, Miriam may actually frame the story of the exodus if the unnamed sister of Moses is also identified with her.[109] In this case Miriam is associated especially with salvation from water. First, she is involved in the rescue of Moses from the river, and second, she provides interpretation of the confrontation at the sea.

15:19 The verse can be read in several ways: as the conclusion to the Song of the Sea, as the introduction to the Song of Miriam, or as an analepsis, which

109. Trible, "Bringing Miriam out of the Shadows," 172-73.

resumes the narrative in Exodus 14. Janzen advocates the latter interpretation, arguing that 15:19 is meant to provide additional information on the narrated events in 14:26-29.[110] But 15:19 could also be the conclusion to the Song of the Sea. In this case the narrative summary in v. 19 provides the reason for the confession of Yahweh's eternal kingship in v. 18. Hebrew *kî*, which opens the verse, would then introduce a causal clause and be translated "for" or "because." Finally, 15:19 could also be the introduction to the Song of Miriam, which would require Hebrew *kî* to be translated "when," signaling that v. 19 is a temporal clause. I have translated v. 19 as a temporal clause, which provides an introduction to the Song of Miriam. The translation is tentative, however, since all three interpretations are possible from the syntax and from the narrative context.

The identification of the author of v. 19 is clear from the motifs. Verse 19 repeats central motifs from the Non-P History. It contains no language from the P History, contra some interpreters.[111] The verse repeats the sequence in the Non-P History in which Pharaoh enters the sea in pursuit of the Israelite people, Yahweh engulfs the Egyptians in the sea, while the Israelites walk through on dry ground (14:16b, 22a, 29a). The splitting of the sea and the walls of water from the P History are absent.

15:20-21a   The imagery changes in these verses from the confrontation at the sea to the role of women in the tradition of the victory song (see the commentary above). The language does not allow for the identification of the author with either the Non-P or the P historian. E. Poethig has clarified that the tradition of women singing victory songs is well established in ancient Israel and not specifically related to the authors of the pentateuchal histories. Meyers has further clarified the extensive role of women as drummers, composers, and performers through a study of archaeological remains, focusing in particular on terra-cottas.[112]

Miriam is first named in the story of the exodus in 15:20. The name may mean "gift" or perhaps "eminence."[113] She is described as a "prophetess" and as "the sister of Aaron." Scholars often judge the two descriptions of her to be in conflict, prompting an emphasis on one over the other. But the combination of both titles is important for interpretation. The prophetic role of Miriam returns in Numbers 12, where the special role of Moses as prophet is confirmed over against the clairvoyance of Miriam and Aaron and all other prophets. Whatever may be the origin of the title "prophet" for Miriam, she embodies the P reinterpretation of a prophet during the postexilic period. The book of Chronicles in-

---

110. Janzen, "Song of Moses," 191.

111. See, e.g., Childs, *Exodus*, 248; Smith, *Pilgrimage Pattern*, 215.

112. C. Meyers, "Miriam the Musician," in *Feminist Companion to Exodus to Deuteronomy*, ed. Brenner, 207-30; idem, *Exodus*, esp. 117-19.

113. See M. Görg, "Mirjam — ein weiterer Versuch," *BZ* 23 (1979): 287-89.

dicates that Levitical singers become prophets in the postexilic period.[114] 2 Chronicle 20 provides a window into this process, when the Levitical temple choir of the Korahites assumes the role of prophets during holy war. The prophecy of the Levitical choir consists of cultic choral music performed with lyres, harps, and cymbals (1 Chr 25:1). The characterization of Miriam as a prophetess provides guidelines for interpreting her song. It is more than an antiphon to the Song of the Sea; it contains its own prophetic interpretation of the exodus.[115]

The identification of Miriam as the sister of Aaron may indicate a clan relationship, as it does in the description of Aaron at the close of the wilderness commission (Exod 4:10-17). But it may also signify a familial relationship, which would place the text within the orbit of the P History. Miriam acquires a central role in the P History. She is one of the three heroes of the exodus along with Moses and Aaron. The three characters are identified as a family in Num 26:59, making Miriam a Levite. The death of Miriam at Kadesh is also specifically noted in the P History. Her death foreshadows the subsequent death of Aaron at Mount Hor (Num 20:22-29) and the death of Moses on Mount Nebo in the Abarim mountain range (Num 27:12-14; Deut 32:48-52; 34:1-8). Noth concluded that the death of Miriam presented the "death of the three family members . . . at the three final stations [of the P itinerary]."[116] The identification of Miriam as the sister of Moses and Aaron in the P genealogy of Num 26:59 also provides an inner-biblical interpretation on the birth story of Moses (2:1-10). Once the P genealogy enters the Pentateuch, Miriam becomes the unnamed sister who rescues Moses in the river. She acts as savior at the outset of the story. She also acquires the last word of interpretation on the exodus with her song in v. 21.

The Song of Miriam is meant to be a prophecy in the P History. The placement of the Song of Miriam provides insight into its function within the P History, and its relationship to the Song of the Sea in the P History. The Song of Miriam creates a repetition, which disrupts the chronology of the Song of the Sea. Moses is no more finished singing about the future conquest of the land than Miriam enters the stage to refocus the reader's attention back on the event at the sea. Her prophetic song provides a countervoice to the prophecy of Moses in the Song of the Sea. It emphasizes that the defeat of Pharaoh in the sea is the decisive event of salvation, unrelated to the future conquest of the land. The P History advances the same interpretation by making the confrontation at the

---

114. See D. L. Petersen, *Late Israelite Prophecy: Studies in Deutero-Prophetic Literature and in Chronicles* (SBLMS 23; Missoula, Mont.: Scholars Press, 1977), 55-87.

115. On the prophetic role of Miriam as representing a prophetic group in the postexilic period see U. Rapp, *Mirjam: Eine feministische-rhetorische Lektüre der Mirjamtexte in der hebräischen Bibel* (BZAW 317; Berlin: de Gruyter, 2002).

116. Noth, *History of Pentateuchal Traditions,* 183.

Red Sea the final events in the land of Egypt, rather than the first event in the wilderness as it is in the Non-P History.

15:21b   The Song of Miriam is a victory song. It opens with the imperative form of the verb, summoning the community to praise: "Sing to Yahweh." The summons is followed by a motive clause, introduced by the particle *kî*: "For he acted supremely." The motive for praise is followed by the description of the divine victory: "horse and his rider he hurled into the sea." B. W. Anderson has underscored the close relationship in form between the Song of Miriam and the hymn of praise, which also includes the summons to praise, the motivation for praise, and an elaboration of the Deity's praiseworthy acts.[117]

---

117. Anderson, "Song of Miriam," 288-90.

PART 2

The Presence of Yahweh in the Wilderness
(15:22–40:38)

Journey (15:22–18:27)

INTRODUCTION

Central Themes

The conflict between Yahweh and Pharaoh in the land of Egypt gives way to the Israelite journey with God in the wilderness. With it the central theme shifts from divine power to divine presence. Images of holy war persist. T. W. Mann has illustrated that Yahweh is idealized and exalted in the wilderness journey, marching before the Israelites as their vanguard.[1] Yahweh even undertakes a holy war against the Amalekites (17:8-16). But the focus is on Yahweh's initial providential care of the Israelites as they journey through the wilderness.

The wilderness setting and the central role of the journey from Egypt to the promised land determine the central themes in this episode: divine guidance and the faith of the Israelite people. The prominence of the journey turns the experience of the Israelite people in the wilderness into a story of pilgrimage, which functions as a rite of passage. A. van Gennep defined the rite of passage as: "Rites which accompany every change of place, state, social position and age." Such transitions are marked by three phases: (1) the act of separation from a social structure or cultural condition; (2) a marginal state, described as "liminal," from the Latin meaning "threshold"; and (3) reincorporation into a new social structure.[2] The three phases in the rite of passage provide a framework for interpreting the three-part structure of salvation history: the exodus from Egypt is

---

1. T. W. Mann, *Divine Presence and Guidance in Israelite Tradition: The Typology of Exaltation* (JHNES; Baltimore: Johns Hopkins University Press, 1977).

2. A. van Gennep, *The Rites of Passage* (trans. M. B. Vizedom and G. L. Caffee; London: Routledge and Kegan Paul, 1909), 15-25.

the act of separation; the wilderness journey is the marginal state; and the promised land represents the reincorporation into a new social structure.

The marginal location of the Israelite people during the wilderness journey is important for the thematic development of the second half of the book of Exodus. The separation from the social structure of slavery in Egypt propels the Israelites into the liminal space of the wilderness where they journey toward the promised land, but are not yet reincorporated into a new social structure in Canaan. V. Turner characterizes liminality as a time of ambiguity, when participants are "betwixt-and-between" recognized social structures, and thus momentarily free of past constraints. The liminal phase in a rite of passage, according to Turner, is a time of trial and testing where participants enter as a tabula rasa in order to undergo initiation, to experience role reversals, and to create community.[3]

The wilderness journey describes the Israelite initiation into a life with Yahweh. The stories explore the themes of divine guidance and care and the need for the people to have faith in Moses and in Yahweh. Individual stories describe the trials and tests of the Israelite people and the structure of their new communal life after their rescue from the Egyptian oppression.[4] Nature plays an important role in the rite of passage. Its forces, however, are no longer weapons of war but resources for nurture and care. Yahweh decontaminates diseased water (15:22-26), rains down food from heaven (chap. 16), and coaxes water from a rock to keep the Israelites alive in the desert (17:1-7). The Song of the Sea signaled this shift when it introduced the pastoral imagery of Yahweh as a shepherd, leading the Israelites to the pastoral abode (15:13-18).

The wilderness also becomes the setting for creating social and religious structures. In the first story of the wilderness journey at Shur (15:22-26), God proposes the possibility of forming a society under divine law. The gift of manna at the wilderness of Sin inaugurates the observance of the Sabbath (chap. 16). The water from the rock at Rephidim introduces the sacred mountain, Horeb (17:6), and the first altar to Yahweh (17:15). The story of Jethro's visit to Moses introduces cultic worship (18:1-12) and a legal system by which to adjudicate divine law in the community (18:13-27).

The wilderness journey also explores the relationship between Yahweh and the Israelite people through a sequence of trials and tests, characterized by Coats as the murmuring stories.[5] The murmuring stories explore the theme of faith as a dynamic relationship between the Israelite people, Moses, and Yah-

---

3. V. Turner, *The Ritual Process: Structure and Anti-Structure* (Ithaca: Cornell University Press, 1969), 94-111.

4. See R. Cohn, *The Shape of Sacred Space: Four Biblical Studies* (AAR Studies in Religion 23; Missoula, Mont.: Scholars Press, 1981), 7-23.

5. Coats, *Rebellion in the Wilderness*, 15ff. passim.

weh. The faith of the Israelite people was introduced in the commission of Moses in the Non-P History (3:1–4:18) and it returned when Yahweh destroyed Pharaoh and the Egyptian army in the Red Sea (14:30-31). The faith of the Israelites is not assumed in Exodus. It must be acquired through their rite of passage in the wilderness journey. The need for faith implies the ability of the Israelites to accept or to reject divine leading and the leadership role of Moses. The theme of the Israelites' faith is central to the wilderness journey. The theme is explored through stories of conflict, hence the title "murmuring stories" or even "protest stories,"[6] in which the people must choose between a secure life in Egypt, albeit as slaves, or the riskier journey with God and Moses through the desert. Thus the murmuring stories trace the complaints by the people about threatening situations in the wilderness. The complaints are directed against Moses. They question the authority of his commission. But they also call into question the salvation of God in leading the Israelites from Egypt into the wilderness.

The murmuring stories are introduced already at the Red Sea, when the Israelites state that slavery in Egypt was preferable to the risk of following Yahweh into the wilderness (14:11-12). The contrast between the Egyptian slavery and the wilderness journey is developed into a sequence of challenges to Moses' leadership, which provides the structure to the wilderness journey in the Pentateuch. There are two sequences of murmuring stories (chaps. 14–18 and Numbers 11–21), separated by the revelation at Mount Sinai (Exodus 19–Numbers 10). The book of Exodus contains only the first sequence of the murmuring stories, which occur on the march from Egypt to Sinai (chaps. 14–18). The Israelites raise three complaints about environmental threats in the wilderness: health (15:22-27), food (chap. 16), and water (17:1-7). The second sequence occurs in Numbers when the people journey from Sinai to the plains of Moab (Numbers 11–21). The second sequence repeats the same complaints of health (21:4-9), food (11:4-35), and water (20:2-13), along with additional conflicts over the promised land (chaps. 13–14) and leadership (chap. 16).[7] The diagram in figure 24 on page 350 illustrates the two-part sequence of the wilderness journey with the revelation of law and the cult at the mountain of God separating the two parts.

The revelation of law, the formation of covenant, and the creation of the Israelite cult at Mount Sinai are pivotal in the interpretation of the wilderness journey, since these events change God's response to the murmuring of the Israelites. Prior to the revelation at Mount Sinai the murmuring stories are "tests." Yahweh tests the Israelites with the crisis of diseased water (Exod 15:22-27) and

---

6. See M. Vervenne, "The Protest Motif in the Sea Narrative," *ETL* 63 (1987): 257-71.

7. Dozeman, "Numbers," 98-100.

Figure 24
Wilderness Journey in the Pentateuch and Stories of Murmuring

Wilderness Journey Murmuring Stories Initial Testing = Positive (Exod 14–18)

14:11-12	Threat	Red Sea
15:22-26	Diseased Water	Shur
15:27–16:36	Food/Manna	Elim/Sin
17:1-7	No Water	Rephidim

Revelation of Law and Cult at the Mountain (Exod 19–Num 10)

32:1-35	Golden Calf	mountain of God

Wilderness Journey Murmuring Stories Lack of Faith = Negative (Num 11–21)

11:1-3	General	Taberah
11:4-35	Food/Meat	Kibroth-hattaavah
13–14	Land	Kadesh/Paran
16	Priesthood	Kadesh/Paran
20:1-13	No Water	Kadesh
21:4-9	General	Red Sea Road

the absence of food (chap. 16). The Israelites, in turn, test Yahweh over the crisis of water (17:1-7). The stories explore initiation. The complaints have a positive role in establishing the relationship between Israel, Moses, and God. Each complaint leads to divine rescue, not punishment.

The revelation of law (chaps. 19–24) and the incident of the golden calf (chaps. 32–34) are pivotal in the story of the wilderness journey. These events indicate that murmuring is no longer a test of faith in the second stage of the wilderness journey (Numbers 11–21), but instances of the lack of faith in Moses and in the salvation of Yahweh. Thus, after the revelation of law and the establishment of the covenant at Mount Sinai, the murmuring stories indicate the rejection of God's salvation. The negative character of the murmuring stories in Numbers 11–21 is highlighted by the two accounts that frame the sequence of the literature: the general complaints at Taberah (Num 11:1-3) and on the Red Sea Road (Num 21:4-9). Both stories lack specific content to account for the complaint of the Israelite people. Numbers 11:1-3 states that the people complained about their "misfortune," while Num 21:4-9 presents the contradictory situation in which the people complain simultaneously about the lack of food and the quality of their food. Numbers 11:1-3 and 21:4-9 are general complaints about the wilderness journey and not responses to a specific crisis. The two stories underscore that the complaints of the Israelite people in Numbers 11–21 are no longer initial tests in the rite of passage, but occasions in which the people lack faith in the leadership of Moses and in the salvation of Yahweh. Consequently, Yahweh's response changes from assistance to judgment, resulting in the death of the first generation of the Israelites (see especially Numbers 13–14; 16; 21:4-9). The geographical notices associated with the murmuring stories even hint at the circularity of the journey of the first generation, when the Red Sea is referred to at the beginning (Exodus 14) and at the end (Num 21:4-9) of the story.

The structure of the murmuring stories in the Pentateuch clarifies that a central theme in the wilderness journey from the Red Sea to Sinai in Exodus 15–18 is testing during the initial rite of passage. There is a quality of innocence and even courtship in the initial segment of the wilderness journey (see Hos 2:14-15). The theme of testing introduces a new element into the book of Exodus, divine law (Exod 15:26). Law tests the Israelite people by raising the question of whether they have the faith to live by divine law in the wilderness. The Israelites, in turn, test God by asking: "Is Yahweh among us or not?" (17:7). The mutual testing between Yahweh and the Israelite people also allows for the character development of Moses as the mediator between the two parties during the rite of passage through the wilderness.

Authors

Wilderness Journey

The wilderness setting dominates the Pentateuch. Coats clarified the extent of the setting: the wilderness is introduced already in the commissioning of Moses (Exodus 3–4); it returns during the exodus (13:18); and it remains the setting for most of the subsequent events in the Pentateuch.[8] Noth underscored the significance of the wilderness journey in the creation of the pentateuchal histories. He concluded that the two traditions at the core of the Pentateuch were the exodus from Egypt and the acquiring of the promised land. Yet, according to him, it was the wilderness journey that related the core traditions, which creates the genre of history. He wrote of the wilderness: "It presupposes in every instance the themes, 'guidance out of Egypt' and 'guidance into the promised land' and depends on both of these."[9] Von Rad agreed with Noth, also concluding that the wilderness journey is necessary for the composition of salvation history, since it

---

8. Coats, "A Structural Transition in Exodus," *VT* 22 (1972): 129-42; idem, "An Exposition for the Wilderness Tradition," *VT* 22 (1972): 288-95.
9. Noth, *History of Pentateuchal Traditions*, 47-51.

relates the exodus and the promised land into a single and continuous story through the imagery of an original desert journey.[10]

Modern interpreters have sought to locate the origin of the wilderness tradition in the history of Israelite religion, as a means for identifying the author(s) of the wilderness journey in the Pentateuch. The early origin of the wilderness tradition was accentuated in late-nineteenth- and early-twentieth-century studies on the nomadic ideal. K. Budde introduced the hypothesis of a nomadic ideal by reconstructing an ancient form of desert Yahwism associated with the Rechabites. In this hypothesis, the wilderness was considered the most ancient tradition in Israelite religion.[11] As the earliest form of Yahwism, it became the ideal for later criticism of Yahwistic religion during the period of the monarchy, when the Israelites established an agricultural life in the settled land. Later interpreters, such as J. W. Flight, expanded the nomadic ideal hypothesis to the point where it became the "taproot" influencing "all the later life and thought of Israel."[12] Thus according to the advocates of the nomadic ideal, the wilderness tradition was always a part of ancient Israelite religion. The composition of the stories of the wilderness journey in the Pentateuch took place already in the initial stages of the monarchical period. The wilderness tradition in the Pentateuch provided glimpses into the earliest traditions of Yahwism, which were formed in the setting of the desert.

Subsequent interpreters have challenged the nomadic ideal in the history of ancient Israelite religion. S. Talmon noted that the desert was not idealized by ancient Israelites. Indeed, he argued just the opposite, that agriculture in the settled land was the ideal vision of life. The desert represented desolation and death, threats to the ideal of an agricultural life style within the settled land.[13] P. A. Riemann reached the same conclusion in his study of the preexilic prophets. He too concluded that the preexilic prophets viewed the wilderness from the perspective of the settled land. In every case they had a pejorative view of the desert as a place of desolation, judgment, and death.[14] Yet, even with the rejection of the hypothesis of the nomadic ideal, interpreters still advocated the

---

10. Von Rad, *Problem of the Hexateuch*, 1-78, esp. 3-13, 41-48.

11. K. Budde, "The Nomadic Ideal in the Old Testament," *New World* 4 (1895): 235-79.

12. J. W. Flight, "The Nomadic Idea and Ideal in the Old Testament," *JBL* 42 (1923): 158-226.

13. S. Talmon, "The 'Desert Motif' in the Bible and in Qumran Literature," in *Biblical Motifs: Origins and Transformations* (ed. A. Altmann; Philip W. Lown Institute of Advanced Judaic Studies, Brandeis University, Studies and Texts 3; Cambridge: Harvard University Press, 1966), 31-61.

14. P. A. Riemann, "Desert and Return to Desert in the Pre-Exilic Prophets" (Ph.D. diss., Harvard, 1964). See also K. Pfisterer Darr, "Breaking through the Wilderness: References to the Desert in Exilic Prophecy" (Ph.D. diss., Vanderbilt, 1984), 11-81.

dating of the wilderness journey accounts in the Pentateuch to the early monarchical period. Riemann postulated a wilderness wandering in an early credo (e.g., Deut 26:4-9) and in a premonarchical epic. Talmon also presumed an account of the wilderness journey in a monarchical history. In both instances the author(s) of the wilderness journey in the Pentateuch were judged to be court historians, writing under the Israelite monarchs or even earlier tradents from the premonarchical period.

The research of Noth and von Rad is especially influential for the early dating of the wilderness wandering tradition and the writing of history. Noth concluded that the wilderness journey was a secondary development in the history of Israelite tradition and literature: "It is obvious that [the wilderness theme] is not a very important or really independent theme." But the secondary development of the wilderness journey did not mean that it was composed late in the history of Israelite religion. On the contrary, Noth concluded that the wilderness theme merged with the exodus and the promise of land already in the premonarchical period of ancient Israel, forming the outline for the genre of history writing in the early monarchical period. Von Rad agreed with Noth. Salvation history, which for von Rad included the related themes of the promise of land to the ancestors, the exodus, the wilderness wandering, and the possession of the land of Canaan, emerged from tribal celebrations of the exodus and was fully developed in the early monarchical period, when it was given written form in the Yahwistic History by court historians under David and Solomon.[15]

The research of Noth and von Rad has provided the framework for more precise identifications of the author(s) of the wilderness journey in the Pentateuch. Coats sought to identify the author by focusing, in particular, on the "murmuring motif" — the repeating leitmotif of complaint by the Israelite people concerning the harsh conditions of life in the desert. He concluded that there was a transformation in the history of composition of the motif from positive stories of testing and divine leading in the earliest writing to negative stories, in which the Israelite people reject the salvation of Yahweh and are punished by the Deity. The origin of the murmuring motif, according to Coats, arose in the Jerusalem cult as a polemic against the northern kingdom after the divided monarchy.[16] V. Fritz pushed the murmuring stories further back in time to the rise of the Davidic monarchy.[17] Childs detected two patterns of murmuring stories already prior to their incorporation into the monarchical J Source: Pattern I focuses on stories of deliverance and Pattern II emphasizes

---

15. Von Rad, *Problem of the Hexateuch*, 41-48.

16. Coats, *Rebellion in the Wilderness*, 249-56.

17. V. Fritz, *Israel in der Wüste: Traditionsgeschichtliche Untersuchung der Wüstenüberlieferung der Jahwisten* (Marburger theologische Studien 7; Marburg: Elwert, 1970).

disobedience.[18] S. J. De Vries sought a literary solution to the positive and negative versions of the murmuring stories in the combination of northern and southern conquest traditions.[19] There are two common threads throughout the diverse studies. The first is the tendency to assume that the contrast between the positive and the negative stories of murmuring provides insight into the history of composition of the wilderness journey. The second is the early dating of the composition of the wilderness journey to the premonarchical and the early monarchical periods.

My identification of the author(s) begins with rejecting the idea that there is a history of composition from positive stories of murmuring to negative stories of punishment. Past research has demonstrated that the wilderness journey in the Pentateuch includes etiological legends that functioned independently from their present narrative context in the Non-P and P Histories. In the commentary I will clarify that the naming of Massah and Meribah (17:1-7), the war with Amalek (17:8-16), and the tradition of Jethro's leadership (chap. 18) are not the creation of either the Non-P or P authors. Thus there is a history of composition in the wilderness journey in the Pentateuch. The distribution of positive and negative stories of murmuring, however, will be interpreted as a literary strategy of the Non-P and P authors, and not as the result of tradition-historical stages of composition. The overview of the murmuring stories in the previous section ("Central Themes") suggests literary design in the wilderness journey. The murmuring of the Israelite people in the journey from the Red Sea to Sinai (chaps. 15–18) represents positive instances of testing between God and the Israelite people. The repetition of the same stories in Numbers 11–21, after the revelation of law at the mountain of God, results in negative stories of disobedience. The hinge between the two perspectives is the revelation of law (Exodus 19–24), the story of the golden calf (chap. 32), and covenant renewal (chap. 34).

I also depart from the past tendency to date the wilderness journey in the Pentateuch to the early monarchical period.[20] The references to the wilderness in the book of Hosea indicate that the development of the wilderness journey in the Pentateuch, as an episode in salvation history linking the exodus from Egypt with the entry into the promised land, cannot be earlier than the late monarchical period and is more likely a literary innovation in the exilic period. Five times in prominent passages the Hebrew *midbār*, "wilderness, steppe,

18. Childs, *Exodus,* 254-64. The two-part pattern of murmuring stories is expanded to three by P. Buis, "Les conflits entre Moïse et Israël dans Exode et Nombres," *VT* 28 (1978): 257-70; see also Vervenne, "Protest Motif," 264-69.

19. S. J. De Vries, "The Origin of the Murmuring Tradition," *JBL* 87 (1968): 51-58.

20. See, in particular, Dozeman, *God on the Mountain;* idem, "Horeb/Sinai and the Rise of Law in the Wilderness Tradition," *SBLASP* 28 (1989): 282-90; idem, *God at War.*

desert," is used in Hosea to describe divine actions toward Israel (Hos 2:3, 14-15 [MT 5, 16-17]; 9:10; 13:4-5, 15). The wilderness journey of the Pentateuch is not presupposed in any of these instances. The book of Hosea employs the wilderness as a metaphor of desolation (2:3; 9:10; 13:15). It also refers to the wilderness as a contrasting location to the settled land (2:14-15; 13:5). But there is no imagery of divine leading from Egypt to the promised land in Hosea, which is crucial to the wilderness journey stories in the Pentateuch.[21] Only once, Hos 2:14-15, is the image of divine leading present in Hosea in association with the wilderness. But in this instance the leading of God is in the reverse direction from the wilderness journey stories in the Pentateuch. God leads from the settled land into the wilderness: "Therefore I [Yahweh] will allure her, and bring her into the wilderness and speak tenderly to her."

The book of Hosea provides important background for identifying the author(s) of the wilderness journey in the Pentateuch. The composition of the Non-P and P Histories is later than the prophet Hosea. The references to the wilderness in Hosea indicate that the stories of the wilderness journey from Egypt to the promised land are not yet written at the time of the fall of the northern kingdom. The framework of salvation history, in which the exodus, the wilderness journey, and the promised land become stages in one story, is evident in literature from Jeremiah, which may have been composed as early as the closing years of the monarchical period, but more likely in the exilic period: "They [the ancestors] did not say, 'Where is Yahweh who brought us up from the land of Egypt; who led us in the wilderness in a land of deserts and pits . . .'" (Jer 2:6). The march of God through the wilderness from Babylon to the land of Canaan is a central motif in the exilic prophet Second Isaiah: "In the wilderness prepare the way of Yahweh, make straight in the desert a highway for our God" (Isa 40:3). The wilderness journey is also prominent in the exilic writing of the prophet Ezekiel, where it provides the framework for a broad view of the history of rebellion (Ezekiel 20).

The wilderness journey in the Pentateuch may be in formation as early as the late monarchical period, thus corresponding to Jeremiah tradition. The elaborate literary structure of the wilderness journey in the Pentateuch, however, with its complex thematic development from testing (Exodus 15–18) to rebellion (Numbers 11–21), would favor a later period for its composition, in the late exilic or the postexilic period. The wilderness journey in the Non-P and P Histories, therefore, is commentary on the experience of the exile and the reformation of the Israelite nation as a "wilderness community" in light of the Dias-

---

21. T. B. Dozeman, "Hosea and the Wilderness Wandering Tradition," in *Rethinking the Foundations: Historiography in the Ancient World and in the Bible: Essays in Honour of John Van Seters* (ed. S. L. McKenzie and T. Römer; BZAW 294; Berlin: de Gruyter, 2000), 55-70.

pora.[22] The experience of the exile ushers in the rite of passage through the wilderness that is proclaimed by Second Isaiah. The stories of the wilderness journey in the Pentateuch provide the paradigm for a new form of community for postexilic Israelites.

The dating of the wilderness journey stories to the late monarchical, exilic, and postexilic periods has increased in recent scholarship. But the identification of the author(s) and the theories of the composition of the wilderness journey vary widely. Most agree that the P historian has contributed in a limited manner to the wilderness journey in Exodus 15–18, especially in the story of manna (chap. 16) and in the itinerary sequence of the travel from the Red Sea to Sinai. W. Johnstone identifies a far greater role for the P author, which includes most of the literature in 15:22–19:2. According to him, the pre-P account of the journey of Israel from the Red Sea to the mountain of God includes only the itinerary notice in 15:22ab*a*, about the departure from the Red Sea, and the additional notice in 19:2, about the arrival at the mountain of God. The result is a three-day journey from Egypt to the mountain of God in the pre-P version of events, which lacks stories of complaint. Johnstone's hypothesis is that the pre-P account of the wilderness journey and the references to it in Deuteronomy were likely authored by the same person or school, and thus the story lines are the same. He identifies this larger body of related literature as the D-work, which includes the pre-P account of the exodus, the wilderness journey, and the revelation at the mountain of God; Deuteronomy; the Deuteronomistic History; and the Deuteronomistic portions of Jeremiah. The absence of stories of complaint from the Red Sea to the mountain of God in Deuteronomy is the reason for the elimination of the wilderness stories in the pre-P version of Exod 15:22–19:2. It is the P redactor, according to Johnstone, who fashions the sequence of stories in 15:22–19:2, which results in a six-week period of travel, rather than the three-day sequence of the pre-P version.[23] I argue that the murmuring stories in chaps. 15–18 are not intended to be stories of rebellion, because they occur before the revelation of law in chaps. 19–24. For this reason the entire episode does not have a point of comparison with

---

22. On the experience of the exile in the formation of the Pentateuch see especially J. Blenkinsopp, *Treasures Old and New: Essays in the Theology of the Pentateuch* (Grand Rapids: Eerdmans, 2004). And for a more focused study on the wilderness journey see R. P. Carroll, "Rebellion and Dissent in Ancient Israelite Society," *ZAW* 89 (1977): 176-204.

23. W. Johnstone, "From the Sea to the Mountain: Exodus 15,22-19,2: A Case Study in Editorial Techniques," in *Chronicles and Exodus: An Analogy and Its Application* (JSOTSup 275; Sheffield: Sheffield Academic Press, 1998), 242-61; idem, "The Use of Reminiscences in Deuteronomy in Recovering the Two Main Literary Phases in the Production of the Pentateuch," in *Abschied vom Jahwisten: Die Komposition des Hexateuch in der jüngsten Diskussion* (ed. J. C. Gertz, K. Schmid, and M. Witte; BZAW 315; Berlin: de Gruyter, 2002), 247-73.

Deuteronomy, which lacks an account of the wilderness journey prior to the Israelites' arrival at Mount Horeb.

The identification of the Non-P author is more widely debated. H. H. Schmid noted parallels between the murmuring stories in the wilderness journey of the Pentateuch and the cycle of rebellion in Judges, which suggest a similar time frame for their composition, perhaps in the Deuteronomic or Deuteronomistic circle of writers.[24] A difference between the two bodies of literature, however, is the absence of intercession in Judges. Van Seters argued that the intercessory role of Moses in the wilderness is modeled after the character of Jeremiah, who takes on an increasingly larger role of intercession in the later Deuteronomistic additions to Jeremiah (i.e., Jer 7:16; 11:14; 14:11; 15:1). The parallels indicate to Van Seters that the pentateuchal account of the wilderness journey is an exilic composition, which he identifies as the exilic Yahwist historian.[25] C. Levin also identifies the author as the Yahwist, who writes in the exile, but he characterizes the method of composition as redaction and not the writing of a historian.[26] Aurelius supports the later dating of the wilderness tradition, by associating the role of Moses as intercessor with late exilic and postexilic traditions of prophetic intercession.[27] Blum also includes the literature in Exodus 15–17 (excluding the P additions in chap. 16) with the *D-Komposition*, the exilic or postexilic pre-P composition.[28]

Non-P and P Histories

The distinct authorship of the Non-P and P Histories in Exodus 15–18 is evident from the motifs in the literature. The most distinctive motifs indicating P authorship occur in the story of manna. These include the designation of the Israelites as the "congregation" (*'ēdâ*, 16:1), the reference to the divine appearance as the Glory of Yahweh (*kĕbôd yhwh*, v. 7), and the recognition formula, which states that the Israelites will acknowledge Yahweh from the event of manna (v. 6). Interpreters have also sought without success to identify the separate authors of the murmuring stories on the basis of the language of complaint. Johnstone attributes the Hebrew *lûn*, "to murmur, complain," to the P author. The word is prominent in the story of manna, where the evidence of P authorship is strong (16:2, 7, 8), and in other murmuring stories in Numbers 11–21 (Num 14:2,

24. Schmid, *Sogenannte Jahwist*, 61-82.
25. Van Seters, *Life of Moses*, 165-75.
26. Levin, *Jahwist*, 348-59.
27. Aurelius, *Fürbitter Israels*, 141-202.
28. Blum, *Studien*, 143-64.

27, 29, 36; 16:11; 17:5 — all P texts).[29] But the term also occurs in narratives with little evidence of P authorship, such as the account of bitter water (Exod 15:24) and the absence of water (17:3).

The sequence of travel in Exodus 15–18 is also different in the Non-P and P Histories. The distinctive use of geography began with the commission of Moses (3:1–7:7) and continued in the confrontation at the Red Sea (13:17–14:31) through the divergent travel notices, where the P author inserted the location of Pi-hahiroth as the setting for the conflict at the sea (see fig. 12 in the introduction to 7:8–15:21). The P author also changes the sequence of travel from the Red Sea to the mountain of God in chaps. 15–18. The travel notices and the geographical locations in 15:22–18:27 include the following:

15:22   And Moses made the Israelites set out from the *Red Sea.*
        And they went out to the *wilderness of Shur.*
        And they walked three days in the wilderness, but they did not
        find water.
15:23   And they approached *Marah.*
        But they were not able to drink the water from *Marah,* because it
        was bitter.
        Therefore one called its name *Marah.*
15:27   And they approached toward *Elim.*
        And there were there twelve springs of water and seventy
        date-palm trees.
        And they camped there by the water.
16:1   And they went out from *Elim.*
        And the entire congregation of the Israelites approached the
        wilderness of Sin, which is between *Elim and Sinai,*
        on the fifteenth day of the second month of their going out of the
        land of Egypt.
17:1   And the entire congregation of the Israelites set out from
        the *wilderness of Sin* by stages according to the mouth of Yahweh.
        And they camped at *Rephidim.*

Interpreters agree that there are signs of P authorship in the travel sequence from the Red Sea to Rephidim. But they disagree on the extent of the P composition. Johnstone attributes all of the travel sequence to the P author except the notice of the Israelite arrival at the wilderness of Shur in 15:22ab.[30] Van Seters, on the other hand, limits the influence of the P author to secondary de-

---

29. Johnstone, *Chronicles and Exodus,* 247-48.
30. Ibid., 242-61.

scriptions of the dating and the characterization of the Israelites as the "congregation" (16:1; 17:1).[31] Thus for Van Seters the entire sequence of travel belongs to the Non-P historian. Other interpreters separate the travel notices more evenly: Cross attributes three travel notices to the P author, Shur (15:22a), Sin (16:1), and Sin (17:1);[32] while M. S. Smith expands the number of P texts to four: Shur (15:22a), Elim (15:27), Sin (16:1), and Sin (17:1a).[33] Lohfink identifies Shur (15:22a*a*), Elim (15:27), and Sin (16:1) as P itinerary stops, which relate to the *tôlĕdôt* of Jacob (see Gen 37:2).[34]

Most interpreters recognize the P authorship of the wilderness of Sin in 16:1 and 17:1 as the setting for the story of manna. Exodus 16:1 states that the Israelites departed from Elim and arrived at the wilderness of Sin. The system of dating in this verse (the designation of month 2, day 15) and the reference to the Israelites as the "congregation" (*'ēdâ*) indicate that the travel notice belongs to the P History. The more precise location of the wilderness of Sin, "between Elim and Sinai," further supports the P authorship of the travel notice. The same literary device repeats in 14:1-4, where the P author also described Pi-hahiroth as being located "between Migdol and the sea." The literature style indicates that the P author introduces a new setting, the wilderness of Sin, to interpret the story of manna.

The travel notice in 17:1a at the close of the story of manna is also the composition of the P author. It connects the wilderness of Sin with Rephidim, noting that the "congregation" departed "by stages as Yahweh commanded." The description of the Israelites as the "congregation" once again identifies the author as the P historian, while the characterization of their journey as taking place "by stages" and "by the command of Yahweh" (*'al-pî yhwh*) repeats the language and technique of the P author in describing the departure from Sinai for the wilderness of Paran, where the Israelites also "set out by stages" and "by the command of Yahweh" (Num 10:12-13).

The P author's insertion of a new itinerary stop at the wilderness of Sin creates a literary tension in the sequence of travel, especially surrounding Elim (15:27). In the present form of the text, Elim is out of place, since it lacks an accompanying narrative. But, with the removal of the P itinerary stop at the wilderness of Sin, Elim becomes the setting of the story of manna in the Non-P History. I explore the meaning of the story of manna in the Non-P History as an

---

31. Van Seters, *Life of Moses,* 154-56. This may also be the position of Davies, "Wilderness Itineraries and Composition," who appears to limit the P itineraries to Exod 19:1; Num 10:12; 20:1a*a*; 22:1.

32. Cross, *Canaanite Myth and Hebrew Epic,* 310-11.

33. Smith, *Pilgrimage Pattern,* 227.

34. N. Lohfink, "The Priestly Narrative and History," in *Theology of the Pentateuch* (trans. L. M. Maloney; Minneapolis: Fortress, 1994), 136-72, esp. 150-55.

Figure 25

Topic	Non-P History	P History
bitter water	15:22-26	—
manna	15:27; 16:4-5, 13b-15, 21b, 27-31, 35a	16:1-3, 6-13a, 16-21a, 22-26, 32-34, 35b, 17:1a
no water	17:1b-7	—
war with the Amalekites	17:8-16	—
Jethro at the mountain	18:1-27	—

event in the lush setting of Elim, as opposed to the desert setting of the wilderness of Sin in the P History.

The chart in figure 25 above illustrates the distribution of literature in the Non-P and P Histories. It indicates that the majority of the literature belongs to the Non-P History. The P History is limited to the story of manna.

Non-P History

The Non-P History contains six stories: diseased water (15:22-26), manna (15:27; 16:4-5, 13b-15, 21b, 27-31, 35a), the miracle of water from the rock (17:1b-7), the war with the Amalekites (17:8-16), and two stories about Moses' Midianite father-in-law — an account of worship on the mountain of God (18:1-12) and the administration of law (18:13-27).

The Non-P History is organized around three locations: the wilderness of Shur, Elim, and Rephidim. The story of diseased water (15:23-26) takes place in the wilderness of Shur after the Israelites set out from the Red Sea (15:22). Elim is the location for the story of manna (15:27). Rephidim may be the setting for a number of events. It is clearly the setting for the crisis of water (17:1b-7), where it is also associated with Horeb, the mountain of God. Rephidim continues to be the setting for the war with the Amalekites (17:8-16). Rephidim may also be the intended setting for the stories of Jethro at the mountain of God (chap. 18), since the departure from Rephidim is not stated until 19:2.

The Non-P History accentuates the theme of law in the journey from the Red Sea to the mountain of God. Law becomes the means by which Yahweh and the Israelites will interact and form a relationship leading to covenant. The relationship between Yahweh and the Israelite people is explored through the motif of testing. The journey begins with the divine proposal of law to the Israelites at the wilderness of Shur. The theme of testing is introduced with the proposal of law, which is also accompanied with the promise of health (15:22-26). The instruction for gleaning manna at Elim is the first instance of law in the wilderness and the initial test of the Israelite people (15:27; 16:1-36*). The Israelites, in turn, test God at Rephidim when they lack water (17:1b-7).

The Non-P History broadens in perspective after the stories of testing to explore the Israelites' relationship to other nations. The Amalekites are an enemy to be exterminated (17:8-16). The Midianites are an ally providing leadership in worship (18:1-12) and in the administration of law (18:13-27). The two perspectives toward these foreign nations are recounted in the story of King Saul in 1 Samuel 15. He wages a holy war against the Amalekites, because of their hostility to the Israelites in the wilderness journey, but he spares the Kenites (= Midianites) because of their hospitality.

The stories of Jethro in Exodus 18 are difficult to place in the structure of the book of Exodus. I have located them within the wilderness journey from Egypt to the mountain of God. But the text states that Moses is already encamped at the "mountain of the God" (*har hā'ĕlōhîm*, 18:5). The stories in chap. 18 lack a travel notice, suggesting that Rephidim and the mountain of God are only loosely associated. The divine mountain, Horeb, is associated with Rephidim in the miracle of water from the rock (17:6). Yet a reference to Rephidim is lacking in chap. 18, and the introduction to the revelation of God on the mountain in chaps. 19–34 clearly separates the two locations, stating that the Israelites leave Rephidim to encamp before the mountain where Moses meets God (19:2). The breakdown in the travel notices and the anachronism of placing Moses and the Israelites at the mountain of God in 18:1-12, before the notice of their arrival at the same location in chap. 19, leads to two conclusions: (1) the story of Jethro is a separate tradition of worship from chaps. 19–34, and (2) the Non-P historian has incorporated the story of Jethro to provide transition to the revelation of God in chaps. 19–34.

There are several indications that the stories of Jethro represent an independent tradition of worship at the mountain of God. First, the names for the divine mountain are different in chap. 18 than in chaps. 19–34. Although the narrative in chaps. 19–34 shares the identification of the sacred mountain as "the mountain of God" (18:5; 24:13), it also names the mountain as Mount Horeb (*har ḥōrēb*, 33:6) and as Mount Yahweh (*har yhwh*, Num 10:33). Second, stories about Moses' father-in-law frame Exodus 19–34. Jethro provides guidance in worship and in law in Exodus 18, and Moses requests the leadership of Hobab (= Jethro) in Num 10:29-32, suggesting that Exodus 18 and Num 10:29-32 were one continuous story at an earlier stage of tradition. Third, the framing of Exodus 19–34 with stories about the leadership of Jethro (Exod 18:1-12 and Num 10:29-32) is reinforced by a similar repetition with regard to the selection of judges. Leaders are selected to administrate law both prior to the revelation of law in Exodus 19–34, when Moses first appoints judges (18:13-27), and after the event, when Moses commissions the seventy elders (Num 11:4-35). The stories that center on judges address the related themes of the burden of leadership for Moses (Exod 18:18; Num 11:14, 17) and the need for a select group to share his responsibility (Exod 18:22; Num 11:17), even though the designation of the judges is different in each story. The result is a clear design in the Non-P History, in which stories about the leadership of Jethro and the need for judges (Exodus 18; Num 10:29–11:35) now frame the account of the revelation of law in Exodus 19–34.

The selection of judges in 18:13-27 repeats in Deut 1:9-18, suggesting a literary relationship between the Non-P History and Deuteronomy. Yet the relationship between the two stories raises questions about tradition history, since the account in Deut 1:9-18 places the events of Exod 18:13-27 after the revelation at Mount Horeb, not before it as is the case in the Non-P History. It is not possible to reconstruct with certainty the tradition-historical process surrounding Jethro or the tradition of judges (see the commentary on 2:15b-22 and 4:18-26). R. Knierim and, more recently, S. Cook have explored possible social developments in the monarchical period that may account for the texts.[35]

The literary tensions surrounding the selection of judges in 18:13-27; Num 11:4-35; and Deut 1:9-18 have prompted scholars to conclude that the stories of Jethro in Exodus 18 belong after the revelation in chaps. 19–34, which leads to the conclusion that Exodus 18 and Num 10:29-32 were once a single story. They argue that the placement of Exodus 18 before chaps. 19–34 accounts for the confusion of geography surrounding Rephidim and the mountain of God. It explains the reappearance of Moses' father-in-law in Num 10:29-32 after he supposedly departed to his own country in Exod 18:27. It also provides an explanation for the repetition of themes in 18:13-27 and Num 11:4-35 about judges to assist Moses.[36]

The tradition-historical analysis also provides insight into the present structure of the Non-P History. I have placed the story of Jethro as the last episode in the journey to the mountain of God. But the setting of the mountain of God (18:5) indicates that the story is also transitional. It could be interpreted as the introduction to the revelation of God in chaps. 19–34. The role of the Midianites in the Non-P History provides support for this conclusion. Stories about the Midianites frame the two accounts of revelation on the divine moun-

---

35. R. Knierim, "Exodus 18 und die Neuordnung der mosäischen Gerichtsbarkeit," *ZAW* 73 (1961): 146-71; S. L. Cook, "The Tradition of Mosaic Judges: Past Approaches and New Directions," in *On the Way to Nineveh: Studies in Honor of George M. Landes* (ed. S. L. Cook and S. C. Winter; ASOR Books 4; Atlanta: Scholars Press, 1999), 286-315.

36. See Sarna, *Exodus*, 97-98; J. Van Seters, "Etiology in the Moses Tradition: The Case of Exodus 18," *HAR* 9 (1985): 355-61; esp. Johnstone, *Chronicles and Exodus*, 257-61.

tain in the Non-P History. The commission of Moses on the mountain of God (3:1–4:17) is preceded by a story of Midianite hospitality (2:15b-22) and followed by a story of Midianite rescue through ritual from the divine attack (4:18-26). The revelation to the Israelites (chaps. 19–34) is also framed by stories about the Midianites. Jethro provides guidance in matters of worship and law on the mountain of God (chap. 18) before his cultic leadership is transferred to Moses in chaps. 19–34. The refusal of Hobab (= Jethro) to lead Moses at the close of the covenant ceremony (Num 10:29-32) sets the stage for a transfer of leadership to God, symbolized by the ark (Num 10:33-36). The Non-P historian idealizes the Midianites as a nation that has knowledge of Yahweh, is hospitable to the Israelites, and mentors them in the rituals and worship of Yahweh, until the Israelites receive their own divine law at the mountain of God (Exodus 19–34), at which time the leadership of Moses' Midianite father-in-law is transferred to the ark of the covenant.

P History

The P History is limited to the story of manna. The P literature consists of 16:1-3, 6-13a, 16-21a, 22-26, 32-34, 35b; 17:1a. The P History changes the location of the story of manna from Elim to the wilderness of Sin. According to 16:1 the Israelites departed from Elim and arrived at the wilderness of Sin. The system of dating in this verse (the designation of month 2, day 15) and the reference to the Israelites as the "congregation" (ʿēdâ) indicate that the travel notice belongs to the P History. Earlier it was also noted that the more precise location of the wilderness of Sin, "between Elim and Sinai," also repeats the technique of the P author from 14:1-4, where Pi-hahiroth was located "between Migdol and the sea." The travel notice in 17:1a at the close of the story of manna connects the wilderness of Sin with Rephidim, noting that the "congregation" departed "by stages as Yahweh commanded." The same language and literary style repeat in the P author's description of the Israelite departure from Sinai for the wilderness of Paran, where the Israelites also "set out by stages" and "by the command of Yahweh" (Num 10:12-13).

The P History reinterprets the story of manna. In the Non-P History manna is a divine test of the Israelite people in the setting of the abundance of Elim. In the P History the story becomes a complaint by the Israelites in a setting of the deprivation of the wilderness of Sin. The change in setting allows the P author to explore in more detail the revelation and meaning of the Sabbath. The P account of manna begins with murmuring (Exod 16:1-3). Two speeches by Moses and Aaron follow. The first (16:6-13a) is a response to the murmuring of the Israelites containing motifs central to the P History — manna will bring the Israelites to the knowledge of Yahweh (see 7:5) and the divine presence is identified as the Glory of Yahweh *(kĕbôd yhwh)*. The P History also expands the providential food to include meat. The second speech focuses on the Sabbath (16:16-21a, 22-26), which is a central theme running throughout the P History (see Gen 2:1-3). The P History concludes by recounting the preservation of an omer of manna for future generations (16:32-34, 35b-36).

LITERARY STRUCTURE

The Non-P History provides the basic outline of the Israelite journey from the Red Sea. The wilderness of Shur is the setting for the story of diseased water. The oasis of Elim is the location of manna. And the Israelites do not clearly depart from Rephidim until 19:2. The influence of the P History is limited to the story of manna. Thus the P History is dependent on the Non-P History. This is most evident in the P itinerary notices. The setting of the wilderness of Sin modifies the sequence of travel in the Non-P History; it does not represent an independent account of the wilderness journey. But the P History does introduce a significant change into the travel route of the Israelites. The P History relocates the story of manna from the lush oasis of Elim to the arid wilderness of Sin. As a result, the setting of Elim loses its function in the canonical form of the text as the location for the story of manna. Many interpreters have pondered the place of Elim in the Israelites' sequence of travel and its apparent lack of function.

The introduction of a new setting to accompany the P interpretation of the story of manna repeats the pattern from the confrontation at the Red Sea, where the P author also changed the setting from Etham (13:20) to Pi-hahiroth (14:1-4). The pattern will occur again. The P author will change the setting of the divine mountain to Mount Sinai for the revelation of P law (Exodus 19–Numbers 10), and, after the revelation on Mount Sinai, the P author will further change the setting of the spy story from Kadesh to Paran (Num 12:16; 13:3, 26) to provide the P interpretation of the loss of the promised land.[37] The change in geography in the P History to accompany new interpretations indicates the theological significance of the geographical setting throughout the Israelites' rite of passage in the wilderness journey.

The overview of the wilderness journey in the "Central Themes" indicated that the travel of Israelite people is not limited to Exodus 15–18, but continues through Numbers 11–21. The result is a two-part development of the wilderness journey: the period of testing in Exodus 15–18 and the period of disobedience in Numbers 11–21. My comments are limited to the first stage of the wilderness journey.

---

37. See Dozeman, "Numbers," 120-28.

I separate the commentary into the following outline:

COMMENTARY

LAW AND HEALTH (15:22-26)

^{15:22}*And Moses made the Israelites set out from the Red Sea. And they went out to the wilderness of Shur. And they walked three days in the wilderness, but they did not find water.* ²³*And they approached Marah. But they were not able to drink the water from Marah, because it was bitter. Therefore one called its name Marah.*

²⁴*And the people complained against Moses, saying, "What will we drink?"*

²⁵*And he cried to Yahweh. And Yahweh showed him a tree. And he threw it in the water. And the water became sweet.*

²⁶*There he placed for them a statute and an ordinance. And there he tested them. And he said, "If you listen carefully to the voice of Yahweh, your God, and what is straight in his eyes you do, and you give ear to his commands, and you observe all of his statutes, then all of the disease that I set in Egypt I will not set on you. For I am Yahweh, your healer."*

Notes

15:22 *and they went out.* The LXX makes Moses the subject, translating, *ēgagen autous*, "he led them out," as does the Sam, "he [Moses] brought them out."

but they did not find water. The LXX adds *hōste piein*, "to drink," indicating more precisely that the Israelites did not find drinkable water, since there was "bitter water" at Marah.

15:23 *and they approached Marah.* The MT *mārātâ* likely derives from the root *mrr*, "to be bitter." The LXX has *Merra*.

because it was bitter. The MT *kî mārîm hēm* is a wordplay on the place name (*mārâ* and *mārātâ*). The LXX *pikron gar ēn* loses the wordplay on Marah (but see next note).

therefore one called its name Marah. The MT *'al-kēn qārā'-šĕmāh mārâ* indicates an etiology, in which an event is associated with the name of a place. The name of the place, Marah, arises from the experience of "bitter *(mārîm)* water." In the LXX the name of the location becomes *Pikria*, the Greek word for "bitter."

15:24 *the people complained.* Hebrew *lûn,* "to complain," in the MT indicates the Israelite act of murmuring against Moses (and God) in the wilderness (e.g., 16:2, 7, 8; 17:3; Num 14:2, 27, 29, 36; 17:10). The LXX translates, *diegongyzen,* "muttered, murmured."

15:25 *and Yahweh showed him.* The MT *wayyôrēhû* indicates instruction, the Hiphil of the verb *yārâ,* "instruct." The LXX translates, *edeixen,* which means "to show forth," but can also indicate instruction, "to explain." The Sam, however, moves in another direction, employing the Hebrew verb *rā'â,* "to see," which does not emphasize any form of teaching.

a statute and an ordinance. Hebrew *ḥōq ûmišpāṭ* is translated in the plural in the LXX: *dikaiōmata kai kriseis,* "ordinances and judgments," which reflects the more common expression in Hebrew, *ḥuqqîm ûmišpāṭîm,* "statutes and ordinances." Weinfeld suggests a parallel between the singular reference to law in 15:25 and Akkadian *mīšaram šakānum,* "to issue a reforming edict."[1]

15:26 *if you listen carefully.* Hebrew *šāmôa' tišma'* intensifies the command to listen, lit. "listening, you listen."

All the disease that I set in Egypt. Since Hebrew *kol-hammaḥălâ* is not used to describe the plagues, the intended reference is ambiguous. The word repeats in 23:25 as a reward for obedience, "I [Yahweh] will take sickness away from you [Israel]," where there is also no reference to the Egyptian plagues.

Commentary

The variety of literary styles in 15:22-26 has prompted debates over the history of composition and the identity of the author. As noted, interpreters debate the author of the itinerary notice in 15:22a assigning it to both the Non-P and the P author. Most interpreters recognize that 15:22a-25a is an etiological story about bitter water at Marah, which reaches a conclusion when the water is sweetened.[2] Noth attributes the story to the older pentateuchal tradition. Yet Aurelius notes the peculiar character of the etiology, since the naming of Marah is given already at the outset of the story (v. 23). For Aurelius this raises the further question of the relationship of Moses' intercession (v. 25) to the original etiology.[3]

The problems of authorship and composition multiply with the ending of the story in 15:25b-26. The distinct literary style of the section indicates either a different author or a new interpretation of the etiological story of Marah. Wellhausen interpreted v. 25b, "there he placed for them a statute and an ordinance, and there he tested them," as poetry providing the basis for his identification of an ancient tradition of lawgiving at Kadesh.[4] Lohfink has questioned

---

1. M. Weinfeld, *Deuteronomy and the Deuteronomic School* (Oxford: Clarendon, 1972), 152.

2. See Childs, *Exodus,* 266-68.

3. Aurelius, *Fürbitter Israels,* 154.

4. Wellhausen, *Prolegomena,* 343.

Wellhausen's reading by noting that v. 25b does not conform to poetic structure and that the insertion of poetic fragments in narrative is noted by some form of quotation, which is absent in this instance. L. Ruppert concluded that v. 25b represents Deuteronomistic teaching on the motif of "testing," noting parallels in Deut 8:2, 16; 13:4; Judg 2:22; and 3:1.[5] Lohfink cautioned that the expression "a statute and an ordinance" in the singular does not conform to Deuteronomistic usage, in which the terms are written in the plural (e.g., Deut 4:1; 5:1; 11:32; 12:1).[6] The singular construction, however, is also used in Josh 24:25, a Deuteronomistic passage where the terms once again refer to a general exhortation.

The relationship between Exod 15:25b and v. 26 presents still further problems of literary style, suggesting separate authors to some interpreters. E. Meyer judged the tradition of Yahweh as healer in v. 26 to be ancient. But subsequent interpreters have underscored the many parallels to Deuteronomistic tradition, including the intensive use of the call to observe, "If you listen carefully to the voice of Yahweh, your God" (Deut 11:13; 15:5; 28:1), and the command to do "what is straight in his eyes" (Deut 6:18; 12:25, 28). But, even in this case, Lohfink identified a post-P author in Exod 15:26, because of the possible blending of legal language from both Deuteronomy and the P legal corpus (e.g., the use of the word "to do" and the designation of God's laws as "commandments").[7]

The story of bitter water at Marah in Exod 15:22-26 clearly includes an older etiological tale that has been refashioned into a story about law and health. The indications of P influence in the composition, noted by Lohfink, are not distinctive enough to attribute the story to the P History, while the literary correspondence to Deuteronomy and the Deuteronomistic History is striking. Thus the first wilderness story after the conflict at the Red Sea will be interpreted as an episode in the Non-P History. The story is intended to relate law and health. A crisis over contaminated water (vv. 22-24) provides the occasion for Yahweh to instruct Moses in the art of purifying water. The miracle leads to a divine proposal of law, in which Yahweh promises the Israelites continued healing in exchange for obedience (vv. 25-26). The episode includes many themes that repeat throughout the wilderness journey, including crisis in the desert, complaint, law, and the role of Moses as mediator.

15:22-24 The Israelite people journey from the Red Sea to the wilderness of Shur. Hebrew *šûr* means "wall." Sarna identifies the location with Egyptian walls of fortification in the eastern Delta of the Nile.[8] Such historical and geographical specificity is difficult to confirm from the details of the story. The

---

5. L. Ruppert, "Das Motiv der Versuchung durch Gott in vordeuteronomischer Tradition," *VT* 22 (1972): 55.

6. Lohfink, *Theology of the Pentateuch*, 43, 55.

7. Ibid., 55-62.

8. Sarna, *Exodus*, 84.

The Presence of Yahweh in the Wilderness (15:22–40:38)

same location also plays a role in the story of Hagar, where it is associated with a spring of water and a theophany (Gen 16:7-14). M. Oblath concludes that all instances of Shur in the Hebrew Bible indicate a location east of Egypt (Gen 20:1; 25:18; 1 Sam 15:7; 27:8).[9] The wilderness of Shur is a three-day journey. The distance fulfills the original request of Moses to Pharaoh that the Israelites journey three days to worship God (Exod 5:3). The motif will return one other time in the Non-P History when the Israelites depart from the Mountain of Yahweh on a three-day journey (Num 10:33).

The story moves quickly and somewhat unevenly. First, the people find no water (v. 22). Then they progress to the location, Marah, where they are confronted with "bitter" or diseased water (v. 23). The location and the crisis of bitter water derive from the same word in Hebrew *(mārâ)*, indicating that the story is an etiology, the naming of a place after an event. The diseased water occasions a complaint against Moses, with the standard word *lûn,* "to murmur." The people want to know: "What will we drink?" The word *lûn* is used in a variety of the murmuring stories, requiring context for interpretation. The act of murmuring has negative meaning in Numbers, where it indicates rejection of Mosaic authority and the salvation of Yahweh. In view of this, Aurelius interprets the same negative meaning in Exod 15:22-26.[10] But the literary design of the murmuring stories argues against the negative interpretation of the word in 15:22-26, as many interpreters have concluded.[11] The murmuring stories are developed as a two-part sequence of events, which progress from an initial period of testing (chaps. 15–18) prior to the revelation of law (chaps. 19–34) to the rejection of divine leading after the revelation (Numbers 11–21).

15:25-26   The crisis of water and the complaint of the Israelite people require that Moses mediate. He cries out *(ṣāʿaq)* to Yahweh. The motif occurred previously in the story of the exodus. Initially the Israelites cried out in general (2:23), then to Pharaoh (5:15), and finally to Yahweh (14:10). The Egyptians also cried out during the death of their firstborn (11:6; 12:30). All of these instances are direct cries from a situation of distress.[12] As Aurelius has noted, Moses is also under distress in this story, since the complaint of the people is directed against him.[13] But the crying out of Moses also has the function of intercession. Only once in the story of the exodus did Moses intercede and it was for Pharaoh, not the Israelites. Moses cried out to Yahweh for Pharaoh during the

9. Oblath, *Exodus Itinerary Sites,* 113-14.

10. Aurelius, *Fürbitter Israels,* 154-55.

11. See, e.g., Coats, *Rebellion in the Wilderness,* 51; Childs, *Exodus,* 268; Lohfink, *Theology of the Pentateuch,* 46.

12. R. N. Boyce, *The Cry to God in the Old Testament* (SBLDS 103; Atlanta: Scholars Press, 1988).

13. Aurelius, *Fürbitter Israels,* 155.

plague of frogs (8:12). The crisis of bitter water is the first time that Moses intercedes for the Israelites (see the other occurrences of Moses "crying out" to Yahweh in 17:4; and Num 12:13). The story of intercession contrasts to 14:11-15, where the complaint of the Israelite people about their present condition prompted a direct reassurance from Moses without intercession, which led to a negative response from Yahweh: "Why do you cry out to me?" In 15:22-26 Yahweh responds to the intercession of Moses in three ways. First, Yahweh instructs Moses in the art of water purification. Second, Yahweh proposes law to the Israelites. Third, God reveals to Moses the power of healing in an additional self-revelation: "I am Yahweh, your healer."

Yahweh instructs Moses in the art of purifying water with wood. The event is miraculous. Either Moses or Yahweh throws the wood into the water and it instantly becomes sweet. The closest parallel is Elisha decontaminating water with salt (2 Kgs 2:19-22). The purification of water is the first event in the wilderness after the crossing of the Red Sea. The context is important; it invites comparison to the cycle of the plagues, in which Yahweh contaminated water and disrupted nature in the land of Egypt. The purification of water at Marah is a reversal of the plagues. It indicates a change in theme from Yahweh's war with Pharaoh to the divine guidance of the Israelite people. The comparison is reinforced in v. 26, when the reference to diseases is interpreted as a contrast to the plagues. The word "disease," *maḥălâ,* however, is not used to describe the plagues in any other text.

The point of emphasis in the story, however, is not the water but law. Past interpreters have concluded that the purification of water at Marah and the revelation of law do not relate well. Childs states: "Verse 25b introduces a subject which has no apparent connection with the preceding story of water except that it had the same geographical setting."[14] But the two themes, health and law, are more related than Childs suggests. The theme of law is indicated already in v. 25a, when Yahweh responds to the cry of Moses by "teaching" *(yārâ)* him the art of purifying water. The verb is related to the noun "Torah" *(tôrâ),* meaning "instruction." It will appear again in the next story (16:4-5). The motif reaches a climax on the mountain of God when Yahweh gives Moses the tablets of stone containing the law (24:12). The divine instruction to Moses about purifying water relates the themes of law and health. It fulfills a divine promise to Moses from his commission that Yahweh would teach Moses (4:12, 15). The purification of diseased water is the occasion for Yahweh's first presentation of law to the Israelites (15:25-26).

The revelation of law is introduced in v. 25 with the statement: "Yahweh placed there a statute and an ordinance for them." Elaboration follows in v. 26 in

---

14. Childs, *Exodus,* 269.

the form of a casuistic law, meaning it is conditional upon obedience ("if, then," see the introduction, "Literature: Individual Genres: Law Codes"). The language of the law is mixed. It begins in the third person in reference to God: "If you [the Israelites] listen . . . to the *voice of Yahweh* . . . and pay attention to *his commands.*" And it concludes in the first person: "[Then] *I will not bring* on you any of the disease *I brought* on the Egyptians." The shift in person is unusual, raising the question of whether Moses or Yahweh is the speaker. The conclusion of the speech, however, with the divine self-revelation, "I am Yahweh your physician," leaves no doubt that Yahweh is the one addressing the people. The blurring of the speakers between Moses (v. 25) and Yahweh (v. 26) certainly accentuates Mosaic authority, a central theme throughout the wilderness journey.

An even more pressing problem in the speech of 15:25-26 is that no specific law is presented. Childs writes: "The writer does not disclose what he means by 'a statute and an ordinance.'"[15] Sarna suggests that the actual law has fallen out of the text.[16] But the absence of a specific law is the key to interpretation. The speech is a proposal for law in general, not the legislation of a particular law. God proposes that law be the means by which the Israelites live with Yahweh in the wilderness. The proposal of law is presented to the Israelite people with emphatic language, *'im-šāmôaʿ tišmaʿ*, "If you listen carefully." The emphasis in the proposal of law is not on any specific legislation, but on the promise of reward, namely that obedience to the law will generate health among the Israelite people. The interweaving of law and health relates the proposal of covenant in vv. 25-26 to the miracle of purifying diseased water in vv. 22-24. A similar proposal of law will reappear in 19:1-8, as an introduction to the establishment of covenant in chaps. 19–24. As in 15:25-26, the emphasis in 19:1-8 will also be on the promise of reward for obedience to law (see the commentary on 19:1-8), and not on any specific laws themselves.

A revelation of the divine name, "I am Yahweh, your healer," provides motivation for the Israelites to accept the proposal of law, further relating law and health. The self-introduction, "I am Yahweh," is a form of theophany already encountered in the P version of the commission of Moses (see 6:2-13). The Non-P author employs the self-introduction to reveal that Yahweh is a physician. The particular content of this self-revelation does not occur again in the Hebrew Bible. The root word *rāpāʾ*, "to heal," may be related to the legendary Rephaim in the Hebrew Bible (e.g., Deut 2:11, 20).[17] J. C. de Moor has probed the history of religions background, noting the god Rapiʾu in the Ugaritic literature, who is a

15. Ibid.

16. Sarna, *Exodus,* 85.

17. See M. Dietrich, O. Loretz, and J. Sanmartín, "Die ugaritischen Totengeister *RPU(M)* und die biblische Rephaim," *UF* 8 (1976): 45-52.

healing god.[18] The prophet Hosea provides the most helpful background within the Hebrew Bible for interpreting the Non-P History. He proclaims that Yahweh is able to heal the diseases of the Israelites (Hos 7:1), including their disloyalty (14:4). But the remedial power of God requires recognition and acknowledgment by the Israelites (6:1; 11:3). The demand for recognition is often implied in the formula of divine self-introduction (12:9; 13:4).

The healing power of God provides a paradigm for the wilderness. It frames the wilderness journey in the Non-P History.[19] The promise of healing in the first wilderness story (Exod 15:22-26) is fulfilled in the last (Num 21:4-9), the story of Nehushtan — the copper serpent. The story of Nehushtan is the final complaint of the Israelites before they enter the plains of Moab. The healing power of Yahweh is fulfilled when Yahweh commands Moses to construct the copper serpent to cure the Israelites who were bitten by snakes as a result of their murmuring. But the medicinal power of Yahweh in Exod 15:26 is broader than the curative role of Nehushtan. Yahweh promises that law itself will heal the Israelites. Lohfink has demonstrated that Deuteronomy 28 provides background for the broader perspective of law and health. It states that obedience to the law will create social health, human fertility, and productive crops.[20] The wisdom tradition expands the relationship between law and health by reflecting upon the curative role of water. Psalm 1:2-3 provides an example. It promises that those following Torah will be healthy, like trees planted by streams of fresh water (see also Ezek 47:1-12). The Non-P historian shares the perspective of sages in Psalm 1 as well as Deuteronomy that obedience to law and human health are inseparable.

The literary context of Exod 15:22-26 in the Non-P History further aids its interpretation. I have noted that the divine proposal in 15:26 repeats in 19:5, with a change of theme from a proposal of law to a proposal of covenant. Yahweh states in 19:5: "If you obey me fully and keep my covenant." But, the proposal of the covenant is not ratified until 24:3-8, when Moses presents the law of the covenant to the people, requiring their acceptance. The Covenant Ceremony in 24:3-8 closes the period of divine proposal. Thus the period between the initial proposal of law (15:22-26) and the ratification of covenant (24:3-8), when Moses proclaims the words of Yahweh and the people accept them as law, is a time of courtship in the Non-P History. This period, 15:22–24:8, is characterized by testing. Exodus 15:25 states that the statutes and the or-

---

18. J. C. de Moor, "Rapi'uma-Rephaim," *ZAW* 88 (1976): 323-45. For a more broadly based discussion of medicine and health in the ancient Near East see J. Hempel, "Ich bin der Herr, dein Arzt," *TL* 11 (1957): 809-18.

19. Dozeman, "Numbers," 163-64.

20. Lohfink, *Theology of the Pentateuch*, 71-80.

dinances are a test *(nāsâ)*. The presence of this motif in 15:22-26 has puzzled interpreters because there is no specific test in the story.

The motif of testing is central to the Non-P History (Gen 22:1; Exod 15:25; 16:4; 17:2, 7; 20:20; Num 14:22). The book of Deuteronomy (Deut 6:16; 8:2, 16; 13:4)[21] provides the starting point for interpreting the Non-P History. Deuteronomy underscores the close relationship between divine testing and the law. Deuteronomy 13:1-16 illustrates that the law is more reliable than a prophet. It states that any prophetic oracle, contrary to the law, is a divine test *(nāsâ)* of the people "to know whether [they] love Yahweh." Thus the motif of testing requires that the people follow the divine commandments over a prophetic teaching to the contrary. Deuteronomy 6:16-17 further reinforces the relationship of testing and law, emphasizing that there is no place for testing God, once law is revealed.[22] Moses states: "Do not put Yahweh your God to the test, as you tested him at Massah." In place of such testing, he urges the people: "You must diligently keep the commands of Yahweh your God." The human testing of God is always a negative act of rebellion in Deuteronomy, because the book presupposes the revelation of law.

The Non-P History also interprets the motif of testing in relationship to law, but, unlike Deuteronomy, it develops the motif in two different time periods, separated by the revelation of law at the mountain of God (Exodus 19–34). The emphasis in the Non-P History, moreover, is the role of testing in the prelaw period of ancient Israelite history (Gen 22:1; Exod 15:25; 16:4; 17:2, 7; 20:20). There is only one occurrence of the motif after the revelation of law in the story of spies (Num 14:22).[23]

The motif of testing first appears in the Akedah (Genesis 22), when God tests Abraham in the command to sacrifice Isaac (Gen 22:1). The command is implied, not stated; it unfolds in the telling of the story. The implied command

21. Deuteronomy 4:34 and 28:56 add little to the study of the motif. The motif of testing is also preserved in the ancient poem "The Blessing of Moses" in Deuteronomy 33. Verse 8 recounts the divine testing of Levi at Massah, which leads to the ordination of the Levites. For interpretation see F. M. Cross and D. N. Freedman, "The Blessing of Moses," *JBL* 67 (1948): 191-210; slightly revised in idem, "The Blessing of Moses," in *Studies in Ancient Yahwistic Poetry,* 97-122. The poem does not reflect the theology of testing in the book of Deuteronomy. Schmid *(Sogenannte Jahwist,* 64-69) also notes the continuation of the motif of testing in Judges 2–3, esp. Judg 2:22; 3:1, 4.

22. The law must be followed even if a new prophecy contradicts the law. Deuteronomy 13:2-7 states that a prophet who contradicts Deuteronomic law by advocating another god is merely a divine test to know whether the people actually love Yahweh.

23. The Non-P version of the spy story in Numbers 13–14 includes: Num 13:17b-20, 22-24, part of 26, 27-30; 14:1b, 3-4, part of 6, 8-10a, 11-25, and 39-45. The P interpretation of the spy story includes: Num 13:1-3, 17a, 21, 25, part of 26, 32-33; 14:1a, 2, 5, part of 6, 7, 10b, 26-38; and the legislation in 15:1-41. See Dozeman, "Numbers," 120-28.

is meant to test the allegiance of Abraham by pitting his "love" for Isaac (22:2) over against his "fear" of God (22:12), which requires obeying or heeding (*šāmaʿ*) the voice (*qôl*) of God. The phrase "to heed the voice of God" infuses the story with a legal background. The phrase repeats in the wilderness journey (Exod 15:26) and in the revelation of law on the divine mountain (19:5; 23:22). It appears again during the story of the spies (Num 14:22) and in Deuteronomy (e.g., Deut 15:5; 28:1), where it is always associated with law.

The motif of testing is prominent in the first part of the wilderness journey (chaps. 15–18). It appears not less than four times in three stories (15:25; 16:4; 17:2, 7). God introduces the theme of testing with the proposal of law (15:25). The proposal of law leads directly into the story of manna in the Non-P History, when God actually tests the Israelites with a specific command associated with the collection of manna (16:4). The people, in turn, test God at Rephidim, questioning whether Yahweh is present with them (17:2, 7). The motif reappears during the revelation of the Decalogue, when the people hear, directly, the divine voice (*qôl*) as law, which Moses explains is a test (20:20) to see if they will "fear" God, recalling the quality of Abraham at the close of the Akedah. The motif occurs one final time in the story of the spies (Num 14:22). This story occurs after the revelation of law in the second phrase of the wilderness journey (Numbers 11–21). The people's testing of God is now judged to be rebellion, since it indicates that "they have not heeded (*šāmaʿ*) the voice (*qôl*) of God."

The distribution of the motif of testing indicates thematic development in the Non-P History. Abraham is idealized as the ancestor who passes the test of God by fearing God and by heeding the voice of God (Genesis 22). The emphasis of the Non-P author is on the initial phase of the wilderness journey from the Red Sea to the mountain of God, which is characterized as a period of courtship before the revelation of law. Exodus 15:22-26 inaugurates the period of courtship, when Yahweh proposes the relationship of law and health. The proposal introduces the theme of the divine testing of the Israelites, thus signaling the beginning of the period of courtship. The first test is the instruction for collecting manna (chap. 16), since it contains a specific command (16:4), which unfolds in the plot of the narrative. In this respect the story of manna recalls the Akedah of Abraham. But, unlike Abraham, who obeys the voice of God, the Israelite people fail the test of manna. In the pre-law period of courtship, however, failure is not rebellion and there is no divine punishment (16:27-31). The peoples' testing of the presence of God in 17:1-7 is also not an act of rebellion, since this story also precedes the revelation of the divine law in the midst of the people. The merging of law and testing is made explicit in the revelation of the Decalogue (20:1-17). Moses instructs the people that the law is the test, which will instill fear in them and thus prompt their obedience to God (20:20).

373

The period of testing, courtship, and failure without consequence stops after the ratification of the covenant (24:3-8). The story of the golden calf (chap. 32) marks the change, even though it does not contain the motif of testing. The final occurrence of testing in the Non-P History is in the story of spies (Num 14:22), which affirms the teaching of Deuteronomy. Numbers 14 underscores that, once law is revealed, human testing of God is an act of rebellion, which leads to the covenant curses of Deut 28:15-68.

DIVINE FOOD AND SABBATH (15:27–16:36)

^{15:27} *And they approached toward Elim. And there were there twelve springs of water and seventy date-palm trees. And they camped there by the water.*

^{16:1} **And they went out from Elim. And the entire congregation of the Israelites approached the wilderness of Sin, which is between Elim and Sinai, on the fifteenth day of the second month of their going out of the land of Egypt.** ² **And the entire congregation of the Israelites complained against Moses and against Aaron in the wilderness.** ³ **And the Israelites said to them, "Would that he gave our death by the hand of Yahweh in the land of Egypt, when we sat by the pot for boiling meat and when we ate bread to fullness. For you brought us out to this wilderness to kill this entire assembly by hunger."**

⁴ *And Yahweh said to Moses, "See, I am raining down for you bread from heaven. And the people will go out and they will collect a day's amount in its day, so that I may test them, whether they walk in my law or not.* ⁵ *And on the sixth day they will prepare what they bring in, and it will be double what they collect day by day."*

⁶ **And Moses and Aaron said to all the Israelites, "Evening, you will know that Yahweh brought you out from the land of Egypt.** ⁷ *And, morning, you will see the Glory of Yahweh in his hearing your complaining against Yahweh — for who are we that you complain against us?"* ⁸ **And Moses said, "When Yahweh gives you in the evening meat to eat and bread in the morning to fullness, when Yahweh hears your complaining, which you complain against him, what are we? Not against us do you complain, but against Yahweh."**

⁹ *And Moses said to Aaron, "Say to all the congregation of the Israelites, 'Draw near before Yahweh, for he has heard your complaining.'"*

¹⁰ **And when Aaron spoke to the entire congregation of the Israelites, they turned to the wilderness. And, indeed, the Glory of Yahweh appeared in a cloud.**

¹¹ **And Yahweh spoke to Moses, saying,** ¹² **"I heard the complaint of the Israelites. Say to them, saying, 'Between the evenings you will eat meat and at morning you will be full with bread. And you will know that I am Yahweh your God.'"**

¹³*And in the evening quail came up and covered the camp;* and in the morning a layer of dew was around the camp. ¹⁴*The layer of dew came up:* Indeed, on the face of the wilderness a fine flakey substance, fine like frost on the earth.

¹⁵*And the Israelites saw and they said each to his brother, "What is that?"* for they did not know what that was.

And Moses said to them, *"It is the bread that Yahweh has given you to eat.* ¹⁶*This is the word that Yahweh commanded, 'Gather from it each to the number eating it, an omer per head. You will take according to the number of persons in each tent.'"*

¹⁷*And the Israelites did so. And they gathered, some more and some less.* ¹⁸*And they measured in the omer. But those gathering more had no surplus, and those gathering less did not lack. They gathered each according to the number eating it.*

¹⁹*And Moses said to them, "Let no one leave any of it until morning."*

²⁰*But they did not listen to Moses. And men left some of it until morning. And it bred worms and it became foul. And Moses was angry with them.*

²¹*And they gathered it morning by morning, each according to the number eating it.* But when the sun grew hot, it melted. ²²*And on the sixth day they gathered double the bread, two omers for the one. When each leader of the congregation approached and reported to Moses,* ²³*he said, "This is what Yahweh said, 'Tomorrow is a Sabbath rest, a holy Sabbath to Yahweh. Bake whatever you bake, and boil whatever you boil. Save for yourselves all the remainder for service until morning.'"*

²⁴*And they saved it until morning as Moses commanded. And it did not grow foul and there were no worms in it.*

²⁵*And Moses said, "Eat it today, for today is a Sabbath to Yahweh. Today you will not find it in the field.* ²⁶*Six days you will gather it. But on the seventh day, the Sabbath, it will not be in it."*

²⁷*On the seventh day some of the people went out to gather, but they did not find.* ²⁸And Yahweh said to Moses, *"How long do you refuse to observe my commandments and my laws?* ²⁹*See! For Yahweh gave you the Sabbath, therefore he is giving you on the sixth day bread for two days. Each of you must remain where you are. Each of you must not go out from his place on the seventh day."*

³⁰*And the people rested on the seventh day.*

³¹*And the Israelites called its name manna. It was like a coriander seed, white, and its taste like a wafer in honey.* ³²*And Moses said, "This is the word that Yahweh commanded, 'Fill an omer of it for service throughout your generations, so that they see the bread with which I fed you in the wilderness, when I brought you out of the land of Egypt.'"*

³³*And Moses said to Aaron, "Take one jar and place there the full omer*

of manna, and set it before Yahweh for service throughout your generations." [34] *As Yahweh commanded Moses, Aaron set it before the testimony for service.*

[35] *So the Israelites ate the manna forty years until their entering the habitable land.* **They ate the manna** *until their entering the border of the land of Canaan.*

[36] *And the omer, it is the tenth of the ephah.*

Notes

15:27 *toward Elim.* The directional ending of the MT *'êlimāh* is absent from the Sam, *'ylym.* The LXX translates, *eis Ailim.*

date-palm trees. Hebrew *tĕmārîm* is translated as both "date" and "palm trees." The LXX reads, *stelechē phoinikōn,* "trunks of date palms."

16:3 *would that he gave our death by the hand of Yahweh.* Hebrew *mî-yittēn mûtēnû* expresses a wish by exclamation in the form of an interrogative (GKC §151.a.1; *IBHS* §40.2.2d). The LXX translates, *ophelon apethanomen,* expressing a contrary-to-fact wish, "would that we died."

16:4 *a day's amount in its day.* Hebrew *dĕbar-yôm bĕyômô* is lit. "the thing of a day on his day." The phrase repeats the command of the taskmasters in 5:13: "Complete your work, a day's work in its day, as when there was straw." The LXX translates the phrase, *to tēs hēmeras eis hēmeran.*

so that I may test them, whether they walk in my law or not. The MT writes the phrase in the singular, *'ănassennû,* "so that I may test him," *hăyelik,* "whether he walks." The translation follows the LXX, *hopōs peirasō autous,* "so that I might test them," *ei poreusontai,* "if they walk."

my law. The LXX translates Hebrew *tôrâ* as *nomos.*

16:5 The Hebrew includes three clauses beginning with the conjunction, *wĕ,* "and": "And on the sixth day. And they will prepare. . . . And it will be double. . . ." The relationship of the three clauses is unclear, raising the question of whether the doubling occurred in the collecting or in the preparation. The LXX continues the confusion: *kai estai tē hēmera tē hektē kai hetoimasousin ho ean eisenenkōsin, kai estai diploun.*

16:8 *when Yahweh hears your complaining, which you complain against him.* The LXX, *dia tō eisakousai ton gongysmon hymōn epi tō theō,* lacks the explicit subject "Yahweh."

16:12 *between the evenings.* The LXX renders Hebrew *bên hā'arbayim* as *hesperan.*

16:14 *on the face of the wilderness a thin flakey substance, thin like frost on the earth.* The Hebrew is difficult. The dew is described with two parallel lines in the structure AB::B'A':

> *'al-pĕnê hammidbār daq mĕḥuspās*
> *daq kakkĕpōr 'al-hā'āreṣ*

A and A' designate the location of the dew: "on the face of the wilderness" (*'al-pĕnê hammidbār*) and "on the earth" (*'al-hā'āreṣ*). B and B' describe the dew by repeating the word *daq*, "thin, scarce, fine," from the root *dqq*. The phrase *daq kakkĕpōr* is an image of frost, "thin or fine like frost *(kĕpōr)*" (see also Job 38:29; Ps 147:16). The phrase *daq mĕḥuspās* is uncertain in meaning, appearing only in this verse in the Hebrew Bible. Cassuto derives Hebrew *mĕḥuspās* from the Ugaritic verb *ḥsp*, "uncover, reveal";[1] GKC §55k translates "peeled off, like scales," from *ḥāsap*, hence the translation "flakey"; Propp follows 1QExod, reading *dq kḥsps*, "fine as rime," thus favoring an image of frost.[2] The LXX includes the description of the dew from 16:31 and provides more of a paraphrase than a translation, *epi prosōpon tēs erēmou lepton hōsei korion leukon hōsei pagos epi tēs gēs*, "on the face of the desert thin like coriander and white like frost on the earth."

16:15 *What is that? for they did not know what that was.* The question in Hebrew, *mān hû'*, employs a primitive form of the interrogative, "what," to provide an etiology for the traditional name "manna." The more common interrogative appears in the concluding clause, "for they did not know what *(mah)* that *(hû')* was."

16:16 *each to the number eating it.* Hebrew *'îš lĕpî 'oklô*, translates more lit. "each to the mouth eating it." The phrase is also used to describe the consumption of the Passover in 12:4.

You will take according to the number of persons in each tent. Wevers notes that the image in the MT is of one person collecting for the entire tent, *'îš la'ăšer bĕ'oholô tiqqāḥû*, "each for those who are in his tent." The LXX changes the command so that all persons in one tent collect together, *hekastos syn tois syskēniois hymōn*, "each of you with your tentmates."[3]

16:22 *double the bread.* The LXX has *ta deonta dipla*, "double what was required."

16:23 *for service until morning.* Hebrew *lĕmišmeret*, "for service," suggests cultic obligations in the preservation of manna through the night (see 16:32). The LXX *eis apothēkēn*, "in storage," loses the cultic meaning of the Hebrew.

16:29 *each of you must remain where you are.* Hebrew *šĕbû 'îš taḥtāyw* translates lit. "sit each one under himself." The LXX interprets the Hebrew as *kathēsesthe hekastos eis tous oikous hymōn*, "remain each of you in your houses."

16:33 *take one jar.* Hebrew *ṣinṣenet* is a hapax legomenon. The LXX also interprets the word as a jar, translating *stamnon*.

16:34 *the testimony.* Hebrew *hā'ēdūt* could also be translated "covenant." It is related to the description of the people as a "congregation" in v. 2, *kol-'ădat bĕnê-yiśrā'ēl*.

16:35 *the land of Canaan.* The LXX departs from the MT by designating the land as Phoenicia, *Phoinikēs*, not Canaan.

16:36 *the ephah.* The LXX changes "ephah" to "three measures" *(tōn triōn metrōn)*. Wevers notes that the "three measures" was used in determining the capacity of oil.[4]

---

1. Cassuto, *Exodus*, 195.
2. Propp, *Exodus 1–18*, 586.
3. Wevers, *Notes*, 251.
4. Ibid., 262.

Commentary

The story of manna in the wilderness separates into the following five sections: (1) the setting (15:27–16:3), (2) the instruction (16:4-12), (3) the event (16:13-21), (4) the Sabbath (16:22-30), and (5) the conclusion (16:31-36). Interpreters have long recognized tensions in the present form of the story that indicate a history of composition. The divine instruction concerning manna repeats in vv. 4-5 and 9-12. The instruction about the Sabbath, as well as the events surrounding it, also repeats in vv. 22-26 and 27-30. The instruction to gather the manna is inconsistent, as is the failure of the Israelites to fulfill the instructions. Do they fail because they hoard manna (v. 20)? Or do they fail because they took the manna for granted (vv. 27-30)? The repetition of the story of manna and quails in Exodus 16 and Numbers 11 adds an additional problem concerning the tradition-historical development of the story of manna and its history of composition. Finally, the relationship of manna and quail is also not clear (see also Numbers 11).

The diagram in figure 26 on page 379 sets out recent trends in the identification of the authors in Exodus 16.[5] Noth illustrates a prominent solution among contemporary interpreters for identifying the authors of Exodus 16. He judged the story of manna in Exodus to be a composition by the P author. He also recognized a history of composition in chap. 16 from the repetitions noted above. But for him the P author has so reworked chap. 16 (15:27; 16:1-3, 6-26, and most likely the conclusion in vv. 31-36) that the Non-P History can no longer be recovered, since only fragments remain. The portions of the Non-P History still evident in the story include the divine announcement that manna would rain from heaven (vv. 4-5) and the statement about the Sabbath (vv. 29-30). Since the Non-P History was an early composition for Noth that preceded the focus on law in Deuteronomy, he judged the references to law in vv. 27-28 to be Deuteronomistic additions to the story. Coats refined the study of Noth, assigning 16:31-32 and 35a to the Non–P J source, while also attributing the motif of testing (v. 4bb) to a Deuteronomistic redactor.

Childs represents the attempt to recover a more complete form of the Non-P History. He agrees with Noth that the divine announcement in vv. 4-5 is from the Non-P author. But he also attributes the appearance of manna and the etiology of its name (vv. 13b-15) to the Non-P History, as well as the additional description that the manna melted with the rising of the sun (v. 21b). The Non-P version of the story is also evident in the conclusion, according to Childs, in

---

5. For a more detailed summary of the history of interpretation of Exodus 16 see Childs, *Exodus*, 274-83; P. Maiberger, *Das Manna* (Ägypten und Altes Testament 6; Wiesbaden: Harrassowitz, 1986), 33-86; Van Seters, *Life of Moses*, 181-91. For the data in fig. 26 see Noth, *Exodus*, 128-37; Coats, *Rebellion in the Wilderness*, 83-127; Childs, *Exodus*, 274-92; Van Seters, *Life of Moses*, 181-91; Propp, *Exodus 1–18*, 588-601.

Figure 26

	Setting 15:27–16:3	Instruction 16:4-12	Event 16:13-21	Sabbath 16:22-30	Conclusion 16:31-36
Noth		J: 4-5		J: 29-30	
	P: 15:27; 16:1-3	P: 6-12 (8?)	P: 13-21	P: 22-26	
				Dtr: 27?-28	
Coats		J: 4aba, 5		J: 29-30	J: 31-32, 35b
	P: 1-3	P: 6-12	P: 13-21	P: 22-26	P: 33-35a
Childs	J: ?	J: 4-5	J: 13b-15, 21b	J: 27-30	J: 31, 35a
	P: 1-3	P: 6-12	P: 13a, 16-21a	P: 22-26	P: 32-35a
		Dtr: 4b?		Dtr: 28?	gloss: 36
Van Seters	J: 15:27; 16:1a, 2-3*	J: 4-7	J: 13b-15	J: 27-30	J: 31, 35a
Propp		J/E: 4-5	J/E: 14-15a, 21b	J/E: 28-30	
	P: 16:2	P: 6-12	P: 13, 15b-21a	P: 22-27	P: 31-35
	R: 15:27; 16:1				P/R: 36?
Dozeman	N-P: 15:27	N-P: 4-5	N-P: 13b-15, 21b	N-P: 27-30	N-P: 31, 35a
	P: 1-3	P: 6-12	P: 13a, 16-21a	P: 22-26	P: 32-34, 35b

the description of manna (v. 31) and in the note that the people ate manna for forty years (v. 35a). Van Seters and Propp represent variations on the approach of Childs. Both agree that more than fragments of the Non-P version of the story can be identified in chap. 16. Propp identifies nearly the same Non-P narrative as Childs, while Van Seters expands the Non-P History to include the murmuring of the Israelite people (16:1a, 2-3*).

I also follow the lead of the interpreters who have departed from the position of Noth. My presupposition is that the Non-P and P Histories can be identified in each of the five sections of the story of manna. The past identification of a separate Deuteronomistic redaction to account for the motif of testing (v. 4b) and law (vv. 27-28) is necessary only if the Non-P History is dated early in the monarchical period, which is not my position. The story of manna in chap. 16, therefore, will be separated between the Non-P and P Histories. The Non-P History is composed of the following material: 15:27; 16:4-5, 13b-15, 21b, 27-31, 35a. And the P History includes: 16:1-3, 6-13a, 16-21a, 22-26, 32-34, 35b; as well as the itinerary notice in 17:1a. The most significant departure in the commentary from past interpretations is the prominent role of geography in the interpretation of the story. The lush oasis of Elim will be interpreted as the setting

Figure 27

Elim Version: Non-P History	Wilderness of Sin Version: P History
Setting: 15:27	Setting: 16:1-3
Instruction: 16:4-5	Instruction: 16:6-12
Miracle: 16:13b-15, 21b	Miracle: 16:13a, 16-20, 21a
Sabbath: 16:27-30	Sabbath: 16:22-26
Conclusion: 16:31, 35a	Conclusion: 16:32-34, 35b-36

for the Non-P History as compared to the arid wilderness of Sin in the P History. The result is the two versions of the story of manna set out in figure 27 above.

15:27–16:3 Setting. There is literary tension in the present form of the text resulting from the itinerary sequence surrounding Elim, the wilderness of Sin, and Rephidim. The chart in figure 28 on page 381 illustrates that the setting of the wilderness of Sin (16:1b and 17:1a) has been inserted between the travel sequence of Elim (15:27) and Rephidim (17:1b). In the commentary I will clarify that the insertion of the wilderness of Sin is the result of the P author, while the setting of Elim is a story in the Non-P History.

The Non-P History places the Israelites at Elim (15:27). The location is obscure, limited to this story and the travel list of Numbers 33, where it occurs before the Red Sea, not after it (Num 33:9).[6] Elim is a lush oasis containing twelve springs of fresh water and seventy palm trees. Numbers 33 also underscores the fertile character of the oasis with the same description. The numbers may be symbolic, twelve representing the tribes and seventy the clans (see the commentary on 1:1-5), meaning there is water and food for all. B. P. Robinson notes the relationship between Elim and the proposal of law in 15:22-26: "The Elim story seems to represent, in respect of the twelve springs, the gift of life that awaits the people should they pass the divine test and obey the Torah."[7] The Israelites face no crises at Elim. The springs supply fresh water, not the diseased water at Marah. And the seventy palm trees provide abundant food, enough for each clan.

The setting of Elim indicates that the miracle of manna in the Non-P History is not at a time of distress. It is for this reason that the Non-P version of the story lacks the motif of murmuring. There is no reason for complaint at Elim. It represents an interlude in the wilderness journey, a moment of security when the Israelites are satisfied. The story of manna in the Non-P History parallels

---

6. Dozeman, "Numbers," 251-53.

7. B. P. Robinson, "Symbolism in Exod. 15:22-27 (Marah and Elim)," *RB* 94 (1987): 385.

Figure 28

15:27   <u>They</u> came to Elim, *there were twelve springs of water, and seventy date-palm trees.* <u>They</u> camped there by the water.

16:1a   **<u>They</u> set out from Elim.**

16:2b   **<u>The whole congregation of Israel</u> came to the wilderness of Sin, between Elim and Sinai, on month 2, day 15, year 1 of the exodus.**

17:1a   **<u>And the entire congregation of the Israelites</u> set out from the wilderness of Sin *by stages according to the mouth of Yahweh.***

17:1b   And <u>they</u> camped at Rephidim. *But there was no water for the people to drink.*

---

aspects of the account of Eden (Genesis 2–3). Both Elim and Eden are gardens, set apart from their surrounding landscape. Each garden contains abundant food. And in each story the profusion of food occasions a divine law to restrict human diet in some way, introducing limitation in the midst of plenty (Gen 2:15-17; Exod 16:4-5).

The P History changes the setting from Elim to the wilderness of Sin, which is specifically located between Elim and Sinai. The P author also dates the story to month 2, day 15 (16:1), one month after the exodus from Egypt (12:1-2, 17-18). The location, Sin, is confined to the story of manna and to the travel list in Numbers 33, where it is the first stopping point after the Red Sea (Num 33:11). The change of setting is central to the interpretation of manna in the P History. The wilderness of Sin is anything but a lush oasis. It is a barren place of deprivation, prompting the Israelites to complain *(lûn)* to Moses about the absence of food (16:2-3). The setting prompts the Israelites to idealize their rations in Egypt, which included meat ("sitting by pots of meat") and bread *(lehem)*. The complaint signals the expansion of the story to include meat, raising questions about the relationship of chap. 16 and Numbers 11. But more importantly the change in setting shifts the dynamics of the story in the P History. Manna and quail are divine rations that rescue the Israelites from starvation, in contrast to the Non-P version, in which manna was food from heaven in a situation already characterized by abundance.

16:4-12 Instruction. The Non-P History consists of the divine instruction to Moses that bread from heaven will test the Israelites (16:4-5). The P History is instruction by Moses and Aaron to the Israelites in response to their complaint (16:6-12).

Yahweh initiates the action in the Non-P History. The divine announcement to Moses is unsolicited (vv. 4-5). Yahweh states that bread will rain down from heaven. The last thing Yahweh rained down from heaven was hailstones, which destroyed the land of Egypt (9:23). The change in setting signals a transition in the character of Yahweh from the warrior in the land of Egypt to the shepherd in the wilderness, who feeds his people.

The "bread from heaven" is difficult to interpret. Scholars have sought any number of naturalistic interpretations identifying the food with desert shrubs or insects.[8] But the description in 16:14, 31, and in Num 11:7-9 emphasizes the supernatural character of the food. The bread does not grow from the earth, but descends from the air (Exod 16:14; Num 11:9). Once on the ground it appears as snow *(měḥuspās)* in the desert (Exod 16:14). Hebrew *měḥuspās* could be a reference to texture, meaning that the heavenly bread crystallized like frost after the dew melted away. But snow in the desert may also be the author's way of underscoring the abnormal character of heavenly bread, defying the natural environment, until it melts from the heat of the sun (16:21b). The closest related words, Ethiopic *ḫśp* and Arabic *ḫśf,* refer to snow. More detailed descriptions also emphasize the supernatural character of the food. The texture of the bread is coriander seed (16:31; Num 11:7). It is white (Exod 16:31) and bdellium (Num 11:7) in color. And it tastes like a honey cake (Exod 16:31) and an oil cake (Num 11:8). Bdellium associates the bread with the mythical land of Havilah in Gen 2:12, where there also exist good gold and onyx stones. Honey indicates its heavenly origin. The Canaanite mythology celebrates the resurrection of the god Baal with the raining down of oil and honey (*CTA* 6.iii.6-7, 12-13). Even the naming of the food, "manna," translated, "What is it?" underscores its otherworldly quality. The Israelites are unable to identify it as food.

Other biblical texts further reinforce the miraculous character of the food. Deuteronomy 8:3 also underscores that manna was unknown to humans before this event. Psalm 78:24 describes manna as the "bread of angels." The Gospel of John takes the tradition even further, equating the bread from heaven with God and promising that one meal will satisfy hunger permanently (John 6:22-40). The portrait of the Israelites eating the food of the gods in the wilderness is reminiscent of the Hyperboreans and the Ethiopians in Herodotus's *Histories,* both of whom also live in liminal lands and eat divine food.[9]

But the bread of heaven is not simply a banquet. Yahweh states that the bread will provide a test to determine whether the Israelites will follow divine law. The people are required to glean the heavenly food daily. But on the sixth day they must glean a double portion, since bread will not fall from heaven on the Sabbath. The test is for the Israelites to gather a double portion of food even

---

8. See the summary by Jacob, *Exodus,* 467-75.
9. Herodotus, *Histories* 3.17-26, 97; 4.13.

though they live in the midst of abundance in Elim. The test requires that the people ration food on the Sabbath, even though their circumstance does not require it. Rationing food in the midst of abundance requires that the Israelite people not take the food for granted, but recognize it as a gift from God. Thus the law of the Sabbath in the Non-P History is a prohibition that requires a limitation in the midst of abundance. The lush setting of Elim, with its seventy palm trees, raises the question of whether the limitation is a restriction of diet to the heavenly bread. Hebrew *lāqaṭ*, "to gather," suggests that the law is primarily about harvesting the heavenly bread (see its repeated use in Ruth 2), not the exclusion of other food.

Deuteronomy 8 also emphasizes the harvesting of the manna. It begins with an interpretation of manna as rescue food: "God humbled you, causing you to hunger and then feeding you with manna (Deut 8:3). The motif of rescue from a situation of deprivation is absent in the Non-P version of Exodus 16. But the emphasis in Deuteronomy 8 is actually on the danger of abundance, which parallels the Non-P version of manna. Deuteronomy 8:6-18 sketches the utopian setting of the promised land. It is lush, like Elim, with flowing streams and bountiful food, including wheat, barley, vines, figs, pomegranates, olive oil, honey, and plenty of bread. No food is forbidden. Lohfink writes of Deut 8:2-6: "Here a situation of natural wealth and fullness is addressed, in complete contrast to the wilderness situation."[10] The point of emphasis of the writer of Deuteronomy is the same as the test of manna in the Non-P History. It is that the abundance of food will create the illusion of self-sufficiency. The Israelites will say: "My power and the strength of my hands have produced this wealth for me" (8:17). In the process they will forget divine law (8:11). The limitation in Deuteronomy 8 is not a restriction of diet to certain foods, but dependence on God for all food. The same is true in the account of heavenly bread in the Non-P History. Bread from heaven is both food and law (Exod 16:4), embodying the truth that humans do not live by bread alone, but on every word that comes from the mouth of Yahweh (Deut 8:3).

The P History changes the dynamic of the story. The Israelites, not Yahweh, initiate the action. Their complaint *(lûn)* about starvation is central (Exod 16:1-3). The wilderness of Sin is a wasteland, not the oasis of Elim. The threat of starvation is stated no less than six times in 16:6-12. Moses states that Yahweh heard the complaint of the Israelites (v. 7). And he questions why they complain to him (v. 7), stating that their complaint is really against Yahweh (v. 8). He informs the Israelites that Yahweh is responding by giving them meat in the evening and bread in the morning (v. 8). Yahweh confirms the message of Moses with a separate speech in v. 12.

10. Lohfink, *Theology of the Pentateuch*, 84-85.

The Israelite complaint even occasions a theophany. The "Glory of Yahweh" *(kĕbôd yhwh)* appears for the first time (16:10) surrounded by the cultic imagery of "the cloud," which requires the cultic ritual of "drawing near to Yahweh." The cultic focus foreshadows the central role of the tabernacle in the P History. The revelation of the divine name, Yahweh, in the commission of Moses indicated a progressive view of revelation in the P History through the names Elohim, El Shaddai, and Yahweh (see the commentary on 6:2–7:7). The Glory of Yahweh may signal yet another progression in the revelation of the name of Yahweh. In addition, the Glory of Yahweh also undergoes its own progression in revelation. The stages include the initial revelation in the wilderness (16:10), the descent to the summit of Mount Sinai (24:16, 17), the further descent into the completed tabernacle (40:34-35), and the invasion into the altar (Lev 9:23). The call of Aaron for the Israelites to "draw near before Yahweh" implies the establishment of the cult, which is not complete until the priests are ordained in Leviticus 9. His summons should be interpreted in the larger design of the P History. In the wilderness of Sin the people merely turn toward the wilderness to witness the revelation in the cloud. They may also hear the divine speech during the theophany, when Yahweh responds directly to their complaint by promising meat in the evening and bread in the morning (v. 12).

The theophany culminates with Yahweh's self-introduction, "I am Yahweh," accompanied by the demand for recognition: "Then you [the Israelites] will know that I am Yahweh your God" (v. 12). The demand for the Israelites to recognize Yahweh frames the entire section, since Moses and Aaron state at the outset that the Israelites will recognize Yahweh as the God of the exodus when they eat meat at dusk (v. 6). The recognition of Yahweh is a central theme in the P version of Moses' commission (see the commentary on 6:2–7:7). The self-identification of God, "I am Yahweh," begins the commission of Moses (6:2), and the demand for recognition concludes it (7:3-5). But the target of recognition during the exodus is Pharaoh and the Egyptians, not the Israelites. Pharaoh or the Egyptians must come to knowledge of Yahweh from the plagues (7:17; 8:10, 22; 9:14, 29) and from the destruction of the Egyptian army in the Red Sea (14:4, 18). The call for the Israelites to recognize Yahweh signals the change of focus in the P History from the polemical revelation of Yahweh at war in the land of Egypt to the sacramental presence of the divine "Glory" in the P tabernacle. The self-introduction of Yahweh and the demand for recognition repeat throughout the formation of the tabernacle cult (29:46; 31:13; frequently in Leviticus).

16:13-21 Miracle. The Non-P History describes how the miracle of the bread from heaven occurred (16:13b-15). The food descends from heaven at dawn like dew. It is described as frost or snow on the desert floor (see the commentary above). And it is named as a result of the Israelites' question, *mān hû'*, "What is it?" Moses answers the question by identifying the flakey snow as bread from God.

The P History brings the story into conformity with the earlier section about the complaint of the Israelites (16:13a, 16-21a); thus meat is included in the miracle (16:13a). But the P historian also changes the dynamic of the story, from a test about limitation in the midst of plenty to a story about manna as rescue food at a time of starvation. The response of Moses to the Israelite complaint voices the P historian's interpretation of manna. First, Moses directs the people on the amount of food that they must collect (16:16-18). The reference to the morning (v. 21a) indicates that the instructions concern the manna, not the quail. Each individual must collect one omer, an unknown measurement. And, regardless of whether one gathered more or less, all end up with the exact amount. In this way the P author extends the miracle of manna to include its collection. Second, Moses cautions the people on the consumption of the manna (16:19-20). No manna could remain until morning. The command recalls the instructions for Passover (12:10). But more importantly the command requires that the Israelites not horde the food, even though they fear starvation. The people fail the command. Some store the food into the next day prompting an angry response from Moses (16:20) and the rotting of the food. Thus the failure of the people in the P interpretation of manna is the opposite of the Non-P History. In the scarce setting of the wilderness of Sin the divine test of the Israelites is that they trust in the providence of God by not hording food even though they fear starvation.

The closing comment, that manna melted from the heat of the sun (16:21b) rather than rotting, likely belongs to the Non-P History since it corresponds to the earlier characterization of the food as snow (16:14).

16:22-30 Sabbath. The revelation of Sabbath as sacred time is a crucial event in the P History (16:22-26). It inaugurates the wilderness journey, which signals the initial reclaiming of the lost structure of creation from Genesis 1. The verbal form of "Sabbath," *šābat*, means "to rest." The seventh day of creation is made holy, *qādaš*, in the creation story of the P History, because God rested *(šābat)* from work (Gen 2:1-3). The P History is a quest to reclaim the lost origin of creation from Genesis 1. The revelation of manna brings the ideal structure of creation into focus for the Israelites, because God does not provide food on the day of divine rest. The six-day rhythm of manna reveals that the seventh day, the Sabbath, is holy to Yahweh, set apart from the other days of the week. Thus the wilderness journey brings the Israelites one step closer to the goal of salvation history. As a result, the location for the recovery of Sabbath is memorialized at the specific setting, the wilderness of Sin.

The date of the manna in the wilderness of Sin is carefully noted, month

2, day 15. The reemergence of Sabbath in human history is accompanied by a new appearance of God as the Glory of Yahweh (see the commentary above). Sabbath will continue to play a central role in the P History. The revelation of the Decalogue (20:8-11) and the formation of the tabernacle cult (31:12-17; 35:2-3) will strengthen the structure of the Sabbath in creation. But even further clarification will be required in the second stage of the wilderness journey in Num 15:32-41.

Exodus 16:27-30 recounts the Non-P version of the Israelite failure to observe the law. The failure is the opposite of the account in the P History, where the people horded the food for the next day (16:20). In the Non-P History the people take the food for granted by not observing the law of limitation, which required that they collect a two-day portion for the Sabbath. In the Non-P History some of the Israelites seek to glean manna on the Sabbath like every other morning (16:27), thus illustrating their assumption that food will always be abundant and that it is not dependent on God. The disobedience, however, is not followed by divine punishment. Instead, Yahweh reiterates the law to Moses (16:28-29) underscoring that the people failed to observe Torah. The story of manna in the Non-P History is the first test of the Israelite people during their period of courtship before the revelation of law in chaps. 19-24. The section concludes with the people resting on the seventh day (16:30).

When the Non-P and P Histories are read together the Israelites break both parts of the law (see 16:4-5). They retain food for two days and they fail to collect a double amount of food for the Sabbath. They are guilty both of the sin of hording the food (the P History) and of taking it for granted (the Non-P History). Both acts violate the command to be dependent on Yahweh in the wilderness journey.

16:31-36 Conclusion. The Non-P History concludes in 16:21 and 35a with three descriptions of the heavenly bread, including (1) its name, manna; (2) a depiction of the food's texture (coriander seed), color (white), and taste (honey wafer); and (3) its duration on earth (forty years). The duration of manna and the time period of the wilderness journey repeat in the Non-P History (Num 14:33-34), Deuteronomy (Deut 2:7; 8:2, 4; 29:5), and the Deuteronomistic History (Josh 5:6). Forty years signals important times of intergenerational transition. Isaac (Gen 25:20) and Esau (Gen 26:34) marry at the age of forty. Caleb (Josh 14:7) spies out the land of Canaan at forty. Ishbaal (2 Sam 2:10) becomes king of the north at forty. A forty-year period also represents a generation. Joshua 5:6 states that the wilderness wandering lasted forty years so that the entire first generation of the Israelites would die in the wilderness. The same thought is carried through in the story of the judges. They tend to rule for forty years (e.g., Othniel, Judg 3:11; Deborah, 5:31; and Gideon, 8:28). The number forty, as the time period of a generation, comes to represent completeness. It is this meaning that is likely intended when the number forty returns to describe the time required for Moses to receive the revelation of law (Exod 24:18) or the length of Jesus' temptation in the wilderness (Mark 1:13).

The P History concludes with cultic instruction in Exod 16:32-34, 35b-36. Moses instructs the people in v. 32. One omer of manna must be preserved for future generations. The measurement is clarified in v. 36 as one-tenth of an ephah. The Israelites must not only hear about the gift of manna, they must also see it. Moses directs Aaron on the preservation of the manna in vv. 33-34. He is to place a jar of manna "before Yahweh" (v. 33) "in front of the testimony" (v. 34). The imagery presupposes the tabernacle cult and the ark. The phrase "before Yahweh" is ritualistic language, implying the approach to God in the sanctuary. The reference to the "testimony" *(hā'ēdūt)* signifies the ark in the P History (25:16, 21, 22; 30:6) as compared to the "ark of the covenant" *('ărôn běrît)* in the Non-P History (Num 10:33), Deuteronomy (Deut 10:8; 31:9), and the Deuteronomistic History (Josh 3:14).

LAWSUIT OVER WATER (17:1-7)

17:1 And the entire congregation of the Israelites set out from the wilderness of Sin by stages according to the mouth of Yahweh. And they camped at Rephidim. But there was no water for the people to drink.

2 And the people quarreled with Moses. And they said, "Give us water, so that we may drink."

And Moses said to them, "Why do you quarrel with me? Why do you test Yahweh?"

3 But the people were thirsty there for water and the people complained to Moses. And they said, "Why did you bring us up out of Egypt to kill me, and my children, and my cattle with thirst?"

4 And Moses cried to Yahweh, saying, "What will I do with this people? Yet a little and they will stone me!"

5 And Yahweh said to Moses, "Cross over before the people. And take with you some of the elders of Israel. And the staff with which you struck the Nile take in your hand and go. 6 Indeed, I am standing before you there on the rock at Horeb. Strike the rock and water will come forth from it. And the people will drink."

And Moses did so before the elders of Israel.

7 And he called the name of the place Massah and Meribah, on account of the quarrel of the Israelites and on account of their testing Yahweh, saying, "Is Yahweh in our midst or not?"

Notes

17:1 *by stages.* The MT *lĕmasʿêhem*, "by stages [or stations]," is rendered in the LXX *kata parembolas autōn*, "according to their encampments."

17:2 *the people quarreled with Moses.* Hebrew *wayyāreb*, "quarreled," is not simply a complaint, but indicates a legal challenge to the authority of Moses. The LXX *eloidoreito*, "to rail at," loses the legal background to the challenge.

17:3 *why did you bring us up out of Egypt.* GKC §150e states that questions introduced by *lāmmâ*, as in this instance, *lāmmâ zeh*, "contain an affirmation and are used to state the reason for a request or warning." Thus the statement is not a question, but part of the legal challenge, the quarrel *(rîb)* that is presented to Moses. Moses employs the same rhetorical strategy with God during the incident of the golden calf (32:12).

17:6 *the people will drink.* The LXX adds a pronoun: *pietai ho laos mou*, "*my* people will drink."

Commentary

The divine testing of the Israelites in the stories of diseased water (15:22-26) and food (15:27–16:36) is reversed when the Israelites test God at Rephidim over the absence of water (17:1-7). The initial travel notice (17:1a), linking the wilderness of Sin with Rephidim, derives from the P author (see the introduction, "Authors"). The P History changed the setting of the story of manna from Elim to the wilderness of Sin (16:1). And 17:1a now notes the departure from Sin. Two literary features identify the travel notice with the P History. The Israelites are described as the "congregation" (see also 16:1). And the people are characterized as "journeying by stages" *(lĕmasʿêhem)*, a phrase also employed by the P author in noting the departure of the Israelites from Mount Sinai (Num 10:12).

The narrative in 17:1b-7 presents a series of literary tensions that have raised questions about the author of the story and the history of composition. Childs summarizes the two most prominent problems: (1) the double name of Massah and Meribah in v. 7a; and (2) the combination of a legal dispute (v. 2) and the murmuring motif (v. 3) in the conflict between Moses and the Israelite people.[1] Van Seters and Aurelius argue correctly that these tensions do not result in the identification of two authors and that the story contains no signs of P authorship.[2] The P interpretation of this story occurs in Num 20:4-13. The testing at Massah and Meribah suggests a more complex tradition-historical development than its composition in the Non-P and P History, which will be examined at the close of the commentary on Exod 17:1-7.

The location of Rephidim is difficult to pin down. Like many of the oases in the Non-P History, Rephidim is limited in its occurrences (see 17:1, 8; 19:2 and the

---

1. Childs, *Exodus*, 306-7.
2. Van Seters, *Life of Moses*, 191-98; Aurelius, *Fürbitter Israels*, 169-70.

summary of travel notices in Num 33:14). The root meaning of Rephidim, from *rāpad,* is "to support, refresh." The verb also means "to spread out," referring most likely to a saddlecloth. Whether the place name Rephidim is associated with either of these meanings is uncertain. Water from the rock certainly supports the Israelites in the wilderness. The story includes other place names along with Rephidim. The testing of the Israelites results in the names Massah (= Test) and Meribah (= Lawsuit). And the rock upon which Yahweh appears is identified as Horeb (v. 6), the mountain of theophany in the Non-P History (3:1; 33:6), Deuteronomy (Deut 1:2, 6, 19), and the Deuteronomistic History (1 Kgs 8:9; 19:8). The names Massah and Meribah are etiological locations, meaning that the events in the story provide the meaning of the place names. These locations may be a secondary addition to an older story now incorporated in the Non-P History. In Deut 9:22 Massah is associated with Taberah and Kibroth-hattaavah, not Meribah, locations that occur after the revelation of Yahweh in chaps. 19–34.[3]

The Israelites initiate the action at Rephidim. They "quarrel" *(rîb)* with Moses about the absence of water (17:2). The Hebrew word translated "to quarrel" means "to conduct a legal case," while the noun often refers to a lawsuit.[4] During the crisis of diseased water Yahweh proposed law as the basis by which the Israelites would interact with God (15:22-26). Yahweh employed law to test the Israelites in the story of manna (chap. 16). The Israelites now exercise their legal rights, presenting God with a lawsuit over the absence of water. The speech of Moses clarifies that the lawsuit is not against him but against God, and that it is, indeed, a test case: "Why do you test *(nāsâ)* Yahweh?" In the next verse the Israelites also complain *(lûn)* to Moses (17:3), questioning the wisdom of the exodus and fearing that they will die in the desert. Neither the lawsuit nor the complaint is an instance of rebellion in the first phase of the wilderness journey, since it is a period of courtship before the revelation of law and the ratification of the covenant (chaps. 19–24; see the commentary in 15:22-26). The murmuring, however, should not be confused with the lawsuit. The complaint, not the lawsuit, will become the occasion for judgment and even death in the wilderness journey (see Num 11:1-3, 4-35; 12:9; 14:11-12, 26-35; 16:21, 45). The lawsuit will return in Num 20:2-13, the P interpretation of Exod 17:1-7, where it does not prompt divine judgment even though Moses interprets the action as rebellion. The misinterpretation by Moses of the lawsuit in Num 20:2-13, as an instance of rebellion, signals his failure as the leader in the P History.[5] In the Non-P version of the story in Exod 17:1-7, Moses responds appropriately to the lawsuit by interceding for the Israelites (17:4; see also 15:25).

---

3. Johnstone, *Chronicles and Exodus,* 244-46.
4. BDB 936; *HALOT* 2:1224-26.
5. See Dozeman, "Numbers," 159-61.

Yahweh responds to the lawsuit in 17:5-6. The divine command that Moses "cross before the people" may be an action to authenticate him. His intercession included the fear of being stoned (v. 4), and Mosaic authority is a central theme in the Non-P History (4:1-17). Moses is accompanied by the elders who assume a leadership role throughout the Non-P History (e.g., 4:1-17; 12:21-27). Yahweh also commands Moses to take his staff, specifically identified as the instrument that polluted the Nile River during Yahweh's war with Pharaoh (see 7:17, 20). Now it will draw fresh water from a rock for the Israelites in the desert. The instructions culminate in a theophany: "Indeed, I am standing before you there on the rock at Horeb." The theophany anticipates the content of the lawsuit stated in the closing verse: "Is Yahweh in our midst or not?" Moses is to strike the rock drawing water from it in the sight of the elders, which will confirm the presence of God with the Israelites.

The story concludes in v. 7 with an etiology. The rock or perhaps its general location in Rephidim is named "Lawsuit" (= Meribah, from Hebrew *rîb,* "to present a legal case") and "Test" (= Massah, from Hebrew *nāsâ,* "to test"). The place, "Lawsuit and Test," is the location in the Non-P History where the Israelites exercised their legal rights against God with the legal brief: "Is Yahweh in our midst or not?" The testing of God does not result in divine punishment during the period of courtship (although Rashi interprets the attack by the Amalekites as punishment).[6] The prophets also leave room for testing God in the lawsuit (Jer 12:1), but with great caution (Isa 45:9-17).

The tradition of testing at Meribah and Massah is far more complex in the Hebrew Bible than its use in the Non-P History. The oldest reference to testing, according to Cross and Freedman, is in the Blessing of Moses in Deuteronomy 33.[7] In this poem God tests Levi at Massah and contends with him at Meribah, which leads to the ordination of the Levites (Deut 33:8-9; see also Ps 81:7). The poem recalls the action of the Levites after the sin of the golden calf, when they slaughter three thousand Israelites (Exod 32:25-29).

The book of Deuteronomy thoroughly reworks the tradition of testing at Massah. The incident is significantly reinterpreted in Deut 6:16-17 from the Blessing of Moses in Deuteronomy 33. The direction of the testing at Massah is reversed. It is no longer from God, but originates with humans who test the Deity. The story is no longer about the Levites, but about the whole nation. And the testing is associated with law, while the act of testing is interpreted negatively. Deuteronomy 9:22 states bluntly that the test at Massah prompted divine wrath, and it associates Massah with Taberah and Kibroth-hattaavah, not Meribah, locations that occur after the revelation of Yahweh in chaps. 19–34. Psalm

---

6. Leibowitz, *Studies in Shemot,* 1:287-88.
7. Cross and Freedman, "Blessing of Moses."

95:8 reinforces the negative interpretation of the testing at Massah, describing the Israelites as hard-hearted in testing God. The author of Hebrews in the NT takes the negative interpretation even further, concluding that testing God is an act of rebellion (Heb 3:7-11).

The Non-P History locates the testing at Massah before the revelation of law and interprets it as a positive story during the period of courtship in the first phase of the wilderness journey (chaps. 15–18). The P History extends the positive interpretation of the lawsuit into the second phase of the wilderness journey (Numbers 11–21; see Num 20:2-13). The result is that there are now two stories that recount a crisis of water at Meribah and the presentation of a lawsuit to Yahweh. In each case the lawsuit does not result in punishment to the Israelite people.[8] The two stories indicate that exercising legal rights with Yahweh is risky but appropriate for a relationship governed by law. One aspect of the sin of Moses in Num 20:2-13 is that he forgets this by judging the Israelites falsely as rebels.[9] The P interpretation is echoed in Ps 106:32 and in Deut 32:51, where only the location, Meribah, is stated in recounting the sin of Moses.

WAR AND REMEMBRANCE (17:8-16)

[17:8] *And Amalek approached and fought with Israel at Rephidim. [9] And Moses said to Joshua, "Choose for us men, go out, and fight with Amalek. Tomorrow I will stand on the top of the mountain, and the staff of God in my hand."*

[10] *And Joshua did so, as Moses said to him, to fight against Amalek.*

But Moses, Aaron, and Hur went up to the top of the hill. [11] And it happened whenever Moses raised his hand, Israel would prevail. And whenever he rested his hand, Amalek would prevail. [12] But the hands of Moses became heavy and they took a stone and they placed it beneath him. And he sat on it. Aaron and Hur held his hands, on this side one and on that side one. And his hands were steady until the entry of the sun.

[13] *And Joshua defeated Amalek and his people with the sword.*

[14] *And Yahweh said to Moses, "Write this memorial in a book and place in the ears of Joshua, that I will eliminate completely the memory of Amalek from under heaven."*

[15] *And Moses built an altar and he called its name, "Yahweh is my banner." [16] And he said, "For a hand is on Yah's banner."*

A war for Yahweh with Amalek from generation to generation.

---

8. See Dozeman, "Numbers," 159-61.
9. Ibid.

Notes

17:9 *choose for us men.* The LXX translates, *epilexon seautō andras dynatous*, "choose for yourself men of valor."

17:10 *to the top of the hill.* Hebrew *rō'š haggib'â* could also be translated "to the top of the mountain." The translation maintains the contrast between *gib'â*, "hill," and *har*, "mountain." See also NRSV "on the top of the hill." The LXX also maintains the contrast, employing *bounos*, "hill," rather than *oros*, "mountain."

17:12 *until the entry of the sun.* The LXX translates, *heōs dysmōn hēliou*, "until the setting of the sun."

17:13 *with the sword.* Hebrew *lĕpî-ḥāreb* translates more lit., "at the mouth of the sword." The LXX intensifies the phrase, *en phonō machairas*, "by the slaughter of the sword."

17:15 *my banner.* The LXX translates Hebrew *nissî* as *mou kataphygē*, "my place of refuge." See the commentary.

17:16 *For a hand is on Yah's banner.* The MT *kî-yād 'al-kēs yāh* is unclear. The ambiguity is with the word *kēs*, which I translate "banner." See the commentary. The Sam renders the phrase, *ky yd 'l ks'*, "for a hand is on the seat/throne." The LXX goes in a different direction, *en cheiri kryphaia polemei kyrios epi Amalēk apo geneōn eis geneas*, "in the concealed hand the Lord fights against Amalek from generation to generation." Wevers notes that the translators of the LXX likely combined the Hebrew words *ks* and *yh* into one word, *ksyh*, "hidden."[1]

Commentary

The initial focus on the relationship between Yahweh and the Israelite people in the stories of testing (15:22-26; 15:27–16:36; 17:1-7) is turned outward when the Amalekites attack. A holy war follows with new characters entering the story: Joshua, Aaron, and Hur assist in waging the war. And Moses also assumes a new role. He guides the Israelites in holy war with the staff of God. In addition, Moses now possesses a book and is able to write. He also constructs an altar to Yahweh for the first time along with a memorial banner.

The story moves quickly through three stages: the attack (v. 8), the war (vv. 9-13), and the remembrance (vv. 14-16). B. P. Robinson detects a more elaborate internal chiastic structure to the story: war with Amalek, A (v. 8), A' (v. 16); instruction, B (vv. 9-10a), B' (vv. 14-15); Joshua fighting Amalek, C (v. 10b) and C' (v. 13); Moses, Aaron, and Hur, D (v. 10c) and D' (v. 12b); with the focus of the narrative on the arm of Moses, E (v. 11) and E' (v. 12a).[2]

There is little debate over the internal unity of the passage. The story is not associated with the P History. Childs assigns the story to an early J author,

---

1. Wevers, *Notes*, 272.

2. B. P. Robinson, "Israel and Amalek: The Context of Exodus 17:8-16," *JSOT* 32 (1985): 15-22, esp. 15-16; see also Schart, *Moses und Israel*, 186-87.

as does Noth.[3] Propp attributes the story to an E author.[4] Blum suggests that v. 14 may be an addition to the story, but he interprets the entire story within the *D-Komposition*.[5] Van Seters assigns the text to the exilic J historian.[6] I will interpret the episode within the Non-P History.

17:8 The attack of the Amalekites is at Rephidim, the same setting as the Israelites' test of God with the question: "Is Yahweh in our midst or not?" (17:1-7). The similar setting suggests a possible relationship between the two stories, which will be explored in the commentary on vv. 14-16. The Amalekites are related to the Israelites through the genealogy of Esau (Gen 36:12, 16), making their attack all the more egregious. The Amalekites are said to dwell in the Negev (Num 13:29) in the spy story. Later in the same story they are associated with the valleys (14:25), but they attack the Israelites from the hills (14:43, 45), defeating them. The emerging portrait of the Amalekites is of a desert-dwelling people. Balaam praises them as the first of the nations, but also dooms them as destined to perish (24:20). Deuteronomy 25:17-19 elaborates on their attack in Exod 17:8. It was from the rear, aimed at stragglers, during a time when the Israelites were weary. The assault demonstrated their disregard of God.[7]

The verb "to fight" *(lāham)* to describe the action of the Amalekites recalls the fear of Pharaoh at the outset of the exodus (1:10) and the proclamation of Moses to the Israelites during the confrontation at the Red Sea (14:14). Pharaoh feared a war with the Israelites. Prior to the confrontation at the Red Sea Yahweh feared that the Israelites were not yet ready for war (13:17). During the confrontation at the Red Sea Moses required the Israelites to be passive, allowing Yahweh to fight alone for them. Now Moses calls for the Israelites to participate actively in holy war for the first time.

17:9-13 Joshua appears without an introduction to wage war at the command of Moses. Joshua is the central character in the conquest of the land, leading the Israelites across the Jordan River (Joshua 1–5) and waging war against the Canaanite city-states (Joshua 6–12). But his appearance in the Pentateuch is sudden and uneven, as though he is written into the wilderness journey in the Non-P History, because of his association with the conquest. His presence with

3. Childs, *Exodus*, 312-13; Noth, *Exodus*, 145-50.

4. Propp, *Exodus 1–18*, 615-16.

5. Blum, *Studien*, 152-53.

6. Van Seters, *Life of Moses*, 198-200.

7. The parallel accounts in Exod 17:8-16 and Deut 25:17-19 raise tradition-historical questions about the Amalekite war. See the discussion in Van Seters, *Life of Moses*, 202-7. L. H. Feldman (*"Remember Amalek!" Vengeance, Zealotry and Group Destruction in the Bible According to Philo, Pseudo-Philo, and Josephus* [Monographs of the Hebrew Union College 31; Cincinnati: Hebrew Union College Press, 2004) traces the continued interpretation of the tradition in the postbiblical period.

Moses during the first instance of holy war at Rephidim certainly reinforces the view of salvation in the Non-P History as including both the exodus and the conquest. Moses and Joshua embody the two themes. The pentateuchal story, which provides the clearest background on Joshua, is the account of the spies, with its focus on the conquest (Numbers 13–14). Joshua is identified in the spy story as an Ephraimite (13:8) who undergoes a change of name from Hoshea (13:16). He is idealized, along with Caleb, for demonstrating unreserved courage to wage war against the more powerful Canaanites (14:6, 30, 38; see also 32:12).

The Non-P History will further expand the role of Joshua with three additional stories in Exodus. Joshua will accompany Moses to receive the revelation of law on the mountain of God (Exod 24:13). He descends the mountain with Moses after the construction of the golden calf, indicating that he is not involved in the sin of idolatry (32:17). His speech to Moses while descending the mountain accentuates his role as a warrior: "There is a noise of war in the camp!" (32:17). And Joshua assumes a cultic role in the tent of meeting (33:11).

The Non-P History further develops the portrait of Joshua in Numbers as a charismatic leader. He is the chosen assistant of Moses, when the seventy elders receive a portion of the Mosaic spirit (Num 11:28) at the tent of meeting. He also receives charisma when the spirit of Moses is transferred to him (27:18, 22). Joshua is only loosely edited into Deuteronomy. But the themes associated with him correspond to those from the Non-P History. Joshua is the leader of the conquest (Deut 1:38; 3:21, 28), he is associated with the tent of meeting (31:14), and he is the successor of Moses (31:3, 23).

The holy war against the Amalekites focuses on Moses and his staff, not Joshua. Moses informs Joshua that he will ascend to the summit of the hill with the staff of God (see the commentary on Exod 4:1-9 and 7:8-9). Moses is accompanied by Aaron and Hur, the latter representing yet another new character to the story. The name Hur is probably Egyptian, meaning Horus. Hur returns one other time to assist Aaron in governing the people, while Moses and Joshua ascend the mountain of God to receive the revelation of law (24:14). The command associates him with the sin of idolatry represented by the golden calf, which takes place while Moses and Joshua are absent. Yet Hur is not specifically mentioned during the construction of the golden calf. He may be associated with iconography in general as the grandfather of the artisan Bezalel (31:2; 35:30). This skill is praised in the P History but not in the Non-P History, which advocates aniconic worship in the tent of meeting (see the commentary on 33:7-11).

The holy war against the Amalekites is regulated at the summit of the hill by the action of Moses with the divine staff. When the hands of Moses were raised (presumably with the staff of God), Joshua prevailed. When his hands were lowered, the tide of the battle turned, and the Amalekites gained the upper hand. The circumstances indicate that the power to wage holy war resides in the magical staff of God, not in Moses, and certainly not in Joshua or the Israelite warriors. The staff of God is like a lightning rod at the summit of the hill channeling power down to the Israelites in the battle. When the antenna is down, the power ceases. The eventual weakness of Moses even to raise his arms underscores further that the power in the battle does not reside with him but with God. Victory is achieved when Aaron and Hur assist Moses by providing a seat of stone and holding up his arms until the setting of the sun.

17:14-16   The first holy war in the wilderness is memorialized in two ways: in writing (v. 14) and in the construction of an altar (vv. 15-16). The writing codifies a divine curse on the Amalekites for all time. L. H. Feldman traces the power of this tradition through the Hellenistic Jewish writers, Philo, Pseudo-Philo, and Josephus. [8] The altar memorializes God's aid in the victory. The meaning of both actions is not altogether clear. The book in which Moses writes is difficult to identify. The memorial regarding the Amalekites could be directed at Joshua or God. And the etiology accompanying the construction of the altar yields several interpretations.

The divine command for Moses to write *(kātab)* in a book *(sēper)* introduces a new motif into the wilderness journey that will become prominent. The earlier proposal of Yahweh, that law become the means by which the Israelites and God interact (15:22-26), laid the foundation for written legislation. As a consequence both God and Moses begin writing, especially during the revelation on the mountain of God. God writes laws on tablets (24:12) and the names of the elect in a book (32:32). In the P History God also writes the architectural plans for the tabernacle (31:18). Moses mirrors the action of God, also writing down laws (24:7). In 17:14 Yahweh commands Moses to write a memorial *(zikkārôn)*. Its content is a divine pledge stated emphatically in the first person: "I will completely blot out *(māḥōh 'emḥeh)* the memory of Amalek from under heaven." The verb "to blot out" indicates the extermination of the Amalekites, but even more, the loss of their memory altogether. The same language returns after the sin of the golden calf, when Moses requests Yahweh to blot out *(māḥâ)* his "name" from the divine book if the God is unable to forgive the Israelites (32:32-33).

But to whom is the memorial directed? It may be Joshua, since Moses is instructed to read the pledge to him. This is the interpretation of Deut 25:17-19. It changes the divine command from the first person ("I will blot out . . .") to the second ("You must blot out . . . Do not forget!"). In this case the divine pledge becomes a law for the Israelites preserved as a memorial (see also Exod 13:9). The divine instruction that Moses "place" *(śîm)* the memorial "in the ear of

8. Feldman, *Remember Amalek.*

395

Joshua" would then obligate him to exterminate the Amalekites (see 24:7, where Moses presents law by "speaking into the ear of the Israelites"). Yet Joshua never exterminates the Amalekites, or even wages war with them. Saul does, but fails to exterminate them when he takes the Amalekite king, Agag, captive (1 Samuel 15), leading to the downfall of his kingship.

Memorials, however, can also be directed to God. The stones in the ephod of the high priest, for example, represent a memorial to God, prompting the Deity to be mindful of the Israelites (Exod 28:12). The emphatic language of the divine pledge in the first person could indicate that the memorial in 17:14 is self-directed, meaning that Yahweh is pledging to exterminate the Amalekites. In this case, the instruction "to place" the memorial "in the ear" is not a law for Joshua, but a proclamation which makes the divine obligation public (see similar instances of proclamation in 10:2; 11:2; and especially Gen 23:13-18, where "speaking in the ears of the people" indicates a public statement by Abraham). The divine pledge to complete the holy war against the Amalekites is then a law for God.

"The book" *(hassēper)* in which Moses writes has also raised questions of interpretation. It is stated with the definite article suggesting a specific object. It may be unrelated to other books in the Pentateuch. Yet scholars have explored a variety of inner-biblical identifications. One solution arises from tradition history. Numbers 21:14 mentions an anthology of war poems entitled "The Book of the Wars of Yahweh." Numbers 21:14-15 even contains a fragmentary poem from this collection. Spinoza identified "the book" in Exod 17:14 with "The Book of the Wars of Yahweh," noting the similarity in theme.[9] This solution is followed by a number of modern interpreters.[10] Cassuto interprets the book to mean an inscription, and he locates it on the altar described in 17:15.[11] The context of the Non-P History provides other choices. Moses writes in "The Book of the Covenant" (24:7), but it is likely a distinct book, which refers to law revealed at the mountain of God (see the commentary). "The book" may also point to Deuteronomy. Moses writes Deuteronomy (Deut 31:9). It is characterized as "a book" (31:24), "this book" (28:58), as well as "the book of Torah" (28:61; 30:10). As noted it also contains an account of the divine pledge reinterpreted as a law for the Israelites (25:17-19).

The story concludes with Moses constructing an altar and providing an etiology to memorialize it (Exod 17:15-16). The altar is the first cultic object constructed by Moses in the Non-P History. He repeats the action only once, during the covenant closing ceremony at the mountain of God (24:3-8), which

9. Spinoza, *Theologico-Political Treatise*, 8.
10. See Durham, *Exodus*, 236-37.
11. Cassuto, *Exodus*, 206-7.

is also associated with a book (24:7). No details of the construction are provided, although Yahweh later provides the directions for the construction of altars in 20:22-26. Altars cannot be icons. They cannot be ascended. And they must consist only of uncut stones.

The point of emphasis in 17:15-16 is not the altar, but the etiology accompanying it. B. O. Long noted that etiologies contain fixed features and that they follow established literary forms.[12] Etiologies include the naming of something, introduced with the Hebrew verb "to call" *(qārā')*. The name in the etiology usually includes a wordplay from the story, often quoting an earlier statement, which is sometimes accompanied with explanations. Etiologies have a prominent role in the Non-P History of the wilderness journey. The author included an etiology in the story of manna. During the appearance of the bread from heaven (16:15), the Israelites ask: "What is it?" *(mān hû')*. Their question provides the basis for the etiology in 16:31. It is introduced with the verb "to call" *(qārā')* and it includes a play on their question. They name the food *mān*. The Israelite test *(nāsâ)* of Yahweh with the lawsuit *(rîb)* in 17:1-7 also concluded with an etiology. Exodus 17:7 states that the location is called *(qārā')* Massah ("Test") and Meribah ("Lawsuit"). A closing line explains the play on words: It is because of the Israelite "lawsuit" and "test" when they said, "Is Yahweh in our midst or not?"

The war against the Amalekites is the third etiology in the wilderness journey of the Non-P History. It follows in general the form of the previous stories, employing the same key words. Exodus 17:15 contains the verb "to call" *(qārā')* when Moses names the altar, "Yahweh is my *nēs*." Hebrew *nēs* means "banner" or "flagpole." Nehushtan, the copper snake, is placed on such a flagpole (Num 21:8). The Israelites must look at it to be healed. The prophet Isaiah underscores the same meaning. The banner of Yahweh is a signal for the Israelites of their rescue from the exile, perhaps also carrying images of war against the nations (Isa 11:12; 13:2; 18:3). Both meanings fit the story. Yahweh is both warrior and rescuer in the war against the Amalekites. B. P. Robinson suggests a conscious parallel between the war with the Amalekites (Exod 17:8-16) and the copper serpent Nehushtan (Num 21:4-9) in the formation of the wilderness journey. The thematic development accentuates the power of Yahweh in the serpent and in the arm of Moses. Both are signaled by the banner *(nēs)*.[13]

Exodus 17:16 provides an explanation of the etiology, interrelating the naming to the events in the story: "Because a hand (is) on the *kēs* of Yah." The reference to "hand" relates the closing explanation with the central role of Moses' hands (and the staff of God) in the story. "Yah" is the shortened form of

12. Long, *Etiological Narrative*.
13. Robinson, "Israel and Amalek," 18.

Yahweh. But the Hebrew word *kēs* is unknown. Any translation requires an emendation. The LXX translates "to cover" from Hebrew *kāsâ*. The NIV translates "throne" from Hebrew *kissē̂*.[14] Cassuto suggests "to count" from Hebrew *kāsas*.[15] Childs and Propp provide the strongest solution, preferring "flagpole" or "banner," from Hebrew *nēs*, changing *k* to *n*, and thus relating the explanation to the name, "Yahweh is my *nēs* ('banner')."[16] Childs understands "the phrase 'Hand on YHWH's banner' as a rallying cry of Moses which was directed to Israel."[17] Propp suggests a secondary meaning through wordplay. Hebrew *nēs* may also be an allusion to the motif of testing, *nāsâ*.[18] In this case, the war against the Amalekites is the divine response to the Israelite test of God: "Is Yahweh in our midst or not?" The defeat of the Amalekites demonstrates the presence of Yahweh in the midst of the Israelites. The raising of Moses' hand with the staff of God during the battle was therefore "the test of Yah."

DIVINE RESCUE AND WORSHIP (18:1-12)

¹⁸:¹ *And Jethro the priest of Midian, the father-in-law of Moses, heard of all that God had done for Moses and for Israel, his people, how Yahweh brought Israel from Egypt.* ² *And Jethro, the father-in-law of Moses, took Zipporah, the wife of Moses, after he had sent her away,* ³ *and his two sons, the name of one, Gershom, for he said, "I am a resident alien in a foreign land,"* ⁴ *and the name of one, Eliezer, for he said, "The God of my father is my help and he saved me from the sword of Pharaoh."*

⁵ *Jethro, the father-in-law of Moses, approached Moses with his sons and his wife in the wilderness, where he was camping at the mountain of God.* ⁶ *And he said to Moses, "I, your father-in-law Jethro, am coming to you with your wife and the two sons with her."*

⁷ *Moses went out to meet his father-in-law. And he bowed down and he kissed him. And each requested of his fellow peace and they entered into the tent.* ⁸ *And Moses told his father-in-law all that Yahweh had done to Pharaoh and to the Egyptians on behalf of Israel, all the hardship that happened to them on the way, and how Yahweh had delivered them.*

⁹ *And Jethro rejoiced over all the good that Yahweh had done for Israel, in rescuing him from the hand of Egypt.* ¹⁰ *And Jethro said, "Blessed be Yahweh who rescued you from the hand of Egypt and from the hand of Pharaoh, in rescuing the*

---

14. Sarna, *Exodus*, 96.
15. Cassuto, *Exodus*, 206-7.
16. Childs, *Exodus*, 312; Propp, *Exodus 1–18*, 620.
17. Childs, *Exodus*, 312.
18. Propp, *Exodus 1–18*, 619.

people from under the hand of Egypt. [11] *Now I know that Yahweh is greater than all the gods, for in the matter they dealt presumptuously against them."* [12] *And Jethro, the father-in-law of Moses, brought a whole burnt offering and sacrifices to God. And Aaron and all the elders of Israel ate bread with the father-in-law of Moses before the God.*

Notes

18:1 *all that God did.* The LXX has *kyrios,* "Lord," as compared to the MT *'ĕlōhîm,* "God."

for Moses. The LXX omits the phrase.

18:2 *after he had sent her away.* The phrase *'aḥar šillûḥeyhā* is usually understood to describe Moses sending Zipporah back to her father for safety. The verb *šillaḥ,* however, can also mean divorce (Deut 22:19). The LXX translates *meta tēn aphesin autēs,* "after her release," which is also a technical term for divorce. But such a reading hardly fits the context. Propp provides yet another reading, "marriage gift," in which case the phrase describes the process of Zipporah becoming Moses' wife, not when Jethro took her back.[1]

18:4 *Eliezer, for he said.* My translation follows the LXX; the MT lacks "he said."

18:6 *And he said to Moses, "I, your father-in-law Jethro, am coming to you.* In the LXX Jethro is not the speaker; instead, the approach of Jethro is reported to Moses.

18:11 *they dealt presumptuously against them.* The subject of the verb "dealt presumptuously" is the Egyptians, although the antecedent is not clear. The LXX translates, *epethento autois,* which Wevers renders, "they set upon them," noting that the phrase has military overtones.[2]

18:12 *a whole burnt offering.* Hebrew *'ōlâ,* "whole burnt offering," is in the plural in the LXX, *holokautōmata.*

Commentary

The meeting between Moses and Jethro (Exodus 18) follows immediately after the defeat of the Amalekites (17:8-16), providing a contrast between the two nations. The former is an eternal enemy and the latter an ally of the Israelite people. Two stories about Moses' Midianite family follow. The first is a celebration of divine rescue (*nāṣal,* 18:4, 8, 9, 10 [twice]), culminating in worship (18:1-12). The second focuses on case law (*dābār,* 18:14, 16, 17, 18, 19, 22 [twice], 23, 26 [twice]), resulting in the selection of judges (18:13-27). The father-in-law of Moses assumes a leadership role in both stories. He is named Jethro in the first story (18:1-12), where he teaches Moses about cultic ritual, and is simply described as the unnamed father-in-law of Moses in the second episode where the focus is the administration of law. Once the knowledge of Moses' father-in-law is passed on to Moses, he assumes a more subordinate role in the story. Exodus 18:27 states

1. Propp, *Exodus 1–18,* 625.
2. Wevers, *Notes,* 280-81.

that he returns to his home. Numbers 10:29-32, however, is more ambiguous. In the account of the departure from the divine mountain, the father-in-law of Moses, here named Hobab, is asked to lead the Israelites to the promised land in exchange for a share of the land. Hobab is reluctant, which allows for the direct leading of Yahweh with the ark of the covenant. But Hobab never answers Moses directly, suggesting that he may have accompanied the Israelites to the promised land, therefore accounting for the presence of his descendants in Judges (1:16; 4:11), where Jael assists in an act of holy war against Sisera.

The limitation of the name Jethro to the first episode suggests that Exod 18:1-12 and 13-27 may be separate stories. The repetition of the selection of judges in 18:13-27 and Deut 1:9-18 reinforces a separate reading of the sacrifice of Jethro (Exod 18:1-12) and the selection of judges (vv. 13-27). But the most pressing problems of composition in Exodus 18 have more to do with its position in the Pentateuch than with tensions in the internal literary structure. Stories about Moses' Midianite father-in-law presently frame the revelation of law in Exodus 19–Numbers 10. The Midianite father-in-law of Moses instructs him in worship and in jurisprudence in Exodus 18 and Moses requests the leadership of his father-in-law in Num 10:29-32. Many interpreters suspect that the stories of Moses' Midianite father-in-law were once one continuous narrative and that Exodus 18 was subsequently placed in its present position by a later author or editor (see the introduction, "Authors"). But scholars have not debated in great detail the composition of Exodus 18. Source critics have tended to attribute the authorship of chap. 18 to the E source, noting the prominence of the divine name Elohim. And this position continues to be reflected in the commentary of Propp.[3] Here I am interpreting the story within the Non-P History, since there is no evidence of P authorship within the narrative. The present position of chap. 18 before the revelation of law in chaps. 19–34 will be interpreted as part of the larger literary design of the Non-P writer, rather than as the work of the P historian, as Johnstone suggests.[4]

The worship at the mountain of God progresses through three scenes, shifting in focus between Jethro (vv. 1-5, 9-12) and Moses (vv. 6-8). The opening scene recounts the journey of Jethro to the mountain of God (vv. 1-5). Moses takes center stage in the second scene, recounting to Jethro the details of the divine rescue (vv. 6-8). The final scene is the climax of the story. Jethro leads Moses and the Israelite elders in their first cultic ritual in the wilderness (vv. 9-12).

18:1-5 The story of Jethro's journey to Moses (vv. 1, 5) frames a description

---

3. Propp, *Exodus 1–18*, 622-35. For a broader review of scholarship see Blum, *Studien*, 153-63; Rose, *Deuteronomist und Jahwist*, 224-63.

4. Johnstone, *Chronicles and Exodus*, 242-61. See also the early work by Winnett, *Mosaic Tradition*, 57-69.

of Moses' Midianite family (vv. 2-3). The story lacks a clear wilderness setting. No travel notice is provided after the war with the Amalekites at Rephidim (see the introduction, "Authors: Non-P History"). The opening verse simply reintroduces Jethro as a Midianite priest and as the father-in-law of Moses (see the commentary on 2:15b-22). Verse 5 states that he meets Moses encamped at the mountain of God *(har hā'ĕlōhîm)*. The land of Midian is associated with the mountain of God in the commission of Moses (3:1), which provides narrative background for the setting of the story. But the setting of the mountain of God at this juncture of the story creates a problem voiced by Ibn Ezra: Moses is encamped at the mountain of God to meet Jethro, but his arrival there does not appear until 19:1-2. The problem of setting is compounded by the worship on the divine mountain. Again Ibn Ezra notes that there is an altar for sacrifice in 18:9-12, but the first mention of such an altar is in 24:4. The problems of setting and chronology have led interpreters to conclude that the story of Jethro in chap. 18 is out of place, and that it originally followed the revelation in chaps. 19–34. Johnstone concludes that the cultic leadership of Jethro (18:1-12) originally preceded Num 10:29-32 at the close of the revelation in chaps. 19–34, accounting for the sacrificial altar and the possible reference to the tent of meeting (18:7).[5] Its placement before the revelation in chaps. 19–34 is the result of a P editor, a solution that I do not follow.

The larger design of the Non-P History provides insight into the present location of 18:1-12, thus accounting for the literary placement of chap. 18. The Non-P historian idealizes the Midianites (see the commentary 4:18-26). Stories about the Midianites frame both accounts of revelation to Moses in 3:1–4:17 and to the Israelites in chaps. 19–34. The Midianites show hospitality to Moses (2:15b-22), setting the stage for his encounter with Yahweh at the mountain of God, and they also transmit religious tradition to him (4:24-26) after his commission. The transmission of religious tradition plays an important role in the Non-P History because the Israelites, including Moses, have lost all memory about God and past tradition (see the commentary on 1:6). The Midianites, Abraham's descendants through Keturah (Gen 25:1-5), play a role in the recovery of religious tradition. Zipporah rescued Moses from the divine attack because she knew the ritual of circumcision. Jethro now returns at the outset of the revelation to the Israelites (chaps. 19–34) to celebrate the rescue from Egypt by leading Moses in cultic ritual. Thus the setting of the story is transitional in the Non-P History to prepare the reader for the revelation of God in chaps. 19–34 and the transfer of cultic leadership to Moses (e.g., 24:3-8).[6] The transition

---

5. Johnstone, *Chronicles and Exodus*, 242-61, esp. 258.

6. E. Carpenter, "Exodus 18: Its Structure, Style, Motifs and Function in the Book of Exodus," in *A Biblical Itinerary: In Search of Method, Form and Content: Essays in Honor of George W. Coats* (ed. E. Carpenter; JSOTSup 240; Sheffield: Sheffield Academic Press, 1997), 91-108.

begins already with the two stories in chap. 17. The theophany of Yahweh on Horeb (17:6) and Moses' construction of an altar after the war with the Amalekites (17:15) set the stage for the initial worship of the Israelite leaders on the mountain of God.

Exodus 18:2-4 describes Moses' Midianite family. Jethro returns with Zipporah, who last appeared traveling toward Egypt with Moses (4:18-26). The story accounts for her absence by stating that Moses "sent her away." The verb can mean divorce (Deut 22:19), but it hardly fits this context. The point of the insertion is not Zipporah but Moses' two sons, mention of whom is a surprise to the reader, since the earlier story of Moses in Midian recounted the birth of only one son, Gershom. Moses' interpretation of the name Gershom repeats information from Exod 2:22, providing commentary on his circumstances when he lived with the Midianites: "I have been an alien in a foreign land." The focus of the text is likely on the new information, about the second son, Eliezer. The name means "My God is help." The interpretation that Moses provides is: "The God of my father was my help and he rescued me *(nāṣal)* from the sword of Pharaoh."

Two themes stand out in Moses' interpretation of Eliezer's name. The first is the identification of Yahweh as the "God of the father," and the second is the declaration of salvation as a divine rescue *(nāṣal)*. Both themes occur in the first revelation of Yahweh to Moses on the mountain of God (3:6-9). The phrase "God of the father" stresses Yahweh's kinship with the Israelites, not the Midianites — an important point of clarification since Jethro will assume the leadership role in worship on the mountain of God. The declaration of divine rescue signals the fulfillment of the exodus from Egypt and, with it, the initial phase of Moses' commission. The setting of the mountain of God (18:5) reinforces this interpretation, recalling the divine sign to Moses during his commission (3:12). The sign was that after the exodus he would "worship God on this mountain." The fulfillment of the divine sign will continue into chaps. 19–34 as the worship leadership of Jethro on the mountain of God is transferred to Moses.

18:6-8 Moses' meeting with Jethro recalls his rendezvous with Aaron in 4:27-31. Both stories take place in the wilderness at the mountain of God (4:27; 18:5). The encounter includes a kiss (4:27; 18:7). And in each case Moses recounts a past experience of God to a family member. But the parallel between the two stories ceases when Moses leads Jethro into "the tent." This may be a reference to his dwelling, emphasizing the domestic setting of the story. Abraham is pictured as dwelling in his tent in Genesis 18. But the reference to the mountain of God may indicate a cultic tent, perhaps even the tent of meeting (see 33:7-11). The tent of meeting is described simply as "the tent," but usually in a context in which there is more specific identification (e.g., Num 11:16, "the tent of meeting"; and Num 11:24, 26, "the tent"). The family setting of the encounter in Exod 18:1-5, the lack of a more specific identification of "the tent," and the initial appearance of the tent of meeting in 33:7-11 favor a domestic rather than a cultic interpretation. But the reference to the mountain of God and the concluding worship do not exclude a cultic interpretation.

Moses recounts Yahweh's actions against Pharaoh in v. 8. His summary includes Yahweh's attack against Pharaoh and the Egyptians ("all that Yahweh had done to Pharaoh and the Egyptians for the sake of the Israelites") and the divine leading of the Israelites in the wilderness ("all the hardships that had beset them on the way"). His summary ends by repeating the theme of deliverance: "Yahweh rescued *(nāṣal)* them."

18:9-12 The conclusion of the story is about Jethro and Yahweh. Exodus 18:1-12 employs two names for God, Elohim (vv. 1, 4, 9, 12) and Yahweh (vv. 1, 8 [twice] 9, 10, 11). The divine name Elohim frames the story. At the outset Jethro hears about the deeds of Elohim (v. 1), and at the conclusion of the story he sacrifices to Elohim (v. 12). But the focus of the story is on the name Yahweh. In the first section of the story (vv. 1-5) Jethro knows the divine name Yahweh. Verse 1 mixes the two names, stating "Jethro heard of the deeds of Elohim," that "Yahweh brought out the Israelites from Egypt." In the second section (vv. 6-8) Moses repeats the divine name Yahweh in his report to Jethro. Jethro concludes the story in vv. 9-12, blessing Yahweh (v. 10), confessing the superiority of Yahweh over all other gods (v. 11), and leading the Israelites in a cultic meal before God (v. 12).

The act of blessing Yahweh is a cultic form of praise. H.-J. Kraus notes its uses in the Psalter both in the song of thanksgiving (Pss 124:6; 144:1) and in the hymn (68:19; 135:21).[7] It is uncommon in the Pentateuch. The ancestors (Seth, Gen 9:26; Abraham, 14:19, etc.) and the Israelite nation (Num 22:12) are blessed, but they in turn do not bless God. The priests receive the power to bestow blessing on the Israelites (Num 6:24-26). But only non-Israelites bless God in the Pentateuch. Melchizedek blesses El Elyon in a hymn (Gen 14:20). The servant of Abraham blesses Yahweh as an act of thanksgiving (Gen 24:27). And Jethro blesses Yahweh, the last occurrence of such an action in the Pentateuch. F. Horst concluded that the act of blessing Yahweh is a way of recognizing his position of power and his claim of greatness.[8] This certainly fits the story of Jethro, who blesses Yahweh for the power demonstrated in the rescue *(nāṣal)* of the Israelite people.

The divine power implied in the act of blessing is made explicit in Jethro's confession in v. 11. It separates into three parts: a statement of new awareness,

7. Kraus, *Psalms 1–59,* 341.
8. F. Horst, "Segen und Segenshandlung in der Bibel," *EvT* 1 (1947): 31.

"Now I know"; a proclamation of the incomparable greatness of Yahweh, "Yahweh is greater than all other gods"; and a reason for the confession: "For in the matter when they [the Egyptians?] dealt presumptuously with them." Each phrase has attracted extensive interpretation. Scholars debate whether the knowledge of Jethro signifies his first encounter with Yahweh. Some argue that the confession of incomparability indicates Jethro's conversion to Yahwism.[9] Yet others contemplate whether the reference to "other gods" is meant to indicate Jethro's polytheism. In addition, the reason for Jethro's confession is unclear.[10] The NIV rendition, "for he [Yahweh] did this to those who had treated Israel arrogantly," is at best a loose paraphrase.

The theme of knowing Yahweh plays a role in both the Non-P and P Histories. Pharaoh denies any knowledge of Yahweh in the initial encounter with Moses in the Non-P History (5:2), setting the stage for the cycle of plagues. And the P History expands the theme with the recognition motif, the divine demand that the Egyptians and Pharaoh acknowledge Yahweh (i.e., 7:5). The confession of Jethro is not an instance of the recognition motif, associating him with Pharaoh. It is, rather, a confession ("Now I know"). The confession lacks the polemical character of the demand for recognition ("You will know that"). Psalm 20 provides liturgical background. The psalm separates into three parts: a petition for the king's safety in battle (vv. 1-5), a confession of God's help (vv. 6-8), and a concluding prayer (v. 9).[11] The petition for the king's safety concludes with the phrase: "May Yahweh grant all your requests" (vv. 1-5). Verse 6 marks a transition from petition to assurance employing the confession of Jethro: "Now I know that Yahweh will help his anointed." The transition is not a new revelation of Yahweh since the petition in vv. 1-5 presupposes knowledge of Yahweh. According to H.-J. Kraus the confession signifies that "Yahweh has notified the praying community that he will bestow [salvation] on the king" through a sign of fulfillment or an oracle of salvation.[12] Thus the confession, "Now I know," in Psalm 20 confirms knowledge of Yahweh already held by the community or by the king. The confirmation is through a new experience of God's presence.

The story of Elijah's resurrection of the widow of Zarephath's son uses the confession in the same manner as Psalm 20. When her son dies the widow of Zarephath knows that Elijah is a man of God. She states: "What have you against me, O man of God?" (1 Kgs 17:18). Yet when Elijah resurrects the boy,

---

9. C. Frevel, "Jetzt habe ich erkannt, dass YHWH grösser ist als alle Götter: Ex 18 und seine kompositionsgeschichtliche Stellung im Pentateuch," *BZ* 47 (2003): 3-22.

10. Childs (*Exodus*, 320) notes that the MT is an anacoluthon, avoided in the LXX, which disregards Hebrew *kî*, "for, because."

11. J. Clinton McCann Jr., "The Book of Psalms: Introduction, Commentary, and Reflections," *NIB* 4:755.

12. Kraus, *Psalms 1–59*, 281.

she confesses: "Now I know that you are a man of God" (17:24). The confession is similar to Psalm 20, signifying established knowledge confirmed by a new experience (see also Judg 17:13). Even Yahweh can have knowledge confirmed by new experience. When Abraham demonstrated his willingness to sacrifice Isaac, the Messenger of Yahweh employs the confession: "Now I know that you fear God" (Gen 22:12).

The confession of Jethro is the same as the widow of Zarephath and the cultic confession in Psalm 20. He knows Yahweh (Exod 18:1). But the report of Moses adds new experience to his knowledge of Yahweh. The divine rescue of the Israelites confirms the incomparability of Yahweh over all other gods. Jethro's confession echoes the refrain in the Song of the Sea, where Yahweh's incomparability to the other gods was also confessed (15:11). C. J. Labuschagne underscored the confessional nature of the statement cautioning against more philosophical interpretations, which seek to discern whether Jethro was a polytheist or a monotheist.[13] The point of the confession is that Jethro's knowledge of Yahweh is deepened by the events of the exodus. His confession is no different than the psalmist who states: "For I know that Yahweh is great; our Lord is above all gods" (Ps 135:5).

Exodus 18:12 describes the first Israelite sacrifice, completing the transfer of cultic ritual from the Midianites to the Israelites. Zipporah transmitted the ritual of circumcision to Moses during his individual journey through the wilderness (4:24-26). Now, in the Israelite journey through the wilderness, Jethro leads the people in cultic ritual, performing two types of sacrifices. Both involved slaughter. The first is the "burnt offering" (*'ōlâ*). It is wholly consumed upon the altar. Its root meaning is "ascending," indicating that the entire sacrifice is given over to God; no portion is consumed by the worshiper. The burnt offering is mentioned in Deuteronomy, especially in the law of cultic centralization (Deut 12:6, 11). And it is described in detail in the P legislation (Leviticus 1; 6:8-13). The second type of sacrifice is the "slaughter" (*zebaḥ*). The word for "altar" in Hebrew, *mizbēaḥ*, derives from the same root. Unlike the burnt offering, the worshiper shares in the consumption of the "slaughter" sacrifice, as, for example, in the Passover rite in Deuteronomy (Deut 16:1-6). Exodus 18:12 employs the plural, perhaps indicating a variety of "slaughter" sacrifices. In his initial encounter with Pharaoh, Moses stated that the "slaughter" sacrifice in the wilderness was a divine requirement of the Israelites (5:3). The motif is repeated throughout the plague cycle (8:26-27) and is now fulfilled on the mountain of God. The scene concludes with Aaron, the elders, and most likely Moses eating the slaughter sacrifice with Jethro in the presence of God.

13. C. J. Labuschagne, *The Incomparability of Yahweh in the Old Testament* (Leiden: Brill, 1966).

ADMINISTRATION OF LAW (18:13-27)

¹⁸:¹³*And on the next day Moses sat to judge the people. And the people stood around Moses from the morning until the evening.*

¹⁴*And Jethro, Moses' father-in-law, saw all that he was doing for the people. And he said, "What is this thing that you are doing to the people? Why do you sit alone and all the people are stationed about you from morning until evening?"*

¹⁵*And Moses said to his father-in-law, "Because the people approach me to inquire of God.* ¹⁶*For whenever they have a matter, they come to me and I judge between a man and his neighbor. And I make known the statutes of the God and his laws."*

¹⁷*And the father-in-law of Moses said to him, "The thing that you are doing is not good.* ¹⁸*You will wear out, both you and this people who are with you, for the matter is too heavy for you, and you are not able to do it alone.* ¹⁹*Now listen to my voice. I will counsel you, and God will be with you: You must be for the people the one facing the God, and you bring the matters to the God.* ²⁰*You will enlighten them concerning the statutes and the laws. And you will make known to them the way in which they will walk and the deeds they will do.* ²¹*But you must perceive from all the people men of valor, God-fearers, men of truth, who hate gain. And you will place them as rulers of thousands, rulers of hundreds, rulers of fifties, and rulers of tens.* ²²*And they will judge the people at all times. And any great matter they will bring to you. But all little matters they will judge them. And it will lighten from upon you, and they will bear with you.* ²³*If you do this thing, and God commands you, you will be able to stand, and all this people will enter his place in peace."*

²⁴*And Moses heard the voice of his father-in-law. And he did all that he said.* ²⁵*Moses chose men of valor from all Israel. And he made them heads over the people, rulers of thousands, rulers of hundreds, rulers of fifties, and rulers of tens.* ²⁶*And they judged the people at all times. The difficult matters they would bring to Moses. And every small matter they would judge them.*

²⁷*And Moses sent out his father-in-law. And he directed him to his land.*

Notes

18:13-27 Hebrew *dābār,* "word, thing, matter, affair," is a leitmotif throughout the narrative, occurring ten times in a variety of contexts (vv. 14, 16, 17, 18, 19, 22 [twice], 23, 26 [twice]; see the commentary). The distinct contexts make it difficult to translate the motif consistently. I render the Hebrew as "thing" (vv. 14, 17, 23) and "matter" (vv. 16, 18, 22, 26). The LXX also provides a range of words, including *rhēma,* "that which is said or spoke, word, saying" (vv. 17, 18, 22, 23, 26), *antilogia,* "disputes" (v. 16), *logous,* "words" (v. 19), and the demonstrative pronoun *ti touto,* "what is this" (v. 14).

18:15 *to inquire of God.* Hebrew *lidrōš 'ĕlōhîm* means "to inquire," but when applied to God it can also take on the meaning of an oracular revelation (Gen 25:22; Isa 8:19). The LXX translates, *ekzētēsai krisin para tou theou,* "to seek judgment from God," emphasizing more the legal setting of the narrative.

18:16 *and his laws.* The LXX translates in the singular, *ton nomon autou,* "his law."

18:18 *you will wear out.* Hebrew *nābōl tibbōl* is intensive, "wearing out you will wear out." The word may also include a judgment on Moses' action as being foolish (see Prov 30:32), thus requiring the wise counsel of Jethro in v. 19. Any play on the wisdom tradition in the Hebrew is lost in the LXX: *phthora kataphtharēsē anypomonētō,* "you will be completely destroyed by an unbearable task."

18:19 *the one facing the God.* Hebrew *mûl hā'ĕlōhîm* translates more lit. "in front of the God." The LXX has a more impersonal translation, *ginou sy tō laō ta pros ton theon,* "you be for the people the things before God."

18:20 *You will enlighten.* Hebrew *wĕhizhartā* means "to warn," but also "to shine," perhaps deriving from a different root (see Dan 12:3).[1] The translation "to enlighten" accentuates the revelatory quality of the judicial process, already suggested in v. 15 with Hebrew *dāraš,* "to inquire." See the commentary. The LXX translates, *diamartyrē,* "you will attest to."

18:21 *But you must perceive.* Hebrew *ḥāzâ,* "perceive," continues the emphasis on clairvoyance in the judicial process. The term also functions as a technical word for prophetic clairvoyance (see Amos 1:1; Isa 1:1). The LXX translates, *skeptomai,* "look about carefully."

18:27 *And he directed him to his land.* The construction in the MT is difficult. The phrase *wayyēlek lô 'el-'arṣô* implies that Moses is the subject of *wayyēlek,* with *lô* referring to Jethro, "He [Moses] directed him [Jethro] to his [Jethro's] country." The LXX makes Jethro the understood subject, *kai apēlthen eis tēn gēn autou,* "and he [Jethro] went to his land."

Commentary

The second story about Moses' Midianite father-in-law at the mountain of God changes theme from divine rescue *(nāṣal)* and worship to the administration of law. Hebrew *dābār,* meaning a "word, thing, matter," and, in a more technical sense, "case law," becomes the central motif. E. Greenstein has demonstrated the literary skill with which the motif is developed.[2] The word first occurs in the previous episode (18:11), when Jethro states in his confession that it is "because of the matter" *(baddābār)* of what the Egyptians did to the Israelites that Yahweh rescued them. The rabbinic interpretation of this difficult phrase is legal. Yahweh was applying the principle of *lex talionis* (measure for measure) to

---

1. See also Wevers, *Notes,* 286.

2. E. L. Greenstein, "Jethro's Wit: An Interpretation of Wordplay in Exodus 18," in *On the Way to Nineveh: Studies in Honor of George M. Landes* (ed. S. L. Cook and S. C. Winter; ASOR Books 4; Atlanta: Scholars Press, 1999), 155-71.

the Egyptians for their oppression of the Israelites.[3] The rabbinic interpretation provides a fitting introduction to the following episode where *dābār* occurs ten times (vv. 14, 16, 17, 18, 19, 22 [twice], 23, 26 [twice]) to describe the administration of case law. The motif also provides an introduction to the revelation of the "words of Yahweh" *(dibrê yhwh)* in chaps. 19–34, which will provide the legal basis for the covenant (see 19:7; 24:3-8; 34:27-28).

The establishment of legal judges in 18:13-27 is also recounted in Deut 1:9-18. In Deuteronomy Moses is the protagonist. He states his inability to judge the people alone, and in view of this limitation he selects judges. In Exod 18:13-27 Moses' unnamed Midianite father-in-law become the protagonist. He clarifies for Moses the need to have legal assistance in judging the people. He also fashions the solution in which there are levels of court proceedings.

18:13-16 The two stories about Moses' Midianite father-in-law are separated temporally. The administration of law takes place the next day. Moses' father-in-law is also unnamed in this episode. Moses is presented as a judge (v. 13). The people surround him with cases to be resolved and the action continues from morning until evening. Moses' father-in-law enters the scene in v. 14 and questions the action of Moses with a pun, "What is the *dābār* that you are doing?" He questions why Moses judges legal cases alone. The opening scene ends with Moses' response in vv. 15-16, indicating his role as judge and mediator. The people inquire of God through Moses. When a legal dispute, a *dābār*, arises, they seek out Moses for a judgment. The verdict is likely some form of an oracle. As a result, Moses promulgates the divine statutes and laws.

18:17-23 Moses' father-in-law condemns the practice in vv. 17-18. He states: "The task, the *dābār*, is not good!" The administration of law is far too large for Moses to undertake alone. He offers two solutions with the assurance of divine approval, "God will be with you." Thus the Midianite father-in-law of Moses transmits divine legal advice in addition to his cultic leadership.

The first point of advice concerns Moses (vv. 19b-20). He should maintain his role as mediator between Yahweh and the people, transmitting divine law to the people. The role of mediator means that Moses both receives divine revelation and transmits law to the people. Both roles are implied in the verb used to describe his task in v. 20. Moses is "to enlighten" *(zāhar)* the people in Torah, thus revealing their life path. Hebrew *zāhar* means "to warn," but it can also mean "to shine," taking on the more revelatory meaning implied in the translation "to enlighten." The central book on Jewish mysticism is entitled *The Zohar*. It contains instruction that enlightens. Moses will instruct and warn the Israelites on the meaning of divine law throughout chaps. 19–34, until he finally embodies the law in his shining face in 34:29-35, indi-

3. *Mekilta de-Rabbi Ishmael,* tractate *Beshallaḥ* VII.19-20.

cating his own enlightenment and mystical union with God, as the transmitter of divine law.

The second recommendation involves a system of judges to apply the divine law transmitted through Moses (vv. 21-22). Moses' father-in-law instructs him to decentralize the administration of justice by selecting "God-fearing" men. Their further characterization as "men of valor" (*'anšê ḥayil*) suggests a military background, but the term may simply indicate charismatic leaders in this story.[4] The process of selection requires charismatic, prophetic power by Moses. The Hebrew verb translated "to select" in v. 21 *(ḥāzâ)* is a technical term for prophetic clairvoyance (see Amos 1:1; Isa 1:1; Mic 1:1). The advice is that Moses "perceive" the qualities of justice and truth in the judges he appoints. Thus their ability to judge is charismatic, not inherited. It derives from Moses' ability to recognize their qualities. The selection of the seventy elders in the related story of Num 11:4-35 also emphasizes charismatic leadership.[5] The system of judges breaks down over groups of thousands, hundreds, fifties, and tens.

The concluding assurance of Moses' father-in-law (v. 23) provides a glimpse into the original social setting of the story before its incorporation into the Non-P History. Moses' father-in-law predicts that the people will return to their homes in peace, implying a social setting in the land of Canaan, not the wilderness. The setting of Canaan, rather than the wilderness, prompted R. Knierim to conclude that the story is an etiology aimed at justifying the reorganization of the judicial system during the monarchical period, thus suspending the previous legal system. Knierim reasoned that the setting of the story in the Mosaic office immediately after the exodus was meant to legitimate the change. The historical and social setting addressed in the story may have been the reorganization under Jehoshaphat, recorded in 2 Chr 19:4-11.[6]

S. Cook broadened the scope of study, relating Exod 18:13-27 with similar stories in Deut 1:9-18 and in Num 11:4-35 as a single tradition, which he describes as "the E-stream tradition," a form of Yahwism with northern roots in Ephraim. The E-stream tradition also includes prophetic literature; of special significance is the critique of the administration of justice in Micah 3. Cook concludes that the E-stream tradition of selecting judges represents a critical evaluation and refinement of the judicial office throughout the monarchical period and that Exod 18:13-27 represents an inner-biblical refinement of Num 11:4-35.[7] The social reconstructions are difficult to confirm. Whatever the social background of the story may have been at an earlier time period in Israelite his-

---

4. For discussion of the possible military background of the story see Knierim, "Exodus 18."

5. See Dozeman, "Numbers," 103-8.

6. Knierim, "Exodus 18."

7. Cook, "Tradition of Mosaic Judges."

tory, the Non-P historian now employs the episode as a transition from the initial phase of the wilderness journey (chaps. 15–18) to the revelation of law on the divine mountain (chaps. 19–34). See the introduction for the interpretation of the literary context in the Non-P History.

18:24-27   The story concludes with Moses implementing the recommendations of his father-in-law. Moses then sends his father-in-law away, meaning perhaps that he escorted him or released him from any more service. The closing portrait is of Moses' father-in-law traveling back to his own country.

Yet additional stories of Moses' father-in-law return after the events in chaps. 19–34, when Moses requests the guidance of "Hobab ben Reuel, his Midianite father-in-law," in the wilderness journey from Mount Yahweh in Num 10:29-32. Moses asks that his father-in-law lead the Israelite people to the promised land in exchange for a portion of the inheritance. Hobab is reluctant and refuses the request, stating that he would return to his own land and his own people (Num 10:30). Moses presses his request a second time, adding that Hobab could be the eyes of the Israelites through the wilderness journey, promising "good" from Yahweh in exchange for his leadership. The text breaks off without providing the response of Hobab. The leading of the ark of the covenant may indicate Hobab's negative response. But reappearance of Hobab the Kenite father-in-law of Moses in Judg 4:11 suggests that he did accompany the Israelites to the promised land. Blum has rightly described the literary context of Num 10:29-32 as occupying an "in-between position" *(Zwischenstellung)* in the *KD,* his designation for the Non-P history.[8] The Midianite identity and the name Reuel of Moses' father-in-law forge a literary relationship with the opening stories of Moses' father-in-law Reuel, the priest of Midian (Exod 2:18), and with the later stories of Hobab, the Kenite father-in-law of Moses (Judg 4:11).

---

8. Blum, *Studien,* 143.

Revelation (19:1–24:11)

INTRODUCTION

CENTRAL THEMES

The central themes in this episode are the setting of the divine mountain, the revelation of law, the establishment of covenant, and the holiness of God. The primary event is the initial descent and revelation of God on the divine mountain. The journey through the wilderness (Exod 15:22–18:27) provides a prologue for the revelation on Mount Sinai. The two episodes share similar motifs, including law, the setting of the cosmic mountain in the wilderness, and theophany. The divine proposal of law at the outset of the journey in the wilderness of Shur (15:26) repeats as a proposal of covenant when the Israelites arrive at the wilderness of Sinai (19:3-6). The pivotal role of the divine mountain throughout chaps. 19–24 is foreshadowed by its appearance in the wilderness episodes leading up to the Israelites' arrival at Mount Sinai. God rescued the Israelites by drawing water from the rock at Horeb, the divine mountain (17:6); and Jethro, the father-in-law of Moses, led the Israelites in worship on the mountain of God (18:1-12).

Holiness of God

The motif of holiness is central to Exodus. Related terms occur over eighty times, mostly in the setting of the mountain of God. The first occurrence is the revelation in the burning bush, when Yahweh cautions Moses about trespassing too closely to the flame, since the divine mountain was "holy ground" (3:5). The firstborn (13:2), Yahweh (15:11), Yahweh's temple (15:13), and the Sabbath (16:23) are declared holy in the course of the events of the exodus and the wilderness journey. The motif returns in a more prominent role when the Israelites arrive at the mountain of God, where Moses first encountered Yahweh in the burning bush. The theme of holiness is introduced as a divine promise to the Israelites immediately upon their arrival at Mount Sinai (19:6). But the transfer of holiness from God to the Israelites is not accomplished in 19:1–24:11. The holiness of God requires careful procedures (19:10, 14) and without them in place Yahweh is unable to descend upon Mount Sinai (19:22-23). The safeguards include the sanctuary for containment, the priesthood for service, and cultic rituals for orchestrating the movement into the realm of holiness. These requirements are achieved in the final episode (24:12–40:38), where terms for holiness occur nearly seventy times in the account of the construction of the tabernacle. The result is the divine descent from Mount Sinai into the sanctuary at the close of Exodus (40:34-38).

Holiness describes Yahweh throughout the Hebrew Bible. "Yahweh is the Holy One of Israel," proclaims the prophet Isaiah (Isa 1:4).[1] The Song of the Sea echoes the words of the prophet, celebrating Yahweh as "majestic in holiness" (Exod 15:11). J. Milgrom states that the holiness of God is the quintessential nature of the Deity.[2] As such, holiness is more than a system of ethical actions — it probes the very character of the Deity. R. Otto called the holiness of God the "numinous," an active force that overwhelms humans with the sense of absolute dependence. Humans cannot know the numinous through intellectual reflection or ethical action, according to Otto. Knowledge of the numinous requires its invasion into the human realm, which produces a primal revelation of the Deity as the experience of something wholly other.[3] Otto describes the human response to the "otherness" of God's holiness as the *mysterium tremendum,* a preethical feeling of awe and dependence.[4] For him the story of the Deity's attack against Moses in Exod 4:24-26 illustrates the primal nature of the numinous. It defies a rational interpretation leaving the reader with the question: What did Moses do to deserve the divine attack? Otto would describe this story as monstrous.[5]

Otto's research underscores that the holiness of God is ineffable and dangerous to humans. As such it is more than a system of ethics. The initial experience of the Israelites during the descent of God on Mount Sinai is an illustration

---

1. See R. W. L. Moberly, "'Holy, Holy, Holy': Isaiah's Vision of God," in *Holiness Past and Present* (ed. S. C. Barton; London: T & T Clark, 2003), 122-40.

2. J. Milgrom, *Leviticus 1–16* (AB 3A; New York: Doubleday, 1991), 617.

3. R. Otto, *The Idea of the Holy: An Inquiry into the Non-Rational Factor in the Idea of the Divine and Its Relation to the Rational* (trans. J. W. Harvey; 2nd ed.; London: Oxford University Press, 1958), 1-10.

4. Ibid., 12-30.

5. Ibid., 31-40.

of the otherness of God and the experience of the *mysterium tremendum*. The descent of God overwhelms the people and they simply "tremble" *(ḥārad)* in the presence of God (19:16). Even the mountain trembles at the presence of God, since it too is part of the earthly realm of humans (19:18). But the holiness of God also gives rise to ritual actions and ethical systems, which allow humans to live in the presence of God. The revelation of God in Exodus 19–24 contains the description of cultic and ethical behavior, which arises from an encounter with divine holiness.[6] D. P. Wright concluded that the ritual and ethical implications of holiness *(qōdeš)* derive from the root meaning "to be separate."[7] M. Douglas adds: "The Hebrew root k-d-sh, which is usually translated as Holy, is based on the idea of separation."[8] The character of holiness as separation provides the starting point for describing its cultic and ethical implications in human life.

Milgrom has clarified that the separation of holiness is of two kinds.[9] The first is the separation between the sacred and the profane. We might call this an ontological distinction. The sacred is the immortal world of God. Holiness is intrinsic to God (Isa 5:24; Ps 89:18) and a characteristic of the region of heaven (Ps 20:6; Deut 26:15). The profane is the mortal world of humans. Holiness is absent from this world.[10] Thus holiness, according to P. Jensen, is associated most closely with the concept of space, marking the separation of heaven and earth.[11] The first creation story (Gen 1:1–2:4a) provides definition. Humans are good, blessed, and even image bearers of the Deity in the utopian world of Genesis 1, but they are not holy (1:26-30). The same is true for the creation: it is good but not holy (1:31). The profane world in the first creation story is separate from the holiness of God. The Hebrew verb *qādaš*, "to be holy," at the close of the first creation story illustrates further the separation between the sacred and the profane: "God blessed the seventh day and *hallowed it*" (Piel of Hebrew *qādaš*; 2:3). Although the verb is correctly translated "to consecrate" or "to make hallowed," the root meaning indicates that God "separated" the Sabbath from the other six days, thus creating a permanent distinction between them. The contrast is between the sacred, the realm of God, and the profane, the world of humans. The focus in the first six days of creation is on the human

6. See D. J. Davies, "The Sociology of Holiness: The Power of Being Good," in *Holiness Past and Present*, ed. Barton, 48-67.

7. D. P. Wright, "Holiness," *ABD* 3:237-49.

8. M. Douglas, *Purity and Danger: An Analysis of the Concepts of Pollution and Taboo* (London: Routledge & Kegan Paul, 1966), 8.

9. See Milgrom, *Leviticus 1–16*, 42-61, 616, *et passim*.

10. See M. Eliade, *The Sacred and the Profane: The Nature of Religion* (trans. W. R. Trask; New York: Harcourt, Brace, 1959).

11. P. Jensen, "Holiness in the Priestly Writing," in *Holiness Past and Present*, ed. Barton, 105-7.

world in all of its complexity. But on the seventh day no act of creation takes place. The focus is instead on God, who is described as resting in the divine realm, prompting worship in the human world.

The demand for a tithe in Lev 27:32 further illustrates the root meaning "to be separate" in the concept of holiness: "All tithes of herd and flock, every tenth one that passes under the shepherd's staff, will be holy [i.e., separated out] to Yahweh." The holy status of the tithe does not arise from any quality within the chosen animal. Rather, in the act of separation the animal leaves the possession of its human owner, enters the realm of God, and becomes a divine possession. As such it is holy. God and the region of heaven are qualitatively distinct from humans and the created world. They are not to be mixed. The need to keep separate the sacred and the profane is underscored negatively at the outset of the flood story (Genesis 6–9). The merging of the two realms through sexual intercourse, resulting in the birth of the Nephilim, is stated as one of the reasons that God seeks to destroy the world through the flood (Gen 6:1-4). The word for the offspring, Nephilim, means "the fallen ones."

The second level of separation is more biological, resulting from sin entering the human world. The origin of the biological distinction between God and humans is described in the shedding of blood in the story of Cain and Abel (Genesis 4). When Cain kills Abel the blood of Abel leaves his body and enters the ground. The blood cries out from the ground because it becomes a contaminate, rather than a life force. The murder of Abel indicates that the source of the virus of sin is "blood out of place." The result for humans is a further distancing from God. The ontological separation between the sacred and the profane is widened to include the distinction between the pure and the impure. After the murder of Abel, humans are not only mortal, they are also diseased, and thus repelled by God, which intensifies the danger between the holiness of God and humans.[12] Douglas concludes that the biological distinction between the pure and the impure contrasts the wholeness and the order of divine holiness to the impure world of disorder and decay occupied by humans.[13] Milgrom extends the contrast to include life and death: God must be quarantined from death (Numbers 19),[14] human disease (Leviticus 13–15),[15] moral disease (Leviticus 19),[16] and disorder (Leviticus 11).[17] The separation between purity and impurity widens the distance between God and humans.

12. See Milgrom, *Leviticus 1–16*, 718-36, 1000-1009.

13. Douglas, *Purity and Danger*, 29-40.

14. See J. Milgrom, *Numbers* (JPS Torah Commentary; Philadelphia: Jewish Publication Society, 1990), 157-62, 438-47.

15. Milgrom, *Leviticus 1–16*, 43-44, 766ff.

16. J. Milgrom, *Leviticus 17–22* (AB 3A; New York: Doubleday, 2000), 1602-1726.

17. Douglas, *Purity and Danger*, e.g., 41-57.

The separation between the sacred and the profane and the pure and the impure makes any contact between God and humans volatile and dangerous. Fire often represents the danger of the sacred. G. E. Mendenhall notes that fire often accompanies deities in the ancient Near East in the form of the *melammū,* a radiant halo surrounding the head of a god.[18] Fire from heaven can also represent divine judgment, as in the plague cycle, when Yahweh, the Storm God, rained down hail and lightning on the Egyptians (Exod 9:13-35). When the two realms of the sacred and the profane do come into proximity humans proceed with great caution. Unregulated contact with holiness results in death to humans regardless of motive. God kills Uzzah when he steadies the ark, regardless of his good intention (2 Sam 6:6-11). The most appropriate human response to holiness is fear. Moses reacts with fear to the holiness of God in the burning bush (Exod 3:5), as does the prophet Isaiah in the Jerusalem temple (Isa 6:1-6).[19] Human sin intensifies the danger of contact between the two realms. God attacks Moses in the wilderness, and Zipporah must rescue him through circumcision and a blood ritual (Exod 4:24-26). Yahweh fears contamination in meeting with the Israelites at Mount Sinai (19:22-23). Even the two sons of Aaron, Nadab and Abihu, are killed by God when they violate rituals associated with the divine fire in the altar (Lev 10:1-2). The two-part separation between God and humans results in a paradoxical situation. Humans need holiness for life and health. But the gift is a two-edged sword — it can kill or heal.

The root meaning of holiness as separation indicates the point of tension and the goal of the narrative in Exod 19:1–24:11. When biblical writers attribute holiness to God, they affirm the separation between God and humans. Yet Yahweh offered the Israelites health at the outset of the wilderness journey (15:22-26); and, upon their arrival at Mount Sinai, God even promises them holiness (19:6). The drama in the revelation at Mount Sinai is to overcome the separation inherent in holiness to fulfill the divine promise.

Law and Covenant

The promise of covenant draws God into the profane world in 19:1–24:11, even though holiness prevents God from taking up residency. The theme of covenant is introduced in the divine proposal of covenant (19:1-8) and in the revelation of covenantal law (20:1-17; 20:22–23:33).[20] The repeated trips by Moses

18. G. E. Mendenhall, "The Mask of Yahweh," in *The Tenth Generation: The Origins of the Biblical Tradition* (Baltimore: Johns Hopkins University Press, 1973), 32-66.

19. For discussion on the fear of the holy (or numinous) see Otto, *Idea of the Holy.*

20. E. W. Nicholson, *God and His People: Covenant and Theology in the Old Testament* (Oxford: Clarendon, 1986).

throughout the episode are dominated by the revelation of law and its codification in the Decalogue and in the Book of the Covenant. The Decalogue (20:1-17) is a public revelation of law to the Israelite people during the experience of theophany. It provides guidelines for living in the sphere of holiness. The private revelation of the Book of the Covenant (20:21–23:33) to Moses draws out the implications of divine law for the Israelites' future life in the land.

The people's acceptance of divine law at the close of the episode establishes the covenant between themselves and God (24:3-8). Mendenhall defines covenant as: "An agreement enacted between two parties in which one or both make promises under oath to perform or refrain from certain actions stipulated in advance."[21] R. Kraetzschmar emphasized that covenant describes obligations imposed upon one or both of the parties.[22] E. Kutsch further reinforced the meaning of covenant as obligation.[23] Yet the fulfillment of the promises or obligations also creates a relationship between the covenant parties, according to S. McKenzie: "Covenant is the main biblical image for the distinctive relationship of the people of Israel with God."[24] Thus the establishment of covenant is one means by which the rule of God can be established on earth. The role of covenant in 19:1–24:11 will require further interpretation in the commentary. But it becomes clear at the outset that the covenant between God and the Israelite people creates tension with the holiness of God. Holiness underscores God's separation from humans, while covenant describes God's commitment to the Israelite people. The tension between covenant and holiness established in the revelation (19:1–24:11) will reach a climax in the story of the golden calf (chap. 32) in the following section on the sanctuary (24:12–40:38).

The theme of covenant and law also develops the role of Moses as mediator between God and the Israelite people. The role of Moses as mediator and as the human author of divine law advances the theme of Mosaic authority. The theme of Mosaic authority was introduced in the wilderness commission of Moses, when Moses objected to his commission, fearing that the elders would not believe in him (4:1-9). The authority of Moses increased at the Red Sea, when the people believed in him and in Yahweh (14:31). Mosaic authority is established further at the mountain of God, when the people hear the voice of God and thus believe in Moses (19:9; 20:18-20). According to M. R. Hauge,

---

21. G. E. Mendenhall, "Covenant," *ABD* 1:1179-1202.

22. R. Kraetzschmar, *Die Bundesvorstellung im Alten Testament in ihrer geschichtlichen Entwicklung* (Marburg: Elwert, 1896). See the discussion by S. L. McKenzie, *Covenant* (Understanding Biblical Themes; St. Louis: Chalice, 2000), e.g., 32, 37.

23. E. Kutsch, *Verheissung und Gesetz: Untersuchungen zum sogenannten 'Bund' im Alten Testament* (BZAW 131; Berlin: de Gruyter, 1973).

24. McKenzie, *Covenant*, 9.

"Moses could represent the ideal religious figure, while the mountain scene provides the framework of the ultimate religious experience."[25]

Mountain of God and Theophany

The setting of the divine mountain is also a central theme in this episode, as the quotation from Hauge indicates. God is associated with the mountain in the opening verses, when Moses ascends to the summit in order to meet God (19:3) while the Israelites encamp below (19:2). The opening portrait indicates the important role of the mountain as the main structuring device throughout the story. In structuring the story the mountain will also define the spatial relationship of the characters. The episode will continue to locate God at the summit of the mountain, the Israelites at its base, while tracing the movement of Moses between both parties, as the drama of covenant unfolds. J. Lotman provides insight into the structuring role of the mountain and its symbolic significance: "Spatial relations [within narrative] turn out to be one of the basic means for comprehending reality." The result is that the "structure of the space of a text becomes a model of the structure of the space of the universe."[26]

Mountains model the world of heaven and earth in ancient Near Eastern culture and religion. R. E. Clements concluded that cosmic mountains became symbols of divine presence in the created world.[27] The entrance of God into the created world is often associated with a "holy mountain of residency." Baal invades the earth by taking up residency on Mount Zaphon. Psalm 99:9 states: "Extol Yahweh our God, and worship at his holy mountain; for Yahweh our God is holy." The divine residency on a sacred mountain is a description of the temple, according to R. J. Clifford, which serves to bridge the gulf between heaven and earth.[28] J. D. Levenson adds that cosmic mountains also disclose "the essential . . . relationship of YHWH to his people."[29] Thus the role of the divine mountain in bridging the worlds of heaven and earth is essential to their symbolic meaning in the ancient Near East. I will explore the close relationship between cosmic mountains and temples in the concluding episode on the sanctuary (24:12–40:38; see the introduction). In the present episode the cosmic

25. M. R. Hauge, *The Descent from the Mountain: Narrative Patterns in Exodus 19–40* (JSOTSup 323; Sheffield: Sheffield Academic Press, 2001), 26.

26. J. Lotman, *The Structure of the Artistic Text* (Michigan Slavic Contributions 7; Ann Arbor: University of Michigan Press, 1977), 217-18.

27. R. E. Clements, *God and Temple* (Philadelphia: Fortress, 1965), 2.

28. Clifford, *Cosmic Mountain,* 20-25.

29. J. D. Levenson, *Sinai and Zion: An Entry into the Jewish Bible* (New York: Winston, 1985), 33.

mountain serves more to underscore the distance between God and humans and the danger of bringing the sacred and profane worlds together, since Yahweh does not take up residency on earth.

The mountain does provide the setting for theophany in 19:1–24:11, meaning the appearance of God (see the introduction, "The Theophany on the Mountain").[30] J. Jeremias concluded that the earliest form of the genre of theophany described the approach of God from the southern region of Edom and its effects on nature (Deut 33:2; Hab 3:3; Ps 68:8). The theophany is often for the purpose of divine rescue in a situation of war.[31] The appearance of God on Mount Sinai reflects a later development of this tradition. It includes a range of technical language associated with the tradition of theophany, including the imagery of fire associated with the Deity, the accompanying cloud, and the language of the divine approach *(bô')* and descent *(yārad)*.[32] But the circumstances of the theophany are different in Exodus 19–24. The Deity does not approach from another region at a time of crisis, but descends upon the mountain to speak to the people, to create a covenant with them, to fashion cultic ritual, and to provide future blessing.[33]

AUTHORS

The revelation of God at the divine mountain contains literature from several different authors and from many different time periods. The appearance of God in a storm on the mountain (19:16-17) and the meal with the Deity at the summit of the mountain (24:10-11) may be independent accounts of theophany (see the introduction, "Individual Genres"; "Theophany on the Mountain"). The Decalogue (20:1-17) and the Book of the Covenant (20:22–23:33) are also independent law codes now incorporated into the revelation of God on Mount Sinai. The combination of the genre of theophany with the law codes has dominated the modern interpretation of the composition of Exodus 19–24, raising literary and tradition-historical questions about the relationship of law and narrative in the formation of the Pentateuch.

---

30. See F. Polak, "Theophany and Mediator: The Unfolding of a Theme in the Book of Exodus," in *Studies in the Book of Exodus: Redaction — Reception — Interpretation* (ed. M. Vervenne; BETL 126; Leuven: Leuven University Press, 1996), 113-47.

31. See Jeremias, *Theophanie*.

32. See Mettinger, *Dethronement of Sabaoth*.

33. Van Seters, *Life of Moses*, 254-70. Van Seters compares the reinterpretation of theophany in Exodus 19–24 to late prophetic texts in the Hebrew Bible and to Neo-Babylonian building inscriptions.

Research

I begin the review of research with a survey of the tradition-historical study of Exodus 19–24 and conclude with an overview of the literary solutions to the composition of Exodus 19–24. Wellhausen will provide the point of departure for both areas of research.

The diverse genres of theophany and law in Exodus 19–24 have set the framework for hypotheses about the origin and development of Israelite religion. Wellhausen focused primarily on the literary development of Exodus 19–24. Yet he also presented a more tradition-historical hypothesis with the conclusion that the promulgation of law was originally associated with the setting of Kadesh, not Sinai. The basis for his conclusion was literary-critical. The revelation at Sinai was a large insertion into the Pentateuch, which separated the legal traditions in Exodus 18 and Num 10:29ff. The earliest version of Exodus 19–24, according to Wellhausen, was an account of the appearance of God, not the promulgation of law. Deuteronomy represents the combination of law, covenant, and narrative, which became the springboard for the P author to make law the primary event at the revelation at Sinai.[34] Thus the prominent role of law in the Pentateuch was a late development in the history of Israelite religion.

Von Rad expanded and transformed the hypothesis of Wellhausen, influencing the interpretation of Exodus 19–24. He argued that the literary break between Exodus 18 and Numbers 10 provided a window into a more profound tradition-historical distinction between the Kadesh cycle of stories associated with the exodus (Exodus 17–18; Numbers 10–14) and the Sinai cycle of stories (Exodus 19–24, 32–34).[35] The two cycles are the result of the separate cultic traditions of the exodus-conquest and the revelation of law at Sinai, which precede the literary formation of the Pentateuch/Hexateuch.[36] The celebration of the exodus-conquest originated in the cultic practice at Gilgal. The tradition was preserved in the historical credos (Deut 6:20-24; 26:5b-9; Josh 24:2b-13). The credos commemorated salvation history with the themes of the promise to the ancestors, the exodus, and the conquest. The tradition of law at Kadesh was an episode in the exodus-conquest tradition. Von Rad concluded that the revelation of law at Sinai was a separate cultic legend, associated with worship at Shechem. Its central themes included the approach of the Deity, the address of God to the people in the form of law, the promise of blessing, and the sealing of the covenant. The hypothesis of von Rad modified the conclusion of Wellhausen, placing law in the earliest stages of Israelite religion.

---

34. Wellhausen, *Composition*, 331-33; idem, *Prolegomena*, 345-47.
35. Von Rad, *Problem of the Hexateuch*, 14-15.
36. Ibid., 1-78; Noth, *History of Pentateuchal Traditions*, 58-59, 115-36.

The focus of von Rad on ancient preliterary traditions influenced the study of Exodus 19–24. Scholars focused on the origin of Israelite tradition in cultic rituals, rather than on the composition of the literature. The focus on the cult gave rise to debate over the setting and function of the Sinai tradition and the relationship of myth and ritual in the formation of the tradition. S. Mowinckel located the cultic legend of Sinai in the New Year Festival in Jerusalem, as opposed to Shechem.[37] H.-J. Kraus argued that the separate cultic legends of salvation history and the revelation at Sinai merged already in the preliterary period as the cultic centers moved during the tribal period.[38] The interest in the early period of Israelite religion also led to hypotheses about the literary composition of Exodus 19–24. Von Rad concluded that the combination of the historical credo and the revelation at Sinai occurred in the literary sources, J and E, during the early monarchical period.[39] Noth identified an even earlier literary composition, which he described as "G," the document that preceded the sources J and E.[40]

The identification of the revelation at Sinai as a separate tradition received further support from the comparative study of ancient Near Eastern legal treaties.[41] Von Rad identified the themes of the revelation at Sinai as the approach of the Deity, the address of God to the people in the form of law, the promise of blessing, and the sealing of the covenant. The work of Mendenhall on the form of international vassal treaties added precision and a broader historical context to the themes of the revelation at Sinai.[42] The structure of the treaties included the identification of the overlord, the historical prologue, the legal stipulations, the provisions for public reading, the blessings and curses, and the ratification. The form of the vassal treaty corresponds to the revelation at Sinai, according to Mendenhall, suggesting that Exodus 19–24 was intended to establish the covenant between Yahweh and Israel patterned on the structure of the vassal treaties. The common form of the vassal treaties also provided an additional window into the early formation of Israelite religion. The cult and the law were inseparable from the very

37. S. Mowinckel, *Le décalogue* (Études d'histoire et de philosophie religieuses 16; Paris: Alcan, 1927).

38. H.-J. Kraus, *Worship in Israel: A Cultic History of the Old Testament* (trans. G. Buswell; Richmond: John Knox, 1965).

39. Von Rad, *Problem of the Hexateuch*, 53.

40. Noth, *History of Pentateuchal Traditions*, 38-41.

41. V. Korošec, *Hithitische Stattsverträge: Ein Beitrag zu ihrer juristiche Wertung* (Leipziger rechtswissenschaftliche Studien 60; Leipzig: Weicher, 1931).

42. G. E. Mendenhall, *Law and Covenant in Israel and the Ancient Near East* (Pittsburgh: Biblical Colloquium, 1955). See also the studies by D. J. McCarthy, *Treaty and Covenant* (AnBib 21; Rome: Pontifical Biblical Institute Press, 1963); K. Baltzer, *The Covenant Formulary in Old Testament, Jewish, and Early Christian Writings* (trans. D. E. Green; Philadelphia: Fortress, 1971).

origin of Israelite religion, according to Mendenhall, and the covenant form "furnished . . . the nucleus about which the historical traditions crystallized in early Israel."[43]

W. Beyerlin represents a synthesis of the tradition-historical and the comparative research on the revelation at Sinai, while also underscoring the weakness of concentrating on the formative role of the cultic traditions over the literary composition. Beyerlin noted a series of problems that resulted from the focus on preliterary cultic traditions. It was not possible to recognize the factors influencing the independent development of the traditions or their combination in the formation of the Pentateuch. As a result, there was a wide range of disagreement on how the traditions of Sinai and the exodus merged and how the Sinai tradition was tied to the cult. Beyerlin concluded that only the literature could be analyzed with any certainty in a quest for the origins and history of the oldest Sinaitic traditions.[44]

Wellhausen also provides the starting point for the literary study of the composition of Exodus 19–24. He identified several authors in the present form of the literature. Three literary criteria were especially important: (1) the distribution of the divine names Yahweh and Elohim, (2) the diverse law codes, and (3) the multiple accounts of Moses ascending the mountain. Wellhausen noted the literary problem of repetition that resulted from Moses repeatedly ascending the mountain, and he correlated the trips with the distinct law codes of the Decalogue (20:1-17), the Book of the Covenant (21:1–23:19), and the legislation of the tabernacle (chaps. 25–31, 35–40).[45] The result was the identification of the authors P, E, and J in chaps. 19–24. The P author is nearly absent from chaps. 19–24, according to Wellhausen, who attributes to P only the notice of the Israelite arrival (19:1-2a) and the ascent of Moses on Mount Sinai (24:15b-18a), though he also assigns to P the legislation of the tabernacle (chaps. 25–31, 35–40).[46]

Wellhausen attributes most of the literature in Exodus 19–24 to the E and J sources. The Elohist includes the theophany (19:10-19) and the revelation of the Decalogue (20:1-20), where the divine name Elohim is prominent. The proposal of covenant (19:3-9) is also in the tradition of E, but may be the composition of a later editor. The E source continues with the divine command that Moses write the law (24:1-2, 11-14; 31:18) and the subsequent story of the golden

---

43. Mendenhall, *Law and Covenant,* 44.

44. W. Beyerlin, *Origins and History of the Oldest Sinaitic Traditions* (trans. S. Rudman; Oxford: Basil Blackwell, 1965).

45. Wellhausen, *Composition,* 83-88. The so-called Ritual Decalogue in Exodus 34 also plays an important role in the source-critical analysis of the law codes. See the discussion in the following section, "Sanctuary," Exodus 24:12–40:38.

46. Wellhausen, *Composition,* 84, 98-99.

calf (Exodus 32; 33:1-11).[47] The J source includes the ascent of Moses (19:20-25), the revelation of the Book of the Covenant (20:23-26; 21-23), and the covenant ceremony (24:3-8).[48] The two sources are expanded, reorganized, and combined by the Yehowistic redactor, an author in the tradition of Deuteronomy, whose literary creativity makes the separation of the E and J sources difficult in the present form of the text.[49]

L. Perlitt signaled a change in the interpretation of Exodus 19–24 by focusing more carefully on the redactor of the literature, who was already identified in the work of Wellhausen as the Yehowist. Perlitt concluded that the entire theme of covenant throughout Exodus 19–24 was the composition of a Deuteronomistic redactor writing at the end of the monarchical period, and not part of the J or E sources. Perlitt based the conclusion on the study of the theme of covenant throughout the Hebrew Bible, which he judged to be a late development in the literature and not an original feature of Israelite religion.[50] Perlitt also compared the language, the literary structure, and the theological outlook of Exodus 19–24 to Deuteronomy. He concluded that Exodus 19–24 was closely related to the presentation of covenant in Deuteronomy, especially in three places: (1) the proposal of covenant (19:3-8), (2) the Decalogue (20:1-17), and (3) the covenant ceremony (24:3-8). Perlitt concluded that the author of the three sections of literature was the Deuteronomist.

Perlitt represents a modification of source criticism, since he continued to assume the presence of separate sources in Exodus 19–24.[51] Subsequent interpreters have built on the research of Perlitt, while also rejecting the hypothesis of source criticism. Blum identifies the Non-P literature in Exodus 19–24 as an episode in what he calls the D-Komposition.[52] Blenkinsopp attributes the Non-P portions of Exodus 19–24 to the Deuteronomic canon, which spans the Enneateuch (Genesis–2 Kings).[53] Van Seters identifies the author of Exodus 19–

47. Ibid., 89-90.

48. Ibid., 89-90, 98.

49. Ibid., 91-97. Wellhausen adjusted his source-critical analysis in light of the research of A. Kuenen. Originally he attributed Exodus 34 to a separate author, but later he assigned this law code to J (pp. 329-35). Subsequent source critics refined the work of Wellhausen. G. Beer assigned the literature to E (Exod 19:2b, 3a, 10, 13b, 14, 16, 17, 19; 20:18-26; 21:1–23:19; 24:1, 3*, 4b-6, 8-12, 13-15a, 18b) and J[2] (Exod 19:9, 11-13a, 15, 18, 20). Beer identified various redactors: R in 23:29-30; R[D] in 19:3b-8; 23:23-25a*a*; R[JE] in 19:20-25; and R[P] in 20:1-17 (*Exodus* [HAT 3; Tübingen: Mohr (Siebeck), 1939]). See the additional review of scholarship in Childs, *Exodus,* 344-47.

50. In this respect Perlitt represents a return to the position of Wellhausen, who also judged the prominent role of law to be a late development in the history of Israelite religion.

51. See also the study of E. Zenger, *Die Sinaitheophanie: Untersuchungen zum jahwistischen und elohistischen Geschichtswerk* (Forschung zur Bibel; Würzburg: Echter Verlag, 1971).

52. Blum, *Studien,* 47-53.

53. Blenkinsopp, *Pentateuch,* 183-97; idem, "What Happened at Sinai?" 163-74.

24 as the exilic Yahwist, who is reinterpreting the account of revelation from Deuteronomy.[54]

More recent redaction-critical studies have followed the trend in dating the composition of the literature to the late monarchical, exilic, and postexilic periods, while also identifying more authors in the composition of Exodus 19–24. B. Renaud traces the formation of Exodus 19–24 from a monarchical account of theophany (19:2b, 3a, 10-11a, 13b, 14-17, 19; 20:18b, 20; 24:9-11), which may have included a shortened form of the Decalogue, through two Deuteronomistic editions. The first edition introduces covenant and accentuates the Decalogue (19:3b-8; 20:1-17*; 24:4-8). The second Deuteronomistic edition idealizes Moses (19:9; 20:1, 18a, 19, 21), accentuates the volcanic imagery of theophany (19:11b, 18), and incorporates the Book of the Covenant (20:22–23:33). The P literature in chaps. 19–24 is a source document (19:1-2a, 20[?]; 24:15ff.), according to Renaud, which includes additions (19:13a, [20?], 21-25; 20:8-11; 24:1-2).[55]

W. Oswald discerns even more authors in the composition of Exodus 19–24.[56] He describes four stages of Deuteronomistic redaction. The first is a mountain of God story that includes the Book of the Covenant (Exod 19:2b, 3a, 10a-11a, 14a-15b, 16-17, 18b, 19a; 20:18b-d, 21bc, 22a; 21:2–23:19; 24:3, 12-13*, 18bc). The second is the inclusion of the Decalogue (20:1, 2-17, 19, 21a). The third redaction centers on the theme of covenant (19:3b-7a, 7c-8, 9-10, 13-14; 20:22b-23; 21:1; 24:4-8). The fourth Deuteronomistic redaction idealizes the elders (24:13a-14), while also incorporating the Messenger of Yahweh (23:20-33). The P literature is limited to 19:1-2a and 24:9-11. But Oswald identifies two additional stages of composition in the formation of the Pentateuch. The first is a pentateuchal redaction, which forges links between the Deuteronomistic and P versions (19:11b-13e, 15, 18a-c, 20-25; 20:18a; 24:1-2; 24:15-18a). The second redaction represents an idealization of Moses and the Torah (19:8f-9e, 19b; 20:20).

The research on authorship indicates a wide variety of views concerning the tradition-historical development and the literary composition of Exodus 19–24. The comparative research in vassal treaties continues to influence the interpretation of the revelation at Sinai. But interpreters have become less confident of recovering the origin of Israelite religion and the cultic practice of the earliest period in Israelite history. L. Rost identified the historical credos as late literary compositions, as opposed to ancient liturgical confes-

---

54. Van Seters, *Life of Moses,* 247-89.

55. B. Renaud, *La théophanie du Sinaï: Ex 19–24: Exégèse et théologie* (CahRB 30; Paris: Gabalda, 1991).

56. W. Oswald, *Israel am Gottesberg: Eine Untersuchung zur Literargeschichte der vorderen Sinaiperikope Ex 19–24 und deren historischen Hintergrund* (OBO 159; Freiburg: Universitäts-verlag, 1998).

sions.[57] Van Seters also questioned the antiquity of the tradition of the revelation of law at Sinai: "It is possible that the giving of divine law was first associated with Moses and the wilderness period of Deuteronomic reformers in the late monarchy, but there is no evidence that this notion rested on cultic tradition of a covenant renewal festival or law making."[58] The quest to describe the origin of Israelite religion and the development of the early cultic legends will not be a focus of interpretation. In the commentary I limit the identification of the authors to the literary composition of Exodus 19–24.

The composition of Exodus 19–24 continues to pose problems for interpreters, giving rise to a variety of literary solutions to account for the present organization of the literature. The identification of sources continues. The role of redactors has expanded beyond the initial research of Wellhausen, and the dating of the literature has shifted from the early monarchical period to the late monarchical, exilic, and postexilic periods. The later dating has prompted interpreters to identify the Non-P composition of Exodus 19–24 more closely with Deuteronomy and the broader development of Deuteronomistic literature in the Hebrew Bible. The complexity of the composition, noted already by Wellhausen, is underscored once again by recent redaction-critical studies, where numerous authors are identified in the present composition of Exodus 19–24. In the commentary I limit the identification of the authors of Exodus 19–24 to the Non-P and P Histories. The recent redaction-critical studies indicate, however, that the Non-P History incorporates a wide range of literature, which is far more loosely organized than the literature assigned to the P History.

Non-P and P Histories

The chart in figure 29 on page 425 identifies the literature of the Non-P and P Histories.

Non-P History

My summary begins with an interpretation of the mountain setting and concludes with an outline of the literary structure and the central motifs in the Non-P History.

---

57. L. Rost, "Das kleine geschichtliche Credo," in *Das kleine Credo und andere Studien zum Alten Testament* (Heidelberg: Quelle & Meyer, 1965), 11-25.

58. J. Van Seters, "'Comparing Scripture with Scripture': Some Observations on the Sinai Pericope of Exodus 19–24," in *Canon, Theology, and Old Testament Interpretation: Essays in Honor of Brevard S. Childs* (ed. G. M. Tucker et al.; Philadelphia: Fortress, 1988), 111-30, esp. 127. For a review of the problem see T. B. Dozeman, "Horeb/Sinai and the Rise of Law in the Wilderness Tradition," *SBLSP* 28 (1989): 282-90.

Figure 29

Topic	Non-P History	P History
Proposal of Covenant (19:1-8a)		
1. Arrival	19:2	19:1
2. Proposal	19:3-5*a*, 6b	19:5b-6a
3. Acceptance	19:7-8a	—
Theophany (19:8a-19)		
1. Preparation	19:8b-11a, 12-15	19:11b
2. Event	19:16-17, 19	19:18
Revelation of Law (19:20–23:33)		
1. Introduction	—	19:20-25
2. Decalogue	20:1-17*	20:8-11
3. Fear of Israel	20:18-20	—
4. Book of the Covenant	20:21–23:33	—
Covenant Ceremony (24:1-11)		
1. Instruction	—	24:1-2*
2. Ceremony	24:3-5, 7	24:6, 8
3. Vision and meal on the mountain		24:9-11*

Setting of the Divine Mountain

The travel notice in the Non-P History signals the prominence of the mountain setting in Exodus 19–24 and its sacred character. The sequence of travel is likely contained in 19:2: the Israelites leave Rephidim, arrive in the wilderness of Sinai, and camp "before the mountain" *(negeb hāhār)*. Verse 3 identifies the unnamed mountain as the divine residence: Moses ascends the mountain to meet God who speaks to him from the summit. The travel notice suggests a definite location, "the mountain" *(hāhār, 19:2-3)*, which repeats throughout the episode (19:2, 3, 12 [twice], 13, 14, 16, 17; 24:4), but it is not clearly identified with a name. The problem in identifying the mountain is compounded by a range of overlapping terms in the Non-P History. The "mountain of God" is the location for Moses' encounter with the burning bush (3:1), his rendezvous with Aaron (4:27), and his meeting with Jethro (18:5). Mount Horeb is the location where Yahweh brought water from the rock (17:6) and perhaps also waged war against the Amalekites (17:6-8). Now the Israelites encounter God at "the mountain" (19:2).

The "mountain of God," "Mount Horeb," and "the mountain" may originate from distinct religious traditions.[59] This was the conclusion of Noth, who identified all references to the mountain of God as a separate tradition of divine revelation.[60] But regardless of their origin the incorporation of the different traditions into a single history forces a loose relationship among the terms in the Non-P History. The mountain of God may be equated with Horeb already in the commission of Moses (3:1). It is certainly equated with the mountain of revelation in chaps. 19–24 at the close of the episode, when the leaders of Israel eat and drink in the presence of the Deity on the mountain of God (24:13). Deuteronomy is explicit in identifying the unnamed mountain of revelation in Exodus 19–24 as Mount Horeb (Deut 1:2, 6, 19; 4:10, 15; 5:2; 9:8; 18:16; 29:1). Deuteronomy states that the revelation of the Decalogue (Deut 4:10; 5:6-21 = Exod 20:1-17), the establishment of covenant (Deut 29:1 = Exod 19:3-8; 24:3-8), and the selection of Moses as mediator (Deut 18:16 = Exod 20:18-20) take place on Mount Horeb. The Non-P historian will also identify the mountain of revelation as Horeb in the following episode (Exod 33:6). The overlapping terminology indicates a close relationship between the account of revelation in the Non-P History and in Deuteronomy.

Structure and Central Themes

The revelation in the Non-P History recounts the successful transfer of holiness from God to the Israelites through the public revelation of law and the creation of covenant. The story progresses through four episodes: the proposal of covenant (19:2-5ba, 6b, 7-8a), the theophany (19:8b-17, 19), the revelation of law (20:1-20*; 20:21–24:1a), and the covenant closing ceremony (24:3-5, 7, 9aa, bb, 10-11).

PROPOSAL OF COVENANT

The proposal of covenant takes place on the divine mountain in the Non-P History, dividing between Moses and Yahweh on the summit (19:2-5ba, 6b) and Moses and the Israelites at the base of the mountain (19:7-8a). Divine speech as law dominates the scene. Yahweh declares (*qārā'*, v. 3) the proposal of covenant to Moses promising the people an exclusive relationship with God (*sĕgullâ*, v. 5ba). The covenant (*bĕrît*, v. 5) requires observing the voice (*qōl*, v. 5) and the words (*dĕbārîm*, v. 6b) that God commands (*ṣwh*, v. 7). Moses approaches (*bô'*,

---

59. See L. Perlitt, "Sinai und Horeb," in *Beiträge zur Alttestamentlichen Theologie: Festschrift für Walther Zimmerli* (ed. H. Donner et al.; Göttingen: Vandenhoeck & Ruprecht, 1977), 302-22.

60. Noth, *History of Pentateuchal Traditions*, 136-41.

v. 7) the people and repeats (*qārā',* v. 7) the divine declaration to the Israelites, who accept the divine words (*děbārîm,* v. 8a).

THEOPHANY

The appearance of God is also an event of divine speech in the Non-P History. Moses returns the words of the people to God (v. 8b), prompting the Deity to state two purposes for theophany (v. 9). The approach *(bô')* of God in the cloud will allow the Israelites to hear divine words *(děbārîm),* and it will also authenticate the commission of Moses (3:1–4:17), with the people believing in him *('āman).* After a period of preparation (19:10-11a, 12-15), Yahweh and the people meet at the divine mountain (v. 17). The appearance of God in the storm (v. 16) evolves into a conversation between God and Moses (v. 19), the content of which is the Decalogue (20:1-17*), thus blurring the transition from theophany to the revelation of law in the Non-P History. The people overhear the conversation, fulfilling the first part of the divine prediction to Moses. The theophany in the Non-P History, therefore, is a public experience of divine law, suggesting the transfer of holiness from God to the people who hear divine speech.

REVELATION OF LAW

The revelation of law progresses from a public event in the words of the Decalogue (20:1-17) to the private revelation of the Book of the Covenant to Moses (20:21–24:1a). The transition from public to private revelation is important to the structure of the Non-P History. It was anticipated in the divine announcement of theophany to Moses (19:9). Thus the revelation of the Decalogue, as a direct speech of God to the people, is part of the experience of theophany in the Non-P History. The people hear divine words as God predicted to Moses. But the people also so fear the divine words that they choose Moses to mediate all future speech by God (20:18-20), fulfilling the second part of the divine prediction to Moses. As a result, Moses emerges as the covenant mediator of all future law. The private revelation of law to Moses is also closely tied to the preceding theophany. It begins with Yahweh affirming that the divine appearance on the mountain was an experience of speech, in which God spoke (Piel of *dābar*) to the Israelites from heaven (20:22). The divine address at the outset of the Book of the Covenant repeats the prophetic messenger speech of Moses from the proposal of covenant: "Thus you will say to . . ." (19:3; 20:22). The language reinforces Moses' authoritative role, idealizing him as a prophetic teacher who is able to convey divine speech to the Israelites. Moses fulfills his new role by receiving the revelation of the Book of the Covenant alone at the summit of the divine mountain (20:21–24:1a).

COVENANT CEREMONY

Moses returns to the people and proclaims the law at the base of the mountain in a covenant ceremony (24:3-5, 7). The episode may end with the leaders of Israel on the divine mountain feasting with God (24:9a*a*, b*b*, 10-11), although this scene advances themes more central to the P History. In his study of covenant theology, Perlitt noted that the covenant ceremony contains many parallels to the proposal of covenant in vocabulary and in structure, including an emphasis on divine speech as law and the verb "to approach" (*bô'*) to describe the movement of Moses on the mountain.[61] Other parallels include Moses presenting the "words" (*dĕbārîm*, 24:3; see 19:7) of God to the Israelites and the people's acceptance of them as covenantal law (24:7; see 19:8a).

But the covenant ceremony also goes beyond the proposal of covenant and the theophany on the mountain. God spoke law to the Israelites during the theophany. But in the covenant ceremony divine speech becomes written law (*kātab*, 24:4) in the Book of the Covenant (*sēper habbĕrît*, 24:7), which Moses proclaims (*qārā'*, 24:7; see 19:7) and reads (Piel of *sāpar*, 24:3) to the people. Thus the revelation in the Non-P History not only progresses from a public experience of all the Israelites to a private experience of Moses, but also evolves from oral to written law and from a proposal of covenant to its codification in a book. The Non-P author concludes the episode with the leaders of Israel seeing God and feasting on the divine mountain (24:10-11).

P History

I begin this summary with an interpretation of the mountain setting and conclude with an outline of the literary structure and the central motifs in the P History.

Setting of the Divine Mountain

Mount Sinai is the mountain of revelation in the P History. The word "Sinai" occurs thirty-five times in the Hebrew Bible in three different forms. Five times the word "Sinai" occurs alone (Exod 16:1; Deut 33:2; Judg 5:5; Ps 68:8, 17). Thirteen times Sinai is described as a region, "the wilderness of Sinai" (Exod 19:1, 2; Lev 7:38; Num 1:1, 19; 3:4, 14; 9:1, 5; 10:12; 26:64; 33:15, 16). And seventeen times Sinai is identified as a specific mountain, "Mount Sinai" (Exod 19:11, 18, 20, 23; 24:16; 31:18; 34:2, 4, 29, 32; Lev 7:38; 25:1; 26:46; 27:34; Num 3:1; 28:6; Neh 9:13).

---

61. L. Perlitt, *Bundestheologie im Alten Testament* (WMANT 36; Neukirchen-Vluyn: Neukirchener Verlag, 1969), 168-99.

The distribution — twenty-eight of the thirty-five occurrences — indicates how important Sinai is in the P History. A summary of the different uses of Sinai will clarify its role as the mountain of revelation in the P History.

The references to Sinai *(sînay)* in the four poetic passages (Deut 33:2; Judg 5:5; Ps 68:8, 17) provide insight into an early Israelite tradition of theophany, according to Albright.[62] The poems are identified as the "March in the South" tradition of theophany, because they associate Yahweh with a variety of southern locations (see also the commentary on 3:1–4:18). Psalm 68 identifies Yahweh with Sinai without indicating a more specific location. Judges 5:4-5 celebrates Yahweh as the "One of Sinai" and locates the Deity in Seir and Edom. Deuteronomy 33:2 also describes Yahweh's march from Sinai, making reference to Seir and Mount Paran. Cross concluded that the poetic texts identify Sinai as a southern region from where Yahweh would appear to rescue the Israelites at a time of crisis.[63] R. J. Clifford confirmed Cross's conclusion: "In the March in the South passages . . . the writer had no specific mountain in mind, but a mountainous territory."[64]

The only other use of the word "Sinai" alone is in the travel notice of Exod 16:1. This travel notice must be distinguished from the poetry. I assigned 16:1 to the P History, noting the use of the "congregation," the date of the Israelite arrival in the wilderness of Sin (month 2, day 15), and the more precise location, "between Elim and Sinai," as the style and language of the P author. The "wilderness of Sinai" *(midbar-sînay)* is a favorite location in the P History. The P author is responsible for ten of the thirteen occurrences, which will be examined momentarily. First it is necessary to examine the role of Sinai in the Non-P History.

Sinai occurs in the Non-P History (19:2) and in the summary of the wilderness journey in Numbers 33 (vv. 15-16). The wilderness of Sinai was likely the location for the unnamed mountain of God already in the Non-P History. The travel notice in the Non-P History states that the Israelites left Rephidim and entered the wilderness of Sinai (Exod 19:2). Although Rephidim and the wilderness of Sinai are clearly separated in the Israelites' journey, both locations occur in stories about the divine mountain, blurring their distinction. Stories about Horeb (Exodus 17) and the mountain of God (chap. 18) take place at Rephidim, while the revelation of God on the mountain occurs in the wilder-

---

62. W. F. Albright, "The Earliest Form of Hebrew Verse," *JPOS* 2 (1922): 69-86; idem, "The Song of Deborah in Light of Archaeology," *BASOR* 66 (1936): 30; idem, "A Catalogue of Early Hebrew Lyric Poems," *HUCA* 23 (1950-51): 14-24; idem, *Yahweh and the Gods of Canaan: A Historical Analysis of Two Contrasting Faiths* (Jordan Lectures; London: University of London, 1968), passim. Habakkuk 3:3-4 is also included in this tradition because of its reference to Mount Paran, which is associated with Sinai in Deut 33:2.

63. Cross, *Canaanite Myth and Hebrew Epic*, 99-105.

64. Clifford, *Cosmic Mountain*, 115 n. 16.

ness of Sinai (chap. 19), raising a question about the relationship of the different divine mountains and the two locations, Rephidim and the wilderness of Sinai (see the introduction to Exodus 19–24, "Authors"). The sequence of travel in 19:2 agrees with the summary of the wilderness journey in Num 33:15-16, where the people also progress from Rephidim to the wilderness of Sinai before moving on to Kibroth-hattaavah, the site for the divine feeding of the Israelites with quails in the Non-P History (see Num 11:34-35). The authorship of Numbers 33 is disputed. The P writer is certainly responsible for portions of the present text, as Noth recognized long ago.[65] But the references to the wilderness of Sinai in vv. 15-16 do not appear to be the work of the P author. Thus the P author does not create the tradition of the wilderness of Sinai but expands it.

The wilderness of Sinai is one of four central locations in the P History along with Pi-hahiroth, the setting for the confrontation at the Red Sea (Exodus 14); the wilderness of Sin, the setting for the story of manna (chap. 16); and the wilderness of Paran, the site where the first generation of the Israelites loses the gift of the land (Numbers 13 15). The wilderness of Sinai is the location for the revelation of sacrifices (Lev 7:37-38), the census of the Israelites (Num 1:1, 19) and the Levites (Num 3:14), as well as the location for the celebration of Passover (Num 9:1, 5).

The identification of the mountain of revelation as Mount Sinai *(har sînay)* is the creation of the P author.[66] All sixteen references to Mount Sinai in the Pentateuch are from the P author. Mount Sinai is identified as the mountain of revelation in the Israelites' preparation for theophany (Exod 19:11b) and in the failed attempt by Yahweh to descend on the summit of the mountain (19:18, 20, 23). Mount Sinai continues to be the mountain of revelation when the Glory of Yahweh *(kĕbôd yhwh)* successfully descends upon its summit. Mount Sinai is also the location where Yahweh reveals the "two tablets of the testimony" (31:18; 34:2, 4, 29, 32), the sacrifices (Lev 7:38), the Sabbatical Year (Lev 25:1), the Holiness Code (Lev 26:46), the remaining laws within Leviticus (Lev 27:34), and the legislation concerning the daily offerings (Num 28:6).

There are surprisingly few references to Mount Sinai outside the P History. It is absent altogether from the preexilic prophetic literature, appearing for the first time in postexilic texts. Mount Sinai is the mountain of revelation in the prayer of Ezra in Neh 9:13, the mountain of revelation in 2 Esd 3:17-19, and it is identified with Mount Horeb in the eulogy to Elijah in Sir 48:7, all late postexilic texts. Mount Sinai provides the setting for the interpretation of holiness in the P History.

---

65. M. Noth, *Numbers* (trans. J. D. Martin; OTL; Philadelphia: Westminster, 1968), 242-46. For discussion see Dozeman, "Numbers," 251-54.

66. See Dozeman, *God on the Mountain*, 120-26; idem, "Horeb/Sinai."

Revelation (19:1–24:11)

Structure and Central Motifs

The P historian changes the details of the revelation in this episode (Exod 19:1–24:11) and in the next episode (24:12–40:38). The changes occur in three texts: (1) in the initial revelation of Yahweh in chap. 19; (2) in the revelation of the Glory of Yahweh in 24:15-18; and (3) in the divine appearance for covenant renewal in chap. 34. The P author employs similar motifs in the three texts. Mount Sinai is introduced as the mountain of revelation (19:11, 18, 20; 24:16; 34:2, 4, 29, 32). There is a divine descent (*yārad* in 19:18, 20; 34:5; or *šākan* in 24:16) to the "top of the mountain" (*'el-rōʾš hāhār;* 19:20; 24:17; 34:2). And there is an emphasis on the role of Moses as mediator to maintain the separation between the sacred and the profane. The P author underscores that Moses alone is called by God to the summit of the mountain (19:20; 24:18; 34:2).

The changes to the revelation of God transform the structure of chaps. 19–24 and force a new interpretation of the episode. The most significant change is that the Decalogue is separated from the Israelites' direct experience of theophany. The Israelite people no longer hear the words of God in the P History. Rather, the Decalogue is communicated to the people through Moses (19:25). As a result, the role of Moses as mediator is less the charismatic teacher of law and more the priest who maintains distance between the sacred and the profane. The effect of the change is that the initial theophany on Mount Sinai fails to transfer holiness to the Israelite people, who neither hear the speech of God nor participate in any sacramental rituals.

PROPOSAL OF COVENANT

The P History adds two motifs to the proposal of covenant. The Israelite arrival in the wilderness of Sinai is dated to month 3 in the year of the exodus (19:1), a common practice of the P historian (e.g., 16:1). And the people are promised holiness in exchange for covenant obedience (19:5b-6a) — a promise that remains unfulfilled in the episode.

THEOPHANY

The theophany of Yahweh takes place on Mount Sinai in the P History (19:11b, 18). It requires a divine descent (*yārad*) to the summit of the mountain, rather than the divine approach (*bôʾ*) in the Non-P History (19:9). The appearance of God results in a visual encounter with fire (19:18), not an auditory experience of divine speech as in the Non-P History (19:19). In the commentary I explore where the P historian may also have included motifs of purification in the preparation of the Israelite people for the theophany.

REVELATION OF LAW

The Decalogue is separated from the experience of theophany in the P History. The people do not hear the Decalogue as a public revelation of law as in the Non-P History (19:19; 20:18-20). Instead, Moses teaches it to them (19:25). The change of status in the communication of the Decalogue is part of the reinterpretation of theophany in the P History. The initial theophany in chap. 19 fails to transfer holiness to the people of Israel, according to the P author. Exodus 19:20-24 states that Yahweh halted the descent on the summit of the mountain because of the need for further sanctification, clearer boundaries between the sacred and the profane, and the divine fear of contamination. The theophany is aborted and the people are restricted from approaching Mount Sinai, thus prohibiting them from hearing any divine speech on Mount Sinai. As a result, the Decalogue becomes a separate teaching by Moses at the base of Mount Sinai (19:25). The P historian also reinterprets the teaching of the Sabbath in the Decalogue (20:8-11) so that it conforms to the creation story in Genesis 1. But the signs of P reinterpretation in the Book of the Covenant (20:21–24:1a) are absent.

COVENANT CEREMONY

The P History emphasizes the role of Moses as a priestly mediator at the close of the revelation of the Book of the Covenant (24:1-2), associating him with Aaron and his two sons, Nadab and Abihu. The P History also includes a blood ritual in the covenant ceremony (24:6, 8) introducing the motif of sanctification first promised to the Israelites in the proposal of covenant (19:6). The ritual creates points of comparison with the sanctification ceremony of the priesthood in Leviticus 8. Finally, the vision of God on the mountain (Exod 24:9-11) may also have been expanded by the P author to provide a transition to the revelation of the tabernacle in Exodus 25–31.

LITERARY STRUCTURE

The stories of the conflict in Egypt and the wilderness journey are organized by repetition. The theme of oppression in Exodus 1–2, for example, is developed through a series of actions by Pharaoh that progress from slave labor to genocide. Pharaoh's repeated action against the Israelites intensifies the theme of oppression. The commission of Moses is also structured as a repetition in 3:1–7:7, occurring first in the wilderness (3:1–4:17) and repeating in the land of Egypt (6:2–7:7). Repetition is also central to the conflict between Yahweh and Pharaoh in 7:8–15:21, through the sequence of the plagues. Hauge writes that the plagues are "presented as a series of stereotyped situations with the same set of actors again and again acting out their roles."[67] The sequence of the plagues pushes the conflict between Yahweh and Pharaoh ahead until it culminates in the death of the Egyptian firstborn and the defeat of the Egyptian army in the Red Sea.

Repetition continues to structure the wilderness journey in 15:22–18:27. The repeated crises in the wilderness at distinct locations move the narrative forward to develop the theme of testing. The central role of repetition in each of the sections of Exodus advances the plot of the story. Repetition in service of plot and chronology creates a narrative characterized as Bildungsroman, according to D. Mickelsen.[68] Such narratives are like a road in which events move in one direction with a clear progression, resulting from the actions of characters. The development of the narrative plot is central in a Bildungsroman.

The revelation on the divine mountain in Exodus 19–24 is also organized by repetition. The story builds through repeated trips by Moses to the summit of the mountain. But unlike the preceding repetitions in Exodus, there is not a clear progression from one scene to the next toward a climax. Once the Israelites arrive at the divine mountain all forward movement ceases. The story appears to lack a plot. The people are stationary at the base of the mountain and God is at the summit, while Moses moves between the two parties. Wellhausen saw the problem of organization, noting that the "natural movement" and "consistent sequence" of earlier narratives give way to a "labyrinth of stories" in chaps. 19–24, which lack a natural progression to the events.[69] Wellhausen's conclusion is certainly correct when we compare the organization of chaps. 19–24 to the previous stories in Exodus. Exodus 19–24 does not conform to the rules of Bildungsroman. B. J. Schwartz confirms the earlier analysis of Wellhausen, noting that the account of revelation cannot be read "without insurmountable problems."[70] B. D. Sommer agrees, concluding that the text "presents a bewildering aggregate of verses describing Moses' ascents and descents on the mountain."[71]

The key for interpreting repetition in Exodus 19–24 is the setting of the mountain, not the development of the plot or the unfolding chronology of the story. The repeated trips by Moses relate the two worlds of heaven and earth in

---

67. Hauge, *Descent from the Mountain*, 21.

68. D. Mickelsen, "Types of Spatial Structure in Narrative," in *Spatial Form in Narrative* (ed. J. R. Smitten and A. Daghistany; Ithaca: Cornell University Press, 1981), 65-67.

69. Wellhausen, *Composition*, 81; idem, *Prolegomena*, 342.

70. B. J. Schwartz, "The Priestly Account of the Theophany and Lawgiving at Sinai," in *Texts, Temples, and Traditions: A Tribute to Menahem Haran* (ed. M. V. Fox et al.; Winona Lake, Ind.: Eisenbrauns, 1996), 111.

71. Sommer, "Revelation at Sinai," 426-27.

the setting of the divine mountain. The result is a narrative that is spatial in form whose aim is to address the central theme of holiness. A spatial-form narrative is like an orange, not a roadway. Individual scenes are organized around the center, focusing on the single subject at the core of the story. The scenes of the story do not progress in one direction, but are juxtaposed to one another, providing a different perspective on the same core event — the revelation of God on the mountain. The result is a narrative in which temporal sequence is replaced by a more circular movement around the central core subject.

The mountain setting is the hub at the center of the narrative. The individual scenes are spokes that provide different perspectives on the core event. The repeated trips by Moses on the mountain allow the biblical writers to present the distinct conceptions of holiness in the Non-P and P Histories. The visual appearance of God on Mount Sinai in the P History and the auditory experience of God as speech in the Non-P History are juxtaposed like segments of an orange, providing different perspectives on the single revelation of God on the one mountain. The result is that the contour of the mountain changes to accommodate the different views of holiness. Although it is presented as the one mountain of revelation, its identity shifts between Mount Sinai, the mountain of God, and Mount Horeb. But whatever its identity in a given scene, the mountain remains central to the organization of the story. Whenever interpretation shifts from the mountain setting to plot in an attempt to find structure, the narrative resists organization, as Wellhausen noted. But when interpretation remains clearly focused on the setting, Levenson rightly concludes that the mountain serves as a "mold into which new experiences could be fit . . . without rupturing the sense of tradition and continuity of historic identity."[72] The mold allows the Non-P and P Histories to be related into a single event of revelation on the one mountain without being harmonized. The result is a spatial-form narrative in which spatial relations on the mountain become "the basic means for comprehending reality."[73] Mount Sinai, Mount Horeb, and even the mountain of God become the one mountain of revelation even though they represent very different visions of the cultic presence of God on earth. Dohmen provides a visual illustration of the spatial-form narrative with the portrait of Mount Horeb and Mount Sinai as two mountains standing side-by-side in the drawing from the *Orientalische Reyss dess Edlen und Vesten Jacob Breuning von und zu Buechenbach* (Strassburg, 1612).[74]

The clearest example of the spatial-form design of Exodus 19–24 is the conflicting presentation of the Decalogue. The P interpretation of the

72. Levenson, *Sinai and Zion*, 18.
73. Lotman, *Structure of Artistic Text*, 217-18.
74. Dohmen, *Exodus 19-40*, 55.

Decalogue, as mediated teaching by Moses, provides the introduction to the law code (19:20-25). The P History separates the Decalogue from the experience of theophany. Yahweh halts the divine descent in fire upon Mount Sinai and commands Moses to descend the mountain in order to teach the law to the Israelites. But at the conclusion of the Decalogue the Israelites react to the direct speech of Yahweh, not the teaching of Moses (20:18-20). The people fear divine speech, and it is only at this point in the story that they choose Moses to mediate all future law for them. Thus in the present form of the text the Decalogue is both mediated teaching by Moses and direct divine speech. The setting of the mountain holds the two different conceptions of theophany, law, and holiness together. The result is a narrative that does not progress clearly in plot or in time. The wilderness stories already demonstrated the same literary structure. The locations of Rephidim and the wilderness of Sinai are clearly separated in the sequence of the Israelite journey. But repeated references to the divine mountain, as Horeb (17:6), the mountain of God (18:5), and Mount Sinai (19:11), raise questions about the distinction between the two locations. In the commentary I explore further instances where the distinct interpretations of the divine revelation on the cosmic mountain are organized spatially in the setting of the mountain. The commentary separates into the following units:

I. 19:1-8a, Proposal of Covenant
II. 19:8b-19, Theophany
III. 19:20–23:33, Revelation of Law
IV. 24:1-11, Covenant Ceremony

COMMENTARY

PROPOSAL OF COVENANT (19:1-8A)

[19:1]*On the third month after the Israelites went out from the land of Egypt, on this very day they entered the wilderness of Sinai.* [2]*And they set out from Rephidim and they entered the wilderness of Sinai, and they camped in the wilderness. And Israel camped there in front of the mountain.*

[3]*Then Moses ascended to the God. And Yahweh called to him from the mountain, saying, "Thus you will say to the house of Jacob and you will declare to the Israelites,* [4]*'You saw what I did to the Egyptians, how I bore you on eagles' wings, and I brought you to me.* [5]*Now if you listen carefully to my voice and you observe my covenant, you will be my personal possession from all the peoples.* **Indeed, all the earth is mine,** [6]**but you will be for me a kingdom of priests and a holy nation.***' These are the words which you will speak to the Israelites."*

⁷ *Then Moses went and called to the elders of the people. And he placed before them all these words, which Yahweh commanded him.*

⁸ᵃ *And all the people answered as one, and they said, "All which Yahweh spoke, we will do."*

Notes

19:1-2 The literary structure of the notice of the Israelites' arrival consists of three repetitions: the date (19:1a), the entrance into the wilderness of Sinai (19:1b-2a), and the encampment in the wilderness before the mountain (19:2b).

19:1 *on the third month . . . on this very day.* Hebrew *baḥōdeš haššĕlîšî* is also translated "on the third new moon" (see NRSV). Noth favored this translation, arguing that when it is read in conjunction with the second phrase, *bayyôm hazzeh*, 19:1 provides a reference to a specific day, the first day of the third month: "The reference in v. 1b to a definite day shows that the first word in v. 1a does not have the general meaning 'month,' but is meant in the special sense of the 'day of the new moon.'"[1] The LXX *tou de mēnos tou tritou . . . tē hēmera tautē* supports this translation, according to Wevers: "The lengthy dating formula ends with τῇ ἡμέρᾳ ταύτῃ which must refer to τοῦ μηνός; i.e. 'on the day of the month' can only refer to the first day; what Exod. [LXX] is saying is that it was the third month to the day, exactly two months, after the exodus of the Israelites from the land of Egypt."[2] A. Dillmann noted the problem with the more specific translation in that one would expect *bĕ'eḥād laḥōdeš* to designate a specific day (see Gen 8:5; Exod 40:2; Num 1:1, 18; 29:12).[3] The use of the nearer demonstrative, "on this very day," in the second temporal clause may emphasize the significance of the event without providing a specific date. The phrase also marks the first day of the flood (Gen 7:11), the sanctification of the priests (Lev 8:34), and the Day of Atonement (Lev 16:30) in addition to the arrival at Sinai (19:1). Childs writes: "The expression *bayyôm hazzeh* or *bĕ'eṣem hayyôm hazzeh*, which is common to P, can follow either an exact date formula (Gen. 7.13) or also refer to a specific day without the precise formulation (Gen. 17.23; Ex. 12.17)."[4]

19:3 *Then Moses ascended to the God.* The LXX states that Moses ascended "the mountain of God," *to oros tou theou.*

And Yahweh called to him from the mountain. The LXX reads, "the God," *ho theos,* instead of "Yahweh."

19:4 *you saw.* The LXX intensifies the statement with the emphatic use of *autoi,* "you yourselves saw."

19:5 *now if you listen carefully to my voice.* See 15:26.

you will be my personal possession. Hebrew *sĕgullâ* may be translated as "personal possession" or as "treasured possession" (see NRSV). The divergent translations re-

1. Noth, *Exodus*, 155.
2. Wevers, *Notes*, 292.
3. A. Dillmann, *Die Bücher Exodus und Leviticus* (KEHAT; Leipzig: S. Hirzel, 1880), 191.
4. Childs, *Exodus*, 342.

flect the debate over whether the Hebrew *sĕgullâ* conveys inherent value or describes a special relationship between Yahweh and the Israelite people (see the commentary). Translations by R. Mosis, J. P. Hyatt, and E. Zenger emphasize the relational quality of the term, "my personal possession."[5] Childs and Noth imply inherent value in the term by translating "special possession."[6] A. H. McNeile and S. R. Driver emphasize the inherent value even further, translating "peculiar treasure."[7] M. Greenberg notes that the related Akkadian word *sikiltum* is an economic term, which he translates, "private accumulation" and "private fund," as it occurs in a last will and testament from Nuzi, detailing the division of property between a wife and son: "whatever oils and copper which Kiraše [the wife] has privately accumulated *(sikiltaša)* are given to her." Greenberg concludes: "A woman's *sikiltu* was . . . her own private property."[8] The notion of private property is also evident in the Ugaritic *sglt*. See the letter to Ammurapi, king of Ugarit, from the Hittite king, in which he is told, "You are his property" ([s]*glth.at, PRU,* V 60:11-12).[9] The LXX translates, *periousios,* meaning "surplus, abundance."

from all the peoples. Hebrew *min,* "from," is used in a separative sense (see GKC §119w); similarly LXX *apo.*

Indeed, all the earth is mine. Hebrew *kî* has an asseverative function.[10] As usual, the LXX renders Hebrew *kî* with *gar.*

19:6 *but you will be for me a kingdom of priests and a holy nation.* Hebrew *waw* at the beginning of the phrase is disjunctive, "but" (GKC §154). See also the use of *de* in the LXX. The attributes "priests" *(kōhănîm)* and "holy" *(qādôš)* have adjectival force in the construct relationship with "kingdom" *(mamleket)* and "nation" *(gôy).* The two descriptions are in a parallel construction describing all Israel as a "kingdom of priests" and a "holy nation."[11] The word order of the MT, *mamleket*

---

5. R. Mosis, "Ex 19,5b.6a: Syntaktischer Aufbau und lexikalische Semantik," *BZ* 22 (1978): 18; Hyatt, *Exodus,* 200; Zenger, *Sinaitheophanie,* 167.

6. Childs, *Exodus,* 341, 367; Noth, *Exodus,* 157.

7. A. H. McNeile, *The Book of Exodus* (Westminster Commentaries; London: Methuen, 1906), 110; S. R. Driver, *The Book of Exodus* (Cambridge Bible for Schools and Colleges; Cambridge: Cambridge University Press, 1911), 170.

8. M. Greenberg, "Hebrew *sᵉgullā*: Akkadian *sikiltu,*" *JAOS* 71 (1951): 173.

9. For discussion of Ugaritic *sglt* see M. Dahood, "Hebrew-Ugaritic Lexicography III," *Bib* 46 (1965): 313; idem, "Hebrew-Ugaritic Lexicography VII," *Bib* 50 (1969): 341.

10. On the asseverative use of *kî* in nominal clauses see the discussion of C. Brockelmann, *Hebräische Syntax* (Neukirchen Kreis Moers: Buchhandlung des Erziehungsvereins, 1956), 31(b). For further discussion see Mosis, "Ex 19,5b.6a," 16; J. Muilenburg, "The Linguistic and Rhetorical Usages of the Particle כי in the Old Testament," in *Hearing,* 220; see also *HALOT* 1:470.

11. See R. B. Y. Scott, "A Kingdom of Priests (Exodus xix 6)," *OTS* 8 (1950): 219; J. B. Bauer, "Könige und Priester, ein heiliges Volk (Ex 19,6)," *BZ* 2 (1958): 285; W. L. Moran, "A Kingdom of Priests," in *The Bible in Current Catholic Thought* (ed. J. L. McKenzie; New York: Herder & Herder, 1962), 7; G. Fohrer, "Priesterliches Königtum, Ex 19,6," *TZ* 19 (1963): 361. This interpretation contrasts with a variety of past attempts to establish a semantic distinction between the two descriptions of Israel. See W. Caspari, "Das priesterliche Königreich," *TBl* 8 (1929): 105-10;

kōhănîm wĕgôy qādôš, is changed in the LXX, *basileion hierateuma kai ethnos hagion*, creating a chiastic construction consisting of adjective + noun; noun + adjective. Wevers concludes that *basileion*, "kingdom," is "descriptive of the body of priests," while the second phrase, *ethnos hagion*, emphasizes that the Israelite nation is "a sacral people especially devoted to God."[12]

19:7 *which Yahweh commanded him.* The LXX uses *ho theos*, "the God," in place of Hebrew *yhwh*.

19:8 *And all the people answered as one.* The LXX renders the Hebrew *yaḥdāw*, "as one," with *homothymadon*, "with one accord."

all which Yahweh spoke, we will do. The LXX uses *ho theos*, "the God," in place of "Yahweh," as in 19:3 and 7.

Commentary

The scene separates into three parts: the arrival of the Israelites in the wilderness of Sinai (vv. 1-2), the ascent of Moses to the summit of the mountain to receive the proposal of covenant from God (vv. 3-6), and his return to the people with the divine offer (vv. 7-8a). The present form of the text includes the work of several authors. Noth concluded that the notice of the Israelite encampment before the mountain and the ascent by Moses in 19:2b-3a may be "a fragment from . . . one of the older sources."[13] Eissfeldt supported this interpretation, noting that 19:3b-6 introduces a divine speech with distinct vocabulary.[14] I interpret the combination of texts as representing the Non-P History. The P History is most noticeable in the date of the Israelite arrival (v. 1) and in the priestly images within the promise of reward (vv. 5b-6a).

19:1-2 The travel notice does not conform to the previous occurrences (12:37; 13:20; etc.). One would expect 19:1-2 to read: "The Israelites journeyed from Rephidim, and they came to the wilderness of Sinai, and they camped in the wilderness." The remnant of this form in v. 2 suggests that it may represent the travel notice in the Non-P History. But the present text has been so thoroughly refashioned by the P author that it is no longer possible to identify the Non-P History with certainty. The dating of the Israelite arrival in v. 1 is a clear indication of the P History (see 12:2; 16:1).

Exodus 19:1-2 contains a series of repetitions establishing the time of the

---

Beyerlin, *Oldest Sinaitic Traditions*, 71-73; H. Cazelles, "Royaume des prêtres et nation consacrée, Exode 19,6," in *Humanisme et foi chrétienne* (ed. C. Kennenigiessar and Y. Marchasson; Mélanges scientifiques du centenaire de l'Institut catholique de Paris; Paris: Beuchesne, 1975), 541-45; J. Coppens, "Exodus, XIX, 6: Un royaume ou une royauté de prêtres?" *ETL* 53 (1977): 185-86.

12. Wevers, *Notes*, 295.

13. Noth, *Exodus*, 157. For further discussion see Th. Booij, "Mountain and Theophany in the Sinai Narrative," *Bib* 65 (1984): 17; Dozeman, *God on the Mountain*, 20-22.

14. O. Eissfeldt, *Die Komposition der Sinai-Erzählung Exodus 19–34* (Sitzungsberichte der Sächsischen Akademie der Wissenschaften zu Leipzig 113/1; Berlin: Akademie-Verlag, 1966), 14.

Israelite arrival (v. 1a), the setting of the wilderness of Sinai (vv. 1b-2a), and the encampment before the mountain (v. 2b). The time is stated with parallel temporal clauses: the people arrive "on the third month" *(baḥōdeš haššĕlîšî)* and "on this very day" *(bayyôm hazzeh)*. The combination of a general reference to a month followed by a specific day creates tension between the two notices. Noth sought to resolve the problem by translating the Hebrew word "month" as "new moon," hence "day of the new moon," indicating a specific day.[15] But if the author intended a specific day, one would expect a different phrase in Hebrew *(bĕ'eḥād laḥōdeš,* "on the first day to the month"; Gen 8:5; 40:2; Num 1:1; etc.). Thus it is best to avoid harmonizing the two temporal causes and interpret them instead as serving different purposes for the P author. The first phrase anchors the arrival of the Israelite people at Sinai within the history of the exodus and the wilderness journey. It is the third month after the Israelites left Egypt (see the previous dates in 12:2; 16:1). The second phrase is more liturgical in meaning. Its distribution emphasizes four events in the P History: the first day of the flood (Gen 7:11), the arrival of the Israelite people in the wilderness of Sinai (Exod 19:1), the sanctification of the priesthood (Lev 8:34), and the Day of Atonement (Lev 16:30). The distribution indicates the pivotal role of Sinai in the P History. The arrival of the Israelites at Sinai sets in motion acts of atonement, administered by a sanctified priesthood, which will provide the antidote to the pollution, which causes the flood. The arrival in the third month may also be anchored in the celebration of law in the P liturgical calendar. Two additional repetitions underscore the wilderness of Sinai as the setting for the following events (vv. 1b-2a), and the encampment of the Israelites before the mountain (v. 2b).

19:3-6 Moses ascends the mountain to God (v. 3a), prompting a divine speech (vv. 3b-6). The discourse separates into four parts: the commissioning of Moses (v. 3b), the call for the Israelites to see a past action of Yahweh (v. 4), the offer of covenant (v. 5a), and the promise of reward (vv. 5b-6).

Already in the nineteenth century, A. Dillmann described the unit as a classical example of OT covenant.[16] In the mid-twentieth century G. E. Mendenhall and K. Baltzer reinforced the interpretation of covenant through comparison to Hittite suzerainty treaties, a form of diplomatic contracts in the ancient Near East between unequal parties.[17] The suzerainty treaty includes (1) the identification of the suzerain or lord, (2) a historical prologue listing the acts of salvation of the suzerain toward the vassal, (3) the treaty stipulations or

15. Noth, *Exodus,* 155.
16. Dillmann, *Exodus und Leviticus,* 194.
17. Mendenhall, *Law and Covenant;* idem, *Tenth Generation;* idem, "Covenant," *ABD* 1:1179-1202; Baltzer, *Covenant Formulary.*

laws required of the vassal, (4) the provisions for reading the treaty, (5) the witnesses to the treaty, and (6) the curses resulting from disobedience and the blessings arising from obedience. The suzerainty treaty provides a framework for interpreting the covenant relationship between Yahweh and the Israelites in Exodus 19–24, Deuteronomy,[18] and in selective prophetic literature.[19] When the form was applied to Exod 19:3-6, the call for the Israelites to see a past action of Yahweh (19:4) was identified as a historical prologue and the offer of covenant (19:5a) as the legal stipulation. Perlitt rightly questioned the comparison to treaty forms in this particular case, noting the truncated form of a historical prologue and the absence of treaty curses.[20]

J. Muilenburg identified 19:3-6 as a covenantal genre on the basis of its literary structure and central themes.[21] He concluded that the emphasis in the divine speech was on the offer of covenant (v. 5a). The interpretation of Muilenburg invites comparison to the proposal of law at the outset of the wilderness journey (15:26). Both texts encourage the Israelites to enter into a relationship with God by listening to the divine voice. Exodus 15:25-26 offers law as a means for the Israelites to acquire health, while 19:3-6 extends the role of law to become the basis of covenant.

But F. B. Knutson argued that the emphasis in 19:3-6 was on the promise of reward (vv. 5b-6) rather than on the covenant law (v. 5a), prompting him to reevaluate the genre of 19:3-6 as a proposal of covenant, not as an actual covenant. Knutson concluded: "The proposal to enter a covenant is quite different from the post-covenantal exhortations to keep the covenant, as 19:4-6a is often interpreted."[22] The offer of covenant would require specific laws for observation, which are absent from 19:3-6.

The interpretation of Knutson clarifies that the opening divine speech to Moses is not a covenant but a proposal with a future orientation and a utopian quality. It introduces the central theme of holiness as a divine promise that is not yet realized. Yahweh describes what the Israelite people could be one day if they enter into a covenant. The characterization of the Israelites as God's private possession, a kingdom of priests, and even a holy nation does not describe their present state, but represents a future hope based upon divine promise.

---

18. See the overview by M. Weinfeld, *Deuteronomy 1–11* (AB 5; New York: Doubleday, 1991), 6-9.

19. D. Hillers, *Treaty-Curses and the Old Testament Prophets* (BibOr 16; Rome: Pontifical Biblical Institute Press, 1969).

20. Perlitt, *Bundestheologie*, 163-67.

21. Muilenburg, "The Form and Structure of the Covenantal Formulations," in *Hearing*, 108-26.

22. F. B. Knutson, "Literary Genres in PRU IV," in *Ras Shamra Parallels II* (ed. L. R. Fisher; AnOr 50; Rome: Pontifical Biblical Institute Press, 1975), 180-94, quotation 194.

The language of the proposal of covenant provides a point of departure for interpretation. The motifs in 19:3-8a indicate a close relationship between the Non-P History and Deuteronomy. The idealization of Moses as the teacher of covenantal law (Exod 19:3) is central to Deuteronomy, which repeatedly presents Moses as teaching (e.g., Deut 4:1, 5, 10, 14). The call for the Israelites to see (*rā'â*) a past event (Exod 19:4) repeats in Deut 4:3, 9; 10:21; 11:7. The form of the offer of covenant, "if you obey my voice" (*'im-šāmôa' tišmĕ'û bĕqōlî*, Exod 19:5a), also occurs in Deuteronomy (Deut 11:13; 15:5; 28:1), as does the emphasis on the "words of Yahweh" (*dibrê yhwh*, Exod 19:6b; see Deut 4:12; 5:5, 22). The divine promise that the Israelites will become God's "personal possession" (*sĕgullâ*, Exod 19:5b) in exchange for covenant loyalty also conforms to a central vision of the people of God in Deuteronomy (Deut 7:6; 14:2; 26:18).

The language of the proposal of covenant (Exod 19:3-8a) repeats in the revelation of the Book of the Covenant (20:22-24:8).[23] The repetitions include the commission of Moses with the words, "thus you will say to" (*kōh tō'mar lĕ*, 19:3; 20:22a), the call to see a past action of Yahweh (*'attem rĕ'îtem*, 19:4; 20:22b), covenant (*bĕrît*, 19:5; *sēper habbĕrît*, 24:7), the "approach" of Moses to the people (*bô'*, 19:7; 24:7), his "declaring" to them (*qārā'*, 19:7; 24:7) "all the words of Yahweh" (*kol-haddĕbārîm*, 19:7; 24:3, 7), to which the people agree unanimously (19:8; 24:3, 7). The chart in figure 30 on page 442 illustrates the similar structure resulting from the repetition of the motifs.

The parallel structure indicates a thematic development in the account of the revelation in chaps. 19–24. The episode opens with the proposal of covenant (19:1-8a), where the focus is on the future promises of God to the Israelites. The offer of covenant (v. 5a) contains no specific laws. The point of focus is on the future promise of reward, which is aimed at the character of the Israelite people should they enter into covenant with God (vv. 5b-6a). The episode closes with a covenant ceremony (20:22–24:8), where the focus shifts to the present time. The offer of covenant now becomes the point of focus, with the Book of the Covenant providing detailed laws to regulate the Israelite people in their covenantal relationship with God (20:23–23:19). In the covenant ceremony the promise of reward shifts from the characterization of the Israelite people to the promise of land (23:20-33). The commentary on the proposal of covenant follows the structure outlined in figure 30 on page 442.

19:3 Commission of Moses. God addresses Moses with the prophetic messenger formula in v. 3: "Thus you will say to . . ." (*kōh tō'mar lĕ*). The address recalls Moses' original encounter with God, when he was commissioned in the

---

23. See Perlitt, *Bundestheologie*, 181, 191-92; Dozeman, *God on the Mountain*, 57-65; L. Schmidt, "Israel und das Gesetz: Ex 19, 3b-8 und 24, 3-8 als literarischer und theologischer Rahmen für das Bundesbuch," *ZAW* 113 (2001): 167-85.

Figure 30

Topic	Proposal of Covenant 19:3-8a	Covenant Ceremony 20:22–24:8
The commission of Moses	19:3, "Thus you will say"	20:22b, "Thus you will say"
Call "to see" a past action of God	19:4, "You have seen what I did to the Egyptians"	20:22b, "You have seen that I spoke to you"
Offer of covenant	19:5a, proposal: "If you obey my voice and keep my covenant . . ."	20:23–23:19, law: Book of the Covenant (24:7)
Promise of reward	19:5b-6a, people: "You will be my personal possession . . ."	23:20-33, land: "I will send my messenger before you . . . to bring you to the place . . ."
Proclamation by Moses	19:7, Moses "called"	24:3a, 7a, Moses "called"
People's acceptance	19:8a, "We will do . . ."	24:3b, 7b, "We will do . . ."

role of the prophetic messenger to the Israelites (3:14, 15). The repetition be-tween 19:3 and 20:22 indicates a progression in the events of chaps. 19–24, from the initial proposal of covenant to the revelation of covenantal law in the Book of the Covenant (20:21–23:33). The identification of the Israelites as the "house of Jacob" echoes similar language from the prophetic literature (e.g., Isa 2:5; Jer 2:4; Amos 3:13; Mic 2:7). Dohmen also traces a literary development in the mo-tif, from Gen 46:27 and Exod 1:1, where the house of Jacob was numbered at seventy persons.[24]

19:4 Call "to See" a Past Action of God. The divine message to the Isra-elites begins in v. 4 with a recounting of salvation as two events: God's action against the Egyptians and the divine guidance to the mountain on the wings of eagles. The divine action against the Egyptians is not specifically stated. But similar language in Deuteronomy suggests that it is a reference to their destruc-tion (Deut 11:7; 29:2). The image of "eagles' wings" is often interpreted as the di-vine care of the Israelites in the wilderness journey, over against the destruction of the Egyptians in Egypt. But the image may be intended to relate the two events. Already in early Mesopotamian art the eagle is contrasted to the ser-pent, likely representing the conflict between good and evil and the power of

24. Dohmen, *Exodus 19–40*, 556.

the eagle to destroy.[25] The destructive power of the eagle is also evident in the Hebrew Bible where the bird is associated with war (Deut 28:49; Jer 48:40; 49:22; Hos 8:1; Lam 4:19). The eagle is wild (Lev 11:13; Deut 14:12) and fierce, swooping down from heaven on its prey (Job 9:26; 39:27). When this image is applied to war, the point of emphasis is the swiftness with which destruction comes (Jer 4:13; Hab 1:8; Obad 4). But as is evident in Exod 19:4, the speed of the eagle and the strength of its wings are also metaphors for swift rescue (2 Sam 1:23; Isa 40:31; Deut 32:11). Both images may be present in Exod 19:4.

The Israelites' direct experience of the Egyptian destruction and their wilderness rescue are indicated in visual terms, as something that they "saw" *(rā'â).* The use of the visual imagery to indicate the direct experience of God is likely rooted in the tradition of theophany, where the emphasis is on the immediacy of the divine appearance. The past reference to "seeing" at the outset of the revelation of God on the mountain indicates that the divine defeat of the Egyptians and the guidance of God through the wilderness are already forms of theophany for the Israelites, in so far as they were experienced firsthand by the people. The speech of Moses at the Red Sea supports this interpretation. He told the people that they would see *(rā'â)* the salvation of God in the destruction of the Egyptians (14:13).

What the Israelites have not yet witnessed firsthand is divine law codified in writing, which is the purpose of the theophany in chaps. 19–24. The introduction of law, as an experience of theophany, sets the stage for the contradictory imagery in 20:22 when Yahweh states that the people have seen divine speech from heaven. The combination of "seeing" and "hearing" will shift the experience of theophany from a visual to an auditory event, a practice that is also prominent in Deuteronomy (Deut 4:9, 12, 15, 19; 5:22). The change in imagery provides the foundation for a theology of Scripture as divine speech. According to B. D. Sommer, *Pirqe Abot* 1:1 illustrates the effects of this process over time: "Moses received Torah at Sinai and passed it on," which is to say, made it tradition. Sommer affirms the merging of revelation and law in this episode: "the authority of Jewish law and the sacred status of the Bible rest on these verbs [God *gave,* Israel *received*]," that is, the revelation in Exodus 19–24.[26] J. Neusner takes the conclusion a step further, writing that revelation, canon, and authority are not simply related in Exodus 19–24 but are one in classical Judaism.[27]

19:5-6 Offer of Covenant and Promise of Reward. The offer of covenant is conditioned upon two things (v. 5a). The people must hear *(šāma')* the divine

25. J. Lundquist, "Babylon in European Thought," *CANE* 1:74-75.

26. B. Sommer, "Revelation at Sinai in the Hebrew Bible and in Jewish Theology," *Journal of Religion* 79 (1999): 425.

27. J. Neusner, "Religious Authority in Judaism: Modern and Classical Modes," *Int* 39 (1985): 374-75.

voice *(qôl)* and observe *(šāmar)* the covenant *(běrît)*. When the metaphors "hearing" and "observing" are contrasted, they outline the plot of chaps. 19–24, in which revelation progresses from an experience of the divine voice in the Decalogue to the codification and observance of the Book of the Covenant. Whether the author intends to outline the overall plot of the episode with the two distinct metaphors is difficult to confirm, since the metaphors are also used as synonymous expressions for observing divine law. Moses calls the people to obey Deuteronomic law with the same mixture of metaphors: "hearing" the divine voice is "observing" the written law (Deut 15:5; 28:1; etc.). The examples from Deuteronomy strengthen the conclusion that the revelation in Exodus 19–24 is intended to establish the authority of written law. The word "covenant" further reinforces the point, since it too can designate a written document with legal authority (Gen 21:27, 32; Deut 5:2; etc.). Psalm 78:10 provides illustration when it repeats the phrase "to observe the covenant" and defines the action as "walking in God's Torah" (see also Ps 103:18).

The language in the offer of covenant (Exod 19:5a) indicates that the revelation in chaps. 19–24 is intended to establish the authority of law. The offer of covenant indicates further that the observance of law will become a means for God to transfer holiness to the people of Israel. The promise of reward (vv. 5b-6) envisions what the Israelites will become if they adhere to divine law. The promise builds on the first wilderness story at Shur (15:22-26), where God initially promised the people health in exchange for the obedience to the law. The promise of healing at the wilderness of Shur focused on the character of God with the self-revelation: "I am Yahweh your healer" (15:26). The promise of reward in 19:5b-6 shifts the focus from God as healer to the results of the divine healing on the people. The ideal character of the Israelite people is presented in three statements: (1) the people will be a personal possession of God separated from the other nations; (2) God rules the entire earth; and (3) the people will be a kingdom of priests and a holy nation. The relationship of the three lines is unclear. The point of tension arises from the first two lines. The exclusive vision of the Israelites as God's personal possession and the divine claim of universal rule make contradictory statements about God, the Israelites, and the world.

The central point of the divine promise in the first line is the word *sĕgullâ* to describe the Israelite people. There is debate whether the term conveys inherent value, "treasured property," in its description of the Israelite people, or simply the quality of their promised relationship with God, "personal possession." Keil and Delitzsch represent the first interpretation: *sĕgullâ* "does not signify property in general, but valuable property."[28] The resulting meaning of the

---

28. C. F. Keil and F. Delitzsch, *Commentary on the Old Testament* (trans. J. Martin; vol. 2; repr. Grand Rapids: Eerdmans, 1981), 96.

divine promise is that "although all the earth belongs to God," the Israelite people are of more value, hence they are "treasured property" (see NIV). Greenberg favors the second choice, noting that Akkadian *sikiltum,* the equivalent of Hebrew *sĕgullâ,* is an economic term designating private property regardless of its value.[29] The same meaning is evident in two economically oriented texts in the Hebrew Bible, where David (1 Chr 29:3) and the Preacher (Eccl 2:8) refer to "private property." The second interpretation emphasizes that the relationship between God and the Israelite people is exclusive, separating the people from all other nations. This interpretation accentuates the tension between the first two lines, which suggests that the claim of the universal rule of God in the second line qualifies the more exclusive vision of the people of Israel in the first line (see NRSV).

I follow the second interpretation, which suggests that there are two visions of the Israelite people in the promise of reward: the first is contained in line one and the second is in lines two and three. The two visions result in the following translation:

> You will be my personal possession from all the peoples.
> Indeed, all the earth is mine,
> but you will be for me a kingdom of priests and a holy nation.

The promise of reward to the Israelite nation in the first line represents the perspective of the Non-P History and Deuteronomy. The presence of holiness among the people of Israel results in an exclusive relationship with God, in which the people are separated from the nations as God's private possession. The same exclusive vision continues in Deuteronomy, where *sĕgullâ* occurs three times to describe the ideal vision of the Israelite people (Deut 7:6; 14:2; 26:18), which also requires their separation from other nations and their gods. The ideal of an exclusive relationship with God can be illustrated in the following manner:

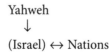

The proclamation of the divine rule over all the earth contrasts a universal perspective of divine rule to the exclusive focus of the opening vision. The new vision is indicated by the translation "Indeed." The universal context changes the ideal of holiness for the people of Israel. The separation from the

---

29. Greenberg, "Hebrew s^egullā," 173.

nations is transformed from geographical or social isolation to a qualitative distinction like that between the priest and the laity. The result is that the entire Israelite nation is envisioned in a priestly role to the nations, as a "kingdom of priests" and a "holy nation" in the following manner:

Yahweh
↓
(Israel)
↓
Nations

The priestly metaphors, "kingdom of priests" and "holy nation," belong to the P History. These images are absent from the Non-P History and from Deuteronomy. The language of the P History recalls late Isaiah tradition (Isa 61:5-6), where the other nations call the Israelites "priests of Yahweh," and Ezekiel (20:41), where the holiness of God is also made known to the nations through Israel. B. J. Schwartz has argued that priestly imagery is out of place in the promise of reward and inappropriate in the P History: "Nothing could be less priestly than the notion that all Israel is as sacred as a priesthood."[30] But the promise of reward is intended to envision the ideal — a future promise, not a present reality. The future ideal in Exod 19:6 is not different from the divine statements to the Israelites in Leviticus: "You shall be holy, for I am holy." Moreover, the ideal vision of the Israelites in a priestly role to the nations does not eliminate the role of the priesthood within the Israelite cult. Rather, it demands it. The P writer will underscore the need for a priesthood during the initial theophany in Exod 19:20-25. The realization of the promise of national holiness will require the revelation and construction of the priestly tabernacle (Exodus 25–31, 35–40), the creation of the sacrificial cult (Leviticus 1–7), and the formation of the priesthood (Leviticus 8–9). Even after the establishment of the cult, the ideal remains a future goal, which is indicated by the continued exhortation: "You are to be holy, for I Yahweh your God am holy" (e.g., Lev 19:2). The exhortation assumes that the people are not in a state of holiness at the present time. The qualification of holiness in the P History contrasts to Deuteronomy, which attributes holiness to the people in the present time (Deut 7:6; 14:2, 21; 26:19; 28:9).

The language in the proposal of covenant (Exod 19:5a) indicates that the revelation in Exodus 19–24 is intended to establish the role of covenantal law as the means by which God will transfer holiness to the people. The promise of reward (vv. 5b-6) contains two visions of what the Israelites will become if they ad-

---

30. Schwartz, "Priestly Account," in *Texts, Temples,* ed. Fox et al., 112-13.

here to divine law. The exclusive vision of the Israelite people as a private possession of God (v. 5b) will require the revelation of the Book of the Covenant on the divine mountain in the Non-P History and, more importantly, the additional revelation of law on Mount Horeb in Deuteronomy. The vision of the Israelite people as a priestly kingdom and a holy nation (Exod 19:6) will require the revelation of the P legislation on Mount Sinai in Exodus 25–31, 35–40, Leviticus, and Numbers 1–10. The two visions of holiness are mythologized as taking place on the separate mountains of Sinai and Horeb. Yet the setting of the divine mountain allows the distinct views of holiness to be held together as one promise of reward in the proposal of covenant, which occurred as a single revelation.

19:7-8a   Proclamation by Moses and the People's Acceptance. The descent of Moses is indicated as an "approach" *(bô')* to the people, not a descent from the mountain. The same verb will be used to describe the approach of God for theophany (19:9), creating a parallel between the movement of God and that of Moses on the divine mountain. Once Moses returns to the people, he repeats the proposal of covenant to the elders, who assumed an important role in his commission (e.g., 3:16, 18). The events move quickly. Moses conveys the divine "words" *(dĕbārîm),* prompting unanimous agreement by the people of Israel to accept the divine proposal of covenant.

THEOPHANY (19:8B-19)

ⁱ⁹:⁸ᵇ*And Moses brought back the words of the people to Yahweh.* ⁹*And Yahweh said to Moses, "Indeed, I am coming to you in the dense cloud so that the people may hear when I speak with you and believe in you forever." And Moses declared the words of the people to Yahweh.* ¹⁰*And Yahweh said to Moses, "Go to the people and consecrate them today and tomorrow. And they must wash their clothes,* ¹¹*and they must be ready on the third day,* **because on the third day Yahweh will descend before the sight of all the people on Mount Sinai.** ¹²*And you will set a border for the people all around, saying, 'Guard yourselves to ascend the mountain or to touch its boundaries. Any one touching the mountain will be put to death.* ¹³*No hand will touch him, but he will be stoned or shot. Whether beast or human he will not live.' When the ram's horn blows, they may ascend the mountain."*

¹⁴*And Moses descended from the mountain to the people and he sanctified the people. And they washed their clothes.* ¹⁵*And he said to the people, "Be ready for three days, do not approach a woman."*

¹⁶*On the third day at dawn, there was thunder and lightning, and a heavy cloud on the mountain, and the sound of the horn was very strong. And all the people in the camp trembled.* ¹⁷*And Moses brought the people out to meet the God from the camp. And they were stationed at the base of the mountain.* ¹⁸**But**

Mount Sinai smoked, all of it, because Yahweh descended on it in fire. And its smoke ascended like the smoke of a kiln. And the entire mountain trembled.
    [19]*And the sound of the horn grew louder and louder. Moses spoke and the God answered in a voice.*

Notes

19:8b *to Yahweh.* The LXX has *pros ton theon,* "to the God" (see also 19:3, 7).
19:9 *Indeed, I am coming to you.* The Hebrew combines the particle *hinnēh* with the participle *bā'* to announce a future action that is imminent (GKC §119p).
in the dense cloud. The Hebrew phrase *bĕ'ab he'ānān* is a hapax legomenon in the MT. The Sam is plural, *b'y h'nn.* The LXX translates, *en stylō nephelēs,* "in a pillar of cloud," reflecting Hebrew *bĕ'ammûd 'ānān,* "pillar of cloud," which leads the people in the wilderness journey (13:21).
19:10 *go to the people.* The LXX expands the command, *katabas diamartyrai,* "go down and instruct the people," which corresponds to the divine instruction to Moses in 19:21.
consecrate them. Hebrew *qiddaštām* is translated in the LXX *hagnison,* emphasizing, according to Wevers, "the state of holiness as one of purification, cleansing."[1]
19:12 *and you will set a border.* The MT *wĕhigbaltā* is translated in the LXX as *aphorieis,* which means "to mark off by boundary," but also carries the meaning "to separate."
for the people. The Sam reads, *'t hhr,* "for the mountain."
guard yourselves. The negative warning is also translated, "be careful not to go up" (NRSV).
will be put to death. The MT *môt yûmāt* expresses an intensive statement (Gen 26:11; Exod 21:12, 15-17). The LXX renders the phrase *thanatō teleutēsei,* "in death he will be completed/brought to an end/killed."
19:13 *but he will be stoned or shot.* The LXX adds *bolidi,* "missile, javelin," as a dative of means, which is reflected in NRSV "shot with arrows."
when the ram's horn blows. The LXX expands and reinterprets the phrase, *hotan hai phōnai kai hai salpinges kai hē nephelē apelthē apo tou orous,* "when the thunder and the trumpets and the cloud depart from the mountain." In the MT the people ascend the mountain while the Deity is on it after approaching in the dense cloud (19:9). In the LXX the people ascend after the Deity departs from the mountain. The LXX suggests a harmonization with the subsequent instruction in 19:20-25.
19:15 *be ready for three days.* Hebrew *hĕyû nĕkōnîm lišlōšet yāmîm* is written differently from the command in 19:11, thus raising a problem of translation and interpretation. Is the command for three full days of preparation or that the people be ready on the third day, as is stated in 19:11 *(wĕhāyû nĕkōnîm layyôm haššĕlîšî)?*[2] The LXX favors the latter interpretation, *ginesthe hetoimoi treis hēmeras.*[3]

1. Wevers, *Notes,* 298.
2. For discussion see Milgrom, *Leviticus 1–16,* 928-29.
3. See Wevers, *Notes,* 301-2.

19:16-19 The text is structured as a chiasm to describe the meeting of the people and Yahweh at the mountain (C, C′). The people and the mountain tremble (B, B′) at the descent of Yahweh. The entire event occurs during the sound of the horn (A, A′).

A The sound of the horn *(qōl šōpār)*		v. 16a
B All the people *(kol-hāʿām)* tremble *(ḥārad)*		v. 16b
C The people approach the mountain		v. 17
C′ Yahweh descends on Mount Sinai		v. 18a
B′ The entire mountain *(kol-hāhār)* trembles *(ḥārad)*		v. 18b
A′ The sound of the horn *(qōl haššôpār)*		v. 19a

A leitmotif throughout the section is the Hebrew *qôl,* "thunder, sound, voice." The motif describes the sound of the horn (vv. 16a, 19a), the thunder on the mountain (v. 16a), and the voice of God (v. 19b).

19:16 *on the third day at dawn.* The dawn *(bōqer)* has functioned as the time when God exhibits acts of power in the plague cycle (blood, flies, hail) and at the Red Sea.

there was thunder. The plural *qōlōt* always means thunder, usually in association with hail (9:23; 28, 29, 33), rain (9:34; 1 Sam 12:17-18), or lightning (20:18). The *qōlōt* also describes the sound of the mythological water *(mayim rabbîm,* Ps 93:4).

and the sound of the horn was very strong. Hebrew *ḥāzaq mĕʾōd,* "was very strong," is translated in the LXX *ēchei mega,* "echoed greatly."

19:18 *because Yahweh descended on it in fire.* The LXX changes MT "Yahweh" to *ton theon,* "the God."

And the entire mountain trembled. The LXX substitutes "all the people" *(pas ho laos)* for "the entire mountain."

19:19 *And the sound of the horn grew louder and louder.* The Hebrew participles *hôlēk wĕḥāzēq,* "grew louder and louder," are *casus adverbialis.* They are meant to describe "more particularly the manner or attendant circumstances . . . under which an action or state has taken place or is taking place" (GKC §144h).

Moses spoke and the God answered in a voice. Hebrew *bĕqôl* can also be translated "thunder" (see NRSV) as is evident in certain psalms (e.g., 18:13 [MT 14]; 29:3). But the singular can also mean "voice" (e.g., Deut 4:10; 5:4). The change from the plural (Exod 19:16) to the singular (v. 19) in the context of a conversation between Moses and God favors the translation "voice." The transition prepares for the Decalogue as divine speech (20:1-17).

Commentary

The account of the divine appearance on the mountain includes the preparation for theophany (vv. 8b-15) and the event (vv. 16-19).

19:8b-15 The preparation for theophany divides between the divine instructions on the summit of the mountain (vv. 8b-13) and Moses' execution of the commands at the base of the mountain (vv. 14-15). Comparison isolates three motifs: Moses must (1) "consecrate" (Piel of *qādaš*; vv. 10, 14) the people; (2) by having them wash *(kābas)* their clothes *(śimlâ*; vv. 10, 14); and (3) be ready *(nĕkōnîm*; vv. 11, 15) for the appearance of God. The requirement to abstain from sex (v. 15b) breaks the symmetry, suggesting a later addition to the text.[4]

The instructions for purification divide between the preparation of the people (vv. 9-11) and the protection of the mountain (vv. 12-13). The literary style suggests a history of commentary, although identification of the different authors remains difficult. Verse 8b states that Moses repeated "the words of the people to Yahweh," prompting the divine announcement of theophany (v. 9). Yet once it is completed the notice repeats: "Moses reported the words of the people to Yahweh." Such repetitions are resumptive and their function is to bracket insertions.[5] The repetition may be an editorial device to isolate the announcement of theophany in v. 9.[6] The repetition also provides transition to the preparation for theophany in 19:10-13.

Verses 10-13 suggest further signs of editorial additions. Noth noted the problem of voice: "The occurrence of Yahweh in the third person [in v. 11b] in the middle of a speech of Yahweh [vv. 10-11a] . . . is striking."[7] He identified v. 11b as an explanatory gloss. But the naming of the mountain as Sinai allows for a more precise identification of the author as the P historian. Questions about authorship continue in vv. 12-13. R. Althann identified vv. 12ab-13 as a clarification of the opening command in v. 12aa: "Put limits for the people around the mountain."[8] The addition includes the danger of touching the cosmic mountain, the penalty of death for trespass, and the method of execution — a trespasser must be stoned to avoid anyone touching the person. The overlay of commentary in 19:9-15 underscores the central place of holiness in the religion of ancient Israel and the important role of purification in the divine revelation on the mountain.

Exodus 19:9-11 focuses on the preparation of the people for theophany. Verse 8b indicates the transition from the proposal of covenant to the account of theophany: "Moses brought back the words of the people to Yahweh."

---

4. See Dozeman, *God on the Mountain*, 22-25, 98-100.

5. C. Kuhl, "Die 'Wiederaufnahme' — ein literarkritisches Princip?" *ZAW* 64 (1952): 1-11.

6. Zenger (*Sinaitheophanie*, 59) identifies v. 9a as older tradition, now isolated by the repetitions in vv. 8b and 9b. F. L. Hossfeld (*Der Dekalog: Seine späten Fassungen, die originale Komposition und seine Vorstufen* [OBO 45; Göttingen: Vandenhoeck & Ruprecht, 1982], 190) and H-. C. Schmitt ("Redaction des Pentateuch im Geiste der Prophetie," *VT* 32 [1982]: 176-77) identify v. 9a as a later redactional insertion.

7. Noth, *Exodus*, 158.

8. R. Althann, "A Note on Exodus 19,12aB-13," *Bib* 57 (1976): 242-46; see also Zenger, *Sinaitheophanie*, 60.

Figure 31

Theophany	*Non-P History: Verse 9*	*P History: Verse 11b*
Movement of God	Approach *(bô')*	Descend *(yārad)*
Presence of God	Auditory: to hear	Visual: to see
Purpose	The people fear Moses	The people see God

Yahweh responds to the agreement with an extended speech in vv. 9-11 in which two announcements of theophany (vv. 9 and 11b) frame the instruction for purification (vv. 10-11a). The announcements introduce the distinct interpretations of theophany in the Non-P and P Histories (see fig. 31 above).

Verse 9 is a first person divine speech to Moses: "I am coming *(bô')* to you on a dense cloud" *(bĕ'ab he'ānān*, lit. "the cloud of the cloud"). The approach *(bô')* of God to the mountain mirrors the movement of Moses in the previous scene (v. 7). The imagery of the cloud as the vehicle for God's appearance is a common motif in the ancient Near East. Mendenhall provides background with his study of Akkadian *melammū*. The *melammū* is a bright disk surrounding a god, a person, or even an object that shares in divine power, much like the halo around Jesus and the saints in Christian art.[9] The *melammū* is similar to the cloud that appears during theophany in the Hebrew Bible. The root of the cloudlike imagery is most likely the sun, especially viewed through mist or at the time of an eclipse, when there is a diffuse radiance around it. The encircling radiance rather than the sun itself is the *melammū*. The enthronement imagery of God in the temple in Ps 97:1-2 illustrates:

> Yahweh is king! Let the earth rejoice;
> let the many coastlands be glad!
> Cloud *('ānān)* and thick darkness *('ărāpel)* are all around him;
> righteousness and justice are the foundation of his throne.

God is not literally seen in this psalm. Yahweh is surrounded by a cloud and thick darkness that conceal the Deity. Yet the psalmist is confident of the divine presence because the radiance of God appears in the form of the cloud. Thus, as T. N. D. Mettinger has noted, the cloud both conceals and reveals the cultic presence of God.[10] The imagery of the cloud underscores the cultic setting of the theophany on the mountain in Exodus 19–24. Sarna quotes Ram-

---

9. Mendenhall, *Tenth Generation*, 32-66.
10. Mettinger, *Dethronement of Sabaoth*, 19-37 *et passim*.

bam: "Mount Sinai assumes the character of a sanctuary for the duration of the theophany."[11]

The approach of God on a cloud even more precisely recalls the storm god Baal in Canaanite religion, who is described as the "rider on the clouds" (*rkb 'rpt; CTA* 2.iv.8; 3.B.40). The Ugaritic word for "cloud" here is the "thick darkness" that appears in conjunction with the "cloud" in Ps 97:1-2 (see also Deut 4:11; Joel 2:2; etc.). Biblical authors also use the imagery of the storm god to indicate the appearance of God, describing Yahweh as "the rider of the swift cloud (*'āb*)" (Isa 19:1; and perhaps also Ps 68:4 [MT 5]). The Song of Deborah celebrates the approach of Yahweh with similar imagery of the thunderstorm: "The clouds poured down rain" (Judg 5:4; see also Psalm 29). The imagery of the thunderstorm reinforces the cultic setting of Exodus 19–24. The language also plays a literary role in the structure of Exodus, relating the theophany on the mountain with the Israelite exodus from Egypt, where Yahweh embodied the power of the storm god in the plague of hail (9:13-35), while also waging war from the cloud at the Red Sea (14:20).

God provides two further descriptions of the theophany in 19:9. Both are part of the literary design of Exodus. First, God states that theophany will be an auditory experience. It will provide an opportunity for the people to hear God speak. The emphasis on hearing God continues from the offer of covenant in 19:5a, where God also encouraged the people to hear the divine voice and to observe covenant law. The motif will return in 19:19 when the theophany is described as a conversation between Moses and God, the content of which is the Decalogue (20:1-17). Exodus 20:18-20 will confirm that the Israelites heard the conversation, thus fulfilling the divine prediction in 19:9.

Second, God states that the people will believe (*'āman*) in Moses forever from the experience of theophany as speech. The authority of Moses was introduced in his commission (4:1-9). Moses feared that the people would not believe (*'āman*) in him and thus not listen to his voice (*qôl*; 4:1). Indeed, his authority has waxed and waned during the changing circumstances of the Israelites in the land of Egypt and in the wilderness journey. The initial belief of the people in Moses as the representative of Yahweh (4:31) faded immediately upon the first signs of resistance from Pharaoh (chap. 5). Again the faith of the people in Moses at the Red Sea (14:31) turned quickly to murmuring in the wilderness journey at the first sign of crisis (15:22-26). But now God states that the divine voice in theophany will so terrify the people that they will elect Moses to mediate all future divine speech, permanently intermingling the voices of God and Moses. The result is that they will believe in him forever (see 20:18-20). T. W. Mann describes this development as the exaltation of Moses on analogy to the exaltation of kings

---

11. Sarna, *Exodus*, 106.

through victory in war within the Assyrian literature.[12] But the merging of divine speech and Mosaic teaching appears rather to lay the groundwork for a theology of law as authored by Moses yet representing the voice of God. It is the central role of law in the religious life of the Israelite people that will ensure their permanent belief in Moses. J. Neusner encapsulates the eternal status of Mosaic authority in law in the following way: "God revealed the Torah to Moses at Mount Sinai. Authority rests upon God's will and word to Moses."[13]

The divine instruction for the purification of the people follows in 19:10-11a. The people must be sanctified or consecrated (Piel of *qādaš*). The form of the verb "to consecrate" means that the people must be in a holy state requiring purification. The command in v. 13 indicates that the purification is to prepare the people to enter the realm of holiness and to meet God on the mountain at the blast of the trumpet. Such language is usually reserved for the priests (Exodus 28–29; Leviticus 8). Purification requires the people to wash their clothes, perhaps for two days, which would be unique in biblical literature.[14] The practice of washing clothes for ablution is described in detail in the P literature with regard to skin disease (Leviticus 13–14) and genital discharge (Leviticus 15). The typical reference to clothing in the P texts is *beged*, a general word for garment, occurring over two hundred times. The reference to clothing in 19:10 is *śimlâ*, an outer garment often translated as "cloak" or "mantle," as compared to the more general "clothes." The "cloak" occurs in ethical laws such as 22:26, which state that even if taken in pawn, a neighbor's cloak must be returned at night for warmth to sleep. The word "cloak" may be tied to the past events of the exodus. The Israelites left Egypt with their kneading bowls wrapped in their "cloaks" (12:34), which were taken from the Egyptians (3:22; 12:35), perhaps accounting for the unique two-day period of ablution. At the end of the period of sanctification, the people are instructed "to be ready," meaning prepared and possibly alert (Josh 8:4) for the theophany of God.

The preparation of the people concludes with a description of theophany in Exod 19:11b, which contrasts to v. 9. As noted above, v. 11b is an insertion, marked by change in voice. Even though the divine speech to Moses continues, the Deity now makes self-references in the third person: "On the third day *Yahweh* [rather than 'I'] will descend (*yārad*) on Mount Sinai in view of all the people." The naming of the mountain as Sinai identifies the author as the P historian. The P author provides a new purpose for theophany: it is for the people to see God as opposed to hearing divine speech (v. 9). The visual emphasis of theophany is accompanied by a new description of the divine movement:

---

12. Mann, *Divine Presence*, 134-38.
13. Neusner, "Religious Authority in Judaism," 374-75.
14. See Milgrom, *Leviticus 1–16*, 974.

Yahweh will "descend" upon Mount Sinai rather than "approach" the people on a cloud (v. 9). The imagery of a divine descent upon Mount Sinai will reappear in the P description of theophany in v. 18, where the visual metaphors of the event will be clarified as fire and smoke on Mount Sinai.

Exodus 19:12-13 shifts the focus from the purification of the people to the holy quality of the mountain. God states that the mountain must be quarantined with boundaries and that the people are forbidden to ascend it. This command is likely intended for the period of purification, since the people are instructed to ascend the mountain at the sound of the trumpet (v. 13). The presupposition of the command is that holiness occupies physical space, and that its properties can be transferred by touch. Conversely the properties of the profane world can also be transferred to holiness through touch, thus polluting it. The fear of defiling holiness through touch is the more common concern (see the P legislation such as Lev 5:2, 3; or Hag 2:11-13). But the contagious property of holiness is also addressed in a limited number of texts all in the P legislation. The holiness of the altar (Exod 29:37; 30:29) and holy food (Lev 6:18, 27) are contagious to touch. The prohibition in Exod 19:12-13 is ambiguous. It could reflect the threat of defilement to holiness or the danger of holiness to humans.

In 19:12-13 God declares the death penalty to any person or animal that trespasses the boundary and touches the mountain. Death is by stoning *(šāqal)*. The Hebrew word often suggests a sin of sacrilege in the Non-P History, Deuteronomy, and the Deuteronomistic History. The word is absent from the P law and narrative. Moses states to Pharaoh during the plagues that the Israelites must sacrifice in the wilderness, rather than in the land of Egypt, because their actions would be offensive, prompting the Egyptians to stone them (8:26). Other sins of sacrilege that require stoning include false prophecy (Deut 13:10), worship of other gods (Deut 17:5), and profaning holy war (Achan in Josh 7:25). Even cattle can be stoned if they kill a human (Exod 21:28-32).

The divine instruction for purification concludes in Exod 19:13 with the command: "When the ram's horn blows, they may ascend the mountain." The ram's horn *(yôbēl)* has liturgical significance in ancient Israel. It is associated with holy war (Josh 6:3-4) and with the Year of Jubilee (Lev 25:9).[15] It may be synonymous with the "trumpet" *(šôpār)*, which describes the appearance of God in 19:16. God states that the ram's horn will signal the moment of encounter on the mountain. Scholars debate who is instructed to meet God on the mountain. Noth suggests the group of people described in 24:1-2, 9-11.[16] An-

---

15. I. H. Jones, "Music and Musical Instruction," *ABD* 4:930-39.

16. Noth, *Exodus*, 158; see the more extended discussion by Oswald, *Israel am Gottesberg*, 37-39 *et passim*.

other possibility emerges at the conclusion of the episode, when "the young men of Israel" are singled out to perform sacrifices (24:4-5).[17] But the command may just as well refer to all the Israelite people, since there was no distinction in the earlier command for purification (19:10).

Verses 14-15 narrate the descent of Moses from the mountain and his fulfillment of the divine command. The repetitions include the sanctification of the people, the washing of their clothes, and their readiness. The additional command for sexual abstinence now completes the process of purification for theophany, although not commanded by God on the mountain. Sexual abstinence is required of holy warriors who are in a state of purity (see Uriah the Hittite in 2 Sam 11:11), especially in the war camp (Deut 23:10-14). The P legislation provides extensive commentary on purification for worship from sexual intercourse or bodily emissions (Leviticus 15).

19:16-19 The appearance of God on the mountain is a foundational event in the literary structure of Exodus. God stated to Moses at the outset of the exodus that the theophany on the mountain was the goal of his commission (3:12). It is not surprising therefore that its description is overlaid with commentary from different authors. Scholars have long since noticed divergent motifs in the description of theophany in vv. 16-19.[18] The primary contrast is between storm and volcanic imagery. The storm imagery includes thunder *(qōlōt)*, lightning *(běrāqîm)*, and the heavy cloud *('ānān)* in vv. 16-17 signaling the divine residence on the mountain. Verse 19 also reflects aspects of the tradition of the storm, but the thunder is reinterpreted as the voice *(qôl)* of God in conversation with Moses. The volcanic imagery consists of fire *('ēš)* and smoke *('āšān)* from a furnace *(kibšān)* at the summit of the mountain in v. 18 resulting from the divine descent upon the mountain.

The distinct motifs identify the authors. Verses 16-17 represent a tradition of theophany as the thunderstorm, in which there are both visual (lightning) and auditory (thunder) images. It is an independent tradition available to the Non-P author (see the introduction, "Literature: Individual Genres: Theophany on the Mountain"). Verses 18-19 represent distinct reinterpretations of the

---

17. Dozeman, *God on the Mountain*, 23-25.

18. Noth (*Exodus*, 158-59) evaluated the contrasting motifs within the framework of the Documentary Hypothesis, concluding that the volcanic imagery in Exod 19:16a*a*, 18, 20 represented the J source and the storm imagery in Exod 19:16a*b*-17, 19 was the E source. Jeremias (*Theophanie*, 103) narrowed the scope of the unit, identifying only v. 18 as J, and as E vv. 16-17, 19. Zenger (*Sinaitheophanie*, 61) identifies v. 19b as a Deuteronomistic redaction. In a more recent study, Oswald (*Israel am Gottesberg*, 74-77) departs from a source-critical analysis to evaluate the description of theophany from the perspective of different typologies: Exod 19:18b is part of a typology that accentuates the descent of Yahweh upon the mountain, while vv. 16-17, 19 reflect a more stationary perspective, in which God dwells upon the mountain.

thunderstorm by the Non-P and P authors. The volcanic imagery of fire in v. 18 is part of the P History in which theophany is a visual experience of the divine descent upon Mount Sinai predicted in v. 11b. The reinterpretation of thunder in v. 19 as the voice of God belongs to the Non-P History, where theophany is an auditory experience of divine speech predicted in v. 9.

The description of the theophany as a thunderstorm in vv. 16-17 separates into three parts: (1) a description of theophany in v. 16a, (2) the people's reaction of fear in v. 16b, and (3) the encounter between God and the people at the mountain in v. 17.

Verse 16a begins the description of theophany with two temporal clauses, "on the third day" *(wayhî bayyôm haššělîšî)* and "in the morning" *(bihyōt habbōqer)*. The NIV harmonizes the two clauses, translating "on the morning of the third day." But Noth is probably correct that the two clauses represent distinct introductions to the theophany. The first emphasizes a two-day period of preparation with theophany on the third day, perhaps extending the period of preparation and theophany from two ("today and tomorrow" in v. 10) to three days (vv. 11, 15a). The second introduction is less definite about the period of time for preparation, emphasizing instead that theophany takes place at dawn. A divine action at dawn continues the motif from the plagues (7:8–10:20) and the defeat of Pharaoh at the Red Sea (10:21–14:31).

The appearance of God in v. 16a is characterized as thunder *(qōlōt)*, the plural form of the word meaning voice *(qôl)* in v. 19. Thunder designates the appearance of God in conjunction with rain (1 Sam 12:17, 18), the storm cloud (Job 28:26; 38:25), or even the mythological "great waters" (Ps 93:4). In Exodus the thundering of God was introduced during the plague of hail, where it was accompanied by rain and hail (Exod 9:13-35) when Yahweh appeared as the Storm God. In 19:16a the thunder is accompanied by lightning and the heavy cloud on the mountain. Lightning can symbolize the power of God to wage war, in which case lightning bolts are likened to God's arrows (Hab 3:11). At other times thunder and lightning characterize the creative power of God to bring forth rain from heaven (Ps 135:7; Jer 10:13). The appearance of God is announced with the sound of the trumpet *(qôl haššôpār)*. Van Seters notes that the trumpet is unusual in the tradition of theophany and more common in cultic liturgies, especially associated with festival occasions.[19] The trumpet announces the procession of the ark into the temple (2 Sam 6:15) and the enthronement of God in the temple (Ps 47:5).

Exodus 19:16b-17 describes the response of the people to the enthronement of God on the mountain. Their trembling *(hārad)* in the camp at the sound of the trumpet connotes fear. The prophet Amos links the response of

---

19. Van Seters, *Life of Moses*, 268.

trembling to the sound of the trumpet as though it were a truism: "Does the trumpet sound in the city without making the people afraid?" (Amos 3:6). At the sound of the trumpet, Moses leads the people out of the camp to the base of the mountain in order to meet God.

Exodus 19:18-19 provides distinct interpretations of the account of the theophany in vv. 16-17. The P author focuses on the mountain in v. 18, stating that Mount Sinai also trembled *(ḥārad)* at the descent of Yahweh upon it. The image is not of an earthquake, but of fear at the approach of God like the people in v. 16b. The personification of Mount Sinai underscores its cosmic quality, which is reinforced by the syntax of v. 18. The mountain is referred to no less than three times: "But Mount Sinai *(har sînay)* smoked, all of it *(kullô)*, because Yahweh descended on it *('ālāyw)* in fire." Such personification is unusual. The LXX changes the text so that it is the people *(pas ho laos)* and not the mountain that trembles. But the prophet Ezekiel provides a parallel describing the isles as trembling over the downfall of Tyre (Ezek 26:18). The imagery of the divine descent fulfills the prediction from Exod 19:11b.

The Non-P author focuses on the "sound of the trumpet" in v. 19, which now signals an ongoing conversation between God and Moses. The NIV, "Then Moses spoke and the voice of God answered him," captures the reinterpretation of the theophany as divine speech. But the NRSV, "Moses would speak and God would answer him," better conveys the immediacy of the conversation and its ongoing nature as opposed to a past event. The Non-P author intends for the content of the conversation in v. 19 to be the revelation of the Decalogue in 20:1-17, which revelation, we are told in 20:18-20, the Israelites heard as direct speech from God. The P author has severed the link between the public conversation in 19:19 and the Decalogue in 20:1-17 by inserting 19:20-25, where God stops the experience of theophany and commands Moses to speak the Decalogue to the Israelites.

REVELATION OF LAW (19:20–23:33)

Introduction to Law

The theophany of God on the mountain provides the occasion for the revelation of law, first as the Decalogue (19:20–20:20) and second as the Book of the Covenant (20:21–23:33). Thus the law is central to the story of the exodus, so central that it continues to the end of the book, including the cultic laws surrounding the tabernacle (chaps. 25–31, 35–40) and the additional law revealed in the setting of the covenant renewal (34:11-26).

Definition of Law

Law in the Hebrew Bible resists a simple definition. It embraces many words and metaphors, including torah *(tôrâ)*, judgment *(mišpāṭ)*, statute *(ḥôq)*, commandment *(miṣwâ)*, testimony *('ēdût)*, and covenant *(běrît)*. The dynamic character of law is conveyed through metaphors of motion and speech. Law is alive, deriving from the words *(děbārîm)* or voice *(qôl)* of God. The words are codified in writing, including the Ten Words *('ăśeret hadděbārîm)*, the Book of Torah *(sēper hattôrâ)* and the Book of the Covenant *(sēper habběrît)*. Once codified the law is anything but static. Rather, it creates a roadway *(derek)* through life upon which humans are able to walk *(hālak)*. The vocabulary indicates the breadth of the subject matter, while the metaphors underscore the dynamic quality of law as a resource for change through time. Jewish legal interpretation employs the metaphor of walking, *halakah*, to underscore the dynamic character of law in ongoing tradition.

Modern scholars have offered more precise sociological definitions of Israelite law. H. J. Boecker defines ancient Israelite law by social function: biblical law served to settle disputes.[1] D. Patrick provides a broader sociological definition of law: "The order of justice and right to which individuals and groups should conform and which judicial authority should enforce." He notes that the definition is intended to be comprehensive. It includes far more than the explicit rules and also embraces the collective conscience of the community.[2] The comprehensive character of law assumed in the definition is a problem in the Bible, for the legal collections in the Hebrew Bible are far from comprehensive. Thus B. S. Jackson cautions that ancient laws function differently than the modern Western model of law, where the legal judgments of the court are comprehensive and clearly expressed in written language available to participants in advance. The ancient legal practice is not tied exclusively to written laws, but depends on the context of a situation to resolve dispute. Jackson underscores the difference between modern and ancient law by describing the latter as "wisdom-laws," where the intent is to evoke typical situations and shared images to provide the context for resolution.[3] The focus on shared experience in the ancient legal tradition underscores the conclusion of the contemporary jurist Oliver Wendell Holmes that the life of law is not logic but experience.

---

1. H. J. Boecker, *Law and the Administration of Justice in the Old Testament and Ancient East* (trans. J. Moiser; Minneapolis: Augsburg, 1980), 37.

2. D. Patrick, *Old Testament Law* (Atlanta: John Knox, 1985), 4.

3. B. S. Jackson, *Studies in the Semiotics of Biblical Law* (JSOTSup 314; Sheffield: Sheffield Academic Press, 2000), 70-92.

Law in the Ancient Near East

The genre of biblical law received further definition by comparison to other ancient Near Eastern law codes. The discovery of law codes from the Sumerian period revealed a legal tradition in the ancient Near East going back to the third millennium, including the Laws of Ur-Nammu, the founder of the Third Dynasty of the city of Ur (ca. 2100 B.C.E.); the Laws of Lipit-Ishtar, ruler of the city of Isin (ca. 1900 B.C.E.); and the Laws of Eshnunna (ca. 1900 B.C.E.).[4] The extensive Code of Hammurabi from the Babylonian period (Hammurabi ruled 1728-1686 B.C.E.) comprises three hundred paragraphs written on a stone monument.[5] Hittite Laws from the fourteenth century B.C.E., Middle-Assyrian Laws from the eleventh century B.C.E., and Neo-Babylonian Laws from the sixth century B.C.E. indicate the continuing tradition of legal writing in the ancient Near East through the period of the Israelite monarchy.[6] As Patrick notes: "No area of biblical studies has benefited more from the recovery of ancient Near Eastern literature than law."[7]

Comparison has yielded a range of insights into the function of law throughout the ancient Near East, including Israelite society. The incompleteness of the biblical law codes is mirrored throughout the ancient Near Eastern counterparts. The law codes also share legal practices and address many similar legal situations, such as the case of an ox goring and killing another ox (Eshnunnu 53 and Exod 21:35), or laws regarding slavery (Eshnunna 34 and Exod 21:2-11). Comparison has also aided in clarifying differences between ancient and modern law. R. Westbrook has elaborated the differences, noting the important role of family status in the ancient legal process, the more limited role of the court in setting limits for revenge, and the ancient concern for pollution as a divine act upon society.[8] Comparison of distinct legal traditions has become so important to the study of ancient law codes that A. Watson rewrote the conclusion of Oliver Wendell Holmes noted above: "The life of the law is not logic, nor is it experience. It is borrowing."[9] But as M. Malul has noted, the com-

---

4. Laws of Ur-Nammu, *ANET*, 523-55; M. T. Roth, *Law Collections from Mesopotamia and Asia Minor* (2nd ed.; SBLWAW 6; Atlanta: Scholars Press, 1997), 13-22; Laws of Lipit-Ishtar, *ANET*, 159-61; Roth, *Law Collections*, 23-35; Laws of Eshnunna, *ANET*, 161-63; Roth, *Law Collections*, 57-70.

5. *ANET*, 163-80; Roth, *Law Collections*, 71-142.

6. Hittite Laws, *ANET*, 188-97; Roth, *Law Collections*, 213-47; Middle-Assyrian Laws, *ANET*, 180-88; Roth, *Law Collections*, 153-209; Neo-Babylonian Laws, *ANET*, 197-98; Roth, *Law Collections*, 143-49. For a summary of the different law codes see Boecker, *Law and Administration*, 53-133.

7. Patrick, *Old Testament Law*, 28.

8. R. Westbrook, *Studies in Biblical and Cuneiform Law* (CahRB 26; Paris: Gabalda, 1988).

9. A. Watson, *Ancient Law and Modern Understanding: At the Edges* (Athens, Ga.: University of Georgia Press, 1998), 3.

parative study of ancient Near Eastern law by biblical scholars has often suffered from a lack of clear method. He argues that any comparison of biblical and ancient Near Eastern law must distinguish a narrower historical comparison from a broader typological one. Comparison must also include an analysis of context, and it must distinguish coincidental similarity from more unique similarities that arise from a shared stream of tradition.[10]

Literary Study of Law

The interpretation of biblical law has tended to isolate individual laws through the examination of their structure and form. Alt's form-critical research in distinguishing casuistic ("if . . . , then . . .") from apodictic ("you shall not") law is an excellent example of this approach.[11] The literary structure of the law codes and their larger narrative context were not a central concern for Alt or for other interpreters of biblical law. Some interest in the larger literary structure of the law codes emerged from the comparative study of law. Scholars noted that ancient Near Eastern law codes often included a prologue and an epilogue that honor the king.[12] But on the whole interpreters did not use literary design as an avenue for the interpretation of biblical law. D. Daube argued that additional laws were often attached to the end of law codes regardless of topic, thus presenting a chaotic structure.[13]

But more recent interpreters are investigating the internal design of the law codes. J. Halbe argued for the compositional unity of the Book of the Covenant.[14] F. Crüsemann has followed the lead of Halbe, concluding that a clear understanding of the internal structure of a law code is necessary for interpreting individual laws and their compositional history.[15] The prominence given to the literary design of the law codes in Exodus by C. M. Carmichael, B. S. Jackson, E. Otto, and L. Schwienhorst-Schönberger indicates the change of paradigm in the study of ancient law.[16]

---

10. M. Malul, *The Comparative Method in Ancient Near Eastern and Biblical Legal Studies* (AOAT 227; Neukirchen-Vluyn: Neukirchener Verlag, 1990).

11. Alt, "Origins of Israelite Law," in *Essays*, 81-132.

12. Roth, *Law Collections*, 4-7.

13. D. Daube, *Studies in Biblical Law* (Cambridge: Cambridge University Press, 1947), 74-101.

14. J. Halbe, *Das Privilegrecht Jahwes Ex 34, 10-26: Gestalt und Wesen, Herkunft und Wirken in vordeuteronomischer Zeit* (FRLANT 114; Göttingen: Vandenhoeck & Ruprecht, 1975), 391-505.

15. F. Crüsemann, *The Torah: Theology and Social History of Old Testament Law* (trans. A. W. Mahnke; Minneapolis: Fortress, 1996).

16. C. M. Carmichael, *The Laws of Deuteronomy* (Ithaca: Cornell University Press, 1974); Jackson, *Studies in Semiotics*, 218-30; E. Otto, *Wandel der Rechtsbegründungen in der Gesell-*

The literary design of law codes is accompanied by more careful study of the narrative context. The literary setting of the Decalogue in 20:1-17 within the larger story of theophany is crucial to its interpretation, as is the progression from the public revelation of the Decalogue to the private revelation of the Book of the Covenant to Moses. J. P. Fokkelman has argued that law and narrative are inseparable for interpreting the themes of Exodus.[17] N. Stahl goes further, suggesting that law is a distinctive literary feature of "foundational biblical narratives," providing transition at liminal moments in the biblical story. In the revelation at Mount Sinai, law celebrates the relationship between God and Israel in covenant. Law gives voice to reservations concerning Israel's capacity to remain faithful to covenant. Law also affirms and calls into question the narrative theme of divine holiness and its transfer to the Israelite people, according to Stahl.[18]

The focus on the literary structure and the narrative context of law is also extended to the study of the inner-biblical relationship between law and narrative. Daube related the genres of law and narrative by examining the legal background of biblical stories. He demonstrated that the account of Joseph's brothers returning his bloodied coat or the closing episode in Moses' life when he is allowed to see the promised land were stories based on laws. According to Daube, the act of Moses seeing the promised land is a legal account of land transfer, while the bloodied coat of Joseph represents a law among shepherds excluding his brothers from responsibility in his loss.[19] Carmichael reverses the inner-biblical relationship between law and narrative, arguing that biblical laws are a literary creation to provide commentary on narratives. The Decalogue provides illustration. The first half of the Decalogue with its focus on the exclusive worship of Yahweh is commentary on the story of the golden calf in Exodus 32, according the Carmichael. The second half of the Decalogue beginning with the command to honor parents is commentary on the story of Adam and Eve, with special focus on Cain. Carmichael concluded that the Decalogue, as well as other law codes in the Hebrew Bible, are the product of didactic and reflective activity by scribes and that they are constructed in conjunction with the narrative.[20]

---

schaftsgeschichte des Antiken Israel: Eine Rechtsgeschichte des "Bundesbuches" Ex XX 22 — XXIII 13 (Studia biblica 3; Leiden: Brill, 1988); L. Schwienhorst-Schönberger, *Das Bundesbuch (Ex. 20,22–23,33): Studien zu seiner Entstehung und Theologie* (BZAW 188; Berlin: de Gruyter, 1990).

17. J. P. Fokkelman, "Exodus," in *The Literary Guide to the Bible* (ed. R. Alter and F. Kermode; Cambridge: Harvard University Press, 1987), 62.

18. N. Stahl, *Law and Liminality in the Bible* (JSOTSup 202; Sheffield: Sheffield Academic Press, 1995), 11-26, 51-73.

19. Daube, *Studies in Biblical Law*, 1-73.

20. C. M. Carmichael, *The Origins of Biblical Law: The Decalogues and the Book of the*

Freedman has recently extended the method by arguing that the Decalogue provides the structure for the entire history of Genesis through 2 Kings.[21] He detects the following correspondence between the laws of the Decalogue and the narratives in Genesis–2 Kings: laws 1 and 2 (no other gods and no images) are the story of the golden calf (Exodus 32); law 3 (the divine name) is the story of blasphemy (Leviticus 24); law 4 (Sabbath) is the story of the man picking up sticks on the Sabbath (Numbers 15); law 5 (honor parents) is the account of the son disrespecting his parents (Deut 21:18-21); law 6 (stealing) is the theft of Achan (Joshua 7); law 7 (murder) is the story of the concubine (Judges 19–21); law 8 (adultery) is the story of David and Bathsheba (2 Samuel 11); law 9 (false witness) is the theft of Naboth's vineyard by Ahaz and Jezebel (1 Kings 21); and law 10 (coveting) is woven into all the previous stories.

Law and Religion

Daube raised important reservations about the equation of law and religion throughout all phases of ancient Israelite history (see the commentary on the Book of the Covenant). But he also concluded that whatever their origin, it is clear that "the authors of the Bible saw law as part of religion."[22] The authors of Exodus leave no doubt that they envisioned law as representing the essence of their religion. God promises the Israelites at the outset of the wilderness journey that the revelation of law will be the source of health for them (Exod 15:22-27). The divine origin of the law is made explicit at the divine mountain, when God states to Moses (24:12): "I will give you the tablets of stone with the law and commandments which I have written for their instruction." S. Greengus notes that the anchoring of law in religion may be unique to the legal tradition of Israel in the ancient Near East.[23] The result according to Z. W. Falk is that law and spirituality become merged into one in the formation of the Hebrew Bible: "The commandments are meant not only as norms of behavior but also as objects of contemplation to lead toward the perception and love of God."[24] The

---

Covenant (Ithaca: Cornell University Press, 1992), 22-73; see also idem, *Law and Narrative in the Bible: The Evidence of the Deuteronomic Laws and the Decalogue* (Ithaca: Cornell University Press, 1985); idem, *The Spirit of Biblical Law* (Athens, Ga.: University of Georgia Press, 1996); idem, *Law, Legend, and Incest in the Bible: Leviticus 18–20* (Ithaca: Cornell University Press, 1997).

21. D. N. Freedman, with J. C. Geoghegan and M. M. Homan, *The Nine Commandments: Uncovering a Hidden Pattern of Crime and Punishment in the Hebrew Bible* (New York: Doubleday, 2000).

22. Daube, *Studies in Biblical Law*, 1.

23. S. Greengus, "Law," *ABD* 4:243-52.

24. Z. W. Falk, "Spirituality and Jewish Law," in *Religion and Law: Biblical Judaic and Islamic Perspectives* (ed. E. B. Firmage et al.; Winona Lake, Ind.: Eisenbrauns, 1990), 130.

exilic prophet Ezekiel gives expression to the merging of spirituality and law by attributing the possibility of a new heart and a new spirit to the observance of law (Ezekiel 18).

The ideal person exhibiting the spirituality of law is not the prophet but Moses, who becomes in Exodus the model of the human who contemplates law and perceives the core of divine love. His direct experience of God in the cave at the mountaintop reveals the essence of divine grace (Exod 34:6-9). His repeated trips to the summit of the mountain will eventually transform his face into divine light (34:29-35). The result is that the contemplation of law and the mystical experience of God become inseparable in the story of Moses. M. Fishbane clarifies the mystical power of law in *Sifre Deuteronomy* (343), which describes God's word as fire moving from his right to left hand and, in the process, encircling the nation before being inscribed on tablets by Moses. The image identifies law with the very essence of God conceived as fire. Fishbane concludes: "The written Law is thus an extension of divine speech — and not merely its inscriptional trace."[25]

An interpretation of law as a dynamic resource for change and spiritual contemplation is less common among Christian interpreters, who selectively read NT literature that views law negatively as a system of religious legalism resistant to change and antithetical to the mystical experience of God. The apostle Paul provides the strongest illustrations of this position when he presents a series of dichotomies in which law is identified with sin, the flesh, and death and contrasted to faith, the Spirit, and life. Law is static in this paradigm, an obstacle to the dynamic change signaled by the ushering in of God's kingdom. Justification in the new kingdom of God is by faith and not by observing the law (Gal 2:16), and the Spirit of God working in humans stems from faith, not from the observance of law (Gal 3:5). Law is an obstacle to change for Paul and a wedge preventing mystical union with God. Paul anchors his view of law in Christology. What the law was powerless to do, God did by sending his own Son (Rom 8:3). The Pauline vision of Jesus liberating religion from law is also embedded in the Gospel tradition. The Prologue to John, for example, states the following contrast: the law was given by Moses, but grace and truth came through Jesus Christ (John 1:17). Those who see the difference are transformed into light and become children of God.

But the NT vision of law and religion is far more complex than the selective texts cited above. Jesus affirms the central role of the law in the Gospel of Matthew: "Do not think that I have come to abolish the Law or the Prophets; I have not come to abolish them but to fulfill them" (Matt 5:17). Paul too appears

---

25. M. Fishbane, *The Exegetical Imagination: On Jewish Thought and Theology* (Cambridge: Harvard University Press, 1998), 9-21.

to quote the law, instructing the Roman Christians not to kill, commit adultery, steal, or covet (Rom 13:8-10). Law is also a resource for change in the NT. Jesus states in the Gospel of Matthew that teachers of the law trained in the kingdom of heaven bring forth old and new treasures (Matt 13:52). Recent scholarship has reinforced the dynamic role of law in NT literature. Daube has demonstrated the thorough dependency of NT writers on biblical and emerging rabbinic law. He notes Paul's use of law in 1 Corinthians to resolve disputes with regard to conversion, marriage, and food consumption, and the role of the Passover Haggadah in the structure of the Gospel of Mark.[26] J. Marcus has added to the legal background of the Gospel of Mark noting the important role of the law throughout the Gospel.[27] E. P. Sanders has moved the discussion of law from the reigning hermeneutical model of "pro" versus "anti" law to an examination of the variety of perspectives toward law in NT literature.[28]

Revelation of Law and Promise of Land

The structure of Exodus suggests that the promulgation of law at the divine mountain is the goal of the story. Once introduced it dominates the narrative both in Exodus and in the Pentateuch as a whole. Such an interpretation, however, appears to conflict with the larger story of the Pentateuch, in which the promise of land, not the revelation of law, is the goal of the story. God promises the ancestors that they will inherit the land of Canaan (e.g., Gen 12:1-10). The promise is guaranteed by God and repeated in the commission of Moses (Exod 3:7-10) and in the events of the exodus (13:5).

The conflict between the revelation of law and the narrative goal of reaching the promised land is more apparent than real, since the content of the divine legislation relates the two themes of law and land. The laws presuppose the Israelites' future life in the land, not their present encampment in the desert. The Decalogue and the Book of the Covenant presuppose the possession of the land in many of the laws (including slave laws, the resident alien, crop damage, etc.). Thus the promulgation of law and the divine gift of the land reinforce each other. The merging of law and land already in the revelation in the wilder-

---

26. On Paul see D. Daube, "Pauline Contributions to a Pluralistic Culture: Re-Creation and Beyond," in *Jesus and Man's Hope* (ed. D. G. Miller and D. Y. Hadidian; 2 vols.; Pittsburgh: Pittsburgh Theological Seminary, 1970-1971), 2:223-45; on Mark see idem, *He That Cometh* (London: Diocesan Council, 1966).

27. J. Marcus, *Mark* (AB; New York: Doubleday, 2000), e.g., 19-21.

28. E. P. Sanders, *Paul, the Law, and the Jewish People* (Philadelphia: Fortress, 1983); idem, *Jesus and Judaism* (Philadelphia: Fortress, 1985); idem, "When Is a Law a Law? The Case of Jesus and Paul," in *Religion and Law: Biblical Judaic and Islamic Perspectives* (ed. E. B. Firmage et al.; Winona Lake, Ind.: Eisenbrauns, 1990), 139-58.

ness gives the legislation at Mount Sinai a dynamic quality and a future orientation. The laws are revealed in the present journey through the wilderness, but their content is about the Israelites' future life in the land. The future orientation of the laws suggests that their observance is a catalyst for change in the salvation history of the Israelite people in the wilderness journey. Observing Torah has a utopian quality. It will aid the Israelites in realizing the divine gift of the land.

Decalogue (19:20–20:20)

^{19:20}*And Yahweh descended on Mount Sinai to the top of the mountain. And Yahweh called Moses to the top of the mountain. And Moses ascended.* ²¹*And Yahweh said to Moses, "Go down and warn the people, lest they break through to Yahweh to see, and many of them fall.* ²²*Even the priests who approach Yahweh must be consecrated, lest Yahweh break through against them."*

²³*And Moses said to Yahweh, "The people are not able to ascend Mount Sinai, for you warned us, saying, 'Set boundaries around the mountain and consecrate it.'"*

²⁴*And Yahweh said to him, "Go and descend, and you ascend and Aaron with you. But the priests and the people may not break through to ascend to Yahweh, lest he break through against them."*

²⁵*And Moses descended to the people, and he said to them,* ^{20:1}*"God spoke all these words, saying,* ²*'I am Yahweh, your God, who brought you out of the land of Egypt from the house of slavery.*

³*You shall have no other gods in my presence.*

⁴*You will not make for yourself a carved image, any likeness of what is in the heavens above or on the earth below, or in the water below the earth.* ⁵*You will not bow down to them and you will not serve them, for I, Yahweh your God, am a jealous God, visiting the iniquities of the fathers on the children to the third and to the fourth generation of those who hate me,* ⁶*but doing steadfast love to the thousandth generation of those loving me and observing my commandments.*

⁷*You may not lift up the name of Yahweh your God in vain, for Yahweh will not acquit the one who lifts up his name in vain.*

⁸*Remember the Sabbath day to keep it holy.* ⁹*Six days you will labor and do all your work.* ¹⁰*But the seventh day is a Sabbath to Yahweh your God. You will not do any work — you, and your son, and your daughter, your male slave, and your female slave, and your cattle, and your resident alien in your gates.* ¹¹*For in six days Yahweh made the heavens and the earth, the sea, and all that is in them. And he rested on the seventh day. Therefore Yahweh blessed the Sabbath day and he sanctified it.*

¹²*Honor your father and your mother, so that your days may be long on the ground that Yahweh your God is giving you.*

¹³*You shall not murder.*

¹⁴*You shall not commit adultery.*

¹⁵*You shall not steal.*

¹⁶*You shall not bear false witness against your neighbor.*

¹⁷*You shall not covet the house of your neighbor. You shall not covet the wife of your neighbor, his male slave, and his female slave, and his ox, and his ass, and anything that is your neighbor's.'"*

¹⁸*And all the people were seeing the thunder, and the lightning, and the sound of the horn, and the mountain smoking. And the people saw and they trembled, and they stood at a distance.* ¹⁹*And they said to Moses, "You speak with us, so that we hear. But do not let God speak with us, lest we die."*

²⁰*And Moses said to the people, "Do not fear; for to test you the God has come and to place his fear on your face, so that you do not sin."*

Notes

19:21 *lest they break through to Yahweh.* Hebrew *pen-yehersû* expresses contingency (*IBHS* §31.6.1), which may also be translated, "not to break through" (NRSV). The particle *pen* (almost always with the imperfect) at the beginning of a clause expresses fear or precaution (GKC §152w). The LXX translates the Hebrew with *mēpote*, "never, on no account," with the aorist subjunctive to convey a prohibition. Hebrew *hāras* means "to throw down, overthrow, ruin." The meaning in 19:21 likely conveys the overthrowing of the boundaries (*gĕbûl;* see the verb in 19:12, 23), indicating trespassing into the sacred space of the mountain. The word repeats in 19:24. The LXX translates Hebrew *hāras* in 19:21 simply as *engisōsin,* "to draw near," but in 19:24 the word *biazesthōsan,* "to use force," more closely conveys the Hebrew. The LXX also refers to the Deity as *ho theos* and *ton theon,* rather than *kyrios,* for MT *yhwh.*

and many of them fall. Hebrew *nāpal* is a reference to death. The LXX translates, *pesōsin,* "to fall," which can also refer to death as "the fallen in battle" (LSJ 1407).

19:22 *even the priests who approach Yahweh.* The reference to priests is proleptic in this context. The LXX adds *tō theō,* "the God," after *kyriō.*

lest Yahweh break through against them. For Hebrew *pen-yiprōṣ* see the translation note on 19:21, though there *hāras* is used for "break through." The threat of the people "breaking through" (*hāras;* 19:21, 24) is countered by the danger of Yahweh "breaking through" (*pāraṣ;* 19:22, 24).

19:23 *set boundaries around the mountain and consecrate it.* The statement of Moses refers to 19:10-13, where the mountain was separated from the people, but the people were sanctified, not the mountain. The emphasis on the mountain corresponds to the P writer's emphasis on Mount Sinai in 19:11b, 18.

19:25 *and he said to them.* Hebrew *wayyō'mer 'ălēhem* suggests the introduction to a speech, "he said to them," and not the reporting of past speech, "he told them"

(NRSV). Verse 25 is not a report of the conversation between Yahweh and Moses in vv. 21-24. See, for example, 19:9, where the reported speech by Moses is signified by the verb *nāgad*. The author of 19:25 fashions the Decalogue (20:1-17) as the speech of Moses, who conveys the divine words to the people.[29]

20:3 *in my presence*. Hebrew *'al-pānāy* translates more lit. "upon my face." Houtman notes that the phrase likely implies the setting of the sanctuary.[30] The LXX translates, *plēn emou*, "besides me." That the MT lacks a *soph pasuq* suggests that vv. 3-6 be read as a single unit (cf. the parallel version in Deut 5:7, which has the *soph pasuq*).

20:4 *a carved image*. Hebrew *pesel*, "carved image," derives from the verb *pāsal*, "to carve." The noun likely refers to cultic images. It is used in conjunction with pillars (*maṣṣēbâ*) in Lev 26:1 and with the molten image (*massēkâ*) in Deut 27:15. The plural *pĕsîlîm* often refers to idols (e.g., NIV "images," Deut 7:25; NIV, NRSV "idols," 12:3).

any likeness. Hebrew *wĕkol-tĕmunâ* is lit. "and any likeness." The conjunction *wĕ* is absent from the parallel version of Deut 5:8, *pesel kol-tĕmûnâ*, suggesting a relationship of apposition, "a carved image, any likeness."[31] Dohmen interprets the conjunction in Exod 20:4 as an expansive interpretation of Deut 5:8 to include the representation of any image in the setting of the cult.[32] Houtman interprets the conjunction more narrowly to indicate emphasis, "indeed, of no one creature."[33]

20:6 *but showing steadfast love*. Hebrew *wĕ'ōśeh ḥesed* translates lit. "and doing steadfast love." The verb *'āśâ* often describes Yahweh's actions toward humans, allowing for the broader translation in this case, "showing."[34]

to the thousandth generation. The Hebrew simply states, "to the thousands," *la'ălāpîm*.

20:7 *you may not lift up the name of Yahweh your God*. Hebrew *tiśśā'*, "to lift up," is unclear in the text. Weinfeld concludes that the verb means "to take upon one's lips" (see 23:1; Ps 15:3; 139:20), which is an idiom for swearing in God's name.[35]

in vain. Hebrew *laššāwĕ'* means "emptiness." Houtman states that the word also denotes deception and falsity.[36] The LXX translates, *epi mataiō*, which when applied to words means "idle."

for Yahweh will not acquit. Hebrew *yĕnaqqeh*, "acquit," carries the meaning of being clean as well as free. The LXX reinforces the meaning of cleanliness and purity with the verb *katharisē*.

20:8 *remember the Sabbath day*. Hebrew *zākôr* is an infinitive absolute used as a legislative command (see *IBHS* §35.5.1). The Sam reads *šmwr*, corresponding to the version of the Decalogue in Deut 5:12.

---

29. See Durham, *Exodus*, 267-78.

30. Houtman, *Exodus*, 3:17.

31. Weinfeld, *Deuteronomy 1–11*, 289-90.

32. C. Dohmen, *Das Bilderverbot: Seine Entstehung und seine Entwicklung im Alten Testament* (2nd ed.; BBB 62; Frankfurt: Athenäum, 1987), 213, 227 *et passim*.

33. Houtman, *Exodus*, 3:32.

34. Houtman, *Exodus*, 1:49-50.

35. Weinfeld, *Deuteronomy 1–11*, 278-79.

36. Houtman, *Exodus*, 3:36.

to keep it holy. Hebrew *lĕqaddĕšô* is composed of the preposition *lĕ,* the infinitive form of the verb, and the pronominal suffix for the direct object. See also the LXX *hagiazein autēn.* Cf. NRSV, "remember the Sabbath day, and keep it holy."

20:10 *you, and your son, and your daughter, your male slave, and your female slave, and your cattle.* The list is expanded in the LXX to include "your ox and your ass" *(ho bous sou kai to hypozygion sou).*

and your resident alien in your gates. Hebrew *gēr* is translated *prosēlytos* in the LXX, which also paraphrases the phrase "in your gates" as "residing among you" *(ho paroikōn en soi).*

20:12 *Honor.* The LXX translates Hebrew *kabbēd* as *tima.*

so that your days may be long on the ground. The Hebrew uses the word *'ădāmâ,* "ground," which designates more precisely the agricultural land. The LXX adds two clauses: "so that it may be well with you" *(hina eu soi genētai),* and "so that you may be a long time in the good land" *(hina makrochronios genē epi tēs gēs tēs agathēs).* The syntax of the LXX with the two result clauses rather than one is closer to the version of the command in Deut 5:16, although the specific content of the two clauses differs.

20:13-15 *You shall not murder. You shall not commit adultery. You shall not steal.* The LXX changes the order of the prohibitions to: adultery, stealing, murder.

20:17 *You shall not covet the house of your neighbor. You shall not covet the wife of your neighbor.* The command in 20:17 employs the same verb twice, *ḥāmad,* "to covet." Deuteronomy 5:21 employs separate verbs, *ḥāmad,* "to covet," and *'āwâ,* "to desire," while also reversing the commands: "You shall not covet the wife of your neighbor. And you shall not desire the house of your neighbor." The LXX follows the order of the two sentences in Deut 5:21, but employs the same verb, *epithymēseis,* "to long for, covet, desire." The Sam significantly expands the conclusion to the Decalogue with literature from Deut 27:2, 5-7; and 11:30.

20:18 *And all the people were seeing.* The Hebrew participle *rō'îm* is intended to convey the immediacy of the experience. J. I. Durham favors the translation "were experiencing," because of the wide range of sensory objects that follow the verb: thunder, lightning, sound of the horn, and smoke.[37] The tension surrounding the theophany, as an event of mixed perception between sight and sound, is also evident in Deuteronomy (e.g., 4:9-14).

And the people saw. The singular MT *wayyar'* is problematic in a context where the other verbs are plural; the LXX *phobēthentes* reflects Hebrew *wayyir'û,* "and they feared."

20:19 *you speak with us, so that we hear.* The Hebrew consists of an imperative, *dabbēr,* "you speak," and a cohortative, *wĕnišmā'â,* "let us listen." The sequence of imperative plus cohortative indicates purpose or result (*IBHS* §36.4).

20:20 *for to test you.* The Hebrew translates more lit. "for in order to test you" *(kî lĕba'ăbûr nassôt).*

on your face. The LXX translates Hebrew *'al-pĕnêkem* as *en hymin,* "in you."

37. Durham, *Exodus,* 301.

Commentary

Introduction

HISTORY OF COMPOSITION

The present form of the Decalogue indicates a history of composition. Individual laws appear to have undergone expansion. This is most evident in the law of the Sabbath, where the command to observe the Sabbath is anchored in extensive commentary on the creation (20:8-11). But other laws also include additional commentary such as the prohibition against images (20:4-6), where the motive to obey the law is carefully delineated with a description of divine punishment and love. The history of commentary is also evident in that the entire law code occurs twice in the Pentateuch, as a revelation on Mount Sinai in 20:1-17 and as a revelation on Mount Horeb in Deut 5:6-21. The addition of motive clauses for the observance of individual laws highlights the difference between the two occurrences of the Decalogue in the Pentateuch, of which Sabbath observance provides the clearest illustration. The motive for Sabbath observance in Exod 20:8-11 is the divine structure of creation, while in Deut 5:12-15 the Sabbath arises from the Israelites' exodus from Egypt.

Scholars have sought to identify the original form and the social location of the Decalogue.[38] S. Mowinckel argued that there was an ancient form of the Decalogue that functioned in an annual New Year liturgy. He recognized allusions to the Decalogue in Pss 50:16-20 and 81:9-10.[39] Alt also interpreted the original setting of the Decalogue to be the cult, tied specifically to the recitation of the law at Shechem. He argued that the original form of the Decalogue consisted of apodictic laws, a categorical form of law, which he judged to be unique to ancient Israel.[40] E. Gerstenberger questioned Alt's identification of the apodictic form of law and the original cultic setting of the Decalogue. He argued that the more original form of law was less rigid than Alt had identified, preferring the description of prohibitive law over apodictic law. The genre of prohibitive law is more varied in style within the individual laws, including the shift

---

38. For more detailed summary of the past scholarship on the Decalogue see E. Nielsen, *The Ten Commandments in New Perspective* (trans. D. J. Burke; 2nd ed.; SBT 2/7; Naperville: Allenson, 1968); J. J. Stamm and M. E. Andrew, *The Ten Commandments in Recent Research* (2nd ed.; SBT 2/2; London: SCM, 1967); W. Harrelson, *The Ten Commandments and Human Rights* (OBT; Philadelphia: Fortress, 1980). Also see M. Noth, *The Laws in the Pentateuch and Other Studies* (trans. D. R. Ap-Thomas; Philadelphia: Fortress, 1966); W. Malcolm Clark, "Law," in *Old Testament Form Criticism* (ed. J. H. Hayes; Trinity University Monograph Series in Religion 2; San Antonio: Trinity University Press, 1974), 99-139; Crüsemann, *Torah.*

39. Mowinckel, *Le décalogue.*

40. Alt, *Essays.*

between positive (vv. 8, 12) and negative (all the rest) laws and the references to God, which change from the first (vv. 1-6) to the third (vv. 7-17) person. Gerstenberger also concluded that the prohibitive laws arose in the setting of clan ethics rather than cultic ritual. Such laws were likely clustered in groups of three or four, not in larger sequences of ten, as in the present form of the Decalogue.[41] A. Phillips represents another attempt to recover the origin of the Decalogue in the setting of preexilic criminal law, which, he concludes, may have been associated with the treaty form identified by Mendenhall.[42] Still other interpreters have sought to reconstruct the original or primitive form of ten laws.[43] For example, according to E. Nielsen each command refers to a concrete object and is unambiguous:

First Command: Thou shalt not bow down before any other god.
Second Command: Thou shalt not make to thyself any idol.
Third Command: Thou shalt not take the name of Yahweh in vain.
Fourth Command: Thou shalt not do any work on the Sabbath day.
Fifth Command: Thou shalt not despise thy father or thy mother.
Sixth Command: Thou shalt not commit adultery with thy neighbour's wife.
Seventh Command: Thou shalt not pour out the blood of thy neighbour.
Eighth Command: Thou shalt not steal any man from thy neighbour.
Ninth Command: Thou shalt not bear false witness against thy neighbour.
Tenth Command: Thou shalt not covet thy neighbour's house.[44]

The quest to recover the origin of the Decalogue has given way to the more limited study of the synoptic tradition of the Decalogue in 20:1-17 and Deut 5:6-21. The traditional view of the history of composition in the modern period is that the Decalogue in Exod 20:1-17 is the parent text for the version of

41. E. Gerstenberger, *Wesen und Herkunft des apodiktischen Rechts* (WMANT 20; Neukirchen-Vluyn: Neukirchener Verlag, 1965).

42. A. Phillips, *Ancient Israel's Criminal Law: A New Approach to the Decalogue* (Oxford: Basil Blackwell, 1970). Phillips later detached his theory from the hypothesis of the treaty form in "The Decalogue: Ancient Israel's Criminal Law," in *Essays on Biblical Law* (JSOTSup 344; Sheffield: Sheffield Academic Press, 2002), 2-24.

43. See H. Schmidt, "Moses und der Dekalog," in *Eucharisterion: Festschrift für H. Gunkel* (ed. H. Schmidt; Göttingen: Vandenhoeck & Ruprecht, 1923), 78-119; K. Rabast, *Das apodiktische Rechte im Deuteronomium und im Heiligkeitsgesetz* (Berlin: Heimat-Dienst, 1948); Harrelson, *Ten Commandments and Human Rights*.

44. Nielsen, *Ten Commandments*, 84-85; see also M. Greenberg, "The Decalogue Tradition Critically Examined," in *The Ten Commandments in History and Tradition* (ed. B.-Z. Segal; Jerusalem: Magnes, 1990), 83-119, esp. 109-14.

the Decalogue in Deut 5:6-21, even though there are clear signs of P editing in Exod 20:1-17.[45] Perlitt reversed the literary relationship, arguing that the setting for the development of the Decalogue is in the tradition of Deuteronomy, not in Exodus. The Decalogue is part of the interpretation of covenant in Deuteronomy that arises at the close of the monarchical period. The insertion of the Decalogue into Exodus is an even later development. Exodus 20:1-17 is a secondary insertion into the book, according to Perlitt, undertaken in conjunction with the emergence of the covenant theology in Deuteronomy. The secondary character of the Decalogue in Exodus is evident from the literary isolation of 20:1-17 in its present narrative context. Perlitt identifies the author of 20:1-17 as a Deuteronomistic redactor.[46]

The thesis of Perlitt was presupposed in the work of Nielsen, and it has been expanded by a number of recent interpreters, including E. W. Nicholson, Blum, and Dohmen.[47] But it is not accepted universally. Weinfeld, Houtman, Levin, A. Graupner, and Johnstone maintain the priority of a version of the Decalogue in 20:1-17. Houtman suggests that Deut 5:6-21 is part of a canonical interpretation of the preceding literature in Exodus.[48] Weinfeld argues that the syntax of the law against idols favors the priority of Exod 20:4 over Deut 5:9.[49] Graupner sees the same direction of reinterpretation from Exodus to Deuteronomy in the status of the wife (Exod 20:17; Deut 5:21).[50] Johnstone concludes that a pre-P Deuteronomistic form of the Decalogue in Exod 20:1-17 provides the basis for the law in Deuteronomy, noting the repeated references to the past promulgation of law in Deuteronomy (e.g., 5:12), which suggested to him a form of the law in Exodus.[51] Levin also favors the priority of Exod 20:1-17 based on the principle that the shorter version must be older.[52]

A number of interpreters follow the framework of Perlitt's thesis, but they attribute the entire composition of 20:1-17 to the P author. Most interpreters identify P composition in the law of the Sabbath in 20:8-11, while attributing the composition of the law code to another author (E in traditional source criticism; the Deuteronomist according to Perlitt; I prefer the Non-P History).

---

45. See, e.g., Beyerlin, *Origins and History.*

46. Perlitt, *Bundestheologie*, 78-99.

47. E. W. Nicholson, *God and His People: Covenant and Theology in the Old Testament* (Oxford: Clarendon, 1986); Blum, *Studien*, 49-50, 93-97; Dohmen, *Exodus 19–40*; W. Johnstone, "The Decalogue and the Redaction of the Sinai Pericope in Exodus," *ZAW* 100 (1988): 361-85 = *Chronicles and Exodus*, 168-97.

48. Houtman, *Exodus*, 3:10-11.

49. Weinfeld, *Deuteronomy 1–11*, 243, 290-91.

50. A. Graupner, "Zum Verhältnis der beiden Dekalogfassungen Ex 20 und Dtn 5," *ZAW* 99 (1987): 308-29, esp. 321-22.

51. Johnstone, "Decalogue and Redaction" = *Chronicles and Exodus*, 168-97.

52. C. Levin, "Der Dekalog am Sinai," *VT* 35 (1985): 165-91.

Winnett departs from this approach by attributing the entire composition of 20:1-17 to the P author on the basis of the clear signs of P authorship in the Sabbath law. The same general line of interpretation is presented in the work of F.-L. Hossfeld and Van Seters, although each author works with distinct views of the composition of the Pentateuch.[53] The result is that the two versions of the Decalogue in the Pentateuch represent the distinct authors P (20:1-17) and D (Deut 5:6-21). The P composition of 20:1-17 also means that the pre-P account of Exodus 19–24 lacks a version of the Decalogue.

History of Interpretation

The perspective on human rights in the Decalogue and its demand for singular allegiance to God echoes throughout Scripture and in ongoing Jewish and Christian tradition. In the overview of the history of composition I have already noted the prominence given to the Decalogue in the Pentateuch.[54] It has become the constitutional statement for covenant in the books of Exodus and Deuteronomy. The full text occurs in Deuteronomy 5, with additional references throughout the book (chaps. 4, 9, 10), including the curses for breaking the covenant in 27:15-26. The Decalogue is also central in the P legislation. The version of the Decalogue in Exodus 20 indicates editing by the P historian, especially in the law of the Sabbath observance (20:8-11). The result is a P (20:1-17) and a D (Deut 5:6-21) version of the constitutional document. The general character of the laws in the Decalogue, such as prohibitions against killing, stealing, and lying, makes it difficult to trace a direct influence on other literature. Yet the influence of the Decalogue in P tradition appears to go beyond Exodus 20. B. J. Schwartz, among others, has argued that the laws pertaining to moral and ritual holiness in Leviticus 19 refer to the Decalogue.[55] The prophets echo the Decalogue in their preaching. The book of Jeremiah lists ethical commands reminiscent of the Decalogue, warning the Israelite people not to steal, murder, commit adultery, swear falsely, or worship other gods (Jer 7:9). Hosea includes swearing, lying, murder, stealing, and adultery as unethical actions opposed to the worship of Yahweh (Hos 4:2). According to the prophet Ezekiel, the sins of Jerusalem include murder, contempt of parents, oppression of the alien, widow, and orphan, slander, adultery, incest, and exploitation of neigh-

---

53. Winnett, *Mosaic Tradition*, 30-42; Van Seters, *Life of Moses*, 248-52; Hossfeld, *Dekalog*, 21-162.

54. See Dohmen, *Exodus 19–40*, 88-91, for an interpretation of the two occurrences of the Decalogue in the present form of the Pentateuch.

55. B. J. Schwartz, "Selected Chapters of the Holiness Code — A Literary Study of Leviticus 17-19" (Hebrew; Ph.D. diss., Hebrew University, 1987). See the review of scholarship on the topic in Milgrom, *Leviticus 17-22*, 1596-1602.

bor (Ezek 22:1-12).[56] The influence of the Decalogue may continue into the Psalms (e.g., Ps 50:16-20) and perhaps also into the book of Job (Job 24:13-17), where the characterization of the wicked relates to many of the laws of the Decalogue.

The influence of the Decalogue continues beyond the Hebrew Bible. It was singled out for daily prayer along with the Shema (Deut 6:4) in Jewish worship already before the Common Era, and it continues in the liturgy of the Feast of Weeks.[57] Philo of Alexandria reinforced its constitutional character, arguing that the Decalogue contained in essence all the other commands.[58] Direct quotation of the Decalogue is less evident in the teaching of Jesus, although he repeatedly mentions the importance of law, referring to many of the commands from the Decalogue in the Sermon on the Mount (Matthew 5). Jesus summarizes the essence of law as love of God above all and love of neighbor as self (e.g., Matt 19:16-19; 22:39; Mark 10:17-20; 12:28-31). The law takes on a more polemical role in the teaching of Paul (see Gal 3:13; 4:24). Yet he too appears to cite the Decalogue in Rom 13:9, listing the prohibitions against adultery, murder, stealing, and coveting, as well as "any other commandment," as actions summed up in the command to love.[59] An interpretation of the Decalogue as natural law in early Christian tradition placed the law code within the world of Hellenistic ethics, where it played a role in shaping Western culture. From Justin and Aquinas, through Luther and Calvin, and into the present time through such work as done by W. Harrelson and P. Lehmann, Christian interpreters have explored the universal truth of the Decalogue for creating a just society.[60] Indeed, the Decalogue has

---

56. Weinfeld, *Deuteronomy 1–11,* 250-57; M. Weiss, "The Decalogue in Prophetic Literature," in *Ten Commandments in History,* ed. Segal, 67-81.

57. *Mishna Tamid* 4:3; 5:1; possibly also the Nash Papyrus, dating 150 B.C.E., where the Shema and the Decalogue appear together. See Weinfeld, *Deuteronomy 1–11,* 267-75; idem, "The Uniqueness of the Decalogue and Its Place in Jewish Tradition," in *Ten Commandments in History,* ed. Segal, 1-44, esp. 21-44; E. E. Urbach, "The Role of the Ten Commandments in Jewish Worship," in *Ten Commandments in History,* ed. Segal, 161-89.

58. Philo, *Decal.* 154. See Y. Amir, "The Decalogue According to Philo," in *Ten Commandments in History,* ed. Segal, 121-60.

59. Dale C. Allison, "Mark 12:28-31 and the Decalogue," in *The Gospels and the Scriptures of Israel* (ed. C. A. Evans and W. Stegner; JSNTSup 104; SSEJC 3; Sheffield: Sheffield Academic Press, 1994), 270-78; R. H. Fuller, "The Decalogue in the New Testament," *Int* 43 (1989): 243-55; Patrick, *Old Testament Law,* 187-222; D. Flusser, "The Ten Commandments and the New Testament," in *Ten Commandments in History,* ed. Segal, 219-46.

60. Harrelson, *Ten Commandments and Human Rights;* P. L. Lehman, *The Decalogue and a Human Future: The Meaning of the Commandments for Making and Keeping Human Life Human* (Grand Rapids: Eerdmans, 1994). It is not possible to cover the rich history of interpretation surrounding the Decalogue. Excellent summaries are provided by Childs, *Exodus,* 431-37; Stamm and Andrews, *Ten Commandments in Recent Research;* Segal, ed., *Ten Commandments in History;* Houtman, *Exodus,* 3:1-16; Janzen, *Exodus,* 250-85.

become so central to Western culture, according to M. D. Coogan, that we are in danger of blurring its religious and secular roles.[61] This is evident in debates over the placement of the Decalogue in civil law courts, where it is argued that the Decalogue represents the core of national law rather than religious law.

Literary Context

The divine promise of law has been a central theme in the wilderness journey. God introduced the theme of law immediately after the crossing of the Red Sea in the wilderness of Shur (15:22-26). God proposed law as the basis for the divine-human relationship, promising the Israelites health in exchange for their obedience. And God guaranteed the promise with a self-revelation: "I am Yahweh, your healer" (v. 26). The divine proposal of law repeats at the mountain of God as the basis for covenant (19:1-8). The promise of health is supplemented with the divine vow that the Israelite people would have a special status in the world as a holy nation (vv. 5-6), if they live by divine law. Both proposals lack specific legislation. The only law revealed to the Israelites in their initial journey through the wilderness has been Sabbath observance in the story of manna (Exodus 16). Thus the Decalogue is the first extended revelation of law, giving it the special status as a charter document. Its importance as a foundational Scripture is indicated by a divine self-revelation in the prologue: "I am Yahweh your God, who brought you out of Egypt" (20:1). The self-revelation provides context for interpreting the Decalogue as an outgrowth of the salvation of the Israelite people. Thus salvation and law become intertwined in Exodus. The revelation of law will dominate the remainder of the book, including the Book of the Covenant (20:21–23:33), the cultic legislation of the tabernacle (chaps. 25–31, 35–40), and the legislation of covenant renewal (34:10-28).

The commentary on the revelation of the Decalogue separates into three parts: an introduction (19:20-25), the revelation of the Decalogue (20:1-17), and the conclusion (20:18-20). The introduction and the conclusion represent distinct interpretations of the Decalogue. The introduction presents the law as mediated speech by Moses, while the conclusion interprets the Decalogue as a direct speech by God to the Israelite people. The revelation of the Decalogue reflects the P interpretation with regard to Sabbath observance (20:8-11), which provides a contrast to the Deuteronomic version of the law of the Sabbath (Deut 5:12-15).

19:20-25 *Introduction.* The introduction to the Decalogue narrates an unexpected ascent of Moses on Mount Sinai (v. 20) during the event of theophany (vv. 16-19). In two speeches Yahweh underscores the danger of holiness to the people (vv. 21-22) and the need to exclude them from ascending the

---

61. M. D. Coogan, "The Ten Commandments on the Wall," *BRev* 15 (1999): 2.

mountain (v. 24). The scene closes with Moses descending the mountain and speaking *('āmar)* to the people (v. 25). The language is from the P historian. The mountain of revelation is Mount Sinai (see 19:11, 18) and the approach of God is a descent *(yārad)* to the summit of the mountain *('el-rō'š hāhār)*. The imagery repeats from the P account of theophany in 19:18 and it will return in the subsequent P account of theophany in 24:15-18.

The section has puzzled interpreters. The divine commands conflict with the preceding instructions for theophany (19:10-15), and the role of Moses as mediator forces a new interpretation of the Decalogue (20:1-17). The exclusion of the people from the mountain (19:23) contradicts the earlier command that they ascend the mountain at the blast of the trumpet (19:13). The new restriction on the people's access to holiness is also carried through the revelation of the Decalogue. With the descent of Moses to the people in v. 25 the Decalogue is no longer a direct address of God to the Israelites as is the case in the Non-P History (19:19; 20:18-20) and in its parallel version in Deuteronomy 4–5.[62] Instead, the revelation is mediated through Moses, who teaches the law code to the people as though it were a priestly Torah:[63] "And Moses descended to the people, and he [Moses] said *('āmar)* to them, 'God spoke all these words, saying, . . .'" (19:25–20:1).

The mediation of the Decalogue by Moses in 19:25 is unexpected. It conflicts so sharply with the fear of the people upon hearing the divine speech at the end of the scene (20:18-20) that interpreters have sought to modify the text. The NIV and NRSV illustrate the tendency to harmonize 19:20-25 with the tradition of the Decalogue as the public revelation of God. Both versions translate the Hebrew verb *'āmar*, "to say," as though it were the verb *nāgad*, "to tell": "So Moses went down to the people and told them." The translations suggest that Moses is communicating the content of the past divine warnings from 19:22-24 to the Israelites, as was the case in 19:9. Dohmen states the problem: Is 19:25 the end of a unit providing a summary conclusion to 19:20-24, or the beginning of a new unit that introduces the Decalogue? He seeks a third solution by interpreting the Decalogue on a metalevel in the narrative as information for the reader, and not as an element in the unfolding plot.[64] But the research of S. A. Meier on the verb *'āmar* suggests that it is more likely introducing the Decalogue as direct discourse by Moses.[65]

---

62. For discussion of the narrative context see Childs, *Exodus*, 387-401; E. W. Nicholson, "The Decalogue as the Direct Address of God," *VT* 27 (1977): 422-33; Dohmen, *Exodus 19–40*, 87-91.

63. J. Begrich, "Das priesterliche Tora," in *Werden und Wesen des Alten Testaments* (ed. P. Volz et al.; BZAW 66; Berlin: Töpelmann, 1936), 63-88.

64. Dohmen, *Exodus 19–40*, 76-77.

65. S. A. Meier, *Speaking of Speaking: Marking Direct Discourse in the Hebrew Bible* (VTSup 46; Leiden: Brill, 1992), esp. 59-140.

Interpreters have long debated the purpose of the scene. Noth judged vv. 20-24 to be a secondary expansion supplementing the theme of holiness, while v. 25, in his judgment, was a fragment without meaning in its present narrative context.[66] W. Beyerlin speculated that perhaps v. 25 was the introduction to a lost speech.[67] The theme of holiness is certainly central to the scene, but v. 25 cannot be so easily separated from vv. 20-24, since Moses is described as ascending the mountain in v. 20, which requires his descent in v. 25. And there is no evidence that a speech is missing from the text.

Childs detected a literary pattern in 19:20-25, in which the citing of a prior command (vv. 11-13) is repeated to support its truth (v. 23). In this case the citation by Moses in v. 23 underscores that the people are indeed unable to ascend Mount Sinai (vv. 11-13).[68] The commands in vv. 11-13 and 23 are certainly related, but they do not state the same thing. Verse 23 changes the command from vv. 11-13, restricting the people from ascending the mountain even at the sound of the trumpet.

W. Rudolph provided a better starting point for interpretation when he argued that vv. 20-24 represent a midrashic expansion of the command in vv. 11-13 about the need for boundaries.[69] Durham has built on the approach of Rudolph and Beyerlin, noting the strong interest in the author to underscore the need for an intercessor between Yahweh and the people.[70]

The Non-P and P authors share a view of holiness as originating from God and as being dangerous to humans. But they disagree on the transfer of holiness to humans. In the Non-P History, the experience of theophany as speech (19:19) results in the transfer of holiness to the people through the direct revelation of the Decalogue. The people experience divine holiness firsthand in the speech of God, they acquire the proper fear of God, and they elect Moses to mediate the revelation of all future law (20:18-20). Deuteronomy agrees with the author of the Non-P History, describing the Israelites as "a holy people" (e.g., Deut 7:6). The P author disagrees with such an immediate and direct transfer of holiness. By placing Exod 19:20-25 between the description of theophany (19:16-19) and the revelation of the Decalogue (20:1-17), the P author qualifies the experience of theophany and the revelation of law by changing the role of Moses. Moses' public conversation with God (19:19) turns private (19:20-24), which requires that he take on the role of a priestly mediator to communicate the Decalogue to the people. Childs rightly describes the literary function of 19:20-25: "Right at the apparent climax of the theophany, the

---

66. Noth, *Exodus*, 160.
67. Beyerlin, *Origins and History*, 8-9.
68. Childs, *Exodus*, 362-63.
69. Rudolph, *Elohist*, 44.
70. Beyerlin, *Origins and History*, 8; Durham, *Exodus*, 272.

scene is interrupted and Moses is again called back up the mountain for further instructions."[71]

The "further instructions" noted by Childs consist of two divine speeches to Moses, vv. 21-22 and v. 24, separated by Moses' reply in v. 23. The two divine speeches provide the P author's view of holiness. Both warn the people about the danger of holiness and the need for a priestly class of mediators. The first speech negates the command from v. 13 that the people ascend the mountain at the sound of the trumpet. God states that the people must not break through (*hāras*), suggesting some kind of fence or barrier around the mountain. The verb indicates the breakdown of walls (Ezek 26:12), altars (Judg 6:25), and cities (2 Sam 11:25), as well as enemies (15:7). The reference to priests appears out of place, anticipating their ordination in Leviticus 8–9. Their mention at this point in the story underscores the P author's view that priests are mediators necessary to approach holiness. The command for a priestly class is stated negatively as a warning. Priests who approach must be sanctified lest Yahweh break out (*pāraṣ*; see the commentary on 1:12) against them. The reply of Moses in 19:23 is a paraphrase of an earlier divine command from v. 12. Moses assures the Deity that trespass is not possible: "You yourself warned us, 'Put limits around the mountain and set it apart as holy.'" The quotation sets the stage for a further reinterpretation of the earlier command, limiting the ascent on the mountain to Moses and Aaron, and thus restricting even the priestly class from the realm of the sacred (v. 24), perhaps in reference to their later ordination in Leviticus 8–9.

The descent of Moses in v. 25 and his teaching the Decalogue to the people, rather than its direct revelation, conforms to the P view of holiness expressed in the two divine speeches. The insertion of 19:20-25 severs the connection between theophany and the revelation of the Decalogue. As a result, the holiness of God is no longer transferred directly to the people because they do not experience the Decalogue as divine speech. Instead, the law is communicated through the priestly mediator, Moses. The transfer of holiness to the people remains a future goal in the P History (Lev 19:2). Although God does appear to the people in the altar after the construction of the tabernacle (Lev 9:22-24), the ritual transfer of holiness to the people is not achieved. It remains a future ideal.

20:1-17 *Decalogue.* The Decalogue inaugurates the revelation of law at the divine mountain. The title "Decalogue" (also rendered in English as the "Ten Commandments") derives from the Hebrew designation of the law code as the "ten words" (*'ăśeret haddĕbārîm*), used at the close of covenant renewal (34:28) and repeated twice in Deuteronomy (4:13; 10:4). The three texts share motifs that underscore the prominence of the law code. The "ten words" derive

71. Childs, *Exodus*, 361.

from God (Deut 4:13). They form the basis for covenant (*běrît*, Exod 34:28; Deut 4:13). And they are written down *(kātab)* on two tablets (*šěnê lūḥōt*, Exod 34:28; Deut 4:13; 10:4), thus forming the core of Scripture. Other references reinforce their divine origin as a handwritten document from God (Exod 32:15). The ongoing cultic significance of the law code is indicated by its placement in the ark (25:16, 21; 40:20). Thus the Decalogue serves as a constitutional law for the Israelites, providing a foundational perspective on God and human relationships that is expanded in subsequent law codes.

The designation of the Decalogue as "ten words," which are written on "two tablets," provides clues to its literary structure. Yet the Hebrew Bible spells out neither the specific laws nor their organization into two sections. The ambiguity has given rise to a history of interpretation, especially concerning the number of the laws in 20:2-6 and in v. 17. In Jewish tradition the self-revelation of God (20:2) is the first commandment. It is interpreted as a demand for faith in the Deity. The prohibition against graven images (20:3-6) is the second law. The distribution of the commands on two tablets is evenly divided between 20:2-12 (five commands) and 20:13-17 (five commands).[72] The cantillation system of the Decalogue is preserved in two forms in Jewish tradition. The lower system of cantillation separates into verses so that long commands, such as the Sabbath, contain several verses. The upper system of cantillation separates the commands into single units, rather than verses.[73] The two systems of cantillation influence Jewish worship. Ashkenazim read the upper system of cantillation only during the Feast of Weeks. Sephardim read the upper system of cantillation at every public reading of the Decalogue.

The early church read the Decalogue differently from the Jewish division of the commandments. Verse 2 became the prologue to the law code, with the prohibition against images the first command (vv. 3-6). The Roman church retained the number ten by interpreting the command against coveting (v. 17) as two laws. The early church also changed the division of the law code. The first tablet was restricted to three commands (vv. 3-11) with seven on the second tablet (vv. 12-17).[74] John Calvin provides yet another interpretation, separating vv. 3-6 into two commands: exclusive worship of Yahweh (v. 3) and no idols (vv. 4-6). He retained the number ten by reading the command against coveting (v. 17) as one law as in Jewish tradition. He also follows the Jewish division of the Decalogue, separating the law code into two tablets of five laws each (vv. 3-12 and 13-17).[75] The weakness of this division of the Decalogue is that the first

72. See Sarna, *Exodus*, 107-14.
73. See M. Breuer, "Dividing the Decalogue into Verses and Commandments," in *Ten Commandments in History*, ed. Segal, 219-46.
74. See Houtman, *Exodus*, 3:4-5.
75. J. Calvin, *Institutes* 2.8.

command, which is to worship Yahweh exclusively (v. 3), is not separated from the command against idols (vv. 4-6) with a *soph pasuq,* which marks the end of a verse in the MT. The diverse history of interpretation regarding the division and number of the laws continues with Houtman, who even limits the commands to nine, interpreting vv. 3-6 as one law.[76] I follow the literary structure proposed by Calvin, while exploring other interpretations in the exegesis of the individual laws.

20:1-2 *Prologue.* The introduction anchors the law code within the literary context of Exodus. The motif of divine "speech" (Piel of *dābar,* "God spoke") in v. 1 fulfills the divine announcement of theophany to Moses: "I am coming to you . . . so that the people will hear me speaking with you" (19:9). The additional reference to "all these words" *(děbārîm)* provides the content of the public conversation between Yahweh and Moses during theophany: "Then Moses spoke and the voice of God answered him" (19:19). The emphasis on a public, divine speech underscores the degree to which 19:20-25 disrupts the context of theophany in the revelation of the Decalogue.

The opening words of God in v. 2 are a self-introduction, "I am Yahweh," a common form by which deities are introduced in the ancient Near East within cultic worship (see the commentary on 6:2-9). The self-introduction indicates that the entire Decalogue is a revelation of the divine name Yahweh, first introduced to Moses in 3:13-15 and expanded by the P author in 6:2-9. The first section (or tablet, 20:3-12) of the Decalogue explores the meaning of the name for the divine-human relationship (e.g., exclusive worship, no images, the power of the name, Sabbath observance, and the role of parents), while the second section (20:13-17) outlines the social implications of the divine name (e.g., no murder, adultery, stealing, lying, or coveting). The structure of the Decalogue, with its progression from cultic to social law, provides a blueprint for the organization of laws throughout the Pentateuch. The P law progresses from cultic (Leviticus) to social (Numbers 1–10) law, as does Deuteronomy according to D. Olson, while Freedman views the Decalogue as a template for the entire history of Genesis–2 Kings.[77]

The self-introduction is followed by the divine claim upon the Israelites: "I am Yahweh, *your God."* The divine ownership of the Israelites is grounded in God's rescue from Egypt, "I brought you out of the land of Egypt," known as the exodus motif (see the commentary on Exodus 13). H. D. Preuss concluded that the exodus motif expresses liberation from slavery. The reference to divine redemption from slavery immediately after the self-introduction underscores

---

76. Houtman, *Exodus,* 3:19. See the summary by Dohmen, *Exodus 19–40,* 98-101.

77. D. Olson, *Deuteronomy and the Death of Moses: A Theological Reading* (OBT; Minneapolis: Fortress, 1994); Freedman, *Nine Commandments.*

how foundational liberation is to understanding the divine name Yahweh. The association was confirmed early in Exodus, when Yahweh was introduced as the God of the Hebrews in the story of the midwives (1:15-21). The image of a "house of slavery" (lit. "slave barracks") further reinforces the imagery of social oppression. The identification of Egypt with a slave house in which humans are bought and sold is repeated throughout Deuteronomy. The motif is a criticism of Egypt, which provides the basis for the exclusive worship of Yahweh (Deut 5:6; 6:12; 7:8; 8:14; 13:5, 10; see also Judg 6:8). Outside the Pentateuch, Yahweh's redemption of the Israelites from the "house of slavery" is the basis for covenant (Josh 24:17) and for social ethics among the Israelites. The call for justice in Micah is grounded in God's liberation of the Israelites from the slave house of Egypt (Mic 6:1-8), as is the Jubilee law demanding release of Hebrew slaves every seventh year (Jer 34:8-22).

The exodus motif ties the Decalogue into the larger literary context of the book of Exodus. The motif first occurred in the commission of Moses as a promise (Exod 3:10-12), which is fulfilled when the Israelites leave Rameses for Succoth during the death of the Egyptian firstborn (12:37). At Succoth the exodus motif becomes the basis for two cultic laws: the Feast of Unleavened Bread (13:3-10) and the divine claim on the firstborn (13:11-16). The Decalogue is now the third law grounded in the divine rescue of the Israelites from Egyptian oppression.

20:3 *First Commandment: No Other Gods.* The worldview of the first commandment is henotheistic, not monotheistic. It neither presupposes nor advocates the belief that Yahweh is the only God. Rather, it presupposes just the reverse, that the world is populated with gods. The law demands monolatry, namely the exclusive worship of Yahweh by the Israelites. The basis of the command arises from the reference to the exodus in the prologue. By redeeming the Israelites from slavery, Yahweh now demands absolute allegiance from the Israelites. They are God's private possession (19:5). As a result, the first commandment forbids the Israelites to worship other gods.

The syntax of the Hebrew has caught the attention of interpreters. The verbal phrase is indefinite and indicates possession in Hebrew, literally: "There will not be to you . . . other gods before my face." The absence of an imperative verb (i.e., "you shall not") has prompted some interpreters to conclude that v. 3 is not a command in itself, but an introduction to the subsequent law against images (vv. 4-6).[78] But even when v. 3 is interpreted as an independent law, Zimmerli concluded that the syntax suggests a broad and general meaning.[79]

---

78. See J. H. Tigay, *Deuteronomy* (JPS Torah Commentary; Philadelphia: Jewish Publication Society, 1996), 63.

79. W. Zimmerli, *Old Testament Theology in Outline* (trans. D. E. Green; Atlanta: John Knox, 1978), 109-24.

The reference to "other gods" (*'ĕlōhîm 'ăḥērîm*) confirms the broad perspective of the law. "Other gods" is a general term for all rival deities. It is used most frequently in Deuteronomy (18 times), the Deuteronomistic History (20 times), and Jeremiah (18 times). The Targums and selective modern interpreters have preferred to translate the plural phrase "other gods" in the singular, "another god," to take away any possible emphasis on the existence of other gods.[80]

Deuteronomy aids in interpreting the henotheistic worldview of the law. It states that many gods have been allotted to the different nations (Deut 29:26). As a result, each god has a distinct cult (8:19), rules over a particular nation (7:4; 13:2, 7, 13), and communicates with different prophetic messengers (18:20). These gods may include the sun, moon, or even the host of heaven (17:3). The first commandment does not require the denial of such gods by the Israelites, as is evident in the rhetoric of Second Isaiah (e.g., Isa 44:6-8; cf. 43:11-13). Rather, Yahweh demands the absolute allegiance of the Israelite people in exchange for having redeemed them from slavery in Egypt. The exodus therefore is less about freedom in a modern democratic sense than it is about transferred slavery from Pharaoh to Yahweh.

The additional phrase "before my face" (NRSV "before me") suggests that the law is focused on worship. To be "before the face of God" indicates divine presence. The divine beings, including the Satan, appear "before the face of God" in the heavenly council in the opening scenes of the book of Job (Job 1:12; 2:7). Humans appear before the face of God in worship. God states in a context of worship: "When you come to appear before me [i.e., 'before my face']" (Isa 1:12). Hannah (1 Sam 1:22) enters the sanctuary at Shiloh to appear before the face of Yahweh. Zechariah 8:21-22 describes a pilgrimage to the Jerusalem temple where worshipers will appear before the face of God. The law of cult centralization in Deuteronomy requires all males to journey to the temple ("the place of the name") to appear before the face of Yahweh (Deut 16:16).

The focus on worship indicates that the first commandment is aimed at monolatry. It states that no other gods can be worshiped in Yahweh's sanctuary. But the phrase also takes on a broader meaning in Scripture. The worldview of henotheism could extend the rule of God from the sanctuary to include the territory of divine rule. Thus when David is forced to flee outside the land of Israel into the wilderness, he describes himself as being "away from the presence of God" (1 Sam 26:20). In a completely different usage, the face of God can even indicate divine anger (Lev 20:3, 5, 6, 17). In view of the range of possible meaning, interpreters have sought to broaden the command beyond the cultic setting, translating "beside me," "over against me," "above me," or even "except me," thus excluding relations with any other Deity in any context. D. Patrick

---

80. See Houtman, *Exodus*, 3:30.

concludes: "Exodus 20:3 . . . forbids any state of relation that might issue in illicit actions."[81]

20:4-6 *Second Commandment: No Idols.* The length of the second command indicates its importance. The prohibition includes three verbs: do not "make," "bow down," or "worship." It also provides an expansive description of the forbidden object as both an idol *(pesel)* and a representation *(těmûnâ)*. It concludes with an extended rationale: "For I Yahweh, your God, am a jealous God." Nielsen may be correct in suggesting a more succinct original command: "You shall not make for yourself an idol *(pesel).*"[82] Dohmen underscores the central problem of interpretation, noting that Hebrew has no single word for "idol" but a range of terms describing different aspects of divine images.[83] The Hebrew word translated "idol," *pesel,* is related to the verb *pāsal,* "to cut" or "to quarry" stone. Moses cuts stone tablets (Exod 34:1, 4; Deut 10:1, 3). Solomon quarries stone for the foundation of the temple (1 Kgs 5:17). Thus as a noun *pesel* indicates a chiseled object of stone or wood, representing a deity, hence its translation "idol" or "carved image." The idol may be covered with metal, either silver or gold, in which case it is described as a molten or metal image (*massēkâ,* e.g., Deut 27:15; from *nāsak,* meaning "to cast" or "to pour").

The idol is not the Deity but represents the channel by which the Deity is present in this world. The function of idols, as channels of divine presence, is not unlike the objects of bread and wine in the Christian Eucharist. The bread and wine are not the risen Christ, nor are they fashioned to represent the Deity. But they provide a partial analogy to the subject in that the objects are channels for the physical presence of Christ in the ritual. The eucharistic prayer provides the interpretation: "Make this bread and wine be for us the body of Christ." The difference, of course, is that idols are more representational. The idol in the Hebrew Bible may be specifically named as, for example, representing the Asherah (2 Kgs 21:7). But more often the identity of the Deity remains general and inclusive in the Hebrew Bible as a polemic against all gods and idols (Deut 4:16, 23, 25). The second command reflects the general and inclusive form of the prohibition.

The second command does not clarify whether the prohibition against idols is aimed at images of Yahweh, of rival deities, or both. The absence of plastic representation of Yahweh in the Hebrew Bible certainly conforms to the command. But H. Th. Obbink long ago noted that the divine reaction of jealousy to the idols made sense only if the iconography was of other gods, not Yahweh.[84] The close relationship between the first two commandments further

---

81. Patrick, *Old Testament Law,* 42.
82. Nielsen, *Ten Commandments,* 84-85.
83. Dohmen, *Exodus 19–40,* 106.
84. H. Th. Obbink, "Jahwebilder," *ZAW* 29 (1929): 264-74.

strengthens the conclusion of Obbink, suggesting that the prohibition is directed against the "other gods," forbidden in the first commandment. Deuteronomy describes the other gods as objects of wood and stone (Deut 28:36, 64). The near equation between idols and rival deities has led Weinfeld to conclude: "'Having no other gods' actually means 'having no images,' and the second commandment, in fact, continues the idea or concretizes the first one."[85]

The history of the law against images in ancient Israel is difficult to recover. The prohibition is distributed widely, appearing in the law code of covenant renewal (Exod 34:17), Deuteronomy (Deut 4:16, 23, 25; 27:15), and the P legislation (Lev 26:1). The law may have deep roots in ancient Israelite tradition. It is firmly established by the time the law codes are written, perhaps as early as the late monarchical period and into the postexilic period. The strong polemic against idols in Jeremiah (Jer 10:1-16), Second Isaiah (Isa 40:19-20; 44:9-20), and Habakkuk (Hab 2:18) indicates that the cult of divine icons was prominent in the exilic period and that it posed a threat to the worship of Yahweh. Jeremiah describes the construction of idols from silver and gold and the lavish clothing on the icons. He concludes that they are false because they have no breath (Jer 51:17). Second Isaiah expands the polemic of Jeremiah even misinterpreting the role of idols by equating them with gods: the workman "bows down to it and worships it; he prays to it and says, 'Save me, for you are my god!'" (Isa 44:17).

Three additions to the second command of the Decalogue reflect the growing concern over idols already evident in the exilic prophetic literature. First, the prohibition against an idol *(pesel)* is expanded in Exod 20:4 to include a "form" or "representation" *(těmûnâ,* v. 4b). Dohmen has concluded from the comparison of the command in 20:4 with Deut 5:8 that the version in Exodus enlarges the scope of Deuteronomy by forbidding any images associated with the cult (see the Notes).[86] Second, additional prohibitions are added forbidding one "to bow down" and "to worship" (v. 5a). Third, a rationale is added describing the jealous character of Yahweh (vv. 5b-6). Although the additions are intended to clarify the law, each also creates a degree of ambiguity in meaning.

First, the word "form" *(těmûnâ)* is added to the word "idol" *(pesel),* raising the question of what is intended. A form is a representation or a likeness. It tends not to be an object, but a template that creates an object, although the two meanings could merge. Thus Yahweh has a "form" that Moses sees (Num 12:8). Psalm 17:15 expresses the hope of the psalmist to see the form of God. Deuter-

85. Weinfeld, *Deuteronomy 1–11,* 288.

86. Dohmen, *Exodus 19–40,* 107-13. See also T. N. D. Mettinger, "Israelite Aniconism: Developments and Origins," in *The Image and the Book: Iconic Cults, Aniconism, and the Rise of Book Religion in Israel and the Ancient Near East* (ed. K. van der Toorn; CBET 21; Leuven: Peeters, 1997), 175-78. Cf. Houtman, *Exodus,* 3:32-33.

onomy 4:12 and 15 underscore that the Israelites did not see the form of God during the theophany on Mount Horeb, but only heard a voice (see also Job 4:16). The second command in Exod 20:4 states that the "form" under discussion is of air, land, and water creatures. The syntax of the parallel law in Deut 5:8 indicates that the "form" is meant to be a further qualification of the forbidden "idols." It conveys this meaning by adding the word "form" to the word "idol" without a conjunction, placing it in apposition as a further description of idols. The idols cannot be in the shape of any air, land, or water creatures. This meaning is repeated in Deut 4:16, 23, 25.

Exodus 20:4 is more ambiguous than the version of the law in Deut 5:8, because the word "form" *(těmûnâ)* is added to the word "idol" *(pesel)* with the Hebrew conjunction *wě,* "and." The result is that the command appears to forbid two things, the making of an idol and any representation of an air, land, or sea creature. The difference is lost in the NIV of Exod 20:4 and Deut 5:8. It is difficult to judge how much emphasis to place on the conjunction. But if the difference between the two commands is intentional, then 20:4 represents a further interpretation of Deut 5:8 prohibiting not only idols, but all visual and representational art. Dohmen and Hossfeld even detect a development in the history of Israelite religion from the more narrow command against idols in Deuteronomy to a broader command against all plastic art in Exodus.[87]

Second, the command against making idols also includes additional prohibitions against bowing down or worshiping them. The combination of the verbs "to bow down" and "to worship" is concentrated in Deuteronomy (4:19; 8:19; 11:16) and in the Deuteronomistic History (Josh 23:7, 16; Judg 2:19; 1 Kgs 9:6; 2 Kgs 17:35; see also Jer 13:10; 25:6). It is aimed at worshiping "other gods" in nearly every case, although Deut 4:19 prohibits the worship of the heavenly bodies. The object of the command in Exod 20:4 is not stated but referred to simply as "them": "You shall not bow down and worship *them.*" The plural object of the prohibition, "them," may refer to the "idol" and the "representation" together, thus accounting for the plural form, even though both nouns, "idol" and "form," are in the singular. Such an interpretation is similar to the command in Deut 4:19 concerning the worship of heavenly bodies. But it is also possible that the plural refers to the "other gods" in v. 3, in which case the first two commandments (no other gods and no idols) are related as one. T. N. D. Mettinger concludes that the present form of the com-

---

87. Dohmen, *Das Bilderverbot;* C. Dohmen and T. Sternberg, eds., *Kein Bildnis machen: Kunst und Theologie im Gespräch* (Würzburg: Echter Verlag, 1987); J. Gutmann, *No Graven Images: Studies in Art and the Hebrew Bible* (New York: Ktav, 1971); R. S. Hendel, "The Social Origins of the Aniconic Traditions," *CBQ* 50 (1988): 365-82; T. N. D. Mettinger, *No Graven Image? Israelite Aniconism in Its Ancient Near Eastern Context* (ConBOT 42; Stockholm: Almqvist & Wiksell, 1995); van der Toorn, ed., *Image and Book.*

mandment in the Decalogue already presupposes the aniconic nature of the cult of Yahweh.[88]

Third, the rationale for the command against idols is the jealousy of Yahweh, "I Yahweh, your God, am a jealous God *('ēl qannā')*." Hebrew *qannā'* is an emotional word rooted in love and marriage. J. H. Tigay states that the root meaning is "to become dark red" and that it is frequently used of "fiery passions such as love, anger, indignation, and jealousy."[89] Weinfeld prefers to translate *'ēl qannā'* as "an impassioned God."[90] The word conveys the passion of an offended lover in the account of the wife suspected of adultery (Num 5:11-31). The husband is described as having a "spirit of jealousy" toward his wife, which is both emotional and potentially violent. The law likely outlines due process to protect the woman from her husband.[91] Love's passion becomes a theological motif to describe the relationship of Yahweh and Israel. The prophet Hosea described the Israelites' rejection of God as an illicit love affair (Hos 2:7, 10-13). In Hosea God, the offended lover, fluctuates between love (2:14) and hate (9:15) toward unfaithful Israel. Phinehas's killing of an Israelite man, Zimri, and a Midianite woman, Cozbi, during the act of sex in order to defend the purity of Israelite religion is praised as an act of divine jealousy. God states: "He [Phinehas] was zealous [jealous] as I am for my honor" (Num 25:11). The book of Hosea and the story of Phinehas indicate that the description of Yahweh as a jealous God implies marriage. The worship of other gods and the construction of their idols in the second commandment are interpreted as adultery. God's response is that of an offended lover. It is both passionate and potentially violent (see also Deut 4:24; 6:13).

The remainder of the rationale intermingles imagery of marriage and treaty relations by outlining God's reaction to idolatry with the contrasting language of love and hate. Those who make idols and worship other gods hate Yahweh. The root meaning of "hate" *(śānē')* is forced separation. When Isaac is driven out of the land of Abimelech he describes it as hate (see Gen 26:27). The separation certainly includes the passion of hostility. Abimelech fears the power of Isaac (see also the hate of Jephthah's brothers in banishing him from the land in Judg 11:7). The notion of forced separation is carried over into divorce law. A spouse declares divorce by publicly proclaiming his or her hatred (Deut 22:13-16; 24:3). The setting of divorce law fits the context for the second command, where the title "jealous God" already indicated marriage. Any Israelite who worships other gods has divorced Yahweh. The act of worship is a

88. Mettinger, "Israelite Aniconism," 176.

89. Tigay, *Deuteronomy*, 65.

90. Weinfeld, *Deuteronomy 1–11*, 295.

91. T. Frymer-Kensky, "The Strange Case of the Suspected Sotah (Numbers V 11-31)," *VT* 34 (1984): 24.

declaration of hatred, which creates guilt *('āwōn)* that is contagious, prompting divine vengeance *(pāqad)* through four generations. As B. M. Levinson has demonstrated, "hate" can also refer to the rebellion of a treaty partner.[92] The reference to four generations may be literal, or it may signify the common span of life (Job 42:16). In either case the law reflects collective, not individual, guilt.

Conversely those who love *('āhab)* Yahweh draw forth a response of love *(ḥesed)* from God. Hebrew *'āhab* continues the imagery of marriage. Love describes the passion of marriage (Gen 24:67; 29:18), and it too becomes a theological motif. The psalmists declare, "I love you, O Yahweh" (Ps 18:1), and encourage fellow worshipers to share the affection: "Love Yahweh, all you his saints" (Ps 33:23). Deuteronomy provides extensive theological reflection on the role of love in community and in covenant with God. God is the source of love in humans. The Israelites are able to love God because Yahweh circumcised their hearts (Deut 30:6), which likely means that God has transformed their character. God's love finds expression in the revelation of law (Deut 7:9; 11:1; 19:9; 30:16). The message of the second command is that when humans express their love for God by following the command against images and idols they prompt still further love *(ḥesed*; see the commentary on 34:6-7) from God (see also Deut 7:13).

20:7 *Third Commandment: The Divine Name.* The significance of the name Yahweh cannot be overestimated in the Hebrew Bible. Divine names in the ancient Near East carry inherent power that provides access to gods. For example, the conclusion to the Babylonian creation myth *Enuma Elish* provides the worshiper with the fifty names of the god Marduk that provide the worshiper with access to Marduk. The same is true in Christian tradition. The revelation of the name Jesus gives all Christians direct access to God through prayer. Thus Christian prayer is punctuated with the closing: "In Jesus' name we pray, Amen." Jacob's wrestling with the night demon or divine messenger at the Jabbok River illustrates the power of naming and of knowing names in ancient Israel (Gen 32:22-32). Jacob wrestles through the night with his opponent and is even prevailing before his hip is put out of joint by the touch of the opponent. When the opponent wishes to escape at dawn, Jacob refuses to release him without receiving a blessing. But the assailant tricks Jacob into giving his name in order to receive a blessing. The result is that Jacob's opponent acquires power over him and even renames him Israel. But when Jacob wishes for the same information his opponent withholds his name and thus does not allow Jacob to gain power over him. A person's name penetrates to his or her very iden-

---

92. B. M. Levinson, "The Human Voice in Divine Revelation: The Problem of Authority in Biblical Law," in *Innovation in Religious Traditions* (ed. M. A. Williams et al.; Berlin: Mouton de Gruyter, 1992), 46.

tity; thus to know the name gives one access and even power over another. Noth concludes: "The bearer of the name is therefore present in some mysterious way in the name."[93] The story of Jacob illustrates Noth's point. When Jacob reveals his name the opponent has the power to rename him and thus change him. Jacob, the trickster, becomes Israel, the God-wrestler. When Jacob demands the name of his opponent in return, he is rebuffed: "Why is it that you ask my name?" Alone, in the morning, Jacob can only speculate on the identity of his opponent, naming the location of his encounter Peniel, "face of God."

All speculation on the identity of God ceases at the outset of Exodus when God reveals the name Yahweh. The book is an extended definition of the name. The revelation of the name Yahweh is central to both the Non-P (Exod 3:13-15) and P (6:2-9) Histories. The self-introduction, "I am Yahweh," reveals the destructive power of the name when it is directed at Pharaoh throughout the plagues. Conversely, the revelation of the name to the Israelites puts them in contact with the divine power of healing (15:22-26). The self-introduction of Yahweh at the outset of the Decalogue (20:2) indicates that the law code is a continuation of the revelation of the name to the Israelites. The name Yahweh means savior ("I brought you out of Egypt"), exclusive allegiance (no other gods), and it may also indicate the absence of plastic images to represent the Deity (no idols).

The third commandment is a warning about the danger of knowing the name, and it cautions the Israelites not to use it in destructive ways. The command shifts from the first person to the third person in referring to God. The rhetorical shift in voice creates distance between Yahweh and the Israelites, which aids in conveying the meaning of the command. The distance between speaker and audience indicates that holiness is not casual. Having access to the very name of God brings with it not only power but also accountability. The command states: "You shall not lift up *(nāśā')* the name in vain *(laššāwĕ')*." The verb "to lift up" likely indicates the making of oaths. In the ancient world such oaths were a self-curse invoking the deity: "May God judge me, if what I say is not true." Similar language of self-cursing continues in our legal tradition: "Do you swear to tell the truth, the whole truth, and nothing but the truth, *so help you God.*" The response, "I do," puts one before the divine judge for better or worse. The third command likely carries the meaning of swearing falsely in a legal setting.

The word *laššāwĕ'*, "in vain," may have broader meaning than the legal context. Flattery is vain (Ps 12:3), as are idols (Ps 31:6). Conjuring up the name Yahweh may also include the magical use of the power of God for evil purposes. Mowinckel concluded that the third command was a prohibition against magic

---

93. Noth, *Exodus*, 163.

and all powers of sorcery that bring about evil (see Isa 59:4; Zech 10:2).[94] Cassuto detected a warning against fortune-telling through the power of the name.[95] Noth extended the magical misuse of the name: "Anyone who knows a divine name can make use of the divine power present in the name to effect blessings and curses, adjurations and bewitchings and all kinds of magical undertakings. To this extent the divine name is comparable with the divine image."[96] Thus the law against misusing the power of the name is broad, ranging from magical abuse to swearing falsely in court. God will not acquit (*nāqâ*, "to go free of punishment") anyone guilty of these offenses.

20:8-11 *Fourth Commandment: Sabbath.* The fourth command separates into three parts: first, a positive command to sanctify the Sabbath; second, the guidelines for fulfilling the command; and, third, its rationale. The Sabbath command in 20:8-11 provides the clearest indication of P authorship in the Decalogue with direct references to the creation story in Gen 1:1–2:4a. The P version of the command diverges from the parallel account in Deut 5:12-15 in many details, indicating the different worldviews of the P History and Deuteronomy (in fig. 32 on page 489 the differences are italicized).

The command (20:8) is that the Israelites remember (*zākar*) the Sabbath. The version in Deuteronomy uses the word "to observe" (*šāmar*), not "to remember."[97] The divergent wording indicates different theological perspectives in the P History and Deuteronomy. In Deuteronomy the content of memory is salvation history and the act of memory is primarily the responsibility of humans. The Israelites must remember their slavery in Egypt (Deut 15:15), what God did to Pharaoh (7:18), how God led them in the wilderness (8:2), the divine anger in the wilderness toward them (9:7), Miriam (24:9), and even the Amalekites (25:17). The Israelites' memory of salvation history is intended to encourage observance of the commandments (6:17), statutes (6:2), words of Torah (17:19), and the covenant (7:12; 29:9). The version of the Sabbath command in 5:12-15 illustrates the difference between the words "remember" and "observe." The Israelites are commanded to remember the past slavery in Egypt (*zākar*, v. 15) and thus to observe Sabbath (*šāmar*, v. 12). Divine memory plays almost no role in Deuteronomy. Its only occurrence is in the intercessory prayer when Moses encourages God to remember the promise to the ancestors as a basis for forgiving the Israelite people (9:27).

Memory in the P History functions differently. Divine and human mem-

94. S. Mowinckel, *The Psalms in Israel's Worship* (trans. D. R. Ap-Thomas; 2 vols.; Nashville: Abingdon, 1962).

95. Cassuto, *Exodus,* 241-43.

96. Noth, *Exodus,* 163.

97. See E. Z. Melammed, "'Observe' and 'Remember' Spoken in One Utterance," in *Ten Commandments in History,* ed. Segal, 191-217.

Figure 32

	Exod 20:8-11 (P)	*Deut 5:12-15 (D)*
Command	v. 8: Remember *(zākôr)* the Sabbath day by keeping it holy	v. 12: Observe *(šāmôr)* the Sabbath day by keeping it holy,
	—	*As Yahweh, your God has commanded you*
Guidelines		
1. Time of Labor	v. 9: Six days you shall labor and do all your work.	v. 13: Six days you shall labor and do all your work.
	v. 10: But the seventh day is a Sabbath to Yahweh your God	v. 14: But the seventh day is a Sabbath to Yahweh your God
2. Scope of the Law	On it you shall not do any work	On it you shall not do any work
	neither you,	neither you,
	nor your son or daughter	nor your son or daughter
	nor your manservant or maidservant	nor your manservant or maidservant
	—	nor *your ox, your donkey,*
	nor your animals	or any of your animals
	nor the alien within your gates	nor the alien within your gates
	—	*so that your manservant and maidservant may rest as you do.*
Rationale	v. 11: For in six days Yahweh made the heavens and the earth, the sea and all that is in them, but he rested on the seventh day.	v. 15: *Remember (zākar) that you were slaves in Egypt and that Yahweh, your God, brought you out of there with a mighty hand and an outstretched arm.*
	Therefore Yahweh blessed the Sabbath day and made it holy.	*Therefore Yahweh your God has commanded you to observe the Sabbath day.*

ory interact with each other. Divine memory is prominent in the P History. It creates salvation history. Divine memory is introduced during the flood (Gen 8:1) and it becomes a prominent motif at the close of the flood (Gen 9:15-16), when God promised to remember the covenant. The divine recognition of the Israelite oppression (Exod 2:24) and the exodus from Egypt (6:5) arise from the divine memory of the covenant. The Israelites' future life in the land is also based on God's memory of the covenant (Lev 26:42). The interaction of divine and human memory allows for the sacramental presence of God in the sanctuary. The priestly breastplate (Exod 28:12, 29) and the trumpets (Num 10:9-10) are intended to prompt divine memory of the people in the sanctuary. In turn the Israelite people are required to remember three things: their ransom from Egypt as a crucial event in salvation history (Exod 12:14; 30:16), the central role of the Sabbath as a time of rest both during the week (20:8) and in the liturgical year (the Day of Atonement, Lev 23:24), and the distinction between the priests and the laity (Num 17:5).

The guidelines for Sabbath observance (Exod 20:9-10) include the proper time for work and rest, and the identification of those covered by the law. H. A. McKay underscores that the command for Sabbath rest in the Decalogue is not a sacred day with worship rituals. The demand is the cessation of work.[98] The two versions (Exod 20:9-10 and Deut 5:13-14) are nearly the same. Each restricts work to six days, with rest on the seventh day. The seventh day of rest would be Saturday, not Sunday, in the Israelite cultic calendar. The command is general and the forbidden work activities are not spelled out. But the Sabbath command does presuppose the Israelites' life in the promised land, not their present situation in the wilderness. It is directed toward property owners. Those included in the command are listed in concentric circles moving from the owner of the property ("you") and the immediate family ("sons and daughters"). Beyond the nuclear family the law also includes human slaves ("manservant and maidservant") and domestic animals. The P version (20:10) provides the general word for domestic animals (*bĕhēmōt,* "cattle"), while Deuteronomy (5:14) specifies the animals as ox and ass. Finally, both versions include the resident alien within the scope of the command (see the commentary on 12:43-51; and Exodus 21–23). The version in Deuteronomy adds a humanitarian conclusion to the section, namely that the slaves must be able to rest from their labor just as the property owner does.

The rationale (Exod 20:11) for the Sabbath command in the P History derives directly from the creation. The creation story ends with God resting on the seventh day from the work of world creation (Gen 2:1-3). It is the ideal

---

98. H. A. McKay, *Sabbath and the Synagogue: The Question of Sabbath Worship in Ancient Judaism* (Religions in the Graeco-Roman World 122; Leiden: Brill, 1994), 11-42.

rhythm of work and rest in the design of creation. The version in Deuteronomy moves in a different direction. It continues the humanitarian argument from the conclusion of the previous section of the law, which stated the guidelines for the Sabbath. The Israelites must remember their social liberation from Egypt. They were once slaves and God rescued them from their oppression with a strong arm. The law of the Sabbath observance with its demand for rest by the Israelites and their slaves actualizes the memory of liberation, as compared to the P version of the Sabbath rest, which allows the Israelites to conform to the structure of creation as God intended.

The origins of the observance of the Sabbath have been extensively re-searched, without firm conclusions.[99] Sabbath observance may be Babylonian in origin *(sab/pattu)* in which case the Sabbath is not a weekly day, but perhaps the day of the full moon.[100] Sabbath does occur in ancient Israel along with reference to the full moon (Amos 8:4-7; Hos 2:11-15; Isa 1:10-14). The Sabbath is mentioned in the story of the ninth-century prophet Elisha (2 Kgs 4:23), and it appears in the books of Amos (Amos 8:5) and Hosea (Hos 2:11), both eighth-century prophets. King Ahaz of Judah is described as dismantling a Sabbath canopy in the temple in the late eighth century. And the Sabbath command appears in the cultic laws of Exod 23:10-12. The authorship and date of each of these texts are debated, yet the distribution suggests the observance of some form of the Sabbath in the monarchical period, although its centrality in that period is not clear.[101] The observance of the Sabbath remains limited in Deuteronomy to the Decalogue (Deut 5:12-15). Sabbath observance takes a more prominent role in the exilic and postexilic prophetic literature. Late Jeremiah tradition (Jer 17:19-27), the exilic prophet Ezekiel (20:8-26; 46:1-12), and postexilic literature in Isaiah (56:2, 6; 58:13; 66:23) forbid work on the Sabbath. The observance of the Sabbath also concludes the postexilic book of Nehemiah (13:15-22). The observance of the Sabbath emerges as a central law in the P History, occurring in both of its cultic calendars (Lev 23:3; Num 28:9-10). The transformation of the Sabbath as a time of worship is evident at Qumran, and it continues to develop in Judaism in the Common Era.[102]

The revelation of the Sabbath in stages in the P History provides structure

99. See N.-E. Andreasen, *The Old Testament Sabbath: A Tradition-Historical Investigation* (SBLDS 7; Missoula, Mont.: Scholars Press, 1972); R. Robinson, *The Origin and Development of the Old Testament Sabbath* (Frankfurt am Main: P. Lang, 1988).

100. E. Kutsch, "Der Sabbat — ursprünglich Vollmondstag?" in *Kleine Schriften zum alten Testament* (Berlin: de Gruyter, 1986), 71-77.

101. T. Veijola, "Die Propheten und das Alter des Sabbatgebots," in *Prophet und Prophetenbuch: Festschrift für Otto Kaiser* (ed. V. Fritz et al.; BZAW 185; Berlin: de Gruyter, 1989), 246-64.

102. See McKay, *Sabbath and Synogogue.*

to the history.[103] The foundation for Sabbath observance is established in creation (Gen 2:1-3). The ideal rhythm of creation is six days of work punctuated by one day of rest. It is lost with the flood and reappears only gradually in the P History, in a similar fashion to the progressive revelation of the divine name (see the commentary on 6:2-8). There are five stages in the revelation of the Sabbath, and each new revelation of the Sabbath is accompanied by a theophany. First, the theophany of the Glory of Yahweh (16:10) in the wilderness of Shur occasions the reappearance of the Sabbath in the cycle of manna (16:22-26). Second, the theophany on Mount Sinai (19:18) advances the revelation of the Sabbath as a law (20:8-11). Sabbath observance in the Decalogue is restricted to life in the promised land, anticipating the time when the Israelites would be property owners. The relationship between the Sabbath and creation is made explicit in the revelation of the law. Third, the additional theophany of the Glory of Yahweh on Mount Sinai (24:15-18) leads to further revelation about the Sabbath (31:12-17). It is an eternal covenant between God and the Israelites. Its observance sanctifies the Israelite people, and its violation carries the death penalty. Fourth, the revelation of covenant renewal (34:1-9) leads to clarification regarding what work is forbidden on the Sabbath. The Non-P law in 23:10-12 and 34:21 already forbad Sabbath work during planting and harvest time. The P author extends forbidden work to include household fires (35:3). Fifth, the P History returns to the topic of Sabbath observance one final time with a special revelation to Moses (Num 15:32-41) in the form of a divine oracle. God clarifies that even when a human picks up sticks on the Sabbath in the wilderness journey, that person is liable for the death penalty. The oracle extends the geographical scope of the law from the promised land to any location. The result is that the Sabbath law is universal for the P author, including Jews in Palestine and in the Diaspora. The Sabbath even takes on larger meaning in the P History through the prominent role of the number seven throughout the history. The number seven organizes the liturgical year and the social vision of the P author. There are seven feasts in the P calendar and seven days of observance for Unleavened Bread and Booths. The seventh month contains the central feasts in the P calendar (New Year, Day of Atonement, and Feast of Booths). The social vision of the Jubilee law is also structured around the number seven, as the fiftieth year completes the cycle of 7×7 (= 49 years).

20:12 *Fifth Commandment: Honoring Parents.* W. Harrrelson notes that the command is aimed at adults, not children.[104] It is concerned with the care of the elderly, a theme that repeats throughout ancient Near Eastern literature. In

---

103. N. Lohfink, "Arbeitswocke und Sabbat in der priesterlichen Geschichtserzählung," *Bibel und Kirche* 52 (1997): 110-18.

104. Harrelson, *Ten Commandments and Human Rights*, 92-95.

the Ugaritic Epic of Aqhat, for example, Danel's son performs a series of duties for him, including feeding, washing clothes, erecting a pillar, and caring for him when he is drunk (*CTA* 17.i.27-34). The Decalogue differs from the Epic of Aqhat by including both father and mother in the command. Honoring parents may have extended to the care of the dead in ancestral worship. The Decalogue is not clear whether the worship of the ancestors is a form of honor. But the present form of the Hebrew Bible is explicit in forbidding the worship of the ancestors (Deut 18:11; Lev 19:31), suggesting that the command in the Decalogue is also focused on the social welfare of parents, rather than the ancestral cult.

The command to honor parents repeats throughout the Hebrew Bible. The law in Exod 20:12 repeats in the P law of Lev 19:3. The writer Ben Sira outlines the extensive duties of a child toward father and mother, including respect, patience, and kindness in their old age (Sir 3:1-16). The rabbinic literature distinguishes between reverence (the qualities listed in Sir 3:1-16) and care (the actions listed in the Epic of Aqhat). Jesus repeats the teaching of the Decalogue in Matt 15:4 reaffirming the penalty of death for lack of observance: "Honor your father and your mother, and whoever speaks evil of father or mother must die."

The command to honor parents provides a transition in the structure of the Decalogue. A number of literary features in the command bridge the focus on God in the first tablet of the law and the more socially oriented commands in the second tablet. First, the linking of two positive commands, observance of the Sabbath and honoring parents, relates the worlds of worship and ethics. Second, the reference to God as Yahweh occurs in the first four commands and ceases after the fifth. Third, commentators note the close relationship between God and parents as an additional feature that intertwines the commands directed to God and the demand to honor parents. The power of creating can be attributed to both. Malachi 3:17 makes the analogy explicit when God states: "I will spare them [the Israelites] as parents spare their children who serve them." Fourth, the language of honor *(kābēd)* continues to intertwine the worlds of worship and social ethics. God is honored in worship (Ps 86:9) and through the gift of firstfruits (Prov 3:9). Fifth, the reward also relates to the commands. It is aimed at the Israelites' life in the promised land. The phrase "the land that Yahweh your God is giving you" is a shortened form of the divine promise of land secured by oath (see the commentary on 13:3-10). The promise of land is made to the ancestors, not to the present generation of Israelites. Its inclusion in the command to honor parents further merges the social responsibility of caring for the elderly with salvation history, especially in realizing the gift of land. The additional promise of long life in the land is a favored expression in Deuteronomy (e.g., Deut 4:40; 5:29; 6:24). The mingling of cultic and social concerns in the demand to honor parents is evident in the divergent divisions of the Decalogue, with the Jewish interpreters including the command in the first tablet of the law and the early church placing it as the initial social command in the second tablet.

20:13 *Sixth Commandment: Murder.* The command forbidding murder is broad. It lacks specific cases or circumstances with regard to killing, and it does not probe the role of motive in killing. The law is stated categorically and does not spell out the consequences for disobedience.

The verb *rāṣaḥ* occurs in prophetic literature to describe intentional murder (Hos 6:9; Isa 1:21). The P author used the same verb in the law of blood vengeance to describe both the intentional and unintentional killing of another human being (Numbers 35). The P author anchors the broad understanding of the law in the instruction concerning sacrifice at the close of the flood (Gen 9:1-7). Humans emerge from the ark carnivorous even though they were created to be vegetarian. God concedes meat to the human diet, but adds that all human blood pollutes creation because the divine image resides in humans. The result is an economics of blood: "Whoever sheds the blood of a human, by a human shall that person's blood be shed." The law is the basis for blood vengeance. It is unclear whether the law against murder forbids both intentional and unintentional murder as well as the practice of bloodguilt. The P author certainly qualifies blood vengeance in later teaching (Numbers 35). The law probably does not forbid war, at least in the Non-P History — war is sanctioned in Deuteronomy 20. But the P author does conclude that the shedding of blood in war is a pollutant, even when God sanctions the war (Numbers 31).[105]

20:14 *Seventh Commandment: Adultery.* The law is stated categorically without indicating the consequences for disobedience, though Lev 20:20 and Deut 22:22 indicate the death penalty for offenders.

The law is aimed against sexual intercourse between a man and the wife or fiancée of another, not against premarital sex. The law regarding premarital sex requires the couple to marry and does not allow for divorce (see Exod 22:16-17; Deut 22:28-29). The social setting of the command is a patrilineal society in which paternity is essential for inheritance law. Thus the penalty of adultery is severe: death by stoning in Deuteronomy (22:24) and death by burning in P (Lev 20:14). Adultery is also used as a metaphor for idolatry (Isa 57:1-13; Jer 3:6-9), providing a literary connection to the second command (Exod 20:4-6).

20:15 *Eighth Commandment: Stealing.* The command forbids the stealing of objects or humans. The rabbis interpreted the law narrowly to include only kidnapping (*b. Sanh.* 86a; see Deut 24:7), as did Alt in the modern period. The more narrow reading, according to Alt, provided a contrast to the tenth commandment against coveting. But few modern interpreters follow this read-

105. See Dozeman, "Numbers," *NIB* 2:244-57.

ing, preferring instead a broad interpretation. The broad interpretation would prohibit the secret taking of any property. The act of stealing concerns social ethics, the taking of a neighbor's property, but also cultic or religious stealing, the taking of property from God (such as spoils of war, Deut 20:14; 21:10-14).

20:16 *Ninth Commandment: False Testimony.* The command is narrow in scope. It forbids false testimony in court, a central prohibition throughout the Hebrew Bible (Exod 23:1; Lev 19:15; Deut 16:19; 19:16). The judicial setting creates some overlap with the third command, forbidding the improper use of the divine name Yahweh in making oaths. The version of the law in Deuteronomy is somewhat broader, forbidding evasive speech in court as well as lying. The law does not specifically address other forms of lying or dishonesty that are evident in later tradition (Matt 19:18; Rom 2:21; 1 Thess 4:4).

20:17 *Tenth Commandment: Coveting.* The final command moves away from a particular action to focus on the danger of misplaced desire and greed. In this way the final command internalizes the law. Hebrew *ḥāmad* has a range of meanings, including to delight, to desire, or to covet, which may lead to the act of taking something. The fruits of the garden (Gen 2:9) and the tree of the knowledge of good and evil (Gen 3:6) are a delight *(ḥāmad)* to the eyes. The use of the verb in Gen 2:9 does not convey the meaning of misplaced desire as is the case in Gen 3:6. The psalmist praises those who desire the law over gold (Ps 19:10). Yet Proverbs repeatedly warns against desire that leads to wicked acts (Prov 12:12). Achan confesses his misplaced desire, which led to his stealing spoils of war (Josh 7:21). The impact of the final command is to focus on the interior emotions and the attitude of humans, particularly men. The forbidden property of the neighbor includes house, wife, slaves, and livestock. The version in Deut 5:21 accentuates coveting another's wife over other forms of property.

20:18-20 Conclusion. The conclusion to the Decalogue underscores the people's direct experience of theophany, which provides a contrast to the introduction to the Decalogue in the P History, where Moses mediates the law to the people (Exod 19:20-25). The conclusion is part of the Non-P History. It is intended to follow from the account of theophany in 19:19 as a public conversation between God and Moses. Van Seters argues that the transition from the experience of theophany (19:19) to the fear of the people (20:18) does not include a version of the Decalogue, but focuses instead on the sound of the horn. The P author, according to Van Seters, has inserted the version of the Decalogue with the addition of 19:20-25 and 20:1-17.[106] Here I interpret the Decalogue within the Non-P History, while also noting the additions by the P author.

The conclusion fulfills the divine prediction to Moses in 19:9 concerning the purposes of theophany, that the Israelites would hear divine speech and ac-

---

106. Van Seters, *Life of Moses*, 248-52.

quire faith in Moses. Exodus 20:18 confirms that the people heard divine speech through the contradictory imagery of their seeing sounds (both the thunder and the trumpet), as well as the visual images of lightning and smoke. The direct experience of theophany creates fear in the people, which prompts them to choose Moses as their future mediator (20:19). Once elected, Moses assumes the role of the reliable interpreter of God's words in 20:20. He conveys the previous speech of God from 19:9 by repeating the technical language of divine approach *(bô')* before instructing the people on the meaning of the event: their fear of God is the proper response to the divine words. Moses also interprets the direct revelation of law as yet another divine test of the Israelite people, a motif that is central to the wilderness journey in chaps. 15–18 (see the commentary on 15:22-26; 16:1-36).

Book of the Covenant (20:21–23:33)

Introduction

The scene separates into three parts: an introduction identifying the revelation of law as a private experience of Moses and the promulgation of the initial laws regarding proper altars (20:21-26); a collection of laws, including casuistic civil law on slavery, communal life, and property rights (22:1-7), apodictic and religious law on the implications of holiness in humans (22:18–23:19); and a conclusion encouraging faithfulness to the law supported by the divine promise of land through conquest (23:20-33). The title "Book of the Covenant" derives from the following scene when Moses is described as reading the "book of the covenant" to the people (24:7). The versification between the English and the MT/LXX differs by one verse throughout Exodus 22 (Eng. 22:1-31 = MT/LXX 21:37–22:30). The references in the commentary follow English versification for the most part (MT/LXX is added where necessary).

HISTORY OF COMPOSITION

The changing literary style in the Book of the Covenant suggests a history of composition. Exodus 20:21-26 includes narrative along with cultic law on the proper altars for worship. Exodus 21:1–22:15 consists of civil law in casuistic form that many interpreters judge to have its own title, *Mishpatim* ("ordinances, rules"). Exodus 22:16–23:19 shifts in style to apodictic law and returns to the topic of religious and cultic legislation as in the first address contained in 20:21-26. Exodus 23:20-33 is not law at all, but homiletical instruction reminiscent of Deuteronomy. Interspersed throughout the law code are theological statements about the nature of Yahweh and the Israelites' experience of salvation (Exod 22:21-24; 23:9).

Interpreters have employed a variety of methodologies to evaluate the distinct literary styles of the Book of the Covenant and to identify the history of composition. Scholars have sought to locate the different styles of law in particular social settings and to describe the process by which they were merged into a single document.[1] The interpretation of the Book of the Covenant has been influenced further by comparison to ancient Near Eastern law and to the other Israelite law codes. The civil character of ancient Near Eastern law has prompted scholars to seek an early version of the Book of the Covenant as a code of civil law rather than religious legislation.[2] The comparison of the law codes within the Hebrew Bible has also been used to determine the history of composition between the Book of the Covenant, the laws in Deuteronomy, and the P legislation in Leviticus and Numbers. The chronology of the composition of the law codes becomes a window into the legal and social history of ancient Israel. The paradigm to emerge from the modern history of interpretation is that the Book of the Covenant contains old law codified before the laws in Deuteronomy and the P legislation in Leviticus and Numbers.[3]

The paradigm for the literary composition of the Book of the Covenant was forged in the late nineteenth and early twentieth centuries, and it continues to be refined into the present time.[4] The background for evaluating the history of composition was the Documentary Hypothesis, which presupposed the early to mid-monarchical period as the time of the writing of the pentateuchal sources. Wellhausen associated the Book of the Covenant with the J source, which accentuated the mediatorial role of Moses in the revelation on the mountain (Exod 19:20-25) and the promulgation of the Book of the Covenant (20:23–22:33). Wellhausen also detected a history of composition in the Book of the Covenant, noting in particular the shift between the use of the singular and the plural, which he identified with a later redactor in the tradition of Deuteronomy.[5]

Subsequent interpreters began to evaluate the internal literary structure of the Book of the Covenant in more detail, advocating its independent history of composition from the present narrative context in the Pentateuch.

---

1. See R. Sonsino, "Forms of Biblical Law," *ABD* 4:252-54.

2. See S. Greengus, "Biblical and ANE Law," *ABD* 4:242-52.

3. See the recent review of the research on the Book of the Covenant by J. Van Seters, *A Law Book for the Diaspora: Revision in the Study of the Covenant Code* (Oxford: Oxford University Press, 2003), 8-46.

4. Childs (*Exodus*, 451-64) and Crüsemann (*Torah*, 109-200) provide helpful summaries of the twentieth-century interpretation of the Book of the Covenant.

5. Wellhausen, *Composition*, 88-93.

B. Bäntsch separated civil *Mishpatim* ("rules, ordinances"; 21:1–22:17) from religious *Debarim* ("words"; 22:18–23:19) laws in the Book of the Covenant. He argued further that the Book of the Covenant was an independent law code, incorporated into the E source during the monarchical period, then into its present narrative context.[6] Alt added the form-critical distinction of casuistic and apodictic law. He anchored the casuistic law of the *Mishpatim* in ancient Near Eastern civil law and judged the apodictic legislation to be unique to the religious institutions of ancient Israel. According to Alt, the *Mishpatim* represent civil law common to the ancient world, while the apodictic laws depart from the ancient Near Eastern model by anchoring law in God, not the king, and by addressing cultic matters, a topic absent from ancient Near Eastern laws. The agrarian setting, the absence of a king, the lack of taxes or any other central organization indicated to Alt that the laws in the Book of the Covenant and their fusion into one law code reflected the social context of premonarchical Israel.[7] Noth gives voice to the view of Alt in his commentary on Exodus: "It is probable that this collection once formed an independent book of law, which has been inserted into the Pentateuchal narrative as an already self-contained entity."[8]

Many of the historical conclusions of Alt have been called into question. For example, F. Crüsemann argues that the law regulating slaves (21:2-11) derives from the monarchical period, not the prestate environment. Yet the paradigm of anchoring the Book of the Covenant at the outset of the ancient Israelites' legal history continues into the present time.[9] For instance, J. W. Marshall concludes from an anthropological study of the Book of the Covenant that the law code "reflects a period in Israelite history between Israel's beginnings as a segmentary society with localized authority and its eventual status as a centralized state."[10] The result of the literary evaluation of the Book of the Covenant is that the parallel laws in Deuteronomy are judged to be later revisions of the legislation in the Book of the Covenant. Thus B. M. Levinson argues that the law of the altar in Exod 20:24-26 is refashioned in Deuteronomy 12 to accentuate the centralization of the cult.[11]

6. B. Bäntsch, *Das Bundesbuch, Ex XX 22-XXIII 33: Seine ursprüngliche Gestalt, sein Verhältnis zu den es umgebenden Quellenschriften und seine Stellung in der alt-testamentlichen Gesetzgebung* (Halle: Max Neimeyer, 1892).

7. Alt, *Essays*, 79-132.

8. Noth, *Exodus*, 173.

9. Crüsemann, *Torah*, 153 *et passim*.

10. J. W. Marshall, *Israel and the Book of the Covenant: An Anthropological Approach to Biblical Law* (SBLDS 140; Atlanta: Scholars Press, 1993), 3-4.

11. B. M. Levinson, *Deuteronomy and the Hermeneutics of Legal Innovation* (Oxford: Oxford University Press, 1997), 3-52.

The paradigm concerning the compositional history of the Book of the Covenant also included literary additions to the laws. Already in the early twentieth century, A. Jirku and A. Jepsen extended the work of Wellhausen, noting the shift between singular and plural laws. The law prohibiting a female sorcerer is written in the second person singular form (22:18 [MT 17]), while the law against oppressing a widow is plural (22:22 [MT 21]). They also highlighted the changing syntax of the laws, as in the use of the participle in 21:12-17. They even noted the blending of casuistic and apodictic forms, of which the opening of the slave law in 21:2 may be an example.[12] Contradictions in content further reinforced a history of composition, which included late literary additions to codified laws. Daube provides an illustration in the law against kidnapping: "He that steals a man and sells him and he is found in his hand shall be put to death" (21:16). The law has internal contradictions. How can a human who is kidnapped and sold still be found in the hand of the kidnapper? The answer according to Daube is that the law is not a single composition. The concluding phrase, "and he is found in his hand," is an addition representing a new development in judicial procedure, in which the death penalty now applies whether or not the kidnapper sells the victim.[13] A central hypothesis in the study of Daube, as well as for Jirku and Jepsen, is that biblical law reflects change over time. As a result, the identification of additions or changes in the law provides insight into the social evolution of ancient Israel's legal history.

The study of revision and interpolation of biblical laws in the Book of the Covenant has blossomed with the contemporary methodology of legal exegesis and inner-biblical interpretation, a form of proto-midrash in which additions to the text are interpreted as attempts by scribes to clarify judicial procedures for a later time. This practice eventually evolved into the legal (or halakic) interpretation in rabbinic tradition. M. Fishbane has provided an extensive study employing the methodology, and Levinson extended the method to interpret the Book of the Covenant as well as the laws in Deuteronomy. These scholars have identified interpolations and legal exegesis, which are intended to expand a law (the law of kidnapping, 21:16), to clarify an ambiguous law (the law against striking a pregnant woman, 21:22), to narrow the scope of a law (the restriction of the *ḥērem* law in Deuteronomy 7 from Exod 23:20-33), to introduce a new law (the distinction between legitimate and illegitimate homicide in the case of housebreaking, Exod 22:1-3), or even to apply one law to another (the designation that a child functions as an adult in the law addressing an ox that

12. A. Jirku, *Das weltliche Recht im Alten Testament* (Gütersloh: Bertelsmann, 1927); A. Jepsen, *Untersuchungen zum Bundesbuch* (Stuttgart: Kohlhammer, 1927).

13. Daube, *Studies in Biblical Law*, 95.

gores, 21:31).[14] The application of inner-biblical exegesis is also extended to a comparison between distinct law codes in the Hebrew Bible, as is evident in the *ḥērem* law noted above. The triple tradition of slave laws in 21:2-11, Deut 15:12-18, and Lev 25:39-54 provides yet another important example of inner-biblical interpretation between law codes. The comparison of distinct law codes has tended to reinforce the paradigm that views the Book of the Covenant as the earliest law code, followed by Deuteronomy and finally the P legislation. Crüsemann gives voice to the dominant view: an "indisputable fact," he concludes, is that "the Book of the Covenant is older than Deuteronomy and so is the oldest law book in the Old Testament."[15]

LITERARY STRUCTURE AND NARRATIVE CONTEXT

The quest for the history of composition of the Book of the Covenant often ignored the literary structure of the law code. Alt separated casuistic and apodictic laws without examining their literary arrangement, which led to the judgment that the Book of the Covenant lacked design.[16] Daube's thesis that additions to laws were attached at the end, often out of context, reinforced the form-critical judgment concerning the lack of literary design.[17] This evaluation has influenced the history of interpretation. For example, Childs evaluated the literary structure of the Book of the Covenant with the following three points: it lacks logical order, its arrangement may be arbitrary, and there appears to be no theological or thematic organization.[18]

But not all agreed with such a negative view of the literary structure of the Book of the Covenant. S. M. Paul concluded his form-critical and comparative study of the Book of the Covenant with a brief examination of the arrangement of the laws in 21:12–22:16, seeking to demonstrate a pattern of "associative reasoning behind the structure."[19] J. Halbe presented a far more thorough analysis of structure as a prerequisite for interpreting both the form and the history of composition of the Book of the Covenant. He identified 22:20 as the center of

---

14. On expansion see M. Fishbane, *Biblical Interpretation in Ancient Israel* (Oxford: Clarendon, 1985), 188-90. On clarification see ibid., 92. To introduce a new law see B. M. Levinson, "The Case for Revision and Interpolation with the Biblical Legal Corpora," in *Theory and Method in Biblical and Cuneiform Law: Revision, Interpolation and Development* (ed. B. M. Levinson; JSOTSup 181; Sheffield: Sheffield Academic Press, 1994), 50-51; see also Levinson, *Deuteronomy and Hermeneutics*. On application see Fishbane, *Biblical Interpretation*, 212.

15. Crüsemann, *Torah*, 109.

16. Alt, *Essays*, 81-132.

17. Daube, *Studies in Biblical Law*, 74-101.

18. Childs, *Exodus*, 459-60.

19. S. M. Paul, *Studies in the Book of the Covenant in the Light of Cuneiform and Biblical Law* (VTSup 18; Leiden: Brill, 1970), 106-11.

the law code: "Whoever sacrifices to any god other than Yahweh must be destroyed." Three concentric rings frame this command. The outermost ring is cultic law, consisting of the altar law (20:22-26) and the festival calendar (23:13-19). The next ring balances the slave (21:2-11) and Sabbath (23:10-12) laws. The innermost ring contrasts the death-penalty laws (21:12-19) with the rights of foreigners (22:21–23:9).[20]

The literary design of the Book of the Covenant has become an important feature in its interpretation. E. Otto evaluates the history of the composition of the Book of the Covenant from an analysis of its present structure, in which the center of the laws in 21:2–22:26 contains the laws of restitution in 21:33–22:15-16. Y. Osumi builds on the work of Halbe and Otto, extending the interpretation of the literary structure to the conclusion in 23:20-33, as has L. Schwienhorst-Schönberger.[21] As a consequence, the literary structure of the Book of the Covenant has emerged as a central feature of interpretation.[22] B. S. Jackson has identified 21:2–22:27 as a chiasmus.[23] C. M. Carmichael has described an internal repetition between 22:20-26 and 23:9-12.[24] J. M. Sprinkle interprets the entire Book of the Covenant based solely on literary structure, eschewing any evaluation of the history of composition in the analysis of literary design.[25] Crüsemann concludes from the growing body of research that an interpretation of structure must "be the starting point for all further analysis."[26] Dohmen suggests the literary design to the Book of the Covenant shown in figure 33 on page 502.[27]

Dohmen has identified a series of frames in the literary design of the Book of the Covenant. The outer frame is the introduction (20:22a) and the conclusion (23:20-33). The next frame includes three motifs in 22:22b-26 and 23:13-19: (1) the reference to God's word (22:22b; 23:13a); (2) the command

20. J. Halbe, *Das Privilegrecht Jahwes Ex 34, 10-26: Gestalt und Wesen, Herkunft und Wirken in vordeuteronomisticher Zeit* (FRLANT 114; Göttingen: Vandenhoeck & Ruprecht, 1975), 413-39; see the diagram on p. 421.

21. Y. Osumi, *Die Kompositionsgeschichte des Bundesbuches Exodus 20,22b-23,33* (OBO 105; Göttingen: Vandenhoeck & Ruprecht, 1991); L. Schwienhorst-Schönberger, *Das Bundesbuch (Ex 20, 22-23,33): Studien zu seiner Entstehung und Theologie* (BZAW 188; Berlin: de Gruyter, 1990).

22. For bibliography see G. C. Chirichigno, *Debt-Slavery in Israel and the Ancient Near East* (JSOTSup 141; Sheffield: Sheffield Academic Press, 1993), 188 n. 2.

23. B. S. Jackson, "Modeling Biblical Law: The Covenant Code," *Chicago-Kent Law Review* 70 (1995): 1745-1827, esp. 1779; idem, *Studies in Semiotics*, 218.

24. C. Carmichael, "A Singular Method of Codification of Law in the *Mishpatim*," ZAW 84 (1972): 19-25.

25. J. M. Sprinkle, *The Book of the Covenant: A Literary Approach* (JSOTSup 174; Sheffield: Sheffield Academic Press, 1994).

26. Crüsemann, *Torah*, 113.

27. Dohmen, *Exodus 19-40*, 150.

Figure 33

20:22a **Introduction and instruction**

> 22:22b   Reference to God's word
> 22:23   Command against images
> 22:24-26 Altar law — cult place

> > 21:1   Title
> > 21:2-11   *Slave law (6/7 years)*

> > > **21:12-17** **Death-penalty law** (v. 13 exception)
> > > 21:18-32   Bodily injury
> > > 21:33–22:14 Questions of imprisonment
> > > 22:15-16   Bodily injury

> > > **22:17-19** **Death-penalty law**
> > > 22:20-26   Social commands
> > > 22:27-30   Religious commands
> > > 23:1-9   Social commands

> > 23:10-12 *Fallow year and Sabbath rest (6/7 years)*

> 23:13a   Reference to God's word
> 23:13b   Command against foreign gods
> 23:14-19 Festival calendar

23:20-33 **Conclusion**

---

against images and foreign gods (22:23; 23:13b); and (3) the cultic law of the altar (22:24-26) and the festivals (23:14-19). The slave law and the Sabbath law provide the next frame (21:2-11 and 23:10-12). The center of the law code contrasts the laws of bodily injury (21:12–22:16) to the social and the religious commands (22:17–23:9), with each section containing death-penalty legislation (21:12-17 and 22:17-19).

Otto illustrates the merging of literary structure and the history of composition in the interpretation of the Book of the Covenant.[28] He identifies 21:2–22:26 and 22:28–23:12 as distinct collections of law, each of which is chiastic in structure. The first corpus, 21:2–22:26, provides illustration. It separates into

---

28. E. Otto, *Wandel der Rechtsbegründungen in der Gesellschaftsgeschichte des antiken Israel: Eine Rechtsgeschichte des "Bundesbuches" Ex XX, 22-XXIII, 13* (StudBib 3; Leiden: Brill, 1988); idem, *Rechtsgeschichte der Redaktionen im Kodex Eshnunna und im 'Bundesbuch'* (OBO 85; Göttingen: Vandenhoeck & Ruprecht, 1989).

three pairs of laws: (1) Protection of Slaves, Aliens, and Poor (21:11A/22:20-26*A'); (2) Capital Punishment (21:12-17 A/22:17-19a A'); and (3) Bodily Harm (21:18-22 C/22:15C'), with the *šallēm* law ("laws of restitution"; 21:33–22:16).

Otto relates the literary structure and the history of composition in the interpretation of each of the small collections. He detects a development in casuistic law from profane legislation, focused on the restitution between family members, to a more systematized criminal law, sanctioned by the cult and aimed at social units larger than the family. The change from profane to cultic law is further advanced when the Jerusalem priesthood relates the four collections of law, adding the altar law (20:24-26), the laws of rape (22:16-17), the laws of capital punishment (22:18-20a), and the laws concerning the resident alien and the poor (22:21-27). Otto concludes that a theology of Yahweh as the king and the protector of the poor became the basis for legitimizing the law during the monarchical period as evidenced in 22:27 with the divine claim to be compassionate.[29] The second corpus of law, 22:29–23:12, also requires an interpretation of literary structure to reveal its history of composition. The framing of the collection with the commands for exclusive loyalty to Yahweh (22:29-30 and 23:10-12) and the command for solidarity with the alien (23:4) at the center of the corpus indicate that the author is rooting the authority of law in a theology of divine transcendence.[30]

The two legal collections, 21:2–22:26 and 22:29–23:12, are brought together in two stages with a clear literary design, according to Otto. The first stage underscores the demand for exclusive loyalty to Yahweh by creating a two-part chiasmus. The outer ring contrasts the slave laws (21:2-11) with the commands for exclusive loyalty to Yahweh (23:10-12). The inner ring is made up of the laws for the protection of the resident alien and the poor (22:21-27) and additional commands regarding the exclusive loyalty to Yahweh (22:29-30). The second stage of literary development is by Deuteronomistic redactors, who anchor the law code in its narrative context, providing an introduction (20:22-23; 21:1), internal editing (22:20ab-b, 21, 23, 30; 23:9), and a conclusion (23:13-33). The additions relate the law code to the events of the exodus, while also developing a covenantal theology based on a transcendent view of God.[31] Otto concludes that the composition of the Book of the Covenant spans the history of ancient Israel and reveals its evolution from profane to sacred law.[32] His study pays less attention to late literary developments either in the form of redaction or the methodology of legal exegesis advanced by Fishbane and Levinson. But

29. Otto, *Wandel,* 8-44.

30. Ibid., 45-51.

31. Ibid., 51-60.

32. See E. Otto, "Aspects of Legal Reforms and Reformulations in Ancient Cuneiform and Israelite Law," in *Theory and Method,* ed. Levinson, 160-96.

that gap is partially filled by Schwienhorst-Schönberger, who builds on Otto's work, while also focusing on the later compositional history of the Book of the Covenant.[33]

RECENT PROPOSALS

Three proposals challenge the paradigm for studying the Book of the Covenant. C. M. Carmichael questions the relationship of the Book of the Covenant to Israel's social and legal history and advocates a new methodology for interpreting the relationship between narrative and law in the Pentateuch. R. Westbrook reevaluates the comparative study of law and the hypothesis that law codes change reflecting the social history of ancient Israel. Van Seters has challenged the literary composition of the Book of the Covenant as an independent law code. He also advocates for a reversal in the chronology of the composition between the Book of the Covenant, the laws in Deuteronomy, and the P legislation.

Carmichael has reevaluated the relationship between law and history in the Book of the Covenant. He has questioned the complex history of composition of the Book of the Covenant developed in the modern period of study, and the ability of interpreters to recover the social and legal history of ancient Israel from a study of the literature. He argues instead that biblical law is a late literary development by scribes. As a result: "Attempts to date the texts must end in frustration because the historical data necessary for the task are simply not available."[34] The focus of the law is not "real-life" issues from the legal history of ancient Israel. The interest of the biblical writers "is on the history of their own national traditions, the very stories and legends available to us in the books of Genesis, Exodus, Numbers, Joshua, Judges, Samuel, and Kings. . . . What the laws focus on is the first-time-ever occurrence of a problem and the recurrence of that problem in subsequent generations."[35] The laws provide commentary on narratives, and conversely the narratives illustrate the impact of the laws. Carmichael interprets many of the laws in the Book of the Covenant as commentary on the story of the exodus or the ancestor Jacob. For example, the altar law (20:23-26) relates to the story of Adam and Eve (Gen 2:4–3:24) and the incident of the golden calf (Exodus 32). The law of slavery must be read in conjunction with the near-slave status of Jacob to his uncle Laban (Gen 27:41–31:55).[36]

Westbrook reevaluates the role of comparative law for the study of the

---

33. Schwienhorst-Schönberger, *Bundesbuch*.
34. C. M. Carmichael, "The Three Laws on the Release of Slaves (Exod 21,2-11; Dtn 15,12-18; Lev 25,39-46)," *ZAW* 112 (2000): 509.
35. Carmichael, *Origins of Biblical Law*, 11-12.
36. Ibid., 74-97.

Book of the Covenant.[37] He concludes that ancient Near Eastern law codes are static in nature; they evince no evolution in thought as a consequence of social change. This conclusion runs counter to the very heart of the more traditional paradigm for interpreting ancient law, which envisions ancient law codes as prescriptive law for social reform. Over against this hypothesis Westbrook concludes that ancient law codes are academic documents, and as such they are conduits for preserving tradition, not instruments for social change. The static and academic nature of ancient Near Eastern law codes means that they did not undergo a process of revision and editing and thus they must be read as clear and coherent statements in their own right regardless of apparent inconsistencies. The more dynamic role of law as a resource for social change did not take place until the late seventh or sixth century B.C.E., according to Westbrook, under the influence of the Greek social and intellectual revolution. The legal codes in the Hebrew Bible reflect both the ancient Near Eastern tradition of static law and the more socially dynamic law springing from the Greek intellectual revolution. The Book of the Covenant is part of the static world of ancient Near Eastern academic law codes, while the laws in Deuteronomy and the P legislation reflect the more dynamic variety. Thus Westbrook eschews any study of the history of composition in the Book of the Covenant: it is "a coherent text comprising clear and consistent law, in the same manner as its cuneiform forbears."[38]

Van Seters has long argued that the narrative account of the revelation in Exodus 19–24 is part of a late exilic history that reinterprets the account of revelation in Deuteronomy. He identified the late composition as the J History. In *Life of Moses* he argues that the J historian created narrative scenes about the account of theophany from what had been hortatory accounts in Deuteronomy, while also reinterpreting the central teaching in Deuteronomy that the Israelite people heard divine speech. For the J historian, the divine speech is not heard by the Israelites but experienced more generally in the sound of the shofar (trumpet). The revelation of the Book of the Covenant is part of the J History, according to Van Seters, although he limits his analysis in *Life of Moses* to the narrative introduction (20:22-23) and the law of altars (20:24-26).[39]

In *Law Book for the Diaspora* Van Seters seeks to demonstrate the late literary character of the Book of the Covenant, again identifying the author as the J historian.[40] Houtman already anticipated the conclusion of Van Seters in part by arguing that the Book of the Covenant is not an independent composition,

---

37. R. Westbrook, *Studies in Biblical and Cuneiform Law* (CahRB 26; Paris: Gabalda, 1988); idem, "What Is the Covenant Code?" in *Theory and Method,* ed. Levinson, 15-36.

38. Westbrook, "What Is the Covenant Code?" 36.

39. Van Seters, *Life of Moses,* 247-89.

40. Van Seters, *Law Book.*

but composed by the author of the narrative of Exodus 19–24. For Houtman this author is responsible for the history extending from Genesis through 2 Kings.[41] Van Seters notes the breakdown of several pillars of the traditional interpretation of the Book of the Covenant as an early and independent law code. The rejection of the Documentary Hypothesis associated with Well-hausen calls into question the dating of the literature to the monarchical period. The research on scribal schools raises the question of whether law codes reflect social change. The absence of parallels between the Book of the Covenant and the Babylonian laws of the second millennium B.C.E. does not support the independent nature or the antiquity of the Book of the Covenant. The Assyrian and Neo-Babylonian law codes provide a closer parallel, according to Van Seters, again suggesting the late composition of the Book of the Covenant. As a result, the Book of the Covenant cannot be assumed to be ancient law reinterpreted by the later legislation in Deuteronomy. It is, rather, composed by the exilic J historian, and as such it is a late reinterpretation of the laws in Deuteronomy. The laws of the Hebrew slave in Exod 21:2-11 provide an example. Van Seters concludes that they represent the latest version of slave law in the Pentateuch, a reinterpretation of the law from Deuteronomy 15, reflecting the social practices of the Second Temple period as preserved in Neh 5:1-13.[42]

The issues surrounding the history of the composition of the Book of the Covenant are noted at points in the commentary. The focus of interpretation remains on the role of the Book of the Covenant in the larger literary context of the Non-P History, which includes Deuteronomy and the Deuteronomistic History. I will compare the different versions of similar laws in the Book of the Covenant and in Deuteronomy 12–26, as well as noting other references to specific laws in the Hebrew Bible. The outline of the commentary follows the three-part structure of the Book of the Covenant, which includes the introduction and altar laws (20:21-26), the law (21:1–23:19), and the conclusion (23:20-33).

Commentary

Introduction and the Law of the Altars (20:21-26)

[20:21]*And the people stood at a distance, but Moses approached the dark cloud where the God was.* [22]*And Yahweh spoke to Moses, "Thus you will say to the Israelites, 'You saw that from heaven I spoke with you.* [23]*Do not make with me gods of*

---

41. C. Houtman, *Das Bundesbuch: Ein Kommentar* (Documenta et Monumenta Orientalis Antiqui 24; Leiden: Brill, 1997); idem, *Exodus*, 3:79-98.

42. J. Van Seters, "The Law of the Hebrew Slave," *ZAW* 108 (1996): 534-46.

*silver, and gods of gold you will not make for yourselves.*²⁴*An altar of earth you will make for me. And you will sacrifice on it your burnt offerings, and your well-being offerings, your sheep and your oxen. In every place where I cause to remember my name, I will come to you and I will bless you.* ²⁵*But if an altar of stones you make for me, you will not build them of cut stone. For if you move your chisel on them, you will profane it.* ²⁶*And you shall not ascend the steps on my altar, that your nakedness may not be exposed on it.*

Notes

20:21 *And the people stood at a distance, but Moses approached the dark cloud.* The people were also described as "standing at a distance" in 20:18 because of their fear of theophany. The repetition in 20:21 introduces a contrast between the people and Moses that signals the beginning of the episode. The Sam follows the MT verbatim in 20:21a after having departed significantly from the MT in 20:18-20. The Sam also adds an extended divine speech in 20:21b in which Yahweh acknowledges the request of the people for Moses to mediate for them and also promises the people blessing. The LXX follows the transition in the MT. The contrast between Moses and the people is represented by *de*, "but." The presence of God in the dark cloud (*'ărāpel*) picks up the imagery from 19:9, which described the cloud of theophany as the thick cloud (*bě'ab he'ānān*). The LXX translates the dark cloud (*'ărāpel*) as *gnophon*, also suggesting a dark storm cloud.

20:22 *And Yahweh spoke to Moses, "Thus you will say to the Israelites."* The MT employs the prophetic messenger form, *kōh tō'mar 'el-běnê yiśrā'ēl*. The LXX *tade ereis* follows the MT, adding "the house of Jacob" to "the Israelites," as in 19:3. The Sam eliminates the prophetic messenger form, employing the imperative "speak" (*dbr*).

20:23 *do not make with me gods of silver, and gods of gold you will not make for yourselves.* The MT punctuation of the verse indicates a different translation: "Do not make with me. Gods of silver and gods of gold you will not make for yourselves." Crüsemann seeks to overcome the problem of the punctuation by reading Hebrew *'ittî*, "with me," as *'ōtî*, "me," translating: "You shall not make me."[43] Houtman notes that the MT punctuation ignores the parallel construction of silver and gold, making the object of the opening command all gods of silver and gold.[44] My translation follows the Sam and LXX, which maintain the parallel between "gods of silver" and "gods of gold."

20:24 *an altar of earth you will make for me.* The MT shifts from the plural "you" (20:22-23) to the singular "you," a regular occurrence throughout the Book of the Covenant. The LXX continues to state the command in the plural. I translate Hebrew *'ădāmâ* as "earth"; it could also be translated "ground," like LXX *gēs*.

your well-being offerings. Hebrew *šělāmeykā* is also translated as "peace offering." The LXX translates, *ta sōtēria*, which has a range of meanings, including deliverance,

---

43. Crüsemann, *Torah*, 198 n. 447.
44. Houtman, *Exodus*, 3:104.

health, and security. When the term is applied to this sacrifice, Wevers suggests the translation "peace offering."[45]

in every place. The statement repeats language from the law of cultic centralization in Deuteronomy 12, raising questions of its meaning. Hebrew *běkol-hammāqôm* could be translated as a statement of cult centralization, "in all the place," or as referring to multiple cultic sites, "in every place." The Sam *bmqwm,* "in the place," favors the centralization of worship to one location. The LXX moves in yet another direction, relating the reference to the cultic site, "in every place" *(en panti topō),* with the preceding sacrifices. Dohmen translates "in all the place" *(am Ganzen Ort),* noting the parallel construction in 34:3 in reference to the mountain.[46]

where I cause to remember my name. The imperfect form of the verb, *'azkîr,* "I cause to remember," is rendered in the past in the Sam, emphasizing a specific place, *'zkrty 't šmy šmh,* "I *caused* my name to be remembered *there,*" again emphasizing the single location *(bmqwm,* "in the place"). The LXX appears to follow the Sam, *hou ean eponomasō to onoma mou ekei,* "then I will declare my name there." God is both the subject and the object of the statement. The causative translation of the MT avoids this construction.[47] Van Seters suggests a change in the MT to the second person, although it is not reflected in any textual tradition: "In every place where you invoke my name."[48]

20:25 *for if you move your chisel on them, you will profane it.* The Hebrew noun *ḥarběkā* in isolation translates "your sword." The verb *nûp,* "move," designates an act of chiseling (see NRSV, "for if you use a chisel upon it"). The word is also used to describe the wave offering (29:24, 26). The LXX renders Hebrew *ḥereb,* "sword," as *encheiridion,* "hand tool," and the verb *hēnaptā,* "move," as *epibeblēkas,* "you brought upon."

20:26 *and you shall not ascend the steps on my altar, that your nakedness may not be exposed on it.* The command is directed to all the Israelite people. In later tradition the verse is narrowed to a command to the priests.[49]

Commentary

The section includes a narrative account of the commissioning of Moses with a law forbidding other gods or idols (vv. 21-23) and the instruction on the proper form of altars (vv. 24-26). The section follows immediately the revelation of the Decalogue (19:20–20:20), providing narrative context for the Book of the Covenant, while also creating a literary progression from the previous scenes, the proposal of covenant (19:1-8a) and the theophany of God on the mountain (19:8b-19).

20:21-23 This section establishes the narrative context for the private

45. Wevers, *Notes,* 319.
46. Dohmen, *Exodus 19–40,* 145.
47. For further discussion see ibid.
48. Van Seters, *Law Book,* 62.
49. Houtman, *Exodus,* 3:109.

revelation of law to Moses. Moses is separated from the people in v. 21 when he approaches the "dark cloud" *('ărāpel)* where God dwells, while the people stand "at a distance." The *'ărāpel* cloud signals the appearance of God (see Deut 4:11; 5:22; Ps 97:1-2) associating the Book of the Covenant with the preceding theophany. The separation of Moses from the people underscores his authority. God had predicted that the public experience of theophany would authenticate Moses to the people of Israel (Exod 19:9). The fear of theophany as a result of the public revelation of the Decalogue (20:1-17) prompted the Israelite people to elect Moses to mediate the revelation of all future law (20:18-20). The introduction to the Book of the Covenant fulfills the divine prediction, when Moses receives the revelation of law privately in the divine cloud.

The divine speech to Moses in v. 22 creates a repetition with the proposal of covenant in 19:1-8a. The parallels include: the commission with the words "thus you will say" (19:3b/20:22a), and the call for the people to recognize a past action of God (19:4/20:22b). God speaks in the first person and addresses the Israelites in the second person plural, which may be a sign that it is a late literary addition to the legislation in Exodus 21–23.[50] In the proposal of covenant God states: "You yourselves have seen what I did to Egypt." After the public revelation of the Decalogue God states: "You have seen for yourselves that I spoke to you from heaven." The repetition signals a progression in events from the exodus to the proposal of covenant (19:3), and from the public revelation of the Decalogue to the private revelation of the Book of the Covenant to Moses (20:22). The two divine speeches relate the themes of salvation from Egypt with the revelation of the law and Mosaic authority.

The divine proclamation "from heaven" is noteworthy, since the preceding events have situated God on the mountain for the revelation of the Decalogue. In view of this Van Seters suggests that the imagery of a voice from heaven is not a reference to the Decalogue at all, but indicates only the abstract sound of the trumpet from the earlier description of theophany (19:16-19).[51] T. D. N. Mettinger has demonstrated that the location of the divine voice in heaven is certainly a more abstract and transcendent view of God than the image of the Deity dwelling on the summit of the mountain.[52] But the similar language between 20:22 and Deut 4:35-40 indicates that the content of the divine voice from heaven is the Decalogue.

The parallel to Deuteronomy 4 is important for interpreting the narrative context of the introduction to the Book of the Covenant in the Non-P History. Deuteronomy 4 represents late tradition in Deuteronomy, where the voice of

---

50. See, e.g., Childs, *Exodus*, 449-50, 465.
51. Van Seters, *Life of Moses*, 275-80.
52. Mettinger, *Dethronement of Sabaoth*, 38-79.

God was also from heaven as compared to the location of God on Mount Horeb in the parallel account of Deuteronomy 5.[53] Deuteronomy 4 stresses the chasm between God and the Israelite people: "From heaven he [God] made you hear his voice to discipline you" (4:36). Several themes are associated with the emphasis on divine transcendence. First, the content of theophany is the revelation of law, more specifically the Decalogue: God "declared to you his covenant, the Ten Commandments" (4:13). Second, the merging of the law and theophany carries with it a demand for an exclusive allegiance to Yahweh: "He has shown you these things so that you might know that Yahweh is God, beside him there is no other" (4:35). Third, faithfulness to the law will lead to the gift of the land through conquest: "God has brought you out of Egypt by his presence and his great strength to drive out before you nations greater and stronger than you and to bring you into the land to give it to you for your inheritance" (4:37-38). Finally, Moses is idealized as a teacher who bridges the gap between God and humans through the role of the lawgiver: "Yahweh directed me at that time to teach you the decree and laws" (4:14). As a result, all law and even the experience of theophany are mediated through Moses in Deuteronomy.

The introduction to the Book of the Covenant includes many of the themes from Deuteronomy 4. The transcendence of God is underscored when the divine voice is also located in heaven in Exod 20:22. The literary context indicates that the content of the divine voice is the Decalogue (20:1-17). The opening proclamation of God to Moses in 20:23 continues the literary relationship with Deuteronomy 4, underscoring the need for an exclusive loyalty to Yahweh: "Do not make [any gods] to be alongside me." Moses also emerges as the idealized teacher who bridges the gap between God and humans when he receives the revelation of the Book of the Covenant privately (Exod 20:21). The only theme of Deuteronomy 4 missing from the introduction to the Book of the Covenant is the promise of land through conquest, which does appear in the epilogue to the Book of the Covenant (23:20-33), making the thematic parallels to Deuteronomy 4 complete. The parallels indicate that the introduction (Exod 20:21-23) and the conclusion (23:20-33) to the Book of the Covenant in the Non-P History share the theology of divine transcendence established in Deuteronomy 4.

The syntax of the demand for exclusive loyalty is ambiguous, giving rise to different interpretations of v. 23. The MT divides the command in two parts: "Do not make with me. Do not make for yourselves gods of silver and gods of

---

53. For discussion of the literary relationship between Deuteronomy 4 and 5, and for the compositional history of the book of Deuteronomy, see A. D. H. Mayes, *Deuteronomy* (NCB; repr. Grand Rapids: Eerdmans, 1981), e.g., 35, 38-41; idem, "Deuteronomy 4 and the Literary Criticism of Deuteronomy," *JBL* 100 (1981): 23-51.

gold." The first line is difficult. It does not express a complete thought, since the verb lacks an object. The NIV represents one solution in which the phrase "any gods" is inserted as the object, "do not make [any gods] to be alongside me." The NRSV represents another solution in which the entire verse is redivided, separating gods of silver from gods of gold: "You shall not make gods of silver alongside me, nor shall you make for yourselves gods of gold." Both solutions present problems. The motifs of gold and silver tend not to be separated in biblical literature, and the insertion of "any gods" lacks textual evidence. In either case it is evident that the instruction is intended to echo the first two commandments of the Decalogue tying the private revelation to Moses in the introduction to the Book of the Covenant with the previous public revelation of the law.

20:24-26 Verses 24-26 consist of two altar laws (v. 24a and vv. 25-26), which frame a theology of divine cultic presence (v. 24b). Each altar law divides between instruction on the proper material for the altar and directions for acceptable ritual. The first altar law is stated positively. The altar is made of earth and intended for sacrifices (v. 24a). The second altar law is stated negatively. The altar of stones cannot have manufactured material, while the ritual command is also one of restriction. The altar cannot have steps allowing someone to ascend the structure.

The designation of an "altar of earth" *(mizbaḥ 'ădāmâ)* in v. 24a is unique in the Hebrew Bible, raising questions about its material construction, the age of the law, the intended social context, and the meaning. H. Cazelles concluded that an earthen altar consisted of loose soil, while D. Conrad suggested baked bricks, noting that such altars have appeared in the archaeological record.[54] Both interpreters agree that the law is ancient, reflecting an early period of Israelite worship. Van Seters disagrees, arguing that the law is late and that it reflects the social situation of the Diaspora. The closest parallels to the law are Deut 27:5-7 and Josh 8:30-31.[55]

E. Robertson is less precise on the material of the altar, suggesting simply that an earthen altar signifies something "natural."[56] Robertson's interpretation is helpful since it places the question of material within the larger framework of its symbolic meaning. Regardless of its origin, the Non-P historian is making a polemical statement about the role of technology and civilization in the Israelites' future life in the land. The call for sacrifices on an altar of earth idealizes nature and the land as a divine gift. The phrase *'ōhēb 'ădāmâ*, for example, in 2 Chr 26:10 provides some context describing Uzziah as a "lover of nature." The

---

54. H. Cazelles, *Études sur le code de l'alliance* (Paris: Letouzey & Ané, 1946), 40; D. Conrad, *Studien zum Altargesetz: Ex 20.24-26* (Marburg: H. Kimbächer, 1968), 21.

55. Van Seters, *Law Book,* 63-64.

56. E. Robertson, "The Altar of Earth (Exodus XX, 24-26)," *JJS* 1 (1948): 18-19.

word "earth" is a recurring motif in the divine promise of land throughout Deuteronomy: "That you may live long in the earth *('ădāmâ)* Yahweh your God gives you" (Deut 4:40 *et passim*).

Sprinkle summarizes the naturalistic interpretation of the altar law: "Those who build altars must use material from the ground as it left the hand of the Creator rather than any humanly manufactured material."[57] S. Olyan reinforces this interpretation indirectly, noting that the requirement for uncut stones in the second altar law also forbids the manufacturing of material. The purpose is to maintain the separation of the sacred and the profane. An altar of earth may reflect the same intent "to preserve the holiness of the deity's space," undefiled by human manufacturing.[58] The same polemic against technology and civilization is evident in the Non-P historian's genealogy of Cain in Gen 4:17-24. The offspring of the first murderer produce manufacturing and the cultural features of civilization, which for the Non-P historian represent the history of violence on earth, culminating in the boast of Lamech when he wantonly kills a boy.

Exodus 20:24b anchors the law of the earthen altar in a theology of divine cultic presence: "In every place *(běkol-hammāqôm)* where I cause to remember *('azkîr)* my name *(šēmî),* I will come to you and I will bless you." The theology of divine cultic presence in v. 24b must be interpreted against the backdrop of the Name Theology in Deuteronomy, in which the cultic presence of God is also identified as the divine "name" *(šēm)* and the cultic site as the "place *(māqôm)* of the name." The Name Theology in Deuteronomy is expressed through precise liturgical formulas. A short form simply states: "The place Yahweh will choose" *(hammāqôm 'ăšer yibḥar yhwh;* Deut 12:14, 18, 26). Two longer liturgical forms make explicit reference to the name: "The place *(hammāqôm)* Yahweh your God will choose as a dwelling for his Name *(lěšakkēn šěmô)*" (16:2; 26:2); and "The place Yahweh your God will choose . . . to put his Name *(lāśûm šěmô)*" (12:5; 14:24). The place of the name is important to the theology of cult centralization in Deuteronomy. There can be only one place of the name, and Deuteronomy 12 commands that an altar be built on that location. Deuteronomy 14 designates the place of the name as the location for tithes. Deuteronomy 16 limits the observance of Passover to the place of the name. Deuteronomy 26 locates the offering of firstfruits to the same cultic location.[59]

Exodus 20:24b also appears to advocate the Name Theology from Deuteronomy by designating the cultic site as the "place" *(māqôm)* and the divine

---

57. Sprinkle, *Book of the Covenant,* 41.

58. S. M. Olyan, "Why an Altar of Unfinished Stones? Some Thoughts on Exod 20,25 and Dtn 27,5-6," *ZAW* 108 (1996): 161-71, esp. 170.

59. For discussion and bibliography see Mettinger, *Dethronement of Sabaoth,* 38-79.

presence as the "name" *(šēm)*. But there are differences in the liturgical form of 20:24b that raise questions about its relationship to Deuteronomy. Childs notes that the phrase "in every place" may not indicate one single cultic site as is advocated in Deuteronomy, but "presupposes a multiplicity of legitimate places of worship."[60] The phrase that refers to the divine memory is also a problem, since the motif of divine memory is nearly absent from Deuteronomy. Only the Israelite people are called upon to remember in Deuteronomy (see the commentary on 20:8-11). The comparisons indicate that the theology of divine cultic presence in 20:24b is not the same as that expressed in Deuteronomy, yet the law is also within the tradition stream of Deuteronomy and thus serves the purposes of the Non-P historian. It is either an older expression of theology than the formulations in Deuteronomy, or it is a literary creation by the Non-P historian to be read in sequence with the more developed theology of the name in Deuteronomy. Levinson provides an interpretation of Exod 20:24-26 as an early law refashioned in Deuteronomy 12.[61] Van Seters argues the reverse, that 20:24-26 advocates multiple cultic sites for Jews living in the Diaspora.[62] In either case the Name Theology in 20:24b is within the stream of tradition of the theology of the name in Deuteronomy. It advocates an aniconic view of divine cultic presence in which the divine word, codified as law, takes precedence over manufactured altars, images, and icons.

20:24-26 The second altar law in 20:24-26 continues the polemic against manufactured cultic material, stating that stone altars must include only uncut rock. The law is at first surprising, since the command for the altar of earth appears to be absolute, giving the law of cut stones in 20:24-26 the character of an exception to the earlier law. The purpose of the Non-P historian for including the law is both literary and theological. The literary reason is that the command for an uncut stone altar repeats in Deut 27:5-7 and Josh 8:30-31. Moses is commanded in Deut 27:5-7 to build an altar of uncut stones on Mount Ebal in the promised land. The uncut stones are described as "complete" or "whole stones" *('ăbānîm šĕlēmôt)*. The altar is the location for whole burnt sacrifices and peace offerings (the sacrifices prescribed for the earthen altar in v. 24a), as well as for the writing down of law. Joshua fulfills the divine command after the destruction of Ai (Josh 8:30-31) and ties the altar at Mount Ebal into the initial revelation about altars. The literary argument is strengthened by noting that Moses also writes law at the altar in Exod 24:3-8 as in the subsequent accounts.

Olyan provides a theological reason for the law by noting that the natural

60. Childs, *Exodus*, 447, 466.
61. Levinson, *Deuteronomy and Hermeneutics*, 32-34.
62. Van Seters, *Law Book*, 61.

state of the stone, described as "whole" or "complete," is meant to safeguard holiness from defilement through human manufacture. Thus the second altar law carries forward the idealization of nature and the polemic against civilization from the first altar law.[63] The two laws are supported by an aniconic theology of the divine cultic presence of the name, which forbids the manufacture of any objects (v. 25b).

The literary context and the polemic against manufacturing provide only a partial interpretation of 20:24-26 because the focus of the command is on its steps *(ma'ălōt)* and the liturgical action of ascending them. This motif is absent from the altar on Mount Ebal. Thus additional religious and symbolic interpretation is required to account for the prohibition against ascending steps and the imagery of exposed nakedness associated with it. One interpretation is religious and cultic. The prohibition against making and ascending the steps is a polemic against Canaanite or other alien cultic practices. Cassuto notes such cultic practices in Sumerian and Egyptian religion.[64] The Hebrew Bible contains different opinions on this matter, however. The prophet Ezekiel envisions steps to the altar in his description of the temple (Ezek 43:13-17). The P author is explicit in forbidding priests to officiate in the nude. They were required to wear breeches to cover themselves (Exod 28:42). The Non-P historian may share the P writer's view concerning nudity. But neither Ezekiel nor the P writer shares the Non-P author's prohibition against manufactured material.

Another interpretation of 20:24-26 is political, not religious, and it arises from Hebrew *ma'ălōt*, "steps." The word is used in a variety of metaphorical ways in the Hebrew Bible. It often signifies ascent, as in the "Songs of Ascents" (Psalms 120–133). It may also designate the course of the sun in its movement forward or backward (2 Kgs 20:9-11; Isa 38:8). But more helpful for the interpretation of Exod 20:26 is Amos 9:6, where steps are associated with God's rule in heaven: "Building his steps *(ma'ălōtāw)* in heaven." The NIV translation of *ma'ălōt* as "palace" suggests monarchical imagery of coronation and exaltation, which finds support in the Hebrew Bible. Six steps are an important feature of the throne of Solomon (1 Kgs 10:19-20; 2 Chr 9:18-19). Jehu assumes the monarchy of the northern kingdom by ascending the steps of the throne: "They hurried and took their cloaks and spread them under him on the bare steps. Then they blew the trumpet and shouted, 'Jehu is king!'" (2 Kgs 9:13). If the imagery of natural material is a polemic against the manufacturing that characterizes civilization, then the prohibition against ascending the stairs may also be a statement against the monarchy. Such a political interpretation is reinforced by the sexual imagery of exposed nakedness. The phrase frequently describes sex-

63. Olyan, "Why an Altar?"
64. Cassuto, *Exodus,* 257.

ual practice, promiscuity, incest, and violence (Lev 18:7, 11, 15, 17; Ezekiel 16, 22; Gen 9:20-27, etc.).[65] But it can also indicate political defeat, exile, and the fall of a monarch. Isaiah 20:4 describes the defeat and the exile of the Egyptians as their nakedness. Isaiah 47:3 uses the phrase from Exod 20:26, "to uncover (*gālâ*) nakedness ('*erwâ*)," to describe the fall of Babylon. The Israelite exile is the great "uncovering" (i.e., Jer 43:3; Ezek 39:28; 2 Kgs 25:11).

The introduction to the Book of the Covenant is in the form of primitive law. But it carries a polemical message that is more conducive to the exile, sharing the religious and political outlook of Deuteronomy. Earthen altars for sacrifice idealize nature and provide a critique of manufacturing. Altars of uncut stone extend the polemic against the power of foreign cults abroad and monarchs at home and instead idealize Moses, the lawgiver. At the center of the two altar laws is a theology of the cultic presence of the name, which, according to v. 23, demands exclusive loyalty to Yahweh and a prohibition against images.

Rules (21:1–23:19)

²¹:¹ *And these are the rules that you will set before them:*

² *When you buy a Hebrew slave, he will serve six years. But in the seventh, he shall go out free without cost.* ³ *If single he came, single he goes out. If he is the husband of a wife, then his wife will go out with him.* ⁴ *If his master gives him a wife, and she bears for him sons or daughters, the wife and her children belong to her master. And he will go out single.* ⁵ *But if the slave says, "I love my master, my wife, and my children, I will not go out free,"* ⁶ *then his master shall bring him to the God. And he will bring him to the door or to the doorpost. And his master will pierce his ear with an awl, and he will serve him for life.*

⁷ *When a man sells his daughter as a slave, she will not go out as the male slaves go out.* ⁸ *If she is displeasing in the eyes of her master who designated her for himself, then he must let her be redeemed. To a foreign people he does not have the right to sell her, since he dealt unfairly with her.* ⁹ *And if he designates her for his son, as the practice with daughters he will deal with her.* ¹⁰ *If he takes another to himself, he may not diminish her food, her clothing, and her sexual intercourse.* ¹¹ *If these three things he does not do for her, she will go out without debt, without payment.*

¹² *Whoever strikes a human and he dies will be put to death.* ¹³ *And if he did not lie in wait, but the God moved his hand, then I will appoint for you a place to which he will flee.* ¹⁴ *But if someone intentionally acts against his neighbor to kill him with forethought, you will take him from my altar to be put to death.*

---

65. J. S. Bergsma and S. W. Hahn, "Noah's Nakedness and the Curse on Canaan (Genesis 9:20-27)," *JBL* 124 (2005): 25-40.

[15] *Whoever strikes his father or his mother shall be put to death.*

[16] *Whoever steals a human and sells him or he is found in his hand shall be put to death.*

[17] *Whoever curses his father or his mother shall be put to death.*

[18] *And when humans quarrel and one strikes his neighbor with a stone or with a fist, and he does not die, yet he is confined to bed,* [19] *if he gets up and walks around outside on his staff, the one striking him will go unpunished, except he will pay him for his lost time and he will arrange for his cure.*

[20] *And when a person strikes a male or female slave with a rod, and he dies under his hand, he must be avenged.* [21] *But if the slave stands for one or two days, he will not be avenged, because he is the master's property.*

[22] *And when people are fighting and they strike a pregnant woman, and they bring forth her child, but there is no deadly accident, he will be fined as the husband of the woman places on him. And he will give according to the arbitration.* [23] *But if there is a deadly accident, you will give life for life,* [24] *eye for eye, tooth for tooth, hand for hand, foot for foot,* [25] *burn for burn, wound for wound, bruise for bruise.*

[26] *When a person strikes the eye of his male slave or the eye of his female slave, and he destroys it, he will send him out free on account of his eye.* [27] *And if he knocks out the tooth of his male servant or the tooth of his female servant, he will send him out free on account of his tooth.*

[28] *And when an ox gores a man or a woman to death, the ox will be stoned, and its flesh will not be eaten. But the owner of the ox is innocent.* [29] *But if an ox was in the habit of goring in the past, and its owner, after having been warned, did not guard it, and it kills a man or a woman, the ox will be stoned, and even its owner will be put to death.* [30] *If a ransom is placed upon him, he must give the ransom money for his life, according to whatever is placed upon him.* [31] *If it gores a son or a daughter, he will be dealt with according to the same ruling.* [32] *If the ox gores a male slave or a female slave, he shall pay thirty shekels of silver to the slave's owner, and the ox will be stoned.*

[33] *And when a person opens a pit or when a person digs a pit, and he does not cover it, and an ox or a donkey falls into it,* [34] *the owner of the pit must pay restitution. He will pay the price to the owner. But the dead animal will be his.*

[35] *And when an ox of one person gores an ox of his neighbor, and it dies, then they will sell the live ox and divide its money. And they will also divide the dead animal.* [36] *If it was known that the ox was in the habit of goring yesterday and the day before, and its owner did not guard it, he will make restitution for the ox. But the dead animal will be his.*

[22:1] (21:37) *When a person steals an ox or a sheep, and slaughters it or sells it, he will pay back five oxen for the ox, and four sheep for the sheep.*

[2] (1) *If when digging the thief is found, and he is beaten, and he dies, there is*

no bloodguilt for him. ³ ⁽²⁾*If the sun rises on him, there is bloodguilt for him. He must make full restitution, but if he is unable, he shall be sold for his theft.*

⁴ ⁽³⁾*If the stolen property is found in his hand alive, whether ox, donkey, or sheep, he will pay double restitution.*

⁵ ⁽⁴⁾*And when a person causes a field or a vineyard to be grazed over, and he sends cattle, and it grazes in another's field, restitution must be made from the best of his field and from the best of his vineyard.*

⁶ ⁽⁵⁾*When fire goes out and spreads to thorns so that stacked grain or the standing grain or the field is consumed, the one starting the fire must make restitution for the fire.*

⁷ ⁽⁶⁾*When a person gives to his neighbor money or vessels to guard, and they are stolen from the house of the person, if the thief is caught, he shall make double restitution.* ⁸ ⁽⁷⁾*If the thief is not found, the owner of the house shall draw near before the God, if he did not send his hand against the goods of his neighbor.*

⁹ ⁽⁸⁾*In any matter of contested property, whether an ox, a donkey, a sheep, clothing, or any other loss in which one says, "This is it," the matter of the two of them will be brought to the God. The one whom God condemns will pay double restitution to his neighbor.*

¹⁰ ⁽⁹⁾*When a person gives his neighbor a donkey, ox, sheep, or any animal to guard and it dies, or is injured, or is carried off, with no one seeing,* ¹¹ ⁽¹⁰⁾*an oath before Yahweh will be between them if he did not send his hand against the goods of his neighbor. Its owner will accept and he will not make restitution.* ¹² ⁽¹¹⁾*If it is stolen from him, he will make restitution to its owner.* ¹³ ⁽¹²⁾*If it was mangled as prey, he will bring it as evidence, and he will not make restitution for the prey.*

¹⁴ ⁽¹³⁾*When a person requests from his neighbor, and it is injured or dies and the neighbor is not with him, he will make full restitution.* ¹⁵ ⁽¹⁴⁾*If its owner is with him, he will not make restitution. If it is hired, he brings its hiring fee.*

¹⁶ ⁽¹⁵⁾*And when a man seduces a virgin who is not betrothed, and lies with her, he must pay the bride-price for her and make her his wife.* ¹⁷ ⁽¹⁶⁾*And if her father refuses to give her to him, he must pay money equal to the bride-price for virgins.*

¹⁸ ⁽¹⁷⁾*A female sorcerer you will not allow to live.*

¹⁹ ⁽¹⁸⁾*Anyone who lies with an animal shall be put to death.*

²⁰ ⁽¹⁹⁾*Anyone who sacrifices to gods, other than Yahweh alone, will be devoted to destruction.*

²¹ ⁽²⁰⁾*And a resident alien you will not wrong and you will not oppress him, for resident aliens were you in the land of Egypt.*

²² ⁽²¹⁾*Any widow or orphan you will not abuse.* ²³ ⁽²²⁾*If you abuse him, when he cries to me, I will indeed hear his cry.* ²⁴ ⁽²³⁾*And my anger will become hot and I will kill you with the sword. And your wives will be widows and your children orphans.*

²⁵ ⁽²⁴⁾*If you lend money to my people, to the poor among you, you will not be to him like a creditor. You will not place on him interest.*

²⁶ ⁽²⁵⁾*If you take your neighbor's cloak in pledge, before the sun sets you must return it to him,* ²⁷ ⁽²⁶⁾*for it is his only covering, it is the cloak for his skin. With what will he lie down? And it will be if he cries to me, I will hear, because I am compassionate.*

²⁸ ⁽²⁷⁾*God you shall not slight. And a leader of your people you shall not curse.*

²⁹ ⁽²⁸⁾*The firstfruits of your fruits and the firstfruits of the wine from your press you shall not delay.*

The firstborn of your sons you will give to me. ³⁰ ⁽²⁹⁾*Thus you will also do with your oxen and with your sheep. Seven days it will be with its mother. On the eighth day you will give it to me.*

³¹ ⁽³⁰⁾*Holy humans you will be to me. And mangled flesh in the field you will not eat. To the dogs you will throw it.*

²³:¹*You shall not lift up a false report. You shall not join your hands with the wicked to be a malicious witness.* ²*You shall not follow the majority to promote violence. You shall not give testimony on a suit to support the majority to pervert justice.* ³*And to the poor you shall not show deference in his lawsuit.*

⁴*When you come upon your enemy's ox or his donkey wandering, you must return it to him.* ⁵*When you see the donkey of one who hates you lying under its burden and you would refrain from helping it, you must assist it.*

⁶*You shall not pervert the rule of your poor in his lawsuit.*

⁷*From a false charge you shall keep far away. The innocent and the righteous one you shall not kill, for I will not acquit the guilty.* ⁸*And a bribe you will not take, for the bribe blinds those who see, and distorts the words of the righteous.*

⁹*And a resident alien you shall not oppress, and you know the life of the resident alien, for resident aliens were you in the land of Egypt.*

¹⁰*Six days you shall sow your land, and you shall gather in its yield.* ¹¹*But the seventh you shall let it rest and lie fallow. And the needy of your people will eat. And what they leave the wild animals will eat. Thus you will do with your vineyard and your olive orchard.* ¹²*Six days you shall do your work. But on the seventh day you shall rest, so that your ox and your ass may rest. Your home-born slave and the resident alien may be refreshed.*

¹³*And in all I have said to you, you must be observant. And the name of other gods you shall not remember, and they shall not be heard on your lips.*

¹⁴*Three times you will hold a festival for me in the year.* ¹⁵*The Feast of Unleavened Bread you will observe. For seven days you will eat unleavened bread, as I commanded you, at the appointed time in the month of Abib, for in it you came out from Egypt. And no one shall appear before me empty-handed.* ¹⁶*And the Festival of Harvest of the firstfruits of your work of what you sow in the field. And the*

Festival of Ingathering at the end of the year, when you gather your work from the field. [17] *Three times in the year all your males shall appear before the Lord, Yahweh.*

[18] *You shall not sacrifice with leaven the blood of my sacrifice. And you shall not let the fat of my festival remain until morning.*

[19] *The first of the firstfruits of your ground you shall bring to the house of Yahweh, your God.*

You shall not boil a kid in the milk of its mother.

Notes

21:1 *the rules.* Hebrew *mišpāṭim* is difficult to translate. The word ranges in meaning to include judgment, decision, custom, right, ordinance, rule, and claim (BDB 1048-49; *HALOT* 1:651-52). Translators debate whether the word designates the general process of judicial ruling or the more precise written legal standards of conduct codified in the form of casuistic law. L. Schwienhorst-Schönberger notes that the problem of translation is often tied to the interpretation of the function of 21:1. Many interpreters view 21:1 as a heading or title translating *mišpāṭim* narrowly to refer to a fixed form of casuistic law in 21:1–22:17 in contrast to the *dĕbārîm* ("words"), which are more apodictically oriented laws in 22:18–23:19. The distinction between the *mišpāṭim* and the *dĕbārîm* does not arise from 21:1–23:33, but from 24:3: "And Moses approached, and he read to the people all the *dibrê yhwh* and all the *mišpāṭim*." Exodus 21:1 may also be interpreted as the promulgation of law, in which case 21:1 would encompass the entire body of law in 21:2–23:19. The syntax of 21:1 parallels most closely the promulgation of law by Moses in Deut 4:44: "And this *(wĕzō't)* is the law *(hattôrâ)* which Moses placed before the Israelites," which suggests more the promulgation of law.[1] The LXX translates, *dikaiōmata*, which carries the same broad range of meaning from pleading to documents.

21:2 *he will serve.* The Sam adds a pronominal suffix, "he will serve *you*" *(y'bdk),* which also appears in the LXX, *soi.*

but in the seventh, he shall go out free without cost. Hebrew *ḥopšî* indicates a person emancipated from debt slavery. The status of the person after six years of service is described further as *ḥinnām,* "in vain, without cause," meaning in this context that all debts are paid in full. J. W. Marshall notes that the designation of the person as "free" may indicate an economically underprivileged class of emancipated slaves.[2] The LXX translates, *eleutheros dōrean,* "free without obligation."

21:3 *if single he came, single he goes out.* Hebrew *bĕgappô* translates more lit. "with his body," meaning alone without wife or family. The LXX translates, *ean autos monos eiselthē,* "if he comes in single."

---

1. Schwienhorst-Schönberger, *Bundesbuch,* 299-301. See also J. M. Sprinkle, *The Book of the Covenant: A Literary Approach* (JSOTSup 174; Sheffield: Sheffield Academic Press, 1994), 32-33.

2. J. W. Marshall, *Israel and the Book of the Covenant: An Anthropological Approach to Biblical Law* (SBLDS 140; Atlanta: Scholars Press, 1994), 122.

21:5 *But if the slave says.* Hebrew *'āmōr yō'mar* is emphatic, perhaps suggesting a situation of taking an oath, "declares emphatically." The LXX translates, *ean de apokritheis eipē ho pais,* "and if answering, the slave says."

21:6 *then his master shall bring him to the God.* Hebrew *'el-hā'ĕlōhîm,* "to the God," is changed in the LXX to "the tribunal place of God" (cf. below). Interpreters debate the meaning, whether the reference is cultic (the sanctuary) or juridical (the magistrates). See the commentary.

and he will bring him to the door or to the doorpost. The LXX reinterprets the setting more precisely: first, the slave is led *pros to kritērion tou theou,* "to the tribunal place of God," and then more specifically, *epi tēn thyran epi ton stathmon,* "to the door, to the doorpost."

21:8 *who designated her for himself.* The Kethib of the Hebrew *lō' yĕ'ādāh* translates, "he [the master] does not designate her," indicating that *lō'* is the negation. My translation follows the Qere, *lô,* "to him," which is closer to the LXX, *hēn hautō kathōmologēsato,* "to whom she is married." Cf. Dohmen, who retains the Kethib, translating, "so dass er sie nicht (zur Frau) bestimmt" ("so that he does not appoint her [for a wife]").[3]

21:13 *And if he did not lie in wait.* Hebrew *'ăšer* is used to introduce the conditional clause (GKC §159cc). Hebrew *lō' ṣādâ,* "he did not lie in wait," is translated in the LXX, *ho de ouch hekōn,* "the one who acts unwittingly."

he will flee. The LXX identifies the one fleeing as "the killer" *(ho phoneusas).*

21:18 *And when humans quarrel.* Hebrew *yĕrîbūn,* "to quarrel," implies a juridical background (see 17:2). The LXX *loidorōntai,* "rebuke, revile," suggests a more general setting of conflict.

21:19 *will go unpunished.* Hebrew *wĕniqqâ* means "to acquit."

he will pay him for his lost time. Hebrew *šibtô yittēn,* "he will give his rest," may mean that a person must take the victim's place, perhaps in work.[4]

and he will arrange for his cure. Hebrew *wĕrappō' yĕrappē'* may be translated, "and he shall be fully healed," in which case the subject of the clause is the injured person. The LXX simply translates, *ta iatreia,* "the healing."

21:20 *and he dies under his hand.* Hebrew *ûmēt taḥat yādô* means that the slave dies immediately from the blow.

21:21 *he stands.* Hebrew *ya'ămōd* means to survive. The LXX translates, *diabiōsē,* "he survives."

because he is the master's property. The words "the master's" are inserted for clarity. The Hebrew states: "He is his property."

21:22 *but there is no deadly accident.* The translation of Hebrew *'āsôn* is debated. The LXX translates with *exeikonizō,* "to be fully formed," and interprets the phrase as a description of the fetus: "The child of her comes out and is not fully formed *(mē exeikonismenon)."* R. Westbrook states that *'āsôn* refers to the one who struck the

---

3. Dohmen, *Exodus 19–40,* 239.

4. See F. C. Fensham, "Exodus XXI, 18-19 in the Light of Hittite Law," *VT* 10 (1960): 333-35.

woman and indicates that the assailant is not identified. His reading is based on the three instances of the word in the story of Joseph (Gen 42:4, 38; 44:29). Thus he translates: "Damage caused by an unknown perpetrator."[5] Houtman argues from the larger context of Exod 21:22-25 that *'āsôn* is directed toward the pregnant woman and not the fetus, and that the word indicates a fatal injury. He translates: "But she herself is not fatally injured."[6] Schwienhorst-Schönberger concludes that *'āsôn* designates damage, but not a fatal injury.[7]

according to the arbitration. The meaning of Hebrew *biplilîm* is uncertain. Hebrew *pālîl* means "judge," and the verb *pālal* means "to arbitrate." The LXX translates, *meta axiōmatos*, "according to the judicial assessment." Houtman translates, "miscarriage," relating the roots *pll* and *npl*, "to fall." In this case "the fallen ones" *(biplilîm)* would be the fetuses who were miscarried.[8]

21:23 *but if there is a deadly accident.* The LXX continues the interpretation of the law with the focus on the fetus. It states that if the fetus is fully formed, the *lex talionis* is applied.

21:26 *and he destroys it.* The LXX translates, *ektyphlōsē*, "and he causes blindness."

21:28 *to death.* Hebrew *wāmēt* is lit. "and he dies."

21:29 *in the habit of goring yesterday and the day before.* The idiomatic phrase in Hebrew, *mitmōl šilšōm*, also appears in 5:14.

21:31 *if it gores.* The Hebrew lacks *'im*, "if."

22:1-4 (21:37–22:3) The order of the laws is rearranged in some translations (NEB, NRSV). The result is the following sequence in the English versification: 22:1, 3b, 4, 2, 3a. The new arrangement results in the laws of theft and restitution (vv. 1, 3b, 4) followed by the laws of bloodguilt (vv. 2-3a).

22:2 (1) *if when digging the thief is found.* Hebrew *bammaḥteret* likely describes the breach made in a wall to enter a house. See also Jer 2:34. The LXX translates, *diorygmati*, "cut, canal."

22:5-6 (4-5) The two laws regarding damage to the field of a neighbor are related by the word *bā'ar*. Schwienhorst-Schönberger notes that the root has three meanings: to burn, to graze over, and to be unreasonable. The first law focuses on the meaning "to graze over; to ravage," and the second law focuses on the meaning "to burn."

22:5 (4) *restitution must be made from the best of his field and from the best of his vineyard.* The Sam and LXX expand the restitution, making the normal yield of crop the standard for compensation.

22:8 (7) *if he did not send his hand against the goods of his neighbor.* Hebrew *'im-lō'* introduces a negative protasis (*IBHS* §38.2d), "if not." The LXX interprets the phrase as an oath, *kai omeitai*, "and he shall swear." Cf. NRSV: "To determine whether or not the owner had laid hands on the neighbor's goods."

5. R. Westbrook, "Lex Talionis and Exodus 21, 22-25," *RB* 93 (1986): 52-69.
6. Houtman, *Exodus*, 3:160, 163, 168.
7. Schwienhorst-Schönberger, *Bundesbuch*, 89-94.
8. Houtman, *Exodus*, 3:162-63.

22:9 (8) *the one whom God condemns.* Hebrew *yaršîʿūn* is plural, suggesting the alternative translation, "they [the gods] condemn."

22:11 (10) *an oath before Yahweh.* Hebrew *šĕbūʿat yhwh* is changed in the LXX: *horkos estai tou theou,* "an oath will be to God."

if he did not send his hand against the goods of his neighbor. See 22:8.

its owner will accept. Hebrew *lāqaḥ,* "to take, accept," is translated in the LXX, *prosdexetai,* "receive favorably, accept."

22:13 (12) *was mangled as prey.* Hebrew *ṭārap,* "to tear apart," occurs three times in the verse: twice as a verb, "was mangled as prey," and once as a noun, "the mauled animal."

he will bring it as evidence. The MT *yĕbīʾēhû* includes the object suffix on the verb, indicating that the accused person will show the mauled animal as evidence. The Sam includes only the verb without object, *ybʾ,* translating, "he will bring a witness." The LXX provides yet another version, *axei auton epi tēn thēran,* "he will take him [the owner of the animal] to the mauled animal."

22:14 (13) *When a person requests from his neighbor.* The MT lacks an object.

22:17 (16) *he must pay money.* Hebrew *yišqōl,* "to weigh," is translated in the LXX, *apotisei,* "to pay restitution," which is given to the father *(tō patri).*

22:18 (17) *a female sorcerer.* Hebrew *mĕkaššēpâ* is restricted to women. The LXX translates, *pharmakous,* "sorcerers," which is not restricted to women.

22:20 (19) *Anyone who sacrifices to gods, other than Yahweh alone, will be devoted to destruction.* The Hebrew word order is different from the translation: "Any one who sacrifices to gods, will be devoted to destruction, except to Yahweh alone." The Sam reads: "Any one sacrificing to other gods will be devoted to destruction" *(zbḥ lʾlhym ʾḥrym yḥrm).*

22:23 (22) *If you abuse him, when he cries to me, I will indeed hear his cry.* The LXX translates in the plural (e.g., "them," "their voice").

22:26 (25) *take your neighbor's cloak in pledge.* NRSV translates Hebrew *ḥābōl taḥbōl* as "to take in pawn."

22:27 (26) *his skin.* Hebrew *ʿōr* means the "bare body." The LXX translates, *aschēmosynēs,* "private parts."

22:28 (27) *you shall not slight.* Hebrew *qālal* could also be translated more strongly, "to curse."

and a leader of your people you shall not curse. Hebrew *nāśîʾ* could also be translated "chieftain" (see NJPS).

22:29 (28) *the firstfruits of your fruits and the firstfruits of the wine from your press you shall not delay.* The translation follows the LXX. The meaning of the MT is unclear.

23:2 *you shall not give testimony on a lawsuit to support the majority to pervert justice.* The Hebrew is difficult. The verb *taʿăneh* in a legal context means "to give testimony." The following phrase, *ʿal-rīb,* is translated, "on a lawsuit." Cf. the LXX, which translates, "with the majority." This is the second occurrence of *nāṭâ* as a Hiphil infinitive, lit. "to cause to extend." In the Hiphil the verb can mean "to twist" justice, which is reflected in the translation, "to pervert justice."

23:5 *when you see the donkey of one who hates you lying under its burden and you would refrain from helping it, you must assist it.* The first part of the law is clear, but the second half of the law is debated. The problem is the threefold use of the Hebrew verb *ʿāzab.* The verb is common in the Hebrew Bible with the meaning "to leave, to abandon." But interpreters have had difficulty maintaining the same meaning for all three instances. A second meaning of the root *ʿzb* has also been identified as "to make, to prepare, to set," corresponding to Ugaritic *ʿdb,* which is reflected in Neh 3:8 and 4:2 (MT 3:34) with the meaning "to rise up."[9] A variety of translations are offered depending on which meaning of the verb is chosen. A. Cooper focuses on the abandonment of the animal: "And you would refrain from leaving *(mēʿăzōb)* it [the donkey], you must leave *(ʿāzōb taʿăzōb)* the animal alone."[10] My translation employs the root meaning "to rise up," which could focus on either the animal or the enemy (see also NRSV and NJPS).[11] Childs presents yet another translation, focusing the law on the enemy and not the animal, and employing both meanings of the verb: "You must by no means abandon him. You must help him with it."[12]

23:7 *for I will not acquit the guilty.* The MT provides a theological explanation with the divine statement in the first person. The LXX states the phrase as a command in the second person: "And you will not acquit the ungodly *(asebē)* for the sake of gifts *(heneken dōrōn).*"

23:13 *you must be observant.* NRSV translates Hebrew *tiššāmērû* as "be attentive."

23:15 *the month of Abib.* Hebrew *ʾābîb* means "ears." The LXX translates, *tōn neōn,* "new grains."

23:16 *and the Festival of Harvest.* Hebrew *qāṣîr,* "harvest, reaping," is translated in the LXX, *therismou,* "harvest, reaping." Hebrew *ḥag,* "festival," means a pilgrimage festival.

the Festival of Ingathering. Hebrew *ʾāsîp,* "harvesting," is from the verb *ʾāsap,* "to gather." The LXX translates, *synteleias,* "consummation, completion," from the verb *synteleō,* "to complete."

at the end of the year. Hebrew *bĕṣēʾt haššānâ* is lit. "in the going out of the year."

23:17 *the Lord, Yahweh.* Hebrew *hāʾādon yhwh,* "the Lord, Yahweh," is unusual. The LXX translates, *kyriou tou theou sou,* "the Lord, your God."

23:18 *you shall not sacrifice with leaven the blood of my sacrifice.* Hebrew *ʿal-ḥāmēṣ* suggests "in conjunction with leaven." The LXX *epi zymē* may indicate location, according to Wevers: "You shall not sacrifice in the presence of or near anything leaven."[13]

23:19 *the first of the firstfruits.* Hebrew *rēʾšît,* "first," can also mean "choicest" (see NRSV).

---

9. See the review in A. Cooper, "The Plain Sense of Exodus 23:5," *HUCA* 59 (1988): 1-22; H. G. Williamson, "A Reconsideration of *ʿzb* II in Biblical Hebrew," *ZAW* 97 (1985): 74-85.

10. Cooper, "Plain Sense," 15-16.

11. See the discussion in Houtman, *Exodus,* 3:244-46.

12. Childs, *Exodus,* 445, 450-51.

13. Wevers, *Notes,* 369.

Commentary

21:1 The opening verse identifies the following laws as "ordinances," "judgments," or "rules" *(mišpāṭîm).* The syntax, "these are the rules" *(wĕ'ēlleh hammišpāṭîm),* suggests a title, even recalling the similar phraseology from the opening verse of Exodus: "These are the names of the sons of Israel" *(wĕ'ēlleh šĕmôt bĕnê yiśrā'ēl).* The rules provide the content of the covenant law from the proposal of covenant (19:1-8a): "These are the words that you will speak to the people of Israel" (19:6). In the present narrative context the *Mishpatim* may include the divine discourse through 23:33. The traditional practice is to limit the *Mishpatim* to the casuistic law in 21:2–22:17, followed by the *Debarim* in 22:18–23:19, and an epilogue in 23:20-33. The separation of the *Mishpatim* from the *Debarim* derives from 24:3, not from the internal structure of the laws. The conclusion in 23:20-33 is more clearly separated from the laws as a series of promises in exchange for obedience. I interpret 21:1–23:19 as one law code in its present form, noting smaller divisions on the basis of content or writing style. I interpret 23:20-33 as the conclusion to the law code.

21:2-11 The central role of debt slavery in ancient Israel is evident in the repetition of slave laws in 21:2-11; Deut 15:12-18; and Lev 25:39-54, and in the multiple accounts of the Israelites' entering debt slavery (e.g., 2 Kgs 4:1; Jer 34:8-22; Neh 5:1-13). The prophet Elisha rescues a widow's two sons from debt slavery by miraculously filling jars with oil (2 Kgs 4:1-7). Jeremiah criticizes the leaders of Judah at the time of King Zedekiah for taking back their male and female Hebrew slaves after performing a covenant ritual of release in the temple (Jer 34:8-11), associated with the seventh year (Jer 34:14). Nehemiah 5 presents an even more complex situation in the postexilic period in which Jewish landowners are selling off their kinsmen to foreigners, requiring Nehemiah to purchase back Jewish slaves from Gentiles.

Scholars have traditionally interpreted the laws of debt slavery as progressing from the Book of the Covenant (Exod 21:2-11), where the laws are different for males and females, to Deuteronomy (15:12-18), where there is no distinction between male and female, and finally to the P legislation (Lev 25:39-54), where the status of debt slavery is changed to that of the resident alien. But Van Seters has reversed the order, suggesting that the prohibition against selling an Israelite woman to a foreigner (Exod 21:8) reflects the postexilic situation of Nehemiah 5.[14] Evaluating the history of slavery in ancient Israel on the basis of the laws is complicated by questions of genre surrounding the nature of ancient Near Eastern law codes. C. M. Carmichael rejects any historical reading of the laws and suggests instead that the multiple accounts are intended to provide commentary on different stories: the Book of the Covenant addresses the near-

---

14. Van Seters, "Law of the Hebrew Slave," 535-46; idem, *Law Book,* 82-95.

slave status of Jacob; Leviticus 25 is commentary on Joseph's slavery in Egypt; Deuteronomy 15 evaluates the Israelite slavery in Egypt.[15]

The slave laws in the ancient Near East provide a broader vantage point for interpreting the role of the slave laws in the structure of the Book of the Covenant. The frequent comparison to Mesopotamian law in the exegesis of Exod 21:2-11 indicates the common culture of the legal tradition regulating slavery in the ancient Near East. In addition to the slave laws cited from Nuzi, the topic is also included in the Laws of Eshnunna (§§16, 22, 23, 31, 34-35, 40, 49-52, 55, 57), the Laws of Lipit-Ishtar (§§12-14, 25-26), the Laws (or Code) of Hammurabi (see below), the Hittite laws (I.1, 3, 8, 12, 14, 16, 18, 20-24, 31-36, 52, 95, 97, 99; II.194, 196), the Middle Assyrian Laws (A.4, 39, 41, 44, 48; C + G.1, 2, 3, 7, 9), and the Neo-Babylonian Laws (§6). M. A. Dandamayev summarizes the prominence of slavery in the ancient Near East: the "institution of slavery had a profound influence on the social structure, ideology, law, social psychology, morals and ethics of the various cultures of the ANE [ancient Near East]."[16] According to H. J. Boecker, ancient society was structured in three levels: independent free persons (landowners and craftsmen), semi-independent serfs (laborers for the palace or temple who might also own property), and slaves (human property or chattel). The slave class was an "essential factor in the economy" of the ancient world.[17]

The most significant law code for understanding slavery in the ancient world is that of Hammurabi, written in the second millennium. The laws regarding male and female slaves are not confined to any one section, but they appear throughout the law code under a variety of topics. A central presupposition is that slaves are property requiring a series of laws on property damage (any free person damaging a slave must pay compensation, §199; see also §§213, 214, 231), warranty (an epileptic attack within one month of purchase negates the sale of a slave, §278), resale (§§118, 119), insurance against improper health care (a surgeon who kills a slave in operation must repay the owner, §219; see also §223), theft (§7), and workplace compensation (a slave owner is owed one-third mina for any slave gored by an ox, §252). Other laws regulate the behavior of slaves stating the punishment for aiding a slave in an escape (§§15-20) or in assisting with the removal of a slave brand (§§226, 227). Still other laws address the circumstances by which a person might move between the different social classes from free to slave (debt slavery, §§117-119) or from slave to free (the laws of redemption, §§32, 116-119). The laws regulating marriage also address the change of status between free persons and slaves (§§144, 146, 147, 175, 176). H. Petschow suggests that slave laws play a role in the structure of the Laws of

---

15. Carmichael, "Three Laws," 509-25.
16. M. A. Dandamayev, "Slavery (ANE), (OT)," *ABD* 6:58-65, quotation 61.
17. Boecker, *Law and Administration,* 77-78.

Hammurabi inaugurating a sequence of themes including slavery, bodily injury, commercial law, and family law.[18]

Scholars suspect the influence of the Laws of Hammurabi on the compiler or author of the Book of the Covenant. The nature of the influence ranges from direct literary dependence (Gressmann, Westbrook) to a more general shared culture of law (Boecker, E. Otto).[19] Following the work of Petschow, V. Wagner argued that the compiler of the Book of the Covenant was working within a school or scribal tradition of law evident in the Laws of Hammurabi that resulted in the sequence: slavery (21:2-11), bodily injury (21:18-32), liability (21:33–22:15), with a small section on marriage (22:16-17).[20] Like the Laws of Hammurabi, slave laws are not confined to one section of the Book of the Covenant. They assume a primary position as the initial legislation in 21:2-11. Laws regulating slaves reappear in three other sections in the Book of the Covenant: the law protecting a slave from abuse (any slave hurt by an owner is given freedom as compensation for the damage, 21:26-27), the property rights of a slave master (if a slave is gored by another person's ox, the slave owner must be compensated for the damaged property, 21:32), and the law of the Sabbath rest for slaves (23:10-12).

The repetition between the Sabbath release of debt slaves (21:2-11) and the law of the Sabbath rest for slaves is striking (23:10-12), suggesting literary design in the composition of the Book of the Covenant (see the outline by Dohmen above). More recent studies have identified additional structures in the distribution of the slave laws in the Book of the Covenant. G. C. Chirichigno concludes that the slave laws organize 21:2-27: the laws of release (21:2-11 and 26-27) form the outer frame, with the law on the assault of slaves (21:20-21) at the center.[21] Otto broadens the literary analysis, interpreting the protection of debt slaves (21:2-11) and the protection of the resident alien and poor (22:21-25) as a frame for the first half of the Book of the Covenant.[22] The psychological identification with the resident alien from the Israelite experience of slavery in Egypt certainly reinforces Otto's interpretation (23:9).

Exodus 21:2-11 consists of two slave laws. Verses 2-6 focus on the condi-

---

18. H. Petschow, "Zur Systematik und Gesetzestechnik im Codex Hammurabi," *ZA* 23 (1965): 146-72.

19. Schwienhorst-Schönberger (*Bundesbuch*, 240-68) provides an excellent overview of the varying positions regarding the cultural and literary relationship between the Book of the Covenant and the Laws of Hammurabi.

20. V. Wagner, "Zur Systematik in dem Codex Ex 21,2–22,16," *ZAW* 81 (1969): 176-82.

21. Chirichigno, *Debt-Slavery*, 196.

22. Otto, *Wandel*, 9-11; idem, *Rechtsgeschichte der Redaktionen im Kodex Ešnunna und im "Bundesbuch:" Eine redaktionsgeschichtliche und rechtsvergleichende Studie zu altbabylonischen und altisraelitischen Rechtsüberlieferungen* (OBO 85; Göttingen: Vandenhoeck & Ruprecht, 1989), 7-14.

tions of service and release of Hebrew males from debt slavery. Verses 7-11 outline the legal rights of a female Hebrew slave bride. Both laws are casuistic in form. The principal case is introduced by the word *kî*, translated "when," and secondary cases are introduced by the word *'im*, translated "if."

The first law, vv. 2-6, focuses on the release of Hebrew male slaves. The principal case is stated in v. 2: "When you buy *(qānâ)* a Hebrew *('ibrî)* slave, he shall serve you for six years. But in the seventh year he shall go out *(yāṣā')* free *(ḥopšî)* without cost." The verb "to buy" indicates the act of purchase, not simply of slaves (Lev 22:11; 25:44-45) but also of other commodities such as land (Gen 25:10; 33:19). The law is addressed to the person buying a slave. The description of the slave as "free" indicates emancipation. Similar language in the Laws of Hammurabi suggests that the purchase of such a slave results from unpaid debt: "If an obligation is outstanding against a man and he sells or gives into debt service his wife, his son, or his daughter, they shall perform service in the house of their buyer or of the one who holds them in debt service for three years; their release shall be secured in the fourth year" (§117).[23] The comparison underscores the lengthening of service in 21:2-6 with the release in the seventh year.

The word "Hebrew" has prompted debate on the scope of the law since the term may indicate social class or ethnicity (see the commentary on 1:8-14). Cassuto interprets the word broadly as social class, thus including native and foreign persons within the law.[24] S. M. Paul reinforces the interpretation on the basis of Nuzi service contracts from the mid-second millennium in which the word *ḥabiru* also indicates a social class consisting of "self-enslaved individuals who, occasionally with their families, served their patrons in return for food and raiment."[25] But Chirichigno cautions against the comparison, noting that there is no money exchange in the Nuzi laws.[26] He argues that the word "Hebrew" in 21:2 refers to an Israelite debt slave. Childs adds support for this interpretation, noting the explicit reference to "foreigner" in 21:8, which suggests that the focus of the slave laws is on Israelites.

The ethnic interpretation of "Hebrew" does not exclude a connotation of social class in the word, at least in view of its broader use in Exodus where the identity of the Israelites as Hebrews is interwoven with slave imagery in the opening chapters. N. Na'aman notes that the term "Hebrew," although designating an ethnic group, is often used in situations of oppression.[27] The literary

---

23. Roth, *Law Collections*, 103.

24. Cassuto, *Exodus*, 266-67.

25. Paul, *Book of the Covenant*, 45-53. See M. P. Maidman, "Nuzi: Portrait of an Ancient Mesopotamian Provincial Town," *CANE* 2:931-47.

26. Chirichigno, *Debt-Slavery*, 92-97.

27. N. Na'aman, "Ḥabiru and Hebrews: The Transfer of a Social Term to the Literary Sphere," *JNES* 45 (1986): 271-88.

relationship between the law of debt slavery and the story of the exodus is further reinforced by the verb "to go out" as the description of release from slavery, "in the seventh year he will go out *(yāṣā')*." Paul adds that the verb is a legal term for the release from slave status.[28] As is evident in the prologue to the Decalogue, the verb is also a central metaphor for the Israelites' salvation from Egypt. God's self-identification interweaves the exodus and slave imagery: "I am Yahweh your God, who brought you out *(yāṣā')* of Egypt, out of the land of slavery."

Verses 3-6 add four conditions to the law of release from debt slavery. The first three describe the circumstances for leaving the status of slavery (vv. 3-4). If an Israelite male enters debt slavery unmarried, he will also leave single. If he entered married, his family will also be released with him. But if an Israelite male entered debt slavery single and was married while a slave, his wife and children cannot leave their slave status. They remain the property of the owner, and only the man is released from debt slavery.

The final condition in vv. 5-6 provides an additional option for the Hebrew male who marries while in debt slavery. It appears to be the point of focus of the conditions for release from debt slavery, outlining the procedures for the man to become a permanent slave and thus remain with his family. Verse 5 provides the oath by which the slave makes public declaration: "I love my master and my wife and children, and I will not go out free." The declaration of love is unique in biblical law. It likely has legal force, as does its antonym, "hate," in divorce law (Deut 22:13-16).

The ceremony in v. 6 is also a public act legalizing the permanent slave status of the man. But the location is debated. The Hebrew law states: "His master will bring him to the God/gods." The meaning of the phrase "to the God/god(s)" *('el-hā'ĕlōhîm)* is debated. One interpretation emphasizes the plural form of the Hebrew, translating "gods." The ceremony according to this interpretation is taking place in the house of the master before the household gods, known as the Ilani in Nuzi adoption law.[29] The ceremony is a ritual for incorporating the slave into the household economy. The second interpretation substitutes the word "judges," as in NIV, "then his master must take him before the judges." The evidence is based on historical conjecture about the age of the law, on the use of the word "judges" in the Targums and the Peshitta, and on 22:8, which pairs the Hebrew *'ĕlōhîm*, "gods," with a plural verb. C. H. Gordon has demonstrated the weakness of this translation.[30] The third and strongest reading is that the ritual

---

28. Paul, *Book of the Covenant,* 47-48.

29. Ibid., 49-51.

30. C. H. Gordon, "אלהים in Its Reputed Meaning of *Rulers, Judges,*" *JBL* 54 (1935): 139-44.

describes an action in the sanctuary "before the God." Z. W. Falk notes that slaves are released through temple rituals in Babylon, suggesting that a ritual of transition from free status to permanent slavery may also have a cultic setting.[31]

The second half of v. 6 describes a ritual whereby the master pierces the ear of the slave, marking his permanent slave status. Slaves were often marked in some physical way in the ancient Near East. The Laws of Hammurabi also indicate that slaves were branded in some way (§§226-227). The relationship of the two halves of v. 6 is unclear. How does the appearance before God and the bringing of the slave to the doorpost relate? Does v. 6 describe a sequence of actions in the temple? Is the doorpost a different setting, perhaps at the home of the master? A. Loretz argues that vv. 5-6 describe one action. The appearance before God and the doweling of the slaves ear occur simultaneously while the slave publicly declares his love for his master.[32]

The second law, vv. 7-11, describes the conditions of a female Hebrew sold as a concubine or slave bride. The principal clause in v. 7 denies release from debt slavery to such a woman: "When a man sells *(mākar)* his daughter as a slave *('āmâ)*, she shall not to go out *(yāṣā')* as the male slaves go out." The focus on a marriage contract, as opposed to nonsexual slave labor, suggests a close literary relationship to the preceding law on male debt slavery, where the emphasis of the conditions was also on marriage. The direct comparison to "male slaves" further strengthens the literary relationship between the two slave laws. The primary difference between the two is the absence of any release for the woman. The daughter has no freedom since she is already a commodity of her father to be sold to another man in a marriage contract. C. Pressler notes the "extensive authority a father has over his daughter. He may sell her into bondage. She is one of his economic assets; her economic worth is, first of all, her sexuality and her reproductive capacity."[33] The sale changes her status from daughter *(bat)* to slave *('āmâ)*. A. Jepsen defines the slave status more precisely: she is an "unfree woman as well as a second wife of a free man and also an unfree woman of an unfree man."[34] Paul notes similar marriage contract laws from Nuzi entitled "document of daughtership and daughter-in-law-ship."[35]

The point of emphasis in the law of the concubine is on the conditions in

---

31. Z. W. Falk, "Exodus XXI:6," *VT* 9 (1959): 86-88; see also A. Viberg, *Symbols of Law: A Contextual Analysis of Legal Symbolic Acts in the Old Testament* (ConBOT 34; Stockholm: Almqvist & Wiksell, 1992), 77-87.

32. A. Loretz, "Ex 21,6; 22,8 und angebliche Nuzi-Parallelen," *Bib* 41 (1960): 167-75.

33. C. Pressler, "Wives and Daughters, Bond and Free," in *Gender and Law in the Hebrew Bible and the Ancient Near East* (ed. V. H. Matthews et al.; JSOTSup 262; Sheffield: Sheffield Academic Press, 1998), 162.

34. A. Jepsen, "*Ama*[h] und *Schiphcha*[h]," *VT* 8 (1958): 293-97.

35. Paul, *Book of the Covenant*, 52.

vv. 8-11, which qualify and even negate the principal law. The result is that the law of the slave women begins to mirror the law of the slave man (cf. the repetition between vv. 2 and 11). The first condition in v. 8 protects the woman against rejection by the purchaser: "If she is displeasing in the eyes of her master who designated *(yā'ad)* her for himself, he must let her be redeemed (Hiphil of *pādâ*)." Three features of the translation require comment: the phrase "for himself," the verb "to designate," and the meaning and scope of redemption. The translation follows the LXX, not the MT. The latter has the word "not" *(lō')*, rather than the prepositional phrase "for himself" *(lô)*. Most interpreters follow the LXX, since the MT reading may be internally contradictory: "If she does not please the master, who has *not* selected her, he must let her be redeemed." If he has not selected her, why would she be in need of redemption? Dohmen resolves the potential contradiction with the translation: "Falls sie ihrem Herrn missfällt, so dass er sie nicht (zur Frau) bestimmt, dann soll er sie auslösen lassen" ("if she displeases her master, so that he does not appoint her [for a wife], then he should let her leave").[36]

Carmichael provides an answer, suggesting a change in the verb from "designate"*(yā'ad)* to "know" *(yāda')*, which often has a sexual meaning in Hebrew. The result is the following translation: "If she does not please the master, who has not had intercourse with her, he must let her be redeemed." Carmichael notes that his reading also resolves a potential conflict between this condition and the last, which advocates the free release of the woman, rather than a financial ransom as is the case here.[37]

The problem with Carmichael's solution is that, according to Paul, the verb "to designate" is likely a technical term describing a type of marriage with parallels in Mesopotamian marriage law.[38] The law stipulates that redemption through ransom is allowed if the master breaks the contract. But the range of persons who are able to redeem the woman is not specified. The law is precise in stating that the slave woman cannot be sold to a "foreigner," a term that in its broadest meaning indicates anyone outside the Israelite community and, in its most narrow meaning, indicates her family.

The second condition in v. 9 outlines the legal rights of a woman who is bought as the wife for a son. Noth suggests that the law follows as a consequence of the previous condition, meaning that she was not redeemed by her family and is now passed on to a son by the original purchaser.[39] The interpretation is certainly possible, but it is just as likely that this law is independent of

---

36. Dohmen, *Exodus 19–40*, 139.
37. Carmichael, *Laws of Deuteronomy*, 57-59.
38. Paul, *Book of the Covenant*, 54.
39. Noth, *Exodus*, 179.

the first condition and simply states another qualification of the principal law in v. 7. The point of the condition is that the status of a woman purchased for marriage to a son must be safeguarded. She is not described as "slave" in this condition. Rather she must have "the rights of a daughter" *(kĕmišpaṭ habbānôt yaʿăśeh-lāh)*. Paul detects a legal background to the phrase, translating, "to treat as a free(-born) woman."[40]

The third condition in v. 10 safeguards the slave wife in cases where the master/husband takes a second wife. The law specifies three requirements in the case of a polygamous marriage: flesh *(šĕʾēr)*, meaning most likely food but may also include physical needs including sex; clothing *(kĕsût)*; and an unknown requirement *(ʿōnāt)* that only occurs in this law. Interpreters conjecture that the last word means sexual intercourse, in which case "flesh" is limited to food.

The fourth condition in v. 11 is a summary about the consequences for the woman should the three previous conditions not be met. The reference to the conditions may be the food, clothing, and sex noted in the previous law, but the intention more likely concerns the previous three conditions in vv. 8, 9, and 10. The final condition negates the principal law in v. 7. It states that if any of the conditions are not met the woman "is to go out free, without any payment of money." The closing condition repeats the principal law of male Hebrew slaves from v. 2, suggesting to Chirichigno an intentional literary design in the arrangement of the two slave laws in vv. 2-6 and 7-11.[41]

21:12-17 The four laws in this section share a similar form. The actions are stated with a participle (i.e., "the one striking"), and each law stipulates the death penalty ("he shall be put to death," *môt yûmāt*). All the laws address the negation of a person, either physically by an act of murder or through the loss of one's personhood (kidnapping) or honor (cursing). Parents loom large; they are singled out in the second (murder or striking) and the fourth (cursing) laws. The death penalty returns in 22:18-20, where three additional actions are also stated with the Hebrew participle: the act of sorcery by a woman (v. 18), sex with an animal (v. 19), and sacrifices to foreign gods (v. 20). The syntactical similarities have raised the question of whether 21:12-17 and 22:18-20 were once a single collection now distributed in two places in the Book of the Covenant. But the vastly different subject matter makes a unified reading difficult.

The offense in v. 12 includes two verbs, "strikes" *(makkeh)* and "he dies" *(mēt)*. The Hebrew verb *nākâ*, "to strike," often signifies "to kill," as it does in the story of Moses striking (i.e., killing) the Egyptian taskmaster (2:12). Thus the two verbs appear redundant. The context of the laws provides some help,

40. Paul, *Book of the Covenant*, 55.
41. Chirichigno, *Debt-Slavery*, 252-54.

since the next law is also against "striking" one's parents, but the second verb, *mût*, "to die," is absent from the offense (v. 15). The context indicates that the Hebrew verb *nākâ* is not restricted to killing in this body of laws. The repetition of only the verb "to strike" may mean that any physical act against a father or mother requires the death penalty. The same narrow meaning of striking without killing also occurs in the law against bodily damage in vv. 18-19.

Verses 13-14 introduce motive as a qualification to the opening law against murder: "If he did not lie in wait" *(ṣādâ)* the death penalty is removed. The only other instance of the verb in the Hebrew Bible is the description of Saul's pursuit of David to kill him (1 Sam 24:11 [MT 12]). The P legislation employs the noun *ṣĕdîyâ*, "malicious intent," to discuss the same topic of premeditated versus accidental death (Num 35:20, 22). Thus "he did not lie in wait" must imply some form of accidental death. The event is attributed to God, not a human: "But the God moved (Piel of *'ānâ*) his hand." The psalmist uses the same verb to describe the overpowering of God: "You have overwhelmed *('ānâ)* me with all your waves" (Ps 88:7).

Accidental death gives rise to the law of asylum. The law is surprising because of its form as first person divine speech: "I will appoint for you a place *(māqôm)* to which he can flee" (Exod 21:13b). The word "place" likely indicates a sanctuary or its altar as the location of asylum. The same word indicated an altar or a sanctuary in 20:24b. Asylum is protection from bloodguilt, the economics of blood that required payment for the shedding of any blood. The story of Adonijah seizing the horns of the altar for protection from Solomon is most likely an illustration of asylum (1 Kgs 1:49-53; 2:28-35). Milgrom writes that the basic premise of asylum is "that those who touch the altar absorb its sanctity and are removed from and immune to the jurisdiction of the profane world."[42] Deuteronomy (4:41-43) and the P legislation (Num 35:9-34) transfer asylum from the sanctuary to designated "Levitical" cities. The issue of intention in the action returns one final time in Exod 21:14 to qualify the law of asylum. If a killing looks to be accidental, but is in fact an intentional murder made to look as though it were not, then the murderer is removed from asylum and executed. The story of Joab provides illustration (see 1 Kgs 2:31-33). He must be forcibly removed from the tent of meeting before he is killed by Benaiah. The Hebrew word for "forethought" is *'ormâ*, the same word used to describe the action of the Gibeonites in Josh 9:4.

The death penalty is also the punishment for kidnapping that has as its aim the trading in slavery. Exodus 21:16 states: "Whoever steals a human and sells him or he is found in his hand shall be put to death." The syntax of the law has puzzled interpreters because of the apparent contradiction between selling,

42. Milgrom, *Numbers*, 504.

yet possessing, a kidnapped victim. Daube argued that the internal contradiction results from an extension of an original law against kidnapping and selling humans. The extension of the law is the middle clause, "or he is found in his hand," which includes the death penalty even if the victim is recovered before being sold into slavery.[43] Levinson states that the syntax indicates contrast, "*whether* the person is sold, *or* is still held in possession" (see also NRSV).[44] Westbrook moves in a different direction on the basis of comparison to ancient Near Eastern law, which he argues follows a "three-cornered" pattern, meaning that legislation is addressed to three different parties: the owner of property (in this case the victim), the thief, and a third party who receives stolen property, either unwittingly or wittingly through purchase. Westbrook concludes that 21:16 undergoes a change in reference so that all three parties are included in the law. The thief receives the death penalty, as does the buyer in the case of slave trade. The law does not distinguish between an Israelite and a foreigner, although it certainly recalls the story of Joseph in Genesis 37–50.

The final death penalty law in the section (v. 17) returns to the parent and child relationship: "Whoever curses (Piel of *qālal*) his father or his mother shall be put to death." Cassuto notes the connection between this law and the Decalogue, which states the command positively: "Honor (Piel of *kābēd*) your father and your mother." He concludes that cursing is the opposite of honoring, noting the divine speech in 1 Sam 2:30: "For those who honor me I will honor, and those who despise me shall be treated with contempt ['cursed,' Piel of *qālal*]."[45] But cursing also functions as the opposite of blessing, thus giving the command the broader context of life and death. God turns Balaam's curse into a blessing according to Deut 23:5 (see also Josh 24:9-10). And Sarah accuses the pregnant Hagar of cursing her, signifying her barrenness (Gen 16:4, 5). Thus cursing parents is not only an act of disrespect but also carries metaphorical meaning, signifying death to parents, who are the source of life. Even an act of metaphorical murder receives the punishment of death.

21:18-36   A variety of laws against bodily harm are listed in this section, separating between damage that occurs directly from a human action (21:18-27) and indirectly through an owner's ox (21:28-36).

The laws of bodily harm from direct human action are organized in a descending order of value from free persons (21:18-19) to slaves (21:20-21) and finally to a fetus (21:22-23). The section ends with prescriptions of value in the form of the *talion* laws, which also distinguish between free persons (21:24-25) and slaves (21:26).

43. Daube, *Studies in Biblical Law,* 95.
44. Levinson, "Case for Revision," 46-47.
45. Cassuto, *Exodus,* 271.

Verses 18-19 outline the law regulating bodily harm from conflict between two free Israelites. The law is about redress if a person intentionally harms another by striking. The reference to stones or the fist likely indicates intention. The verb "to strike" *(nākâ)* is clear in signifying injury rather than the expected meaning of death. If the victim of a blow is bedridden for a time, but then is able to walk outside with a cane, the perpetrator is free from guilt *(nāqâ)*, presumably meaning the death penalty through blood vengeance, although it is not clearly stated. The ability to walk, according to Jackson, indicates a "degree of recovery so that any subsequent death cannot be attributed to the original assailant."[46] The perpetrator is responsible to pay for the inactivity of the victim and his health care costs.

Verses 20-21 change in focus from two free Israelites in conflict to a master and a slave. Again the law is about intentional acts of violence. Any master who strikes his male or female slave with a rod causing their death must be punished. The dead slave must be avenged *(nāqam)*. Mendenhall argues that the reference to vengeance is not bloodguilt in this case, but legal retribution.[47] Sprinkle concluded that the content of vengeance is death.[48] But who exercises the punishment if it is not bloodguilt? The answer depends in part on the status of the slave. If the person is an indentured Israelite slave, then the family would be responsible for exercising judgment, suggesting that the vengeance may be bloodguilt (see the details for exercising bloodguilt in Numbers 35). If the slave is a non-Israelite, the statement may not be a law at all, but a moral prescription without explicit punishment. Any slave not dying from a beating does not give rise to vengeance, because he or she is the property of the owner.

Exodus 21:22-23 addresses the legal status and the economic value of a fetus. The law presupposes a fight between two men in which a pregnant woman is unintentionally hit with the result that "her child goes out" *(wĕyāṣĕʾû yĕlādeyhâ)*. The phrase is ambiguous, indicating either premature birth or miscarriage. That similar laws throughout the ancient Near East focus on miscarriage suggests the same meaning in the Book of the Covenant. The Law of Hammurabi §209 provides an example: "If a person *(awilu)* strikes a woman of the *awilu*-class and thereby causes her to miscarry her fetus, he shall weigh and deliver 10 shekels of silver for her fetus."[49] An additional qualification to the law in 21:22-23 states: "but there is no deadly accident." The lack of a clear object creates ambiguity, but it is likely that the qualification is directed toward the woman, meaning she did not die in the miscarriage. In such a circumstance the

---

46. Jackson, *Studies in Semiotics*, 84-85.
47. Mendendall, *Tenth Generation*, 69-104.
48. Sprinkle, *Book of the Covenant*, 101.
49. See *ANET*, 175. See also Middle Assyrian Laws §§21, 51, 52; and Hittite Laws §§17, 18.

offender is required to pay a sum of money determined by the husband and confirmed by a public standard. The exact economic value of the fetus is not stated in the law, but its compensation is monetary, not an exchange of life.

The second part of the law, v. 23, qualifies the penalty in case of death, most likely to the woman: "But if there is a deadly accident, you will give life for life." The law is known as the *lex talionis*, the law of equal restitution or retaliation. The concept of *talion* already appears in the Laws of Hammurabi (§§196-197, 200), and it reappears in other biblical law codes. Deuteronomy 19:19 applies the law against a false witness: the judge who finds a witness guilty must "do to him as he intended to do to his brother." Leviticus 24:17-22 also applies the principle of *lex talionis* to a range of crimes, from death to bodily injury. The *lex talionis* is often interpreted as a harsh and even barbaric penalty of equivalence. The negative judgment of the law appears to receive confirmation in the teaching of Jesus as recorded in the Sermon on the Mount: "You have heard that it was said, 'Eye for eye, and tooth for tooth.' But I tell you, Do not resist an evil person. If someone strikes you on the right cheek, turn to him the other also" (Matt 5:38-39).

The negative interpretation of the *lex talionis* may have influenced the translation "life for life" *(nepeš taḥat nāpeš)*. Jackson states that the translation is too theoretical, suggesting an abstract principle of equivalence, whereas Hebrew *nepeš* is more personal. Jackson prefers the translation "person for person."[50] He adds that the verb *nātan* does not mean "to take," but the reverse, "to give." The personal character of the law, along with the focus on the one who committed the act, suggests that the context for the penalty is self-initiating and that the content of the law is substitution. In case of death to the woman the law calls for the substitution of another: "But if there is a deadly accident, you shall give person for person." J. J. Finkelstein and S. M. Paul have also argued that the *lex talionis* is an advance in justice whether it intends substitution or equal punishment.[51] The ethical advance is the transfer of wrongful death from civil law, in which the perpetrators could buy their way out of the crime, to criminal law, which held the perpetrators to a higher standard of accountability and thus also provided better protection to the victim. W. F. Albright goes so far to conclude that the *"lex talionis . . .* is . . . the principle of equal justice for all!"[52]

The law of *talion* is extended in 21:24-26. Verses 24-25 provide more detailed application of the *lex talionis* between free persons. But the details do not fit the present context. The legal case in v. 23 is concerned with the death to a

---

50. Jackson, *Studies in Semiotics,* 271-97.

51. J. J. Finkelstein, "Ammiṣaduqa's Edict and the Babylonian 'Law Codes,'" *JCS* 15 (1961): 91-104; Paul, *Book of the Covenant,* 72-77.

52. W. F. Albright, *History, Archaeology, and Christian Humanism* (New York: McGraw-Hill, 1964), 74.

woman through premature labor, not whether she loses a body part. Scholars speculate that perhaps the instance of the *lex talionis* in the case of the woman attracted the more complete statement of the law in vv. 24-25. The *lex talionis* in vv. 24-25 may be intended as a summary statement on the topic in the Hebrew Bible, since it combines similar legislation from Deut 19:16-21 and Lev 24:17-22. Exodus 21:24 includes the four parts of the body (eye, tooth, hand, and foot) from Deut 19:21. Exodus 21:25 shifts the application of the law from body parts to types of injuries (burn, wound, and bruise), as is the case in Lev 24:20: "As he has injured the other, so he is to be injured." The synthetic character of the *lex talionis* in Exod 21:24-25 suggests that it is the latest statement on the law in the Hebrew Bible, not the earliest.

Exodus 21:26-27 extends the *lex talionis* to male and female slaves. If a master destroys an eye or knocks out the tooth of a slave, the compensation is freedom. The repetition of the first two body parts, eye and tooth, suggests that the extension of the *lex talionis* in 21:24-25 is aimed at the law of the slaves (21:26-27), not the previous law about the death to the free Israelite woman through premature labor (21:22-23). The application of the *lex talionis* to violent acts against slaves fills out the slave laws from 21:20-21. The murder of a slave requires unspecified punishment of the master (v. 20). The beating of a slave requires health care, but the absence of any permanent damage does not violate the law (v. 21). The law in vv. 26-27 now addresses instances of permanent damage to a slave. The mutilation of a male or a female slave results in his or her freedom.

Verses 28-36 address a range of liability laws regarding an ox. There is debate on the boundaries of this section, whether the unit constitutes one section of law or two, with the separation between vv. 28-32 and 33-36. The debate arises from the subject matter. The topic of an "ox" continues throughout the unit, but the legal discourse shifts from human injury (vv. 28-32) to property damage (vv. 33-36). Finkelstein and more recently Otto interpret the shift in law to signify two different sections.[53] But Jackson favors a unified interpretation with three distinct topics: vv. 28-32 addresses laws governing injury to humans caused by an ox (ox vs. human); vv. 33-34 are laws governing injury to an ox caused by a human (human vs. ox); and vv. 35-36 are laws governing injury to an ox by an ox (ox vs. ox). He notes the same principle of arrangement in reverse order in the Laws of Hammurabi: an ox is killed by another animal (§244), an ox is killed or injured by its hirer (§§245-249), and an ox kills a man (§§250-252).[54]

---

53. J. J. Finkelstein, *The Ox That Gored* (Transactions of the American Philosophical Society 71/2; Philadelphia: American Philosophical Society, 1981), 27-29; Otto, *Wandel*, 12-31.

54. Jackson, *Studies in Semiotics*, 189.

The principal law regarding an ox that gores a human is stated in v. 28: "When an ox gores a man or a woman to death, the ox shall be stoned to death and its flesh will not be eaten. But the owner of the ox is innocent." Two features of the law are distinct from a similar law in the Laws of Hammurabi (§250), which has no punishment to either the owner or the ox as compared to the death of the ox in 21:28 (although Westbrook questions this comparison as an argument from silence in §250).[55] The Israelite law also requires the ox to be stoned and its meat not consumed. The distinctive features of the Israelite law have been interpreted in two different directions, one religious and the other civil.

The religious interpretation is that the goring ox has acquired bloodguilt from killing a human. Paul refers to Gen 9:5-6 as the background to the law in which God demands an accounting of blood for the shedding of blood, especially in the death of a human who bears the divine image. The condition of bloodguilt accounts for the unusual act of killing the animal in which the community participates in the death through stoning. The prohibition against eating the meat is because it has become taboo.[56] Finkelstein adds a variation on the religious interpretation by suggesting that the ox violates the hierarchy of creation in killing a human, and thus is guilty not simply of murder but of treason or insurrection. This accounts for death by stoning, which is the punishment for treason against God and king, and the prohibition against eating since treason places the animal under the "ban."[57]

The civil interpretation is utilitarian. Jackson states that the stoning of the animal is a form of community protection.[58] Westbrook moves in a slightly different direction, agreeing with the civil interpretation of Jackson that a goring ox is a threat to the community requiring death to the animal. The reason for the prohibition against eating the meat of the animal is twofold, according to Westbrook. The animal is not fit for sacrifice, now blemished by the act of goring; and the slaughter of the animal does not take place at a cultic site, which is a requirement for meat consumption.[59]

Exodus 21:29-32 provides three conditions to the law. First, if the ox has habitually gored, the owner becomes responsible for the death and thus receives the death penalty along with the ox. The law includes a caveat for the owner, whose life may be ransomed, although no price is fixed. The second

55. Westbrook, *Studies in Biblical and Cuneiform Law,* 83-88.

56. Paul, *Book of the Covenant,* 79-80; see the review of interpretation in Schwienhorst-Schönberger, *Bundesbuch,* 131-36.

57. Finkelstein, *Ox That Gored,* 27-29.

58. B. S. Jackson, "The Goring Ox," in *Essays in Jewish and Comparative Legal History* (SJLA 10; Leiden: Brill, 1975), 108-16.

59. Westbrook, *Studies in Biblical and Cuneiform Law,* 83-86.

condition states that children are given the same consideration as adults. Thus the death of a son or daughter is the same as any other person. The third condition states that the death of a slave from goring requires a fine of thirty shekels and the death of the ox. Variations of these conditions also appear in the Laws of Hammurabi (§§244-252).

The laws in 21:33-36 explore two other situations in which there is damage to an ox. Verses 33-34 legislate the fine if a human kills an ox or another animal through negligence, by not covering a pit. The penalty is a fine equaling the value of the animal. The guilty person is allowed to eat the meat of the death animal. Verses 35-36 outline the penalty when one ox kills another. The principal law requires the equal division of both animals between the owners. The live animal is sold and the money is divided, while the meat of the dead animal is also shared. If, however, the ox was accustomed to goring and not penned by the owner, the fine is nearly the same as negligence in vv. 33-34. The owner of the ox that gored must pay the full price of the dead animal, while receiving its meat in return. There is no stipulation about killing the ox that gored.

22:1-17 There are seven laws in the section, if the particie *kî* indicates each new law: (1) 22:1-4, the penalties for theft; (2) v. 5, the destruction to crops from animal grazing; (3) v. 6, the destruction of crops from fire; (4) vv. 7-9, additional laws of theft; (5) vv. 10-13, the laws regulating wrongful possession; (6) vv. 14-15, the laws regulating leasing or borrowing; and (7) vv. 16-17, the law regulating the seduction of a virgin. The final two laws stand out in form by employing the conjunction with the particle, *wĕkî,* translated "and if." Y. Osumi notes that the laws are held together loosely by the repetition of the verb "to repay" (Piel of *šālam*) in five of the seven laws. The term does not appear in the law regulating the destruction to crops from grazing (22:5) or the seduction of a virgin (22:16-17). He also notes that the phrase "his neighbor" (*rē'ēhû*) repeats in three of the four laws (theft [22:7-9], wrongful possession [22:10-13], and leasing/borrowing [22:14-15]).[60] But the partial overlap of terms has given rise to debate over the structure and boundaries of the unit. Otto extends the section to include 21:33-36 as further examples of liability law, since these laws also include the verb "to repay." He eliminates the law against seduction because it does not include the motif of repayment. He also interprets 22:9, the requirement to appear before God/the judge to determine guilt and innocence, as the central point in the literary structure of the section.[61] Sprinkle reduces the division of the laws from seven to five: 22:1-4, theft; 22:5-6, destruction of crops; 22:7-13, theft; 22:14-15, leasing/borrowing; 22:16-17, seduction of a virgin daughter.[62]

60. Osumi, *Kompositionsgeschichte des Bundesbuches,* 122-26.
61. Otto, *Wandel,* 13-19.
62. Sprinkle, *Book of the Covenant,* 129.

The law against theft in 22:1-4 is in an illogical order. The principal law is stated in 22:1: "When a person steals an ox or a sheep, and slaughters it or sells it, he shall pay back five oxen for the ox, and four sheep for the sheep." Verse 3b follows the principal law in subject matter, addressing the problem of restitution should the thief have no money to pay the penalty: "He shall be sold for his theft." Verses 2-3a disrupt the law, changing the topic from theft to bloodguilt should the thief be killed in the act of stealing. If the thief is killed at night, there is no bloodguilt. But if the killing takes place during the day, the property owner is responsible for bloodguilt. The law ends in v. 4 by returning to the punishment for theft, this time stipulating a twofold penalty if the animal is found alive in the possession of the thief.

The solutions to the law against theft vary. The NRSV resolves the problem of logic by changing the order of the text: (1) the principal law requiring four- or fivefold restitution for sale or slaughter (v. 1); (2) the problem of restitution should the thief have no money (v. 3b); (3) the provision about bloodguilt (vv. 2-3a); and (4) the penalty for stolen property that is recovered with the animal still alive (v. 4). Cassuto understands the interpolation of the bloodguilt, vv. 2-3a, to be the central topic because of the focus on human life.[63] Daube explains the lack of order to be the result of editorial techniques in ancient law, in which additions were attached to the end of a law, rather than in their proper place within the argument. Westbrook presents a broad comparative study of ancient Near Eastern law to conclude: "Theft is a three-cornered affair involving the owner, the thief who is also the seller, and the receiver of the stolen goods from him"[64] (see the laws of theft in Hittite Laws §§57-71 and in the Laws of Hammurabi §§8, 9-11, 265). The threefold focus explains the arrangement of the law. The principal law in v. 1 is addressed to the thief, "who faces multiple damages according to the type of animal." The explicit mention of slaughter or sale, according to Westbrook, is to "show that the original thief is meant: the animal is no longer in his possession." The damages of four- and fivefold payment are not simply a fine, but a ransom for the life of the thief whose act of breaking in to the property of the victim is a crime of violence, worthy of the death penalty. The laws of bloodguilt in vv. 2-3a address the limits of ransom in the case of theft. The twofold penalty in the law of 22:4 is directed not to the thief but to the possessor of the stolen animals, who unwittingly bought them from the thief. The one receiving stolen property is not innocent, but liable for a lesser payment.[65]

Verses 5-6 address two instances of negligence. The first law, v. 5, stipu-

---

63. Cassuto, *Exodus,* 282-83.
64. Westbrook, *Studies in Biblical and Cuneiform Law,* 115.
65. Ibid., 111-28.

lates the punishment if an owner's cattle graze on another's property. The owner of the cattle must make restitution. The Laws of Hammurabi provide a similar solution (§57). The second law, v. 6, changes the subject from grazing to fire. If a human starts a fire that progresses to another's land and destroys grain, the one starting the fire must make full restitution.

Verses 7-13 concern situations of bail in which entrusted property is stolen or in the case of livestock injured or killed. The central problem throughout the section of the law is the lack of evidence for wrongdoing requiring a judgment about guilt and innocence in a cultic/legal procedure. Verses 7-9 focus on inanimate property, silver or other movable goods, while verses 10-13 address livestock.

The principal law governing bail in the form of money or goods is stated in v. 7: "When a person gives his neighbor silver or vessels to guard, and they are stolen from the house of the person, if the thief is caught, he shall make double restitution." The penalty for stealing money or objects is twice the value of the property. The law continues the focus on the "neighbor" *(rēʾēhû)* and the motif of restitution (Piel of *šālam*) from the previous section. The focus of the law is on the further conditions outlined in vv. 8-9, which arise when the thief is not caught. The problem is the lack of evidence to resolve the crime. Verse 8 states that in such cases the owner of the house (i.e., the bailee or the one entrusted with the victim's property) must appear before "the God" *(hāʾĕlōhîm)*. The NIV translates "the god" to designate a judge, following the rabbinic tradition (see also 21:6). Sprinkle rightly notes that the meaning "judges" is not clearly attested for Hebrew *hāʾĕlōhîm*.[66] The text likely refers to a cultic setting, in which the bailee swears his innocence before God.

The process of determining guilt or innocence is not spelled out; 22:9 is likely an addition that makes a more general claim about the process involved with allegations of theft or disputes over ownership. The law states that in all cases of dispute over possession in which a victim states, "This is it!" both parties must appear before "the God" *(hāʾĕlōhîm)*. The one whom "God" *(ʾĕlōhîm)* declares guilty must pay double the value of the disputed property. Again there is debate over the translation of "god/s." It is surprising that the verb "to declare guilt" *(rāšāʿ)* is plural. Sprinkle lists other texts in which God is coupled with a plural verb (Gen 20:13; 31:53).[67]

Exodus 22:10-13 continues the topic of the legal responsibility of bailees, but shifts the subject matter from money to animals. The law moves immediately to situations in which there is no evidence, thus requiring a cultic/legal solution: "When a person gives his neighbor a donkey, ox, sheep, or any animal to

---

66. Sprinkle, *Book of the Covenant*, 145-46.
67. Ibid., 146.

guard and it dies, or is injured, or is carried off, with no one seeing, an oath before Yahweh will be between them if he did not send his hand against the goods of his neighbor." The person required to take the oath is the bailee, who states that he did not take the victim's property. The procedure is not described in the law. The law simply states that if innocent, the victim must accept the verdict and, if the animal was stolen, the bailee must make restitution to the owner. The law concludes in v. 13 by requiring the bailee to present the carcass of any livestock killed by wild animals. The evidence frees the bailee from liability.

Verses 14-15 state the legal responsibility involved in borrowing an animal (see Laws of Hammurabi §§242-244). The principle of the law is that the responsibility of an animal rests with the borrower. In case of injury or death the borrower is responsible to make restitution. This law completes the sequence of laws addressing restitution. The presence of the owner of an animal at the time of an accident is an exception to the law of responsibility. In such cases the owner is responsible for any injury or death to his property. The final clause is likely focused on the animal as the "hire." This clause shifts the focus of the law from the one borrowing to the one leasing, stating that in such cases the price of rent covered any damages to the animal.

Verses 16-17 describe the penalty for seducing a virgin. The law is transitional in the structure of the Book of the Covenant. The penalty regulating the seduction of a virgin is monetary, the bride-price, whether or not the man marries the woman. The principal law also requires marriage so that the woman obtains the status of wife. But the father of the daughter has final say on whether the marriage requirement is executed. In either case the father receives the bride-price because of the loss of virginity to his daughter and the financial consequences of this should he seek another suitor. The monetary focus places the law with the previous laws of restitution, even though the specific word *šālam* is absent. At the same time, the topic of sexual intercourse and marriage anticipates the sexual law in v. 19 forbidding bestiality. Verses 16-17 are certainly not intended to provide comprehensive marriage law. This incompleteness is underscored by comparison to more detailed laws on sex and marriage in Leviticus 18 and 20 and in Deut 21:10-17; 22:13-29; 24:1-4; 25:5-12.

22:18–23:1 The legal formulations change in this section. The predominance of casuistic law in 21:1–22:17 gives way to a more varied style, including casuistic law, apodictic law, and first person divine speech. Divine speech in the first person occurred in 21:13: "Then I will appoint for you a place to which he will flee." But the legislation in 21:1–22:17 is stated for the most part in an impersonal third person style. In 22:18–23:19 God breaks in, promising to hear the cry of the oppressed ("I will hear," 22:23, 27) and to respond directly ("I will kill you," 22:24). The shift in style has prompted interpreters to distinguish between the *Mishpatim* (Rules) in 21:1–22:17 and the *Debarim* (Words) in 22:18–23:19. The

Debarim are organized loosely around two phrases, God's self-declaration of mercy and the divine demand for holiness in the people. The divine self-revelation in 22:27, "because I am compassionate" *(kî-ḥannûn 'ānî)*, provides the basis for the Israelites to be just and merciful in their dealings with each other and with the alien. The divine demand for holiness in 22:31, "Holy humans you will be to me" *(wĕ'anšê-qōdeš tihyûn lî)*, prompts laws of exclusive loyalty to Yahweh. A more detailed structure to 28:18–23:19 is difficult to identify.

22:18-20   This section consists of three commands, prohibitions against sorcery (v. 18), bestiality (v. 19), and sacrifice to any other gods than Yahweh (v. 20). The three commands stand out from their present narrative context in form. Each is stated categorically in apodictic form. The forbidden action is identified with a participle (lit. "the one undertaking sorcery," "the one lying down," and "the one sacrificing"). And the offense in each case requires the death penalty. The form is similar to the laws in 21:12-17, suggesting a possible literary relationship between the two sections. The similarity in form and in punishment raises the question of whether the three laws are also related in content or theme. Cassuto suggests: "The factor common to the three transgressions . . . is that they are all connected, directly or indirectly, with idolatry and its usages."[68] Sarna relates all three laws to the threat of foreign practices that are subversive to the religion of Israel.[69]

Exodus 22:18 states the prohibition against sorcery. The Hebrew word describing the forbidden activity is *mĕkaššēpâ*, a Piel feminine singular participle, usually translated as "sorceress" (see also Deut 18:10). The precise meaning is difficult to discern. Definitions based on etymology relate to some form of divination, including the activity of cutting oneself to influence a deity, as in the case of the prophets of Baal in 1 Kings 18. The term also indicates a pharmaceutical activity involving drugs or herbs, or some form of magical rite to compel a deity to act.[70] Exodus 7:11 described "sorcerers" as one of the three Egyptian groups called to resist Moses and Aaron along with the wise men and the magicians, suggesting a positive role in Egyptian society. Magic was a normal part of life both in Egypt and in Mesopotamia. A similar group of sorcerers is noted in Dan 2:2, along with magicians, conjurers, and Chaldeans (= astrologers?). But most references to sorcerers in the Hebrew Bible are negative. Micah 5:12; Mal 3:5; 2 Chr 33:6; and 2 Kgs 9:22 all reflect the negative perspective of Exod 22:18, condemning sorcery and associating it with fornication (2 Kgs 9:22) and false worship (Mic 5:12). The most extensive condemnation is Deut 18:10, which lists

---

68. Cassuto, *Exodus,* 289.

69. Sarna, *Exodus,* 136.

70. For review see T. Witton Davies, *Magic, Divination, and Demonology: Among the Hebrews and Their Neighbours* (New York: Ktav, 1969), 47-50; Schwienhorst-Schönberger, *Bundesbuch,* 329-30.

a variety of forms of divination, including Hebrew *mĕkaššēp*, where NIV translates it "witchcraft" and NRSV "sorcerer." The identification of "sorcery" as a foreign practice is reinforced in Isa 47:9, 12, and Nah 3:4.

The limitation of the law to women creates further difficulty in identifying the activity of sorcery, since the other condemnations of sorcery in the Hebrew Bible are directed toward both men and women. Does the author of the law have a particular magical practice in view that is employed only by women? Or does the law reflect a changing social environment in ancient Israel where women are singled out as particularly dangerous practitioners of black magic?[71] The text does not supply enough information to answer the questions. Van Seters notes that the idea of sorcery as a feminine activity parallels the term "harlotry" *(zĕnûnîm)* as a metaphor for worshiping foreign gods (see 2 Kgs 9:22).[72] If the law is late and related to a fear of foreign influence in the Israelite cult, it may relate to the forced divorce of a foreign wife in Ezra 9–10, a phenomenon that D. Janzen characterizes as a witch hunt for the purpose of maintaining purity and social boundaries.[73]

The narrow focus of the law on women has certainly influenced the history of translation. The KJV translators rendered Hebrew *mĕkaššēpâ* as "witch" in order to find biblical support for the practice of witch hunts in England. Opponents of the witch trials debated the translation, stating that OT witches were not devil worshipers but merely wizards and diviners, thus creating a false analogy between biblical and contemporary law. On the basis of the KJV translation of 22:18, John Wesley countered: "Giving up witchcraft, is, in effect, giving up the Bible."[74]

Verse 19 forbids bestiality. Similar laws repeat in Deut 27:21, Lev 18:23, 20:15-16, and in the Hittite Laws (II.187-188, 199-200a). The Hittite Laws demand the death penalty for any person having sex with cattle or sheep (II.187-189). The death penalty may also, but need not, be imposed for sex with a pig or a dog (II.199). But sex with a horse or a mule (and foreign women) is not against the law (II.200a). Deuteronomy 27:21 forbids sex with any animal as a cursed activity, without stating the punishment. Leviticus 18:23 forbids both men and women from having sex with animals, declaring that such persons "must be cut off from their people" (Lev 18:29). Leviticus 20:15-16 intensifies the punishment as death for both the animal and the man or woman.

71. See M. G. Marwick, "Witchcraft," *ER* 15:414-28.

72. Van Seters, *Law Book*, 104-5.

73. For discussion of Ezra 9–10 see D. Janzen, *Witch-Hunts, Purity and Social Boundaries: The Expulsion of the Foreign Women in Ezra 9–10* (JSOTSup 350; Sheffield: Sheffield Academic Press, 2002).

74. See K. Thomas, "The Decline of Witchcraft Prosecutions," in *Witchcraft and Sorcery* (ed. M. Marwick; 2nd ed.; London: Penguin, 1982), 158-59.

One reason for the prohibition against bestiality is the mixing of kinds, which goes against "natural law" according to the biblical writers. The P author states in Genesis 1 that all things are created according to their kind, implying that such boundaries and divisions must be maintained. The creation story of Adam in the garden of Eden may carry the same message. He was unable to find a suitable partner from any of the created animals (Gen 2:19-20). The violation of natural law in the account of sex between gods and humans prompts the implosion of the natural order by means of the flood (Gen 6:1-4).

The story of sex between gods and humans in Gen 6:1-4 may provide another reason for the prohibition in Exod 22:19, the potential creation of mixed forms of life. The offspring of the gods and humans in Gen 6:1-4 were Nephilim, "fallen ones," freaks of nature that existed to be destroyed (Num 13:33). The law against bestiality may be intended to safeguard the natural order against further mixing in the creation, which would result in human-animal creatures. Hybrid creatures, who walk on two legs, are associated with demons in the ancient Near East, as compared to monsters, who walked on four legs.[75] A demonic interpretation of the law against bestiality may provide a link to the previous law against women sorcerers, conceived as witches, whose power is associated at times with hybrid demonic creatures. It is also possible that marriage with foreign women may be conceived as a form of bestiality. In this case the law of bestiality would reinforce the social boundaries of exclusive marriage as it is stated in Ezra 9–10.

Exodus 22:20 completes the three apodictic laws by forbidding sacrifice to any god but Yahweh. There is likely a progression in the intensity of the three laws, signaled by the language requiring the death penalty. The sorceress is "not allowed to live" (v. 18).[76] The person practicing bestiality "must be put to death" (v. 19). The one sacrificing to another god must be destroyed under the "ban," requiring total annihilation of person and property (v. 20). The biblical law of the ban *(ḥērem)* means that all property is given over to God through "destruction," signifying total annihilation.[77]

22:21–23:9 This section contains a collection of social and religious laws organized loosely around the law of the resident alien, which frames the section in 22:21 and in 23:9: "And a resident alien *(gēr)* you will not wrong/op-

---

75. See J. Black, A. Green, and T. Richards, *Gods, Demons and Symbols of Ancient Mesopotamia: An Illustrated Dictionary* (Austin: University of Texas Press, 1992), 63-65. But, as O. Keel and C. Uehlinger (*Gods, Goddesses, and Images of Ancient Israel* [trans. T. H. Trapp; Minneapolis: Fortress, 1998], 252-56) demonstrate, hybrids can also take on a protective role.

76. Van Seters (*Law Book,* 104) notes that the phrase, "you will not allow to live," may indicate the death penalty (see Ezekiel 18).

77. See P. D. Stern, *The Biblical Ḥerem: A Window on Israel's Religious Experience* (BJS 211; Atlanta: Scholars Press, 1991); N. Lohfink, *"ḥāram," TDOT* 5:180-99.

press."[78] "Resident alien" is also translated at different times as "stranger" and "sojourner." The category of a resident alien presupposes the Israelites' life in the land, since the resident alien was defined as a foreign-born person who resided permanently in the land of Israel but did not own property. The resident alien assumed an intermediate position in society between a foreigner *(nokrî)* and a native-born Israelite *('ezrāḥ)*. Such persons lacked the support of clan or the inalienable right to property, making them vulnerable in the social structure of ancient Israel.

The motif of the resident alien is woven into the exodus story. Moses identified himself as a "resident alien" during his sojourn in Midian (2:15b-22). The rights of the resident alien were also addressed in the Passover legislation (12:43-51) as well as in the law of the Sabbath (20:8-11). Exodus 22:21 and 23:9 legislate the rights of the resident alien against oppression. But the laws do not list what those rights may be. Instead the laws are aimed at native-born Israelites, and their intent is more psychological than legal. They demand that the Israelites not oppress the resident alien because native-born Israelites know such oppression firsthand, having themselves been resident aliens in Egypt (22:21; 23:9). The style of the laws, with their psychological identification with the oppressed and the vulnerable, is not characteristic of the casuistic laws (21:1–22:17), which tended to be stated in the more impersonal legislative style of third person discourse. The change in style, the call for psychological identification, and the absence of specific legal rights for the resident alien suggest that 22:21 and 23:9 are more theological statements than law, setting the tone for the social legislation aimed at the poor and the practice of lending. The psychological identification with the resident alien is developed further in Deuteronomy as the basis for charity during the harvesting of grain and grapes (Deut 24:19-22). The legal relationship between the native-born Israelite and the resident alien is outlined in the Jubilee laws of Leviticus 25, where the focus is more on the protection of native-born Israelites than on the rights of the resident alien.

Exodus 22:22-25 contains laws protecting the widow, the orphan, and the poor with regard to lending practices. The subject matter of the widow, the orphan, and the poor returns in 23:1-3 and 6-8 to address court proceedings. The repetition of laws concerning the widow, the orphan, and the poor provides an inner frame to the laws of the resident alien in 22:21 and 23:9.

Exodus 22:22-24 forbids the mistreatment of the widow and the orphan. The triad resident alien, widow, and orphan signifies the disenfranchised in ancient Israelite society, the *personae miserabiles* according to Noth.[79] As was the

---

78. See C. van Houten, *The Alien in Israelite Law* (JSOTSup 107; Sheffield: Sheffield Academic Press, 1991), 52-58.

79. Noth, *Exodus,* 186.

case with the law of the resident alien, the laws protecting the poor are more a statement of theology than jurisprudence. The statements are aimed at the Israelite people in general without listing the rights of the disenfranchised. The point of emphasis is the supplement in vv. 23-24, where God identifies with the widow and the orphan and repeats the language of lament from the opening chapters of Exodus: "I will certainly hear their cry" (see 2:23-25; 3:7, 9). God promises to execute the punishment for oppression personally: "I will kill you with the sword" (22:24). The statement is an instance of the *lex talionis,* since the punishment results in the wife of the oppressor becoming a widow and the children becoming orphans.

The personal character of the legislation to protect the poor continues in 22:25-27 with the law against money lending at interest. Similar laws regulating lending are stated in Lev 25:35-38; Deut 23:20-21; and 24:10-13, with Deut 23:20-21 allowing for interest payment in the case of foreigners. The law against interest is followed by the demand to return at sunset a coat taken in pledge. The prophet Amos criticizes the northern Israelites for not adhering to this law, when he states that the poor are trampled upon when lenders use their cloaks taken in pledge "to lie down beside every altar" (Amos 2:8). Deuteronomy 24:12-13 describes the return of a cloak at sunset as a righteous action before Yahweh.

The ethical requirements toward the poor are grounded in divine grace in Exod 22:27. God promises to hear the cry of the oppressed person, stating in the first person: "Because I am compassionate" *(kî ḥannûn 'ānî).* Only God is described as being *ḥannûn,* "compassionate," in the Hebrew Bible. Verse 27 is the initial revelation of this divine quality in the Hebrew Bible. Otto judges this declaration to be so important that it provides the center of the Book of the Covenant.[80] The compassion (or grace) of Yahweh issues from the quality of the divine character. It is a spontaneous gift that can exist only in the relationship between God and humans or between humans who mirror the character of God. It is not a possession or a commodity. Proverbs 22:1 states: "Favor [Hebrew *ḥēn,* 'compassion'] is better than silver or gold."

The relationship created by grace is most often between unequal parties in the Hebrew Bible. A person of superior rank bestows grace on a subordinate. The book of Proverbs reflects the social hierarchy between the sages and the poor by repeatedly urging the pupil to be gracious to the poor. Proverbs 14:21 states: "Those who despise their neighbors are sinners, but happy are those who are kind [Hebrew *mĕḥônēn,* 'show grace'] to the poor" (see also 14:31; 28:8). Such acts of grace are grounded theologically: "Whoever is kind to the poor lends to Yahweh, and will be repaid in full" (19:17).

80. Otto, *Wandel,* 10.

The law in Exod 22:27 indicates that human lament draws out the compassion of God. God will hear the cry of the poor and respond with grace. The structure of the law corresponds with the psalms of lament in which the gracious attitude of God toward Israel is also the foundation for humans to entreat God in lament. Repeatedly the psalmist states: "Be gracious to me, O LORD" (Pss 4:1; 6:2; 9:13; 25:16; 31:9; 56:1; 57:1; etc.; cf. 123:3). The gift of grace may be rescue from an enemy (6:2); healing (41:4); forgiveness, including deliverance from divine punishment (Neh 9:17, 31; Joel 2:13); or an act of justice (Amos 5:15), as it is in Exod 22:27. The gracious character of Yahweh will be developed further during the story of the golden calf (Exodus 32) and in the events immediately following (chaps. 33–34).

Exodus 22:28-31 changes the hierarchical relationships by outlining the requirements of the Israelites toward those in a superior position, not their social responsibility to the poor and disenfranchised. The change in perspective is indicated by two declarations in v. 28: God cannot be taken lightly (Piel of *qālal*) and the "leader" *(nāsî')* cannot be cursed *('ārar)*. Cassuto interprets the first part of the command to be a prohibition against cursing God, reading the two statements about God and the leader as synonymous declarations. But the first command about God may have a broader meaning, demanding that God not be taken for granted or "treated lightly." Jeremiah provides an example of this broader meaning when he criticizes the Israelite people for not evaluating their present circumstances carefully enough: "They dress the wound of my people as though it *were not serious.* 'Peace, peace,' they say, when there is no peace" (Jer 6:14; 8:11). The reference to a leader in the second statement is not the word for "king" *(melek),* but a more general designation for a leader, ruler, or perhaps even a tribal chief. The designation has prompted debate over the date of the law, suggesting to some its premonarchical origin and to others an antimonarchical outlook reflecting the postmonarchical period.

The laws in Exod 22:29-31 may provide the content or guidelines for the demand to respect God and the ruler in 22:28. Verse 29 demands the prompt offering of two things, the *mĕlē'â* and the *dema'*. The first word is related to the Hebrew verb *mālē'*, "to be full." The noun occurs in only two other places in the Hebrew Bible. In Num 18:27 it may be associated with juice from the wine- or olive press, and in Deut 22:9 it may also refer to the vineyard. The second word may be related to the verb "to shed tears." It occurs as a noun only in Exod 22:28, perhaps also indicating the flow of wine or oil. The law demands prompt payment of the tithe.

Verses 29-30 extend the divine claim from produce or wine to firstborn humans and cattle (see the commentary on 13:1-2 for discussion of the divine claim on firstborn humans). The divine claim on firstborn animals requires their sacrifice, which is not acceptable until they have lived with their mother for one week (see also Lev 22:27). Exodus 22:31 states the demand of holiness, recalling a similar promise from the proposal of covenant (19:6), even echoing the syntax: "you will be to me." The perspective on holiness, however, is different. Exodus 19:6 is a future promise stating that the Israelites will be a "holy nation." Exodus 22:31 presupposes the holiness of the people. It demands that the Israelites be a "holy people." The consequence of the demand for holiness is that the Israelites may not eat meat killed and torn by another animal. Such meat is ritually impure and fit only for dogs because of the absence of proper sacrifice.

Exodus 23:4-5 interrupts the laws of judicial procedure (vv. 1-3, 6-8) and care for the alien (v. 9) with two casuistic laws that recall the laws from 21:1–22:17. Both laws demand acts of kindness toward one's enemy. The first requires the return of an enemy's ox or donkey if it wanders away (v. 4). The second may go further, demanding all Israelites to aid someone who may hate them: if an Israelite sees the donkey of another struggling with their load, they must aid the person in their time of need, even though that person may hate them (v. 5). According to this interpretation there is progression in the two laws. The second goes beyond the simple return of an animal to an enemy to require more personal assistance. The same two laws repeat in Deut 22:1-4 and in the Sermon on the Mount (Matt 5:43-48). A. Cooper disagrees with this interpretation, suggesting that the Hebrew verb *'āzab* demands that a neighbor avoid contact with the animal (see the translation note to 23:5).[81]

Exodus 23:6-8 demands justice for the poor through fair court proceedings that exclude false witnesses and bribery. The law echoes the same demand from 23:1-3, which also forbids false reports and favoritism toward either the crowd or perhaps even the powerful *(rabbîm)*. It also forbids favoritism toward the poor. Leviticus 19:15 states the same principle: "Do not pervert justice; do not show partiality to the poor or favoritism to the great, but judge your neighbor fairly."

23:10-13   This section contains two different laws on the Sabbath. Verses 10-11 advocate a rest for the land every seventh year, and v. 12 reiterates the weekly Sabbath rest introduced in the story of manna (chap. 16) and codified in the Decalogue (see the commentary on 20:8-11). The motivation for the weekly Sabbath rest is to provide rest for slaves; this point conforms more closely to the version of the Decalogue in Deut 5:12-15 than to the P rendition in Exod 20:8-11.

The sabbatical year may have played a role in ancient Near Eastern religion and culture. Baal's second conflict with Mot, the god of death, takes place in the seventh year: "A day, days passed, from days they passed into months, from months into years. Then in the seventh year divine Mot [   ] to mightiest Baal; he lifted up his voice and cried, 'Because of you, Baal, I have suffered

---

81. Cooper, "Plain Sense."

abasement, because of you I have suffered splitting with the sword" (*CTA* 6.v.7-13). The reference to the seventh year in the speech of Mot is cryptic, but it suggests some form of liturgical activity associated with a seven-year agricultural cycle in Canaanite religion.

The law for sabbatical rest in 23:10-11 demands that the fields and the vineyard be left fallow every seventh year. The motivation is not religious or cultic but ethical. Any produce arising in the seventh year is food for the poor and the wild animals. The focus on the poor continues the theme of care for the needy stated in the law of lending money (22:25) and in the command for fair legal processes (23:3, 6). The giving over of the land to the "wild animals" is a new motif. It may simply indicate that the land is uncultivated during the Sabbatical Year. But wild animals also take on a larger role in the Hebrew Bible. They are often seen as a threat to the Israelites (Deut 7:22) or as an instrument of divine punishment (Lev 26:22; Hos 2:12). Neither meaning fits the law in Exod 23:10-11. The grazing of wild animals can also take on a utopian quality as in the divine promise of covenant in Hos 2:18, in which there is a harmony of nature, bringing together the domestic and the wild, and resulting in peace and safety (see the reverse in Hos 4:3). The demand for a Sabbatical Year may share in the utopian vision of Hosea describing an ideal state of land, people, and nature. The utopian vision is expanded in the P tradition with the Jubilee Year, the fiftieth year at the end of seven cycles of Sabbatical Years (Lev 25:8-55), which signals liberty for Israelites and restoration of the land. The P vision is central to the NT writer's interpretation of the mission of Jesus and its consequences for society and nature (see especially Luke 4:16-30, citing the year of release from Isaiah 61).[82]

The Sabbatical Year in Exod 23:10-11 is more explicit with regard to its ethical motivation than to its theological grounding — it is a welfare system for the poor. But even the ethical focus in the law raises questions. The feeding of the poor every seventh year is hardly practical care for the disenfranchised. Leviticus 25:2-7 provides a firmer theological grounding for the Sabbatical Year as a rest of the land to Yahweh. Leviticus 25 also expands the scope of those who can eat the produce of a fallow field to include the landowner and his household (the resident alien, slaves, and domestic livestock) as well as the poor and wild animals. Deuteronomy 15 moves in yet another direction, developing the ethical and humanitarian component of the Sabbath Year to include release from debt (15:1-3) and debt slavery (15:12-18; see Exod 21:2-11).

23:14-17 This section provides regulations on worship and cultic seasons, shifting in perspective from the weekly cycle of the Sabbath rest (23:12) and

---

82. See S. Ringe, *Jesus, Liberation, and the Biblical Jubilee: Images for Ethics and Christology* (Philadelphia: Fortress, 1985); C. J. H. Wright, "Jubilee, Year of," *ABD* 3:1025-30.

the larger seven-year period of the Sabbatical Year (23:10-11) to the yearly cycle of the annual festivals. The calendar continues the focus on the land established in the Sabbath laws (23:10-14), suggesting a structural coherence to 23:10-19.[83] Three annual festivals are identified. Each festival is closely tied to the agricultural cycle of Canaan. All three festivals require a pilgrimage of males to a central cult site, where they appear before Yahweh, who is described as the sovereign (23:14, 17). The calendar lacks three central festivals: the Passover in the spring, Rosh Hashanah (New Year) in the fall, and Yom Kippur (the Day of Atonement) in the fall. The absence of these central festivals suggests that the calendar represents an early stage in the yearly worship cycle of the Israelites.[84]

The Festival of Unleavened Bread *(ḥag hammaṣṣôt)* is the first yearly feast (23:15). The dates of the festivals are not firmly established in the calendar because of the agricultural focus. The only set date in the entire calendar is the month Abib, as the time for the observance of the Feast of Unleavened Bread. The name Abib is noteworthy because it is a Canaanite word for the month, as compared to the more frequent Babylonian reckoning (i.e., Nisan). The month of Abib is unknown from other sources outside the Hebrew Bible. It also appears in 13:4 as the month in which the Israelites left Egypt; in 34:18 in a similar use to 23:14-17; and in Deut 16:1 in an expanded cultic calendar. Abib may translate "green heads of grain," or perhaps "milky grain," which reinforces the agricultural focus of the calendar. Abib designates a spring month in March/April.

The Festival of Unleavened Bread takes place for seven days. It requires the eating of unleavened bread, a pilgrimage *(ḥag)* to a cultic site, and some form of sacrifice ("no one is to appear before me [Yahweh] empty-handed"). In the present form of the text the festival is associated with the exodus, but it is not combined with the Passover as in the account of the exodus in Exodus 12–13 or in the cultic calendars of Deuteronomy (chap. 16) and the P legislation (Leviticus 23; Numbers 28–29). The absence of the Passover suggests that the calendar is older than the combination of these festivals. It is possible that even the historicizing of the agricultural feast with the exodus is an editorial addition within the Book of the Covenant so that the original calendar focused only on the relationship of the Festival of Unleavened Bread with the agricultural year.

The Festival of the Harvest *(ḥag haqqāṣîr)* is described in Exod 23:16a. The Festival of Harvest is of the firstfruits of planting. The cultic calendar in 34:22 describes the same observance as the Festival of Weeks *(ḥag šābūʿōt)*, identifying it as the firstfruits of the wheat harvest. The time of observance of

83. See A. Cooper and B. R. Goldstein, "The Festivals of Israel and Judah and the Literary History of the Pentateuch," *JAOS* 110 (1990): 21.
84. See the discussion of Levinson, *Deuteronomy and Hermeneutics*, 53-97, esp. 65-68.

the Festival of Harvest is not stated in 23:16a, but determined simply by the ripening of the first planting. The author of Deuteronomy specifies the date more precisely as seven weeks from the moment when the sickle is put to the grain (Deut 16:9-12). The P author fixes the observance even more precisely as fifty days from the day after the Sabbath of Passover, prompting the Jews of the Diaspora to name the festival Pentecost, the Greek work for fifty, which is also the name for the festival in Christian tradition. In later Judaism the Feast of Weeks becomes the occasion to celebrate the revelation of Torah on Mount Sinai, while in Christian tradition it signifies the outpouring of the Holy Spirit upon the church. The Festival of Harvest, like the Festival of Unleavened Bread, requires a pilgrimage to a central cult location.

The Festival of Ingathering *(ḥag hā'āsīp)* is described in Exod 23:16b. The observance is tied to the agricultural cycle, without a specific date. The Festival of Ingathering takes place when the crops are gathered from the field at the "going out" or end of the year, suggesting a fall date. Exodus 34:22 describes the same festival as taking place at the fall equinox *(tĕqûpat haššānâ,* "turn of the year"). The festival is identified as Sukkoth (Booths) in Deut 16:13-15 and Lev 23:33-43. No duration for the festival is stated in Exod 23:16b, although the calendars in Deuteronomy 16 and Leviticus 23 specify a seven-day observance. The Festival of Ingathering requires a pilgrimage to a central cult location without further instruction as to its observance. Its ritual practice undergoes significant transformation as the Festival of Sukkoth, when it is historicized to recall the wilderness period, which required the construction of booths.

23:18-19　This section completes the legislation in the Book of the Covenant with four stipulations on sacrifice: the prohibition against leaven in a blood sacrifice (v. 18a), the command against preserving sacrificial fat until morning (v. 18b), the requirement that firstfruits be brought to the temple (v. 19a), and the restriction against boiling a kid in its mother's milk (v. 19b). Interpreters have sought to relate the commands to the festival calendar in 23:14-17. The command against leaven recalls the Festival of Unleavened Bread, and the requirement for firstfruits corresponds to the Feast of Weeks. But a complete correlation is difficult. The command against fat and the prohibition against boiling a kid in its mother's milk do not correspond with any of the three festivals. Interpreters have also sought to use the repetition of the sacrificial laws in 34:25-26 to aid in the interpretation of 23:18-19, especially in identifying the first two commands with Passover, since it is specifically mentioned in 34:25 in the prohibition against retaining fat until the morning. But there is no mention of Passover in 23:18.

The prohibition against mixing leaven in the blood sacrifice (23:18a) repeats in the instructions for the grain offering (Lev 2:11; 6:17). Milgrom concludes that the fermentation of leaven was understood as decay, thus account-

551

ing for the prohibition.[85] The same root in Hebrew (*ḥms*) also forms the word for "vinegar," which supports Milgrom's interpretation. Vinegar is viewed as sour and corrosive. It takes on negative metaphorical meaning in Proverbs, where vinegar on the teeth is compared to a sluggard (Prov 10:26; see also 25:20). Surprisingly, however, leaven returns as a proper ingredient for the peace offering (Lev 7:13) and for the sacrifice of the Feast of Weeks (Lev 23:17).

The prohibition against leaving the fat of a sacrifice until morning (Exod 23:18b) recalls the Passover command from 12:10, and 34:25 makes the correlation explicit. The parallels have prompted interpreters to identify the fat of the sacrifice in 23:18b as the Passover lamb. But the law does not make the connection to the Passover. Hebrew *ḥēleb* is the layer of fat beneath the surface of the skin and around the organs given over to God in the act of sacrifice. Thus the prohibition need not refer specifically to the Passover. The laws in Leviticus 3 identify different kinds of sacrificial fat, which are not distinguished in Exod 23:18b.[86]

Verse 19 contains two laws. The first requires that the firstfruits of the land be brought to the sanctuary of Yahweh. The second is the prohibition against boiling a kid in its mother's milk. The latter law is obscure, but clearly important, repeating in 34:26 and Deut 14:21, but absent from the P legislation. The law may have a polemical focus against some form of Canaanite practice, although there is no evidence for such a practice. *CTA* 23.14 may describe the mixing of coriander in milk, but there appears to be no mention of meat or a kid.[87] Philo introduced a humanitarian interpretation, stating that cooking a kid in its mother's milk was cruel and thus forbidden (*Virt.* 134, 143-44).[88] More recent interpretations have sought to uncover a social taboo in the law such as incest, or an act against the cosmic order in which the image of a mother suckling her young was a symbol of divine order in the world.[89] Carmichael argued that the prohibition addressed life and death.[90] Milgrom agrees, arguing that the life force of mother's milk could not be used in the death of a kid.[91] The rabbis reinforce the cosmic dimension to the law, using it as the basis for the prohibition against mixing milk and meat in Jewish dietary laws (i.e., *m. Ḥul.* 8:4).

---

85. Milgrom, *Leviticus 1–16*, 188-89.

86. See ibid., 205-7.

87. Cassuto, *Exodus*, 305.

88. See M. Haran, "Seething a Kid in Its Mother's Milk," *JSS* 20 (1979): 24-35.

89. For the former see F. Martens, "Diététhique ou la cuisine de Dieu," *Communications* 26 (1977): 16-45; for the latter see O. Keel, *Das Böcklein in der Milch seiner Mutter und Verwandtes* (Freiburg: Universitätsverlag, 1980).

90. C. M. Carmichael, "On Separating Life and Death: An Explanation of Some Biblical Laws," *HTR* 69 (1976): 1-7.

91. Milgrom, *Leviticus 1–16*, 737-42.

Conclusion (23:20-33)

23:20*I am sending the Messenger before you to guard you on the way and to bring you to the place that I have prepared.* 21*Be attentive to him and listen to his voice. Do not rebel against him, for he will not pardon your offenses, since my name is in him.* 22*For if you listen carefully to his voice and you do all that I say, then I will be an enemy to your enemies and a foe to your foes.*

23*When my Messenger goes before you and brings you to the Amorites, the Hittites, the Perizzites, the Canaanites, the Hivites, and the Jebusites, I will annihilate them.* 24*You shall not bow down to their gods, and you shall not serve them, and you shall not do as they do, for you will tear them down and you will thoroughly shatter their pillars.* 25*You will serve Yahweh, your God, and he will bless your bread and your water. And I will remove sickness from your midst.* 26*No woman will miscarry and be barren in your land. I will fill the number of your days.*

27*I will send my terror before you, and I will throw into panic all the people to whom you approach. And I will make all of your enemies turn their backs to you.* 28*I will send the pestilence in front of you. And it will drive out the Hivites, the Canaanites, and the Hittites before you.* 29*I will not drive them out from before you in one year, lest the land become desolate and the wild animals multiply on it.* 30*Little by little I will drive them out from before you until you increase and possess the land.* 31*And I will set borders from the Red Sea to the Sea of the Philistines, and from the wilderness to the Euphrates. For I will give into your hand all the inhabitants of the land, and you will drive them out from before you.* 32*You shall not cut a covenant with them or with their gods.* 33*And they must not dwell in the land, lest they cause you to sin against me, for you will serve their gods and it will be to you a snare.*

Notes

23:20 *the place.* Hebrew *hammāqôm* could refer to a cult site or the land, as in LXX *tēn gēn.*

23:21 *do not rebel against him.* The MT vocalization suggests the root *mrr*, "bitter." My translation is based on the root *mrh*, "rebel." The LXX *apeithei*, "to be disobedient," also suggests the root *mrh*.

23:25 *you will serve Yahweh, your God, and he will bless your bread and your water. And I will remove sickness from your midst.* The Hebrew shifts between the plural and the singular and between third person and first person in reference to the Deity.

23:26 *I will fill the number of your days.* The Hebrew phrase indicates long life. NRSV translates: "I will fulfill the number of your days"; cf. NJPS: "I will let you enjoy the full count of your days."

23:27 *my terror.* Hebrew *ʾêmātî* is translated in the LXX, *ton phobon*, "the fear."
turn their backs to you. The Hebrew phrase *ʾēleykā ʿōrep* is lit. "to your neck." The im-

age suggests that the enemy turns to run away from the Israelite people. See NJPS: "Your enemies turn tail before you." The LXX reinterprets the Hebrew as *dōsō pantas tous hypenantious sou phygadas,* "I will make all your enemies fugitives."

23:28 *the pestilence.* The meaning of the Hebrew *haṣṣir‘â* is uncertain. Many translate "hornet" based on the LXX *sphēkias,* "wasp."

23:33 *for you will serve their gods and it will be to you a snare.* The Hebrew consists of two *kî* clauses, "for you will serve . . . for you will be."

Commentary

The style of this section changes from legislation to a more sermonic discourse, when God promises to give the Israelites the land of Canaan in exchange for obedience to the law. Westbrook notes that ancient Near Eastern law codes are framed with prologues and epilogues.[1] The Laws of Hammurabi begin with an extended prologue anchoring the authority of the king in the world of the gods, and they conclude with an epilogue describing the ideal nature of society, the just character of the king, and the power of the gods to support Hammurabi in executing justice. The Book of the Covenant conforms to the ancient Near Eastern pattern. Exodus 20:21-22 is the prologue establishing the divine authority of the law, and 23:20-33 is the epilogue envisioning an ideal life of blessing in the promised land. The content of 20:22, "You have seen that I spoke with you," indicates that the entire account of revelation on the divine mountain is intended to provide the prologue for the revelation of law in the Book of the Covenant. The opening words of the epilogue, "I am sending a Messenger ahead of you to guard you along the way and to bring you to the place I have prepared," indicate the change of theme from the divine authority of the law in the prologue to the promise of land as a reward for obedience.

The promise of land in 23:20-33 is couched in the language of holy war. H. Ausloos notes that the motifs of the Messenger (v. 20), terror (v. 27), confusion (v. 27), the hornet (v. 28), the imagery of the enemy turning and running (v. 28), as well as the giving of the enemy into the hand (v. 31) and driving the enemy out (vv. 29, 31) are all the language of war. The imagery repeats throughout a wide range of texts, including Exodus 14, Joshua 10, Judges 4, and 1 Samuel 7.[2] But the first person divine speech, the theme of holy war, the demand for exclusive loyalty to Yahweh, and the requirement that the Israelites separate themselves and exterminate the indigenous nations recall in particular Deuteronomy 7. It too contains a divine promise to drive out the indigenous nations, the demand that the Israelites exterminate the indigenous nations, and the need for the people to remain exclusively loyal to Yahweh. The thematic parallels include many similar motifs on holy war, for example, the gradual process of con-

1. R. Westbrook, "Biblical and Cuneiform Law Codes," *RB* 92 (1985): 251.
2. H. Ausloos, "Exod 23, 20-33 and the 'War of YHWH,'" *Bib* 80 (1999): 557.

quest to protect the Israelite people from wild animals and prohibitions against iconic forms of worship. The nature of the inner-biblical relationship and the chronology of the two texts are debated, with some interpreters arguing for the priority of the epilogue in Book of the Covenant and others reversing the relationship.[3] The similarity in language and motifs indicates a close literary relationship between the epilogue of the Book of the Covenant in the Non-P History and Deuteronomy regardless of the exact chronology of composition.

The theology of holy war in 23:20-33 is developed through the motif of the "Messenger." The identification of the "Messenger" is difficult, since it represents a range of divine embodiments. The account of the "Messenger of Yahweh" cursing Meroz for not coming to the aid of Yahweh in a situation of war in Judg 5:23 may contain a glimpse into the tradition-historical roots of the term. T. H. Gaster argues that the story is about a professional diviner and not the mythological personification of God.[4] Even when the Messenger is clearly associated with the Deity it is described with a variety of terms, including "the Messenger of Yahweh" (Gen 16:7-14; 22:11, 15; Exod 3:2; Num 22:22-35), "the Messenger of God" (Gen 21:17; 31:11; Exod 14:19; Judg 13:6, 9; 1 Sam 29:9; 2 Sam 14:17, 20; 19:27), or simply "the Messenger" (Exod 23:20, 23; 32:34; 33:2). Interpreters have sought to identify distinct authors from the different descriptions of the Messenger. Source critics attribute the Messenger of Yahweh to the J source and the Messenger of God to the E source.[5] More recently Blum has identified the tradition of the Messenger with a late post-P redaction of the Pentateuch.[6] In the commentary I interpret all the references to the Messenger within the Non-P History. The motif is absent from the P History. All the different terms for the Messenger occur in the Non-P historian's account of the exodus and the wilderness journey to the mountain of God. The "Messenger of Yahweh" *(mal'ak yhwh)* appears to Moses in the theophany on the divine mountain (3:2). The "Messenger of the God" *(mal'ak hā'ĕlōhîm)* travels before the Israelite people at the Red Sea (14:19). The term "Messenger" is used alone in the epilogue to the Book of the Covenant (23:20, 23) and again in the context of the golden calf (32:34; 33:2).

The Messenger is a medium for revelation in the Pentateuch and in the Deuteronomistic History. The Messenger communicates to Hagar (Gen 16:7-14), Moses (Exod 3:2), Balaam (Num 22:22-35), Gideon (Judg 6:11-24), the parents of Samson (Judges 13), David (2 Samuel 24), and Elijah (1 Kings 19). A

---

3. See ibid., 555-63; Fishbane, *Biblical Interpretation,* 200-203; Van Seters, *Law Book,* 67-81.

4. T. H. Gaster, *Myth, Legend, and Custom in the Old Testament* (New York: Harper & Row, 1969), 419.

5. See, e.g., Childs, *Exodus,* 51-53, 220.

6. Blum, *Studien,* 361-82.

closer examination of the setting in which the Messenger appears indicates two distinct functions, as guide in the wilderness journey and as the holy warrior in the promised land. The holy war function of the Messenger comes to the foreground when the Israelites are in the vicinity of the land (Numbers 22) or when they are settled in the land (Judg 2:1-7; 1 Sam 29:9; 2 Sam 24:15-17 = 1 Chr 21:14-17; 2 Kgs 19:35 = 2 Chr 32:21).[7] The Messenger protects the sanctity of the promised land through holy war. The Messenger can wage war against Israel's enemies (2 Kgs 19:35) or against the Israelites themselves if they are unfaithful (Judg 2:1-7). The role for the Messenger as the wilderness guide is first evident in the story of Hagar, who is rescued in the wilderness (Gen 16:7-14; 21:17). The Messenger as wilderness guide is central in the Israelites' journey from Egypt to Canaan (Exod 3:2; 14:19; 23:20; 32:34; 33:2; Num 20:16). The Messenger continues in the role of guide in the narrative of Elijah, who is also rescued in the wilderness and brought to Mount Horeb (1 Kgs 19:5, 7). The divine promises associated with the Messenger in Exod 23:20-33 include both the role of the wilderness guide and the holy warrior in the promised land. Exodus 23:20 characterizes the Messenger as the wilderness guide of the Israelite people. Exodus 23:23 changes the imagery of the Messenger to the holy warrior who will exterminate the indigenous population of the promised land.

The hortatory and repetitive style of 23:20-33 resists a simple outline. The theme of unconditional promise, according to Childs, yields a three-part structure: vv. 20-22, 23-26, and 27-33.[8] If we narrow the language of promise to the phrase, "I will send . . . before you," a two-part structure emerges between vv. 20-26 and 27-33. Verse 20 begins the first section with the divine promise: "See I am sending *(šālah)* a Messenger *(mal'āk)* before you *(lĕpāneykā)*." Verses 27-28 mark the transition to the second section with the twofold divine promise: "I will send *(šālah)* my terror *('êmātî)* before you *(lĕpāneykā)*," and "I will send *(šālah)* the pestilence *(haṣṣir'â)* before you *(lĕpāneykā)*." The metaphors of terror and pestilence interpret the holy war imagery of the Messenger from v. 23. Although the promise of land runs throughout the epilogue, relating the two sections, the change of topic from the Messenger as wilderness guide to the divine terror indicates a development in theme from journey to conquest. The initial promise of the Messenger encourages the Israelites to be faithful in their pilgrimage to the land (vv. 20-26), while the subsequent promise of divine terror demands faithfulness in the conquest of the land (vv. 27-33). The conclusion to the Book of the Covenant indicates the thematic development from guidance to conquest.

7. For an overview of the different functions of the Messenger *(mal'āk)* see G. von Rad, "angelos," *TDNT* 1:76-80; Blum, *Studien,* 58-60, 361-82, esp. 365-78.

8. Childs, *Exodus,* 486.

23:20-26 The opening section centers on the divine promise of a "Messenger" *(mal'āk)*. The first person divine speech gives the divine promise immediacy. The particle *hinnēh,* "see," is combined with the pronoun and participle *'ānōkî šōlēaḥ,* "I am sending." The Non-P historian employs the same form in other central divine predictions, including the death of the Egyptian firstborn ("See, I am killing your firstborn sons," 4:23); the theophany to the Israelites ("See, I am coming to you in a dense cloud," 19:9); and the establishment of covenant ("See, I am making a covenant with you," 34:10). The promise in 23:20-26 is that the Messenger will be the wilderness guide for the Israelite people. Verse 20 states that the Messenger will lead the Israelite people to the place that Yahweh has prepared for them. There is imagery of conquest in the section (vv. 23-24), but the focus remains on the leading of the Messenger, which will require careful observance by the Israelite people (vv. 21-22) and result in the benefits of health (vv. 25-26).

The leading of the Messenger will be through divine law. The reference to the voice of the Messenger in v. 22 recalls the divine voice as law in the theophany (19:19). The command that the Israelite people listen to the voice of the Messenger repeats the earlier exhortations to observe the law, which was stated at the outset of the wilderness journey (15:26) and at the mountain of God (19:5): "If you listen carefully to his voice" (*'im-šāmōaʻ tišmaʻ bĕqōlî,* 23:22). Exodus 23:25-26 promises that faithful observance of law in the wilderness journey will lead to the health of the Israelite people in the promised land. If the Israelites obey divine law by separating themselves from the worship practices of the indigenous nations, God promises to give the people health (food, water, no disease or miscarriages), reiterating the divine promise from the outset of the wilderness journey: "If you listen carefully to the voice of Yahweh, your God . . . all the disease that I set in Egypt I will not set on you. For I am Yahweh, your healer" (15:26).

23:27-33 The Messenger becomes an agent of holy war in 23:27-33. The section describes the conquest of the land through two divine promises. God states: "I will send my terror *('êmâ)* before you." The terror of God is a holy war motif. It seizes the Canaanites in the Song of the Sea (15:16) and in the conquest story of Joshua (Josh 2:9). The result of God's terror is that the nations are frozen into "panic" or "confusion" *(hāmam),* which is the same reaction of the Egyptians in the middle of the Red Sea (Exod 14:24), when they recognized the power of God against them. The second divine promise, 23:28, reinforces the image of conquest as a divine war against the nations. God states: "I will send the pestilence *(ṣirʻâ)*." The image is likely that of hornets (see also Deut 7:20; Josh 24:12). The result of the hornets is that the indigenous nations will be driven out *(gāraš;* Exod 23:28, 29, 30, 31; 33:2) of the land, including the Amorites, Hittites, Perizzites, Canaanites, Hivites, and Jebusites (see the commentary on 3:4b-9).

The image of God driving out the nations is a motif of divine war from the story of the exodus (11:1; 12:39). The same imagery occurs in Canaanite mythology (*CTA* 1.iv.24; 2.iv.12) and in the Moabite Inscription, in which the god Chemosh is praised for "driving out" the Israelites from the land of Moab.[9]

The divine promises of holy war serve an ideological and theological role for the Non-P author. The demand for exclusive loyalty to Yahweh provides insight into the theological motivation. The identity of the Israelites, as people who are not indigenous to the land of Canaan, fuels the theological demand that the Israelite nation be culturally and religiously separate from other nations in the land of Canaan and from their religious traditions. K. Schmid has noted that the exclusive vision of life in the land through invasion contrasts to the portrait of the patriarchs in Genesis — they are indigenous to the land and make covenant with their neighbors. The contrast provides the basis for Schmid's conclusion that the story of the patriarchs in Genesis and Moses in Exodus–Numbers represent distinct origin traditions now combined in the Non-P History (for Schmid this combination is first accomplished by the P historian).[10] D. Sperling characterizes the biblical conquest tradition as a political allegory to support the utopian goal of religious exclusion.[11] The theme of exclusivity arose in the first section of the epilogue (Exod 23:20-26), when God demanded that the Israelite people not worship indigenous gods, focusing in particular on the destruction of their cultic objects (23:24-25). It returns in the second section of the epilogue, when God forbids all covenants with foreign gods (23:32). The separate commands reinforce the first two commandments of the Decalogue, which also demand that the Israelites serve no other gods than Yahweh (20:3 = 23:32) and that they refrain from the worship of idols (20:4-6 = 23:24-25).

The epilogue concludes with a survey of the boundaries of the promised land in 23:31. Geographical descriptions of the promised land are an established genre of literature in Israelite history writing. They must not be confused with the historical geography of ancient Israel. Z. Kallai has clarified that the written tradition of the geographical boundaries of the land serves ideological purposes for ancient Israelite scribes and historians. It provides a framework to address such themes as covenant, the relationship of the Israelites to their neighbors, and the divine right of land.[12] All of these themes are present in the

9. See *ANET*, 320-21.

10. Schmid, *Erzväter und Exodus*. For Schmid the combination of the two origin traditions is a later literary achievement first accomplished by the P historian.

11. D. Sperling, *The Original Torah: The Political Intent of the Bible's Writers* (New York: New York University Press, 1998).

12. Z. Kallai, "The Patriarchal Boundaries, Canaan and the Land of Israel: Patterns and Application in Biblical Historiography," *IEJ* 47 (1997): 69-82; idem, "Territorial Patterns, Biblical Historiography and Scribal Tradition — A Programmatic Survey," *ZAW* 93 (1981): 431.

epilogue to the Book of the Covenant. The ideological use of geography means that the different boundaries for the land reflect the particular social circumstances of an author, as well as changing worldviews about the relationship of the Israelites to their neighbors. Some biblical writers include portions of the land east of the Jordan within the territory of the promised land, others do not.[13] The distinct boundaries imply different points of view about the relationship of the Israelite people to the Edomites and Ammonites who occupy this territory. The divergent views of the geography of the promised land in the Non-P and P Histories even influence the different accounts of the wilderness journey east of the Jordan (Numbers 20–21).[14]

The enormous size of the promised land is noteworthy in Exod 23:31. It reaches from the Egyptian Red Sea to the Euphrates River and from the Mediterranean Sea (the Sea of the Philistines) to the desert region. Thus the promised land includes the ancient kingdoms of Phoenicia, Syria, Edom, Ammon, as well as large sections of the Mesopotamian empire of the Assyrians and the later Neo-Babylonians. At no time in the history of the Israelite monarchy did the nation encompass the territory described in 23:31. The vision of the land is again serving an ideological and theological purpose for the Non-P author. The aim of the author is likely to indicate the territory in which the newly revealed law of Yahweh is authoritative. There are other echoes of the same tradition of geography in the Hebrew Bible. The rule of Solomon is idealized once as including the same territory envisioned in 23:31 (1 Kgs 4:21). Abraham also receives a promise of land that resembles Exod 23:31. It too stretches from Egypt to the Euphrates River (Gen 15:18-19). The size of the land promised to Abraham requires a list of ten nations to encompass the geopolitical scope of the indigenous population, rather than the more common list of six or seven nations.

The large boundaries of the promised land correspond to the administrative district "Across the River," first established by the Neo-Assyrians and continuing as a geopolitical region under the rule of the Neo-Babylonians and the Persians.[15] The district Across the River assumes a central role in the books of Ezra and Nehemiah, when it provides the territory for the legal authority of the Torah of Moses, most likely to embrace the Jews of the Diaspora within the world of divine Torah (Ezra 7:12-26). The Non-P historian shares the worldview of the author of Ezra–Nehemiah. Exodus 23:31 indicates the same broad region,

---

13. See Kallai, "Patriarchal Boundaries, Canaan," 69-82; and now his collected essays, *Biblical Historiography and Historical Geography: Collection of Studies* (BEATAJ 44; Frankfurt am Main: Peter Lang, 1998).

14. Kallai, *Biblical Historiography*, 165-74; B. MacDonald, *"East of the Jordan": Territories and Sites of the Hebrew Scriptures* (ASOR 6; Boston: American Schools of Oriental Research, 2000).

15. A. Rainey, "The Satrapy 'Beyond the River,'" *AJBA* 1 (1969): 51-78.

known as the Across the River district, to describe the geographical scope in which the Book of the Covenant functions as authoritative law.

COVENANT CEREMONY (24:1-11)

²⁴:¹ *But to Moses he said, "Ascend to Yahweh, you and Aaron, Nadab and Abihu, and the seventy elders of Israel. And you will worship from a distance. ² And Moses will draw near to Yahweh alone. But these will not draw near. And the people will not ascend with him."*

³ *And Moses approached and he read to the people all the words of Yahweh and all the rules. And all the people answered with one voice and they said, "All the words that Yahweh spoke we will do."*

⁴ *And Moses wrote all the words of Yahweh. And he arose early in the morning, and he built an altar at the base of the mountain, and twelve pillars for the twelve tribes of Israel.* ⁵ *And he sent the young men of Israel and they offered burnt offerings and they sacrificed sacrifices of well-being to Yahweh with oxen.* ⁶ ***And Moses took half of the blood and he placed it in basins, and half of the blood he sprinkled on the altar.*** ⁷ *And he took the book of the covenant and he read it aloud to the people.*

And they said, "All that Yahweh spoke we will do and we will obey."

⁸ ***And Moses took the blood and he sprinkled on the people. And he said, "This is the blood of the covenant that Yahweh cut with you according to all these words."***

⁹ ***And Moses and Aaron, Nadab and Abihu, and the seventy elders of Israel went up.*** ¹⁰ ***And they saw the God of Israel, and under his feet there was the likeness of pavement of sapphire stone, like the very heaven for purity.*** ¹¹ ***But against the leaders of the Israelites he did not send his hand. And they beheld the God, and they ate and they drank.***

Notes

24:1 *But to Moses he said.* Hebrew *wě'el-mōšeh* is disjunctive, "but." The absence of a subject for the verb *'āmar,* "he said," is unusual, most likely relating the instruction in the introduction to the Book of the Covenant in 20:21-22.

ascend to Yahweh, you and Aaron, Nadab and Abihu, and the seventy elders of Israel. The Sam adds Eliezar and Ithamar along with Nadab and Abihu, completing the list of Aaron's sons.

And you will worship from afar. The LXX changes the command from the second to the third person, *proskynēsousin,* "they will worship," and specifies the object of worship as *tō kyriō,* "to the Lord."

24:2 *to Yahweh.* The LXX reads *pros ton theon,* "to God."

with him. The LXX reads *met' autōn*, "with them."

24:3 *all the words that Yahweh spoke we will do.* The LXX adds *akousometha*, "and we will hear."

24:4 *twelve pillars.* The MT *maṣṣēbâ* is changed to "stones" in the LXX *(lithous)* and in the Sam *('bnym).*

24:5 *the young men of Israel.* The meaning of Hebrew *na'ărê běnê yiśrā'ēl* is unclear. The phrase could be determinate, "the young men," or indeterminate, "young men" (see NRSV). The word *na'ar* designates a young male. But the term can also identify an attendant, such as "the attendants of David" (1 Sam 25:9, 12, 25). The translation "the attendants of the Israelites" suggests a more defined group functioning in the priestly role of sacrificing.[16] The LXX provides no clarity, translating *tous neaniskous tōn huiōn Israēl*, "the youth of the sons of Israel."

sacrifices of well-being. The absolute construction of Hebrew *zĕbāḥîm šĕlāmîm* as the designation of a sacrifice appears only one other time in the Hebrew Bible (1 Sam 11:15). Rendtorff argues that *zĕbāḥîm* is an addition to the text, while E. Zenger suggests the opposite, that *šĕlāmîm* is a later addition.[17] The closest parallel to the Hebrew is the *zebaḥ šĕlāmîm* or *zibḥê šĕlāmîm* sacrifice in the P tradition (29:28; Lev 3:1, 3, 6, 9; 4:10; 7:11-21, 29, 34; 9:18; 10:14). The LXX translates, *thysian sōtēriou*, "peace offering."

with oxen. Hebrew *pārîm*, "oxen," lacks the preposition.

24:6 *basins.* Hebrew *'aggānōt* also occurs in Cant 7:3 and Isa 22:24. See also *CTA* 23.15, 31, 36. The LXX translates, *kratēras*, "bowls."

24:7 *and he read it aloud to the people.* Hebrew *wayyiqrā' bĕ'oznê hā'ām* is lit. "he called into the ears of the people."

24:8 *this is the blood of the covenant.* Hebrew *hinnēh dam-habbĕrît* is lit. "See, the blood of the covenant."

24:9 *and Moses and Aaron, Nadab and Abihu, and the seventy elders of Israel went up.* Hebrew *wayya'al* is singular, "he went up."

24:10 *and they saw the God of Israel.* Hebrew *wayyir'û 'ēt 'ĕlōhê yiśrā'ēl* indicates a direct perception of the Deity. Cf. LXX, *eidon ton topon hou heistēkei ekei ho theos tou Israēl*, "they saw the place where the God of Israel stood."

sapphire stone. Hebrew *sappîr*, "a sapphire-like stone," denotes lapis lazuli.

purity. Hebrew *lāṭōhar* could also be translated "clearness" (see NRSV).

24:11 *the leaders of the Israelites.* The identity of the Hebrew *'aṣîlê běnê yiśrā'ēl*, "the leaders of the Israelites," is unclear. The LXX translates, *tōn epilektōn*, "a select group."

---

16. See already C. Steuernagel, "Der jehovistische Bericht über den Bundesschluss am Sinai," *TSK* 72 (1899): 319-50, esp. 348-49.

17. R. Rendtorff, *Studien zur Geschichte des Opfers im Alten Israel* (WMANT 24; Neukirchen-Vluyn: Neukirchener Verlag, 1967), 41, 98-99, 150-51; Zenger, *Sinaitheophanie*, 75, 150.

Commentary

Exodus 24:1-11 is a literary montage recounting two events, a covenant ceremony (24:3-8) and a theophany with festal meal on the divine mountain (24:1-2, 9-11). Both events are fashioned around independent traditions. C. Steuernagel noted already at the end of the nineteenth century that the sacrifices by "the young men of Israel" (24:4-5) rest uneasily within a larger ritual focused on Moses, whose writing and reading of law forms a covenant between God and the Israelite people (24:3-8).[18] Similarly, E. W. Nicholson notes that the direct vision of God by "the leaders of the Israelites" (24:10-11) creates tension with the divine command in vv. 1b-2 that only Moses ascend the mountain to approach God.[19]

The authorship of 24:1-11 also separates between the Non-P and P historians. The Non-P historian composed the covenant ceremony (24:3-8) repeating motifs from the proposal of covenant (19:1-8a). The parallels include Moses' presentation of the divine words to the people (19:7; 24:3) and their unanimous acceptance of them (19:8a; 24:3, 7). The repetition advances the theme of covenant from a divine offer (19:5) to its ratification in a book (24:7). The Non-P account of the revelation at the mountain in chaps. 19–24 includes the proposal of covenant (19:1-8a), the public revelation of God including the Decalogue (19:8b-19; 20:1-20), and the private revelation to Moses of the Book of the Covenant (20:21–23:33), which concludes with the covenant ceremony (24:3-8). Wellhausen recognized the structure long ago when he concluded that the ceremony in 24:3-8 was meant to be a formal closing for the promulgation of law.[20] The vision of God in 24:9-11 may also represent a covenant meal if it was used by the Non-P historian.

It is more likely, however, that the P historian incorporated the vision of God (24:1-2, 9-11) and included a purification ritual with blood (24:6, 8) into the covenant ceremony. The sprinkling of blood on both the altar and the participants has only one parallel in the Hebrew Bible, which is in the ordination ceremony of the priests (Lev 8:22-30). The divine speech to Moses in Exod 24:1-2, in which an initial command for a large group to approach God (v. 1a) is restricted to Moses (vv. 1b-2), recalls the literary technique from 19:20-24, where the P author also restricted access to the sacred through a divine speech to Mo-

---

18. Steuernagel, "Jehovistische Bericht," 348-49. See also Beyerlin, *Oldest Sinaitic Traditions*, 39; Driver, *Exodus*, 253; Perlitt, *Bundestheologie*, 196-97; E. W. Nicholson, "The Covenant Ritual in Exodus XXIV 3-8," *VT* 32 (1982): 74-86.

19. See E. W. Nicholson, "The Interpretation of Exodus xxiv 9-11," *VT* 25 (1975): 77-97; idem, "The Antiquity of the Tradition in Exodus xxiv 9-11," *VT* 26 (1976): 148-60; Th. C. Vriezen, "The Exegesis of Exodus xxiv 9-11," *OTS* 17 (1972): 100-133; Dozeman, *God on the Mountain*, 28, 113-16.

20. Wellhausen, *Composition*, 82.

ses. The vision of God in 24:9-11 shows little sign of P composition, beyond perhaps the large cast of characters (24:1a, 9), suggesting that the description of God in vv. 10-11 is an independent tradition of theophany. But the theme of the vision of God provides transition for the P author to the revelation of the tabernacle in chaps. 25–31. The result, as noted by Wellhausen, is that the formal closing of the promulgation of law becomes an intermezzo for additional revelation and legislation.[21]

The present form of the text is the result of the P historian, who frames the covenant ceremony (24:3-8) with the story of theophany by using the technique of divine command (24:1-2) and fulfillment (24:9-11). The command in 24:1-2 introduces a new theme of theophany into the divine instruction of the Book of the Covenant. The setting for the revelation of the Book of the Covenant is of Moses on the divine mountain alone with God (20:21). This setting continues into 24:1-11, but there is a change in focus and in subject matter. The Book of the Covenant is divine law addressed to the people of Israel. Yahweh states to Moses: "Thus you will say to the people of Israel *('el-běnê yiśrā'ēl)*" (20:22). Exodus 24:1 marks a transition from the legislation governing the people to more specific instruction for Moses concerning an additional theophany: "But to Moses *(wě'el-mōšeh)* he [God] said, 'Ascend to Yahweh.'" The new command pushes the story ahead from the revelation of law and the establishment of covenant to an additional theophany. The result is that the vision of God in the heavenly temple (24:9-11) provides transition to the appearance of the Glory of Yahweh on Mount Sinai (24:15-18), which is the setting for the revelation of the tabernacle (chaps. 25–31).

24:1-2 These verses conclude the divine instruction that began in 20:22. In v. 1a God directs Moses to select a group of leaders and to ascend the divine mountain for worship. Verses 1b-2 qualify the command. God instructs Moses to ascend alone to the summit of the mountain, separating him from the leaders, who must remain at a lower point on the mountain. The people are restricted from the mountain altogether. The command recalls the previous restrictions from 19:20-24, while comparison indicates progression in the drama of theophany. God demanded the exclusion of all the Israelite people and the leaders from the mountain in 19:20-24. Now God allows the leaders to ascend the mountain. They include Aaron and his two eldest sons, Nadab and Abihu, as well as seventy of the elders of Israel. The characters separate into two groups, representing the models of leadership in the Non-P and P Histories.

The elders have played a significant role in the Non-P History. They were the focus of Moses' commission (3:16, 18). Their belief in Moses was crucial for establishing his authority (4:1, 5, 8, 9, 31), and their loyalty was a central theme

---

21. Ibid., 83.

in the opening confrontation between Pharaoh and Moses (5:1-21). The elders emerged as worship leaders during the Passover (12:21-27) and as judges in the initial stages of the wilderness journey (18:1-12). The inclusion of the elders on the divine mountain for the theophany further confirms their leadership role. The identification of seventy elders suggests an even more select group whose authority the Non-P historian will develop further in Numbers 11, when they receive a portion of Moses' spirit and thus become inspired scribes. The social and religious role of the seventy elders is difficult to describe.[22] The prophet Ezekiel provides some evidence that such a group assumed a leadership role in worship during the exilic period that the prophet strongly opposed (Ezek 8:11).

Aaron and his sons Nadab and Abihu represent the priestly leadership advocated in the P History. Aaron is a central character in the P History. The genealogy in Exod 6:14-27 identifies Aaron as the brother of Moses, and Nadab and Abihu as his two eldest sons. In the plague cycle Aaron assumes an important role, representing the power of Yahweh over against the Egyptian magicians (chaps. 7–10). The ordination of Aaron and his sons emerges as a crucial theme in the P History to overcome the separation of divine holiness. The ordination of the Aaronide priesthood is announced by God in Exodus 29 and accomplished in Leviticus 8–9. The inclusion of Nadab and Abihu is particularly noteworthy, since God kills them immediately after their ordination because of improper leadership in worship (Lev 10:1-2). The result is the continuation of the Aaronide priesthood through Eleazar and Ithamar. R. de Vaux rightly notes that the exclusion of certain of Aaron's sons from the priesthood likely reflects social and political developments in the exilic and the postexilic periods.[23] The appearance of Nadab and Abihu in Exod 24:1-2, 9-11, and Lev 10:1-2 anticipates a thematic development in the P History, from the theophany on the mountain of God in Exodus 24 to the theophany on the altar in Leviticus 8–10 (see the commentary on 24:9-11 and 24:12-18).

24:3-8 Moses approaches the people with the divine legislation to perform the covenant ceremony. The description of Moses' ascent as an "approach," his proclamation of "all the words of Yahweh," and the unanimous acceptance of the people to obey divine law in 24:3-4 create parallels to the proposal of covenant in 19:7-8a. But the additional notice in v. 4a that Moses wrote down the divine words is a new motif relating divine speech and Scripture. The codification of a divine law allows the revelation at the mountain to progress from the proposal of covenant (19:1-8a) to a closing ceremony (24:3-8),

---

22. See Dozeman, *God on the Mountain*, 180-92; J. L. Ska, "Le repas de Ex 24,11," *Bib* 74 (1993): 305-27.

23. R. de Vaux, *Ancient Israel: Its Life and Institutions* (trans. J. McHugh; 2 vols.; 1961; repr. New York: McGraw-Hill, 1965), 2:372-86, 396-97.

which includes a sacrificial ritual (vv. 4b-6), a public reading of law (v. 7), and a covenant ceremony (v. 8).

That the sacrificial ritual in 24:4b-5 fits loosely into its present narrative suggests its original independence. It begins at dawn with the construction of an altar at the base of the mountain and the establishment of twelve pillars representing the twelve tribes of Israel. The objects suggest some form of a covenant ceremony. A pillar provides the witness to a covenant between Jacob and Laban in Gen 31:45-54. Twelve stones return as a memorial to the crossing of the Jordan (Joshua 4). The central role of the young men of Israel, rather than Moses, indicated to Steuernagel that the sacrificial ritual was independent of its present narrative context.[24] He may be correct. A more specific role of the "young men of Israel" is not possible to discern in the Hebrew Bible. In this text they are responsible for burnt offerings (*ʿōlōt*), a sacrifice in which the victim is wholly consumed on the altar. They also offer "sacrifices of well-being (*zĕbāḥîm šĕlāmîm*) to Yahweh."

The meaning of the second sacrifice, *zĕbāḥîm šĕlāmîm* (lit. "sacrifices, well-being sacrifices"), is unclear and even ungrammatical (see also 1 Sam 11:15 and the translation note on 24:5). The first term, "sacrifices" (*zĕbāḥîm*), is a general term for offerings, and the "well-being" (*šĕlāmîm*) offering was a communal meal between the worshiper and God. Rendtorff identifies "sacrifices" as an addition, resulting in the original combination of "burnt offerings" and "well-being sacrifices."[25] The repetition of the same two offerings in the story of the golden calf (Exod 32:6) supports this reading, providing a reversal between the establishment of covenant and the breaking of it. But the pairing of "burnt offerings" and "sacrifices" also occurs in the Non-P History. Moses informs Pharaoh during the plagues that Yahweh requires "burnt offerings and sacrifices" of the Israelites (10:25), which Jethro performs for Moses and the leaders of Israel (18:12). The offering of the same sacrifices by the young men of Israel would fulfill the demand of Yahweh first stated by Moses and taught to the Israelites by Jethro. The P "sacrifice of well-being" *(zebaḥ šĕlāmîm)* provides the closest parallel to the present form of 24:5 (see the translation note on 24:5).[26]

The sacrifice provides the context for a blood ritual of three stages in 24:6-8: the sprinkling of blood on the altar (v. 6); the reading of the Book of the Covenant to the people, who accept its authority (v. 7); and the sprinkling of blood on the people with the pronouncement that it is the "blood of the covenant" (v. 8). The blood ritual begins when Moses halves the blood, sprinkling one portion on the altar and placing the remaining half in a vessel, an *ʾaggānōt*,

---

24. Steuernagel, "Jehovistische Bericht," 319-50.
25. Rendtorff, *Studien zur Geschichte*, 41, 98-99, 150-51.
26. See Milgrom, *Leviticus 1–16*, 217-25.

a form of cultic bowl also appearing in Ugaritic myths (*CTA* 23.15, 31, 36) as well as in Isa 22:24 and Cant 7:3. The sprinkling of blood on the altar does not appear in Deuteronomy, but is a ritual in the P legislation, suggesting the P historian incorporates the ritual in Exod 24:6 and 8. The halving of blood and its sprinkling on both the altar and the participants repeats only in the ordination of the Aaronide priesthood in Lev 8:22-30. Milgrom interprets the sprinkling of blood on the priests in Leviticus 8 as a means of decontaminating and purifying them.[27] The sprinkling of blood on the people may also be functioning as a form of purification for the covenant.

The motif of covenant repeats twice in the ceremony. First the Non-P historian recounts that the people hear the Book of the Covenant and accept its authority (Exod 24:3-4a). The expression "Book of the Covenant" occurs in only one other context in the Hebrew Bible: Josiah's finding it in the temple prompts his religious reform (2 Kgs 23:2, 21). The repetition creates a literary relationship between the Jerusalem temple, the Book of the Covenant, and the foundational ceremony of covenant in the wilderness at the divine mountain. Interpreters debate whether the Non-P historian intended the Decalogue as part of the Book of the Covenant.[28] The structure of the Non-P History separates the Book of the Covenant from the Decalogue. God, not Moses, will write the Decalogue on the tablets of stone (Exod 24:12-15) in the concluding episode. The central point is that revelation is codified, becoming authoritative law for the Israelite people (v. 4b). The motif of covenant appears a second time in the concluding blood ritual (v. 8). The people are sprinkled with the "blood of the covenant." The ritual may function as a way of sealing the covenant. But the parallel to Lev 8:22-30 underscores the purifying role of the ritual, preparing the people to live in proximity to holiness.

The purification of the people allows the drama of theophany to progress beyond Exod 19:16-19, when Yahweh ceased the divine descent because of the lack of safeguards to protect holiness (19:20-24). The purging of the people with the "blood of the covenant" does not allow them to feast with God on the divine mountain (24:9-11), but it does prepare them to see the Glory of Yahweh on the mountain (24:12-18), and eventually in the altar before the tabernacle (Lev 9:23-24). The expression "blood of the covenant" repeats once in the Hebrew Bible. The prophet Zechariah develops the theme of purification and theophany into an eschatological vision of salvation when the "blood of the covenant" prompts God to refashion the creation and, in the process, to rescue the Israelite people from slavery (Zech 9:9-13). NT writers incorporate the purification ritual into the passion of Jesus, whose sacrificial blood becomes "the blood of the cove-

---

27. Ibid., 528-29.
28. See Childs, *Exodus*, 505.

nant" (Matt 26:28; Mark 14:24), memorialized in the Eucharist. Paul (1 Cor 11:25) and the author of the Gospel of Luke (22:20) emphasize more the eschatological character of the text, describing the "blood of the covenant" as "new," employing imagery from Jer 31:31-34.

24:9-11 Theophany takes center stage in this section. Comparison to 19:16-19 indicates development of the theme. The initial theophany included the primary motifs of the genre: fire, thunder, lightning, and the dense cloud. Yet the event itself was unstable and lacked clear rituals of sanctification for the people and a sanctuary to contain divine holiness. Exodus 24:3-8 introduced initial rituals of purification for the people. Verses 9-11 begin the process of addressing the need for a sanctuary by introducing the image of the heavenly temple as the model for an earthly sanctuary to contain the holiness of God.

Verse 9 lists the characters who experience the vision of the divine temple: Moses, Aaron, Nadab, Abihu, and the seventy elders, a repetition from v. 1b. Verses 10-11 provide the content of their experience as a direct vision of the "God of Israel." But the text immediately gives way to temple imagery, "under his feet was something like a pavement made of sapphire *(libnat hassapîr),* pure *(ṭōhar)* as the heaven itself *(ûkĕʿeṣem haššāmayim lāṭōhar)*." The "sapphire-like stone" under the feet of God is the precious stone, lapis lazuli, used in temple construction in the ancient Near East.[29] The prophet Ezekiel envisions the throne of God with the same material (Ezek 1:26; 10:1). E. Ruprecht adds to the image, noting that the blue color of lapis lazuli could also refer to the pinnacle of the temple. The blue of the temple pinnacle symbolized the connection between heaven and earth that allows for the descent of God into the earthly sanctuary.[30] Thus the vision is of the divine temple. The additional description of the vision, "like the very heaven for purity," requires interpretation. Hebrew *ûkĕʿeṣem* literally means "and like bone," but can also express absolute identity, "bone of my bone" (Gen 2:23). The translation "like the very heaven for purity" indicates that the veil between heaven and earth is momentarily lifted.

The word *ṭōhar* has two meanings, "clear" and "pure." Both meanings may be functioning in Exod 24:10-11, where the imagery suggests that the vision of God on the heavenly throne is "clear," meaning unobstructed. It also indicates that the "pure" environment of heaven has also momentarily engulfed the participants. Ugaritic texts describe Baal's heavenly temple with the same language (*CTA* 4.v.81-82, 95-97). The experience is so surprising and dangerous

---

29. See Eliade, *Sacred and Profane,* 36-40; and the qualification by J. Z. Smith, *To Take Place: Toward Theory in Ritual* (Chicago: University of Chicago Press, 1987).

30. E. Ruprecht, "Exodus 24,9-11 als Beispiel lebendiger Erzähltradition aus der Zeit des babylonischen Exil," in *Werden und Wirken des Alten Testaments: Festschrift für Claus Westermann* (ed. R. Albertz et al.; Neukirchen-Vluyn: Neukirchener Verlag, 1978), 138-73, esp. 146-51.

that it requires a footnote. The writer clarifies that no one was killed: "But against the leaders of the Israelites he did not send his hand." Instead of death, the participants acquire clairvoyant vision: "They beheld *(ḥāzâ)* the God." Hebrew *ḥāzâ* often signifies prophetic insight. The direct vision of the Deity is accompanied by a meal on the divine mountain, a repetition from 18:12 when Jethro led the participants in worship. A similar meal is also mythologized by the prophet Isaiah in Isa 25:6-8, which has become a standard Easter lection in Christian tradition. But the heavenly temple in Exod 24:9-11 lacks an earthly counterpart, providing the central theme for the remainder of the book of Exodus: the construction of a temple on earth.

Sanctuary (24:12–40:38)

INTRODUCTION

CENTRAL THEMES

The central theme of the final episode is the presence of God on earth, dwelling within a sanctuary in the midst of the Israelite people. The theme of divine presence assumed center stage already in the wilderness journey to the mountain of God (15:22–18:27), when the Israelites began to glimpse the nearness of God through manna, the rhythm of Sabbath, the gift of water, and the promise of health. The theme intensified upon the arrival at the divine mountain (19:1–24:11), where holiness underscored the separation between God and humans, heaven and earth, the sacred and the profane, and even the pure and the impure (see the introduction to 19:1–24:11). The problem of the separation between God and humans continues into the final episode. But the means for bridging the two worlds evolves from the revelation of law and the establishment of covenant (chaps. 19–24) to the construction of a sanctuary and the creation of cultic rituals (chaps. 25–40; Leviticus; Numbers 1–10). The vision of the heavenly temple in 24:9-11 signals the change in theme. The construction of the sanctuary will replicate the heavenly temple on earth and thus allow a holy God to dwell safely in the midst of the Israelites.

Temple and Cosmic Mountain

The symbolism of the temple in ancient Near Eastern religion creates a web of related themes that influence the interpretation of 24:12–40:38. The theological meaning of the temple is rooted in its association with the mythology of the cosmic mountain. G. van der Leeuw represents the interpretation of the cosmic mountain as a *Weltberg* ("a world mountain"): "The mountain, the hard stone, was regarded as a primal and permanent element of the world: out of the waters of Chaos rose the primeval hill from which sprang all life; . . . it was looked upon as the navel of the earth, as its focal point and beginning."[1] M. Eliade clarified the mythological view of the cosmic mountain as a *Weltberg* and its relationship to the temple with two conclusions. First, the cosmic mountain connects heaven and earth, and in that role it represents both the temporal origin of the world ("the primeval hill") and its spatial center (the *Axis Mundi* and the Navel). Second, the temple is assimilated into the cosmic mountain and thus it also joins heaven and earth, participating in the mythology of the "center."

The comprehensive claims of the mythology of the *Weltberg* has been criticized and qualified by subsequent researchers. J. Z. Smith rightly concludes that the mythology of the *Weltberg*, especially in the role of the primeval hill, does not exist in Mesopotamian religion or in Canaanite mythology.[2] Yet even with these qualifications, the association of the temple and the mythology of the divine mountain remain important insights into the religious world of the ancient Near East. R. J. Clifford agrees that the cosmic mountain and the temple do not represent the cosmological center envisioned by the *Weltberg*. Yet he recognizes the theological significance of the association of the cosmic mountain and the temple.[3] Foremost, a cosmic mountain represents the meeting place between heaven and earth and hence the residency of God within the temple. The Canaanite god Baal invades the created world by taking up residency in his temple on Mount Zaphon. The same is true of Yahweh, who takes up residency on Mount Zion (Ps 76:2), which is equated at times with Mount Zaphon (Psalm 48). As the location of holiness in the profane world, the sacred mountain and its temple provide the resource for health, water, and fertility. Psalm 65 describes Yahweh sending forth water from his temple residence on Mount Zion. Living water also flows from the throne of God in Ps 46:4 and in Ezek 47:1-12. The cosmic mountain is also the location from where God wages war against enemies. Habakkuk 3 envisions Yahweh warring against his enemies from the divine mountain Teman. Psalm 76:2-3 represents the more common development, in which the cosmic mountain, the temple, and a royal city merge in the image of war. It describes Yahweh waging a fierce war from his temple home on Mount Zion in the royal city of Jerusalem. Psalm 2 envisions

---

1. G. van der Leeuw, *Religion in Essence and Manifestation* (trans. J. E. Turner; 2 vols.; Princeton: Princeton University Press, 1963), 1:55-56.

2. J. Z. Smith, *To Take Place: Toward Theory in Ritual* (Chicago: University of Chicago Press, 1987), 13-23.

3. R. J. Clifford, *The Cosmic Mountain in Canaan and the Old Testament* (HSM 4; Cambridge: Harvard University Press, 1972).

the earthly king joining in the war from Zion. Finally the cosmic mountain is also the source for divine governance of the world, including the location from where God issues divine decrees: Torah goes forth from Mount Zion according to the prophet Isaiah (Isa 2:2-4).

The preceding examples indicate the role of the Jerusalem temple and Mount Zion in the mythology of the cosmic mountain. Biblical writers never cease to return to the subject of Zion. The construction of the Jerusalem temple repeats in the Deuteronomistic History (1 Kings 5–9) and in the Chronicler's History (1 Chronicles 17–2 Chronicles 8). It reappears in the stories of restoration in Ezra and in Nehemiah. It also provides the focal point for the preaching of Haggai and the visions of Ezekiel (chaps. 40–48) and Zechariah (chaps. 1–8). G. T. R. Hayward traces the continuing influence of the mythology of Zion in a host of nonbiblical writers, including Hecataeus of Abdera, Ben Sira, *Jubilees,* as well as Philo and Josephus.[4]

The symbolism of the divine mountain and the temple also informs the building of the sanctuary in Exod 24:12–40:38. Two motifs are especially prominent. The sanctuary in the wilderness will connect heaven and earth, providing a safe means for Yahweh to take up residency with the Israelite people. The sanctuary also stores the covenant tablets, indicating that it is the location from where God issues the divine decrees. But the absence of a royal city as the location for Yahweh's sanctuary, so central to the mythology of the Jerusalem temple, is equally important for interpretation.[5] It indicates the antimonarchical orientation of both the Non-P and P Histories. Both historians replace the royal imagery of Mount Zion with the symbols of Mount Horeb and Mount Sinai, and the permanent temple in the royal city of Jerusalem with the movable tent shrines, the tent of meeting (33:7-11) in the Non-P History and the tabernacle (chaps. 25–31, 35–40) in the P History.

Literary Tradition of Temple Building

V. Hurowitz describes the impact of temple symbolism in the literary tradition of the ancient Near East. The mythology of the temple is evident in building inscriptions. Hurowitz notes that already in the earliest sources the building inscriptions support a royal ideology, which interweaves temple, city, law, and

4. G. T. R. Hayward, *The Jewish Temple: A Non-Biblical Sourcebook* (London: Routledge, 1996); see also C. R. Koester, *The Dwelling of God: The Tabernacle in the Old Testament, Intertestamental Jewish Literature, and the New Testament* (CBQMS 22; Washington, DC: Catholic Biblical Association, 1989).

5. See B. Ollenburger, *Zion, the City of the Great King: A Theological Symbol for the Jerusalem Cult* (JSOTSup 41; Sheffield: JSOT Press, 1987).

king, infusing them with divine authority. The inscriptions indicate that the center of the royal ideology is the idealization of the king as a temple builder for the gods, and that the divine temple in turn gives authority to a royal city.[6] A cylinder inscription of King Gudea of Lagash provides an early example, describing the king as receiving a revelation from the god Ningirsu to build the temple Eninnu.[7] The account, according to Hurowitz, reflects a conventional pattern of six parts that continues to structure reports of temple building throughout the history of the ancient Near East. The pattern includes (1) the reason for temple construction with the consent of the gods; (2) the preparation for construction, including the acquisition of all supplies; (3) the construction; (4) the dedication; (5) the prayer and the blessing to ensure prosperity; and (6) the conditional blessings and curses to ensure temple repair by future kings.[8] The literary pattern and the royal ideology inform the story of Solomon (1 Kings 5–9), who builds Yahweh's temple in his royal city Jerusalem.[9]

The building inscriptions are taken up into other literary genres in the ancient Near East.[10] The Laws of Hammurabi illustrate how the account of temple construction gives divine authority to law. The prologue anchors the authority of Hammurabi (and his law code) in the gods, because of the divine origin of his city Babylon and because of Hammurabi's care for and restoration of the temples in Babylon (Prologue).[11] The creation myth *Enuma Elish* illustrates an even more complex development of the building account, as the climax of creation resulting from the divine victory over chaos. Marduk's victory over Tiamat and his enthronement as the divine king are intertwined in *Enuma Elish* (tablet IV). Once he is victorious over chaos Marduk creates the cosmos, including the sun, moon, and all the heavenly constellations (tablet V). But cosmological creation is unstable until the Anunnaki gods build Babylon (tablet VI), linking world creation, the city, and the divine sanctuary. Marduk authorizes the building: "Construct Babylon. . . . Let its brickwork be fashioned. You shall name it 'The Sanctuary'" (VI.57-58). After two years of construction, the Anunnaki present Marduk with his sanctuary city, proclaiming: "This is Babylon, the place that is your home!" (VI.72).[12] The story illustrates that the temple in *Enuma Elish* is not the primeval starting point of creation, but its capstone.

---

6. V. Hurowitz, *I Have Built You an Exalted House: Temple Building in the Bible in Light of Mesopotamian and Northwest Semitic Writings* (JSOTSup 115; Sheffield: Sheffield Academic Press, 1992), 312-13.

7. Ibid., 33-57.

8. Ibid., 311 *et passim*.

9. Ibid., 131-310.

10. Ibid., 91-92.

11. See *ANET*, 164-65.

12. See *ANET*, 68, 69.

The construction of the sanctuary in Exodus follows many of the patterns of temple construction from the ancient Near Eastern literary tradition. The two parts of Exodus are fashioned after the model of the god victorious over chaos, who builds a temple after achieving victory in war. Exodus 1:1–15:21 recounts the divine victory over the chaotic opponent. Revelation in the first part of the story of Exodus is in the form of the destructive plagues. Exodus 15:22–40:38 narrates the subsequent journey to the divine mountain for temple construction. The same pattern also structures the Canaanite mythology of Baal, whose victory over chaotic sea (*CTA* 2) also progresses to temple construction (*CTA* 3–4).

The building of the tabernacle is similar to *Enuma Elish* in that its construction is part of world creation, and, like the temple in Babylon, the tabernacle does not represent the primeval origin of creation but a significant addition to the process of world creation. There is also a contrast to Marduk's construction of his sanctuary in Babylon. The wilderness setting and the theme of a future enthronement of Yahweh in the promised land (15:17-18) indicate that the tabernacle is not the capstone of creation. The splitting of the Red Sea (14:21), the reemergence of Sabbath in the wilderness (chap. 16), and the six-day period of preparation for the revelation of the tabernacle on the seventh day (24:15-18) all suggest that the construction of Yahweh's sanctuary on earth is part of a process of world creation (or perhaps better, world re-creation). It is not the primeval event, nor even the capstone of creation. Rather, it represents a new era in creation marked by the New Year (40:2, 17). Hurowitz even discerns the ancient Near Eastern pattern of temple construction in the story of the tabernacle, including the revelation to Moses (24:15–31:18), the preparation of material (35:20–36:7), the construction (36:8–39:32), the consecration (Exodus 40; Leviticus 8), and the blessing (Lev 9:22-23).[13]

But there are significant differences between the building of the sanctuary in Exodus and the ancient Near Eastern literary tradition of temple construction. The wilderness sanctuary does not support the royal ideology so central to the ancient Near Eastern tradition. The builder and cult founder is not a king. Moses is a complex character in Exodus, embodying the roles of liberator, teacher, and priest. But at no time is he idealized as a king. Only once is Moses' leadership associated with monarchical imagery, in the opening story of his adult life, immediately after he murders the Egyptian (Exod 2:11-15). The image arises when one of the two Hebrews who is fighting describes Moses as a "prince" (*śar*, 2:14), while wondering if Moses intends to kill him. The imagery is thoroughly negative, far removed from the heroic projection of the king in the royal ideology. Not even the association of Moses with divine law in the

---

13. Hurowitz, *I Have Built*, 110-13.

previous episode (19:1–24:11) corresponds to the royal model as it is reflected in the Laws of Hammurabi. The lawgiver at the divine mountain is not a king, but a mediator and a scribe.

The imagery of the wilderness sanctuary also departs from the royal ideology of temple construction. It is not associated with a royal city or, for that matter, with any city. Thus unlike Babylon in *Enuma Elish* or Jerusalem in the royal ideology of Solomon, the presence of God in the wilderness sanctuary cannot be equated with a capital city. The absence of monarchical imagery in the idealization of Moses indicates that the construction of the sanctuary in 24:12–40:38 is an antimonarchical story. The separation of the divine residency from a royal city further confirms, as T. E. Fretheim has argued, that the tabernacle of the P History is anti-temple, if by temple we mean the king's royal sanctuary.[14]

Wilderness Sanctuary as Sacred Place

The revelation and construction of the wilderness sanctuary participate fully in the mythology of the cosmic mountain. The sanctuary connects heaven and earth on the divine mountain. It provides the location for the divine decrees of covenant, which, according to J. D. Levenson, disclose "the essential . . . relationship of YHWH to his people," thus creating value and meaning.[15] The humanistic geographer Yi-Fu Tuan clarifies the insight of Levenson with the geographical metaphors of space and place providing commentary on the setting of the wilderness: "Space is more abstract than place. What begins as undifferentiated space becomes place as we get to know it better and endow it with value. . . . If we think of space as that which allows movement, then place is pause; each pause in movement makes it possible for location to be transformed into place."[16] Tuan's description is commentary on the plot structure of the second half of Exodus. The Israelites begin their journey into the impersonal space of the wilderness, accumulating fleeting experiences of God at successive oases, until they pause at the divine mountain. The revelation of covenant law and the eventual residency of God in the sanctuary transform the abstract space of the wilderness into a place of value filled with meaning.

The revelation and construction of the wilderness sanctuary also critically evaluate the ancient Near Eastern literary tradition of temple building. The sanctuary certainly transforms the space of the wilderness into a place of

---

14. T. E. Fretheim, "The Priestly Document: Anti-Temple?" *VT* 18 (1968): 313-29.

15. Levenson, *Sinai and Zion*, 33.

16. Yi-Fu Tuan, *Space and Place: The Perspectives of Experience* (Minneapolis: University of Minnesota Press, 1977), 6; see also Smith, *To Take Place*, 24-46.

value. But the portable character of the wilderness sanctuary also resists a nationalistic interpretation, in which the residency of God is identified with and confined to a royal city. The introduction to the Book of the Covenant in the Non-P History draws out one implication of what it means to loosen the sanctuary from a single, royal cult site: "In every place *(māqôm)* where I cause to remember my name, I will come to you and I will bless you" (Exod 20:24). The location of the divine residency on earth in a movable shrine means that any impersonal space in the wilderness has the potential of becoming a personal place of value, a *māqôm* where God resides on earth. The closing verses of Exodus from the P History state the same insight with the imagery of travel: "In all the travels of the Israelites, whenever the cloud lifted from above the tabernacle, they would set out. But if the cloud was not taken up, they would not journey until the day that it was taken up. For the cloud of Yahweh was on the tabernacle by day, and a fire was on it by night before all the entire house of Israel throughout their journey" (40:36-38). Once God is loosened from a fixed temple in a royal city, the Deity is able to dwell with the Israelites "throughout their journey," rather than in a royal city. The separation of the wilderness sanctuary from a capital city and a king suggests further that both the Non-P and P historians reject the mythology of the sanctuary as the *Axis Mundi*. The tabernacle is not the center of world creation. Instead the Israelites journey toward the center, symbolized as the future rule of God in the promised land (15:17-18). In this respect Exodus and the Pentateuch as a whole are structured with an eye on the future, not the present. Both histories suggest the religious worldview of Diaspora Jews. The fulfillment or realization of the law revealed at Mount Sinai is a future ideal in the promised land.

AUTHORS

Research

There are broad areas of continuity in the identification of the authors of 24:12–40:38 in the modern period of interpretation. Wellhausen identified the author of the cultic law and ritual as P. This literature includes 25:1–31:17 and chaps. 35–40, and continues through Leviticus 1–27 and Num 1:1–10:28. He identified the ascent of Moses in Exod 24:15-18 as the narrative introduction to the legal corpus, which followed immediately from the arrival of the Israelites at the divine mountain (19:1-2a). Wellhausen also recognized a history of composition within the P legislation that subsequent scholars have developed.[17]

---

17. See the summary by Pola, *Die ursprüngliche Priesterschrift.*

Wellhausen concluded that the Non-P literature included the instruction for Moses and Joshua to receive the tablets in 24:12-14 and 31:18, the story of the golden calf in chap. 32, the intercession of Moses in chap. 33, and the renewal of the covenant in chap. 34. The Non-P literature comprised the work of several authors, including the sources J and E, perhaps an additional author in chap. 34, as well as redactional additions by JE, an editor that Wellhausen also identified as the Jehowist.

Wellhausen interpreted two different views of the cult in the P and the Non-P literature. The P author idealized the cult as the only way in which God is revealed at Sinai. This is evident by the revelation of the cult (chaps. 25–31) before the story of the golden calf (chap. 32). The Non-P authors (J and E) place the revelation of the cult after the sin of the golden calf (chaps. 33–34) as a compromise to the weakness of the people.[18]

The identification of the Non-P authors in chaps. 32–34 has been widely debated. The history of interpretation will be examined in the subsequent sections of the commentary. The boundaries of the P literature have remained more constant in the modern period of interpretation. Interpreters debate the composition of the narrative introduction to the P law in 24:15-18. Noth limited the introduction to 24:15b-18 and placed the ascent of Moses in v. 15a with vv. 12-14.[19] Beyerlin illustrates the tendency to separate the notice of Moses' forty-day stay on the mountain in 24:18b from the P source.[20] Van Seters notes the connections that emerge in the Non-P literature between 24:12-15a, 18b, 31:18*, and the introduction to the golden calf in 32:1-6. According to this line of interpretation, the P literature would then consist of 24:15b-18a and 25:1–31:17.[21]

There is disagreement about the presence of the P literature in chaps. 32–34. Interpreters agree that there are few signs of P literature in chaps. 32–33. Johnstone sees the presence of the P author in the reference to the "tablets of testimony" in 31:18 and 32:15.[22] The authorship of chap. 34 is more debated. Johnstone provides a recent example. He notes the emphasis on hierarchy and ritual purity in 34:2-3 as a sign of the P author, which provides a parallel to 19:12-13a and 20-25, where the same themes emerge.[23] M. Haran has also assigned the story of Moses' shining face to the P author, noting the connection to

---

18. Wellhausen, *Composition*, 81-98.

19. Noth, *Exodus*, 199-200.

20. Beyerlin, *Oldest Sinaitic Traditions*, 14-18.

21. Van Seters, *Life of Moses*, 292-93.

22. W. Johnstone, "Reactivating the Chronicles Analogy in Pentateuchal Studies, with Special Reference to the Sinai Pericope in Exodus," in *Chronicles and Exodus: An Analogy and Its Application* (JSOTSup 275; Sheffield: Sheffield Academic Press, 1998), 142-67, esp. 156-57.

23. Johnstone, "The Decalogue and the Redaction of the Sinai Pericope in Exodus," in *Chronicles and Exodus*, 168-97.

Figure 34

Topic	Non-P History	P History
Loss of Stone Tablets		
1. Ascent of Moses	24:12-15a, 18b; 31:18*	24:15b-18a
2. Revelation of tabernacle	———	25:1-31:17, 18*
3. Golden calf	32	32:15
Intercession of Moses in Tent of Meeting		
1. Retreat of God	33:1-6	———
2. Tent of meeting	33:7-11	———
3. Ritual of intercession	33:12-23	———
Recovery of Stone Tablets		
1. Mercy of God	34:1, 4*, 5-9	34:2-3, 4*
2. New tablets	34:10-28	34:29a
3. Moses' face	34:29b-35	34:32*
4. Construction of tabernacle	———	35:1–40:38

the motif of splendor in Num 27:20.[24] The debates over authorship will receive more detailed review in the commentary.

Non-P and P Histories

The chart in figure 34 above identifies the literature of the Non-P and P Histories. The subsequent sections provide an overview of their distinctive motifs and divergent interpretations of the wilderness sanctuary.

A range of contrasting motifs allows for the identification of the Non-P and P Histories. The most important distinction is the description of the divine sanctuary as the "tent of meeting" (33:7-11) in the Non-P History and as the "tabernacle" (chaps. 25–31, 35–40) in the P History. The tent of meeting represents the oracular and aniconic cultic presence of God. Joshua functions as its priestly custodian. The revelation of God is in the form of direct speech to Moses. The P History transforms the tent of meeting into the tabernacle, with complex architecture and furnishings. Aaron and his sons replace Joshua as the

---

24. M. Haran, "The Shining of Moses' Face: A Case Study in Biblical and Ancient Near Eastern Iconography," in *In the Shelter of Elyon: Essays on Ancient Palestinian Life and Literature in Honor of G. W. Ahlström* (ed. W. B. Barrick and J. Spencer; JSOTSup 31; Sheffield: JSOT Press, 1984), 159-73.

priestly custodians. The revelation of God as speech in the tent of meeting also becomes the appearance of the Glory of Yahweh in the tabernacle (24:15b-18a; 40:34-38; Lev 9:22-24). Moreover, the sanctuaries are located on distinct mountains. The tent of meeting is associated with Mount Horeb (33:6), while the tabernacle is revealed on Mount Sinai (24:15b-18a; 34:2-3, 4*, 29a, 32). The plot structure of the two histories is also organized around divergent tablets. The "tablets of stone" (*lūḥōt hā'eben,* 24:12; 31:18*; 34:1, 4*, 28) in the Non-P History become the "tablets of testimony" (*lūḥōt hā'ēdūt,* 31:18*; 32:15; 34:29) in the P History. The "tablets of stone" limit the divine words to the Decalogue, thus emphasizing the presence of God as speech. The "tablets of testimony," by contrast, contain the entire architectural plans of the tabernacle and its instructions for cultic rituals.

The comparisons indicate that the Non-P and P Histories present conflicting views of the proper sanctuary to contain the presence of God on earth. The Non-P History idealizes the presence of God as speech. The tent of meeting, the tablets of stone, and the setting of Mount Horeb conform to the account of theophany in the Non-P History, when God speaks directly to the people in issuing the Decalogue (19:9, 19; 20:1-20). The P History emphasizes more the visual presence of God. The tabernacle, the tablets of testimony, and the setting of Mount Sinai provide location and structure for the fiery Glory of Yahweh to reside on earth. Wellhausen may also be correct that the P History emphasizes the importance of the cult by providing its revelation before the story of the golden calf.

What holds the Non-P and P Histories together is their rejection of the golden calf as representing the cultic presence of Yahweh on earth. The shared tradition of the Decalogue in the Non-P and P Histories provides religious grounding for their condemnation. Both agree that the Decalogue leaves no room for other gods or images (20:3-6; Deut 5:7-10). The inner-biblical interpretation of the golden calf as representing the cult of Jeroboam (1 Kgs 12:25-33) provides a shared political grounding for the two histories in rejecting the royal ideology of the cult and the king. As political allegories, the Non-P and P Histories agree that the merging of the king and the cult is the most dangerous sin of all. It is a form of idolatry that is able to stop the history of salvation altogether.

Non-P History

Moses' reading of the Book of the Covenant to the Israelites and their acceptance of its authority (Exod 24:7) are followed immediately with the divine instruction that Moses ascend the mountain of God to receive the "tablets of stone" (24:12-13). These events are the transition to the final episode in the

Non-P History. The fate of the "tablets of stone" provides the structure for the episodes in the Non-P History.

LOSS OF STONE TABLETS

Exodus 24:12-15a, 18a; 31:18*; 32:1-35 narrate the ascent of Moses and Joshua to receive the tablets of stone, most likely the Decalogue. Their composition will require forty days, prompting Moses to instruct the elders to seek direction from Aaron and Hur in his absence. The scene shifts immediately to the Israelite people in chap. 32, who request the golden calf to replace Moses in his absence and possibly also God. The scene swings wildly between the base of the mountain (vv. 1-6) and its summit (vv. 7-14), highlighting the separation between God and the Israelites created by the golden calf and the divine desire to destroy the nation. The two worlds collide when Moses descends the mountain and, upon seeing the golden calf, he acts out the divine anger, destroying the tablets (vv. 15-19), the calf (vv. 20-24), and even many of the people (vv. 25-29). The scene closes on an ominous note, in which the mediation of Moses for the remaining people ends only with the divine promise of future punishment, not forgiveness (vv. 30-35).

INTERCESSION OF MOSES IN TENT OF MEETING

The centerpiece of the scene is the appearance of the tent of meeting in 33:7-11. It is most likely an independent unit of literature incorporated by the Non-P historian. There is no etiology for the construction of the tent of meeting in the Non-P History. Moses does not build it; he only names it. He would "call it the tent of meeting" (v. 7). The tent of meeting simply appears during the crisis of the golden calf as a cultic site outside the Israelite camp, where God would descend in a cloud to speak with Moses face-to-face.

The tent of meeting represents the wilderness sanctuary in the Non-P History. It is the alternative to the golden calf. It appears at a time of crisis and represents the rejection of religious and political idolatry. It exists precariously at the margins of the people's life, outside the camp, suggesting that it may function as a temporary cultic site in the Non-P History. Yet even in this fragile situation the tent of meeting provides a location for Moses to intercede with God over the fate of the Israelites. His mediation for the continued life of the people is the ideal of cultic leadership, drawing God into the outskirts of the camp through intercession and thus creating hope for the future. The rhetoric of Moses' mediation as persuasive prayer (33:12-23) models the liturgy of the tent of meeting. It is a form of intercession that Moses first learned at the summit of the mountain when he was with God in 32:7-14.

RECOVERY OF STONE TABLETS

The persuasive power of Moses to intercede for the people is confirmed when God agrees to write new tablets of stone in Exodus 34. The issuing of new tablets (34:10-28) is preceded by a theophany, in which God reveals new qualities of compassion and mercy that allow for divine forgiveness (34:1, 4*, 5-9). The revelation of divine mercy and the writing of new covenant tablets signal the completion of the events at the divine mountain. In the Non-P History, the literature in Exodus concludes by returning to the cultic role of Moses in 34:29b-35. The author states that the face of Moses becomes infused with divine glory during his intercessions with God, allowing him to continue to speak with God in the tent of meeting even after the Israelites leave the divine mountain. As a result, Moses is required to mask his face outside the cult at all times upon leaving the divine mountain.

The Non-P History proceeds beyond Exodus. The next episode, Num 10:29–12:16, continues to describe the tent of meeting. Numbers 10:29-36 identifies the ark of the covenant as the central furnishing in the tent of meeting, which is also introduced without an etiology of origin. Numbers 11–12 recount the cultic role of the seventy elders of Israel, who receive a portion of Moses' spirit in the tent of meeting, and the conflict over cultic leadership between Aaron, Miriam, and Moses. The role of Joshua as the custodian of the tent of meeting noted in 33:7-11 returns when he is commissioned as Moses' successor in Deut 31:14-23, relating the Non-P History and Deuteronomy.

P History

The point of departure for the P History is not the codification of the Book of the Covenant (Exod 24:7), but the divine command in 24:1b-2 that Moses ascend the summit alone. It allows for another theophany in 24:15b-18a, setting the stage for the revelation of the tabernacle cult and the inscription of its plans on the "tablets of testimony."

LOSS OF TABLETS OF TESTIMONY

The ascent of Moses in 24:15b-18a allows for a new revelation of the Glory of Yahweh on Mount Sinai, in which Moses receives the architectural plans of the tabernacle in chaps. 25–31. They are written on distinct tablets in the P History, the "tablets of testimony" (31:18*), the same word used to describe the worshiping congregation in the tabernacle (e.g., Num 1:2-3). The P History constructs the episode around the story of the golden calf, making only one addition, which is the clarification that the broken tablets were "the tablets of testimony"

(Exod 32:15). Thus according to the P History Moses destroys the plans for the tabernacle when he becomes enraged at the sight of the calf.

INTERCESSION OF MOSES IN TENT OF MEETING

The P historian makes no additions to the account of Moses interceding in the tent of meeting. But the framing of this event with the revelation (Exodus 25–31) and construction (chaps. 35–40) of the tabernacle underscores the temporary nature of the tent of meeting (33:7-11). The location of the tent of meeting on the margins of the camp, as a site where Moses intercedes for the presence of God, is clearly transitional and limited to the crisis of the golden calf. The tent of meeting in chap. 33 provides a bridge to the subsequent construction of the tabernacle in the midst of the Israelite camp (chaps. 35–40).

RECOVERY OF TABLETS OF TESTIMONY

The P historian transforms the mountain of covenant renewal into Mount Sinai (34:2-3, 4*, 32) and continues to identify the new tablets as "the tablets of testimony." Verse 29a summarizes the interpretation of this event in the P History: "When Moses came down from Mount Sinai . . . he had . . . the two tablets of testimony in his hands." The reissuing of the tablets of testimony leads to temple construction in chaps. 35–40 and the descent of the Glory of Yahweh from the summit of Mount Sinai into the tabernacle at the base of the mountain (40:34-38). Thus the tabernacle, not the tent of meeting, combats the idolatry of the golden calf in the P History. This event marks a new year in the liturgical dating of the P History (40:1-2, 17).

The P History proceeds beyond Exodus. The construction of the tabernacle in chaps. 35–40 is followed by the creation of a cultic system (Leviticus 1–7) and the ordination of the Aaronide priesthood (Leviticus 8–10). These events allow for the further descent of the Glory of Yahweh into the midst of the Israelite people from the tabernacle to the altar (Lev 9:22-24). The presence of the Glory of Yahweh in the altar leads to further laws promoting holiness among the Israelites (Leviticus 11–27) and a utopian vision of the community within the camp (Numbers 1–10).

LITERARY STRUCTURE

The theme of revelation has been crucial throughout the entire book of Exodus, providing thematic development for the construction of the sanctuary in Exod 24:12–40:38. The revelation of God in the land of Egypt is a destructive force in the first half of Exodus (1:1–15:21). The absence of God in the opening episode of the book (Setting, 1:1–2:25) sets the stage for a series of divine revelations as Yahweh enters the story to rescue the Israelites from their oppression in Egypt. After the initial self-revelation of Yahweh to Moses on the divine mountain (Characters, 3:1–7:7), the focus of the divine revelation is on Pharaoh and the Egyptian people (Conflict, 7:8–15:21). The revelation of Yahweh in the land of Egypt creates a volatile mixture resulting in darkness and devastation. The plagues are epiphanies of destruction that mark the approach of Yahweh into the land of Egypt, where the aim of the Deity is not to take up residency but to defeat Pharaoh and thus to break his hold upon the Israelites. Yahweh provides the interpretation, repeatedly underscoring the revelatory power of the plagues to Pharaoh: "so that you may know that there is no one like me in all the land" (9:14). But Pharaoh's refusal to acknowledge the revelation results in the ruin of the land, the death of the Egyptian firstborn at midnight, and the annihilation of the Egyptian army in the Red Sea.

The revelation of God in the wilderness becomes a constructive force for life and health in the second half of Exodus (15:22–40:38). The reason is that the goal of revelation is no longer the defeat of an enemy, but the divine residency with the Israelites. The transition from war to residency is marked by the change in setting from the land of Egypt to the wilderness. It is signaled by a new form of revelation from the destructive plagues to divine holiness (for the definition of holiness see the introduction to 19:1–24:11). The Song of the Sea punctuates the transition celebrating Yahweh as a holy God (15:11), whose aim is not the destruction of earth but residency within it: "you guided [the people] in your strength to your holy abode" (15:13).

The themes of the revelation of God, holiness, and the divine residency on earth dominate the second half of Exodus. The themes undergo development that culminates in the construction of an earthly sanctuary for Yahweh. The themes begin with the recovery of the Sabbath as a holy day (16:23) in the initial wilderness journey of the Israelites (Journey, 15:22–18:27). The revelation of God is in the form of the Glory of Yahweh, not the plagues (16:10). The goal of revelation is life-giving food, not pestilence (16:11). The recovery of the Sabbath through the cycle of manna is intended to reveal the power of God to the Israelites. Yahweh states: "You will know that I am Yahweh your God" (16:12). The result is the initial sign of holiness on earth, not in a specific location, but in the flow of time. The recovery of the Sabbath introduces a day of rest for humans, rather than the oppression from the land of Egypt.

The revelation of God on the divine mountain (19:1–24:11) advances the theme of divine residency on earth. The theme of holiness appears as a divine promise to the Israelites: "you will be for me a kingdom of priests and a holy nation" (19:6). But the theophany of God (19:16-19), which was intended to transfer holiness and to realize the divine promise, accentuates the separation between heaven and earth, and between divine holiness and humans. The focus on the separation between God and humans is confirmed when the Deity aborts the divine descent to earth (19:20-24). But the story does not end here. The revelation of divine law (the Decalogue and the Book of the Covenant) and the establishment of covenant between God and the people of Israel (24:3-8) hold promise that holiness may one day be transferred from heaven to earth. The scene ends on a note of promise with a vision of the divine sanctuary in heaven, not its construction on earth (24:9-11).

The final episode (Sanctuary, 24:12–40:38) is crucial to the story of the book of Exodus. It recounts how the heavenly vision of the temple becomes an earthly reality, allowing God to dwell on earth in the midst of the people of God. The Non-P History provides the structure for the final episode with the theme of the tablets of stone. The account of the golden calf establishes the central problem, namely the threat of religious and political idolatry surrounding the establishment of a divine temple on earth. The solution is a divine dwelling detached from kings and royal cities. The Non-P History proposes the tent of meeting. But it is the P description of the tabernacle that now dominates the episode, not the tent of meeting. Within the present structure of the episode, the tent of meeting provides transition between the revelation and construction of the tabernacle. It is a temporary sanctuary, in which Moses draws out the new qualities of divine grace and mercy that allow for the construction of the tabernacle. The extended description of the tabernacle, its cult, and the camp in the larger design of the Pentateuch further serve to marginalize the tent of meeting as the solution to the golden calf, so much so that the return of stories about the tent of meeting in Num 10:29–12:16 now appears out of context. I will interpret the episode on the sanctuary (24:12–40:38) in the following units:

I. Loss of Tablets (24:12–32:35)
II. Intercession of Moses (33:1-23)
III. Recovery of Tablets (34:1–40:38)

COMMENTARY

Loss of Tablets (24:12–32:35)

The section separates into three parts: the ascent of Moses (24:12-18), the revelation of the tabernacle (chaps. 25–31), and the story of the golden calf (chap. 32).

Ascent of Moses (24:12-18)

24:12 *And Yahweh said to Moses, "Ascend the mountain to me and stay there, and I will give you the tablets of stone and the torah and the commandment, which I have written to teach them."* 13 *And Moses arose, and Joshua his assistant, and Moses ascended to the mountain of God.* 14 *But to the elders he said, "Wait here for us until we return to you. Aaron and Hur are with you. Whoever has a dispute, let him bring it to them."*

15 *And Moses ascended the mountain.* **And the cloud covered the mountain.** 16 **And the Glory of Yahweh settled on Mount Sinai. And the cloud covered it six days. And he called to Moses on the seventh day from the midst of the cloud.** 17 **But the appearance of the Glory of Yahweh was like a consuming fire on the summit of the mountain before the eyes of the Israelites.** 18 *And Moses entered the midst of the cloud, and he ascended the mountain.* *And Moses was on the mountain forty days and forty nights.*

Notes

24:12 *and stay there.* Hebrew *wehyēh-šām,* lit. "be there," is followed by the Sam, *whwy šm,* and LXX, *isthi ekei.*

and I will give you the tablets of stone and the torah and the commandment. The MT refers to the "tablets of stone" *('et-lūḥōt hā'eben)* in the singular, adding a conjunction to the following phrase, "and the torah and the commandment" *(wěhattôrâ wěhammiṣwâ).* The syntax suggests a distinction between the tablets of stone and the torah and the commandment. The Sam has the plural, *lwḥt h'bnym,* "the tablets of stones," while eliminating the conjunction in the following phrase *(htwrh whmṣwh).* The syntax places the phrase in apposition, suggesting that the tablets of stones and the torah and the commandment are the same. The LXX most likely reflects the Sam, *ta pyxia ta lithina, ton nomon kai tas entolas.* The contrast between the textual witnesses creates a problem of interpretation, whether the tablets contain the Ten Commandments or the more extended law in the Book of the Covenant. See the summary of the problem in Childs, who concludes that the present form of the MT includes "a later expansion [*wěhattôrâ* . . .] which has confused the syntax."[1]

which I have written to teach them. The antecedent to the pronominal suffix "them" is absent from the text.

24:13 *And Moses arose, and Joshua his assistant, and Moses ascended to the mountain of God.* The LXX writes the verbs in the plural, indicating that Moses and Joshua ascended.

24:14 *whoever has a dispute.* The MT *mî-ba'al děbārîm* is an idiom employing an adjectival genitive, "whoever is a possessor of words" (*IBHS* §9.5.3.a). Cf. LXX *ean tini symbē krisis,* "if a case of judgment happens to someone."

1. Childs, *Exodus,* 499.

24:15 *And Moses ascended the mountain.* The LXX has "Moses and Joshua."

24:16 *And the Glory of Yahweh settled on Mount Sinai.* Hebrew *kĕbôd-yhwh* could also be left untranslated, "Kebod Yahweh," since it describes a specific manifestation of the Deity (see the commentary). The LXX has *hē doxa tou theou*, "the Glory of God." The LXX translates Hebrew *wayyiškōn*, "to dwell, settle," as *katebē*, "to come down." Wevers noted that this is the only place in the LXX where Hebrew *šākan* is translated in this manner.[2] See the commentary for discussion.

And he called to Moses. The MT lacks a subject for the verb "to call." The context suggests the Glory of Yahweh or perhaps Yahweh. The LXX adds *kyrios*, "Lord," as the subject.

24:17 *like a consuming fire.* Hebrew *kĕ'ēš 'ōkelet* is translated "devouring fire" in NRSV. The LXX translated, *pyr phlegon*, "a flaming fire."

24:18 *And Moses was on the mountain.* The LXX includes *ekei*, "there": "he was there on the mountain."

Commentary

The Non-P and P Histories are interwoven in the scene. The Non-P History includes 24:12-15a, 18b. The context of the Non-P History is the covenant ceremony (vv. 3-5), in which Moses writes the laws of the Book of the Covenant and reads them to the people, who agree to their authority: "All that Yahweh spoke we will do and we will obey" (v. 7). Verses 12-15a, 18b are the divine response to the covenant ceremony. They continue the emphasis on written law developed in the Non-P History. God commands Moses to ascend the mountain to receive the "tablets of stone," the name for the divine law code in the Non-P History. The central characters in the scene include Moses, Joshua, Aaron, Hur, and the elders, all of whom play a role in other stories in the Non-P History. The appearance of God is signified by the "cloud," which will become associated with the tent of meeting (33:7-11). The inscription of the tablets requires forty days and nights, setting the stage for the people's request to Aaron to replace Moses with the golden calf in his absence (32:1-6).

The P History is 24:15b-18a. The context of the P History reaches back to the failed attempt at theophany in 19:20-24, when God aborted the divine descent because of inadequate safeguards for holiness. The divine instruction to Moses in 24:1-2 relates the scenes. Yahweh restricts the leaders of the people from the mountain: "The others must not come near. And the people may not come up" (24:2b). The restriction of characters on the mountain is preceded by the focus on Moses with the command: "Moses alone is to approach Yahweh" (v. 2a). The focus on Moses establishes the narrative context for his ascent in vv. 15b-18a. The purging of the people through the blood rite (vv. 6, 8) and the vision of God in the heavenly temple (vv. 9-11) also address the inadequate safe-

2. Wevers, *Notes*, 388.

guards for holiness from 19:20-24, further preparing for the theophany in 24:15b-18a. The appearance of God as the Glory of Yahweh, the identification of the mountain as Sinai, and the references to the creation story in Genesis 1 further anchor the theophany in the P History as the introductory event for the revelation of the tabernacle.

The Non-P and P Histories are related spatially as events that transpire at three different altitudes on the mountain. The covenant ceremony (24:7, the Non-P History) and the purification of the people (vv. 6, 8, the P History) occur at the base of the mountain, setting the stage for three distinct events at increasingly higher elevations on the mountain signaled by the repetition of the verb "to ascend" (*'ālâ*) in vv. 12, 13, 15, 16, 18. The spatial organization recalls the architecture of the sanctuary, in which gradations of holiness also result in three areas of ever more restrictive access: the altar, the outer sanctuary ("the holy place"), and the inner sanctuary ("the holy of holies").[3] See the diagram of the tabernacle (fig. 39) in the commentary on chaps. 25–31.

The first event on the mountain is the vision of the heavenly sanctuary and the meal with God in 24:9-11. The location for this event is unclear. There is no divine command that the participants ascend the mountain. The text simply states that they "went up" and that they had a vision of God. The imagery of feasting with God, however, suggests the sacrificial rituals surrounding the altar. The cast of characters at this elevation on the mountain is large, including Moses, Aaron, his sons Nadab and Abihu, and the seventy elders. The second event on the mountain is the issuing of the tablets of stone in vv. 12-14. It is signaled by a divine command to ascend the mountain, now identified as the mountain of God. The cast of characters at this elevation narrows to Moses and Joshua, who leave behind Aaron, Hur, and the elders. The third event on the mountain is the appearance of the Glory of Yahweh on the summit in vv. 15-18. At this altitude the mountain is identified as Sinai, and its access is restricted to Moses alone, who encounters the presence of the Deity described as a consuming fire.

24:12-14 The central event in this section is the divine command that Moses ascend the mountain to receive "the tablets of stone" *(lūḥōt hā'eben).* The motif of the tablets organizes the episode reappearing in four other contexts in the Non-P History in slightly different expressions. God completes the writing of the tablets (31:18). Moses descends the mountain with the "tablets" *(lūḥōt),* breaking them upon seeing the golden calf (32:15-16). He chisels "two tablets of stones" *(šĕnê-lūḥōt hā'ăbānîm)* like the first for covenant renewal (34:1, 4). After a period of forty days and nights, he descends the mountain with

---

3. See P. P. Jenson, *Graded Holiness: A Key to the Priestly Conception of the World* (JSOTSup 106; Sheffield: JSOT Press, 1992).

the "tablets" (*lūḥōt*; 34:29). The "tablets," the "tablets of stone," and the "two tablets of stones" are related in the Non-P History, as they are in Deuteronomy,
where Moses also receives the tablets of stone (Deut 9:11), breaks them (9:15-17),
and acquires new tablets for covenant renewal (10:1-4).

The content of the tablets is the Decalogue in the Non-P History and in
Deuteronomy. The plot of the Non-P History indicates that Moses has already
inscribed the Book of the Covenant (Exod 24:4, 7), leaving only the previously
revealed Decalogue to be written. The descent of Moses for covenant renewal
in 34:27-29 confirms the content as the Decalogue, describing the tablets of
stone as the "ten words." Deuteronomy supports the Non-P History. Deuteronomy 4:13 also equates the tablets of stone with the "ten words." The version of
the Decalogue in Deuteronomy (5:6-21) concludes with the statement that their
inscription was by God on the "tablets of stone."

Deuteronomy adds to the interpretation of the "two tablets of stones," as
the "tablets of the covenant" (Deut 9:9, 15), which were placed in the ark (10:5).
The further description of the legislation in Exod 24:12, "and the torah and the
commandment" *(wĕhattôrâ wĕhammiṣwâ)*, is puzzling. It can be read in two
ways. If the Hebrew *waw* connects the phrase "the torah and the commandment" to the "tablets of stone," then the legal terms are further description of
the Decalogue; this interpretation would conform to Deuteronomy.[4] The translation would be explicative, "the tablets of testimony, that is, the torah and the
commandment." But if the *waw* is read as a conjunction, "the tablets of stone
and the torah and the commandment," then other legislation besides the
Decalogue may be included on the tablets.[5] The identification of law as "torah"
appears only infrequently in Exodus to describe the Passover (12:49), Unleavened Bread (13:9), manna (16:4, 28), and the judicial instruction of the elders
(18:16, 20). Perhaps the additional description of the law in 24:12 is intended to
include these other laws, but this is unlikely. The phrase may also point to Deuteronomy, since it is frequently described as the "torah" (e.g., Deut 4:8; 17:18;
33:4) and its individual laws as the "commandments" (e.g., 6:25; 8:1; 11:8).

The address of Moses to the elders in Exod 24:13-14 continues their central role in the Non-P History (see 3:16-20). But it is the other characters in the
scene, Joshua, Aaron, and Hur, who are noteworthy. E. Zenger identifies the author as the P historian on the basis of the characters.[6] But the same cast of characters has already played a role in the Non-P History. This is the second story in
which Joshua, Aaron, and Hur appear with Moses (for interpretation of Joshua

---

4. On the explicative use of the conjunction see GKC 484 n. 1(b).
5. See GKC §154a; Childs, *Exodus*, 499; Noth, *Exodus*, 199-200; Zenger, *Sinaitheophanie*,
77.
6. Zenger, *Sinaitheophanie*, 217.

and Hur see 17:8-16; for Aaron, 4:15-17). The first was the war against the Amalekites (17:8-16). Both stories are structured around the setting of a mountain, which serves to separate Aaron and Hur from Joshua. Both stories also focus on writing and memory. In the war against the Amalekites, Aaron and Hur accompany Moses to the top of the mountain, assisting him in raising his hands while Joshua wages holy war at its base. All the characters fulfill their assigned roles, resulting in the first altar and the first instance of writing a divine command. The record is a remembrance directed to Joshua. He is "to blot out" the memory of the Amalekites forever. The characters reverse their positions in 24:12–32:35. Joshua accompanies Moses on the mountain, while Aaron and Hur remain at its base to govern the people. The story is a tragedy aimed at the failure of Aaron and the loss of written divine commands when Moses destroys the tablets. The failure of Aaron and the divine desire to destroy the Israelites also reverse the role of Moses from the author of divine curses aimed at "blotting out" a nation to a mediator who offers to have his own name "blotted out" from God's book for the sake of a nation (32:32).

24:15-18   The P account of theophany in 24:15b-18a is the central event in this section. The scene begins by placing Moses within the cloud in v. 15: "And Moses ascended the mountain. And the cloud covered the mountain." The appearance of the cloud may tie this event to the earlier divine announcement of theophany in 19:9: "I am coming to you in the dense cloud so that the people may hear when I speak with you." The literary relationship suggests that all of v. 15 may be part of the Non-P History. But the imagery of the cloud and its association with the Glory of Yahweh move in a different direction, highlighting the visual appearance of God as fire in the P History, instead of the auditory emphasis on divine speech in the Non-P History. The imagery of the cloud indicates that v. 15b is part of the P History.

C. Westermann describes the structure of 24:15b-18 and 25:1 as two symmetrical units that separate into a three-part sequence:

> A   Approach of Yahweh (24:15b-16a𝖆): And the cloud (ʿānān) covered the mountain. And the Glory of Yahweh (kĕbôd-yhwh) settled (šākan) on Mount Sinai.
> B   Dwelling on the Mountain (24:16a𝖇): And the cloud covered it six days.
> C   Word of Yahweh (24:16b): And he called to Moses on the seventh day from the midst of the cloud.
> 24:17   But the appearance of the Glory of Yahweh was like a consuming fire on the summit of the mountain before the eyes of the Israelites.
> A′   Approach of Moses (24:18a): And Moses entered the midst

of the cloud and he ascended the mountain.

B′ Dwelling on the Mountain (24:18b): And Moses was on the mountain forty days and forty nights.

C′ Word of Yahweh (25:1): And Yahweh said to Moses . . .

The structure indicates that the theophany is organized around the movement of Moses and Yahweh toward the mountain. Westermann concludes: "The two movements go in opposite directions: the movement from above descends on the mountain; and movement from under (where the people are located) ascends the mountain. The movements come together as a *mô'ēd*, which makes possible the promulgation of the words to the mediator."[7] The conclusion of Westermann builds on the earlier insight of G. von Rad that the theology of divine presence in the P History is the result of God and humans meeting in the cultic site, rather than the view of the Deity dwelling permanently in the sanctuary. At the center of the two sequences is the people's new experience of theophany as the Glory of Yahweh.[8] The new perception of the people provides a point of contrast to the first appearance of God in 19:18, when Yahweh sought to descend *(yārad)* to the summit of the mountain before aborting the theophany (19:20-24).

The P History describes the theophany on Mount Sinai as transpiring over the period of one week, which recalls the divine act of creation from Genesis 1. For six days the cloud hovers over the mountain until God calls out to Moses on the seventh day (24:16). The imagery of creation repeats in the description of the tabernacle when the Sabbath returns in 31:12-17 and 35:1-3. The two central descriptions of God in the week-long theophany are crucial for interpretation. They are the appearance of God as the "Glory of Yahweh" *(kĕbôd-yhwh)* and presence of God on the mountain as "settling" *(šākan)*. Both terms provide contrast to and qualification of the theophany in 19:16-19, which is judged a failure in the P History (19:20-24). The qualifications allow for the successful appearance of God on the divine mountain to all the Israelites.

The appearance of Yahweh in 19:16-19 is qualified as the Glory of Yahweh in 24:16. The term *kābôd*, "glory," has a long history in ancient Israel signaling the power of God in the thunderstorm (Psalm 29) or the enthronement of Yahweh as king in the Jerusalem cult (Psalm 96). The term also appears in the Non-P History when Moses mediates to see God's glory (Exod 33:18). But the term "Glory of Yahweh" acquires a more technical meaning in the P History as a

---

7. C. Westermann, "Die Herrlichkeit Gottes in der Priesterschrift," in *Wort — Gebot — Glaube: Beiträge zur Theologie des Alten Testaments: Walther Eichrodt zum 80. Geburtstag* (ed. H. J. Stoebe; ATANT 59; Zurich: Zwingli, 1970), 227-47, esp. 231-32.

8. G. von Rad, "Deuteronomy's 'Name' Theology and the Priestly Document's 'Kabod' Theology," in *Studies in Deuteronomy* (trans. D. Stalker; SBT 1/9; Chicago: Regnery, 1953), 37-44.

particular representation of Yahweh. The relationship between Yahweh and the "Glory of Yahweh" is difficult to describe, as is the "Messenger of Yahweh" in the Non-P History (e.g., 3:2; see the commentary on 23:20-33). That the Glory of Yahweh clearly represents the presence of God on earth prompts interpreters to describe it as a divine attribute, although the authors of the Hebrew Bible do not employ such language.[9] The prophet Ezekiel shares features of the theology of the P History, also describing the presence of God in the temple as the Glory of Yahweh (e.g., Ezek 1:28; 43:2, 4, 5; 44:4). Whatever the exact relationship, the Glory of Yahweh introduces a safeguard between God and humans that was absent from the original theophany of Exod 19:16-19, allowing God to take up residency on earth in a qualified and thus in a less direct and dangerous form.[10]

The descent of the Glory of Yahweh into the midst of the Israelites organizes the P History. It embodies the power of God to re-create the world and to purge humans. The Glory of Yahweh first appeared to the Israelites as a cloud in the wilderness on the distant horizon during the story of manna (16:10). Its appearance is accompanied by the revelation of the Sabbath, which was lost to the world since the original act of creation in Gen 1:1–2:4a. The Glory of Yahweh appears to the Israelites more intensely as a consuming fire on Mount Sinai (Exod 24:17) within the structure of the Sabbath week. In this appearance it is accompanied by the revelation of the tabernacle cult (Exodus 25–31). The Glory of Yahweh will increase in intensity at the conclusion of Exodus when it takes up residency on earth by entering the tabernacle (40:36-38), signaling a New Year (and a new era) in world history (40:2, 17). The sacrificial cult and the consecration of the priesthood will draw the Glory of Yahweh even closer to the people, allowing it to move from the tabernacle into the altar (Lev 9:22-24) in the sight of all the Israelites. Thus the appearance of the Glory of Yahweh frames the revelation and the construction of the tabernacle, its cultic rituals, and its personnel, appearing at the summit of Mount Sinai in Exod 24:17 and in the altar in Lev 9:22-24.

Exodus 24:16 characterizes the presence of God on the mountain as "tabernacling," or "settling" *(šākan)*: "And the Glory of Yahweh settled on Mount Sinai." The quality of divine presence indicated by the verb šākan becomes the name of the tent shrine in the P History, "the tabernacle" *(miškān)*. Thus the verb is important to the cultic theology of the P History, and interpreters debate its precise meaning. The problem is that the verb occurs in P and Non-P descriptions of the cult, raising debate whether šākan in the P History represents a distinctive theology of divine presence or a continuation of the royal theology of the monarchy.

---

9. Mettinger, *Dethronement of Sabaoth,* 97-105.
10. See ibid., 97-115.

The enthronement of Yahweh in the royal ideology of Jerusalem is conveyed with the Hebrew verb *yāšab,* "to dwell." According to T. N. D. Mettinger, "The word *yāšab* . . . is the key expression recurring in significant contexts to express the presence of God in the Temple and on Zion."[11] Solomon declares at the dedication of the Jerusalem temple: "I have indeed built a magnificent temple for you [Yahweh], a place for you to dwell in *(yāšab)* forever" (1 Kgs 8:13).[12] The verb *yāšab* indicates the permanent presence of God enthroned in the temple. When Yahweh dwells in the cultic site, it is "forever." The poem is coupled with the additional line: "Yahweh has said that he would settle *(šākan)* in thick darkness" (1 Kgs 8:12). The use of the verbs "to dwell" *(yāšab)* and "to settle" *(šākan)* in 1 Kgs 8:12-13 may indicate the same quality of divine cultic presence, suggesting a continuity in meaning between the two terms. The NRSV translates both verbs the same: "Yahweh has said that he would dwell *(šākan)* in thick darkness. I have built you an exalted house, a place for you to dwell *(yāšab)* in forever." Isaiah 8:18 supports an interpretation of *šākan* as representing the permanent presence of Yahweh in the Jerusalem cult: "Yahweh Sabaot who dwells *(šākan)* on Mount Zion" (see also Pss 78:60; 135:21). The citations suggest that the P theology of divine cultic presence in the tabernacle may be a continuation of the enthronement tradition from the monarchical period. When Yahweh settles on Mount Sinai and eventually enters the tabernacle, the cultic presence of God is permanent.[13]

The P historian employs the verb "to dwell" *(yāšab)* to describe the residency of humans in a variety of contexts (e.g., Gen 13:12; 16:3; 45:10; Lev 18:3; Num 35:2, 3). But the P author never uses the term in the more technical and theological sense to describe the presence of God in the tabernacle. The absence of the verb *yāšab* suggests that the P author presents a distinctive view of divine cultic presence from the royal theology of Zion, either by reusing older tradition or through a new theological formulation. F. M. Cross interprets the verb *šākan* in the P History to represent a point of departure from the cultic theology of Jerusalem, signifying the temporary presence of God in the sanctuary.[14] The description of the "cloud" in Exod 24:15b-18a and in 40:34-35 as also "settling" *(šākan)* and "ascending" *(ʿālâ)* suggests the same meaning for the Glory of Yahweh as an impermanent presence.[15]

---

11. Ibid., 28.

12. See, e.g., M. Görg, "Die Gattung des sogenannte Tempelweispruches (I Kgs 8:12f.)," *UF* 6 (1974): 55-63.

13. See Mettinger, *Dethronement of Sabaoth,* 90-91; R. Schmitt, *Zelt und Lade als Thema alttestamentlicher Wissenschaft* (Gütersloh: Gütersloher Verlagshaus, 1972), 219-21.

14. Cross, *Canaanite Myth and Hebrew Epic,* 245, 299, 313; idem, "The Priestly Tabernacle," *BARead* 1:201-28.

15. Dozeman, *God on the Mountain,* 129-30.

The description of the sanctuary with the related term *miškān*, "tabernacle," indicates a qualification of divine cultic presence in the P History. Yahweh is no longer permanently enthroned in the cultic site, as Solomon proclaimed with regard to the Jerusalem temple. Instead the Glory of Yahweh is more mobile, having the ability to descend into and to leave the tabernacle. The introduction of the verb *šākan* plays a role in the literary development of the P History. It represents a further qualification of the divine presence from the failed theophany in 19:16-19, where Yahweh was described as "descending" *(yārad)* on Mount Sinai in fire (19:18).[16] The verb "to settle" indicates that the Glory of Yahweh dwells only temporarily in the cult, not permanently as in the royal ideology associated with the temple. In addition, the verb indicates that God is not confined to a single place but is able to move with the people of God. The closing verses of Exodus provide a glimpse into the mobile character of God. The Glory of Yahweh and its cloud are able to journey with the Israelites in their wilderness journey (40:34-38). This new quality of divine presence revealed on Mount Sinai now characterizes the sanctuary in the P History as the tabernacle *(miškān)*.

Revelation of the Tabernacle (25:1–31:18)

Introduction

The divine instructions for building the sanctuary follow immediately from the P writer's account of theophany in 24:15b-18a. The content of the instruction is broad in scope and in detail. It includes the materials for construction (25:1-7), the purpose of the sanctuary (25:8-9), the architectural plans for the tabernacle (26:1-37), the altar (27:1-8), the courtyard (27:9-19), and all the furnishings (25:10-40; 30:1-10, 17-21), as well as the selection of the builders (31:1-11). The instructions also include the design of the priestly vestments (28:6-43), the ritual for the ordination of the priesthood (29:1-46), the ritual practices of the priesthood on behalf of the people (chap. 30), and further instruction on Sabbath observance (31:12-17).

COMPOSITION OF LITERATURE ON THE TABERNACLE

For the purpose of this commentary, I interpret the description of the tabernacle in Exodus 25–31 and 35–40 within the literary context of the P History.

---

16. See F. Schnutenhaus, "Das Kommen und Erscheinen Gottes im Alten Testament," *ZAW* 36 (1964): 1-21, esp. 5-6, 12-14.

Figure 35

	P Literature	Supplement to P
Revelation of tabernacle	25:1–29:46	
		30:1–31:17
	31:18	
Construction of tabernacle	35:1a, 4b, 5-10, 20-27, 29-31a, 32, 33	35:1b-4a, 11-19, 28, 31b, 34, 35
	36:2-7	36:1
	36:8-38	
	37:1-24	37:25-29
	38:1-7, 9-22, 24-31	38:8, 23
	39:1-32, 43	39:33-42
	40:1, 2, 9, 17-25, 28, 29a, 33	40:3-8, 10, 16, 26, 27, 29b, 30-32, 34-38

There are no signs of composition from the Non-P History, except for the closing reference to the tablets in 31:18. Even though the material is traditionally assigned to the P History, interpreters have debated the unity of the literature and its tradition-historical development. The vocabulary associated with the sanctuary is unique in biblical literature, as is the focus on rituals of atonement.

Wellhausen judged the description of the tabernacle to be a historical fiction from the exilic period based on the Jerusalem temple. The description of the cultic practice was theoretical reflection by priests on past practice, a process that continues in the literature of the postexilic period, as is evident in Jubilees and in the NT book of Hebrews. In addition, Wellhausen questioned the unity of the literature, noting that the instruction for the altar of incense in Exodus 30 was out of place. The legislation would fit better in chaps. 25–27, which describe the furnishings of the tabernacle. The altar of incense itself was an invention, according to Wellhausen, unknown to the history of sacrifice in ancient Israel during the monarchical period.[1] Subsequent interpreters continue to debate the literary unity of the P legislation on the tabernacle, with many identifying a history of composition within P tradition. Noth provides an example, which I put in tabular form in figure 35 above.[2]

The fictional portrayal of the tabernacle suggested by Wellhausen has

---

1. Wellhausen, *Composition*, 137-47; idem, *Prolegomena*, 52-82, esp. 63-67.
2. Noth, *History of Pentateuchal Traditions*, 18; for further discussion of Pg and Ps literature see Pola, *Ursprüngliche Priesterschrift*.

come under scrutiny as interpreters have explored the historical roots of the cultic objects, the ritual practices, and the role of sacred tents in Israel and in the ancient Near East. The cultic objects such as the Urim and Thummim, the altar, as well as the ritual role of the priests provide insight into the worship practices of Israel in the monarchical period.[3] As a result, Rendtorff and K. Koch have argued that the P description of the tabernacle includes collections of ritual material from the history of Israelite worship.[4] Sacred tents have a larger role in the ancient Near East than Wellhausen assumed. J. Morgenstern compared the tabernacle with the bedouin kubbe, indicating the antiquity of the tradition.[5] R. E. Friedman anchors the tradition of the tabernacle in the premonarchical period, when it was erected at Shiloh (Josh 18:1; 19:51) and eventually incorporated into the Jerusalem temple.[6] Houtman notes historical parallels for the tabernacle with the Persian royal tents, which functioned as movable palaces.[7] M. M. Homan has catalogued a range of comparative information on tent shrines in the ancient Near East, ranging from bedouin tents, Ugaritic and Hittite mythologies in which a deity dwells in the tent, Egyptian funeral tents, and Semitic tents from the Negev.[8] Weinfeld and D. P. Wright have provided comparative studies that place the P ritual system in the broader context of ancient Near Eastern cultic practice.[9] As a result, the P law is no longer viewed as fiction, but as the compilation of ritual material, a position not unlike Wellhausen's conclusion with regard to the sacrificial legislation in Leviticus 1–7.

The unity of the literature on the tabernacle continues to be debated. The repetition of the tabernacle material in Exodus 25–31 and 35–40 has received extensive attention. The Legend of Keret in the Ugaritic literature provides an example of repetition in composition, which is similar in style to the descrip-

---

3. M. Haran, "The Complex of Ritual Acts Performed in the Tabernacle," *ScrHier* 8 (1961): 272-302; idem, *Temples and Temple-Service*; B. Levine, "The Descriptive Tabernacle Texts of the Pentateuch," *JAOS* 85 (1965): 307-18.

4. Rendtorff, *Problem*; Koch, *Priesterschrift*.

5. J. Morgenstern, *The Ark, the Ephod, and the "Tent of Meeting"* (Henry and Ida Krolik Memorial Publications 2; Cincinnati: Hebrew Union College Press, 1945), 55-77.

6. R. E. Friedman, *Who Wrote the Bible?* (New York: Summit Books, 1987); idem, "Tabernacle," *ABD* 6:292-300.

7. Houtman, *Exodus*, 3:328-29.

8. M. M. Homan, *To Your Tents, O Israel! The Terminology, Function, Form, and Symbolism of Tents in the Hebrew Bible and the Ancient Near East* (Culture and History of the Ancient Near East 12; Leiden: Brill, 2002), 91-128.

9. M. Weinfeld, "Social and Cultic Institutions in the Priestly Source against Their ANE Background," in *Proceedings of the Eighth World Congress of Jewish Studies* (Jerusalem: World Union of Jewish Studies, 1983), 95-125; D. P. Wright, *The Disposal of Impurity: Elimination Rites in the Bible and in Hittite and Mesopotamian Literature* (SBLDS 101; Atlanta: Scholars Press, 1987).

tion of the tabernacle.[10] But the repetition of the tabernacle presents additional problems of style and literary consistency that have prompted interpreters to identify more than one author in the composition of Exodus 25–31 and 35–40. Wellhausen entertained the hypothesis that the repetition was the result of separate authors.[11] But it was J. Popper who provided an extensive study arguing that the author of chaps. 36–40 was not the same as the writer of chaps. 25–31, and that 36:8–38:20 formed the core of the second tabernacle account.[12] This section, according to Popper, was the latest addition to the MT. The views of Popper were expanded by A. Kuenen and A. H. McNeile, both of whom judged chaps. 35–40 to be a later literary composition than chaps. 25–31.[13]

The problems of composition are compounded in the LXX textual tradition, which departs from the MT at many points in chaps. 35–40.[14] The change of order in the LXX account of chaps. 35–40 is particularly problematic. The MT describes the construction of the furniture of the tabernacle and the altar (37:1–38:8) before the courtyard (38:9-20). The LXX reverses the order, describing the construction of the courtyard (37:7-18) before the furnishings (38:1-26). In addition, the description of the priestly vestments in the MT of 39:1-31 occurs already in the LXX of 36:8-38. Wevers concludes that 36:8–39:32 is the most problematic section of literature in the comparison of the MT and LXX. In figure 36 on page 596 I have tabulated his list of the differences in the order of the MT and LXX in chaps. 36–39.[15] M. L. Wade has concluded from a comparison of lexical equivalents between the two sections that the LXX versions of chaps. 25–31 and 35–40 were undertaken by different translators. Yet she also notes that the different order between the MT and the LXX remains a problem with regard to the compositional history of the tabernacle literature.[16]

The debate on the authorship of chaps. 25–31 and 35–40 continues into the present time. I. Knohl, for example, has argued that the description of the tabernacle includes two levels of composition, the earlier Priestly Torah and a later revision by the Holiness School. According to him, the description of the tabernacle in chaps. 25–30 derives for the most part from the Priestly Torah,

10. M. Lichtenstein, "A Note on the Text of I Keret," *JANES* 2 (1970): 94-100.

11. Wellhausen, *Composition*, 142.

12. J. Popper, *Der biblische Bericht über die Stiftshütte* (Leipzig: Heinrich Hunger, 1862).

13. A. Kuenen, *An Historical-Critical Inquiry into the Origin and Composition of the Hexateuch (Pentateuch and Book of Joshua)* (trans. P. H. Wiksteed; London: MacMillan, 1886), 76-80; McNeile, *Exodus*, 226.

14. See D. W. Gooding, *The Account of the Tabernacle: Translation and Textual Problems of the Greek Exodus* (Contributions to Biblical and Patristic Literature 6; Cambridge: Cambridge University Press, 1959).

15. Wevers, *Notes*, 596-97.

16. M. L. Wade, *Consistency of Translation Techniques in the Tabernacle Accounts of Exodus in the Old Greek* (SBLSCS 49; Atlanta: Scholars Press, 2003).

Figure 36

MT	LXX
36:8-9	37:1-2
36:10-34	no parallel
36:35-38	37:3-6
37:1-10a	38:1-11
37:10b-15	no parallel
37:16-17a	38:12-17
37:17b-28	no parallel
37:29	38:25
38:1-7	38:22-24
38:8	38:26
38:9-23	37:7-21
38:24-31	39:1-10a
39:1	39:13
39:2-31	36:9-40
39:32	39:10b-11
39:33	39:14
39:34	no parallel
39:35	39:15-16a
39:36	39:18
39:37-38	39:16a-17
39:40	39:20-21
39:41	39:19
39:42-43	39:22-23

where the revelation of the tabernacle is directed to Moses alone, with the people playing no role in its construction or in its cultic rituals. A later tradition, the Holiness School, broadens the focus of the revelation of the tabernacle to include the entire Israelite people within the scope of holiness so that the people assist in the construction of the sanctuary. The additions of the Holiness School include the requirement that the people provide materials for construction (25:1-7), the stated purpose of the sanctuary for God to dwell with the people (25:8-9; 29:38-46), the ritual atonement of the people (30:10), the people's provision of oil (27:20-21), their participation in the construction of the sanctuary and cult (the vestments, 28:3-5; the sanctuary, 31:1-11; chaps. 35–40), the observance of Sabbath (31:12-17), and the tablets of testimony (31:18). According to Knohl, the editing of the Holiness School indicates a transformation in holiness within the P tradition from a narrow focus on ritual purity in the sanctuary to a broader focus on moral purity in the people and in the camp.[17] H. Utzschneider provides his own assessment of the history of composition, noting that the editing creates ambiguity with regard to the building of the tabernacle.[18]

SANCTUARY NAMES

The English "temple" translates Hebrew *hêkal*, as in the phrase "the temple of Yahweh" to describe the cultic site at Shiloh (1 Sam 1:9). The Hebrew term is usually connected to the Sumerian *é-gal*, meaning "great house." C. Meyers concludes: "When used with the name of the deity, it indicates that the building is conceived of as a residence for that deity."[19] A more common name for the temple in the Hebrew Bible builds on the imagery of the divine house, as in the phrase "house of Yahweh" *(bêt yhwh)* to describe Solomon's temple (1 Kgs 7:12). The speech of Solomon provides further interpretation, when he states to Yahweh: "I have built you a house of dominion *(bêt zĕbūl)*, a place *(mākôn)* for you to dwell *(yāšab)* permanently" (1 Kgs 8:13). The statement reflects the royal ideology of the temple and the idealization of the king as the temple builder. The temple is a "house of dominion," where the Deity has taken up permanent residency, immobile in the center of the royal city, Jerusalem. The earthly king represents the heavenly Deity in maintaining dominion, as is illustrated in Psalm 2. The royal imagery is absent in the P description of the sanctuary in Exodus 25–31.

The P writer describes the cultic center in Exodus 25–31 as the tabernacle *(miškān)* twenty times and as the tent of meeting *('ōhel mô'ēd)* an additional sixteen times. Interpreters have long debated the use of these terms by the P author, whether they reflect similar or different concepts of the cultic site in chaps. 25–31. The debate is ancient, as is evident from the LXX translators, who often merge the terms into one designation. It has become clear that the terms have a distinct tradition-historical background (see the commentary on the tent of meeting in 33:7-11) and that the P author has taken over the older tent of meeting tradition in the description of the tabernacle.[20] But the debate contin-

---

17. I. Knohl, *The Sanctuary of Silence: The Priestly Torah and the Holiness School* (Minneapolis: Fortress, 1995), e.g., 175ff.

18. H. Utzschneider, *Das Heiligtum und das Gesetz: Studien zur Bedeutung der Sinaitischen Heiligtumstexts (Ex 25–40; Lev 8–9)* (OBO 77; Göttingen: Vandenhoeck & Ruprecht, 1988), 19-79, esp. 85-88. Utzschneider provides an overview of the past theories of composition in the P legislation, including the most recent by Weinberg, *Citizen-Temple Community*, who associates the law with the citizen-temple community of the Persian period (see the commentary on Exod 6:14-27).

19. C. Meyers, "Temple, Jerusalem," *ABD* 6:351.

20. For a summary of the research on the tent of meeting see Mettinger, *Dethronement of Sabaoth*, 81-87.

ues whether the terms represent distinct conceptions of the cult, perhaps even reflecting distinct authors.[21]

The distribution of the terms provides insight into the literary strategy of the P author. The two terms are used separately in the description of the sanctuary in chaps. 25–31. The tabernacle is limited to the description of the sanctum, including the architecture of the sanctuary and its furnishings in 25:1–27:19 (25:9; 26:1, 6, 7, 12, 13, 15, 17, 18, 20, 22, 23, 26, 27 [twice], 30, 35; 27:9, 19). It is replaced by the term "tent of meeting" when the subject matter shifts to the rituals of the sanctuary and the ordination of the priesthood in 27:20–31:11 (27:21; 28:43; 29:4, 10, 11, 30, 32, 42, 44; 30:16, 18, 20, 26, 36; 31:7; and once as the tent in 31:7). The separation provides insight into the theology of divine cultic presence in the P History and the literary structure of chaps. 25–31. The distribution of the terms "tabernacle" and "tent of meeting" reinforce the conclusion of Dohmen that chaps. 25–31 divide between 25:1–27:19 and 27:20–31:11. He notes that the first section describes the sanctuary structure, while the second focuses on the cultic practice of the people and takes on a more future orientation about the relationship of Yahweh and the Israelites.[22]

The word "tabernacle" describes the cultic site from the point of view of the Deity. It characterizes the earthly sanctuary from the perspective of God's heavenly dwelling as sanctum. When the Deity enters the sanctuary, it is a tabernacle, not a tent of meeting. Hebrew *miškān,* "tabernacle," derives from the verb *šākan,* "to settle," indicating the descent of God and the quality of divine presence in the cultic site as temporary and movable (see the commentary on 24:15b–18a). The initial occurrence of the term in 25:8-9 establishes the point of view. The tabernacle is identified as a "copy" or "pattern" (*tabnît,* 25:9) of the heavenly dwelling and as a "holy place" or "sanctuary" (*miqdāš,* 25:8). The perspective contained in the word "tabernacle" is of the Deity entering the sanctuary. This point of view is carried through the remaining occurrences. The tabernacle describes the architectural structure, including the curtains (26:1-6), the outer tent (26:7-14), the frames (26:15-25), the crossbars (26:26-29), the curtain separating the holy place from the most holy place or holy of holies (26:31-36), and the courtyard (27:1-19). Thus when the word *'ōhel,* "tent," is used in 26:7-14, it indicates a specific outer covering to protect the holiness of God in the tabernacle. It is not a general term for the sanctuary as is the case with the tent of meeting, when the perspective shifts from the entrance of God into the sanctuary to the entrance of humans.

The phrase "tent of meeting" describes the cultic site from the perspective of humans who participate in rituals. J. Milgrom describes the rituals of the

---

21. See the summary of interpretation in Houtman, *Exodus,* 3:319-20.
22. Dohmen, *Exodus 19-40,* 241.

sanctuary as "sancta-in-action."[23] When humans enter the sanctuary it becomes a tent of meeting, not a tabernacle. The tent of meeting is the identity of the cultic site in the Non-P History (33:7-11), where it indicates the communication between God and Moses through the cloud. The P writer does not share the charismatic and auditory theology of cultic presence in the Non-P History. Rather, the P author employs the term to identify the ritual practices in the sanctuary and the ordination of the priesthood that allow humans to enter the realm of holiness and to communicate with God. The tent of meeting is introduced in the divine command that the Israelites provide oil for the lampstand (27:20-21). It further describes the entrance into the sanctuary by the Aaronide priests (28:43), and their location for ordination (chap. 29). The tent of meeting continues to identify the sanctuary from the perspective of ritual practice (30:11-38). Finally, the craftsmen Bezalel and Oholiab are described as constructing the tent of meeting (31:7), not the tabernacle.

The two names, tabernacle and tent of meeting, indicate the meeting of God and humans in the sanctuary. The descent of God into the tabernacle and the approach of priestly representatives into the tent of meeting bridge the gap between the sacred and the profane, which was not possible during the original theophany on Mount Sinai (19:16-19, 20-24). The diagram in figure 37 on page 600 provides the structure of chaps. 25–31 and the distribution of the different terms that are used to describe the P view of the sanctuary.

B. D. Sommer rightly notes the tension that arises when the two names for the sanctuary are related. The tension is accentuated when one recalls that the tent of meeting exists outside the camp in the Non-P History, not at its center. He concludes that the two orientations for the sanctuary create a dynamic tension between the presence of God at the center of the Israelites' life, as opposed to the periphery.[24] The tabernacle embraces the presence of God in the midst of the people, while the tent of meeting in the Non-P History envisions divine immanence as a utopian goal on the horizon at the edge of the camp. The P Historian locates the tensions between the sacred and the profane at the center of the camp by creating contrasting points of view about the sanctuary with the terms "tabernacle" and "tent of meeting." The tension recalls the insight of Dohmen that the focus in the second part of the description of the sanctuary (27:20–31:11, where the designation of the sanctuary is "tent of meeting") takes on a future orientation. The tension underscores further the important role of divine movement with the people of God as they journey through the wilderness toward the goal of the promised land.

23. Milgrom, *Leviticus 23–27,* 2085.
24. B. D. Sommer, "Conflicting Constructions of Divine Presence in the Priestly Tabernacle," *BibInt* 9 (2001): 40-63.

Figure 37

Outline	Revelation of Tabernacle	Description of Sanctuary
PART I: TABERNACLE		
Material	25:1-7	
Purpose	25:8-9 to dwell	25:8 sanctuary (*miqdāš*) 25:9 tabernacle (*miškān*)
Furnishings:		
1. Ark	25:10-22	
2. Table	25:23-30	
3. Lampstand	25:31-40	
Architecture		
1. Tabernacle	26:1-37	tabernacle (18 times)
2. Altar	27:1-8	
3. Courtyard	27:9-19	27:9, 19 tabernacle
PART II: TENT OF MEETING		
Oil	27:20-21	27:21 tent of meeting (*'ōhel mô'ēd*)
Material	28:1-5	
Priestly Vestments		
1. Ephod	28:6-14	
2. Breastplate	28:15-30	
3. Robe	28:31-35	
4. Plate	28:36-38	
5. Tunics and undergarments	28:39-43	28:43 tent of meeting
Priestly Ordination	29:1-43	29:10, 30 tent of meeting 29:4, 11, 32, 42 Door of tent of meeting
Purpose	29:44-46 to know	29:44 tent of meeting
Priestly Rituals		
1. Altar of incense and Day of Atonement	30:1-10	
2. Census and tax	30:11-16	30:16 tent of meeting
3. Basin for washing	30:17-21	30:18, 20 tent of meeting
4. Anointing oil	30:22-33	30:26 tent of meeting
5. Incense for holy of holies	30:34-38	30:36 tent of meeting
PART III: BUILDERS	31:1-11	31:7 tent of meeting

LITERARY STRUCTURE

Past interpreters have identified different structures to the revelation of the tabernacle in Exodus 25–31.[25] Fretheim clarified a variety of ties to creation, including the reference to the spirit of God (31:1-11; Gen 1:2), the revelation of Sabbath (Exod 31:12-17; Gen 2:1-3), and an emphasis on intricate design (Exod 36:37; Gen 1:11-12, 20).[26] P. Kearney noted further ties to creation, identifying seven speeches of Yahweh: "And Yahweh said/spoke to Moses" (Exod 25:1; 30:11, 17, 22, 34; 31:1, 12). The seven speeches repeat the seven-day theophany in 24:15-18 and the seven days of creation in Gen 1:1–2:4a. But they are concentrated in the final chapters, leaving Exodus 25–30 as one large section,[27] which R. Knierim has demonstrated is presented as a single narrated speech.[28]

The speech in Exodus 25–30 also breaks into small units and changes in perspective. The names of the sanctuary provide the clue to the smaller structure since they indicate a division between the tabernacle (25:1–27:19), which describes the architecture and the furnishings, and the tent of meeting (27:20–31:11), which focuses on ritual practices. The Sabbath command (31:12-17) and the notice about the tablets (31:18) conclude the revelation. The result is a four-part structure to the revelation of the sanctuary in chaps. 25–31 of varying lengths: the tabernacle (25:1–27:19), the tent of meeting (27:20–31:11), the Sabbath (31:12-17), and the tablets (31:18).

The most striking literary feature of the tabernacle in Exodus is the extended repetition between its revelation (chaps. 25–31) and its construction (chaps. 35–40). The problems that this repetition creates for interpreting the history of composition have been noted above. The repetition also creates a literary problem in the present composition of Exodus: the overwhelming role of the tabernacle in the final episode, which comprises thirteen of the last sixteen chapters of Exodus. The dominance of this repetition prompts interpreters to compare chaps. 25–31 and 35–40 when interpreting the revelation of the tabernacle. But the comparison quickly indicates that the repetition between chaps. 25–31 and 35–40 is only partial. The counterpart for the revelation of the taber-

---

25. See, e.g., G. Steins, "'Sie sollen mir ein Heiligtum machen': Zur Struktur und Entstehung von Ex 24,12-31,18," in *Vom Sinai zum Horeb: Stationen alttestamentlicher Glaubensgeschichte* (Festschrift E. Zenger; ed. F.-L. Hossfeld; Würzburg: Echter Verlag, 1989), 145-67.

26. Fretheim, *Exodus*, 269-71.

27. P. Kearney, "Creation and Liturgy: The P Redaction of Ex 25–40," *ZAW* 89 (1977): 375-87.

28. R. Knierim, "Conceptual Aspects in Exodus 25:1-9," in *Pomegranates and Golden Bells: Studies in Biblical, Jewish, and Near Eastern Ritual, Law, and Literature in Honor of Jacob Milgrom* (ed. D. P. Wright, D. N. Freedman, and A. Hurvitz; Winona Lake, Ind.: Eisenbrauns, 1995), 113-23.

Figure 38

Revelation of the Tabernacle and Its Cultic Rituals on Mount Sinai (Exod 25–31)	Building the Tabernacle and Institution of Its Cultic Rituals at Mount Sinai (Exod 35–Num 10)
PART I: TABERNACLE	
Material: 25:1-7	35:4-29
Purpose: 25:8-9 "to dwell"	40:34-35/Lev 9:22-24/Num 7:89
Furnishings	
1. Ark: 25:10-22	37:1-9
2. Table: 25:23-30	37:10-16
3. Lampstand: 25:31-40	37:17-24/Lev 24:1-3/Num 8:1-4
Architectural Plans	
1. Tabernacle: 26:1-37	36:8-38/40:1-33/Num 7:1
2. Altar: 27:1-8	38:1-7
3. Courtyard: 27:9-19	38:9-20
PART II: TENT OF MEETING	
Oil for Light: 27:20-21	Lev 24:1-3
Appointment of Priestly Mediators	
A. Vestments	
1. Material: 28:1-5	39:1
2. Ephod: 28:6-14	39:2-7

nacle in chaps. 25–31 is not its construction in chaps. 35–40, but the larger story of the institution of the cult and the ordination of the priesthood in Leviticus, as well as the formation of the camp in Numbers 1–10.

The purpose of the tabernacle that is stated in Exod 25:8-9 is for God to dwell in the sanctuary. This theme undergoes development in Exodus 35–Numbers 10. The Glory of Yahweh enters the sanctuary in Exod 40:34-38, progresses to the altar in Lev 9:22-24, until Moses finally speaks with God in Num 7:89. The tabernacle is also assembled twice, in Exod 40:1-33 and in Num 7:1. The material for the cultic rituals repeats in Exod 39:1 and perhaps also in Num 7:1-88. The oil for the menorah in Exod 27:20-21 is not presented until Lev 24:1-3. And the census and temple tax also repeat in Exod 38:21-31 and in Num 1:1-54. The repetitions indicate that the interpretation of the revelation of the tabernacle in Exodus 25–31 requires the larger context of the P legislation in Exodus 35–Numbers 10. The diagram in figure 38 above and on page 603 provides the out-

Revelation of the Tabernacle and Its Cultic Rituals on Mount Sinai (Exod 25–31)	Building the Tabernacle and Institution of Its Cultic Rituals at Mount Sinai (Exod 35–Num 10)
3. Breastplate: 28:15-30	39:8-21
4. Robe: 28:31-35	39:22-26
5. Plate: 28:36-38	39:30-31
6. Priestly clothing: 28:39-43	39:27-29
B. Rite of ordination: 29:1-46	Lev 8-9
1. Material: 29:1-3	
2. Vestments: 29:4-9	
3. Bull of sin offering: 29:10-14	
4. Ram of Burnt Offering: 29:15-18	
5. Ram of ordination: 29:19-41	
6. Cultic presence of God: 29:42-46	
C. Rituals of mediation	
1. Altar of incense: 30:1-9	37:25-28
2. Day of Atonement: 30:10	Lev 16:1-34
3. Census and tax: 30:11-16	38:21-31/Num 1:1-54
4. Basin of water: 30:17-21	38:8
5. Anointing oil and incense: 30:22-38	37:29
Builders: 31:1-11	35:30-35; 36:1-7; 38:21-23
PART III: SABBATH: 31:12-17	35:1-3
PART IV: TABLETS: 31:18	

line of the revelation of the tabernacle and its cult in Exodus 25–31 and the instances where the divine commands are fulfilled in Exodus 35–Numbers 10.

Commentary

TABERNACLE (25:1–27:19)

The focus in 25:1–27:19 is on the construction of the sanctuary. The purpose is to allow for the divine descent to earth. The sanctuary is identified throughout as the tabernacle (see the commentary above). The section separates into four parts. Exodus 25:1-7 is a divine command that Moses collect materials for the construction of the sanctuary. Verses 8-9 state the purpose of the sanctuary. Verses 10-40 describe the furnishings of the tabernacle, moving from the center, where the holiness of God is most intense, outward in three stages: from the most holy object, the ark (vv. 10-22), to the table (vv. 23-30), and finally to the lampstand (vv. 31-40). Exodus 26:1–27:19 contains the architectural plans for the tabernacle, which like the furnishings progress in three stages of holiness from the tabernacle (26:1-37), to the altar (27:1-8), and finally to the courtyard (27:9-19).

Material (25:1-7; 35:4-29)

25:1-7

[1]And Yahweh spoke to Moses, saying, [2]"Speak to the Israelites. They are to take for me a contribution. From every person whose heart moves him, you will give my dedication offering. [3]And this is the contribution which you will take from them,

gold and silver and copper,

[4]blue, purple, and crimson yarn and linen,

goat's hair, [5]the skin of rams from red, and the skin of dolphins, and acacia wood,

[6]oil for lamps, spices for the anointing oil, and the perfumed incense,

[7]stones of onyx, and stones for setting in the ephod and in the breastplate."

(Tabernacle: 26:1-37)

(Ark: 25:10-22)

(Table: 25:23-30)

(Lampstand: 25:31-40)

35:4-29

[4]And Moses said to the entire congregation of the Israelites, saying, "This is the word that Yahweh commanded, saying,[5]'Take from among you a contribution to Yahweh. Whoever is of a generous heart will bring the contribution of Yahweh:

gold, silver, and copper,

[6]blue, purple, and crimson yarn and linen,

[7]goat's hair, and skin of rams from red, and the skin of dolphins, and acacia wood,

[8]oil for lamps, and spices for the anointing oil, and the perfumed incense,

[9]and stones of onyx, and stones for setting in the ephod and in the breastplate.'

[10]And whoever is skilled of heart among you shall approach and make all that Yahweh commanded.

[11]The tabernacle: its tent, and its covering, its clasps, and its frames, its bars, its pillars, and its bases.

[12]The ark: and its poles, the cover, and the curtain of the screens.

[13]The table: and its poles, and all its vessels, and the bread of Presence.

[14]The lampstand for lighting: and its vessels and its lamps, and the oil for lighting.

(Altar of incense: 30:1-9)
(Oils: 30:22-38)

¹⁵The altar of incense: and its poles, and the oil of anointing, and the fragrant incense, and the screen of the door to enter the tabernacle.

(Altar of burnt offering: 27:1-8)

¹⁶The altar of burnt offering: and grating of copper to it, its poles, and all its vessels, the laver and its stand.

(Courtyard: 27:9-19)

¹⁷The hangings of the enclosure: and its pillars, and its bases, and the screen for the gate of the court. ¹⁸The pegs of the tabernacle: and the pegs of the enclosure, and their cords.

(Vestments: 28:1-43)

¹⁹The vestments of service for officiating in the sanctuary: the holy vestment for Aaron, the priest, and the vestments of his sons for priestly service."

²⁰And the entire congregation of the Israelites went out from before Moses. ²¹And each person whose heart was lifted up, and everyone whose spirit was incited brought the contribution of Yahweh for the work of the tent of meeting, and for its service and for the holy vestments. ²²Men and women came, all whose hearts were willing brought brooches, and earrings, and rings, and pendants.

²³And every person with whom was found blue, purple, and crimson yarn and linen, and goat's hair, and skin of rams from red, and the skin of dolphins brought them.

²⁴Everyone who was able to raise up a contribution of silver and copper brought the contribution of Yahweh. And everyone with whom was found acacia wood for any work of the service brought it.

²⁵And all the women skilled of heart spun with their hands, and they

brought what they had spun, the blue, the purple, the crimson yarns, and the linen.

²⁶ And all the women whose hearts rose up in wisdom spun the goat's hair.

²⁷ And the leaders brought the stones of onyx and the stones for setting in the ephod and the breastplate, ²⁸the spices, the oil for the light, and the anointing oil, and the fragrant incense.

²⁹ All the men and women whose heart was incited brought all the work that Yahweh commanded to be done by the hand of Moses. The Israelites brought [it] as a freewill offering to Yahweh.

Notes

25:2 *a contribution.* Hebrew *tĕrûmâ,* "dedication offering," may derive from the verb *rûm,* "to raise up." Milgrom notes that the word designates separation.[29] The LXX *aparchas* can mean "the beginning of a sacrifice" or "firstfruits."

whose heart moves him. The Hebrew phrase *yidbennû libbô* indicates a spontaneous gift. The LXX employs the verb *dokeō,* "to think, intend."

25:3 *copper.* Hebrew *nĕḥōšet* is also translated "bronze." The LXX *chalkon* can also designate either copper or bronze.

25:4 *crimson.* Hebrew *wĕtôlaʿat šānî* refers to the worm that produces the red color *(coccus ilicus).*

25:5 *the skin of dolphins.* The meaning of Hebrew *taḥaš* is debated. Modern translations render the term as "dolphin skins" (NJPS), "fine leather" (NRSV), and "sea cow" (BDB 1065). The LXX translates, *huakinthina,* "blue."

25:7 *stones of onyx.* The meaning of the Hebrew *šōham* is uncertain. Akkadian *sāmtu* means red stone, most likely carnelian (see also *HALOT* 2:1424). The LXX translates, *sardiou.* "This stone was of two kinds, the transparent-red or female being our carnelian, the transparent-brown or male our sardine" (LSJ 1584). The LXX is not consistent in its translation. In 28:9 it has *smaragdou,* "a green stone, including emerald" (LSJ 1619). In 28:20 it translates *beryllion,* "a gem of sea green color" (LSJ 314).

35:5 *whoever is of a generous heart.* Hebrew *kōl nĕdîb libbô* indicates a freewill gift. The phrase repeats in 35:21 and 29. The NJPS translates: "Everyone whose heart so moves him." The parallel phrase in 25:2 is *yidbennû libbô,* "whose heart moves him."

29. Milgrom, *Leviticus 1–16,* 415-16.

35:10 *and whoever is skilled of heart among you.* Hebrew *wĕkol-ḥăkam-lēb bākem* indicates a skilled craftsperson. The NRSV translates: "All who are skillful among you." A similar phrase describes the women weavers in 35:25, *wĕkol-'iššâ ḥakmat-lēb bĕyādeyhā.*

35:11-19 In the list of items for the tabernacle, the author identifies eight different items or cultic objects, repeating the same syntax. The subject matter is introduced with the direct object marker *('et),* followed by more detailed items associated with the subject. The tabernacle provides an example: "The tabernacle *('et-hammiškān):* its tent *('et-'ohŏlô).* . . ." The translation combines the hangings (v. 17) and the pegs (v. 18) into one paragraph, although they may represent separate subject matter. The order of the cultic items departs from their revelation in chaps. 25–31 with regard to the altar of incense and the oils (35:15; see 30:1-9, 22-38). The placement of the altar of incense at the conclusion of the divine instruction to Moses (30:1-9) led Wellhausen to conclude that it was a late addition to the literature.[30]

Commentary

Yahweh lists the material required for the construction of the tabernacle and its cult in 25:1-7. The fulfillment of the command is a more extended narrative in 35:4-29. Moses addresses the entire congregation of the Israelites to request building materials for the tabernacle and the necessary skilled artisans. The section divides between command (35:4-19) and fulfillment (35:20-29), a common literary device in the P History (see, e.g., the revelation of the tabernacle in chaps. 25–31 and its construction in chaps. 35–40). But the content indicates the spontaneous motivation of the people to provide the material and the labor for the tabernacle as a freewill gift. Exodus 35:5 states that all material gifts are voluntary, "everyone is willing *(nĕdîb libbô).*" The section consists primarily of the list of materials, which are described as a "contribution *(tĕrûmâ)* to Yahweh" (35:5). Milgrom clarifies the meaning of *tĕrûmâ* as "to set apart." The function of the *tĕrûmâ* is to transfer the ownership of an object from the human realm to the sacred world of God by setting it apart from one's other possessions. The transfer of an object takes place without ritual, outside a sanctuary, when the owner gives the gift to the priest, which is exactly the situation in 35:4-29.[31]

The tabernacle, its furnishings, and the courtyard are illustrated in figure 39 on page 608.

---

30. Wellhausen, *Composition,* 137-39.
31. Milgrom, *Leviticus 1–16,* 415-16.

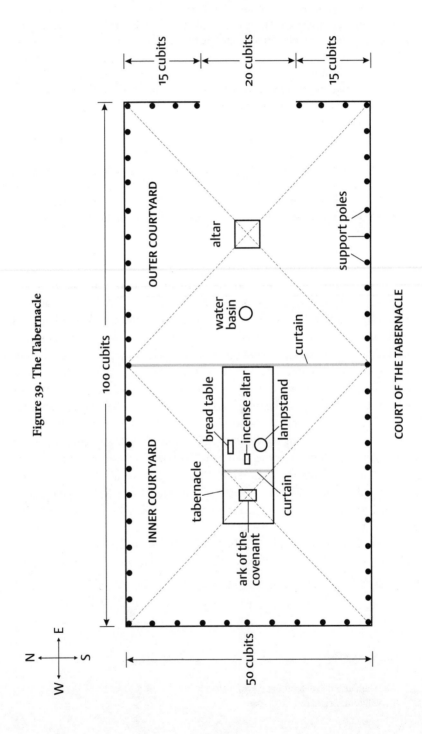

Figure 39. The Tabernacle

Purpose (25:8-9; 40:34-35)

25:8-9

⁸"And they shall make for me a sanctuary, and I will settle in their midst. ⁹According to all that I am showing to you, including the pattern of the tabernacle and the pattern of all its vessels, so you will do."

40:34-35

³⁴And the cloud covered the tent of meeting and the Glory of Yahweh filled the tabernacle. ³⁵But Moses was not able to enter the tent of meeting, because the cloud settled on it and the Glory of Yahweh filled the tabernacle.

(The Glory of Yahweh in the Altar: Lev 9:22-24)

Notes

25:8 *a sanctuary*. Hebrew *miqdāš*, "sanctuary, holy place," is translated in the LXX as *hagiasma*.

and I will settle in their midst. Hebrew *šākan* translates "to settle, tent, encamp," according to F. M. Cross.³² The translation "to settle" indicates movement and descent in the description of the divine presence in the tabernacle in contrast to the more static presence of God in the temple that is indicated by the verb *yāšab*, "to dwell, sit." The LXX reads, *ophthēsomai en hymin*, "I will be seen among you."

25:9 *according to all that I am showing to you*. The Sam adds, *bhr*, "on the mountain," which is also reflected in the LXX.

the pattern of the tabernacle and the pattern of all its vessels. Hebrew *tabnît*, "pattern," is also translated "image" (Deut 4:16-18), "model" (2 Kgs 16:10), and "architect's plan" (1 Chr 28:19). Cf. LXX *to paradeigma*, "the paradigm." Hebrew *miškān*, "tabernacle," is translated in the LXX as *skēnēs*, "tent."

Commentary

The theological significance of the tabernacle is stated in this section. God commands Moses in v. 8 to make a "sanctuary" *(miqdāš)*. The word *miqdāš* underscores the holy quality of the building; it derives from the verb *qādaš*, "to be holy." The conclusion to the Song of the Sea (15:17) also describes Yahweh's temple as a sanctuary, which is constructed by God, not humans. The designation of the cultic center as a *miqdāš* does not occur again in chaps. 25–31, and only infrequently in the P literature: any priest with a physical defect is restricted from the sanctuary (Lev 21:23; see also Num 19:20); the Aaronide priests are responsible for the care of the sanctuary (Num 3:38; see also 18:1); and the Kohathites are responsible for carrying the sanctuary (10:21).

God describes the tabernacle and its furnishings in Exod 25:9 as a "pattern"

---

32. Cross, "Priestly Tabernacle," *BAR* 1:201-28. See also M. Görg, *Der Zelt der Begegnung* (BBB 27; Bonn: Hanstein, 1967), 114-15.

(tabnît) "shown" *(mar'eh)* to Moses on Mount Sinai. The meaning of the text is difficult. The word *tabnît* translates as "form, structure, shape," while *mar'eh* indicates a "vision" or even the "form" of an object. A *tabnît* describes blueprints for the Jerusalem temple in 1 Chr 28:11: "Then David gave his son Solomon the plans *(tabnît)* for the portico of the temple." It may even describe the replica of the temple in 1 Chr 28:19: "He [God] gave me understanding in all the details of the plan *(tabnît)*" (see also 2 Kgs 16:10, where *tabnît* may indicate the replica of an altar). In Num 8:4 Yahweh shows Moses a form or perhaps a copy *(mar'eh)* of the lampstand. The examples indicate that Moses receives the plans of the tabernacle from God, certainly in the form of a blueprint. Their purpose is to instruct Moses in the building process. The additional meaning of *tabnît* as replica and of *mar'eh* as the form of an object may indicate that the tabernacle is also a copy of the heavenly dwelling. The setting of the cosmic mountain supports this interpretation; in this case the tabernacle provides a holy place on earth, a sanctuary *(miqdāš),* which replicates the heavenly temple, thus allowing God to dwell on earth.

The presence of God in the sanctuary is characterized as "tabernacling" or "settling," from Hebrew *šākan:* "I will settle *(šākan)* among them" (Exod 25:8). The word also occurred in the theophany of the Glory of Yahweh on Mount Sinai (24:15b-18a). The meaning of the verb *šākan* indicates a more movable view of God's presence in the sanctuary: God is able to leave the tabernacle to lead the people or to retreat from them in case of pollution or sin (see the commentary in 24:15b-18a). The focus of the divine presence is not on the sanctuary, however, but on the people. The sanctuary will allow God to reside in the midst of the people, "among them." The theme of divine presence in the midst of the people is developed throughout the P History. The Glory of Yahweh enters the tabernacle (40:34-38), then the altar (Lev 9:22-24), before Moses speaks with God in the most holy place (Num 7:89). The progression underscores the power of God to heal and to purify the people, thus allowing them to live in the sphere of holiness. Yet the Glory of Yahweh can also be a destructive force. The destructive power of divine presence in the midst of the people is illustrated in the story of the spies, when the people reject the gift of the land (Num 14:10, 21). The destructive force of the Glory of Yahweh continues in the rebellion of Korah (16:19), prompting the people to complain (16:42). The healing power of the Glory of Yahweh returns in 20:6, when it provides life-giving water to the people at the close of the wilderness journey.

FURNISHINGS (25:10-40)

Verses 10-40 describe the furnishings of the tabernacle, moving from the center of holiness outward in three stages: from the most holy object, the ark (25:10-22), to the table (25:23-30), and finally to the lampstand (25:31-40).

Ark (25:10-22; 37:1-9)

25:10-22

10"They shall make an ark of acacia wood; two and a half cubits its length, and one and a half cubits its width, and one and a half cubits its height. 11You shall overlay it with pure gold, inside and outside you shall overlay it. And you shall make a border of gold around. 12And you shall cast for it four rings of gold, and you shall place them on its four feet, two rings on its one side and two rings on its second side. 13And you shall make poles of acacia wood, and overlay them with gold. 14And you shall place the poles in the rings on the sides of the ark to lift the ark with them. 15The poles will be in the rings of the ark. They will not be removed from it.

16"You shall put into the ark the testimony, which I will give you.

17"You shall make a cover of pure gold, two and a half cubits its length, and one and a half cubits its width. 18And you shall make two cherubim of gold. You shall make them of hammered work at the two ends of the cover. 19Make one cherub at one end and one cherub at the other end. From the cover you shall make the cherubim on the two ends of it. 20The cherubim shall have their wings spread out above, with their wings hiding the cover and their faces one to the other. The faces of the cherubim shall be turned toward the cover.

21"You shall place the cover on the ark from above, and you shall put the testimony, which I will give you, in the ark.

37:1-9

1And Bezalel made the ark of acacia word; two and a half cubits its length, and one and a half cubits its width, and one and a half cubits its height. 2And he overlay it with pure gold, inside and outside. And he made for it a border of gold around. 3And he cast for it four rings of gold on its four feet, two rings on its one side and two rings on its second side. 4And he made poles of acacia wood, and he overlay them with gold. 5And he placed the poles in the rings on the sides of the ark to lift the ark.

(Tablets of Testimony: 40:20)

6And he made a cover of pure gold, two and a half cubits its length and one and a half its width. 7And he made two cherubim of gold. He made them of hammered work at the two ends of the cover. 8One cherub at one end and one cherub at the other end. From the cover he made the cherubim on the two ends of it. 9And the cherubim had their wings spread out above, with their wings hiding the cover, and their faces one to the other. The faces of the cherubim were turned toward the cover.

(Tablets of Testimony in the Ark of the Testimony: 40:20)

²²"I will meet you there. And I will   (Meeting with Moses: Num 7:89)
speak with you from above the cover,
between the two cherubim that are
on the ark of the covenant, all that I
command you concerning the
Israelites."

Notes

25:11 *You shall overlay it with pure gold, inside and outside you shall overlay it. And you shall make a border of gold around it.* The second person commands are for the most part in the singular addressed to Moses alone (but not exclusively; see v. 19).

25:14 *And you shall place the poles.* Hebrew *wĕhēbēʼtā* means "to approach, bring."

25:16 *You shall put into the ark the testimony.* Hebrew *wĕnātatā*, "you shall put," is the verb usually translated "to give." The use of the verb to indicate placement repeats in v. 21. The LXX writes, *embaleis*, "you throw/place in." The Hebrew *hāʻēdūt*, "the testimony," can also be translated "treaty" (see NRSV mg.) and "Pact" (NJPS). The LXX translates, *ta martyria*, "the witness, testimony."

25:17 *a cover of pure gold.* Hebrew *kappōret* is translated "cover" (NJPS) and also "mercy seat" (NRSV). See the commentary. The LXX translates *hilastērion*, "mercy seat."

25:19 *from the cover you shall make the cherubim on the two ends of it.* The Hebrew suggests that the cherubim and the cover are one piece. The NRSV translates: "Of one piece with the mercy seat."

25:20 *hiding the cover.* Hebrew *sōkĕkîm* can also mean "overshadow" (so NRSV; LXX *syskiazontes*) and "make unapproachable." Cf. NJPS "shielding the cover."

the faces of the cherubim shall be turned toward the cover. Hebrew *ʼel-hakkapōret yihyû pĕnê hakkĕrūbîm* is lit. "Toward the cover will be the faces of the cherubim."

25:22 *I will meet you there.* Cf. LXX *kai gnōsthēsomai soi ekeithen*, "and I will make myself known to you there."

Commentary

The word *ʼārōn*, "ark," means chest. It is used to describe a collection box in the temple (2 Kgs 12:9-11) and it also designates a coffin (Gen 50:26). Exodus 25:10-22 and 37:1-9 contain the most detailed information on the "ark" in the Hebrew Bible as a central sacramental object, signifying the presence of Yahweh in the Israelite cult. The closest analogy to the ark as a sacramental object in Christian tradition is the Eucharist, in which bread and wine signify the presence of the risen Christ in worship. Like the Christian Eucharist, the ark undergoes a complex history of interpretation and cultic transformation as the worship life and the political circumstances of the Israelites change.

C. L. Seow provides glimpses into the early meaning of the ark as a sacred object associated with holy war.[33] The poem in Num 10:35-36 about the leading

---

33. C. L. Seow, "Ark of the Covenant," *ABD* 1:386-93.

of Yahweh may describe the ark as a sacred war palladium, although the word "ark" is not in the poem. The cultic legends about the crossing of the Jordan at Gilgal (Joshua 4–5) and the warring against the Philistines at Shiloh (1 Samuel 4–6) may also provide a window into the role of the ark as representing the sacramental presence of "Yahweh Sabaoth, enthroned upon the cherubim" (1 Sam 4:4), especially in times of war (see also Judg 20:27). The ark is also associated with the Jerusalem temple through the cultic legend of David processing with the ark to Jerusalem (2 Samuel 6), where it may have functioned as the footstool of the enthroned God (Pss 99:5; 132:7; see also 1 Chr 28:2).

The cultic legends repeatedly underscore the power and danger of the ark as a sacred object. It controls nature (the stopping of the Jordan River and the infertility of the Philistines), and it kills humans who encroach, regardless of their motive (Joshua 4–5; 1 Sam 6:9; 2 Sam 6:6-8). The multiple references to the ark suggest its early and important role in the Israelite cult. But the refashioning of the cultic legends by later writers makes a firm interpretation of the early cultic traditions of the ark difficult, especially in view of the surprising absence of the ark in prophetic literature. The only reference to the ark in the entire prophetic corpus is Jer 3:16, an exilic or postexilic declaration about the restoration of Zion.

The most prominent cultic role of the ark is its function as the container for the tablets of law. The Non-P History identifies the ark as "the ark of the covenant of Yahweh" (*'ǎrôn běrît-yhwh*) when the Israelites depart from Mount Yahweh (Num 10:33) and once again in the failed war against the Amalekites and the Canaanites, when "the ark of the covenant" remained in the camp rather than accompanying the people in battle (Num 14:39-45). The name "ark of the covenant" derives from the "tablets of the covenant" (Exod 34:28) in the chest, also described as the "two tablets of stone" (24:12-14). The construction of the ark is recounted in Deut 10:1-5, but not in the Non-P History of Exodus 19–34. The ark is a chest made of acacia wood, devoid of iconography. The sacramental character of the ark results from the presence of the tablets within it, not from any inherent quality of the chest. T. N. D. Mettinger suggests that the emphasis on the tablets as sacred objects, rather than the ark, is intended to play down a cultic theology of divine enthronement associated with the monarchy.[34]

The P History shares the rejection of divine enthronement reflected in the theology of the Non-P History and Deuteronomy. Thus the sacred character of the ark in the P History also derives from its function as the container of divine law. God instructs Moses: "Put in the ark the testimony (*'ēdût*), which I will give you" (25:21). The "testimony" means the tablets of the law. But the ark acquires a new name in the P History, "the ark of the testimony" (*'ǎrōn hā'ēdût*,

---

34. Mettinger, *Dethronement of Sabaoth*, 50-52.

25:22) to reflect the different content of the tablets, as documents containing the revelation of the tabernacle and its cult (see 31:18; 32:15; 34:29).

The ark of the testimony is introduced as the central cultic object in the tabernacle in the revelation of the cult to Moses (25:1-22; 26:33-34; 30:6, 26; 31:7). It is the place where God promises to meet with Moses and to give instruction to the people (25:22), which is fulfilled in Num 7:89. Exodus 37:1-9 describes its construction. The ark of the testimony is anything but a simple wooden box, devoid of iconography. The structure of the ark remains acacia wood, with the dimensions 2½ cubits long × 1½ cubits wide × 1½ cubits high (about 3¾ feet long × 2¼ feet wide × 2¼ feet high). But it is lavished in pure gold both inside and outside of the box with an additional molding of gold. The outside includes gold rings, two on each side, and wooden poles, also covered in gold, which are used to carry the ark. Pure gold is also used to fashion the top of the ark, described as the atonement cover *(kappōret)*, sometimes translated "mercy seat," from the rite of atonement that takes place at the ark on the Day of Atonement (Lev 16:2). The dimensions of the *kappōret* are 2½ cubits long × 1½ cubits wide, matching the chest.

Two cherubim are sculpted into the *kappōret* from hammered, or manufactured, gold. They face each other with wings "spread upward, overshadowing the cover with them" (Exod 37:9). Cherubim are hybrid creatures, according to O. Keel and C. Uehlinger, including an array of different features, such as a lion's body, the wings of birds, and a human face.[35] They represent power in the human world, and they are often presented as the bearers of the throne in the ancient world and as guards (Gen 3:24). Two massive cherubim are associated with the throne of Yahweh in the Jerusalem temple (1 Kgs 6:23-28), while the walls of the temple also included their representation (1 Kgs 6:29), like the curtains in the tabernacle. The two cherubim in the P History probably no longer represent the throne of God, but they continue to stand guard over the law, placed in the ark of the testimony after its completion (Exod 40:3, 5, 20-21).[36] Numbers 7:89 describes the ongoing revelation of Yahweh as a speech to Moses that originates from between the two cherubim.

The Kohathite Levites are charged with the care of the ark during the wilderness journey (Num 3:31; 4:5).

---

35. O. Keel and C. Uehlinger, *Gods, Goddesses, and Images of God in Ancient Israel* (trans. T. H. Trapp; Minneapolis: Fortress, 1998), 168-69.
36. C. Meyers, "Cherubim," *ABD* 1:899-900.

Table (25:23-30; 37:10-16)

25:23-30	37:10-16
²³"And you shall make a table of acacia wood, two cubits its length, and one cubit its width, and one and a half cubits its height. ²⁴And you shall overlay it with pure gold. And you shall make for it a border of gold around. ²⁵And you shall make a rim a hand's breadth around it, and you shall make a border of gold for its rim around. ²⁶And you shall make for it four rings of gold, and you shall place the rings on the four corners, which are at its four feet. ²⁷The rings shall be next to the rim used for the poles to carry the table. ²⁸And you shall make poles of acacia wood, and you shall overlay them with gold. The table will be carried by these. ²⁹And you shall make its platters, its saucers, its jars, and its bowls, with which to offer libation. You shall make them of pure gold. ³⁰And you will place on the table the bread of the Presence to be before me continually."	¹⁰And he made the table of acacia wood, two cubits its length, and one cubit its width, and a cubit and a half its height. ¹¹And he overlaid it with pure gold. And he made for it a border of gold around. ¹²And he made for it a rim of a hand's breadth around, and it made a border of gold for its rim around. ¹³And he cast for it four rings of gold, and he placed the rings on the four corners, which are at its four feet. ¹⁴The rings were next to the rim used for the poles to carry the table. ¹⁵And he made the poles of acacia wood, and he overlay them with gold to carry the table. ¹⁶And he made vessels for the table of pure gold, its platters, its saucers, its jars, and the bowls to offer libation.

Notes

25:26 *and you shall place the rings on the four corners, which are at its four feet.* The LXX envisions a somewhat different table in which the rings are attached lower on the legs.

25:29 *and you shall make its platters, its saucers, its jars, and its bowls, with which to offer libation.* The vessels include: *qĕʿārōt*, "plates, platters" (NRSV "plates"; NJPS "bowls"); *kappōt*, "saucers" (NRSV "dishes for incense"; NJPS "ladles"); *qĕśôt*, "jars" (NRSV "flagons"; NJPS "jars"); and *mĕnaqqîyōt*, "bowls" (NRSV "bowls"; NJPS "jugs"). The LXX translates, *ta tryblia*, "dishes"; *tas thuiskas*, "censers"; *ta spondeia*, "bowls"; and *tous kuathous*, "cups."

25:30 *the bread of the Presence to be before me.* Hebrew *leḥem pānîm*, "bread of the Presence," is lit. "bread of the face," creating a wordplay with the following phrase, "before my face *(lĕpānay)*."

37:16 *its platters, its saucers, its jars, and the bowls to offer libation.* The first three utensils are written with the pronominal suffix, translated "its." The final utensil, "the bowls," is written without a suffix, suggesting that only these bowls are used for the offering of libation.

Commentary

M. Haran writes that the furnishings of the tabernacle with their related complex of ritual acts were intended to give the tabernacle "the character of a dwelling place of the Deity."[37] The story of the Shunammite women and Elisha mentions the furnishings required to make a home. They include a bed, table, chair, and lamp (2 Kgs 4:10). Yahweh, the God of Israel, neither slumbers nor sleeps, hence requires no bed. But the tabernacle does include a table with utensils and food, a lamp, and perhaps also a chair, if the imagery of a throne still lingers in the iconography of the cover on the ark.

The table in the tabernacle is made of acacia wood. Its dimensions are 2 cubits long × 1 cubit wide × 1½ cubits high (=about 3 feet long × 1½ feet wide × 2¼ feet high). Like the ark it is covered lavishly with pure gold, and then overlaid with a gold mold and an additional gold rim. Four golden rings are attached to the four corners for the poles, used to carry the table. The utensils for the table were also made of gold, including plates or bowls *(qĕʿārōt),* ladles *(kappōt),* perhaps another bowl of some sort *(mĕnaqqîyōt),* and pitchers *(qĕśôt)* for a drink offering. The function of the table as the location for a drink offering is not explored further in the P History. Exodus 26:35 locates the table in the Holy Place on the north wall opposite the lampstand.

Exodus 25:30 states the "the bread of the Presence" must be on the table at all times. Leviticus 24:5-9 describes the ingredients of the bread, their arrangement on the table in two rows of six loaves each, the significance of the loaves as a sign of the covenant, and the ritual cycle of their replacement every Sabbath; it also authorizes the priests to eat the bread. The detailed description of the table and the bread of the Presence is confined, for the most part, to the P History (Exod 25:23-30; 26:35; 30:27; 31:8; 35:13; 37:10-16; 39:36; 40:4, 22, 24; Lev 24:5-9; Num 3:31; 4:7). Yet the table and the bread of the Presence are also associated with the Jerusalem temple of Solomon (1 Kgs 7:48). David is described as eating cultic bread from the sanctuary at Nob (1 Sam 21:5-7). The psalmist speaks of a cultic table in Ps 23:5: "You prepare a table before me in the presence of my enemies." But the imagery is likely not in reference to the table and bread of the Presence in the P tabernacle.

The symbolic meaning of the table is difficult to determine. It may represent food for Yahweh. The table prepared with food may also represent hospitality, especially that of a king toward subjects, as in the story of David's hospitality toward Mephibosheth (2 Sam 9:9-13). The imagery of feasting with

37. Haran, *Temples and Temple-Service,* 216-21, esp. 218.

Yahweh on the cosmic mountain has already appeared in Exodus (18:12; 24:11), and the table in the tabernacle may represent a way of ritualizing the imagery, while restricting the experience to the priesthood who will become the only ones allowed to eat the food from Yahweh's table (Lev 24:5-9).

Lampstand (25:31-40; 37:17-24)

25:31-40

[31]"And you will make a lampstand of pure gold. The lampstand will be made of hammered work, its base, its shaft, its cups, its bulbs, and its buds will be from it. [32]Six shafts will go out from its sides, three shafts of the lampstand from its one side, and three shafts of the lampstand from its second side. [33]Three cups like almond blossoms will be on one shaft, with bulb and bud; and three cups like almond blossoms on the other shaft, with bulb and bud, so six shafts were going out of the lampstand. [34]On the lampstand there will be four cups like almond blossoms, with its bulbs and its buds. [35]A bulb from it will be under two shafts, a bulb from it under two shafts, and a bulb from it under two shafts for the six shafts to go out from the lampstand. [36]Their bulbs and their shafts will be from it, the whole of it one hammered work of pure gold.

[37]"You shall make its seven lamps. The lamps shall be set up, and it will give light on the space in front of it. [38]And its tongs and its trays you will make of pure gold. [39]From a talent of pure gold you shall make all of these vessels. [40]And see that you make them according to the pattern, which was shown you on the mountain."

37:17-24

[17]And he made the lampstand of pure gold. He made the lampstand of hammered work, its base, its shaft, its cups, its bulbs, and its buds from it. [18]Six shafts went out from its sides, three shafts from the lampstand from its one side, and three shafts from its second side. [19]Three cups like almond blossoms were on one shaft, with bulb and bud; and three cups like almond blossoms on the other shaft, with bulb and bud, so six shafts were going out of the lampstand. [20]On the lampstand there were four cups like almond blossoms, with its bulbs and buds. [21]A bulb from it was under two shafts, a bulb from it under two shafts, and a bulb from it under two shafts for the six shafts to go out from the lampstand. [22]Their bulbs and their shafts were from it, the whole of it one hammered work of pure gold.

[23]And he made its seven lamps,

its tongs, and its trays of pure gold. [24]From a talent of pure gold he made it and all its vessels.

Notes

25:31 *a lampstand.* Hebrew *hammĕnōrâ* is from the root *nwr,* "to shine, light"; LXX has *lychnian,* "lampstand."

its base, its shaft, its cups, its bulbs, and its buds. The imagery of the lampstand is likely botanical. Hebrew *yĕrēkāh,* "its base," is lit. "its thigh." In reference to the lampstand, it can be translated "shaft" or "stem," as is evident in the LXX, *ho kaulos.* Hebrew *wĕqānāh,* "its shaft," refers to a reed or stalk. C. Meyers reads the phrase *yĕrēkāh wĕqānāh* as referring to one item, "thickened shaft," which contains botanical imagery from the Egyptian reed plant.[38] R. Hachlili translates *qāneh* as "reed," meaning a "hollow tube," which carries no botanical imagery.[39] The LXX translates, *hoi kalamiskoi,* "reeds" or "branches." Hebrew *gĕbî'eyhā,* "cups," is translated in the LXX, *hoi kratēres,* "bowls." Hebrew *kaptōreyhā,* "its bulbs," can also describe a knob. The NRSV and NJPS translate "calyxes," which refers to the green leafy part of the flower. Hebrew *ûperāḥeyhā,* "its buds," could also be translated "blossom" or "pedal." The LXX translates, *ta krina,* "lilies."

will be from it. This is a literal translation of Hebrew *mimmennâ yihyû;* it indicates that the lampstand is of one piece. Cf. NRSV "will be of one piece with it."

25:35 *A bulb from it will be under two stems, a bulb from it under two stems, and a bulb from it under two stems for the six stems to go out from the lampstand.* The Hebrew is awkward, repeating the same phrase three times. The NRSV translates: "There shall be a calyx of one piece with it under the first pair of branches, a calyx of one piece with it under the next pair of branches, and a calyx of one piece with it under the last pair of branches — so for the six branches that go out of the lampstand."

25:37 *The lamps shall be set up, and it will give light on the space in front of it.* The MT *wĕhe'ĕlâ* is written in the third person singular. The Sam *wh'lyt* and the LXX *epithēseis* change the verb to the second person, "you will set up." The singular verb in the MT, *wĕhē'îr,* "it will give light," is changed to the plural in the Sam, *wh'yrw,* and in the LXX, *phanousin.*

25:38 *you will make.* The verb is absent from the MT and Sam but provided in the LXX, *poiēseis.*

25:40 *and see that you make them according to their pattern, which was shown you on the mountain.* The syntax of the Hebrew is unusual, consisting of an imperative with conjunction, *ûrĕ'ēh,* followed by another imperative, *wa'ăśēh.* The LXX translates, *hora poiēseis,* "see that you do."

Commentary

The lampstand or menorah *(mĕnōrâ)* is revealed to Moses in 25:31-40, where it is described as a copy *(tabnît;* see the commentary on 25:8-9), indicating per-

---

38. C. Meyers, *The Tabernacle Menorah: A Synthetic Study of a Symbol from the Biblical Cult* (ASORDS 2; Missoula, Mont.: Scholars Press, 1976), 19-21.

39. R. Hachlili, *The Menorah, the Ancient Seven-Armed Candelabrum: Origin, Form and Significance* (JSJSup 68; Leiden: Brill, 2001), 29-33.

haps that it is a replica of a heavenly form. The lampstand is constructed in 37:17-24 and its ritual practice is described in Num 8:1-4. The location of the menorah is on the south wall of the tabernacle, opposite the table. Numbers 8:1-4 indicates that its light is directed toward the altar of incense.

The construction of the menorah is detailed in botanical imagery, yet obscure in its dimensions and proportions. The quantity of one talent (about 75 pounds) of pure gold suggests a large object. The menorah is manufactured, that is, hammered. According to C. Meyers, its iconography suggests a stylized tree of life, symbolizing fertility in nature and the life-giving power of God.[40] The botanical imagery begins with the shaft of the menorah, called a stem (*qāneh*), perhaps indicating a reed.[41] The receptacles for lamps are branches (*qānîm*), to which are attached "cups shaped like almond flowers with buds and blossoms" (37:19). The result is a stylized tree. The seven branches represent completeness. The almond tree symbolizes wakefulness in the call of Jeremiah (Jer 1:11-12) and may have a similar meaning here. The imagery is likely directed to Yahweh, whose wakeful eyes are represented by the menorah. This is the interpretation offered in Zechariah's fifth vision, which equates the menorah with the eyes of God (Zechariah 4).

The tree of life is common throughout the ancient Near East. Ten lampstands are part of the temple of Solomon, but there is no indication that they represent the botanical imagery of the menorah. The construction and imagery of the tabernacle menorah point in particular to the influence of Egyptian craft techniques, according to Meyers.[42] When the focus is narrowed to the Hebrew Bible, the menorah invites comparison to the tree of life in the garden of Eden (Gen 3:22-24). It relates the divine presence in the tabernacle to creation and holds out hope that Yahweh is able to restore fertility even in the wilderness. R. Hachlili disagrees with the interpretation of the menorah as a stylized tree, interpreting Hebrew *qāneh* instead as a hollow pipe or tube. She concludes that the menorah is "a unique form" in the ancient Near East, and that its inherent symbolism is of light, not plant life.[43]

ARCHITECTURAL PLANS (26:1–27:19)

Exodus 26:1–27:19 contains the architectural plans for the tabernacle; like the furnishings, these plans progress in three stages of holiness: from the tabernacle (26:1-37) to the altar (27:1-8) and finally to the courtyard (27:9-19).

40. C. Meyers, "Lampstand," *ABD* 4:141-43; see the drawings in idem, *Tabernacle Menorah*, 205-21.
41. Meyers, *ABD* 4:142.
42. Meyers, *Tabernacle Menorah*, e.g., 188-91.
43. Hachlili, *Menorah*, 7-37.

Tabernacle (26:1-37; 36:8-38)

26:1-37

Exterior Curtains of Yarn

¹"And the tabernacle you will make with ten curtains of fine twisted linen of blue, purple, and crimson yarns. You will make them with a cherubim skillfully worked in. ²The length of one curtain will be twenty-eight cubits, and the width of one curtain will be four cubits. One measurement will be for all the curtains. ³Five curtains will be joined to one another, and five curtains will be joined to one another.

⁴"You will make loops of blue on the edge of the outer curtain of one set, and do the same on the edge of the curtain of the second set. ⁵You shall make fifty loops on the one curtain, and you shall make fifty loops on the edge of the curtain in the second set; the loops will be opposite one to the other. ⁶You shall make fifty clasps of gold, and you will join the curtains one to the other with the clasps, so that the tabernacle is one.

Exterior Curtains of Goat's Hair

⁷"You will make curtains of goat's hair for the tent on the tabernacle. You will make eleven curtains. ⁸The length of each curtain will be thirty cubits, and the width of one curtain four cubits. One measurement will be for the eleven curtains. ⁹You will join five of the curtains by themselves and six of the curtains by themselves. And you will fold double the sixth curtain at the front of the tent.

36:8-38

⁸And all the skilled of heart among those undertaking the work made the tabernacle of ten curtains, of fine twisted linen of blue, purple, and crimson yarn. Cherubim were skillfully worked into them. ⁹The length of one curtain was twenty-eight cubits, and the width of one curtain was four cubits. One measurement was for all the curtains. ¹⁰He joined five curtains to one another, and five curtains he joined to one another.

¹¹And he made loops of blue on the edge of the outer curtain of one set, so he did on the outer end of the curtain of the second set. ¹²Fifty loops he made in the one curtain, and fifty loops he made on the edge of the curtain in the second set. The loops were opposite one to the other. ¹³And he made fifty clasps of gold. And he joined the curtains one to the other with the clasps, so the tabernacle was one.

¹⁴And he made curtains of goat's hair for the tent on the tabernacle. He made eleven curtains. ¹⁵The length of each curtain was thirty cubits, and the wide of one curtain four cubits. One measurement was for the eleven curtains. ¹⁶He joined five curtains by themselves, and six curtains by themselves.

¹⁰"You shall make fifty loops on the edge of the outer curtain of one set, and fifty loops on the edge of the curtain of the second set. ¹¹And you shall make fifty copper clasps, and you will place the clasps in the loops. And you will join the tent, and it will be one.

¹²"The overhang of the surplus in the curtain of the tent, the half of the surplus curtain, you will overhang on the back of the tabernacle. ¹³The cubit on one side and the cubit on the other side in the length of the curtain of the tent will be the overhang on the sides of the tabernacle, on this side and on that side, to cover it.

Exterior Curtains of Tanned Ram Skins and Dolphin Skins

¹⁴"You shall make for the tent a covering of the skin of rams from red and a covering of the skin of dolphins.

Structure

¹⁵"You are to make the boards for the tabernacle of acacia wood, upright. ¹⁶The board will be ten cubits in length, a cubit and a half in width for each board. ¹⁷There will be two pegs for each board to fit one to the other, so you will make for every board of the tabernacle. ¹⁸And you shall make the boards for the tabernacle: twenty boards for the south side. ¹⁹And forty bases of silver you will make under the twenty boards, two bases under the first board for its two pegs, and two bases under the other board for its two pegs, ²⁰and for the second side of the tabernacle on the north side twenty boards. ²¹And forty bases of silver you will make under the twenty boards, two bases under the first board for its two pegs, and two bases under the other board.

¹⁷And he made fifty loops on the edge of the outer curtain of one set, and fifty loops on the edge of the curtain of the second set. ¹⁸And he made fifty copper clasps to join the tent to be one.

¹⁹And he made a covering for the tent, skin of rams from red, and a covering of the skin of dolphins.

²⁰And he made boards for the tabernacle of acacia wood, upright. ²¹The board was ten cubits in length, a cubit and a half in width for each board. ²²There were two pegs for each board to fit one to the other, so he made every board of the tabernacle. ²³And he made the boards for the tabernacle, twenty boards for the south side. ²⁴And forty bases of silver he made under the twenty boards, two bases under each board for its two pegs, and the two bases under the other boards for its two pegs. ²⁵And for the second side of the tabernacle on the north side he made twenty boards, ²⁶forty bases of silver, two bases under the first board, and two bases under the other board.

²²"And for the rear of the tabernacle on the west you will make six boards. ²³And two of the boards you will make for the corners of the tabernacle in the rear. ²⁴And they will be identical at the bottom and they will be together at the top in the first ring. So it will be for both of them. They shall form the two corners. ²⁵And there shall be eight boards, and their bases of silver, sixteen bases, two bases under one board, and two bases under another board.

²⁶"And you will make bars of acacia wood, five for the boards of one side of the tabernacle, ²⁷and five for the boards of the second side of the tabernacle, and five bars for the boards of the side of the tabernacle at the rear to the west. ²⁸The center bar in the middle of the boards will extend from end to end. ²⁹The boards you will overlay with gold, and their rings you will make of gold as holders for the bars. You will overlay the bars with gold.

³⁰"And you will raise up the tabernacle, according to the manner of it, which you were shown.

Interior Curtain

³¹"And you will make a curtain of blue, purple, and crimson yarns, and fine twisted linen. It will be made with cherubim skillfully woven in it. ³²And you will place it on the pillars of acacia overlaid with gold, with hooks of gold on four bases of silver. ³³And you will place the curtain under the clasps, and you will set there behind the curtain the ark of the testimony. The curtain will divide for you between the holy place and the holy of holies.

²⁷And for the rear of the tabernacle on the west, he made six boards. ²⁸And two boards he made for the corners of the tabernacle in the rear. ²⁹And they were identical at the bottom and they were together at the top in the first ring. So he made two of them for the two corners. ³⁰And there were eight boards and their bases of silver, sixteen bases, two bases under each board.

³¹And he made bars of acacia wood, five for the boards of one side of the tabernacle, ³²and five for the boards of the second side of the tabernacle, and five bars for the boards of the tabernacle at the rear to the west. ³³And he made the center of the bar to extend in the middle of the boards from end to end. ³⁴The boards he overlay with gold, and the rings he made of gold as holders for the bars. And he overlay the bars with gold.

(Assembly 39:32-43)

³⁵And he made the curtain of blue, purple, and crimson yarns, and fine twisted linen. He made it with cherubim skillfully woven. ³⁶And he made for it four pillars of acacia. And he overlaid them with gold, with hooks of gold. He cast for them four bases of silver.

Holy of Holies

³⁴"You shall set the cover on the ark
of the testimony in the holy of holies.

Holy Place

³⁵"You will set the table outside of the
curtain, and the lampstand opposite
the table on the south side of the
tabernacle. The table you will place
on the north side.

Screen for the Entrance

³⁶"You shall make a screen for the
door of the tent of blue, purple, and
crimson yarns, and of fine twisted
linen, worked in embroidery. ³⁷You
shall make for the screen five pillars
of acacia. And you shall overlay them
with gold, and their hooks of gold.
And you shall cast for them five bases
of copper."

³⁷And he made a screen for the door
of the tent of blue, purple, and
crimson yarns, and fine twisted linen,
worked in embroidery, ³⁸and the five
pillars and its hooks. He overlaid
their tops and their bands with gold,
and their five bases were copper.

Notes

26:1 *and the tabernacle you will make with ten curtains of fine twisted linen of blue, purple, and crimson yarns.* Hebrew *miškān* derives from the verb *šākan,* "to settle, dwell." The designation *miškān* contrasts to another description of the wilderness sanctuary as the *'ōhel mō'ēd,* "tent of meeting." See the commentary for discussion and interpretation. For discussion of the colors see 25:4.

you will make them with cherubim skillfully worked in. Hebrew *ma'ăśēh ḥōšēb,* "work of reflection," is unclear. The verb *ḥāšab* means "to think, to devise," and even "to invent." It appears frequently in the description of the tabernacle and its cultic objects (26:1, 31; 28:6, 15; 31:4); here it may indicate the technical and artistic ability to weave and embroider. Cf. NRSV: "With cherubim skillfully worked into them." The NJPS translates the word as a description of the "design" of the cherubim, rather than the activity of weaving: "With a design of cherubim worked into them." The LXX translates, *cheroubim ergasia hyphantou,* "cherubim in work of weaving."

26:7 *for the tent on the tabernacle.* Hebrew *lě'ōhel,* "for the tent," does not signify the "tent of meeting" (*'ōhel mō'ēd*), but a covering over the tabernacle. The LXX notes the distinction, translating "tent" in this verse as *skepēn,* "covering, shelter," in contrast to the tabernacle/tent of meeting, which is translated *skēnē,* "booth, tent."

26:9 *and you will fold double the sixth curtain at the front of the tent.* Hebrew *wěkāpaltā,* "to fold double," suggests the imagery of the sixth curtain providing a cover to the front of the tent. The NJPS translates: "And fold over the sixth cloth at the front of the tent." Cassuto identifies the sixth curtain as the first curtain on the eastern side of the tabernacle closest to the entrance. He concludes that the curtain was folded in the middle along its length, doubling the thickness of the first curtain for the purpose of protecting the sacred space.[44]

26:12 *the overhang of the surplus in the curtain of the tent, the half of the surplus curtain, you will overhang on the back of the tabernacle.* Cassuto quotes *b. Shab.* 98 to describe the overhanging curtain: "What did the tabernacle resemble? A woman walking in the street with her train trailing behind her."[45]

26:14 *the skin of rams from red and a covering of the skin of dolphins.* See 25:5.

26:15 *the boards for the tabernacle.* Hebrew *qĕrāšîm,* "boards," is also translated as "planks" (NJPS), "frames" (NRSV), and "poles" (LXX *stylous*). The only occurrence outside the tabernacle description is Ezek 27:6, where *qereš* describes part of a ship. Cassuto suggests "boards," as did Philo (*Moses* 2.18).[46]

26:24 *And they will be identical at the bottom and they will be together at the top in the first ring.* The meaning of the Hebrew is uncertain. The Hebrew *tō'ămîm* means "double" or "twin," suggesting that the two boards are the same. See NJPS: "They shall match at the bottom." Cf. NRSV: "They shall be separate beneath." The description of the two boards at the top is even less certain. Hebrew *tammîm* means "complete, whole." One image arising from the translation is a triangular shaped frame, with the boards separated at the bottom and joined at the top. The Sam repeats the first term *(t'mym),* suggesting the same relationship at the bottom and the top of the boards. On the basis of comparison to Egyptian wooden structures, M. M. Homan writes: "'Double from below' (תֹאֲמִם) and 'complete above' (תַמִּים) in 26:24 are synonymous wood-working terms for fusing boards."[47]

26:30 *according to the manner of it.* Hebrew *kĕmišpāṭô,* "according to the manner of it," is translated in NRSV: "according to the plan for it," which accentuates a literary relationship with the phrase in 25:40, "according to the pattern *(tabnît)* for them." The LXX translates Hebrew *mišpāṭ* as *eidos,* "form, figure, shape," which also suggests a close relationship with 25:40, *kata ton typon,* "according to the pattern/ model."

26:31 *a curtain.* Hebrew *pārōket,* "curtain," separating the holy place from the holy of holies, is distinct from the other interior curtains, *yĕrî'ōt* (26:1ff.), and the exterior curtains, *qĕlā'îm,* "hangings" (27:9-19).

26:33 *between the holy place and the holy of holies.* Hebrew *bên haqqōdeš ûbên qōdeš haqqodošîm* are definite, prompting the translation, "the Holy Place and the Most Holy Place" (Houtman),[48] or "the Holy and the Holy of Holies" (NJPS), or "the holy place from the most holy" (NRSV).

36:38 *He overlaid their tops and their bands with gold.* Hebrew *rō'šêhem,* "their tops," is translated in NRSV, "capitals." Hebrew *waḥăšûqêhem,* "and their bands," derives from the verb *ḥāšaq,* "to become attached to, to love." The Piel form of the verb in

44. Cassuto, *Exodus,* 352.

45. Ibid., 353.

46. Ibid., 357; for discussion of the translation "boards" see Homan, *To Your Tents,* 142-47.

47. Homan, *To Your Tents,* 148.

48. Houtman, *Exodus,* 3:436.

38:28 means "to join together." The Pual participle in this verse and in 27:17 likely means "joints" or "bands" that hold the pillars together.

Commentary

The construction of the tabernacle begins with its curtain coverings (26:1-14), followed by the frame (26:15-30), and it concludes with a description of two additional curtains, the one separating the most holy place and the holy place (26:31-35), and the screen at the entrance of the tabernacle (26:36-37).

Three layers of curtains cover the tabernacle in 26:1-14. The emphasis on the number three continues the practice in the P History of separating the sacred and the profane in three stages. The architecture of the tabernacle moves from the most holy place to the holy place and finally to the courtyard. The selection of cultic personnel results in three classes of people, the Aaronide priests, the Levites, and the laity. The coverings of the tabernacle also provide three layers of separation between the inside and the outside of the tabernacle.

The first level of curtain (26:1-6) is closest to the holiness of God. It is made of linen in the colors of blue (a sky blue),[49] purple, and scarlet, with cherubim iconography. This layer consists of ten curtains, 28 cubits long × 4 cubits wide (about 42 feet × 6 feet), joined into two units of five curtains each. Fifty loops of blue and fifty golden clasps are attached to the two panels of curtain, creating a secure seal and covering for the tabernacle.

The second layer of curtain (26:14-18) is goat's hair. It consists of eleven curtains, 30 cubits long and 4 wide (about 45 feet × 6 feet), joined in two panels of five and six each, with fifty loops and fifty bronze clasps. The slightly larger size allows the curtain to hang over the rear of the tabernacle and to cover more completely the sides: "The overhang of the surplus in the curtain of the tent, the half of the surplus curtain, you will overhang on the back of the tabernacle" (26:12). The sixth curtain on the one panel allows for a double covering at the front: "And you will fold double the sixth curtain at the front of the tent" (26:9).

The third layer of curtain (26:14) consists of two different materials, ram's skin dyed red, most likely limited to the sides, and the skin of a sea mammal placed "above" *(milmā'lâ),* apparently on the top of the structure. But the verse is anything but clear. My interpretation follows Maimonides and is reflected in the reconstruction of M. Levine.[50] But the skin of the sea mammal may also be a fourth covering or, as Cassuto suggests, a protective covering for transit (see Num 4:6).[51] The ambiguity illustrates the tension in the description of the ta-

---

49. See Levine, *Tabernacle,* 38.
50. Ibid., 64-67.
51. Cassuto, *Exodus,* 354.

bernacle between what appears upon first reading to be exact details, yet upon closer examination is surprisingly incomplete.

Exodus 26:15-30 describes the structure of the tabernacle. Verses 15-16 begin with the upright frames or "boards" *(qĕrāšîm)* made of acacia wood. Forty-eight boards make up the walls of the tabernacle, each 10 cubits long × 1½ cubits wide (about 15 feet × 2¼ feet). The longest walls on the north and south contain twenty boards each, and the west wall consists of six boards, with two additional boards for the corners. Each board is anchored in two silver bases, resulting in forty silver bases for the north and south walls, and sixteen for the rear or west wall. Verse 17 indicates that the boards were attached to the silver bases by tenons or supports *(yādôt,* lit. "hands").

Verses 26-29 describe poles or bars *(bĕrîḥīm)* that fasten to the boards of the tabernacle to make them more secure and stable. They are covered in gold. Five bars are described as supporting each of the three walls, with the center bar extending from end to end at the middle of the frames (see also 36:31-34). The text does not allow for a more detailed description of where the bars were attached (on the outside or inside wall), or how the bars functioned on the walls.

The resulting area of the tabernacle, when the boards stand flush against one another, is 10 cubits × 30 cubits (about 15 feet × 45 feet). The width of 10 cubits is not specifically stated, but results from the six boards (9 cubits) and the two corner boards (making up the extra cubit). The measurement for the tabernacle is noteworthy since it is half the size of Solomon's temple, described as 20 cubits × 60 cubits (see 1 Kings 6). The correlation prompted Wellhausen to interpret the description of the tabernacle as a literary genre from the exilic or postexilic period, providing commentary on the destroyed temple from the monarchical period, rather than preserving the description of an ancient cult site.[52] The prophet Ezekiel's extended description of the rebuilt Jerusalem temple from the exilic period provides a similar example of this genre of literature. K. R. Stevenson concluded that the temple of Ezekiel was also not intended to be built.[53] R. E. Friedman disagrees with a purely literary interpretation of the architecture, materials, and design of the tabernacle. He has argued that the tabernacle was originally a shrine in the Jerusalem temple located beneath the wings of the cherubim, whose span allowed precisely for a tent shrine of 20 cubits long, 10 cubits high, and less than 10 cubits wide.[54]

The debate over literary genre and historical representation surrounding the Priestly tabernacle illustrates the tension and the ambiguity facing inter-

---

52. Wellhausen, *Prolegomena,* 36-38 *et passim.*

53. K. R. Stevenson, *Vision of Transformation: The Territorial Rhetoric of Ezekiel 40–48* (SBLDS 154; Atlanta: Scholars Press, 1996).

54. R. E. Friedman, "Tabernacle," *ABD* 6:292-300, esp. 295-96; idem, "The Tabernacle in the Temple," *BA* 43 (1980): 241-48.

preters, when what appears upon first reading to be exact details of a concrete sanctuary becomes more and more elusive as one continues to read. The P History is presenting a utopian picture of divine holiness in the midst of the Israelites, not a historical account of a lost sanctuary.

The enigma of utopian literature like the tabernacle, writes P. Ricoeur, is the exhaustive listing of items.[55] The reader is so flooded with minutiae that the wealth of details is able to break through the present reality of the reader and offer an alternative world. The alternative utopian world is both a place of refuge and a source for critically evaluating the present social structures. This is certainly how the tabernacle functions in Exodus. It provides a refuge for the Israelites of the exilic and postexilic period. It is located in the wilderness outside the social structures of the geopolitical world, providing a critical perspective on power, politics, the sacred, and leadership. Its vision of God provides a resource for rejecting the close ties between temple construction and the royal ideology of the king, which is represented in Exodus through the golden calf (Exodus 32).

The literary description of the tabernacle is certainly intended to influence the cultic practice in the postexilic period, and in this way it does become concrete in the religious and political life of the Israelites. The tendency of the literature toward concreteness continues to influence subsequent interpreters. Thus although the P author is writing a cultic theology of holiness in describing the architectural plans of the tabernacle, the details of the description, like holiness itself, push the interpreter toward concreteness, not abstraction. M. Levine provides an exquisite example of this tendency in a historical reproduction, while B. O. Long illustrates the same powerful tendency in North American religious folklore with the reproduction of the tabernacle in Eureka Springs, Arkansas.[56]

Exodus 26:31-37 describes the curtains that partition the different areas of the tabernacle. The *pārōket* curtain is traditionally interpreted as a screen separating the interior of the tabernacle into two areas, the most holy place and the holy place. The resulting area of both rooms is not provided, but tradition concludes the most holy place as a perfect square, 10 cubits × 10 cubits (about 15 feet × 15 feet), and the holy place a rectangle, 10 cubits × 20 cubits (about 15 feet × 30 feet). The most holy place contained the ark of the testimony. The holy place includes the lampstand, the incense altar, and the table. The *pārōket* curtain is made of nearly the same material as the first layer of curtain over the tabernacle, and it also has the cherubim as iconography. The curtain was hung on four pillars of acacia work, covered with gold and fixed on silver bases. R. E.

55. P. Ricoeur, *Lectures on Ideology and Utopia* (ed. G. H. Taylor; New York: Columbia University Press, 1986). Ricoeur notes the writing of Fourier as an example of the use of extreme details and exhaustive lists in utopian writing (pp. 301-7).

56. Levine, *Tabernacle*; B. O. Long, *Imagining the Holy Land: Maps, Models, and Fantasy Travels* (Bloomington: Indiana University Press, 2003), 43-87.

Friedman provides a different reading, interpreting the *pārōket* as a tent over the ark, a sukkah, rather than a curtain.[57] Verses 36-37 describe the curtain or "screen" *(māsāk)* serving as the door of the tabernacle. The curtain is made of the same material as the *pārōket*, but the process of its construction is embroidery, and it is hung on five pillars, covered in gold and set in bronze pedestals.

Altar of Burnt Offering (27:1-8; 38:1-7)

27:1-8	38:1-7
[1]"You shall make an altar of acacia wood, five cubits in length, and five cubits in width. The altar will be square, and its height three cubits. [2]You shall make its horns on its four corners. Its horns will be from it, and you will overlay it with copper. [3]You shall make its pots for clearing away its ashes, and its shovels, its basins, its forks, and its firepans. You will make all of the vessels of copper. [4]And you shall make for it a grating, a network of copper. And you shall make on the network four copper rings on its four corners. [5]You shall place it under the ledge of the altar, and the network will be halfway down the altar. [6]And you shall make poles for the altar, poles of acacia wood. And you will overlay them with copper. [7]The poles will be placed in the rings, and the poles will be on the two sides of the altar when it is carried. [8]Hollowed of boards you shall make it as it was shown to you on the mountain, so shall they be made.	[1]And he made an altar of burnt offering of acacia wood, five cubits its length, five cubits its width, square, and three cubits its height. [2]And he made its horns on its four corners. Its horns were from it. And he overlaid it in copper. [3]And he made all the vessels of the altar, the pots, the shovels, the basins, the forks, and the firepans, all of its vessels he made of copper. [4]And he made for the altar a grating, a network of copper under its ledge, extending below halfway down. [5]He cast four rings on the four corners of the copper grating to hold the poles. [6]And he made the poles of acacia wood, and he overlaid them with copper. [7]And he placed the poles in the rings on the sides of the altar to carry it with them.
	Hollowed of boards he made it.

Notes

27:3 *you shall make its pots for clearing away its ashes.* The LXX departs from the MT, *kai poiēseis stephanēn tō thysiastēriō*, "and you shall make an edge [or border] to the altar."

and its shovels, its basins, its forks, and its firepans. The MT *wĕyāʿāyw*, "its shovels," is

---

57. Friedman, "Tabernacle," 295.

translated in the LXX, *kalyptēra autou*, "its cover"; the MT *ûmizrĕqōtāyw*, "its basins," is translated in the LXX, *phialas autou*, "its bowls"; the MT *ûmizlēgōtāyw*, "its
forks," is translated in the LXX, *kreagras autou*, "its forks"; and, finally, the MT
ûmaḥtōtāyw, "its firepans," is translated in the LXX, *pyreion autou*, "its censer."

27:4-5 *a grating, a network of copper. . . . You shall place it under the ledge of the altar.*
Three terms are used to describe aspects of the altar. It has a grating *(mikbār)*, a
network *(rešet)*, and a ledge *(karkōb)*. The reference to the grating is limited to the
description of the altar in the tabernacle (27:4; 35:16; 38:4, 5, 30; 39:39). The grating
and network are related; cf. NJPS: "grating of meshwork in copper." The ledge may
have encircled the altar. The LXX envisions a different altar, translating "ledge" as
"hearth" *(eschara)*.

27:8 *Hollowed of boards you shall make it.* Cf. LXX, *koilon sanidōton*, "hollow, made of
planks."

38:1 *an altar of burnt offering.* The altar is described with the additional qualification,
mizbaḥ hā'ōlâ, "altar of burnt offering," as compared to 27:1: "altar."

Commentary

A second altar is described as the altar of burnt offering *(mizbaḥ hā'ōlâ)*. Its location is not stated in either 27:1-8 or 38:1-7. But its location in the courtyard of
the tabernacle is indicated in 30:18 and again in 40:6-7, 29-30, where it is set up
in front of the tabernacle. The name, "altar of burnt offering," derives from the
burnt offering sacrifice performed upon it. The altar is large, 5 cubits long × 5
cubits wide × 3 cubits high (about 7½ feet long × 7½ feet wide × 4½ feet high).
Like the altar of incense, it is made of acacia wood and it is four-horned in
structure. But unlike the altar of incense it is covered in bronze, not gold, indicating its further distance from the presence of God within the sanctuary. The
exact construction is unclear, especially with regard to a bronze grate located
halfway up the altar. The altar of burnt offering also included bronze rings and
poles for its transportation, and it had an array of utensils for sacrifice, pots,
shovels, sprinkling bowls, meat forks, and firepans.

Altars for the purpose of sacrifice have functioned throughout the story
of the exodus. The exodus of the Israelites from Egypt was for the purpose of
sacrificing to Yahweh in the desert (8:27). Moses built an altar after the victory
over the Amalekites, but no sacrifices are described (17:15). Jethro offers burnt
offerings on the mountain of God, but no altar is mentioned (18:12). Moses sacrifices burnt offerings on an altar for the covenant ceremony (24:4-5), which
likely conforms to the instructions for altars in 20:25-26, in which they consist
of only earth, no cut stones, and no steps. The P History does not share the
strict prohibition against iconography evident in the Non-P History. Its altar of
burnt offering does not conform to 20:25-26. It is clearly manufactured, and it is
not limited to earth and uncut stones, but includes bronze. It may even include
steps, although it is also possible that the priest ascended the altar on a ramp.

Courtyard (27:9-19; 38:9-20)

27:9-19

27:9 "And you shall make the court of the tabernacle.

"On the south side, the hangings for the court of fine twisted linen, one hundred cubits in length for one side, 10its twenty pillars and its twenty bases of copper, the hooks of the pillars and their bands of silver.

11"And so it will be on the north side in length, one hundred hangings in length, and its twenty pillars and its twenty bases of copper, and the hooks of the pillars and their bands of silver.

12"And the width of the courtyard on the front of the west side, there shall be fifty cubits of hangings, its ten pillars and its ten bases.

13"And the width of the court on the front, the east side, fifty cubits, 14and fifteen cubits of hangings on one side, with their three pillars and their three bases. 15For the second side there will be fifteen cubits of hangings, its three pillars and its three bases.

16"And for the gate of the court there will be a screen of twenty cubits of blue, purple, and crimson yarns and fine twisted linen, made with embroidery, its four pillars and its four bases.

38:9-20

38:9 And he made the court.

On the south side, the hangings of the court of fine twisted linen, one hundred cubits, 10its twenty pillars, and its twenty bases of copper, and the hooks of the pillars and their bands of silver.

11And to the north, one hundred cubits, its twenty pillars, and its twenty bases of copper, and the hooks of the pillars and their bases of silver.

12And to the west side fifty cubits of hangings, its ten pillars and its ten bases, and the hooks of the pillars and its bases of silver.

13And to the east on the front, fifty cubits, 14hangings for fifteen cubits on the side, its three pillars and its three bases, 15and fifteen cubits of hangings for the second side. For each side of the gate of the court there were hangings of fifteen cubits for the side, its three pillars and its three bases. 16All the hangings around the court were of fine twisted linen. 17And the bases for the pillars were of copper, and the hooks of the pillars and its bands of silver, and the overlaying of its tops of silver. And all the pillars of the court were banded with silver.

18And the screen of the gate of the court was made of embroidery of blue, purple, and crimson yarns and fine twisted linen.

It was twenty cubits in length, and the height in width five cubits according to the hangings of the court. ¹⁹There were four pillars, and its four bases of copper, and its hooks of silver, and the overlay of its tops and its bands of silver.

¹⁷"All the pillars of the court around will be banded with silver, their hooks with silver, and their bases of copper.

¹⁸"The length of the court shall be one hundred cubits, and the width fifty, and the height five cubits, with hangings of fine twisted linen and bases of copper.

¹⁹"All the vessels of the tabernacle for all its work, and all its pegs, and all the pegs of the court shall be copper." ²⁰And all the pegs for the tabernacle and for the court all around were of copper.

Notes

27:9 *the court of the tabernacle.* Hebrew *ḥāṣēr* can mean either a settlement without walls (2 Sam 17:18; Neh 8:16) or an enclosure around a building, as in the case of the tabernacle. Cf. NJPS "enclosure"; LXX *aulēn*, "courtyard."

on the south side. Hebrew *negeb-têmānâ*, "toward the south side," is changed in the LXX to *pros liba*, "to the west." See the commentary.

the hangings for the court. Hebrew *qĕlāʿîm*, "hangings," could also be translated "curtains." The translation "hangings" contrasts the outer *qĕlāʿîm* with the interior *yĕrîʿōt*, which I render "curtains" (26:1ff.).

27:11 *on the north side.* Hebrew *ṣāpôn* is changed in the LXX to *pros apēliōtēn*, "to the east." See the commentary.

27:12 *the west side.* Hebrew *yām*, "west," is translated in the LXX, *kata thalassan*, "toward the sea," which means north when it is contrasted to v. 13. See the commentary.

27:13 *the east side.* Hebrew *qēdĕmâ*, "toward the east," is changed in the LXX to *pros noton*, "to the south." See the commentary.

27:16 *a screen.* Hebrew *māsāk* is a "screen" or "covering."

38:18 *and the height in width.* Hebrew *wĕqômâ bĕrōḥab*, "the height in width," is unclear. The NJPS translates "its height — or width," noting textual problems in the MT. The NRSV translates "along the width of it."

Commentary

The enclosure of the tabernacle is revealed to Moses in 27:9-19 and constructed in 38:9-20. The courtyard was clearly marked off as a rectangular area. According to the description in the MT the north and south walls of the courtyard measured 100 cubits (about 150 feet). The walls were supported with twenty posts and twenty bronze bases. The walls were made of linen curtains, attached

Figure 40

	MT	LXX
Length, v. 9	South	West
Length, v. 11	North	East
Width, v. 12	West	North
Width, v. 13	East	South

with silver hooks. The west wall was 50 cubits (about 75 feet). It was supported by ten posts and ten bronze bases, and it was made of linen curtains. The east wall, toward the sunrise, was the entrance to the courtyard. Its width was also 50 cubits (about 75 feet). The door of the courtyard was centered in the east wall, and on each side there was a curtain of 15 cubits (about 22½ feet), supported by 3 posts and 3 bases. The door consisted of a curtain, 20 cubits in length (about 30 feet long) and 5 cubits high (about 7½ feet). The curtain was made of blue, purple and scarlet yarn and linen, supported by four posts and four bronze bases, with silver hooks.

The comparison of the MT and the LXX indicates two distinct orientations for the courtyard of the tabernacle. The comparison of the two textual traditions results in the geographical descriptions set out in figure 40 above. The MT orients the length of the tabernacle and its courtyard on the north-south axis so that the front of both the tabernacle and the courtyard face east, representing the Palestinian perspective (for description of the tabernacle see 26:18-22). The LXX follows the MT in the orientation of the tabernacle in 26:18-22, but it departs from the MT in the orientation of the courtyard in 27:9-13. The LXX turns the courtyard so that the axis of its length is east-west, rather than north-south, which represents the Alexandrian point of view. The change in the geographical orientation is likely intentional according to Wevers: "That [the LXX] intentionally changed the orientation over against MT is clear from the orientation of the tabernacle in 26:18-22 where [the LXX] uses πρὸς βορρᾶν and πρὸς νότον for 'northward' and 'southward,' and πρὸς θάλασσαν for 'westward' in agreement with MT." The geographical orientation may provide insight into the role of symbolic geography in the description of the tabernacle and its courtyard, though according to Wevers: "It is possible that the Alexandrian translators were subtly saying something about the relation of Jerusalem to the diaspora in placing a Jerusalem oriented σκηνή [tabernacle] within an Alexandrian oriented αὐλή [courtyard], but this should not be pressed."[58]

58. Wevers, *Notes*, 434-35.

TENT OF MEETING (27:20–31:11)

The section focuses on the appointment of the priests and the ritual practice of mediation within the sanctuary, which will allow humans to approach God and to live in the sphere of holiness. The sanctuary is identified throughout as the "tent of meeting" (see the commentary above) as compared to the "tabernacle" in 25:1–31:10. The tent of meeting separates into three parts. The opening and closing scenes focus on the Israelites. Exodus 27:20-21 signals the transition from the tabernacle to the tent of meeting with the demand that the Israelites furnish oil for the lampstand, while 31:1-11 concludes the section by underscoring the role of the Israelites in the construction of the tent of meeting. The middle section, 28:1–30:38, contains the divine instruction for the appointment of the Aaronide priesthood.

Oil for Light (27:20-21)

27:20-21	Lev 24:1-3
[20]"And you will command the Israelites that they bring you pure beaten olive oil for lighting, so that a lamp may be set up continually. [21]In the tent of meeting outside of the curtain before the testimony Aaron and his sons will arrange it from evening until morning before Yahweh, as a continuing statute throughout their generations by the Israelites."	[1]And Yahweh spoke to Moses, saying, [2]"Command the Israelites that they bring to you pure beaten olive oil for lighting, so that a lamp may be set up continually. [3]From outside of the curtain of the tent of meeting Aaron will arrange it from evening until morning before Yahweh, as a continuing statute throughout your generations."

Notes

27:20 *pure beaten olive oil.* The Hebrew phrase *šemen zayit zāk kātît* is used only one other time in the MT, in the parallel passage in Lev 24:2. The LXX *elaion ex elaiōn atrygon katharon* describes the olive oil as unpressed and pure.

so that a lamp may be set up continually. Hebrew *lĕhaʿălōt*, "to cause to set up," implies the burning of the lamp. See NJPS: "For kindling lamps regularly."

27:21 *will arrange.* The MT *yaʿărōk* is translated in the LXX as *kausei*, "will burn."

as a continuing statute throughout their generations by the Israelites. The Hebrew is ambiguous, particularly with the closing phrase, *mēʾēt bĕnê yiśrāʾēl*, "by the Israelites." It is possible to interpret *lĕdōrōtām*, "throughout their generations," as a reference to the Israelites who are commanded to bring oil (so Houtman), or as a reference to Aaron and sons who are required to tend the lamp (so Cassuto).[1] The third

---

1. Cf. Houtman, *Exodus*, 3:464; Cassuto, *Exodus*, 370.

person suffix in the MT favors the reference to Aaron and his sons. The LXX translates in the second person, *eis tas geneas hymōn,* "your generations," favoring a reference to the Israelite people.

Commentary

God commands the Israelites to provide olive oil for the lampstand. The command appears out of place upon first reading. It is removed from the description of the lampstand (25:31-40), and it occurs abruptly between the detailed architectural plans of the tabernacle cult (25:1–27:19) and the subsequent focus on the priesthood (chaps. 28–30). Noth judged the verses to be a later addition, which for him meant that the section lacked clear function in the present structure of the text.[2] But Durham rightly notes that the present position of the command is to provide transition to the subject of the priesthood.[3]

Exodus 27:20-21 provides a transition in the structure and in the theological perspective of the revelation in chaps. 25–31 from the tabernacle, as the location for the divine descent to earth (25:1–27:19), to the tent of meeting as the site where humans encounter God through ritual (27:20–31:11). The opening words of the divine command focus on the Israelite people, not the priesthood: "Command the Israelites to bring you pure beaten olive oil." Milgrom clarifies that the emphasis in the passage is on the oil, not the lampstand, and the role of the people to provide it. Exodus 27:20-21 is inserted into its present location to signal the transition in chaps. 25–31 from a description of the tabernacle (the sancta) to its rituals (the sancta-in-action). The point, according to Milgrom, is "to emphasize that the oil used by the priests must stem from the people-at-large."[4]

The transition in perspective is marked by a new name for the sanctuary, the "tent of meeting," which becomes the designation for the sanctuary throughout the subsequent description of the priesthood and their ritual responsibilities.

The oil provides the fuel for a continual light during the night in the tent of meeting. The symbolism of the command, according to the rabbinic interpretation, is one of teaching (*Shemot Rabbah* 36:3). The Torah is light to the individual (Prov 6:23). The teaching of Torah also influences the Israelites collectively so that they become a light to the world (Isa 60:3).[5] The imagery provides commentary on the promise of reward in 19:5-6, when Yahweh promised the Israelites that they would become a "kingdom of priests" and a "holy nation."

---

2. Noth, *Exodus,* 217.
3. Durham, *Exodus,* 380.
4. Milgrom, *Leviticus 23–27,* 2085.
5. See Liebowitz, *Studies in Shemot,* 2:508-23.

APPOINTMENT OF PRIESTLY MEDIATORS (28:1–30:38)

The establishment of the Aaronide priesthood is crucial for the tabernacle to function as a tent of meeting. The appointment of the priesthood is structured in three parts to underscore their role as ritual mediators between God and the people. The three parts also reflect degrees of holiness from the priestly vestments (chap. 28) to the ordination of the priests when they are invested with the holy garments (chap. 29) and, finally, to the role of the priests in mediating for the people through rituals (chap. 30).

Vestments (28:1-43)

28:1-43

Material

1"And you will bring near to yourself Aaron and his sons with him from among the Israelites to be his priest for me, Aaron, Nadab, Abihu, Eleazar, and Ithamar, the sons of Aaron. ²And you shall make holy garments for Aaron your brother for glory and distinction. ³And you shall speak to everyone who is wise of heart, whom I have filled with a spirit of wisdom. And they will make the garments of Aaron to consecrate him to his priesthood for me. ⁴And these are the garments that they shall make: a breastplate, an ephod, a robe, a checkered tunic, a turban, and a sash. And they shall make the holy garments for Aaron your brother and for his sons for his priesthood to me. ⁵They shall receive the gold, the blue, purple, and crimson yarns and the fine linen."

Ephod

6"And they shall make the ephod of gold, of blue, purple, and crimson yarns, and of fine twisted linen skillfully worked.

39:1-31

¹And from the blue, purple, and crimson yarns they made the garments of service for ministering in the sacred place. And they made the garments of holiness, which were for Aaron as Yahweh had commanded Moses.

²And he made the ephod of gold, blue, purple, and crimson yarns, and of fine twisted linen. ³They hammered out plates of gold. And he cut threads to work into the blue,

⁷It will have two attaching shoulders. They will be attached at its ends. ⁸And its decorated band will be like it, from gold, blue, purple, and crimson yarns and of fine twisted linen. ⁹And you shall take two onyx stones, and you shall place on them the names of the Israelites, ¹⁰six of their names on one stone, and the names of the remaining six on the second stone, according to their birth. ¹¹The work of a stonecutter — an engraver of seals — you shall engrave the two stones with the names of the Israelites. You shall set them in frames of gold. ¹²You shall place the two stones on the shoulders of the ephod as stones of remembrance for the Israelites. And Aaron will raise up their names before Yahweh on his two shoulders as a remembrance. ¹³And you shall make settings of gold. ¹⁴Two chains of pure gold, twisted like cords; and you shall place the corded chains to the setting."

Breastplate

¹⁵"You shall make a breastplate of judgment, skillfully designed like the work of the ephod. They will make it of gold, blue, purple, and crimson yarns, and of fine twisted linen you will make it. ¹⁶It shall be square and doubled, a span in its length and a span in its width. ¹⁷You shall set in it four rows of settings of stone, a row of carnelian, chrysolite, and emerald will be the first row. ¹⁸The second row will be turquoise, sapphire, and amethyst; ¹⁹the third row jacinth, agate, and crystal, ²⁰and the fourth

purple, and crimson yarns and into the fine twisted linen, skillfully worked in.

⁴They made for it attaching shoulders, attached on its two ends. ⁵And the decorated band on it was made like it of gold, blue, purple, and crimson yarns and of fine twisted linen as Yahweh commanded Moses. ⁶And they made the stones of onyx bordered in gold settings,

engraved with the names of the Israelites, like an engraver of seals.

⁷And he set them on the shoulders of the ephod as stones of remembrance for the Israelites, as Yahweh commanded Moses.

⁸And he made the breastplate skillfully designed like the work of the ephod of gold, blue, purple and crimson yarns, and of fine twisted linen. ⁹It was square. They made the breastplate doubled, a span its length and a span its width, doubled. ¹⁰And they set in it four rows of stone, a row of carnelian, chrysolite, and emerald was the first row. ¹¹The second row was turquoise, sapphire, and amethyst; ¹²and the third row jacinth, agate, and crystal, ¹³and the fourth row beryl, onyx, and jasper.

row beryl, onyx, and jasper. They shall be set in gold in their settings. ²¹And the stones will be according to the names of the Israelites, twelve, corresponding to their name. They shall be engraved like seals, each with its name for the twelve tribes.

²²"And you shall make on the breastplate twisted chains, a work of cord of pure gold. ²³You shall make on the breastplate two rings of gold. And you will place the two rings on the two ends of the breastplate. ²⁴And you shall place the two golden cords on the two rings at the ends of the breastplate. ²⁵And the two ends of the two cords you shall place on the two settings. And you shall place them on the shoulders of the ephod in the front of it. ²⁶And you shall make two rings of gold, and you shall place them on the two ends of the ephod on its inner edge, next to the ephod. ²⁷And you shall make two rings of gold, and place them on the lower part of the two shoulders of the ephod, in the front at its seam above the decorated band. ²⁸They will attach the breastplate with its rings to the rings of the ephod with a blue cord so that the breastplate is on the decorated band, and the breastplate does not come loose from the ephod.

²⁹"And Aaron will raise up the names of the Israelites in the breastplate of judgment on his heart when he enters the holy place as a continual remembrance before Yahweh.

³⁰"And you shall place on the breastplate of judgment the Urim and the Thummin. And they will be on

They were enclosed around in their setting of gold. ¹⁴And the stones were according to the names of the Israelites. They were twelve corresponding to their names, engraved like seals, each with its name for the twelve tribes.

¹⁵And they made on the breastplate twisted chains, a work of cord of pure gold. ¹⁶And they made two settings of gold and two rings of gold on the two ends of the breastplate. ¹⁷And they placed the two cords of gold on the two rings at the ends of the breastplate. ¹⁸And the two ends of the two cords they placed on the two settings. And they placed them on the shoulders of the ephod in the front. ¹⁹And they made two rings of gold, and they placed [them] on the two ends of the breastplate on its inner edge, next to the ephod. ²⁰And they made two rings of gold and placed them on the two shoulders of the ephod in front of its seam above the decorated band.

²¹And they attached the breastplate with its rings to the rings of the ephod with a blue cord so that it was on the decorated band of the ephod. And the breastplate would not loosen from the ephod, as Yahweh commanded Moses.

the heart of Aaron when he enters before Yahweh. And Aaron will raise up continually the judgment of the Israelites on his heart before Yahweh."

Robe

[31] "You shall make the robe of the ephod all of blue. [32] And it will have an opening for the head in its middle, the opening shall have a binding of woven work around like the opening in a coat of mail so that it does not tear. [33] And you will make on its hem pomegranates of blue, purple, and crimson yarns, all around its hem, and bells of gold between them all around: [34] a golden bell and a pomegranate, a golden bell and a pomegranate all around the hem of the robe.

[22] And he made the robe of the ephod a woven work all of blue, [23] and the opening of the robe in the middle of it was like the opening in a coat of mail, a binding around so that it did not tear. [24] And they made on the hem of the robe pomegranates of blue, purple, and crimson yarns, twisted. [25] And they made bells of pure gold and they placed the bells between the pomegranates, around the middle on the hem of the robe, [26] a bell and a pomegranate, a bell and a pomegranate on the hem of the robe all around to minister as Yahweh commanded Moses.

[35] "And it will be on Aaron when he ministers, and its sound will be heard when he enters into the holy place before Yahweh, and when he goes out. And he will not die."

Plaque

[36] "And you shall make a plaque of pure gold. And you will engrave on it, like the engraving of a seal, 'Holy to Yahweh.' [37] And you will set it on a cord of blue, and it will be on the turban. It will be on the front of the turban. [38] And it will be on the forehead of Aaron, and Aaron will raise up the guilt of the holiness, which the Israelites consecrate in all the gifts of their consecration. And it will be on his forehead continually to make them acceptable before Yahweh."

[30] And they made the plaque of the sign of consecration of pure gold. And they wrote on it the engraved seal, "Holy to Yahweh." [31] And they placed on it a blue cord to attach to the turban above, as Yahweh commanded Moses.

Priestly Clothing

³⁹"And you shall weave the tunics of fine linen. And you shall make the turban of fine linen. And the sash you shall make a work of embroidery.

⁴⁰For the sons of Aaron you shall make tunics. And you shall make for them sashes. And you will make for them headdresses for glory and honor.

⁴¹And you will wash them, Aaron your brother and his sons with him. And you will anoint them, you will fill their hands, and you will consecrate them. And they will be priest for me.

⁴²And make for them linen breeches to cover their naked flesh. From the hips to the thighs they will be.

⁴³And they will be on Aaron and his sons when they enter into the tent of meeting or when they approach the altar to minister in the holy place, so that they do not lift up guilt and die. This shall be an eternal statute for you and for your offspring after you."

²⁷And they made the tunics of fine linen, of woven work, for Aaron and for his sons, ²⁸and the turban of fine linen, and the decorated headdresses of fine linen,

and the linen breeches of fine twisted linen, ²⁹and the sash of fine twisted linen of blue, purple, and crimson yarn, made in embroidery as Yahweh commanded Moses.

Notes

28:1 *to be his priest for me.* The MT includes the third person suffix on the phrase *lĕkahănô-lî*, "to be his priest for me," suggesting that the priesthood of Aaron's sons is related to his ordination. The Sam eliminates the suffix, *lkhn*. The LXX reflects the Sam, *hierateuein moi*.

28:2 *holy garments.* The LXX translates Hebrew *bigdê-qōdeš* as *stolēn hagian*, "holy clothes/stoles." In English the "stole" continues to designate an ecclesiastical garment, a long narrow band worn around the neck.

28:4 *a checkered tunic.* Hebrew *tašbēṣ*, which describes the tunic (*kĕtōnet*), is a hapax legomenon. Syriac *šebaṣ* means "to mix." Thus the term may indicate a type of weave or embroidery. NJPS "a fringed tunic" reflects the LXX *chitōna kosymbōton*, "a tunic with fringe."

a turban. NJPS translates Hebrew *miṣnepet* as "headdress."

28:6 *the ephod of gold, of blue, purple, and crimson yarns, and of fine twisted linen skill-fully worked.* The LXX eliminates the list of colored yarns and gold, describing the material of the ephod simply as "fine-spun linen" *(ek byssou keklōsmenēs).*

28:7 *They will be attached at its ends.* The MT concludes the verse with a separate clause, *wĕḥubār,* "and it will be joined." The Sam translates in the imperfect, *yḥbr,* without a separate clause. The LXX *epi tois dysi meresin exērtēmenai,* "the two parts will be attached," is probably following the Sam.

28:11 *You shall set them in frames of gold.* The LXX lacks this clause.

28:13 *And you shall make settings of gold.* The LXX omitted this phrase in v. 11. The LXX translates *mišbĕṣōt,* "settings," as *aspidiskas,* "small shields."

39:3 *They hammered out plates of gold.* The LXX (36:10) eliminates this clause.

28:15 *a breastplate of judgment.* Hebrew *ḥōšen mišpāṭ* is translated in the LXX, *logeion tōn kriseōn,* emphasizing the oracular function of the breastplate.

28:17 *carnelian.* Hebrew *'ōdem* suggests a stone of red color, hence the reddish quartz stone carnelian in the translations and LXX *sardion;* but the identification is not clear. Cf. NIV "ruby."

chrysolite. Hebrew *piṭdâ* may refer to yellow if the term is related to Sanskrit *pita.* The LXX translates, *topazion.* Cf. NIV "topaz."

emerald. Hebrew *bāreqet* is translated in the LXX as *smaragdos.* Cf. NIV "beryl."

28:18 *turquoise.* Hebrew *nōpek* is translated in the LXX as *anthrax,* perhaps referring to ruby.

sapphire. See 24:10, where sapphire or lapis lazuli describes the vision of the Deity.

amethyst. Hebrew *yāhălōm* is translated in the LXX as *iaspis.* The amethyst stone is purple.

28:19 *jacinth.* Hebrew *lešem* is translated in the LXX as *ligyrion,* a yellowish or perhaps a brownish stone. Jacinth is a gem more the color of orange.

agate. Hebrew *šĕbô* is translated in the LXX as *achatēs.* The agate is a quartz-like stone whose colors are arranged in strips.

crystal. Hebrew *'aḥlāmâ* is translated in the LXX as *amethystos,* a blue-violet crystal. Cf. NIV "amethyst."

28:20 *beryl.* Hebrew *taršîš* is translated in the LXX as *chrysolithos,* suggesting a yellow or gold colored stone. Beryl can occur in yellow as well as green, pink and even white. Cf. NIV "chrysolite."

onyx. See 25:7.

jasper. Hebrew *yošpēh* is translated in the LXX as *onychion.* Jasper can be a variety of colors, although green is prominent.

28:23-28 The order of the MT is changed in the LXX. The description of Aaron representing the Israelites before Yahweh in v. 29 is placed immediately after v. 22 in the LXX.

28:30 *the Urim and the Thummim.* The LXX translates Hebrew *hā'ûrîm,* "the Urim," as *dēlōsin,* "revelation," and Hebrew *hattummîm,* "the Thummim," as *alētheian,* "truth."

28:31 *all of blue.* Hebrew *kĕlîl tĕkēlet* may also be translated, "of pure blue" (see Ezek 27:3).

28:32 *like the opening in a coat of mail.* The meaning of Hebrew *taḥrā'* is uncertain. The word is limited to the description of the robe. Some form of protective or strong clothing is likely suggested. The LXX provides a different interpretation, *tēn symbolēn synphasmenēn ex autou,* "with the binding interwoven with it," suggesting a strong fabric that cannot rip.

28:33 *and you will make on its hem pomegranates of blue, purple, and crimson yarns.* The Sam adds "fine twisted linen" to the fabric. The LXX clarifies the metaphorical nature of the pomegranates, *hōsei exanthousēs rhoas rhoiskous,* "knobs as of a blooming pomegranate."

28:36 *and you shall make a plaque of pure gold.* Hebrew *ṣîṣ* means "blossom" and "front ornament." The LXX translates, *petalon,* "plate" or "leaf."

28:38 *and Aaron will raise up the guilt of the holiness.* Hebrew *wĕnāśā' 'ahărōn 'et-'ăwōn haqqŏdošîm* likely means that Aaron "bears/takes away the guilt of the holiness." The LXX translates, *exarei Aarōn ta hamartēmata tōn hagiōn,* "Aaron lifts up/removes the sins of holiness."

to make them acceptable. The antecedent of "them" in both the Hebrew *(lĕrāṣôn lāhem)* and the Greek *(dekton autois)* is ambiguous. It could refer to the gifts or to the Israelites.

39:30-31 The order of the plaque and the tunics is reversed in 39:27-31 from the divine instructions in 28:36-43. The instructions begin with the plaque (28:36-38) and end with the tunics (28:39-43). But in the fulfillment of the divine instruction the weaving of the tunics and the turban of Aaron (39:27-29) precede the engraving of the plaque (39:30-31).

28:39 *a turban of fine linen.* Hebrew *miṣnepet* is limited in all instances but one to the P legislation (28:4, 37, 39; 29:6; 39:38; Lev 8:9; 16:4), where it designates Aaron's hat as compared to the headdresses of the priests, which are described as *migbā'ōt* (see 28:40). The LXX does not maintain the distinction between the two types of headdress, using *kidaris* and *mitra* interchangeably. The lone occurrence of *miṣnepet* outside the P literature is in Ezek 21:26 (MT 31), where it suggests royal imagery, since it is used in the same context as a royal crown. I follow NRSV in translating *miṣnepet* as "tunic" and *migbā'ōt* as "headdresses." But compare NJPS, which reverses the translation, rendering the *miṣnepet* of Aaron as "headdress" and the *migbā'ōt* of the priests as "turbans."

28:40 *And you will make for them headdresses.* See 28:39.

28:41 *you will fill their hands.* The Hebrew phrase indicates ordination; thus NRSV: "you shall ordain them."

Commentary

The ordination of the Aaronide priesthood is grounded in their selection by God to wear holy clothing. The opening divine command that Moses separate Aaron and his sons from the Israelite people to serve as priests (28:1) is followed immediately in v. 2 with the instruction that Moses "make sacred garments" *(bigdê-qōdeš).* Sacred garments are crucial in the formation of the priesthood.

The office of priest is inseparable from the vestments. They serve to protect the priest in the presence of God, much like the gear of firefighters protects them from the heat of a blaze. Thus when God selects Aaron and his sons to be priests, separating them from the Israelite people in general, he also makes provisions for holy clothing to protect them as they work in close proximity to God. The importance of vestments is further reinforced in the ritual of ordination in the following chapter, which centers on the dress of the priests. In putting on the garments Aaron and his sons become ordained, allowing them to mediate in the sanctuary between God and the Israelite people.

About ritual clothing, J. E. Vollmer states: "Special clothes are used to transform the priest into a ritual celebrant," who is "capable of bridging the gap between the physical world and the world of the spirits."[6] Moreover, ritual clothing is shaped by theology, a view of ordination, and liturgical practice. The more the clergy is seen as a priesthood, according to D. H. Kraak, the greater will be the visual distinction in clothing between the religious leaders and the laity.[7] This is certainly the case with the priestly vestments in chap. 28. The clothing of Aaron as the high priest is the most distinctive, because it signifies his holy status. Most of the sacred vestments focus on the high priest, including the ephod, the breastplate, the Urim and Thummim, the robe, and the turban (28:6-38). The vestments of the general priesthood also separate them from the laity, but in a less distinctive way. Their sacred garments include the tunic and the undergarment (28:39-43). The elaborate dress of the high priest contrasts to the vestments of the twelve disciples in the Gospel of Mark, who upon receiving power from Jesus to heal and to exorcise are clothed with a staff, sandals, and one tunic, not two (Mark 6:6b-13). The worldview of the Gospel of Mark is not the same as that of the P author of the tabernacle, and the clothing of the twelve disciples is meant to convey that message.[8]

The ordination of the Aaronide priesthood is noncharismatic, meaning that their selection does not arise from the power of their individual personalities (see the commentary on 6:2–7:7). The authority of their office is hereditary, residing in the holy clothing and the access that it affords them to God. Such a view of ordination contrasts with a more charismatic orientation, in which prophetic leaders are invaded directly by the power of God's spirit, as in the words of the prophet Third Isaiah: "The spirit of Yahweh is on me, because Yahweh has anointed me to preach good news to the poor" (Isa 61:1). The spirit of God does not seize Aaron and his sons in Exodus 28. Nor does their power arise from the persuasive rhetoric of the prophetic preacher. They exercise the power

6. J. E. Vollmer, "Religious Clothing in the East," *ER* 3:537-40.
7. D. H. Kraak, "Religious Clothing in the West," *ER* 3:340-46.
8. Marcus, *Mark*, 382-91.

of their office in rituals, which they are able to perform, in part, because they are invested with holy clothes. The death of Nadab and Abihu illustrates the protective power of vestments. When the divine fire destroys them because of their abuse of office, it is as though their tunics lose the power to protect them. The divine fire burns the men, but not their tunics (Lev 10:1-2). Leviticus 10:5 describes the removal of their carcasses from the altar: "They came and carried them [Nadab and Abihu], still in their tunics, outside the camp." The authority of holy clothes is also evident in the office of the high priest, since it is passed on through the sacred garments (29:29-30). Whoever puts on the sacred garments becomes the next high priest.

28:1-5   The introduction serves as an interpretation of the ordination of the priesthood. Verse 1 identifies the priests as Aaron and his four sons, Nadab, Abihu, Eleazar, and Ithamar. We have already seen that the two eldest sons, Nadab and Abihu, die during the opening ceremony in Lev 10:1-2, leaving the families of Eleazar and Ithamar to fulfill the priestly role in the tent of meeting. The genealogy of the priesthood in 6:14-25 indicates further that the house of Eleazar carries on the role of high priest. Numbers 20:22-29 recounts the first transfer of the office with the divine command: "Remove Aaron's garments and put them on his son Eleazar" (Num 20:26). The emphasis in the initial selection of the priesthood is on Moses: "And you will bring near to yourself." Moses also performs the first transition in the office of high priest from Aaron to Eleazar (Num 20:26-27).

The subject changes from the priests to their vestments in Exod 28:2-5. The primary description of the garments is that they are "holy" *(qōdeš)*, indicating clothing from the realm of heaven, not earth. The purpose of the clothing is for "glory" *(kābōd)*, the same word used to describe the presence of God on the mountain (24:15-18), and for "beauty" *(tip'āret)*. There is undoubtedly an aesthetic quality to *tip'āret*, indicating the lavish character of the vestments. The term also contains royal imagery, indicating power and sovereignty, and it even overlaps with *kābōd*, "glory." Psalm 96:6 describes the enthronement of God in the temple with the words "splendor and majesty are before him; strength and glory *(tip'eret)* are in his sanctuary." Thus, as Houtman concludes, the garments are meant to empower for ministry, transforming the wearer into cultic officials.[9] Verse 3 describes the transformation as "his" sanctification *(lĕqaddĕšô)*, probably referring to Aaron. The result of the sanctification is the transfer of the priesthood from the profane world to the sacred world in service to God.

The introduction includes a list of the vestments and the description of the material and fabrics used in their tailoring. Six items are listed: breastplate, ephod, robe, tunic, sash, and turban. The material is extravagant, gold, blue, pur-

---

9. Houtman, *Exodus,* 3:473.

ple, and crimson wools, as well as fine linen, further separating the clothing of the priesthood from that of ordinary Israelites. The construction of holy garments, moreover, requires divine inspiration. Only those who are wise of heart and filled with the spirit of wisdom are able to weave the vestments. A wise heart is attributed to God in Job 9:4 and praised in humans in Proverbs (e.g., 10:8; 16:21).

28:6-14 The ephod (*'ēpōd*) is an outer apron worn by the high priest Aaron. In other contexts the ephod appears to be a cultic object. Gideon makes an ephod, which is worshiped (Judg 8:27). In the story of Micah and his priest, the ephod again appears to be an object: "Now this man Micah had a shrine, and he made an ephod and some idols and installed one of his sons as his priest" (Judg 17:5; see also 18:14, 17, 18, 20). The sword of Goliath is also stored behind the ephod in the sanctuary at Nob, again suggesting a cultic object (1 Sam 21:9). But other texts also describe the ephod as something that is worn. Samuel wears an ephod as a young boy in ministering before Yahweh (2:18), as does Eli (2:28; see also 14:3). The function of the ephod appears to be divination. David requests the ephod from Abiathar, the priest, to inquire from God whether to pursue the Amalekites (30:7). The relationship of the ephod apron of Aaron to these examples is unclear, although similarities arise. The ephod is always associated with the cult, and it functions as a source of divination.

The apron of the ephod likely encircled the lower body of Aaron and was held in place with two shoulder straps. The material was costly, indicating its symbolic value. The apron included the range of blue, purple, and crimson yarns, as well as fine linen. These fabrics were woven together with gold, a material usually reserved for the statues of the gods in the ancient Near East. The two straps of the ephod each held an onyx stone at the point where the straps touched the shoulder of the high priest. The stones were engraved with the names of the twelve tribes of the Israelites. They functioned as a memorial (*zikkārōn*) for Yahweh. When Aaron enters the presence of Yahweh in the sanctuary, God will see the stones and be mindful of the Israelites (see also Exod 17:14-16). Thus the priest functions to prompt divine memory, which in the P History is tied to the covenant.

The establishment of covenant and the burden of memory rest with God in the P literature, not with humans. The theme of covenant is introduced at the close of the story of the flood in Gen 9:8-17, when God states to Noah: "I now establish my covenant" (9:9). Covenant in the P literature is self-imposed by God: "I now establish." The content of the covenant is that "never again shall all flesh be cut off by the waters of the flood, and never again shall there be a flood to destroy the earth" (9:11). There are no conditions or time limits on the covenant. God states that it exists "for all future generations" (9:12).

The covenant in the P literature is a free action of God to restrict the divine use of destructive power against the profane world. Although it is self-imposed, God loses freedom in making covenant. God gives up the power to destroy the impurity of the profane world through the flood. God states to Noah: "I will maintain my covenant" (Gen 9:11). God does not say that Noah must observe the covenant. Indeed, the covenant does not require any particular observance by Noah. It only restricts God, especially how the Deity will exercise power in the profane world. The covenant with creation at the close of the flood forces God to nurture a relationship with the profane world while trying to purify it, even though impurity repels God. The Deity makes a similar covenant with humans when God states to Abraham in Gen 17:7: "I will establish my covenant between me and you, and your offspring after you throughout their generations, for an everlasting covenant, to be God to you and to your offspring after you."

The divinely self-imposed restrictions of covenant with creation and with Abraham put the burden of memory on God in the P literature, not on humans. In the P literature, God must continually remember the covenant, and thus maintain a relationship between the sacred and the profane. Signs accompany the covenant in the P literature to remind God of obligations. The rainbow is the sign in the covenant with creation, while circumcision is the sign with Abraham. The signs prompt God, not the people, to remember the covenant. God states at the close of the flood: "I have set my bow in the clouds, and it shall be a sign of the covenant between me and the earth. When I bring clouds over the earth and the bow is seen in the clouds, I will remember my covenant . . . and the waters shall never again become a flood to destroy all flesh" (Gen 9:13-15). The speech underscores that it is God who must remember the covenant through time. In the same way the covenant with Abraham places the obligation of memory on God. Yahweh states to Moses at the outset of the exodus: "I have heard the groaning of the Israelites whom the Egyptians are holding as slaves, and I have remembered my covenant" (Exod 6:5; see also 2:24-25).

The covenant and divine memory provide the basis for sacramental rituals in the P literature. One result of the performance of rituals is that God is reminded of past promises, allowing the power of holiness to be transmitted through the ritual. The bread of the Presence in the tabernacle is a remembrance for Yahweh (Lev 24:7), as is the blowing of trumpets: "They shall serve as a reminder on your behalf before Yahweh your God" (Num 10:10). The interpretation of covenant and divine memory in the P literature defines the purpose of the priestly ordination. The task of the priest is to prompt divine memory of the covenant and salvation through ritual actions. The stones in the breastplate of Aaron (Exod 28:12, 29; 39:7) are meant to arouse God's memory of covenant promises of salvation. The divine memory is aroused when the priest approaches God through rituals; this memory insures the healing power of holiness in the sacramental rites.

Figure 41

Carnelian	Chrysolite	Emerald
Turquoise	Sapphire	Amethyst
Jacinth	Agate	Crystal
Beryl	Onyx	Jasper

28:15-30 The breastplate, *ḥōšen*, may be related to Arabic *ḥaṣanu*, "to enclose," or to Aramaic *ḥsn*, "to possess."[10] Neither etymology is certain. The breastplate is described in three ways: its construction (vv. 15-21), its attachment to the ephod (vv. 22-28), and its function in the cult as the container for the Urim and the Thummim (vv. 29-30).

The construction of the breastplate is similar to the ephod. It is made from the same materials, gold, blue, purple, and crimson yarn, as well as fine linen. Its dimensions are square, one span in Hebrew, roughly the equivalent of nine inches. It is folded over, creating a strong fabric for the inset stones and perhaps also a pouch to contain the Urim and the Thummim (see vv. 29-30). The breastplate, like the ephod, represents the Israelites before God. Whereas the ephod contained the names of the twelve tribes on two onyx stones, the breastplate represents the twelve tribes with distinct stones, arranged in four rows of three stones, and embedded in the fabric (see fig. 41 above).

The Hebrew words for the stones are uncertain in some cases, as are their meaning and correspondence to the twelve tribes. The breastplate was attached to the ephod with golden chains and rings (vv. 22-28). Two chains from the breastplate connected the object to the shoulder straps and another two attached to the waist of the ephod.

The function of the breastplate, like that of the ephod, is to be a memorial for Yahweh (28:29). The breastplate, however, is not limited to its role in representing the Israelites before God. It also takes on the more specific function of divination. The full title of the vestment is literally "breastplate of judgment" (*ḥōšen mišpāṭ*; 28:15, 29). *Mišpāṭ* takes on a wide variety of meanings in the Hebrew Bible. The title for the Book of the Covenant includes the same word in the plural, which I translated "rules." The meaning of the word in the present context is more about rendering a decision. The NIV underscores this meaning of judgment by translating "breastplate for making decisions." The LXX reinforces the role of divination by translating the Hebrew phrase as *logeion tōn kriseōn*, "a speaking-place of judgment/decision."

The placement of the Urim and the Thummim in the pocket of the

---

10. Cf. *HALOT* 1:362.

breastplate further reinforces its role of communication. Little is known of these cultic objects or, indeed, whether they are one or two distinct items. But they function as a means of communication with God. The Levites are entrusted with the "Thummim and Urim" in the Blessing of Moses (Deut 33:8). The qualities associated with the Levites in the poem are their absolute allegiance to God even over family, their ability to guard the covenant, to protect the law, and to teach the people (Deut 33:8-11). The emphasis on law in the poem suggests that the oracular function of the Urim and the Thummim in the breastplate of the high priest may also be to provide decisions or priestly teachings in response to those seeking divine counsel. C. Van Dam notes that the decision to war often requires an inquiry with the Urim and the Thummim (i.e., Num 27:21; 1 Sam 28:6), as does the determination of legitimate priests (Ezra 2:63; Neh 7:65).[11] Exodus 28:30 concludes the section, underscoring the oracular function of the high priest in the cult: "And Aaron will raise up continually the judgment of the Israelites on his heart before Yahweh."

28:31-35 The robe of the ephod, *mĕʿîl hāʾēpôd*, is the garment worn immediately beneath the ephod and breastplate. It is a vestment only for the high priest. The robe is described as a singular piece of blue cloth with an opening for the head and with pomegranates and bells on the hem. The LXX translates Hebrew *mĕʿîl*, "robe," as *podērēs*, indicating a full-length garment to the feet, although the Hebrew does not convey the length of the garment. The pomegranates on the hem of the garment likely have symbolic significance, but interpreters struggle to uncover their meaning. The function of the bells, however, is stated. They protect Aaron as he enters and leaves the holy place of the sanctuary. Thus their sound is apotropaic, perhaps also signifying a ritual act associated with entering and exiting the presence of God. Failure to perform the actions results in death for Aaron.

28:36-38 The "plate of pure gold" (*ṣîṣ zāhāb ṭāhôr*) shifts the focus of the vestments from the robe to the headgear. Hebrew *ṣîṣ* means "blossom" or "flower," perhaps also conveying the sense of luster and brightness. The same object is described as *nēzer* in 39:30 and in Lev 8:9, translated "diadem" or "crown." The translation "plate" derives from the LXX *petalon*, meaning "leaf." The image of a flower may symbolize life. The plate is attached to the front of Aaron's turban, so that it is on his forehead.

Engraved on the object are the words, "Holy to Yahweh." The inscription is likely aimed at Aaron, stating that he belongs to Yahweh in his role as high priest. It is more difficult to determine the function of the plate. It may, as Noth suggests, protect Aaron in case the rituals of the high priest are not performed

---

11. C. Van Dam, *The Urim and Thummim: A Means of Revelation in Ancient Israel* (Winona Lake, Ind.: Eisenbrauns, 1997), 177-93 *et passim*.

exactly.[12] The text states that Aaron bears the iniquity of the Israelites' sacred gifts, making them acceptable to Yahweh even when cultic infractions occur.

28:39   The final vestments reserved only for the high priest include the tunic *(kutōnet)*, the turban *(miṣnepet)*, and the sash *('abnēṭ)*. The *kutōnet* describes both cultic and profane (Gen 3:21; 37:3) dress in the Hebrew Bible. The material is of linen, but the shape is unclear from the text. The turban of the high priest is not described with regard to shape or size. It is made of linen and it is different from the headwear of the priests called "headbands" *(migbā'ôt)*. The sash or girdle is not described.

28:40-42   All priests are invested with holy garments, including a tunic *(kutōnet)*, a sash *('abnēṭ)*, a headdress *(migbā'â)*, and undergarments *(miknĕsê-bād)*. The headdress derives from the word "hill," suggesting a cone-shaped turban. The linen undergarments may be intended to prevent defilement from perspiration. The purpose of the vestments repeats the statement from 28:2, to glorify and to provide beauty among the priests. Finally 28:41 outlines the two-step process of ordination: first the priests are clothed in the sacred vestments and second they are anointed for service.

Rite of Ordination (29:1-46)

Material (29:1-3)
[29:1] *"And this is the matter that you shall do to them to consecrate them to serve as priest for me. Take one young bull and two rams without blemish, [2] and unleavened bread, and unleavened cakes mixed with oil, and unleavened wafers spread with oil. You shall make them of choice wheat flour. [3] You shall place them in one basket. And you shall bring near the basket, the bull, and the two rams."*

Vestments (29:4-9)
[4] *"Aaron and his sons you shall bring near to the door of the tent of meeting, and you shall wash them with water. [5] You shall take the garments and you shall clothe Aaron with the tunic, the robe of the ephod, the ephod, the breastplate, and gird on him the band of the ephod. [6] And you will place the turban on his head and place the plaque on the turban. [7] And you shall take the anointing oil and pour it on his head and anoint him. [8] And his sons you shall bring near and clothe them with tunics, [9] and gird them with the sash, Aaron and his sons. And you shall bind the headdresses on them. And the priesthood will be theirs as a perpetual statute. You shall fill the hand of Aaron and his sons."*

---

12. Noth, *Exodus*, 225-26.

Bull of Sin Offering (29:10-14)

[10] *"And you will bring near the bull in front of the tent of meeting. And Aaron and his sons will lay their hands on the head of the bull.* [11] *And you shall slaughter the bull before Yahweh at the door of the tent of meeting.* [12] *And you shall take from the blood of the bull and place it on the horns of the altar with your finger. And all of the blood you shall pour on the base of the altar.* [13] *And you shall take the fat that covers the entrails, the appendage of the liver, and the two kidneys with the fat on them, and turn them into smoke on the altar.* [14] *But the flesh of the bull, its skin, and its dung you shall burn in fire outside the camp. It is a sin offering."*

Ram of Burnt Offering (29:15-18)

[15] *"And one of the rams you will take. And Aaron and his sons will lay their hands on the head of the ram.* [16] *And you shall slaughter the ram and take its blood and dash it around the altar.* [17] *And the ram you will cut in its pieces, and you shall wash its entrails and its legs. And you will place its pieces and its head,* [18] *and you will turn the entire ram into smoke on the altar. It is a burnt offering to Yahweh, a pleasing odor, an offering of fire to Yahweh."*

Ram of Ordination (29:19-41)

[19] *"And you shall take the second ram. And Aaron and his sons shall lay their hands on the head of the ram.* [20] *And you shall slaughter the ram and take from its blood and place it on the lobe of Aaron's right ear and on the lobe of his son's right ear, on the thumbs of their right hands, and on the big toes of their right feet. And you shall dash the blood around the altar.* [21] *And you shall take from the blood, which is on the altar and from the anointing oil and sprinkle it on Aaron, his garments, his sons, and on the garments of his sons with him. And he will be holy, and his garments, his sons, and the garments of his sons with him.*

[22] *"And you shall take the fat from the ram, and the tail, and the fat that covers the entrails, and the appendage of the liver, and the two kidneys, and the fat that is on them, and the right thigh for it is the ram of ordination,* [23] *and one loaf of bread, one cake of bread made with oil, and one wafer from the basket of unleavened bread that is before Yahweh.* [24] *And you shall place all of it on the palms of Aaron and on the palms of his sons. And you shall raise them as an elevation offering before Yahweh.* [25] *And you will take them from their hands and turn them into smoke on the altar on the burnt offering, as a pleasing odor before Yahweh, an offering of fire to Yahweh.*

[26] *"And you shall take the breast of the ram of ordination for Aaron and raise it as an elevation offering before Yahweh. And it shall be your portion.* [27] *And you shall consecrate the breast as the elevation offering and the thigh as the dedication offering, which is raised and offered from the ram of ordination of Aaron and his sons.* [28] *And it will be for Aaron and for his sons a perpetual statute from*

the Israelites. For this is the dedication offering, and the dedication offering will be from the Israelites from their sacrifices of well-being, their dedication to Yahweh.

²⁹ "The sacred garments, which belong to Aaron, will be for his sons after him to anoint them and to ordain them. ³⁰ The son who is priest in his place, who enters the tent of meeting to minister in the holy place, shall wear them seven days.

³¹ "The ram of ordination you shall take and boil its flesh in a holy place. ³² And Aaron and his sons shall eat the flesh of the ram and the bread in the basket at the door of the tent of meeting. ³³ And they will eat them, only those who are atoned by them for their ordination and their consecration. A stranger may not eat them, because they are holy.

³⁵ "And you shall do to Aaron and his sons all that I have commanded you. For seven days you shall ordain them. ³⁶ A bull of sin offering you shall offer every day for the atonement. You shall offer a sin offering on the altar when you make atonement on it. And you shall anoint it to consecrate it. ³⁷ Seven days you shall make atonement on the altar. And you shall consecrate it, and the altar shall be most holy. Whatever touches the altar will be consecrated.

³⁸ "And this is what you shall offer on the altar: two lambs one year of age each day, regularly. ³⁹ One lamb you shall offer in the morning, and the second lamb you shall offer at twilight. ⁴⁰ A tenth of a measure of choice flour mixed with one-fourth of a hin of beaten oil mixed in and a libation of one-fourth of a hin of wine will be with the one lamb. ⁴¹ And the second lamb you shall offer at twilight, as in the offering of the morning, you shall offer it with its libation as a pleasing odor, an offering of fire to Yahweh."

Cultic Presence of God (29:42-46)

⁴² "There will be a regular burnt offering throughout your generations at the door of the tent of meeting before Yahweh, where I will appear to you to speak with you there. ⁴³ I will appear there to the Israelites and it will be consecrated by my glory. ⁴⁴ And I will consecrate the tent of meeting and the altar. And Aaron and his sons I will consecrate to be priests for me. ⁴⁵ And I will settle in the midst of the Israelites. And I will be their God. ⁴⁶ And they will know that I am Yahweh, their God, who brought them out from the land of Egypt so that I might settle in their midst. I am Yahweh, their God."

Notes

29:1 *And this is the matter.* Hebrew *wĕzeh haddābār* indicates a ritual law or command. The phrase is common in P (e.g., 16:16, 32). Leviticus 8:5 likely refers to Exodus 29 as a command: "This is what *(haddābār)* Yahweh has commanded *(ṣiwwâ)*." Cf. LXX *kai tauta estin,* "and this is."

one young bull. Hebrew *par 'eḥād ben-bāqār* is translated in the LXX as *moscharion ek boōn,* "a calf of an ox."

29:2 *and unleavened bread, and unleavened cakes mixed with oil, and unleavened wafers spread with oil.* The MT lists three distinct forms of unleavened bread. The LXX combines the first two types into one, *artous azymous pephyrmenous en elaiō,* "unleavened bread mixed in oil."

29:6 *And you will place the turban on his head and place the plaque on the turban.* For discussion of the headdress of Aaron and the priests see 28:39. Hebrew *nēzer,* "plaque," is translated as "diadem" in the NJPS and NRSV. The LXX translates *petalon,* "leaf," the same word used to translate *ṣîṣ,* describing it further as "holy" (*hagiasma*). Milgrom notes that the root meaning of Hebrew *nāzar* is "to keep apart," signifying "dedication, consecration." He concludes that *nēzer* and *ṣîṣ* (28:36) are synonyms, which is reinforced by the LXX translation.[13] For this reason I have translated it "plaque." M. Görg argues for an Egyptian etymology, *nzt.t,* meaning "the snake goddess," which describes the uraeus that protrudes from the crown of the pharaoh providing protection.[14] In this case the turban of Aaron the high priest contains royal imagery.

29:9 *you shall fill the hand of Aaron and his sons.* See 28:41. The LXX translates *teleiōseis tas cheiras,* "to validate the hands." Wevers writes of the Greek translation: "The verb is also associated with the mysteries in the sense of being initiated, to become an initiate in the mystery religions, a τέλειος."[15]

29:12 *from the blood. . . . And all of the blood.* Hebrew *middam,* "from the blood," and *we'et-kol-haddām,* "all of the blood," can also be translated "some of the blood" and "the remainder of the blood" (see NRSV, NJPS). The LXX follows the latter translation, *to de loipon pan haima,* "but all the remaining blood."

29:13 *And you shall take the fat that covers the entrails, the appendage of the liver, and the two kidneys with the fat on them.* Three parts of the bull are sacrificed. (1) The fat of the entrails (*'et-kol-haḥēleb hamkasseh 'et-haqqereb*) is translated in the LXX as *to stear to epi tēs koilias,* "the fat on the stomach or intestines." Milgrom translates the fat as "suet," the hard fat around the kidneys and loins.[16] (2) The appendage of the liver (*hayyōteret 'al-hakkābēd*). The appendage or lobe is also known as *ubānu* in Akkadian, which functioned to predict future events. The LXX translates *ton lobon tou hēpatos,* "the lobe of the liver." (3) The two kidneys (*šĕtê hakkĕlāyōt*) with then fat are also considered to be suet. The LXX may separate the two kidneys and their fat as distinct parts of the animal: *kai tous dyo nephrous kai to stear to ep' autōn.*

and turn them into smoke on the altar. Hebrew *wĕhiqṭartā* is translated in the LXX as *epithēseis.* Wevers writes of the Greek verb: "It represents an old understanding of the verb as a technical term for the presentation of an offering on an altar."[17] Mil-

---

13. Milgrom, *Leviticus 1–16,* 512-13.

14. M. Görg, "Die Kopfbedeckung des Hohenpriesters," *BN* 3 (1977): 24-26; idem, "Weiteres zu *nzr* ("Diadem")," *BN* 4 (1977): 7-8. For more general discussion of Wadjyt, the protective goddess on the headdress of Pharaoh, see S. Quirke, *Ancient Egyptian Religion* (London: British Museum, 1992), 31-32.

15. Wevers, *Notes,* 469.

16. Milgrom, *Leviticus 1–16,* 525.

17. Wevers, *Notes,* 471.

grom comments on the Hebrew: "Turning the offering into smoke was considered, originally, the only way of reaching the celestial gods."[18] Thus the verb always has the Deity as an object. In this respect *hiqṭîr* must be distinguished from *śārap*, "to burn," which describes nonsacrificial incineration, as in v. 14.

29:14 *you shall burn in fire outside the camp.* See 29:13.

It is a sin offering. Hebrew *lammaḥăneh ḥaṭṭāʾt hûʾ* is translated ambiguously in the LXX as *hamartias gar estin,* "for it is sin." Milgrom suggests the translation "purification offering" as opposed to "sin offering." He notes that Hebrew *ḥaṭṭāʾt* is the language of purification.[19]

29:16 *and dash it.* Hebrew *wĕzāraqtā* means "to sprinkle." The translation "to dash" provides a contrast to *nāzâ* in 29:21, "to sprinkle, splatter," which describes a similar action with the blood on Aaron and his sons. The LXX maintains the distinction in the verbs with different imagery, describing the action on the altar in v. 16 as "pouring" *(proscheeis)* and the action on Aaron and his sons as in v. 21 "sprinkling" *(rhaneis).*

around the altar. Cf. NRSV: "against all sides of the altar."

29:17 *And you will place its pieces and its head.* The clause is part of the following verse, implying that they are the parts of the animal that are placed on the altar. Hebrew *wĕʾal-rōʾšô,* "and its head," is translated "with its head" *(syn tē kephalē)* in the LXX.

29:18 *a burnt offering.* Hebrew *ʿōlâ* is also translated "whole burnt offering," which is more clearly indicated in LXX *holokautōma.* See Milgrom: "*ʿōlâ* literally means 'that which ascends,' which implies that the offering is entirely turned to smoke."[20]

a pleasing odor. Hebrew *rēaḥ nîhôaḥ* is translated in the LXX as *eis osmēn euōdias,* "into a fragrant aroma." The idiom indicates the Deity's favor toward a sacrifice, not the act of atonement.[21]

an offering of fire to Yahweh. Hebrew *ʾiššeh lyhwh hûʾ* lacks the word "offering." The translation assumes that *ʾiššeh* derives from *ʾēš,* "fire." The phrase is likely a synonym to the previous idiom, "a pleasing odor." The LXX does not translate the word "fire," but instead reads *thysiasma kyriō estin,* "it is a sacrifice to the Lord." Milgrom argues that Hebrew *ʾiššeh* most likely derives from Ugaritic *iṯṯ,* "gift," and thus should be translated "food gift."[22]

29:21 *and sprinkle it on Aaron.* See 29:16.

and he will be holy. Hebrew *wĕqādaš* is the Qal rather than the Piel or the Hiphil, "to consecrate" (see, e.g., 28:38; 29:27).

29:22 *for it is the ram of ordination.* Hebrew *milluʾîm* means "filling." It derives from the description of ordination as "filling the hands" (see 28:41; 29:9).

29:24 *And you shall raise them as an elevation offering before Yahweh.* Hebrew *wĕhēnaptā,* "and you shall raise," is also translated "wave" in the KJV, and the offering, *tĕnûpâ,* is translated "wave offering," to reflect the back and forth movement

18. Milgrom, *Leviticus 1–16,* 160-61.
19. Ibid., 253-92.
20. Ibid., 172.
21. See ibid., 162-63.
22. Ibid., 162.

of the cultic action.[23] The LXX translates the verb as *aphorieis,* "to separate," and the sacrifice as the *aphorisma,* "the state of being separated." The LXX translators do not appear to envision a wave offering. According to Milgrom, "*těnûpâ* transfers the offering from the domain of the offerers to the domain of the Lord."[24] The ritual action therefore signifies the dedication and the transfer of the priests to the possession and realm of God. In this respect it is similar to a well-being offering. The translation "raise" and "elevation offering" indicates the act of transfer.

29:26 *portion.* Hebrew *lěmānâ* designates the prebend of the priests. It is the portion that they receive for officiating at the cultic site. The LXX *meridi* also means "part" or "portion."

29:27 *you shall consecrate the breast as the elevation offering and the thigh as the dedication offering.* Hebrew *těrûmâ* means "dedication offering" or "contribution." The verb used to describe the action is *rûm,* "to be high, exalted." Y. Muffs notes that Akkadian *rēmūtu* means "to be kind, charitable," suggesting that the action associated with the *těrûmâ* offering may mean "to give a gift," which in the Hiphil would mean "to dedicate."[25] Milgrom states that the function of the *těrûmâ* is to transfer an object from the human to the Deity, and in this respect it is similar to the *těnûpâ* (evelation offering). The distinction between the two acts of transfer is that the *těnûpâ* is restricted to the sanctuary since the action is performed "before Yahweh." The *těrûmâ* can take place outside the cultic site since the action is performed "to Yahweh."[26]

29:33 *And they will eat them, only those who are atoned by them for their ordination and their consecration.* The Hebrew is ambiguous. The main clause is clear: *wě'oklû 'ōtām,* "and they [the priests] will eat them [the items of food listed in v. 32]." The ambiguity arises with the relative clause: *'ǎšer kuppar bāhem lěmallē' 'et-yādām lěqaddēš 'ōtām.* Most translations interpret the relative clause as a description of the food, not the priests. Examples include NRSV: "They themselves shall eat the food *by which atonement is made*"; Durham: "They are to eat these gifts *by which atonement was made for their ordination*"; Childs: "Only they for whose atonement these things were used to ordain"; Houtman: "Only they may eat the food *by which their sin was removed.*" But the passive form of *kuppar* suggests that the description is of the priests and their present state of ordination and consecration. The LXX *hagiasthēsan,* "having been made holy," favors a description of the priests rather than their food. See also NJPS: "These things shall be eaten only by those for whom expiation was made with them."

atoned. The root meaning of Hebrew *kuppar* is "to rub, wipe." Milgrom reviews a variety of ancient Near Eastern texts that describe the ritual actions of wiping off or of rubbing on a substance to purge an object or person. The transfer of impurity from the object to the wiping material is at the root of the notion of ransom. A common

---

23. Durham, *Exodus,* 393.

24. Milgrom, *Leviticus 1–16,* 465.

25. Y. Muffs, *Studies in the Aramaic Legal Papyri from Elephantine* (Leiden: Brill, 1969), 132-35; Milgrom mentions Muffs's work in *Leviticus 1–16,* 475.

26. Milgrom, *Leviticus 1–16,* 415-16, 473-81.

translation for designating this action is "to purge." The Pual (passive) form of the verb occurs elsewhere only in Num 35:33; Isa 6:7; 22:14; 27:9; 28:18; Prov 16:6. The form may suggest a more abstract use of the verb, which points to a direct action of the Deity.

A stranger may not eat them because they are holy. Hebrew *zār* takes on a wide range of meanings in the Hebrew Bible, including "foreign," "illegitimate." It can refer to other gods (Hos 8:12) or to illegitimate cultic practices (Lev 10:1). In the present context it likely designates the laity as opposed to the priests. See NJPS: "They may not be eaten by a layman."

29:36 *sin offering.* Hebrew *ḥaṭṭā't* is also translated "purification offering" to differentiate the ritual process, in which case the *ḥaṭṭā't* removes impurity from the altar to prepare the way for expiation or atonement.[27] The LXX translates, *tēs hamartias,* "the sin offering."

every day for the atonement. Hebrew *layyôm 'al-hakkippurîm* indicates a series of sacrifices. The LXX translates, *tou katharismou,* "cleansing," and understands the act to take place only once, *tē hēmera,* "in the day of cleansing." The nominal form *kippurîm* is infrequent in the Hebrew Bible, occurring most notably to describe the Day of Atonement in the Priestly ritual calendars, where it occurs twice in Lev 23:27-28 and once in Num 29:11. In the Priestly calendars "the sin offering of atonement" is prescribed for the tenth day of the seventh month (i.e., the Day of Atonement). The same phrase, "sin offering of atonement," also describes the cultic role of Aaron once a year, presumably on the Day of Atonement (Exod 30:10). The Day of Atonement is also associated with the Jubilee (Lev 25:9). The atonement of the altar in the ordination of the priests appears to have no relation to the Day of Atonement, yet it suggests a similar ritual practice to the purging of the sanctuary on the Day of Atonement. Two additional references to *kippurîm* are the "money of atonement" to describe the contribution of the Israelites to the sanctuary (Exod 30:16) and the "ram of atonement" to make reparation to the priest in cases where an injured party is unable to receive restitution (Num 5:8).

29:39 *at twilight.* The dual of the Hebrew "evening" (*'ereb*) in the phrase *bên hā'arbāyim,* "between the two evenings," indicates dusk or twilight.

29:42 *where I will appear.* Hebrew *'iwwā'ēd* is the Niphal of *yā'ad,* "to meet," as in the designation of the sanctuary/tent of meeting (*mô'ēd*). The root *y'd* appears four times in vv. 42-44, creating a network of motifs to describe the meeting between Yahweh and the Israelites. Twice the root *y'd* describes the sanctuary as the tent of meeting (*mô'ēd,* vv. 42, 44). And twice the Niphal form of the verb is used to describe the appearance of Yahweh in the cultic site (vv. 42, 43). The translation "to appear" reflects the passive voice of the Niphal. Cf. NRSV: "Where I will meet with you." The LXX translates with a future passive, *gnōsthēsomai soi,* "I will be known to you."

29:45 *and I will settle in the midst of the Israelites.* See the commentary on 24:12-18 for the translation of Hebrew *šākan* as "to settle."

---

27. See ibid., 253-54, 290, *et passim.*

Figure 42

Topic	Instruction: Exodus 29	Fulfillment: Leviticus 8
Material	29:1-3	8:1-5
Vestments	29:4-9	8:6-13
Bull of Sin Offering	29:10-14	8:14-17
Ram of Burnt Offering	29:15-18	8:18-21
Ram of Ordination	29:19-41	8:22-36
Cultic Presence of God	29:42-46	9:23-24/Num 7:89

Commentary

The instructions for the vestments set the stage for the rite of ordination. The rite calls for one bull, two rams, unleavened wheat, and oil (29:1-3); and it requires seven days to complete, reinforcing again the importance of seven in the P History. The ritual is structured into four stages. First, Aaron and his sons put on the vestments (29:4-9). Second, a bull is sacrificed as a sin offering (29:10-14). Third, a ram is offered as a whole burnt offering (29:15-18). Fourth, another ram is offered as the sacrifice of ordination, which also includes a meal with God (29:19-41). The three sacrifices follow the same structure: (1) the location at the door of the tent of meeting is stated; (2) the priests lay their hands on the animal; (3) the animal is slaughtered; (4) there is a blood ritual; (5) followed by the sacrifice of the animal. The sacrifice of ordination departs from the previous two sacrifices by progressing to a ritual meal, identified as a well-being sacrifice (29:28). As B. Levine notes, the sequence of the sacrifices also represents a liturgy: the sin offering purifies the altar; the burnt offering provides an invocation to God; and the well-being offering is a sacred meal between the priests and God.[28] Exodus 29:42-46 concludes the rite with an interpretation of the ordination of the priests, repeating the introduction to the instructions for the vestments in 28:1-5. The ordination of the Aaronide priests is fulfilled in Lev 8:1-36.

The chart in figure 42 above illustrates the process for the ritual in Exodus 29 and the corresponding structure in Leviticus 8. The interpretation of the ordination in Exod 29:42-46 is partially fulfilled in Lev 9:23-24 when the Glory of Yahweh enters the altar, and it is completed in Num 7:89 when God speaks to Moses in the tabernacle.

29:1-3 The rite of ordination is a *dābār,* meaning a law. The same word is used by Jethro to describe the judicial action of Moses (Exod 18:13-27). The

---

28. B. Levine, *Numbers 1–20* (AB 4A; New York: Doubleday, 1993), 263-64.

content and aim of the law is to sanctify Aaron and his sons to be priests to Yahweh. The young bull and the two rams must be perfect. The unleavened wheat and oil must be baked into two kinds of bread, thick bread *(ḥallōt maṣṣōt)* and thin bread *(rĕqîqê maṣṣôt),* before being placed in a basket and, most likely, brought to the entrance of the tent of meeting.

29:4-9 The first step in the ordination of Aaron and his sons is the investiture of the sacred garments. They are brought to the "door of the tent of meeting" *(petaḥ 'ōhel mô'ēd)* to be clothed. The entrance of the tent of meeting probably designates the area between the altar and the tabernacle (see the diagram in fig. 39 above at 25:1-7). The priests performed many of their ritual duties in this area, from which lay Israelites were restricted. In Lev 8:1-5 the congregation of the Israelites is summoned to observe the ordination of the priests. They are likely located in front of the altar, where they later see the theophany of the Glory of Yahweh in the fire on the altar (Lev 9:23-24).

The process of clothing Aaron and his sons requires three stages. First, they are washed to purify their bodies before putting on the vestments (Exod 29:4). The text is unclear about the process. The ritual bathing could have included their entire body or, as Ibn Ezra suggests, only the hands and feet. The washing for ablution was likely from the water in the basin located between the tabernacle and the altar. Second, they are clothed, Aaron initially (vv. 5-6) and then his sons (vv. 8-9). Third, Moses anoints Aaron with oil (v. 7). The anointing of the other priests is not stated, even though God directs Moses to do so in 28:41. The act of anointing with oil is also a form of cleansing that bestows a special status on the person. Thus both kings and prophets can be anointed with oil (e.g., Jehu and Elisha, respectively, 1 Kgs 19:16).

29:10-14 The second step in the ordination of Aaron and his sons is the sin offering of the bull. Aaron and his sons lay their hands on the bull as they do with each of the three animals sacrificed in the ordination ritual. The sin offering *(ḥaṭṭāʾt)* is meant to decontaminate or purify the altar from any pollution that may result from Aaron and his sons. For this reason, Milgrom prefers the term "purification offering" rather than the more common "sin offering." Exodus 29:35-37 indicates that the bull offering to purify the altar is repeated seven times: "A bull of sin offering you shall offer every day for the atonement" (29:36). The purification is aimed at the altar: "You shall offer a sin offering on the altar when you make atonement on it. And you shall anoint it to consecrate it" (29:36). The bull sacrifice purifies in two ways. The impurity of Aaron and his sons is transferred to the bull, whose fat of the inner organs is sacrificed on the altar to propitiate God. Also, as B. Levine notes, the hide is taken from the camp as a ritual of riddance, removing further impurity.[29] The result is that the

29. Levine, *Leviticus,* 20-22.

altar becomes "most holy. Whatever touches the altar will be consecrated" (29:37). The purification of the altar prepares it for the subsequent acts of expiation.[30] The blood rites underscore the focus on the altar. The blood of the bull is placed on the four horns of the altar and poured at its base, signifying its complete purification.

29:15-18 The first of the two rams is sacrificed as a burnt offering (*ʿōlâ*). The sacrifice is a whole burnt offering given over completely to God. "Turn the entire ram into smoke on the altar," demands God (29:18). The purpose of the burnt offering is to expiate the one sacrificing in order to evoke a favorable response from God. Thus there is a shift in focus in the ordination ritual from the purification of the altar with the sacrifice of the bull to the expiation of Aaron and his sons with the sacrifice of the first ram. The result is a "pleasing odor" to Yahweh. The phrase indicates that God is satisfied with the sacrifice and thus the one sacrificing is able to approach the divine. The Epic of Gilgamesh illustrates the meaning. Utnapishtim, the survivor of the flood, describes his sacrifice to the gods:

> The gods smelled the savor,
> The gods smelled the sweet savor,
> The gods crowded like flies about the sacrifice.

The P author employs this phrase to indicate that an offering is accepted by God, and hence will draw forth power from God (see also Leviticus 1–3; Num 15:3, 7, 10, 13, 14).

29:19-41 The second ram is the ordination sacrifice: "It is the ram of ordination (*ʾēl milluʾîm*)" (29:22). The Hebrew phrase translates literally "ram of filling"; "to fill the hands" indicates the ordination of the priests. The meaning is acted out in v. 24, when the two kinds of bread and the sacrificial victim are placed in the hands of Aaron and his sons before being sacrificed. The sacrifice of ordination follows the structure of the previous two sacrifices: the laying on of hands, the slaughter, a blood rite, and the sacrifice. But it also builds in intensity in three ways.

The first sign of intensification is the blood rite (commanded in 29:19-21 and fulfilled in Lev 8:22-24). In contrast to the exclusive focus on the altar with the blood of the bull and the ram, the blood of the ordination ram is sprinkled on the altar and the priests. The ritual recalls the blood rite in 24:6, 8, where the altar and the Israelites were sprinkled with the blood of the sacrifice. In this ritual the people entered a covenant relationship with Yahweh followed by a meal with God on the divine mountain (24:9-11). But they are not conse-

---

30. Milgrom, *Leviticus 1–16*, 253-56, 261-64, *et passim*.

crated. The blood ritual with the priests will transform them from the realm of the profane to the sacred. The ritual is also more exact than the action in 24:6, 8. Blood is placed on the extremities of the priests, their right ear lobe, thumb, and large toe. The same procedure is followed after a person is cured from skin disease (Leviticus 14), suggesting that the ritual signifies purification. Furthermore the blood ritual is performed twice. Initially only the blood of the ram is used to daub Aaron and his son. Then a mixture of blood and oil is again sprinkled on Aaron, his sons, and their garments. God states the results: "And he [Aaron] will be holy, and his garments, his sons, and the garments of his sons" (29:21).

Second, the sacrifice of the ram includes new rituals (commanded in 29:22-26 and fulfilled in Lev 8:25-28). The two types of unleavened bread are combined with the inner parts of the ram and placed in the hands of the priests as an elevation offering *(těnûpâ)*. The elevation offering derives from the Hebrew verb *rûm,* "to lift, raise." The rite of the elevation offering is a separate sacrifice in which the offering is raised and presented to God for acceptance. It signifies the transfer of the sacrifice from the human owner to the realm of God. In the ordination ritual the elevation offering is not performed alone. It precedes the burning of the inward parts of the ram and the bread.

Third, the sacrifice is followed by a meal in the entrance to the tent of meeting (commanded in Exod 29:27-34 and fulfilled in Lev 8:29, 31-36). God declares that the breast and the thigh of the ram are the portion of food for the priests. The food is sacred and any portion remaining after the meal must be burned up before morning. The progression from a sacrifice and blood ritual to a meal recalls the sequence of Exodus 24, where the sprinkling of blood on the people (24:6, 8) is also followed by a meal with God on the mountain (24:9-11). The meal of the Aaronide priests takes place in the tent of meeting rather than on the divine mountain, signaling a progression in the descent of God on earth. The focus on the priests (29:27-28) and their sacred meal (29:31-34) is interrupted in 29:29-30 by a reaffirmation of the sacred quality of the vestments. The insertion underscores that the sacred garments of Aaron must be passed on to his sons, and that whoever wears the garments for seven days in the tent of meeting becomes the next high priest.

Verses 35-42 summarize the duration of the rite and the daily sacrfices required to complete the ordination. The ritual takes seven days (v. 35). The sin offering of a bull is required each day to atone and to consecrate the altar (vv. 36-37). In addition there are daily sacrifices of two lambs, one in the morning and another at twilight, with the following ingredients: one-tenth ephah of fine flour (about 2 quarts); 1 hin of olive oil (about 1 quart); and one-quarter hin of wine. Yahweh commands that the burnt offering continue with future generations, and the Deity also promises to meet or appear *(yāʿad)* to the people of Israel and to speak with Moses. The verb *yāʿad* is from the same root used for the *ʾōhel môʿēd,* "tent of meeting." The fulfillment of the divine promise to speak with Moses occurs in Num 7:89.

29:43-46   God broadens the promise of presence in the conclusion. The promise opens with the verb "to appear/meet," reinforcing the sanctuary as a tent of meeting. The result of the divine presence is the consecration of the sanctuary by means of the Glory of Yahweh. The consecration includes the tent of meeting, the altar, as well as Aaron and his sons. The promise of consecration does not include the people of Israel. Instead God promises "to settle" *(šākan)* in the midst of the people and to be their God. The result of the divine presence in the midst of the people is knowledge, which is expressed with the combination of the recognition formula, "so that you may know," and the divine self-introduction, "I am Yahweh." Verse 46 states: "They will know that I am Yahweh, their God." The ordination of the Aaronide priesthood will allow God to enter the sanctuary and it will also bring the Israelites to the knowledge of God's power and presence. The power of God will be revealed in their knowledge of the exodus. They will know that Yahweh brought them out from the land of Egypt. The purpose of the exodus is for Yahweh to settle in the midst of the Israelites.

The promise of divine presence in the cult is crucial to the development of the P History. The P author employed the recognition formula throughout the story of the exodus (see the commentary on Exodus 7–14) as an address to Pharaoh and to the Egyptians. The plagues and the defeat of the Egyptian army at the Red Sea were events aimed at bringing the Egyptians to the knowledge of Yahweh. The Israelites must also know the power of Yahweh in the destructive events of the exodus. But they will acquire this knowledge through the safeguard of the mediated presence of God in the tabernacle and through the priesthood. The mediation of the divine presence through the ritual actions of the priesthood is the topic of instruction in Exodus 30.

RITUALS OF MEDIATION (30:1-38)

Exodus 30 describes the rituals of priestly mediation. Houtman prefers the word "institution" to describe the appointment of the priestly mediators, because the consecration of the Aaronide priests involves the creation and maintenance of the entire cultic ritual system and not just the ordination of the priests.[31] Houtman is certainly correct. The establishment of the Aaronide priesthood allows for a wide range of rituals, allowing the tabernacle to function as a tent of meeting.

31. Houtman, *Exodus* 3:526.

The appointment of the priesthood is structured into three parts to underscore their role as ritual mediators between God and the people. The three parts reflect degrees of holiness, from the priestly vestments (chap. 28), to the ordination of the priests when they are invested with the holy garments (chap. 29), and finally to the role of the priests in mediating for the people through rituals (chap. 30). The rituals of mediation in chap. 30 include a mixture of cultic objects necessary for maintaining the purity of the priests (the altar of incense, the basin of water, the anointing oil), instruction concerning the support of the cult by the people (the census and tax), and selective ritual actions and ointments (the Day of Atonement and the incense).

Altar of Incense and Anointing Oil (30:1-9; 37:25-29)

30:1-9

¹"And you shall make an altar of incense. You shall make it of acacia wood. ²It will be a cubit its length, a cubit its width, square, and two cubits its height, its horns from it. ³You shall overlay it with pure gold, its top and its sides around, and its horns. And you shall make for it a border of gold around. ⁴And two rings of gold you shall make for it under its border. And it will house the poles with which to carry it. ⁵And you shall make the poles of acacia wood, and you shall overlay them with gold. ⁶And you shall place it before the curtain that is above the ark of the testimony, before the curtain that is above the testimony, where I will appear to you there. ⁷And Aaron will burn fragrant incense; every morning when he tends the lamps he shall burn it. ⁸And when Aaron sets up the lamps at twilight he shall burn it, a continual incense offering before Yahweh throughout your generations. ⁹You shall not offer on it strange incense, a burnt offering, or a meal offering. And you shall not pour a libation on it."

37:25-28

²⁵And he made the altar of incense of acacia wood, a cubit its length, and a cubit its width, square, and two cubits its height. Its horns were from it. ²⁶He overlaid it with pure gold; its top, its sides around, and its horns. And he made for it a border of gold around. ²⁷Two gold rings he made for it under its border on its two sides, on two opposite sides of it to house the poles with which to carry it. ²⁸And he made the poles of acacia wood, and he overlaid them with gold.

Notes

The Sam changes the location of the altar of incense, placing it after the description of the tabernacle (26:1-37). See the introduction for discussion of the location of the altar of incense in the MT and the theories of composition associated with its present location.

30:6 *and you shall place it before the curtain that is above the ark of the testimony, before the curtain that is above the testimony, where I will appear to you there.* The Sam has shortened the MT by eliminating the phrase, "before the curtain that is above the testimony" *(lipnê hakkappōret 'ăšer 'al-hā'ēdūt).* The LXX follows the Sam.

30:7 *every morning.* The repetition in Hebrew, *babbōqer babbōqer,* lit. "in the morning in the morning," means "every morning." The LXX follows the Hebrew: *prōi prōi.*

30:9 *you shall not offer on it strange incense.* For discussion of Hebrew *zārâ,* "strange," see 29:33. In this context "strange" likely indicates cultic practices that are foreign to Yahwism as conceived by the P author. The story of Nadab and Abihu provides an illustration of the violation (Lev 10:1-2).

Commentary

The altar of incense *(mizbēaḥ miqṭar)* is revealed to Moses in 30:1-6. The revelation also includes ritual instruction for its daily use (30:7-9) and for its yearly use on the Day of Atonement (see the commentary on 30:10), as well as the ingredients for the incense of the perfume, which is burned on the altar (30:34-38). Scholars puzzle over the placement of the instructions in 30:1-9 after the requirements for the priestly ordination (27:20–29:46), which is far removed from the description of the other cultic objects for the tabernacle in 26:1–27:19. The reason is likely to include the ritual instructions for its care in 30:7-10 by Aaron in the role of the high priest. He is instructed to burn incense daily, both in the morning and in the evening. The altar of incense also plays an important role in cleansing the sanctuary on the Day of Atonement, outlined in Leviticus 16. The emphasis of the altar of incense is its function in ritual mediation, rather than on the object itself. For this reason the altar of incense is part of the section on the tent of meeting where the focus is on ritual mediation as a means for humans to meet God, rather than the section on the tabernacle where the approach of God into the sanctuary is described.

The construction of the altar of incense and the mixing of the perfume is recounted in 37:25-29. The altar of incense is a small object made of acacia wood with square dimensions, 1 cubit long × 1 cubit wide × 2 cubits high (about 1½ feet long × 1½ wide × 3 feet high). The altar is covered with pure gold and it also has a gold molding. Two golden rings on two sides of the altar allow for its transportation with two wooden poles, which are also covered in gold. The location of the altar of incense within the tabernacle is not stated, but it was likely positioned in the holy place, in front of the *pārōket* curtain, perhaps in the middle of the room. Numbers 8:1-4 indicates that the light of the menorah shone on the altar of incense.

The distinctive feature of the altar of incense is its horns. S. Gitin notes the prominence of four-horned altars throughout the ancient Near East, tracing the form to roof sacrifices in the Late Bronze Age that are evident in terracotta-tower models from Emar, Mumbaqat, and Tell Faq'ous in the Syrian Middle Euphrates region: "The long-term use of the form of the tower-shaped altar to symbolize the roof tops on which offerings were made, reflects the well-established ancient Near Eastern tradition of the roof ritual, which was an integral element of East and West Semitic cultic practices." According to Gitin, the four-horned altar came to represent an intrinsic quality of sanctity.[32] The Jerusalem temple had such an altar (1 Kgs 8:64), which also functioned as a place of asylum (1 Kgs 2:28-35). The prophet Ezekiel envisioned a four-horned altar (Ezek 43:15). Further examples have been discovered at Megiddo, Dan, and Beer-sheba.[33]

Day of Atonement (30:10)

[30:10] *And Aaron shall make atonement on its horns once a year from the blood of the sin offering of atonement. Once a year he shall make atonement on it throughout your generations. It is most holy to Yahweh.*

Notes

30:10 *sin offering of atonement.* For discussion of this phrase see 29:33.

Commentary

The ritual of the Day of Atonement concludes the instructions for the altar of incense. The altar of incense is located in the tabernacle before the curtain separating the holy place and the most holy place. Only Aaron is allowed to burn the incense on the altar when he lights the lampstand. The burning of incense on the altar most likely symbolizes the presence of God in the sanctuary. Incense probably represents the cloud that surrounds and hides the divine glory, as in 24:15-16: "When Moses went up on the mountain, the cloud covered it, and the Glory of Yahweh settled on Mount Sinai." The Christian church continues the practice by employing incense to fill the sanctuary at the moment in which Christ enters the bread and wine in the liturgy of the Eucharist. The

---

32. S. Gitin, "The Four-Horned Altar and Sacred Space: An Archaeological Perspective," in *Sacred Time, Sacred Place: Archaeology and the Religion of Israel* (ed. B. M. Gittlen; Winona Lake, Ind.: Eisenbrauns, 2002), 95-99, quotation 99.

33. Y. Aharoni, "The Horned Altar of Beer-Sheba," *BA* 37 (1974): 1-6.

burning of incense is crucial for maintaining the presence of the Glory of Yahweh in the tabernacle. Once present in the tent of meeting the Glory of Yahweh must be shielded by the cloud of incense.

The instructions for the altar of incense conclude with reference to the Day of Atonement or Yom Kippur, which is described in Leviticus 16. Yom Kippur is a ritual of riddance intended to purge the sanctuary of impurity that accumulates during the year from the transgressions of the Israelites and, more importantly, from the priesthood who were responsible for maintaining the purity of the sanctuary. If the priests did not maintain the purity of the cult on a regular basis, God would be driven away from the sanctuary. Thus the instructions for the construction and maintenance of the altar also include the process by which it is to be purified once a year on the Day of Atonement. Only the high priest can remove the impurity of the people and of the priesthood from the altar of incense. The detergent is the blood of the sin offering from the sacrifice of the bull and the goat on the Day of Atonement. The sacrifice is described in Lev 16:11-17 and the ritual of riddance performed on the altar of incense is outlined in Lev 16:18-19.

Census and Temple Tax (30:11-16; 38:21, 24-31)

30:11-16

[11]And Yahweh spoke to Moses, saying, [12]"When you take a census of the Israelites according to their regiments, each person shall give a ransom for his life to Yahweh when registering them. [13]This is what each one passing into the regiment shall give: a half-shekel according to the shekel of the sanctuary (twenty gerahs to the shekel), a half-shekel is a dedication offering to Yahweh. [14]Each one passing into the regiment from twenty years old and upward shall give the dedication offering of Yahweh. [15]The rich shall not pay more and the poor shall not pay less than the half-shekel to present the dedication offering of Yahweh for the ransom of your lives. [16]You shall take the money of atonement from the Israelites and you shall give it for the

38:21, 24-31

[21]And these are the administrative records of the tabernacle, the tabernacle of the testimony, which were recorded by the command of Moses. . . . [24]All the gold used for the work in all the work of the sanctuary, it was gold of the elevation offering, was twenty-nine talents and seven hundred thirty shekels according to the shekel of the sanctuary. [25]The silver of the regiments of the testimony of those recorded was one hundred talents and one thousand seven hundred seventy-five shekels, according to the shekel of the sanctuary. [26]A beqa per head, that is, a half-shekel according to the shekel of the sanctuary, for everyone passing into the regiment from twenty years old and upward, for six hundred three thousand five hundred fifty

work of the tent of meeting. And it will be for the Israelites a remembrance before Yahweh for the atonement of their lives."

men. ²⁷ And the one hundred talents of silver were for casting the bases of the sanctuary and the bases of the curtain, one hundred bases for the one hundred talents, a talent for a base. ²⁸ And of the one thousand seven hundred and seventy-five shekels he made hooks for the pillars, and overlay for their tops, and bands for them. ²⁹ The copper from the elevation offering was seventy talents and two thousand four hundred shekels. ³⁰ And he made of it the bases of the door of the tent of meeting, the copper altar, the copper grating for it, and all the utensils of the altar, ³¹ the bases around the court, the bases of the gate of the court, all the pegs of the tabernacle, and all the pegs around the court.

Notes

30:12 *When you take a census of the Israelites.* Hebrew *kî tiśśā' 'et-rō'š běnê-yiśrā'ēl*, lit. "when you lift the head of the Israelites," indicates a poll or census. The LXX translates, *Ean labēs ton syllogismon tōn huiōn Israēl*, "When you take a calculation of the Israelites."

according to their regiments. Hebrew *lipqūdêhem* derives from the verb *pāqad*. A form of this word occurs fives times in the instruction on the census (vv. 12 [3 times], 13, 14). The verb has a range of meanings, "to look after, to see, to take care of, to pass in review, to muster." It certainly indicates registration in the present context. See NRSV: "When you take a census of the Israelites to register them." B. Levine notes that there is a military meaning to the verb *pāqad*, evident in the derivative noun *pěqudîm*. This is especially evident when the terms reappear in the census of Numbers 1, where military service is explicitly stated *(yōṣē' ṣābā')*. The translation "regiments" reflects the military background of the census, even though the focus in Exod 30:11-16 is on the temple tax. The LXX translation, *episkopē*, emphasizes more the act of inspecting, perhaps with a more ecclesiastical focus.

each person shall give a ransom for his life to Yahweh when registering them. Hebrew *kōper* appears thirteen times in the Hebrew Bible, and it is usually translated "ransom" (see, however, NRSV "bribe" in Amos 5:12; 1 Sam 12:3; Prov 6:35). The law of the ox that gores in Exod 21:30 provides an example: "If a ransom *(kōper)* is placed upon him, he must give the ransom money *(pidyōn)* for his life." The noun *kōper* derives from the root *kpr*, meaning "atone." The meaning of atonement is emphasized in the present context when the tax is described in v. 16 as "the money of atonement" *(kesep hakkippurîm)*. The interpretation of the temple tax as an atonement may account for the placement of the altar of incense (30:1-10) and the census and tax (30:11-16) in the same context. The LXX translates *lytra*, "ransom."

30:13 *each one passing into the regiment.* Hebrew *kol-hā'ōbēr 'al-happĕqudîm* is translated in the LXX, *hosoi an paraporeuōntai tēn episkepsin*, "anyone who passes along under review." E. Speiser translates: anyone who "emerges as 'one who is entered among the enrolled.'"[34]

30:15 *to present the dedication offering of Yahweh.* For discussion of the *tĕrûmâ* see 29:27.

30:16 *the money of atonement.* See 29:36.

38:24 *elevation offering.* Hebrew *tĕrûmâ* is translated in the LXX as *aparchas*, "firstfruit."

36:25 *according to the shekel of the sanctuary.* The phrase is absent from the Sam.

Commentary

The Israelite people are responsible for the financial resources of the tabernacle cult. Exodus 30:11-16 introduces the divine command for a temple tax of a half shekel per person, thus requiring a census. A shekel is a unit of weight, not a coin. The average weight of a shekel is 11.4 grams, according to Sarna.[35] Exodus 38:25-28 provides the results of the census commanded in 30:11-16. It specifies that the census is limited to males twenty years of age and older. The number of Israelite males in this age group is 603,550. The topic of a census returns in Numbers 1. It is related to the census in Exod 30:11-16 and 38:25-28. It too numbers males only twenty years of age and older (30:14; 38:26; Num 1:3). It uses the verb "to consider" or "to muster" *(pāqad)* to describe the registration of the males (Exod 30:12; Num 1:3), and it arrives at the same number, 603,550 (Exod 38:26; Num 1:46).[36]

The number of males is large. G. B. Gray estimates that the total population of Israelites would be over two million.[37] The number likely has symbolic value for the P author. But deciphering the meaning is difficult. The enormous size of the community may indicate the fulfillment of the blessing to Abram (Gen 12:1-3). The large number may also represent the strength of the nation, since the P author described the nation as going out of Egypt as a "host" (Exod 12:41), as an "army in five parts" (13:18), and with a high hand (14:8). More precise interpretations of the numbers have also been offered. P. J. Budd ties the num-

34. E. A. Speiser, "Census and Ritual Expiation in Mari and Israel," in *Oriental and Biblical Studies* (Philadelphia: University of Pennsylvania Press, 1967), 171-86, esp. 182.

35. Sarna, *Exodus*, 196.

36. See the discussion of these texts by M. Fishbane, "Census and Intercession in a Priestly Text (Exodus 30:11-16) and in Its Midrashic Transformation," in *Pomegranates and Golden Bells*, ed. Wright et al., 103-11.

37. G. B. Gray, *A Critical and Exegetical Commentary on Numbers* (ICC; Edinburgh: T. & T. Clark, 1903), 9-15.

bers to the dimensions of the tabernacle.[38] G. Fohrer speculates that the numerical figures represent gematria, a process in which letters from the alphabet have a numerical value. The value of the Hebrew phrase *běnê yiśrā'ēl* (lit. "sons of Israel") is 603, which when multiplied by 1,000 results in the figure 603,000. He suggests further that the number 550 results from the numerical value of the phrase *kl r'š*, "all the heads" (rounded down from 551), which is used repeatedly in the census from Numbers 1.[39] M. Barnouin looks instead to Babylonian astronomy as the key for the numbering system: the aim of the P writers is to place the wilderness community in the universal setting of the empire.[40]

The census of the people is a dangerous topic in the Hebrew Bible. Numbering the people carries the threat of divine wrath through a plague, even though God may command the action. The tension is also apparent in the story of David. When he first counted the people in 2 Samuel 24, God judged it to be a sin, necessitating a divine punishment. The reason for the divine wrath is that counting the people is related to war in ancient Israel as in the rest of the ancient Near East. It is why the census is limited to males twenty years of age and older. It may also be the reason for the military imagery that is associated with the word *pĕqudîm,* which can mean both the recording of persons and also the military regiment (see the translation note on 30:12).

The danger in a census is that it turns the focus from faith in God as the resource of the people in war to the inherent strength of the nation; such a turn is a sin in ancient Israel. It is the reason why David and the entire Israelite nation are punished in 2 Samuel 24. Victory in war results from Yahweh's action, not from the Israelites or the power of their king. Deuteronomy 9:3 illustrates the teaching: "Be assured today that Yahweh your God is the one who goes across ahead of you like a devouring fire. He will destroy them [the nations of the land]." Deuteronomy 8:17-18 provides further commentary: "Do not say to yourself, 'My power and the strength of my hands have produced this wealth for me.' But remember Yahweh, your God, for it is he who gives you the ability to produce wealth, and so confirms his covenant."

The word "to muster" in Exod 30:12 and Num 1:3 still carries the overtones of military action. The noun deriving from the word indicates a military garrison (see Numbers 1 and the note to 30:12 above). Thus even when the census is focused on the temple the danger of divine wrath in numbering the people lingers. The result is a monetary payment of atonement or ransom. The danger of divine wrath must be appeased through a temple tax: "each person

38. P. J. Budd, *Numbers* (WBC 5; Waco: Word, 1984), 8-9.

39. G. Fohrer, *Introduction to the Old Testament* (trans. D. E. Green; Nashville: Abingdon, 1968), 184.

40. M. Barnouin, "Les recensements du livre des Nombres et l'astronomie babylonienne," *VT* 27 (1977): 280-303.

shall give a ransom for his life to Yahweh when registering them" (Exod 30:12). Moreover, the tax is not graduated according to wealth, but is an equal amount for the rich and the poor. The effect of the tax is that it becomes a memorial to Yahweh, reminding God that the lives of the numbered males have been ransomed even though they were counted.

Basin of Water (30:17-21; 38:8)

30:17-21

¹⁷And Yahweh spoke to Moses, saying, ¹⁸"You shall make a basin of copper and its stand of copper for washing. And you shall place it between the tent of meeting and the altar. And you shall put water in it. ¹⁹And Aaron and his sons shall wash from it their hands and their garments. ²⁰And when they enter the tent of meeting they will wash with water so that they will not die, or when they approach the altar to minister to turn into smoke an offering of fire to Yahweh. ²¹And they will wash their hands and their garments, so that they will not die. And it will be for them a perpetual statute, for him and for his offspring throughout their generations."

38:8

⁸And he made the basin of copper and its stand of copper from mirrors of the women who performed tasks at the entrance of the tent of meeting.

Notes

30:18 *a basin of copper.* Hebrew *kîyôr,* "basin," is also translated "laver" (see NJPS). The LXX translates *loutēra,* "washtub, basin."

30:20 *to turn into smoke an offering of fire to Yahweh.* The LXX translates, *anapherein ta holokautōmata kyriō,* "to bring up a whole burnt offering to the Lord."

38:8 *from mirrors.* Hebrew *bĕmar'ōt* usually means a "vision," as in the experience of Samuel in the temple (1 Sam 3:15) or the statement of Yahweh to Moses, Miriam, and Aaron (Num 12:6). But this translation hardly works in the present verse, since the basin and its stand are constructed from the *mar'ōt.* The LXX (38:26) translates, *ek tōn katoptrōn,* "out of the mirrors," which I follow. The use of the Hebrew preposition *bĕ* in the phrase *bĕmar'ōt* indicates that the basin and its stand are made out of the *mar'ōt,* not with them.

of the women who performed tasks at the entrance of the tent of meeting. The description of the women is obscure in Hebrew: *haṣṣōbĕ'ōt 'ăšer ṣābĕ'û.* Hebrew *ṣābā'* means to fight in war. The word describes the men who are numbered in the census of Numbers 1 (v. 3). The image of war corresponds to the role of Miriam and the women during the war at the Red Sea (15:21-22). But the image of war does not easily fit the present context, nor does it aid in interpreting the *mar'ōt*. The same women appear in 1 Sam 2:22: "They [the sons of Eli] lay with the women who served *('et-hannāšîm haṣṣōbĕ'ôt)* at the entrance of the tent of meeting." The motif of sexual intercourse in this passage raises further questions about the cultic role of the women, although the focus of 1 Sam 2:22 is on the role of Eli's sons, not the women. The LXX (38:26) interprets the role of the women as that of fasting *(hai enēsteusan),* and it further defines the mirrors as objects used in fasting *(tōn nēsteusasōn).*

Commentary

Exodus 30:17-21 describes the construction of a basin or laver. Lavers are associated with cooking pots (1 Sam 2:14) and also with cultic purification and washing. The temple of Solomon has ten large lavers (1 Kgs 7:27-39). The P tabernacle has a single laver or basin, located between the altar of burnt offering and the door of the tabernacle. The exact size is not stated, but its material is identified as bronze.

The function of the basin is solely for the purification of the priests. They are commanded to wash their hands and feet upon entering the tabernacle and when they approach the altar to administer offerings (30:20-21). Failure to purify themselves results in death. The function of water for purification, especially of priests, is common in the ancient Near East. Egyptian priests wash twice each day and twice each night according to Herodotus. H. te Velde notes rites of water purification by Egyptian priests three times a day corresponding to their daily services in the temple.[41] The ritual of cleansing took place in stone basins at the entrance of the temple, a similar location to the basin of water in the court of the tabernacle. In addition to the daily ministry in the tabernacle and at the altar, the purification ritual is also associated with the ordination of the Aaronide priests in Lev 8:11.

Exodus 38:8 states that the bronze material for the basin of water came from the mirrors of the women who served at the door of the tent of meeting. The statement is obscure and clearly anachronistic in its present literary context, since whoever the women may be, there is as yet no tabernacle in Exodus 38. Interpreters struggle to identify the women (see the translation notes). P. A. Bird concludes that the description "serving women" *(haṣṣōbĕ'ōt)* suggests at least work in service to the sanctuary.[42] A similar phrase in Num 4:23 may also sug-

---

41. Te Velde, *CANE* 3:1733.

42. P. A. Bird, *Missing Persons and Mistaken Identities: Women and Gender in Ancient Israel* (OBT; Minneapolis: Fortress, 1997), 42, 63, 91, 97.

gests a cultic context. A more precise identification of the women has ranged widely without success. The women are mentioned in 1 Sam 2:22, which states that the sons of Eli slept "with the women who served at the entrance of the tent of meeting." But the parallel provides little assistance in identification. The comparative study of ancient Near Eastern literature has yielded little further information. R. de Vaux compared the women to pre-Islamic girls who guarded the *qubba,* a small sacred tent.[43] The sexual activity noted in 1 Sam 2:22 may indicate some form of sexual role for the women, but the text is anything but clear.

The point of focus in Exod 38:8, however, is on the mirrors, not the women. E. L. Greenstein notes that the mirrors are not gifts, but taken from the women and destroyed to provide material for the basin of water.[44] Copper mirrors were manufactured in Egypt and may represent foreign worship, according to M. Görg.[45] U. Winter associates possible sexual imagery with the mirrors.[46] The destruction of the mirrors to build the basin of water indicates that the activity of the women is rejected in the tabernacle cult of the P History. Even more pointedly, the mirrors of the women become the source material for priestly purification with the basin of water. Greenstein notes a parallel to the destruction of the censers of the Korah group in Numbers 16–17.[47]

Anointing Oil and Incense (30:22-38; 37:29)

30:22-38

[22]And Yahweh spoke to Moses, saying, [23]"You take for yourself the finest spices: flowing myrrh five hundred weight, fragrant cinnamon half of it, two hundred and fifty, and cane spice two hundred and fifty, [24]cassia five hundred of the sanctuary shekel, and a hin of olive oil. [25]And you shall make of it sacred anointing oil blended as by a perfumer. It will

37:29

[29]And he made the holy anointing oil and the pure fragrant incense, blended as by a perfumer.

43. R. de Vaux, *Ancient Israel,* vol. 2: *Religious Institutions* (New York: McGraw-Hill, 1965), 296-97.

44. E. L. Greenstein, "Recovering the Women Who Served at the Entrance," in *Studies in Historical Geography and Biblical Historiography Presented to Zecharia Kallai* (ed. G. Galel and M. Weinfeld; Leiden: Brill, 2000), 172.

45. M. Görg, "Der Spiegeldienst der Frauern," *BN* 23 (1984): 9-13.

46. U. Winter, *Frau und Göttin: Exegetische und ikonographische Studien zum weiblichen Gottesbild im Alten Israel und in dessen Umwelt* (OBO 53; Göttingen: Vandenhoeck & Ruprecht, 1983), 58-65.

47. Greenstein, "Recovering the Women," 172-73.

be a sacred anointing oil. ²⁶And you
will anoint with it the tent of   (40:9-15)
meeting, and the ark of the testimony,
²⁷and the table, and all its utensils,
and the lampstand, and its utensils,
and the altar of incense, ²⁸and the
altar of burnt offering, and all of its
utensils, and the basin, and its stand.
²⁹And you shall consecrate them.
And they will be most holy; whatever
touches them will be consecrated.

³⁰"And Aaron and his sons you shall
anoint, and you shall consecrate them
to be priest for me.

³¹"And to the Israelites you shall
speak, saying, 'Holy anointing oil this
will be for me throughout your
generations.' ³²It shall not be rubbed
on the flesh of a human; and you
must not make anything like it in its
composition. It is holy; holy it shall
be to you. ³³Any person who mixes
any like it or who places any of it on
a stranger shall be cut off from his
people.'"

³⁴And Yahweh spoke to Moses, "Take
for yourself paste, stacte, onycha, and
galbanum, spices with pure
frankincense, it will be an equal part
of each. ³⁵And you shall make it into
incense blended as by a perfumer,
salted pure and holy. ³⁶And you shall
beat some of it into powder, and put
part of it before the testimony in the
tent of meeting where I will appear to
you there. It will be most holy to you.
³⁷But the incense that you will make,
according to this composition, you
shall not make for yourself. Holy to
Yahweh it will be for you. ³⁸Any
person who makes anything like it to
smell like it shall be cut off from his
people."

Notes

30:23 *the finest spices.* Hebrew *běśāmîm* refers to the balsam tree, which is characterized by aromatic resinous oil. The plural form in this verse is a general term referring to the following list of spices or oils, qualified as the "finest" *(rō'š)*. The LXX
translates, *hēdysmata*, "seasoning," "aromatic spices."

flowing myrrh. Hebrew *mār* is a gum resin of yellowish brown and reddish brown
color from the *Commiphora abyssinica* tree. The description of it as *děrôr*, "flowing," is uncertain. It may describe its liquid form. The LXX translates differently, *to
anthos smyrnēs eklektēs*, "the best of flowering myrrh." The word *eklektēs* describes
the myrrh rather than the spices in general, while the myrrh itself is "flowering,"
not "flowing." Wevers suggests a metaphorical meaning to indicate the finest
myrrh.[48]

fragrant cinnamon. The cinnamon is qualified as *beśem*, "fragrant," or perhaps "spice."
See the plural form earlier in this verse.

cane spice. Hebrew *qěnēh* may refer to the aromatic root of calamus or perhaps cymbi-
dium, a tropical plant producing boat-shaped flowers. The LXX translates
kalamou, "calamus."

30:24 *cassia.* Hebrew *qiddâ* is an aromatic substance often related to cinnamon. The
LXX translates, *ireōs*, "iris."

30:25 *blended as by a perfumer.* The LXX translates, *technē myrepsou*, "in the craft of
the perfumer."

30:33 *a stranger.* For discussion of Hebrew *zār* see 29:33; 30:9.

shall be cut off from his people. The penalty of *kārēt*, "to be cut off," from Hebrew *kārat*,
is common in the P History. The meaning of the penalty is disputed. It may signify
the death penalty, early death, childlessness, the loss of an afterlife, or excommunication from the congregation (*'ēdâ*). There are four cases of *kārēt* in Exodus (12:15,
19; 30:33, 38). Milgrom concludes that the term signifies a divine penalty referring
to the termination of the offender's line, which may include the loss of an afterlife.[49]

30:34 *paste.* Hebrew *sammîm* describes a type of resin, "paste," "perfume," or perhaps
"spice."

stacte. Hebrew *nāṭāp* is a hapax legomenon deriving from the verb "to drop, drip," and
is translated "drops of stacte." The translation "stacte" derives from LXX *staktēn*.
LSJ 1630 defines the noun *staktē* as "oil of myrrh" and the adjective *staktos* as "ooz-
ing out in drops."

onycha. Hebrew *šěḥēlet* is a hapax legomenon. It may refer to a vegetable husk of
wheat or barley or to a mollusk. The LXX translation, *onycha*, "a cloven hoof," may
favor the reference to a mollusk, since "cloven" may describe the shell of a mollusk.[50]

galbanum. Hebrew *ḥelběnâ* is a hapax legomenon. The word may be associated with

48. Wevers, *Notes*, 499.
49. Milgrom, *Leviticus 1–16*, 457-60.
50. See Houtman, *Exodus*, 1:170-71, who favors the association with a vegetable rather
than mollusk.

"milk" *(ḥālāb)*. It is considered to be the resin of the ferula, a plant in the carrot family that produces gum resin. The LXX translates, *chalbanum*, "the resinous juice of all-heal, *Ferula galbaniflua*" (LSJ 1971).

frankincense. Hebrew *lĕbōnâ* refers to the *Boswellia Carteri* tree in Arabia and East Africa. The word is associated with "white" *(lābān)*, suggesting a white-colored resin. The LXX translates *libanon*, "frankincense."

Commentary

The oil for anointing (30:22-33) and the incense (30:34-38) are specified in this section, as well as their use, power, and restrictions among the Israelites.

The four ingredients of the anointing oil are listed in 30:22-25. The first is myrrh, a yellowish brown or reddish brown gum resin from the tree *Commiphora abyssinica*. Its taste was bitter, but its aroma was pungent. The myrrh was congealed into drops weighing five hundred shekels (a shekel is about 11.4 grams). The next two ingredients are a fragrant form of cinnamon *(qinnĕmān)* and cane *(qĕnēh)*, each valued at 250 shekels. The fourth is likely a coarse cinnamon bark, but Hebrew *qiddâ* is unknown. Five hundred shekels are required. The four ingredients are mixed together with olive oil.

The recipe is used to anoint the sanctuary, its furnishings (30:25-29), and the priests (30:30-33). The anointing consecrates the tent of meeting and the furnishings, making the objects holy and even contagious to touch. The same is true with the priests. The oil is prohibited from use by lay Israelites. Anyone who makes a similar recipe for noncultic use is expelled from the community or perhaps even executed.

The incense for burning on the altar in the tent of meeting is made from four different spices (30:34-38): *nāṭāp*, a gum resin; *šĕḥēlet*, an unknown substance translated as *onycha* in the LXX; *ḥelbĕnâ*, another gum resin; and *lĕbōnâ*, frankincense (the Hebrew word means "white"). The incense has the same power and restrictions as the anointing oil. It is sacred and prohibited from profane use upon penalty of the user being "cut off" from the people.

The exact nature of many of the perfumes is difficult to identify. The incense for burning in 30:34 includes three hapax legomena. The ingredients are not indigenous to Syria-Palestine, indicating a developed trading system as far away as India. V. H. Matthews notes that the manufacture of many of the spices required pounding and that the pulverized form was blended with different oils, the very process described in 30:25 and 35.[51] The emphasis in 30:22-38 is on the purification of the sanctuary, but the same spices also had medicinal qualities. Thus they may also have been associated with the healing power of Yahweh (see 15:25-26).

---

51. V. H. Matthews, "Perfumes and Spices," *ABD* 5:226-28.

Builders (31:1-11; 35:30–36:7; 38:21-23)

31:1-11

¹And Yahweh spoke to Moses, saying, ²"See, I have called by name Bezalel son of Uri son of Hur of the tribe of Judah. ³And I have filled him with the spirit of God in wisdom, in understanding, and in knowledge in every kind of work, ⁴to design plans in order to craft in gold, in silver, and in copper, ⁵in the cutting of stone, and in the carving of wood to craft in every kind of work. ⁶And I have given him Oholiab son of Ahisamach of the tribe of Dan. And in the heart of all who are skillful I have given wisdom. They will make everything that I command you: ⁷the tent of meeting, the ark of the testimony, the cover that is on it, all the utensils of the tent, ⁸the table, its utensils, the pure lampstand, all its utensils, the altar of incense, ⁹the altar of burnt offering, all its utensils, the basin, and its stand; ¹⁰the woven garments, the sacred garments of Aaron the priest, the garments of his sons for their service as priests; ¹¹the anointing oil and the fragrant incense for the holy place. They shall do according to everything that I commanded you."

35:30–36:7; 38:21-23

³⁰And Moses said to the Israelites, "See, Yahweh has called by name Bezalel son of Uri son of Hur of the tribe of Judah. ³¹He has filled him with the spirit of God in wisdom, in understanding, in knowledge in every kind of work, ³²to design plans in order to craft in gold, in silver, and in copper, ³³in the cutting of stone and in the carving of wood to craft every kind of work. ³⁴And he has given in his heart to teach, he and Oholiab son of Ahisamach of the tribe of Dan. ³⁵And he has filled them with a wise heart to do all the work of engraving, designing, embroidery in blue, purple, and crimson yarns, and in fine linen, and the work of the weaver. ³⁶:¹Bezalel, Oholiab, and all persons of a wise heart to whom Yahweh has given wisdom, understanding, and knowledge to do all the work in the construction of the sanctuary shall do the work according to everything that Yahweh commanded."

²And Moses called to Bezalel and to Oholiab, and to every person whom Yahweh had given wisdom in his heart. And each lifted up his heart to undertake the work and to do it. ³And they received from Moses all the dedication offering that the Israelites brought for the work of the service of the sanctuary. And they brought to him freewill offerings morning after morning.

⁴All the wise ones who were making all the work of the sanctuary, each according to the task in which he was working, ⁵said to Moses, saying, "The people are bringing more than enough service for the work."

⁶And Moses commanded, and the word was spread throughout the camp, saying, "Let no man or woman make any further work for the dedication offering of the sanctuary."

And the people ceased from bringing. ⁷The work was more than enough for all the work to be completed. . . .

³⁸:²¹And these are the administrative records of the tabernacle, the tabernacle of the testimony, which were recorded by the command of Moses, the work of the Levites by the hand of Ithamar the son of Aaron the priest. ²²And Bezalel the son of Uri son of Hur of the tribe of Judah made all that Yahweh commanded Moses; ²³and with him was Oholiab son of Ahisamach of the tribe of Dan, engraver, designer, and embroiderer in blue, purple, and crimson yarns, and in fine linen.

Notes

31:2 *I have called by name.* Hebrew *qārā'tî běšēm* means to name or to summon. The phrase likely underscores the special status of Bezalel. In 33:17 the Deity states to Moses: "I will also do this thing that you have asked; for you have gained my favor and I know you by name" *(wā'ēdā'ăkā běšēm).* The LXX conveys the favored status of Bezalel by translating the verb in the middle voice, *anakeklēmai ex onomatos,* "I have called out for myself by name."

Bezalel son of Uri son of Hur of the tribe of Judah. J. A. Fager states that the name *běṣal'ēl* may mean "in the shadow (protection) of El (God)."⁵² In 1 Chr 2:19-20 Bezalel is a descendant of Caleb: "When Azubah died, Caleb married Ephrath, who bore him Hur. Hur became the father of Uri, and Uri became the father of

52. J. A. Fager, "Bezalel," *ABD* 1:717; idem, "Uri," *ABD* 6:767.

Bezalel." The relation of this Hur to the Hur who functions as the assistant of Moses (Exod 17:10, 12; 24:14) is not clear.[53]

31:4 *to design plans in order to craft.* Hebrew *laḥšōb maḥăšābōt* is translated in *HALOT* 1:360: "to devise, invent artistic designs."

31:5 *to craft in every kind of work.* See NRSV, "in every kind of craft."

31:6 *Oholiab son of Ahisamach of the tribe of Dan.* The name Oholiab, *'ohŏlî'āb* is limited to the P description of the tabernacle. The name may be a literary metaphor to provide commentary on his role as the father *('āb)* of the tent *('ōhel)*, that is, the one who fashions it. Noth also detects aspects of West Semitic nomenclature, which also raises the possibility of the preservation of a particular individual.[54]

31:10 *the woven garments.* Hebrew *haśśĕrād* may indicate a type of woven fabric. See NJPS "the service vestments," and NRSV "the finely worked vestments." The LXX lacks the phrase.

Commentary

In the introduction I noted that kings were often temple builders in the ancient Near East. King Gudea of Lagash built the temple for the god Ningirsu; and, in ancient Israel, King Solomon built the Jerusalem temple for Yahweh Sabaoth. Gods could also build their own temples. The Song of the Sea states that Yahweh will build his own temple (Exod 15:17). Psalm 147:2 extends the building power of Yahweh from the temple to the city of Jerusalem. The building of a temple is also attributed to specific craftsmen gods in the ancient Near East. Ptah is the craftsman god in Egypt. His home is in Memphis. In the Canaanite mythology the craftsman god is Kothar-wa-Hasis *(ktr-w-ḥss)*, meaning "skillful and clever." His home is also located in Memphis. Kothar-wa-Hasis is able to make the magical clubs, Yagrush ("chaser") and Ayyamir ("expeller"), that defeat the chaos god Yamm for Baal (*CTA* 2.iv.7-11). When Baal desires a temple after his victory over Yamm, he sends for Kothar-wa-Hasis in the city of Memphis to build his home (*CTA* 3.F.18-21; 4.v.103). After seven days of smelting Kothar-wa-Hasis presents Baal with a temple made of gold and silver, to which Baal responds: "I have built my mansion" (*CTA* 4.vi.36). The construction of Baal's temple is accompanied by conquest over the surrounding nations and by the building of an empire over which Baal rules.

The construction of the priestly tabernacle departs from the ancient Near Eastern model. God plans the priestly tabernacle, but does not build it. Moses oversees the architectural plans, but even he does not build it. Instead God endows two humans with divine wisdom to build the divine home on earth. The main builder is Bezalel, the son of Uri and the grandson of Hur.

53. E. A. Knauf, "Hur," *ABD* 3:334.
54. Noth, *Exodus*, 240.

This may be the same Hur who accompanied Aaron on the mountain in the war against the Amalekites (17:8-16) and who governed the people with Aaron when Moses and Joshua received the tablets of stone (24:13-14). He is from the tribe of Judah. Bezalel is divinely inspired, filled with the "spirit of God" *(rûaḥ 'ĕlōhîm)*, a form of charismatic divine power that infuses a person directly. Saul, for example, is possessed by the spirit of God, causing him to prophesy when he is initially anointed king (1 Sam 10:10) and later tormenting him into insanity (1 Sam 16:15, 16, 23).

Bezalel acquires three qualities from his divine inspiration: wisdom *(ḥokmâ)*, understanding *(tĕbûnâ)*, and knowledge *(da'at)*. All are qualities associated with the wisdom school. Yet the most striking parallel to Bezalel is the portrait of the ideal messianic king in Isa 11:2, who will also be from the tribe of Judah, the branch of Jesse. The prophet proclaims: "The spirit of Yahweh *(rûaḥ yhwh)* will rest on him, the spirit of wisdom *(ḥokmâ)* and of understanding *(bînâ)*, the spirit of counsel and of power, the spirit of knowledge *(da'at)* and of the fear of Yahweh." The builder of the tabernacle may not be a king, but he certainly possesses messianic qualities. His assistant is Oholiab the son of Ahisamach from the northern tribe of Dan. He too possesses wisdom *(ḥokmâ;* NIV "skill"). These divinely inspired master craftsmen are responsible for all aspects of the tabernacle cult, the tent of meeting, its furnishings, the vestments, and even the anointing oil and incense.

SABBATH (31:12-17; 35:1-3)

31:12-17

¹²And Yahweh said to Moses, saying, ¹³"You shall speak to the Israelites, saying, 'Indeed, my Sabbath you must observe, for it is a sign between me and you throughout your generations to know that I am Yahweh the one consecrating you. ¹⁴You shall observe the Sabbath, for it is holy to you. The one profaning it will be put to death; for anyone doing work on it, that life will be cut off from among the people. ¹⁵Six days work will be done, but on the seventh day there shall be a Sabbath of complete rest. It is holy to Yahweh. Anyone doing work on the Sabbath day will be put to death.

35:1-3

¹And Moses assembled the entire congregation of the Israelites, and he said to them, "These are the words that Yahweh commanded you to do.

²Six days work will be done, but on the seventh day there shall be a holy Sabbath of complete rest to Yahweh. Anyone doing work on it shall be put to death.

¹⁶The Israelites shall observe the
Sabbath, undertaking the Sabbath
throughout their generations. It is a
perpetual covenant. ¹⁷It is a sign
between me and Israel forever, for in
six days Yahweh made the heaven
and the earth, and on the seventh day
he rested and was refreshed."

³You shall kindle no fire in any of
your dwellings on the Sabbath day."

Notes

31:17 *he rested and was refreshed.* Hebrew *šābat,* "he rested," is translated *epausato* in
the LXX. The second verb, *wayyinnāpaš,* "he was refreshed," is unusual, especially
as a description of the Deity. The Sabbath command in 31:12 attributes the quality
of being refreshed on Sabbath to the resident alien. David is refreshed at the Jordan
River after his flight from Absalom in 2 Sam 16:14. The LXX avoids the description
of the Deity needing to be refreshed from the work of creation by translating,
katepausen, "he left off [the work of creation]."

35:1 *the words that Yahweh commanded.* Hebrew *děbārîm,* "words," could also be
translated "things" (see NRSV). The LXX translates, *hoi logoi.*

35:2 *complete rest.* NRSV translates Hebrew *šabbat šabbātôn* as "solemn rest." The LXX
translates, *sabbata anapausis,* "a making to rest."

Commentary

The Sabbath law structures the P History. It is embedded in the creation of the
world (Gen 1:1–2:3), but lost with the flood. The Sabbath structure returns in the
wilderness (Exodus 16) and emerges as a law at Mount Sinai (see the commentary on 20:8-11). The P author returns to the Sabbath law when he concludes the
revelation of the tabernacle; here he further explores the power of the law in the
life of the Israelites. Yahweh states to Moses that the Sabbath is holy and that it is
a sign that will reveal to the Israelites that God is also sanctifying them when
they observe it as a day of rest. Thus the Sabbath brings the knowledge of God to
the Israelites. God also intensifies the consequences of disobedience. Failure to
observe Sabbath rest during the gift of manna resulted in spoiled food. The
Decalogue stated only the positive demand that the Israelites observe the Sabbath to reclaim the rhythm of creation. The Sabbath command following the
construction of the tabernacle is now described as an "eternal covenant," carrying the death penalty to anyone who breaks the law. Profaning the Sabbath is
now a capital offense against the sanctuary. Those who are guilty must die.

There may also be an allusion to ancient Near Eastern mythology in the
sequence of temple building and rest. V. Hurowitz notes that the relation of tem-

ple building and divine rest is a common motif in ancient Near Eastern religion. Gods rest after they construct their temples.[1] Nabonidus prays to Shamash, calling Ebabaar the "residence of your rest." Also Enlil and Ea "dwell on a restful dais in a pure dwelling." B. Batto extends the metaphor by noting that the sleeping God is also part of the mythology of divine rest.[2] The relationship of temple building and rest may also have influenced the P author, although the focus shifts from the rest of God to that of the people. The Israelites are commanded to build Yahweh's sanctuary, and they are also required to rest at its completion.

TABLETS (31:18; 34:29)

31:18

[18] And he gave to Moses when he finished speaking to him **on Mount Sinai the two tablets of testimony,** the tablets of stone written with the finger of God.

34:29

[29] **And Moses descended from Mount Sinai, and the two tablets of testimony were in the hand of Moses** when he descended from the mountain. But Moses did not know that the skin of his face shone in his speaking with him.

Notes

31:18 *when he finished.* The LXX translates Hebrew *kĕkallōtô* as *katepausen,* the same word used in the previous verse to describe God at the conclusion of creation.

Commentary

Exodus 31:18 is a combination of literature from the Non-P and P Histories. The version of 31:18 in the Non-P History states: "And he [God] gave to Moses when he finished speaking to him the tablets of stone written with the finger of God." This verse follows immediately from 24:12-15a, 18b, when God commanded Moses to ascend the mountain to receive the tablets of stone. The repetition of the same term, "tablets of stone," indicates the continuation of the Non-P History. The forty-day period of writing is complete and provides a transition to the story of the golden calf in chap. 32, when Moses destroys the tablets of stone upon descending the mountain. The completion of the tablets of stone in 31:18 heightens the faithlessness of the Israelites in building the golden calf. Their request for the idol is at the very moment when Moses receives the tablets of stone and is about to return to the camp.

The P History changes the name of the tablets and the location of their

---

1. Hurowitz, *I Have Built,* 330-31.
2. B. F. Batto, "The Sleeping God: An Ancient Near Eastern Motif of Divine Sovereignty," *Bib* 68 (1987): 153-77.

revelation by adding the middle phrase of the verse: "on Mount Sinai the two tablets of testimony." Mount Sinai is the mountain of revelation in the P History (see the introduction to 19:1–24:11, "Authors: P History"), and the "two tablets of testimony" *(šĕnê lūḥōt hā῾ēdūt)* is the name for the tablets in the P History. F. M. Cross notes that ῾*ēdūt* is frequently the designation of cultic law in the P literature (25:16, 21, 22; 26:33, 34; 27:21; 30:6, 36), and it is also used to describe the worshiping congregation in the tabernacle (i.e., Num 1:2-3).[3] The result of the addition is an awkward sentence, in which reference to the tablets is repeated with different words.

The identification of the tablets as "the two tablets of testimony" is important to the P History. It changes the content of the revelation from the Decalogue in the Non-P History (the two tablets of stone) to the revelation of the tabernacle and its cult in Exod 25:1–31:17 (the two tablets of testimony). The P author will continue to identify the content of the tablets as the tabernacle and its cult throughout the final episode. When Moses descends from the mountain in 32:15 the tablets will once again be identified as "the tablets of testimony." When God writes new tablets for Moses in 34:27-29, the P author again adds the phrase, "tablets of testimony."

The result of the distinct names for the tablets is that two interpretations of law are interwoven in 24:12–40:38 without being harmonized, the "tablets of stone" in the Non-P History and the "tablets of testimony" in the P History. Thus Moses receives both the Decalogue of the Non-P History and the tabernacle cult of the P History. The content of the two systems of law is different. But both systems of law are equally threatened by the cult of the golden calf, and both systems of law are also restored through covenant renewal.[4]

GOLDEN CALF (32:1-35)

[32:1] *And when the people saw that Moses delayed to descend from the mountain, the people assembled against Aaron. And the people said to Aaron, "Arise, make for us gods who will go before us, because this Moses, the man who brought us up from the land of Egypt, we do not know what has happened to him."*

[2] *And Aaron said to them, "Take off the gold rings that are on the ears of your wives, your sons, and your daughters, and bring them to me."*

[3] *And all the people took off the gold rings that were on their ears, and they brought them to him.*

[4] *And he took from their hands and he fashioned it with a graving tool. And he made it into a molten calf.*

3. Cross, *Canaanite Myth and Hebrew Epic*, 313.
4. See Dozeman, *God on the Mountain*, 168-73.

And they said, "These are your gods, Israel, who brought you from the land of Egypt."

⁵ And Aaron saw, and he built an altar before it. And Aaron called and said, "A festival to Yahweh tomorrow."

⁶ And they rose early the next day and they sacrificed whole burnt offerings, and they brought near well-being offerings. And the people sat to eat and to drink. And they rose to revel.

⁷ And Yahweh spoke to Moses, "Go and descend, for your people whom you brought up from the land of Egypt are corrupted. ⁸ They have turned aside quickly from the way that I commanded them. They have made for themselves a molten calf, and they have bowed down to it and sacrificed to it. And they have said, 'These are your gods, Israel, who brought you up from the land of Egypt.'" ⁹ And Yahweh said to Moses, "I have seen this people. And indeed a people of stiff neck it is. ¹⁰ And now let me alone that my anger may burn hot against them, so that I consume them. And I will make you into a great nation."

¹¹ And Moses made entreaty before the face of Yahweh his God. And he said,

"Why, Yahweh, does your anger burn hot against your people whom you brought out of the land of Egypt with great power and with a strong hand? ¹² Why should the Egyptians say, 'For evil he brought them out to kill them in the mountains and to exterminate them from the face of the ground.' Turn from your hot anger and repent of the evil against your people. ¹³ Remember Abraham, Isaac, and Israel your servants, to whom you swore by yourself and you spoke to them, 'I will increase your offspring like the stars of heaven, and all this land of which I said that I would give to your seed, they will inherit forever.'"

¹⁴ And Yahweh repented of the evil that he spoke to do to his people.

¹⁵ And Moses turned and he descended from the mountain, **and the two tablets of testimony were in his hand,** the tablets written on their two sides. On the one side and on the other they were written. ¹⁶ And the tablets were the work of God. The writing was the writing of God, engraved on the tablets.

¹⁷ And Joshua heard the voice of the people as a shout, and he said to Moses, "There is a sound of war in the camp." ¹⁸ But he said,

"It is not the sound of the cry of victory;
nor the sound of the cry of defeat;
the sound of singing I am hearing."

¹⁹ And when Moses drew near to the camp and he saw the calf and the dancing, Moses' anger became hot and he threw the tablets from his hand and he shattered them at the base of the mountain. ²⁰ And he took the calf that they made, and he burned it in fire, he ground it to powder, he scattered it on the water, and he made the Israelites drink it.

²¹ Moses said to Aaron, "What did this people do to you that you brought on it a great sin?"

²² And Aaron said to Moses, "Let not the anger of my lord be hot. You know the people, that it is bent on evil. ²³ They said to me, 'Make for us gods, who will go before us because this Moses, the man who brought us up from the land of Egypt, we do not know what happened to him.' ²⁴ And I said to them, 'Whoever has gold must take it off and give to me.' And I threw it in the fire, and this calf came out."

²⁵ And Moses saw the people, that it was out of control, for Aaron let them out of control to the derision of those who would rise against them. ²⁶ And Moses stood at the gate of the camp and he said, "Whoever is for Yahweh come to me." And all the Levites gathered to him. ²⁷ And he said to them, "Thus said Yahweh the God of Israel, 'Each place his sword on his side. Go back and forth from gate to gate in the camp and kill each his brother, his neighbor, and his kin.'" ²⁸ And the Levites did according to the word of Moses, and about three thousand of the people fell on that day. ²⁹ And Moses said, "Your hands are filled today for Yahweh — each at the cost of his son and his brother — who gives you today a blessing."

³⁰ And on the next day Moses said to the people, "You have sinned a great sin. And now I will ascend to Yahweh. Perhaps I can atone for your sin."

³¹ And Moses returned to Yahweh and he said, "Alas, this people has sinned a great sin. They have made for themselves gods of gold. ³² And now, if you will, lift up their sin, but if not, please blot me from your book in which you write."

³³ And Yahweh said to Moses, "Whoever sinned against me I will blot out from my book. ³⁴ And now go and lead the people where I spoke to you. Indeed, my Messenger will go before you. And on the day of my visitation, I will visit on them their sin."

³⁵ And Yahweh sent a plague on the people because they made the calf, which Aaron made.

Notes

32:1 *And when the people saw.* Hebrew *rā'â* provides the point of view throughout the narrative: the perception of the people in v. 1, Aaron in v. 5, the Deity in v. 9, and Moses in v. 19. The LXX translates the perception of the people (v. 1) and Aaron (v. 5) with *idōn*. The perception of the Deity (v. 9) and that of Moses (v. 19) are absent from the LXX.

Moses delayed. Hebrew *bōšēš* may derive from the root *bwš*, "be put to shame," or a distinct root with the meaning "to delay." The same meaning of the word likely occurs in Judg 5:28: "Out of the window she peered, the mother of Sisera gazed through the lattice: 'Why is his chariot so long in coming *(bōšēš)*? Why tarry the hoof beats of his chariots?'" The LXX translates, *kechroniken,* "to delay."

the people assembled against. The Hebrew phrase *qhl 'al* indicates a confrontation (see also Num 16:3).

Arise, make for us gods who will go before us. Hebrew *'ĕlōhîm* could be interpreted as singular or plural. But the verb *yēlĕkû*, "will go," in the plural suggests that the plural form of the noun is intended, creating a problem of meaning in the context of Exodus 32. The LXX, *poiēson hēmin theous hoi proporeusontai hēmōn*, follows the MT. The reference to the "gods" repeats in 32:4, 8, 23. The plural form is required in each case from the larger literary context. Verse 23 is the only text that combines a plural *(yēlĕkû)* and a singular *(he'ĕlānû)* verb in referring to the *'ĕlōhîm*. Cf. Houtman, who reads all the references to *'ĕlōhîm* in the singular, thus changing every verb.[1]

32:2-3 *bring them. . . . they brought them.* The MT lacks the object "them."

32:4 *and he fashioned it with a graving tool.* Hebrew *wayyāṣar 'ōtô baḥereṭ* is unclear. The verb *wayyāṣar* may derive from *ṣārar*, "to tie up, press"; from *ṣûr*, "to confine, bind"; or from *yāṣar*, "to form, shape." Hebrew *yāṣar* is used to describe the making of an idol in Isa 44:9. The object *'ōtô* most likely refers to the golden rings in v. 3, even though the form is in the singular and the golden rings are in the plural. The word *ḥereṭ* indicates a graving tool in Isa 8:1. Another proposal is the word *ḥārîṭ*, meaning "pouch, bag," which in the present context suggests a container or mold for making the golden calf. My translation follows the LXX, *eplasen auta en tē graphidi*, "and he formed them [plural] with a graving tool."

a molten calf. Hebrew *'ēgel massēkâ* is interpreted in two distinct ways. *Massēkâ* can be derived from *nāsak*, "to cast," resulting in the translation "molten calf." Dohmen has argued that the word describes instead a process of hammering, from the root *nsk*; hence what is described is the plating of an object in gold.[2] The LXX translates, *moschon chōneuton*, "molten calf."

And they said. The MT *wayyō'mĕrû* is in the plural, indicating that Aaron and the Israelites are speaking, or perhaps only the Israelites. The LXX changes the phrase to the singular, *eipen*, indicating that Aaron is the speaker.

32:6 *to revel.* Hebrew *ṣāḥaq* has a range of meanings. It can be translated "to laugh," especially in the Qal form of the verb (e.g., Prov 1:26; 29:9; Job 5:22; 30:1). Ugaritic parallels support this meaning (e.g., *CTA* 3.B.25; 6.ii.28-37). The word also has sexual meaning, especially in the Piel form of the verb (Gen 19:14; 21:9; 26:8; 39:14, 17; Judg 16:25). For example, when Isaac's action with Rebekah is described with the Piel of *ṣāḥaq*, Abimelech's response is to recognize that they are married, even though Isaac has sought to deceive him in stating that they are not married. The text is not explicit, but something sexual is implied in the action. The same is true when Sarah sees Ishmael "playing" (Gen 21:9); she fears the loss of inheritance, suggesting again sexual activity. A sexual meaning is also likely in Exod 32:6. The sexual orgy of the Israelites on the altar before the golden calf should likely be read in conjunction with the law against the altar in 20:22-26. Both are Non-P texts. The actions of the

---

1. Houtman, *Exodus*, 3:631-32.
2. Dohmen, *Exodus 19-40*, 291.

Israelites in reveling at the altar of the golden calf have likely exposed (uncovered) their nakedness (20:26), an action explicitly forbidden by the Deity, which means, according to J. S. Bergsma and S. W. Hahn, "sexual intercourse."[3]

32:7 *are corrupted.* Hebrew *šiḥēt* in the Niphal describes the spoiled state of something such as the land of Egypt after the invasion of the flies (8:24 [MT 20]). The Hiphil can describe the act of spoiling, hence the meaning "to destroy" (e.g., Gen 6:13; and the "destroyer" in Exod 12:13, 23). The Piel is more difficult to translate, since it can describe the act of destroying or the state of being spoiled. Either meaning fits the context of 32:7. The translation emphasizes the present state of the people after having built and worshiped the golden calf. The LXX emphasizes more the action of the people, employing *ēnomēsen*, "to act lawlessly."

32:9-10 *And Yahweh said to Moses, "I have seen this people. And indeed a people of stiff neck it is. And now let me alone that my anger may burn hot against them, so that I consume them."* The syntax of the divine speech is reminiscent of the divine address to Moses in 3:6-10. It begins with a statement of revelation ("I have seen") and progresses to a commission introduced by *wĕʿattâ* ("And now let me alone"). The syntax underscores that Moses disobeys the divine commission in his act of intercession (vv. 11-13).

And indeed a people of stiff neck it is. The Hebrew makes the statement in the singular, *hûʾ,* "it," referring to people (*ʿām*). The NRSV translates in the plural, "how stiff-necked they are." Verse 9 is absent from the LXX.

let me alone. Hebrew *hannîḥâ,* the Hiphil of the verb "to rest," is translated in the LXX *eason me,* "permit me."

And I will make you into a great nation. The MT repeats the promise to Abram from Gen 12:2a. The Sam adds a sentence emphasizing the divine anger against Aaron and Moses' intercessory prayer for Aaron, *wbʾhrn htʾnp yhwh mʾd lhšmydw wytpll mšh bʿd ʾhrn,* "Yahweh was angry enough with Aaron to destroy him. And Moses prayed for Aaron." The addition is quite close to Deut 9:20.

32:11 *made entreaty.* Hebrew *ḥālâ* is also translated "to implore" (see NRSV, NJPS). The LXX translates, *edeēthē,* "he asked, begged, prayed." K. R. Suomala notes that the idiom, "to make entreaty, implore," is difficult to capture in English, yet it is essential in understanding the relationship between Yahweh and Moses throughout his intercessory dialogues. "Moses' entire discourse is colored by the deference implied in this phrase."[4]

32:11-12 *Why, Yahweh, . . . Why should.* Hebrew *lam(m)â,* "why," is used by Moses to intercede for the Israelites. "Of very frequent occurrence also are questions introduced by לָמָה, which really contain an affirmation and are used to state the reason for a request or warning" (GKC §150c).

and with a strong hand. The MT *ûbĕyād ḥăzāqâ* is changed in the Sam to *wbzrwʿ nṭwyh,* "an outstretched arm."

---

3. Bergsma and Hahn, "Noah's Nakedness," 25-40, esp. 37-39.

4. K. R. Suomala, *Moses and God in Dialogue: Exodus 32–34 in Postbiblical Literature* (Studies in Biblical Literature 61; New York: Peter Lang, 2004), 23.

to exterminate them. Hebrew *ûlĕkallōtām* is also translated "to consume them" (NRSV) and "to annihilate them" (NJPS).

repent. Hebrew *wĕhinnāḥēm* implies a change in the divine character. The LXX transforms the imagery: *hileōs genou epi tē kakia tou laou sou,* "be merciful toward the evil of your people."

32:13 *remember Abraham, Isaac, and Israel.* The three patriarchs are normally referred to as Abraham, Isaac, and Jacob, as is the case in the Sam and LXX.

they will inherit forever. The Sam adds the object "it" on the verb, *wnḥlwh,* as compared to the MT *wĕnāḥălû.*

32:17 *a shout.* Hebrew *bĕrē'ōh* derives from *rēa',* "shouting, cheering." The verb *rû'* means "to shout, raise an alarm." The term can be connected with war (Josh 6:5, 10, etc.) or simply a cultic festival (Pss 47:1; 95:1).

32:18 *it is not the sound of the cry of victory; nor the sound of the cry of defeat; the sound of singing I am hearing.* There are several difficulties in translating the poem. The first is the meaing of *'ānâ.* The first and second lines employ the Qal infinitive construct *'ănôt,* and the third line employs the Piel *('annôt).* Interpreters debate whether the root meaning is "to answer" *('ānâ* I) or "to sing" *('ānâ* II).[5] A second problem is the meaning of the Piel form of *'ānâ* in the third line. F. I. Andersen interprets *'annôt* "as a technical cult term derived from *'ny* 'answer.'" In this case it may describe a person who directs antiphonal singing in worship, which may be reflected in the Ugaritic literature.[6] R. Edelmann and A. Deem move in a different direction, suggesting that *'annôt* is an instance of paronomasia, referring to the Canaanite goddess Anat.[7] In this interpretation, the third line would be translated: "The voice of Anat I am hearing." This translation is not a description of what Moses hears in the camp, but a commentary on the role that he is about to take on in defending Yahweh against the golden calf, when his destruction of the golden calf in v. 20 parallels Anat's destruction of Mot in the Ugaritic mythology. The text very likely carries both meanings.

32:19 *from his hand.* The MT *mîyādāw* is singular, "from his hand." The LXX is plural.

32:22 *You know the people, that it is bent on evil.* Hebrew *'attâ yāda'tā 'et-hā'ām kî bĕrā' hû'* is lit. "you, you know the people that it is in evil." The LXX interprets the Hebrew: *sy gar oidas to hormēma tou laou toutou,* "for you know the evil inclination of this people." For the last clause the Sam has *ky prw' hw',* "because it is out of control."

32:25 *it was out of control.* Hebrew *pārua'* means "to let loose." The passive form likely indicates a situation out of control. The LXX translates, *dieskedastai,* "was dispersed."

---

5. For the first see F. I. Andersen, "A Lexicographical Note on Exodus XXXII 18," *VT* 16 (1966): 108-12. For the second see Houtman, *Exodus,* 1:387-88; idem, *Exodus,* 3:654-56.

6. Andersen, "Lexicographical Note"; similarly J. Makujina, "Additional Considerations for Determining the Meaning of *'Ănôt* and *'Annôt* in Exod XXXII 18," *VT* 55 (2005): 39-46.

7. R. Edelmann, "Exodus 32:18: קוֹל עַנּוֹת אָנֹכִי שֹׁמֵעַ," *JTS* 1 (1950): 56; A. Deem, "The Goddess Anath and Some Biblical Cruces," *JSS* 23 (1978): 25-30; R. N. Whybray, "'annôt in Exodus 32:18," *VT* 17 (1967): 122.

to the derision of those who would rise against them. The meaning of Hebrew *lĕšimṣâ* is uncertain in this context; it usually means "to whisper." My translation follows the LXX *epicharma,* "laughingstock." Hebrew *bĕqāmêhem,* "who would rise against them," can also be translated "their enemies" (NRSV).

32:27 *Go back and forth.* Hebrew *ʿibrû wāšûbû* is lit. "cross through and return."

his brother, his neighbor, and his kin. The three different relationships are *ʾāḥ,* "brother"; *rēaʿ,* "neighbor, friend, companion"; and *qārōb,* "one who is near in relationship, kin." Cf. NRSV: "your brother, your friend, and your neighbor."

32:29 *Your hands are filled.* The phrase "to fill the hands" indicates ordination. See 28:41.

32:30 *Perhaps I can atone for your sin.* Hebrew *ʾûlay,* "perhaps," followed by the cohortative, *ʾăkappĕrâ,* "I can atone," expresses the wish or hope of the speaker. The LXX is more definite in its translation, *hina exilasōmai peri tēs hamartias hymōn,* "so that I can make atonement for your sin."

32:31 *Alas, this people has sinned a great sin.* The exclamation *ʾānnāʾ* in this verse (and *nāʾ* in v. 32) underscores the entreaty of Moses. Suomala notes only five other occurrences of this pattern in the MT, four in addresses to the Deity (Neh 1:5-6, 11; Ps 118:25; Dan 9:4, 16) and once in the address of the brothers to Joseph (Gen 50:17).[8]

32:32 *And now, if you will, lift up their sin, but if not.* Hebrew *nāśāʾ,* "to lift up," in this context means "to forgive." The MT, however, is an ellipsis, which is completed in the Sam with the addition of *śʾ:* "If you will lift up their sin, then lift it up." The LXX is similar to the Sam.

32:34 *lead the people where I spoke to you.* For Hebrew *ʾăšer,* "where," the LXX has, *eis ton topon hon,* "to the place of which."

on the day of my visitation, I will visit on them their sin. Hebrew *pāqad,* "to visit," is also translated "punish" (NRSV) and "account" (NJPS). The LXX departs from the repetition in the Hebrew: *an hēmera episkeptōmai epaxō ep' autous tēn hamartian autōn,* "on the day I make a visitation I will bring their sin on them."

32:35 *And Yahweh sent a plague on the people because they made the calf, which Aaron made.* The Hebrew is unclear. It states the construction of the calf twice: once by the people and once by Aaron. Childs suggests that the last phrase, "which Aaron made," may be an addition to the text.[9]

Commentary

Central Themes

The story of the golden calf is "the nearest equivalent to the concept of original sin" in postbiblical Jewish literature, according to M. Aberbach and L. Smolar.[10]

---

8. Suomala, *Moses and God,* 41 n. 39.

9. Childs, *Exodus,* 557.

10. M. Aberbach and L. Smolar, "The Golden Calf Episode in Postbiblical Literature," *HUCA* 39 (1968): 91-116; idem, "Aaron, Jeroboam, and the Golden Calves," *JBL* 86 (1967): 129-40.

The placement of the event in Exodus and its role throughout the Hebrew Bible support this conclusion. The construction of the golden calf in Exodus 32 occurs at the very moment when God is handing the tablets of the law to Moses and establishing the covenant with the people. The golden calf signifies the Israelites' rejection of covenant, and it prompts the divine desire to destroy the nation. Yahweh states to Moses: "Now leave me alone so that my anger may burn against them and that I may destroy them." Deuteronomy 9 returns to the topic, when Moses recounts the event to the second generation of Israelites. He exhorts the people never to forget the sin of the calf, where "at Horeb [the people] aroused Yahweh's wrath so that he was angry enough to destroy [them]." The psalmist echoes the teaching of Moses, also stating: "At Horeb they made a calf . . . and exchanged their glory for an image of a bull, which eats grass" (Ps 106:19-20).

The extreme nature of the sin of the golden calf could not be clearer in Exodus 32. Yahweh is so angry with the Israelites that he is even willing to begin the story of salvation anew with Moses: "I will make you into a great nation." It is more difficult, however, to interpret the content of the sin. The golden calf represents the sin of idolatry, which, according to rabbinic and NT interpretation, is a form of human greed — the desire to possess and to control God.[11] But the human desire to control God is so complex and multifaceted that the identification of the golden calf as idolatry merely adds to the uncertainty of the "original sin."

The Israelites and Aaron provide an immediate interpretation of the golden calf at the moment of its construction: "These *('ēlleh)* are your gods, O Israel, who brought you up out of Egypt" (32:4). Their statement indicates the original sin to be the equation of the calf with "gods." The proclamation reappears in the Former Prophets (Joshua–2 Kings); 1 Kings 12 recounts the emergence of the monarchy in the northern kingdom under Jeroboam. Following the pattern of kings as temple builders, the rule of Jeroboam is accompanied by the construction of two cult sites, one in Dan and another in Bethel (12:26-32). The temple complexes include the institution of a non-Levitical priesthood, a liturgical calendar and festival, cultic objects, and altars (12:31-32). The central cultic object at each site is a golden calf, which Jeroboam interprets for the northern Israelites: "Here are your gods, O Israel, who brought you up out of Egypt" (12:28), a near repetition of the words of Aaron and the people in Exod 32:4. In the present structure of the Hebrew Bible, the proclamation of

11. The interpretation of idolatry as a form of greed is stated with reference to Balaam in *m. 'Abot* 5:18 and in 2 Pet 2:15. For further discussion see J. R. Baskin, *Pharaoh's Counselors: Job, Jethro, and Balaam in Rabbinic and Patristic Tradition* (BJS 47; Chico, Calif.: Scholars Press, 1983); M. S. Moore, *The Balaam Traditions: Their Character and Development* (SBLDS 113; Atlanta: Scholars Press, 1990).

Jeroboam is an inner-biblical quotation, relating the golden calf in the wilderness with the cultic sites in Dan and Bethel. Thus Jeroboam is presented as repeating the original sin of the golden calf.

But a closer look at the context indicates that the inner-biblical quotation moves in the other direction: the construction of the golden calf in the wilderness is meant to be an interpretation of the story of Jeroboam. His statement, "Here are your gods, O Israel, who brought you up out of Egypt," is written in the plural, "gods," because there are two golden calves, one in Dan and another in Bethel. The statement fits the narrative context of 1 Kings 12. But the proclamation by Aaron and the Israelites, which also refers to the golden calf in the plural, "these (*'ēlleh*) are your gods," does not conform to the narrative context of Exodus 32, where there is only one calf. The inner-biblical quotation moves from Jeroboam to the wilderness community, and it indicates how crucial the rise of the northern monarchy is for interpreting the "original sin" of the golden calf in the Non-P History. It is so important that the inner-biblical quotation takes precedence over narrative logic in Exodus 32. This fact did not escape the eye of the author of Nehemiah, who corrects the grammar so that Ezra prays: "Therefore you [God] did not desert them even when they cast for themselves an image of a calf and said, 'This (*zeh*) is your god, who brought you up out of Egypt'" (Neh 9:17-18). The Non-P historian, unlike the author of Nehemiah, is willing to sacrifice grammar and narrative context to insure that monarchy looms in the background of any interpretation of the golden calf in Exodus 32. As a result, an interpretation of the original sin of the Israelites requires an interpretation of the two golden calves in the Deuteronomistic History.

The golden calves are a religious and political metaphor in the Deuteronomistic History. They represent the apostasy of Jeroboam I (1 Kgs 12:26-32), and, indeed, of all monarchs — even reforming kings like Jehu, who destroyed Baal worship, but continued "the worship of the golden calves at Bethel and Dan" (2 Kgs 10:29). The golden calves are the reason for the destruction of the northern kingdom (2 Kgs 17:7-23). It fell because "they forsook all the commands of Yahweh their God and made for themselves two idols cast in the shape of calves" (2 Kgs 17:16). The two calves are also at the center of a range of forbidden worship practices in the Deuteronomistic History, including the Asherah, astrology, child sacrifice, sorcery, and high places. The prophet Hosea echoes the same criticism of the north (Hos 8:5-6; 13:2), providing a glimpse into the cultic practices of the northern kingdom. Hosea proclaims the sin of Ephraim with the words: "People are kissing the calves!" The prophet also provides the divine judgment: "Your calf is rejected, O Samaria." In the Deuteronomistic History the golden calves and the accompanying cultic practices are not limited to a critique of the cultic practices of the north. The calves become a metaphor for rejecting Yahweh, and the criticism of the calves is also extended to the south. Judah too "followed the practices Israel had introduced." As a result, Yahweh "rejected all the people of Israel; he afflicted them and gave them into the hands of plunderers, until he thrust them from his presence" (2 Kgs 17:19-20). Van Seters is certainly correct when he concludes: "The Jeroboam apostasy has become a model for the whole people and for their ultimate fate, even of Judah."[12]

The Former Prophets provides a backdrop for interpreting the idolatry of the golden calf in Exodus 32 as a political and religious allegory about the inherent conflict between Yahweh and kings. The inner-biblical quotation by Aaron (and the Israelites) of Jeroboam signals that on one level the golden calf in the wilderness is the taproot, which will inevitably lead to the political idolatry associated with monarchy in the promised land. The content of the idolatry is worshiping the power of the king over Yahweh. On another level the Non-P historian elaborates on the nature of idolatry as any manufactured icon, thus reinforcing the aniconic cultic theology of the Name (see the commentary on 19:1–24:11). Both the Decalogue and the Book of the Covenant introduce a rigid prohibition against any representation of the Deity, or, for that matter, any other icons.

Authors

The composition of Exodus 32 has been extensively researched in the modern period. Two literary problems are central in identifying the author(s) of the story of the calf. The first is the unity of chap. 32, including the larger composition of chaps. 32–34. The motif of the tablets and the thematic structure of sin and forgiveness indicate that chaps. 32–34 have been fashioned into an overarching story. But the identification of the author is hindered by dislocations in the flow of events, suggesting to many a composite text of several authors. The second problem is the relationship between Exodus 32, Deut 9:7-10:11, and 1 Kgs 12:26-32. The three stories are clearly related, even sharing specific motifs. Yet the inner-biblical interpretation of Exodus 32 has tended to focus individually on either Deut 9:7-10:11 or 1 Kgs 12:26-32; only rarely are all three texts read together.[13]

The inseparable nature of the two literary problems of Exodus 32 provides the point of departure for identifying the author. Traditionally the history

---

12. Van Seters, *Life of Moses*, 300.

13. For a recent review of the literary problems in Exodus 32–34 and a summary of the history of interpretation see K. Schmid, "Israel am Sinai: Etappen der Forschungsgeschichte zu Ex 32–34 in seinen Kontexten," in *Gottes Volk am Sinai: Untersuchungen zu Ex 32–34 und Dtn 9-10* (ed. M. Köckert and E. Blum; VWGT 18; Gütersloh: Chr. Kaiser, 2001), 9-39.

of composition of Exodus 32 has preceded the inner-biblical interpretation of the three stories of the calves, yielding an early version of Exodus 32 as the parent text for Deut 9:7–10:11 and 1 Kgs 12:26-32.[14] Van Seters has questioned the traditional literary relationship between Exodus 32, Deuteronomy 9–10, and 1 Kgs 12:26-32, suggesting instead that Exodus 32 represents the latest version of the story of the golden calf. An interpretation of the three stories in their present form lends support to his conclusion.[15] The identification of the author of Exodus 32 will begin with a comparison of the stories of the calf in 1 Kings 12 and Deuteronomy 9–10.

1 Kgs 12:26-32 and Deut 9:7–10:11   First Kings 12 narrates the rise of Jeroboam as king of the northern kingdom. Verses 1-20 describe the selection of Jeroboam to rule the northern kingdom. Verses 25-32 recount the initial building projects of Jeroboam, including cities (v. 25) and new cultic centers (vv. 26-32).[16] Verse 33 provides a transition to the condemnation of the cultic practice of Jeroboam by the man of God in 1 Kings 13. 1 Kings 12:25-32 likely includes source material, such as the notice that Jeroboam built Shechem and Penuel (v. 25).[17] The reference to the calves may reflect the cultic practice of the northern kingdom (v. 28), since it corresponds to the prophet Hosea's criticism of the "calf of Samaria" (Hos 8:5-6). The prophet's reference to Samaria, rather than Bethel or Dan, however, also raises questions about the tradition-historical background of the reference to these cultic sites (1 Kgs 12:29), suggesting to

14. See the review of interpretation by J. Hahn, *Das "Goldene Kalb": Die Jahwe-Verehrung bei Stierbildern in Geschichte Israels* (2nd ed.; EHS 154; Frankfurt: Bern, 1987).

15. Van Seters, *Life of Moses*, 290-318.

16. G. N. Knoppers (*Two Nations Under God: The Deuteronomistic History of Solomon and the Dual Monarchies* [2 vols.; HSM 52; Atlanta: Scholars Press, 1993], 2:13-14) summarizes the following tensions in the chapter, which suggest a history of composition: 1 Kgs 12:1-20 is pro-Jeroboam, while vv. 26-33 are critical of him; 1 Kgs 12:1-20 is anti-Judah, while vv. 21-24 are pro-Judah. The literary tensions prompted Wellhausen (*Composition*, 279-80) to separate the chapter into three parts: vv. 1-24 (of which vv. 21-24 were a late addition), vv. 25-31, and vv. 32-33 (as part of 1 Kings 13). E. Würthwein (*Das Erste Buch der Könige, Kapitel 1–16* (ATD 11/1; Göttingen: Vandenhoeck & Ruprecht, 1977], 150) represents a more complex history of composition: (1) vv. 2, 20a, 25 are an annalistic report about Jeroboam; (2) vv. 1, 2b-19* are a narrative about Rehoboam; (3) vv. 21-24 are a legend in the style of the Chronicler; (4) vv. 26-30 are a criticism of Jeroboam's cultic practices from the perspective of the Jerusalem temple; and (5) vv. 31-33 are a late addition about the problem of Jeroboam's cultic practices. For additional interpretation see H. D. Hoffmann, *Reform und Reformen: Untersuchungen zu einem Grundthema der deuteronomistischen Geschichteschreibung* (ATANT 66; Zurich: Theologischer Verlag, 1980), 64-69; Van Seters, *Life of Moses*, 296; S. L. McKenzie, *The Trouble with Kings: The Composition of the Book of Kings in the Deuteronomistic History* (VTSup 42; Leiden: Brill, 1991), 51.

17. See, e.g., M. Noth, *Könige* (2nd ed.; BKAT IX/1; Neukirchen-Vluyn: Neukirchener Verlag, 1983), 280-81.

H. D. Hoffmann that the entire episode is a historical fiction.[18] What is clear is that in its present form the story provides the springboard for the critique of the northern monarchy in the Deuteronomistic History.

First Kings 12:26-32 recounts Jeroboam's construction of the cult of the golden calves at Bethel and Dan and the worship practices associated with these sites. The story begins with a problem (vv. 26-27), the threat to Jeroboam of the cult of Yahweh in Jerusalem. The literary style of this section is unusual; it provides psychological insight into the motives of Jeroboam, which underscores his self-serving intention. The Deuteronomist has Jeroboam acknowledge that Yahweh is worshiped in Jerusalem: "If this people continues to go up to offer sacrifices in the house of Yahweh in Jerusalem. . . ." Yet he fears that the worship of Yahweh in Jerusalem will threaten his power and even his life: "The heart of this people will turn . . . they will kill me and return to King Rehoboam of Judah."[19] The problem is solved in vv. 28-30 with the construction of the two calves along with their cultic sites at Bethel and Dan. The resolution is noted through the progression from private reflection in vv. 26-27 to the public declaration in vv. 28-30. The progression moves from Jeroboam's personal fear about the worship of Yahweh in Jerusalem to the public proclamation about "gods" in Bethel and Dan: "These are your gods, O Israel, who brought you up out of the land of Egypt" (v. 28). Immediately after Jeroboam's speech, the narrator evaluates the two calves as "sin" (v. 30).

The proclamation of Jeroboam about the golden calves is the central theme in 1 Kgs 12:26-32. All the additional motifs in the story relate to the cult of the calves, as Hoffmann has demonstrated through the study of the literary structure.[20] The motifs include the prominent role of the king in the cult, the foreign worship practices associated with the cultic sites, the creation of a new festival, and the exclusion of the Levites in the formation of the cultic system. In the process, Jeroboam violates a range of laws from Deuteronomy, including the making of iconic images (chap. 5), the demand for a single cultic location (12:5), the worship of one God (6:4), the exclusive ordination of the Levitical priesthood (18:1-8), and the proper worship calendar (16:15).[21]

The story lacks the dynamic character of sin and forgiveness. The golden calves are presented as a past event of "sin," whose construction seals the destiny of the northern kingdom: "This matter became sin to the house of Jeroboam, so as to cut it off and to destroy it from the face of the earth" (1 Kgs 13:34).

18. It may be possible to read the reference to Beth-aven in Hos 10:5 as Bethel. See Hoffmann, *Reform und Reformen*, 73.

19. See Würthwein, *Könige*, 162.

20. Hoffmann, *Reform und Reformen*, 63-70; see also Knoppers, *Two Nations under God*, 2:33-34.

21. See Hahn, *Goldene Kalb*, 304.

The story serves as the pivotal judgment on the northern kingdom in the Deuteronomistic History.[22] The criticism of Jeroboam is introduced immediately in the following story about the man of God who predicts the destruction of the altar (1 Kings 13), which is fulfilled in the reform of Josiah (2 Kings 23). Between these stories, the criticism of Jeroboam and his "sin" are repeatedly applied to successive monarchs in the north, until the kingdom is destroyed.[23]

Modern interpreters debate the central theme, the literary structure, and the history of composition of Deut 9:7–10:11. The point of departure for interpretation has tended to be the account of the golden calf in Exodus 32, which is judged to be the literary source for the formation of Deut 9:7–10:11. This presupposition has influenced all aspects of interpretation. Interpreters identify a series of authors in the formation of each text who change the theme and the structure of Deut 9:7–10:11.[24] E. Talstra questioned this approach, arguing instead that a synchronic study of form, syntax, and style should precede a diachronic analysis of composition.[25]

The design of Deut 9:7–10:11 is obscured by the lack of clear plot development and the repetition of motifs.[26] The prayers of Moses do not clearly follow each other (9:25-28; 10:10), nor is it possible to locate Moses on the mountain at different times in the story (9:18-19; 10:5, 10). A series of repetitions, including

22. See Knoppers, *Two Nations Under God*, 2:15: "Inasmuch as the Deuteronomist derives royal and national fate from cultic praxis, the very description of Jeroboam's cultus casts doubt upon the long-term prospects for the northern kingdom."

23. 1 Kgs 14:16, 22; 15:3, 26, 30, 34; 16:2, 13, 19, 26, 31; 2 Kgs 3:3; 13:2, 6, 11; 14:24; 15:9, 18, 24, 28; 17:22.

24. See, e.g., S. Lehming, "Versuch zu Ex XXXII," *VT* 10 (1960): 16-50; P. Weimar, "Das Goldene Kalb: Redaktionskritische Erwägungen zu Ex 32," *BN* 38-39 (1987): 117-60; J. Vermeylen, "L'affaire du veau d'or (Ex 32-34): Une clé pour la 'question deutéronomiste,'" *ZAW* 97 (1985): 1-23; Hahn, *Goldene Kalb*; C. Begg, "The Destruction of the Calf (Exod 32,20 and Deut 9,21)," in *Das Deuteronomium* (ed. N. Lohfink; Leuven: Leuven University Press, 1985), 208-51; idem, "The Destruction of the Golden Calf Revisited (Exod 32,20/Deut 9,21)," in *Deuteronomy and Deuteronomic Literature: Festschrift C. H. W. Brekelmans* (ed. M. Vervenne and J. Lust; BETL 133; Leuven: Leuven University Press, 1997), 469-79; S. Boorer, *The Promise of the Land as Oath: A Key to the Formation of the Pentateuch* (BZAW 205; Berlin: de Gruyter, 1992), 203-325; N. Lohfink, "Deuteronomium 9,1-10,11 und Exodus 32–34: Zu Endtextstruktur, Intertextualität, Schichtung, und Abhängigkeit," in *Gottes Volk am Sinai*, ed. Köckert and Blum, 41-47; M. Franz, *Der barmherzige und gnädige Gott: Die Gnadenrede vom Sinai (Exodus 34, 6-7) und ihre Parallelen im Alten Testament und seiner Umwelt* (BWANT 160; Stuttgart: Kohlhammer, 2003), 176-93.

25. E. Talstra, "Deuteronomy 9 and 10: Synchronic and Diachronic Observations," in *Synchronic or Diachronic? A Debate on Method in Old Testament Exegesis* (ed. J. C. de Moor; OTS 34; Leiden: Brill, 1995), 187-210.

26. Talstra (ibid., 194-95) identifies the boundaries of Deut 9:7–10:11, noting that the imperatives "to hear" in 9:1 and "to remember" in 9:7 indicate a transition in the text. Cf. Lohfink, "Deuteronomium 9,1-10,11," 42-45, who begins the unit at 9:1.

the forty-day period of intercession (9:9, 11, 18, 25; 10:10), the giving of the tablets (9:10, 11), the mediation of Moses (9:18, 20, 26-29), and the sin of the people (9:12, 13), further complicate the flow of the narrative. The style presented an impenetrable literary problem for G. Seitz, who resolved the lack of consistency by identifying several authors.[27] Many interpreters have expanded the work of Seitz, identifying a multiauthored composition in 9:1–10:11. For example, A. D. H. Mayes identified a seventh-century B.C.E. composition at the time of the Josianic reform (9:1-7a, 13-14, 26-29; 10:10-11) that accentuates the wrath of God in the wilderness. The story in Deuteronomy is expanded in the exile by Deuteronomistic redactors (9:9-12, 15-19, 21, 25; 10:1-5), who introduce the motif of the tablets and the role of the calf.[28] E. Aurelius also identifies an original story of intercession by Moses in the wilderness (9:1-7a, 13-14, 26a*, 27-28, 10:11) that undergoes a two-stage process of expansion. The first redactor relocates the story from the general setting of the wilderness to Mount Horeb (vv. 8-9), introduces the motif of the tablets and the calf (vv. 11-12, 15-17, 21), and accentuates the intercessory role of Moses (vv. 26, 29). An additional redaction emphasizes the Decalogue (9:10), the tablets (10:1-5), and further idealizes the intercessory role of Moses (9:18-19).[29] These readings suggest that there is little literary consistency to the present form of 9:7–10:11.

N. Lohfink provided a way forward by noting that the repetition of Moses interceding for a period of forty days was not an obstacle to the organization of the text, but the key to its design.[30] Lohfink concluded that the five occurrences of the motif (9:9, 11, 18, 25; 10:10) mark the introduction to a new scene, separating the story into five parts: (1) the close of the covenant (9:9-10); (2) the breaking of the covenant (9:11-17); (3) the intercession of Moses to repair the broken covenant (9:18-21); (4) the renewal of the covenant (9:25–10:9); and (5) the new beginning with the command to journey to the land (10:10-11).[31] The motif of the forty-day period of intercession is the key to the literary structure of 9:7–10:11. But, rather than the five episodes that were identified by Lohfink, the motifs yield a three-part story (9:7-17, 18-29; 10:1-11), which develops the role of Moses as intercessor.[32]

27. G. Seitz, *Redaktionsgeschichtliche Studien zum Deuteronomium* (BWANT 13; Stuttgart: Kohlhammer, 1971), 51-69. Seitz identifies four levels of composition: "Dtn Speech" (Deut 9:1-7a, 13-14, 26-29; 10:10), "Connecting Material" (9:8, 10, 25), "Continuation of Horeb Experience" (9:9, 11-12, 15-17, 18-19, 21; 10:1-5, 11), and "Late Additions" (9:7b, 20, 22-24; 10:6-9).

28. A. D. H. Mayes, *Deuteronomy* (NCB; repr. Grand Rapids: Eerdmans, 1981), 34-55.

29. Aurelius, *Fürbitter Israels*, 8-56.

30. N. Lohfink, *Das Hauptgebote: Eine Untersuchung literarischer Einleitungstragen zu Dtn 5-11* (Rome: Pontifical Biblical Institute, 1963), 207; idem, "Deuteronomium 9,1–10,11," 50-51.

31. See also Mayes, *Deuteronomy*, 195; M. Weinfeld, *Deuteronomy 1–11* (AB 5; New York: Doubleday, 1991), 427.

32. Cf. Lohfink ("Deuteronomium 9,1–10,11," 57), who argues that Deut 9:1–10:11 narrates two trips up the mountain by Moses. Interpreters have offered a variety of solutions to the liter-

The first scene sets the stage for Moses to mediate (9:7-17). It begins with Moses on the mountain for a forty-day period (9:9, 11) while he receives the tablets of the covenant. During this period the people construct a molten image (9:12), prompting Yahweh's desire to destroy them (9:13-14). The scene closes when Moses descends the mountain (9:15), sees the sin of the molten calf (9:16), and destroys the tablets (9:17), signifying the breaking of the covenant.

The second scene describes the mediation of Moses in the wake of the broken covenant (9:18-29). The scene is framed by the account of Moses' intercession for a second forty-day period (9:18-19 and 25-28). Verses 18-19 describe Moses prostrate before the Deity and the anger of God during the period of mediation, while 9:26-29 provides the words of Moses' mediation. Thus the two accounts of Mosaic intercession for forty days are not separate episodes, as Lohfink argued.[33] Instead, they are one event whose two-part description frames the account of Moses' destruction of the calf (9:21). Scholars note the ambiguity of the setting throughout this scene.[34] Moses is described as lying prostrate before Yahweh, without a clear location on the mountain. The ambiguity of the setting has prompted many interpreters to argue for multiple authors, in which one writer emphasizes the more general setting of the wilderness, while another narrows the story to the setting of Mount Horeb.[35] But this approach overlooks the important role of setting throughout the three scenes of the story. The ambiguous setting in the second scene (9:18-29) contrasts to the clear setting of the mountain in the first (9:7-17) and third (10:1-11) scenes. It is intentional. The ambiguous setting in the second scene reflects the fragile nature of Mosaic intercession during the threat of the calf. Moses cannot be clearly located on the mountain with God, while the people have cast a molten calf for themselves.

The third scene recounts the writing of new tablets (10:1-11). The setting of the mountain is once again clarified, when Moses is commanded to ascend the mountain (10:1) and when he later descends the mountain with the tablets

---

ary structure of Deut 9:1–10:11 in addition to the five-part sequence in the work of Lohfink. M. Zipor ("The Deuteronomic Account of the Golden Calf and Its Reverberation in Other Parts of the Book of Deuteronomy," *ZAW* 108 [1996]: 20-33) suggests the following structure: 9:1-3 (God goes before Israel into the land) and 9:4–10:11 (the sin of the people). The latter section separates further into 9:4-6 (theoretical debate) and 9:7–10:11 (accusations and proof). The accusations and proof include three episodes: 9:7-25 (acts that provoked God's wrath); 9:26-29 (reconciliation efforts); and 10:1-11 (reconciliation and acceptance). Cf. Talstra, "Deuteronomy 9 and 10," 196-200, who divides 9:7–10:11 into two portraits: 9:7-24 (Israel as a rebellious people, which yields a negative itinerary); and 9:25–10:11 (the intercession by Moses, which yields a positive itinerary).

33. Lohfink, "Deuteronomium 9,1–10,11," 50-51.
34. See already Seitz, *Redaktionsgeschichtliche Studien*, 51-69.
35. See, e.g., Aurelius, *Fürbitter Israels*, 8-40.

(10:5), which repeats his action from the first scene (9:15). The clarity of the setting in the third scene indicates the success of Mosaic intercession in the second scene. The third scene also emphasizes further the role of Moses as a mediator, which, once again, frames the scene (10:1-4, 10-11). Verses 1-4 describe Moses on the mountain with God, while vv. 10-11 provide the content of Moses' mediation during the final forty-day period. Verses 10-11 provide a summary conclusion to the story of Moses' intercession. The reference to a prior forty-day period in v. 10 relates the third scene to the first (9:7-17), when Moses initially received the tablets: "I stayed on the mountain forty days and forty nights, as I had done the first time." The additional statement, that Moses interceded further for the people while receiving the new tablets, relates the final scene to the second: "And once again Yahweh listened to me. Yahweh was unwilling to destroy you."

There are likely editorial additions to the story of Mosaic intercession in 9:7–10:11. The reference to Moses' intercession for Aaron (9:20), the rebellion of the people at a variety of wilderness locations (9:22-24), as well as the notice of the death of Aaron and the succession of Eleazar (10:6-7) are additions that introduce Priestly concerns into the story.[36] But the structure and the setting of 9:7–10:11 do not suggest a complex history of composition. The literary style reinforces a unified composition, since the second person plural references to the people dominate the episode. G. Minette de Tillesse identified the second person plural sections of Deuteronomy with Noth's Deuteronomist.[37] H.-C. Schmitt has more recently argued that the author is post-Deuteronomistic.[38] Mayes notes that the author of 9:7–10:11 is also responsible for the Decalogue in chap. 5, since it recounts the establishment of the covenant that is broken in the story: "The theme of chs. 9f., that of covenant breaking and renewal, presupposes an earlier account of covenant making, which is to be found in ch. 5."[39]

The prominent role of the forty days of intercession indicates that the central theme in 9:7–10:11 is the mediation of Moses, not the rebellious character of the people or the sin of making the calf.[40] The motif of the calf provides

---

36. See, e.g., Seitz, *Redaktionsgeschichtliche Studien*, 51-69; Mayes, *Deuteronomy*, 195-96; Van Seters, *Life of Moses*, 302; Talstra, "Deuteronomy 9 and 10," 203-4.

37. G. Minette de Tillesse, "Sections 'tu' et sections 'vous' dans le Deutéronome," *VT* 12 (1962): 29-87.

38. H.-C. Schmitt, "Die Erzählung vom Goldenen Kalb Ex 32* und das Dtr Geschichtswerk," in *Rethinking the Foundations: Historiography in the Ancient World and in the Bible: Essays in Honour of John Van Seters* (ed. S. L. McKenzie and T. Römer; BZAW 294; Berlin: de Gruyter, 2000), 244-50.

39. Mayes, *Deuteronomy*, 195.

40. Cf. Zipor, "Deuteronomic Account," who concludes that the central theme of Deut 9:1–10:11 is the calf.

important background to the story, since it represents the rejection of the covenant with Yahweh, which propels Moses into the role of intercessor. But the calf itself is not the point of focus. In fact, very little information is provided about the calf. The initial reference to it is indirect: 9:12 simply refers to "a molten object." Verse 16 specifies that the object is, indeed, "a molten calf." Verse 21 describes the destruction of "the calf," without making reference to its molten character. The three references to the calf provide such a loose inner-biblical relationship to the golden calves of Jeroboam that one may rightly question whether the texts are related. The author of 9:7–10:11 does not describe the construction of the calf, its theological significance, or the cultic ritual that accompanies it, all of which dominate 1 Kgs 12:26-32. Rather, the calf signifies the rejection of the covenant from Deuteronomy 5, which provides the necessary condition for Moses to intercede for the people in successive forty-day periods. Even the way in which the text lingers on Moses' destruction of the calf (v. 21) further highlights his central role in the story, not that of the calf. The actions of Moses in burning, crushing, grinding, and reducing the calf to dust signify its total destruction.[41] The destruction of the calf aids in authenticating Moses during his mediation in the second scene.

Two additional descriptions of the molten calf do suggest that the story of Moses' intercession at Horeb is written in conjunction with the account of the two golden calves of Jeroboam. First, the calf is described as a "sin" three times in Deut 9:18, 21, 27. C. Begg notes that the qualification of the calf as a "sin" relates the two stories, since the narrator in 1 Kings 12 also judges the calves of Jeroboam as a sin: "And this thing became a sin" (1 Kgs 12:30). Begg notes further that the sin of Jeroboam becomes a leitmotif throughout the Deuteronomistic History.[42] Thus the "sin" of the calf relates the intercession of Moses to the broader history of the monarchy. Second, Moses' destruction of the calf in Deuteronomy 9 anticipates the actions of Josiah against the foreign altars in 2 Kings 23. Minette de Tillesse noted that the pulverizing of the calf and the throwing of its dust into the brook (Deut 9:21) is repeated by Josiah in his reform of the Jerusalem cult, when he too throws the dust of the altars into the Kidron brook (2 Kgs 23:12).[43]

The inner-biblical interpretation of 1 Kgs 12:26-32 and Deut 9:7–10:11 highlights the distinctive themes of the two stories. The cultic practice associated with the golden calves is the point of focus in 1 Kgs 12:26-32, whose construction by Jeroboam is presented as a story of fate, which seals the destruction of the northern kingdom. Deuteronomy 9:7–10:11 employs the motif of the calf but associates the sin with the entire nation, not solely with the king, while

---

41. See Begg, "Destruction of the Calf," 213-14.
42. Ibid., 233-35.
43. Minette de Tillesse, "Sections," 60.

also modifying the fateful outcome of the sin of the calf through the motif of intercession. The intercession of Moses for the entire nation introduces the possibility of divine forgiveness, allowing for a more open-ended future for the Israelites. The inner-biblical interpretation suggests that the portrayal of Moses as a mediator in Deut 9:7–10:11 is a Deuteronomistic composition, which is intended to introduce a way forward for the nation in the wake of the exile.

Composition of Exodus 32   The traditional solution to the composition of Exodus 32 has been to identify an early form of the story as the first version of the golden calf, which has undergone supplementation and revision. The supplementation of Exodus 32, in turn, provides insight into the subsequent composition of Deut 9:1–10:11 and of 1 Kgs 12:26-33. Wellhausen illustrates the general consensus concerning the composition of Exodus 32.[44] He noted a series of problems with the organic unity of chap. 32. The intercession of Moses in 32:7-14 was especially troublesome. In this section the Deity informs Moses of the sin of the people on the summit of the mountain, yet Moses only discovers the sin of the calf in 32:15-20. In addition, the successful intercession of Moses in vv. 7-14 also conflicts with his subsequent anger (32:15-20), the punishment of the people (32:25-29), and the failed intercession of Moses (32:30-34). These literary problems prompted Wellhausen to identify an original story of the golden calf in the E source consisting of 3:1-6, 15-21, 35. This story includes the construction of the golden calf (vv. 1-6), its destruction by Moses (vv. 15-21), and the plague (v. 35). The intercession of Moses (vv. 7-14), the exchange between Moses and Aaron (vv. 22-24), the role of the Levites (vv. 25-29), and the unsuccessful mediation of Moses (vv. 30-34) are either independent stories or later additions to the original story of the golden calf.

The analysis of chap. 32 has undergone modification since Wellhausen,[45] yet the broad outline of his identification of the original story has endured.[46] The most significant innovation has been the identification of Deuteronomistic literature in the portrayal of Moses as mediator, relating the intercession of Moses in vv. 7-14 with Deut 9:7–10:11.[47] H.-C. Schmitt illustrates a recent develop-

---

44. Wellhausen, *Composition*, 91-92.

45. For review see Hahn, *Goldene Kalb*, 101-43.

46. Hahn (*Goldene Kalb*, 143) arrives at a similar position to that of Wellhausen, identifying Exod 32:1-6, 15, and most likely 35 as the original story of the golden calf, remaining unsure of the authorship of vv. 17-18, 19-20, 21-24. See also Boorer (*Promise of Land*, 231-62), who identifies the original story as vv. 1-6, 15-20, (21-24?), 30-35; and Aurelius (*Fürbitter Israels*, 60-68): vv. 1-6, 15a*, 19-20, 30-34. See the additional studies of Lehming, "Versuch zu Ex XXXII"; Weimar, "Goldene Kalb"; Vermeylen, "L'affaire du veau d'or."

47. See, e.g., Noth, *Exodus*, 244; L. Perlitt, *Bundestheologie im Alten Testament* (WMANT 36; Neukirchen-Vluyn: Neukirchener Verlag, 1969), 204-11.

ment of this thesis, identifying three stages in the composition of Exodus 32: (1) an original story of the golden calves, which is dependent on the Bethel tradition preserved in 1 Kings 12 (Exod 32:1-6, 15a*, 19-20, 30-34); (2) a post-P redaction concerning the tablets (31:18a; 32:15-16); and (3) a late Deuteronomistic redaction by the same author as Deut 9:7–10:11 emphasizing the mediation of Moses (Exod 32:7-14, 17-18, 25-29).[48] The problem with the identification of multiple authors in Exodus 32 is that it does not resolve the literary problems in the present form of the chapter, which prompted Wellhausen's identification of the authors in the first place. The identification of distinct authors in chap. 32 leaves unexplained why Moses destroys the tablets (vv. 15-20) and purges the camp (vv. 25-29) after he successfully interceded for the people (vv. 7-14).

It is possible to account for the present form of Exodus 32 when the narrative is read as the combination of Deut 9:7–10:11 and 1 Kgs 12:26-33 by a single author. The interpretation of Exodus 32 as an inner-biblical composition acquires support when we note that the distinct compositions of Exodus 32 separate, for the most part, between Deut 9:7–10:11 and 1 Kgs 12:26-33. Wellhausen's original version of the golden calf relates to the story of Jeroboam in 1 Kgs 12:26-33, while the intercession of Moses in Exod 32:7-14 relates to Deut 9:7–10:11. The literary relationship between Exodus 32 and 1 Kgs 12:32-34 is established most clearly in the similar statements of Aaron/Israel and Jeroboam: "These are your gods, O Israel, who brought you up out of the land of Egypt" (Exod 32:4; 1 Kgs 12:28). The lack of context for the plural reference to "gods" in Exodus 32 indicates that it is meant to be commentary on 1 Kings 12. The inner-biblical relationship also includes the motif of sin to describe the worship of the calf (Exod 32:21, 30; 1 Kgs 12:30), cultic sacrifices (Exod 32:6; 1 Kgs 12:32), a new festival (Exod 32:5; 1 Kgs 12:32), and non-Levitical worship (Exod 32:25-29; 1 Kgs 12:31).[49] The literary relationship between Exodus 32 and Deut 9:7–10:11 includes the intercessory prayer of Moses (Exod 32:7-14; Deut 9:26-29), the reception and the smashing of the tablets (Exod 32:15-16, 19; Deut 9:9-10, 17), and the destruction of the calf (Exod 32:20; Deut 9:21). The larger context of Exodus 32–34 also includes the motif of the forty-day period of intercession (Exod 34:28; Deut 9:9, 11, 18, 25; 10:10; cf. also Exod 24:18).

The motif of the forty-day period of intercession indicates that Exodus 32–34 follows the three-part structure of Deut 9:7–10:11: (1) the destruction of the tablets (Exod 24:12–32:35; Deut 9:7-17); (2) the intercession of Moses (Exodus 33; Deut 9:18-29); and (3) the reissuing of new tablets (Exodus 34; Deut

48. Schmitt, "Erzählung vom Goldenen Kalb," 237-38.

49. For examination of the literary relationship between these texts see Aberbach and Smolar, "Aaron, Jeroboam"; G. N. Knoppers, "Aaron's Calf and Jeroboam's Calves," in *Fortunate the Eyes That See: Essays in Honor of David Noel Freedman in Celebration of His Seventieth Birthday* (ed. A. Beck et al.; Grand Rapids: Eerdmans, 1995), 92-104.

10:1-11). The three episodes share the same ambiguity of setting, in which Moses is clearly located on the mountain in the first and third episodes, but not in the second episode while he mediates with the Deity. Moses is on the mountain with God inititally to receive the tablets (Exod 24:12-14; 32:1-14) and to receive the new tablets (Exodus 34). But he is not on the mountain with the Deity in Exodus 33, as is also the case in Deut 9:18-29. The comparison indicates that Exodus 32–34 is an expansion and a reinterpretation of Deut 9:7–10:11. The expansion includes the incorporation of the golden calves of Jeroboam into the narrative (Exod 32:1-6) and the prolonged mediation of Moses in the second (Exodus 33) and third (Exodus 34) episodes. Exodus 33 provides an extended dialogue between Moses and Yahweh about the continued presence of God and the favored status of Moses, while Exodus 34 includes the private theophany of Moses as the setting in which he receives the new tablets and also seeks divine forgiveness.[50]

The differences between Exodus 32–34 and Deut 9:7–10:11 indicate a reinterpretation of the nature of the sin of the calf and the role of mediation. In Deut 9:7–10:11 the sin of the calf results in corporate guilt. Thus the construction of the calf need not be narrated in the first scene, because all Israel was equally responsible for the sin of the calf (Deut 9:7-17). The intercession of Moses in the second (Deut 9:18-29) and third (Deut 10:1-11) scenes also remains corporate in nature. All are guilty of the sin of the calf and all are included in the covenant of the new tablets. Exodus 32–34 introduces individual responsibility for the sin of the calf. The author develops the new theme through four changes to the narrative of Exodus 32 from Deut 9:7–10:11: (1) the inclusion of the construction of the calf (Exod 32:1-6); (2) the sequence of Mosaic intercession (32:7-14); (3) the introduction of the motif of a water ordeal that leads to the Levitical purging of the guilty from the camp (32:20b, 25-29); and (4) the inability of Moses to atone corporately for the nation (32:30-35). A closer examination of the literary design of Exodus 32 will clarify the strategy of the author.

The author of Exodus 32 narrates the construction of the golden calf through an inner-biblical interpretation of the calves of Jeroboam. Verses 1-6 narrate the demand of the people for the calf, its construction by Aaron, the establishment of a new festival, and the sacrifices to the calf, all motifs from 1 Kgs 12:26-32. The account of the construction of the calf provides the foundation for

---

50. See further J. Blenkinsopp, "Structure and Meaning in the Sinai-Horeb Narrative (Exodus 19–34)," in *A Biblical Itinerary: In Search of Method, Form and Content: Essays in Honor of George W. Coats* (ed. E. E. Carpenter; JSOTSup 240; Sheffield: Sheffield Academic Press, 1997), 109-25; idem, "Deuteronomic Contribution to the Narrative in Genesis–Numbers: A Test Case," in *Those Elusive Deuteronomists: The Phenomenon of Pan-Deuteronomism* (ed. Linda S. Schearing and Steven L. McKenzie; JSOTSup 268; Sheffield: Sheffield Academic Press, 1999), 84-115, esp. 101-15.

the author to explore individual guilt. The construction of the calf prompts the question: Who are "the people" that demand the calf (Exod 32:1)? And in its construction what is the role of Aaron, who, unlike the people, proclaims a feast to Yahweh (32:4-5)?

The successful intercession of Moses follows immediately in 32:7-14, while Moses is still on the mountain with Yahweh. This is a significant departure from Deut 9:7–10:11. In Deut 9:7–10:11 the motif of divine destruction (9:13-14) and the intercession of Moses (9:25-29) are removed from each other in the development of the story. Yahweh wishes to destroy the nation in the opening scene (9:13-14). Moses does not intercede for the nation until the second scene (9:25-29), after he destroys the calf (9:21). The intercession of Moses leads to the corporate forgiveness of the people, since the following scene begins with the divine command for new tablets (10:1-4). In Exodus 32 Moses mediates immediately as a response to the divine anger. Thus the intercession of Moses in 32:7-14 is not about divine forgiveness after the destruction of the calf. It is, rather, aimed at qualifying divine anger and corporate punishment. The intercession of Moses in 32:11-13 is a response to the divine desire to destroy the entire nation indiscriminately for the sin of the golden calf (32:9-10). Moses seeks to temper the divine anger. The success of his mediation is noted in v. 14, when Yahweh repents of the evil of corporate punishment: "And Yahweh repented of the evil that he spoke to do to his people."

The destruction of the calf in 32:20 also departs from Deut 9:21. Both accounts employ motifs that signify the total destruction of the cultic object. Moses burns, grinds, and scatters the calf on the water.[51] But Exod 32:20 extends the actions of Moses by adding the water ordeal.[52] After Moses scatters the powder of the golden calf on the water, he makes the Israelites drink it. The last motif is absent from Deut 9:21, and it indicates that Exod 32:20 is an inner-biblical interpretation that has expanded its parent text. The water ordeal develops the theme of individual guilt. It provides the means for identifying which people demanded the calf in the opening section. The water ordeal leads to the purging of the camp by the Levites in 32:25-29. The purging of the camp of foreign worship relates Exodus 32 to 1 Kgs 12:26-32, where the priests of the calves were also non-Levitical (1 Kgs 12:31). The prominent role of the Levites authenticates their cultic leadership, which is also noted in Deut 10:8-9. The unique aspect of the Levites in Exod 32:25-29, however, is their role in purging the camp of the guilty. The action of the Levites in killing three thousand persons further advances the theme of individual guilt. The selective punishment of the

---

51. See Begg, "Destruction of the Calf."

52. Noth (*Exodus,* 249) is certainly correct in reading this motif as a "water of cursing," which introduces divine judgment.

three thousand by the Levites, rather than the destruction of the entire nation, corresponds to Yahweh's early repenting of corporate punishment.

The closing scene in 32:30-35 explores individual guilt from the perspective of intercession and atonement, thus qualifying the nature of Mosaic intercession. It contains material that is absent from Deut 9:7–10:11. The scene opens with Moses suggesting that he will atone for the nation: "Perhaps I can atone for your sin." The Deity firmly rejects Moses' attempt to atone for the many and thus refuses to forgive in an indiscriminate manner. The failed attempt of Moses to atone further clarifies the theme of individual guilt in Exodus 32. The opening intercession of Moses (32:7-14) qualified the divine anger. The divine repentance of evil means that the entire nation will not be held guilty for the sin of the few. The purging of the camp by the Levites (32:25-29) provides the new paradigm of individual guilt, in which three thousand are singled out for the sin of the golden calf. The closing intercession of Moses now qualifies the nature of mediation within the framework of individual guilt. Just as the many are not guilty for the few, so also the one cannot atone for the many. Thus the request of Moses to represent the nation as a whole is rejected. The Deity legislates the law of individual guilt: "Whoever sinned against me I will blot out from my book."

The comparison of the three stories of the golden calf allows for the identification of the author of Exodus 32 as the Non-P historian. The Non-P author merges Deut 9:7–10:11 and 1 Kgs 12:26-32 into one story. Thus Exodus 32 is not an early tradition but a late composition. The literary context for the composition of Exodus 32 is the Enneateuch. The inner-biblical relationships indicate that the Non-P author intends for the story of the golden calf in the wilderness to be read in the larger context of the history of the failed monarchy. The theme of corporate guilt either in the form of the king (1 Kgs 12:26-32) or the nation (Deut 9:7–10:11) is qualified in Exodus 32, providing a new basis for hope. The author explores the implications of individual guilt for divine anger, the maintenance of purity in the camp, and the nature of mediation. The commentary on Jeroboam, the idealization of Moses as a mediator, the prominence of the Levites as priests, and the shared vocabulary indicate that the Non-P author is closely related to the Deuteronomist.[53] The P author adds only minimal commentary concerning the description of the tablets (Exod 32:15-16).[54]

---

53. See, e.g., Schmitt ("Erzählung vom goldenen Kalb"), who identifies the author of Exod 32:7-14, 17-18, 25-29 with the author of Deut 9:7–10:11; cf. Van Seters, *Life of Moses*, 290-318, who identifies the author as the post-Deuteronomistic Yahwist.

54. Cf. J. Gertz ("Beobachtungen zu Komposition und Redaktion in Exodus 32–34," in *Gottes Volk am Sinai*, ed. Köckert and Blum, 88-106) who sees closer literary ties between Exodus 32 and the P account of the tabernacle.

Literary Structure

In the commentary I follow the outline of Exodus 32 that emerged from the comparison with Deut 9:7–10:11 and 1 Kgs 12:26-32:

    I. Absence of Moses and Construction of the Golden Calf (32:1-6)
    II. Intercession of Moses and Destruction of the Calf (32:7-20)
    III. Purging the Camp of Foreign Worship (32:21-29)
    IV. Failed Intercession of Moses to Atone for the People (32:30-35)

Additional structuring devices are also evident in Exodus 32. The incident of the golden calf is examined from different points of view, signaled by the verb *rā'â*, "to see." The initial construction of the calf is told from the perspective of the people (v. 1) and Aaron (v. 5), before shifting to Yahweh's point of view on the summit of the mountain (v. 9). The concluding events are told through the eyes of Moses (v. 19). The episode is also structured into a three-day period, signaled by the time word *māḥār*, translated "tomorrow" in v. 6 and "the next day" in v. 30. The events begin with the construction of the calf on the first day (vv. 1-6). The second day includes the new festival before the calf, the divine response on the summit of the mountain, and the destruction of the tablets by Moses (vv. 7-29). On the third day Moses begins to intercede for the presence of God in the aftermath of the "original sin" (vv. 30-35), leaving the immediate events of the golden calf behind. The intercession of Moses on the third day functions more as an introduction to the dialogue between Moses and Yahweh in Exodus 33 than as an integral part of the story of the golden calf, suggesting that the incident of the golden calf is confined to 32:1-29. The transitional role of 32:30-35 is further supported by the absence of this story from Deuteronomy 9–10 and 1 Kgs 12:26-32. Cassuto and R. W. L. Moberly are likely correct when they combine Exod 32:30-35 with the intercession of Moses in Exodus 33, although the reservations of Childs are also noteworthy, since there is a new introduction in 33:1 with a change in emphasis.[55]

32:1-6 The scene describes the Israelites at the base of the mountain, at the very moment Moses is receiving the tablets on the summit. The story begins from the people's point of view: "And when the people saw." In quick succession the reader gains insights into their perception of Moses.

First, the people perceive that "Moses delayed to descend from the mountain." The Hebrew is unusual. The word *bōšēš*, "delayed," is the Pilpel form of the Hebrew verb *bôš*, "to be ashamed." Shame describes a situation in which the

---

55. Cassuto, *Exodus*, 425-27; R. W. L. Moberly, *At the Mountain of God* (JSOTSup 22; Sheffield: Sheffield Academic Press, 1983), 56-63; Childs, *Exodus*, 587.

opposite of what was intended occurs. It is unclear whether the connotation of shame is part of the Israelites' perception of Moses. This form of the verb occurs in only one other text in the Hebrew Bible, to describe the mother of Sisera, waiting for the return of her son: "Why is his chariot so long in coming (*bōšēš*)? Why is the clatter of his chariots delayed?" (Judg 5:28). If there is the connotation of shame in Exod 32:1, then the phrase conveys both a lengthy absence and the people's sense of failure on the part of Moses.

Second, the people "assembled against" Aaron, indicating confrontation. The Niphal of *qhl* plus *ʿal*, "to assemble/gather against," also describes the challenge of Korah, Dathan, and Abiram to the leadership of Moses and Aaron (Num 16:3) and the complaint of the people when they lacked water in the desert (Num 20:2). The confrontation recalls the instruction of Moses in Exod 24:14: "Wait here for us until we return to you. Aaron and Hur are with you. Whoever has a dispute, let him bring it to them." The absence of Hur is noteworthy but unexplainable. Hur has functioned in a number of stories in the Non-P History (Exodus 17, 24). Rabbinic interpretation solves the problem of his absence by suggesting that he was killed by the people (e.g., *b. Sanh.* 7a). Aaron's response to the complaint indicates his failure of leadership.

Third, the people request "gods" to replace Moses, suggesting that the story about the golden calf is as much about Mosaic authority as it is about the rule of Yahweh over the people. Moberly suggests that the Hebrew *ʾĕlōhîm* is a polemical reference to foreign deities and should be translated in the singular, "god": "For it is not plurality of gods but a false conception of the one God that the writer is conveying."[56] But this is unlikely. The plural reference to "gods" is confirmed by the plural form of the demonstrative pronoun "these" and by the plural form of the verb (see the translation note on v. 1).

Fourth, the phrase, "we do not know what has happened to him [Moses]," foreshadows a tragic story, recalling Pharaoh's similar declaration of ignorance to Moses regarding Yahweh, "I do not know Yahweh" (Exod 5:2). Such ignorance leads to destruction in Exodus, or at least to the threat of it.

Aaron responds to the people in 32:2-5. Verses 2-4 describe his construction of the calf, and v. 5 concludes the section with his perception of the calf, providing a contrast to the people's point of view in v. 1. The confrontational mood of the people, gathering against Aaron, is carried over into his response: "Take off (*pāraq*) the gold rings that are on the ears of your wives, your sons, and your daughters" (32:2). The Hebrew is more violent than the translation suggests. "Tear off" is closer to the meaning of the Hebrew. The same word describes the theophany to Elijah on Mount Horeb, when a powerful wind "tore (*pāraq*) the mountains apart and shattered the rocks" (1 Kgs 19:11). Thus Aaron

---

56. Moberly, *At the Mountain of God*, 48.

instructs the people to rip off their earrings, which they do willingly (Exod 32:3), setting the tone of reckless violence that will culminate in the orgy before the calf (v. 6).

The construction of the calf in v. 4 has given rise to extensive interpretation, reviewed, for example, by Houtman.[57] The problems of interpretation arise from the Hebrew phrase, *wayyāṣar 'ōtô baḥeret* (see the translation note on 32:4). The verb "to fashion" or "to shape" may derive from Hebrew *yāṣar* or from *ṣûr*. Both words suggest the process of shaping and molding. Some interpreters also suggest *ṣārar*, meaning "to wrap" or "to tie up." The object of Aaron's action, "it," may refer to the golden earrings of the people or to the calf. The tool employed by Aaron could be a graving device *(ḥeret)* or some kind of container, perhaps even a pouch *(ḥārît)*. The exact details of the process remain uncertain. He either wrapped the earrings in a container or fashioned the material into the calf. In either case the text is clear that Aaron is manufacturing an object, a definite violation of the altar laws in 20:22-26.

The result of Aaron's action is "a molten calf," a translation of the Hebrew *'ēgel massēkâ*. The calf *('ēgel)* is a symbol of power and fertility. It is further qualified as "molten" *(massēkâ)*, from the verb "to pour out" *(nāsak,* Gen 35:14; Num 28:7; see the translation note for the suggestion by Dohmen indicating a process of hammering). The phrase "molten calf" suggests construction from a manufacturing process, which includes melting down gold and pouring it into a form. The creation of the calf concludes with its interpretation: "These are your gods, Israel, who brought you up out of Egypt" (see the commentary above). The context suggests that Aaron is the speaker, but the plural verb, "then they said," indicates a proclamation by all the people of Israel. The identification of the calf with the exodus is incompatible with the self-revelation of Yahweh at the outset of the Decalogue, where Yahweh was identified with the exodus: "I am Yahweh, your God, who brought you out of the land of Egypt" (20:2). The self-revelation of Yahweh in the Decalogue leads immediately to the laws forbidding other gods and images (20:3-5). The references to the Decalogue indicate that what began in 32:1 as a confrontation about Mosaic authority evolves quickly in 32:4 into a challenge about the very rule of Yahweh.

The construction of the golden calf in Exodus 32 is a story that is critical of Aaron. Moses charged him, along with Hur, with the governance of the people in 24:13-14. The opening scene illustrates how, upon the first indication of a dispute, Aaron gives in to the complaint of the people. He does not uphold Mosaic authority by forcing the people to wait for the return of Moses. Instead he builds the calf, which, at the very least, is intended to replace Moses. Yet v. 5 separates Aaron from the people by presenting his perception of the golden

---

57. Houtman, *Exodus*, 3:636-38.

calf, as compared to the people in v. 1. The orientation of Aaron is signaled once again by the verb "to see" *(rā'â)*, "and Aaron saw." What Aaron perceives in the golden calf is a "feast to Yahweh," requiring that he build an altar before it. In proclaiming a new festival for Yahweh, Aaron reflects Jeroboam in 1 Kgs 12:26-32, who also institutes a new cultic festival to accompany the golden calves at Bethel and Dan. In the story of Jeroboam, the new festival is never associated explicity with Yahweh. In fact, the festivals of Jeroboam at Bethel and Dan contrast to the worship of Yahweh in Jerusalem. Aaron provides a contrast to Jeroboam in that he identified the new festival with Yahweh. Aaron is certainly not a heroic character in the Non-P History. But v. 5 indicates that he is also not a villain. Rather, according to the Non-P author, he represents a bygone era of idols and icons, reminiscent of the monarchy (see the discussion above on 1 Kings 12). His vision of Yahwism is now incompatible with Mosaic authority grounded in the new revelation of law codified on tablets (Exod 32:15-16), whose leaders are recorded in a book (32:32-33).

Verse 6 describes the worship of the golden calf. The worship commences in a familiar manner, with sacrifices that have already appeared in Exodus. But it quickly devolves into ritual chaos, suggesting a sexual orgy. The "festival to Yahweh" announced by Aaron begins with the familiar burnt offering *('ōlâ)*, followed by the well-being sacrifice *(šĕlāmîm)*. The same two sacrifices are prescribed in 20:24 and celebrated in 24:4-5. The well-being sacrifice contains a meal, which is also included in the worship of the calf, when the people sit to eat and to drink, recalling a similar meal on the mountain (24:9-11). But events quickly spin out of control.

The concluding sentence, "And they rose to revel" *(wayyāqūmû lĕṣaḥēq)*, introduces a new motif. There is debate on the nature of the activity in part because of the range of meaning of *ṣāḥaq* (see the translation note). The word means "laugh" in the birth story of Isaac, forming the basis of his name (Hebrew *yiṣḥāq*). Abraham (Gen 17:17) and Sarah (Gen 18:12, 15; 21:6) laugh when told that they would have a child in their old age. A related word, *śāḥaq*, indicates sport and dancing, prompting some to translate, "they rose to dance/sport."[58] The meanings "laughter" and "dance" underscore the noise of the festival, a prominent motif from ancient Near Eastern mythology often prompting divine anger. In the Mesopotamian version of the flood, *Atra-Hasis*, the noise of humans so angers Enlil, keeping him from sleep, that it becomes the reason for the flood.[59] The motif of the noisy festival returns in the descent of

---

58. J. M. Sasson, "Bovine Symbolism in the Exodus Narrative," *VT* 18 (1968): 380-87; idem, "The Worship of the Golden Calf," in *Orient and Occident: Essays Presented to Cyrus H. Gordon on the Occasion of His Sixty-Fifth Birthday* (ed. H. A. Hoffner Jr.; AOAT 22; Neukirchen-Vluyn: Neukirchener Verlag, 1973), 151-59.

59. *ANET*, 104-6; see *Atra-Hasis* A.II.i.2-8.

Moses and Joshua, when both hear the clamor of the feast before they ever see it (Exod 32:17-18).

The Piel of *ṣāḥaq*, as in 32:6, also takes on sexual meaning. When Ishmael is described with this form of the verb in his interaction with Isaac, Sarah drives him and Hagar from the camp in the fear that he will inherit (Gen 21:9). When Isaac performs the same activity with Rebekah, Abimelech realizes that they are husband and wife, not brother and sister (Gen 26:8). The use of the same verb in the accusation of Potiphar's wife against Joseph is accompanied by the claim that he attempted to have sex with her (Gen 39:14, 17). The sexual connotation of the verb goes beyond the motif of noise, indicating that what begins as an orderly ritual of burnt offerings and the well-being sacrifice evolves into an orgy. The manufacturing of the golden calf already violated the altar laws in 20:22-26. Now the sexual orgy of the people further violates the more specific prohibition against ascending an altar, lest one's nakedness is uncovered (20:26). Exodus 32:25 adds to the chaos of the ritual, describing the people as "out of control" *(pārūaʿ).*

32:7-20 The second day includes two actions at different locations on the mountain. The episode begins at the summit, where Yahweh judges the people while Moses intercedes on their behalf (vv. 7-14). The scene shifts to the base of the mountain, where Moses destroys the tablets and executes the divine judgment on the calf and the people (vv. 15-29). This division of the scene follows Cassuto.[60] Noth separates the events into three parts: the intercession of Moses, including his initial descent (vv. 7-16); the exchange between Joshua and Moses on the mountain (vv. 17-19); and the destruction of the calf and the people in the camp (vv. 20-29).[61] Childs, Beyerlin, and F. C. Fensham divide the scene even further between the intercession of Moses (vv. 7-14), the destruction of the calf (vv. 15-20), the rebuke of Aaron (vv. 21-24), and the purging of the camp by the Levites (vv. 25-29).[62] H. Brichto also identifies the anger of Yahweh (vv. 7-8) and the intercession of Moses (vv. 9-14) as distinct scenes.[63]

The scene cuts immediately from the worship of the golden calf (v. 6) to the summit of the mountain (vv. 7-14). A divine speech to Moses in vv. 7-8 provides the transition, setting the stage for Yahweh's perception of the event in vv. 9-10. Yahweh relates the events below to Moses in vv. 7-8, judging the golden calf to be a violation of the recently revealed law: "They have turned aside quickly from the way that I commanded them." God also describes the people as "corrupted" *(šiḥēt),* recalling the condition of humanity and the earth at the time of

60. Cassuto, *Exodus,* 410.

61. Noth, *Exodus,* 247-50.

62. Childs, *Exodus,* 564-72; Beyerlin, *Oldest Sinaitic Traditions,* 20, 191; F. C. Fensham, "The Burning of the Golden Calf and Ugarit," *IEJ* 16 (1966): 213.

63. H. Brichto, "Worship of the Golden Calf," *HUCA* 54 (1983): 4-20.

the flood (Gen 6:12). The divine point of view of the event targets the people in Exod 32:9-10, not the calf: "I have seen *(rāʾâ)* this people." The demonstrative *hazzeh,* "this," functions to underscore the distance between the Yahweh and the people. The demonstrative pronoun is used throughout the narrative to under-score distance and alienation between characters. In v. 1 the pronoun is used by the people in referring to Moses ("this Moses") when they request gods to re-place him; in v. 9 the demonstrative pronoun in the speech of Yahweh indicates alienation between the Deity and the people ("this people"); in v. 21 Moses refers to "this people" in describing their sin; in v. 24 Aaron distances himself from the calf with the words "this calf"; and finally in v. 31 Moses once again refers to the people with the demonstrative pronoun in his speech to Yahweh where he notes their "great sin": "Alas, this people has sinned a great sin."

The divine speech to Moses provides further interpretation of the people: "And indeed a people of stiff neck it is." The meaning of "stiff-necked" is "stub-born" (see Jer 17:23). Proverbs 29:1 provides commentary: "A human who re-mains stiff-necked after many rebukes will suddenly be destroyed — without remedy." The threat of destruction from Prov 29:1 is conveyed in Exod 32:9-10 through imagery of the flood. God wishes to destroy the people, like the gener-ation of the flood, and create a new nation from Moses, like Noah: "I will make you [Moses] into a great nation." Even the divine demand for rest, "let me alone" *(hannîḥâ,* "give rest"), recalls the name Noah *(nōaḥ,* "rest"), while also playing off the motif of noise noted above.

Moses ceases the analogy to the flood in vv. 11-13. He does so by interced-ing for the people as Abraham did for Sodom (Gen 18:16-33), rather than prepar-ing for his own survival like Noah in the flood (Genesis 6–9). The opening phrase in Exod 32:11 signals the intercession of Moses: "And Moses made en-treaty before the face of Yahweh his God" *(wayḥal mōšeh ʾet-pĕnê yhwh ʾĕlōhāyw).* The translation is disputed, especially the meaning of the verb *ḥālâ,* whether it derives from a root meaning "to be weak," or another meaning "to be pleasant."[64] But when combined with reference to the divine face *(pānîm)* the phrase indicates persuasive prayer. The phrase is even used with the verb "to pray" in the story of the man of God: "Then the king said to the man of God, 'In-tercede *(ḥal-nāʾ ʾet-pĕnê . . .)* with Yahweh your God and pray *(wĕhitpallēl)* for me'" (1 Kgs 13:6). God hears such prayer (2 Kgs 13:4), which at times is even able to persuade God to change the course of events by "repenting of evil" (Jer 26:19).

The content of Moses' prayer on the summit provides the model for inter-cession, which will be expanded at the base of the mountain as the liturgy for the tent of meeting in Exodus 33. Moses raises two questions in his prayer using the interrogative "Why" *(lam[m]â)* in vv. 11-12a. Both questions are meant to dis-

---

64. See BDB 317-18; Houtman, *Exodus,* 647-48.

suade Yahweh from destroying the Israelites by presenting God with an affirmation (see the translation note). The questions are followed by two imperatives in vv. 12b-13 that seek to influence God to change behavior. Moses first asks God: "Why *(lāmâ)*, Yahweh, does your anger burn hot against your people whom you brought out of the land of Egypt with great power and with a strong hand?" (v. 11). The question reaffirms that the Israelites are indeed Yahweh's people, not Moses' people, as God has stated earlier (v. 7). The second question concerns the Egyptians: "Why *(lāmmâ)* should the Egyptians say, 'For evil he brought them out to kill them'?" This question explores the effect of the exodus on the nations, not just on the Israelites. The reputation of Yahweh among the Egyptians is a central motif in the first half of Exodus, to which Moses now returns. The book of Jonah provides further commentary on the important role of God's reputation among the nations and its power to persuade God to change a decree of judgment. To the dismay of Jonah, Yahweh saves the evil city of Nineveh when the king and the residents repent. The prophet responds to Yahweh with a bitter complaint about Yahweh's ability "to repent of evil" (Jon 4:2).[65]

Moses follows the questions in Exod 32:11-12a with petitions in vv. 12b-13. First, he implores Yahweh to change the course of events by "repenting of the evil against your people." Divine repentance, writes Fretheim, "is the reversal of a direction taken or a decision made."[66] The phrase, "to repent of evil," indicates that Yahweh is a God of change in the Hebrew Bible. The divine ability to change provides the basis for intercessory prayer, illustrated by Moses in this story, and expanded upon in prophetic literature like Jonah (4:2) and Joel (2:13).[67] Second, Moses invokes God to remember past promises to the ancestors, specifically the promise of land (Exod 32:13). Verse 14 concludes the exchange, underscoring the initial success of Moses. Yahweh indeed "repented of the evil that he spoke to do to his people," allowing the story to continue.

Verses 15-20 describe the descent of Moses into the camp. The account begins with the central point of the story, the incompatibility of the golden calf with the newly revealed divine law inscribed on the tablets. The text lingers on this point in vv. 15-16, so much so that the description of the tablets becomes grammatically awkward. The Hebrew states: "Moses turned and descended from the mountain. And the two tablets of testimony *(ûšěnê lūḥōt hā'ēdūt)* were in his hands. Tablets *(lūḥōt)* having been written on their two sides, they were written on one side and the other. The tablets *(wěhallūḥōt)* they were the work of God. And the writing *(wěhammiktāb)*, it was the writing of God engraved on

---

65. T. B. Dozeman, "Inner-Biblical Interpretation of Yahweh's Gracious and Compassionate Character," *JBL* 107 (1989): 207-23.

66. Fretheim, *Exodus*, 286.

67. See Dozeman, "Inner-Biblical Interpretation."

the tablets." Part of the reason for the awkward description of the tablets is their identification as "the two tablets of testimony," which continues the interpretation of the P historian from 31:18. The insertion of the phrase by the P historian reminds the reader once again that Moses is carrying the architectural plans for the tabernacle and its cultic furnishings on the tablets, in addition to the Decalogue in the Non-P historian's account (see the introduction to 24:12–40:38, "Authors"). The extended description of the tablets in the Non-P History emphasizes two points. First, the tablets contain divine law, whose words are even engraved by God. Second, their fate at this juncture of the story is in the hands of Moses, not God. Moses has departed from the summit of the mountain and God has allowed him to leave with the divine law code in his possession. The successful intercession of Moses before the destruction of the tablets and the golden calf departs from the account in Deuteronomy 9–10. The change in the plot indicates the more complex characterization of Moses in the Non-P History, where his impulsive temper has played a role from the outset of his story in his killing of the Egyptian (Exod 2:11-15).

Exodus 32:15-20 explores the character of Moses, especially his violent anger as he responds to the golden calf. The descent of Joshua and Moses and their exchange on the mountain in vv. 17-18 sets the stage for the subsequent events. Joshua hears the roaring of the people in the camp and misinterprets it as war, reflecting his function as a holy warrior (see 17:8-16). The statement of Joshua allows Moses to correct the interpretation of the noise from the camp with a poem in 32:18:

> It is not the sound of the cry (*qôl 'ănôt*) of victory;
> nor the sound of the cry (*qôl 'ănôt*) of defeat;
> it is the *qôl 'annôt* I am hearing.

The function of the poem, according to H. Gressmann, is to stop action momentarily and to emphasize the moment.[68] E. Greenstein adds that the structure of the poem is a weak form of staircase parallelism, which consists of three lines that build to a climax in the final line.[69] Thus the action is momentarily stopped to emphasize the final line of the poem, which provides Moses' initial interpretation of the noise.

The key for interpreting the poem is the phrase *qôl 'annôt* in the third line. Upon first reading, the phrase "sound of the cry" appears to weave the three lines together and to carry forward the meaning of the poem. Hebrew *qôl* is "sound," also translated as "voice" in certain contexts (e.g., 19:19); and *'ănôt* is

---

68. Gressmann, *Mose und seine Zeit*, 202.

69. E. Greenstein, "Two Variations of Grammatical Parallelism in Canaanite Poetry and Their Psycholinguistic Background," *JANESCU* 6 (1974): 97.

"cry," most likely from the verb *ʿānâ*, "to sing" (see the translation note). Thus the phrase could be translated as I have, "the sound of singing." But a closer look at the poem indicates that the phrase is not the same in all three lines. In the first two lines the word *ʿănôt*, "cry," has only one *n*, indicating that the infinitive construct *ʿănôt* is in the Qal form. The phrase is also qualified as either "victory" or "defeat." In the third line, the word *ʿannôt* has two *n*s, indicating that the infinitive construct is in the Piel form. The syntax is also different, since there is no qualification to the phrase as in the first two lines ("cry *of victory*" and "cry *of defeat*"). In view of these differences, interpreters are unsure of the meaning of the third line, even though as Greenstein noted it carries the meaning of the poem.

Scholars propose a number of solutions for reading the final line. Those who focus on the problem of syntax suggest a word is missing. Gressmann proposed the phrase, "the cry of prostitution" *(zĕnûnîm)*, underscoring the orgy, while Houtman tentatively suggests, "the cry of the feast *(ḥag)*," or "the sound of partying."[70] Others focus on the unique form of Hebrew *ʿannôt*. Andersen suggests that a particular form of cultic music is intended.[71] J. Makujina suggests parallels to the story of holy war against the Amalekites.[72]

More attractive is an interpretation from comparative religion, in which the final line could also be translated, "the voice of Anat," the Canaanite goddess. The reference may be negative, as M. Delcor argues, associating the cult of the golden calf in some way with the goddess, who has replaced Moses.[73] She is identified as a heifer in Ugaritic mythology (*CTA* 6.ii.28). But the intent of the analogy may also be positive, characterizing Moses' loyalty to Yahweh on analogy of Anat's loyalty to Baal. Anat is Baal's ally and defender throughout Ugaritic mythology. She supports Baal in his quest for a temple (*CTA* 3–4). Her character is often excessive and violent, like that of Moses. And her heart is bonded to Baal like a heifer for her calf (*CTA* 6.ii.28-30). Her devotion is most evident when she defends Baal against his opponent, Mot, the god of death. If the third line of the poem is translated, "the voice of Anat I am hearing," then Moses is describing himself, particularly his role as Yahweh's loyal defender. This translation suggests that the poem explores the character of Moses.

The interpretation favoring a positive analogy between Anat and Moses acquires strength in 32:19-20, when Moses reaches the camp. The story is told from his point of view: "when Moses drew near to the camp and he saw *(rāʾâ)* the calf" (32:19). His first action is one of rage, underscoring his volatile person-

---

70. Gressmann, *Moses und seine Zeit*, 202; Houtman, *Exodus*, 3:656, 654, respectively.
71. Andersen, "Lexicographical Note."
72. Makujina, "Additional Considerations," 39-46.
73. M. Delcor, "Une allusion à ʿAnath déesse guerrière en Ex. 32:18?" *JJS* 33 (1982): 145-60.

ality from the opening chapters of Exodus (see 2:11-15). He shatters the tablets, whose preservation he had only just secured through mediation. The commentators have puzzled over the abrupt change in his personality, from the defender of the people to the one waging holy war against them. Some suggest the combination of different stories. This may very well be the case, since Exodus 32 is a combination of Deuteronomy 9–10 and 1 Kgs 12:26-32. But there is also a strategy in the Non-P author's construction of the story. The abrupt shift in character signals that Moses' loyalty to Yahweh will now take precedence in his character development over his previous role as mediator for the people. The distinctive acts of Moses take place at different settings on the mountain. Thus at the base of the mountain, Moses takes on the divine anger, and he utterly destroys the calf. He burns *(wayyiśrōp)* it in fire. He grinds *(wayyiṭḥan)* it to powder. Finally, he scatters *(wayyizer)* it on the water. His actions are contradictory and confusing, especially in imagining how the golden calf can be both burnt in fire and ground to powder in that order. But the intent of the Non-P historian is not the verisimilitude of Moses' actions, but his similarity to the goddess Anat. She performs the same sequence of actions against Mot, the god of death, out of her loyalty to Baal, the god of life. Mot boasts to Anat that he has consumed Baal. In response Anat wages holy war against him by also burning *(tšrpnn)*, grinding *(tṭḥnn)*, and scattering *(tdrʿnn)* Mot *(CTA* 6.ii.32-36).

In the Ugaritic myth the holy war actions of Anat against Mot are intended to purge the earth of death in order to prepare the world for a new cycle of life, which is evident when Baal assumes an active role after Anat's destruction of Mot *(CTA* 6.iii-v). The actions of Moses are also intended to purge the camp of the influence of the golden calf. O. Hvidberg-Hansen interprets the purging to include the ritual of the last grain during harvest, in which case the story is aimed at the worship life of the Israelites during the monarchical period.[74] But in the story of Moses the purging of the camp goes beyond the golden calf to the people and the failed leadership of Aaron in 32:21-29. The story of the golden calf in chap. 32, therefore, need not be limited to the threats of agricultural worship during the time of the monarchy. C. Begg has clarified that the destructive actions of Moses are formalized motifs throughout ancient Near Eastern literature to signify the total destruction of a cultic object. He notes further that this motif repeats in the Deuteronomistic History in the actions of Josiah against the cultic objects in Jerusalem.[75]

32:21-29   The Non-P History contains a criticism of Aaron and the iconic form of worship he represents. The criticism is presented through the

---

74. O. Hvidberg-Hansen, "Die Vernichtung des Goldenen Kalbes und der Ugaritische Ernteritus," *AcOr* 33 (1971): 5-46, esp. 22-23.

75. Begg, "Destuction of the Calf," 208-37.

juxtaposition of Aaron (32:21-25) and the Levites (32:26-29). First, Moses addresses Aaron (32:21-25) about his failed leadership, which provides the background for the call of the Levites to service in purging the camp (32:26-29). Thus the etiological story of the rise of the Levites to a leadership position functions in the Non-P History as a replacement to the leadership of Aaron. In the introduction to this section I indicated the inner-biblical relationship between the non-Levitical worship practices of Jeroboam in 1 Kgs 12:26-32 and the active role of the Levites in Exod 32:26-29. The Levites earn their ordination through this action of loyalty. This is certainly not the case in the P History, where the Levites assume an intermediate role between the Aaronide priests and the people as substitutes for the firstborn (Numbers 1–8).

The address of Moses to Aaron in Exod 32:21-25 maintains the distinction between him and the people first established in vv. 1-5. Aaron repeats the events from vv. 1-5 with an important omission. In his version of the story, the calf emerges from the fire. It does not result from his manufacturing of it. But the statement in v. 25, that the people are "out of control," is unequivocal in placing the blame of the golden calf on Aaron's leadership. The closing phrase in v. 25, "for Aaron let them out of control to the derision of those who would rise against them," is out of place, since there are no enemies at the mountain of God. H. Valentin is likely correct in detecting political commentary on the fate of the northern kingdom, if not the entire history of the monarchical period.[76]

The Levites emerge as the defenders of Yahweh in 32:25-29. But the Non-P History presents an ambivalent portrait of the Levites. The stories surrounding them accentuate violence in service to Yahweh. Levi and Simeon destroy the family of Shechem in order to avenge the defilement of their sister, Dinah (Gen 34:25-31). This action is cursed in the last words of Jacob (Gen 49:5-7). The patriarch characterizes it as uncontrolled and denies the Levites land in Canaan because of their violence. The Levites now return in the story of the golden calf, where their singular allegiance to Yahweh and their violence become heroic. They answer the prophetic call to war by Moses: "Thus said Yahweh the God of Israel, 'Each place his sword on his side. Go back and forth from gate to gate in the camp and kill each his brother, his neighbor, and his kin.'" The Levites kill three thousand Israelites to purge the camp from the sin of worshiping the golden calf.

The action of the Levites is praised in the Song of Moses (Deut 33:8-11), which attributes their priestly status (as the ones who consult the Thummim and the Urim) to their loyalty to Yahweh, even at the cost of family and children. When read together, these stories account for the special status of the Levites as priests (Deuteronomy 33) who are without land in Canaan (Genesis 49).

---

76. Valentin, *Aaron*, 248, 268.

Their special role is rooted in violence, which is motivated by allegiance to God. The Non-P History contains traditions that both praise (Deut 33:8-11) and curse (Gen 49:5-7) their fanaticism. But the story of the golden calf falls squarely on the side of praising them. Moses even conveys a divine blessing on them for killing their own sons and brothers. The purging of the camp by the Levites concludes the story of the golden calf.

32:30-35   This episode provides a bridge between the story of the golden calf (vv. 1-29) and the theme of mediation (chap. 33). The central problem in 32:30-35 is no longer the threat of the calf, but the absence of divine presence (vv. 34-35). Verses 30-33 begin on a new day, with Moses stating his intention to the people: "Perhaps I can atone for your sin." The episode explores the corporate nature of sin and forgiveness. The corporate consequence of sin is central in the early chapters of Exodus, where the sin of Pharaoh affects all Egyptians and even the land of Egypt. The opening statement of Moses to the people, "you have sinned a great sin," also suggests the corporate nature of the sin resulting from the golden calf. This background allows for the focus of the story on the question of whether a single person can make atonement for the many.

The Non-P historian does not believe that it is possible for the one to atone for the many. Moses requests forgiveness for the people in vv. 31-32. He states to the Deity that if it is not possible for God to forgive the people corporately, then he wishes his name be removed from the divine record book. Yahweh's response to Moses is abrupt, underscoring the requirement of individual responsibility for sin: "Whoever sinned against me, I will blot out from my book" (v. 33). Suomala has argued that the failure of Moses to intercede in vv. 30-35 is because Moses takes the initiative in the process of mediation, as compared to his more deferential role in vv. 7-14.[77] But the failure of Moses is not his role in mediation, but the theme of corporate versus individual punishment. Yahweh rejects Moses' solution concerning sin and forgiveness. Individuals responsible for an action must atone for their own sin. The P author will extend the Non-P author's theology of individual responsibility for sin beyond the people in general to the character of Moses. In the P History Moses will lose the gift of the promised land because of his own sin (Num 20:1-13), not because of the sin of the nation.

Exodus 32:34-35 returns to the theme of divine presence, but on an ominous note, providing transition to the central themes of chap. 33. Yahweh commands Moses to lead the people from the mountain, noting that the Messenger will provide guidance. The motif of the Messenger recalls the earlier appearance from the outset of Exodus, where the close identity between the Messenger and Yahweh was emphasized. The Messenger appeared to Moses on the

---

77. Suomala, *Moses and God,* 26-28.

mountain (3:1-2), led and then guarded the people at the Red Sea (14:19), and was promised to the people at the close of the Book of the Covenant (23:20-33; see the commentary). Exodus 32:34 departs from the previous passages by emphasizing the difference between Yahweh and the Messenger. The leading of the Messenger is not the same as the day of Yahweh's visitation. The separation between Yahweh and the Messenger provides the setting for Moses' further mediation in chap. 33 for the presence of Yahweh. But before the further intercession of Moses takes place, the story gives way momentarily in v. 35 to the theme of punishment, which is partially realized with a plague.

INTERCESSION OF MOSES (33:1-23)

³³:¹*And Yahweh spoke to Moses, "Go and ascend from here, you and the people whom you brought up from the land of Egypt, to the land that I swore to Abraham, Isaac, and Jacob, saying, 'To your offspring I will give it.'"* ²*And I will send before you a Messenger. And I will drive out the Canaanites, the Amorites, and the Hittites, and the Perizzites, the Hivites, and the Jebusites,* ³*to a land flowing with milk and honey. But I will not go up in the midst of you because a people of stiff neck are you, lest I exterminate you in the way."*

⁴*And the people heard this evil word and they mourned. And no one put on ornaments.*

⁵*And Yahweh said to Moses, "Say to the Israelites, 'You are a people of stiff neck. If for one moment I would go up in the midst of you, I would exterminate you. Now take off your ornaments from on you, so that I may know what I will do to you.'"*

⁶*And the Israelites despoiled themselves of their ornaments from Mount Horeb onward.*

⁷*But Moses would take the tent and he pitched it outside the camp at a distance from the camp. And he named it the tent of meeting. And everyone who sought Yahweh would go out to the tent of meeting, which was outside the camp.* ⁸*And whenever Moses went out to the tent, all the people would rise, and each would stand at the door of his tent, and watch after Moses until he entered the tent.* ⁹*And whenever Moses entered the tent, the pillar of cloud descended and stood at the door of the tent, and he spoke with Moses.* ¹⁰*And all the people saw the pillar of cloud standing at the door of the tent. And all the people rose and worshiped, each at the door of his tent.* ¹¹*And Yahweh spoke to Moses face-to-face as a man speaks to his friend. And when he returned to the camp, his young assistant Joshua, son of Nun, would not depart from the tent.*

¹²*And Moses said to Yahweh, "See, you say to me, 'Bring up this people.' But you have not made known to me whom you will send with me. And you said, 'I*

know you by name and you have indeed found favor in my eyes.' ¹³*Now if indeed I have found favor in your eyes, make known to me, please, your way, so that I may know you and that I may find favor in your eyes. See also that this nation is your people."*

¹⁴*And he said, "My face will go and I will give you rest."*

¹⁵*And he said to him, "If your face is not going, do not bring us up from here.* ¹⁶*For how shall it be known that I have found favor in your eyes, I and your people, if not in your going with us? Then we will be separate, I and your people, from all the people who are on the face of the earth."*

¹⁷*And Yahweh said to Moses, "Even this word that you spoke I will do because you have found favor in my eyes and I know you by name."*

¹⁸*And he said, "Show me, please, your glory."*

¹⁹*And he said, "I will make all my goodness pass before your face. And I will call before your face the name Yahweh. And I will grant favor to whom I will grant favor and I will show mercy to whom I will show mercy."* ²⁰*And he said, "You will not be able to see my face, for a human cannot see me and live."* ²¹*And Yahweh said, "There is a place near me. You will station yourself on the rock.* ²²*And when my glory passes by, I will place you in the cleft of the rock, and I will cover my hand on you until my passing.* ²³*Then I will remove my hand and you will see my back. But my face shall not be seen."*

Notes

33:2 *and I will send before you a messenger.* The MT *mal'āk* is indefinite, raising a question about the relationship of this messenger to past appearances of the messenger (see the commentary). The messenger is definite in the LXX, *ton angelon.*

the Canaanites, the Amorites, and the Hittites, and the Perizzites, the Hivites, and the Jebusites. The order of the indigenous nations differs slightly in the LXX, which omits the Canaanites and includes the Girgashites: Amorites, Hittites, Perizzites, Girgashites, Hivites, and Jebusites.

33:3 *to a land flowing with milk and honey.* The phrase is awkward in the MT and in the Sam. It is likely a continuation of the statement: "I will send before you a messenger." The LXX rewrites the phrase as a sentence, *kai eisaxō se eis gēn,* "I will bring you to the land."

33:4 *and they mourned.* Hebrew *wayyit'abbālû,* "and they mourned," may be described in more detail in the LXX, *katepenthēsan en penthikois,* if the latter phrase indicates "mourning garments" (see LSJ 1360). Wevers reads the phrase as a cognate free infinitive, "they mourned bitterly."[1]

And no one put on ornaments. The LXX omits this phrase.

33:5 *And Yahweh said to Moses.* The divine address is directly to the people in the LXX, *kai eipen kyrios tois huiois Israēl.*

---

1. Wevers, *Notes,* 542.

If for one moment I would go up in the midst of you. The LXX departs from the MT, *horate mē plēgēn allēn epaxō egō eph' hymas,* "see, lest I bring on you another plague," which most likely refers to 32:25.

Now take off your ornaments from on you, so that I may know what I will do to you. Hebrew includes an imperative, *hôrēd,* and a cohortative, *wĕ'ēd'â,* which is translated as purpose, "so that I may know" *(IBHS §34.5.2).* The LXX departs from the Hebrew: *nyn oun aphelesthe tas stolas tōn doxōn hymōn kai ton kosmon kai deixō soi ha poiēsō soi,* "now take off your robes of glory and the decorations, and I will show you what I will do to you."

33:6 *and the Israelites despoiled themselves of their ornaments.* The LXX continues with the reference to robes and decorations.

from Mount Horeb onward. Hebrew *mēhar ḥôrēb* is both locative, indicating the location of Mount Horeb as the cosmic mountain of revelation in the Non-P History and in Deuteronomy; and temporal, indicating that from this instance onward Israelite worship is characterized as being aniconic.[2] The LXX translates, *apo tou orous tou chōrēb.*

33:7 *Moses would take the tent.* The prefixed form of the Hebrew verb *yiqqaḥ* most likely expresses frequentative action (GKC §112e). Verses 7-11 therefore are meant to describe the ongoing worship practices associated with the tent of meeting. The LXX changes the text in two ways. The action of Moses is stated with a participle and an aorist form of the verb, *labōn Mōusēs . . . epēxen,* which does not suggest the customary action of the Hebrew. The tent is also identified as Moses' own tent, *tēn skēnēn autou,* rather than "the tent," Hebrew *hā'ōhel.*

he pitched it outside the camp at a distance from the camp. The antecedent for Hebrew *lô,* "it," is debated. The problem of translation is related to the history of composition, raising the question of whether the word should be located in its present literary context or as part of an independent narrative. Some interpreters read the unit independently from its context to suggest a reference to the ark.[3] Others interpret "for himself," suggesting that the tent is Moses' own or at least specially reserved for him, as is the case in the LXX.[4] My translation follows those who translate as *dativus commodi,* referring to the tent.[5]

33:9 *and he spoke with Moses.* The subject is not stated.

33:12 *And Moses said to Yahweh, "See, you say to me, 'Bring up this people.' But you have not made known to me whom you will send with me."* The motif of sight *(rā'â)* is central to the structure of 33:12-23, separating the episode between a dialogue that is dominated by Moses (vv. 12-17) and another that is dominated by the divine response (vv. 18-23). The motif of sight is employed by Moses two times in vv. 12-17 to call upon Yahweh to see divine promises and obligations. In v. 12 Moses focuses on his relationship with the Deity: "See, you say to me." In v. 13 he extends the di-

---

2. See Houtman, *Exodus,* 3:692.

3. See already Wellhausen, *Composition,* 108-10. For more extensive bibliography see Haran, *Temples and Temple-Service,* 263 n. 5.

4. Haran, *Temples and Temple-Service,* 264.

5. See Childs, *Exodus,* 584; Houtman, *Exodus,* 3:693.

vine obligation to the people: "See also that this nation is your people." Moses' third use of the motif advances the story to a new level of theophany in v. 18: "Show me *(har'ēnî)*, please, your glory." This request provides a transition to an extended divine speech in which the motif of sight *(rā'â)* occurs four times. Yahweh states twice in v. 20 that humans cannot see *(rā'â)* the face of God. The motif returns in the closing verse (v. 23), when Yahweh concedes a theophany of his back to Moses: "You will see *(rā'â)* my back." The entire dialogue between Moses and Yahweh however ends with the emphatic statement: "But my face shall not be seen *(yērā'û)*."

33:13 *your way.* The MT *děrākekā* is singular. The Sam is plural, *drkyk,* "your ways."

see also that this nation is your people. The LXX reinterprets the argument from a focus on Yahweh to Moses. In the LXX Moses now wishes to know that the people are indeed Yahweh's and that they are a great nation, *hina gnō hoti laos sou to ethnos to mega touto.*

33:16 *then we will be separate.* Hebrew *wěniplênû* is also translated "distinct, distinguished" (NRSV, NJPS). The LXX translates *endoxasthēsomai egō te kai ho laos sou,* "then I and your people will be glorified." Wevers suggests that the LXX reflects the word *npl'nw* rather than *nplynw.*[6] See the interplay of these terms in 33:16 and 34:10.

33:19 *And I will call before your face the name Yahweh.* Hebrew *qārā'* could also be translated, "I will proclaim" (NRSV). The LXX presents a somewhat different picture, *egō pareleusomai proteros sou tē doxē mou* [as compared to the divine goodness in the Hebrew] *kai kalesō epi tō onomati mou Kyrios enantion sou,* "I will pass before you in my glory and I will call in/through my name Lord before you."

And I will grant favor to whom I will grant favor and I will show mercy to whom I will show mercy. The statement is in the form of the *idem per idem.*[7] The construction emphasizes the verbal idea, which in this case is divine favor and mercy. The formula can also be used in some cases to terminate debate. Whether this function is present in 33:19 depends in part on the syntactical relationship between vv. 19a and 19b. Three interpretations are possible. The first is that v. 19b is intended to halt the dialogue between Moses and Yahweh. The second is that the merciful character of Yahweh in v. 19b is the cause for the proclamation of the name in v. 19a. The third interpretation is that v. 19b is a further revelation of the name Yahweh proclaimed in v. 19a.

Commentary

Central Theme

The interpretation of the central theme in Exodus 33 is difficult for two related reasons. First, Exodus 33 contains a variety of literary motifs. The following mo-

6. Wevers, *Notes,* 550.
7. Lundbom, "God's Use."

tifs occur in Exodus 33. The divine promise of land plays a central role in the chapter. Yahweh instructs Moses to leave the divine mountain and to journey to the promised land, the possession of which is assured by the promise to the ancestors (vv. 1-3). Yahweh also repeats the promise of the Messenger as a guide (v. 2) from 23:20-33, but separates the leading of the Messenger from the divine presence: "I will not go up in the midst of you" (v. 3). The people respond to the retreat of God as their guide with ritual mourning accompanied by the removal of ornaments (vv. 4-6). The ritual action of the people is juxtaposed with an account of the tent of meeting outside the camp as the setting where Moses meets God (vv. 7-11). The remainder of the chapter explores the intercessory role of Moses (vv. 12-23), presumably in the setting of the tent of meeting, although there are no explicit literary connections to the tent of meeting (vv. 7-11). The intercession of Moses progresses in two parts with distinct themes. In vv. 12-17 Moses requests the presence of God on the journey to the promised land, continuing the theme from vv. 1-3. In vv. 18-23 Moses requests a new revelation of Yahweh.

Second, chap. 33 cannot be read in isolation. Exodus 33 bridges the story of the golden calf and the destruction of the tablets (chap. 32) with the account of covenant renewal and the reissuing of new tablets (chap. 34). Thus the intertwining of themes in chap. 33 blurs the literary boundaries between chap. 32, especially vv. 30-35, and 34:1-10. The guidance of the Messenger appears in 32:30-34 and 33:1-3, and the theme of theophany in the second request of Moses (vv. 18-23) provides a bridge to the events in chap. 34.

The overview of the literary segments indicates two central themes in chap. 33, the divine guidance in the wilderness and the revelation of God at the mountain. The two themes are held together by the account of the tent of meeting at the center of the chapter and the mediation of Moses. Interpreters accentuate one theme or the other, depending on which portion of the chapter they judge to be most prominent. J. Muilenburg, for example, focused on the intercessory role of Moses, isolating 33:1a and 12-17 as an instance of covenant mediation, in which the role of Moses modeled a cultic liturgy.[8]

H. Gressmann judged the central theme in chap. 33 to be the guidance of the Israelites in the wilderness. It introduces the chapter (vv. 1-6) and continues in the first part of Moses' intercession (vv. 12-17). Gressmann also noted that the theme of guidance relates a series of texts, including 23:20-33; 33:1-6, 12-23; 34:5b-9; and Num 10:29-36. The account of the tent of meeting was not original to the narrative, according to Gressmann. He also judged the theme of theophany or the cultic presence of God to be unimportant to the story.[9] Instead

8. J. Muilenburg, "The Intercession of the Covenant Mediator (Exodus 33:1a, 12-17)," in *Hearing,* 170-92.

9. Gressmann, *Mose und seine Zeit,* 218-19.

the theme of divine guidance in the wilderness was most prominent, becoming associated with the ark in Num 10:29-36.

Noth concluded that the central theme was "the presence of God in the midst of his people." The prominent role of this theme was evident in that it "plays some part in all of [the literary units]."[10] Noth concluded that the theme of the presence of God is first established in 32:34a: "And now go and lead the people where I spoke to you. Indeed, my Messenger will go before you." Exodus 32:34a certainly introduces the theme of divine presence after the incident of the golden calf. But the more important text for developing this theme is the account of the tent of meeting (33:7-11), since it describes the cultic presence of God and suggests that it is the setting both for the mourning of the Israelites (vv. 4-6) and for the intercession of Moses (vv. 12-23). I follow the lead of Noth and interpret the central theme of chap. 33 as the presence of God in the midst of the people.

Childs also underscores the crucial role of the tent of meeting in the present form of Exodus 33: "In terms of topical sequence vv. 7-11 serve as a connection between what precedes and what follows by combining Moses, God, and the people within one activity."[11] He has clarified the pivotal role of the tent of meeting in developing the theme of divine presence in the present form of chap. 33. Dohmen adds support for this conclusion, noting that the tent of meeting is anything but "superfluous" to the story. The tent of meeting accentuates the intercessory role of Moses, which is crucial for resolving the central problem of the presence of the God in the midst of the people.[12]

The introduction of the tent of meeting in 33:7-11 not only addresses the immediate crisis of the golden calf and its aftermath but also provides the cultic setting for theophany in the Non-P History. The broader literary role of the tent of meeting is evident from parallels to the original theophany in 19:16-17. The location of the tent of meeting outside the camp recalls the original theophany, which also took place outside the camp: "Moses brought the people out of the camp to meet God" (19:17).[13] In both stories the Israelites also overhear the conversation between Yahweh and Moses (19:19; 33:4). The insight of Gressmann also indicates that the divine presence of God in the tent of meeting is not limited to the theophany at the divine mountain, but continues to function in the larger narrative when the tent of meeting and the ark become closely associated with each other as the Israelites journey toward the promised land.

---

10. Noth, *Exodus*, 253.

11. Childs, *Exodus*, 592.

12. Dohmen, *Exodus 19-40*, 322.

13. See M. Haran, "The Nature of the ʿ*ōhel mô ʿēdh*' in Pentateuchal Sources," *JSS* 5 (1960): 50-65, esp. 57.

Authors

The composition of Exodus 33 is debated in the modern period. Many interpreters have argued that the P author plays little or no role in the composition of the chapter. Syntactical problems in 33:1-3 may indicate a history of composition: 33:1 repeats the command from 32:34, the insertion of the Messenger in 33:2-3a fits only loosely, and the closing line in v. 3b lacks a verb.[14] But there are no clear signs of P authorship associated with any of these problems. Moreover, the P account of the tabernacle in chaps. 25–31 creates a distinct portrait of the cult from the tent of meeting in 33:7-11, which argues further against attributing this text to the P author.[15] The dialogue between Yahweh and Moses in 33:12-17 is tightly woven, suggesting a single author.[16] The central motifs of knowledge (*yādaʿ*), face *(pānîm)*, finding favor in the eyes of God, rest *(nûaḥ)*, and the emphasis on charismatic persuasion in mediation do not point to the P author. Since 33:18-23 lacks the central motifs of vv. 12-17, it may be a distinct composition, intended to qualify the face-to-face encounter between Yahweh and Moses stated in v. 11.[17] But the change in theme from divine leading to theophany would account for the distinctive language between vv. 12-17 and 18-23, and the qualification of the face-to-face encounter in vv. 7-11 could be attributed to the Non-P author as well as to the P author, since neither author would agree with this portrayal of theophany. W. Johnstone has argued that the motif of glory *(kābôd)* in v. 18 indicates P authorship, but the association of the motif with God's "goodness" *(ṭôb,* v. 19) does not point to the more technical development of the Glory of Yahweh *(kĕbôd yhwh)* in the P History (e.g., 24:17).[18]

I attribute the composition of Exodus 33 to the Non-P author. The juxtaposition of literary units suggests that the author is incorporating an independent tradition of the tent of meeting (33:7-11) as the central text for exploring Mosaic intercession. The theme of Mosaic intercession in chap. 33 and its relationship to chaps. 32 and 34 suggests that the Non-P author is basing the story on the intercession of Moses in Deuteronomy 9–10 (see the commentary on

14. See Blum, *Studien,* 57-60.

15. Cf. W. Johnstone ("From the Mountain to Kadesh with Special Reference to Exodus 32.30–34.29*," in *Chronicles and Exodus: An Analogy and Its Application* [JSOTSup 275; Sheffield: Sheffield Academic Press, 1998], 262-80, esp. 276), who attributes a much more prominent role to the P author in shaping Exodus 32–34. The criteria for identifying P authorship in Exodus 32–34 are language and differences in structure from Deuteronomy 9–10. Johnstone concludes that the P author is responsible for the command to depart from the mountain (Exod 33:1-6), the insertion of the tent of meeting (33:7-11), and the second intercession of Moses (33:17-23), which qualifies the statement that Moses spoke to the Deity face-to-face (33:11).

16. See esp. Muilenburg, "Intercession."

17. Van Seters, *Life of Moses,* 322-23; Blum, *Studien,* 64-65.

18. Johnstone, *Chronicles and Exodus,* 275.

Exodus 32). A comparison to Deuteronomy 9–10 indicates that the mediation of Moses is significantly expanded in Exodus 33. Deuteronomy 9–10 is structured around the motif of Moses interceding with God for a forty-day period. The motif occurs four times (Deut 9:9, 18, 25; 10:10), resulting in a four-part story (see the outline in the commentary on Exodus 32). Moses receives the tablets on Mount Horeb (Deut 9:8-11), the tablets are destroyed (9:12-20), the calf is destroyed (9:21-29), and new tablets are issued to Moses (10:1-10). The four-part intercession of Moses concludes with the command to journey to the promised land (10:11).

Exodus 33 provides detailed commentary on the final intercession of Moses in Deut 10:1-10, when Yahweh issues the new tablets. The Non-P author's expansion of the story includes more than Exodus 33. The episode begins already in 32:30-35 and continues into 34:1-10. The author departs from the strict structure of forty-day intervals to mark the transitions in the intercession of Moses, transitions that are central to Deuteronomy 9–10. The intercession of Moses in Exodus 33 is refashioned around the concluding command in Deut 10:11 that Moses lead the Israelites to the promised land. The result is that the command to leave Mount Horeb now occasions the final intercession of Moses in Exodus 33. The dialogue between Moses and Yahweh over divine presence and guidance in 32:30–34:10 also takes place in a more indefinite period of time. The expanded story provides a far more complex portrayal of Moses as intercessor, including the liturgical model for intercessory prayer (32:30-34; 33:12-23; 34:8-9). The liturgy is accompanied by a more subtle theology of divine grace and forgiveness, which explores the process by which the Deity is able to repent of evil (32:30-34; 33:18-23; 34:6-7). In addition, the Non-P author provides a cultic setting for Mosaic intercession in the tent of meeting (33:7-11) that is lacking in Deuteronomy 9–10. The result is a nuanced reflection on atonement, forgiveness, and cultic intercession. The conclusion of the Non-P historian is that Moses is not able to atone for the many (Exod 32:30-34). Individual responsibility emerges as the highest moral value in the wake of the golden calf (32:33). But Moses is able to intercede for the many, and in so doing he is able to persuade Yahweh to change his intention (33:18-23; 34:6-9).

Literary Structure

The central text in Exodus 33 concerns the tent of meeting, the designation for the sanctuary in the Non-P History. The sanctuary tent and its rituals are presented through three scenes, providing the structure for the chapter. First, 33:1-6 establishes the setting of crisis in the aftermath of golden calf. The Israelites have lost the presence of God, which loss prompts a mourning ritual that also includes imagery of unfaithfulness in marriage, illicit sex, and divorce when

God strips the people of ornaments. The action of God provides the etiology for aniconic worship at Mount Horeb. Second, in 33:7-11 the imagery of divorce (or at least separation) continues when the tent of meeting is introduced as a sanctuary outside the camp. It represents the presence of God at the fringe of the people's life. The scene focuses on the ritual behavior of the Israelites, portraying their actions at the doors of their tents while Moses processes to the tent of meeting outside the camp. Third, 33:12-23 outlines the central ritual of intercession within the tent of meeting. The scene recounts an intercessory prayer of Moses for the presence of God, repeating the form of intercession from the summit of the mountain (32:11-13). The repetition indicates that for the Non-P historian the tent of meeting bridges the gap between heaven and earth at the time of crisis. The ritual means for connecting heaven and earth is persuasive prayer, a form of intercession that Moses learned at the summit of the mountain with God. The goal of Moses' intercession is to regain the lost presence of God symbolized by the destruction of the tablets.

33:1-6   The aftermath of the golden calf creates a situation of crisis. God retreats from the people (vv. 1-3), they mourn by not putting on jewelry (v. 4), God commands them not to wear jewelry (v. 5), and the narrator concludes the section by describing the Israelites as "despoiled" (v. 6).

The divine speech to Moses in vv. 1-3 repeats many of the central themes of the book: the exodus from Egypt, the promise of land to the ancestors, and the future conquest of the indigenous nations. God commands Moses to leave the mountain, repeating the exodus motif (see the commentary on chap. 13), but with Moses as the subject: "Go and ascend from here, you and the people whom *you* brought up from the land of Egypt." The identification of the exodus with Moses' leadership, not God's, repeats the divine statement from 32:7, where Yahweh judged the people to be corrupt. The exodus motif is coupled with the divine promise of land (see the commentary on chap. 13). Moses is to lead the people "to the land [God] promised . . . to Abraham, Isaac, and Jacob." Finally God even underscores the leading of a "Messenger" to conquer the indigenous nations (see the commentary on chaps. 3 and 23), adding a description of the utopian character of the land, "flowing with milk and honey" (see the commentary on chap. 3).

But God refuses to accompany the people: "I will not go up in the midst of you." The refusal introduces a separation between God and the Messenger that did not exist in the previous occurrences (cf. 3:2; 14:19; 23:20-33). The reference to the Messenger is also indefinite, "a Messenger," as compared to the definite identification in the past occurrences. These problems have prompted questions about the authorship of 33:2-3a. E. Blum suggests a later addition to the text at this point.[19] The problem of authorship does not resolve the chal-

19. Blum, *Studien*, 58-59.

lenge of interpretation, especially with regard to the identity of the Messenger in this case. Past references to the Messenger underscore the close relationship to Yahweh. The present indefinite reference indicates separation from Yahweh and perhaps a closer identification with Moses. The central point of the opening speech, however, is the divine retreat from the people. God will remain faithful to the ancestral promises, but the people have become incompatible with divine holiness. Their "stiff-necked" character has repelled God, creating a crisis situation in which God is now absent.

Exodus 33:4 provides a parallel to 19:19. Both texts indicate that the people are able to hear God speak with Moses during the theophany. The people fear God in the first theophany (20:18). In 33:4 the people react to the divine retreat with a ritual of mourning: "They mourned" (*'ābal*). The mourning rite is associated with funerals. It is performed for seven days at the death of Jacob (Gen 50:10) and for thirty days at the death of Moses (Deut 34:8). Joab's advice to the wise woman of Tekoa provides insight into the ritual practice: "Pretend you are in mourning. Dress in mourning clothes, and don't use any cosmetic lotions. Act like a woman who has spent many days grieving for the dead" (2 Sam 14:2). The description of the people, not putting on any "ornaments" (*'ădî*), underscores their ritual of mourning over the absence of God. The LXX makes the mourning ritual more explicit by including the reference to clothing.

Immediately after the description of the people not wearing ornaments (33:4), Yahweh demands that they remove their ornaments (*'ădî*). The juxtaposition of the seemingly contradictory statements has raised questions of authorship, suggesting to some a doublet that indicates two authors. But the dual reference to ornaments may also signal a different use of the motif in the divine command than in the ritual of mourning. The divine demand to strip off ornaments introduces the themes of marriage, illicit sex, and perhaps also Yahweh's desire to divorce the people. Brides put on jewelry in preparation for their wedding in the Hebrew Bible: "A bride adorns herself with her jewels" (Isa 61:10). The practice acquires a theological interpretation throughout the prophetic literature to describe Yahweh's love for Israel, as well as the marriage between God and the people. Second Isaiah writes of the salvation of Zion: "As surely as I live, declares Yahweh, you will wear them [your sons] all as ornaments; you will put them on, like a bride" (49:18). Ezekiel also describes Yahweh's love for Jerusalem as marriage through a detailed description of the jewelry and ornaments with which God clothed the city: "When I looked at you and saw that you were old enough for love, I spread the corner of my garment over you and covered your nakedness. . . . I adorned you with jewelry: I put bracelets on your arms and a necklace around your neck" (Ezek 16:8-14).

Conversely, the stripping off of jewelry signifies judgment and even divorce. The background for this image is unfaithfulness, when the ornaments of marriage are used to attract other lovers. The sin of Jerusalem, according to Ezekiel, is that the city put on jewelry for strangers (Ezek 23:40). The judgment is that God in a rage will strip the city naked; and more, even her lovers will return to strip away her fine jewelry (16:35-42). Hosea uses the same violent imagery of rage and jealousy to describe his reaction to the prostitution of Gomer and his desire to divorce her (Hosea 2). Yahweh's demand in Exod 33:5 that the Israelites strip off their ornaments introduces the motif of marriage into the story of the golden calf and the violent rage of an offended lover from the literature of divorce in the prophetic corpus. Given the violence associated with the motif, the retreat of God from the people, as a momentary reprieve from judgment, is surprising: "If for one moment I would go up in the midst of you, I would exterminate you" (33:5).

The Non-P historian employs the imagery of marriage, unfaithfulness, and divorce as background to forbid any icons in worship. Verse 6 indicates that the scene is meant to be an etiology for imageless worship: "And the Israelites despoiled themselves of their ornaments from Mount Horeb onward." One consequence of the golden calf, according to the Non-P historian, is that jewelry, ornaments, and fine metals such as gold and silver become associated with foreign gods. Their use in the Israelite cult implies unfaithful sexual relations by the Israelites with other gods, making Yahweh the offended spouse. The Non-P historian leaves open the possibility that in a utopian world "good gold" may be possible, as it exists in the mythical land of Havilah (Gen 2:11-12). But in the present state of the world gold is incompatible with divine holiness. Jacob is the first to realize this (Gen 35:1-4). The Decalogue makes the revelation clear to all Israelites (Exod 20:3-6). The golden calf illustrates its danger (chap. 32). Deuteronomy provides extensive theological reflection on the problem (Deuteronomy 4–5, 9–10). The story of Achan places gold under the ban (Joshua 6–7).

The jewels and ornaments used by the Israelites to fashion the golden calf are their undoing, according to the Non-P historian. The people "despoil themselves" (Hithpael of *nāṣal*) of their ornaments, and thus they lose the booty acquired in leaving Egypt (see the commentary on 3:21-22; 11:2-3; 12:35-36). The absence of ornaments establishes the paradigm of imageless worship, symbolized by Mount Horeb in the Non-P History and in Deuteronomy. The tent of meeting represents the sanctuary for aniconic worship in the Non-P History. It is introduced abruptly in 33:7-11, and it must be contrasted to the tabernacle/tent of meeting (chaps. 25–31; 35–40) in the P History, where gold was lavished on the sanctuary furnishings and woven into the priestly vestments.

33:7-11 The Non-P History is vague about the origins of the tent of meeting. It is introduced simply as "the tent" *(hā'ōhel),* suggesting its existence before the incident of the golden calf. There are echoes of the tent of meeting in the presentation of Abraham sitting at the door of his tent, where he receives divine revelation (Genesis 18). The literary relationship is not spelled out in the Non-P History, and the origin of the tent of meeting is left unexplained. Thus unlike the tabernacle in the P History, Moses does not make the tent shrine, but he does name it. Exodus 33:7 states that Moses removed the tent from the camp, placed it outside the camp, and called it *'ōhel mô'ēd,* "tent of meeting," from Hebrew *yā'ad,* "to appoint," "to meet," or "to gather by appointment." The noun *mô'ēd* can take on religious meaning, signifying appointed times and places, when God and humans meet. Appointed times are sacred festivals, such as the Passover (Num 9:2), and the tent of meeting is a sacred place where God and humans meet.

R. J. Clifford provides insight into the history of religions background of the tent of meeting. He notes parallels to the Canaanite tradition of El's tent dwelling.[20] El's tent shrine is located on his cosmic mountain (*CTA* 1.iii.21-24), at the source of the Two Rivers (*CTA* 3.E.13-16). The tent is the location for divine assembly (i.e., "meetings," *CTA* 1–2) and for authoritative decrees (*CTA* 3.E.38 41). A direct relation between the two shrines cannot be determined, but the parallels indicate that the tent of meeting at Mount Horeb participates in the mythology of the cosmic mountain. It symbolizes the cult site where God is present on earth and where Yahweh issues divine degrees, establishing the rituals of aniconic worship.

V. Hurowitz provides further insight into the setting and function of the tent of meeting, noting a tradition of temporary dwellings for deities in the ancient Near East.[21] Nabonidus places Shamash in a temporary dwelling while restoring Ebaddar. Enlil takes up residence in a temporary shrine when Ekur was destroyed. Hurowitz adds that mourning rituals often accompany the move of a deity to a temporary dwelling. The tradition of a temporary tent in ancient Near Eastern religious practice raises the question of whether the tent of meeting is also intended to be a provisional shrine in the Non-P History, providing yet another perspective on the mourning rites of the Israelites.

The location of the tent of meeting at the fringes of camp, rather than its center, encourages its interpretation as a temporary cultic site. The impermanent nature of the tent of meeting becomes more apparent when the Non-P History is read in conjunction with Deuteronomy and the Former Prophets (Joshua–2 Kings). The tent of meeting returns in Numbers 11–12 to clarify the leadership role of the seventy elders and the prophetic authority of Moses over against Aaron and Miriam. It occurs one other time in the Pentateuch, as the

---

20. R. J. Clifford, "The Tent of El and the Israelite Tent of Meeting," *CBQ* 33 (1971): 221-27; see further D. E. Fleming, "Mari's Large Public Tent and the Priestly Tent Sanctuary," *VT* 50 (2000): 484-98.

21. Hurowitz, *I Have Built,* 328-29.

location for the transfer of leadership from Moses to Joshua at the close of Deu-teronomy (Deut 31:14-23), relating the Non-P History and Deuteronomy. After the conquest of Canaan Joshua is envisioned as distributing the land to the tribes from the tent of meeting at Shiloh (Josh 18:1), relating the Non-P History with the Deuteronomistic History. The tradition of a temporary dwelling for Yahweh is evident in the Deuteronomistic History, according to Hurowitz.[22] The ark is placed in a house after it is rescued from the Philistines (1 Sam 7:1), and later David erects a tent for the ark (2 Sam 6:17). But in neither case is the tent of meeting mentioned. The temporary housing of the ark is associated with the tent of meeting, however, in the inauguration of the Jerusalem temple, when Solomon summons a procession to Jerusalem including the ark, the tent of meeting, and its furnishings (1 Kgs 8:1-4), to signal the new and permanent home of God in Jerusalem.

The tradition-historical background of the tent of meeting is complex, es-pecially its relationship to the Shiloh cult, and its function, if any, in the Jerusa-lem temple.[23] The present literary structure of the Non-P History, Deuteron-omy, and the Deuteronomistic History is clear, however. It presents the tent of meeting as a temporary shrine for Yahweh, to be replaced by the Jerusalem temple (1 Kings 8), even though it is the Deity's preferred residence (2 Sam 7:6-7). The P History further accentuates the temporary nature of the tent of meet-ing by framing Exodus 33 with the revelation (chaps. 25–31) and construction (chaps. 35–40) of the tabernacle. The result is that in the present form of Exo-dus the tent of meeting provides the bridge between the revelation (chaps. 25–31) and the construction (chaps. 35–40) of the tabernacle. The persuasive prayer of Moses for the presence of God in the tent shrine on the outskirts of the camp leads to the presence of God in the midst of camp in the P tabernacle.

The tent of meeting represents the auditory presence of God on earth lo-cated on the cosmic mountain, Horeb. The theophany of God is represented by the pillar of cloud *('ammûd he'ānān)*, which first appeared on the journey from Egypt (see 13:20-21). The pillar of cloud descends to the door of the tent *(petaḥ hā'ōhel)*, where the presence of God is indicated by speech: "he [Yahweh] spoke with Moses" at the entrance of the tent (v. 9). In the P History the door of the ta-bernacle/tent of meeting is where the priests officiated, performing sacrificial rituals for the people (chaps. 28–30). In 33:7-11 the door of the tent is the loca-tion for an auditory revelation, suggesting its influence from the prophetic tra-dition, according to M. Haran.[24] The emphasis on revelation as divine speech

22. Ibid.
23. See B. Halpern, "Shiloh," *ABD* 5:1213-15; R. E. Friedman, "Tabernacle," *ABD* 6:292-300.
24. Haran, *Temples and Temple-Service*, 271.

continues the account of theophany on the mountain in the Non-P History (19:19; 20:18-20). Just as the Decalogue was heard by all the Israelites, so now all the people see the descent of the pillar of cloud (v. 10).

The tent shrine is also available to all persons: "everyone who sought Yahweh would go out to the tent of meeting, which was outside the camp" (v. 7). In view of this, Haran suggests that the tent is "not a cultic institution housing the deity in its focal centre, but a tent where the solitary worshipper might receive divine inspiration from outside its empty interior." In other words, according to Haran, 33:7-11 does not describe "the deity's permanent 'abode,' but a place appointed for a fleeting prophetic vision."[25] Haran's conclusion may reflect the tradition-historical background of the tent of meeting. The role of the tent of meeting in the Non-P History certainly indicates a central (albeit temporary) shrine, with restricted access. Moses processes to the shrine without the people, and only Joshua dwells in it.

The ritual activity in 33:7-11 underscores the role of the tent of meeting as a central shrine. The focus is not on the people's access to God, but on the role of Moses. The Non-P historian separates Moses from the people, creating parallel rituals in which the people stand at the door of their tents in the camp, while Moses processes to the door of the tent of meeting outside the camp. The people worship at the doors of their tents, while Moses speaks to God at the door of the tent of meeting. The effect, according to A. M. Cooper and B. R. Goldstein, is to accentuate and to idealize the authority of Moses.[26] Only he speaks to God, and he does so "face-to-face," as friends speak to each other. All cultic activity takes place before the face of God (see the priestly blessing in Num 6:22-26). But the phrase "face-to-face" expresses a more intimate encounter of a direct and charismatic inspiration. Jacob realizes that he has seen God "face-to-face" only after he physically wrestles with God all night at the Jabbok River (Gen 32:30). Gideon comes to the same realization after his commission by the Messenger of Yahweh (Judg 6:22). Deuteronomy 5:4 attributes the same experience to the Israelite people, stating that they heard God speak the Decalogue to them "face-to-face," which is qualified in the following verse (5:5). It is Moses, however, who most clearly embodies the experience of speaking to God face-to-face, always within the tent of meeting. Deuteronomy 34:10 uses this experience to separate Moses from all other prophets, while Num 12:6-8 provides further commentary on Moses' unique status. God states: "With him [Moses] I speak face-to-face [lit. 'mouth-to-mouth'], clearly and not in riddles; he sees the form of Yahweh." Joshua is also

---

25. Ibid., 266.

26. A. M. Cooper and B. R. Goldstein, "At the Entrance to the Tent: More Cultic Resonances in Biblical Narrative," *JBL* 116 (1997): 201-15, esp. 205-6.

separated from the people in Exod 33:7-11, as the assistant of Moses who resides in the tent of meeting.

33:12-23 The scene recounts an intercessory prayer of Moses in the tent of meeting in two stages: first, Moses intercedes for the presence of God to guide the people (vv. 12-17), and then he requests to see God (vv. 18-23). The external rituals surrounding the tent, especially the procession of Moses outside the camp and the parallel action of the people at their tents (33:7-11), set the stage for a description of the ritual practice within the tent of meeting, or, as Haran suggests, at the door of the tent.[27] Exodus 32:30-35 provides the background for interpretation, when Moses stated to the people after the sin of the golden calf: "Perhaps I can make atonement for your sin." God firmly rejected the proposal of Moses, underscoring the inability of one human to atone for the many. Exodus 33:12-23 now returns to the theme, qualifying somewhat the earlier conclusion. Moses may not be able to atone for the many, but he can mediate for the many, especially in the context of covenant, as J. Muilenburg noted.[28] The mediation of Moses in the tent shrine repeats the form of his prayer at the summit of the mountain during the crisis of the golden calf (32:11-13). It is a prayer based on persuasion. The repetition of this form of prayer draws God in to the edges of the Israelite camp.

Exodus 33:12-17 is an intercession for the renewed presence of God with the Israelites. The prayer is persuasive. It influences the decision of God. The power of the prayer to influence God is not in external rituals of sacrifice, but in the charisma of Moses that arises from his personal relationship with God, as one who speaks to God face-to-face (33:11). The prayer builds upon Moses' special status as a human who has "found favor" in the eyes of God (33:12, 13, 16, 17). The intercession for the renewed presence of God begins with Moses' charisma. On the basis of his favor, he coaxes God to return and to lead the Israelites. E. Aurelius has demonstrated the roots of this form of intercession in the prophetic tradition, for example in the prayer of Amos for the people during his visions (Amos 7–9).[29] The prayer is based upon the fact that Moses is known by God, and it is also motivated by Moses' quest for additional knowledge of God (33:12, 13, 16, 17). Muilenburg probes the complex role of the motif of knowledge in vv. 12-17. He concludes that knowledge in the passage "implies a personal relationship" within the larger context of covenant.[30]

According to Muilenburg, the prayer is based on the "personal inward relation" between Moses, conceived as a charismatic hero, and Yahweh.[31] K. R.

27. Haran, *Temples and Temple-Service,* 266.
28. Muilenburg, "Intercession."
29. Aurelius, *Fürbitter Israels,* 82-83, 93.
30. Muilenburg, "Intercession," 187-91, quotation from 188.
31. Ibid., 188.

Suomala concurs, noting that the dialogue between God and Moses "moves into a more personal realm."[32] The prayer itself models the influence of the charismatic person to persuade God to change the course of future events. The persuasive power of the prayer is conveyed through its rhetoric. The prayer is structured in three petitions, each with a divine response. The first petition begins in the past, when Moses recounts his commission to lead the Israelites, noting also his favored status with God (vv. 12-14). The second petition shifts to the present crisis, when Moses requests that God lead the people of Israel (vv. 15-17). The third petition turns to the future, when Moses seeks a new revelation of the divine name Yahweh (vv. 18-23), where the motifs change from divine leading to theophany. The success of Moses' intercession is indicated by the shifting discourse from Moses to God. The speech of Moses dominates in the first two sections of the prayer (vv. 12-14, 15-17), but gives way to divine speech at the conclusion (vv. 18-23). The shift in discourse is accompanied by a change in theme from divine absence at the outset to the preparation for a new theophany at the end.

Verses 12-14 contain the first petition. Verse 12 begins in the past, when Moses quotes two divine promises made to him personally, not to the Israelites in general. The first quotation, "you say to me, 'Bring up this people,'" recalls the commission of Moses (chap. 3). The second, "you said, 'I know you by name and you have indeed found favor in my eyes,'" does not refer to a previous divine promise, yet it becomes the point of emphasis in the prayer. Moses opens the intercession in the tent of meeting by establishing his special status before Yahweh in the second quotation. The phrase, "to be known by name," most likely signifies intimacy. Moses is probably claiming a special relationship with God, which the LXX translates, "I know you above all" *(para pantas)*. The content of Moses' special status is that he "has found favor ['grace'] in the eyes of God." The only other human to have the same status before God is Noah (Gen 6:8), and the connection between Moses and Noah continues in the story of the golden calf (Exod 32:7-14). The phrase introduces the central theme of the prayer, divine "grace" *(ḥēn)*. The goal of Moses' intercession is not to confirm his own status with God, but to draw out the divine grace already bestowed upon him to the entire Israelite nation.

Moses makes a personal petition in 33:13, grounded in his special status before God: "Now if indeed I have found favor *(ḥēn)* in your eyes, make known to me, please, your way." The petition of Moses is to know God's way(s) *(derek)*. The request may be for a revelation of God's "essential personality," as N. Sarna suggests.[33] The prayer certainly moves to this point by the third petition (vv. 18-

---

32. Suomala, *Moses and God*, 32.
33. Sarna, *Exodus*, 212-13.

23), but the opening petition focuses more on the divine guidance to the promised land. Moses opens the prayer by recalling the divine promise of leading: "See, you say to me, 'Bring up this people.' But you have not made known to me whom you will send with me" (v. 12). The request to know God's "way" continues the theme of divine guidance toward the land. K. Koch notes that the theological content of the term *derek,* "way," in the prophetic literature is the harmonious life of a person in the land: "*Derek* on one's own land, given to the patriarchs by God, counts as the precondition which makes a successful and harmonious life possible."[34] The initial petition of Moses is grounded in his commission to lead the Israelites from Egypt to Canaan. But by the close of the petition Moses shifts the focus from himself to the people: "See also that this nation is your people" (v. 13). The divine reply in v. 14 ignores the larger focus on the nation and focuses only on Moses. Yahweh promises to accompany Moses and to give him rest.

The second petition in vv. 15-17 also begins with Moses' favored status before Yahweh, but it focuses more explicitly on the people. Moses petitions again for divine guidance: "If your face is not going, do not bring us up from here." The argument of Moses, however, focuses more on the distinctiveness of the Israelites from the other nations than on his favored status: "Then we will be separate [Niphal of *pālâ*], I and your people, from all the people who are on the face of the earth" (v. 16). The Hiphil of *pālâ,* "to separate, distinguish," occurs in the plague stories, where God first separated the land of Goshen, the residence of the Israelites, from the land of Egypt in the plagues of flies (8:22 [MT 18]) and the death of cattle (9:4), then separated the Israelites themselves from the Egyptians in the death of the Egyptian firstborn (11:7). The special status of the Israelites with God also recalls the divine promise in the proposal of covenant that they would become a private possession of God's in contrast to the other nations (19:5). God responds favorably to Moses' request, and also shifts the focus back to Moses' favored status away from the distinctive character of the people: "My face will go and I will give you rest" (33:14).

The third petition in vv. 18-23 is often judged to be a separate unit, since it includes new themes.[35] Yet it also builds on the divine response to Moses in v. 17, where Yahweh underscored Moses' favored status. The final request of Moses is abrupt and personal: "Show me, please, your glory." The request moves the prayer from the earlier petition for guidance to the desire for a new level of enlightenment into the very character of God. The progression in the prayer is indicated by the repetition of syntax from v. 13, where Moses requested guidance, "Make known to me, please, your way" *(hôdīʿēnî nāʾ ʾet-*

---

34. K. Koch, *The Prophets,* vol. 1: *The Assyrian Period* (trans. M. Kohl; Philadelphia: Fortress, 1982), 45-46.

35. See, e.g., Van Seters, *Life of Moses,* 323.

děrākekā), to v. 18, where Moses seeks new insight into the character of God, "Show me, please, your glory!" *(har'ēnî nā' 'et-kěbōdekā).* The divine glory in the Non-P History designates the inner character of God, revealed in the divine name Yahweh (3:13-15). It must be distinguished from the more technical "Glory of Yahweh" in the P History (see 24:15-18). The divine glory is further described in v. 19 as God's "face" and "goodness." Cassuto interprets the latter term as divine virtue, whose essential characteristic is grace.[36] Childs builds on the insight of Cassuto, noting that the goodness of God "signifies his benefits which are experienced by Israel" (Hos 3:5; Jer 31:12).[37]

The speech of Yahweh dominates in the final petition of Moses, including vv. 18-23. The focus on the revelation of the divine name Yahweh is made explicit in v. 19, when God states to Moses: "I will call before your face the name Yahweh." The proclamation is followed by the announcement that God will bestow grace on whomever he sees fit. The syntax of this statement indicates the close relationship between Moses' request to see the divine glory and the initial revelation of the divine name Yahweh during his commission (3:13-15). In the commission of Moses, Yahweh reveals the divine name by employing the *idem per idem* formula, in which the same verb repeats in the first person, connected by the relative pronoun, "I am who I am" *('ehyeh 'ăšer 'ehyeh).* The same syntax repeats in the revelation of the divine name in v. 19, "I will have grace on whom I will have grace, and I will have mercy on whom I will have mercy" *(wěhannōtî 'et-'ăšer 'āḥōn wěriḥamtî 'et-'ăšer 'ăraḥēm).* Comparison indicates an evolution in the revelation of the name Yahweh from God's initial involvement in the liberation of the Israelites (3:13-15) to the bestowing of divine grace on the people (33:19), a quality of the divine that Moses has already experienced. The revelation of divine grace in the name Yahweh is a reversal from the divine promise of punishment to Moses' initial intercession for the people after the sin of the golden calf: "Whoever sinned against me I will blot out from my book" (32:33).

The intercessory prayer of Moses in the tent of meeting concludes in 33:20-23 with divine instructions for theophany in response to Moses' request to see the divine glory. The change in theme from the request for guidance to theophany indicates the success of Moses' intercession, providing transition from the tent of meeting to the mountain of God in the final scene. The content of theophany in 34:1-9 will explore further the new insight into the name Yahweh as embodying the qualities of grace and mercy. The divine instructions for theophany in vv. 20-23 seek to qualify the direct experience of God stated in 33:11. God informs Moses that no human can see the face of God and survive (v. 20), and that as a consequence his encounter with divine glory will be qualified. Mo-

36. Cassuto, *Exodus,* 435.
37. Childs, *Exodus,* 596.

ses will be placed in a cave, similar to the experience of the prophet Elijah on Mount Horeb (1 Kings 19). Furthermore God will cover the eyes of Moses while passing by, removing his hands only to reveal the back side of God. Thus the appearance of the divine glory will both conceal and reveal God to Moses, sparing his life yet invading his face with divine light (see Exod 34:29-35).

Recovery of the Tablets (34:1–40:38)

Introduction

The successful mediation of Moses in the tent of meeting (Exodus 33) propels the story ahead to a new revelation on the mountain, concluding Exodus. The scene separates into four parts. First, 34:1-9 is a theophany that begins with the divine instruction to Moses: "Carve for yourself two tablets of stone like the first, and I will write on the tablets the words that were on the first tablets that you shattered." God reveals the gracious character of the divine name Yahweh, providing the context to reissue the lost and broken tablets. Second, 34:10-28 outlines the new covenant represented by the tablets. Third, 34:29-35 describes the descent of Moses with the tablets and his subsequent cultic role of mediation, symbolized by his shining face. Fourth, chaps. 35–40 conclude Exodus with the construction of the tabernacle.

The Non-P History provides the basic structure of the scene. The revelation of divine grace (34:1, 4-9), the reissuing of the covenant law on the new "tablets of stone" (34:10-28), and the cultic role of Moses in the tent of meeting (34:29b-35) conclude the events at the divine mountain. The next scene in the Non-P History is the departure of the Israelites from the divine mountain, named "Mount Yahweh," in Num 10:29-36, followed by additional stories about the tent of meeting (Numbers 11–12).

The P History identifies the mountain of revelation as Mount Sinai (Exod 34:2-3, part of vv. 4, 29a, and 32) and the tablets as "the two tablets of testimony" (34:29a), signifying their content as the blueprint for the tabernacle. The P History also includes the lengthy description of the tabernacle and its cult (Exod 35:1–Num 10:28), presently inserted between the story of Moses' shining face (Exod 34:29b-35) and the departure of the Israelites from Mount Yahweh (Num 10:29-36). In its present form, Exodus concludes with the P author's account of the construction of the tabernacle in chaps. 35–40, but the description of the tabernacle continues into the books of Leviticus and Numbers. The sacrificial cult, the ordination of the priesthood, and the laws of holiness surrounding the cult of the tabernacle are described in Leviticus, while the social formation of the Israelites around the tabernacle, as a temple community, is outlined in Num

1:1–10:10. The P History includes its own version of the departure from Mount Sinai in Num 10:11-28, before the Non-P story of the Israelites leaving Mount Yahweh (Num 10:29-36).

Gracious Character of Yahweh (34:1-9)

³⁴:¹*And Yahweh said to Moses, "Carve for yourself two tablets of stone like the first, and I will write on the tablets the words that were on the first tablets that you shattered.* ²***And be ready in the morning, and you will ascend Mount Sinai and you will be stationed there before me on the top of the mountain.*** ³***No one will ascend with you, and no one else shall be seen on the entire mountain. Even flocks and herds shall not graze in front of that mountain."***

⁴*And he carved two tablets of stone like the first, and Moses rose early in the morning,* ***and he ascended on Mount Sinai as Yahweh commanded him.*** *And he took in his hand the two tablets of stone.*

⁵*And Yahweh descended in the cloud and was stationed there with him. And he proclaimed the name Yahweh.* ⁶*And Yahweh passed before him and he proclaimed,*

> *"Yahweh, Yahweh, God merciful and gracious,*
> *slow to anger,*
> *great in steadfast love and truth,*
> ⁷*keeping steadfast love to the thousandth generation,*
> *lifting up iniquity, transgression, and sin.*
> *Yet by no means does he acquit,*
> *visiting the iniquity of the fathers on the children to the third and fourth generation."*

⁸*And Moses quickly bowed to the earth and he worshiped.* ⁹*And he said, "Please, if I have found favor in your eyes, my Lord, please, my Lord, walk in our midst. Although that is a people of stiff neck, pardon our iniquity and our sin, and possess us as an inheritance."*

Notes

34:1 *like the first.* The LXX adds here, *anabēthi pros me eis to oros,* "and come up to me on the mountain," then continuing as in MT: "and I will write. . . ."

34:2 *and you will be stationed there before me.* Hebrew *wĕniṣṣabtā lî,* a Niphal, means "wait for me" according to Houtman.[1] Dohmen notes the repetition from 33:21.[2] The LXX renders, *stēsē moi,* "you shall set yourself to me."

34:3 *in front of that mountain.* Hebrew *'el-mûl hāhār hahû',* "in front of that moun-

---

1. Houtman, *Exodus,* 3:705-6.
2. Dohmen, *Exodus 19–40,* 321.

tain," is translated in NJPS, "at the foot of this mountain." The LXX translates, *plēsion tou orous ekeinou,* "near that mountain."

34:4 *he carved.* The Sam names Moses as the subject.

he took in his hand. The LXX names Moses as the subject.

34:5 *And he proclaimed the name Yahweh.* The subject of Hebrew *wayyiqrā' běšēm,* "he proclaimed the name," is unclear. M. Franz notes that there is confusion over the location of Yahweh on the mountain in the present form of the text, and that the absence of the phrase, "and Yahweh descended in the cloud," would suggest that Moses is the subject.[3] Childs summarizes briefly the history of the debate over this problem. My translation assumes that Yahweh is the subject. As Childs writes: "In the present context of the whole chapter in which v. 5 is read in light of v. 6, Yahweh is most naturally the subject of the proclamation."

34:6 *And Yahweh passed before him and he proclaimed, "Yahweh, Yahweh, God merciful and gracious."* The ambiguity of the subject of *wayyiqrā',* "and he proclaimed," continues (see 34:5). Franz concludes that the syntax suggests no change in the subject between the clauses "And Yahweh passed before him" and "and he proclaimed."[4] An alternative translation is: "And Yahweh proclaimed, 'Yahweh, God merciful and gracious.'" The singular occurrence of the name may be reflected in Num 14:17. The doubling of a name for emphasis occurred in 3:4, "Moses, Moses." See other instances of the repetition with Abraham (Gen 22:11), Jacob (Gen 46:2), and Samuel (1 Sam 3:10). The LXX translates, *kai ekalesen Kyrios ho theos oiktirmōn,* "And the Lord proclaimed, 'The God compassionate.'"

slow to anger. Hebrew *'erek 'appayim* translates lit. "long of nostrils," indicating patience. Franz detects monarchical imagery of the wise king.[5] The LXX translates, *makrothymos,* "patient, long-suffering."

34:7 *lifting up.* Hebrew *nōśē',* "lifting up," is translated "forgiving" in NRSV and NJPS.

Yet by no means does he acquit. Hebrew *wěnaqqēh lō' yěnaqqeh* is emphatic. Waltke and O'Connor translate the negative use of the infinitive absolute in this instance: "Yet he will by no means leave the guilty unpunished" (*IBHS* 35.2.2). The Sam makes the statement positive, *wnqh lw ynqh,* "he will acquit him."

34:9 *my Lord, please, my Lord.* The LXX does not translate the first Hebrew *'ǎdōnāy.*

and possess us as an inheritance. The LXX translates, *kai esometha soi,* "and we shall be yours."

Commentary

34:1-3 Houtman notes the uncertainty of the setting of the divine instructions to Moses in vv. 1-3.[6] Although the focus is on a new theophany, Mo-

---

3. M. Franz, *Der barmherzige und gnädige Gott: Die Gnadenrede vom Sinai (Exodus 34,6-7) und ihre Parallelen im Alten Testament und seiner Umwelt* (BWANT 160; Stuttgart: Kohlhammer, 2003), 163.

4. Ibid., 164.

5. Ibid., 123.

6. Houtman, *Exodus,* 3:705.

ses is not yet on the mountain. Instead the scene continues the mediation of Moses in the tent of meeting from 33:12-23, prompting some interpreters, such as Durham, to combine the theophany in 34:1-9 with the mediation of Moses in 33:12-23.[7] The scenes are certainly woven together. But the change in the divine speech, from the earlier decision to retreat from the Israelites to the new instructions for theophany, signals a new scene. The change of theme is from divine absence to the renewed presence of God, symbolized by the reissuing of the tablets for covenant renewal.

The command in 34:1 to prepare new tablets signals the success of Moses' mediation in the tent of meeting. It also indicates the central role of "the two tablets of stone" as cultic icons in the Non-P History (see the commentary on 24:12-14). God instructs Moses "to chisel" or "to carve" *(pāsal)* the two tablets like the first ones. The cutting and manufacture of stone for altars is prohibited in 20:25; and *pesel,* the nominal form from the verb "to carve," means "idol," indicating the excessive form of iconography that is condemned in the Decalogue (20:4; Deut 5:8; see also Deut 4:16, 23, 25, etc.). The divine command to Moses in Exod 34:1 limits iconography in the Non-P History to the abstract "tablets of stone," containing the words of God (see also Deut 10:1, 3). The imagery surrounding the tablets of stones suggests that recording the law itself has become the only acceptable form of iconography in the Non-P History.

Exodus 34:2-3 changes the focus from the tablets to the danger of the divine mountain, Sinai, a central theme in the P History. God also commands Moses to ascend to the top of the mountain alone, repeating earlier themes from the P History (19:20-25; 24:15b-18a). The designation of the mountain as Mount Sinai, the separation of Moses from the people, and the emphasis on the holiness of the mountain as well as its need for protection indicate that the literature is a composition of the P author.

34:4-9   The section clarifies that the setting has shifted from the tent of meeting in Exodus 33 to the mountain. The central motifs of theophany return. The transition in setting is indicated when Moses fulfills the divine instruction in v. 4. He chisels two new tablets of stone and ascends to the summit of the mountain. The theophany of God is introduced in v. 5: "And Yahweh descended in the cloud." The descent of the cloud repeats the earlier imagery of theophany from the Non-P History, first described to Moses in 19:9, "I am coming to you in the dense cloud," and repeated in the setting of the tent of meeting as the pillar of cloud in 33:9: "And whenever Moses entered the tent, the pillar of cloud descended and stood at the door of the tent." The content of theophany remains on the auditory experience of divine speech, as in the previous accounts: he (Yahweh?) "was stationed there with him. And he proclaimed the name

---

7. Durham, *Exodus,* 450-55.

Yahweh." Hyatt suggests that Moses is the subject of the sentence and that he calls upon the name Yahweh, which then prompts a further revelation of God in vv. 6-7 (see also the translation note).[8] But the proclamation of the name is more likely a self-introduction of Yahweh, leading to the extended revelation of divine grace in vv. 6-7. According to R. W. L. Moberly, the use of the divine self-introduction is unique to this passage: "Elsewhere it is always used of the worshipper calling upon Yahweh (cf. Gen. 4:26, etc.)."[9] In the same way the further revelation of the gracious character of God in vv. 6-7 also becomes a confession of worshipers to God in its other occurrences within the Hebrew Bible (e.g., Joel 2:13).

Exodus 34:6-7 provides an extended interpretation of the name Yahweh, with a liturgical formula emphasizing the gracious character of God. Verse 6a introduces the liturgy. It reaffirms the setting of theophany: "And Yahweh passed before him." It also indicates that the focus of revelation is on the divine name Yahweh: "And he [God] proclaimed *(wayyiqrā')*, 'Yahweh, Yahweh.'" The repetition of the divine name is unique in the Hebrew Bible. Such repetition is used in several places when the Deity addresses humans, such as in the initial commission of Moses (3:4; see the translation note). One could translate, "Yahweh proclaimed, 'Yahweh . . . ,'" thus eliminating the repetition. But the repetition may be intentional, perhaps for emphasis, marking the moment of the original revelation of the gracious character of God. Houtman adds that the repetition, "Yahweh, Yahweh," could be translated "as a nominal clause: 'YHWH is and remains YHWH.'"[10] This translation emphasizes the larger context of Exodus, where the proclamation of the divine name Yahweh is a direct response to the request of Moses to see God's glory (33:18), and the content of the revelation is an extension of the original revelation of the name in the commission of Moses (3:13-15).

Interpreters debate the origin of the formula in 34:6-7. Franz provides an extensive review of the language of the formula in ancient Near Eastern literature. He notes that Egyptian literature indicates a strong hope in the reality of grace, the close ties to the deity, and the profound role in personal piety. Mesopotamian literature also includes hymns, personal names, key words, and the imagery of the king as a channel for grace. Franz notes in particular the relationship of the gracious character of Marduk, the king, and events in *Enuma Elish* that provide some comparison to the development of Yahweh's gracious character in Exodus 32–34. The gracious character of the deity is also prominent in Ugaritic literature especially in association with El, the merciful god.

8. J. P. Hyatt, *Exodus* (NCB; repr. Grand Rapids: Eerdmans, 1983), 322.
9. Moberly, *At the Mountain of God*, 77.
10. Houtman, *Exodus*, 3:708 n. 191.

The gracious character of the Deity also appears in Hebrew inscriptions, including references to Yahweh in the prayers at Kuntillet ʿAjrud and at Khirbet Beit-Lei, which provide an especially close parallel to 34:6b-7. The personal names of Yahweh, reflecting divine grace, indicate that the *ḥnn*-name is ancient in Israel and part of the larger religious practice in the ancient Near East.[11]

The liturgical formula that is contained in 34:6-7 presents a series of distinct problems for interpretation. Scholars debate whether the present text has combined two distinct cultic formulas, the proclamation of divine grace in v. 6 and the retribution of God in v. 7. J. Scharbert argued for distinct formulas, as have K. Sakenfeld and L. Perlitt,[12] noting that the statement of divine retribution in v. 7 repeats the prohibition against idols in the Decalogue (20:4-6; Deut 5:8-10), which suggests its independence from the confession of divine grace in v. 6. R. C. Dentan disagrees, arguing for the unity of the liturgy already in the early cultic development of ancient Israel.[13] Van Seters follows Dentan but dates the liturgy much later in the exilic period.[14] Comparison to the Decalogue suggests that 34:6-7 is a unified confession, fashioned in the Non-P History to reinterpret the prohibition against idolatry in the Decalogue (20:4-6) and the subsequent law against abusing the divine name Yahweh (20:7). A summary of the law against idolatry will provide the starting point for interpreting the revelation of divine grace in 34:6-7 as an inner-biblical transformation of the Decalogue.[15]

The command against idolatry in 20:4-6 is framed negatively and stated in the absolute terms of love or hate, and of obedience or punishment. There is only one consequence for idolatry in the Decalogue, violent rejection by God. Yahweh grounds the command in a self-introduction of the divine name (see the commentary on 6:2-8; 20:1-2): "For I am Yahweh (*ʾānōkî yhwh*), your God." This is followed by a new revelation of the divine character, as "a jealous God," *ʾēl qannāʾ*. The jealous nature of God reveals the divine passion for the Israelites, arising from their new covenant relationship. The passion is conveyed with the imagery of marriage, but the focus of the command is on the violent emotions of an offended lover. The divine jealousy results in "visiting (*pōqēd*) the iniquities (*ʿāwōn*) of the fathers on the children to the third and to the fourth

---

11. Franz, *Barmherzige und gnädige Gott*, 43-93.

12. J. Scharbert, "Formgeschichte und Exegese von Ex 34, 6f und seiner Parallelen," *Bib* 38 (1957): 130-50; K. Sakenfeld, *The Meaning of Hesed in the Hebrew Bible* (HSM 17; Missoula, Mont.: Scholars Press, 1978), 118-19; Perlitt, *Bundestheologie*, 213-14.

13. R. Dentan, "The Literary Affinities of Exodus XXXIV 6f," *VT* 13 (1963): 35-36.

14. Van Seters, *Life of Moses*, 345-51.

15. See also R. Scoralick, "'JHWH, JHWH, ein gnädiger und barmherziger Gott . . .' (Ex 34,6): Die Gottesprädikationen aus Ex 34, 6f. in ihrem Kontext in Kapitel 32 34," in *Gottes Volk am Sinai*, ed. Köckert und Blum, 141-56.

generation of those who hate me." Only at the end of the command does the language of love emerge, as the divine emotion toward those who refrain from making idols: "but doing steadfast love *(ḥesed)* to the thousandth generation of those loving me and observing my commandments." Thus God is capable of both love and hate toward the Israelites as a result of entering into covenant with them. But both the vengeance and the love of God are automatic responses triggered by the actions of love and hate in humans toward God. The formulation of divine jealousy in the Decalogue allows for no change in how God responds to humans.

The revelation of divine grace in 34:6-7 introduces change into the character of God, which is necessary if covenant with the Israelites is to continue after the sin of the golden calf. The ability of Yahweh to change is signaled by a new revelation of the divine character, echoing the language and the syntax of the law against idolatry in 20:5. Yahweh, the jealous God *('ēl qannā'),* now becomes Yahweh, the merciful and gracious God *('ēl raḥûm wĕḥannûn).* The repetition suggests that the newly revealed qualities of mercy and grace in 34:6 presuppose the earlier revelation of divine jealousy from the Decalogue. This is important for interpretation. It underscores that grace builds on jealousy, it does not replace it. M. Aurelius goes further, stating that divine jealousy is the ground and presupposition for divine grace.[16] The revelation of grace means that Yahweh will not act immediately and automatically with the emotional rage of an offended lover, often indicated in Hebrew as hot breath, especially through one's nostrils, as in the case of the divine response to the golden calf. The idol made God's nose hot *(wĕyiḥar-'appî),* prompting God to seek the immediate annihilation of the Israelites (32:10). With the new revelation of divine grace, the spontaneous rage of jealousy is tempered by patience. God's nose or nostrils are no longer *('erek 'appayim)* making the Deity prone to anger. In Hebrew "patience" means that God is willing to withhold the immediate rage of jealousy, even though God may be an offended lover, as in the case of the Israelite worship of the golden calf.

The result of divine patience is a new prominence to the quality of steadfast love *(ḥesed)* in God. This quality was already present in the revelation of the Decalogue. But it is reserved for the conclusion of the law against idolatry (20:6), after the vengeance of God against idol makers was spelled out (20:5). Now it acquires a leading role in 34:7, preceding the vengeful character of God. The revelation of divine mercy and grace accentuates Yahweh's ability to "keep steadfast love to the thousandth generation," and even more to "lift up iniquity, transgression, and sin." Steadfast love in the Decalogue was reserved only for those who obey God. Now the forgiveness of God broadens the scope of stead-

16. Aurelius, *Fürbitter Israels,* 125.

fast love to include both the obedient and the disobedient, indicating Yahweh's ability to change emotions toward disobedient Israel, a quality that was absent from the Decalogue's prohibition against idolatry.

The vengeance of God appears at the close of the liturgy in v. 7 with new meaning. It no longer signifies the spontaneous emotion of a jealous God. Now it becomes a means to safeguard divine grace from abuse: "Yet by no means does he acquit, visiting the iniquity of the fathers on the children to the third and fourth generation." The punishment directed to the fourth generation is a quotation from the law against idols (20:5). But the opening phrase, "yet by no means does he acquit," is from the law of the divine name in the Decalogue (20:7), not the law against idols (20:4-6). The law of the divine name warns the Israelites not to misuse the gift of the divine name Yahweh in destructive ways (20:7). The consequence of such abuse is that "Yahweh will not acquit *(nāqâ)* the one who lifts up his name in vain." The revelation of divine grace in 34:6-7 concludes with the same warning from the Decalogue: "Yet by no means does he [Yahweh] acquit" *(wĕnaqqēh lō' yĕnaqqeh)*. The new revelation of divine mercy is not automatic amnesty, because grace only functions in relationship with jealousy. There is forgiveness, but God also reserves the right to punish to the fourth generation, as in the Decalogue.

The new revelation of the name Yahweh is filled with pathos. The mercy *(raḥûm)* of God denotes physical emotion, a feeling of affection for another. The meaning of *raḥûm* derives from *reḥem,* "womb." The role of the womb in birthing gives rise to a metaphorical use, signifying God's intimate attachment and strong emotion toward the Israelites. The gracious character of God *(ḥannûn)* extends the emotional imagery of the metaphor, indicating the unique charismatic quality of God to bestow the gifts of peace and blessing upon humans, as in the Priestly Benediction (Num 6:24-26). The qualities of mercy and grace temper divine anger. God becomes "slow to anger," producing steadfast love *(ḥesed),* a central theological term to describe God in the Hebrew Bible. K. Sakenfeld emphasizes the spontaneity of steadfast love, prompting a mutual response from the one who receives it. The result is an enduring relationship, "so great in faithfulness that he [God] is willing even to forgive breach of relationship."[17] N. Glueck also notes the legal background, in which *ḥesed* means loyalty within the context of making an oath or of establishing a covenant.[18]

Once revealed, the gracious character of Yahweh becomes the starting point for intercession. Moses establishes the paradigm immediately in 34:8-9, requesting divine forgiveness for the sin of the people, and he repeats the pro-

---

17. Sakenfeld, *Meaning of Hesed,* 119.
18. N. Glueck, *Ḥesed in the Bible* (trans. A. Gottschalk; ed. E. L. Epstein; Cincinnati: Hebrew Union College Press, 1967), 38-55.

cess in Num 14:17-19 after the people's rejection of the promised land. The gracious character of Yahweh continues as the source for intercession and forgiveness in the prophetic literature (Jon 4:2; Joel 2:13), in the Psalms (Pss 86:15; 103:8; 111:4; 112:4; 145:8), and in the wisdom literature (Sir 2:11).[19] Joel 2:13 encourages repentance from the Israelites even during the threat of the Day of Yahweh as judgment, because Yahweh is gracious. The prophet Jonah complains to Yahweh about divine grace when it is extended to the people of Nineveh, indicating the broad limits of divine grace. The Psalms provide a range of models for requesting the grace of God.

Law of Covenant Renewal (34:10-28)

[34:10] *And he said, "Indeed, I will make a covenant before all your people, and I will do wonders that have not yet been created on earth among any nation. And all people in whose midst you live will see the work of Yahweh; for it is awesome what I am doing with you.*

[11] *"Observe what I am commanding you today. I am indeed driving out from before you the Amorites, and the Canaanites, and the Hittites, and the Perizzites, and the Hivites, and the Jebusites.* [12] *Be vigilant, lest you make a covenant with those dwelling in the land in which you are entering, lest it become a snare in your midst.* [13] *For their altars you will tear down, and their pillars you will smash, and his Asherah you will cut down.* [14] *For you will not worship another god, because Yahweh, whose name is Jealous, is a jealous God,* [15] *lest you make a covenant with those dwelling in the land. And they will prostitute themselves after their gods and they will sacrifice to their gods. And one will call to you, and you will eat from his sacrifice.* [16] *And you will take from his daughters for your sons. And his daughters will prostitute themselves after their gods. And they will cause your sons to prostitute themselves after their gods.*

[17] *"You shall not make molten gods for yourself.*

[18] *"The Festival of Unleavened Bread you shall observe. Seven days you shall eat unleavened bread as I commanded you at the appointed time of the month of Abib, for in the month of Abib you went out from Egypt.*

[19] *"Every first opening of a womb will belong to me, all of your male livestock that open a womb, cattle or sheep.* [20] *The first opening of a donkey you shall redeem with a sheep. And if you do not redeem, you must break its neck. All the firstborn of your sons you shall redeem. No one will appear before my face empty-handed.*

[21] *"Six days you shall work. But on the seventh you shall rest. At plowing time and at harvest time you shall rest.*

---

19. See Fishbane, *Biblical Interpretation*, 335-50; Dozeman, "Inner-Biblical Interpretation."

[22] "And the Festival of Weeks you shall observe, the firstfruits of the wheat harvest, and the Festival of Harvest at the end of the year. [23] Three times in the year all your males shall appear before the face of the Lord, Yahweh, the God of Israel. [24] For I will dispossess nations before you. And I will widen your borders. No one will covet your land when you go up to appear before the face of Yahweh, your God, three times in the year.

[25] "You shall not offer the blood of my sacrifice with leaven. And the sacrifice of the Festival of Passover shall not remain until the morning.

[26] "The first of the firstfruits of your ground you will bring to the house of Yahweh, your God.

"You shall not boil a kid in its mother's milk."

[27] And Yahweh said to Moses, "Write these words, for on the basis of these words I cut a covenant with you and with the Israelites."

[28] He was there with Yahweh forty days and forty nights. Bread he did not eat, and water he did not drink. He wrote on the tablets the words of the covenant, the ten words.

Notes

34:10 *before all your people.* Hebrew *neged kol-ʿammĕkā* identifies the people as belonging to Moses, suggesting a continuation of the distance between God and the Israelites from the story of the golden calf (32:7). Childs notes that the verse raises problems of literary structure, since it functions both as a response to Moses' request for divine forgiveness (v. 9) and as an introduction to the following law (v. 11).[20]

have not yet been created. Hebrew *nibrĕʾû* is the Niphal of *bārāʾ*, which is reserved for divine acts of creation (e.g., Gen 1:1). The LXX translates *gegonen*, "which has not yet happened," rather than *epoiēsen* (as in Gen 1:1). The use of *gegonen* may indicate a weakening of the statement or it may simply be stylistic, since the verb *poieō* was used in the previous line, *poiēsō endoxa*: "I will do wonders."

and all people in whose midst you live will see the work of Yahweh; for it is awesome what I am doing with you. The emphasis of the divine statement is on the public nature of the wonders that Yahweh will do for the Israelites.

34:11-16 The literary structure of the section is formed by the two imperatives in vv. 11-12 (observe and be vigilant), followed by three instances of the particle *pen*, "lest" (two in v. 12, and the third in v. 15), providing warnings: lest you make a covenant, lest it become a snare, lest you make a covenant. The repetition of the warning, "lest you cut a covenant," indicates two sections, prohibitions against foreign worship in vv. 12-14 and prohibitions against foreign marriage in vv. 15-16.

34:11-12 *Observe . . . be vigilant.* The Hebrew repeats the verb *šāmar* as an imperative, first in the Qal form and second in the Niphal. In each case the verb is followed by *lĕkā*, "for yourself." The LXX translates both commands as *proseche*, "pay atten-

---

20. Childs, *Exodus*, 612-13.

tion." In the first command the LXX changes Hebrew *lĕkā* from the dative to the nominative, *sy*; while the second follows the Hebrew syntax, employing *seautō*.

34:13 *for their altars you will tear down, and their pillars you will smash, and his Asherah you will cut down.* The verse repeats in Deut 7:5 with the additional phrase: "and burn their idols with fire." The LXX translation here reflects Deut 7:5, including the phrase, *kai ta glypta tōn theōn autōn katakausete en pyri,* "the carvings of their gods you will burn in fire." The translation "his Asherah" reflects the MT *'ăšērāyw,* where the suffix is in the singular as compared to the plural suffixes in the references to the altars and pillars. The Sam *(w'šryhm)* and the LXX *(ta alsē autōn)* employ the plural suffix. Hebrew *'ăšērâ* is also rendered "sacred poles" (NRSV, NJPS). The LXX translates *ta alsē,* "sacred groves."

34:14 *because Yahweh, whose name is Jealous, is a jealous God.* The LXX translates, *ho gar kyrios ho theos zēlōtōn onoma, theos zēlōtēs estin,* "for the Lord the God is a jealous name, a jealous God."

34:15 *they will prostitute.* The NJPS translates Hebrew *wĕzānû* as "they will lust after." The LXX underscores the sexual imagery with the translation *ekporneusōsin,* "they will commit sexual sin."

34:17 See 32:4.

34:18 See 23:15.

34:19-20 See 13:12-13.

34:21 See 23:12.

34:22 See 23:16.

34:23 See 23:17.

34:24 *I will dispossess.* Hebrew *'ôrîš* could also be translated "disinherit." Cf. NRSV "cast out" and NJPS "drive out," both of which lose the meaning of land possession as inheritance. I have reserved the translation "to drive out" for Hebrew *gāraš* (e.g., 11:1). Cf. LXX *ekbalō,* "I will drive out," which is also used to translate Hebrew *gāraš.*

covet. Hebrew *yaḥmōd* could also be translated "desire." The same verb is used in the Decalogue (20:17).

34:25 See 23:18.

34:26 See 23:19.

34:27 *on the basis of.* Hebrew *'al-pî* is lit. "according to the mouth of" (see *IBHS* §11.3.1).

34:28 *he was there with Yahweh.* The LXX identifies the subject as Moses.

Commentary

The revelation of divine mercy (34:1-9) is followed by the announcement of covenant (34:10) and the promulgation of a law code (34:11-26), identified as the "ten words" and the new "tablets of the covenant" (34:27-28).

The interpretation of 34:10-28 in the modern period has been dominated by the striking repetition of the laws in the Book of the Covenant, and, to a lesser degree, in the Decalogue. The Sabbath law (34:21) repeats in the Book of the Covenant (23:12). The festivals of Unleavened Bread, Weeks, and Ingathering (34:18, 22) repeat in the Book of the Covenant (23:15-16). The prohibitions against mixing blood and yeast (34:25) and boiling a kid in its mother's milk (34:26), as well as the law of firstfruits (34:26) also repeat nearly verbatim in the Book of the Covenant (23:18-19). The laws against worshiping any other god (34:14-16) and the prohibition against making idols (34:17) correspond to the two opening commandments of the Decalogue (20:2-6).

Scholars debate the nature and direction of the inner-biblical relationships among the different bodies of law. They also seek to determine whether 34:11-26 is an early and independent law code influencing the formation of subsequent law, or a later literary creation designed specifically for its present narrative context.[21] Wellhausen represents the majority view in the modern period, which goes back at least to Goethe.[22] Wellhausen identified 34:14-26 as a distinct and ancient law code, which he further characterized as the cultic Decalogue because of the focus on worship and ritual.[23] Thus according to Wellhausen there were two Decalogues, the older cultic version in 34:11-26, and the more recent ethical rendition in 20:1-17. The interpretation represented by Wellhausen was compelling, in part, because the law code is described as the "ten words" in 34:28. Although Wellhausen originally attributed the law code to an unknown author, his later revision of its composition in the wake of A. Kuenen's research reinforced the presupposition of the Documentary Hypothesis, which encouraged a J and E version of the law (see the introduction, "Authors: Documentary Hypothesis"). Wellhausen's reconstruction of the history of composition provided a clear history of ancient Israelite law, even though it was not possible to isolate ten laws.[24]

The interpretation of 34:11-26 as a Decalogue continues into contemporary scholarship, even with the breakdown of the Documentary Hypothesis. Noth continued to presuppose an original Decalogue,[25] building on the research

21. D. Carr ("Method in Determination of the Direction of Dependence: An Empirical Test of Criteria Applied to Exodus 34,11-26 and Its Parallels," in *Gottes Volk am Sinai*, ed. Köckert and Blum, 107-40) broadens the study of comparison from the laws in the Pentateuch to include later editions of the law such as the Sam and 4QRP.

22. See B. M. Levinson, "Goethe's Analysis of Exodus 34 and Its Influence on Wellhausen," *ZAW* 114 (2002): 212-23.

23. Wellhausen, *Composition*, 83 *et passim*; idem, *Prolegomena*, 439.

24. See, e.g., Eissfeldt, *Introduction*, 215-16 *et passim*. For the history of interpretation see F.-E. Wilms, *Das jahwistische Bundesbuch in Exodus 34* (SANT 32; Munich: Kösel, 1973); for an overview see Blum, *Studien*, 67-70. See also H.-C. Schmitt, "Das sogenannte jahwistische Privilegrecht in Ex 34, 10-28 als Komposition der spätdeuteronomistischen Endredaktion des Pentateuch," in *Abschied vom Jahwisten: Die Komposition des Hexateuch in der jüngsten Diskussion* (ed. J. C. Gertz, K. Schmid, and M. Witte; BZAW 315; Berlin: de Gruyter, 2002), 158-62.

25. Noth, *Exodus*, 260-62; idem, *Laws in the Pentateuch*, 20-21.

of G. Beer, who identified the following ten laws: (1) No worship of other gods (v. 14); (2) No idols (v. 17); (3) Firstborn (v. 19a); (4) Redemption of firstborn sons (v. 20bb); (5) Sabbath (v. 21); (6) Three yearly festivals (v. 23); (7) No blood sacrifice with leaven (v. 25a); (8) Passover sacrifice (v. 25b); (9) Firstfruits (v. 26a); and (10) Not boil a kid in its mother's milk (v. 26b).[26] In his recent introduction to the Pentateuch, Blenkinsopp also entertains the hypothesis of Noth: "A Decalogue has also been identified in Ex 34:13-26, though in its present form the covenant contains either eleven articles or twelve if v. 13 is included."[27]

But many interpreters have departed from the quest to structure the law code as a Decalogue. J. Halbe focused instead on the festivals as representing the original structure, which were later refashioned around the theme of pilgrimage. Thus 34:10-27, which Halbe described as the "privilege law of Yahweh," is an independent law code, but it is not a Decalogue. Even though there are clear signs of later redaction in the present form of 34:11-26, the antiquity of the core laws in the corpus makes it the source for the laws in the Book of the Covenant, providing a key to the history of law in ancient Israel. Variations of the methodology of Halbe are evident in a number of recent studies, in which a core of ancient laws is identified in 34:11-26 along with subsequent redactions.[28] Crüsemann builds on the work of Halbe, placing the earliest form of the law code in the ninth or eighth century B.C.E. Crüsemann, like Halbe, identifies a history of composition in the present form of 34:11-26, resulting in literary tensions such as the shift between the first (34:11, 18, 19, 20) and third (34:14, 23, 24, 26) person in the divine promulgation of the laws. But he also identifies an early form of the law code, which addresses the conflict associated with an emerging interpretation of Yahwism in the northern kingdom that emphasized the exclusive claims of the religion, which conflict is similar to the religious struggle in Hosea.[29]

Perlitt questioned the interpretation of 34:11-26 as an old and independent law code, noting that the language was Deuteronomistic, and thus a later exilic composition.[30] Aurelius builds on the work of Perlitt, cataloguing many correspondences in language to the exilic and postexilic Deuteronomistic literature.[31] The later dating favored an interpretation of 34:11-26 as a literary creation by the same author(s) who composed the late stages of Deuteronomy. S. L. McKenzie provides an example: "The mandate to 'observe what I command you today'

---

26. Beer, *Exodus*, 161.

27. Blenkinsopp, *Pentateuch*, 206.

28. See, e.g., the introductory study by Patrick, *Old Testament Law*, 36-37; and the more detailed examination by Osumi, *Kompositionsgeschichte des Bundesbuches*, 10-11, 70-80.

29. Crüsemann, *Torah*, 115-43.

30. Perlitt, *Bundesbuch*, 216 *et passim*; for criticism see Crüsemann, *Torah*, 116-19.

31. Aurelius, *Fürbitter Israels*, 116-26.

(v. 11) occurs nearly word for word throughout Deuteronomy (4:40; 6:6; 7:11; etc.). In fact, the passage as a whole is very similar to Deuteronomy 7."[32]

The later dating of the literature is accompanied by divergent opinions on the composition of the laws and their incorporation into Exodus. A. Toeg suggested that individual laws in 34:10-27 may be intended to recite past law, thus reversing the literary relationship between the repetitions of law in the Book of the Covenant and the "privilege Law of Yahweh."[33] D. Carr concluded from a study of textual traditions (including the Samaritan Pentateuch and Qumran manuscripts such as 4QRP) that the literary techniques in 34:10-27 indicate its late composition and dependence on other law codes in Exodus (esp. 20:10-19). He noted the tendency in 34:10-27 toward expansion of material, the filling in of logical gaps, the conflation of motifs into one context, and the shift to divine speech, all of which are common practices in literature that is dependent on early material.[34] Moberly notes the important role of context for interpreting 34:10-27: "The laws were compiled specifically for the present narrative context, largely out of other laws already contained within the tradition (i.e., Ex. 20–23)."[35] Blum expanded the scope of the inner-biblical connections, suggesting that 34:11-26 is part of a late stratum of literature related to a larger corpus of texts surrounding the divine Messenger.[36] H.-C. Schmitt broadens the literary connections even further, arguing that 34:10-27 is a late Deuteronomistic redaction that spans literature from Genesis 1 through 2 Kings 25.[37]

I interpret 34:10-27 as a composition by the Non-P historian, which is fashioned for its present literary context in the Non-P History. There may be a more complex history of composition surrounding the formation of the individual laws, and H.-C. Schmitt and others have clearly demonstrated the broad literary relationships between the law code, Deuteronomy, and the Deuteronomistic History. But the focus of interpretation will remain limited to the present form of the law code and its inner-biblical relationship to the literature in Exodus. Exodus 34:10-28 repeats the themes, motifs, and laws from Exodus, as shown in figure 43 on page 745.

32. S. L. McKenzie, *Covenant* (Understanding Biblical Themes; St. Louis: Chalice, 2000), 21. For a detailed study of the language see H. Cazelles, *Autour de l'Exode* (Sources bibliques; Paris: Gabalda, 1987), 175-85.

33. A. Toeg, *Lawgiving at Sinai: The Course of Development of the Traditions Bearing on the Lawgiving at Sinai within the Pentateuch, with a Special Emphasis on the Emergence of the Literary Complex in Exodus xix-xxiv* (Hebrew; Jerusalem: Magnes, 1977).

34. Carr, "Method in Determination."

35. Moberly, *At the Mountain of God*, 131-35, esp. 133.

36. Blum (*Studien*, 67-70, 369-76) attributed the composition of Exod 34:11-26 to the postexilic *D-Komposition* (see the introduction, "Authors").

37. Schmitt, "Sogenannte jahwistische Privilegrecht," 157-71.

Figure 43

34:11-28	*Second Tablets*	*Book of Exodus*
34:10	Covenant	Proposal of Covenant (19:5)
		Covenant Ceremony (24:7)
34:10	Promise of Wonders	Commission of Moses (3:20)
34:11-13	Expulsion of Indigenous Nations	
	and Rejection of Foreign Worship	Book of the Covenant (23:27-33)
34:14-16	No Other God	Decalogue (20:3)
34:17	No Cast Idols	Decalogue (20:4-6)
		Golden Calf (32:4, 8)
34:18	Feast of Unleavened Bread	Book of the Covenant (23:15)
		Instruction at Succoth (13:3-10)
34:19-20	Law of Firstborn	Instruction at Succoth (13:11-16)
34:21	Sabbath	Book of the Covenant (23:12)
34:22a	Festival of Weeks/Firstfruits	Book of the Covenant (23:16a)
34:22b	Festival of Ingathering	Book of the Covenant (23:16b)
34:23-24	Three Festival Appearances	Book of the Covenant (23:14)
34:25a	No Blood Sacrifice with Yeast	Book of the Covenant (23:18)
34:25a	Passover	Instruction at Rameses (12:21-27)
34:26a	Law of Firstfruits	Book of the Covenant (23:19a)
34:26b	No Boiling a Kid in Mother's Milk	Book of the Covenant (23:19b)
34:27	Authorship of Moses	Curse of the Amalekites (17:14)
		Covenant Ceremony (24:4)
34:28	Forty-Day Period	Ascent for the First Tablets (24:18b)

In the commentary on 34:1-9 I underscored the inner-biblical relationship between the revelation of divine grace, "Yahweh is a God *('ēl)* merciful *(raḥûm)* and gracious *(ḥannûn),*" in 34:6 and the revelation of God's jealousy in the Decalogue, Yahweh is a "jealous *(qannā')* God *('ēl)*" in 20:4-6. My interpretation also indicated that the revelation of divine grace does not eliminate divine jealousy but tempers it, allowing for forgiveness. On the basis of this new revelation, Moses petitions Yahweh to forgive the sin of the people (34:9). Moses states the positive content of divine forgiveness with the request in 34:9: "possess us as an inheritance." The request introduces the theme of the promised land. The word "to inherit" *(nāḥal)* is a central theological motif in the Pentateuch, but it occurs infrequently in Exodus (15:17; 23:30; 32:13), always in association with the land.[38] The Song of the Sea identifies the inheritance of God with the divine temple in the midst of the land (15:17). The epilogue to the Book of the Covenant equates inheritance with the land: "You will inherit *(nāḥal)* the land." And during the crisis of the golden calf Moses reminds God of the divine promise to the ancestors that the land "they will inherit *(nāḥal)* forever" (32:13).

The request of Moses that Yahweh forgive, and thus renew the original promise of the land to the ancestors, provides the focus for the new law in 34:10-27. It is aimed only at the Israelites' future life in the land, not on the guidance of God in the wilderness journey. The guidance of the Israelites through the wilderness journey has already been secured in the previous intercession of Moses, when Yahweh promised the continued leading of the Messenger (32:34; 33:1-3). The fulfillment of this promise accounts for the absence of the divine Messenger in 34:10-27, which has puzzled interpreters, who note that the Messenger is prominent in 23:20-33, where many of the parallel laws to 34:10-27 are located. Thus the absence of the Messenger from 34:10-27 is the result of literary context and the change in theme. The focus of the law in 34:10-27 is the relationship of Yahweh to the Israelites in the promised land. The central theme for exploring the relationship of Yahweh and the Israelites in the promised land is not the new revelation of divine grace, but the jealous character of Yahweh first revealed in the Decalogue (20:4-6). Exodus 34:14 states: "For you will not worship another god, because Yahweh, whose name is Jealous, is a jealous God."

The meaning of divine jealousy in the land is explored in four parts: the central role of covenant (34:10), prohibitions against foreign worship and intermarriage (34:11-16), guidelines for proper worship (34:17-26), and the importance of written law (34:27-28).

34:10   This verse introduces the theme of covenant after the destruction of the tablets by Moses. The theme of covenant first appeared in the proposal of covenant (19:5), and it was established in the covenant ceremony (24:7). The appearance of the theme in 34:10 indicates the successful intercession of Moses for the presence of God (chap. 33), prompting interpreters to describe the episode as covenant renewal. The divine announcement indicates that covenant renewal rests solely with Yahweh, "Indeed *(hinneh),* I *('ānōkî)* will make/cut *(kōrēt)* a covenant *(běrît)*." The expression echoes previous divine announcements of salvation, revelation, and guidance in the Non-P History, including the salvation of the Israelites, "Indeed *(hinneh),* I *('ānōkî)* come *(bā')* to the Israelites" (3:13); the theophany on the mountain, "Indeed *(hinneh),* I *('ānōkî)* come

---

38. See C. J. H. Wright, *God's People in God's Land: Family, Land, and Property in the Old Testament* (Grand Rapids: Eerdmans, 1990).

(*bā'*) to you in the dense cloud" (19:9); and the guidance of the Messenger, "In-deed *(hinneh)*, I *('ānōkî)* am sending *(šōlēaḥ)* the Messenger" (23:20).

The divine proclamation of covenant reaches back to the original com-mission of Moses by repeating the promise of "wonders" (see 3:20). In both texts the divine wonders are aimed more at the nations than at the Israelites. In the commission of Moses, Yahweh states that the Egyptians will experience the divine wonders (3:20). Now Yahweh promises that the indigenous nations will also experience the wonders of God, most likely in their expulsion from the land (v. 11). The focus on the indigenous nations corresponds to the emphasis on the inheritance of the land in 34:10-27.

34:11-16 This section begins with the divine announcement of the ex-pulsion of the indigenous nations, "I am indeed *(hinĕnî)* driving out *(gōrēš)* from before you the Amorites. . . ." But the focus is more on the Israelites and the danger they face, living in covenant with Yahweh within the promised land. The law accentuates the jealousy of God (34:14), revealed in the Decalogue (20:5). Divine jealousy requires exclusive loyalty by the people. The section ex-plores the meaning of exclusive loyalty in two distinct but related ways. The first half explores the implication of Yahweh's jealous character with regard to foreign worship (vv. 11-14), while the second part shifts to the problem of inter-marriage (vv. 15-16). Both sections are punctuated with the warning: "lest you make a covenant with those dwelling in the land" (vv. 12, 15).

Verses 11-13 repeat the epilogue from the Book of the Covenant, where God demanded the expulsion of the indigenous nations and the rejection of their worship practices (see the commentary on 23:27-33). Verse 14 echoes the opening commandment of the Decalogue, repeating the law against other gods, but in the singular. The Israelites are forbidden to worship "any other god." The singular "god" rather than the plural "gods" from the Decalogue (20:3) may be a reference to the golden calf. The further prohibition against "molten idols" in 34:17 is even more explicit in referring to the golden calf, which is twice de-scribed as the "molten calf" (32:4, 8). Divine jealousy, arising from covenant, requires exclusive loyalty to Yahweh, meaning the expulsion of other people and their gods from the land, and the absence of images in the Israelites' wor-ship practice.

The social implications of the jealous character of Yahweh are explored in the laws against common meals and intermarriage in 34:15-16. The command is stated in two parts. Verse 15 forbids social meals with the indigenous nations in the setting of sacrifice. The prohibition provides a link to the previous command against worshiping foreign gods (vv. 11-14). The implications of such meals are spelled out in v. 16 in the law against intermarriage. The law is focused only on the daughters of the indigenous nations, who are characterized with the sexual metaphor of prostitution. The sexual imagery underscores both the seduction of the foreign women and the danger of intermarriage. The emphasis on clear boundaries between Israelite men and foreign women brings to mind the law against the female sorcerer in 23:18, which is also linked with the prohibition against sacrificing to other gods (23:20). Both require the death penalty. The inner-biblical connection raises the further question of whether the indigenous women are the "beasts" with whom no Israelite was allowed to have sex (22:19).

34:17-26   The section turns from warnings against improper worship to a list of the proper forms of worship in the promised land. Verse 17 provides a transition with the prohibition against molten idols, most likely a reference to the golden calf. Verses 18-26 outline the proper forms of worship in the promised land. The instructions are similar to the worship practices outlined in the Book of the Covenant. The similarities include an emphasis on Sabbath (34:21; 23:10-13), the demand to worship three times each year (34:23-24; 23:14, 17), the three festivals of Unleavened Bread, Firstfruits/Weeks, and Ingathering, as well as their order of observance (34:18, 22; 23:15-16); and the three sacrificial laws prohibiting the mixing of blood and yeast, the requirement of firstfruits, and the command against boiling a kid in its mother's milk (34:25-26; see the commentary on 23:18-19). Moreover, many of the repetitions are verbatim, suggesting a close inner-biblical relationship between the Book of the Covenant and the law of covenant renewal.

But there are also differences, indicating that the law of covenant renewal goes beyond the prescribed worship practice of the Book of the Covenant. Two differences stand out. The first is the inclusion of the law of the firstborn in 34:19-20, which repeats the instruction about the firstborn at Succoth recorded in 13:3-10. The repetition suggests that the Non-P author wishes to include additional law from Exodus within the legislation of covenant renewal. The second difference is the Passover in 34:25. The Passover instruction in the Non-P History occurs in 12:21-27, and its incorporation in 34:25 may also be for the purpose of including it in the law of covenant renewal.

There are still further questions of interpretation surrounding the law of Passover in 34:25. It is surprising that the Passover is clustered with the other sacrifices and separated from the Feast of Unleavened Bread. The separation raises the question of how closely the two festivals are related in the Non-P History as compared to the P History, where Passover and the Festival of Unleavened Bread are clearly merged into one feast. The law of Passover also includes new information. The original instruction in the Non-P History indicated that Passover is a sacrifice (12:27). Exodus 34:25 now clarifies that the Passover sacrifice must be consumed in one night. This teaching is included in the P History (12:10), where Passover is not considered a sacrifice. It also reappears in the cultic calendar of Deuteronomy 16 (see v. 4), suggesting a literary relationship between the law of covenant renewal and Deuteronomy.

34:27-28   The section describes the writing of the new tablets. The chiseled tablets represent the appropriate form of iconography within the tent of meeting according to the Non-P History. They also signal the central role of law in Israelite worship practice within the promised land. Interpreters note the contradiction regarding the divine and Mosaic authorship of the tablets, as well as problems surrounding their content. Exodus 34:1 states that God wrote the tablets. God commands Moses at the outset to chisel new tablets and states: "I will write on them the words that were on the first tablets." But 34:27-28 concludes the revelation of law, stating that Moses, not God, wrote the tablets: "He [Moses] wrote on the tablets the words of the covenant — the ten words." There is also ambiguity regarding the content of the tablets. Verse 28 explicitly states that Moses wrote the Decalogue (see the commentary on 24:12-14). But this raises questions about the recording of the law of covenant renewal (34:11-26). Some interpreters suggest that there is more than one law code in the events at the divine mountain.[39]

The ambiguity of authorship and of the content of the tablets, however, may be the point of emphasis. It blurs the distinction between divine and Mosaic authorship, as well as any qualitative difference in the revelation of law at the divine mountain. The P author adds to the ambiguity by including the blueprints for the tabernacle as the content of the tablets (see 34:29). The meshing of divine and Mosaic authority has been a central theme throughout the Non-P History from the commission of Moses (3:16–4:18). It remained a central concern in the revelation at the divine mountain (19:9). It will become the point of focus in the following scene (34:29-35), when Moses' face is infused with divine light, further intermingling his authority with God's.

Moses' Shining Face and Mosaic Authority (34:29-35)

[34:29] *And Moses descended from Mount Sinai, and the two tablets of testimony were in the hand of Moses* when he descended from the mountain. But Moses did not know that the skin of his face shone in his speaking with him. [30] *And Aaron and all the Israelites saw Moses. And indeed the skin of his face shone. And they feared from approaching him.* [31] *And Moses called to them, and Aaron and all the leaders of the congregation returned to him. And Moses spoke to them.* [32] ***And afterward all the Israelites approached, and he commanded them all that Yahweh spoke with him on Mount Sinai.*** [33] *And when Moses completed speaking with them, he placed on his face a veil.* [34] *And when Moses would enter before Yahweh to speak with him he would remove the veil until his coming out. And when he came out he would speak to the Israelites what he was commanded.*

---

39. See Schmitt, "Sogenannte jahwistische Privilegrecht," 159-62.

[35] *And the Israelites would see the face of Moses, that the skin of the face of Moses shone. And Moses would return the veil on his face until his going to speak with him.*

Notes

34:29 *And when Moses descended from Mount Sinai, and the two tablets of testimony were in the hand of Moses when he descended from the mountain.* The Hebrew syntax is awkward, with two temporal clauses indicating the descent of Moses ("when . . . when"). The LXX smooths out the repetition by interpreting the second temporal clause as modifying Moses. The LXX also refers only to *tou orous*, "the mountain," not specifying Mount Sinai, and has the plural "hands of Moses," rather than MT's singular.

the skin of his face shone. Hebrew *qāran*, "shone," is a denominative verb from *qeren*, "horn." The noun has prompted translations of the verb as "to sprout horns." This translation is evident in the Vulgate, *cornuta esset facies sua.* The Vulgate influenced the history of Western art, as is evident in da Vinci's sculpture of Moses in the Church of St. Peter in Chains (Rome). More recent interpretations include an illusion to the horned crown associated with kings, facial scarring from exposure to the divine fire, or a horned mask perhaps representing the bull.[40] A related meaning is evident in Ps 69:31 (MT 32): "This will please Yahweh more than an ox, or a bull with horns *(maqrin)* and with hoofs." The translation "to shine" finds support in Hab 3:4: "The brightness was like the sun; rays *(qarnayim)* came forth from his hand."[41] The LXX translates, *dedoxastai*, "was glorified" (see the commentary).

in his speaking with him. Hebrew *bĕdabbĕrô 'ittô* does not clarify either the subject or the object in the phrase. My translation interprets Moses as the subject of the speaking and Yahweh as the object (see also NRSV). Houtman reverses the role of the characters: "while he (YHWH) was talking with him."[42] This translation corresponds to v. 32, which states that Yahweh spoke with Moses on Mount Sinai.

34:33 *a veil.* Hebrew *masweh* is a hapax legomenon translated as "veil" and occasionally as "mask" (see the commentary).

34:34-35 *when Moses would enter . . . he would remove. . . . And when he came out, he would speak to the Israelites what he was commanded. And the Israelites would see. . . . And Moses would return the veil. . . .* Childs notes that the verbs shift to the frequentative in these verses to describe ongoing cultic practice rather than a sin-

---

40. For the crown see J. M. Sasson, "Bovine Symbolism in the Exodus Narrative," *VT* 18 (1968): 380-87, esp. 384. For the scarring see W. Propp, "The Skin of Moses' Face — Transfigured or Disfigured?" *CBQ* 49 (1987): 375-86, esp. 384. For the horned mask see A. Jirku, "Die Gesichtsmaske des Mose," *ZDPV* 67 (1944): 43-45; K. Jaroš, "Die 'strahlende Haut,'" *ZAW* 88 (1976): 275-80.

41. Haran, "Shining of Moses' Face," in *In the Shelter of Elyon*, ed. Barrick and Spencer, 159-73; S. L. Sanders, "Old Light on Moses' Shining Face," *VT* 52 (2002): 400-406. For review see T. B. Dozeman, "Masking Moses and Mosaic Authority in Torah," *JBL* 119 (2000): 21-45.

42. Houtman, *Exodus*, 3:727.

gular event.[43] Wevers writes of the LXX: "MT opens with a בְּ + bound infinitive which [LXX] renders by ἡνίκα δ' ἂν + an imperfect verb εἰσεπορεύετο; this correctly interprets the collocation as one of customary action, also accented by the imperfect περιῃρεῖτο of the apodosis: 'whenever he would enter . . . he would remove.'"[44]

Commentary

The descent of Moses to the people with the new tablets is a two-part story focused on Moses' cultic authority as the mediator for the Israelites. Exodus 34:29-33 recounts the final descent of Moses from the mountain, and 34:34-35 shifts from the historical past to describe the continual ritual practice of Moses, most likely in the tent of meeting. The central theme, Mosaic authority, is explored through two symbols, Moses' shining skin and his veil.

Verses 29-33 begin with an account of Moses' descent from the mountain with shining skin (*qāran 'ôr pānāyw*, v. 29), of which he is unaware. The leaders react with fear at the sight of Moses' face (v. 30), but return upon hearing his voice (v. 31). Moses then mediates divine law (v. 32), and, upon completion, covers his face with a veil (*masweh*, v. 33). The episode continues the emphasis on revelation as an experience of divine speech, first introduced in the account of theophany in the Non-P History (19:9, 19; 20:18-20). The authority of Moses is complete in his final descent from the mountain when the light of God infuses his face, signifying to all the Israelites his unique role as the mediator of the law. The idealization of Moses as mediator reinforces an aniconic form of worship, since 34:30-31 underscores that the leaders of Israel respond to the voice of Moses, not to his shining face. Thus even though the shining face of Moses is a central symbol, the details of the story indicate that the authority of Moses is not in his appearance, but in his voice.

Verses 34-35 are a story about the continual ritual practice of Moses. It presupposes a cultic setting, most likely the tent of meeting (33:7-11). The episode clarifies that whenever Moses would enter to speak with Yahweh, he would remove his veil to receive revelation and to communicate it to the Israelites and, in the process, enlighten the people with divine law. Once the divine law was mediated, Moses would again cover his face with the veil. The account of the continual ritual practice of Moses suggests that the Israelites never again see his profane character. They see the shining skin of Moses during cultic revelation and his veil at all other times. The loss of personal identity is an important feature in establishing Mosaic authority in the Hebrew Bible.

Both ancient and modern interpreters have struggled with the puzzling

43. Childs, *Exodus*, 604.
44. Wevers, *Notes*, 572.

nature of this episode, even while sensing its significance in the characteriza-tion of Moses and in the development of Mosaic authority. The problems of in-terpretation begin with the translation of Moses' "shining skin" *(qāran 'ôr)* and his "veil" *(masweh)*. Interpreters debate the meaning of the Hebrew verb *qāran*, used to describe Moses' face. A traditional translation is "the sprouting of horns," from the Hebrew noun *qeren*, evident in the Vulgate, and reappearing in the history of painting, when Moses is represented with horns.[45] R. W. L. Moberly even suggests a possible allusion to the golden calf.[46] Propp prefers the meaning "disfigurement," perhaps alluding to leathery skin.[47] Childs argues for the translation "ray of light," which is reflected in the LXX, Philo, and Paul.[48] It is also the preferred reading in rabbinic literature.[49] The occurrence of the verb *qāran* in Hab 3:4 as "rays of light," along with comparison to the *melammū*, the halo surrounding gods in ancient Near Eastern iconography, favors the imagery of light, rather than horns, as the description of Moses.[50] Thus the imagery in-dicates that the divine glory, represented as light, has invaded the face of Moses on the summit of the mountain, and that it continues to dwell in him when he descends the mountain.

The Hebrew noun *masweh*, translated "veil," is equally problematic. The word is confined to this one episode, and there are no other related stories of this particular mask or veil in the Hebrew Bible.[51] It may derive from the root *swh*, which perhaps means "covering." A noun that may be related is *sûtōh*, used in parallel with *lĕbūšô* ("his garment") in Gen 49:11 to describe Judah, suggest-ing some form of coat or clothing: "He [Judah] washes his garments in wine and his robe *(sûtōh)* in the blood of grapes." The imagery of clothing from Gen

---

45. "When Moses went down from Mount Sinai, he was holding the two tablets of the testimony, and he did not know that his face was horned as a result of his speaking with God." See A. Jirku, "Die Gesichtsmaske des Moses," *ZDPV* 67 (1945): 43-45; E. L. Flynn, "Moses in the Visual Arts," *Int* 44 (1990): 265-76.

46. Moberly, *At the Mountain of God*, 108-9.

47. Propp, "Skin of Moses' Face."

48. Childs, *Exodus*, 609; see also Cassuto, *Exodus*, 448. LXX: "When Moses went down from the mountain, and the two tablets were in his hands, as he was descending from the moun-tain Moses did not know that the skin of his face had become glorified." Philo: "He [Moses] went down and his appearance was far more beautiful than when he had gone up, so that those who saw him were filled with awe and amazement; their eyes could not continue to stand the brightness that flashed from him like the brilliance of the sun" (*Moses* 2.70). Paul: "The Israelites could not look steadily at the face of Moses because of its glory" (2 Cor 3:7).

49. See Leibowitz, *Studies in Shemot*, 2:629-43; Kugel, *Bible As It Was*, 435-37.

50. G. Mendenhall, "The Mask of Yahweh," in *The Tenth Generation: The Origins of the Biblical Tradition* (Baltimore: Johns Hopkins University Press, 1973), 32-66.

51. See K. van der Toorn, "The Significance of the Veil in the Ancient Near East," in *Pomegranates and Golden Bells*, ed. Wright et al., 327-39.

49:11 has reinforced a translation of *masweh* in Exod 34:29-35 as "veil," which conforms to the function of covering the shining skin of Moses.

Verses 29-35 play a central role in the Non-P History, with only minimal additions by the P historian, including the identification of the mountain as Sinai in vv. 29 and 32, and the tablets as the "two tablets of testimony" in v. 29. Childs probed the prehistory of the story, noting its unusual problems with regard to form and function, and concluded in the end that a preliterary origin of the tradition was untraceable.[52] Coats rightly identifies the purpose of the story as a description of Mosaic authority, resulting from Moses' exposure to God on the mountain.[53] M. Haran adds that the story is unique, "unmentioned elsewhere in the Hebrew Bible."[54] Gressmann sought to explain the function of the story and the process by which Moses acquires authority, interpreting the veil as a mask that transforms the wearer and represents God in cultic ritual.[55] The result of such a reading, according to Coats, is that the masking of Moses is his transfiguration.[56]

Gressmann is certainly correct in identifying the importance of cultic masking in the story as the key for interpreting Mosaic authority. But the role of masking begins already with his shining face and is not limited to his veil, which suggests two masks associated with Moses, his shining skin and the veil.[57] H. Pernet notes that direct changes to the face fit a wider definition of masks as objects that conceal the identity of the wearer in order to reveal the power of God.[58] The shining skin of Moses fulfills the definition. It represents God. Moses' radiant face also obscures his identity to the leaders of Israel, which also conforms to Pernet's definition of the mask (34:30). Thus, like ritual masks in general, the shining skin of Moses both conceals his everyday identity while it also represents the Deity.[59] This is the foundation of Mosaic authority, predicted by God during the theophany (19:9). Moses' shining skin indicates Moses' transformation, concealing his profane identity in order to reveal the presence of God in him during cultic mediation.

But the transformation of Moses is peculiar in two ways. First, the story

---

52. Childs, *Exodus,* 609-10.

53. G. W. Coats, *Moses: Heroic Man, Man of God* (JSOTSup 57; Sheffield: JSOT Press, 1988), 173-74.

54. Haran, "Shining of Moses' Face," 159.

55. Gressmann, *Mose und seine Zeit,* 247-48.

56. Coats, *Moses,* 173-74.

57. Dozeman, "Masking Moses."

58. H. Pernet, "Masks: Theoretical Perspectives," *ER* 9:261; see also R. L. Grimes, "Masking: Toward a Phenomenology of Exteriorization," *JAAR* 43 (1975): 509-16.

59. See L. Lommel, *Masks: Their Meaning and Function* (New York: Excalibur Books, 1981); J. Campbell, *The Masks of God: Primitive Mythology* (New York: Viking, 1959).

makes clear that God has invaded the person of Moses without his knowing it, suggesting that the charisma of Moses cannot account for Mosaic authority. Thus even though the speech of God and of Moses merge into one voice at the divine mountain, the power of Mosaic authority does not arise from the profane character of Moses. S. Dean McBride captures the dynamic of Mosaic authority when he states that Moses should not be interpreted as a popular hero like David, whose exploits accentuate his personal power.[60] That Moses is unconscious of the invasion of divine light into his face indicates, instead, that God is the hero in Moses' life and teaching.

Second, the divine possession of Moses is permanent. It does not fade, contrary to Paul's argument in 2 Cor 3:7.[61] The light never leaves his face, requiring that Moses veil himself outside the cult. Thus the veil of Moses is also important for understanding Mosaic authority. It too is a mask, but of a different kind. Its primary role is to conceal Moses' everyday identity outside cultic situations. The concealing of Moses' profane identity has the opposite function as his shining skin, which served to represent God in the setting of the sacred. R. L. Grimes notes that masks of concealment, like the veil of Moses, accentuate the authority of the wearer by setting the person apart in the profane world.[62] The veil of Moses is a mask of concealment intended to set him apart from the Israelites in their social interactions, giving him the social authority that was also promised by God (Exod 3:16–4:17; 19:9).

An analogy to the veil of Moses is the judicial wig in British jurisprudence. Crüsemann is helpful at this point. He states that the study of the judicial system is necessary to interpret the figure of Moses.[63] The veil symbolizes unification and consolidation of judicial authority in Moses. It designates Moses as the lawgiver who administrates divinely revealed legislation into the life of the Israelites. Yet the veil also represents more than social and judicial authority, since it covers the divine light that has permanently invaded him. If removed, the veil would reveal only the divine light, not the profane face of Moses, indicating that Moses' social authority resides in God having invaded Moses' face, not in his profane personality. Thus the two masks relate the sacred and the profane role of law in Mosaic authority. The veil connects the revelation of God to Moses in the sanctuary with his legal authority within Israelite society.

60. S. Dean McBride, "Transcendent Authority: The Role of Moses in Old Testament Traditions," *Int* 44 (1990): 229-39.

61. For discussion of the midrashic interpretation of the apostle Paul as an example of inner-biblical echoing see R. B. Hays, *Echoes of Scripture in the Letters of Paul* (New Haven: Yale University Press, 1989), 122-53.

62. Grimes, "Masking," 513.

63. Crüsemann, *Torah*, 62.

The shining face of Moses and his veil define Mosaic authority in the Hebrew Bible. Although Moses' authority is grounded in his person, the two masks underscore that this authority does not acquire power from his personality. The shining skin indicates that the foundational power of Mosaic authority arises from the cultic revelation of law through Moses, while the veil extends the authority of religious law to Israelite society. J. Neusner captures this view of Mosaic authority with these words: "God revealed the Torah to Moses at Mount Sinai. Authority rests upon God's will and word to Moses."[64] But in the merging of God's will and the speech of Moses, the personality of Moses becomes subsumed in divine Torah. The subordination of Moses' profane character paradoxically makes him the most authoritative person in all of Scripture. He is the only one who speaks with God face-to-face (Num 12:6-8).

The story of Moses' shining face and veil is crucial to the thematic development of Mosaic authority in the Non-P History. The theme was introduced in his commission (Exodus 3–4) and increased in intensity during the revelation at the mountain of God. God promised Moses authority as a result of the initial divine revelation (19:9; 20:18-20). The authority of Moses to speak with God acquired intensity after the incident of the golden calf with the establishment of a cultic setting in the form of the tent of meeting (33:7-11). The direct encounter between Moses and God in 34:34-35 likely implies the setting of the tent of meeting, providing a literary connection to the mediation of Moses in chap. 33 and a resolution for Moses' request to see God's glory (33:12-23). The scene concludes the literature of the Non-P historian in Exodus. But the theme of Mosaic authority in the tent of meeting continues in the Non-P History into the subsequent stories of Numbers 11–12, where the tent of meeting remains the setting for further definition of the social (Numbers 11) and the cultic (Numbers 12) authority of Moses.

The P historian makes additions to the story of Moses' shining face, bringing it into conformity with the themes of the P History, including the setting of Mount Sinai (Exod 34:29, 32), the reference to the "congregation" (34:31), and the name of the tablets as the "two tablets of testimony" (34:29). The P historian also reinterprets Mosaic authority, subordinating the mediation of Moses in the tent of meeting so that it becomes the introduction to the construction of the tabernacle (chaps. 35–40). The framing of the tent of meeting with the revelation (chaps. 25–31) and construction (chaps. 35–40) of the tabernacle emphasizes its transitional character.

The P author also transfers the role of Moses as mediator in the tent of meeting (34:34-35) to the tabernacle in Num 7:89, when Moses enters the most holy place to receive divine revelation. The transition is emphasized through

---

64. J. Neusner, "Religious Authority in Judaism," *Int* 39 (1985): 374-75.

repetition. The cultic role of Moses in Exod 34:34-35 begins: "Whenever Moses entered the presence of Yahweh to speak with him . . ." *(ûběbō' mōšeh lipnê yhwh lĕdabbēr 'ittô)*. The statement repeats in Num 7:89: "Whenever Moses entered the tent of meeting to speak with him" *(ûběbō' mōšeh 'el-'ōhel mô'ēd lĕdabbēr 'ittô)*. The phrase "to speak with him" fits the context of Exod 34:34-35, but is less clear in Num 7:89, suggesting that the latter text is intended to be an inner-biblical interpretation in the P History.

The context of Num 7:89 indicates that the tent of meeting has become identified with the tabernacle (Num 7:1, 5), now located at the center of the Israelite camp. In Numbers 7 Moses mediates in the tabernacle. The thematic changes between Exod 34:34-35 and Num 7:89 leave little doubt that the portrait of Moses mediating revelation in the tent of meeting in Exod 34:29-35 is provisional. Numbers 7:89 indicates the end of this period of the tent of meeting by locating Moses within the camp in the inner sanctum of the tabernacle.

The oracular character of revelation continues in Num 7:89, but the imagery of revelation is now associated with the iconography of the tabernacle's inner sanctum, rather than with the person of Moses. Moses remains idealized as the one who speaks with God, but the P historian clarifies that the voice of Yahweh originates from between the two cherubim covering the ark. The material following 7:89 further clarifies that the content of revelation concerns the ritual role of the Aaronide priesthood in the tabernacle (8:1-4) and the protective role of the Levites outside it (8:5-26). Priests and Levites assume the social responsibility of Mosaic authority in the P History, as compared to the seventy elders in the Non-P History (Numbers 11).

Construction of the Tabernacle (35:1–40:38)

The building of the tabernacle in the P History concludes the literature in Exodus. The account of building repeats many of the instructions from the revelation in chaps. 25–31. The process of construction separates into six parts: (1) the law of Sabbath, 35:1-3; (2) the building of the sanctuary and its furnishings, 35:4–38:31; (3) the making of the vestments, 39:1-31; (4) the inspection of the work by Moses, 39:32-43; (5) the assembly on New Year's Day, 40:1-33; and (6) the theophany of the Glory of Yahweh in the completed tabernacle, 40:34-38. The diagram in figure 44 on page 757 provides an outline of the construction of the tabernacle and its correspondence to the revelation in chaps. 25–31.

Figure 44

Topic (following Exod 35–40)	Construction of Tabernacle and Priestly Vestments (Exod 35–40)	Revelation of Tabernacle and Its Cultic Rituals (Exod 25–31)
PART I: SABBATH	35:1-3	31:12-17
PART II: ARCHITECTURE AND FURNISHINGS		
Material: Offerings	35:4-29	25:1-7
Builders	35:30–36:7	31:1-11
Construction		
A. Tabernacle	36:8-38	26:1-37
1. Ark	37:1-9	25:10-22
2. Table	37:10-16	25:23-30
3. Lampstand	37:17-24	25:31-40
4. Incense altar	37:25-28(a)	30:1-9
B. Altar	38:1-7	27:1-8
C. Basin of water	38:8	30:17-21
D. Courtyard	38:9-20	27:9-19
Material: Census/Tax	38:21-31	30:11-16
PART III: VESTMENTS		
A. Material	39:1	28:1-5
B. Ephod	39:2-7	28:6-14
C. Breastplate	39:8-21	28:15-30
D. Robe	39:22-26	28:31-35
E. Tunics	39:27-29	28:39-43
F. Plate	39:30-31	28:36-38
PART IV: INSPECTION	39:32-43	————
PART V: ASSEMBLY	40:1-33	————
PART VI: THEOPHANY	40:34-38	24:15b-18a; 25:8-9

SABBATH

31:12-17

[12]And Yahweh said to Moses, saying, [13]"You shall speak to the Israelites, saying, 'Indeed, my Sabbath you must observe, for it is a sign between me and you throughout your generations to know that I am Yahweh the one consecrating you. [14]You shall observe the Sabbath for it is holy to you. The one profaning it will be put to death, for anyone doing work on it, that life will be cut off from among the people. [15]Six days work will be done, but on the seventh day there shall be a Sabbath of complete rest. It is holy to Yahweh. Anyone doing work on the Sabbath day will be put to death. [16]The Israelites shall observe the Sabbath, undertaking the Sabbath throughout their generations. It is a perpetual covenant. [17]It is a sign between me and Israelites forever, for in six days Yahweh made the heavens and the earth, and on the seventh day he rested and was refreshed.'"

35:1-3

[1]And Moses assembled the entire congregation of the Israelites, and he said to them, "These are the words that Yahweh commanded you to do.

[2]Six days work will be done, but on the seventh day there shall be a holy Sabbath of complete rest to Yahweh. Any one doing work on it shall be put to death.

[3]You shall kindle no fire in any of your dwellings on the Sabbath day.

Notes

35:1 *These are the words that Yahweh commanded you to do.* Hebrew *děbārîm,* "words," could also be translated "things" (see NRSV). The LXX translates *hoi logoi.*

35:2 *a holy Sabbath of complete rest to Yahweh.* Hebrew *šabbat šabbāton,* "complete rest," is translated in NRSV, "solemn rest." The LXX translates, *sabbata anapausis,* "a making to rest."

31:17 *he rested and was refreshed.* Hebrew *šābat,* "he rested," is translated *epausato* in the LXX. The second verb, *wayyinnāpas,* "he was refreshed," is unusual especially as a description of the Deity. The Sabbath command in 23:12 attributes the quality of being refreshed on the Sabbath to the resident alien. David is refreshed at the Jordan River after his flight from Absalom in 2 Sam 16:14. The LXX avoids the description of the Deity needing to be refreshed from the work of creation by translating *katepausen,* "he left off (the work of creation)."

Commentary

The law of Sabbath is central to the P History. It is introduced immediately in the wilderness journey in the story of manna (Exodus 16), revealing the lost structure of creation (Gen 1:1–2:3). The law of Sabbath repeats in the Decalogue, again tied to the structure of creation (Exod 20:8-11). The revelation of the tabernacle concludes with the Sabbath law (31:12-17). Now, the construction of the tabernacle begins with a reiteration of the law (35:1-3). I. Knohl detected a pattern in the appearance of Sabbath law in the P History, in which instances of revelation at Mount Sinai are followed by the proclamation of the Sabbath law.[65] First, the theophany in 19:16-25 is followed by the Sabbath law in the Decalogue (20:8-11). Second, the appearance of the Glory of Yahweh on Mount Sinai (24:15–31:11) concludes with the Sabbath law (31:12-17). Now, the Sabbath law in 35:1-3 follows the story of Moses' mediation in the tent of meeting (34:29-35). Revelation and Sabbath law are inseparable in the P History.

The repetitions also explain the scope of the law. The Sabbath is introduced in the story of manna as an inherent feature of the structure of creation (chap. 16). Sabbath observance is reformulated into a law in the Decalogue, without punishment (20:8-11). The conclusion to the revelation of the tabernacle introduces the death penalty for violators of the Sabbath law (31:12-17). The introduction to the construction of the tabernacle extends the law further, forbidding domestic fires (35:1-3). And the story of the man picking up sticks in the wilderness on the Sabbath will underscore that the law is universal, applying to all Israelites in the Diaspora and not just to those living in the land of Canaan (Num 15:32-36).[66]

ARCHITECTURE, FURNISHINGS, AND VESTMENTS (35:4–39:31)

The building of the tabernacle separates into four parts: 35:4-29 lists the building materials presented as a freewill offering by the people; 35:30–36:7 identifies the builders; 36:8–38:20 recounts the construction of the tabernacle and its furnishings; 38:21-31 states the census and a tax levy to support the tabernacle cult, and 39:1-31 lists the vestments. These passages are discussed with their parallels at 25:1–31:11.

INSPECTION (39:32-43)

39:32 *And all the work of the tabernacle of the tent of meeting was completed. And the Israelites made according to everything that Yahweh commanded Moses, so they did.* **33** *And they brought the tabernacle to Moses, the tent, and all its*

65. Knohl, *Sanctuary of Silence*, 66-67.
66. Dozeman, "Numbers," *NIB* 2:128.

vessels, its clasps, its frames, its bars, its pillars, and its bases, [34] the covering of the red-dyed skins of rams, and the covering of the skin of dolphins, and the curtain for the screen, [35] the ark of the testimony and its poles and cover, [36] the table, and its poles, and the bread of the Presence, [37] the pure lampstand, its lamps, lamps arranged, and all its vessels, and the oil for the lamp, [38] the golden altar, the oil for anointing, and the fragrant incense, and the screen for the door of the tent, [39] the copper altar, and its grating of copper for it, its poles, and all its vessels, the laver and its basin and its stand, [40] the hangings of the court, its pillars, and its bases, and the screen for the gate of the courtyard, its cords, its pegs, and all the vessels of the work of the tabernacle for the tent of meeting, [41] the garments of service for ministering in the holy place, the holy garments for Aaron, the priest, and the garments of his sons to serve as priests. [42] According to all that Yahweh commanded Moses, thus the Israelites did all the work. [43] And Moses saw all the work and indeed they made it according to everything that Yahweh commanded, so they did. And Moses blessed them.

Notes

39:32-43 The list of the material and the objects for the tabernacle is framed in vv. 32 and 42-43 with similar statements of completion, emphasizing the work of the people. The conclusion in vv. 42-43 shifts the focus back to Moses, who blesses the people.

39:32 *all the work of the tabernacle of the tent of meeting.* Both terms for the wilderness sanctuary are combined in vv. 32 and 40. The LXX eliminates any reference to the sanctuary, simply stating that the people completed the work according to the divine commands given to Moses (39:10).

39:37 *its lamps, lamps arranged.* Hebrew *nērōt hamma'ărākâ* indicates the arrangement of the lamps. This is the only place where this description of the lampstand occurs. The LXX (39:16) translates, *lychnous tēs kauseōs,* "lamps of burning."

Commentary

The central theme in the section is the completion of work on the tabernacle, its furnishings, and the priestly vestments. The section separates into three parts: 39:32 states that the work was completed; 39:33-41 lists the material that the Israelites bring to Moses; and 39:42-43 repeats the statement that the work was completed, noting the inspection by Moses and his blessing.

The completion of the tabernacle conforms to a larger literary tradition in the ancient Near East. V. Hurowitz notes that accounts of building projects conclude with a summary statement, indicating the successful completion of the temple.[67] Tiglath-pileser I reports the building of the Anu and Adad temple:

67. Hurowitz, *I Have Built,* 235-41. He cites Tiglath-pileser from E. A. W. Budge and L. W. King, *Annals of the Kings of Assyria* (London: British Museum, 1902), 97-98, VII 90-97.

"The pure temple . . . I planned, I exerted myself, I built, I completed." Hurowitz includes further examples from Sennacherib, Esarhaddon, Ashurbanipal, Nebuchadnezzar, and Nabonidus. Each king concludes his building project with some form of the phrase: "I built and I completed." The same is true of Solomon: "So Solomon built the temple and completed it" (1 Kgs 6:14). The pattern emphasizes the central role of the king in temple building.

The construction of the tabernacle follows the ancient Near Eastern literary tradition, with slight changes. The initial statement of the tabernacle's completion is attributed to the people in Exod 39:32, not to Moses: "And all the work of the tabernacle of the tent of meeting was completed. And the Israelites made according to everything that Yahweh commanded Moses, so they did." The repetition in 39:42 reinforces the same point: "According to all that Yahweh commanded Moses, thus the Israelites did all the work." Moses takes on the role of inspector. He blesses the people and their work upon seeing the tabernacle (39:43). Moses is also credited with assembling the tabernacle in 40:1-33, which ends with a formula of completion, "And Moses completed the work" (see also Num 7:1). The people build the tabernacle in the P History. It is not a king's sanctuary. W. P. Brown states: "The Israelites as a whole are cast in the role of collaborative cocreators in the tabernacle's construction."[68]

Blenkinsopp also demonstrated the close relationship between world creation and the construction of the tabernacle in the P History. He noted the similar actions and phrases to describe God at the completion of creation, and Moses at the end of the construction of the tabernacle (fig. 45 on p. 762).[69]

J. D. Levenson characterizes the tabernacle as representing a microcosm of world creation,[70] to which Brown adds spatial correspondences, progressing from holiness (Sabbath in creation and the most holy place in the tabernacle) to chaos (the watery darkness of creation and the wilderness surrounding the tabernacle).[71] Blenkinsopp may be correct when he concludes: "The construction of the sanctuary is the completion of the work begun in creation."[72] T. Pola goes further to conclude that the construction of the tabernacle completes the original P source.[73] But the further repetition of the formula of completion in Josh 19:51, "So they finished dividing the land," raises the question of whether the construction of the tabernacle in the wilderness is not the end of

---

68. W. P. Brown, *The Ethos of the Cosmos: The Genesis of Moral Imagination in the Bible* (Grand Rapids: Eerdmans, 1999), 84.

69. Blenkinsopp, *Pentateuch,* 218; also idem, "The Structure of P," *CBQ* 38 (1976): 275-92.

70. J. D. Levenson, *Creation and the Persistence of Evil: The Jewish Drama of Divine Omnipotence* (San Francisco: Harper & Row, 1988), 86.

71. Brown, *Ethos of the Cosmos,* 83-85 *et passim.*

72. Blenkinsopp, *Pentateuch,* 218.

73. Pola, *Ursprüngliche Priesterschrift.*

Figure 45

Creation of the world	Construction of the sanctuary
And God saw everything that he had made, and behold, it was very good (Gen 1:31)	And Moses saw all the work, and behold, they had done it (Exod 39:43)
Thus the heavens and the earth were finished (Gen 2:1)	Thus all the work of the tabernacle and the tent of meeting was finished (Exod 39:32)
God finished his work which he had done (Gen 2:2)	So Moses finished the work (Exod 40:33)
So God blessed the seventh day (Gen 2:3)	So Moses blessed them (Exod 39:43)

the story. The P History may also envision the tabernacle as one day residing in the land of Canaan, which could then accentuate the divine promise of land to the ancestors.

ASSEMBLY OF THE TABERNACLE (40:1-33)

40:1 And Yahweh spoke to Moses, saying, 2 "On the first day of the first month you shall set up the tabernacle of the tent of meeting. 3 You shall place there the ark of the testimony, and you shall screen the ark with the curtain. 4 You shall bring in the table and you shall arrange its setting. And you shall bring in the lampstand and you shall raise its lamps. 5 And you shall put the golden altar for incense before the ark of the testimony. And you shall place the screen of the door for the tabernacle. 6 And you shall put the altar of burnt offering before the door of the tabernacle of the tent of meeting. 7 And you shall put the basin between the tent of meeting and the altar. And you shall put there water. 8 And you shall place the court all around. And you shall put in the screen of the gate of the courtyard. 9 And you shall take the oil of anointing and anoint the tabernacle and all that is in it. And you shall consecrate it and all its vessels. And it will be holy. 10 And you shall anoint the altar of burnt offering and all of its vessels. And you shall consecrate the altar and the altar will be most holy. 11 And you shall anoint the basin and its stand. And you shall consecrate it.

12 "And you shall bring near Aaron and his sons to the door of the tent of meeting. And you shall wash them with water. 13 You shall clothe Aaron with the sacred garments and you shall anoint him, and you shall consecrate him so that he may serve me as priest. 14 And his sons you shall bring near, and you shall clothe them with tunics. ¹⁵ You shall anoint them as you anointed their father so that they may serve me as priests. Their anointing will be for them an everlasting priesthood throughout their generations."

¹⁶ And Moses did according to everything that Yahweh commanded him, so he did. ¹⁷ In the first month of the second year the tabernacle was set up. ¹⁸ Moses set up the tabernacle. He put in its bases. He placed its frames. He put in its bars. And he set up its poles. ¹⁹ He spread the tent on the tabernacle. He placed the cover of the tent on top of it as Yahweh commanded Moses. ²⁰ And he took and he put the testimony in the ark. And he placed the poles on the ark. And he put the cover on the top of the ark. ²¹ And he brought the ark into the tabernacle and he placed the curtain for screening. And he screened the ark of the testimony as Yahweh commanded Moses. ²² And he put the table in the tent of meeting on the north side of the tabernacle outside the curtain. ²³ And he arranged on it the setting of bread before Yahweh as Yahweh commanded Moses. ²⁴ And he placed the lampstand in the tent of meeting opposite the table on the south side of the tabernacle. ²⁵ And he raised the lights before Yahweh as Yahweh commanded Moses. ²⁶ And he placed the golden altar in the tent of meeting before the curtain. ²⁷ And he burnt fragrant incense on it as Yahweh commanded Moses. ²⁸ And he placed the screen for the door of the tabernacle. ²⁹ The altar of burnt offering he placed at the door of the tabernacle of the tent of meeting. He offered on it the burnt offering and the grain offering as Yahweh commanded Moses. ³⁰ He placed the basin between the tent of meeting and the altar, and he put there water for washing. ³¹ And Moses, Aaron, and his sons would wash their hands and feet from it ³² when they would enter the tent of meeting. And when they would draw near to the altar they would wash as Yahweh commanded Moses. ³³ And he set up the court all around for the tabernacle and for the altar. And he put in the screen for the gate of the courtyard. And Moses completed the work.

Notes

40:2 *on the first day of the first month.* Hebrew *bĕʾeḥād laḥōdeš* is a common expression for designating the month in the P History (see Gen 8:5; Num 1:1, 18; 29:1). The LXX translates, *tou mēnos tou prōtou noumēnia,* "the first month in the new moon." The reference to the "new moon" underscores the first day. The repetition is lacking in the LXX translation of 40:17.

40:4 *you shall arrange its setting.* Hebrew *wĕʿāraktā ʾet-ʿerkô* is lit. "you shall arrange its arrangement," meaning the twelve loaves of bread in two rows (see 25:30).

you shall raise its lamps. Hebrew *wĕhaʿălêtā* is lit. "and you shall ascend," meaning most likely that the lamps must be lit.

40:7 This verse is absent from the LXX. The description of the basin is placed at the conclusion of Exodus 38 in the LXX, where its construction is noted in conjunction with the washing of the priests (MT 40:30-32 = LXX 38:27).

40:11 This verse is absent from the LXX.

40:20 *And he took and he put the testimony in the ark*. The reference to the "testimony" is "the tablets of testimony" in the P History.

40:28 This verse is absent from the LXX.

40:31-32 *would wash . . . when they would enter. . . . And when they would draw near . . . they would wash*. The description is frequentative to describe future ongoing cultic practice (see the same frequentative syntax in 34:34-35 with regard to Moses). The practice is first enacted in Leviticus 8–9. The description of the washing of the priests in the LXX is in Exod 38:27.

40:33 *Moses completed the work*. The LXX and Sam add "all" to modify "the work."

Commentary

Yahweh commands Moses to set up the tabernacle. The section follows the pattern of divine command (40:1-15) and fulfillment (40:16-33). The point of emphasis in the assembly of the tabernacle is the date, New Year's Day of the second year after the exodus (40:1, 17). The emphasis on New Year's Day further reinforces the correspondence between creation (month 1, day 1, year 1) and the construction of the tabernacle (month 1, day 1, year 2667) in the liturgical dating of the P History (see the introduction, History and Exodus). This suggests that the assembly of the tabernacle marks a new era in world history, similar to the new era of humanity after the flood (Gen 8:13).

The divine command to Moses in Exod 40:1-15 extends beyond the literature in Exodus for its completion. Verses 2-11 consist of directions for Moses to set up the sanctuary and its furnishings, while vv. 12-15 are instructions for the ordination of the Aaronide priests, but these are not fulfilled until Leviticus 8–9. Thus as is the case in the revelation of the tabernacle in Exodus 25–31, so also the instructions for assembly of the tabernacle presuppose the larger body of literature on the tabernacle and its cult in Leviticus and in Numbers 1–10.

The book of Exodus concludes with an account of Moses assembling the tabernacle on New Year's Day. The assembly includes the structure (40:17-19) and its furnishings (40:20-32), which are also consecrated. First, the ark is placed in the most holy place with the tablets of testimony (40:20-21). Second, the furniture for the holy place is positioned, including the table (40:22-23), the lampstand (40:24-25), and the altar of incense (40:26-28). Finally, the altar of burnt offering (40:29) and the basin for washing (40:30-32) are positioned within the larger setting of the courtyard (40:33).

Theophany in the Tabernacle (40:34-38)

⁴⁰:³⁴ *And the cloud covered the tent of meeting and the Glory of Yahweh filled the tabernacle.* ³⁵ *But Moses was not able to enter the tent of meeting, because the cloud settled on it and the Glory of Yahweh filled the tabernacle.*

³⁶ *In all the journeys of the Israelites, whenever the cloud was taken up from above the tabernacle, they would journey.* ³⁷ *But if the cloud was not taken up, they would not journey until the day that it was taken up.* ³⁸ *For the cloud of Yahweh was on the tabernacle by day, and a fire was on it by night before all the entire house of Israel throughout their journey.*

Notes

40:34-35 The distinction between the tabernacle and the tent of meeting in the P History is illustrated in vv. 34-35 (see the introduction). When the Deity (in the form of the Glory of Yahweh) enters the sanctuary it is the tabernacle (v. 34). When the human (Moses) enters (or in this case attempts to enter) the sanctuary it is the tent of meeting (v. 35).

40:34 *covered.* The LXX translates Hebrew *waykas* as *ekalypsen.*

40:35 *settled.* The LXX translates Hebrew *šākan* as *epeskiazen,* "overshadowed."

40:38 *the cloud of Yahweh.* Hebrew *'ānān yhwh* is used only twice in the Hebrew Bible, once by the P author in this verse and a second time in the account of the Israelites' departure from the mountain in the J History in Num 10:34 (see Num 10:29-36).[74] The LXX refers only to "cloud" *(nephelē).*

Commentary

The book of Exodus ends with a theophany of the Glory of Yahweh in the tabernacle. The theophany divides between the description of the Glory of Yahweh in the newly assembled tabernacle (40:34-35) and a preview of the leading of the cloud in the Israelites' wilderness march (40:36-38).

The theophany within the tabernacle in 40:34-35 indicates the further descent of the Glory of Yahweh into the midst of the Israelites. It repeats the imagery of theophany from the summit of Mount Sinai in 24:15b-18a, when the Glory of Yahweh appeared to all the Israelites and Moses ascended into the cloud to receive the plans for the tabernacle. But the dynamic of the theophany in 40:34-35 recalls the original appearance of God on Mount Sinai (19:20-25), where the appearance of God was a dangerous event, requiring the people to stay away from the mountain.

The point of emphasis in 40:34-35 is that without proper rituals to approach God, or a qualified priesthood to mediate holiness, the cultic presence of God is dangerous and unapproachable. Not even Moses is able to enter the sanc-

---

74. Dozeman, "Numbers," *NIB* 2:93-96.

tuary. By concluding Exodus with a cultic theophany that repels people, the P author points the reader ahead to the ordination of the priesthood in Leviticus 8–9, commanded by Yahweh in Exodus 29 and 40:12-15. Once the Aaronide priesthood is firmly in place, the Glory of Yahweh will appear in the altar before all the Israelites (Lev 9:22-24). The theme of theophany will return one final time at Mount Sinai, when the tabernacle is assembled in the midst of the Israelite camp in Num 7:1-88, at which time Moses enters the sanctuary and experiences the revelation of Yahweh as speech from the ark of the testimony (Num 7:89).

The closing image of the presence of God in Exod 40:36-38 is not of the stationary Glory of Yahweh in the cult, but of the divine cloud leading the Israelites in their wilderness march toward the promised land of Canaan. The cloud provides rhythm to the life journey of the Israelites. It determines when the people march and when they rest. It hovers over the tabernacle by day, while at night the divine fire within it appears.

The theology of the cloud, its relationship to the tabernacle, and its role in leading the Israelites is developed further in Num 9:15 23, which provides a parallel to Exod 40:34-38. In both texts the P author relates two aspects of divine presence, the presence of God as divine Glory in the tabernacle (40:34-35; Num 9:15-16) and the cloud as a guide in the Israelites' journey (Exod 40:36-38; Num 9:17-23).

The P author's theology of the cloud as wilderness guide is established in the theophany on Mount Sinai in Exod 24:15b-18a. Three aspects of the cloud emerge from this story. First, the Glory of Yahweh resides in the cloud. When Moses ascends Mount Sinai to receive plans for the tabernacle, the cloud surrounds the divine Glory (24:16). Second, the Glory of Yahweh is a divine fire. The appearance of the Glory of Yahweh was like a consuming fire on the top of Mount Sinai (24:17). Third, the cloud and the Glory of Yahweh are not the same thing. The cloud first covers Mount Sinai (24:15), before the Glory of Yahweh settles on it (24:16).

The separation of the cloud and the Glory of Yahweh continues in the theophany within the tabernacle, allowing the cloud to take on the role of wilderness guide in 40:36-38. Numbers 9:15-23 provides further commentary on the relationship of the Glory of Yahweh and the cloud, greatly expanding the role of the cloud as wilderness guide. The text emphasizes the variation in the routine of travel. Rest periods may include one night (Num 9:21), days, a month, or even longer periods of time (Num 9:22). The imagery of travel with periods of unequal rest may refer to the Priestly cultic calendar (Leviticus 23; Numbers 28–29), where distinct feasts require different periods of rest. Observing these festivals through the liturgical year is how the Israelites follow the cloud. It has the ability to lead them ahead in their journey to the promised land, while it is also able to bring them back to the Glory of Yahweh in the tabernacle for rest and renewal in order to continue the journey.

Bibliography

Aberbach, M., and L. Smolar. "Aaron, Jeroboam, and the Golden Calves." *JBL* 86 (1967): 129-40.

—————. "The Golden Calf Episode in Postbiblical Literature." *HUCA* 39 (1968): 91-116.

Achenbach, R. *Die Vollendung der Tora: Studien zur Redaktionsgeschichte des Numeribuches im Kontext von Hexateuch und Pentateuch.* BZABR 3. Wiesbaden: Harrassowitz, 2002.

Ackerman, J. S. "The Literary Context of the Moses Birth Story (Exodus 1–2)." Pages 74-119 in *Literary Interpretations of Biblical Narratives.* Edited by K. R. R. Gros Louis et al. Nashville: Abingdon, 1974.

Ackerman, S. "Why Is Miriam Also Among the Prophets? (And Is Zipporah Among the Priests?)" *JBL* 121 (2002): 47-80.

Ackroyd, P. R. *Exile and Restoration: A Study of Hebrew Thought of the Sixth Century B.C.* OTL. Philadelphia: Westminster, 1968.

Addinall, P. "Exodus iii 19b and the Interpretation of Biblical Narrative." *VT* 49 (1999): 289-300.

Aharoni, Y. "The Horned Altar of Beer-Sheba." *BA* 37 (1974): 1-6.

Ahlström, G. W. *The History of Ancient Palestine.* Minneapolis: Fortress, 1993.

Albertz, R. "Exodus: Liberation History against Charter Myth." Pages 128-43 in *Religious Identity and the Invention of Tradition: Papers Read at a Noster Conference in Soesterbert, January 4-6, 1999.* Edited by J. W. Van Henten and A. Houtepen. Studies in Theology and Religion 3. Assen: Van Gorcum, 2001.

Albright, W. F. "A Catalogue of Early Hebrew Lyric Poems." *HUCA* 23 (1950/51): 14-24.

—————. "The Earliest Form of Hebrew Verse." *JPOS* 2 (1922): 69-86.

—————. *History, Archaeology, and Christian Humanism.* New York: McGraw-Hill, 1964.

—————. "Jethro, Hobab and Reuel in Early Hebrew Tradition." *CBQ* 25 (1963): 1-11.

—————. "The Name of Yahweh." *JBL* 43 (1924): 370-78.

—————. "The Psalm of Habakkuk." Pages 1-18 in *Studies in Old Testament Prophecy Presented to Theodore H. Robinson.* Edited by H. H. Rowley. Edinburgh: T. & T. Clark, 1950.

—————. "The Song of Deborah in Light of Archaeology." *BASOR* 66 (1936): 26-31.

————. *Yahweh and the Gods of Canaan: A Historical Analysis of Two Contrasting Faiths.* 1968. Repr. Garden City, N.Y.: Doubleday, 1969.

Alexander, T. D. "The Composition of the Sinai Narrative in Exodus xix 1-xxiv 11." *VT* 49 (1999): 2-20.

Allen, L. *Psalms 101–150.* WBC 21. Waco: Word, 1983.

Allison, D. "Mark 12:18-31 and the Decalogue." Pages 270-78 in *The Gospels and the Scriptures of Israel.* Edited by C. A. Evans and W. Stegner. JSNTSup 104; SSEJC 3. Sheffield: Sheffield Academic Press, 1994.

————. *The New Moses: A Matthean Typology.* Minneapolis: Fortress, 1993.

Alt, A. *Essays on Old Testament History and Religion.* Translated by R. A. Wilson. Oxford: Basil Blackwell, 1966.

Alter, R. *The Art of Biblical Narrative.* New York: Basic Books, 1981.

————. *The Art of Biblical Poetry.* New York: Basic Books, 1985.

Althann, R. "A Note on Exodus 19:12ab-13." *Bib* 57 (1976): 242-46.

Amir, Y. "The Decalogue According to Philo." Pages 121-60 in *The Ten Commandments in History and Tradition.* Edited by B.-Z. Segal. Jerusalem: Magnes, 1990.

Andersen, F. I. "A Lexicographical Note on Exodus XXXII 18." *VT* 16 (1966): 108-12.

Andersen, F. I., and D. N. Freedman. *Amos.* AB 24A. Garden City, N.Y.: Doubleday, 1989.

Anderson, B. W. "The Song of Miriam Poetically and Theologically Considered." Pages 285-96 in *Directions in Biblical Hebrew Poetry.* Edited by E. R. Follis. JSOTSup 40. Sheffield: Sheffield Academic Press, 1987.

Anderson, G. "Sacrifice and Sacrificial Offerings (OT)." Pages 872-86 in vol. 5 of *Anchor Bible Dictionary.* Edited by D. N. Freedman. 6 vols. New York: Doubleday, 1992.

Anderson, G., and S. M. Olyan, eds. *Priesthood and Cult in Ancient Israel.* JSOTSup 125. Sheffield: Sheffield Academic Press, 1991.

Andreasen, N.-E. A. *The Old Testament Sabbath: A Tradition-Historical Investigation.* SBLDS 7. Missoula, Mont.: Scholars Press, 1972.

Assmann, J. *Moses the Egyptian: The Memory of Egypt in Western Monotheism.* Cambridge: Harvard University Press, 1997.

Auerbach, E. *Moses.* Amsterdam: G. J. A. Ruys, 1953.

Auffret, P. "Essai sur la structure littéraire d'Ex 14." *EstBib* 41 (1983): 53-82.

————. "Remarks on J. Magonet's Interpretation of Exodus 6.2-8." *JSOT* 27 (1983): 69-71.

Auld, A. G. *Joshua, Moses and the Land: Tetrateuch-Pentateuch-Hexateuch in a Generation since 1938.* Edinburgh: T. & T. Clark, 1980.

Aurelius, E. *Der Fürbitter Israels: Eine Studie zum Mosebild im Alten Testament.* ConBOT 27. Lund: Almqvist & Wiksell, 1988.

Ausloos, H. "Deuteronomi(sti)c Elements in Exod 23,20-33? Some Methodological Remarks." Pages 481-500 in *Studies in the Book of Exodus: Redaction — Reception — Interpretation.* Edited by Marc Vervenne. BETL 126. Leuven: Leuven University Press, 1996.

————. "Exod 23, 20-33 and the 'War of YHWH.'" *Bib* 80 (1999): 555-63.

Avalos, H. "Exodus 22:9 and Akkadian Legal Formulae." *JBL* 109 (1990): 116-17.

Avishur, Y. "The Narrative of the Revelation at Sinai (Exod 19–24)." Pages 197-214 in *Studies in Historical Geography and Biblical Historiography: Presented to Zecharia Kallai.* Edited by G. Galil and M. Weinfeld. VTSup 81. Leiden: Brill, 2000.

Bach, A. "Dreaming of Miriam's Well." Pages 151-58 in *Exodus to Deuteronomy*. Edited by A. Brenner. FCB 2/5. Sheffield: Sheffield Academic Press, 2000.

Bäntsch, B. *Das Bundesbuch: Exod. xx 22-xxiii 33. Seine ursprüngliche Gestalt, seine Verhältnis zu den es umgebenden Quellenschriften und seine Stellung in der alttestamentlichen Gesetzgebung*. Halle: Max Niemeyer, 1892.

―――. *Exodus–Leviticus–Numeri*. HKAT. Göttingen: Vandenhoeck & Ruprecht, 1903.

Bailey, L. R. "The Golden Calf." *HUCA* 42 (1971): 97-115.

Balentine, S. E. *The Hiding of the Face of God in the Old Testament*. New York: Oxford University Press, 1983.

Baltzer, K. *The Covenant Formulary in the Old Testament, Jewish and Early Christian Writings*. Translated by D. E. Green. Philadelphia: Fortress, 1971.

Barnouin, M. "Les recensements du livre des Nombres et l'astronomie babylonienne." *VT* 27 (1977): 280-303.

Bar-On, S. "The Festival Calendars in Exodus xxii 14-19 and xxxiv 18-26." *VT* 48 (1998): 161-95.

―――. "Zur literarkritischen Analyse von Ex 12, 21-27." *ZAW* 107 (1995): 18-31.

Barr, J. "Theophany and Anthropomorphism in the Old Testament." *VT* 7 (1959): 31-38.

Barré, M. L. "My Strength and My Song in Exod 15:2." *CBQ* 54 (1992): 623-37.

Barstad, H. M. *A Way in the Wilderness: The "Second Exodus" in the Message of Second Isaiah*. JSSM 12. Manchester: Manchester University Press, 1989.

Barth, Chr. "Zur Bedeutung der Wüstentradition." Pages 14-23 in *Volume du Congrès: Genève 1965*. VTSup 15. Leiden: Brill, 1966.

―――. "Theophanie, Bundesschliessung und neuer Anfang am dritten Tage." *EvT* 28 (1968): 521-33.

Baskin, J. R. *Pharaoh's Counselors: Job, Jethro, and Balaam in Rabbinic and Patristic Tradition*. BJS 47. Chico, Calif.: Scholars Press, 1983.

Batto, B. F. "Red Sea or Reed Sea: How the Mistake Was Made and What *Yam Sûp* Really Means." *BAR* 10/4 (1984): 57-63.

―――. "The Reed Sea: *Requiescat in Pace*." *JBL* 102 (1983): 27-35.

―――. *Slaying the Dragon: Mythmaking in the Biblical Tradition*. Louisville: Westminster/John Knox, 1992.

―――. "The Sleeping God: An Ancient Near Eastern Motif of Divine Sovereignty." *Bib* 68 (1987): 153-77.

Bauer, J. B. "Könige und Priester, ein heiliges Volk (Ex 19,6)." *BZ* 2 (1958): 283-86.

Beer, G. *Exodus*. HAT 3. Tübingen: Mohr (Siebeck), 1939.

Begg, C. T. "The Destruction of the Calf (Exod 32,20/Deut 9,21)." Pages 208-51 in *Das Deuteronomium: Entstehung, Gestalt und Botschaft*. Edited by N. Lohfink. BETL 68. Leuven: Leuven University Press, 1985.

―――. "The Destruction of the Golden Calf Revisited (Exod 32,20/Deut 9,21)." Pages 469-79 in *Deuteronomy and Deuteronomic Literature: Festschrift C. H. W. Brekelmans*. Edited by M. Vervenne and J. Lust. BETL 133. Leuven: Leuven University Press, 1997.

Begrich, J. "Berīt: Ein Beitrag zur Erfassung einer alttestamentlichen Denkform." Pages 55-66 in *Gesammelte Studien zum Alten Testament*. Edited by W. Zimmerli. TBü 21. Munich: Chr. Kaiser, 1964.

———. "Das priesterliche Heilsorakel." *ZAW* 52 (1934): 81-92.

———. "Das priesterliche Tora." Pages 63-88 in *Werden und Wesen des Alten Testaments.* Edited by P. Volz et al. BZAW 66. Berlin: Töpelmann, 1936.

Bergant, D. "An Anthropological Approach to Biblical Interpretation: The Passover Supper in Exodus 12:1-20 as a Case Study." *Semeia* 67 (1994): 43-62.

Berge, K. *Reading Sources in a Text: Coherence and Literary Criticsm in the Call of Moses: Models, Methods, Micro-Analysis.* Arbeiten zu Text und Sprache in Alten Testament 54. St. Ottilien: EOS Verlag, 1997.

———. *Die Zeit des Jahwisten: Ein Beitrag zur Datierung jahwistischer Vätertexte.* BZAW 186. Berlin: de Gruyter, 1990.

Bergsma, J. S., and S. W. Hahn. "Noah's Nakedness and the Curse of Canaan (Genesis 9:20-27)." *JBL* 124 (2005): 25-40.

Beyerlin, W. *Origins and History of the Oldest Sinaitic Traditions.* Translated by S. Rudman. Oxford: Basil Blackwell, 1965.

———. "Die Päranese im Bundesbuch und ihre Herkunft." Pages 9-29 in *Gottes Wort und Gottes Land: Hans-Wilhelm Hertzberg zum 70. Geburtstag.* Edited by H. G. Reventlow. Göttingen: Vandenhoeck & Ruprecht, 1965.

Birch, B. "Divine Character and the Formation of Moral Community in the Book of Exodus." Pages 119-35 in *The Bible in Ethics: The Second Sheffield Colloquium.* Edited by John W. Rogerson et al. JSOTSup 207. Sheffield: Sheffield Academic Press, 1995.

Bird, P. *Missing Persons and Mistaken Identities: Women and Gender in Ancient Israel.* OBT. Minneapolis: Fortress, 1997.

Black, J., and A. Green. *Gods, Demons and Symbols of Ancient Mesopotamia: An Illustrated Dictionary.* Austin: University of Texas Press, 1992.

Blendis, M. "The Horns of Moses." *Jewish Bible Quarterly* 27 (1999): 254-50.

Blenkinsopp, J. "Deuteronomic Contribution to the Narrative in Genesis–Numbers: A Test Case." Pages 84-115 in *Those Elusive Deuteronomists: The Phenomenon of Pan-Deuteronomism.* Edited by L. S. Schearing and S. L. McKenzie. JSOTSup 268. Sheffield: Sheffield Academic Press, 1999.

———. *A History of Prophecy in Israel: From the Settlement in the Land to the Hellenistic Period.* Philadelphia: Westminster, 1983.

———. *The Pentateuch: An Introduction to the First Five Books of the Bible.* ABRL. New York: Doubleday, 1992.

———. "Structure and Meaning in the Sinai-Horeb Narrative (Exodus 19–34)." Pages 109-25 in *A Biblical Itinerary: In Search of Method, Form and Content: Essays in Honor of George W. Coats.* Edited by E. E. Carpenter. JSOTSup 240. Sheffield: Sheffield Academic Press, 1997.

———. "The Structure of P." *CBQ* 38 (1976): 275-92.

———. *Treasures Old and New: Essays in the Theology of the Pentateuch.* Grand Rapids: Eerdmans, 2004.

———. *Wisdom and Law in the Old Testament: The Ordering of Life in Israel and Early Judaism.* London: Oxford University Press, 1983.

Blum, E. "Israël à la montagne de Dieu: Remarques sur Ex 19–24; 32–34 et sur le contexte littéraire et historique de sa composition." Pages 271-95 in *Le Pentateuque en ques-*

tion: *Les origines et la composition des cinq premiers livres de la Bible à la lumière des recherches récentes.* Edited by A. de Pury et al. MdB. Geneva: Labor et Fides, 1989.

———. *Die Komposition der Vätergeschichte.* WMANT 57. Neukirchen-Vluyn: Neukirchener Verlag, 1984.

———. "Die literarische Verbindung vom Erzvätern und Exodus: Ein Gespräch mit neueren Endredaktionshypothesen." Pages 119-56 in *Abschied vom Jahwisten: Die Komposition des Hexateuch in der jüngsten Diskussion.* Edited by J. C. Gertz, K. Schmid, and M. Witte. BZAW 315. Berlin: de Gruyter, 2002.

———. "Das sog. 'Privilegrecht' in Exodus 34,11-26: Ein Fixpunkt der Komposition des Exodusbuches?" Pages 347-66 in *Studies in the Book of Exodus: Redaction — Reception — Interpretation.* Edited by Marc Vervenne. BETL 126. Leuven: Leuven University Press, 1996.

———. *Studien zur Komposition des Pentateuch.* BZAW 189. Berlin: de Gruyter, 1990.

Boecker, H. J. *Law and the Administration of Justice in the Old Testament and Ancient East.* Translated by J. Moiser. Minneapolis: Augsburg, 1980.

Boling, R. G., and G. E. Wright. *Joshua.* AB 6. Garden City, N.Y.: Doubleday, 1982.

Booij, Th. "Mountain and Theophany in the Sinai Narrative." *Bib* 65 (1984): 1-26.

Boorer, S. *The Promise of the Land as Oath: A Key to the Formation of the Pentateuch.* BZAW 205. Berlin: de Gruyter, 1992.

Borghouts, J. F. "Witchcraft, Magic, and Divination in Ancient Egypt." Pages 1775-85 in vol. 3 of *Civilizations of the Ancient Near East.* Edited by J. M. Sasson. 4 vols. New York: Scribner's, 1995.

Bori, P. C. *The Golden Calf and the Origins of the Anti-Jewish Controversy.* Translated by D. Ward. SFSHJ 16. Atlanta: Scholars Press, 1990.

Botterweck, G. J., H. Ringgren, and H.-J. Fabry, eds. *Theological Dictionary of the Old Testament.* Translated by G. W. Bromiley, D. E. Green, D. W. Stott, and J. T. Willis. 15 vols. Grand Rapids: Eerdmans, 1974-2006.

Boyce, R. N. *The Cry to God in the Old Testament.* SBLDS 103. Atlanta: Scholars Press, 1988.

Braaten, C. E., and C. R. Seitz, eds. *I Am the Lord Your God: Christian Reflections on the Ten Commmandments.* Grand Rapids: Eerdmans, 2005.

Braulik, G. *Das Deuteronomium.* 2 vols. NEB 15, 28. Würzburg: Echter Verlag, 1986-1992.

———. *Die Mittel deuteronomischer Rhetorik: Erhoben aus Deuteronomium 4,1-40.* AnBib 68. Rome: Pontifical Biblical Institute Press, 1978.

———. *Studien zur Theologie des Deuteronomiums.* Stuttgarter Biblische Aufsatzbände Altes Testament 2. Stuttgart: Katholisches Bibelwerk, 1988.

Brekelmans, Chr. "Die sogenannten deuteronomistischen elemente in Genesi bis Numeri: Ein Beitrag zur Vorgeschichte des Deuteronomiums." Pages 89-96 in *Volume du Congrès: Genève 1965.* VTSup 15. Leiden: Brill, 1966.

Brenner, A., ed. *Exodus to Deuteronomy.* FCB 2/5. Sheffield: Sheffield Academic Press, 2000.

———, ed. *A Feminist Companion to Exodus to Deuteronomy.* FCB 1/6. Sheffield: Sheffield Academic Press, 1994.

Brenner, M. J. *The Song of the Sea: Ex 15:1-21.* BZAW 195. Berlin: de Gruyter, 1991.

Brettler, M. Z. *The Creation of History in Ancient Israel.* London: Routledge, 1995.

———. "The Many Faces of God in Exodus 19." Pages 353-67 in *Jews, Christians, and the*

Theology of the Hebrew Scriptures. Edited by A. Ogden Bellis and J. S. Kaminsky. SBLSymS 8. Atlanta: Society of Biblical Literature, 2000.

Breuer, M. "Dividing the Decalogue into Verses and Commandments." Pages 219-46 in *The Ten Commandments in History and Tradition.* Edited by B.-Z. Segal. Jerusalem: Magnes, 1990.

Brichto, H. C. "Worship of the Golden Calf." *HUCA* 54 (1983): 1-44.

Bright, J. *A History of Israel.* 3rd ed. Philadelphia: Westminster, 1981.

Brin, G. *Studies in Biblical Law: From the Hebrew Bible to the Dead Sea Scrolls.* Translated by J. Chipman. JSOTSup 176. Sheffield: Sheffield Academic Press, 1994.

Brinkman, J. *The Perception of Space in the Old Testament: An Exploration of the Methodological Problems of Its Investigation, Exemplified by a Study of Exodus 25 to 31.* Kampen: Kok Pharos, 1992.

Brockelmann, C. *Hebräische Syntax.* Neukirchen Kreis Moers: Buchhandlung des Erziehungsvereins, 1956.

Brodie, L. T. "Again the Golden Calf: Shades of Hosea." *ExpTim* 91 (1979): 19-20.

Brooks, R. *The Spirit of the Ten Commandments: Shattering the Myth of Rabbinic Legalism.* San Francisco: Harper & Row, 1990.

Brown, J. P. *Israel and Hellas.* BZAW 231. Berlin: de Gruyter, 1995.

Brown, R. E. *The Birth of the Messiah: A Commentary on the Infancy Narratives in the Gospels of Matthew and Luke.* ABRL. New York: Doubleday, 1993.

Brown, W. P. *The Ethos of the Cosmos: The Genesis of Moral Imagination in the Bible.* Grand Rapids: Eerdmans, 1999.

———, ed. *The Ten Commandments: The Reciprocity of Faithfulness.* Louisville: Westminster John Knox, 2004.

Brueggemann, W. "The Book of Exodus." Pages 675-981 in vol. 1 of *New Interpreter's Bible.* Edited by L. E. Keck. Nashville: Abingdon, 1994.

———. "The Kerygma of the Priestly Writers." Pages 101-13 in Brueggemann and H. W. Wolff, *The Vitality of Old Testament Traditions.* 2nd ed. Atlanta: John Knox, 1982.

———. "Pharaoh as Vassal: A Study of Political Metaphor." *CBQ* 57 (1995): 27-51.

———. "A Response to 'The Song of Miriam' by Bernhard Anderson." Pages 297-302 in *Directions in Biblical Hebrew Poetry.* Edited by E. R. Follis. JSOTSup 40. Sheffield: Sheffield Academic Press, 1987.

Buber, M. *Kingship of God.* 3rd ed. New York: Harper & Row, 1967.

———. *Moses.* Oxford: Oxford University Press, 1946.

Budd, P. J. *Numbers.* WBC 5. Waco: Word, 1984.

Budde, K. "Bemerkungen zum Bundesbuch." *ZAW* 11 (1891): 99-114.

———. "The Nomadic Ideal in the Old Testament." *The New World* 4 (1895): 235-79.

Budge, E. A. W., and L. W. King. *Annals of the Kings of Assyria.* London: British Museum, 1902.

Buis, P. "Les conflits entre Moïse et Israël dans Exode et Nombres." *VT* 28 (1978): 257-70.

Burns, R. J. *Has the Lord Indeed Spoken Only through Moses? A Study of the Biblical Portrait of Miriam.* SBLDS 84. Atlanta: Scholars Press, 1987.

Butler, T. C. *Joshua.* WBC 7. Waco: Word, 1983.

———. "'The Song of the Sea': Exodus 15:1-18: A Study in the Exegesis of Hebrew Poetry." Ph.D. diss. Vanderbilt University, 1971.

Caloz, M. "Exode, XIII, 3-16 et son rapport au Deutèronome." *RB* 75 (1968): 5-62.

Calvin, J. *The Four Last Books of Moses Arranged in the Form of a Harmony.* Translated by C. W. Bingham. Vol. 1. Grand Rapids: Eerdmans, 1950.

Camp, C. V. *Wise, Strange and Holy: The Strange Woman and the Making of the Bible.* JSOTSup 320. Sheffield: Sheffield Academic Press, 2000.

Campbell, J. *The Masks of God: Primitive Mythology.* New York: Viking, 1959.

Carmichael, C. M. *Law and Narrative in the Bible: The Evidence of the Deuteronomic Laws and the Decalogue.* Ithaca: Cornell University Press, 1985.

———. *Law, Legend, and Incest in the Bible: Leviticus 18–20.* Ithaca: Cornell University Press, 1997.

———. *The Origins of Biblical Law: The Decalogues and the Book of the Covenant.* Ithaca: Cornell University Press, 1992.

———. "A Singular Method of Codification of Law in the *Mishpatim*." *ZAW* 84 (1972): 19-25.

———. *The Spirit of Biblical Law.* Athens: University of Georgia Press, 1996.

Carpenter, E. E. "Exodus 18: Its Structure, Style, Motifs and Function in the Book of Exodus." Pages 91-108 in *A Biblical Itinerary: In Search of Method, Form, and Content: Essays in Honor of George W. Coats.* Edited by E. E. Carpenter. JSOTSup 240. Sheffield: Sheffield Academic Press, 1997.

Carr, D. "Genesis in Relation to the Moses Story: Diachronic and Synchronic Perspectives." Pages 273-95 in *Studies in the Book of Genesis: Literature, Redaction and History.* Edited by A. Wénin. BETL 155. Leuven: Leuven University Press, 2001.

———. "Method in Determination of the Direction of Dependence: An Empirical Test of Criteria Applied to Exodus 34,11-26 and Its Parallels." Pages 107-40 in *Gottes Volk am Sinai: Untersuchungen zu Ex 32–34 und Dtn 9–10.* Edited by M. Köckert and E. Blum. VWGT 18. Gütersloh: Gütersloher Verlagshaus, 2001.

———. *Reading the Fractures of Genesis: Historical and Literary Approaches.* Louisville: Westminster John Knox, 1996.

Carrol, R. P. "The Aniconic God and the Cult of Images." *ST* 31 (1977): 51-64.

———. "Rebellion and Dissent in Ancient Israelite Society." *ZAW* 89 (1977): 176-204.

———. "Strange Fire: Abstract of Presence Absent in the Text Meditations on Exodus 3." *JSOT* 61 (1994): 39-58.

Case-Winters, A. *God's Power: Traditional Understandings and Contemporary Challenges.* Louisville: Westminster/John Knox, 1990.

Caspari, W. "Das priesterliche Königsreich." *TBl* 8 (1929): 105-10.

Cassuto, U. *A Commentary on the Book of Exodus.* Translated by I. Abrahams. Jerusalem: Magnes, 1967.

Cathcart, K. J. "Day of Yahweh." Pages 84-85 in vol. 2 of *Anchor Bible Dictionary.* Edited by D. N. Freedman. 6 vols. New York: Doubleday, 1992.

Cazelles, H. "Alliance du Sinaï, alliance de l'Horeb et renouvellement de l'alliance." Pages 69-79 in *Beiträge zur Alttestamentlichen Theologie: Festschrift für Walther Zimmerli.* Edited by H. Donner, Robert Hanhart, and Rudolf Smend. Göttingen: Vandenhoeck & Ruprecht, 1977.

———. *Autour de l'Exode (Études).* Sources bibliques. Paris: Gabalda, 1987.

———. "Royaume des prêtres et nation consacrée, Exode 19,6." Pages 541-45 in *Humanisme et foi chrétienne.* Edited by C. Kennenigiessar and Y. Marchasson;

Mélanges scientifiques du centenaire de l'Institut catholique de Paris. Paris: Beauchesne, 1975.

————. "La Théophanie au désert: Montagne de Dieu, Sinaï, Horeb." Pages 19-32 in *Tradició i Traducció de la Paraula.* Edited by Frederic Raurell et al. Scripta et Documenta 47. Montserrat: Associació Biblica de Catalunya — Publicacions de l'Abadia de Montserrat, 1993.

Černý, P. L. *The Day of Yahweh and Some Relevant Problems.* Facultas Philosophica Universitatis Carolinae Progensis 53. Prague: Nakladem Filosofické Fakuty University Karlovy, 1948.

Childs, B. S. *The Book of Exodus: A Critical, Theological Commentary.* OTL. Philadelphia: Westminster, 1974.

————. "Deuteronomic Formulae of the Exodus Traditions." Pages 30-39 in *Hebräische Wortforschung: Festschrift zum 80. Geburtstag von Walter Baumgartner.* Edited by B. Hartmann et al. VTSup 16. Leiden: Brill, 1967.

————. "A Traditio-Historical Study of the Reed Sea Tradition." *VT* 20 (1970): 406-18.

Chirichigno, G. C. *Debt-Slavery in Israel and the Ancient Near East.* JSOTSup 141. Sheffield: Sheffield Academic Press, 1993.

Clark, W. Malcolm. "Law." Pages 99-139 in *Old Testament Form Criticism.* Edited by J. H. Hayes. Trinity University Monograph Series in Religion 2. San Antonio: Trinity University Press, 1974.

Clements, R. E. *God and Temple.* Philadelphia: Fortress, 1965.

Clifford, R. J. *The Cosmic Mountain in Canaan and the Old Testament.* HSM 4. Cambridge: Harvard University Press, 1972.

————. "Cosmogonies in the Ugaritic Texts and in the Bible." *Or* 53 (1984): 183-201.

————. "The Tent of El and the Israelite Tent of Meeting." *CBQ* 33 (1971): 221-27.

Coats, G. W. "Conquest Traditions in the Wilderness Theme." *JBL* 95 (1976): 177-90.

————. "Despoiling the Egyptians." *VT* 18 (1968): 450-57.

————. *Exodus 1–18.* FOTL IIA. Grand Rapids: Eerdmans, 1999.

————. "An Exposition for the Conquest Theme." *CBQ* 47 (1985): 47-54.

————. "An Exposition for the Wilderness Traditions." *VT* 22 (1972): 288-95.

————. *Moses: Heroic Man, Man of God.* JSOTSup 57. Sheffield: JSOT Press, 1988.

————. "Moses versus Amalek: Aetiology and Legend in Exod. XVII 8-16." Pages 29-41 in *Congress Volume: Edinburgh 1974.* VTSup 28. Leiden: Brill, 1975.

————. *Rebellion in the Wilderness: The Murmuring Motif in the Wilderness Traditions of the Old Testament.* Nashville: Abingdon, 1968.

————. "The Song of the Sea." *CBQ* 31 (1969): 1-17.

————. "A Structural Transition in Exodus." *VT* 22 (1972): 129-42.

————. "The Traditio-Historical Character of the Reed Sea Motif." *VT* 17 (1967): 253-65.

————. "The Wilderness Itinerary." *CBQ* 34 (1972): 135-52.

Cody, A. *A History of Old Testament Priesthood.* AnBib 35. Rome: Pontifical Biblical Institute, 1969.

Cohen, C. "Studies in Early Israelite Poetry 1: An Unrecognized Case of Three-Line Staircase Parallelism in the Song of the Sea." *JANES* 7 (1975): 13-17.

Cohn, H. H., ed. *Jewish Law in Ancient and Modern Israel.* New York: Ktav, 1971.

Cohn, R. L. *The Shape of Sacred Space: Four Biblical Studies.* AAR Studies in Religion 23. Missoula, Mont.: Scholars Press, 1981.

Collins, J. "The Development of the Exodus Tradition." Pages 144-55 in *Religious Identity and the Invention of Tradition: Papers Read at a Noster Conference in Soesterbert, January 4-6, 1999.* Edited by J. W. Van Henten and A. Houtepen. Studies in Theology and Religion 3. Assen: Van Gorcum, 2001.

Conrad, E. W. *Fear Not, Warrior: A Study of 'al tîrā' Pericopes in the Hebrew Scriptures.* BJS 75. Chico, Calif.: Scholars Press, 1985.

Coogan, M. D. "The Ten Commandments on the Wall." *BRev* 15 (1999): 2.

Cook, S. L. "The Tradition of Mosaic Judges: Past Approaches and New Directions." Pages 286-315 in *On the Way to Nineveh: Studies in Honor of George M. Landes.* Edited by S. L. Cook and S. C. Winter. ASOR Books 4. Atlanta: Scholars Press, 1999.

Cooper, A. "The Plain Sense of Exodus 23:5." *HUCA* 59 (1988): 1-22.

Cooper, A., and B. R. Goldstein. "Exodus and *Maṣṣôt* in History and Tradition." *Maarav* 8 (1992): 15-37.

Coote, R. B. *In Defense of Revolution: The Elohist History.* Minneapolis: Fortress, 1991.

Coote, R. B., and D. R. Ord. *The Bible's First History.* Philadelphia: Fortress, 1988.

———. *In the Beginning: Creation and the Priestly History.* Minneapolis: Fortress, 1991.

Coppens, J. "Exode, XIX,6: Un royaume ou une royauté de prêtres?" *ETL* 53 (1977): 185-86.

Cortese, E. *Josua 13–21: Ein priesterschriftlicher Abschnitt im deuteronomistischen Geschichtswerk.* OBO 94. Göttingen: Vandenhoeck & Ruprecht, 1990.

Craigie, P. C. "The Poetry of Ugarit and Israel." *TynBul* 22 (1971): 3-31.

———. *The Problem of War in the Old Testament.* Grand Rapids: Eerdmans, 1978.

———. *Psalms 1–50.* WBC 19. Waco: Word, 1983.

Croatto, J. S. *Exodus: A Hermeneutics of Freedom.* Translated by S. Attanasio. Maryknoll, N.Y.: Orbis, 1978.

Cross, F. M. *The Ancient Library of Qumran.* 3rd ed. Minneapolis: Fortress, 1995.

———. *Canaanite Myth and Hebrew Epic: Essays in the History of Religion.* Cambridge: Harvard University Press, 1973.

———. *From Epic to Canon: History and Literature in Ancient Israel.* Baltimore: Johns Hopkins University Press, 2000.

———. "The Priestly Tabernacle." Pages 224-27 in vol. 1 of *Biblical Archaeologist Reader.* Edited by G. E. Wright and D. N. Freedman. Garden City, N.Y.: Doubleday, 1961.

Cross, F. M., and D. N. Freedman. "The Blessing of Moses." *JBL* 67 (1967): 191-210.

———. "The Song of Miriam." *JNES* 14 (1955): 237-50.

———. *Studies in Ancient Yahwistic Poetry.* SBLDS 21. Missoula, Mont.: Scholars Press, 1975.

Crüsemann, F. *Studien zur Formgeschichte von Hymnus und Danklied in Israel.* WMANT 32. Neukirchen-Vluyn: Neukirchener Verlag, 1969.

———. *The Torah: Theology and Social History of Old Testament Law.* Translated by A. W. Mahnke. Minneapolis: Fortress, 1996.

Dahood, M. "Exodus 15,2 'anwĕhû and Ugaritic šnwt." *Bib* 59 (1978): 260-61.

———. "Hebrew-Ugaritic Lexicography III." *Bib* 46 (1965): 313.

Damrosch, D. *The Narrative Covenant: Transformations of Genre in the Growth of Biblical Literature.* New York: Harper & Row, 1987.

Dandamayev, M. A. "Slavery (ANE), (OT)." Pages 58-65 in vol. 6 of *Anchor Bible Dictionary*. Edited by D. N. Freedman. 6 vols. New York: Doubleday, 1992.

Darr, K. Pfisterer. "Breaking Through the Wilderness: References to the Desert in Exilic Prophecy." Ph.D. diss., Vanderbilt University Press, 1984.

Daube, D. *The Exodus Pattern in the Bible*. All Souls Studies 2. London: Faber & Faber. 1963.

———. "Pauline Contributions to a Pluralistic Culture: Re-Creation and Beyond." Pages 223-45 in vol. 2 of *Jesus and Man's Hope*. Edited by D. G. Miller and D. Y. Hadidian. 2 vols. Pittsburgh: Pittsburgh Theological Seminary, 1970-1971.

———. *Studies in Biblical Law*. Cambridge: Cambridge University Press, 1947.

Davies, D. J. "The Sociology of Holiness: The Power of Being Good." Pages 48-67 in *Holiness Past and Present*. Edited by S. C. Barton. London: T & T Clark, 2003.

Davies, G. F. *Israel in Egypt: Reading Exodus 1–2*. JSOTSup 135. Sheffield: JSOT Press, 1992.

Davies, G. I. "The Composition of the Book of Exodus: Reflections on the Theses of Erhard Blum." Pages 71-85 in *Texts, Temples, and Traditions: A Tribute to Menahem Haran*. Edited by Michael V. Fox et al. Winona Lake, Ind.: Eisenbrauns, 1996.

———. "*KD* in Exodus: An Assessment of E. Blum's Proposal." Pages 407-20 in *Deuteronomy and the Deuteronomic Literature: Festschrift C. H. W. Brekelmans*. Edited by M. Vervenne and J. Lust. BETL 133. Leuven: Leuven University Press, 1997.

———. "The Theology of Exodus." Pages 137-52 in *In Search of True Wisdom: Essays in Old Testament Interpretation in Honour of Ronald E. Clements*. Edited by E. Ball. JSOTSup 300. Sheffield: Sheffield Academic Press, 1999.

———. *The Way of the Wilderness: A Geographical Study of the Wilderness Itineraries in the Old Testament*. SOTSMS 5. Cambridge: Cambridge University Press, 1979.

———. "The Wilderness Itineraries: A Comparative Study." *TynBul* 25 (1974): 46-81.

———. "The Wilderness Itineraries and Recent Archaeological Research." Pages 161-75 in *Studies in the Pentateuch*. Edited by J. A. Emerton. VTSup 41. Leiden: Brill, 1990.

———. "The Wilderness Itineraries and the Composition of the Pentateuch." *VT* 33 (1983): 1-13.

Davies, T. W. *Magic, Divination, and Demonology Among the Hebrews and Their Neighbours*. Repr. New York: Ktav, 1969.

Day, J. "Baal." Pages 545-49 in vol. 1 of *Anchor Bible Dictionary*. Edited by D. N. Freedman. 6 vols. New York: Doubleday, 1992.

———. *God's Conflict with the Dragon and the Sea: Echoes of a Canaanite Myth in the Old Testament*. University of Cambridge Oriental Studies 35. Cambridge: Cambridge University Press, 1985.

Deem, A. "The Goddess Anath and Some Biblical Cruces." *JSS* 23 (1978): 25-30.

Delcor, M. "Une allusion à ʿAnath déesse guerrière en Ex. 32:18?" *JJS* 33 (1982): 145-60.

Dentan, R. "The Literary Affinities of Exodus XXXIV 6f." *VT* 13 (1963): 34-51.

De Vries, S. J. "The Origin of the Murmuring Tradition." *JBL* 87 (1968): 51-58.

———. "Temporal Terms as Structural Elements in Holy-War Tradition." *VT* 25 (1975): 80-105.

Dietrich, M., O. Loretz, and J. Sanmartín. "Die ugaritischen Totengeister *Rpu(m)* und die biblische Rephaim." *UF* 8 (1976): 45-52.

Dillmann, A. *Die Bücher Exodus und Leviticus*. KEHAT. Leipzig: S. Hirzel, 1880.

Dion, P. E. "The 'Fear Not' Formula and Holy War." *CBQ* 32 (1970): 565-70.

Dohmen, C. *Das Bilderverbot: Seine Entstehung und seine Entwicklung im Alten Testament.* BBB 62. Bonn: Königstein, 1985.

———. *Exodus 19-40.* Herders theologischer Kommentar zum Alten Testament. Freiburg: Herder, 2004.

Douglas, M. *Purity and Danger: An Analysis of the Concepts of Pollution and Taboo.* London: Routledge and Kegan Paul, 1966.

Dozeman, T. B. "The Book of Numbers." Pages 1-268 in vol. 2 of *New Interpreter's Bible.* Edited by L. E. Keck. Nashville: Abingdon, 1998.

———. *God at War: Power in the Exodus Tradition.* New York: Oxford University Press, 1996.

———. *God on the Mountain: A Study of Redaction, Theology and Canon in Exodus 19-24.* SBLMS 37. Atlanta: Scholars Press, 1989.

———. "Horeb/Sinai and the Rise of Law in the Wilderness Tradition." *SBLSP* 28 (1989): 282-90.

———. "Hosea and the Wilderness Wandering Tradition." Pages 55-70 in *Rethinking the Foundations: Historiography in the Ancient World and in the Bible: Essays in Honour of John Van Seters.* Edited by S. L. McKenzie and T. Römer. BZAW 294. Berlin: de Gruyter, 2000.

———. "Inner-Biblical Interpretation of Yahweh's Gracious and Compassionate Character." *JBL* 108 (1989): 207-23.

———. "The Institutional Setting of the Late Formation of the Pentateuch in the Work of John Van Seters." *SBLSP* 30 (1991): 253-64.

———. "Moses: Divine Servant and Israelite Hero." *HAR* 8 (1984): 45-61.

———. "The Song of the Sea and Salvation History." Pages 94-113 in *On the Way to Nineveh: Studies in Honor of George M. Landes.* Edited by S. L. Cook and S. C. Winter. ASOR Books 4. Atlanta: Scholars Press, 1999.

———. "Spatial Form in Exod 19:1-8a and in the Larger Sinai Narrative." *Semeia* 46 (1989): 87-101.

——— "The *yam-sûp* in the Exodus Tradition and in the Crossing of the Jordan River." *CBQ* 58 (1996): 407-16.

Driver, G. R. "The Original Form of the Name 'Yahweh': Evidence and Conclusions." *ZAW* 46 (1928): 7-25.

Driver, S. R. *The Book of Exodus.* Cambridge Bible for Schools and Colleges. Cambridge: Cambridge University Press, 1911.

Duggan, C.-K. "Divine Puppeteer: Yahweh of Exodus." Pages 75-102 in *Exodus to Deuteronomy.* Edited by A. Brenner. FCB 2/5. Sheffield: Sheffield Academic Press, 2000.

Dumermuth, F. "Josua in Ex. 33:7-11." *TZ* 19 (1963): 161-68.

———. "Moses strahlendes Gesicht." *TZ* 17 (1961): 241-48.

Durham, J. I. *Exodus.* WBC 3. Waco: Word, 1987.

Dus, J. "Die Analyse zweier Ladeerzählungen des Josuabuches (Jos 3-4 und 6)." *ZAW* 72 (1960): 107-34.

Eakin, F. E. "The Plagues and the Crossing of the Sea." *RevExp* 74 (1977): 473-82.

———. "The Reed Sea and Baalism." *JBL* 86 (1967): 378-84.

Eaton, J. H. *Kingship and the Psalms.* 2nd ed. Bible Seminar. Sheffield: JSOT Press, 1986.

Edelman, D. "Clio's Dilemma: The Changing Face of History-Writing." Pages 247-55 in *Congress Volume: Oslo 1998*. Edited by A. Lemaire and M. Sæbø. VTSup 80. Leiden: Brill, 2000.

Edelmann, R. "Exodus 32:18: קוֹל עֲנוֹת אנכי שׁמע." *JTS* 1 (1950): 56.

———. "To עֲנוֹת Exodus XXXII 18." *VT* 16 (1966): 355.

Eissfeldt, O. *Die Komposition der Sinai-Erzählung Ex 19–34*. Sitzungsberichte der Sächsischen Akademie der Wissenschaften zu Leipzig 113/1. Berlin: Akademie-Verlag, 1966.

———. *The Old Testament: An Introduction*. Translated by P. R. Ackroyd. New York: Harper & Row, 1965.

Eliade, M. *The Sacred and the Profane: The Nature of Religion*. Translated by W. R. Trask. New York: Harcourt, Brace, 1959.

Elliger, K. "Ich bin der Herr — euer Gott." Pages 211-31 in *Kleine Schriften zum Alten Testament*. Edited by H. Gese and O. Kaiser. TB 32. Munich: Chr. Kaiser, 1966.

———. "Sinn und Ursprung der priesterlichen Geschichtserzählung." *ZTK* 49 (1952): 121-43.

Emerton, J. A. "The Priestly Writer in Genesis." *JTS* 39 (1988): 381-400,

Engnell, I. *A Rigid Scrutiny: Critical Essays on the Old Testament*. Translated by J. T. Willis. Nashville: Vanderbilt University Press, 1969.

Eric, A. L. *The Lord Rose Up from Seir: Studies in the History and Traditions of the Negev and Southern Kingdom*. ConBOT 25. Lund: Almqvist & Wiksell, 1987.

Eslinger, L. "Freedom or Knowledge? Perspective and Purpose in the Exodus Narrative (Exodus 1–15)." *JSOT* 52 (1991): 43-60.

Everhart, J. "Serving Women and Their Mirrors: A Feminist Reading of Exodus 38:8b." *CBQ* 66 (2004): 44-54.

Exum, J. C. "'You shall let every daughter live': A Study of Exodus 1:8–2:10." *Semeia* 28 (1983): 63-82.

Eyre, J. "The Agricultural Cycle, Farming, and Water Management in the Ancient Near East." Pages 175-89 in vol. 1 of *Civilizations in the Ancient Near East*. Edited by J. M. Sasson. New York: Scribner's, 1995.

Fabry, H.-J. "Spuren des Pentateuchredaktors in Jos 4, 21ff.: Anmerkungen zur Deuteronomismus-Rezeption." Pages 351-56 in *Das Deuteronomium: Entstehung, Gestalt und Botschaft*. Edited by N. Lohfink. BETL 68. Leuven: Peeters, 1985.

Fager, J. A. "Bezalel." Page 717 in vol. 1 of *Anchor Bible Dictionary*. Edited by D. N. Freedman. 6 vols. New York: Doubleday, 1992.

———. "Uri." Page 767 in vol. 6 of *Anchor Bible Dictionary*. Edited by D. N. Freedman. 6 vols. New York: Doubleday, 1992.

Falk, Z. W. "Exodus XXI:6." *VT* 9 (1959): 86-88.

———. *Hebrew Law in Biblical Times*. Jersualem: Wahrmann, 1964.

———. "Hebrew Legal Terms." *JSS* 5 (1960): 350-54.

———. "Spirituality and Jewish Law." Pages 127-38 in *Religion and Law: Biblical-Judaic and Islamic Perspectives*. Edited by E. B. Firmage et al. Winona Lake, Ind.: Eisenbrauns, 1990.

Feldman, L. H. *"Remember Amalek!" Vengeance, Zealotry, and Group Destruction in the Bi-*

ble According to Philo, Pseudo-Philo, and Josephus. Monographs of the Hebrew Union College 31. Cincinnati: Hebrew Union College Press, 2004.

Feliks, Y. "The Incense of the Tabernacle." Pages 125-49 in *Pomegranates and Golden Bells: Studies in Biblical, Jewish, and Near Eastern Ritual, Law, and Literature in Honor of Jacob Milgrom.* Edited by D. P. Wright et al. Winona Lake, Ind.: Eisenbrauns, 1995.

Fensham, F. E. "The Burning of the Golden Calf and Ugarit." *IEJ* 16 (1966): 191-93.

———. "Exodus XXI: 18-19 in Light of Hittite Law." *VT* 10:1960: 333-35.

———. "New Light on Exod 21:6 and 22:7 from the Laws of Eshnunna." *JBL* 78 (1959): 160-61.

———. "The Role of the Lord in the Legal Sections of the Covenant Code." *VT* 26 (1976): 262-74.

Finkelstein, J. J. "Ammiṣaduqqa's Edict and the Babylonian 'Law Codes.'" *JCS* 15 (1961): 91-104.

———. *The Ox That Gored.* Transactions of the American Philosophical Society 71/2. Philadelphia: American Philosophical Society, 1981.

Finley, M. I. "Introduction." Pages 9-32 in Thucydides, *History of the Peloponnesian War.* Penguin Classics. London: Penguin, 1972.

Fischer, G. "Exodus 1–15 — Eine Erzählung." Pages 149-78 in *Studies in the Book of Exodus: Redaction — Reception — Interpretation.* Edited by Marc Vervenne. BETL 126. Leuven: Leuven University Press, 1996.

———. "Keine Priesterschrift in Ex 1–15?" *ZKT* 117 (1995): 203-11.

———. *Jahwe Unser Gott: Sprache, Aufbau und Erzähltechnik in der Berufung des Moses (Ex 3–4).* OBO 91. Göttingen: Vandenhoeck & Ruprecht, 1989.

Fishbane, M. *Biblical Interpretation in Ancient Israel.* Oxford: Clarendon, 1985.

———. "Census and Intercession in a Priestly Text (Exodus 30:11-16) and in Its Midrashic Transformation." Pages 103-11 in *Pomegranates and Golden Bells: Studies in Biblical, Jewish, and Near Eastern Ritual, Law, and Literature in Honor of Jacob Milgrom.* Edited by D. P. Wright et al. Winona Lake, Ind.: Eisenbrauns, 1995.

Fitzpatrick-McKinley, A. *The Transformation of Torah from Scribal Advice to Law.* JSOTSup 287. Sheffield: Sheffield Academic Press, 1999.

Fleming, D. E. "Mari's Large Public Tent and the Priestly Tent Sanctuary." *VT* 50 (2000): 484-98.

———. "The Biblical Tradition of Anointing Priests." *JBL* 117 (1998): 401-14.

Flight, J. W. "The Nomadic Idea and Ideal in the Old Testament." *JBL* 42 (1923): 158-226.

Flusser, D. "The Ten Commandments and the New Testament." Pages 219-46 in *The Ten Commandments in History and Tradition.* Edited by B.-Z. Segal. Jerusalem: Magnes, 1990.

Flynn, E. L. "Moses in the Visual Arts." *Int* 44 (1990): 265-76.

Fohrer, G. *Introduction to the Old Testament.* Translated by D. E. Green. Nashville: Abingdon, 1968.

———. "Priesterliches Königtum,' Ex 19,6." *TZ* 19 (1963): 359-62.

———. *Überlieferung und Geschichte des Exodus: Eine Analyse von Ex 1–15.* BZAW 91. Berlin: Töpelmann, 1964.

Fokkelman, J. P. "Exodus." Pages 36-55 in *The Literary Guide to the Bible.* Edited by R. Alter and F. Kermode. Cambridge: Harvard University Press, 1987.

Follis, E. R., ed. *Directions in Biblical Hebrew Poetry.* JSOTSup 40. Sheffield: Sheffield Academic Press, 1987.

Foote, T. C. "The Ephod." *JBL* 21 (1902): 1-47.

Foresti, F. "Composizione e redazione deuteronomistica in Ex 15,1-18." *Lateranum* 48 (1982): 41-69.

Forsyth, N. *The Old Enemy: Satan and the Combat Myth.* Princeton: Princeton University Press, 1987.

Frankel, D. "The Destruction of the Golden Calf: A New Solution." *VT* 44 (1994): 330-39.

————. *The Murmuring Stories of the Priestly School: A Retrieval of Ancient Sacerdotal Lore.* VTSup 89. Leiden: Brill, 2002.

Frankfort, H. *Kingship and the Gods.* 1948. Repr. Chicago: University of Chicago Press, 1978.

Franz, M. *Der barmherzige und gnädige Gott: Die Gnadenrede vom Sinai (Exodus 34, 6-7) und ihre Parallelen im Alten Testament und seiner Umwelt.* BWANT 160. Stuttgart: Kohlhammer, 2003.

Freedman, D. N. "Canon of the OT." Pages 130-36 in *Interpreter's Dictionary of the Bible Supplementary Volume.* Edited by K. Crim. Nashville: Abingdon, 1976.

————. "The Name of the God of Moses." *JBL* 79 (1960): 151-56.

————. "Pentateuch." Pages 711-27 in vol. 3 of *Interpreter's Dictionary of the Bible.* Edited by G. A. Buttrick. 4 vols. Nashville: Abingdon, 1962.

————. *Pottery, Poetry, and Prophecy: Studies in Early Hebrew Poetry.* Winona Lake, Ind.: Eisenbrauns, 1980.

————. "Temple without Hands." Pages 21-30 in *Temples and High Places: Proceedings of the Colloquium in Honor of the Centennial of Hebrew Union College–Jewish Institute of Religion.* Edited by A. Biran. Jerusalem: Nelson Glueck School of Biblical Archaeology, 1977.

————, with J. C. Geoghegan and M. M. Homan. *The Nine Commandments. Uncovering a Hidden Pattern of Crime and Punishment in the Hebrew Bible.* Edited by A. B. Beck. New York: Doubleday, 2000.

Frerichs, E. S., and L. H. Lesko. *Exodus: The Egyptian Evidence.* Winona Lake, Ind.: Eisenbrauns, 1997.

Fretheim, T. E. *Exodus.* Interpretation. Louisville: John Knox, 1991.

———— "The Plagues as Ecological Signs of Historical Disaster." *JBL* 110 (1991): 385-96.

———— "The Priestly Document: Anti-Temple?" *VT* 18 (1968): 313-29.

———— "The Reclamation of Creation: Redemption and Law in Exodus." *Int* 45 (1991): 354-65.

———— "Suffering God and Sovereign God in Exodus: A Collision of Images." *HBT* 11 (1989): 31-56.

Frevel, C. "'Jetzt habe ich erkannt, dass YHWH grosser ist als alle Götter': Ex 18 und seine kompositionsgeschichtliche Stellung im Pentateuch." *BZ* 47 (2003): 3-22.

————. *Mit Blick auf das Land die Schöpfung erinnern: Zum Ende der Priestergrundschrift.* Herders Biblische Studien 23. Freiburg: Herder, 2000.

Friedman, R. E. *The Exile and Biblical Narrative: The Formation of the Deuteronomistic and Priestly Works.* HSM 22. Chico, Calif.: Scholars Press, 1981.

————. *The Hidden Book in the Bible.* San Francisco: HarperCollins, 1998.

———. "Tabernacle." Pages 292-300 in vol. 6 of *Anchor Bible Dictionary*. Edited by D. N. Freedman. 6 vols. New York: Doubleday, 1992.

———. "The Tabernacle in the Temple." *BA* 43 (1980): 241-48.

———. *Who Wrote the Bible?* New York: Summit Books, 1987.

Fritz, V. "Das Geschichtsverständnis der Priesterschrift." *ZTK* 84 (1987): 426-39.

———. *Israel in der Wüste: Traditionsgeschichtliche Untersuchung der Wüstenüberlieferung des Jahwisten*. Marburger theologische Studien 7. Marburg: Elwert, 1970.

———. *Tempel und Zelt: Studien zum Tempelbau in Israel und zu dem Zeltheiligtum der Priesterschrift*. WMANT 47. Neukirchen-Vluyn: Neukirchener Verlag, 1977.

Frymer-Kensky, T. "The Strange Case of the Suspected Sotah (Numbers V 11-31)." *VT* 34 (1984): 11-26.

Fuchs, E. "A Jewish-Feminist Reading of Exodus 1-2." Pages 307-27 in *Jews, Christians, and the Theology of the Hebrew Scriptures*. Edited by A. Ogden Bellis and J. S. Kaminsky. SBLSymS 8. Atlanta: Society of Biblical Literature, 2000.

Fuller, R. H. "The Decalogue in the New Testament." *Int* 43 (1989): 243-55.

Fuss, W. *Die deuteronomistische Pentateuchredaktion in Exodus 3-17*. BZAW 126. Berlin: de Gruyter, 1972.

Galling, K. *Die Erwählungstraditionen Israels*. BZAW 48. Giessen: de Gruyter, 1928.

García-Treto, F. O. "Servant and ʾAmah in the *Mishpatim* of the Book of the Covenant." Pages 25-42 in *Trinity University Studies of Religion XI in Honor of Guy Harvey Ranson*. Edited by W. O. Walker. San Antonio: Trinity University Press, 1982.

Gaster, T. H. *Myth, Legend, and Custom in the Old Testament: A Comparative Study with Chapters from Sir James G. Frazer's Folklore in the Old Testament*. New York: Harper & Row, 1969.

———. *Thespis: Ritual, Myth, and Drama in the Ancient Near East*. 2nd ed. New York: Norton, 1953.

George, A. R. *The Temples of Ancient Mesopotamia*. Mesopotamian Civilizations. Winona Lake, Ind.: Eisenbrauns, 1993.

Gerleman, E. "Was heisst פֶסַח?" *ZAW* 88 (1976): 409-13.

Gerstenberger, E. *Wesen und Herkunft des apodiktischen Rechts*. WMANT 20. Neukirchen-Vluyn: Neukirchener Verlag, 1965.

Gertz, J. C. "Abraham, Mose und der Exodus: Beobachtungen zur Redaktionsgeschichte von Gen 15." Pages 63-81 in *Abschied vom Jahwisten: Die Komposition des Hexateuch in der jüngsten Diskussion*. Edited by J. C. Gertz, K. Schmid, and M. Witte. BZAW 315. Berlin: de Gruyter, 2002.

———. "Beobachtungen zu Komposition und Redaktion in Exodus 32–34." Pages 88-106 in *Gottes Volk am Sinai: Untersuchungen zu Ex 32–34 und Dtn 9–10*. Edited by M. Köckert and E. Blum. VWGT 18. Gütersloh: Gütersloher Verlagshaus, 2001.

———. "Mose und die Anfänge der jüdischen Religion." *ZTK* 99 (2002): 3-20.

———. *Tradition und Redaktion in der Exoduserzählung: Untersuchungen zur Endredaktion des Pentateuch*. FRLANT 186. Göttingen: Vandenhoeck & Ruprecht, 2000.

———, K. Schmid, and M. Witte, eds. *Abschied vom Jahwisten: Die Komposition des Hexateuch in der jüngsten Diskussion*. BZAW 315. Berlin: de Gruyter, 2002.

Gese, H. "Bemerkungen zur Sinaitradition." *ZAW* 79 (1967): 137-54.

Gevirtz, S. "West-Semitic Curses and the Problem of the Origins of Hebrew Law." *VT* 11 (1961): 137-58.

Gibson, J. C. L. *Canaanite Myths and Legends.* 2nd ed. Edinburgh: T. & T. Clark, 1978.

Gilmer, H. W. *The If-You Form in Israelite Law.* SBLDS 15. Missoula, Mont.: Scholars Press, 1975.

Ginzberg, L. *The Legends of the Jews.* 7 vols. Translated by Henrietta Szold et al. Philadelphia: Jewish Publication Society, 1909-1938.

Gitin, S. "The Four-Horned Altar and Sacred Space: An Archaeological Perspective." Pages 95-123 in *Sacred Time, Sacred Place: Archaeology and the Religion of Israel.* Edited by B. M. Gittlen. Winona Lake, Ind.: Eisenbrauns, 2002.

Glueck, N. "The Theophany of the God of Sinai." *JAOS* 56 (1936): 462-71.

Gnuse, R. *Heilsgeschichte as a Model for Biblical Theology: The Debate Concerning the Uniqueness and Significance of Israel's Worldview.* College Theology Society Studies in Religion 4. Lanham, Md.: University Press of America, 1988.

————. *No Other Gods: Emergent Monotheism in Israel.* JSOTSup 241. Sheffield: Sheffield Academic Press, 1997.

————. "Redefining the Elohist." *JBL* 119 (2000): 201-20.

Goldin, J. *The Song of the Sea.* New Haven: Yale University Press, 1971.

Good, E. M. "Exodus XV 2." *VT* 20 (1970): 358-59.

————. "The Just War in Ancient Israel." *JBL* 104 (1985): 385-400.

Good, R. M. "Exodus 32.18." Pages 137-42 in *Love and Death in the Ancient Near East: Essays in Honor of Marvin H. Pope.* Edited by J. H. Marks and R. M. Good. Guilford, Ct.: Four Quarters, 1987.

Gooding, D. W. *The Account of the Tabernacle: Translation and Textual Problems of the Greek Exodus.* Contributions to Biblical and Patristic Literature 6. Cambridge: Cambridge University Press, 1959.

Gordon, C. H. "אלהים in Its Reputed Meaning of *Rulers, Judges.*" *JBL* 54 (1935): 139-44.

Görg, M. "Die Gattung des sogenannte Tempelweispruches (1 Kgs 8:12f.)." *UF* 6 (1974): 55-63.

————. "Die Kopfbedeckung des Hohenpriesters." *BN* 3 (1977): 24-26.

————. "Mirjam — ein weiterer Versuch." *BZ* 23 (1979): 285-89.

————. "Der Spiegeldienst der Frauern." *BN* 23 (1984): 9-13.

————. "Weiteres zu *nzr* ('Diadem')." *BN* 4 (1977): 7-8.

————. *Der Zelt der Begegnung.* BBB 27. Bonn: Hanstein, 1967.

Gorman, F. H., Jr. *The Ideology of Ritual: Space, Time and Status in the Priestly Theology.* JSOTSup 91. Sheffield: Sheffield Academic Press, 1990.

Gottlieb, I. B. "Law, Love, and Redemption: Legal Connotations in the Language of Exodus 6:6-8." *JANES* 26 (1998): 47-57.

Gottwald, N. K. *The Tribes of Yahweh: A Sociology of the Religion of Liberated Israel, 1250-1050 B.C.E.* Maryknoll, N.Y.: Orbis, 1979.

Gowan, D. E. *Theology in Exodus: Biblical Theology in the Form of a Commentary.* Louisville: Westminster John Knox, 1994.

Grabbe, L. L. "Who Were the First Real Historians? On the Origins of Critical Historiography." Pages 156-81 in *Did Moses Speak Attic? Jewish Historiography and Scripture in the Hellenistic Period.* Edited by L. L. Grabbe. JSOTSup 317; ESHM 3. Sheffield: Sheffield Academic Press, 2001.

Gradwohl, R. "*Niṣṣal* and *hiṣṣîl* als Rechtsbegriffe im Sklavenrecht." *ZAW* 111 (1999): 187-95.

Graupner, A. *Der Elohist: Gegenwart und Wirksamkeit des transzendenten Gottes in der Geschichte.* WMANT 97. Neukirchen-Vluyn: Neukirchener Verlag, 2002.

———. "Zum Verhältnis des beiden Dekalogfassungen Ex 20 und Dtn 5." *ZAW* 99 (1987): 308-29.

Gray, G. B. *A Critical and Exegetical Commentary on the Book of Numbers.* ICC. Edinburgh: T. & T. Clark, 1903.

Gray, J. *The Biblical Doctrine of the Reign of God.* Edinburgh: T. & T. Clark, 1979.

———. "The Day of Yahweh in Cultic Experience and Eschatological Prospect." *SEA* 39 (1974): 5-37.

———. "The Desert Sojourn of the Hebrews and the Sinai-Horeb Tradition." *VT* 4 (1954): 148-54.

———. *Joshua, Judges and Ruth.* NCB. London: Nelson, 1967.

Green, A. *The Role of Human Sacrifice in the Ancient Near East.* ASORDS 1. Missoula, Mont.: Scholars Press, 1977.

Greenberg, M. "The Decalogue Tradition Critically Examined." Pages 83-119 in *The Ten Commandments in History and Tradition.* Edited by B.-Z. Segal. Jerusalem: Magnes, 1990.

———. "Hebrew *sᵉgullā*: Akkadian *sikiltu.*" *JAOS* 71 (1951): 172-74.

———. "The Redaction of the Plague Narrative in Exodus." Pages 243-52 in *Near Eastern Studies in Honor of William Foxwell Albright.* Edited by H. Goedicke. Baltimore: Johns Hopkins University Press, 1971.

———. *Understanding Exodus.* Melton Research Center Series 2. New York: Behrman House, 1969.

Greengus, S. "Biblical and ANE Law." Pages 242-52 in vol. 4 of *Anchor Bible Dictionary.* Edited by D. N. Freedman. 6 vols. New York: Doubleday, 1992.

———. "Some Issues Relating to the Comparability of Laws and the Coherence of the Legal Tradition." Pages 60-87 in *Theory and Method in Biblical and Cuneiform Law. Revision, Interpolation, and Development.* Edited by B. M. Levinson. JSOTSup 181. Sheffield: Sheffield Academic Press, 1994.

Greenstein, E. L. "The First-Born Plague and the Reading Process." Pages 555-68 in *Pomegranates and Golden Bells: Studies in Biblical, Jewish, and Near Eastern Ritual, Law, and Literature in Honor of Jacob Milgrom.* Edited by D. L. Wright et al. Winona Lake, Ind.: Eisenbrauns, 1995.

———. "Jethro's Wit: An Interpretation of Wordplay in Exodus 18." Pages 155-71 in *On the Way to Nineveh: Studies in Honor of George M. Landes.* Edited by S. L. Cook and S. C. Winter. ASOR Books 4. Atlanta: Scholars Press, 1999.

———. "Recovering 'The Women Who Served at the Entrance.'" Pages 165-73 in *Studies in Historical Geography and Biblical Historiography Presented to Zecharia Kallai.* Edited by G. Galil and M. Weinfeld. VTSup 81. Leiden: Brill, 2000.

———. "Two Variations of Grammatical Parallelism in Canaanite Poetry and Their Psycholinguistic Background." *JANESCU* 6 (1974): 87-105.

Greifenhagen, F. V. *Egypt on the Pentateuch's Ideological Map: Constructing Biblical Israel's Identity.* JSOTSup 361. Sheffield: Sheffield Academic Press, 2002.

Grelot, P. "Études sur le 'Papyrus Pascal' d'Éléphantine." *VT* 4 (1954): 349-84.

────. "Sur le 'Papyrus Pascal' d'Éléphantine." Pages 163-72 in *Mélanges bibliques et orientaux en l'honneur de M. Henri Cazelles.* Edited by A. Caquot and M. Delcor. AOAT 212. Neukirchen-Vluyn: Neukirchener Verlag, 1981.

Gressmann, H. *Mose und seine Zeit: Ein Kommentar zu den Mose-Sagen.* FRLANT 1. Göttingen: Vandenhoeck & Ruprecht, 1913.

────. *Der Ursprung der israelitisch-jüdischen Eschatologie.* Göttingen: Vandenhoeck & Ruprecht, 1905.

Grimes, R. L. "Masking: Toward a Phenomenology of Exteriorization." *JAAR* 43 (1975): 508-16.

Grosby, S. *Biblical Ideas of Nationality Ancient and Modern.* Winona Lake, Ind.: Eisenbrauns, 2002.

Gross, B. "Exodus 19,18 in the Biblical Redaction." Pages 41-43 in *"Lasset und Brücken bauen . . ." Collected Communications to the XVth Congress of the Organization for the Study of the Old Testament, Cambridge 1995.* Edited by K.-D. Schunck and M. Augustin. BEATAJ 42. Frankfurt am Main: Lang, 1998.

Gross, W. "Der Glaube an Mose nach Exodus (4.14.19)." Pages 57-65 in *Wort — Gebot — Glaube: Beiträge zur Theologie des Alten Testaments: Walther Eichrodt zum 80. Geburtstag.* Edited by H. J. Stoebe et al. ATANT 59. Zurich: Zwingli, 1970.

────. "Die Herausführungsformel — Zum Verhältnis von Formel und Syntax." *ZAW* 86 (1974): 425-53.

Gunkel, H. *The Folktale in the Old Testament.* Translated by M. D. Rutter. Sheffield: Almond, 1987.

Gunn, D. M. "The 'Hardening of Pharaoh's Heart': Plot, Character and Theology in Exodus 1–14." Pages 72-96 in *Art and Meaning: Rhetoric in Biblical Literature.* Edited by D. J. A. Clines et al. JSOTSup 19. Sheffield: JSOT Press, 1982.

Gunneweg, A. H. J. "Das Gesetz und die Propheten: Eine Auslegung von Ex 33,7-11; Num 11,4-12,8; Deut 31,14f.; 34:10." *ZAW* 102 (1990): 169-80.

────. "Moses in Midian." *ZTK* 61 (1964): 1-9.

Gutmann, J. *No Graven Images: Studies in Art and the Hebrew Bible.* New York: Ktav, 1971.

Haag, H. "Das 'Buch des Bundes' (Ex 24,7)." Pages 226-33 in *Das Buch des Bundes: Aufsätze zur Bibel und zu ihrer Welt.* Edited by B. Lang. Düsseldorf: Patmos, 1980.

Habel, N. "The Form and Significance of the Call Narratives." *ZAW* 77 (1965): 297-323.

Hachlili, R. *The Menorah, the Ancient Seven-Armed Candelabrum: Origin, Form and Significance.* JSJSup 68. Leiden: Brill, 2001.

Hadas, M. *A History of Greek Literature.* New York: Columbia University Press, 1950.

Haelvoet, M. "La théophanie du Sinaï: Analyse littéraire des récits d'Ex. XIV-XXIV." *ETL* 29 (1953): 374-97.

Hahn, J. *Das "Goldene Kalb": Die Jahwe. Verehrung bei Stierbelden in Geschichte Israels.* EHS 154. Frankfurt: Bern, 1987.

Halbe, J. "Erwägungen zur Ursprung und Wesen des Massotfestes." *ZAW* 87 (1975): 324-46.

────. "Passa-Massot im deuteronomischen Festkalender: Komposition, Entstehung und Programm von Dtn 16, 1-8." *ZAW* 87 (1975): 147-68.

────. *Das Privilegrecht Jahwes Ex 34,10-26: Gestalt und Wesen, Herkunft und Wirken in vordeuteronomischer Zeit.* FRLANT 114. Göttingen: Vandenhoeck & Ruprecht, 1975.

Halbertal, M. *People of the Book: Canon, Meaning, and Authority.* Cambridge: Harvard University Press, 1997.

Halpern, B. *The Constitution of the Monarchy in Israel.* HSM 25. Chico, Calif.: Scholars Press, 1981.

———. "The Exodus and the Israelite Historians." *Eretz Israel* 24 (Avraham Malamat volume; 1993): 92-109.

———. *The First Historians: The Hebrew Bible and History.* San Francisco: Harper & Row, 1988.

———. "Kenites." Pages 17-22 in vol. 4 of *Anchor Bible Dictionary.* Edited by D. N. Freedman. 6 vols. New York: Doubleday, 1992.

Hanson, P. D. "The Theological Significance of Contradiction within the Book of the Covenant." Pages 110-31 in *Canon and Authority.* Edited by G. W. Coats and B. O. Long. Philadelphia: Fortress, 1977.

———. "War and Peace in the Hebrew Bible." *Int* 38 (1984): 341-62.

Haran, M. "Behind the Scenes of History: Determining the Date of the Priestly Source." *JBL* 100 (1981): 321-33.

———. "Exodus, The." Pages 304-10 in *Interpreter's Dictionary of the Bible Supplementary Volume.* Edited by K. Crim. Nashville: Abingdon, 1976.

——— "The Nature of the ''ōhel mô'ēdh' in Pentateuchal Sources." *JSS* 5 (1960): 50-65.

———. "The Passover Sacrifice." Pages 86-116 in *Studies in the Religion of Ancient Israel.* VTSup 23. Leiden: Brill, 1972.

——— "Seething a Kid in Its Mother's Milk." *JJS* 30 (1979): 23-35.

———. "The Shining of Moses' Face: A Case Study in Biblical and Ancient Near Eastern Iconography." Pages 159-73 in *In the Shelter of Elyon: Essays on Ancient Palestinian Life and Literature in Honor of G. W. Ahlström.* Edited by W. B. Barrick and J. R. Spencer. JSOTSup 31. Sheffield: JSOT Press, 1984.

———. *Temples and Temple-Service in Ancient Israel: An Inquiry into the Character of Cult Phenomena and the Historical Setting of the Priestly School.* Oxford: Clarendon, 1978.

Harrelson, W. "Calf, Golden." Pages 488-89 in vol. 1 of *Interpreter's Dictionary of the Bible.* Edited by G. A. Buttrick. 4 vols. Nashville: Abingdon, 1962.

———. *The Ten Commandments and Human Rights.* OBT. Philadelphia: Fortress, 1980.

Harrington, H. K. *Holiness: Rabbinic Judaism and the Graeco-Roman World.* Religion in the First Christian Centuries. London: Routledge, 2001.

Harris, M. *Exodus and Exile: The Structure of the Jewish Holidays.* Minneapolis: Fortress, 1992.

Hartenstein, F. "Das 'Angesicht Gottes' in Exodus 32–34." Pages 157-83 in *Gottes Volk am Sinai: Untersuchungen zu Ex 32–34 und Dtn 9–10.* Edited by M. Köckert and E. Blum. VWGT 18. Gütersloh: Gütersloher Verlagshaus, 2001.

Hauge, M. R. *The Descent from the Mountain: Narrative Patterns in Exodus 19–40.* JSOTSup 323. Sheffield: Sheffield Academic Press, 2001.

———. "On the Sacred Spot: The Concept of the Proper Localization before God." *SJOT* 1 (1990): 30-60.

Haupt, P. "Der Name Jahwe." *OLZ* 12 (1909): 211-14.

———. "Moses' Song of Triumph." *AJSL* 20 (1904): 149-72.

Hauser, A. J. "Two Songs of Victory: A Comparison of Exodus 15 and Judges 5." Pages 265-84 in *Directions in Biblical Hebrew Poetry.* Edited by E. R. Follis. JSOTSup 40. Sheffield: Sheffield Academic Press, 1987.

Hays, R. B. *Echoes of Scripture in the Letters of Paul.* New Haven: Yale University Press, 1989.

Hayward, C. T. R. *The Jewish Temple: A Non-Biblical Sourcebook.* London: Routledge, 1996.

Heinische, P. *Das Buch Exodus.* HSAT 1. Bonn: Peter Hanstein, 1934.

Hempel, J. "Ich bin der Herr, dein Arzt." *TLZ* 82 (1957): 809-26.

Hendel, R. S. "Aniconism and Anthropomorphism in Ancient Israel." Pages 205-28 in *The Image and the Book: Iconic Cults, Aniconism, and the Rise of Book Religion in Israel and the Ancient Near East.* Edited by K. van der Toorn. CBET 21. Leuven: Peeters, 1997.

———. "Sacrifice as a Cultural System: The Ritual Symbolism of Exodus 24,3-8." *ZAW* 101 (1989): 366-90.

———. "The Social Origins of the Aniconic Traditions." *CBQ* 50 (1988): 365-82.

Hertog, C. den. "Concerning the Sign of Sinai (Ex. 3:12): Including a Survey of Prophetic and Call Signs." Pages 33-41 in *Unless Someone Guide Me . . . Festschrift for Karel A. Deurloo.* Edited by J. W. Dyk. ACEBTSup 2. Maastricht: Shaker, 2001.

Hertzberg, H. W. *Die Bücher Josua, Richter, Ruth.* ATD 9. Göttingen: Vandenhoeck & Ruprecht, 1959.

Hesse, F. *Das Verstockungsproblem im Alten Testament.* BZAW 74. Berlin: Töpelmann, 1955.

Hiers, R. H. "Day of Judgment." Pages 79-82 in vol. 2 of *Anchor Bible Dictionary.* Edited by D. N. Freedman. 6 vols. New York: Doubleday, 1992.

———. "Day of the Lord." Pages 82-83 in vol. 2 of *Anchor Bible Dictionary.* Edited by D. N. Freedman. 6 vols. New York: Doubleday, 1992.

Hillers, D. *Treaty-Curses and the OT Prophets.* BibOr 16. Rome: Pontifical Biblical Institute, 1969.

Hoffman, Y. "The Day of the Lord as a Concept and a Term in the Prophetic Literature." *ZAW* 93 (1981): 37-50.

Hoffmann, H. D. *Reform und Reformen: Untersuchungen zu einem Grundthema der deuteronomistischen Geschichteschreibung.* ATANT 66. Zurich: Theologischer Verlag, 1980.

Hoffmeier, J. K. "The Arm of God versus the Arm of Pharaoh in the Exodus Narratives." *Bib* 67 (1986): 378-87.

———. *Israel in Egypt: The Evidence for the Authenticity of the Exodus Tradition.* New York: Oxford University Press, 1997.

Hoftijzer, J. "Exodus XXI 8." *VT* 7 (1957): 388-91.

Homan, M. M. "The Divine Warrior in His Tent: A Military Model for Yahweh's Tabernacle." *BRev* 16 (2000): 22-33, 55.

———. *To Your Tents, O Israel! The Terminology, Function, Form, and Symbolism of Tents in the Hebrew Bible and the Ancient Near East.* Culture and History of the Ancient Near East 12. Leiden: Brill, 2002.

Honeycutt, R. L., Jr. "Aaron, the Priesthood, and the Golden Calf." *RevExp* 74 (1977): 523-35.

Horowitz, W. *Cosmic Geography*. Mesopotamian Civilizations 8. Winona Lake: Eisenbrauns, 1998.

Horst, F. "Zwei Begriffe für Eigentum (Besitz)." Pages 141-56 in *Verbannung und Heimkehr: Festschrift für Wilhelm Rudolph*. Edited by A. Koschke. Tübingen: Mohr (Siebeck), 1961.

Hosch, H. "Exodus 12:41: A Translational Problem." *HS* 24 (1983): 11-15.

Hossfeld, F.-L. *Der Dekalog: Seine späten Fassungen, die originale Komposition und seine Vorstufen*. OBO 45. Göttingen: Vandenhoeck & Ruprecht, 1982.

Houten, C. van. *The Alien in Israelite Law*. JSOTSup 107. Sheffield: JSOT Press, 1991.

Houtman, C. *Das Bundesbuch: Ein Kommentar*. Documenta et Monumenta Orientalis Antiqui 24. Leiden: Brill, 1997.

———. *Exodus*. 3 vols. Historical Commentary of the Old Testament. Kampen: Kok, 1993-2000.

———. "On the Function of the Holy Incense (Exodus XXX 34-8) and the Sacred Anointing Oil (Exodus XXX 22-33)." *VT* 42 (1992): 458-65.

———. "'YHWH Is My Banner' — 'A Hand on the Throne of YH': Exodus xvii 15b, 16a and Their Interpretation." *OTS* 25 (1989): 110-20.

Howell, M. "Exodus 15,1b-18. A Poetic Analysis." *ETL* 65 (1989): 5-42.

Huddlestun, J. R. "Red Sea." Pages 633-42 in vol. 5 of *Anchor Bible Dictionary*. Edited by D. N. Freedman. 6 vols. New York: Doubleday, 1992.

Huffmon, H. B. "The Exodus, Sinai, and the Credo." *CBQ* 27 (1965): 101-13.

Hughes, J. *Secrets of the Times: Myth and History in Biblical Chronology*. JSOTSup 66. Sheffield: Sheffield Academic Press, 1990.

Huizenga, J. "A Definition of the Concept of History." Pages 1-10 in *Philosophy and History: Essays Presented to Ernst Cassirer*. Edited by R. Klibansky and H. J. Paton. Oxford: Clarendon, 1936.

Hulst, A. R. "Der Jordan in den alttestamentlichen Überlieferungen." *OTS* 14 (1965): 162-88.

Humbert, P. "Dieu fait sortir: Hiphil de *yāṣā'* avec Dieu comme sujet." *TZ* 18 (1962): 357-61, 433-36.

Hurowitz, V. *I Have Built You an Exalted House: Temple Building in the Bible in Light of Mesopotamian and Northwest Semitic Writings*. JSOTSup 115. Sheffield: JSOT Press, 1992.

———. "The Priestly Account of Building the Tabernacle." *JAOS* 105 (1985): 21-30.

Hurvitz, A. *A Linguistic Study of the Relationship between the Priestly Source and the Book of Ezekiel: A New Approach to an Old Problem*. CahRB 20. Paris: Gabalda, 1982.

Hvidberg-Hansen, O. "Die Vernichtung des Goldenen Kalbes und der Ugaritische Ernteritus." *AcOr* 33 (1971): 5-46.

Hyatt, J. P. *Exodus*. NCB. 1971. Repr. Grand Rapids: Eerdmans, 1983.

Isbell, C. "Exodus 1–2 in the Context of Exodus 1–14: Story Lines and Key Words." Pages 37-61 in *Art and Meaning: Rhetoric in Biblical Literature*. Edited by D. J. A. Clines et al. JSOTSup 19. Sheffield: Sheffield Academic Press, 1982.

Ishida, T. "The Structure and Historical Implications of the Lists of the Pre-Israelite Nations." *Bib* 60 (1979): 461-90.

Isser, S. "Two Traditions: The Law of Exodus 21:22-23 Revisited." *CBQ* 52 (1990): 30-45.

Jackson, B. S. *Essays in Jewish and Comparative Legal History*. SJLA 10. Leiden: Brill, 1975.

————. "Modeling Biblical Law: The Covenant Code." *Chicago-Kent Law Review* 70 (1995): 1745-1827.

————. "The Problem of Exod. XXI 22-5 (Ius talionis)." *VT* 23 (1973): 273-304.

————. *Studies in the Semiotics of Biblical Law.* JSOTSup 314. Sheffield: Sheffield Academic Press, 2000.

————. *Theft in Early Jewish Law.* Oxford: Clarendon, 1972.

Jackson, J. J. "The Ark and Its Making." *HBT* 17 (1995): 117-22.

Jacob, B. *The Second Book of the Bible: Exodus.* Translated by W. Jacob. Hoboken, N.J.: Ktav, 1992.

Jacobsen, T. "The Graven Image." Pages 15-32 in *Ancient Israelite Religion: Essays in Honor of Frank Moore Cross.* Edited by P. D. Miller Jr. et al. Philadelphia: Fortress, 1987.

Jagersma, H. "Structure and Function of Exodus 19:3b-6." Pages 43-48 in *Unless Someone Guide Me . . . Festschrift for Karel A. Deurloo.* Edited by J. W. Dyk. ACEBTSup 2. Maastricht: Shaker, 2001.

Jamieson-Drake, D. *Scribes and Schools in Monarchic Judah.* JSOTSup 109. Sheffield: Sheffield Academic Press, 1991.

Janowski, B. "Tempel und Schöpfung: Schöpfungstheologische Aspeckte der priesterschriftlichen Heiligtumskonzeption." *Jahrbuch für biblische Theologie* 5 (1990): 37-69.

Janzen, D. *Witch Hunts, Purity and Social Boundaries: The Expulsion of the Foreign Women in Ezra 9–10.* JSOTSup 350. Sheffield: Sheffield Academic Press, 2002.

Janzen, J. G. "The Character of the Calf and Its Cult in Exodus 32." *CBQ* 52 (1990): 597-607.

————. "Song of Moses, Song of Miriam: Who Is Seconding Whom?" Pages 187-99 in *A Feminist Companion to Exodus to Deuteronomy.* Edited by A. Brenner. FCB 1/6. Sheffield: Sheffield Academic Press, 1994. (Originally published in *CBQ* 54 [1992]: 211-20.)

Janzen, W. *Exodus.* Believers Church Bible Commentary. Waterloo, Ont.: Herald, 2000.

Jaroš, K. "Des Mose 'strahlende Haut': Eine Notiz zu Ex 34:29, 30, 35." *ZAW* 88 (1976): 275-80.

Jeffers, A. "The Magical Element in Ancient Israelite Warfare." Pages 35-41 in *Proceedings of the Irish Biblical Association 13.* Edited by K. J. Cathcart. Dublin: Columba, 1990.

Jenks, A. W. "Elohist." Pages 478-82 in vol. 2 of *Anchor Bible Dictionary.* Edited by D. N. Freedman. 6 vols. New York: Doubleday, 1992.

————. *The Elohist and North Israelite Traditions.* SBLMS 22. Missoula, Mont.: Scholars Press, 1977.

Jenni, E. "'Kommen' im theologischen Sprachgebrauch des Alten Testaments." Pages 251-61 in *Wort — Gebot — Glaube: Beiträge zur Theologie des Alten Testaments: Walther Eichrodt zum 80. Geburtstag.* Edited by H. J. Stoebe et al. ATANT 59. Zurich: Zwingli, 1970.

Jenson, P. P. *Graded Holiness: A Key to the Priestly Conception of the World.* JSOTSup 106. Sheffield: JSOT Press, 1992.

————. "Holiness in the Priestly Writing." Pages 93-121 in *Holiness Past and Present.* Edited by S. C. Barton. London: T & T Clark, 2003.

Jepsen, A. "Ama^h und Schiphcha^h." *VT* 8 (1958): 293-97.

————. *Untersuchungen zum Bundesbuch.* BWANT III/5. Stuttgart: Kohlhammer, 1927.

Jeremias, J. *Das Königtum Gottes in den Psalmen: Israels Begegnung mit dem kanaanäischen*

Mythos in den Jahwe-König-Psalmen. FRLANT 141. Göttingen: Vandenhoeck & Ruprecht, 1987.

―――. *Theophanie: Die Geschichte einer alttestamentlichen Gattung.* WMANT 10. Neukirchen-Vluyn: Neukirchener Verlag, 1965.

Jirku, A. "Die Gesichtsmaske des Moses." *ZDPV* 67 (1945): 43-45.

―――. *Das weltliche Recht im Alten Testament.* Gütersloh: C. Bertelsmann, 1927.

Johnson, A. R. *Sacral Kingship in Ancient Israel.* 2nd ed. Cardiff: University of Wales Press, 1967.

Johnstone, W. *Chronicles and Exodus: An Analogy and Its Application.* JSOTSup 275. Sheffield: Sheffield Academic Press, 1998.

―――. "The Decalogue and the Redaction of the Sinai Pericope in Exodus." *ZAW* 100 (1988): 361-85.

―――. *Exodus.* Old Testament Guides. Sheffield: JSOT Press, 1990.

―――. "The Exodus as Process." *ExpTim* 91 (1979/80): 358-63.

―――. "The Two Theological Versions of the Passover Pericope in Exodus." Pages 160-78 in *Text and Pretext: Essays in Honour of Robert Davidson.* Edited by R. P. Carroll. JSOTSup 138. Sheffield: JSOT Press, 1992.

―――. "The Use of Reminiscences in Deuteronomy in Recovering the Two Main Literary Phases in the Production of the Pentateuch." Pages 247-73 in *Abschied vom Jahwisten: Die Komposition des Hexateuch in der jüngsten Diskussion.* Edited by J. C. Gertz, K. Schmid, and M. Witte. BZAW 315. Berlin: de Gruyter, 2002.

Jones, G. H. "Holy War or Yahweh War?" *VT* 25 (1975): 642-58.

Jones, I. H. "Music and Musical Instruction." Pages 930-39 in vol. 4 of *Anchor Bible Dictionary.* Edited by D. N. Freedman. 6 vols. New York: Doubleday, 1992.

Jones, L. *The Hermeneutics of Sacred Architecture.* 2 vols. Harvard Center for the Study of World Religions. Cambridge: Harvard University Press, 2000.

Kaiser, O. *Die mythische Bedeutung des Meeres in Ägypten, Ugarit und Israel.* 2nd ed. BZAW 78. Berlin: Töpelmann, 1962.

Kallai, Z. *Biblical Historiography and Historical Geography: Collection of Studies.* BEATAJ 44. Frankfurt am Main: Peter Lang, 1998.

Kang, S.-M. *Divine War in the Old Testament and in the Ancient Near East.* BZAW 177. Berlin: de Gruyter, 1989.

Kapelrud, A. S. "Temple Building: A Task for Gods and Kings." *Or* 32 (1963): 56-62.

Kearney, P. "Creation and Liturgy: The P Redaction of Ex 25–40." *ZAW* 89 (1977): 375-87.

Keel, O., and C. Uehlinger. *Gods, Goddesses, and Images of God in Ancient Israel.* Translated by T. H. Trapp. Minneapolis: Fortress, 1998.

Kegler, J. "Zu Komposition und Theologie der Plagenerzählungen." Pages 55-74 in *Die Hebräische Bibel und ihre zweifache Nachgeschichte: Festschrift für Rolf Rendtorff.* Edited by E. Blum, et al. Neukirchen-Vluyn: Neukirchener Verlag, 1990.

Keil, C. F., and F. Delitzsch. *Biblical Commentary on the Old Testament.* Vol. 1: *The Pentateuch.* Translated by J. Martin. Repr. Grand Rapids: Eerdmans, 1981.

Keller, C. A. "Über einige alttestamentliche Heiligtumslegenden II." *ZAW* 68 (1956): 85-97.

Kensky, A. "Moses and Jesus: The Birth of the Savior." *Judaism* 165 (1993): 43-49.

Kingsbury, E. C. "The Theophany *Topos* and the Mountain of God." *JBL* 86 (1967): 205-10.

Kirk, G. S. *Myth: Its Meaning and Functions in Ancient and Other Cultures*. Cambridge: Cambridge University Press, 1970.

Kitchen, K. A. "The Desert Tabernacle: Pure Fiction or Plausible Account?" *BRev* 16 (2000): 14-21.

Kittel, G., and G. Friedrich, eds. *Theological Dictionary of the New Testament*. Translated and edited by G. W. Bromiley. 10 vols. Grand Rapids: Eerdmans, 1964-1976.

Klein, R. W. "Back to the Future: The Tabernacle in the Book of Exodus." *Int* 50 (1996): 264-76.

Kloos, C. *Yhwh's Combat with the Sea: A Canaanite Tradition in the Religion of Ancient Israel*. Leiden: Brill, 1986.

Knauf, E. A. *Midian: Untersuchungen zur Geschichte Palästinas und Norarabiens am Ende des 2 Jahrtausens v. Chr.* Wiesbaden: Harrassowitz, 1988.

Knierim, R. "The Composition of the Pentateuch." *SBLSP* 24 (1985): 393-415.

—————. "Conceptual Aspects of Exodus 25:1-9." Pages 569-80 in *Pomegranates and Golden Bells: Studies in Biblical, Jewish, and Near Eastern Ritual, Law, and Literature in Honor of Jacob Milgrom*. Edited by D. P. Wright et al. Winona Lake, Ind.: Eisenbrauns, 1995.

—————. "Exodus 18 und die Neuordnung der mosäischen Gerichtsbarkeit." *ZAW* 73 (1961): 146-71.

Knight, D. A. "Village Law and the Book of the Covenant." Pages 163-79 in *A Wise and Discerning Mind: Essays in Honor of Burke O. Long*. Edited by S. M. Olyan and R. C. Culley. BJS 325. Providence: Brown Judaic Studies, 2000.

Knight, G. A. F. *Theology as Narration: A Commentary on the Book of Exodus*. Grand Rapids: Eerdmans, 1976.

Knohl, I. "The Priestly Torah Versus the Holiness School: Sabbath and the Festivals." *HUCA* 58 (1987): 65-117.

—————. *The Sanctuary of Silence: The Priestly Torah and the Holiness School*. Minneapolis: Fortress, 1995.

Knoppers, G. N. "Aaron's Calf and Jeroboam's Calves." Pages 92-104 in *Fortunate the Eyes That See: Essays in Honor of David Noel Freedman in Celebration of His Seventieth Birthday*. Edited by A. B. Beck, A. H. Bartelt, P. R. Raabe, and C. A. Franke. Grand Rapids: Eerdmans, 1995.

—————. *Two Nations under God: The Deuteronomistic History of Solomon and the Dual Monarchies*. 2 vols. HSM 52. Atlanta: Scholars Press, 1993.

Knutson, F. B. "Literary Genres in PRU IV." Pages 180-94 in *Ras Shamra Parallels II*. Edited by L. R. Fisher. AnOr 50. Rome: Pontifical Biblical Institute Press, 1975.

Koch, K. "Die Eigenart der priesterschriftlichen Sinaigesetzgebung." *VT* 37 (1958): 36-51.

—————. "P — Kein Redaktor! Erinnerung an zwei Eckdaten der Quellenscheidung." *VT* 37 (1987): 447-67.

—————. *Die Priesterschrift von Exodus 25 bis zu Leviticus 16: Eine überlieferungsgeschichtliche und literarkritische Untersuchung*. FRLANT 71. Göttingen: Vandenhoeck & Ruprecht, 1959.

—————. *The Prophets*. Translated by Margaret Kohl. 2 vols. Philadelphia: Fortress, 1982-1984.

Köckert, M. "Wie kam das Gesetz an den Sinai?" Pages 13-27 in *Vergegenwärtigung des*

Alten Testaments: Beiträge zur biblischen Hermeneutik — Festschrift für Rudolf Smend zum 70 Geburtstag. Edited by C. Bultmann, W. Dietrich, and C. Levin. Göttingen: Vandenhoeck & Ruprecht, 2002.

Köckert, M., and E. Blum, eds. *Gottes Volk am Sinai: Untersuchungen zu Ex 32–34 und Dtn 9–10.* VWGT 18. Gütersloh: Gütersloher Verlagshaus, 2001.

Koester, Craig R. *The Dwelling of God: The Tabernacle in the Old Testament, Intertestamental Jewish Literature, and the New Testament.* CBQMS 22. Washington, DC: Catholic Biblical Association of America, 1989.

Kohata, F. "Die Endredaktion (Rp) der Meerwundererzählung." *AJBI* 14 (1988): 10-37.

————. *Jahwist und Priesterschrift in Exodus 3–14.* BZAW 166. Berlin: de Gruyter, 1986.

Korošec, V. *Hithitische Stattsverträge: Ein Beitrag zu ihrer juristische Wertung.* Leipziger rechtswissenschaftliche Studien 60. Leipzig: Weicher, 1931.

Kosmala, H. "The So-Called Ritual Decalogue." *ASTI* 1 (1962): 31-61.

Kotter, W. R. "Gilgal." Pages 1022-24 in vol. 2 of *Anchor Bible Dictionary.* Edited by D. N. Freedman. 6 vols. New York: Doubleday, 1992.

Kraak, D. H. "Religious Clothing in the West." Pages 340-46 in vol. 3 of *The Encyclopedia of Religion.* Edited by M. Eliade. 15 vols. New York: Macmillan, 1986.

Kraetzschmer, R. Die *Bundesvorstellung im Alten Testament in ihrer geschichtlichen Entwicklung.* Marburg: Elwert, 1896.

Kramer, P. "Miriam." Pages 104-33 in *Exodus to Deuteronomy.* Edited by A. Brenner. FCB 2/5. Sheffield: Sheffield Academic Press, 2000.

Krašovec, J. "Unifying Themes in Ex 7,8–11,10." Pages 47-66 in *Pentateuchal and Deuteronomistic Studies: Papers Read at the XIIIth IOSOT Congress, Leuven 1989.* Edited by C. Brekelmans and J. Lust. BETL 94. Leuven: Leuven University Press, 1990.

Kratz, R. G. "Der Dekalog im Exodusbuch." *VT* 44 (1994): 205-38.

Kraus, H.-J. *Geschichte der historisch-kritischen Erforschung des Alten Testaments.* 3rd ed. Neukirchen-Vluyn: Neukirchener Verlag, 1982.

————. "Gilgal: Ein Beitrag zur Kultusgeschichte Israels." *VT* 1 (1951): 181-99.

————. "Das heilige Volk: Zur alttestamentlichen Bezeichnung 'am qādōš." Pages 50-61 in *Freude am Evangelium: Alfred de Quervain zum 70. Geburtstag.* Edited by J. J. Stamm and E. Wolf. BevT 44. Munich: Chr. Kaiser, 1966.

————. *Psalms.* 2 vols. Translated by H. C. Oswald. Continental Commentary. Minneapolis: Augsburg, 1988-1989.

————. *Worship in Israel: A Cultic History of the Old Testament.* Translated by G. Buswell. Richmond: John Knox, 1966.

Kuenen, A. *An Historical-Critical Inquiry into the Origin and Composition of the Hexateuch (Pentateuch and Book of Joshua).* Translated by P. H. Wiksteed. London: Macmillan, 1886.

Kugel, J. L. *The Bible as It Was.* Cambridge: Belknap Press of Harvard University, 1997.

Kuhl, C. "Die 'Wiederaufnahme' — ein literarkritisches Princip?" *ZAW* 64 (1952): 1-11.

Kuhrt, A. "Israelite and Near Eastern Historiography." Pages 257-79 in *Congress Volume: Oslo 1998.* Edited by A. Lemaire and M. Sæbø. VTSup 80. Leiden: Brill, 2000.

Kunin, S. D. *God's Place in the World: Sacred Space and Sacred Place in Judaism.* Cassell Religious Studies. London: Cassell, 1998.

Kutsch, E. "Erwägungen zur Geschichte der Passafeier und des Massotfestes." *ZTK* 55 (1958): 1-35.

———. *Verheissung und Gesetz: Untersuchungen zum sogenannten 'Bund' im Alten Testament.* BZAW 131. Berlin: de Gruyter, 1973.

Laaf, P. *Die Pascha-Feier Israels: Eine literarkritische und überlieferungsgeschichtliche Studie.* BBB 36. Bonn: Peter Hanstein, 1970.

Labuschagne, C. J. *The Incomparability of Yahweh in the Old Testament.* Leiden: Brill, 1966.

———. "The Meaning of $b^e y\bar{a}d$ $r\bar{a}m\bar{a}$ in the Old Testament." Pages 143-48 in *Von Kanaan bis Kerala: Festschrift für J. P. M. van der Ploeg.* Edited by W. C. Delsman et al. AOAT 211. Neukirchen-Vluyn: Neukirchener Verlag, 1982.

Langlamet, F. *Gilgal et les récits de la traversée du Jourdain (Jos. III-IV).* CahRB 11. Paris: Gabalda, 1969.

Larocca-Pitts, E. C. *"Of Wood and Stone": The Significance of Israelite Cultic Items in the Bible and Its Early Interpreters.* HSM 61. Winona Lake, Ind.: Eisenbrauns, 2001.

Larsson, G. *Bound for Freedom: The Book of Exodus in Jewish and Christian Traditions.* Peabody, Mass.: Hendrickson, 1999.

Lateiner, D. *The Historical Method of Herodotus.* Toronto: University of Toronto Press, 1989.

———. "Historiography (Greco-Roma)." Pages 212-19 in vol. 3 of *Anchor Bible Dictionary.* Edited by D. N. Freedman. 6 vols. New York: Doubleday, 1992.

Lauha, A. "Das Schilfmeermotiv im Alten Testament." Pages 32-46 in *Congress Volume: Bonn 1962.* VTSup 9. Leiden: Brill, 1963.

Lehman, P. L. *The Decalogue and a Human Future: The Meaning of the Commandments for Making and Keeping Human Life Human.* Grand Rapids: Eerdmans, 1994.

Lehming, S. "Versuch zu Ex. XXXII." *VT* 10 (1960): 16-50.

Leibowitz, N. *Studies in Shemot: The Book of Exodus.* Translated by A. Newman. 2 vols. 1976. Repr. Jerusalem: World Zionist Organization, 1981.

Lemche, P. "Ḫabiru, Ḫapiru." Pages 6-10 in vol. 3 of *Anchor Bible Dictionary.* Edited by D. N. Freedman. 6 vols. New York: Doubleday, 1992.

———. "The 'Hebrew Slave': Comments on the Slave Law, Ex xxi,2-11." *VT* 25 (1975): 129-44.

———. "The Old Testament — A Hellenistic Book?" Pages 287-318 in *Did Moses Speak Attic? Jewish Historiography and Scripture in the Hellenistic Period.* Edited by L. L. Grabbe. JSOTSup 317. ESHM 3. Sheffield: Sheffield Academic Press, 2001. (Slightly revised from *SJOT* 7 [1993]: 163-93.)

Lemmelijn, B. "The Phrase וּבָעֵצִים וּבָאֲבָנִים in Exod 7,19." *Bib* 80 (1999): 264-68.

———. "The So-called 'Priestly' Layer in Exod 7,14–11,10: 'Source' and/or/nor 'Redaction'?" *RB* 109 (2002): 481-511.

Leneman, H. "Miriam Re-Imagined, and Imaginary Women of Exodus in Musical Settings." Pages 134-50 in *Exodus to Deuteronomy.* Edited by A. Brenner. FCB 2/5. Sheffield: Sheffield Academic Press, 2000.

Levenson, J. D. *Creation and the Persistence of Evil: The Jewish Drama of Divine Omnipotence.* San Francisco: Harper & Row, 1988.

———. *The Death and Resurrection of the Beloved Son: The Transformation of Child Sacrifice in Judaism and Christianity.* New Haven: Yale University Press, 1993.

———. "Exodus and Liberation." *HBT* 13 (1991): 134-74.

———. "From Temple to Synagogue: 1 Kings 8." Pages 143-92 in *Traditions in Transformation: Turning Points in Biblical Faith.* Edited by B. Halpern and J. D. Levenson. Winona Lake, Ind.: Eisenbrauns, 1981.

———. *Sinai and Zion: An Entry into the Jewish Bible.* New York: Winston, 1985.

———. "Zion Traditions." Pages 1098-1102 in vol. 6 of *Anchor Bible Dictionary.* Edited by D. N. Freedman. 6 vols. New York: Doubleday, 1992.

Levin, C. "Der Dekalog am Sinai." *VT* 35 (1985): 165-91.

———. *Der Jahwist.* FRLANT 157. Göttingen: Vandenhoeck & Ruprecht, 1993.

Levine, B. A. "The Descriptive Tabernacle Texts of the Pentateuch." *JAOS* 85 (1965): 307-18.

———. *In the Presence of the Lord.* SJLA 5. Leiden: Brill. 1974.

———. *Leviticus.* JPS Torah Commentary. Philadelphia: Jewish Publication Society, 1989.

———. *Numbers 1-20.* AB 4A. New York: Doubleday, 1993.

———. "Priestly Writers." Pages 683-87 in *Interpreter's Dictionary of the Bible: Supplementary Volume.* Edited by K. Crim. Nashville: Abingdon, 1976.

Levine, M. *The Tabernacle: Its Structure and Utensils.* 4th ed. London: Soncino, 1989.

Levinson, B. M. *Deuteronomy and the Hermeneutics of Legal Innovation.* New York: Oxford University Press, 1997.

———. "The Human Voice in Divine Revelation: The Problem of Authority in Biblical Law." Pages 35-71 in *Innovation in Religious Traditions.* Edited by M. A. Williams et al. Berlin: Mouton de Gruyter, 1992.

———. "Goethe's Analysis of Exodus 34 and Its Influence on Wellhausen: The Pfropfung of the Documentary Hypothesis." *ZAW* 114 (2002): 212-23.

———, ed. *Theory and Method in Biblical and Cuneiform Law: Revision, Interpolation and Development.* JSOTSup 181. Sheffield: Sheffield Academic Press, 1994.

Lévi-Strauss, C. *The Raw and the Cooked: Introduction to a Science of Mythology.* Translated by J. and D. Weightman. New York: Harper & Row, 1969.

Lewis, B. *The Sargon Legend.* ASORDS 4. Cambridge: ASOR, 1980.

Lewy, I. "The Story of the Golden Calf Reanalyzed." *VT* 9 (1959): 316-22.

Lichtenstein, M. "A Note on the Text of I Keret." *JANES* 2 (1970): 94-100.

Lind, M. C. *Yahweh Is a Warrior: The Theology of Warfare in Ancient Israel.* Scottdale, Pa.: Herald, 1980.

Lingen, A. Van Der. *Les guerres de Yahvé: L'implication de YHWH dans les guerres d'Israël selon les livres historiques de l'Ancien Testament.* LD 139. Paris: Cerf, 1990.

Littauer, M. A., and J. H. Crouwel. "Chariots." *ABD* 1:888-92.

Lockshin, M. I., ed. *Rashbam's Commentary on Exodus: An Annotated Translation.* BJS 310. Atlanta: Scholars Press, 1997.

Loewenstamm, S. E. *The Evolution of the Exodus Tradition.* Translated by B. J. Schwartz. Jerusalem: Magnes, 1992.

———. "The Lord Is My Strength and My Glory." *VT* 19 (1969): 464-70.

———. "The Making and Destruction of the Golden Calf." *Bib* 48 (1967): 481-90.

Lohfink, N. "Arbeitswoche und Sabbat in der priesterlichen Geschichtserzählung." *Bibel und Kirche* 52 (1997): 110-18.

———. "Deuteronomium 9,1-10,11 und Exodus 32-34: Zu Endtextstruktur, Intertextualität, Schichtung, und Abhängigkeit." Pages 41-87 in *Gottes Volk am Sinai: Unter-*

suchungen zu Ex 32–34 und Dtn 9–10. Edited by M. Köckert and E. Blum. VWGT 18. Gütersloh: Gütersloher Verlagshaus, 2001.

———. "'Gewalt' als Thema alttestamentlicher Forschung." Pages 15-50 in *Gewalt und Gewaltlosigkeit im Alten Testament.* Edited by N. Lohfink. QD 96. Freiburg: Herder, 1983.

———. *Das Hauptbegot: Eine Untersuchung literarischer Einleitungsfragen zu Dtn 5-11.* AnBib 20. Rome: Pontifical Biblical Institute, 1963.

———. "Literatureverzeichnis." Pages 225-47 in *Gewalt und Gewaltlosigkeit im Alten Testament.* Edited by N. Lohfink. QD 96. Freiburg: Herder, 1983.

———. "Poverty in the Laws of the Ancient Near East and of the Bible." *TS* 52 (1991): 34-50.

———. "Die priesterschriftliche Abwertung der Tradition von der Offenbarung des Jahwenamens an Moses." *Bib* 49 (1968): 1-8.

———. "The Priestly Narrative and History." Pages 136-72 in *Theology of the Pentateuch.* Translated by L. M. Maloney. Minneapolis: Fortress, 1994.

———. "The Song of Victory at the Red Sea." Pages 67-86 in *The Christian Meaning of the Old Testament.* Translated by R. A. Wilson. Milwaukee: Bruce, 1968.

———. "The Strata of the Pentateuch and the Question of War." Pages 173-226 in *Theology of the Pentateuch.* Translated by L. M. Maloney. Minneapolis: Fortress, 1994.

———. *Studien zum Pentateuch.* Stuttgarter Biblische Aufsatzbände 4. Stuttgart: Katholisches Bibelwerk, 1988.

———. *Theology of the Pentateuch: Themes of the Priestly Narrative and Deuteronomy.* Translated by L. M. Maloney. Minneapolis: Fortress, 1994.

Lommel, A. *Masks: Their Meaning and Function.* New York: Excalibur, 1981.

Long, B. O. *Imagining the Holy Land: Maps, Models, and Fantasy Travels.* Bloomington: Indiana University Press, 2003.

———. *The Problem of Etiological Narrative in the Old Testament.* BZAW 108. Berlin: de Gruyter, 1968.

Loomer, B. "Two Conceptions of Power." *Criterion* 15 (1976): 12-29.

Loretz, O. "Ex 21,6; 22,8 und angebliche Nuzi-Parallelen." *Bib* 41 (1960): 167-75.

———. "Ugarit-Texte und Israelitische Religionsgeschichte: The Song of the Sea." *UF* 6 (1974): 245-47.

Lotman, J. *The Structure of the Artistic Text.* Michigan Slavic Contributions 7. Ann Arbor: University of Michigan Press, 1977.

Loza, J. "Les catéchèses étiologiques dans l'Ancien Testament." *RB* 78 (1971): 481-500.

———. "Exode 32 et la rédaction JE." *VT* 23 (1973): 31-55.

Lundbom, J. R. "God's Use of the *Idem per Idem* to Terminate Debate." *HTR* 71 (1978): 193-201.

Lundquist, J. "Babylon in European Thought." Pages 67-80 in vol. 1 of *Civilizations of the Ancient Near East.* Edited by J. M. Sasson. New York: Scribner's, 1995.

Lust, J. "Exodus 6,2-8 and Ezekiel." Pages 209-24 in *Studies in the Book of Exodus: Redaction — Reception — Interpretation.* Edited by Marc Vervenne. BETL 126. Leuven: Leuven University Press, 1996.

Luyster, R. "Wind and Water: Cosmogonic Symbolism in the Old Testament." *ZAW* 93 (1981): 1-10.

Luz, U. *Matthew 1–7: A Commentary.* Translated by W. C. Linss. Minneapolis: Augsburg, 1989.

MacDonald, B. *'East of the Jordan': Territories and Sites of the Hebrew Scriptures.* ASOR Books 6. Boston: American Schools of Oriental Research, 2000.

Magonet, J. "The Rhetoric of God: Exodus 6.2-8." *JSOT* 27 (1983): 56-67.

Maiberger, P. *Das Manna.* Ägypten und Altes Testament 6. Wiesbaden: Harrassowitz, 1986.

Maidman, M. P. "Nuzi: Portrait of an Ancient Mesopotamian Provincial Town." Pages 45-53 in vol. 2 of *Civilizations of the Ancient Near East.* Edited by J. M. Sasson. New York: Scribner's, 1995.

Maier, J. *Das altisraelitische Ladeheiligtum.* BZAW 93. Berlin: Töpelmann, 1965.

Makujina, J. "Additional Considerations for Determining the Meaning of ʿĂnôt and ʿAnnôt in Exod XXXII 18." *VT* 55 (2005): 39-46.

Malul, M. *The Comparative Method in Ancient Near Eastern and Biblical Legal Studies.* AOAT 227. Neukirchen-Vluyn: Neukirchener Verlag, 1990.

Mandell, S., and D. N. Freedman. *The Relationship between Herodotus' History and Primary History.* SFSHJ 60. Atlanta: Scholars Press, 1993.

Mann, T. W. *Divine Presence and Guidance in Israelite Traditions: The Typology of Exaltation.* JHNES. Baltimore: Johns Hopkins University Press, 1977.

———. "The Pillar of Cloud in the Reed Sea Narrative." *JBL* 90 (1971): 15-30.

Marcus, J. *Mark.* AB 27. New York: Doubleday, 1999.

Margulis, D. "The Plagues Tradition in Ps 105." *Bib* 50 (1969): 491-96.

Marriott, W. B. *Vestiarium Christianum: The Origin and Gradual Development of the Dress of Holy Ministry in the Church.* London: Rivingtons, 1868.

Marshall, J. W. *Israel and the Book of the Covenant: An Anthropological Approach to Biblical Law.* SBLDS 140. Atlanta: Scholars Press, 1993.

Martens, F. "Diététhique ou la cuisine de Dieu." *Communications* 26 (1977): 16-45.

Martin-Achard, R. *Essai biblique sur les fêtes d'Israël.* Geneva: Labor et Fides, 1974.

Marwick, "Witchcraft." *ER* 15: 414-28.

Mastin, B. A. "Was the *šāliš* the Third Man in the Chariot?" Pages 125-54 in *Studies in the Historical Books of the Old Testament.* Edited by J. A. Emerton. VTSup 30. Leiden: Brill, 1979.

Matthews, V. H. "The Anthropology of Slavery in the Covenant Code." Pages 119-35 in *Theory and Method in Biblical and Cuneiform Law: Revision, Interpolation, and Development.* Edited by B. M. Levinson. JSOTSup 181. Sheffield: Sheffield Academic Press, 1994.

———. "Perfumes and Spices." Pages 226-28 in vol. 5 of *Anchor Bible Dictionary.* Edited by D. N. Freedman. 6 vols. New York: Doubleday, 1992.

May, H. G. "Some Cosmic Connotations of *Mayim Rabbîm*, 'Many Waters.'" *JBL* 74 (1955): 9-21.

Mayes, A. D. H. *Deuteronomy.* NCB. 1979. Repr. Grand Rapids: Eerdmans, 1981.

———. *The Story of Israel Between Settlement and Exile: A Redactional Study of the Deuteronomistic History.* London: SCM, 1983.

McBride, S. Dean. "Transcendent Authority: The Role of Moses in Old Testament Traditions." *Int* 44 (1990): 229-39.

McCann, J. C. "The Book of Psalms: Introduction, Commentary, and Reflections." Pages

641-1280 in vol. 4 of *New Interpreter's Bible*. Edited by L. E. Keck. Nashville: Abingdon, 1996.

———. "Exodus 32:1-14." *Int* 44 (1990): 277-81.

McCarter, P. Kyle, Jr. *II Samuel*. AB 9B. Garden City, N.Y.: Doubleday, 1984.

McCarthy, D. J. "Exodus 3:14: History, Philology and Theology." *CBQ* 40 (1978): 311-22.

———. "Moses' Dealings with Pharaoh: Exodus 7.8–10.27." *CBQ* 27 (1965): 336-47.

———. "Plagues and the Sea of Reeds: Exodus 5–14." *JBL* 85 (1966): 137-58.

———. *Treaty and Covenant: A Study in Form in the Ancient Oriental Documents and in the Old Testament*. 2nd ed. AnBib 21a. Rome: Pontifical Biblical Institute, 1978.

McEvenue, S. E. *Interpreting the Pentateuch*. Old Testament Series 4. Collegeville, Minn.: Liturgical Press, 1990.

———. *The Narrative Style of the Priestly Writer*. AnBib 50. Rome: Pontifical Biblical Institute Press, 1971.

———. "The Speaker(s) in Ex 1–15." Pages 220-36 in *Biblische Theologie und gesellschaftlicher Wander: Für Norbert Lohfink, SJ*. Edited by G. Braulik et al. Freiburg: Herder, 1993.

McKay, H. *Sabbath and Synagogue: The Question of Sabbath Worship in Ancient Judaism*. Religions in the Graeco-Roman World 122. Leiden: Brill, 1994.

McKay, J. W. "The Date of Passover and Its Significance." *ZAW* 84 (1972): 435-47.

———. "Exodus XXIII 1-3, 6-8: A Decalogue for the Administration of Justice in the City Gate." *VT* 21 (1971): 311-25.

———. "Psalms of Vigil." *ZAW* 91 (1979): 229-47.

McKenzie, S. L. *Covenant*. Understanding Biblical Themes. St. Louis: Chalice, 2000.

———. *The Trouble with Kings: The Composition of the Book of Kings in the Deuteronomistic History*. VTSup 42. Leiden: Brill, 1991.

McKenzie, S. L., and T. Römer, eds. *Rethinking the Foundations: Historiography in the Ancient World and in the Bible: Essays in Honour of John Van Seters*. BZAW 294. Berlin: de Gruyter, 2000.

McKnight, S. *A Light among the Gentiles: Jewish Missionary Activity in the Second Temple Period*. Minneapolis: Fortress, 1991.

McNeile, A. H. *The Book of Exodus*. Westminster Commentaries. London: Methuen, 1906.

McNutt, P. *The Forging of Israel: Iron Technology, Symbolism, and Tradition in Ancient Society*. Social World of Biblical Antiquity Series 8. Sheffield: Almond Press, 1990.

Meier, S. A. *Speaking of Speaking: Marking Direct Discourse in the Hebrew Bible*. VTSup 46. Leiden: Brill, 1992.

Melammed, E. Z. "'Observe' and 'Remember' Spoken in One Utterance." Pages 191-217 in *The Ten Commandments in History and Tradition*. Edited by B.-Z. Segal. Jerusalem: Magnes, 1990.

Mendels, D. *Identity, Religion and Historiography: Studies in Hellenistic History*. JSPSup 24. Sheffield: Sheffield Academic Press, 1998.

Mendenhall, G. "Covenant." Pages 1179-1202 in vol. 1 of *Anchor Bible Dictionary*. Edited by D. N. Freedman. 6 vols. New York: Doubleday, 1992.

———. *Law and Covenant in Israel and the Ancient Near East*. Pittsburgh: Biblical Colloquium, 1955.

———. "Midian." Pages 815-18 in vol. 4 of *Anchor Bible Dictionary.* Edited by D. N. Freedman. 6 vols. New York: Doubleday, 1992.

———. *The Tenth Generation: The Origins of the Biblical Tradition.* Baltimore: Johns Hopkins University Press, 1973.

Mettinger, T. N. D. *The Dethronement of Sabaoth: Studies in the Shem and Kabod Theologies.* ConBOT 18. Lund: Gleerup, 1982.

———. "Israelite Aniconism: Developments and Origins." Pages 173-204 in *The Image and the Book: Iconic Cults, Anticonism, and the Rise of Book Religion in Israel and the Ancient Near East.* Edited by K. van der Toorn. CBET 21. Leuven: Peeters, 1997.

———. *No Graven Image? Israelite Aniconism in Its Ancient Near Eastern Context.* ConBOT 42. Stockholm: Almqvist & Wiksell, 1995.

Metzger, M. "Himmlische und irdische Wohnstatt." *UF* 2 (1970): 9-55.

Meyers, C. "Cherubim." Pages 899-900 in vol. 1 of *Anchor Bible Dictionary.* Edited by D. N. Freedman. 6 vols. New York: Doubleday, 1992.

———. *Exodus.* NCBC. Cambridge: Cambridge University Press, 2005.

———. "Lampstand." Pages 141-43 in vol. 4 of *Anchor Bible Dictionary.* Edited by D. N. Freedman. 6 vols. New York: Doubleday, 1992.

———. "Miriam the Musician." Pages 207-30 in *A Feminist Companion to Exodus to Deuteronomy.* Edited by A. Brenner. FCB 1/6. Sheffield: Sheffield Academic Press, 1994.

———. "Realms of Sanctity: The Case of the 'Misplaced' Incense Altar in the Tabernacle Texts of Exodus." Pages 33-46 in *Texts, Temples, and Traditions: A Tribute to Menahem Haran.* Edited by M. V. Fox et al. Winona Lake, Ind.: Eisenbrauns, 1996.

———. *The Tabernacle Menorah: A Synthetic Study of a Symbol from the Biblical Cult.* ASORDS 2. Missoula, Mont.: Scholars Press, 1976.

———. "Temple, Jerusalem." Pages 351-69 in vol. 6 of *Anchor Bible Dictionary.* Edited by D. N. Freedman. 6 vols. New York: Doubleday, 1992.

Michaeli, F. *Le livre de l'Exode.* CAT 2. Paris: Delachaux et Niestlé, 1974.

Michel, D. *Tempora und Satzstellung in den Psalmen.* Abhandlungen zur evangelischen Theologie 1. Bonn: Bouvier, 1960.

Mickelsen, D. "Types of Spatial Structure in Narrative." Pages 64-67 in *Spatial Form in Narrative.* Edited by J. R. Smitten and A. Daghistany. Ithaca: Cornell University Press, 1981.

Milgrom, J. *Leviticus 1–16.* AB 3. New York: Doubleday, 1991.

———. *Leviticus 17–22.* AB 3A. New York: Doubleday, 2000.

———. *Leviticus 23–27.* AB 3B. New York: Doubleday, 2001.

———. *Numbers.* JPS Torah Commentary. Philadelphia: Jewish Publication Society, 1990.

———. "Priestly ('P') Source." Pages 454-61 in vol. 5 of *Anchor Bible Dictionary.* Edited by D. N. Freedman. 6 vols. New York: Doubleday, 1992.

Miller, P. D., Jr. *The Divine Warrior in Early Israel.* HSM 5. Cambridge: Harvard University Press, 1973.

———. "Two Critical Notes on Psalm 68 and Deuteronomy 33." *HTR* 57 (1964): 240-43.

Minette de Tillesse, G. "Sections 'tu' et sections 'vous' dans le Deutéronome." *VT* 12 (1962): 29-87.

Miscall, P. D. "Biblical Narrative and Categories of the Fantastic." *Semeia* 60 (1992): 39-51.

Moberly, R. W. L. *At the Mountain of God: Story and Theology in Exodus 32–34*. JSOTSup 22. Sheffield: JSOT Press, 1983.

———. "'Holy, Holy, Holy': Isaiah's Vision of God." Pages 122-40 in *Holiness Past and Present*. Edited by S. C. Barton. London: T & T Clark, 1991.

Möhlenbrink, K. "Josua im Pentateuch." *ZAW* 59 (1942-43): 140-58.

———. "Die Landnahmesagen des Buches Josua." *ZAW* 15 (1938): 254-58.

Momigliano, A. *The Classical Foundations of Modern Historiography*. Sather Classical Lectures 54. Berkeley: University of California Press, 1990.

———. *The Development of Greek Biography*. Cambridge: Harvard University Press, 1993.

Moor, J. C. de. *New Year with Canaanites and Israelites*. 2 vols. Kampen: Kok, 1972.

———. "Rāpi'ūma — Rephaim." *ZAW* 88 (1976): 323-45.

———. *The Rise of Yahwism: The Roots of Israelite Monotheism*. BETL 41. Leuven: Leuven University Press, 1990.

———. *The Seasonal Pattern in the Ugaritic Myth of Ba'lu*. AOAT 16. Kevelaer: Butzon & Bercker, 1971.

Moore, M. S. *The Balaam Traditions: Their Character and Development*. SBLDS 113. Atlanta: Scholars Press, 1990.

Moran, W. L. "The End of the Unholy War and the Anti-Exodus." *Bib* 44 (1963): 333-42.

———. "The Hebrew Language in Its Northwest Semitic Background." Pages 54-72 in *The Bible and the Ancient Near East: Essays in Honor of William Foxwell Albright*. Edited by G. E. Wright. Garden City, N.Y.: Doubleday, 1967.

———. "A Kingdom of Priests." Pages 7-20 in *The Bible in Current Catholic Thought*. Edited by J. L. McKenzie. New York: Herder & Herder, 1962.

Morgenstern, J. *The Ark, the Ephod, and the "Tent of Meeting."* Henry and Ida Krolik Memorial Publications 2. Cincinnati: Hebrew Union College Press, 1945.

———. "Biblical Theophanies." *ZA* 25 (1911): 139-93; 28 (1914): 15-60.

———. "The Book of the Covenant, Parts 1-4." *HUCA* 5 (1928): 1-51; 7 (1930): 19-258; 8-9 (1931-32): 1-150; 33 (1962): 59-105.

———. "The Despoiling of the Egyptians." *JBL* 68 (1949): 1-28.

———. *The Fire upon the Altar*. Leiden: Brill, 1963.

———. "The Gates of Righteousness." *HUCA* 6 (1929): 1-37.

———. "Moses with the Shining Face." *HUCA* 2 (1925): 1-27.

Morrow, W. "A Generic Discrepancy in the Covenant Code." Pages 136-51 in *Theory and Method in Biblical and Cuneiform Law: Revision, Interpolation, and Development*. Edited by B. M. Levinson. JSOTSup 181. Sheffield: Sheffield Academic Press, 1994.

Mosis, R. "Ex 19,5b.6a: Syntakischer Aufbau und lexikalische Semantik." *BZ* 22 (1978): 1-25.

Mowinckel, S. *Le décalogue*. Études d'histoire et de philosophie religieuse 16. Paris: Alcan, 1927.

———. "Drive and/or Ride in O.T." *VT* 12 (1962): 278-99.

———. *The Psalms in Israel's Worship*. 2 vols. Translated by D. R. Ap-Thomas. Nashville: Abingdon, 1962.

———. *Tetrateuch — Pentateuch — Hexateuch: Die Berichte über die Landnahme in den drei altisraelitischen Geschichtswerken*. BZAW 90. Berlin: Töpelmann, 1964.

———. "Die vermeintliche 'Passahlegende' Ex. 1–15 in Bezug auf die Frage: Literarkritik und Traditionskritik." *ST* 5 (1951): 66-88.

Muffs, Y. *Studies in the Aramaic Legal Papyri from Elephantine.* Leiden: Brill, 1969.

Mühlenbrink, K. "Die levitischen Überlieferung des Alten Testament." *ZAW* 12 (1934): 184-231.

Muilenburg, J. *Hearing and Speaking the Word: Selections from the Works of James Muilenburg.* Edited by T. F. Best. Scholars Press Homage Series. Chico, Calif.: Scholars Press, 1984.

Müller, H.-P. "History Oriented Foundation Myths in Israel and Its Environment." Pages 156-68 in *Religious Identity and the Invention of Tradition: Papers Read at a Noster Conference in Soesterbert, January 4-6, 1999.* Edited by J. W. Van Henten and A. Houtepen. Studies in Theology and Religion 3. Assen: Van Gorcum, 2001.

Na'aman, N. "Ḫabiru and Hebrews: The Transfer of a Social Term to the Literary Sphere." *JNES* 45 (1986): 271-88.

Nasuti, H. "Identity, Identification and Imitation: The Narrative Hermeneutics of Biblical Law." *Journal of Law and Religion* 4 (1986): 11-29.

Nelson, F. A. J. *The Tragedy in History: Herodotus and the Deuteronomistic History.* JSOTSup 251. Sheffield: Sheffield Academic Press, 1997.

Neusner, J. "Religious Authority in Judaism: Modern and Classical Modes." *Int* 39 (1985): 373-87.

Nicholson, E. W. "The Antiquity of the Tradition in Exodus XXIV 9-11." *VT* 25 (1975): 69-79.

———. "The Covenant Ritual in Exodus XXIV 3-8." *VT* 32 (1982): 74-86.

———. "The Decalogue and the Direct Address of God." *VT* 27 (1977): 422-33.

———. *Exodus and Sinai in History and Tradition.* Growing Points in Theology. Richmond: John Knox, 1973.

———. *God and His People: Covenant and Theology in the Old Testament.* Oxford: Clarendon, 1986.

———. "The Interpretation of Exodus XXIV 9-11." *VT* 24 (1974): 77-97.

———. "The Origin of the Tradition in Exodus XXIV 9-11." *VT* 26 (1976): 148-60.

———. "P as an Originally Independent Source in the Pentateuch." *IBS* 10 (1988): 192-206.

Nicolsky, N. M. "Pascha im Kulte des jerusalemischen Tempels." *ZAW* 45 (1927): 171-90, 241-53.

Niditch, S. *War in the Hebrew Bible: A Study in the Ethics of Violence.* Oxford: Oxford University Press, 1993.

Nielsen, E. "Moses and the Law." *VT* 32 (1982): 87-98.

———. *The Ten Commandments in New Perspective: A Traditio-Historical Approach.* Translated by D. Burke. SBT 2/7. London: SCM, 1968.

Noegel, S. B. "Moses and Magic: Notes on the Book of Exodus." *JANES* 24 (1996): 45-59.

Nöldeke, Th. *Untersuchungen zur Kritik des Alten Testaments.* Kiel, 1869.

Norin, S. I. L. *Er spaltete das Meer: Die Auszugsüberlieferung in Psalmen und Kult des Alten Israel.* ConBOT 9. Lund: Gleerup, 1977.

North, R. "Perspective of the Exodus Author(s)." *ZAW* 113 (2001): 481-504.

Noth, M. *Das Buch Josua.* HAT 7. Tübingen: Mohr (Siebeck), 1938.

———. *Exodus: A Commentary.* Translated by J. S. Bowden. OTL. Philadelphia: Westminster, 1962.

———. *A History of Pentateuchal Traditions.* Translated by B. W. Anderson. Englewood Cliffs, N.J.: Prentice-Hall, 1972.

————. *The Laws in the Pentateuch and Other Studies.* Translated by D. R. Ap-Thomas. Philadelphia: Fortress, 1966.

————. *Numbers.* Translated by J. D. Martin. OTL. Philadelphia: Westminster, 1968.

————. "Der Wallfahrtsweg zum Sinai." *PJ* 36 (1940): 5-28.

————. "Zur Anfertigung des 'Goldenen Kalbes.'" *VT* 9 (1959): 419-22.

Obbink, H. Th. "Jahwebilder." *ZAW* 29 (1929): 264-74.

Oblath, M. D. *The Exodus Itinerary Sites: Their Locations from the Perspective of the Biblical Sources.* Studies in Biblical Literature 55. New York: Peter Lang, 2004.

Ollenburger, B. "Introduction: Gerhard von Rad's Theory of Holy War." Pages 1-33 in *Holy War in Ancient Israel.* Translated and edited by M. J. Dawn. Grand Rapids: Eerdmans, 1990.

————. *Zion, the City of the Great King: A Theological Symbol for the Jerusalem Cult.* JSOTSup 41. Sheffield: JSOT Press, 1987.

Olson, D. T. *Deuteronomy and the Death of Moses: A Theological Reading.* OBT. Minneapolis: Fortress, 1994.

————. "The Jagged Cliffs of Mt. Sinai: A Theological Reading of the Book of the Covenant (Exod 20:22–23:19)." *Int* 50 (1996): 251-63.

————. *Numbers.* Interpretation. Louisville: John Knox, 1996.

————. "Power and Leadership: Moses and the Manna Story." *PSB* 25 (2004): 316-31.

Olyan, S. M. "Exodus 31:12-17: The Sabbath according to H, or the Sabbath according to P and H?" *JBL* 124 (2005): 201-9.

————. "Why an Altar of Unfinished Stones? Some Thoughts on Ex 20,25 and Dtn 27,5-6." *ZAW* 108 (1996): 161-71.

Osumi, Y. *Die Kompositionsgeschichte des Bundesbuches Exodus 20.22b–23.33.* OBO 105. Göttingen: Vandenhoeck & Ruprecht, 1991.

Oswald, W. *Israel am Gottesberg: Eine Untersuchung zur Literargeschichte der vorderen Sinaiperikope Ex 19–24 und deren historischen Hintergrund.* OBO 159. Freiburg: Universitätsverlag, 1998.

Otto, E. "Aspects of Legal Reforms and Reformulations in Ancient Cuneiform and Israelite Law." Pages 160-96 in *Theory and Method in Biblical and Cuneiform Law: Revision, Interpolation, and Development.* Edited by B. M. Levinson. JSOTSup 181. Sheffield: Sheffield Academic Press, 1994.

————. *Das Deuteronomium im Pentateuch und Hexateuch: Studien sur Literaturgeschichte von Pentateuch und Hexateuch im Lichte des Deuteronomiumrahmens.* FAT 30. Tübingen: Mohr Siebeck, 2000.

————. "Erwägungen zum überlieferungsgeschichtlichen Ursprung und 'Sitz im Leben' des jahwistischen Plagenzyklus." *VT* 26 (1976): 3-27.

————. *Das Mazzotfest in Gilgal.* BWANT 7. Stuttgart: Kohlhammer, 1975.

————. "Die nachpriesterschriftliche Pentateuchredaktion im Buch Exodus." Pages 61-111 in *Studies in the Book of Exodus: Redaction — Reception — Interpretation.* Edited by Marc Vervenne. BETL 126. Leuven: Leuven University Press, 1996.

————. *Theologische Ethik des Alten Testaments.* Theologische Wissenschaft Sammelwerk für Studium und Beruf 3/2. Stuttgart: Kohlhammer, 1994.

————. *Wandel der Rechtsbegründungen in der Gesellschaftsgeschichte des Antiken Israel:*

Eine Rechtsgeschichte des 'Bundesbuches' Ex XX 22 — XXIII 13. StudBib 3. Leiden: Brill, 1988.

Otto, E., and T. Schramm. *Festival and Joy*. Translated by J. L. Blevins. Biblical Encounters Series. Nashville: Abingdon, 1980.

Otto, R. *The Idea of the Holy: An Inquiry into the Non-Rational Factor in the Idea of the Divine and Its Relation to the Rational*. Translated by J. W. Harvey. 2nd ed. 1950. Repr. London: Oxford, 1958.

Owczarek, S. *Die Vorstellung von Wohnen Gottes inmitten seines Volkes in der Priesterschrift: Zur Heiligtumstheologie der priesterschriftlichen Grundschrift*. EHS Reihe XXIII, Theologie 625. Frankfurt am Main: Lang, 1998.

Park, C. C. *Sacred Worlds: An Introduction to Geography and Religion*. London: Routledge, 1994.

Parker, S. B. "Exodus XV 2 Again." *VT* 21 (1971): 373-79.

Parkinson, R. B. *Voices from Ancient Egypt: An Anthology of Middle Kingdom Writing*. Oklahoma Series in Classical Culture. Norman: University of Oklahoma Press, 1991.

Patai, R. *Man and Temple: In Ancient Jewish Myth and Ritual*. New York: Ktav, 1967.

Patrick, D. "The Covenant Code Source." *VT* 27 (1977): 145-57.

———. *Old Testament Law*. Atlanta: John Knox, 1985.

———. "Traditio-History of the Reed Sea Account." *VT* 26 (1976): 248-49.

———. "Who Is the Evolutionist?" Pages 152-59 in *Theory and Method in Biblical and Cuneiform Law: Revision, Interpolation, and Development*. Edited by B. M. Levinson. JSOTSup 181. Sheffield: Sheffield Academic Press, 1994.

Paul, S. M. "Exodus 1:21. 'To Found a Family' — A Biblical and Akkadian Idiom." *Maarav* 8 (1992): 139-42.

———. *Studies in the Book of the Covenant in Light of Cuneiform and Biblical Law*. VTSup 18. Leiden: Brill, 1970.

Pedersen, J. *Israel: Its Life and Culture*. 4 vols. in 2. London: Oxford University Press, 1926-1940.

———. "Passahfest und Passahlegende." *ZAW* 52 (1934): 161-75.

Perdue, L. G. "The Making and Destruction of the Golden Calf — A Reply." *Bib* 54 (1973): 237-46.

Perlitt, L. *Bundestheologie im Alten Testament*. WMANT 36. Neukirchen-Vluyn: Neukirchener Verlag, 1969.

———. "Sinai und Horeb." Pages 302-22 in *Beiträge zur alttestamentlichen Theologie: Festschrift für Walther Zimmerli*. Edited by H. Donner, Robert Hanhart, and Rudolf Smend. Göttingen: Vandenhoeck & Ruprecht, 1977.

Pernet, H. "Masks: Theoretical Perspectives." *ER* 9:261.

Petersen, D. L. *Late Israelite Prophecy: Studies in Deutero-Prophetic Literature and in Chronicles*. SBLMS 23. Missoula, Mont.: Scholars Press, 1977.

Petschow, H. "Zur Systematik und Gesetzestechnik im Codex Hammurabi." *ZA* 23 (1965): 146-72.

Phillips, A. *Ancient Israel's Criminal Law: A New Approach to the Decalogue*. New York: Schocken, 1970.

———. "A Fresh Look at the Sinai Pericope." *VT* 34 (1984): 39-52.

———. "The Laws of Slavery: Exodus 21:2-11." *JSOT* 30 (1984): 51-66.

————. "The Origin of 'I Am' in Exodus 3,14." *JSOT* 78 (1998): 81-84.

Pixley, G. *On Exodus: A Liberation Perspective*. Maryknoll, N.Y.: Orbis, 1983.

Plastaras, J. *Creation and Covenant*. Milwaukee: Bruce, 1968.

————. *The God of the Exodus: The Theology of the Exodus Narratives*. Milwaukee: Bruce, 1966.

Poethig, E. "The Victory Song Tradition of the Women of Israel." Ph.D. diss. Union Theological Seminary, New York, 1985.

Pola, T. *Die ursprüngliche Priesterschrift: Beobachtungen zur Literarkritik und Traditionsgeschichte von PG*. WMANT 70. Neukirchen-Vluyn: Neukirchener Verlag, 1995.

Polak, F. "Theophany and Mediator: The Unfolding of a Theme in the Book of Exodus." Pages 113-47 in *Studies in the Book of Exodus: Redaction — Reception — Interpretation*. Edited by Marc Vervenne. BETL 126. Leuven: Leuven University Press, 1996.

Polzin, R. *Moses and the Deuteronomist: A Literary Study of the Deuteronomic History*. Part 1. New York: Seabury, 1980.

Popper, J. *Der biblische Bericht über die Stiftshütte: Ein Beitrag zur Geschichte der Composition und Diaskeue des Pentateuch*. Leipzig: Hunger, 1862.

Porten, B., and A. Yardeni. *Textbook of Aramaic Documents from Ancient Egypt*. Vol. 1: *Letters*. Winona Lake, Ind.: Eisenbrauns, 1986.

Pressler, C. "Wives and Daughters, Bond and Free: Views of Women in the Slave Laws of Exodus 21:2-11." Pages 147-72 in *Gender and Law in the Hebrew Bible and the Ancient Near East*. Edited by V. H. Matthews et al. JSOTSup 262. Sheffield: Sheffield Academic Press, 1998.

Preuss, H. D. *Old Testament Theology*. Translated by L. G. Perdue. 2 vols. OTL. Louisville: Westminster John Knox, 1995-1996.

Pritchard, J. B., ed. *Ancient Near Eastern Texts Relating to the Old Testament*. 3rd ed. Princeton: Princeton University Press, 1969.

Propp, W. H. *Exodus 1–18*. AB 2. New York: Doubleday, 1999.

————. *Exodus 19–40*. AB 2A. New York: Doubleday, 2006.

————. "The Skin of Moses' Face — Transfigured or Disfigured?" *CBQ* 49 (1987): 375-86.

————. *Water in the Wilderness: A Biblical Motif and Its Mythological Background*. HSM 40. Atlanta: Scholars Press, 1987.

Pury, A. de. "Abraham: The Priestly Writer's 'Ecumenical' Ancestor." Pages 163-82 in *Rethinking the Foundations: Historiography in the Ancient World and in the Bible: Essays in Honour of John Van Seters*. Edited by S. L. McKenzie and T. Römer. BZAW 294. Berlin: de Gruyter, 2000.

————. "Le cycle de Jacob comme legende autonome des origins d'Israël." Pages 78-96 in *Congress Volume: Leuven 1989*. Edited by J. A. Emerton. VTSup 43. Leiden: Brill, 1991.

————. "Osée 12 et ses implications pour le débat actuel sur le Pentateuque." Pages 175-207 in *Le Pentateuque: Débats et recherches*. Edited by P. Haudebert. LD 151. Paris: Cerf, 1992.

————. "Yahwist ('J') Source." Pages 1012-20 in vol. 6 of *Anchor Bible Dictionary*. Edited by D. N. Freedman. 6 vols. New York: Doubleday, 1992.

————, ed. *Le Pentateuque en question: Les origines et la composition des cinq premiers livres de la Bible à la lumière des recherches récentes.* MdB. Geneva: Labor et Fides, 1989.

Pury, A. de, and T. Römer. "Le Pentateuque en question: Position du probléme et brève histoire de la recherche." Pages 9-80 in *Le Pentateuque en question: Les origines et la composition des cinq premiers livres de la Bible à la lumière des recherches récentes.* Edited by A. de Pury. MdB. Geneva: Labor et Fides, 1989.

Quirke, S. *Ancient Egyptian Religion.* London: British Museum Press, 1992.

Rabast, K. *Das apodiktische Rechte im Deuteronomium und im Heiligkeitsgesetz.* Berlin: Heimatdienst, 1948.

Rabenau, K. von. "Die Beiden Erzählungen vom Schilfmeerwunder in Exod. 13,17–14,31." Pages 9-29 in *Theologische Versuche.* Edited by P. Watzel. Berlin: Evangelische Verlag, 1966.

Rabinowitz, I. "*'āz* Followed by Imperfect Verb-Form in Preterite Contexts: A Redactional Device in Biblical Hebrew." *VT* 34 (1984): 53-62.

Rad, G. von. "Beobachtungen an der Moseerzählung Exodus 1–14." *EvT* 31 (1971): 579-88.

———. *Deuteronomy.* Translated by D. Barton. OTL. Philadelphia: Westminster, 1966.

———. "The Form-Critical Problem of the Hexateuch." Pages 1-78 in *The Problem of the Hexateuch and Other Essays.* Translated by E. W. Trueman Dicken. New York: McGraw-Hill, 1966.

———. *Holy War in Ancient Israel.* Translated and edited by M. J. Dawn. Grand Rapids: Eerdmans, 1991.

———. *Old Testament Theology.* Translated by D. M. G. Stalker. 2 vols. New York: Harper & Row, 1962-1965.

———. "The Origin of the Concept of the Day of Yahweh." *JSS* 4 (1959): 103-8.

———. *Die Priesterschrift im Hexateuch: Literarisch untersucht und theologisch gewertet.* BWANT 65. Stuttgart: Kohlhammer, 1934.

———. *Studies in Deuteronomy.* Translated by D. Stalker. SBT 1/9. Chicago: Regnery, 1953.

Rainey, A. "The Satrapy 'Beyond the River.'" *AJBA* 1 (1969): 51-78.

Rapp, U. *Mirjam: Eine feministisch-rhetorische Lektüre der Mirjamtexte in der hebräischen Bibel.* BZAW 317. Berlin: de Gruyter, 2002.

Rashkow, I. "Oedipus Wrecks: Moses and God's Rod." Pages 59-74 in *Exodus to Deuteronomy.* Edited by A. Brenner. FCB 2/5. Sheffield: Sheffield Academic Press, 2000.

Redford, D. B. *Egypt, Canaan, and Israel in Ancient Times.* Princeton: Princeton University Press, 1992.

———. "An Egyptological Perspective on the Exodus Narrative." Pages 137-61 in *Egypt, Israel, Sinai: Archaeological and Historical Relationship in the Biblical Period.* Edited by A. Rainey. Tel Aviv: Tel Aviv University Press, 1987.

———. "Exodus I 11." *VT* 13 (1963): 401-18.

———. "Pithom." Columns 1054-58 in *Lexicon der Ägyptologie.* Edited by W. Helck and W. Westendorf. Wiesbaden: Harrassowitz, 1982.

Reichert, A. "Israel, the Firstborn of God: A Topic of Early Deuteronomic Theology." Pages 341-49 in vol. 1 of *Proceedings of the Sixth World Congress of Jewish Studies.* Edited by A. Shinan. 3 vols. Jerusalem: World Union of Jewish Studies, 1977.

Renaud, B. *L'alliance, un mystère de miséricorde: Une lecture d'Exode 32–34.* LD 169. Paris: Cerf, 1998.

————. *La théophanie du Sinaï, Ex 19–24: Exégèse et théologie*. CahRB 30. Paris: Gabalda, 1991.

Rendsburg, G. "The Egyptian Sun-God Ra in the Pentateuch." *Hen* 10 (1988): 3-15.

————. "Late Biblical Hebrew and the Date of P." *JANESCU* 12 (1980): 65-80.

Rendtorff, R. "The Concept of Revelation in Ancient Israel." Pages 25-53 in *Revelation as History*. Translated by D. Granskou. Edited by W. Pannenberg. New York: Macmillan, 1968.

————. *The Problem of the Process of Transmission in the Pentateuch*. Translated by J. J. Scullion. JSOTSup 89. Sheffield: Sheffield Academic Press, 1990.

————. "Der Text in seiner Endgestalt: Überlegungen zu Exodus 19." Pages 459-70 in *Ernten was man sät: Festschrift für Klaus Koch zu seinem 65. Geburtstag*. Edited by D. R. Daniels et al. Neukirchen-Vluyn: Neukirchener Verlag, 1991.

————. "The 'Yahwist' as Theologian? The Dilemma of Pentateuchal Criticism." *JSOT* 3 (1977): 2-9.

Richter, W. "Beobachtungen zur theologischen Systembildung in der alttestamentlichen Literatur anhand des 'Kleinen geschichtlichen Credo.'" Pages 175-212 in vol. 1 of *Wahrheit und Verkündigung: Michael Schmaus zum 70. Geburtstag*. Edited by L. Scheffczyk et al. 2 vols. Paderborn: Schoningh, 1967.

Ricoeur, P. *Lectures on Ideology and Utopia*. Edited by G. H. Taylor. New York: Columbia University Press, 1986.

Riemann, P. A. "Desert and Return to Desert in the Pre-Exilic Prophets." Ph.D. diss. Harvard, 1966.

Ringe, S. *Jesus, Liberation and the Biblical Jubilee: Images for Ethics and Christology*. Philadelphia: Fortress, 1985.

Rivard, R. "Pour une Relecture d'Ex 19 et 20: Analyse sémiotique d'Ex 19,1-8." *ScEs* 33 (1981): 335-56.

Robertson, D. A. *Linguistic Evidence in Dating Early Hebrew Poetry*. SBLDS 3. Missoula, Mont.: Scholars Press, 1972.

Robertson, E. "The Altar of Earth (Ex 20,24-26)." *JSS* 1 (1948): 12-21.

Robinson, B. P. "Israel and Amalek: The Context of Exodus 17:8-16." *JSOT* 32 (1985): 15-22.

————. "Symbolism in Exod. 15:22-27 (Marah and Elim)." *RB* 94 (1987): 376-88.

————. "Zipporah to the Rescue: A Contextual Study of Exodus IV 24-26." *VT* 36 (1986): 447-61.

Robinson, R. *The Origin and Development of the Old Testament Sabbath*. Frankfurt am Main: P. Lang, 1988.

Rogerson, J. W. *Myth in the Old Testament*. BZAW 134. Berlin: de Gruyter, 1974.

————. *W. M. L. de Wette, Founder of Modern Biblical Criticism: An Intellectual Biography*. JSOTSup 126. Sheffield: Sheffield Academic Press, 1992.

Römer, T. "Das Buch Numeri und das Ende des Jahwisten Anfragen zur 'Quellenscheidung' im vierten Buch des Pentateuch." Pages 215-32 in *Abschied vom Jahwisten: Die Komposition des Hexateuch in der jüngsten Diskussion*. Edited by J. C. Gertz, K. Schmid, and M. Witte. BZAW 315. Berlin: de Gruyter, 2002.

————. "Competing Magicians in Exodus 7-9: Interpreting Magic in the Priestly Theology." Pages 12-22 in *Magic in the Biblical World: From the Rod of Aaron to the Ring of Solomon*. Edited by T. E. Klutz. JSNTSup 245. London: T. & T. Clark, 2003.

―――. *Israels Väter: Untersuchungen zur Väterthematik im Deuteronomium und in der deuteronomistischen Tradition.* OBO 99. Göttingen: Vandenhoeck & Ruprecht, 1990.

―――. *The So-Called Deuteronomistic History: A Sociological, Historical and Literary Introduction.* London: T. & T. Clark, 2005.

Romm, J. *Herodotus.* Hermes Books. New Haven: Yale University Press, 1998.

Rooke, D. W. *Zadok's Heirs: The Role and Development of the High Priesthood in Ancient Israel.* Oxford Theological Monographs. Oxford: Oxford University Press, 2000.

Rose, M. *Deuteronomist und Jahwist: Untersuchung zu den Berührungspunkten beider Literaturwerke.* ATANT 67. Zurich: Theologischer Verlag, 1981.

―――. "Empoigner le Pentateuque par sa fin! L'investite de Josué et la mort de Moïse." Pages 129-47 in *Le Pentateuque en question: Les origines et la composition des cinq premiers livres de la Bible à la lumière des recherches récentes.* Edited by A. de Pury. MdB. Geneva: Labor et Fides, 1989.

Rost, L. *Das kleine Credo und andere Studien zum Alten Testament.* Heidelberg: Quelle & Meyer, 1965.

―――. "Weidewechsel und altisraelitischer Festkalender." *ZDPV* 66 (1943): 205-15.

Roth, M. T. *Law Collections from Mesopotamia and Asia Minor.* 2nd ed. SBLWAW 6. Atlanta: Scholars Press, 1997.

Rouillard, H. *La péricope de Balaam (Nombres 22–24): Le prose et les "oracles."* Fondation Singer-Polignac. Paris: Gabalda, 1985.

Rowley, H. H. *Worship in Ancient Israel: Its Forms and Meaning.* London: SPCK, 1967.

Rozelaar, M. "The Song of the Sea: Exodus XV, 1b-18." *VT* 2 (1952): 221-28.

Rudolph, W. "Der Aufbau von Exodus 19–34." Pages 41-48 in *Werden und Wesen des Alten Testaments.* Edited by P. Volz et al. BZAW 66. Berlin: Töpelmann, 1935.

―――. *Der "Elohist" von Exodus bis Josua.* BZAW 68. Berlin: Töpelmann, 1938.

Ruppert, L. "Das Motiv der Versuchung durch Gott in vordeuteronomischer Tradition." *VT* 22 (1972): 55-63.

Rupprecht, K. "עלה מן הארץ (Ex 1 10 Hos 2 2): 'Sich des Landes bemächtigen'?" *ZAW* 82 (1970): 442-47.

Ruprecht, E. "Exodus 24,9-11 als Beispiel lebendiger Erzähltradition aus der Zeit des babylonischen Exils." Pages 138-73 in *Werden und Wirken des Alten Testaments: Festschrift für Claus Westermann.* Edited by R. Albertz et al. Neukirchen-Vluyn: Neukirchener Verlag, 1978.

Rylaarsdam, J. C. "The Book of Exodus." Pages 833-1099 in vol. 1 of *Interpreter's Bible.* Edited by G. A. Buttrick. Nashville: Abingdon, 1952.

―――. "Passover and Feast of Unleavened Bread." Pages 663-68 in vol. 3 of *Interpreter's Dictionary of the Bible.* Edited by G. A. Buttrick. 4 vols. Nashville: Abingdon, 1962.

Sæbø, M. "Priestertheologie und Priesterschrift: Zur Eigenart der priesterlichen Schicht im Pentateuch." Pages 357-74 in *Congress Volume: Vienna 1980.* Edited by J. A. Emerton et al. VTSup 32. Leiden: Brill, 1981.

Sakenfeld, K. D. *The Meaning of Hesed in the Hebrew Bible: A New Inquiry.* HSM 17. Missoula, Mont.: Society of Biblical Literature, 1978.

Sanders, E. P. *Jesus and Judaism.* Philadelphia: Fortress, 1985.

―――. *Paul, the Law, and the Jewish People.* Philadelphia: Fortress, 1983.

Bibliography

————. "When Is a Law a Law? The Case of Jesus and Paul." Pages 139-58 in *Religion and Law: Biblical-Judaic and Islamic Perspectives*. Edited by E. B. Firmage et al. Winona Lake, Ind.: Eisenbrauns, 1990.

Sanders, J. A. *From Sacred Story to Sacred Texts*. Philadelphia: Fortress, 1987.

Sanders, S. L. "Old Light on Moses' Shining Face." *VT* 52 (2002): 400-406.

Sanderson, J. E. "War, Peace, and Justice in the Hebrew Bible: A Representative Bibliography." Pages 135-66 in G. von Rad, *Holy War in Ancient Israel*. Translated and edited by M. J. Dawn. Grand Rapids: Eerdmans, 1990.

Sarna, N. M. *Exodus*. JPS Torah Commentary. Philadelphia: Jewish Publication Society, 1991.

————. *Exploring Exodus: The Heritage of Biblical Israel*. New York: Schocken, 1986.

Sasson, J. M. "Bovine Symbolism in the Exodus Narrative." *VT* 18 (1968): 380-87.

————. "Ritual Wisdom? On 'Seething a Kid in Its Mother's Milk.'" Pp. 294-308 in *Kein Land für sich allein: Studien zum Kulturkontakt in Kanaan, Israel/Palästina und Ebirnâri für Manfred Weippert zum 65. Geburtstag*. Edited by U. Hübner and E. A. Knauf. OBO 186. Freiburg: Universitätsverlag, 2002.

————. "The Worship of the Golden Calf." Pages 151-59 in *Orient and Occident: Essays Presented to Cyrus H. Gordon on the Occasion of His Sixty-fifth Birthday*. Edited by H. A. Hoffner Jr. AOAT 22. Neukirchen-Vluyn: Neukirchener Verlag, 1973.

————, ed. *Civilizations of the Ancient Near East*. 4 vols. New York: Scribner's, 1995.

Sauer, G. "Vom Exoduserleben zur Landnahme: Theologische Erwägungen." *ZTK* 80 (1983): 26-32.

Sauter, G. "'Exodus' and 'Liberation' as Theological Metaphors: A Critical Case-Study of the Use of Allegory and Misunderstood Analogies in Ethics." *SJT* 34 (1981): 481-507.

Scharbert, J. "Formgeschichte und Exegese von Ex. 34, 6f und seiner Parallelen." *VT* 18 (1968): 130-50.

————. "Das 'Schilfmeerwunder' in den Texten des Alten Testaments." Pages 395-417 in *Mélanges bibliques et orientaux en l'honneur de M. Henri Cazelles*. Edited by A. Caquot and M. Delcor. AOAT 212. Neukirchen-Vluyn: Neukirchener Verlag, 1981.

————. "Der Sinn der Toledot-Formel in der Priesterschrift." Pages 45-56 in *Wort — Gebot — Glaube: Beiträge zur Theologie des Alten Testaments: Walther Eichrodt zum 80. Geburtstag*. Edited by H. J. Stoebe et al. ATANT 59. Zurich: Zwingli, 1970.

Schart, A. *Mose und Israel im Konflikt: Eine Redaktionsgeschichtliche Studie zu den Wüstenerzählungen*. OBO 98. Göttingen: Vandenhoeck & Ruprecht, 1990.

Schenker, A. "Les sacrifices d'alliance, Ex XXIV, 3-8 dans leur portée narrative et religieuse — Contribution a l'étude de la berit dans l'Ancien Testament." *RB* 101 (1994): 481-94.

Schley, D. G. *Shiloh: A Biblical City in Tradition and History*. JSOTSup 63. Sheffield: Sheffield Academic Press, 1989.

Schmid, Hans Heinrich. *Der sogenannte Jahwist: Beobachtungen und Fragen zur Pentateuchforschung*. Zurich: Theologischer Verlag, 1976.

Schmid, Herbert. *Die Gestalt des Mose: Probleme alttestamentlicher Forschung unter Berücksichtigung der Pentateuchkrise*. EdF 237. Darmstadt: Wissenschaftliche Buchgesellschaft, 1986.

————. *Mose: Überlieferung und Geschichte*. BZAW 110. Berlin: Töpelmann, 1968.

Schmid, K. *Erzväter und Exodus: Untersuchungen zur doppelten Begründung der Ursprung*

Israels innerhalb der Geschichtsbücher des Alten Testaments. WMANT 81. Neukirchen-Vluyn: Neukirchener Verlag, 1999.

———. "Israel am Sinai: Etappen der Forschungsgeschichte zu Ex 32–34 in seinen Kontexten." Pages 9-40 in *Gottes Volk am Sinai: Untersuchungen zu Ex 32–34 und Dtn 9–10.* Edited by M. Köckert and E. Blum. VWGT 18. Gütersloh: Gütersloher Verlagshaus, 2001.

Schmidt, H. "Das Meerlied: Ex 15, 2-19." *ZAW* 49 (1931): 59-66.

Schmidt, J. M. "Erwägungen zum Verhältnis von Auszugs- und Sinaitradition." *ZAW* 82 (1970): 1-31.

Schmidt, L. *Beobachtungen zu der Plagenerzählung in Exodus VII 14–XI 10.* StudBib 4. Leiden: Brill, 1990.

———. "Israel und das Gesetz Ex 19,3b-8 und 24,3-8 als literarischer und theologischer Rahmen für das Bundesbuch." *ZAW* 113 (2001): 167-85.

Schmidt, W. H. *Exodus 1–6.* BKAT II/1. Neukirchen-Vluyn: Neukirchener Verlag, 1988.

———. *Exodus, Sinai und Mose: Erwägungen zur Ex 1–19 und 24.* EdF 191. Darmstadt: Wissenschaftliche Buchgesellschaft, 1983.

Schmitt, H. Chr. "Die Erzählung vom Goldenen Kalb Ex. 32* und das Deuteronomistische Geschichtswerk." Pages 235-50 in *Rethinking the Foundations: Historiography in the Ancient World and in the Bible: Essays in Honour of John Van Seters.* Edited by S. L. McKenzie and T. Römer. BZAW 294. Berlin: de Gruyter, 2000.

———. "Die Geschichte vom Sieg über die Amalekiter Ex 17,8-16 als theologische Lehrerzählung." *ZAW* 102 (1990): 335-44.

———. "'Priesterliches' und 'prophetisches' Geschichtsverständnis in der Meerwundererzählung Ex 13,17-14,31: Beobachtungen zur Endredaktion des Pentateuch." Pages 139-55 in *Textgemäss: Aufsätze und Beiträge zur Hermeneutik des Alten Testaments: Festschrift für E. Würthwein.* Edited by A. H. J. Gunneweg and O. Kaiser. Göttingen: Vandenhoeck & Ruprecht, 1980.

———. "Redaktion des Pentateuch im Geiste der Prophetie." *VT* 32 (1982): 171-89.

———. "Das sogenannte jahwistische Privilegrecht in Ex 34, 10-28 als Komposition der spätdeuteronomistischen Endredaktion des Pentateuch." Pages 157-71 in *Abschied vom Jahwisten: Die Komposition des Hexateuch in der jüngsten Diskussion.* Edited by J. C. Gertz, K. Schmid, and M. Witte. BZAW 315. Berlin: de Gruyter, 2002.

Schmitt, R. *Exodus und Passa: Ihr Zusammenhang im Alten Testament.* 2nd ed. OBO 7. Göttingen: Vandenhoeck & Ruprecht, 1982.

———. *Zelt und Lade als Thema alttestamentlicher Wissenschaft.* Gütersloh: Gütersloher Verlagshaus, 1972.

Schnutenhaus, F. "Das Kommen und Erscheinen Gottes im Alten Testament." *ZAW* 76 (1964): 1-22.

Scholz, S. "The Complexities of 'His' Liberation Talk." Pages 20-40 in *Exodus to Deuteronomy.* Edited by A. Brenner. FCB 2/5. Sheffield: Sheffield Academic Press, 2000.

Schramm, B. "Exodus 19 and Its Christian Appropriation." Pages 327-52 in *Jews, Christians, and the Theology of the Hebrew Scriptures.* Edited by A. Ogden Bellis and J. S. Kaminsky. SBLSymS 8. Atlanta: Society of Biblical Literature, 2000.

Schreiner, J. "Exodus 12:21-23 und das israelitische Pascha." Pages 69-90 in *Studien zum Pentateuch: Festschrift für W. Kornfeld.* Edited by G. Braulik. Vienna: Herder, 1977.

Schrijver, G. de. "The Exodus Motif in the Theologies of Liberation: Changes of Perspective." Pages 169-90 in *Religious Identity and the Invention of Tradition: Papers Read at a Noster Conference in Soesterbert, January 4-6, 1999*. Edited by J. W. Van Henten and A. Houtepen. Studies in Theology and Religion 3. Assen: Van Gorcum, 2001.

Schwally, F. *Der heilige Krieg im alten Israel*. Semitische Kriegsaltertümer 1. Leipzig: Dieterich, 1901.

Schwartz, B. J. "The Priestly Account of the Theophany and Lawgiving at Sinai." Pages 103-34 in *Texts, Temples, and Traditions: A Tribute to Menahem Haran*. Edited by M. V. Fox et al. Winona Lake, Ind.: Eisenbrauns, 1996.

Schwienhorst-Schönberger, L. *Das Bundesbuch (Ex 20,22–23,33): Studien zu seiner Entstehung und Theologie*. BZAW 188. Berlin: de Gruyter, 1990.

Scoralick, R. "'JHWH, JHWH, ein gnädiger und barmherziger Gott . . .' (Exod 34,6): Die Gottesprädikationen aus Ex 34, 6f. in ihrem Kontext in Kapitel 32-34." Pages 141-56 in *Gottes Volk am Sinai: Untersuchungen zu Ex 32–34 und Dtn 9–10*. Edited by M. Köckert and E. Blum. VWGT 18. Gütersloh: Gütersloher Verlagshaus, 2001.

Scott, R. B. Y. "A Kingdom of Priests (Exodus xix 6)." *OTS* 8 (1950): 213-19.

Seebass, H. *Numeri*. BKAT IV/2. Neukirchen-Vluyn: Neukirchener Verlag, 2003.

Seely, J. A. H. "Succoth." Pages 217-18 in vol. 6 of *Anchor Bible Dictionary*. Edited by D. N. Freedman. 6 vols. New York: Doubleday, 1992.

Segal, B.-Z., ed. *The Ten Commandments in History and Tradition*. Jerusalem: Magnes, 1990.

Segal, J. B. *The Hebrew Passover from the Earliest Times to A.D. 70*. London Oriental Series 12. London: Oxford University Press, 1963.

Seitz, C. "The Call of Moses and the 'Revelation' of the Divine Name: Source-Critical Logic and Its Legacy." Pages 145-61 in *Theological Exegesis: Essays in Honor of Brevard S. Childs*. Edited by C. Seitz and K. Greene-McCreight. Grand Rapids: Eerdmans, 1999.

Seitz, G. *Redaktionsgeschichtliche Studien zum Deuteronomium*. BWANT 13. Stuttgart: Kohlhammer, 1971.

Seow, C. L. "Ark of the Covenant." Pages 386-93 in vol. 1 of *Anchor Bible Dictionary*. Edited by D. N. Freedman. 6 vols. New York: Doubleday, 1992.

Setel, D. O'Donnel. "Exodus." Pages 26-35 in *The Woman's Bible Commentary*. Edited by C. A. Newsom and S. H. Ringe. Louisville: Westminster/John Knox, 1992.

Shils, E. *Tradition*. Chicago: University of Chicago Press, 1981.

Simons, J. *The Geographical and Topographical Texts of the Old Testament: A Concise Commentary in XXIII Chapters*. Leiden: Brill, 1959.

Singer, I. "Egyptians, Canaanites, and Philistines in the Period of the Emergence of Israel." Pages 282-338 in *From Nomadism to Monarchy: Archaeological and Historical Aspects of Early Israel*. Edited by I. Finkelstein and N. Na'aman. Jerusalem: Israel Exploration Society, 1994.

Ska, J.-L. "Exode xiv contient-il un récit de 'guerre sainte' de style deutéronomistique?" *VT* 33 (1983): 454-67.

———. "Ex 19,3-8 et les paréneses deutéronomiques." Pages 307-14 in *Biblische Theologie und gesellschaftlicher Wandel: Für Norbert Lohfink, SJ*. Edited by G. Braulik et al. Freiburg: Herder, 1993.

———. "Exode 19,3b-6 et l'identité de l'Israël postexilique." Pages 289-317 in *Studies in the*

Book of Exodus: Redaction — Reception — Interpretation. Edited by Marc Vervenne. BETL 126. Leuven: Leuven University Press, 1996.

———. *Le passage de la mer: Étude de la construction, du style et de la symbolique d'Ex 14, 1-31.* AnBib 109. Rome: Biblical Institute Press, 1986.

———. "La place d'Ex 6,2-8 dans la narration de l'exode." *ZAW* 94 (1982): 530-48.

———. "Les plaies d'Égypte dans le récit sacerdotal (P^g)." *Bib* 60 (1979): 23-35.

———. "Quelques remarques sur Pg et la dernière rédaction du Pentateuque." Pages 95-125 in *Le Pentateuque en question: Les origines et la composition des cinq premiers livres de la Bible à la lumière des recherches récentes.* Edited by A. de Pury. MdB. Geneva: Labor et Fides, 1989.

———. "La sortie d'Egypte (Ex 7-14) dans le récit sacerdotal (P^g) et la tradition prophétique." *Bib* 60 (1979): 191-215.

Smend, R. "Essen und Trinken — Ein Stuck Weltlichkeit des Alten Testaments." Pages 336-59 in *Beiträge zur alttestamentlichen Theologie: Festschrift für Walther Zimmerli.* Edited by H. Donner, Robert Hanhart, and Rudolf Smend. Göttingen: Vandenhoeck & Ruprecht, 1977.

———. *Yahweh War and Tribal Confederation: Reflections upon Israel's Earliest History.* Translated by M. G. Rogers. 2nd ed. Nashville: Abingdon, 1970.

Smith, J. Z. *To Take Place: Toward Theory in Ritual.* Chicago: University of Chicago Press, 1987.

Smith, M. S. *The Early History of God: Yahweh and the Other Deities in Ancient Israel.* San Francisco: Harper & Row, 1990.

———. "The Literary Arrangement of the Priestly Redaction of Exodus: A Preliminary Investigation." *CBQ* 58 (1996): 25-50.

———. "Myth and Mythmaking in Canaan and Ancient Israel." Pages 2031-41 in vol. 3 of *Civilizations of the Ancient Near East.* Edited by J. M. Sasson. New York: Scribner's, 1995.

———. *The Ugaritic Baal Cycle.* Vol. 1: *Introduction with Text, Translation and Commentary of KTU 1.1-1.2.* VTSup 55. Leiden: Brill, 1994.

———, with contributions by Elizabeth M. Bloch-Smith. *The Pilgrimage Pattern in Exodus.* JSOTSup 239. Sheffield: Sheffield Academic Press, 1997.

Snaith, N. H. "יַם־סוֹף. The Sea of Reeds: The Red Sea." *VT* 15 (1965): 395-98.

Soggin, J. A. "Gilgal, Passah und Landnahme: Eine neue Untersuchung des kultischen Zusammenhangs der Kap. III-IV des Josuabuches." Pages 263-277 in *Volume du Congrès: Genève 1965.* VTSup 15. Leiden: Brill, 1966.

———. *Joshua.* OTL. Translated by R. A. Wilson. Philadelphia: Westminster, 1970.

———. "Kultätiologische Sagen und Katechese im Hexateuch." *VT* 10 (1960): 341-47.

———. "Das Wunder am Meer und in der Wüste (Exodus, cc. 14-15)." Pages 379-85 in *Mélanges bibliques et orientaux en l'honneur de M. Mathias Delcor.* Edited by A. Caquot et al. AOAT 215. Neukirchen-Vluyn: Neukirchener Verlag, 1985.

Sommer, B. D. "Conflicting Constructions of Divine Presence in the Priestly Tabernacle." *BibInt* 9 (2001): 41-63.

———. "Revelation at Sinai in the Hebrew Bible and in Jewish Theology." *JR* 79 (1999): 422-51.

Sonsino, R. "Forms of Biblical Law." Pages 252-54 in vol. 4 of *Anchor Bible Dictionary*. Edited by D. N. Freedman. 6 vols. New York: Doubleday, 1992.

———. *Motive Clauses in Hebrew Law*. SBLDS 45. Chico, Calif.: Scholars Press, 1980.

Sparks, K. "The Problem of Myth in Ancient Historiography." Pages 269-80 in *Rethinking the Foundations: Historiography in the Ancient World and in the Bible: Essays in Honour of John Van Seters*. Edited by S. L. McKenzie and T. Römer. BZAW 294. Berlin: de Gruyter, 2000.

Speiser, E. A. "Census and Ritual Expiation in Mari and Israel." Pages 171-86 in *Oriental and Biblical Studies: Collected Writings of E. A. Speiser*. Edited by J. J. Finkelstein and M. Greenberg. Philadelphia: University of Pennsylvania Press, 1967.

Sperling, D. *The Original Torah: The Political Intent of the Bible's Writers*. New York: New York University Press, 1998.

Spieckermann, H. *Heilsgegenwart: Eine Theologie der Psalmen*. FRLANT 148. Göttingen: Vandenhoeck & Ruprecht, 1989.

Spinoza, B. de. *A Theologico-Political Treatise Containing Certain Discussions Wherein Is Set Forth That Freedom of Thought and Speech Not Only May, Without Prejudice to Piety and the Public Peace, Be Granted; But Also May Not, Without Danger to Piety and the Public Peace, Be Withheld*. Translated by R. H. M. Elwes. New York: Dover, 1951.

Sprinkle, J. M. *"The Book of the Covenant": A Literary Approach*. JSOTSup 174. Sheffield: Sheffield Academic Press, 1994.

Stahl, N. *Law and Liminality in the Bible*. JSOTSup 202. Sheffield: Sheffield Academic Press, 1995.

Stähli, H.-P. *Solare Elemente in Jahweglauben des Alten Testaments*. OBO 66. Freiburg: Universitätsverlag, 1985.

Stamm, J. J., and M. E. Andrews. *The Ten Commandments in Recent Research*. 2nd ed. SBT 2/2. Naperville: Allenson, 1967.

Steingrimsson, S. Ö. *Vom Zeichen zur Geschichte: Eine literar- und formkritische Untersuchung von Ex 6,28–11,10*. ConBOT 14. Lund: Gleerup, 1979.

Steins, G. "Priesterherrschaft, Volk von Priestern oder was sonst? Zur Interpretation von Ex 19,6." *BZ* 45 (2001): 20-36.

Stek, J. H. "What Happened to the Chariot Wheels of Exodus 14:25?" *JBL* 105 (1986): 293-94.

Stern, M., ed. *Greek and Latin Authors on Jews and Judaism*. Vol. 1: *From Herodotus to Plutarch*. 2nd ed. Jerusalem: Israeli Academy of Sciences and Humanities, 1976.

Stern, P. D. *The Biblical Ḥerem: A Window on Israel's Religious Experience*. BJS 211. Atlanta: Scholars Press, 1991.

Sternberg, M. *Hebrews between Cultures: Group Portraits and National Literature*. Indiana Studies in Biblical Literature. Bloomington: Indiana University Press, 1998.

Steuernagel, C. "Der jehovistische Bericht über den Bundesschluss am Sinai." *TSK* 72 (1889): 319-50.

Stevenson, K. R. *Vision of Transformation: The Territorial Rhetoric of Ezekiel 40–48*. SBLDS 154. Atlanta: Scholars Press, 1996.

Stolz, F. *Jahwes und Israels Kriege: Kriegstheorien und Kriegserfahrungen im Glauben des alten Israels*. ATANT 60. Zurich: Theologische Verlag, 1972.

Stone, L. "The Revival of Narrative: Reflections on a New Old History." *Past and Present* 85 (1979): 3-24.

Strauss, H. "Das Meerlied des Mose — ein 'Siegeslied' Israels?" *ZAW* 97 (1985): 103-9.

Struppe, U. *Die Herrlichkeit Jahwes in der Priesterschrift: Eine semantische Studie zu kᵉbôd YHWH.* ÖBS 9. Klosterneuburg: Österreichisches Katholisches Bibelwerk, 1988.

Suhr, E. G. "The Horned Moses." *Folklore* 74 (1963): 387-95.

Suomala, K. R. *Moses and God in Dialogue: Exodus 32–34 in Postbiblical Literature.* Studies in Biblical Literature 61. New York: Peter Lang, 2004.

Talmon, S. "The 'Desert Motif' in the Bible and in Qumran." Pages 31-63 in *Biblical Motifs: Origins and Transformations.* Edited by A. Altmann. Philip W. Lown Institute of Advanced Judaic Studies, Brandeis University Studies and Texts 3. Cambridge: Harvard University Press, 1966.

———. *King, Cult and Calendar in Ancient Israel.* Jerusalem: Magnes, 1986.

———. "Wilderness." Pages 946-49 in *Interpreter's Dictionary of the Bible Supplementary Volume.* Edited by K. Crim. Nashville: Abingdon, 1976.

Talstra, E. "Deuteronomy 9 and 10: Synchronic and Diachronic Observations." Pages 187-210 in *Synchronic or Diachronic? A Debate on Method in Old Testamament Exegesis.* Edited by J. C. de Moor. OTS 34. Leiden: Brill, 1995.

Tarragon, J.-M. de. "Witchcraft, Magic, and Divination in Canaan and Ancient Israel." Pages 2071-82 in vol. 3 of *Civilizations of the Ancient Near East.* Edited by J. M. Sasson. New York: Scribner's, 1995.

Taruskin, R. *Stravinsky and the Russian Traditions: A Biography of the Works Through "Mavra."* Berkeley: University of California Press, 1996.

Tengström, S. *Die Hexateucherzählung: Eine literaturgeschichtliche Studie.* ConBOT 7. Lund: Gleerup, 1976.

———. *Die Toldedotformel und die literarische Struktur der priesterlichen Erweiterungsschicht im Pentateuch.* ConBOT 17. Lund: Gleerup, 1981.

Terrien S. *The Elusive Presence: The Heart of Biblical Theology.* Religious Perspectives 26. New York: Harper & Row, 1978.

te Velde, H. "Theology, Priests, and Worship in Ancient Egypt." Pages 1731-49 in vol. 3 of *Civilizations of the Ancient Near East.* Edited by J. M. Sasson. New York: Scribner's, 1995.

Thomas, K. "The Decline of Witchcraft Prosecutions." Pages 158-73 in *Witchcraft and Sorcery.* Edited by M. Marwick. 2nd ed. London: Penguin, 1982.

Thompson, R. J. *Moses and the Law in a Century of Criticism since Graf.* VTSup 19. Leiden: Brill, 1970.

Thompson, T. L. *Early History of the Israelite People: From the Written and Archaeological Sources.* Studies in the History of the Ancient Near East 4. Leiden: Brill, 1992.

———. "Historiography (Israelite)." Pages 206-12 in vol. 3 of *Anchor Bible Dictionary.* Edited by D. N. Freedman. 6 vols. New York: Doubleday, 1992.

———. "How Yahweh Became God: Exodus 3 and 6 and the Heart of the Pentateuch." *JSOT* 68 (1995): 57-74.

———. *The Origin Tradition of Ancient Israel I: The Literary Formation of Genesis and Exodus 1–23.* JSOTSup 55. Sheffield: JSOT Press, 1988.

Tigay, J. *Deuteronomy.* JPS Torah Commentary. Philadelphia: Jewish Publication Society, 1996.

Todorov, T. *The Fantastic: A Structural Approach to a Literary Genre.* Translated by R. Howard. Ithaca: Cornell University Press, 1975.

Toeg, A. *Lawgiving at Sinai: The Course of Development of the Traditions Bearing on the Lawgiving at Sinai within the Pentateuch, with Special Emphasis on the Emergence of the Literary Complex in Exod xix-xxiv.* (Hebrew.) Jerusalem: Magnes, 1977.

Toorn, K. van der. "The Exodus as Charter Myth." Pages 113-27 in *Religious Identity and the Invention of Tradition: Papers Read at a Noster Conference in Soesterbert, January 4-6, 1999.* Edited by J. W. Van Henten and A. Houtepen. Studies in Theology and Religion 3. Assen: Van Gorcum, 2001.

————. "The Significance of the Veil in the Ancient Near East." Pages 1327-39 in *Pomegranates and Golden Bells: Studies in Biblical, Jewish, and Near Eastern Ritual, Law, and Literature in Honor of Jacob Milgrom.* Edited by D. P. Wright et al. Winona Lake, Ind.: Eisenbrauns, 1995.

————, ed. *The Image and the Book: Iconic Cults, Aniconism and the Rise of Book Religion in Israel and in the Ancient Near East.* Leuven: Peeters, 1997.

Tournay, R. J. "Recherches sur la chronologie des Psaumes." *RB* 65 (1958): 321-57.

————. *Seeing and Hearing God with the Psalms: The Prophetic Liturgy of the Second Temple in Jerusalem.* Translated by J. E. Crowley. JSOTSup 118. Sheffield: JSOT Press, 1991.

Towers, J. R. "The Red Sea." *JNES* 8 (1959): 150-53.

Trible, P. "Bringing Miriam out of the Shadows." Pages 166-86 in *A Feminist Companion to Exodus to Deuteronomy.* Edited by A. Brenner. FCB 1/6. Sheffield: Sheffield Academic Press, 1994.

————. "Depatriarchalizing in Biblical Interpretation." *JAAR* 41 (1973): 34-45.

————. "Subversive Justice: Tracing the Miriamic Traditions." Pages 99-109 in *Justice and the Holy: Essays in Honor of Walter Harrelson.* Edited by D. A. Knight and P. J. Paris. Scholars Press Homage Series. Atlanta: Scholars Press, 1989.

Tuan, Y.-F. *Space and Place: The Perspectives of Experience.* Minneapolis: University of Minnesota Press, 1977.

Turner, V. *The Ritual Process: Structure and Anti-Structure.* Ithaca: Cornell University Press, 1969.

Urbach, E. E. "The Role of the Ten Commandments in Jewish Worship." Pages 161-91 in *The Ten Commandments in History and Tradition.* Edited by B.-Z. Segal. Jerusalem: Magnes, 1990.

Utzschneider, H. *Das Heiligtum und das Gesetz: Studien zur Bedeutung der Sinaitischen Heiligtumstexts (Ex 25–40; Lev 8–9).* OBO 77. Göttingen: Vandenhoeck & Ruprecht, 1988.

————. "Die Renaissance der alttestamentlichen Literaturwissenschaft und das Buch Exodus: Überliegungen zu Hermeneutik und Geschichte der Forschung." *ZAW* 106 (1994): 197-223.

Valentin, H. *Aaron: Eine Studie zur vor-priesterschriftlichen Aaron-Überlieferung.* OBO 18. Göttingen: Vandenhoeck & Ruprecht, 1978.

Van Dam, C. *The Urim and Thummim: A Means of Revelation in Ancient Israel.* Winona Lake, Ind.: Eisenbrauns, 1997.

VanderKam, J. C. "Calendars: Ancient Israelite and Early Jewish." Pages 814-20 in vol. 1 of *Anchor Bible Dictionary.* Edited by D. N. Freedman. 6 vols. New York: Doubleday, 1992.

van der Leeuw, G. *Religion in Essence and Manifestation.* Translated by J. E. Turner. 2 vols. Princeton: Princeton University Press, 1963.

van Dijk-Hommes, F. "Some Recent Views on the Presentation of the Song of Miriam." Pages 200-206 in *Feminist Companion to Exodus to Deuteronomy.* Edited by M. J. Brenner. FCB 1/6 Sheffield: Sheffield Academic Press, 1994.

Van Gennep, A. *The Rites of Passage.* Translated by M. B. Vizedom. London: Routledge and Kegan Paul, 1909.

Van Henten, J. W., and A. Houtepen, eds. *Religious Identity and the Invention of Tradition: Papers Read at a Noster Conference in Soesterbert, January 4-6, 1999.* Studies in Theology and Religion 3. Assen: Van Gorcum, 2001.

Van Seters, J. *Abraham in History and Tradition.* New Haven: Yale University Press, 1975.

———. "'Comparing Scripture with Scripture': Some Observations on the Sinai Pericope of Exodus 19–24." Pages 111-30 in *Canon, Theology, and Old Testament Interpretation: Essays in Honor of Brevard S. Childs.* Edited by G. M. Tucker et al. Philadelphia: Fortress, 1988.

———. "Confessional Reformulation in the Exilic Period." *VT* 22 (1972): 448-59.

———. "A Contest of Magicians? The Plague Stories in P." Pages 569-80 in *Pomegranates and Golden Bells: Studies in Biblical, Jewish, and Near Eastern Ritual, Law, and Literature in Honor of Jacob Milgrom.* Edited by David P. Wright et al. Winona Lake, Ind.: Eisenbrauns, 1995.

———. "Cultic Laws in the Covenant Code (Exodus 20,22–23,33) and Their Relationship to Deuteronomy and the Holiness Code." Pages 319-45 in *Studies in the Book of Exodus: Redaction — Reception — Interpretation.* Edited by Marc Vervenne. BETL 126. Leuven: Leuven University Press, 1996.

———. "Etiology in the Moses Tradition: The Case of Exodus 18." *HAR* 9 (1985): 355-61.

———. *In Search of History: Historiography in the Ancient World and the Origins of Biblical History.* New Haven: Yale University Press, 1983.

———. *A Law Book for the Diaspora: Revision in the Study of the Covenant Code.* New York: Oxford University Press, 2002.

———. "The Law of the Hebrew Slave." *ZAW* 108 (1996): 534-46.

———. *The Life of Moses: The Yahwist as Historian in Exodus-Numbers.* Louisville: Westminster John Knox, 1994.

———. "Myth and History: The Problem of Origins and Tradition and History: History as National Tradition." Pages 49-74 in *Histoire et conscience historique dans les civilisations du Proche-Orient Ancien.* Edited by A. de Pury. Cahiers du Centre d'Études du Proche-Orient Ancien 5. Leuven: Peeters, 1989.

———. "The Place of the Yahwist in the History of Passover and Massot." *ZAW* 95 (1983): 167-82.

———. "The Plagues of Egypt: Ancient Tradition or Literary Intention." *ZAW* 98 (1986): 31-39.

————. *Prologue to History: The Yahwist as Historian in Genesis.* Louisville: Westminster/ John Knox, 1992.

————. "The So-Called Deuteronomistic Redaction of the Pentateuch." Pages 58-77 in *Congress Volume: Leuven 1989.* Edited by J. A. Emerton. VTSup 43. Leiden: Brill, 1991.

Vater, A. "A Plague on Both Our Houses: Form and Rhetorical Critical Observations on Exodus 7–11." Pages 62-71 in *Art and Meaning: Rhetoric in Biblical Literature.* Edited by D. J. A. Clines et al. JSOTSup 19. Sheffield: Sheffield Academic Press, 1982.

Vaux, R. de. *Ancient Israel.* Translated by J. McHugh. 2 vols. Repr. New York: McGraw-Hill, 1965.

————. *The Early History of Israel.* Translated by D. Smith. Philadelphia: Westminster, 1978.

Veijola, T. "Die Propheten und das Alter des Sabbatgebots." Pages 246-64 in *Prophet und Prophetenbuch: Festschrift für Otto Kaiser.* Edited by V. Fritz et al. BZAW 185. Berlin: de Gruyter, 1989.

Vermeylen, J. "L'affaire du veau d'or (Ex 32–34): Une clé pour la 'question deutéronomiste.'" *ZAW* 97 (1985): 1-23.

————. "La formation du Pentateuque à la lumière de l'exégèse historico-critique." *Revue théologique de Louvain* 12 (1981): 324-46.

Vervenne, M. "Current Tendencies and Developments in the Study of the Book of Exodus." Pages 21-59 in *Studies in the Book of Exodus: Redaction — Reception — Interpretation.* Edited by Marc Vervenne. BETL 126. Leuven: Leuven University Press, 1996.

————. "The 'P' Tradition in the Pentateuch: Document and/or Redaction? The 'Sea Narrative' (Ex 13,17–14,31) as a Test Case." Pages 67-90 in *Pentateuchal and Deuteronomistic Studies: Papers Read at the XIIIth IOSOT Congress, Leuven 1989.* Edited by C. Brekelmans and J. Lust. BETL 94. Leuven: Leuven University Press, 1990.

————. "The Protest Motif in the Sea Narrative (Ex 14,11-12): Form and Structure of a Pentateuchal Pattern." *ETL* 63 (1987): 257-71.

————. "The Question of 'Deuteronomic' Elements in Genesis to Numbers." Pages 243-68 in *Studies in Deuteronomy: In Honour of C. J. Labuschagne on the Occasion of His 65th Birthday.* Edited by F. García Martínez et al. VTSup 53. Leiden: Brill, 1994.

————, ed. *Studies in the Book of Exodus: Redaction — Reception — Interpretation.* BETL 126. Leuven: Leuven University Press, 1996.

Viberg, A. *Symbols of Law: A Contextual Analysis of Legal Symbolic Acts in the Old Testament.* ConBOT 34. Stockholm: Almqvist & Wiksell, 1992.

Vink, J. G. "The Date and Origin of the Priestly Code in the Old Testament." Pages 1-144 in Vink et al., *The Priestly Code and Seven Other Studies.* OTS 15. Leiden: Brill, 1969.

Vogt, E. "Die Erzählung vom Jordanübergang." *Bib* 46 (1965): 125-48.

Volkwein, B. "Masoretisches 'ēdūt, 'edwōt, 'ēdōt — 'Zeugnis' oder 'Bundesbestimmungen'?" *BZ* 13 (1969): 18-40.

Vollmer, J. E. "Religious Clothing in the East." Pages 537-40 in vol. 3 of *The Encyclopedia of Religion.* Edited by M. Eliade. New York: Macmillan, 1986.

Vriezen, Th. C. "'Ehje 'ašer 'ehje." Pages 498-512 in *Festschrift Alfred Bertholet.* Edited by W. Baumgartner et al. Tübingen: Mohr, 1950.

————. "The Exegesis of Exodus xxiv 9-11." *OTS* 17 (1972): 100-133.

————. "Exodusstudien: Exodus I." *VT* 17 (1967): 334-53.

————. "A Reinterpretation of Exodus 3, 21-22 and Related Texts, Exod 11:2f., 12:35f., and Ps. 105:37f. (Gen 15:4b)." *Jaarbericht . . . Ex oriente lux* 23 (1973/74): 389-401.

Wade, M. L. *Consistency of Translation Techniques in the Tabernacle Accounts of Exodus in the Old Greek.* SBLSCS 49. Atlanta: Scholars Press, 2003.

Wagenaar, J. A. "The Cessation of Manna: Editorial Frames for the Wilderness Wandering in Exodus 16,35 and Joshua 5,10-12." *ZAW* 112 (2000): 192-209.

Wagner, V. "Zur Systematik in dem Codex Ex 21:2–22:16." *ZAW* 81 (1969): 176-82.

Waldman, N. "A Comparative Note on Exodus 15:14-16." *JQR* 66 (1975): 189-92.

Walsh, J. P. M. *The Mighty from Their Thrones: Power in the Biblical Tradition.* OBT 21. Philadelphia: Fortress, 1987.

Walsh, J. T. "From Egypt to Moab: A Source Critical Analysis of the Wilderness Itinerary." *CBQ* 39 (1977): 20-33.

Waltke, B. K., and M. O'Connor. *An Introduction to Biblical Hebrew Syntax.* Winona Lake, Ind.: Eisenbrauns, 1990.

Walzer, M. "Exodus 32 and the Theory of Holy War: The History of a Citation." *HTR* 61 (1968): 1-14.

Wambacq, B. N. "Les origines de la *Pesaḥ* israélite." *Bib* 57 (1976): 206-24, 301-26.

————. "Les *Maṣṣôt.*" *Bib* 61 (1980): 31-53.

————. "*Pesaḥ-Maṣṣôt.*" *Bib* 62 (1981): 499-518.

Ward, W. A. "The Semitic Biconsonantal Root *SP* and the Common Origin of Egyptian *ČWF* and Hebrew *SÛP*: Marsh(-Plant)." *VT* 24 (1974): 339-49.

Watson, A. *Ancient Law and Modern Understanding: At the Edges.* Athens: University of Georgia Press, 1998.

Watts, J. D. W. "The Song of the Sea — Ex. XV." *VT* 7 (1957): 371-80.

Watts, J. W. *Psalm and Story: Inset Hymns in Hebrew Narrative.* JSOTSup 139. Sheffield: JSOT Press, 1992.

————. "Public Readings and Pentateuchal Law." *VT* 45 (1995): 540-57.

Weber, H.-R. *Power: Focus for a Biblical Theology.* Geneva: WCC Publications, 1989.

————. "Power: Some Biblical Perspectives." *Ecumenical Review* 38 (1986): 265-79.

Weber, M. *Ancient Israel.* Translated by H. H. Gerth and D. Martindale. New York: Macmillan, 1952.

Weeks, K. R. "Medicine, Surgery, and Public Health in Ancient Egypt." Pages 1787-98 in vol. 3 of *Civilizations of the Ancient Near East.* Edited by Jack M. Sasson. New York: Scribner's, 1995.

Weems, R. J. "The Hebrew Women Are Not Like the Egyptian Women: The Ideology of Race, Gender and Sexual Reproduction in Exodus 1." *Semeia* 59 (1992): 25-34.

Weimar, P. *Die Berufung des Mose: Literaturwissenschaftliche Analyse von Exodus 2,23–5,5.* OBO 32. Göttingen: Vandenhoeck & Ruprecht, 1980.

————. *Die Meerwundererzählung: Eine redaktionskritische Analyse von Ex 13,17–14,31.* Ägypten und Altes Testament 9. Wiesbaden: Harrassowitz, 1985.

————. "Struktur und Komposition der priesterschriftlichen Geschichtsdarstellung." *BN* 23 (1984): 81-134; 24 (1984): 138-62.

————. "Die Toledot-Formel in der priesterschriftlichen Geschichtsdarstellung." *BZ* 18 (1974): 65-93.

————. *Untersuchungen zur priesterschriftlichen Exodusgeschichte.* FB 9. Würzburg: Echter Verlag, 1973.

————. "Zum Problem der Entstehungsgeschichte von Ex 12,1-14." *ZAW* 107 (1995): 1-17.

Weimar, P., and E. Zenger. *Exodus: Geschichten und Geschichte der Befreiung Israels.* SBS 75. Stuttgart: Katholisches Bibelwerk, 1975.

Weinberg, J. *The Citizen-Temple Community.* Translated by Daniel L. Smith-Christopher. JSOTSup 151. Sheffield: Sheffield Academic Press, 1992.

Weinfeld, M. "The Decalogue: Its Significance, Uniqueness, and Place in Israel's Tradition." Pages 1-44 in *The Ten Commandments in History and Tradition.* Edited by B.-Z. Segal. Jerusalem: Magnes, 1990. Also pages 3-48 in *Religion and Law: Biblical-Judaic and Islamic Perspectives.* Edited by E. B. Firmage et al. Winona Lake, Ind.: Eisenbrauns, 1990.

————. *Deuteronomy and the Deuteronomic School.* Oxford: Clarendon, 1972.

————. "Deuteronomy, Book of." Pages 168-83 in vol. 2 of *Anchor Bible Dictionary.* Edited by D. N. Freedman. 6 vols. New York: Doubleday, 1992.

————. *Deuteronomy 1–11.* AB 5. New York: Doubleday, 1991.

————. *The Place of the Law in the Religion of Ancient Israel.* VTSup 100. Leiden: Brill, 2004.

Weiss, M. "The Decalogue in Prophetic Literature." Pages 67-81 in *The Ten Commandments in History and Tradition.* Edited by B.-Z. Segal. Jerusalem: Magnes, 1990.

Wellhausen, J. *Die Composition des Hexateuchs und der historischen Bücher des Alten Testaments.* 3rd ed. Berlin: Reimer, 1899.

————. *Israelitische und jüdische Geschichte.* 5th ed. Berlin: Reimer, 1904.

————. *Prolegomena to the History of Ancient Israel.* Translated by A. Menzies and J. Sutherland Black. 1883. Repr. New York: Meridian, 1957.

Wenham, G. J. *Genesis 1–15.* WBC 1. Waco: Word, 1987.

Wente, E. F. "Rameses." Pages 617-18 in vol. 6 of *Anchor Bible Dictionary.* Edited by D. N. Freedman. 6 vols. New York: Doubleday, 1992.

Wessner, M. D. "Toward a Literary Understanding of Moses and the Lord 'Face to Face' in Exodus 33:7-11." *ResQ* 44 (2002): 109-16.

Westbrook, R. *Property and the Family.* JSOTSup 113. Sheffield: Sheffield Academic Press, 1991.

————. *Studies in Biblical and Cuneiform Law.* CahRB 26. Paris: Gabalda, 1988.

————. "What Is the Covenant Code?" Pages 15-36 in *Theory and Method in Biblical and Cuneiform Law: Revision, Interpolation, and Development.* Edited by B. M. Levinson. JSOTSup 181. Sheffield: Sheffield Academic Press, 1994.

Westermann, C. "Die Herrlichkeit Gottes in der Priesterschrift." Pages 227-47 in *Wort — Gebot — Glaube: Beiträge zur Theologie des Alten Testaments: Walther Eichrodt zum 80. Geburtstag.* Edited by H. J. Stoebe et al. ATANT 59. Zurich: Zwingli, 1970.

————. *Praise and Lament in the Psalms.* Translated by K. R. Crim and R. N. Soulen. 2nd ed. Atlanta: John Knox, 1981.

Wette, W. M. L. de. *Beiträge zur Einleitung in das Alte Testament.* Halle: 1806-1807.

————. *Dissertatio critico-exegetica qua Deuteronomium a prioribus Pentateuchi Libris diversum, alius cuiusdam recentioris auctoris opus esse monstratur: quam . . . auctoritate amplissimi philosophorum ordinis pro venia legendi* AD XXVII. Jena, 1805.

Wevers, J. W. *Notes on the Greek Text of Exodus.* SBLSCS 30. Atlanta: Scholars Press, 1990.

Whybray, R. N. *The Making of the Pentateuch: A Methodological Study.* JSOTSup 53. Sheffield: Sheffield Academic Press, 1987.

Wifall, W. "The Sea of Reeds as Sheol." *ZAW* 92 (1980): 325-32.

Wijngaards, J. N. M. "עַנּוֹת in Exodus XXXII:18." *VT* 17 (1967): 122.

———. *The Dramatization of Salvific History in the Deuteronomic Schools.* OTS 16. Leiden: Brill, 1969.

———. *The Formulas of the Deuteronomic Creed (Dt. 6/20-23; 26/5-9).* Pontificia Universitas Gregoriana. Tilburg: A. Reijnen, 1963.

———. "הוֹציא and העלה: A Twofold Approach to the Exodus." *VT* 15 (1965): 91-102.

Wilcoxen, J. A. "Narrative Structure and Cult Legend: A Study of Joshua 1–6." Pages 43-70 in *Transitions in Biblical Scholarship.* Edited by J. C. Rylaarsdam. Essays in Divinity 6. Chicago: University of Chicago Press, 1968.

Wildberger, H. "'Glauben' im Alten Testament." *ZTK* 65 (1968): 129-59.

———. *Jahwes Eigentumsvolk: Eine Studie zur Traditionsgeschichte und Theologie des Erwählungsgedankens.* Zurich: Zwingli, 1960.

Williamson, H. G. M. *1 and 2 Chronicles.* NCB. Grand Rapids: Eerdmans, 1982.

———. "A Reconsideration of עזב II in Biblical Hebrew." *ZAW* 97 (1985): 74-85.

Willi-Plein, I. "Ort und literarische Funktion der Geburtsgeschichte des Mose." *VT* 41 (1991): 110-18.

Wilms, F. E. *Das jahwistische Bundesbuch in Exodus 34.* SANT 32. Munich: Kösel-Verlag, 1973.

Wilson, R. R. *Genealogy and History in the Biblical World.* New Haven: Yale University Press, 1977.

———. "The Hardening of Pharaoh's Heart." *CBQ* 41 (1979): 18-36.

Winnett, F. V. *The Mosaic Tradition.* Near and Middle East Series 1. Toronto: University of Toronto Press, 1949.

———. "Re-examining the Foundations." *JBL* 84 (1965): 1-19.

Winter, U. *Frau und Göttin: Exegetische und ikonographische Studien zum weiblichen Gottesbild im alten Israel und in dessen Umwelt.* OBO 53. Göttingen: Vandenhoeck & Ruprecht, 1983.

Witvliet, T. "Exodus in the African-American Experience." Pages 191-205 in *Religious Identity and the Invention of Tradition: Papers Read at a Noster Conference in Soesterbert, January 4-6, 1999.* Edited by J. W. Van Henten and A. Houtepen. Studies in Theology and Religion 3. Assen: Van Gorcum, 2001.

Wolff, H. W. *Joel and Amos.* Translated by W. Janzen, S. D. McBride Jr., and C. A. Muenchow. Hermeneia. Philadelphia: Fortress, 1977.

———. "The Kerygma of the Yahwist." Translated by W. A. Benware. *Int* 20 (1966): 129-58. Repr. in pp. 41-66 of W. Brueggemmann and H. W. Wolff, *The Vitality of Old Testament Traditions.* 2nd ed. Atlanta: John Knox, 1982.

Wolters, A. "Not Rescue but Destruction: Rereading Exodus 15:8." *CBQ* 52 (1990): 223-40.

Wright, C. J. H. *God's People in God's Land: Family, Land, and Property in the Old Testament.* Grand Rapids: Eerdmans, 1990.

Wright, D. P. *The Disposal of Impurity.* SBLDS 101. Atlanta: Scholars Press, 1987.

———. "Holiness (OT)." Pages 237-49 in vol. 3 of *Anchor Bible Dictionary.* Edited by D. N. Freedman. 6 vols. New York: Doubleday, 1992.

———. "The Laws of Hammurabi as a Source for the Covenant Collection (Exodus 20:23–23:19)." *Maarav* 10 (2003): 11-87.

———. "The Spectrum of Priestly Impurity." Pages 150-81 in *Priesthood and Cult in Ancient Israel.* Edited by G. A. Anderson and S. M. Olyan. JSOTSup 125. Sheffield: Sheffield Academic Press, 1991.

Wright, G. R. H. "The Passage of the Sea." *Göttinger Miscellen* 33 (1979): 55-68.

Würthwein, E. *Das Erste Buch der Könige, Kapital 1-16.* ATD 11/1. Göttingen: Vandenhoeck & Ruprecht, 1977.

Wyatt, N. "The Development of the Tradition in Exodus 3." *ZAW* 91 (1979): 437-42.

Wynn-Williams, Damian J. *The State of the Pentateuch: A Comparison of the Approaches of M. Noth and E. Blum.* BZAW 249. Berlin: de Gruyter, 1997.

Zenger, E. *Einleitung in das Alte Testament.* 5th ed. Studienbücher Theologie 1/1. Stuttgart: Kohlhammer, 2004.

———. *Die Sinaitheophanie: Untersuchungen zum jahwistischen und elohistischen Geschichtswerk.* FB 3. Würzburg: Echter Verlag, 1971.

———. "Le thème de la 'sortie d'Égypte.'" Pages 301-31 in *Le Pentateuque en question: Les origines et la composition des cinq premiers livres de la Bible à la lumière des recherches récentes.* Edited by A. de Pury. MdB. Geneva: Labor et Fides, 1989.

———. "Tradition und Interpretation in Exodus XV 1-21." Pages 452-83 in *Congress Volume: Vienna 1980.* Edited by J. A. Emerton. VTSup 32. Leiden: Brill, 1980.

———, ed. *Der neue Bund im alten: Studien zur Bundestheologie der beiden Testamente.* QD 146. Freiburg: Herder, 1993.

Zevit, Z. "Converging Lines of Evidence Bearing on the Date of P." *ZAW* 94 (1982): 481-511.

———. "The Earthen Altar Laws of Exodus 20:24-26 and Related Sacrificial Restrictions in Their Cultural Context." Pages 53-62 in *Texts, Temples, and Traditions: A Tribute to Menahem Haran.* Edited by Michael V. Fox et al. Winona Lake, Ind.: Eisenbrauns, 1996.

———. "The Priestly Redaction and Interpretation of the Plague Narrative in Exodus." *JQR* 66 (1975): 193-211.

———. "Three Ways to Look at the Ten Plagues." *BRev* 6 (1990): 16-23.

Ziegler, J. "Die Hilfe Gottes 'am Morgen.'" In *Alttestamentliche Studien: Friedrich Nötscher zum 60. Geburtstag.* Edited by H. Junker and J. Botterweck, Pages 281-88. BBB 1. Bonn: Peter Hanstein, 1950.

Zimmerli, W. *I Am Yahweh.* Translated by D. W. Stott. Edited by W. Brueggemann. Atlanta: John Knox, 1982.

———. *Old Testament Theology in Outline.* Translated by D. E. Green. Atlanta: John Knox, 1978.

Zipor, M. A. "The Deuteronomic Account of the Golden Calf and Its Reverberation in Other Parts of the Book of Deuteronomy." *ZAW* 108 (1996): 20-33.

Zlotnick-Sivan, H. "Moses the Persian? Exodus 2, the 'Other' and Biblical 'Mnemo-history.'" *ZAW* 116 (2004): 189-205.

Index of Subjects

Index of Authors

Index of Hebrew Words

Index of Scriptural and Ancient Texts

The references to single half verses in the Commentary (e.g., Exod 4:20b)
are indexed as whole verses (e.g., Exod 4:20).

845

33:23	486	93–99	328	3:9	493
41:4	547	93:4	449, 456	6:23	634
46	204	94:9	142	6:35	664
46:4	570	94:13	340	8:27-29	299
46:5	216, 257	95:1	684	10:8	644
47:1	684	95:8	391	10:26	552
47:5	456	96	589	12:12	495
48	6, 123, 570	96:6	642	14:21	546
48:2	5, 123	97:1-2	451, 452, 509	14:31	546
50:16-20	469, 473	98:1	139	16:21	644
56:1	547	99:3	236	19:17	546
57:1	340	99:5	613	22:1	546
51:7	274	99:9	417	24:32	214
63	204, 216	103:8	739	25:20	552
65	570	103:18	444	28:8	546
68:4	452	104	220	29:1	706
68:7	295	104:9	220	29:2	92
68:8	418, 429	105	208, 209	29:9	682
68:9	123	105:5-7	209		
68:17	429	105:27	209	**Job**	
68:18	123	105:32	237	1:12	481
68:19	403	106:19-20	686	2:7	481
69:31	750	106:32	391	4:16	484
72:18	139	110:1	340	5:22	682
73:17	340	111:4	739	7:12	212, 299
74:12-14	299	111:9	226	9:4	644
76:2-3	570	112:4	739	9:13	299
78	208, 209	114	300	9:26	443
78:2-4	209	118:14	321, 337	10:10	324, 338
78:2	209	118:25	685	13:26	269
78:10	444	120–133	514	24:13-27	473
78:13	324	123:3	547	30:1	682
78:24	382	124:6	403	38	235
78:40-55	209	130:7	226	38:2-4	142
78:48	237	132:5	340	38:4-5	142
78:60	591	132:7	613	38:22	237
81:7	390	135:5	405	39:27	443
81:8-9	469	135:7	456	42:16	486
86:9	493	135:21	403, 591		
86:15	739	139:11-12	246	**Song of Songs/Canticles**	
88:7	532	139:20	467	7:3	561, 566
89:8	299	141:10	340		
89:9-10	299	144:1	403	**Ruth**	
89:11	299	145:8	739	2	383
89:18	413	147:2	675	1:1	11
90:14	257				
91:5	257	**Proverbs**		**Lamentations**	
91:6	257	1:26	682	1:4	92